PRENTICE HALL
PORTFOLIO EDITIONS

Prentice Hall is pleased to introduce *Making a Nation: The United States and Its People, Portfolio Edition*. Prentice Hall Portfolio Editions feature a collection of concise textbooks on a variety of subjects. Written in classic narrative form, these books allow for the flexibility to incorporate the use of other material such as primary source documents, readings, and technology resources. As you use *Making a Nation, Portfolio Edition*, complete your portfolio by selecting one of many Prentice Hall resources to enhance your course:

Included with *Making A Nation, Portfolio Edition*

U.S. History Documents CD-ROM. *Provided at no additional charge with this textbook,* the U.S. History Documents CD-ROM enables one to access over 300 primary source documents relevant to the study of American history.

The Study Portfolio

Includes *Practice Tests* and *Evaluating Online Resources for History 2003 with Research Navigator.* Free when bundled with the text.

The Penguin Portfolio

Adopters of *Making a Nation, Portfolio Edition* can receive significant discounts when orders for the text are bundled with Penguin titles in American history. As a special offer from Prentice Hall, Thomas Paine's, *Common Sense* and Upton Sinclair's, *The Jungle* are available for free when bundled with *Making a Nation, Portfolio Edition*.

The Technology Portfolio

Includes the *Mapping American History* CD-ROM and the *Exploring America: Interactive Learning Activities from the Sixteenth Century to the Present* CD-ROM. Free when bundled with the text.

Create your own portfolio. Customize any of these portfolio options to suit your specific needs and interests. For additional details, please see the Preface or contact your local Prentice Hall representative.

D0061297

MAKING
A
NATION

The United States and Its People

MAKING A NATION

The United States and Its People
Combined Edition

Jeanne Boydston
University of Wisconsin

Nick Cullather
Indiana University

Jan Ellen Lewis
Rutgers University, Newark

Michael McGerr
Indiana University

James Oakes
The Graduate Center, The City University of New York

PEARSON

Prentice Hall

Upper Saddle River, New Jersey 07458

Library of Congress Cataloging-in-Publication Data

Making a nation: the United States and its people / Jeanne Boydston . . . [et al.]. — Brief ed.
    p. cm.
    "Combined volume."
    Includes bibliographical references and index.
    ISBN 0-13-111454-9
    1. United States—History. 2. United States—Economic conditions. I. Boydston, Jeanne.
  E178.1.M22 2003
  973—dc21

                          2002035905

Editorial Director: Charlyce Jones-Owen
Senior Acquisitions Editor: Charles Cavaliere
AVP, Director of Production and Manufacturing:
  Barbara Kittle
Editor in Chief of Development: Rochelle Diogenes
Development Editor: Elaine Silverstein
Production Editor: Jan H. Schwartz
Prepress and Manufacturing Manager: Nick Sklitsis
Prepress and Manufacturing Buyer: Sherry Lewis
Media Editor: Deborah O'Connell

Marketing Managers: Claire Rehwinkel,
  Heather Shelstad
Creative Design Director: Leslie Osher
Interior and Cover Design: Nancy Wells
Line Art Supervisor: Guy Ruggiero
Editorial Assistant: Adrienne Paul
Cartographer: CartaGraphics
Cover Photos: Leonard Freed/Magnum
  Photos, Inc.

This book was set in 10/11 New Baskerville by TSI Graphics, Inc. and was printed and bound by R.R. Donnelly, Inc. The cover was printed by Phoenix Color Corporation.

 © 2004 by Pearson Education
Upper Saddle River, New Jersey 07458

All rights reserved. No part of this book may be reproduced, in any form or by any means, without permission in writing from the publisher.

Printed in the United States of America
10 9 8 7 6 5 4 3 2 1

ISBN 0-13-111454-9

PEARSON EDUCATION LTD.
PEARSON EDUCATION AUSTRALIA PTY. Limited
PEARSON EDUCATION SINGAPORE, Pte. Ltd.
PEARSON EDUCATION NORTH ASIA Ltd.
PEARSON EDUCATION CANADA, Ltd.
PEARSON EDUCATION DE MEXICO, S.A. de C.V.
PEARSON EDUCATION—Japan
PEARSON EDUCATION MALAYSIA, Pte. Ltd.

BRIEF CONTENTS

CONTENTS

5. The Eighteenth-Century World, 1700–1775 99

6. Conflict on the Edge of the Empire, 1713–1774 123

15. A War for Union and Emancipation, 1861–1865   343

16. Reconstructing a Nation, 1865–1877   369

MAPS

FIGURES AND TABLES

PREFACE

Every human life is shaped by a variety of different relationships. Cultural relations, diplomatic relations, race, gender, and class relations, all contribute to how an individual interacts with the larger global community. This was the theme of the full-length version of *Making a Nation*. For this concise edition, the authors have worked hard to retain the theme while reducing some of the illustrious material. This allows us to retain our emphasis on the relationships that have historically shaped and defined the identities of the American people. So, for example, to disentangle the identity of a Mexican American woman working in a factory in Los Angeles in the year 2000 is to confront the multiple and overlapping "identities" that define a single American life. There are many ways to explore these and similar relationships. *Making a Nation* views them through the lens of *political economy*.

In March of 1776, a few months before American colonists declared their independence from Great Britain, Adam Smith published his masterpiece, *The Wealth of Nations*. Smith had delayed publication of his work for a year so that he could perfect a lengthy chapter on Anglo-American relations. Thus *The Wealth of Nations*, one of the most important documents in a new branch of knowledge known as political economy, was written with a close eye to events in the British colonies of North America, the colonies that were soon to become the United States.

What did Smith and his many American followers mean by political economy? They meant, firstly, that the economy itself is much broader than the gross national product, the unemployment rate, or the twists and turns of the stock market. They understood that economies are tightly bound to politics, that they are therefore the products of history rather than nature or accident. And just as men and women make history, so too do they make economies—in the way they work and organize their families as much as in their fiscal policies and tax structures.

Political economy is a way of thinking that is deeply embedded in American history. To this day we casually assume that different government policies create different "incentives" shaping everything from the way capital gains are invested to how parents raise their children, from how unmarried mothers on welfare can escape from poverty, to how automobile manufacturers design cars for fuel efficiency and pollution control. Political economy is the art and science that traces these connections between government, the economy, and the relationships that shape the daily lives of ordinary men and women. But that connection points in different directions. Politics and the economy do not simply shape, but are in turn shaped by, the lives and cultural values of ordinary men and women.

Put differently, political economy establishes a context that allows students to see the links between the particular and the general, between large and seemingly abstract forces such as "globalization" and the struggles of working parents who find they need two incomes to provide for their children. *Making a Nation* shows that such relationships were as important in the seventeenth and eighteenth centuries as they are today.

In a sense, globalization has been a theme in American history from its earliest beginnings. As the opening chapters demonstrate, Europe, Africa and the Americas were linked to each other in an Atlantic world across which everything was exchanged, deadly diseases along with diplomatic formalities, political structures and cultural assumptions, African slaves and Europeans servants, colonists and commodities.

In subsequent chapters *Making a Nation* traces the development of the newly formed United States by once again stressing the link between the lives of ordinary men and women to the grand political struggles of the day. Should the federal government create a centralized bank? Should it promote economic development by sponsoring the construction of railroads, turnpikes and canals? At one level, such questions exposed competing ideas about what American capitalism should look like and what the implications of those ideas were for American democracy. But a closer look suggests that those same political quarrels were propelled by the concerns that farmers, workers, and businessmen were expressing about the pace and direction of economic change.

Similarly, the great sectional struggle over slavery and freedom is told as the story of dramatic political maneuvers and courageous military exploits, as well as the story of women who created the modern profession of nursing by caring for civil war soldiers and of runaway slaves who helped push the United States government into a policy of emancipation. The insights of political economy likewise frame the way *Making a Nation* presents the transition from slave to free labor in the South after the Civil War. In the twentieth century, as America became a global power, the demands of the new political economy of urban and industrial America inform our examination of both U.S. diplomacy and domestic affairs. It was no accident, for example, that the civil rights leader A. Philip Randolph took advantage of the crisis of the Second World War to threaten Franklin Roosevelt's administration with a march on Washington. For Randolph, the demand for racial equality was inseparable from the struggle for a more equitable distribution of the rewards of a capitalist economy.

The United States victory in World War II, coupled with the extraordinary burst of prosperity in the war's aftermath, gave rise to fantasies of omnipotence that were tested and shattered by the American experience in Vietnam. Presidents, generals, and ordinary soldiers alike shared in the illusion of invulnerability. America's was the greatest democracy and the most powerful economy on earth. Thus did Americans in Southeast Asia in the late twentieth century find themselves in much the same place that Christopher Columbus had found himself centuries before: halfway around the world, face to face with a people whose culture he did not fully understand. And even today, the unparalleled military might and economic power of the Unites States have not proved enough to make ordinary Americans feel secure from recession at home and deadly attack from abroad. History cannot provide lessons on how to navigate this paradox, but a fuller understanding of the present begins with a better understanding of the past. We trust that this concise edition of *Making a Nation* will help make that possible.

TOPICS AND COVERAGE

Because *Making a Nation* was written from the very beginning with an organizing theme in mind, we have been able to incorporate many topics relatively smoothly within the larger narrative. For example, this textbook includes some of the most extensive coverage of Indian and western history available, but because our coverage is integrated into the larger narrative, there is no need to provide a separate chapter on either topic. At the same time, the theme of political economy allows us to cover subjects that are often missed in standard texts. For example, *Making a Nation* includes more than the usual coverage of environmental history, as well as more complete coverage of the social and cultural history of the late twentieth century than is available elsewhere. And in every case the politics of globalization and environmentalism, of capitalist development and democratic reform, of family values and social inequality are never far from view. *Making a Nation* also provides full coverage of the most recent American history, from the end of the Cold War to the rise of a new information economy and on to the terrorist attacks against the World Trade Center and the Pentagon in September 2001. Here, again, the organizing theme of political economy provides a strong but supple interpretive framework that helps students understand developments that are making a nation in a new century.

STUDENT LEARNING AIDS

To assist students in their appreciation of this history, we have added several distinctive features and pedagogical aids.

Chapter-Opening Vignettes
The vignettes that open each chapter are intended to give specificity as well as humanity to the themes that follow. From the witchcraft trials in Salem to the Trumps' American dream, students are drawn into each chapter with compelling stories that illustrate the organizing factor of political economy.

Chronologies
Found at the end of each chapter, chronologies organize key events into sequential order for quick review.

Further Readings
An annotated list of helpful books related to the key topics of each chapter is located at the end of each chapter.

U.S. History Documents CD-ROM
Bound in every new copy of *Making a Nation, Portfolio Edition*, and organized according to the main periods in American history, the U.S. History Documents CD-ROM contains over 300 primary-sources in an easily-navigable PDF file. Each document is accompanied by essay questions that allow students to read important sources in U.S. history via the CD-ROM and respond online.

Appendix
In addition to providing several key documents in United States history, the Appendix presents demographic data reflecting the 2000 census. An extensive Bibliography offers an expanded compilation of literature, arranged by chapter.

SUPPLEMENTARY MATERIALS

Making a Nation comes with an extensive package of supplementary print and multimedia materials for both instructors and students.

Instructor's Resource Manual and Test-Item File
The Instructor's Resource Manual contains chapter outlines, detailed chapter overviews, discussion questions, lecture strategies, essay topics, and tips on incorporating Penguin titles in American history into lectures. The Test-Item File includes over 1000 multiple-choice, true-false, essay, and map questions, organized by chapter.

Practice Tests (Volumes I and II)
Free when packaged with the text, Practice Tests provide students with chapter outlines, map questions, sample exam questions, analytical reading exercises, collaborative exercises, and essay questions.

American Stories: Biographies in United States History
This two-volume collection of sixty-two biographies in U.S. history is free when packaged with *Making a Nation*. Introductions, prereading questions, and suggested readings enrich this attractive and useful supplement.

Transparencies
 This collection of over 150 full-color transparencies provides maps, charts, and graphs for classroom presentations.

Retrieving the American Past 2003 Edition (RTAP)
RTAP enables instructors to tailor a custom reader whose content, organization, and price exactly match their course syllabi. Edited by historians and educators at the Ohio State University, this online database offers instructors the freedom and flexibility to choose selections of primary and secondary source readings—or both—from 81 (8 new) chapters. Contact your local Prentice Hall

representative for details about RTAP. Discounts apply when copies of RTAP are bundled with *Making a Nation*.

Prentice Hall and Penguin Bundle Program

Prentice Hall and Penguin are pleased to provide adopters of *Making a Nation* with an opportunity to receive significant discounts when orders for *Making a Nation* are bundled together with Penguin titles in American history. Please contact your local Prentice Hall representative for details.

Reading Critically about History

This brief guide provides students with helpful strategies for reading a history textbook and is available free when packaged with *Making a Nation*.

Understanding and Answering Essay Questions

This helpful guide provides analytical tools for understanding different types of essay questions and for preparing well-crafted essay answers. It is available free when packaged with *Making a Nation*.

MULTIMEDIA SUPPLEMENTS

Companion Web site™

The Companion Web site™ for *Making a Nation* is available at www.prenhall.com/boydston and offers students one of the most comprehensive Internet resources available. Organized around the primary subtopics of each chapter, the Companion Web site™ provides detailed summaries, multiple-choice, true-false, essay, identification, map labeling, and document-based questions. Unique Web Connections, directly tied to the content of the text, combine primary sources, interactive maps, audio clips, and numerous visuals to explore key topics in depth. The Faculty Module contains a wealth of material for instructors, including an online instructor's manual and maps, charts, and graphs that can be imported into electronic presentations.

Exploring America CD-ROM

The new Exploring America CD-ROM features thirty-one activities that drill down to explore the impact of key episodes and developments in United States history. Each activity combines primary sources, illustrations, graphics, audio clips, and interactive maps to provide opportunities to further explore the key themes of *Making a Nation*. Available free when packaged with *Making a Nation*.

Research Navigator™

Prentice Hall's new Research Navigator™ helps students make the most of their research time. From finding the right articles and journals, to citing sources; drafting and writing effective papers, and completing research assignments, Research Navigator™ simplifies and streamlines the entire process. Complete with extensive help on the research process and three exclusive databases full of relevant and reliable source material including EBSCO's ContentSelect Academic Journal Database, *The New York Times* Search by Subject Archive, and "Best of the Web" Link Library, Research Navigator™ is the one-stop research solution for students. Research Navigator™ is free when packaged with any Prentice Hall textbook. An Access Code for Research Navigator™ is provided in every copy of Prentice Hall's Evaluating Online Resources guide. Contact your local representative for more details or take a tour on the web at http://www.researchnavigator.com.

Maps and Graphics CD-ROM

Available in Windows and Mac formats for classroom presentations, this CD-ROM includes the maps, charts, tables, and graphs from *Making a Nation*.

Course Management Systems

As the leader in course-management solutions for teachers and students of history, Prentice Hall provides a variety of online tools. Contact your local Prentice Hall representative for a demonstration, or visit www.prenhall.com/demo.

ACKNOWLEDGEMENTS

We would like to express our thanks to the reviewers whose thoughtful comments and insights were of great value in finalizing *Making a Nation*:

Tyler Anbinder, George Washington University
Debra Barth, San Jose City College
James M. Bergquist, Villanova University
Robert Brandfon, College of the Holy Cross
Stephanie Camp, University of Washington
Mark T. Carleton, Louisiana State University
Jean Choate, Northern Michigan University
Martin B. Cohen, George Mason University
Samuel Crompton, Holyoke Community College
George Daniels, University of South Alabama
James B. Dressler, Cumberland University
Elizabeth Dunn, Baylor University
Mark Fernandez, Loyola University of New Orleans
Willard B. Gatewood, University of Arkansas
James Gilbert, University of Maryland at College Park
Richard L. Hume, Washington State University
Frederic Jaher, University of Illinois at Urbana-Champaign
Glen Jeansonne, University of Wisconsin-Milwaukee
Constance Jones, Tidewater Community College
Laylon Wayne Jordan, University of Charleston
Peter Kirstein, St. Xavier University
John D. Krugler, Marquette University
Mark V. Kwasny, Ohio State University-Newark
Gene D. Lewis, University of Cincinnati
Glenn Linden, Southern Methodist University
Robert McCarthy, Providence College
Andrew McMichael, Vanderbilt University
Dennis N. Mihelich, Creighton University

Patricia Hagler Minter, Western Kentucky University
Joseph Mitchell, Howard Community College
Reid Mitchell, University of Maryland Baltimore County
Carl Moneyhon, University of Arkansas at Little Rock
James M. Morris, Christopher Newport University
Earl Mulderink III, Southern Utah University
Alexandra Nickliss, City College of San Francisco
Chris S. O'Brien, University of Kansas
Peter Onuf, University of Virginia
Annelise Orleck, Dartmouth College
Richard H. Peterson, San Diego State University
Leo R. Ribuffo, George Washington University
Kenneth Scherzer, Middle Tennessee State University
Sheila Skemp, University of Mississippi
Kevin Smith, Ball State University
Michael Topp, University of Texas at El Paso
Gregory J. W. Urwin, University of Central Arkansas
Paul K. Van der Slice, Montgomery College
Jessica Weiss, California State University of Hayward
James A. Wilson, Southwest Texas State University
John Wiseman, Frostburg State University
Andrew Workman, Mills College

We also wish to thank the reviewers whose feedback on the concise edition was invaluable:
J. Christopher Arndt, James Madison University
Edward Baptist, University of Miami
Laura Graves, South Plains College
Raymond M. Hyer, James Madison University
Timothy Koerner, Oakland Community College

The authors would like first to acknowledge their co-authors: Without the patience, tenacity, and intellectual support we received from each other, we could scarcely have continued to the end. And we are grateful of course to our families, friends, and colleagues who encouraged us during the planning and writing of *Making a Nation*.

The authors would like to thank the editors, staff, and freelance support at Prentice Hall, especially our acquisitions editor, Charles Cavaliere; editorial director and vice president, Charlyce Jones-Owen; development editor, Elaine Silverstein; editor-in-chief of development, Rochelle Diogenes; production editor, Jan Schwartz; marketing managers, Claire Bitting and Heather Shelstad; and designer, Nancy Wells. We have benefited at each stage from their patience, their experience, and their commitment to this project. Thanks also to Maria Piper who formatted the line art; Nick Sklitsis, manufacturing manager; Sherry Lewis, manufacturing buyer; and Jan Stephan, managing editor; and many other people behind the scenes at Prentice Hall, for helping make the book happen.

ABOUT THE AUTHORS

Jeanne Boydston is Professor of History at the University of Wisconsin-Madison. She is the author of *Home and Work: Housework, Wages, and the Ideology of Labor in the Early American Republic,* coauthor of *The Limits of Sisterhood: The Beecher Sisters on Women's Rights and Woman's Sphere,* co-editor of *The Root of Bitterness: Documents of the Social History of American Women* (second edition), as well as author of articles on the labor history of women in the early republic. Professor Boydston teaches in the areas of early republic and antebellum United States history and United States women's history to 1870. Her BA and MA are from the University of Tennessee, and her PhD is from Yale University.

Nick Cullather is Associate Professor at Indiana University, where he teaches courses on the history of United States foreign relations. He is on the editorial boards of *Diplomatic History* and the *Encyclopedia of American Foreign Policy,* and is the author of *Illusions of Influence* (1994), a study of the political economy of United States-Philippines relations, and *Secret History* (1999), which describes a CIA covert operation against the government of Guatemala in 1954. He received his AB from Indiana University and his MA and PhD from the University of Virginia.

Jan Ellen Lewis is Professor of History and Director of the Graduate Program at Rutgers University, Newark. She also teaches in the history PhD program at Rutgers, New Brunswick and was a Visiting Professor at Princeton University. A specialist in colonial and early national history, she is the author of *The Pursuit of Happiness: Family and Values in Jefferson's Virginia* (1983), and co-editor of *An Emotional History of the United States* (1998) and *Sally Hemings and Thomas Jeffer-son: History, Memory, and Civic Culture* (1999). She is currently completing an examination of the way the Founding generation grappled with the challenge presented to an egalitarian society by women and slaves and a second volume of the Penguin *History of the United States.* She received her AB from Bryn Mawr College, and MAs and PhD from the University of Michigan.

Michael McGerr is Associate Professor of History and Associate Dean for Graduate Education in the College of Arts and Sciences at Indiana University-Bloomington. He is the author of *The Decline of Popular Politics: The American North, 1865–1928* (1986). With the aid of a fellowship from the National Endowment for the Humanities, he is currently writing a book on the rise and fall of Progressive America. Professor McGerr teaches a wide range of courses on modern American history, including the Vietnam War, race and gender in American business, John D. Rockefeller, Bill Gates, and the politics of American popular music. He received his BA, MA, and PhD degrees from Yale University.

James Oakes is Graduate School Humanities Professor and Professor of History at the Graduate Center of the City University of New York, and has taught at Purdue, Princeton, and Northwestern. He is author of *The Ruling Race: A History of American Slaveholders* (1982) and *Slavery and Freedom: An Interpretation of the Old South* (1990). In addition to a year-long research grant from the National Endowment for the Humanities, he was a fellow at the Center for Advanced Study in the Behavioral Sciences in 1989–90. His areas of specialization are slavery, the Civil War and Reconstruction, and the history of American political thought. He received his PhD from The University of California at Berkeley.

CHAPTER

1

Worlds in Motion

1450–1550

Christopher Columbus: World Traveler • The Worlds of Christopher
Columbus • The World of the Indian Peoples
Worlds in Collision • The Biological Consequences
of Conquest • Onto the Mainland • Conclusion

CHRISTOPHER COLUMBUS: WORLD TRAVELER

Christopher Columbus had been preparing all his adult life for his journey across the Atlantic to find a western route to Asia. Columbus and his crew of 89 men—divided among three ships: the *Santa María*, the *Niña*, and the *Pinta*—departed the Spanish port of Palos on August 3, 1492. They reached what he mistakenly thought was an island off the coast of China but was actually an island the Indians called Guanahaní, on October 12. Over the course of his four voyages to the region, he continued to believe it was Asia; hence he called the islands the Indies and the inhabitants Indios (Indians). In a pattern he would repeat again and again, Columbus and his crew disembarked, gave the island a Spanish name, and claimed it for the king and queen of Spain. When the residents gathered to see the strangers, he gave them gifts of red caps and glass beads, and they reciprocated with parrots, balls of cotton thread, and javelins. Columbus described these men and women as generous but poor and concluded that they would make good servants and easy converts to Christianity.

Columbus's arrival in the Western Hemisphere dramatically and irreversibly changed the worlds into which he and the Indians had been born. The encounter in effect fused their two worlds into one Atlantic world that Europeans and Indians—as well as Africans, who were brought forcibly to the Caribbean as early as 1500—would inhabit and transform together.

In many ways, Columbus was an unlikely character to inaugurate such profound changes in the history of the world. With neither privilege nor education, his opportunities were sharply limited. Moreover, he shared fully in the prejudices of his age, but he was well-read and remarkably well-traveled for his time. By the time Columbus sailed to the New World for Spain, he had explored much of the Mediterranean world, as well as Portugal and her Atlantic colonies.

Columbus had traveled even further through his reading. He had read geography books as well as Marco Polo's thirteenth-century account of his travels to Asia. He knew that Polo had mentioned at least 1,378 islands off the coast of Asia. He was also evidently entranced by Polo's description of the empire of the great Kublai Khan and a magnificent island called Cipango (Japan), 1,500 miles off the coast of China. When Columbus left the island of Guanahaní, it was to search for gold and "to see if I can find the island of Cipango." Everywhere he went among the islands inhabited by the Taino Indians, Columbus asked where he could find spices and gold. He was convinced that the large island that the natives called Cuba was really Cipango and that its king "was at war with the Grand Khan."

Columbus was bold and restless in a world that suddenly valued such qualities. Dramatic changes in the political economy of Europe, in particular the expansion of trade and the consolidations of small principalities into powerful nation-states, set men such as Columbus in search of trade and the wealth it would bring. In the process they helped create a truly global economy that transformed the worlds of all the peoples of the globe and continues to transform them still.

THE WORLDS OF CHRISTOPHER COLUMBUS

Imagine a world in which most people live in small villages, where they eat the food that they hunt or raise themselves and never travel more than a few miles from home. At the same time, other people are on the move, especially traders, warriors, and men and women displaced by war and famine. The traders push at the boundaries of the known world, looking for better goods and new markets. The warriors aim at conquest. They seize land that others inhabit, pushing them aside, so that their own people can move in. The traders and the warriors set the world in motion and the population of the world shifts.

Columbus came to the Americas as a trader and became a conqueror. In the process he introduced the ways of the Old World into the New World, changing both of them forever. The modern history of America begins in 1492 with the movement of all of these peoples, from the Old World and the New, on American terrain.

The Political Economy of Europe

In 1492, Europe as we know it did not yet exist. Many of what later became major European nations—Spain, Italy, Germany—were collections of small principalities. Indeed, Spain and Portugal had only recently been liberated from the Moors, a North African people who practiced the Muslim religion and who had invaded the Iberian Peninsula in 711. European nation-states were being consolidated, each under the rule of a single leader, a hereditary monarch. In fact, not until a nation was unified under a strong leader could it turn away from internal struggles and focus on the world beyond. As the first nations to be unified, Portugal and Spain were the first to explore and conquer foreign lands. Holland, France, and England, unified about a century later, then followed the Spanish and Portuguese lead. The consolidation of the European nations unleashed enormous energy and put the peoples of Europe in motion. The world's peoples have always traded with one another. However, the period between 1450 and 1750 witnessed the establishment of new trade patterns. In the preceding centuries, powerful empires had dominated trade in their regions (see Map 1–1). In the middle of the fifteenth century, Islamic traders, for example, linked parts of Europe, Africa, and Asia.

Once western Europe began to dominate world trade after 1450, it began to shape not only the world economy, but global social and political structures as well. The nations of western Europe established global trade networks, linking Europe, Africa, Asia, and the Americas. The inequalities between nations were heightened as wealth flowed first to Spain and Portugal and then to England, France, and Holland. As western European nations became wealthier and their economies more complex,

Map 1–1   World Trade on the Eve of Discovery
For a thousand years, world trade centered on the Mediterranean. European, Arab, and Asian traders criss-crossed much of the Eastern Hemisphere, carrying spices, silks, and cottons from Asia; linens, woolens, and wine from Europe; and gold and slaves from Africa.

those areas of America, Africa, and (to a lesser extent) Asia that were conquered or colonized became economically dependent on western trade. They supplied the raw materials that made Europe wealthy. Increasingly, their own populations were exploited and even enslaved, to turn out gold, silver, sugar, and tobacco to quench the insatiable appetites of Europe.

When Christopher Columbus sailed west looking for Asia, he was trying to reestablish a European trade that had been disrupted by the Black Death. The bubonic plague had arrived in Europe in 1347, brought by a trade caravan from Asia. Until that time, the Italians in particular had engaged in commerce as far east as the Mongol empire in China. Marco Polo, the son of an Italian merchant, had written a book that described his stay in China and India between 1275 and 1292. In the middle of the fifteenth century, as Europe began to recover from the plague, its population began to grow, the economy began to expand, and merchants, especially along the Mediterranean, began to look for new markets.

The vast majority of Europeans were peasants, many living close to destitution. Still, an increasingly prosperous elite (both the nobility and the affluent members of the urban middle classes) developed a taste for luxury items such as sugar, spices, fabrics, and precious metals. Marco Polo's descriptions of Asian temples roofed in gold had dazzled Italian readers since the end of the thirteenth century. The desire for luxury goods sent European explorers off in search of new routes to Asia.

By the middle of the fifteenth century, new technologies made it possible for Europeans to travel far from home. Some of these innovations were adapted from other regions of the world—for example, gunpowder from China and the navigational compass from the Arabs. Others came from Europe, including better maps; stronger metal that could be turned into guns and cannons; and the caravel, a light, swift ship that was well suited for navigating along the coast of Africa.

Europe was on the move by the end of the fifteenth century. The Portuguese had begun exploring the Atlantic coast of Africa, searching for a water route to Asia. Portugal had recently driven out its Muslim conquerors. It was a small nation (about 1.5 million inhabitants, compared to almost 10 million for Spain), but it had achieved political unification under a strong king almost a century earlier. The combination of political unity, a strong monarchy interested in extending its power and wealth, and an aggressive merchant class looking for new markets enabled Portugal to become the first of the modern European imperial nations. By 1475, Portuguese explorers had reached the thriving kingdom of Benin on the lower Guinea coast (the modern country of Nigeria) and had established trading posts along the northwestern coast of the continent. In exchange for European goods such as horses, cloth, and wheat, the Portuguese traded for African luxury products such as ivory, and especially gold, that could be sold in Europe.

Earlier in the fifteenth century, the Portuguese had begun raiding the Sahara coast for slaves. Once they opened up the new trade with sub-Saharan Africa, however, they discovered that they could exchange European goods directly with African kings and be provided with slaves. The Portuguese then resold the slaves, primarily for use as servants, in Africa or Europe. With the opening of plantations (first in the Canary Islands, which the Spanish had completed conquering in 1496), the slave trade became an important part of the Portuguese economy.

The World of the West African Peoples

Starting with the Portuguese, European traders reached the west coast of Africa in the fifteenth century. There they found much of the population living in powerful

Between 1534 and 1542, King Francis I of France financed Jacques Cartier to make three expeditions to seek a route through North America and to look out for any riches along the way. All three came to naught. On the first trip, the French only explored the coastline, but on their second, they sailed up the St. Lawrence River as far as the town of Hochelaga (near present-day Montréal). The Iroquois who lived there spoke of a wealthy land to the west. Although the Iroquois may well have been trying to deceive the French, it is possible that the shiny metal they spoke of was the copper that the Hurons to the west mined and traded. The winter was brutal, and the river was frozen solid. Even with food and attentive nursing from the Indians, at the end of the winter almost a quarter of the party was dead. The French found that their survival depended on the native peoples.

The subsequent expeditions failed as badly. The French quarreled with their Indian hosts and fought among themselves. Moreover, the region was so remote that no one could yet fathom why they were even bothering. Although all these early attempts at colonization failed, the French were demonstrating that European claims to the Americas would rest on exploration, conquest of the natives, and colonization. Needless to say, this principle of European colonialism was established without the consent of the Indians who inhabited the land.

Spanish Outposts

Throughout the sixteenth century, European nations jockeyed for power on the continent. Because most of these nations were at war with each other, North America was often a low priority. But when the fighting in Europe abated, the Europeans looked across the Atlantic in hopes of gaining an advantage over a rival nation or finding a new source of wealth.

Soon the French and English, who found no gold or jewels when they explored along the coastline, discovered an easier source of wealth—stealing from the Spanish. Every season, Spanish ships laden with treasure that they had seized in Mexico and South America made their way through the Caribbean, into the Atlantic south of Florida, and along the coast until they caught the trade winds to take them east across the Atlantic. By the middle of the sixteenth century, French ships were lying in wait off Florida or the Carolinas. Because it was cheaper than exploration, preying on Spanish ships became a national policy.

To put a stop to these costly acts of piracy, King Felipe II established a series of forts along both coasts of Florida. At the same time, a group of Huguenots (French Protestants) established a colony, Fort Caroline, near present-day Georgia. For the new Spanish commander, Pedro Menéndez de Avilés, the first order of business was to destroy the French settlement, which was doubly threatening to the Spanish for being both French and Protestant. At dawn on a rainy September morning in 1565, 500 Spanish soldiers surprised the French at Fort Caroline. Although the French surrendered and begged for mercy, Menéndez ordered their slaughter. In this way, the religious and nationalist conflicts of Europe were transplanted to North America.

Menéndez established a string of forts; one of them, St. Augustine, settled in 1565, is the oldest continuously inhabited city of European origin on the United States mainland. As was true of many ambitious European explorers and conquerors, Menéndez's aspirations exceeded those of his nation. Most of his plans for Spanish settlements were undermined by local Indians whom the Spanish alienated. After attacks by the Orista Indians in 1576 and England's Francis Drake a decade later, the Spanish abandoned all of their Florida forts except St. Augustine.

The Huge Geographical Barrier

In 1522 Ferdinand Magellan's expedition completed the first round-the-world voyage for Spain, proving finally that one could get to the East by heading west. Other nations then became interested in finding a way through, rather than around, North America. Two years after Magellan's voyage, another Italian, Giovanni da Verrazano, sailed for France. He explored the North American coast from South Carolina to Maine, and he and his crew were the first Europeans to see New York harbor. As far as Europeans were concerned, however, all that Verrazano had discovered was that North America was a huge barrier between Europe and Asia (see Map 2–1).

That "huge barrier" of the North American continent was populated by Indians, some wary and some friendly. Unfamiliar with Indian customs, Europeans often could not distinguish hospitality from malice. In the early years of exploration, the survival of a venture often depended on local Indians, yet because the French were looking either for treasure or a Northwest Passage, they tended to focus on cultural differences rather than similarities. Europeans noticed similarities only when political economic objectives such as trade or alliance were in the forefront.

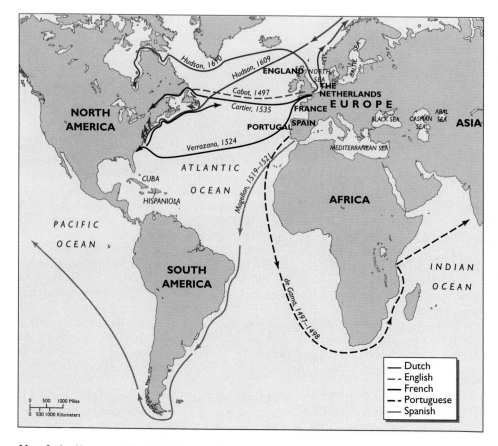

Map 2–1   Voyages of Exploration
In a little over a century after Columbus's first voyage, European explorers had circled the world and charted most of the North American coastline.

PURSUING WEALTH AND GLORY ALONG THE NORTH AMERICAN SHORE

The forces that propelled the Spanish across the Atlantic soon brought other European nations to the Americas in search of wealth and national prestige. As the English explorer Sir Walter Raleigh explained the principles of political economy, "Whosoever commands the sea commands the trade; whosoever commands the trade of the world commands the riches of the world, and consequently the world itself." Most of the North American colonies established by European nations in the first half of the seventeenth century were outposts in the global economy. There were significant differences among these colonies, reflecting the different political economies of their parent nations, but all shared certain factors: First, they were intended to bring in the greatest amount of revenue at the lowest cost. Second, success depended on harmonious relations with—or elimination of—local Indians. Third, colonial societies slowly developed their own distinctive patterns, depending on which route they followed to prosperity.

European Objectives

At first Europeans believed that Columbus had reached Asia by an Atlantic route. By the time they understood that he had discovered a new land, the Spanish were well on their way to conquering native peoples and stripping them of their wealth. Their success inspired other European nations to search for new sources of gold and silver in the regions Spain had not yet claimed. They also continued to seek a path through the Americas to Asia. Colonization was not a goal for almost a century, and even then colonies were designed to provide a quick return on investment, not to transplant Europeans onto foreign soil.

For many years the nations of northern Europe were unwilling to invest in permanent settlements. A foreign colony was costly. It involved procuring a ship, provisioning it, providing a settlement with food and equipment—and resupplying it until it could turn a profit. Spain had been lucky: Isabel and Fernando had been willing to take a considerable risk, which paid off relatively soon. The northern European nations could not afford such expeditions, and, except for the most adventurous souls, exploration for its own sake had little appeal.

Tales of wealth and adventure in New Spain spread throughout Europe, however. Would-be explorers and *conquistadores* began to sell their services to the highest bidder. John Cabot, who sailed for England, was, like Columbus, born in Genoa, Italy. Before coming to England, he had spent time in Muslim Arabia, Spain, and Portugal, apparently looking for sponsors for a voyage to Asia. He found them in the English port city of Bristol, from whence he sailed in 1497. He landed somewhere in North America, possibly at Newfoundland, and claimed the territory for England.

Although England was slow to follow up this claim to American territory, soon both England and France sent fishing expeditions to the waters off Newfoundland. The population of northwestern Europe exploded in the sixteenth and seventeenth centuries, creating an increased demand for fish.

The French colony of New France, planted in the St. Lawrence River region of Canada, grew out of the French fishing venture off Newfoundland. Early French explorers discovered neither gold nor a Northwest Passage to Asia. French fishermen, however, found that the Indians were willing to trade beaver pelts at prices so low that a man could make a fortune in a few months' time.

later, when there were only priests and no soldiers on the voyage, Don Luís had no trouble locating his homeland.

Less than a week after the Jesuits and their Indian convert had settled in Virginia, Don Luís returned to the customs of the Powhatans. He scandalized the Jesuits by taking several wives, a privilege of Indian men of high rank. The Jesuits had expected Don Luís to act as an intermediary with his people, securing them supplies and favorable treatment, but they had misjudged him. Soon they exhausted their supply of food and had to beg from Don Luís. But Don Luís was being pressured by his own people to prove his loyalty. They were suspicious of someone who had been away so long.

Don Luís had to make a choice, and he chose his own people. Powhatans killed eight of the nine missionaries. According to Indian custom, one of the victims, a young Spaniard named Alonso, was spared, although Don Luís argued for his death also. Knowing that the Spanish would someday return, he wanted no witnesses. As Don Luís predicted, the Spanish came back a year and a half later. They retrieved Alonso, ordered Don Luís to appear for an inquest, and began trying and executing other Indians when he failed to appear.

In 1607 the English planted their first permanent colony on the mainland at Jamestown among Don Luís's people. Don Luís, who was very young when he had been abducted by the Spanish, might well have been alive to greet these new foreigners. Throughout the seventeenth century, the English heard rumors about a Powhatan Indian who had spent time in the Spanish colonies.

Whether or not Don Luís lived to see the English take the place of the Spanish, it is clear that the memory of the Europeans lived on among the Powhatans. Before they established settlements, the English, French, and Spanish all explored the North American coastline. In the process, Indians and Europeans learned each other's languages and customs. During this period of American history, no sharp geographic or cultural line separated the Indians and Europeans. Indians such as Don Luís lived among the Europeans, and Europeans such as Alonso spent time with the Indians. As a result, even before permanent colonies were established, each group knew the other moderately well.

After the middle of the sixteenth century, Spain, France, the Netherlands, and England all established outposts in the United States. These early colonies were small and vulnerable to foreign or Indian attack. In these early years, success depended more on the ability to come to an accommodation with the Indians than any other factor. When the number of Europeans settling north of the Rio Grande was small, relations between Indians and Europeans were fluid. Individuals such as Don Luís and Alonso, world travelers who had lived in other cultures and learned their ways, left their mark on their world. They became cultural brokers, working out the accommodations from which an entirely new world was born.

2

Colonial Outposts

1550–1650

Don Luís de Velasco Find His Way Home • **Pursuing Wealth
and Glory Along the North American Shore** • **Spanish Outposts**
New France: An Outpost in the Global Political Economy
New Netherland: The Empire of a Trading Nation
England Attempts an Empire • **Conclusion**

DON LUÍS DE VELASCO FINDS HIS WAY HOME

The Spanish gave him the name of Don Luís de Velasco. His own people, the Powhatan Indians of the Virginia coast, knew him as Paquiquineo. The son of a chieftain, he was a young man when the Spanish picked him up in 1561 somewhere south of his home. The Europeans often abducted young Indians and took them back to their own nations so that they could serve as translators and guides on subsequent expeditions. Sometimes the process worked the other way around: Europeans learned the Native Americans' language and customs and became valuable interpreters. In the early years of colonization, those men and women who had learned the ways of another culture gained influence far out of proportion to their actual numbers.

Don Luís did not see his own people again for ten years. First the Spanish took him to Mexico, where Dominican friars baptized and educated him. The young convert was taken to Spain and then back across the Atlantic to Havana, where he persuaded the priests to let him establish a Christian mission among his own people on the North American mainland. In 1566 Don Luís set sail on a Spanish ship with two priests and 37 soldiers, but he was unable to find the Chesapeake. Four years

1513	Spanish *Requerimiento* promises freedom to all Indians who accept Spanish authority
	Spanish conquer Cuba
	Ponce de Léon reaches Florida
	The Laws of Burgos attempt to regulate working conditions of Indians
1518	Spanish introduce smallpox to New World
1521	Ponce de León returns to Florida
	Cortés lands on Yucatán coast
1519–1522	Ferdinand Magellan's crew sails around the world
1521	Tenochtitlán falls to the Spanish
1526	Ayllón explores South Carolina coast and establishes fort in Georgia
1528	Narváez explores Florida
1539	Estevanico arrives at Zuni
1539–1543	De Soto and his party explore Southeast, arriving at Mississippi, devastating the Indians and their land
1540–1542	Coronado explores Southwest
1542	The New Laws ban further enslavement of Indians

John Thornton, *Africa and Africans in the Making of the Atlantic World, 1400–1680* (1998). A provocative interpretation that places West Africa within an Atlantic context and emphasizes its active participation in the Atlantic world.

David Weber, *The Spanish Frontier in North America* (1992). Both a comprehensive survey of the history of Spanish North America and an interpretation, which shifts the focus of colonial history to the Spanish frontier.

 Please refer to the document CD-ROM for primary sources related to this chapter.

CHRONOLOGY

c. 12,000 B.C.E.	Indian peoples arrive in North America
711 C.E.	Moors invade Iberian peninsula
1275–1292	Marco Polo travels in Asia
1347	Black Death (bubonic plague) arrives in Europe
1434	Portuguese arrive at West Coast of Africa
1488	Bartolomeo Dias rounds Cape Horn
1492	Spanish complete the *reconquista*, evicting Moors from Spain Jews expelled from Spain Columbus's first voyage to America
1493	Columbus's second voyage
1494	Treaty of Tordesillas divides New World between Spain and Portugal
1496	Spanish complete conquest of Canary Islands
1498	Vasco da Gama reaches India Columbus's third voyage to America, reaches South American coast
1500	Portuguese arrive in Brazil
1504	Columbus's fourth voyage to America ends
1508	Spanish conquer Puerto Rico

FURTHER READINGS

Inga Clendinnen, *Aztecs* (1991). A remarkable description of the Aztec world, written from the Aztec point of view.

Alfred Crosby, Jr., *The Columbian Exchange: Biological and Cultural Consequences of 1492* (1972). An eye-opening introduction to environmental and biological history.

J. H. Elliot, *Imperial Spain, 1469–1716* (1963). The definitive history of Spain in this period.

Stuart J. Fiedel, *Prehistory of the Americas*, 2nd ed. (1992). A comprehensive and authoritative survey of the development of Native American civilizations in the Americas.

William D. Phillips, Jr., and Carla Rahn Phillips, *The Worlds of Christopher Columbus, 1400–1680* (1992). A short, readable introduction to Christopher Columbus and his world.

posts, such as St. Augustine, were established to protect the more valuable Spanish territories to the south. To prevent rival nations from claiming the northern reaches of its empire, Spain did not disclose the geographical information it had secured from expeditions like de Soto's. This weakened Spain's claim to the region, which depended on prior exploration.

The impact of the expedition on the Mississippian Indians is hard to determine. The Mississippian towns had begun to decline in the middle of the fifteenth century, before the arrival of Europeans. European diseases certainly hastened the process. Perhaps as significant, the Spanish seriously disrupted the Mississippian political economy. Hernando de Soto's custom of capturing chieftains effectively undermined their leadership, and the losses incurred in battles made it impossible for the rulers to command lower status tribe members to produce the food surplus and build the huge mounds that sustained the social order. After the appearance of the Spanish, no Indian civilizations would be able to match the power and sophistication of the Mississippians.

Coronado and the Pueblo Indians

At the same time that de Soto was attempting to conquer the Southeast, another group of Spaniards was setting out for the Southwest. They had heard tales of a city of Cíbola, supposedly larger than Tenochtitlán, where temples were decorated with gems. In May 1539, a party led by the Moorish slave Estevanico, one of four survivors of the Narváez expedition, reached the city, which was actually the pueblo of Zuni in New Mexico. The inhabitants recognized him as hostile and killed him. The survivors of the party did not contradict the popular belief that Cíbola was filled with treasure, however, and a year later, another aspiring *conquistador*, Francisco Vázquez de Coronado, arrived at Zuni, with 300 Spanish, 1,000 Indian allies from Mexico, and 1,500 horses and pack animals. They took the pueblo by force, and later traveled as far west as the Grand Canyon and as far east as Wichita, Kansas.

CONCLUSION

Within a half-century after Columbus's arrival in the New World, both the world he had come from and the one he had reached had been transformed, as both were drawn into a new, global political economy. Spain, the first of the major European states to achieve unity, dominated exploration, colonization, and exploitation of the New World during this period. The wealth that Spain extracted from her New World colonies encouraged rival nations to enter into overseas ventures as well. Eventually France, England, the Netherlands, Sweden, and Russia also established New World colonies, but because Spain (along with Portugal, which claimed Brazil) had such a head start, rival nations, if they did not want to challenge Spain directly, would have to settle for the lands she left unclaimed. Spain and Portugal had demonstrated that great wealth could be obtained from the New World.

In the shadow of this dream of great and unprecedented wealth, a new global economy was established, linking the Old and the New Worlds. The gold and silver extracted from the Spanish empire sustained that nation's rise to power, and the plantation crops of the New World would make many Europeans wealthy. From the beginning, the Spanish enslaved Indians to work the mines, farms, and plantations. As the native populations were depleted and the morality of enslaving native populations was questioned, the Spanish turned to African slaves.

the southern tip of South America to halfway up what is now the United States, ex-cepting only the Portuguese colony of Brazil and some of the Caribbean islands. Fi-nally the Spanish had found the precious metals they craved, and when the Indians' stores ran out, the Spanish began using slave labor to mine more.

After silver and gold, sugar was the next most important product of the New World, and as its cultivation spread, so did the demand for labor. By the second half of the sixteenth century, Indian laborers were replaced by African slaves. In this way, Africans became yet another commodity to be transported across the seas, transforming the New World, robbing Africa of its population, and making the Old World rich.

Once other European nations saw the great wealth the Spanish were extracting from their colonies, they too were attracted to the New World, where they estab-lished their own colonies that came into conflict with the Spanish. The permanent settlements that the Spanish established in the north (e.g., St. Augustine, San Antonio, Santa Fe, and San Francisco) were relatively small communities. In 1522, as the Spanish completed the conquest of Mexico, this territory was still unex-plored, and no European yet knew whether another awe-inspiring civilization might yet be found.

The Return to Florida

The Spanish resumed their exploration of Florida with heightened expectations. There were several ventures, but the two most significant were led by Lucas Vázquez de Ayllón and Hernando de Soto. Ayllón sailed from Hispaniola in 1526. He ex-plored the South Carolina coast and established a short-lived town on the coast of Georgia.

Over the next several decades, the Spanish continued to explore the southern portions of North America. In 1528, Pánfilo de Narváez landed near Tampa Bay with 400 men and the king's commission to explore, conquer, and colonize Florida. Eight years later, a Spanish slaving expedition working in northwest Mexico found the only four survivors of the failed expedition.

The Spaniard who left the greatest mark on the southeastern part of the United States was a *conquistador* of the classic style. Hernando de Soto had participated in the assault on the Inca empire in Peru, which provided him with a small fortune and the belief that more wealth could be found in Florida. He and his forces landed near Tampa Bay in 1539 to explore and settle the region. His party spent four years explor-ing the southeastern part of the continent. They were the first Europeans to see the Mississippi River, plundering regions densely populated by Mississippian tribes. Hernando de Soto came equipped for conquest. He brought with him 600 young sol-diers, a few women and priests, horses, mules, attack dogs, and a walking food supply of hundreds of pigs. He took whatever food, treasure, and people he wanted as he proceeded on his journey. Some Indian communities fought the Spanish fiercely, while others attempted to placate the invaders. In this way de Soto made his way through the Southeast, plundering and battling, his forces slowly diminishing. In May 1542, de Soto himself took sick and died. It was almost a year and a half, however, before the remnants of the expedition, 300 men and one female servant, made their way back to Mexico.

The Spanish never found the great sought-after treasure, and because the land did not seem suitable for the large-scale agriculture of the *encomienda*, Spain never colonized most of the territory that de Soto had explored. Instead, military out-lifted. From that point on, the pace of human sacrifice quickened; the more victims the Aztec sacrificed, the greater their empire seemed to become, and the more they made war against neighboring peoples. The Aztec demanded tribute from conquered peoples, who both feared and resented the Aztec, making them eager allies for the Spanish.

Hernando Cortés came with conquest in mind. He landed on the Yucatán coast with 500 men in February of 1519. After the Tabasco Indians were defeated, they gave him all their gold and 20 slave women, one of whom, Malinche, became Cortés's translator and mistress. As Cortés marched toward Tenochtitlán, he picked up so many Indian allies that they greatly outnumbered his own troops. When they reached the Aztec capital, the ruler, Moctezuma, welcomed them, probably because it was the Aztec custom to offer hospitality to visiting emissaries. The foreigners soon placed Moctezuma under house arrest and laid Tenochtitlán under siege. After three months, in August 1521, the victorious Spanish entered the city, but the proud Aztec refused either to fight or to submit to the Spanish who had starved them. Frustrated, angry, and unable to understand these now-gaunt people, Cortés and his troops killed 12,000 and let their Indian allies slaughter 40,000 more. Then Cortés turned his cannons on the remaining huddled masses of starving Aztec. By the time they surrendered, the once-glittering city was in ruins.

The Establishment of a Spanish Empire

The ruined city became the center of a Spanish empire, with a new political economy based on the extraction of silver and gold and the production of plantation crops. In the next decades, the Spanish defeated another rich and complex civilization, the Inca of Peru, as well as many other tribes of Indians. Spanish rule now extended from

The first meeting of Cortés and his translator and mistress, Malinche, whom the Spanish called Marina. When Europeans encountered Native Americans, women often acted as cultural brokers, negotiating between the two peoples.

The First Florida Ventures

Ambitious Spaniards continued the search for paths to the Orient and cities of gold. As the Spanish moved rapidly through a region in the quest for wealth, they disrupted local political economies by spreading disease and undermining political structures.

Juan Ponce de León was the first European explorer to set foot on the mainland later to be called the United States. In March 1513 Ponce de León reached the Atlantic shore of the land he named Florida, which he mistakenly thought was an island. He and his men sailed around Florida to its gulf coast, encountering hostile Indians who already knew about Spanish slave traders. On the west coast of Florida, he encountered the Calusa, the most powerful tribe in the region. When Ponce de León returned to Florida in 1521 to attempt to establish a village, the Calusa attacked. Ponce de León was wounded by an arrow, and he returned to Cuba to die.

As the Spanish entered Florida, the diseases that they brought with them struck the densely settled agriculturalists particularly hard. Subsequent explorers routinely pillaged local villages and enslaved the Indians, thereby destroying native populations in another way. There were hundreds of small tribes, each with its own history, culture, and political and economic relationships with their neighbors. In this setting, the Spanish at first appeared to the Indians to be either another enemy or a potential ally in their struggles with other tribes.

The Conquest of Mexico

Although the Spanish had continued to believe that vast and wealthy civilizations were to be found in the New World, until 1519 the only peoples they had encountered were small sedentary or semisedentary tribes, who lived in villages of what the Spanish described as huts. They heard tales, however, of the glittering Aztec empire of central Mexico.

The Aztec people had moved into the valley of Mexico only two centuries earlier, but by the time the Spanish appeared, their empire encompassed perhaps 10 or 20 million people, making its population possibly twice as large as Spain's. In several ways, the Aztec resembled the Spanish: They were fierce and warlike and at the same time deeply religious. Despite many differences in culture, the Spanish recognized in the Aztec signs of a complex civilization and distinctive political economy. The Aztec had built many splendid temples and palaces for the nobility. Aztec society was rigidly hierarchical, with a nobility of warriors and priests at the top and slaves (usually captives of war or debtors) at the bottom. Sex roles were rigid as well, with women of all classes expected to remain in the home. Boys and girls attended separate schools, with the boys learning the arts of war and the girls practicing the skills of the homemaker. The Aztec were literate, writing in a form of hieroglyphics on folded animal hide. Only a few of these codices, as the inscribed hides are called, survived the conquest.

The capital city of Tenochtitlán was built on a lake, and it was traversed with canals. With a population of 200,000, it was more than three times the size of Spain's largest city of Seville. Its whitewashed stone pyramids, temples glittering in the sunlight and reflected water, and clean straight avenues made this city a stark contrast to the cramped and dirty streets of a typical Spanish town.

The Aztec believed that the universe was dangerous and unpredictable and that their gods must always be appeased. In the midst of a serious drought about 1450, the Aztec feared that their god Huitzilopochtli was angry with them. When they offered him human hearts, cut out of the living with obsidian knives, the drought

Map 1–2   The Columbian Exchange
The exchanges of plants, animals, and diseases dramatically changed both the Old World and the New.

The Old World also was transformed as plants were introduced from the Americas. Some plants that we associate with Europe came from the Americas. We might identify potatoes with Ireland, tomatoes with Italy, and paprika with Hungary, but none of these foods was produced in Europe before the sixteenth century. Moreover, the cultivation of American foods in the Old World, particularly potatoes, both white and sweet, and maize (corn), which Europeans have generally used as fodder for their livestock, might well have made possible the dramatic growth in world population of the past five centuries.

Onto the Mainland

In a little more than a quarter of a century, the islands inhabited by the Taino had been virtually emptied of their native populations. The Spanish began raiding the islands of the Lesser Antilles and seizing Caribs, transporting them back to the Spanish colonies as slaves. At the same time, other *conquistadores* pushed onto the mainland of America in search of treasure. Indians learned to tantalize the Spanish with accounts of glittering empires just a little further down the trail or up the river, just far enough away to get the Spanish out of their territories. Eventually, the Spanish found the Aztec empire in Mexico and the Inca empire in Peru, which rivaled the most fantastic images from literature and legend.

Hispaniola in 1518, the process was hastened: Soon no more than a 1,000 of the island's original inhabitants survived. Disease soon worked the same terrible destruction on the nearby islands of Cuba, Puerto Rico, and Jamaica. Disease followed the Spanish and other Europeans every place they went in the Americas, making the work of conquest that much easier.

Europeans did not set out to kill off the native inhabitants of the Americas, but that is exactly what the diseases they brought with them did. Isolation had protected the native peoples from the diseases of the Old World, whereas several centuries of trade among Europe, Asia, and Africa had enabled people from the three continents to share and acquire some natural biological defenses. Without such natural immunities, Indians were overcome by wave after wave of European disease. After smallpox came typhus and influenza, which destroyed entire communities and left the survivors weak and demoralized.

These terrible European diseases challenged Native American belief systems. The Cakchiquel Indian Hernández Arana described the spread of a plague in his native Guatemala in 1521 that killed a substantial proportion of the community: "After our fathers and grandfathers succumbed, half of the people fled to the fields. . . . The mortality was terrible. Your grandfathers died, and with them died the son of the king and his brothers and kinsmen. So it was that we became orphans, oh, my sons! . . . We were born to die!" The shock turned Indians against their traditional gods and prepared them to accept the God of the Spaniards.

The transmission of disease was by no means one way, although most diseases seemed to spread from the Old World to the New World. Because syphilis, or at least a particularly virulent strain, first appeared in Europe shortly after Columbus and his crew made their first return voyage in 1493, historians have suggested that Europeans carried this disease back to the Old World. The disease spread rapidly through the world in the late fifteenth and early sixteenth centuries, from Spain to India, China, and Japan. The disease, which killed millions and incapacitated many more, became a legacy of the European age of exploration as it followed traders and armies throughout the world.

The Columbian Exchange

In what historians have called the Columbian exchange, plants and animals, as well as human beings and their diseases, were shared between the two worlds that were connected in 1492, eventually transforming the environments of the Old World and the New. Along with the 1,500 Spaniards that Columbus brought with him on his second voyage, he also carried pigs, cattle, horses, sheep, and goats, as well as sugar cane, wheat, and seeds for fruits and vegetables (see Map 1–2). European animals reproduced rapidly, overrunning the lands that had once been farmed by Indians.

The introduction of these new plants and animals also dramatically transformed the American landscape. Lands once farmed by native agriculturalists were overrun by herds of Old World animals, which trampled old farmlands and grassy regions, leading to their replacement by scrub plants. Indians adapted Old World life forms to their own purposes. American Southwestern and Plains Indian tribes took readily to the horse, which changed their way of life, making them more productive as hunters and more mobile and hence more dangerous as enemies. Mounted Indians could easily kill more buffalo than they needed for their own subsistence, providing them with a surplus that they could trade with Europeans for European goods.

were subjected to overwork and abuse, even if they could not legally be bought and sold as slaves. Spanish settlers' desire to realize a profit in the New World led to a new political economy and with it a form of exploitation unknown in Europe.

The *Requerimiento* and the Morality of Conquest

Throughout the period that Spain maintained a New World empire, there were tensions between the colonizers, who wished to increase their wealth and enhance their power, and the Crown, which wanted to limit the settlers' autonomy. Moreover, both the Spanish Crown and the clergy continued to be troubled by the treatment of the Indians. To clarify the legal basis for the enslavement of hostile Indians, in 1513 the Spanish Crown issued the *Requerimiento* or "Requirement," a document drafted by legal scholars and theologians. The *Requerimiento* promised the Indians that if they accepted the authority of Christianity, the Pope, and the monarchs of Spain, the *conquistadores* would leave them in peace. If, however, the Indians resisted the peaceful imposition of Spanish rule, the *conquistadores* would make war against them and enslave them. Henceforth, each *conquistador* (conqueror) was required to carry a copy of this document with him and to read it to every new group of Indians he encountered.

There is evidence that the *conquistadores* complied with the letter, but not the spirit, of the *Requerimiento*, by mumbling it in Spanish to groups of uncomprehending Indians or reading it from the decks of ships, far from hearing distance. Moreover, the Crown provided no means of enforcement other than the good faith of the *conquistador* or *encomendero* (owner of an *encomienda*). Considering the profits that might be reaped by the subjugation of the population, perhaps what is most surprising is not the failure of the Spanish Crown to protect the Indians, but that it kept trying.

THE BIOLOGICAL CONSEQUENCES OF CONQUEST

Some of the most important changes produced by contact between Europeans and Native Americans were wholly unintentional. Each continent had its own diseases, its own plants, and its own animals. The arrival of Europeans tipped a delicate preindustrial balance in which everyone's effort was often needed to provide a food supply. The Europeans also introduced new diseases that spread like wildfire. If the biological effects of human contact were felt immediately, however, the consequences of plant and animal exchange took much longer. New breeds of animals were introduced from Europe into the Americas, and plants were exchanged between the continents. The face of the American landscape was changed, as domestic animals trampled grasslands and increasing acreage was turned over to the cultivation of Old World crops.

Demographic Decline

Although the *encomienda* system satisfied Spanish settlers, it proved a disaster for the Indians. The agricultural methods of sedentary Indians such as the Taino could not produce the surplus that was necessary to support the Spanish. As soon happened to Indian communities throughout the Americas, the dislocation of their normal way of life proved demoralizing, and the birthrate began to fall.

Within a few years after the appearance of Europeans, the Native American population began to decline, and with the introduction of the smallpox virus to be sold as slaves and distributed another 600 or so among the Spanish settlers on the island of Hispaniola.

Once again a pattern of New World development had been established. The European quest for wealth led to the subjugation of native peoples. Each European nation reacted somewhat differently to this movement toward enslavement. Generally, the Spanish rulers tried to restrain their New World colonizers and protect their new Indian subjects. In 1493, Pope Alexander VI confirmed Spanish dominion over all the lands that Columbus had explored, and he commanded the Spanish "to lead the peoples dwelling in those islands and countries to embrace the Christian religion." The papal bull also established the Church's interest in the spiritual welfare of the Native Americans. A subsequent treaty between Spain and Portugal, the Treaty of Tordesillas of 1494, divided all lands already discovered or to be discovered between Spain and Portugal, along an imaginary line 370 leagues west of the Azores. This treaty formed the basis for Portugal's subsequent claim to Brazil, which her explorers reached in 1500.

As the monarch who had driven the Muslims out of Spain, Isabel took seriously her responsibilities to evangelize her Indian subjects. Isabel and her successors also had political and economic goals, all of which they attempted to reconcile by insisting that the Indians who inhabited the islands seized by the Spanish were vassals, subjects of the Spanish Crown. In this way, Isabel attempted to fit the Indians into the Spanish political economy.

Like other vassals in Spain and its growing empire, the Indians were technically free, although they could be required to both work and pay tribute to the Crown. Isabel instructed the governor to impose on them a European-style civilization. Humane treatment, and with it freedom from slavery, thus would be dependent on the Indians' willingness to abandon their religion and customs and adopt those of the Spanish. It is easy to be cynical about Isabel's motives, but her approach was considerably more benevolent than that of those who were engaged in the colonizing process.

With the Spanish monarchy refusing to sanction the enslavement of friendly Indians, settlers had to devise an alternate means of getting labor from the Native Americans. Out of this struggle a New World political economy emerged. For the first several years, the Spanish simply demanded tribute from the Tainos. Many of the Spanish found this arrangement insufficiently lucrative, and they began to spread across the island of Hispaniola, subduing individual caciques and compelling their villages to work for the Spanish. The Spanish settlers owned neither the land, which had to be obtained through separate grants from Spanish officials, nor the Indians who worked for them. They possessed only the right to compel a particular group of Indians to work. This system, called the *encomienda*, was unique to the New World. Technically it complied with Isabel's insistence that friendly Indians be made vassals of the Crown rather than slaves.

We do not know precisely how the system developed, although there is some evidence that Spanish men first seized native women as their concubines, and that the village men subsequently worked for the Spanish. We often picture the encounter between Indians and Europeans as armed conflict between groups of men. In truth, women often played a critical role in establishing the shape of a biracial society, whether as captives or as willing participants in a European way of life.

Columbus appears to have sanctioned this new system of labor, and it eventually received begrudging support from the monarchs in Spain. Although the system paid due regard to the Indians' legal rights and spiritual requirements, Native Americans

Taino customs. (left) A young man introducing himself to the family of the young woman he wants to marry. (right) The Taino raising their crops in small, carefully-kept gardens. These illustrations come from a manuscript thought to have been written by a Frenchman who traveled to the West Indies with Sir Francis Drake in the sixteenth century.

direction from their cacique; hence it was not long before the Spanish coerced the Tainos into working for them. Although the Tainos sometimes fought among themselves, they were generally peace-loving people.

The Caribs were more aggressive. At the time of Columbus's arrival, the Caribs were moving north from the South American coast into the island chains of the Atlantic. If the energies of the Tainos were directed toward agriculture and the practice of religion, the Caribs focused on trade and warfare. Men and women lived separately, and because Carib men often obtained their wives by raiding other villages, over time they came to treat their own women as if they were captives of war. Because the Caribs were a maritime people whose men were skilled warriors, it is not surprising that they came into conflict with another maritime people practiced in the arts of war, the Spanish.

Although the Spanish, like all the Europeans who followed them into the Americas, depicted themselves as civilized and the Indians as either gentle but primitive or savage and inhuman, the differences between Europeans and natives were not that great. Seven centuries of warfare with the Moors had made the Spanish a fierce people, and they believed that practices that later generations would condemn as cruel were justified for people at war. Once the Spanish decided that the Caribs were an enemy, they began to treat them harshly.

The Origins of a New World Political Economy

As early as Columbus's second voyage of 1493, it became clear that the vast treasures he had anticipated were not readily at hand. His crew, however, expected to be rewarded for their services, and the queen and king who had financed his expedition expected profits. Therefore, Columbus packed off more than 500 Indians to size and configuration of the lands to the east. There was, however, great curiosity about them, fueled by the search for wealth and national power. It was only a matter of time until Europeans headed west and bumped into America while attempting to circumnavigate the globe.

No private individual had the resources to finance such an expedition, so Columbus sought royal patronage. The king of Portugal turned him down, and Columbus departed for Spain, where he sought patronage from Isabel and Fernando. Even though two scientific commissions cast doubt on his geographical assumptions and calculations, the monarchs were intrigued by his vision of a western route to Asia.

The monarchy agreed to finance most of Columbus's trip (paying for it not, as legend has it, by pawning Isabel's jewels, but by the much more modern method of deficit spending) and granted him a number of powers and privileges. Columbus would realize his lifelong ambition of being made a member of the nobility. Columbus was to be named admiral, viceroy, and governor general of all the lands that he might find. After deducting for expenses, Columbus would get to keep one-tenth of the income from the enterprise, with the monarchy retaining the rest. The small amount spent on Columbus's voyages proved in time to be one of the shrewdest investments in the history of nations.

Columbus Finds a New World

The quest for wealth took Columbus back and forth across the Atlantic four times between 1492 and 1504. In those voyages he planted the Spanish flag throughout the Caribbean region, on the islands of Cuba, Hispaniola, and Puerto Rico, as well as on the mainland at Honduras and Venezuela. Ten years later Columbus was still as obsessed by gold as ever: "O, most excellent gold! Who has gold has a treasure with which he gets what he wants, imposes his will on the world, and even helps souls to paradise." The Spaniards who followed him onto the mainland eventually found among the Aztec of Mexico and the Inca of Peru riches to match their most fantastic dreams. By then the patterns that shaped the next century of Spanish–Indian interaction in the Americas had been established.

Late-medieval Europeans tended to view the world in terms of opposites, which led them to exaggerate differences rather than see similarities or complexities. Columbus and subsequent explorers typically described the lands they visited as an earthly paradise, even in the face of contrary evidence. By the time Columbus returned to Hispaniola on his second voyage, accompanied by 1,500 Spaniards, it was clear that his hopes of easy wealth and harmonious relations with the natives were not to be realized. Columbus had left 39 men on the island among the Taino Indian inhabitants and returned to find them all dead, the first of many casualties to the European colonial experience. According to the Taino chieftain, the sailors set off on a spree of gold-seeking and debauchery, fighting among themselves and becoming easy victims for a rival Indian chieftain.

The Spanish could not see the death of their sailors as a predictable response to their behavior. Instead, they fit it into the Europeans' growing perception that all Indians could be divided into two groups: friendly, peace-loving, unsophisticated, "good" Indians, such as the Tainos, and fierce, savage, man-eating "bad" Indians, for whom they used the Taino term "Caribs."

Historians and anthropologists have identified the Tainos and Caribs as two separate tribes, each with different histories and customs. The Tainos, who inhabited the islands of Cuba and Hispaniola, were sedentary farmers whose agriculture could sustain a population as dense as that of Spain. Taino farmers were accustomed to taking works of art such as totem poles and masks. Periodically, these Indians held potlatch ceremonies in which they gave away or even destroyed all their possessions. When Europeans first encountered this practice, they found it bizarre and even dangerous, so contrary was it to the doctrines of capitalism.

The Great Civilizations of the Americas

Although the Indian peoples north of the Rio Grande River were primarily agriculturalists or hunter-gatherers, several of those to the south developed much more complex political economies, technologies, and urban cultures. The splendid Maya civilization, which had developed both a writing system and mathematics, had dominated southern Mexico and Central America from the fourth to the tenth centuries. Historians do not know for certain why the Maya cultural centers declined, but the causes may have been a change in climate or ecology that made it impossible for Maya agriculture to support so large a population.

The next great empire in the region was that of the Toltecs, whose influence extended from central Mexico as far north perhaps as the cliff-dwelling Anasazi of the American Southwest. After the Toltec empire was destroyed in the middle of the twelfth century by invaders from the north, the Aztec people dominated the region until their own defeat at the hands of a Spanish and Indian alliance.

Worlds in Collision

Columbus's voyages to the Americas marked the beginning of a new era. The world was made immeasurably smaller, and peoples who had lived in isolation from one another were brought into close contact. In this great age of European exploration, Bartolomeo Dias rounded the African cape in 1488, Vasco da Gama reached India in 1498, and an expedition led by Ferdinand Magellan (Fernão Magalhães in Portuguese) sailed around the world between 1519 and 1522. These explorers were seeking not to discover new lands but to find faster routes to old ones. They were propelled by an expanding Europe's desire for trade and for spreading the Christian religion. For the first time in human history, all of the world's great urban civilizations, from Tenochtitlán to Cathay, knew of one another's existence. Moreover, despite the obvious differences in language, dress, architecture, art, and customs, Europeans, Africans, and Native Americans lived in political and economic organizations similar enough to make trade and diplomacy possible. Europeans drew the entire world into their trade network, and the Christian religion was spread by both force and persuasion.

Christopher Columbus Finds a Patron

Between 1492 and 1504, Columbus made four voyages to America, sailing for Queen Isabel and King Fernando of Spain. Born in 1451 in the Italian city-state of Genoa, Columbus first went to sea on merchant ships that sailed the Mediterranean. In the 1470s, he began sailing to Portuguese outposts such as the Madeiras. Within a decade, Columbus had decided to seek support for a voyage to China and Japan, which he had read about in Marco Polo's book.

Columbus's ambitions were shaped by his reading and his extensive experience as a mariner, which had already taken him thousands of miles from the place of his birth. By Columbus's time, it was generally known that the world was round, but its precise dimensions had not been determined, nor were Europeans certain about the almost entirely on persuasion rather than force. The requirement of the consent of all concerned, women included, made the Iroquois particularly cohesive: By the time the Europeans arrived, the Iroquois were able to subdue internal violence, direct it outward at the interlopers, and keep them at bay for more than two centuries.

The Indians of the Plains

The popular image of the Plains Indian comes from Westerns: the brave on horseback, hunting bison. Plains Indians, however, did not have horses until after the Spanish reintroduced horses to the Great Plains in the sixteenth century (they had died out at the end of the Pleistocene era). Like Indians east of the Mississippi, Plains Indians became agriculturalists after the end of the Archaic era. Women were responsible for raising maize and other crops, while men traveled periodically to hunt buffalo. Hunters stampeded buffalo into enclosures, where they ambushed them or forced them to jump over steep cliffs to their death.

After the Spanish brought horses to the Plains, these Indians became nomadic, abandoning their multifamily lodges for tipis that could be carried from one campsite to the next. Buffalo then became a more important part of their diet. With this shift, women's prestige decreased and men's grew.

The Indians of the Deserts

The arid landscape of the desert in the West and Southwest shaped the Indian cultures in those regions. Over the centuries, Indians learned to make maximum use of native plants and to cultivate increasingly productive strains of maize. The population remained relatively small, but by about 200 C.E., villages began to appear. At that time, southwestern Indians began to construct pithouses, round dwellings carved about a foot and a half into the ground with walls and roofs constructed out of mud-covered wooden frameworks.

After 700 C.E., as the population grew, southwestern Indians moved out of these pit houses into adobe pueblos. These huge complexes must have required the labor of well-organized work forces. Abandoned pithouses were turned into kivas, chambers for the practice of religious ceremonies, sometimes reserved exclusively for men.

Like the cities of the eastern mound builders, the Anasazi Indian communities at Chaco Canyon, Mesa Verde, and several other sites simply disappeared, Chaco sometime after 1100 C.E. And Mesa Verde in the last quarter of the thirteenth century. Archaeologists are not certain why, but recent theories for the abandonment of Mesa Verde suggest a combination of prolonged drought, the need to fight off outsiders, and a new and attractive religion that pulled people to the south, away from the dry climate and hostile neighbors.

The Indians of the Pacific Coast

Along the California and Northwest Pacific coast, plentiful fish, game, and edible plants permitted the population to grow even in the absence of agriculture. In California, the variety of local environments meant that each of 500 local cultures could concentrate on its own specialties, which it traded with its neighbors. The Northwest coastal environment was more uniform, but no less lush, and its inhabitants enjoyed a surplus of food. With so little work needed to supply the food needs of the community, Northwest Coast Indians were able to build up surpluses and create magnificent and the Iroquois were matrilineal (tracing descent through the woman) and matrilocal (with husbands moving into their wives' clans), but in many other ways, the two cultures were similar. The Iroquois and Algonquians south of Canada practiced a slash-and-burn method of agriculture: clearing and burning forests for corn and other vegetables, planting them intensively, exhausting the soil, and then moving on to more fertile regions, where clearings once again were burned. This method of agriculture could not sustain as large a population as the fertile river valley cultivation of the mound builders; nonetheless, farming became increasingly efficient, making hunting less important. Because almost all agriculture was the work of women, their prestige in their villages increased.

The Iroquois and Algonquians were fierce people, more violent than the Mississippians, although scholars are not certain why. One theory suggests that as agriculture became more efficient and women's prestige increased, men resorted to warfare to maintain their own prestige. By the eve of European settlement, many Iroquois tribes had banded together in a confederacy to limit infighting and to strengthen them against external enemies. Political influence within these cultures depended

The community at Cahokia, as reconstructed by an artist. The town was surrounded by a stockade, which enclosed the mounds, plazas, temples, and homes.

to hunt smaller game that ranged over a much smaller region than their huge predecessors, and therefore the tribes became less nomadic. They established base camps to which they returned periodically. Their tools became more sophisticated, and they began storing some food, which gave them the ability to survive shortages.

As the Archaic Indians became more efficient in their hunting and gathering, they began to adapt the environment to their needs, for example by periodically burning undergrowth to create an ideal environment for deer. By 3,000 B.C.E., some groups were beginning to cultivate native plants. The population in North America grew to perhaps 1 million. Although the Archaic Indians still lived in small groups of probably no more than 500, they became less egalitarian.

Changes in the North American climate during the Archaic period led to other, more significant differences among Native American's political economies. While the Eastern Woodlands area (generally, east of the Mississippi River) was moist and hence hospitable to agriculture, the Plains region (between the Mississippi River and the Rocky Mountains) was arid. Plains Indians lived in small, highly mobile bands and pursued big game such as bison, elk, bear, and deer.

Further west, in the desert-like Great Basin and Southwest regions, Indians subsisted on small game and seeds. These peoples learned how to use the little moisture available to them, and they domesticated several crops, including maize (corn) and chiles. Some groups became sedentary, building pueblos and cliff dwellings as permanent homes.

On the California coast and in the Pacific Northwest, Archaic hunter-gatherers made use of the abundant natural resources, particularly fish. They also began to develop striking artwork. Another regional culture began to develop south of the Arctic Circle, where Native Americans began to develop the boats, weapons, and tools necessary to hunt whales and seals. Out of these regional environments—Eastern Woodlands, Plains, Great Basin and Southwest, California and Pacific Coast, and Subarctic—developed the distinctive Indian cultures that European explorers later encountered. By the time of Columbus's voyage, these Indian peoples were as different from one another as the peoples of Europe.

The Indians of the Eastern Woodlands

A distinctive Eastern Woodlands Indian culture had developed by 700 B.C.E., when Indians in this area began to cultivate crops. A succession of cultures inhabited the Mississippi and Ohio River valleys and the southeastern quadrant of the United States between 700 B.C.E. and about 1500 C.E., distinguished by the areas in which they lived, the increasing complexity of their crafts, the extent of their trade networks, and their increasing capacity to support large populations from their agriculture. All of them built mounds in which to bury their dead and as platforms for temples and other public structures.

These Indian societies were increasingly hierarchical in their political and social organizations. Some offices were probably hereditary, and large cities such as Cahokia (with a population of between 10,000 and 30,000) dominated smaller ones. When powerful people died, they were buried with huge stores of luxury goods gathered through trade routes that stretched throughout the continent. Because Woodlands Indians buried these goods with the dead, rather than passing them on from generation to generation, they had to keep trading for new supplies. They also crafted exquisite objects out of metal and stone to bury with their dead and to trade to distant tribes.

In the Eastern Woodlands, the Iroquois occupied the southern Great Lakes region, and the Algonquians covered much of eastern Canada and the northeastern United States, as far south as Virginia. These two groups spoke different languages,

By focusing the attention and energy of their nobles against a non-Christian opponent, Isabel and Fernando forged a Christian Spanish national identity that transcended regional loyalties. Herself an exceedingly devout Christian, Isabel had earlier inaugurated an Inquisition, a Church tribunal authorized by the Pope, to root out converted Jews and others who seemed insufficiently sincere Christians. By the time the Inquisition was complete, several hundred Spanish people had been burned at the stake and several thousand more imprisoned. Spain finally conquered the Moorish province of Granada in the spring of 1492. Militant Christians soon insisted on a forcible conversion and baptism of those Moors who chose to remain in the region. The Christian conquest of the Moors led swiftly to the eviction of another religious minority, the Jews. Less than three months after the fall of Granada, Isabel and Fernando signed an edict calling for the expulsion of the approximately 150,000 Jews who resided in their kingdom. The Spanish colonization of the Americas and the subjugation of their native peoples were simply the next chapters in the reign of Isabel and Fernando, the rulers of a nation whose identity was defined by its ability to vanquish those they defined as infidels.

It would be a mistake, however, to conclude that Spain was shaped by militarism and intolerance alone. In 1492, Spain was in the middle of its golden age. It was the most dynamic nation in Europe, and it soon became the most powerful. It welcomed and absorbed foreign influences, including Moorish art, science, and customs; Flemish art and architecture; and Italian humanism. Under the patronage of Queen Isabel, Spain became a center of this Renaissance intellectual movement, known as humanism.

Spain's foray into the New World was both a commercial venture and a religious crusade. It was also fueled by the humanist spirit of discovery. In establishing colonies in the New World, Spain spread her religion, her language, and her culture, creating a new political economy in the process.

THE WORLD OF THE INDIAN PEOPLES

At the end of the fifteenth century, America comprised several large and powerful states, as well as a number of peoples who lived in less complex social organizations, each with different political economies, traditions, cultures, and values. This diversity had its origins at least 12,000 years earlier when people known as the Archaic or Paleo-Indians crossed from Siberia into Alaska. By the time of Columbus's voyage, there were hundreds of separate Indian cultures, speaking 375 different languages. The total native population of America north of the Rio Grande might have been as high as 18 million (with that of Europe perhaps five or six times higher).

The Archaic Indians

The first Americans were hunter-gatherers who followed the mammoth and other huge animals across the land bridge from Asia. Once they had dispersed throughout America, they lived in small bands of perhaps two dozen people who occasionally interacted with other bands. Social and political relations among the Paleo-Indians were probably highly egalitarian, except for differences based on age or gender. Work, for example, was assigned by gender, with men hunting the large game and women gathering nuts, berries, and other foods. The Paleo-Indians did not plant or store food, and hence they lived close to the edge of extinction.

With the end of the Ice Age, around 10,000 B.C. E., America's Paleo-indians had to adapt to a world without the huge animals that had been their prey. They learned

As in Europe, slavery had been practiced in Africa from ancient times, although its character was different because of Africa's different political economy. In Europe, land was the primary form of private, wealth-creating property. In Africa, however, land was owned collectively, and the primary form of private, wealth-creating property was slaves. European law entitled the land owner to everything that was produced on the land, while African law entitled the slave owner to everything that the slave produced.

The African continent was divided among a number of different states that sustained a vigorous internal slave trade. In addition, as the Islamic empire spread in the eighth century, Muslim merchants bought slaves in Africa, usually women and children, for export to other regions of the empire. The African slave trade thus had two components: an internal trade within the continent and an external trade, run primarily by the Muslims. When the Portuguese entered the slave trade, they participated in both components.

Western and central Africans were accustomed to selling slaves, and they entered willingly into the global slave trade. By the seventeenth century, the high prices that Europeans were willing to pay for slaves stimulated the African slave trade and stripped the continent of much of its population.

The Golden Age of Spain

Portugal was the first nation in western Europe to achieve political unity, and hence it was the first to embark on exploration in search of trade. Spain was the second. Until the end of the fifteenth century, the Iberian Peninsula was divided into five independent kingdoms. At one time, the entire Iberian Peninsula had been dominated by Muslims, who had invaded the region from North Africa in 711. Islamic culture exerted a powerful influence in the region. Many Spanish people intermarried with the Muslims, adopting their religion and customs, such as the seclusion of women.

At the time of the invasion, Arab civilization was more sophisticated than that of the people they conquered. Through the Muslims, Greek science was reintroduced into a region that had lost touch with much ancient learning. Muslim, Christian, and Jewish communities generally were able to co-exist. Local leaders, however, for reasons that were political and economic as well as cultural and religious, contested the rule of the Muslims and entered into a 700-year period of intermittent warfare known as the *reconquista* or "reconquest."

Warfare became a normal and expected part of life on the Iberian Peninsula, and it shaped society accordingly. The surest path to wealth and honor lay in plunder and conquest, and a *hidalgo*'s (gentleman's) honor was defined by his capacity to vanquish the Muslims and seize their land and wealth. The Spanish hoped that the *reconquista* would be able to evict from their country those they considered infidels.

By the time Christopher Columbus arrived in Spain in 1485, the Muslims had been ousted from all of Spain except Granada. Castile and Aragon had recently been joined by the marriage of Isabel, princess of Castile, and her cousin Fernando, prince of Aragon. Although Isabel was only 18 at the time of her marriage (and her husband a year younger), she had already demonstrated herself to be a woman of boldness and determination. Because the match was more in Aragon's interest than in Castile's, Isabel was able to dictate the terms of the marriage contract, making it clear that she would play the leading role in governing. Having consolidated their power and asserted their authority over their territories, Isabel and Fernando turned their attention to the final stage of the *reconquista*.

and well-organized kingdoms, much like the European states. Some of those states, especially those just south of the Sahara such as Mali and Songhay, had been deeply influenced by Islam and had adopted its written language. Others, such as the central African Yoruba kingdoms, were complex city-states that produced glorious works of art in bronze and ivory. The population density in the Lower Guinea region was higher than that of Europe.

Not all African peoples lived in states, however. Many were members of villages or family groupings without rulers or bureaucracies. Despite this political diversity, religious beliefs were similar among the African cultures, with Africans recognizing a supreme creator and numerous lesser deities. Gender relations among the African peoples were similar, too, with most people living in extended, male-led families and clans. Although men performed most of the heavy labor and women attended to domestic chores and childrearing, both men and women engaged in farming. Men dominated government and commerce, but on occasion women from prominent families exercised power. Women were active as merchants as well.

Powerful kingdoms dominated commerce and welcomed trade with Europe, which supplied them with prestigious goods. Although Africans themselves manufactured cloth, for example, European textiles found a ready market in Africa. In fact, it was precisely those regions of Africa that already had thriving markets that were most eager to trade with Europeans. Soon African nations willingly entered a global market.

As in Europe, at any given moment in Africa some kingdoms were increasing their dominance while others were in eclipse. But such normal political developments took on new meaning after the appearance of Europeans. In 1591 the defeat of the Songhay empire by Moroccan invaders created instability in West Africa that offered unique opportunities for Europeans to profit.

Slavery Before 1500

The institution of slavery had a long history in both Europe and Africa. In general, slavery had been of limited importance in Europe, except in ancient Rome. The Roman Empire enslaved a number of the peoples it conquered, using them to raise food for the densely populated center of the empire in Italy. Unlike modern slavery, Roman slavery was not based on race, and Roman slaves came from a great variety of ethnic groups.

By the time Portugal opened its trade with West Africa, slavery had disappeared from northwestern Europe, although some slaves were being used in parts of Christian Europe along the Mediterranean. The Muslims who invaded Spain and other regions along the Mediterranean in the eighth century had brought their form of slavery with them. In addition to working as domestic servants, these slaves were used in the production of sugar.

Several centuries later, when European merchants expanded their trade into regions controlled by the Muslims, they also began plying the trade in human beings. Slavery had been a relatively minor institution in Portugal, Spain, Sicily, Cyprus, and other regions of Europe that touched the Mediterranean. However, once Portugal took over the Atlantic island of Madeira and Spain controlled the Canary Islands, the cultivation of sugar brought into being the much larger systems of plantation slavery. At first the Europeans enslaved native islanders, and soon after, they imported Africans. Hence Europeans such as Columbus who lived and sailed along the Mediterranean would have been familiar with the slave trade and would have associated slavery with plantation agriculture.

New France: An Outpost in the Global Political Economy

The Spanish had given up hopes of an empire along the Atlantic coast of North America, but they had succeeded in scaring off the French. After the massacre at Fort Caroline, the French focused their interest on the St. Lawrence region. By the beginning of the seventeenth century the French had discovered a new way to make a profit in North America. French fishing crews, working off the coast of New-foundland, traded for beaver pelts with the coastal Abenaki Indians. These pelts found a ready market in Europe, where they were turned into felt hats. A trade that began almost as an accident soon became the basis for the French empire in Canada. The French were drawing the Indians into a global economy, a process that dramatically changed not only the political economy of the North Americans, but that of the Europeans as well.

The Indian Background to French Settlement

The French intruded on a region where warfare among Indian tribes had been wide-spread and prevalent, although limited in scope. Eastern Woodlands clans and tribes of both the Algonquian and Iroquois culture groups were almost always at war, but the total casualties, unlike those in the European wars, were generally light. These fights were blood feuds called mourning wars. When a member of a clan was lost in battle, his tribesmen, encouraged by his tribeswomen, sought revenge on the enemy clan, either killing or seizing a warrior, who was adopted into the tribe to replace the dead clan member. If the clan's grief was particularly great, many captives might be necessary to repair the emotional loss. Such warfare was accompanied by rituals that mourned the loss of the clan member, prepared warriors for battle, and integrated captives into their new clan. It also focused violence outward. The cruelty that Indi-ans practiced on their enemies shocked Europeans, whose own societies were quite brutal. Unlike in European society, violence within the clan was almost unknown.

By the fifteenth century, the mourning war was taking too great a toll among the Iroquois of northern New York. Sometime after 1400 (and perhaps as late as 1600), the five tribes that lived south of the St. Lawrence River and east of Lake Ontario, primarily in what is now upper New York state, created an alliance called the Five Nations or Great League of Peace (see Map 2–2). The league strengthened the Iroquois when they encountered their traditional enemies such as the Algonquians and Hurons, a powerful Iroquoian tribe that was not a member of the league, and their new adversary, the French.

Champlain Encounters the Hurons

After Cartier's last voyage in 1541, the French waited more than half a century before again attempting to plant a settlement in Canada, because they were preoccupied with a brutal civil war. In 1594, Henry of Navarre, a Huguenot, emerged the victor, converted to Catholicism, and in 1598 issued the Edict of Nantes, which granted lim-ited religious toleration to the Huguenots. The bloodshed over, France could once again look outward to North America.

The French had continued to fish off Newfoundland, and entrepreneurs began sending ships to the mainland to trade for beaver pelts. The French Crown now realized that commerce with the Indians could increase its power and wealth. Several early ventures to establish a permanent settlement failed, but in 1608,

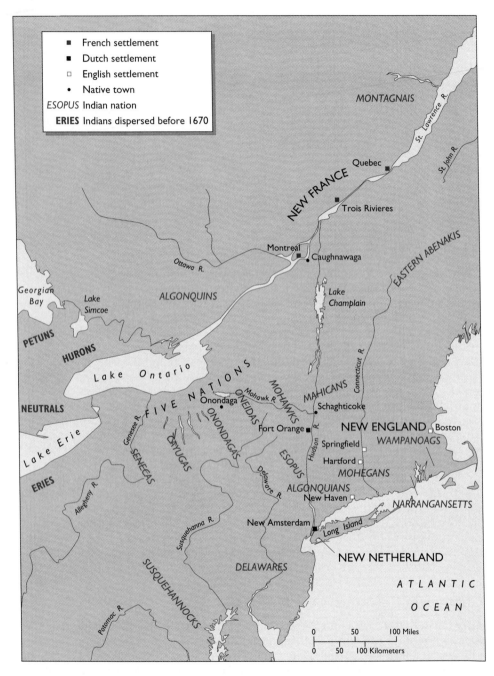

Map 2–2   The Iroquois Region in the Middle of the Seventeenth Century

By the middle of the seventeenth century, the French, Dutch, and English had all established trading posts on the fringe of the Iroquois homeland. In the Beaver War (c. 1648–1660), discussed later in the chapter, the Iroquois lashed out at their neighbors, dispersing several Huron tribes.

Source: Matthew Dennis, Cultivating a Landscape of Peace (New York: Cornell University Press, 1993), p. 16.

Samuel de Champlain and a small band retraced Cartier's route up the St. Lawrence River and established a post at Quebec (see Map 2–3). Champlain created a trading network along the St. Lawrence River and learned how to live among people with a culture different from his own.

The French government provided little support for Champlain's expedition to New France beyond a temporary monopoly on trade with the Indians. Without significant support from France, Champlain's party depended on their Montagnais Indian (an Algonquian tribe) hosts. The price they had to pay to survive in New France was adapting to Indian customs and assisting their Indian benefactors in wars against their enemy.

Over the next several years, Champlain established a fur trade in the St. Lawrence region, linking the French and the Indians in a transformed global political economy. Peasants were transplanted to New France in 1614 to raise food for the traders; Catholic priests were sent to convert the Native Americans. The missionaries were more successful than the peasants. The persistence of the Catholic missionaries, their willingness to adapt to a strange environment, and their ability to translate their religion into terms that were meaningful to Native Americans eventually gained them numerous converts.

Map 2–3 French Exploration and Settlement, 1603–1616
Between 1603 and 1616, Samuel de Champlain and other French explorers made numerous trips up the St. Lawrence River and along the New England coast as far south as Cape Cod. They established several settlements, and they traded with local Indians and fought with them as well.

After Champlain's original monopoly expired, his group competed with other Frenchmen in the fur trade. To maintain a competitive edge, each summer Champlain pushed further up the St. Lawrence River from his base at Quebec to intercept the Indian tribes who were bringing pelts to the east. Each winter he also sent some of his men to live among the western Hurons and Algonquians, to learn their languages and customs and to strengthen the trading partnerships that had been established. These Indians already engaged in an extensive trade in corn, fish, nets, wampum, and other items. As French traders and Huron and Algonquian hunters created a trade network, each group became dependent on the other.

Creating a Middle Ground in New France

Indians and French traders proved able to accommodate each other's cultural practices. Together Indians and French traders on the frontier created a middle ground out of two different traditions.

As the French drew the Native Americans into a vast global trade network, the Indians began to hunt more beaver than they needed for their own purposes, depleting the beaver population. Some historians believe that the introduction of European goods and commerce into Native American cultures destroyed them from within by making them dependent on those goods and inducing them to abandon their own crafts. Others have pointed out that the trade had different meanings for the French and for the Indians. For the French, trade was important for its cash value; for the Indians, trade goods were important both for the uses to which they could be put and for their symbolic value in religious ceremonies.

This drawing depicts the torture of a war captive. The French thought that Indian forms of warfare, including torture, were barbaric, not because Europeans did not practice torture, but because they did not torture other soldiers.

Indians integrated European goods into their traditional practices, breaking up brass pots, for example, into small pieces that could be made into jewelry. Iron tools enabled Indian craftspeople to create more detail in their decorative arts. Just as the Indians were pulled into an international trade network centered in Europe, the French were drawn into the Indians' style of life and political and economic concerns. Traders and priests learned to sleep on the cold ground without complaint and to eat Indian foods. Many French traders found Indian wives. Both the Indians and the French believed that mixed marriages provided a strong foundation for trading and military alliances.

The French were drawn into their Huron and Algonquian allies' political economy as well. To keep the furs flowing east, they had to take part in war parties, usually against the Iroquois, to finance their allies' battles, and to purchase their loyalty with annual payments, which the Indians considered "presents." As long as the French maintained a presence in this region of North America, they attempted to manipulate their Indian allies for their own benefit, just as those tribes tried to maneuver the French to serve their own needs. There were costs and benefits on both sides.

The arrival of the French stimulated competition among the regional tribes for the positions of brokers between the French and the other Indian tribes who had furs to trade. The pace and nature of Indian warfare, which had always been fierce, now changed dramatically, for a new motive had been introduced; control of the lucrative fur trade. With a combination of honed diplomatic skill and liberal dispensing of presents, French officials were usually able to quell the infighting among their allies. Because they were attentive to Indian customs and willing to accommodate them, the French were the best diplomats in North America, and their Indian allies were the most loyal.

An Outpost in a Global Political Economy

New France began as a tiny outpost. By the end of the seventeenth century, it had increased in both size and importance. The French population in North America reached 2,000 in 1650 and 19,000 in 1714, and the primary focus of New France remained the fur trade. In the 1630s, missionaries began to arrive in significant numbers, making the conversion of Indians to Catholicism the second most important endeavor in the colony. At the same time, the Huron population decreased dramatically. A series of epidemics cut the population in half, carrying off many of Huronia's leaders. The result was internal conflict and political instability that left the Hurons vulnerable to their Indian enemies and increasingly dependent on their French allies. At the same time, the French depended on the Hurons and Algonquians to keep bringing them furs. The Hurons, in fact, operated as middlemen, not trapping beaver themselves, but acquiring beaver pelts from other tribes.

By the middle of the seventeenth century, the supply of beaver in the regions closest to European settlements began to diminish. Before the arrival of the French, the Indians had trapped only enough for their own use. The huge European demand for beaver, however, led Indians to kill more beaver than could be replaced by natural reproduction. As a result, Europeans (or to be more precise, the Indians who acted as middlemen) extended their trade routes farther and farther north and west. This expansion drew increasing numbers of Indians into the global economy.

The European demand for beaver pelts was insatiable. To provide more trade goods, the French increased domestic manufacturing of cloth, metal implements, guns, and other goods that were attractive to the Indians. This pattern, in which the mother country produced goods to be sold or traded in foreign colonies for raw materials, was replicated in England and Holland. None of these nations found the treasures in the Americas that Spain had located in Mexico and Peru. Instead, they found new products, such as beaver pelts, for which there was a growing demand in Europe.

A new economic theory called mercantilism developed to guide the growth of European nation-states and their New World colonies. Mercantilism's objective was to strengthen the nation-state by making the economy serve its interests. According to the theory, the world's wealth, measured in gold and silver, could never be increased. As a result, each nation's economic objective must be to secure as much of the world's wealth as possible. One nation's gain was necessarily another's loss. The role of colonies was to provide raw materials and markets for manufactured goods for the mother country. Hence national competition for colonies and markets was not only about economics, but about politics and diplomacy as well. The strength of the nation was thought to depend on its ability to dominate international trade.

NEW NETHERLAND: THE EMPIRE OF A TRADING NATION

In many ways, the Dutch venture into North America resembled that of France. It began with an intrepid explorer in quest of a Northwest Passage and a government that was unwilling to invest in a North American colony. Unlike the French, however, the Dutch government assigned the task of establishing a trading settlement almost entirely to a private company. And because Holland was a Protestant nation, there were no activist Catholic priests in New Netherland to spread their religion and oppose the excesses of a commercial economy. Even more than the French and Spanish colonies, then, New Netherland was shaped by the forces of commerce.

Colonization by a Private Company

Much like England, the other major commercial power at the time, the Netherlands was rising to power as a merchant nation. The nation had secured its independence from Spain after a long and bloody war, which ended in 1648. The Netherlands was Protestant, committed to a market economy, and sustained by a thriving middle class. Indeed, Amsterdam was the center of the world's economy. The Netherlands had a distinctive political economy, with neither a powerful aristocracy nor an oppressed peasantry. Its government and economy were dominated by prosperous merchants.

Holland was the home of the Renaissance humanist Erasmus, and his values of toleration and moderation permeated society. Jews who had been expelled from Spain found a home in the Netherlands alongside strict Calvinists (Protestants who believed in predestination). The spirit of tolerance enabled the Dutch to put aside religious and political conflict and turn their attentions to trade.

It was an accident that the Dutch and not the British claimed the Hudson River valley. Henry Hudson, an English explorer, sailed three times for the English, testing his theory that a Northwest Passage could be found by sailing over the North Pole. Hudson also provided the Dutch with a claim to the Hudson River valley. In 1609 he persuaded a group of Dutch merchants who traded in Asia, the Dutch East India Company, to finance another venture. Sailing on the *Halve Maen* (*Half Moon* in English), Hudson and his crew headed toward the Chesapeake Bay, which he believed offered a passage to the Pacific. He sailed along the coast, anchoring in New York harbor and trading with the local Algonquian Indians. He pushed up the Hudson as far as Albany, where he discovered that the river narrowed, apparently disproving his theory about a water passage through North America.

Within two years of Hudson's "discovery" of the river that still bears his name, Dutch merchants returned to the region, and in 1614 a group of merchants calling themselves the New Netherland Company secured a temporary monopoly for trade between the Delaware and Connecticut Rivers. The trade was so profitable that other merchant groups were attracted to the region. In 1621 the Dutch West India Company obtained a monopoly for trade with both the Americas and Africa that also entitled it to establish colonies in "fruitful and unsettled parts." The only way investors or settlers could be attracted to a remote colony was by the promise of profits. Within a few years, the Dutch West India company established settlements at Fort Orange (present-day Albany) and New Amsterdam (present-day New York City) and purchased the entire island of Manhattan from local Algonquian Indians for a meager 60 florins' worth of merchandise. The first 30 families arrived in 1624. Settlers were supposed to serve the fur trade, either by trading with the regional Indians (the Iroquois to the north and the Delaware to the south) or by providing support for the traders. All the profits were reserved for the Company, with the settlers given small salaries.

Until the Company was willing to offer better terms to settlers, the colony grew very slowly. There were 270 inhabitants in 1628, 500 in 1640, and fewer than 9,000 in 1664. It was difficult to attract settlers from a prosperous nation that permitted its people greater religious and political freedom than was customary in most European countries.

The Company experimented with a number of policies to draw colonists to New Netherland. In 1629, it offered huge plots of land (18 miles along the Hudson River) and extensive governing powers to patroons, men who would bring 50 settlers to the new colony. It also offered smaller grants of land to individuals who would farm the land and return to the Company one-tenth of what they produced. Both approaches placed restrictions on land ownership and self-government, and neither was successful. In 1640, the Company offered greater rights of self-government and 200 acres to anyone who brought over five adult immigrants. This policy worked better, and only a few decades into its existence New Netherland had become a magnet for peoples from a wide variety of cultures and nations. As the colony grew in population, it expanded up the Hudson, out from the island of Manhattan into New Jersey and Long Island, and as far south as the Delaware River.

In most European nations at the time, social order was maintained by a combination of state authority and cohesive religious structures and values. Where the religious or government order was fractured, as in France, bloody civil war was the result. In New Netherland, however, not only religious structure, but also the force of government was relatively weak. The governors were caught between the Company, which expected to earn a profit, and the settlers, who wanted to prosper themselves. Peter Stuyvesant, governor from 1647 until the English takeover in 1664, was the most successful of the governors, but even he could not fully control New Netherland's disorder.

In one year alone, at a time when the population numbered less than 1,000, there were 50 civil suits and almost as many criminal prosecutions. The rate of alcohol consumption seems to have been higher in New Netherland than in any other colony on the North American mainland. In 1645, there were between 150 and 200 houses in New Amsterdam—and 35 taverns! As a consequence, one of Stuyvesant's first acts as governor was to shut the bars at nine o'clock at night. There were also complaints of sexual promiscuity, bar brawls, and mischief caused by sailors on shore leave.

Stuyvesant met with no more success in regulating the economy. He attempted to set prices on such commodities as beer and bread, but he was overruled by the Company, which feared that controls on economic activity would thwart further immigration. In a pattern that would eventually prevail in all of the North American colonies settled by the Netherlands and England, commerce triumphed.

Slavery and Freedom in the Dutch Political Economy

The desire to enrich by commerce the colony, the Company, and the nation led eventually to the introduction of African slavery into New Netherland. The fur trade did not prove as lucrative as investors had hoped, and the Company found that European agricultural workers "sooner or later apply themselves to trade, and neglect agriculture altogether." The Company decided that the primary function of New Netherland should be to provide food for its more lucrative plantation colonies in Brazil and the Caribbean. Earlier in the century, the Dutch had seized a portion of northern Brazil from Portugal, introduced a sugar-plantation slave economy, and transplanted that economy to islands in the Caribbean. By that time they had also entered the transatlantic slave trade.

In the context of the Netherlands' lucrative trade in sugar and slaves, the colony at New Netherland was only a sideshow. Hoping to make the colony profitable, the Company turned to enslaved Africans. By 1664, there were perhaps 700 slaves in the colony, and slaves made up a considerable portion (about 8 percent) of New Netherland's population.

Holland was perhaps the most tolerant nation of its day, and the Dutch Reformed Church accepted Africans as well as Indians as converts, provided they could demonstrate their knowledge of the Dutch religion. The Dutch Reformed Church did not oppose the institution of slavery, however. Moreover, the strict nature of Dutch Calvinism placed limits on the Church's toleration.

The primary force for tolerance in New Netherland was the Dutch West India Company, which saw religious toleration as necessary to commercial prosperity. When the head of the Dutch Reformed Church in New Netherland and Governor Stuyvesant attempted to prevent the entry of 23 Dutch Jews whom the Portuguese had expelled from northern Brazil, they were reversed by the Company. The directors, some of whom were Jews, clarified the relationship between religious tolerance and commercial prosperity: "You may . . . allow everyone to have his own belief, as long as he behaves quietly and legally, gives no offence to his neighbors and does not oppose the government."

The Company also advocated a policy of fairness to the local Indian tribes. They insisted that land must be purchased from its original owners before Europeans could settle on it. Because some individual settlers were coercing Indians to sell their land cheap, in 1652 Stuyvesant forbade purchases of land without government approval.

It might appear puzzling that the Dutch officials and merchants whose policies encouraged toleration of religious minorities and justice toward Native Americans would also introduce and encourage slavery in North America. The Dutch were not motivated, however, by abstract ideals of toleration or equality. The primary goal of the founders of New Netherland was profit through trade. Toleration of religious and cultural diversity, amicable relations with local Indians, and African slavery all served that end.

The Dutch–Indian Trading Partnership

In the 40 years that the Dutch maintained their colony of New Netherland, its most profitable activity was the fur trade. As the French had done to the north, the Dutch disrupted the balance among regional Indian tribes. The arrival of the Europeans, rather than uniting the Indians, heightened long-standing local animosities. Tribes came to rely on their European allies not only for goods but also for weapons and even soldiers to fight their enemies.

Both the Indians and Europeans were playing a dangerous game, that required a constant low level of violence to prevent outsiders from moving in on an established trade. Yet if the violence escalated into full-fledged warfare, it disrupted the very trade it was designed to protect. As a result, the trade frontier between Indians and Europeans was always filled with peril.

The Dutch began trading in the Albany region around 1614 and built Fort Orange there a decade later. This small outpost was in the middle of a region inhabited by the Mahican tribe, an Algonquian people who gave the Dutch access to the furs trapped by other Algonquian tribes to the north. The Dutch began assisting the Mahicans in their trade rivalry with the Mohawks (an Iroquois nation) only to find themselves attacked—and defeated—by the Mohawks. The Mohawks asked for peace: Their objective was not to eliminate the Dutch, but to secure them as trade partners.

By 1628 the Mohawks had defeated the Mahicans and forced them to move east, into Connecticut, establishing the Mohawks as the most powerful force in the region. Kiliaen van Rensselaer, the patroon of a vast estate next to Fort Orange, complained that "the savages, who are now stronger than ourselves, will not allow others who are hostile and live farther away and have many furs to pass through their territory." The Dutch and the Mohawks abandoned their former hostility for a generally peaceful trading partnership.

The Dutch did what was necessary to maintain their lucrative trade. Sometimes that meant giving the Indians gifts, including liquor. At other times, it meant cutting off enterprising individuals who set out on their own, attempting to intercept Indian traders. Despite such efforts, by the 1660s New Netherland was in serious economic trouble. The underlying problem was an oversupply of wampum, beads made from the shells of clams. Indians had placed a high value on wampum well before the arrival of Europeans, and the Dutch introduced iron tools to their Indian trading partners and taught them how to mass-produce wampum in small, uniform beads that could be strung together into ropes and belts. They also helped the Indians establish a trade in wampum itself, in which southern New England Algonquians manufactured wampum and traded it to the Dutch for European goods. The Dutch then exchanged the wampum for furs from the Mohawks and other Indians near Fort Orange and conveyed the furs to the Netherlands for more European goods.

By the 1640s English traders in New England had cornered the market in the beads, just when New Englanders were ceasing to use them as money. The traders then dumped them into the Dutch market by buying up huge quantities of European goods. The price of trade goods skyrocketed and the value of wampum fell, leaving the Dutch with too few of the former and too much of the latter. Competition among Dutch traders increased, the pressure on Iroquois trade partners mounted, and profits fell. The economic crisis tipped the delicate balance of violence on the frontier and precipitated a major war with serious consequences.

The Beaver Wars

As the economic position of the Dutch faltered, the balance of power among many northeastern tribes collapsed. The Iroquois, who depended on the Dutch for a steady supply of guns, were now vulnerable. The Iroquois tribes in the west came under assault from the Susquehannocks, a tribe to the south, while the Mohawks faced renewed pressure from the Mahicans to the east. Simultaneously, the Hurons had cut the Iroquois off from trade with the French to the north. Faced with these pressures, the Iroquois lashed out in hostilities, known as the Beaver Wars, which raged between 1648 and the 1660s. In these conflicts, the Iroquois attacked almost all of their Indian neighbors and succeeded in pushing the few surviving French-allied Hurons to the west.

This warfare was horrendous, not only for the enemies of the Iroquois, but also for the Iroquois themselves. As Indian fought Indian, Europeans gained the upper hand. The Iroquois were the technical winners in the Beaver Wars, but their victory was only temporary. Although the Huron had been pushed west and dispersed, the Iroquois could not secure the French as trade partners. Once the Huron were gone, the French began trading with other Algonquian tribes to the east. Although the Iroquois remained a powerful force until almost the end of the eighteenth century, the Beaver Wars marked an important turning point. The Indians were never able to replace the population they lost to warfare, even by raiding other tribes. By the middle of the seventeenth century, however, the pace of European colonization was increasing. Waves of Europeans came to North America to fill the land once hunted by Indians.

Even before the English conquered New Netherland in 1664, the Iroquois were looking for new trade partners. They found them in the English. The transition in New Netherland from Dutch to English rule was relatively quiet. The Dutch had established the colony hoping to make money through trade. Having failed in that objective, they had little incentive to fight for control of the North American colony.

ENGLAND ATTEMPTS AN EMPIRE

England came late to the business of empire building, but by the time the process was completed, that nation dominated not only North America but also much of the world. Although England's search for an overseas empire was motivated primarily by a search for wealth and power, it is impossible to separate these drives from the religious impulse. All of the great imperial nations of this era—Portugal, Spain, France, and England—believed that they conquered for God and country; hence nationalism was always tinged with religious fervor.

The Origins of English Nationalism

England did not achieve the political unity necessary for empire building until the second half of the sixteenth century. Between 1455 and 1485, England was torn by a dynastic struggle, the War of the Roses. King Henry VII and his son, Henry VIII, spent their reigns consolidating the power of the state by crushing recalcitrant nobles. When the Pope refused to let Henry VIII terminate his sonless marriage to Catherine of Aragon, the king made Protestantism the official religion of the nation, banned Catholicism, and confiscated the land and wealth of the Catholic Church. Henry's daughter Mary, who reigned from 1553 through 1558, took the nation back to the Catholic religion, burning Protestants at the stake and throwing the nation into turmoil. Order was finally established under the rule of Henry's other daughter, Elizabeth I (reigning from 1558–1603), who re-established the Anglican Church, subdued internal dissent, and built on the strong state that her grandfather and father had consolidated.

Queen Elizabeth, although the most ardent of nationalists, was unwilling to risk money on North American adventures. Other English nationalists, however, were convinced that a New World empire could lead to wealth and glory for the nation. By the end of the sixteenth century nationalist propagandists, such as two cousins both named Richard Hakluyt, were setting out the case for an overseas empire. The Hakluyts united nationalism, mercantilism, and militant Protestantism. They argued that if England had colonies to supply it with raw materials and provide markets for manufactured goods, it could free itself from economic dependency on France and Spain. Moreover, colonies could drain off the growing numbers of the unemployed. The Hakluyts also believed that North American Indians could be relatively easily converted to English trade and religion, which they would much prefer to Spanish "pride and tyranie." The English could simultaneously strike a blow against the Spanish and advance "the glory of God."

Raiding Other Empires

Elizabeth I was unpersuaded by the arguments of the Hakluyts and other colonial propagandists. Like most European monarchs, Elizabeth was most concerned about international power politics in Europe, so she was willing to let individual Englishmen try to poach on the Spanish. Her goal was to weaken Spain more than to establish a North American empire.

As early as 1562, John Hawkins tried to break into the slave trade but the Spanish forced him out. The English moved on to privateering, that is, state-sanctioned piracy. In 1570 Sir Francis Drake set off for the Isthmus of Panama on a raiding expedition. Drake was motivated equally by dreams of glory and a conviction that his Protestant religion was superior to all others. He had his start in Hawkins' slaving expedition, from which he had acquired a hatred of the Spanish.

In years to come, Drake led the second expedition ever to sail around the world, crossed the Atlantic many times, helped defeat a huge Spanish fleet, the Armada, and became an architect of England's colonial strategies. Personally brave and militantly Protestant, Drake was the English version of the *conquistador*. His venture into Panama failed to produce the hoped-for treasure, but it inspired a group of professional seamen, aggressive Protestants and members of Elizabeth's court, to formulate plans for an English colonial empire. This group successfully pressured the cautious queen for support.

The success of Drake's round-the-world expedition (1577–1580) spurred further privateering ventures. He brought back to England not only enough treasure to pay for the voyage, but also proof that the Spanish empire was vulnerable. From 1585 to 1604, the English government issued licenses to privateers, sometimes as many as 100 per year. Each venture was financed by a joint-stock company, a relatively new form of business organization that was the forerunner to the modern corporation. These companies brought together merchants who saw privateering as a way to broaden their trade and gentlemen who saw it as a way to increase their incomes.

Rehearsal in Ireland

At the end of the sixteenth century, England embarked on a campaign to bring Ireland, which had long been in its possession, under its full control. The conquest of Ireland between 1565 and 1576 became the model for England's subsequent colonial ventures.

England not only subdued the Irish leaders and their people, but also forcibly removed some of them to make way for loyal Englishmen, who were given land as a reward for their service to the queen. Paying her followers with someone else's land and financing military expeditions from joint-stock companies made the conquest of Ireland relatively cheap. These methods provided useful precedents to a queen who was never convinced that the establishment of colonies on the edge of the known world was in England's national interest. If, however, these ventures could be paid for by privateering, charters to individuals, or joint-stock companies, she was willing to permit them.

The English conquest of Ireland provided not only practical experience in how to organize and finance a colonial venture, but also a set of attitudes about cultural difference that were applied to the Indians. Although the Irish were Catholics and hence Christians, the English thought that people who behaved as the Irish did must be barbarians. According to the English, the Irish "blaspheme, they murder, commit whoredome, hold no wedlocke, ravish, steal, and commit all abomination without scruple of conscience." Without a shred of evidence, the English also accused the Irish of cannibalism, a mark of the barbarian.

These attitudes became the justification for an official English policy of terrorism. The English Governor, Sir Humphrey Gilbert, ordered that the heads of all those killed resisting the conquest be chopped off and placed along the path leading to his tent so that anyone coming to see him "must pass through a lane of heads." The English justified such harsh policies by the supposed barbarism of the Irish people. These ideas, which were quite similar to early Spanish depictions of the Indians of the Americas, were carried to the New World.

The Roanoke Venture

Roanoke, England's first colony in what became the United States, was a military venture, intended as a resupply base for privateers raiding in the Caribbean. In 1584 Walter Raleigh received a charter to establish a colony in North America. Only 30 years old at the time, Raleigh had been a soldier since the age of 14. Elizabeth agreed to let Raleigh establish a combination colony and privateering base north of Spain's northernmost settlement at St. Augustine. Raleigh's scouting party had already found a potential site, at Roanoke Island, on the Outer Banks of North Carolina. Elizabeth gave the enterprise some modest support, even investing in it herself. She knighted Raleigh but refused to let the hotheaded young soldier lead the expedition himself.

The Roanoke expedition left Plymouth in early April 1585, under the command of Sir Richard Grenville, an aristocrat and soldier. Half of the crew of 600 were probably recruited or impressed (i.e., forcibly seized) from the unemployed poor of Britain. Little value was attached to the lives of such poor men. They were expendable, and so ultimately would be the entire population of Roanoke.

It turned out that Roanoke was a poor port, dangerous for small ships and inadequate for larger ones. When the primary ship in the fleet was almost wrecked and a major portion of the food supply lost, Grenville and the fleet departed for England and fresh supplies. Colonel Ralph Lane, a veteran of the war in Ireland, was left in charge as governor. He was supposed to look for a better port, build a fort, and find food for the 100 men who were left under his command.

The first settlers of Roanoke were ill-equipped to build a self-sustaining colony. Half soldiers and gentlemen, and half undisciplined and impoverished young men, no one knew how to work. Unable to provide for themselves, the colonists turned to the local Roanoke Indians (an Algonquian tribe), whom they soon alienated.

The Roanokes were familiar with Europeans and ready to trade with them. The English tendency to resort to force and their need for more food than the natives could easily supply, however, led to conflict. Thinking that one of the Indians had stolen a silver cup, the English retaliated by burning an empty village and the surrounding cornfields. In the light of such actions, the Indians had to balance the benefits brought by trade against the costs of English hostility. After an attempted ambush failed, the Roanokes decided to withdraw from Roanoke Island, leaving the English to starve. When Lane learned of this plan, he attacked the Roanokes, beheading their chieftain. Thomas Hariot, one of the colonists, later placed most of the blame for the deterioration of Indian–English relations on his countrymen. Such was the result of leaving colonization in the hands of military men such as Lane.

Not all the colonists, however, treated the Roanokes as an enemy to be conquered. Much of what we know about the Roanoke colony and its Indian neighbors is due to the work of two sympathetic colonists. John White, a painter, and Thomas Hariot were sent to survey the region and describe its inhabitants and natural features. Their illustrations, maps, and descriptions provide the most accurate information about this region and its inhabitants before the arrival of large numbers of Europeans.

By June 1585, it was clear that Roanoke had failed in its mission. When Sir Francis Drake and his fleet appeared on their way back from a year-long looting party in the Caribbean, the colonists decided to return to England. So great was their haste to clear out that they left behind three men who were on an expedition into the interior. They were never heard from again. Apparently, Drake also dropped off several

Portrait of an Algonquian mother by John White. This beautiful picture illustrates the indulgence of Algonquian mothers and the sensitivity of the English artist who painted her.

hundred Caribbean Indian and African slaves that he had liberated while picking up booty. Freeing slaves was one of his ways to hurt the Spanish. All of these abandoned people (the three Englishmen and Drake's liberated Indians and Africans) probably melted into the Native Indian population, according to the Indian tradition of adoption. When Raleigh's supply ship arrived at Roanoke shortly thereafter, and then Grenville two weeks after that, the colonists had sailed with Drake and the others had disappeared. Grenville dropped off 15 men and returned to England.

The English advocates of colonization were not yet ready to give up. The original plan for a military-style base and a new vision of colonization would now be tried. John White, the painter, assembled a group of settlers that was the forerunner of all future successful English colonies. It included 110 people— men, women, and children who were prepared to raise their own crops—and one loyal Roanoke Indian, Manteo. In return for their investment in the enterprise, Raleigh granted each man 500 acres of land. The new expedition arrived at Roanoke in July 1587. The plan was to pick up the men Grenville had left and proceed north to the Chesapeake, for a superior harbor. The pilot of the fleet, who was more interested in privateering than colony-making, refused to take the colonists any further, however.

The second attempt to establish a colony at Roanoke was probably doomed by the poisoned relations with the Indians. White soon found that Grenville's men had been attacked by Roanokes. The colonists found themselves estranged from their Indian hosts. The survival of the colony now depended on continued support from England. Hence the colonists, who included White's own daughter and granddaughter, sent White back to act as their agent in England. No European ever saw any of these colonists again.

The Abandoned Colony

No one had planned to abandon the little colony. It was mostly a matter of priorities. Raleigh assembled a supply fleet the next spring. A sea war with the Spanish Armada was looming, however, and Elizabeth did not let the ships leave. Raleigh himself became busy with the war against the Spanish and with sending colonists to his plantations in Ireland. In 1588, White secured two ships, but the crews set off in search of treasure instead of Roanoke. In 1589, the supply mission never got beyond the planning stage. In 1590, White arranged with a privateering fleet to drop him at Roanoke. He arrived in mid-August, only to find that everyone was gone. There were signs of an orderly departure, and the word CROATOAN, Manteo's home island, was carved in a post. White assumed that was where the entire group had gone. Short of water, the fleet decided to return to the Caribbean for the winter and not to proceed on to Croatoan until the next spring. They never got there.

What happened to the abandoned colonists? Twenty years after White had last seen them, the English returned to the region, this time establishing a permanent colony at Jamestown, on the Chesapeake. In 1608, English men heard that Roanoke colonists had made their way up to Virginia and settled among the friendly Chesapeake Indians. Indeed, the main body of colonists at Roanoke had intended to seek out the Chesapeake. Perhaps the remainder went to Croatoan, leaving White the message carved into the post.

Those who moved north seem to have become victims of the Powhatans, a powerful and expansionist tribe. At just about the time that the English were arriving, their chief, also named Powhatan, ordered the slaughter of the Chesapeakes and the English who lived among them. There were reports that seven English people had

CHRONOLOGY

1275–1292	Marco Polo travels in Asia
1400–1600	Five Iroquois Nations create the Great League of Peace
1455–1485	War of the Roses in England
1497	John Cabot arrives in North America
1519–1522	Magellan expedition sails around the world for Spain
1522	Giovanni da Verrazano explores North American coast for France
1534–1542	Jacques Cartier makes three trips to Canada for France
1561	Spanish abduct Don Luís de Velasco
1562	John Hawkins tries to break into the slave trade
1565	Spanish establish settlement at St. Augustine Spanish destroy French settlement at Fort Caroline
1565–1576	The English conquer Ireland
1570	Don Luís de Velasco returns home to Virginia
1577–1580	Francis Drake sails around the world for England
1584	Walter Raleigh receives charter to establish colony at Roanoke
1585	First settlement at Roanoke established
1587	Second attempt to found colony at Roanoke
1590	English settlers at Roanoke have disappeared
1607	English establish permanent colony at Jamestown
1608	Samuel de Champlain establishes a fort at Quebec
1609	Henry Hudson arrives at New York, sailing for the Netherlands
1614	Dutch begin trading in Albany region French settlers arrive in New France
1621	Dutch West India Company established
1624	First Dutch families arrive at Manhattan
1648–1660s	Beaver Wars fought
1664	English take over New Amsterdam

escaped, and for years local Indians told tales about people who lived in two-story stone houses and domesticated turkeys. The English at Jamestown eventually came to believe that the survivors of Roanoke were living 50 miles away, but no effort was made to find them. Almost 20 years after the abandonment of Roanoke, the English finally established a permanent North American colony. By that time the Spanish Empire was sinking into its slow decline. In theory at least, the English would be able to provide better support for subsequent New World colonies. As their willingness to abandon the colonists at Roanoke demonstrated, however, they had limited interest in colonies that did not return a profit. Moreover, because the English settlers, with few exceptions, antagonized their Indian hosts, the English could not rely on the Indians for food. As a result, the success of the English colonies would depend on their capacity to grow their own food. In addition, the architects of English imperial policy concentrated more on trade with the English inhabitants of the New World than with Native Americans. Consequently, the history of the English in North America is by and large that of the growth of the English population and the steady decline of the original Indian inhabitants.

CONCLUSION

European nations established colonies to achieve a political or economic advantage over their rivals. The distinctive experience and political economy of each nation shaped its relations with the Indians it encountered, just as the distinctive experience of the Indian nations shaped their interactions with Europeans. The Spanish came prepared for a new *reconquista* and poured huge and well-armed forces into the New World. The French sent small numbers of military officers who quickly found Indian allies and became entangled in the Indians' own conflicts. The English used another military model, that of the pacification of Ireland. Some nations, in particular France and Spain, were comparatively willing to reach out to alien cultures by sending missionaries to convert the Indians. The Dutch also recognized that the goodwill of the Indians was vital if a flourishing trade were to be maintained. The English proved the least interested in accommodating Indian cultures and the most interested in transplanting their own. Out of these different experiences, a North Atlantic political economy began to emerge, shaped by the forces of trade and the quest for national power.

The early years of American colonial history were shaped by vast impersonal forces that built empires and subjugated peoples. But they were also given a lasting imprint by individuals, many of them world travelers. Some set out to find new worlds, while others were forced into them by those with imperial ambitions. Captives such as Don Luís Velasco and Manteo; intrepid explorers such as Jacques Cartier and Henry Hudson; ruthless soldiers such as Sir Francis Drake and Samuel de Champlain; the poor who were dragooned into sailing for Roanoke and left there to die; Africans liberated from the Spanish only to be abandoned on the North Carolina shore, perhaps melting into the Indian population; and Huron women who took French traders as their husbands: All of them left their mark on the New World.

FURTHER READINGS

W. J. Eccles, *France in America* (1990). The standard introduction to the history of New France, succinct and authoritative.

Michael Kammen, *Colonial New York: A History* (1975). A readable survey of colonial New York's history.

Karen Ordahl Kupperman, *Roanoke: The Abandoned Colony* (1984), and David Beers Quinn, *Set Fair for Roanoke: Voyages and Colonies, 1584–1606* (1985). Two excellent histories of the Roanoke colony. Kupperman expertly places the colony in its fullest context, while Quinn offers a more comprehensive narrative.

David Beers Quinn, ed., *New American World: A Documentary History of North America to 1612* (1979). A five-volume collection of documents, indispensable for the study of early explorations of North America.

Daniel K. Richter, *The Ordeal of the Longhouse: The Peoples of the Iroquois League in the Era of European Colonization* (1992). An extraordinary introduction to the history of the Iroquois peoples that shows what early American history looks like when the focus is shifted from European settlers to the original inhabitants.

Helen C. Rountree, *Pocahontas's People: The Powhatan Indians of Virginia Through Four Centuries* (1990). A superb introduction to the history of this southeastern tribe, written by an anthropologist.

 Please refer to the document CD-ROM for primary sources related to this chapter.

CHAPTER

3

The English Come to Stay

1600–1660

The Adventures of John Rolfe • The First Chesapeake Colonies
The Political Economy of Slavery Emerges
A Bible Commonwealth in the New England Wilderness
Dissension in the Puritan Ranks • Conclusion

THE ADVENTURES OF JOHN ROLFE

John Rolfe was an adventurer. In 1609, at the age of 25, he and his wife set sail for the new English colony at Jamestown. Their ship was blown off course and wrecked off the island of Bermuda. It was not until a year later that Rolfe reached Virginia, having survived a mutiny and the death of his infant daughter. Rolfe's wife herself died shortly after their arrival at Jamestown.

Soon Rolfe was experimenting with tobacco, trying to find a strain that would produce a fragrant leaf in Virginia's soil. Walter Raleigh's men had introduced tobacco to England, where the addictive pleasures of smoking soon created a market. The English imported their tobacco from the Spanish West Indies, but with the founding of their colony at Jamestown, they hoped for their own source. Rolfe tried planting West Indian tobacco seeds and produced a successful crop. By 1617, Virginians were exporting Rolfe's variety of tobacco to England. It was not as sweet as the West Indian product, but it was a great deal cheaper. Tobacco proved the economic salvation of Virginia, making many men and women rich and robbing others of their freedom. Like other foreign colonies, Virginia achieved prosperity by feeding European cravings for luxury goods such as tobacco, sugar, coffee, and tea.

Relations with the local Powhatan Indians were tense from the moment of the colonists' arrival. In the spring of 1613, the English captured Pocahontas, daughter of the chieftain Powhatan, and brought her to Jamestown. By summer, John Rolfe had fallen in love with her. He asked permission of the English authorities to marry her, realizing that his countrymen would disapprove of his attachment to "one whose education hath been rude, her manners barbarous, her generation accursed." In John Rolfe, the traditional ethnocentrism of the English was at war with love. Love won out, yet the marriage established an alliance between two peoples that brought an end to warfare.

In 1616, Rolfe took his wife and their young son to England, where Pocahontas adopted the dress of an English lady. Her transformation suggested to the English that Indians could easily be Europeanized. When Rolfe said it was time to return to Virginia, Pocahontas wished to remain in her new home. Before the ship set sail she took ill and died, as a Christian.

By the time that Rolfe returned to Virginia in 1617, tobacco dominated the economy and tobacco-planting settlers encroached on the Powhatans' land. On March 22, 1622, the new leader of the Powhatan Confederacy, Opechancanough, orchestrated attacks on all the plantations along the James River. By the time they were finished, nearly one-third of all the Virginia colonists had been killed. John Rolfe was one of the victims.

John Rolfe had imagined that English and Indians could live together in harmony. He was wrong. Once he developed a marketable strain of tobacco, the English could not be stopped from turning Powhatan lands into tobacco fields. European demand for tobacco doomed not only the Indians who were driven from their homeland but also generations of European indentured servants and, eventually, African slaves. A new kind of society based on the political economy of plantation slavery took shape. Rarely in history is one person so directly responsible for the demise of his own dreams.

THE FIRST CHESAPEAKE COLONIES

In 1607, 20 years after the abandonment of the Roanoke colony, the English returned to North America. They had learned little from their failure in Roanoke, and although their colony at Jamestown was better financed, it was poorly planned. The difference between survival and extinction was tobacco. With the development of this cash crop, for which there was demand in Europe, Virginia began to prosper. Once John Rolfe had developed a palatable strain of tobacco, the primary requirements were land and labor. The English settlers' desire for land led them into warfare with the Powhatans; their desire for cheap labor led them to import indentured servants and African slaves.

Planning Virginia

When Queen Elizabeth died in 1603, she was succeeded by King James I, who signed a treaty with Spain, ending decades of warfare. In 1606, James granted charters to two groups of English merchants and military men, one in London and the other in Plymouth. The Plymouth group was permitted to colonize New England, and the Londoners the Chesapeake region. Each operation was chartered as a private company, which would raise money from shareholders and finance, populate, and regulate each colony that it established. Although both the Virginia and Plymouth Companies reported to a Royal Council, these ventures were fundamentally private operations, subject to little governmental control.

Just before Christmas 1606, the Virginia Company of London sent out three ships under the leadership of Captain Christopher Newport. When the ships arrived at Virginia on April 26, 1607, and the company's sealed orders were opened, the 104 colonists learned that they were to be governed by a council of seven men. Unfortunately, two of them, Edward Maria Wingfield, an original investor in the company but "an arrogant man of no special capacity," and Captain John Smith, an equally arrogant but considerably more capable soldier of fortune, already despised each other, and Smith had been put under arrest early in the voyage. As a result, the early years of the new colony at Jamestown were marked by internal wrangling. Soon external conflict developed as well, as the colonists antagonized their Indian hosts. Indeed, almost everything that could go wrong did.

The English hoped to find a land like Mexico that would provide them with gold and less glamorous raw materials. Whatever limited manufacturing was needed could be performed either by English criminals, who were sent over to work as their punishment, or by indentured servants, English men and women drawn from the lowest ranks of society who agreed to work for a set period of time to pay their transportation expenses. The colonists expected to strike up a trade with the local Indians, who would be the primary suppliers of food.

The Company planned to get the colony up and running within seven years. During that period all the colonists would work for the Company, which would give them food and shelter. At the end of that period, all of the colonists would receive grants of land. The Company evidently thought that such a colony would need a great deal of direction, for more than one-third of the original settlers were gentlemen, that is, members of the elite. In its first years, the proportion of elite in Jamestown's population was six times as great as it was in England.

The Company also sent skilled laborers, many with skills for which there was little use in the new colony, such as tailors, goldsmiths, and a perfumer. Some were thought necessary for the upkeep of the gentlemen. Others were supposed to work with the gold and precious gems the colonists hoped to find. Farmers and ordinary laborers, on the other hand, were in short supply.

Starving Times

Poor planning and bad luck placed the colonists on swampy ground with bad water. The concentrations of salt in the James River were high enough to poison those who drank the water. In addition, in summer the water became a breeding ground for the micro-organisms that cause typhoid and dysentery. Some historians have argued that these diseases left the survivors too weak to plant food, while others note that many of the healthy seemed to prefer prospecting for gold. Whatever the reason, the colonists depended on the resentful Powhatans for food. Malnutrition and even starvation made the effects of disease worse. This combination of factors, along with conflicts with the Powhatan Indians, led to appallingly high mortality rates. As late as 1616, the English population was only 350, although more than five times that number had emigrated from England (see Table 3–1).

By September 1607, half of the 104 Jamestown colonists were dead, and by the next spring only 38 were still alive. Although the Company sent over more colonists, they continued to die off at extraordinary rates. Most who died were victims of malnutrition and disease. The lack of food was so great that over the winter of 1609–1610, the inhabitants were reduced to eating roots, acorns, and even human

TABLE 3–1

English Population of Virginia, 1607–1640

Population in Virginia Colony	Immigration to Virginia Colony
104 (April 1607)	104 (April 1607)
38 (January 1608)	
	120 (January 1608, 1st supply)
130 (September 1608)	
	70 (September 1608, 2nd supply)
200 (late September 1608)	
100 (Spring 1609)	
	300 (Fall 1609, 3rd supply)
	540 (1610)
450 (April 1611)	
	660 (1611)
682 (January 1612)	
350 (January 1613)	
	45 (1613–1616)
351 (1616)	
600 (December 1618)	
	900 (1618–1620)
887 (March 1620)	
	1,051 (1620–1621)
843 (March 1621)	
	1,580 (1621–1622)
1,240 (March 1622)	
	1,935 (1622–1623)
1,241 (April 1623)	
	1,646 (1623–1624)
1,275 (February 1624)	
1,210 (1625)	
	9,000 (1625–1634)
4,914 (1634)	
	6,000 (1635–1640)
8,100 (1640)	Total: 23,951

Although about 24,000 men and women immigrated to Virginia between 1607 and 1640, in 1640 the population stood at only 8,100. Most of the inhabitants fell victim to disease, although the Indian uprising of 1622 took 347 lives.

Source: Data from Earle, Geographical Inquiry and American Historical Problems *(1992) and Bernhard, "Men, Women, and Children at Jamestown: Population and Gender in Early Virginia, 1607–1610,"* Journal of Southern History, *LVIII (1992).*

excrement. For centuries this starvation has perplexed historians. The land was fertile and abounded with game, and the James River was teeming with fish. The colonists should have been able to raise enough to keep themselves alive. Captain John Smith blamed the starvation on the laziness of the colonists, who preferred searching for riches to planting grain. When he served as president of the Council from 1608 to 1609, only a handful of colonists died. He imposed military-style discipline and required all the colonists to work four hours a day. Disease and malnutrition, however, were probably more to blame than laziness. Moreover, seeing so many die around them only increased survivors' sense of despair. They probably suffered from depression.

Decisions by the leadership made the plight worse. John Smith, an effective but hated disciplinarian, returned to England in 1609 after an injury, possibly the result of an assassination attempt. The new rulers unwisely split up the settlement, sending a group of men down the James River to establish a fort and two other parties to establish settlements in spots already inhabited by Indians. In both cases the English were attacked and suffered heavy losses. The colonists who survived were "distracted and forlorn," in many ways resembling modern prisoners of war. They had begun to abandon the colony when they were stopped by the arrival of Lord De La Warr, the new governor who came to impose harsh martial law.

Troubled Relations with the Powhatans

In Virginia, the English encountered one of the most powerful Indian tribes on the continent, the Powhatans, a confederacy of Algonquian tribes who, under their chieftain Powhatan, were bringing less powerful Algonquians under their control. At the time Powhatan's confederacy included about 20,000 Indians, divided into about three dozen tribes. Each group, English and Indian, tried at first to get the other to accept the status of an allied but subordinate tribe. At one point, the English pushed the aging Powhatan down to the ground and put a fake crown on his head, imitating the ceremonies in which feudal princes pledged allegiance to a king. Powhatan held Captain John Smith captive and tried to bully him and other English leaders into acknowledging his supremacy. In the context of these political maneuverings, English bullying sometimes yielded food from the Indians, but it also led to increased animosity, as did English settlement on Indian land.

English leadership also made the tensions between the two peoples worse. Some of the early English leaders had hoped for a biracial society in which the Native Americans would become loyal subjects and trading partners. Frustrated by

Powhatan and English Dwellings. These are reconstructions of typical English and Powhatan Indian homes, c. 1607. Both are dark and low to the ground.

Powhatan's Mantle. This deerskin mantle, decorated with seashells, is supposed to have belonged to Powhatan.

their inability either to produce food or get it from the Indians, Jamestown's leaders came increasingly to think of all Indians as enemies.

Lord De La Warr set out to subjugate the Indians. He ordered Powhatan to return English captives and equipment. When Powhatan refused, De La Warr ordered an attack on an Indian village. The English killed about 75 of the inhabitants, burned the town and its cornfields, and took as captives the wife of a chieftain and her children, whom they brutally killed. This was the opening battle of the First Anglo-Powhatan War, the first in a series of three conflicts between 1610 and 1646. The first ended in 1614, when the marriage between Pocahontas and John Rolfe cemented a truce. In permitting his daughter to marry an Englishman, Powhatan was adapting a means he had used to establish his powerful confederacy. He himself had an unusually large number of wives, selected from throughout his realm, as a means of tightening his dominion. Each of Powhatan's wives represented an important link between Powhatan's tribe and her own. After each of his wives had borne him a child, she and the child were sent back to her home village, allowing Powhatan to maintain a presence there. Sometimes, Powhatan also appointed his own son or son-in-law as chief of a village, bringing the village more tightly under his control and undermining the customary right of Algonquian women to participate in the selection of leaders. By tradition, chiefs, or *werowances*, were the kinsmen of *werowansqua* (tribal queens). At the same time that Powhatan was consolidating his personal leadership, he was enhancing patriarchal authority in the tribes he controlled.

The marriage of John Rolfe and Pocahontas ushered in a brief period of peace. The English were so pleased with the new alliance that they soon asked for another one of Powhatan's daughters as a bride for one of their councilors. Powhatan refused, fearing that, as with Pocahontas, he would lose a daughter rather than gain a powerful and loyal English son-in-law. Powhatan had failed in his objective of turning the English into his vassals.

Toward a New Political Economy

The tide turned against the Powhatans because the English finally found a way to make money in Virginia. John Rolfe's improved strain of tobacco found a ready market in England that stimulated the Virginia economy, transforming it almost overnight into a different sort of society than the one the Virginia Company had planned. Within three years of Rolfe's first cargo, Virginia was shipping 50,000 pounds of tobacco to England per year. Suddenly Virginia experienced an economic boom. By 1619, a man working by himself was making £200 in one crop, and a man with six indentured servants, could make £1000. Once fortunes this large could be made, the race to Virginia was on.

All that was needed to make money in Virginia was land and people to work it. In 1616 the Virginia Company, which had plenty of land but no money, offered land as dividends to its stockholders. Moreover, those already living in Virginia were given land, and anyone who came over (or brought another person over) was to be granted 50 acres a head (called a headright). The Company was taking an important step in the direction of private enterprise, away from the corporate, company-directed economy of the early years. It became far easier to obtain land in Virginia than in England.

As another means of attracting settlers, the Company replaced martial law with English common law, which guaranteed the colonists all the rights of the English people. The colonists were also granted greater rights to self-government than were enjoyed by those who lived in England at the time. The first elected representative government in the New World, the Virginia General Assembly, met in Jamestown on July 30, 1619.

These inducements attracted 3,500 settlers to Virginia in three years, three times as many as had come in the past ten years. By accident more than planning, Virginia had found the formula for a successful English colony. It was a model that all the other colonies generally followed: Colonists would have to be offered greater opportunities to make money and greater rights of self-government than they had at home. These changes came too late, however, to rescue the Virginia Company, which went bankrupt in 1624. King James I dissolved the Company and turned Virginia into a royal colony under direct royal control.

Toward the Destruction of the Powhatans

As the new colonists spread out, establishing private plantations, English settlers claimed all the Indians' prime farmland on both sides of the James River and began to move up the river's tributaries (see Map 3–1). At the same time, the Powhatans became increasingly dependent on English goods such as metal tools. Moreover, as the English population began to grow its own food, it had less need of Indian food, the only commodity the Indians had to trade. The Indians slowly accumulated a debt to the English and lost their economic independence.

After Powhatan died, his more militant brother, Opechancanough, decided to get rid of the English interlopers. On the morning of March 22, 1622, the Indians struck at all the plantations along the James River. By the time they were finished, one-third of the colonists had been killed, including John Rolfe. The Second Anglo-Powhatan War, which continued for another ten years, had begun.

This war marked a turning point in English policy. Although some of the English recognized that the Indian attack had been caused by "our own perfidiouse dealing," most decided that the Indians were untrustworthy and incapable of being

Map 3–1 English Encroachments on Indian Land, 1613–1652
After John Rolfe's development of a marketable strain of tobacco, the English spread out through the Chesapeake region, encroaching steadily on Indian land. Tobacco planters preferred land along the rivers, for casks filled with tobacco bound for England were more easily transported by ship.

Source: Frederic Gleach, Powhatan's World and Colonial Virginia (Lincoln: University of Nebraska Press, 1997), and James Horn, Adapting to a New World: English Society in the Seventeenth-Century Chesapeake (Chapel Hill: University of North Carolina Press, 1994).

converted to the English way of life. Therefore, a policy of extermination was justified. John Smith concluded that the massacre "will be good for the Plantation, because now we have just cause to destroy them by all meanes possible." Until this point, the English had claimed only land the Indians were not farming. Now they seized territory the Indians had cleared and planted. In only 15 years' time, the English and Indians in Virginia had become implacable enemies.

Indian resistance made the English more determined to stay, and with the tobacco economy booming, settlers continued to pour into Virginia. They spread across the Chesapeake to the Eastern Shore and as far north as the Potomac River. The aged Opechancanough, determined to make one final push, struck again on April 18, 1644, killing 400 English people and taking many prisoners.

The Third Anglo-Powhatan War ended, however, in the Indians' total defeat two years later. Opechancanough was seized and killed. The English took complete possession of the land between the James and York Rivers. The land north of the York River was to be reserved for the Indians, making it the first American Indian reservation. In a few years' time, English settlers moved into that region, too.

A New Colony in Maryland

Virginia's original plan was to make money from trading with the local Indians, but when the tobacco boom began, colonists became more interested in the Indians' land. As tobacco prices dipped in the 1620s, however, trade became more attractive. By the late 1620s, an outpost had been established at the northern end of Chesapeake Bay to obtain beaver furs from the Susquehannocks. Sir George Calvert, the first Lord Baltimore and a Catholic, saw the commercial potential of this region and in 1632 persuaded King Charles I, a Catholic sympathizer, to grant him the land north of the Potomac and south of the Delaware that was "not yet cultivated and planted." This territory became Maryland, the first proprietary colony, that is, a colony that was owned by an individual and his heirs. (Virginia was originally a charter colony, one that was held by a group of private shareholders. In charter and proprietary colonies, the English Crown turned over both financing and management to the shareholders or proprietors.)

As the first proprietary colony, Maryland established a pattern. The proprietor had extensive powers to grant land and make laws by himself, but he agreed to the establishment of a representative assembly. In 1649 that assembly passed the Act of Toleration, which said that no one would be "compelled to the beliefe or exercise of any other Religion against his or her consent." Even though religious toleration was extended only to those who professed a belief in Jesus Christ, Maryland was among the most tolerant places in the world at that time. Moreover, this right was explicitly extended to women as well as men.

Although it would be a number of decades before Maryland's population increased substantially, the familiar political economy emerged early. As in Virginia, attracting colonists to the New World required greater opportunities and freedoms—of self-government and of religion—than they enjoyed in England. Throughout the period of conflict with the Powhatan Confederacy, the booming tobacco economy drew settlers to Virginia and, after about 1650, to Maryland as well. Although they had separate governments, Virginia and Maryland had similar political economies, based on tobacco. The defeat of the Indians made more land in the Chesapeake region available for cultivation; the colonies needed only people to work it.

THE POLITICAL ECONOMY OF SLAVERY EMERGES

Chesapeake society in the first half of the seventeenth century was shaped by four forces: weak government, the market for tobacco, the availability of land, and the need for labor. Because government was weak, the forces of plantation agriculture were unchecked, and the profit motive operated without restraint. Those who could take advantage of these opportunities—male and female both—profited wildly, while the poor, both white and African, were without defense. Artificial distinctions such as social status counted for little in comparison to willpower, physical strength, and ruthlessness. Even gender roles were undermined as women worked in the fields and wealthy widows controlled large estates. In this environment the political economy of slavery took root.

The Problem of a Labor Supply

Once the crises of the early years had passed, the Chesapeake's greatest problem was securing laborers to produce tobacco. As soon as John Rolfe brought in his first successful crop, the Virginia governor began pressing England to send him its poor. The Virginia Company also encouraged the emigration of women. No matter how many colonists came, however, the demand for labor always outstripped the supply. By 1660, 50,000 Britons, most single men in their 20s, had migrated to the Chesapeake, but the population was still only a little over 35,000. Because of the poor water supply and disease, the death rate remained extraordinarily high.

The profits from tobacco were so great and the risk of death so high that landowners squeezed out every penny of profit as quickly as they could. Those who obtained land and servants to work it could become rich overnight. Great wealth, however, could be achieved only by the labor of others. The demand for labor was almost insatiable. Perhaps 90 percent of those who migrated to the Chesapeake in the seventeenth century came as servants, and half died before completing their term of service. Servants were worked to the point of death. In England, custom and law both afforded servants some basic protections. In Virginia, working conditions were brutal. In 1623, Richard Frethorne, a young servant, wrote back to his parents in England complaining about life in Virginia. "With weeping tears," he begged them to send food. "We must work early and late for a mess of water gruel and a mouthful of bread and beef."

Servants might be beaten so severely that they died, or they might find their indentures (the contract that bound them to service for a period of usually seven years) sold from one master to another. Their treatment was brutal, and they found little protection from the Virginia or Maryland courts. They would become free if they outlived their period of indenture; they retained all of the rights of English people, and their servitude was not hereditary. But, they were far worse off than servants in England.

The Origins of Slavery in the Chesapeake

Other New World plantation societies where labor was in short supply had already turned to slavery. Historians do not know precisely when slavery was first practiced in the Chesapeake colonies, but Africans first arrived in Virginia in 1619, when a Dutch ship sailing off course sold its cargo of "twenty Negars" to the Virginians. It is not clear, however, if these Africans were indentured servants or lifelong slaves. As long as life expectancy was low, it was more profitable for a planter to purchase an indentured servant for a period of seven years than a slave for life. Not until life expectancy improved toward the end of the seventeenth century were significant numbers of African slaves imported into the Chesapeake.

All of the English plantation colonies followed the same pattern in making the transition from white servitude to African slavery. The shift toward African slavery was quick in some places and slow in others; in Virginia, it took about three-quarters of a century. The primary factors dictating how quickly English colonists adopted African slavery were the need for plantation laborers and the availability of African slaves at a good price. The association between slavery and plantation economies was strong, and all the British colonies eventually practiced slavery.

Even before they had substantial contact with African people, the English and other northern Europeans probably harbored prejudice against dark-skinned people. By the second half of the sixteenth century, the English were depicting Africans in derogatory terms. They said that Africans were unattractive, with "dispositions most savage and brutish." Although these views were not used to justify slavery, they formed the basis for the racism that would develop along with the slave system.

During the seventeenth century, African slavery and white and African servitude existed side by side, and laws to enforce slavery appeared piecemeal. The Chesapeake was a society with slaves, but it was still not a slave society. In 1639 the Maryland Assembly passed a law guaranteeing "all the Inhabitants of this Province being Christians (Slaves excepted)" all the rights and liberties of "any naturall born subject of England." The first Virginia law recognizing slavery, passed in 1661, said that any English servant who ran away with an African would have to serve additional time not only for himself but for the African as well. Historians presume that such Africans were already slaves for life and hence were incapable of serving any additional time.

Such laws and legal proceedings show the great familiarity that existed between white and black servants. Slaves and white servants worked together, enjoyed their leisure together, had sexual relations with each other, and ran away together. As late as 1680, most of the labor on plantations was still being performed by white indentured servants. There is no evidence that they were kept separate from Africans by law or inclination.

As long as the black population remained small, the color line was blurry. Not until late in the seventeenth century were laws passed that restricted free African Americans. In fact, in 1660, Anthony Johnson, an African who had arrived in Virginia as a servant in 1621, owned both land and African slaves. In the 40 years that he had been in Virginia, slavery had become institutionalized and recognized by the law, but laws separating the races had yet to be enacted.

Gender and the Social Order in the Chesapeake

The founders of England's New World colonies hoped to replicate the social order they had known at home. For that reason, as early as 1619, the Virginia Company began to bring single women to the colony to become brides of the unmarried planters. As in England, it was expected that men would perform all the "outside" labor, including planting, farming, and tending large farm animals. Women would do all the "inside" work, including preserving and preparing food, spinning and weaving, making and repairing clothing, and gardening. In English society, a farmer's wife was not simply a man's sexual partner and companion; she was also the mistress of the household economy, performing work vital to its success. Both men and women were vital to the social and economic order that the English wanted to create in the Chesapeake.

However, the powerful tobacco economy transformed both the economy and society of the New World. With profits from tobacco so high, women worked in the tobacco fields instead of the kitchen. When children were born, as soon as they could work, they were in the fields, too. Only when a man became wealthy did he hire a servant—often a woman—to replace his wife in the fields. As a result, for many years, Virginia society lacked the "comforts of home" that women produced, such as prepared food and homemade clothing. Tobacco was everything.

The circumstances of colonial society weakened patriarchal controls. Far from their own fathers, living in a remote part of the world where the government was relatively weak, women in the Chesapeake found themselves unexpectedly liberated from traditional restrictions. Although women without the protection of fathers were certainly vulnerable to exploitation in seventeenth-century plantation societies, where men outnumbered women three or four to one, women often found themselves in a position of relative power. The first generation of women to immigrate to the Chesapeake region married relatively late—in their mid-20s. Many had to wait out their periods of service until they could marry. As a result, they had relatively few children, and it was many decades before Chesapeake society reproduced itself naturally. With disease taking a huge toll, perhaps half of all children born in the colony died in infancy, and one marriage partner was also likely to die within seven years of marriage. At least until 1680 or so, to be a widow, widower, or orphan was the normal state of affairs. In such a society, widows who inherited their husbands' possessions were powerful and in demand on the marriage market. Children, however, were especially vulnerable, often losing their inheritances to a stepparent.

A BIBLE COMMONWEALTH IN THE NEW ENGLAND WILDERNESS

In 1620, 13 years after the founding of the Virginia colony, England planted another permanent North American colony at Plymouth, and nine years after that, one at Massachusetts Bay. In many ways the Virginia and Massachusetts colonies could not have been more different. The primary impetus behind the Massachusetts settlement was religious. Both the Pilgrims at Plymouth and the much more numerous Puritans at Massachusetts Bay moved to New England to escape persecution and to establish new communities based on God's law as they understood it. The Puritans and Pilgrims were middle class, and their ventures were well financed and capably planned. The environment was much healthier than that of the Chesapeake, and the population reproduced itself rapidly. In addition, relations with the Indians were better than in the Chesapeake. Nonetheless, the Puritan movement was a product of the same developing political economy that led to the European exploration of the New World. Both grew out of the consolidation and growth of national states in Europe and the expansion of commerce.

The English Origins of the Puritan Movement

In Europe during the sixteenth century, ordinary people and powerful monarchs had vastly different reasons for abandoning the Roman Catholic Church in favor of one of the new Protestant churches. In England, these differing motives led to 130 years of conflict, including a revolution and massive religious persecution. In the 1530s, Henry VIII established his own state religion in England, the Church of England, for political rather than for pious reasons. After many years of marriage to Catherine of Aragon, Henry still did not have a male heir. With one of Catherine's ladies-in-waiting, Anne Boleyn, already pregnant, Henry pressed the Pope for an annulment of his marriage to Catherine. In 1533, the Pope refused the annulment, and Henry removed the Catholic Church as the established religion of England, replacing it with his own Church of England.

Henry's replacement of the Catholic Church did not bring stability, however. His successors alternated between adherence to Protestantism and persecution of Catholics, and support of Catholicism and persecution of Protestants. Under the reign of Catherine's daughter Mary, hundreds of Protestants left the country to avoid being burned at the stake.

When Mary's Protestant sister, Elizabeth I, ascended the throne, these exiles returned, having picked up the Calvinist doctrine of predestination on the continent. John Calvin, the Swiss Protestant reformer, insisted that even before people were born, God foreordained "to some eternal life and to some eternal damnation." Although the Church of England adopted Calvin's doctrine of predestination, it never held to it thoroughly enough or followed through on other reforms well enough to please the Puritans, those who desired further reforms. And because the monarchs viewed challenges to the state religion as challenges to the state itself, religious dissenters were frequently persecuted for their beliefs.

What Did the Puritans Believe?

Like all Christians, Puritans believed that humanity was guilty of the original sin committed by Adam and Eve when they disobeyed God in the Garden of Eden. They believed that God's son, Jesus Christ, had given his life to pay (or atone) for the original sin, and that as a consequence, all faithful Christians would be forgiven their sins and admitted to heaven after they died. Calvinism differed from other Christian religions primarily in its followers' insistence that there was nothing that men or women could do to guarantee that God would save them by an act of grace from eternal punishment in hell.

Protestants rejected the hierarchy of the Catholic Church, maintaining that the relationship between God and humanity was direct, "unmediated." Because every person had direct access to the inspired word of God through the Bible, Protestants promoted literacy and biblical translation. As Calvinists, Puritans wanted to "purify" the Church of England of all remnants of Catholicism. Anglicans had reduced the number of sacraments; Puritans wanted to eliminate them all. Anglicans retained some church rituals and a church hierarchy; Puritans rejected all rituals and all priestly hierarchy.

Finally, Anglicans had increasingly come to think that believing Christians could earn their way to heaven by good works. Puritans, in contrast, believed that salvation was the free gift of God and that human beings could not force His hand. All that individuals could do was to prepare for grace, by reading and studying the Bible, so that they understood God's plan, and by attempting to live as good a life as they could in the meantime. Because they could never know for certain whether they had been saved, Puritans always lived with anxiety.

Puritanism contained a powerful tension between intellect and emotion. On the one hand, Puritanism was a highly rational religion. It required all of its followers to read and study the Bible, as well as to listen to long sermons that explored fine points of theology. As a result, Puritanism led to high rates of literacy among its followers, both male and female. On the other hand, Puritans believed that no amount of book learning could get a person into heaven and that saving grace was as much a matter of the heart as of the mind. Puritans believed that church membership was only for those who could demonstrate that they were saved. As they were persecuted for their faith, they came to believe that, like the Israelites of old, they were God's chosen people, that they had a covenant or agreement with God, and that if they did His will, He would make them prosper.

The Puritans first attempted to reform the Church of England. Once it became evident to them that the Church of England would resist further reformation and would continue moving away from the Calvinist principle of predestination, some Puritans began to make other plans.

The Pilgrim Colony at Plymouth

The first Puritan colony in North America was established in 1620 at Plymouth, by a group of Puritans known as the Pilgrims, Separatists who had given up all hope of reforming the Church of England. The Pilgrims had already moved to Holland, thinking its Calvinist religion would offer them a better home. It was hard for the Pilgrims to fit themselves into Holland's highly structured economy, however, and they found their children seduced from strict religion by "the manifold temptations of the place."

By 1620 the Pilgrims were ready to accept the Virginia Company of London's offer of land in America for any English people who would pay their own way. With the colony at Jamestown floundering, the Company was looking for other opportunities for profit. To that end, the Company filled the two ships in the expedition, the *Mayflower* and the *Speedwell*, with non-Pilgrims who were willing to pay their own way, Separatists who had not gone to Holland, as well as Pilgrims.

The *Speedwell* leaked so badly it turned back, but the *Mayflower* arrived at Plymouth, Massachusetts, in November 1620, far north of its destination and outside the jurisdiction of the Virginia Company. Because the Pilgrims had landed in territory that had no lawful government, the adult men on board signed a document known as the Mayflower Compact before disembarking. The men bound themselves into a "Civil Body Politic" to make laws and govern the colony and also to recognize the authority of the governor.

Only half of the party survived the harsh first winter. Years later the second governor, William Bradford, remembered the Pilgrims' arrival in a strange land and their early ordeals. The Indians, he claimed, were "savage barbarians . . . readier to fill their sides full of arrows than otherwise." And their new home was "a hideous and desolate wilderness, full of wild beasts and wild men."

In fact, the Plymouth colony would never have survived had it not been for the assistance of friendly Indians. Like the French in New France and in contrast to the English at Jamestown, the Pilgrims were able to establish diplomatic relations both because they were better diplomats and because the local Indians needed foreign allies. Until shortly before the Pilgrims' arrival, Plymouth Bay had been inhabited by as many as 2,000 Indians, with ten times as many in the surrounding region. Then European fishermen and traders introduced some fatal disease, which was carried as far as the trading network reached. Former villages were filled with the skulls and bones of the unburied dead. So recently had Patuxet and Pokanoket Indians inhabited the region that the Pilgrims were able to supplement their meager supplies by rummaging Indian graves, homes, and hidden stores of grain.

The world was vastly changed for those Native Americans who survived. Squanto, a Patuxet warrior, had spent the plague years in Europe, having been kidnapped by an English ship's captain. In London, Squanto praised the virtues of his native land in the hopes that the English would take him home. Once back in Massachusetts, Squanto abandoned the English exploring party that had returned him. He found that his own tribe, the Patuxet, had almost entirely disappeared. The once-powerful Pokanoket, led by Massasoit, were now paying tribute to the Narragansett, who had escaped the deadly disease. Squanto cast his lot with Massasoit, and they decided that the English might prove effective allies against the Narragansett. Thus in the spring of 1621, Squanto and Samoset, a member of another local band, offered the Pilgrims their assistance and showed them how to grow corn.

From the Indian perspective, this assistance was not so much an act of charity as a diplomatic initiative. The two Indians helped negotiate a treaty between the

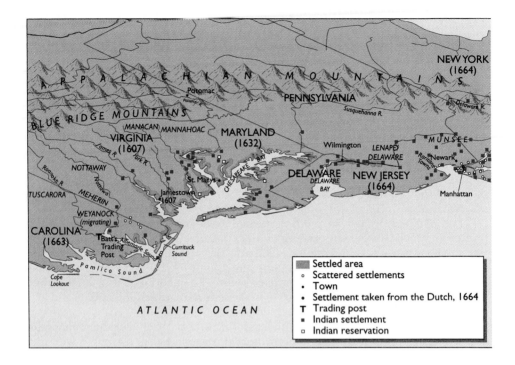

Pokanoket and the Pilgrims. Unlike the powerful Powhatan in Virginia, Massasoit agreed to submit himself to the English. By the time Squanto died of a fever in 1622, he had helped secure the future of the Plymouth colony. The Pilgrim colony at Plymouth grew slowly and proved a disappointment to its investors, who eventually sold their shares to the Pilgrims. Plymouth remained a separate colony until 1691, when it was absorbed into Massachusetts, which was larger and more influential. Socially and religiously similar to the Massachusetts Bay colony, Plymouth was economically somewhat less diverse. Plymouth demonstrated that New England could be inhabited by Europeans and that effective diplomatic relations with local Indians were critical for a colony's survival.

The Puritan Colony at Massachusetts Bay

In 1629, the Massachusetts Bay Company, a group of London merchants, received a charter from King Charles I to establish a colony. The plan was similar to that on which Virginia had been founded. The investors in the joint-stock company would have full rights to a swath of land reaching from Massachusetts Bay west across the entire continent. Along with a number of Puritans who were looking for a new home, the company included some who hoped to turn a profit from trade. The Puritans' objective was to make the colony entirely self-governing, with the directors of the Company and the governors of the colony being one and the same.

The expedition began in 1630, and by the end of that year Boston and ten other towns had been founded. By the early 1640s, between 20,000 and 25,000 Britons had migrated to the Puritan colonies of Plymouth, Massachusetts Bay, Connecticut, Rhode Island, and New Hampshire. Although fewer than half as many people migrated to New England as to the Chesapeake region, by 1660 both had populations of a similar size—around 35,000 (see Map 3–2).

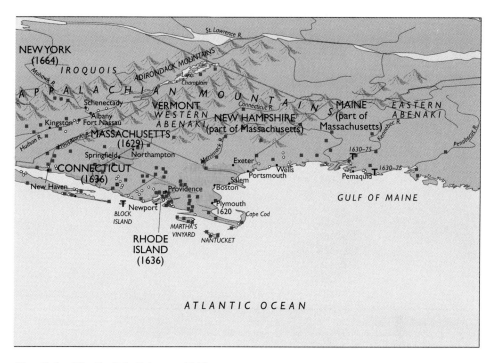

Map 3–2   The English Colonies, 1660
By 1660, English settlements dotted the East Coast, but most of the population was concentrated in two regions: New England and the Chesapeake.
Source: Helen Hornbeck Tanner, ed., Settling North America (New York: Macmillan, 1995), pp. 46–47.

New England was able to catch up and keep pace with the Chesapeake for two reasons. First, New England was a much healthier region than the Chesapeake. The long, cold winters killed the mosquitoes that carried fatal diseases, the water supply was good, and food was plentiful. Second, Puritans migrated as families. Ninety percent came as part of a family group. This pattern was almost exactly the reverse of that in the Chesapeake. In the healthy environment of New England, the population soon reproduced itself.

The Puritans came to stay. Before leaving England, they sold their property. Most were prosperous members of the middle range of society. Many of the men were professionals—doctors, lawyers, and ministers. Others were craftsmen. By and large, these people were profiting from the changes in the English economy of the late sixteenth and early seventeenth centuries. Once again, the contrast with the Chesapeake was dramatic. There, the vast majority of migrants were people with few skills and dim prospects.

The New England Way

The Puritans were men and women with a mission. Their first governor, John Winthrop, set out the vision of a Bible commonwealth in a sermon he preached aboard the *Arbella* in the spring of 1630, even before the ship docked at Boston. God, Winthrop said, had entered into a covenant with the Puritans, just as they had entered into a covenant with one another. Together they had taken enormous risks and

TABLE 3–2

Distribution of Land in Rowley, Massachusetts, 1639–1642

Rowley, 1639–c. 1642

Acres	No. of Grants
Over 400	
351–400	
301–350	
251–300	
201–250	1
151–200	1
101–150	
51–100	7
21–50	22
20 or less	63
No record	1
Total	95

Between 1639 and 1642, the town of Rowley, Massachusetts, distributed a little over 2,000 acres to 95 families—an average of just 23 acres per family—even though the grant to the town was for many thousand acres. Although most grants were for less than 20 acres, some families received considerably more. The founders of Rowley wanted to re-create the hierarchical social order they had known in England.

Source: David Grayson Allen, In English Ways: The Movement of Societies and the Transferal of English Local Law and Custom to Massachusetts Bay in the Seventeenth Century *(Chapel Hill: University of North Carolina Press, 1981), p. 32.*

begun an extraordinary experiment to see whether they could establish a society based on the word of God: "We shall be as a city upon a hill, the eyes of all people are upon us. So that if we shall deal falsely with our God in this work we have undertaken, and so cause Him to withdraw his present help from us, we shall be made a story and a by-word through the world." Although not all those who migrated to New England were Puritans, and there were significant variations among the Puritans themselves, this vision shaped the development of New England's society and political economy.

This communal vision made early New Englanders exceptionally cohesive. Each town was created by a grant of land by the Massachusetts General Court (the name given to the legislature) to a group of citizens. The settlers in turn entered into a covenant with one another to establish a government and distribute the land they held collectively.

At first, the newly established towns divided up only a portion of the land that they held, reserving the rest for newcomers and the children of the original founders. The land was distributed according to social status and family size (see Table 3–2). Although in absolute terms New England society was relatively egalitarian, the Puritans set out to create a social hierarchy. As Winthrop explained, "God Almighty . . . hath so disposed of the condition of mankind as in all times some must be rich, some poor; some high and eminent in power and dignity, others mean and in subjection." The rich and powerful were supposed to take care of the poor, and, indeed, Puritan towns developed mechanisms for assisting all those who could not care for themselves, such as the disabled, widows, and orphans. Each town administered itself through a town meeting, a gathering of the adult male property owners who met periodically to attend to the town's business. In the interim, the town was governed by a small group of selectmen elected at the town meeting. In the past historians pointed to the democratic elements in the town meeting, finding in it the source of American democracy. More recently, historians have emphasized undemocratic elements. Participation was restricted to adult male property holders, who were perhaps 70 percent of the men, but only 35 percent of the adult residents, once women are considered. In addition, the habit of deference to those who were powerful, prosperous, and educated was so strong that a small group of influential men tended to govern each town. Moreover, Puritans abhorred conflict, so great social pressure was used to ensure harmony and limit dissent. However, even with all these restrictions, the New England town meeting was far more democratic than any form of government in England at the time, where the vast majority of men, not to mention women, were excluded from political participation.

Changing the Land to Fit the Political Economy

The Puritans' corporate social vision was generally compatible with a capitalist political economy. Although land was distributed to towns, once those towns transferred parcels of the land to individual farmers, the farmers were free to leave it to their heirs, to sell it to whomever they pleased, and to buy more land from others. Any improvements that people made on their land (from clearing away trees to building homes, fences, dams, or mills) remained the property of the owners. These practices followed English law.

The contrast with Indian patterns of land use was dramatic. Indians held their land communally, not individually. When it was sold, the entire group had to consent to its transfer. Moreover, Indians recognized not the right of exclusive ownership, but rather the right to particular uses of land. Hence they might allow the Puritans to build a village, to plant, and to hunt, while they retained similar rights over the same parcel of land. Therefore, Indians believed that they could sell the right to use the land to several groups of Europeans at once.

The Puritans' notion of exclusive land rights was a cornerstone of their political economy. Because a man could profit from the improvements he and his family made on his land and pass those improvements on to his heirs, he had incentives to increase the value of his land. Moreover, not only the land but its products became commodities to be sold. As a result, like other Europeans, the Puritans turned their Indian neighbors into commercial hunters. For centuries, the Indians had taken only as many beaver as they needed, but soon they were overhunting, which led to the disappearance of beaver in the region. The Puritans themselves cleared the forests of trees. They found a ready market for timber in England, as New England's trees were much taller and straighter than any known in Europe at the time. Although the bounty of the land had seemed limitless, by 1800 much of southern New England had been stripped of its forests and native wildlife.

Prosperity did not come to Massachusetts immediately. For the first decade, the colony maintained a favorable balance of trade with England only by sending back the money that new immigrants brought with them in return for goods imported from the mother country. New England's rocky soil meant that it would never develop a cash crop such as tobacco. In the 1640s and 1650s, the government encouraged local manufacturing (to cut down on imports) and export of raw materials. Through a combination of government policy and individual initiative, New Englanders eventually profited from selling timber, wood products, and fish, and by acting as merchants.

The Puritan Family

Like most early modern western Europeans, Puritans thought of the family as the society in microcosm. As they put it, "a family is a little Church, and a little commonwealth." There was no sharp distinction between home and the wider world. Although Harvard College was founded in 1636 (to train ministers) and the Massachusetts General Court established a system of public education in 1647, most early instruction and virtually all vocational teaching took place at home. Indeed, parents were required to teach their children to read the Bible.

The family was also a place of business, the center of the Puritans' economy. Farmers, of course, worked at home, as did almost all craftsmen. Women also performed tasks critical to the economic survival of the family. Although tasks were assigned by gender, in the absence of her husband a woman could assume his responsibilities, selling the products he had made or even picking up a gun to fight off Indians. The family, like society, was a hierarchy, with the husband at the top and his wife as his "deputy."

Puritans believed that both men and women were equally capable of preparing for and receiving God's grace. Puritans distrusted the passion of love, because they thought it could lead to impulsiveness and disorder. They had great respect, however, for the natural affection that grew between a man and a woman over the course of their marriage. The poems of Anne Bradstreet and the letters that John Winthrop exchanged with his wife give ample testimony to the Puritan capacity for love.

So successful were the early Puritans in establishing tight-knit communities that only two years after the great migration to America had begun, the Reverend Thomas Welde could write proudly back to England that "here I find three great blessings, peace, plenty, and health. . . . I profess if I might have my wish in what part of the world to dwell I know no other place on the whole globe of the earth where I would be rather than here."

DISSENSION IN THE PURITAN RANKS

The Puritan movement embodied tensions that inevitably made for individual and social turmoil. Puritans had difficulty finding a balance between emotion and intellect, between the individual and the community, between spiritual equality and social hierarchy, between anxiety over salvation and the self-satisfaction of thinking yourself one of a chosen people.

Furthermore, the Puritans had no mechanisms for channeling or accommodating dissent, which they interpreted as a replay of Adam and Eve's original sin. The migration to a new and strange land, populated by people they thought of as savages, as well as the pressure of thinking that the whole world was watching them, only increased the Puritans' desire to maintain a strict order.

Roger Williams and Toleration

The Massachusetts Bay colony was only a year old when trouble appeared in the person of Roger Williams, a brilliant and obstinate young minister. No sooner had he landed than he announced that he would not accept appointment at a church unless it repudiated its ties to the Church of England. Massachusetts Bay was already walking a fine line between outward obedience to the laws of England and inner rejection of the English way of life. The leadership considered an explicit repudiation of England's established church an act of political suicide.

Without a church of his own, Williams began preaching to those who would listen. Saying that the king had no right to grant land owned by the Indians, he questioned the validity of the Massachusetts charter and argued for strict separation of church and state as well as strict separation of the regenerate (those who had had a conversion experience) and the unconverted. Williams went so far as to advocate religious toleration, with each congregation or sect governing itself completely free from state interference.

These doctrines were heresy to the Puritan church and state both. In 1635 when Williams violated an order to stop preaching his unorthodox views, the magistrates decided to ship him immediately to England, where he might be imprisoned or executed for his religious notions. John Winthrop warned Williams of his impending fate, giving him time to sneak away to Narragansett Bay, outside the jurisdiction of Massachusetts Bay. Some of Williams's followers joined him, and they established the new colony of Rhode Island, which received a charter in 1644. The colony soon became a refuge for dissenters of all sorts.

Anne Hutchinson and the Equality of Believers

One of Puritanism's many tensions concerned the position of women. By insisting on the equality of all true believers before God and the importance of marriage, Protestantism and especially its Puritan branch undermined the starkly negative image of women that prevailed in sixteenth-century Europe. When Puritan ministers preached that women and men were both "joynt Heirs of salvation" and that women, rather than being a "necessary evil," were in fact "a necessary good," they were directly criticizing both the Catholic legacy and common folk belief.

At the same time that Puritanism extended women, respect, it also insisted that they be subordinate to men. In the strictly hierarchical Puritan society, woman's position was clearly beneath that of man. "Though she be . . . a Mistress, yet she owns that she has a Master." It was never easy, however, for Puritanism to find the balance between women's spiritual equality and their earthly subordination: Although most Puritan women were deferential to male authority, others took advantage of the opportunity that Puritanism seemed to offer. Without exception, the Puritan authorities put them back in their place.

Anne Hutchinson was just over 40 when she, her husband, and their 12 surviving children followed the Reverend John Cotton to Massachusetts Bay. Cotton was a popular preacher who placed particular emphasis on the doctrine of predestination. Hutchinson pushed that doctrine to its logical, if unsettling, conclusion. Hutchinson claimed that she had experienced several direct revelations, one telling her to follow Cotton to Boston. At informal Bible discussion meetings at her Boston home, which even the new governor, Henry Vane, attended, Hutchinson challenged Puritan doctrine. If God had truly chosen those whom He would save, it was unnecessary for Puritans to prepare themselves for saving grace by leading sin-free lives. Nor was good behavior a reliable sign that a person had been saved. It was not that Hutchinson favored sin. She simply thought that her neighbors were deluding themselves into thinking that good works would save them. Hence, she accused them of the heresy of Arminianism. For her part, by claiming that the Holy Spirit spoke directly to her, Hutchinson opened herself to charges of another heresy, *antinomianism.*

Hutchinson's views became extremely popular, and her opponents mounted a campaign against her. In 1637 they moved the site of the election for governor outside Boston, where her strength was greatest, so that John Winthrop could win. At that point, both church and state moved against her and her allies. In November, after her most prominent ally among the ministers had been banished, Hutchinson was put on trial for slandering the ministry. She almost surely would have been acquitted had she not asserted that God had revealed to her that He would punish her persecutors. This was a dangerous heresy: The Puritans believed divine revelations had stopped in biblical times. Hutchinson was convicted and ordered to leave the colony. Followed by 80 other families, she and her family found refuge in Roger Williams's Rhode Island. The fact that Hutchinson's ideas came from a woman made them even more dangerous to the Massachusetts leadership. John Winthrop suggested that she might be a witch. Without any evidence at all of sexual misconduct, ministers such as John Cotton asserted that Hutchinson and her female followers were driven by lust and that unless they were punished, it would lead to communal living, open sex, and the repudiation of marriage.

It is sometimes asserted that Puritans came to New England in search of religious freedom, but they never would have made that claim. They wanted the liberty to follow their own religion but actively denied that opportunity to others. Puritans insisted on their right to keep out nonbelievers. "No man hath right to come into us," John Winthrop wrote, "without our consent."

Puritan Indian Policy and the Pequot War

The Puritan dissidents, despite the diversity of their beliefs, were all critical of the Puritans' Indian policy. Roger Williams insisted on purchasing land from the Indians instead of simply seizing it, and the men in the Hutchinson family refused to fight in the Pequot War of 1637. The Puritans had been fortunate in beginning their settlement in a region where the Indian population had recently been decimated and in having the English-speaking Squanto's diplomatic services. The Puritan communities expanded so rapidly, however, that they soon intruded on land populated by Indians who had no intention of giving New Englanders exclusive rights to it.

Within a few years of the founding of the Massachusetts Bay colony, small groups of Puritans were spreading out in all directions (see Map 3–3). The Reverend John Wheelwright, Anne Hutchinson's brother-in-law and most ardent supporter, took a party into what is now New Hampshire. Others settled in Maine. In 1638, New Haven, Connecticut, was founded by the Reverend John Davenport and a London merchant, Theophilus Eaton, who purchased land from the local Indians. Four years earlier, the first Puritan settlers had reached the banks of the Connecticut River in western Massachusetts. In 1636 the Reverend Thomas Hooker led his followers to the site of Hartford, Connecticut. Many were drawn by the fertile soil of the region, although religious differences played a role too. Puritan Congregationalism encouraged individual ministers and their followers to interpret church teachings in a variety of ways.

The Pequot War grew out of conflicts among Europeans about who would govern the Connecticut River valley and among Native Americans about who would trade with the Europeans. Until the arrival of the English, the Dutch had controlled trade along the Connecticut River. They had granted trading privileges to the Pequots, which frustrated other tribes, who could trade only through these middlemen. When the English arrived, the Pequots' enemies attempted to attract them to the valley as trading rivals to the Dutch. The Pequots, afraid of losing their trade monopoly, made the mistake of inviting Massachusetts Bay to establish a trading post in the region.

As hundreds of settlers led by Thomas Hooker poured in, the Pequots became alarmed. They appealed to their one-time enemies, the Narragansetts, to join with them to get rid of the English. The Narragansetts, however, had already been

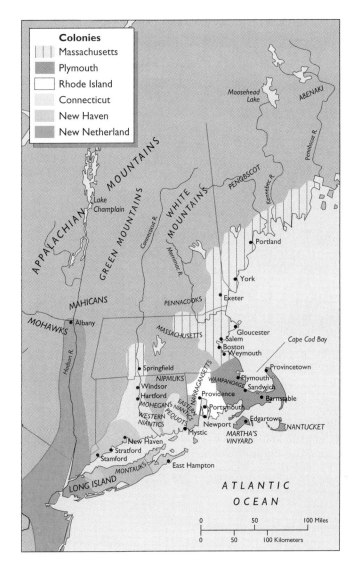

Colonies
	Massachusetts
	Plymouth
	Rhode Island
	Connecticut
	New Haven
	New Netherland

Map 3–3 New England in the 1640s

This map shows the land settled by each of the New England colonies, the regions inhabited by Indian tribes, and the region of Dutch settlement.

Source: John Murrin et al., Liberty, Equality, Power (Harcourt College Publishers, 1st. ed., 1995), p. 73.

approached by the Puritans to join them in fighting the Pequots. That is where the Narragansetts calculated that their long-term advantage lay.

The Pequots were caught in a rivalry between the parent colony at Massachusetts and the new offshoot in Connecticut, both of which wanted to dominate the Pequots' land. The Connecticut group struck first, avenging an attack by the Pequots, which in itself was in revenge for an attack upon their allies. At dawn on May 26, 1637, a party of 90 Connecticut men accompanied by 500 Narragansett allies attacked a Pequot village at Mystic filled with women, children, and old men. As the raiders knew, most of the warriors were away from home. As his men encircled the village, the commander, Captain John Mason, set a torch to the wigwams. Those Pequots who escaped the fire ran into the ring of waiting Englishmen. Mason's party killed between 300 and 700 Indians, while losing only two of their own men. The Narragansetts' allies were so horrified by the brutality of the attack that they refused to participate in it.

The Attack on Mystic Fort. On the inner ring are the New Englanders, attacking the palisaded Indian village.

Deeply demoralized, the remainder of the Pequot tribe was easily defeated. By 1638, the Puritans could declare the Pequot tribe dissolved, and in 1639 Connecticut established its dominance over the Pequots' land. In that year Connecticut established its own government, modeled after that of Massachusetts.

CONCLUSION

At the middle of the seventeenth century, the New England and Chesapeake colonies could hardly have appeared more different. Although the forces of capitalism, launched by people such as John Rolfe, shaped each region, other factors left their distinctive imprints: the objectives of the founders, disease, demographic patterns, and relations with local Indians. The early history of New England was shaped by the extraordinary energy and cohesiveness of the Puritans, which made them uniquely successful in the history of colonial ventures. If New England achieved settlement within a few years, unsettlement was the norm. That was particularly true of the Chesapeake colonies, which were still raw colonial outposts long after New England had achieved a secure order.

All of the North American colonies except those of New England were outposts in the global political economy, created to enrich their mother countries and enhance their power. Indeed, had the Virginia Company known that the Puritans wanted to create a religious refuge rather than a money-making venture, it probably would not have given them a charter. So successful was New England in achieving a stable society that we sometimes forget that it was the exception and not the rule.

CHRONOLOGY

1533	Henry VIII breaks with Roman Catholic Church, establishes Church of England
1603	Queen Elizabeth I dies, succeeded by King James I
1606	James I grants two charters for North American settlement to Virginia Company
1607	English found Jamestown
1608	John Smith named President of Virginia's Council
1609	John Smith returns to England
1610–1614	First Anglo-Powhatan War
1612–1617	John Rolfe develops a marketable strain of tobacco
1614	John Rolfe and Pocahontas marry
1616	Virginia Company offers 50-acre headrights to each immigrant
1619	First meeting of Virginia General Assembly
	First Africans arrive in Virginia
	Virginia Company pays for transportation of women to Virginia
1620	Pilgrims found colony at Plymouth; Mayflower Compact signed
1622–1632	Second Anglo-Powhatan War
1624	Virginia Company dissolved; Virginia becomes a royal colony
1625	James I dies, succeeded by King Charles I
1629	Massachusetts Bay Company receives charter to establish colony in North America
1630	Massachusetts Bay colony founded
1632	George Calvert receives charter for Maryland
1636	Harvard College founded
	Roger Williams exiled from Massachusetts
1637	Anne Hutchinson and her followers exiled
	Pequot War
1638	New Haven founded
1639	First law mentioning slavery, in Maryland
	Connecticut establishes its government
1644	Rhode Island receives charter
1644–1646	Third Anglo-Powhatan War
1647	Massachusetts establishes system of public education
1649	Act of Toleration passed in Maryland
1661	First Virginia law mentioning slavery
1691	Plymouth colony absorbed into Massachusetts

FURTHER READINGS

Kathleen M. Brown, *Good Wives, Nasty Wenches, and Anxious Patriarchs* (1996). A provocative interpretation of colonial Virginia that puts gender at the center.

William Cronon, *Changes in the Land: Indians, Colonists, and the Ecology of New England* (1983). A comparison of the ways that Indians and New Englanders used, lived off, and changed the land.

John Demos, *A Little Commonwealth: Family Life in Plymouth Colony* (1970). Brief and beautifully written, this book helped revolutionize the writing of American social history by showing how much could be learned about ordinary people from a sensitive reading of a wide variety of sources.

Jack P. Greene, *Pursuits of Happiness: The Social Development of Early Modern British Colonies and the Formation of American Culture* (1988). An interpretive overview of colonial development that argues that the Chesapeake was the most American region of all.

Ivor Noël Hume, *The Virginia Adventure: Roanoke to James Towne: An Archaeological and Historical Odyssey* (1994). A detailed and well-written history of the early Chesapeake settlements with a focus on archaeology.

Stephen Innes, *Creating the Commonwealth: The Economic Culture of Puritan New England* (1995). Argues that the Puritans were capitalists.

Francis Jennings, *The Invasion of America: Indians, Colonialism, and the Cant of Conquest* (1975). A highly critical history of Puritan Indian policy that may be read along with Alden T. Vaughan, *New England Frontier: Puritans and Indians, 1620–1675* (1979), which is more sympathetic to the Puritans.

Karen Ordahl Kupperman, *Indians and English: Facing Off in Early America* (2000). An insightful account of the encounter between Indians and English along the Atlantic coast in the seventeenth century, emphasizing mutual attempts—and failures—at understanding.

Edmund S. Morgan, *American Slavery, American Freedom: The Ordeal of Colonial Virginia* (1975). A powerful and magnificently written history of Virginia that argues that racism was intentionally cultivated by elites to keep poor blacks and whites from uniting.

Edmund S. Morgan, *Visible Saints: The History of a Puritan Idea* (1963). A brilliant explanation of one of Puritanism's key ideas.

 Please refer to the document CD-ROM for primary sources related to this chapter.

CHAPTER

4

Creating the Empire

1660–1720

Tituba Shapes Her World and Saves Herself • The Plan of Empire
New Colonies, New Patterns • The Transformation of Virginia
New England Under Assault • The Empire Strikes • Massachusetts
in Crisis • French and Spanish Outposts • Conquest, Revolt, and
Reconquest in New Mexico • Conclusion

TITUBA SHAPES HER WORLD AND SAVES HERSELF

*H*er name was Tituba. Some say she was African, a Yoruba, others that she was an Arawak Indian from Guyana. Had she not been accused of practicing witchcraft in Salem, Massachusetts, in 1692, she surely would have been forgotten by history. Whether she came from South America or Africa, she had been torn away from her home and sent to work on a sugar plantation on the Caribbean island of Barbados, which the English had colonized almost 50 years before. Whatever her origins, Tituba lived in an African-majority society and absorbed African customs.

Tituba was probably a teenager when she was taken, once again as a slave, to Massachusetts in 1680. She had been purchased by a young, Harvard-educated Barbadian, Samuel Parris. Parris's father had failed as a planter, and now he himself abandoned commerce for the ministry. In 1689 Parris moved his wife, their three children, Tituba, and her slave husband John Indian to Salem Village, where he had been appointed minister.

In 1692, one of Parris's daughters, Betty, and her cousin Abigail followed the folk custom of trying to see their futures in the white of an egg dropped into a glass of water. Soon several girls and young women were playing with magic. Then Betty began to experience strange and seemingly inexplicable pains, which spread to others. When neither doctors nor ministers could cure her, a neighbor asked Tituba to bake a "witchcake" out of rye flour and the girls' urine. This was "white magic," intended to uncover the identity of the witch who was thought to be bewitching Betty and the others. Their suffering, however, only got worse. Parris now questioned the girls: Who was bewitching them? This time the girls had an answer: two older, rather marginal white women—and Tituba.

The three women were charged with the capital offense of witchcraft. Under duress, the first woman, Sarah Good, implicated the second, Sarah Osborne. Osborne steadfastly denied her guilt—and was returned to jail. Finally, Tituba was summoned. As a slave, she was particularly vulnerable. Perhaps calculating the odds carefully, Tituba slowly began to embroider a story. She named only two names—Sarah Good and Sarah Osborne. She talked about a tall, white-haired man in Boston who made her sign a mysterious book and conspiring with other, unnamed witches.

Responding to the hints of her Puritan interrogators, Tituba confirmed that she had made a covenant with the devil, the tall man in Boston. But she also added elements that came from African and Indian culture, such as a "thing all over hairy, all the face harye & a long nose . . . " Tituba's tales of witches' meetings, flying to Boston on a broomstick, and wolves and birds and hairy imps persuaded her interrogators that their colony was beset by witches. A children's game spiraled into panic, but Tituba escaped with her life. Having spent her life as a prisoner in other people's lands, she had combined their cultures with her own, crafting them into a strategy for survival.

Colonial America in the second half of the seventeenth century was shaped by conflicting cultures and economic currents. In some ways, Tituba was a victim of political economy. She was in Salem because Samuel Parris failed as a merchant, unable to succeed in the global economy. By melding her own culture and those of her captors, Tituba was able to save herself when the dislocations of the late seventeenth century brought her to face accusations of witchcraft. Tituba's story is like that of many Americans of the late seventeenth century. Caught in the cross-currents of culture and economic transformation, they adapted their cultural inheritances to new circumstances.

THE PLAN OF EMPIRE

Trying to make sense out of the haphazard development of Britain's American colonies, the English political theorist Edmund Burke explained in 1757, "[O]ur colonies . . . were formed, grew, and flourished, as accidents, the nature of the climate, or the dispositions of private men happened to operate." In comparison with the tight direction the Spanish and French governments gave their overseas colonies, the English government did comparatively little to shape the colonies. As expressions of Britain's political economy, all of the colonies were private ventures by individuals or groups, chartered by the British government but given little supervision or material support.

Turmoil in England

In the middle decades of the seventeenth century, the British government was thrown into turmoil as Parliament and the king struggled over the future direction of the nation. Two fundamental and overlapping issues were at stake: religion and royal power. The uneasy balance that Elizabeth I had established between Puritans and Anglicans collapsed under her successors, James I (1603–1625) and Charles I (1625–1649). Archbishop of Canterbury William Laud moved the Church of England away from the Calvinist belief in predestination, brought back worship ceremonies that smacked of Catholicism, and persecuted Puritans, prompting Presbyterian Scotland to revolt.

Parliament refused to appropriate the funds that King Charles requested to quash the revolt. Instead, in 1628, Parliament passed the Petition of Right, which reasserted those freedoms that Britons held dear, including no taxation except by act of Parliament, no arbitrary arrest or imprisonment, and no quartering of soldiers in private homes. In 1642 Charles raised an army and moved against the recalcitrant Parliament, beginning the English Civil War, which concluded in 1647 with Parliament's victory. Two years later, Charles was beheaded. Oliver Cromwell, a Puritan, ruled as Lord Protector until his death in 1658. When Cromwell's son and successor proved an inept leader, Charles II was invited to reclaim the crown in 1660.

Although the monarchy had been restored, its authority had been diminished. Britain had been transformed into a constitutional monarchy in which the power of the Crown was balanced by that of Parliament. In addition, Britain once again found a middle way between a Calvinist Protestantism and Catholicism. When the Catholic King James II (1685–1688) tried to fill the government with Catholics and to rule without the consent of Parliament, he was removed in a bloodless revolution, known as the Glorious Revolution (1688). It brought Mary, James's Protestant daughter, and her equally Protestant husband, William of Orange (Holland) to the throne.

The Political Economy of Mercantilism

After the reassertion of Parliament's authority in 1688, the British state became increasingly strong and centralized. Britain then embarked on a course that would make it the world's most powerful nation by the early nineteenth century.

Throughout the political turmoil of the seventeenth century, Britain's economic policies were guided by a theory called mercantilism, which held that the chief object of a nation's economic policies was to serve the state. Mercantilism's theorists considered the economy and politics both as zero-sum games; one side's gain could come only by another's loss. Mercantilism defined wealth exclusively as hard money, that is, gold and silver. Since there was only a finite amount of gold and silver in the world, a nation could best improve its position by capturing a share of other nations' money. Mercantilism thus led to rivalry between nations. Its chief expression was the regulation of foreign trade.

Between 1651 and 1696, the British government, following mercantilist theories, passed a series of trade regulations, the Navigation Acts, requiring that all goods shipped to England and her colonies be carried in ships owned and manned by Englishmen (including colonists). In addition, all foreign goods going to the colonies had to be shipped via Britain, where they could be taxed. Certain colonial products (tobacco, sugar, indigo, and cotton, with others added later) had to be sent first to England before they could be shipped elsewhere. According to mercantilist doctrine, the mother country was to produce finished products, and the colonies, raw materials. Hence, when the colonies began to manufacture items such as woolen cloth and hats, Parliament passed legislation to restrict those industries.

NEW COLONIES, NEW PATTERNS

In the second half of the seventeenth century, two important new English colonies, Pennsylvania and South Carolina, were established, and New Netherland was seized from the Dutch. As a rule, the most successful colonies offered the most opportunity to free white people and the greatest amount of religious toleration.

New Netherland Becomes New York

By the middle of the seventeenth century, the British were ready to challenge their chief trade rival, the Dutch. The two nations fought three wars between 1652 and 1674, and the English emerged victorious. The Navigation Acts cut the Dutch out of international trade, and Britain began to challenge Dutch dominance of the slave trade. In 1663 King Charles II chartered the Royal Africa Company to carry slaves out of Africa to the British West Indies. At the same time, Britain made a move for New Netherland.

James, the Duke of York and King Charles II's younger brother, persuaded Charles to grant him the territory between the Connecticut and Delaware Rivers (present-day Pennsylvania, New Jersey, New York, and part of Connecticut), which was occupied by the Netherlands. In 1664 James sent over a governor, 400 troops, and several warships that easily conquered the small colony of New Amsterdam. In 1665 James gave away what is now New Jersey to two of his royal cronies, Lords John Berkeley and George Carteret, and in 1667 New York's governor gave the territory on the western side of the Connecticut River to Connecticut. New Netherland had become New York.

The new colony was part Dutch (in New York City and along the Hudson) and part English (on Long Island, where New England Puritans had migrated). The first governors attempted to satisfy both groups. On the one hand, the governors confirmed Dutch landholdings, including the huge estates along the Hudson, and guaranteed the Dutch the freedom to follow their own religion. On the other, the governors distributed 2 million more acres of land, most of it in enormous chunks called manors. The owners of these manors, like feudal lords, rented out land to tenants and set up courts on their estates.

If religious toleration attracted diverse peoples to the region, feudal land policies and England's failure to restore self-government kept others away. Without an elective legislature to raise taxes, the governors, following English mercantilist policy, used customs duties to raise the revenue necessary to run the colony and send back a profit to James. These attempts to regulate trade and direct the economy angered local merchants and harmed the economy. For example, New York's fur production declined between 1660 and 1700. Eventually, James gave in to popular discontent, and in 1683 he allowed New York to have an elective assembly.

At its first meeting, this small group of English and Dutch men passed a "Charter of Libertyes and Priviledges," which, had the king approved it, would have guaranteed New Yorkers both a number of civil liberties and the continuing right to self-government by its elected assembly. The charter was an expression of the principles of liberalism that were beginning to spread through both Britain and the Netherlands. The charter guaranteed all freemen the right to vote and to be taxed only by their elective representatives. It also provided for trial by jury, due process, freedom of conscience for Christians, and certain property rights for women, the latter two items reflecting Dutch practices. However, James, who became king in 1685, refused to approve the charter on two grounds: It would give New Yorkers more rights than any other colonists and the New York assembly might undermine the power of Parliament. Without a secure form of self-government, New Yorkers fell to fighting among themselves, and political instability in combination with feudal land holdings slowed New York's population growth.

Diversity and Prosperity in Pennsylvania

Pennsylvania demonstrated the potential of a colony that offered both religious toleration and economic opportunity. Its founder, William Penn, was a Quaker and the son of one of King Charles II's leading supporters. After his restoration to the throne, Charles had a number of political debts to repay, and giving away vast chunks of North America was a cheap way of doing it. As a Quaker, Penn was eager to get out of England. In 1661 alone, 4,000 English Quakers were jailed, and Penn himself was imprisoned four times. The Quakers were a radical sect of Protestants who believed that God offered salvation to all and placed an "inner light" inside each man and woman. A hard-working, serious, and moral people, Quakers rejected violence as a means of resolving disputes and hence refused to serve in the military or pay taxes for its support. Once they arrived in America, they endeavored to live peaceably with the Indians.

Penn received his charter in 1681. To raise money for his venture, Penn sold land to a group of wealthy Quaker merchants. In return for their investment, he promised them government positions and granted economic concessions. Penn also sought to attract ordinary settlers. He promised self-government (although stacked in favor of the merchant elite), freedom of religion, and reasonably priced land.

In 1682, when Penn arrived at Philadelphia (Greek for the "city of brotherly love"), the colony already had 4,000 inhabitants. Penn had clear ideas about how he wanted his colony to develop. He expected the orderly growth of farming villages, neatly laid out along Pennsylvania's rivers and creeks. He mapped out the settlement of Philadelphia along a grid pattern, with each house set far enough from its neighbors to prevent the spread of fires. He sought and achieved orderly and harmonious relations with the local Indians.

Penn's policies attracted a wide variety of Europeans to his colony. Soon Pennsylvania was populated by self-contained communities, each speaking a different language or practicing a different religion. Although this diversity eventually led to a certain amount of factionalism in government, Pennsylvania's early history was characterized by rapid growth and widespread prosperity. However, this growth and prosperity undermined Penn's plans for a cohesive, hierarchical society. People lived where and how they wanted, pursuing the economic activities they found most profitable.

While moving away from the inequalities of the Old World, Pennsylvania replicated those of the New World. A high proportion of the Europeans who came to the colony were indentured servants or *redemptioners*, people who worked for a brief period to pay back the ship's captain for the cost of transportation to the colony. And by 1700, the Pennsylvania assembly had passed laws recognizing slavery, although not without opposition. That the institution could take root in a colony where some questioned its morality suggests both the force of its power in shaping early America and the weakness of the opposition.

Indians in the Political Economy of Carolina

Like Pennsylvania and Maryland, South Carolina was a proprietary colony. One of the proprietors, Anthony Ashley Cooper, the Earl of Shaftesbury, and his secretary John Locke drafted the Fundamental Constitutions for the new colony. Locke later became a leading political philosopher, and the Constitutions reflect the liberal, rights-guaranteeing principles that he later developed more fully.

The Constitutions made provisions for a representative government and widespread toleration of religion. At the same time, the document embodied the traditional assumption that liberty could be guaranteed only in a hierarchical society. Shaftesbury and Locke attempted to set up a complex hierarchy of landholders at the top and hereditary serfs at the bottom. The Fundamental Constitutions also recognized African slavery. Carolina was the first colony that introduced slavery at the outset. The Constitutions never went into full effect, for the first Carolina representative assembly rejected many of the provisions. The first settlers arrived at Charles Town (later moved and renamed Charleston) in 1670. The area had a semitropical climate with wonderfully fertile soil, 50 inches of rain a year, and a growing season of up to 295 days. The region had once been explored by the Spanish, who still claimed it. It was inhabited by mission Indians, that is, Indians who had converted to Catholicism.

As happened so often when Europeans entered a region, Indian tribes competed to trade with them, and rival groups of Europeans struggled to dominate the trade. Carolina Indian traders quickly established their control over the entire Southeast. In 1680, in the Westo War, the Carolina traders sent their allies, the Savannah Indians, out to destroy the Westos, who were the Virginians' link to the Native American trade of the Southeast. The Carolinians vanquished the Spanish by sending in other Indian allies to destroy the mission towns. In this way, the Carolina traders eliminated their European rivals and established their dominance over all the regional Indians.

In the colonial period, Indian wars usually pitted one group of Europeans and their Indian allies against another group of Europeans and their native allies, with the Indians doing most of the fighting. Such wars were an extension of Europe's market economy: Indians fought for access to European goods, and Europeans fought to achieve a monopoly over Indian products. The English were particularly successful in achieving dominance because of their sophisticated market economy. London's banks had perfected the mechanisms of credit, which financed a fur trade in the forests half a world away.

At the same time that Carolina traders were exchanging European goods for southeastern deerskins, they had found an even more valuable commodity on the southeastern frontier, Indian slaves. In fact, until about 1690, slaves were the most valuable commodity produced by the Carolina colony.

The Barbados Connection

Carolina was part of a far-flung Atlantic political economy based on trade, plantation agriculture, and slavery. Many of the early Carolina settlers had substantial experience with African slavery in Barbados, a small island in the Caribbean that was settled in 1627 and within a decade became a major source of the world's sugar. By that time, it had an African majority, making it Britain's first slave society. By the end of the seventeenth century, Barbados was the most productive of all Britain's colonies. As a result, per-person income was much higher in Barbados than in England.

This income was not shared equally among the inhabitants of the island, however. Those who owned the largest plantations became fabulously wealthy, and even lesser planters enjoyed a high standard of living. Conditions for African slaves, however, were brutal. As in their other slave societies, the British magnified the differences between Europeans and Africans to enhance the distinction between landowners and slaves. Barbadians were the first to portray Africans as beasts. The racism of Caribbean planters was intense, and the slave codes were the harshest of any in the Atlantic world. The laws prescribed that male slaves convicted of crimes could be burned at the stake, beheaded, starved, or castrated. When Caribbean slavery was imported into Carolina, these attitudes came with it. The Carolina slave code, enacted in the 1690s, was the harshest on the North American continent. At the same time that laws and attitudes separated whites from blacks, differences among Europeans were minimized. Despite early restrictions against Irish Catholics and Jews, after Barbados became a slave society, some of those restrictions were lifted. In 1650, the Council in Barbados allowed the immigration of Jews and other religious minorities, six years before similar legislation was passed in England. As in the Chesapeake, increasing freedom for Europeans developed in tandem with the enslavement of Africans.

The sugar plantations of Barbados, and later Britain's other Caribbean islands, made their extraordinary profits from the labor of African slaves. British planters worked Africans harder than they would work European indentured servants. Profits came from keeping labor costs down, as well as from the growing demand for sugar. It is important to remember that the New World slave system would not have grown as it did without European demand for plantation crops.

African slaves were imported into Carolina from the outset of the colony's existence, but only after 1690 did the colony develop a staple crop—rice—that increased the demand for slave labor. Africans probably taught their masters how to cultivate the crop, for they had raised it in their native lands. Soon rice became the region's major cash crop, and African slaves became more valuable. By 1720, Africans comprised more than 70 percent of Carolina's population. With a black majority and wealth concentrated in the hands of an elite, Carolina resembled the Caribbean islands more than it did the other English colonies on the mainland. In only a few decades, Carolina had become a slave society, not simply a society with slaves: Slavery stood at the center of the political economy and gave shape to society.

THE TRANSFORMATION OF VIRGINIA

At the same time that a newly invigorated England was planting new colonies, those established earlier were reshaped. In the final quarter of the seventeenth century, the older colonies experienced political and sometimes social instability, followed by the establishment of a lasting order. In Virginia, the transition was marked by a violent insurrection known as Bacon's Rebellion. Significantly, the rebels sought not to overthrow the social and political order but to secure economic opportunity and a legitimate government that protected that opportunity. In its aftermath, Virginia became a slave society.

Social Change in Virginia

As Virginia entered its second half-century, the health of its population finally began to improve. Apple orchards had matured, so Virginians could drink cider instead of impure water. Ships bringing new servants arrived in the fall, a healthy time of year. Increasingly, these men and women lived to serve out their period of indenture and set out on their own to plant tobacco. However, most of the best land in eastern Virginia had already been claimed, and the land to the west was occupied by Indian tribes that had entered into peace treaties with the English. In addition, the government was in the hands of a small clique of men who were using it as a means of getting rich. For example, Virginia's legislators voted themselves payments 200 times as high as representatives in New England were getting. Taxes, assessed in tobacco, were extraordinarily high, and as taxes rose, the price of tobacco began to fall. Ordinary planters were caught in a squeeze. Many went to work for others as tenants or overseers.

Despite these circumstances, servants kept coming to the colony, most from the low ranks of society. A restless and unhappy set of men and women, these servants participated in a series of disturbances beginning in the middle of the century. The elite responded by lengthening the time of service and stiffening the penalties for running away.

Bacon's Rebellion and the Abandonment of the Middle Ground

When the revolt came, it was led not by one of the poor or landless but by a member of the elite. Nathaniel Bacon was young, well-educated, wealthy, and a member of a prominent family. Bacon made an immediate impression on Virginia's ruling clique, and Gov-

Interior of a freedman's house and interior of a middling planter's house, mid-seventeenth century Chesapeake. By the middle of the seventeenth century, middling planters were able to furnish their homes with chairs, tables, pewter dishes, tablecloths, and candles and candlesticks (left). The standard of living for freedmen was much more stark. Without chairs, the family either sat on benches or storage chests at mealtime or ate leaning against a wall. Without candles, once the sun went down at night, the only light came from the fire in the fireplace (right).

ernor Berkeley invited him to join the colony's Council of State. For reasons that are unclear, however, Bacon cast his lot with Berkeley's enemies among the elite. At that time, the instability of colonial elites gave rise to political factions in a number of colonies. When ruling elites, such as Berkeley's in Virginia, levied exorbitant taxes and ignored the needs of their constituents, they left themselves vulnerable to challenge.

The contest between Bacon and Berkeley might have remained an ordinary faction fight had not Bacon capitalized on the discontent of the colony's freedmen (men who had served out their indentures). In 1676, the conflict known as Bacon's Rebellion was triggered by a routine episode of violence on the middle ground inhabited by Indians and Europeans. Seeking payment for goods they had delivered to a frontier planter, a band of Doeg Indians killed the planter's overseer and tried to steal his hogs. Over the years, Europeans and Indians who shared the middle ground had adapted the Indian custom of providing restitution for crimes committed by one side or the other. Although this practice resulted in sporadic violence, it also helped maintain order. But this time, the conflict escalated, as Virginians sought revenge, prompting further Indian retaliation.

Soon an isolated incident had escalated into a joint Maryland and Virginia militia expedition with 1,000 men, an extraordinarily large force at the time. For six weeks the war party laid siege to the reservation of the Susquehannocks, who escaped and avenged themselves on settlers on the frontier.

When Berkeley refused to commission an expedition against the Susquehannocks, the frontier planters were infuriated. They complained that their taxes went into the pockets of Berkeley's clique instead of being used to police the frontier. Planter women were particularly upset, and they used their gossip networks to tell "hundreds" that Berkeley was "a greater friend to the Indians than to the English."

With his wife's encouragement, Nathaniel Bacon agreed to become the leader in a wholesale war on "all Indians whatsoever." Bacon's rebels went off in search of Susquehannocks and settled for massacring some hitherto friendly Occaneecchees. Bacon then marched on the government at Jamestown with 400 armed men, demanding an immediate commission to fight "all Indians in general, for that they were all Enemies." Berkeley consented, then changed his mind, but it was too late. Bacon was effectively in control, and Berkeley fled to the eastern shore.

By the time a Royal Commission and 1,000 soldiers arrived in January 1677 to put down the disorder, Bacon had died and Berkeley had regained control. Twenty-three leaders of the rebellion were executed, and the king removed Berkeley from office. Support for Bacon's Rebellion had been broad but shallow. Berkeley estimated that upwards of 14,000 Virginians had backed Bacon, but after his death, that support quickly dissipated.

After Bacon's Rebellion, the government remained in the hands of the planter elite, but the rebels had achieved their primary objective. The frontier Indians had been dispersed and their land was now free for settlement. Those in power became more responsive to the needs of white members of society. Other factors, not directly related to the revolt, also improved economic conditions. Tobacco prices began a slow climb, and planters replaced indentured servants with slaves.

Virginia Becomes a Slave Society

No one had planned for Virginia to become a slave society. With the new colonies like New York and Pennsylvania offering greater opportunity to poor whites, the supply of European indentured servants to the Chesapeake dried up just when more Africans were becoming available. Britain entered the slave trade at the end of the seventeenth century, authorizing private merchants to carry slaves from Africa to North America in 1698. Planters could not get enough slaves to meet their needs. In 1680, only 7 percent of Virginia's population was African in origin, but by 1700 the proportion had increased to 28 percent, and half the labor force was enslaved (Table 4–1). Within two decades, Virginia had become a slave society, in which slavery was central to the political economy and the social structure. With the bottom tier of the social order enslaved and hence unable to compete for land or wealth, opportunity for all whites necessarily improved.

As the composition of Virginia's labor force changed, so did the laws to control it. Although all slave societies had certain features in common, the specifics varied from place to place, as governments enacted slave codes to maintain and define the institution. By 1705, Virginia had a thorough slave code in place.

All forms of slavery have certain elements in common: perpetuity, kinlessness, violence, and the master's access to the slave's sexuality. First, slavery is a lifelong condition. Second, a slave has no legally recognized family relationships. Because kinship is the basis of most social and political relationships in society, a slave is socially "dead," outside the bounds of the larger society. Third, slavery rests on violence or its threat, including the master's sexual access to the slave.

American slavery added several other elements. First, slavery in all the Americas was hereditary, passed on from a mother to her children. Second, compared to other slave systems, including that of Latin America, *manumissions*—the freeing of slaves—in the American South were quite rare. Finally, slavery in the South was

TABLE 4–1

Population of British Colonies in America, 1660 and 1710

Colony	1660			1710		
	White	Black	Total	White	Black	Total
Virginia	26,070	950	27,020	55,163	23,118	78,281
Maryland	7,668	758	8,426	34,796	7,945	42,741
Chesapeake	**33,738**	**1,708**	**35,446**	**89,959**	**31,063**	**121,022**
Massachusetts	22,062	422	22,484	61,080	1,310	62,390
Connecticut	7,955	25	7,980	38,700	750	39,450
Rhode Island	1,474	65	1,539	7,198	375	7,573
New Hampshire	1,515	50	1,565	5,531	150	5,681
New England	**33,006**	**562**	**33,568**	**112,509**	**2,585**	**115,094**
Barbados	**26,200**	**27,100**	**53,300**	**13,000**	**52,300**	**65,300**
New York	4,336	600	4,936	18,814	2,811	21,625
New Jersey				18,540	1,332	19,872
Pennsylvania				22,875	1,575	24,450
Delaware	510	30	540	3,145	500	3,645
Middle Colonies	**4,846**	**630**	**5,476**	**63,374**	**6,218**	**69,592**
North Carolina	980	20	1,000	14,220	900	15,120
South Carolina				6,783	4,100	10,883
Lower South	**980**	**20**	**1,000**	**21,003**	**5,000**	**26,003**
Totals	**98,770**	**30,020**	**128,790**	**299,845**	**97,166**	**397,011**

Source: Adapted from Jack P. Greene, Pursuits of Happiness (Chapel Hill: University of North Carolina, 1988), p. 178–179.

racial. Slavery was reserved for Africans, some Indians, and their children, even if the father was white. The line between slavery and freedom was one of color, and it was this line that the slave codes defined.

Slave codes also defined gender roles. Two of the earliest pieces of legislation denied African women the privileges of European women (Table 4–2). A 1643 statute made all adult men and African women taxable, assuming that they (and not white women) were performing productive labor in the fields. Nineteen years later, another law specified that children were to inherit the status of their mother.

TABLE 4–2

Codifying Race and Slavery

1640—Masters are required to arm everyone in their households except Africans (Virginia)

1643—All adult men and African women are taxable, on the assumption that they are working in the fields (Virginia)

1662—Children follow the condition of their mother (Virginia)

1662—Double fine charged for any Christian who commits fornication with an African (Virginia)

1664—All slaves serve for life; that is, slavery is defined as a lifelong condition (Maryland)

1664—Interracial marriage banned; any free woman who marries a slave will serve that slave's master until her husband dies, and their children will be enslaved (Maryland)

1667—Baptism as a Christian does not make a slave free (Virginia)

1669—No punishment is given if punished slave dies (Virginia)

1670—Free blacks and Indians are not allowed to purchase Christian indentured servants (Virginia)

1680—To prevent "Negroes Insurrections," no slave may carry arms or weapons; no slave may leave his or her master without written permission; any slave who "lifts up his hand" against a Christian will receive 30 lashes; any slave who runs away and resists arrest may be killed lawfully (Virginia)

1682—Slaves may not gather for more than four hours at other than owner's plantation (Virginia)

1691—Owners are to be compensated if "negroes, mulattoes or other slaves" are killed while resisting arrest (Virginia)

1691—Forbidden is all miscegenation as "that abominable mixture"; any English or "other white man or woman" who marries a "negroe, mulatto, or Indian" is to be banished; any free English woman who bears a "bastard child by any negro or mulatto" will be fined, and if she can't pay the fine, she will be indentured for five years and the child will be indentured until the age of 30 (Virginia)

1691—All slaves who are freed by their masters must be transported out of the state (Virginia)

1692—Special courts of "oyer and terminer" are established for trying slaves accused of crimes, creating a separate system of justice (Virginia)

1705—Africans, mulattoes, and Indians are prohibited from holding office or giving grand jury testimony (Virginia)

1705—"Christian white" servants cannot be whipped naked (Virginia)

1723—Free blacks explicitly excluded from militia (Virginia)

1723—Free blacks explicitly denied the right to vote (Virginia)

Slavery is a creation of law, which defines what it means to be a slave and protects the master's rights in his slave property. Slave codes developed piecemeal in the Chesapeake, over the course of the seventeenth century. Legislators in the Chesapeake colonies defined slavery as a racial institution, appropriate only for Africans, and protected it with a series of laws, which, in the process, also created a privileged position for whites.

The same set of laws that created and sustained racial slavery also increased the freedom of whites. This increase in freedom was the product of several sorts of policies. First, it depended on the widespread availability of cheap land. As we have already seen, whites could obtain this land only by dispossessing the Indians who inhabited it. Second, it depended on policies of the British government, such as permitting self-government in the colonies. As we have seen, colonies offered this right as a means of attracting immigrants. Third, it depended on specific laws that improved the conditions of whites, often at the same time limiting the freedom of blacks. For example, in 1705 Virginia made it illegal for white servants to be whipped without an order from a justice of the peace.

New England Under Assault

As the New England colonies prospered, their prosperity led to problems, both internal and external. How would a religion that had been born in adversity cope with good fortune? A combination of conflicts among the New England colonies and a growing population that encroached on Indian lands led to the region's deadliest Indian war in 1675. At almost the same time as Bacon's Rebellion, the New England colonies were thrown into turmoil.

Social Prosperity and the Fear of Religious Decline

In many ways, the Puritan founders of the New England colonies saw their dreams come true. Although immigration came to a virtual halt as the English Revolution broke out, natural increase kept the population growing, from about 23,000 in 1650 to more than 93,000 in 1700. Life expectancy was higher than in England, and families were larger

Most New Englanders enjoyed a comfortable, if modest, standard of living. By the end of the century, the simple shacks erected by the first settlers had been replaced by two-story frame homes. Fireplaces were more efficient, making homes warmer in winter, and glass windows replaced oiled paper, letting light into rooms on sunny days. By our standards, these homes would still have been almost unbearably cold in the winter, when indoor temperatures routinely dropped into the 40s. Still, by the end of the century New Englanders were beginning to enjoy the sort of prosperous village life their ancestors had once known in England.

For Puritans, such good fortune presented a problem. Prosperity became a cause for worry, as people turned their minds away from God to more worldly things. In the 1660s and 1670s, New England's ministers preached a series of *jeremiads*, lamentations about spiritual decline. They criticized problems ranging from public drunkenness and sexual license to land speculation and excessively high prices and wages. If New Englanders did not repent and change their ways, the ministers predicted, "Ruine upon Ruine, Destruction upon Destruction would come, until one stone were not left upon another."

Most of the churches were embroiled in controversy in the 1660s concerning who could be members. The founders had assumed that most people, sooner or later, would have the conversion experience that entitled them to full church membership. By the third generation, however, many children and grandchildren of full church members had not had the deeply emotional experience of spiritual rebirth. In 1662 a group of New England ministers adopted the Half-Way Covenant, which set out terms for church membership and participation. Full church membership was reserved for those who could demonstrate a conversion experience. Their offspring could still be "half-way" members of the church, receiving its discipline and having their children baptized. The ministers were resisted by those who wanted to maintain the purity and exclusivity of the church. Rather than settling this question, the Half-Way Covenant aggravated tensions that were always present in the Puritan religion.

King Philip's War

Although New England's colonies developed along a common path, conflicts among them were intense. In fact, the region's deadliest Indian war grew out of one of these conflicts. As in Bacon's Rebellion, the underlying cause of the war was the steady encroachment of English settlers on land inhabited by Native Americans. In the 1660s, Rhode Island, Massachusetts, and Plymouth all claimed the land occupied by the Wampanoags, Massasoit's tribe, now ruled by his son Metacom, known by the colonists as King Philip. By 1671, the colonies had resolved their dispute and ordered King Philip and his people to submit to the rule of Plymouth. King Philip prepared for war, as did the colonists of all the colonies except Rhode Island, which attempted to mediate. In June 1675 King Philip's men attacked the Plymouth village of Swansea.

Over the course of the next year, New Englanders attacked entire villages of noncombatants, and the Indians retaliated in kind. At the beginning of the war, New Englanders looked down on their opponents' traditional methods as evidence of Indian depravity, saying they fought "more like wolves than men." By the end of the war, however, they too were practicing "the skulking way of war." Both sides committed brutalities, including scalpings and putting their victims' heads on stakes. That was the fate of King Philip himself. His wife and nine-year-old son were sold into slavery, along with hundreds of captives.

The New Englanders won King Philip's War, but the cost was enormous. About 4,000 Indians died, many of starvation, after the New Englanders destroyed their

King Philip (Metacom's) Map, 1668. A map of the lands that Metacom (known by New Englanders as King Philip) sold in 1668. Note that Metacom's understanding of what it meant to "sell" land differed from English conceptions of property ownership. He insisted that the Indians who were living on the land could continue to do so.

cornfields. The war eliminated any significant Native American presence in southeastern New England and killed 2,000 English settlers (one out of every 25). The Indians pushed to within 20 miles of Boston, attacked more than half of New England's towns, and burned 1,200 homes. It took the region decades to rebuild.

Moreover, the Puritans owed their victory to the Anglican colony of New York, its governor Edmund Andros, and his Mohawk allies. Andros worked effectively with local Indians, not because of any natural sympathy, but because he kept his eye on the big picture. In the long run, he believed, the British empire would be best served by maintaining peace among its various colonies and the regional Indians, leaving the British in a better position to fight their true enemies, the French and the Dutch. Andros was also determined to secure his own colony's best interest, and in 1676 that meant putting an end to the warfare in New England. Over the protest of New England, Andros encouraged the Mohawk, one of the five Iroquois tribes who made their home in New York, to attack King Philip's forces. Once the Mohawk entered the war, the tide was turned.

Indians and the Empire

New England's relations with Indian tribes were not simply a local concern. They were of deep interest to the British empire, as Andros's participation demonstrated. The British government had to balance the desires of its colonists against the empire's larger geopolitical objectives. As the French expanded their presence in North America, using friendly Indians to check their advance became one of those objectives. In 1673 the French explorers Jacques Marquette and Louis Joliet had traveled down the Mississippi River as far south as the Arkansas River, and nine years later LaSalle reached the mouth of the river and named the surrounding territory Louisiana, in honor of King Louis XIV. Biloxi was founded in 1699, New Orleans in 1718, and the forts at Cahokia and Kaskaskia several years later. Through their trade partnerships, the French and their Indian allies controlled the Great Lakes region and the eastern shore of the Mississippi all the way to its mouth, while the British were confined to the East Coast.

This geopolitical reality dictated Britain's Indian policy. Andros saw a role for Native Americans as trade partners and allies in Britain's continuing conflict with the French. His role in achieving victory enabled him to dictate the terms of the peace at the end of King Philip's War. He welcomed the Indian survivors of the conflict into New York and refused to send them back to New England for execution and enslavement, thus becoming the "father" who offered protection to his Indian "children." The British and the Iroquois, who dominated all the other tribes in the region, joined in a strong alliance known as the Covenant Chain, which enhanced the positions of both New York and the Iroquois. The Iroquois became the middlemen between other tribes in the area and the merchants at Albany and were allowed to push as far north and west against French-allied tribes as they could.

With New York exercising the dominant role in the British–Indian alliance, the New England colonies were effectively hemmed in. New York used the Mohawk to make a claim to Maine and blocked New England's movement to the west. Moreover, Albany became the undisputed center of the Indian trade. In every way, King Philip's War proved exceedingly costly for the New England colonies.

THE EMPIRE STRIKES

While the Glorious Revolution that removed King James II from the British throne secured constitutional government for Britain's subjects on both sides of the Atlantic, it also made Britain strong and stable enough to challenge France for world supremacy. Between 1689 and 1763, the Anglo–French rivalry drew the colonies into four international wars that shaped them in important ways.

The Dominion of New England

When James II ascended the throne, he decided to punish New England for its disloyalty to the Crown during the Puritan Revolution. Moreover, there were continuing reports that New Englanders were defying the Navigation Acts by smuggling. Across the English Channel in France, Louis XIV had centralized his administration and brought both his nation and his empire under firm control, and James decided to try similar tactics. In North America, he began unilaterally to revoke the charters of the colonies. By 1688, Massachusetts, Plymouth, Connecticut, New York, New Jersey, New Hampshire, and Rhode Island had been joined together into the Dominion of New England, and Edmund Andros was named its governor.

Before James II and Andros were deposed by the Glorious Revolution of 1688, considerable havoc was wreaked in New England, and Massachusetts, New York, and Maryland had all suffered revolts. James's attempt to centralize administration of the empire and tighten control over the colonies failed, but it marked a turning point: the colonies' last period of significant political instability before the eve of the Revolution.

James's attempt to tighten control over the colonies affected Massachusetts most seriously. He ordered it to tolerate religious dissenters; some feared that he would impose Catholicism on the colony. He took away liberties that residents had enjoyed for over half a century: Juries were to be appointed by sheriffs, town meetings were limited to once a year, and town selectmen could serve no more than two two-year terms. All titles to land had to be reconfirmed, with the holder paying Andros a small fee for the privilege. Andros claimed the right to levy taxes on his own and began seizing all common lands. Some Boston merchants allied themselves with Andros, hoping to win his favor. This alliance revealed a growing rift in New England between those who welcomed commerce and a more secular way of life and those who wished to preserve the old ways. By and large, however, most people in Massachusetts despised Andros and feared the road he was leading them down.

The Glorious Revolution in Britain and America

The Glorious Revolution made it clear that Parliament, not an autocratic monarch, would henceforth play the leading role in government. It also determined, after almost a century and a half of conflict, that the Anglican religion would prevail. The Glorious Revolution ushered in a period of political stability that enabled Britain to become the world's most powerful nation.

In the next century Britain's North American colonies looked to this moment in British history as a model of constitutional government. Their understanding of events in Britain was shaped by political philosopher John Locke's *Two Treatises of Government* (1690). Since the time that he and Shaftesbury had written Carolina's Fundamental Constitutions more than 20 years earlier, Locke had become increasingly radical. The *Treatises* boldly asserted fundamental human equality and universal rights and provided the political theories that would justify a revolution.

Locke argued that governments were created by people, not by God. Man was born "with a Title to perfect Freedom," or "natural rights." When people created governments, they gave up some of that freedom in exchange for the rights (called "civil rights") that they enjoyed in society. The purpose of government was to protect the "Lives, Liberties," and "Fortunes" of the people who created it, not to achieve glory or power for the nation or to serve God. Moreover, should a government take away the civil rights of its citizens, they had a "right to resume their original Liberty." This right of revolution was Locke's boldest and most radical assertion. Because he argued that there was a systematic connection among social institutions, such as the family, political institutions, and the rights of property, he became the first theorist of political economy as well.

Once news of the Glorious Revolution reached Massachusetts, its inhabitants poured into the streets, seized the government, and threw the despised Andros in jail. They proclaimed loyalty to the new king and lobbied for the return of their charter. Rhode Island and Connecticut soon got their charters back, but Massachusetts, which was perceived as too independent, in 1691 was made a royal colony with a royal governor. Although Massachusetts lost some of its autonomy and was forced to tolerate dissenters, the town meeting was restored. In addition, Massachusetts was allowed to absorb both Maine and Plymouth. At the same time, New Hampshire became a royal colony.

The citizens of Maryland and New York also took the opportunity presented by the Glorious Revolution to evict their royal governors. In Maryland, tensions between the tobacco planters and the increasingly dictatorial proprietor, Charles Calvert, Lord Baltimore, had been building for several decades. Although the price of tobacco had fallen, Baltimore refused to lower the export duty. Four-fifths of the population was Protestant, but the colony's government was dominated by Catholics, who allocated to themselves the best land. When Protestant planters protested, Baltimore imposed a property qualification for voting and appointed increasingly dictatorial governors. When news of the Glorious Revolution reached Maryland in 1689, a group led by John Coode, a militia officer, took over the government in a bloodless coup (known as Coode's Rebellion), proclaimed loyalty to William and Mary, and got the new government in Britain to take away Baltimore's proprietorship. In 1691, Maryland also became a royal colony.

New York's rebels were less successful in achieving their aims. There, a group of prosperous Dutch traders led by Jacob Leisler took over the government. Unlike Coode in Maryland, Leisler was not willing to turn the reins of government over to the new king's appointees. As a result, once the new governor assumed power, he put the rebel leaders on trial, and Leisler and his son-in-law were executed, their bodies decapitated and quartered.

This brutal conclusion to a bloodless revolt did not bring political stability to New York, however. The ethnic and regional divisions ran too deep. In the other colonies, by the end of the seventeenth century the elite had consolidated their position by accepting British authority, on the one hand, and providing opportunity and self-government for their fellow colonists, on the other. In New York, however, the top tier of the English elite competed for leadership with the second, Dutch tier, keeping the colony in political turmoil.

The Rights of Englishmen

Although the Glorious Revolution restored self-government to Britain's North American colonies, the colonists and their British governors interpreted that event somewhat differently. In the minds of the colonists, it gave them all the rights of Englishmen. These rights were of two sorts. First came civil rights, from trial by jury to freedom from unreasonable searches. Equally important were the fundamental rights of self-government: taxation only by their own elected representatives, self-rule, and civilian rather than military rule. The colonists believed that their own legislatures were the local equivalent of Parliament, and that just as the citizens of Britain were governed by Parliament, so they should be governed by their own elective legislatures.

The British government held a different set of assumptions. First, it believed that the colonies were children of the mother country, dependents who needed a parent's protection and who owed that parent obedience. Second, the good of the empire as a whole was more important than that of any one of its parts. The worth of a colony was established by how much it contributed to "the gain or loss of this Kingdom." Third, just as the colonies were subordinate to the empire, the colonial governments were subordinate to the British government. Finally, the British government had complete jurisdiction over every aspect of colonial life. Even if the government chose not to exercise this power, it could still do so if it wished. Later, when events required the colonists to compare their idea of how the empire should operate with Britain's, they discovered how radically their viewpoints had diverged.

Conflict in the Empire

Between 1689 and 1713, Britain fought two wars against France and her allies, King William's War (1689–1697) and Queen Anne's War (1702–1713). At the same time, competition for the allegiance of Indian tribes and the struggle among individual colonies over trade and territory made the borders between European and Indian settlements uncertain and dangerous.

King William's War and Queen Anne's War followed a similar pattern in North America. Each was produced by a European struggle for power, and each resulted in a stalemate. The North American phase of each war began with a Canadian–Indian assault on isolated British settlements on the northern frontier (see Map 4–1). King William's War commenced with the capture of the British fort at Pemaquid, Maine, and the burning of Schenectady, New York, and Falmouth, Maine. Queen Anne's War began in North America in 1704 with a horrific raid on Deerfield, Massachusetts. Half the town was torched, almost one-fifth of its population of 300 was killed, and another third were carried north as captives.

The British colonies responded with massive retaliation. They sent out their own raiding parties and poured resources into ambitious and ultimately unsuccessful attacks on Quebec. In May 1690 Massachusetts governor Sir William Phips conquered the French privateering base at Port Royal, Acadia, then determined to seize Quebec in a two-pronged attack by land and sea. The failed expedition cost 1,000 lives and £40,000. Unable to defeat the French, the American colonies remained vulnerable on the northern frontier, and settlers retreated.

Queen Anne's War followed much the same course. Canadian–Indian attacks on frontier villages were met with raids on Indian villages. Once again, New England attempted a two-pronged attack on Quebec. When 900 troops (and 35 female camp followers) were killed as their ships ran aground in the foggy St. Lawrence River, the commander canceled the expedition. Like King William's War, Queen Anne's War ended in disillusionment for New Englanders who had been eager to remove the twin threats of Catholicism and French-backed Indians to the north.

The imperial wars merged with and were survived by long-standing conflicts with Indian tribes. In North America, rival European powers almost never confronted each other directly but instead mobilized their Indian allies and made war on those of their adversaries. These tactics, in addition to the expansion of the colonial population and the attempt of Native American tribes to secure trade monopolies, made conflict on the frontiers endemic.

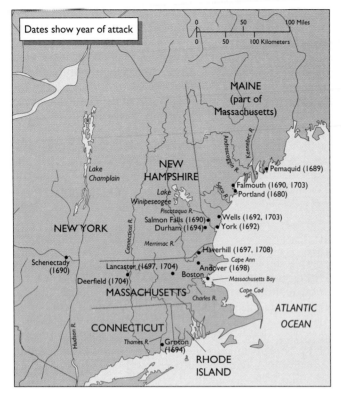

Map 4–1 Frontier Warfare During King William's and Queen Anne's Wars

During these international conflicts, the New England frontier was exposed to attack by French Canadians and their Indian allies.

Source: Adapted from Alan Gallay, ed., Colonial Wars of North America, 1512–1763 (New York: Garland, 1996), p. 247.

MASSACHUSETTS IN CRISIS

If the imperial wars provide a window onto international tensions, the Salem witchcraft trials provide a window onto a society in crisis, one coping with economic development; the conflict between old and new ways of understanding the world; and the threats presented by political instability, imperial war, and conflict with the Indians. In 1692 Massachusetts executed 20 people who had been convicted of witchcraft in Salem. Even in a society that believed in witchcraft, the execution of so many people at once was an aberration that revealed deep tensions.

The Social and Cultural Contexts of Witchcraft

Although the majority of New England's colonists were Puritan, many probably believed in magic. At the same time that they subscribed to such tenets of Puritanism as predestination, they also believed that they could make use of supernatural powers to predict the future, protect themselves from harm, and hurt their enemies. Although the ministry identified the use of magic with the devil, Tituba's folk religion and that of New Englanders were not incompatible. Before the development of scientific modes of explanation for such catastrophes as epidemics, droughts, and sudden death, people looked for supernatural causes.

In 1692, the inhabitants of Massachusetts were unusually anxious. They were without an effective government because they had not yet received their new charter. The opening battles of King William's War had just begun, with the French Catholics of

Frontispiece to Joseph Glanvill, Saducismus Triumphatus; *or,* Full and Plain Evidence Concerning Witches *(1689). Books such as this combined folklore and Christian theology, providing graphic representations of Satan and witches alongside standard religious doctrine.*

Canada and their Algonquian Indian allies raiding settlements on the northern and eastern frontiers. Slaves reported that the French were planning to recruit New England's Africans to join a force of Indians and French soldiers. These immediate sources of stress increased underlying tensions, many of which concerned gender. Although men and women both attempted to use magic, the vast majority of those who were accused of witchcraft in seventeenth-century New England were women. Almost 80 percent of the 355 persons officially accused of practicing witchcraft were women, as were an even higher proportion of the 103 persons actually put on trial. Most of these women had neither sons nor other male heirs. They were thus an anomaly in Puritan society, women who controlled property. By the end of the seventeenth century, land was an increasingly scarce commodity in New England, and any woman who controlled it could be perceived as threatening to the men who wanted it.

In addition, declining opportunity also disrupted the social order that the Puritans had worked so hard to maintain. Because land was scarce, it became difficult for young couples to start out. Consequently the age of marriage increased, and the number of women who were pregnant on their wedding day began to climb. The number of women who gave birth without marrying at all began to grow, and courts less frequently insisted that fathers pay for the support of their babies. Instead, courts increasingly shifted responsibility to the young mothers. By the end of the seventeenth century, New Englanders were even more inclined than previously to hold women responsible for sin.

Witchcraft at Salem

In this context of social strain and political anxiety, on February 29, 1692, magistrates John Hathorne and Jonathan Corwin went to Salem to investigate accusations of witchcraft. By the time the investigation and trials ended, 156 people had been jailed and 20 executed. As in previous witchcraft scares, most of the accused were women past the age of 40, and most of the accusers were women in their late teens and 20s.

Most of the accused fell into several categories that revealed the stresses in Puritan society. Many, like Sarah Good, were the sort of disagreeable women who had always attracted accusations of witchcraft. Others had ties to Quakers or Baptists. Several were suspiciously friendly with the Indians. A significant number of the accusers had been orphaned or displaced by the recent Indian wars, and it is not surprising that they described the devil as "a Tawney, or an Indian color." As a dark-skinned woman from an alien culture, Tituba (whose story was told at the beginning of this chapter) was also vulnerable. In addition, most of the accusers lived in Salem Village, an economic backwater, while most of the accused lived in or had ties to Salem Town, a more prosperous merchant community several miles to the east. The pattern of accusations suggested resentment, perhaps unconscious, about the increasing commercialization of New England's economy.

By late September, accusations were falling on wealthy and well-connected men and women such as Lady Phips, the wife of the governor. The original accusers were taken from town to town to root out local witchcraft, while other people were drawn to Salem like medieval pilgrims, looking for explanations for their problems. At that point, the leading ministers of Boston, most of whom believed in witchcraft but had been skeptical of the Salem trials, stepped in, and Governor Phips ordered the court adjourned. No one was ever convicted of witchcraft in New England again.

The End of Witchcraft

Although New Englanders and other colonists continued to believe in witchcraft, magic, and the occult, by the end of the seventeenth century they came to believe that the universe was orderly and that events were caused by natural, and hence knowable forces. By the eighteenth century, educated people took pride in their rational understanding of natural phenomena, such as weather and diseases, and they disdained a belief in the occult. This change in thinking reflected a new faith not only in human reason but also in the capacity of ordinary men and women to shape their lives. More and more people, especially those who were well-educated, prosperous, and lived in cities, believed that they could control their destinies and were not at the mercy of invisible evil forces. The seed of individualism had been planted in New England's rocky soil.

As individualism slowly spread (it would not triumph for more than another century) and communities became larger, the cohesion of Puritan communities necessarily waned. The eighteenth century also brought new attitudes toward women that stripped them of their symbolic power to do harm.

The witchcraft trials also marked the conclusion of New England's belief in itself as a covenanted society with a collective future. Because Puritans had believed that God had chosen them for a special mission, they read a providential meaning into every event, from a sudden snowstorm to an Indian attack. By the eighteenth century, however, people began to evaluate events separately, rather than as part of God's master plan.

FRENCH AND SPANISH OUTPOSTS

At the end of the seventeenth century in the territory that became the United States, Britain was the only European power that had established a substantial presence (see Map 4–2). The French and Spanish both had outposts on the American

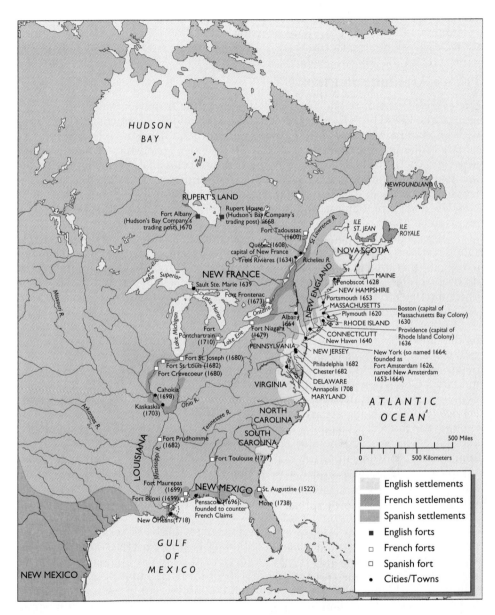

Map 4–2 Colonial North America, East of the Mississippi, 1720

This map shows the expansion of European settlement. English settlement was concentrated in a strip down the East Coast from Maine to North Carolina, with pockets of settlement in Canada and Carolina. French settlements formed a ring along the St. Lawrence River, from the Great Lakes south along the Mississippi, and along the Gulf Coast. The Spanish had outposts along the Gulf and in Florida.

Source: Adapted from Geoffrey Barraclough, ed., The Times Concise Atlas of World History (Maplewood, NJ: Hammond, 1994), p. 67.

mainland north of the Rio Grande River, but these European nations concentrated their resources on more valuable colonies, for the Spanish, Mexico and Latin America, and for the French, the West Indies. Largely irrelevant to the political economies of their parent nations, Spanish and French settlements developed slowly, each taking its own course.

France Attempts an Empire

France's civil wars of religion had ended early in the seventeenth century, leaving France free to establish foreign colonies. Until the middle of the century, its efforts were haphazard, but after 1664, France's minister Jean Baptiste Colbert tried to establish a coherent imperial policy, directed from Paris. He envisioned a series of settlements, each, in accordance with mercantilist principles, contributing to the wealth of the nation, through the fur trade and fishing in North America and plantation agriculture in the West Indies. France tried to direct the development of its New World empire, but it lacked the resources and capacity to control small settlements so far away.

Colbert attempted to control every aspect of life in the colony of Quebec. He subsidized emigration and had the backgrounds of female migrants investigated to make sure that they were healthy and morally sound. To encourage reproduction, dowries were offered to all men who married by the age of 20. Agriculture developed and the population grew, more from natural increase than immigration. Most of the immigrants from France returned home after a brief stay in Quebec.

Colbert's attempt to make Quebec a hierarchical society on the Old World model failed, however. Native Americans were more successful in shaping the fur trade, the mainstay of the Quebec economy, than was Colbert. The French depended on their Indian trading partners to supply them with furs and serve as military allies. When Indians tried to trade their furs to the British, the French established—at considerable cost—forts to intercept them. At the same time, French traders smuggled beaver pelts to the British in return for British-made fabrics that the Indians preferred to inferior French goods. Moreover, to maintain the allegiance of their Algonquian allies, the French supplied them with gifts of ammunition, knives, cloth, tobacco, and brandy. When the declining revenues from the fur trade are balanced against the cost of these presents and the maintenance of forts and a military, it is questionable whether Canada was of any economic benefit to France. In fact, France maintained the fur trade more for political than for economic reasons.

It was for political reasons as well that France established a series of outposts in present-day Louisiana and Mississippi, including Fort Biloxi (1699), Fort Toulouse (1717), and New Orleans (1718), all in the territory named Louisiana. When the French explorer LaSalle reached the mouth of the Mississippi River in 1682 and claimed it for France, the Spanish mainland empire was cut in two and the British faced a western rival. British traders in Carolina had pushed into the lower Mississippi region looking for deerskins and Indian slaves. By the time the French arrived, tribes such as the Choctaws and Mobilians were looking for allies to protect them from the British and their allies. In return for the customary "presents," even the Chickasaws, who had recently lost 800 men in warfare, were willing to ally themselves with the French. Within several decades, the French had established trading posts as far north as Kaskaskia and Cahokia in the Illinois territory.

The early history of the Louisiana colony resembled that of the British settlement at Jamestown. The French shifted authority back and forth between the state and private investors. As in Virginia, the first settlers were ill-suited to the venture, top heavy with military personnel and Caribbean pirates. Louisiana was so unattractive a destination that it could not attract colonists wanting to better their lives, so France began deporting criminals to the colony. Debilitated by the unhealthy environment, colonists could not even grow their own food. Caught up in wars on the continent, the French could not or would not provide adequate support for the colony, so its survival depended on the generosity of local Indians. Without a secure economic base, the leaders of the Louisiana colony began clamoring for African slaves. As early as 1699, one of the founders of the colony asked for permission to import slaves from Africa. A few years later, another suggested trading Indian slaves, who routinely deserted back to their tribes, for Africans. When these requests were rejected, they began smuggling slaves in from the Caribbean. In 1719, France permitted the importation of African slaves, but even as the African population grew, the colony still floundered.

Unlike the Chesapeake, colonial Louisiana never developed a significant cash crop. Because the colony was not important to French economic interests, French mercantilist policies protected Caribbean plantations at the expense of those in Louisiana. Deerskins purchased from the Indians often rotted in the steamy weather. Although Louisiana had a slave majority by 1727, the settlement was not a slave society. Louisiana's economy was one of frontier exchange among Europeans, Indians, and Africans, rather than one of commercial agriculture. As it was marginal to France's political economy, Louisiana was largely left to itself. Europeans, Indians, and Africans all depended on each other for survival. They intermarried and worked together to maintain an exchange economy. Despite Louisiana's leaders' hopes of creating a hierarchical order based on plantation agriculture, social and economic relations in the colony remained fluid.

The Spanish Outpost in Florida

Like France's colony at Louisiana, Spain's settlement at St. Augustine, Florida, was intended to be a self-supporting military outpost. Unable to attract settlers and costly to maintain, Florida too grew slowly and unsteadily. At the beginning of the seventeenth century, the Spanish considered abandoning the colony and moving the population to the West Indies.

Once the British established their colony at Carolina, however, Florida once again became important to Spain—and it gained a new source of settlers in runaway slaves. The British and Spanish began attacking each other, usually using Indian and African surrogates. Spanish raiders seized slaves from Carolina plantations. The Spanish paid these Africans wages and introduced them to Catholicism. Soon, as Carolina's governor complained, slaves were "running dayly" to Florida. In 1693, Spain's king offered liberty to all British slaves who escaped to Florida.

The border between the two colonies was a place of violence—and also, for Africans, a place of opportunity. Africans gained valuable military experience and, in 1738, about 100 former slaves established the free black town of Gracia Real de Santa Teresa de Mose (Mose, for short), two miles from St. Augustine. Mose's leader was the Mandinga captain of the free black militia, Francisco Menéndez. A former slave who had been re-enslaved, he persisted in petitioning for his freedom. Spain freed Menéndez and other Africans like him and reiterated the policy that all British slaves who escaped to Florida should be free. Thus, the persistence of Menéndez and the other escaped slaves led to the establishment of the first free black community on the North American continent.

CONQUEST, REVOLT, AND RECONQUEST IN NEW MEXICO

In the western half of the continent, New Mexico developed into a colonial outpost on the edge of a world empire, far from centers of power and irrelevant to Spain's political economy. Early in the seventeenth century, the Spanish considered abandoning the settlement, but Franciscan missionaries persuaded Spain to stay so the priests could minister to the Native Americans. In the eastern half of the continent, regional Indians could play the European powers against each other, but in the western part, Spain was the only European nation with a presence, reducing the Pueblo Indians' leverage. Nor were there African slaves to complicate local power structures. When the Pueblo Indians rose up against the Spanish at the end of the seventeenth century, the survival of New Mexico was in doubt.

The Conquest of Pueblo Society

Spain established its colony in New Mexico by conquest. Although Coronado's party had explored the Southwest from Arizona to Kansas (1541–1542), it had not planted a permanent settlement. In 1598, Juan de Oñate was appointed governor and authorized to establish a colony. Much like Cortés, in some places Oñate persuaded the local Pueblos to accept him as their ruler. In other places, he overcame them by force. His harsh means proved effective, and the Spanish soon dominated the entire Southwest. In 1610 they established their capital at Santa Fe, and the colony, called New Mexico, began to grow slowly. The primary purpose of the New Mexico colony was to serve as an outpost of the Spanish Empire in North America, protecting its northern border from the French, just as St. Augustine was established to defend against the English. The most important "business" in the colony was to convert the Pueblo Indians to Catholicism. Indeed, official Spanish policy held that "preaching the holy gospel . . . is the principal purpose for which we order new discoveries and settlements to be made."

Franciscan priests established a series of missions in New Mexico. Although there were never more than 50 or so Franciscans in New Mexico at any time, they claimed to have converted about 80,000 Indians in less than a century. Most of these conversions, however, were in name only. In hindsight it is clear that the Indians deeply resented the priests' attempts to change their customs and beliefs. By assuming the traditional roles of both fathers and mothers in Pueblo society and by forcing the Indians to adopt European sex roles and sexual mores, the Franciscans undermined not only Pueblo religion, but also their society.

The Pueblo Revolt

Spanish rule fell harshly on the Pueblos. Although Spanish law forbade enslavement of conquered Indians, some Spanish settlers openly defied that law. More common was the *encomienda* system. Oñate rewarded a number of his lieutenants by naming them *encomenderos*, which entitled them to tribute from the Indians who lived on the land they had been awarded. Some *encomenderos* demanded labor or personal service. Women working in Spanish households were vulnerable to sexual abuse by their masters. Suffering under such burdens, the Indian population declined from about 40,000 in 1638 to only 17,000 in 1670.

A combination of Spanish demands for labor and tribute and a long period of drought that began around 1660 left the Pueblos without the food surpluses that

The Pueblo at Acoma. The Acoma pueblo sits atop a mesa that rises 400 feet above ground. In January 1699, Spanish soldiers destroyed the pueblo and killed 800 of its inhabitants, in retaliation for the killing of a dozen soldiers. All the male survivors over the age of 12 and all female survivors were sentenced to 20 years of servitude to the Spanish, and the men over the age of 25 each had a foot cut off as well. The pueblo was rebuilt after its destruction.

they had been selling to the nomadic Apache and Navajo to the west. As a consequence, the nomadic tribes began to raid the Pueblos, taking by force that which they could no longer get by trade. Under these pressures, Pueblos turned once again to their own tribal gods and religious leaders.

When the Spanish punished the Indians who returned to their traditional religion, they pushed the Pueblos into revolt. A medicine man named Popé united the leaders of most of the region's Pueblos and sent messengers out to carry his message, promising that if the Indians threw out the Spanish and prayed once again to their ancient gods, food would be plentiful once more. Nor would the Indians ever have to work for the Spanish again, he said, and Indian customs would be restored.

Popé's revolt began on August 10, 1680, just before the resupply caravan from Mexico arrived, and when the Spanish were low on supplies. First, the Indians seized all the horses and mules, preventing the Spanish from notifying other settlements quickly or engaging in mounted warfare. Next, they blocked the roads to Santa Fe. Then they systematically destroyed all the Spanish settlements, one at a time. By the end of the day, more than 400 Spanish had been killed, about a fifth of the Spanish population. The Pueblos laid siege to Santa Fe, eventually forcing the Spanish survivors to abandon the town. In the most successful Indian revolt that North America would ever see, the Spanish had been driven from New Mexico.

Reconquest and the Creation of Spanish Colonial Society

The Pueblos held off the Spanish for 13 years, until 1696, but the ongoing struggles took a heavy toll. Contrary to Popé's promise, the drought continued. Warfare took additional lives, and the population continued to drop.

The revolt taught the Spanish several lessons. The new Franciscans who came to minister to the Indians were far less zealous than their predecessors. The *encomienda* was not re-established, and levels of exploitation were significantly lower. Slowly the Spanish colony began rebuilding. The population was divided into four

CHRONOLOGY

1598	Juan de Oñate colonizes New Mexico for Spain
1610	Santa Fe established
1627	Barbados settled
1628	Parliament passes Petition of Right
1642–1647	English Revolution
1649	King Charles I beheaded
1652–1674	Three Anglo-Dutch Wars
1656	Britain seizes Jamaica from Spain
1651–1696	Navigation Acts passed to regulate trade
1660	British monarchy restored, Charles II crowned king
1662	Half-Way Covenant
1664	British seize New Netherland, renaming it New York
1665	New Jersey established
1669	Fundamental Constitutions written for South Carolina
1670	Carolina settled
1673	Marquette and Joliet explore Mississippi for France
1675–1676	King Philip's War
1676–1677	Bacon's Rebellion
1680	Pueblo Revolt in New Mexico re-establishes Indian rule Westo War, Carolina defeats the Westos

social groupings, ranging from a small nobility at the top to enslaved Indians at the bottom. The nobility, a hereditary aristocracy of between 15 and 20 families, included government officials. In all societies with hereditary aristocracies, those groups develop codes of honor to distinguish themselves from the lower orders. This group prided itself on its racial purity, considering whiteness of skin a clear sign of superiority, and scorned those of mixed blood, many of whom, of course, were the illegitimate children of elite Spanish men and the Indian women they raped or seduced. Aristocratic men placed a high value on the personal qualities of courage, honesty, and loyalty, as well as sexual virility. Female honor consisted of extreme modesty and sexual purity.

1681	William Penn granted charter for Pennsylvania
1683	New York's assembly meets for first time
1685	King Charles II dies and James, Duke of York, becomes King James II
1686	Massachusetts, Plymouth, Connecticut, Rhode Island, and New Hampshire combined in Dominion of New England; New York and New Jersey added two years later
1688	Glorious Revolution
1689	Leisler's Rebellion in New York, Coode's Rebellion in Maryland William and Mary become King and Queen of Britain; Dominion of New England overthrown
1689–1697	King William's War
1690	Publication of John Locke's *Two Treatises of Government*
1691	Massachusetts made a royal colony Maryland made a royal colony New Hampshire made a royal colony
1692	Salem witchcraft trials
1696	Reconquest of New Mexico
1702–1713	Queen Anne's War
1706	Spanish establish settlement at Albuquerque
1718	French establish settlement at New Orleans

The second group in the Spanish society in New Mexico were landed peasants, most of them *mestizos*, half-Spanish and half-Indian. In this highly color-conscious society, the *mestizos* prized the Spanish part of their heritage and scorned the Indian. Next came the Pueblo Indians, living in their own communities.

At the bottom were the *genízaros*, conquered Indians who had been enslaved. This lower class of slaves was joined by Indians who left their tribes and moved to Spanish settlements. Often these immigrants were outcasts from their own tribe, such as women who had been raped by Spanish men and were now shunned by their own society. A century after their first conquest, the Pueblo Indians had begun to adopt the values of their conquerors.

CONCLUSION

By the end of the seventeenth century, almost all of the British North American colonies had developed the political economies that they would maintain until the American Revolution. For the most part, the colonies were prosperous, with a large middle class. The efforts to replicate a European hierarchical order had largely failed. Each region had found a secure economic base: farming and shipping in New England, mixed farming in the middle colonies, and single-crop planting in the southern ones. The southern colonies had become slave societies, although slavery was practiced in every colony.

The contrast with New Mexico, which remained a frontier outpost without a secure economic base, was dramatic. Although the British colonies and New Mexico had all undergone political turmoil in the final quarter of the century, that unrest led in different directions. New Mexico had established an exaggerated version of a European hierarchical society, with a hereditary aristocracy. The English colonies had failed to plant Old World hierarchies and had struggled to achieve political order in their absence. Yet this failure was the source of their ultimate success. The new sorts of societies they created were developing in ways that would lead to the American Revolution.

FURTHER READINGS

John Putnam Demos, *Entertaining Satan: Witchcraft and the Culture of Early New England* (1982). A fascinating exploration, from a variety of perspectives, of witchcraft in New England life.

Richard Godbeer, *The Devil's Dominion: Magic and Religion in Early New England* (1992). Shows the ways in which occult and folk religion were an integral part of New England's culture.

Ramón A. Gutiérrez, *When Jesus Came the Corn Mothers Went Away: Marriage, Sexuality, and Power in New Mexico, 1500–1856* (1991). A brilliant analysis of the role of gender and sexuality in structuring colonial New Mexican society.

James Horn, *Adapting to a New World: English Society in the Seventeenth-Century Chesapeake* (1994). A bold interpretation that argues for the influence of English patterns and values in colonial Chesapeake society.

Winthrop D. Jordan, *White Over Black: American Attitudes Toward the Negro, 1550–1812* (1968). Slightly dated, but still the most comprehensive account of the development of American racism.

Jill Lepore, *The Name of War: King Philip's War and the Origins of American Identity* (1998). A provocative new interpretation of King Philip's War that emphasizes the cultural distance between Puritans and Indians.

Wilcomb E. Washburn, *The Governor and the Rebel: A History of Bacon's Rebellion in Virginia* (1957). A highly readable account of Bacon's Rebellion.

 Please refer to the document CD-ROM for primary sources related to this chapter.

CHAPTER

5

The Eighteenth-Century World

1700–1775

George Whitefield: Evangelist for a Consumer Society
The Population Explosion of the Eighteenth Century
The Transatlantic Political Economy: Producing and Consuming
The Varieties of Colonial Experience • The Head and the Heart in
America: The Enlightenment and Religious Awakening
Conclusion

GEORGE WHITEFIELD: EVANGELIST FOR A CONSUMER SOCIETY

In 1740 there were no more than 16,000 people living in Boston, but on October 12, some 20,000 men and women filled the Common to hear an English minister preaching. Everywhere he went, the crowds were unprecedented—8,000 in Philadelphia, 3,000 in the little Pennsylvania village of Neshaminy. Those who could not see the evangelist in person read about him in the newspapers. If there was one binding experience for the American people in the decades before the Revolution, it was George Whitefield's ministry.

No one would have guessed that Whitefield would become one of the most influential preachers in the history of Christianity. He had trouble with his studies and preferred the theater, romance novels, and fancy clothes. Because of the growth of the market economy, men and women on both sides of the Atlantic could now participate in a consumer culture that offered many ways to spend money and leisure time. To those schooled in a traditional Calvinist religion, the consumer society was both attractive and frightening. Could one serve God and oneself at the same time?

At the age of 17, when Whitefield discovered that he had no aptitude for trade, he faced a personal crisis. Then, one morning, he blurted out the words that had just come into his mind: ". . . God intends something for me which we know not of." Whitefield then set out to prepare himself for the ministry. He became friendly with the Methodists, a group of religious young men who were planning a mission to the new English colony of Georgia. Under their influence, Whitefield turned his back on the attractions of consumer culture. Now, "whatsoever I did, I endeavoured to do all to the glory of God." Whitefield was determined to share what he had learned with all who would hear.

Whitefield helped create a mass public. Before his ministry, each minister or priest typically addressed only his own congregation. The crowds Whitefield attracted were often too large for any building to hold, so he preached outdoors. Although Whitefield spoke directly to the heart of each individual, he also drew together entire communities in a way no one had ever done before.

Whitefield embodied the great contradictions of his age without threatening the political or economic order that sustained them. He appealed to men as well as women, to the poor as well as the rich, to slaves as well as their masters, and to those who were suffering from capitalism as well as those who were benefiting from it. Whitefield's strategy was to criticize the individual without attacking the system. He showed men and women who were adrift in the new political economy how to acquire the personal self-discipline that would enable them either to succeed in a competitive market or to bear failures with Christian resignation. He helped them experience religion as an intense personal feeling. He showed people how to find meaning for their lives in a time of rapid economic transformation.

THE POPULATION EXPLOSION OF THE EIGHTEENTH CENTURY

George Whitefield could speak to the hearts of the American colonists because he understood their world. Increasingly, the American colonies were tied into a political economy that spread across the North Atlantic world and brought dramatic changes. One of the most important changes was the increase in population.

The Dimensions of Population Growth

The population in the American colonies grew at a rate unprecedented in human history. In 1700 there were just over 250,000 people living in the colonies, but by 1750 the population had grown to more than 1 million. The rate of growth was highest in the free population in the prosperous farming regions, but it was rapid everywhere, even among slaves, in spite of their harsh living conditions.

Much of the colonies' population growth was caused by their unquenchable thirst for labor. The colonies attracted an extraordinary number of immigrants, and when free labor did not satisfy the demand, unfree labor (slaves, indentured servants, and redemptioners) filled the gap. In fact, when the number of Africans who came in chains is added to the Europeans who came as indentured servants and redemptioners, 90 percent of the immigrants to the British colonies between 1580 and 1775 were unfree at the time of their arrival.

Increasingly, these immigrants reflected the broad reach of the North Atlantic political economy. At the beginning of the eighteenth century, the population of the American colonies was primarily English in origin. By the beginning of the American Revolution, the population had changed significantly. There were small numbers of people with Finnish, Swedish, French, Swiss, and Jewish heritage. There were also large numbers of Welsh, Scotch-Irish, Germans, Dutch, and Africans. The foundation for the subsequent diversity of the American population had been laid.

Bound for America: European Immigrants

A significant portion of the colonies' population increase came from immigration. In the eighteenth century, substantial numbers of people came from Scotland, Northern Ireland, Wales, and Germany. In all, about 425,000 Europeans migrated to the colonies in the eighteenth century.

The largest number of European immigrants were Scotch-Irish; that is, Scottish people who had moved to Northern Ireland to escape famine in their own country. As many as 250,000 came to seek a better life in the British colonies. At first, Massachusetts invited the Scotch-Irish to settle on its borders, as a buffer between the settled region of the colony and the Indians. Once the Scotch-Irish began to arrive in large numbers, however, the English inhabitants worried that they would have to provide for the impoverished newcomers. In 1729 a Boston mob turned away a shipload of Scotch-Irish immigrants, and in 1738 the Puritan inhabitants of Worcester burned down a Presbyterian church. Thereafter, the vast majority of Scotch-Irish immigrants headed for the middle colonies and the South.

Going where land was the cheapest, the Scotch-Irish settled between the English settlements along the seaboard and the Indian communities to the west, from Pennsylvania to Georgia (see Map 5–1). As the Scotch-Irish population increased, it pressed against the Indians, seizing, for example, a 15,000-acre tract that the Penn family had set aside for the Conestoga Indians. Like the Scotch-Irish, most German migrants settled in the back country from Pennsylvania to the Carolinas. Between 1700 and the start of the Revolution, more than 100,000 Germans moved to the American colonies, and by 1775, a third of the population of Pennsylvania was German. The Germans were diverse, including not only Lutherans and Catholics but also Quakers, Amish, and Mennonites. German immigrants established prosperous farming communities wherever they settled.

A large proportion of eighteenth-century migrants were skilled but relatively impoverished artisans drawn to America by the demand for skilled labor. As African slaves began to fill the demand for agricultural workers, especially in the South, the colonists eagerly sought skilled workers.

The majority of European migrants to the colonies were unfree, not only indentured servants and redemptioners but also the 50,000 British convicts whose sentences were commuted to a term of service in the colonies. Most English and Welsh migrants were single men between the ages of 19 and 23 who came as indentured servants. The Scotch-Irish migration included a larger number of families,

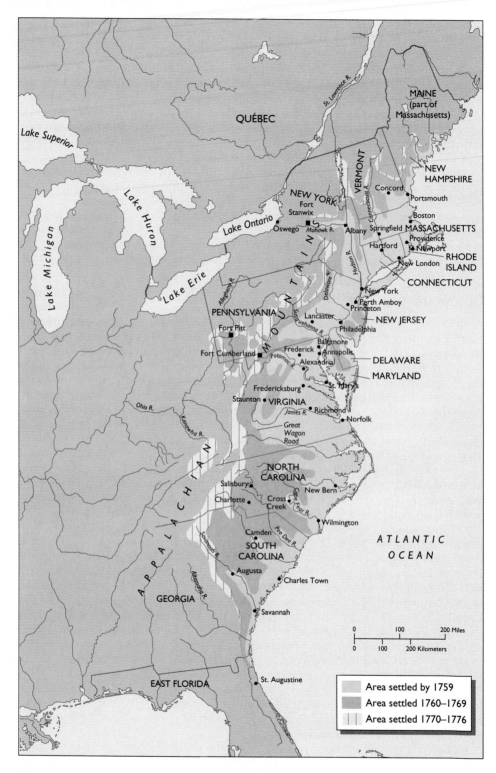

Map 5–1 Expansion of Settlement, 1720–1760

By 1760, the colonial population made up an almost continuous line of settlement from Maine to Florida and was pushing west over the Appalachian Mountains.

Source: Adapted from Bernard Bailyn, Voyagers to the West (New York: Knopf, 1986), p. 9.

and three-fourths of the Germans came in family groups. For all immigrants, the passage to America, which could take three months or more, was grueling. Gottlieb Mittelberger described the afflictions of the journey: "The ship is full of pitiful signs of distress—smells, fumes, horrors, vomiting, various kinds of sea sickness, fever, dysentery, headaches, heat, constipation, boils, scurvy, cancer, [and] mouth-rot." Once the migrants arrived, the servants and convicts were sold for terms of service in auctions that resembled those held for African slaves.

Bound for America: African Slaves

The increase in the African population was even more dramatic than that of Europeans. In 1660 there were only 2,920 African or African-descended inhabitants of the mainland colonies. A century later they numbered more than 300,000. The proportion of Africans grew most rapidly in the southern colonies, where it stood at almost 40 percent on the eve of the Revolution. By 1720 South Carolina had an African majority. Most of the increase in the African population came from the slave trade. By 1808, when Congress closed off the importation of slaves to the United States, about 523,000 African slaves had been imported into the nation (see Figure 5–1). The African slave trade was a profitable and well-organized segment of the world economy.

Until the eighteenth century, when demand from the New World increased, the transatlantic slave trade was controlled by Africans who set the terms, including the prices, of the trade. Generally, Europeans were not allowed into the interior of Africa, so slaves were brought to the coast for sale. Many African nations taxed the

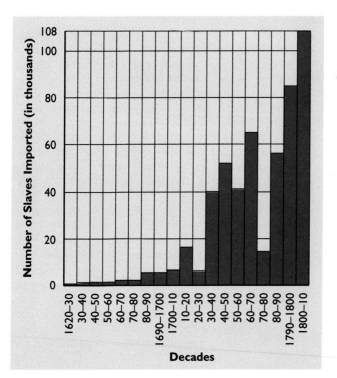

Figure 5–1   The Importation of Slaves into the Colonies, 1620–1810

Source: Helen Hombeck Tanner, The Settling of North America (New York: Macmillan, 1995), p. 51.

sale of slaves and regulated the trade in other ways. Some nations supplied a steady stream of slaves, while others offered them intermittently, suggesting that participation in the trade was a matter of conscious policy. Most slaves were captives of war, and as the New World demand for slaves increased, the tempo of warfare in Africa intensified in response. The New World preferred male slaves, leaving most of the female captives to the African slave market, where they became domestic slaves or plural wives to wealthier Africans.

As bad as the voyage to America was for indentured servants, the trip for enslaved Africans was worse. Perhaps 10 percent died before reaching the African coast. Until they arrived at the coast, many had never seen an ocean or a white man, and both sights terrified them. They were confined in pens or forts for as long as half a year while waiting for a ship to take them to the New World.

The voyage, or "middle passage," proved lethal to many. Male slaves were shackled and confined below deck for most of each day. Chained together and without enough room to stand up, many were unable to reach the large buckets that served as latrines. One ship's doctor reported that the slaves' deck "was so covered with the blood and mucus which had proceeded from them in consequence of the flux, that it resembled a slaughterhouse." The women were left unshackled, but their relative freedom left them prey to the sailors' lust. As the slave trade became more efficient in the eighteenth century, the mortality rate dropped, from perhaps 20 percent to half that amount.

The Great Increase of Offspring

Most of the increase in the colonies' population came not from immigration or the slave trade but from natural increase. The rate of population growth for both Europeans and Africans in the colonies was extraordinary.

For Euro-Americans the main source of population increase was a lower age of marriage for women and a higher proportion of women who married. In England, for example, as many as 20 percent of women did not marry by age 45, compared to only 5 percent in the colonies. The age of marriage for women in the colonies was also considerably lower, with women marrying in their late teens or early 20s, compared to the late 20s in England. Therefore they bore more babies, on average seven or eight each, with six or seven surviving to adulthood. As a rule, the more economic opportunity, the earlier the age of marriage for women and men, and the more children. Likewise, the healthier the climate, the more children survived to adulthood, but compared to today, child mortality rates were high. Still, the rate of population growth in the colonies was phenomenal.

In many ways, the African-American population resembled the Euro-American population, for both suffered from the dislocations of moving to a new land. Those slaves who were born in the colonies married young and established families as stable as slavery permitted. By the time they were 18, most slave women usually had their first child. Following African custom, they might not form a lasting union with the father, but within a few years many settled into long-lasting relationships with the men who would father the rest of their children. Slave women bore between six and eight children, on average. With child mortality even higher for African Americans than for Euro-Americans, between 25 percent and 50 percent of these slave children died before reaching adulthood. Even so, the slave population more than reproduced itself.

THE TRANSATLANTIC POLITICAL ECONOMY: PRODUCING AND CONSUMING

In the eighteenth century, the colonies became capitalist societies, tied increasingly into an Atlantic trade network. Increasingly, people produced for the market, so that they could buy the goods the market had to offer. Throughout the Atlantic world, ordinary people reoriented their economic lives so they could buy more goods. Historians talk about two economic revolutions in this period: a consumer revolution, a slow and steady increase in the demand for, and purchase of, consumer goods; and an industrious revolution, in which people worked harder and organized their households (their families, servants, and slaves) to produce goods for sale, so that they would have money to pay for items they wanted. Income went up only slightly in the eighteenth century, yet people were buying more. In the process, they created a consumer society.

The Nature of Colonial Economic Growth

Throughout human history, population growth has usually led to a decline in standard of living as more people compete for fewer resources. In the American colonies, however, population growth led to an expansion of the economy, as more of the continent's abundant natural resources were brought under human control. The standard of living for most free Americans probably improved, although not dramatically. As the economy matured, a small segment of the economy—urban merchants and owners of large plantations—became wealthy. At the same time, the urban poor and tenant farmers began to slip toward poverty.

All of these changes took place, however, without any significant changes in technology. Most wealth was made from shipping and agriculture. Eighty percent of the colonies' population worked on farms or plantations, areas with no major technological innovations. Virtually all gains in productivity came instead from labor: More people were working, and they were working more efficiently.

The economy of colonial America was shaped by three factors: abundance of land and shortages of labor and capital. The plantation regions of the South and the West Indies were best situated to take advantage of these circumstances, and the small-farm areas of New England were the least suitable. Tobacco planters in the Chesapeake and rice and indigo planters in South Carolina sold their products on a huge world market. Their large profits enabled them to purchase more land and more slaves to work it.

Because northern farmers raised crops and animals that were also produced in Europe, profits from agriculture alone were too low to permit them to acquire large tracts of land or additional labor (see Table 5–1). Northerners who hoped to become wealthy had to look for other opportunities. They found them in trade.

The Transformation of the Family Economy

In colonial America, the family was the basic economic unit. From the time they were able, all family members contributed to the family economy. Work was organized by gender. On farms, women were responsible for the preparation of food and clothing, child care, and care of the home. Women grew vegetables and herbs, provided dairy products, and transformed flax and wool into clothing. The daughters in the family worked under their mother's supervision, perhaps spinning extra yarn to be sold for a profit.

TABLE 5–1

How Wealthy Were Colonial Americans?

Property-Owning Class	New England	Mid-Atlantic Colonies	Southern Colonies	Thirteen Colonies
Men	£169	£194	£410	£260
Women	£42	£103	£215	£132
Adults 45 and older	£252	£274	£595	£361
Adults 44 and younger	£129	£185	£399	£237
Urban	£191	£287	£641	£233
Rural	£151	£173	£392	£255
Esquires, gentlemen	£313	£1,223	£1,281	£572
Merchants	£563	£858	£314	£497
Professions, sea captains	£271	£241	£512	£341
Farmers only, planters	£155	£180	£396	£263
Farmer-artisans, ship owners, fishermen	£144	£257	£801	£410
Shop and tavern keepers	£219	£222	£195	£204
Artisans, chandlers	£114	£144	£138	£122
Miners, laborers	£52	£67	£383	£62

Source: Alice Hanson Jones, Wealth of a Nation to Be: The American Colonies on the Eve of the Revolution (New York: Columbia University Press, 1980), p. 224.

Men performed the work on the rest of the farm. They raised grain and maintained the pastures. They cleared the land, chopped wood for fuel, and built and maintained the house, barn, and other structures. They took their harvested crops to market. Men's and women's work were complementary, and both were necessary for the family's economic survival. For example, men planted apple trees, children picked apples, and women made them into cider. Men herded the sheep whose wool women sheared, carded, spun, and dyed. When a husband was disabled, ill, or away from home, his wife could fill in for him, performing virtually all of his tasks as a sort of "deputy husband." Men whose wives died remarried quickly to have someone to take care of the household and children.

The industrious revolution transformed the family economy: When people decided to produce goods to sell, they changed their family economies. Historians believe that increased production in this period came primarily from the labor of women and children, who worked harder and longer than they had before.

Sources of Regional Prosperity

The South, the most productive region, accounted for more than 60 percent of colonial exports (see Map 5–2). Tobacco remained the region's chief cash crop. Next came cereals such as rice, wheat, corn, and flour, and then indigo, a plant used to dye fabric.

Slave labor accounted for most of the southern agricultural output, and the slave labor force was organized to produce for the market. When profits from tobacco began to slip because of falling prices and the depletion of the soil,

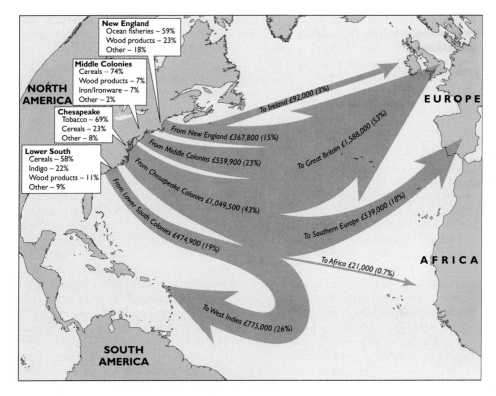

New England
Ocean fisheries – 59%
Wood products – 23%
Other – 18%

Middle Colonies
Cereals – 74%
Wood products – 7%
Iron/Ironware – 7%
Other – 2%

NORTH AMERICA

Chesapeake
Tobacco – 69%
Cereals – 23%
Other – 8%

Lower South
Cereals – 58%
Indigo – 22%
Wood products – 11%
Other – 9%

EUROPE

To Ireland £92,000 (3%)

From New England £367,800 (15%)

From Middle Colonies £559,900 (23%)

To Great Britain £1,588,000 (53%)

From Chesapeake Colonies £1,049,500 (43%)

From Lower South Colonies £474,900 (19%)

To Southern Europe £539,000 (18%)

To Africa £21,000 (0.7%)   **AFRICA**

To West Indies £775,000 (26%)

SOUTH AMERICA

Map 5–2   Exports of the Thirteen Colonies, c. 1770
Almost two-thirds of the exports from the colonies came from the South, and more than one-half went to Great Britain alone. Tobacco and grains were the most important exports of all.
Source: Jacob Cooke, ed., Encyclopedia of North American Colonies (New York: Scribner's, 1993), I, 514.

planters worked their slaves harder and, in the Chesapeake, began to plant corn and wheat. By diversifying their crops, planters were also able to keep their slaves busy throughout the year. Successful planters made maximum use of their slave labor force.

The work routine of slaves depended on the crops that they tended. On tobacco plantations, where careful attention to the plants was necessary to ensure high quality, planters or white overseers worked the slaves in small gangs. Each gang was carefully selected and arranged to maximize productivity. The strongest field hand, for example, would be put at the head of a row of hoers, and all the other slaves would be made to work at his pace.

In the rice-growing regions of the lower South, slaves required far less supervision than they did on tobacco plantations. Because many Africans had grown rice in Africa, it is likely that they taught Europeans how to grow it in America. Under these circumstances, rice planters let the slaves set their own pace. Once the slaves had finished their task for the day, they could use their time as they pleased. Many planted gardens to supplement their own diets or to earn a small income. Slaves trafficked in a wide range of products, not only rice, corn, chickens, hogs, and catfish, but also canoes, baskets, and wax.

The inhabitants of the middle colonies grew prosperous by raising wheat and other grains to sell on the market. The ports of Baltimore, Philadelphia, Wilmington, and New York became thriving commercial centers that collected grain from regional farmers, milled it into flour, and shipped it to the West Indies, southern Europe, and other American colonies. Farmers relied on indentured servants, cottagers, and slaves to supplement the labor of family members. *Cottagers* were families who rented out part of a farmer's land, which they worked for wages.

As long as land was cheap and easy to obtain, the middle colonies enjoyed an evenly shared prosperity. Most inhabitants fell into the comfortable middle class, with the gap between the richest and the poorest relatively small. Pennsylvania, which had both religious toleration and relatively simple procedures for the purchase of land, was particularly prosperous. Gottfried Mittleberger, who endured a horrendous journey to Pennsylvania, described his new home as a sort of paradise: "Our Americans live more quietly and peacefully than the Europeans; and all this is the result of the liberty which they enjoy and which makes them all equal."

When land became expensive or difficult to obtain, however, conflict might have ensued. In the 1740s and 1750s, both New Jersey and New York experienced land riots when conflicting claims made land titles uncertain. In other regions, such as the Chesapeake and southeastern Pennsylvania, increasing land prices drove the poorest inhabitants into tenancy or to the urban centers. The widespread prosperity of the eighteenth century led Americans to expect that every family who wanted a farm would be able to own one. Unlike in Europe, land ownership was the rule, not the exception, and any deviation from this norm produced tension and anger.

Like the middle colonies, New England was primarily a farming region. However, indentured servants, cottagers, and slaves were far less common there. Instead, most farm labor was provided by male family members. Although farms in some regions, such as the Connecticut River valley, produced surpluses for the market, most New England farm families had to look for other sources of income to pay for consumer goods.

Town governments in New England encouraged enterprise, sometimes providing their inhabitants with gristmills, sawmills, and fields on which cattle could graze. As a result the region prospered, and New Englanders came to expect that government should act to enhance the economy. The primary exports of the region were fish, wood and wood products, and ships built from New England timbers.

Merchants and Dependent Laborers in the Transatlantic Economy

Almost all regions of the colonies participated in a transatlantic economy. In each region, those who were most fully committed to a capitalist economy were those with the most resources: large planters in the southern colonies, owners of the biggest farms in the middle colonies, and urban merchants. The wealthiest colonists enhanced their incomes from activities such as speculating in land, practicing law, lending money, and running a gristmill or sawmill.

If some economic development was spurred from above, by enterprising individuals or by governments, much also developed from the aspirations of ordinary men and women. New England's mixed economy of grain, grazing, fishing, and lumbering required substantial capital improvements such as gristmills, sawmills, and tanneries if the inhabitants were to turn a profit. By the beginning of the eighteenth century, shipbuilding was a substantial part of the economy. By 1775, one-third of the English merchant fleet had been built in the colonies.

The shipbuilding industry, in turn, spurred further economic development. In a process called linked economic development, shipbuilding stimulated other activities, such as lumbering, and the availability of ships made trade possible. The profits generated by shipbuilding and trade were reinvested in sawmills to produce more lumber, in gristmills to grind grain into flour, and, of course, in more trading voyages. The growth of shipping in port cities such as Boston, Newport, New York, Philadelphia, and Charleston led to the emergence of an affluent merchant class. Trading was a risky business, and although many tried it, few rose to the top. One ship lost to a storm could ruin a merchant, as could a sudden turn in the market. In 1759 two enterprising Philadelphians, Daniel Wister and Owen Jones, with just over £4,000 between them, persuaded English merchants to send them £94,000 worth of goods. For two years the partnership prospered, but when the market went sour in 1761, Wister was left bankrupt while Jones struggled to pick up the pieces. With an average of ten times the capital of colonial merchants, English merchants could weather such reverses. Because capital was scarce in the colonies, merchants took great risks, seeking to turn a quick profit during wartime or gambling on a sudden spurt in the price of wheat.

The seafaring trades were at the forefront of capitalist development. The developing capitalist economy created a wealthy, risk-taking merchant class as well as that other distinguishing mark of a capitalist economy, a wage-earning class. As long as there was a labor shortage in the colonies, workers had an advantage. By the beginning of the eighteenth century, however, rapid population increase led to a growing supply of labor in towns such as Salem and Marblehead in Massachusetts. Although they were free to shop around for the best wages, workers became part of

"Commerce Moves All," according to this certificate of membership in a sailmakers' society. Here we see not only linked economic activities such as sailmaking (lower right-hand corner) and trade but also the moral benefits that were imagined to flow from commerce—charity (upper right-hand corner) and abolition of slavery (upper left-hand corner).

a wage-earning working class, dependent on others for their employment and income. Although only a small portion of the American population was working for wages on the eve of the Revolution, it was a sign of things to come.

Consumer Choices and the Creation of Gentility

Under the British mercantilist system (see Chapter 4, "Creating the Empire"), the colonies were supposed to export raw materials to the empire and import finished products from the empire. Thus the colonies sent sugar (from the West Indies), tobacco, wheat, lumber, fish, and animal pelts to Britain and imported cloth and iron. Yet within this general pattern, individual men and women made choices about what to buy.

On both sides of the Atlantic, demand for both plantation products and consumer goods was insatiable. At first only the wealthy could afford such luxuries as sugar and tobacco. But as more and more labor was organized to produce for the market, ordinary men and women found themselves with added income, which they used to purchase luxury products. Tea, imported into both Britain and the colonies from Asia, became, like tobacco and sugar, a mass-consumed luxury. Demand for these plantation products led directly to the traffic in African slaves.

As plantation products flowed east across the Atlantic, so manufactured goods came back to the colonies. Consumer behavior on both sides of the Atlantic was similar: Consumers were smoking tobacco; sweetening their tea with sugar; and buying more clothing, more household goods, more books, and more of every sort of manufactured goods.

The consumer revolution was not a product of higher wages. Instead, people chose to work harder, chose work that brought in money, and chose to buy particular items. In seventeenth-century America, extra income was spent on items of lasting value, such as tablecloths and bed linens kept folded away in a chest, to pass on to one's children. In the eighteenth century, men and women bought more clothing made out of cheaper and less durable fabrics. Until this time, most people had only a few outfits of clothing. The wealthy, of course, always had large wardrobes made from fine fabrics. In the eighteenth century, however, fabric prices fell, and new, cheaper fabrics were manufactured to satisfy growing consumer demand.

People became increasingly interested in how they appeared to others. Ordinary people began to pay attention to the latest fashions, which had once been a concern only of the wealthy. By 1700, two new items made it easier for those who had the time and money to attend to their appearance: the dressing table and the full-length mirror. For the first time, people could see how they appeared to others, head to toe. Washing and styling one's hair or periwig became standard rituals for all who hoped to appear "genteel."

In the eighteenth century, prospering people on both sides of the Atlantic created and tried to follow the standards of a new style of life, gentility. Gentility represented all that was polite, civilized, refined, and fashionable. Gentility meant not only certain sorts of objects, such as a dressing table or a bone china teapot, but also the manners needed to use such objects properly. Standards of gentility established boundaries between the genteel and the vulgar. Those who considered themselves genteel looked down on those whose style of living seemed unrefined, and they became uncomfortable when circumstances required them to associate with their social inferiors.

Yet if gentility erected a barrier between the genteel and the vulgar, it also showed the vulgar how to become genteel. All they needed to do was acquire the right goods and learn how to use them. Throughout the colonies, ordinary people began to purchase consumer goods that established their gentility. Even relatively poor people often owned a mirror, a few pieces of china, or a teapot. This mass consumption and widespread distribution of consumer goods created and sustained the consumer revolution.

The consumer revolution had another egalitarian dimension: It encouraged sociability. Throughout the Atlantic world, men and women, particularly those with a little leisure and money (perhaps half the white population) began to cultivate social life. Many believed that the purpose of life was the sort of society that men and women created in their parlors when they met with friends and family for an evening of dining and conversation.

To put all of their guests on an equal footing, men and women began to purchase matching sets of dinner plates, silverware, glasses, and chairs. Until the eighteenth century, the most important people at the table—the man of the house, his wife, and high-ranking men—got the best chairs. Children, servants, and those of lower social standing sat on stools, benches, or boxes, or they stood. Dishes, utensils, and mugs rarely matched. Matched sets of tableware and chairs underscored the symbolic equality of all dinner guests.

The newest and most popular consumer goods made their way quickly to America—forks, drinking glasses, and teapots. Each new implement and style had its own etiquette. Such rules were daunting for the uneducated, but once they were mastered, a person could enter polite society anywhere in the Atlantic world and be accepted. The eighteenth-century capitalist economy created a trade not only in goods and raw materials, but one in styles of life as well.

Historians debate the effects of the consumer revolution, but on balance it was a democratic force. As one Bostonian put it in 1754, the poor should be allowed to buy "the Conveniencies, and Comforts, as well as Necessaries of Life . . . as freely as the Rich." After all, "I am sure we Work as hard as they do . . . ; therefore, I cannot see why we have not as good a natural Right to them as they have."

THE VARIETIES OF COLONIAL EXPERIENCE

Although the eighteenth-century industrial and consumer revolutions tied the peoples of the North Atlantic world together, climate, geography, immigration, patterns of economic development, and population density made for considerable variety. Although the vast majority of Americans lived in small communities or on farms, an increasing number lived in cities that played a critical role in shaping colonial life. Farming regions, both slave and free, were maturing, changing the character of rural life, and the growing population continued to push at the frontiers, leading to the founding of Georgia.

Creating an Urban Public Sphere

At the end of the seventeenth century, none of the colonial towns—except Boston, with 7,000 people—was much more than a rural village. By 1720, Boston's population had grown to 12,000, Philadelphia had 10,000 inhabitants, New York had 7,000, and Newport and Charleston were home to almost 4,000 each. Forty years later, a number of other urban centers had sprung up, each with populations around 3,000—Salem, Marblehead, and Newburyport in Massachusetts; Portsmouth, New Hampshire; Providence, Rhode Island; New Haven and Hartford, Connecticut; Albany, New York; Lancaster, Pennsylvania; Baltimore, Maryland; Norfolk, Virginia; and Savannah, Georgia. All of these cities were either ports or centers for the fur trade.

Philadelphia seen from the southeast, looking across the harbor.

Social life in colonial cities was characterized by two somewhat contradictory trends. On the one hand, nowhere in the colonies was social stratification among free people more pronounced. By the eve of the American Revolution, each city had an affluent elite, made up of merchants, professionals, and government officials, who established a refined style of life. Each city also had indigent poor. On the other hand, urban life brought all classes of society together at theaters, in taverns, and at religious revivals. Civic life became one of the seedbeds of the Revolution because it provided a forum for the exchange of ideas.

Affluent city dwellers created a life as much like that of London as they could. They imported European goods and established English-style institutions. Urban elites founded social clubs, dancing assemblies, and fishing and hunting clubs. Although many of these associations were for men only, some brought men and women together. By the middle of the eighteenth century, half of Philadelphia's merchant families belonged to the Dancing Assembly.

Urban associations reflected the ideals of the Enlightenment. Some, such as the Masons, espoused the ideal of universalism, that all people were by their nature fundamentally the same. Other institutions advocated self-improvement. Whereas some urban institutions separated out the elite and others challenged the ruling hierarchy, still others brought together all members of society in a "public sphere." City dwellers could see stage plays in Williamsburg by 1716, Charleston and New York by the 1730s, and Philadelphia and Boston by the 1740s. Taverns brought all ranks into even closer proximity. Taverns not only served food and drink but also became true public institutions where people could meet and discuss the issues of the day.

Newspapers also played a critical role in creating a public sphere and extending it beyond the cities. The first newspaper was the *Boston News-Letter,* which appeared in 1704. By the time of the Revolution, 39 newspapers were being published, and the chief town in each colony except Delaware had at least one newspaper.

Strict libel laws prohibited the printing of opinions critical of public officials, or even the truth if it cast them in a bad light. John Peter Zenger, editor of the *New-York Weekly Journal,* was tried in 1735 for criticizing the governor. Zenger's flamboyant attorney, Andrew Hamilton, persuaded the jury that they should rule not simply on the facts of the case (Zenger had criticized the governor) but on whether the law itself was just. When the jury ruled in Zenger's favor, cheers went up in the courtroom. The Zenger case was a milestone in the developing relationship between the public and government officials. The verdict expressed the belief that in the contest between the people and government officials, the press spoke for the people, and hence it was the people themselves, not government, that would hold the press accountable.

City dwellers came to think of themselves as a "public." Not only successful artisans such as Benjamin Franklin and Paul Revere but less affluent craftsmen and mechanics all thought of themselves as part of a public that had certain rights or liberties, such as making their views known and enjoying a fair price for their goods. At times, working people, acting as a public, used mob action to assert their political views. Mobs in both New York and Boston reacted violently to press gangs that scoured the waterfront for additional hands for the Royal Navy. By the time of the Revolution, city dwellers had a long history of asserting their rights in public.

The Diversity of Urban Life

Periodic downturns in the urban economy, especially after the middle of the century, led to increased activism on the part of workers and the urban poor. By the middle of the eighteenth century, the increasing wealth of those at the top and the appearance of a small class of permanently poor at the bottom of the economic hierarchy began to undermine the assumption that all city dwellers shared a common interest and that, consequently, the wealthy and well-educated could be trusted to govern for the benefit of everyone.

Although by today's standards the colonial population, even in the cities, was remarkably equal, in the eighteenth century it became more stratified than it had been. At the beginning of the eighteenth century, none of the cities had a substantial number of poor people. Over the course of the eighteenth century, however, colonial wars sent men home disabled and left many women widowed and their children orphaned. Each city responded to the growth in poverty by building almshouses for the poor who could not support themselves and workhouses for those, including women and children, who could. In Philadelphia and New York about 25 percent of the population was at or below the poverty level for the time, and in Boston perhaps as much as 40 percent of the population was living at or near subsistence. Many colonists feared that colonial cities were coming to resemble London, with its mass of impoverished and desperate poor.

All the major cities had slaves, and in some the black population was considerable. By 1746, 30 percent of New York City's working class consisted of slaves. After a serious slave revolt in 1712 and a rumored revolt in 1741, the white population responded with harsh punishments (but without halting the slave trade). In the wake of the 1712 revolt, which had left nine white men dead, city officials executed 18 convicted rebels, some by torture. Six more committed suicide. The response to a rumored slave insurrection in 1741 resembled Salem's witchcraft trials: 18 slaves and four whites were hanged, and 13 slaves were burned at the stake.

New York enacted a stringent slave code after the 1712 revolt, and Boston and Pennsylvania imposed significant import duties on slaves. Nonetheless, the importation of slaves continued into all the port cities, where they were in demand as house servants and artisans. Almost all of Boston's elite owned at least one slave, as did many members of the middle class. Wealthy white artisans often purchased slaves instead of enlisting free whites as apprentices.

In Charleston, where more than half the population was enslaved, many masters let their slaves hire themselves out in return for a portion of their earnings. Such slaves set their own hours, chose their own recreational and religious activities, and participated in the consumer economy by selling their products and making purchases with the profits. Although white city dwellers were troubled by the impudence and relative freedom of urban slaves, urban slavery flourished. Even in northern cities, the advantages of the institution outweighed its dangers in the minds of most whites.

The Maturing of Rural Society

Population increases had a different impact in rural areas than in cities. During the eighteenth century, some long-settled regions became relatively overcrowded. Land that had once seemed abundant had been carelessly farmed and had lost some of its fertility. This relative overcrowding, which historians call *land pressure*, led to a number of changes in colonial society, felt most acutely in New England. Population density increased, and with no additional farmland available, migration from farms to newly settled areas and cities increased. Both the concentration of wealth and social differentiation increased, dividing the farm community into rich and poor.

Such broad economic changes had a direct impact on individual men and women. Families with numerous children to provide for were hard pressed if the original plot of land could not be divided into homesteads large enough for each son. (Daughters were given movable property such as farm animals, household equipment, and slaves.) Some sons migrated to cities, looking for employment. Others worked on other men's farms for wages or, in the South, became tenant farmers. Daughters became servants in other women's households. In such older settled regions, the average age of marriage crept upward. In Middlesex County, Virginia, by 1740, women were marrying at age 22, two years older than before. By the time of the Revolution, women in Andover, Massachusetts, were, on average, 24 before they married, a year or two older than in the previous century.

As young men and women in long-settled regions had to defer marriage, increasing numbers had sexual relations before marriage. In some towns, by the middle of the eighteenth century, between 30 percent and 50 percent of brides bore their first child within eight months of their wedding day. The growing belief that marriage should be based primarily on love probably encouraged some couples to become intimate before they married, especially if poverty required them to postpone marriage. Young women who engaged in sexual relations before marriage took a risk. If their lovers declined to marry them they would be disgraced and their futures would be bleak.

The World That Slavery Made

The rural economy of the South depended on slave labor. Whites and their black slaves formed two distinct cultures, one in the black-majority lower South and the other in the Chesapeake region. In both regions, the most affluent slave masters sold their crops on the international market and used the profits to buy elegant furniture and the latest London fashions. Like their affluent English counterparts, planters aimed for moderation in all things—from the measured cadences of the minuets they liked to dance to and highly stylized love letters, to restrained mourning on the death of a loved one.

Chesapeake planters modeled themselves after English country gentlemen, while low country planters imitated the elite of London. Chesapeake planters designed their plantations to be self-sufficient villages, like English country estates. Because slaves produced most of the goods and services the plantation needed, planters such as William Byrd II imagined themselves living "in a kind of independence on everyone but Providence."

South Carolina planters used their wealth to build elegant homes in Charleston and other coastal cities, where they spent as much time as possible and established a flourishing urban culture. By the eve of the Revolution, the area around Charleston was the most affluent in the mainland colonies. In spite of their affluence, the southern planter elite never achieved the secure political power enjoyed by its English counterpart. In England the social elite dominated government. With noble rank inherited and voting rights limited to male property owners, the English government was remarkably stable. The colonial elite, however (in the northern colonies as well as the southern ones), was cut off from the top levels of political power, which remained in England. The colonists were at the mercy of whichever officials the Crown happened to appoint.

Unable to count on support from above, the colonial elite needed to guarantee the loyalty of those below them. In Virginia, the elite acted as middlemen for lesser planters, advancing them credit and marketing their tobacco. In general, they wielded their authority with a light hand, and punishments for crimes committed by whites were light. Finally, they enhanced their authority by the use of ritual. Actions were calculated for the effect they would produce on both peers and social inferiors. Sitting astride his horse, dressed elegantly, and wearing a wig, a planter was an imposing figure on the landscape. Members of the gentry tried to distance themselves from their slaves, whom they considered "vulgar." Eighteenth-century racial views notwithstanding, some whites crossed in a dramatic way. Some historians believe that sexual relations between whites and blacks were common. Several prominent Virginians acknowledged and supported their mulatto children. Some interracial relationships were affectionate; others were coerced. All the resulting offspring were in a vulnerable position; like all slaves they were dependent on the will of whites.

In the low country, plantation slaves had an unusual degree of autonomy. Living in a region where they were in the majority, slaves were better able to retain their own religions, languages, and customs than were those in the Chesapeake. The Gullah language, still spoken today on the Sea Islands off the coast of South Carolina and Georgia, combined English, Spanish, Portuguese, and African languages.

The mainland colonies' bloodiest slave revolt, the Stono Rebellion, took place in 1739, only a year after the founding of the Spanish free black outpost of Mose in Florida. The uprising was led by about 20 slaves born in Kongo (present-day Angola). Early in the morning of September 9, the rebels broke into a store near the Stono Bridge, taking weapons and ammunition and killing the storekeepers. The rebels moved south toward St. Augustine, killing whites and gathering blacks into their fold. Although the main body of the rebels was dispersed that evening, and many were executed on the spot, skirmishes took place for another week, and the last of the ringleaders was not captured for three years.

The authorities reacted with predictable severity, putting dozens of slave rebels "to the most cruel Death" and revoking many liberties the slaves had enjoyed. A prohibitive duty was placed on the importation of slaves, and attempts were made to encourage the immigration of white Europeans. Although slave imports dropped significantly in the 1740s, by 1750 they rose to pre-Stono levels.

Georgia: From Frontier Outpost to Plantation Society

Nowhere was the white determination to create and maintain a slave society stronger than in Georgia. It is sometimes said that the colonies became slave societies slowly, as individual planters purchased slaves, but without the society as a whole ever committing itself to slavery. Although there is some truth to this analysis, it is not accurate for Georgia, where the introduction of slavery was a purposeful decision.

The establishment of the English colony at South Carolina had, of course, made the Spanish nervous because of its proximity to their settlement at St. Augustine. With the French founding of New Orleans (1718) and Fort Toulouse (1717), Carolinians felt increasingly threatened. They were therefore eager for the English to establish a colony to the south, which would both serve as a buffer between Florida and South Carolina and, if extended far enough west, cut the French colonial empire in two.

The British Crown issued a 21-year charter to a group of trustees led by James Oglethorpe, who had achieved prominence by bringing about reforms in England's debtors' prisons. The colony, Georgia, was designed as a combination philanthropic venture and military-commercial outpost. Its colonists, who were to be drawn from Britain's "deserving poor," were supposed to protect South Carolina's borders and to make the new colony a sort of Italy-on-the-Atlantic, producing wine, olives, and silk.

Unfortunately, Oglethorpe's humanitarianism was not coupled with an understanding of the world political economy. By that time it was well known that excessive indulgence in alcohol was undermining the cohesion of many Indian tribes. Consequently, Oglethorpe had banned liquor from the colony. However, without a product to sell, the colony could not prosper. South Carolina's wharves, merchants, and willingness to sell rum enabled it to dominate the trade with local Indians. Oglethorpe had also banned slavery for humanitarian reasons (making it the only colony expressly to prohibit slavery). As a result, Georgia farmers looked enviously across the Savannah River at South Carolinians growing rich off slave labor. Finally, contrary to common practice in the colonies, the trustees made no provision for self-government. Georgia, despite its founders' noble intentions, lacked everything that the thriving colonies enjoyed: a cash crop or product, large plots of land, slaves to work the land, and laws of its own devising.

Never able to realize their dream of a colony populated by small and contented farmers, the trustees surrendered Georgia back to the Crown a year early, in 1752. With Oglethorpe's laws repealed and slavery introduced, the colony soon resembled the plantation society of South Carolina. Savannah became a little Charleston, with its robust civic and cultural life, and its slave markets as well.

THE HEAD AND THE HEART IN AMERICA: THE ENLIGHTENMENT AND RELIGIOUS AWAKENING

American life in the eighteenth century was shaped by two movements, the Enlightenment and a series of religious revivals known as the Great Awakening. In many ways, these movements were separate, even opposite, appealing to different groups of people. The Enlightenment was a transatlantic intellectual movement that held that the universe could be understood and improved by the human mind. The Great Awakening was a transatlantic religious movement that held that all people were born sinners, that all could feel their own depravity without the assistance of ministers, and that all were equal in the eyes of God. Although the movements might seem fundamentally opposite, with one emphasizing the power of the human mind and the other disparaging it, both criticized established authority and valued the experience of the individual. Both contributed to the humanitarianism that emerged at the end of the century, and both were products of capitalism.

The Ideas of the Enlightenment

The roots of the Enlightenment can be traced to the Renaissance and the spirit of inquiry that led explorers like Columbus halfway around the globe. But the gloomy mysticism of Columbus and the belief in the supernatural held by virtually all the early explorers and colonists disappeared in the bright light of the Renaissance. Men and women of the Enlightenment contrasted the ignorance, oppression, and suffering of the middle or "dark" ages, as they called them, and their own enlightened time. Enlightened thinkers believed fervently in the power of rational thinking and scoffed at superstition.

People of the Enlightenment believed that God and his world were knowable. "Your own reason," Thomas Jefferson told his nephew, "is the only oracle given you by heaven." Rejecting revelation as a guide, the Enlightenment looked instead to reason. Jefferson's "trinity of the three greatest men the world had ever produced" included not Jesus Christ but Isaac Newton, the scientist responsible for modern mathematics and physics; Francis Bacon, the philosopher who outlined the scientific method; and John Locke, the political philosopher of democracy.

Enlightenment thinkers were more interested in what all people had in common than in what differentiated them. No passage in the Bible was more important to the Enlightenment than Genesis 1:27: "So God created man in his own image." It was the basis not only for overcoming Calvinism's belief in humanity's innate depravity but also for asserting the principle of human equality.

Chief among human duties, according to Benjamin Franklin, was "doing good to [God's] other children." In fact, people served God best not by praying, which, as Thomas Paine put it, "can add nothing to eternity," but "by endeavouring to make his creatures happy." Scientific inquiry and experiments such as Franklin's with electricity all had as their object the improvement of human life.

Although the eighteenth century had seen a number of improvements in the quality of life, the world was still violent and filled with pain. The Enlightenment responded to the pain and violence of its world in two ways. First, it attempted to alleviate and curtail them. Scientists eagerly sought cures for diseases. The Reverend Cotton Mather of Boston learned about the procedure of inoculating against smallpox (using a small amount of the deadly virus) from a scientific article and from his African slave Onesimus, who knew of its practice in Africa. An epidemic that began in 1721 gave him an opportunity to try out the technique. The revulsion against pain and suffering also encouraged humanitarian reform, such as James Oglethorpe's reform of English debtors' prisons and, eventually, the anti-slavery movement.

Men and women of the Enlightenment also cultivated a stoic resignation to the evils that they could not change, and a personal ideal of moderation, so that they would neither give nor receive pain. The gentility and politeness of the urban elite was an expression of this ideal of moderation.

The Enlightenment and the Study of Political Economy

Enlightenment thinkers began to study the connections among society, politics, and the economy. John Locke was the first to link these in a theory of political economy. He argued that there was a systematic connection between social institutions (such as the family), political institutions, and property rights. He began with the claim that each person has the right to life and the right to preserve that life. To sustain their lives, people form families, and to support themselves and their families, they labor. The basic right to life thus gives people the right to the product of their labor—property. To protect their lives and their property, people create governments. They give up some of their liberty, but receive protection of their lives and property in return.

Locke also developed a new economic theory. He said that money has no intrinsic value. His idea was a departure from mercantilism, which said that the value of money was fixed. In the second half of the eighteenth century, Scottish philosophers such as Francis Hutcheson and Adam Smith carried Locke's ideas even further, arguing that human beings should be free to value the things that made them happy. They developed a full-scale defense of consumption.

Using happiness as their standard for human life, the Scots argued that people should be free to produce. Adam Smith's influential *The Wealth of Nations* (1776) was both a critique of mercantilism and a defense of free markets and free labor. For Smith and other Enlightenment theorists, the best incentive to hard work was the increased wealth and comforts it would bring. Human beings were happiest, they said, when they lived under free governments, which protected private property but left the market largely unregulated. These ideas became increasingly popular around the time of the Revolution.

Enlightened Institutions

The Enlightenment spurred the creation of institutions that embodied its principles. Humanitarianism led to the building of the Pennsylvania Hospital in 1751 and the Eastern State Mental Hospital at Williamsburg in 1773. Benjamin Franklin played a central role in organizing institutions. In 1743 he proposed a society of learned men, modeled after the Royal Society of London, to study and share information about science and technology. He also helped establish the Library Company of Philadelphia in 1731, the first lending library in the colonies. By the time of the Revolution, Newport, New York, Charleston, and Savannah all had libraries.

The Enlightenment had a significant effect on organized religion as well. The Anglicans, in particular, were receptive to its ideals of moderation and rationalism. In England, John Tillotson, the Archbishop of Canterbury, preached a comforting and simple Christianity: God was "good and just" and required nothing "that is either unsuitable to our reason or prejudicial to our interest . . . nothing but what is easy to be understood, and is as easy to be practiced by an honest and willing mind."

This message became popular in the colonies, even among Congregationalist ministers. John Wise, the minister of Ipswich, Massachusetts, insisted that "to follow God and to obey Reason is the same thing." Arminianism, the belief that salvation was partly a matter of individual effort rather than entirely God's will, enjoyed a new popularity. Harvard became a hotbed of liberal theology, and in response, religious conservatives founded Yale in New Haven, Connecticut, in 1701, to guarantee that New England's ministers could get a proper Calvinist education.

Origins of the Great Awakening

The problem with rational religion was that it was not emotionally fulfilling. Popular demand for more and better religion led to a series of revivals, known as the Great Awakening, that swept through the colonies between 1734 and 1745. At first, church leaders looked with pleasure on the stirrings of spiritual renewal. In the winter of 1734–1735, some of the rowdiest young people in Northampton, Massachusetts, men and women who carried on parties for "the greater part of the night," began seeking religion at the church of a brilliant young minister, Jonathan Edwards. Everyone rejoiced at these signs of spiritual awakening.

The Grand Itinerant

When George Whitefield arrived in Philadelphia in 1739, the local ministers, including officials of Whitefield's own Anglican church, welcomed him. Whitefield drew audiences in the thousands everywhere he spoke. In the 15 months of his grand tour, he visited every colony from Maine to Georgia, met all the important ministers, and was heard at least once by most of the inhabitants of Massachusetts and Connecticut. He spoke to the entire community—rich, poor, slave, free, old, young, male, and female—acting out simple scripts based on biblical stories. The message was always the same, the sinfulness of man and the mercy of God.

In a calculated move, perhaps intended to increase his audiences, Whitefield began speaking out against some in the ministry, accusing them of being unconverted. He started with the deceased Archbishop of Canterbury, John Tillotson, and went on to criticize some of the clergymen who were alive and preaching. Even ministers sympathetic to the revival were shocked by these accusations, which turned their congregations against them and split their churches. Ministers such as Charleston's Anglican Commissary Alexander Garden and Boston's Congregationalist Charles Chauncy, who already had reservations about the revivalists because of their emotional style, now condemned the revival. Such accusations only made the revivalists more popular and attracted larger crowds.

Cultural Conflict and Challenges to Authority

The Great Awakening walked a fine line between challenging authority and supporting it, which no doubt explains its widespread appeal. It antagonized the top tier of the elite, those with the most power and arrogance, but did not challenge the fundamental structures of colonial society. By attacking the ministers, but not government officials, the revivalists criticized authority without suffering any real consequences.

The Great Awakening appealed to all classes of people throughout the colonies. Its greatest impact, however, was in areas that had experienced the greatest change, in particular, cities (especially among the lower orders), the frontier, and older towns that were beginning to suffer from overcrowding. In these places lived the people whose lives were most disrupted by economic changes. Disturbed by the increasing competitiveness of society, men and women were attracted to the democratic fellowship of the revivalist congregation.

While criticizing the materialism and competitiveness of eighteenth-century society, the revival told men and women to look inside themselves for change, not to the structures of society. For example, Sarah Osborn, who heard Whitefield preach at Newport, Rhode Island, blamed herself for her woes, which she thought were punishment for her sinful singing and dancing. After her spiritual rebirth, she trusted in God and reconciled herself to her poverty. Spiritual rebirth provided such men and women with joy and fulfillment that their competitive and changing world had been unable to supply.

The revival also walked a fine line in its treatment of slavery. Early in his travels to the colonies, Whitefield spoke out against the cruelties of slavery and harangued slaveholders. At the same time, however, Whitefield maintained a slave plantation in South Carolina. Like many slaveowners after him, Whitefield argued that it was immoral to enslave Africans, but not to own them, provided that one treated them well and Christianized them. By linking humanitarianism, Christianity, and slavery, the Great Awakening anchored slavery in the South, at least for the time being.

Although it is hard to say if slaves were treated more humanely on the plantations of evangelicals, beginning in the 1740s large numbers of slaves were converted to Christianity. Although some may have converted to please their masters and to get Sundays off, blacks were attracted to evangelical religion for the same reason that whites were. It offered them a way to order their lives and believe that their lives were meaningful.

To a great extent, poor whites and slaves, especially in the South, had been left out of the society that more prosperous people had created. Evangelical religion placed the individual in a community of believers. It offered slaves the opportunity for church discipline and personal responsibility on almost the same terms as whites and gave some blacks the possibility of leadership in a biracial community. Africans grafted some of their religious practices, such as shouting and ecstatic visions, onto the Christian revival, so that worship in southern Baptist and Methodist churches became a truly African-American phenomenon.

What the Awakening Wrought

In general, the Great Awakening took colonial society in the direction in which it was already heading: It encouraged individualism. Church after church split into evangelical and traditional factions, and new denominations appeared. Which religion to follow became a matter of personal choice, and colonies with established churches tolerated dissenters. Religion itself, as a general force, was strengthened, making the colonies simultaneously the most Protestant and the most religiously diverse culture in the world.

The Great Awakening also spurred the establishment of educational institutions. Princeton, chartered in 1748 as the College of New Jersey, grew out of an evangelical seminary. Next came Dartmouth, Brown, and Rutgers, chartered in 1766, to advance "true religion and useful knowledge." Columbia, chartered in 1754, represented the Anglicans' response. The focus of higher education was slowly shifting from the preparation of the ministry to the training of leaders. The Great Awakening diminished the power of ministers while increasing the influence of personal religion.

The Great Awakening was hardly a battle of the pious against the godless or the well-educated against the uninformed. Jonathan Edwards, one of the greatest minds of his age, drew from the Enlightenment as well as Calvinist ideas. He praised both Locke and Newton. For Edwards, however, reason and good habits were not enough. Reason must be supplemented by emotion, in particular the emotion of God's grace. By insisting that religious salvation and virtue were more matters of the heart than the head, Edwards opened the way for a popular religion that was democratic, intensely personal, and humanitarian.

CONCLUSION

Eighteenth-century America was part of an expanding world market and a capitalist political economy. A growing population sustained a vigorous economy, one that produced for and purchased from the world market. As participants in an "industrious revolution," white Americans worked themselves and their slaves harder to

CHRONOLOGY

1693	College of William and Mary founded
1701	Yale founded
1704	First newspaper, *Boston News-Letter*, published in colonies
1712	Slave revolt in New York City
1717	French build Fort Toulouse
1718	French found New Orleans
1731	Library Company, first lending library in colonies, erected in Philadelphia
1733	Georgia founded King of Spain guarantees freedom to English slaves who run away
1734	Great Awakening begins
1735	John Peter Zenger acquitted of libeling New York's governor
1739	Stono Rebellion George Whitefield begins his American tour
1741	35 executed in New York City after slave revolt scare
1748	College of New Jersey (Princeton) founded
1751	Pennsylvania Hospital built in Philadelphia
1752	Georgia becomes a Crown colony
1754	Columbia College founded
1755	Philadelphia College (University of Pennsylvania) founded
1766	Queens College (Rutgers) founded
1773	Eastern State Mental Hospital built in Williamsburg

purchase consumer goods. These new goods enabled people to live more genteely and to cultivate a social life. Especially in the cities, this new emphasis on social life spawned an array of institutions where people could acquire and display learning and gentility. The benefits of the economy were not shared equally, however. Slaves produced for the market economy but were denied its rewards. The increasing stratification of urban society and land pressures in rural regions meant that a growing segment of the population was too poor to profit from the expanding economy.

The eighteenth-century world spawned two different but related intellectual responses, the Enlightenment and the Great Awakening. The Enlightenment led some to believe that rational thought and the scientific method would conquer human ills. At the same time, the Great Awakening reminded men and women that life was short and ultimately beyond their control. In different ways, then, the Enlightenment and the Great Awakening both encouraged the individualism that would become a distinguishing characteristic of American life.

FURTHER READINGS

Richard Bushman, ed., *The Great Awakening: Documents on the Revival of Religion, 1740–1745* (1989). There is no better introduction to the Great Awakening than this collection of sermons and first-person accounts.

Cary Carson, et al., *Of Consuming Interests: The Style of Life in the Eighteenth Century* (1994). An important introduction to the material culture of eighteenth-century consumer culture.

Cornelia Hughes Dayton, *Women Before the Bar: Gender, Law, and Society in Connecticut, 1639–1789* (1995). Uses court records to reveal the lives of ordinary women and their deteriorating position in the eighteenth century.

Thomas M. Doeflinger, *A Vigorous Spirit of Enterprise: Merchants and Economic Development in Revolutionary Philadelphia* (1986). Describes the lives and aspirations of this important segment of the colonial population while providing an excellent introduction to the period's economic history.

David Eltis, *The Rise of African Slavery in the Americas* (2000). A bold new interpretation of the development of slavery that places it in a global context and emphasizes the role of Africans in shaping the slave trade.

Richard Hofstadter, *America at 1750: A Social Portrait* (1971). A beautifully written description of America's peoples and regions that suggests that the Great Awakening made a middle-class society even more so.

Rhys Isaac, *The Transformation of Virginia, 1740–1790* (1982). A magnificent description of the different cultures of Virginia's elite and poor, showing how religious revivals changed them forever.

Philip D. Morgan, *Slave Counterpoint: Black Culture in the Eighteenth-Century Chesapeake and Low Country* (1998). A learned and comprehensive study of slave life in the colonial South.

Gary B. Nash, *The Urban Crucible: Social Change, Political Consciousness, and the Origins of the American Revolution* (1979). Detailed, comprehensive, and indispensable for understanding the social and political world of urban working men.

Please refer to the document CD-ROM for primary sources related to this chapter.

CHAPTER

6

Conflict on the Edge of Empire

1713–1774

Susannah Willard Johnson Experiences the Empire • The Wars for
Empire • The Victory of the British • Enforcing the Empire
Rejecting the Empire • A Revolution in the Empire • Conclusion

SUSANNAH WILLARD JOHNSON EXPERIENCES THE EMPIRE

Today the town is Charlestown, New Hampshire, but then it was "No. 4," a small farming village on the northern frontier of Massachusetts. In 1754 Susannah Willard Johnson and her husband James lived there, having taken advantage of a break in the near-constant struggle between Britain and France for North America by moving up to the frontier. At 24, Susannah had been married for seven years and already had three children, with another due any day. James, a native of Ireland, had commenced his life in America as a servant indentured to Susannah's uncle Josiah. After working for Josiah for ten years, he purchased the remainder of his time, married Susannah, and made his way by a combination of farming and shopkeeping. James also became a lieutenant in the militia.

The region's Abenaki Indians—Algonquians who were allied with the French and had their own grievances against the encroaching settlers—presented both danger and opportunity. At first the settlers at No. 4 were so frightened that they stayed in the fort. However, Susannah later reported, "hostility at length vanished— the Indians expressed a wish to traffick, the inhabitants laid by their fears . . ." James

Johnson was part of the consumer revolution, selling goods to his fellow settlers and to the Abenakis, who gave him furs in return.

Susannah Johnson described her family's life as "harmony and safety," and "boasted with exaltation that I should with husband, friends, and luxuries, live happy in spite of the fear of savages." By the summer of 1754, however, there were rumors of impending warfare with France, which would make the frontier village a target of France's Abenaki allies.

On August 30, 1754, just before daybreak, a neighbor who was coming to work for the Johnsons appeared at the door. As the Johnsons opened the door for him, the neighbor rushed in, 11 Abenaki men following him. Soon, Susannah said, they were "all over the house, some upstairs, some haling my sister out of bed, another had ahold of me, and one was approaching Mr. Johnson, who stood in the middle of the floor, to offer himself up."

The Abenakis tied up the men and gathered the women and children around them. They took plunder and then marched the party to the north. They marched hard, even though Susannah, who had lost her shoes, had bloody feet. On the second day of her captivity, Susannah went into labor. Attended by her sister and husband, Susannah gave birth to a daughter, whom she named Captive.

The French and Indian War had begun on the northern frontier, and the Indians were manipulating it to their advantage. In peacetime they traded furs for manufactured goods, but in wartime they seized British settlers, took them to Canada, and sold them to the French, who either ransomed them back to the British or traded them for prisoners of war. What to others might look like an imperial struggle, Susannah Johnson experienced as a terrifying assault at dawn that took her from her home and eventually her family. The consumer revolution that gave settlers such as the Johnsons the opportunity to live a good life on the frontier was rooted in an imperial struggle between France and England, two empires competing over both the markets the consumer revolution was creating and the lands it was populating. As families such as the Johnsons pushed at the frontiers, they became actors on a global stage.

THE WARS FOR EMPIRE

From 1689 to 1763, Britain and France were at war more than half of the time. All of these wars had their roots in a struggle for world dominance between the two powerful empires. To a great extent, colonial and imperial objectives coincided. Both Britain and the colonies would benefit from securing the empire's borders and from expanding British markets. Yet the imperial wars also exposed the growing divergence between the political economy of the colonies and that of the mother country. When the growing empire and its wars threatened to increase the British government's power over the colonists, raise their taxes to pay for the empire, and station among them a permanent army, the colonists resisted and finally rebelled.

An Uneasy Peace

After the conclusion of Queen Anne's War in 1713 (see Chapter 4, "Creating the Empire"), England and France were at peace until 1739. It was an uneasy peace for the British North American colonies, however. On the north, New Englanders continued to fight with the Abenakis, forcing that tribe into a closer alliance with the French. At the same time, the French attempted to stabilize alliances with their Algonquian allies. The most common method was by providing "gifts" of trade goods.

Worried about their ability to control their Indian allies and about the expansion of the British colonies, the French built new forts: Fort Toulouse (1717), Louisbourg (1720), Fort Niagara (1720), Fort St. Frédéric (1731), and the town of New Orleans (1718). French settlement of the lower Mississippi valley led to conflict with the Natchez Indians, whom they conquered and sold into slavery. Unsuccessful French attacks on the Chickasaw drove that tribe into a closer alliance with its British trading partners.

The British, however, were unable to establish peaceful relations with Indians in the Southeast. In 1711, the Tuscarora Indians attacked settlers in western North Carolina. The short and brutal war ended in the defeat of the Tuscaroras. The survivors made their way north, where they joined the Iroquois confederacy. Although the Yamasees had been reliable trading partners for 40 years and had fought with the British in Queen Anne's War, South Carolina traders cheated them out of their land and enslaved their women and children. In retaliation, the Yamasees attacked, picking up Indian allies along the way and getting within 12 miles of Charleston, stopped by the crumbling of the Indian alliance. The Yamasee War (1715–1716) claimed the lives of 400 white South Carolinians, forced South Carolina to abandon frontier settlements, and revealed the precariousness of the entire South Carolina settlement. When international war commenced again in 1739, the frontier regions were, as they had been a quarter of a century earlier, dangerous and unstable for settlers, traders, and Indians alike.

New War, Old Pattern

Another round of international warfare broke out in 1739 and continued for nine years. In the first phase, the War of Jenkins's Ear (1739–1744), Britain attempted to expand into Spanish territories and markets in the Americas. Urged on by the merchants, and with the approval of colonists who wanted to eliminate Spain as a rival, the British found an excuse for declaring war against the Spanish: A ship's captain, Robert Jenkins, turned up in Parliament in 1738 with an ugly stump on one side of his head, holding in his hand what he claimed was his ear, severed by the Spanish seven years earlier in the Caribbean. In 1741, 3,600 colonists, mostly poor young men lured by the king's promise that they could share Spanish plunder, joined 5,000 Britons in a failed attack on Cartagena, Colombia. More than half the colonial contingent died.

Another ambitious attempt to seize part of the Spanish empire failed in 1740: James Oglethorpe and settlers hired by South Carolina, accompanied by Cherokee and Creek allies, failed to seize the Spanish outpost at St. Augustine and left the southern border vulnerable. When Oglethorpe and his troops repulsed a Spanish attack in 1742, however, Spain's plan to demolish Georgia and South Carolina was thwarted.

Just as the War of Jenkins's Ear ended in stalemate, so did King George's War (1744–1748), a conflict between Britain and Austria, on one side, and France and

Prussia on the other, over succession to the Austrian throne. In North America, a French raid on a fishing village in Nova Scotia met with a huge retaliation by the British. Troops from Massachusetts, subsidized by Pennsylvania and New York and supported by the British Navy, captured the French fort at Louisbourg. Finally, a joint British–colonial venture had succeeded. But, true to the old form, a planned two-pronged attack on Quebec was called off when the British fleet failed to arrive. At the end of the war, Britain returned Louisbourg to France and warned the colonists that they had to maintain the peace. Events in North America, however, were out of European control. The British blockade of French ports cut off trade to Canada, including the all-important presents to Indian allies and trade partners. Without these gifts, the French–Indian empire began to crumble.

War and Political Economy

Successive rounds of warfare had a significant impact on politics and society in British North America. Although the colonists identified strongly with the British cause, decades of warfare were a constant drain on the colonial treasury and population.

Wars are expensive. Generally, rates of taxation in colonial America were low, except when wars had to be financed (see Figure 6–1). In a rehearsal for the conflicts that would lead to the American Revolution, the British government complained that the colonists were unwilling to contribute their fair share to the imperial wars. As a rule, colonial legislatures were willing to go only so far in raising taxes to pay for imperial wars or expeditions against Indians. Then they simply issued paper money. Inevitably, the currency depreciated, making even worse the boom-and-bust cycles that war economies always produce.

No colony did more to support the imperial war efforts than Massachusetts, but the result was heightened political conflict at home. Royal governors, eager to ingratiate themselves with officials in London, pushed the colony to contribute to the imperial wars. Meeting the need for money and manpower also required centralization of government, which in turn inspired a vigorous popular opposition. In 1747 Boston mobs rioted for three days to resist the Royal Navy's attempt to

Figure 6–1   Tax Rates in Boston, 1645–1774
The per capita tax rate in Boston followed the course of imperial war in 1713, increasing during the War of Jenkins's Ear (1739–1748) and rising to unprecedented heights to support the French and Indian War (1754–1763).

Source: Data from Gary B. Nash, The Urban Crucible (Cambridge, MA: Harvard University Press, 1974), p. 403.

"impress" (or force) men into service, and the local militia refused to restore order. For the first time, Bostonians began to speak about a right to resist tyranny.

Much more than in Europe, civilians in America became victims of war. By the eighteenth century, conventions of "civilized" warfare held that civilians should be spared, but this belief broke down in America for two reasons. First, without a transportation system to bring supplies to the Army, troops often relied on plunder. As New England soldiers marched north through Canada to Louisbourg in 1745, they stole chickens, wine, and livestock from French farmers along the way. Second, frontier Indians, adapting their traditional mourning war (see Chapter 2, "Colonial Outposts"), routinely attacked villages, seizing captives to replenish their populations and ransom to the French. Between 1675 and 1763, with war more common than peace, frontier settlers such as Susannah Johnson were often at risk. During that period, Indians took more than 1,600 New England settlers as captives, more than 90 percent during times of war.

Almost half the colonists who were seized eventually returned home. Others died during the arduous march north to Canada. Sometimes Indians killed those they thought were too weak to survive the journey. Many died of disease, and a few, typically girls between 7 and 15, remained with their captors voluntarily. On occasion, a captive escaped.

THE VICTORY OF THE BRITISH EMPIRE

Each imperial war was ignited by a political episode, but the fundamental issues were economic and imperial, matters of political economy, as Europe's great powers contended to dominate markets and assure themselves a steady supply of food and raw materials. The period between the conclusion of King George's War in 1748 and the beginning of the French and Indian War in 1754 was tense, especially on the frontier, and Britain and France were drawn into a war because of events that no one in London or Paris could control.

The French Empire Crumbles From Within

In the years after King George's War, a change in French policy offered a small band of Miami Indians the chance to gain an advantage over rivals. In the process, they started a chain of events that led to the French and Indian War.

Although King George's War had ended in a stalemate, the French position in North America was weaker at the war's conclusion than at the beginning. The British blockade, combined with the need to divert resources to the military effort, had forced the French to cut back on their presents to allied Algonquian tribes, especially in the Ohio River valley. In addition, to raise revenue, the French sharply increased their charges for the lease of trading posts; in turn, traders raised the prices that they charged the Indians for trade goods. These changes significantly weakened the French hold over their Indian allies, creating political instability that was the underlying North American cause of the French and Indian War.

The Ohio River valley was inhabited by a number of small, refugee tribes (see Map 6–1). As long as the French could provide liberal presents and cheap trade goods, they maintained a loose control. Once that control ended, however, each tribe sought to increase its advantage over the others. Moreover, at just this moment the British recognized the strategic and economic importance of the region.

The temporary power vacuum afforded a small group of Miamis, led by a chieftain called La Demoiselle, an opportunity to play one group of colonists off another.

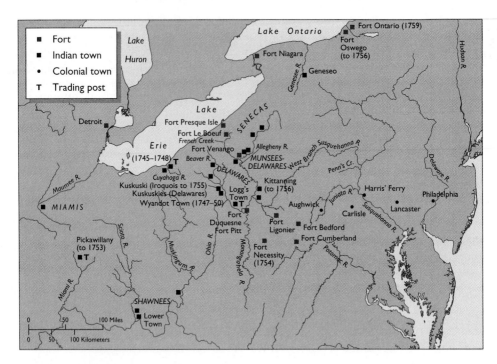

Map 6–1   The Ohio River Valley, 1747–1758

This territory, inhabited by a number of small bands of Indians, was coveted by both the French and the British, not to mention several competing groups of colonial land speculators. The rivalries between the imperial powers, among the Indian bands, and between rival groups of speculators, made this region a powder keg.

Source: Adapted from Michael McConnell, A Country Between (Lincoln: University of Nebraska, 1992), pp. 116–117.

The chain of events that led to the French and Indian War began in 1748 when La Demoiselle's group moved east from their home to establish a new village, Pickawillany, near the head of the Miami River. La Demoiselle welcomed English traders from Pennsylvania, because their trade goods were better and cheaper, and their terms were less demanding, than those of the French. He hoped to trade with the British unencumbered by political or military obligations.

La Demoiselle's move threatened not only the balance of power between Britain and France but also that between the colonies of Pennsylvania and Virginia. The Pennsylvanians welcomed trade with the Miamis, for it gave them a claim to western lands that Virginians sought. At the same time, La Demoiselle was challenging a number of rival chieftains who wished to establish dominance in the area. He used his access to British traders to attract small bands to his village, and within a year his following had grown from 50 warriors to 400 families.

Alarmed, the French set out to re-establish their control of this region. In 1749, the French sent a small expedition to cow their former Indian allies back into submission; when it failed, the French shifted their policy away from trade to force. They began to raid dissident Indian encampments and planned to establish a fort in the Ohio River valley. With this change in French policy, Indians in the region seemed to have two options: to gather Indian allies (La Demoiselle's tactic), or to make alliances with the British (the strategy of a refugee Iroquois chieftain named

Tanacharison). Neither route offered the Indians any real security, but the chaos these bids for advantage created drew the French and British into war.

In 1752, Tanacharison agreed to cede to Virginia not only the 200,000 acres claimed by the Ohio Company, a group of Virginia speculators, but also all the land between the Susquehannah and Allegheny Rivers (that is, present-day Kentucky, West Virginia, and the western half of Pennsylvania). In return, Virginia promised Tanacharison's people trade and protection from their enemies. However, La Demoiselle had miscalculated. With no European or Indian power dominant in the region, conflicts broke out, encouraged by the French, who hoped to use still-loyal Indians to weaken La Demoiselle's alliance, which is precisely what happened. In a raid on Pickawillany, 250 pro-French Ottawas and Chippewas killed La Demoiselle. The village was destroyed, and the demoralized Miamis returned to the French fold, asking for protection. For the moment, the French regained the ascendancy, but by shifting their policy from trade to force, they put themselves on a course that would lead to the loss of their North American empire.

The Virginians Ignite a War

Both France and Virginia now claimed the Ohio River valley, and they raced to establish forts that would secure their claims. Virginia entrusted the job to a well-connected 21-year-old with almost no qualifications for the post: George Washington. Washington was tied to the powerful Fairfax clan, a British family that owned 5 million acres in Virginia and held a share in the Ohio Company. In the Anglo-American political and social world, advancement came through such interlocking ties of family and patronage. As Washington himself recognized, "It was deemed by some an extraordinary circumstance that so young and inexperienced a person should have been employed on a negotiation with which subjects of the greatest importance were involved."

In the spring of 1754, the French and Virginians scrambled to see who could build a fort first at the forks of the Ohio (present-day Pittsburgh). The previous year, the French had constructed three forts to the north. The force that Virginia sent to the region, with Washington as second in command, was pathetically small. Although the French Army numbering 1,000 was only 50 miles away, a combined Virginia–Indian band led by Washington recklessly attacked and defeated a small French reconnaissance party. The French and Indian War (known in Europe as the Seven Years' War) had begun.

The Virginians had bitten off more than they could chew. Fort Necessity, built by Washington and his men, was reinforced by British regulars but quickly deserted by the Indian allies, who recognized it as indefensible. The French overwhelmed the fort, sending Washington and his troops scrambling back to Virginia. Although war was not officially declared in Europe until May 1756, fighting soon spread throughout the frontier, leading to raids such as the one that seized Susannah Johnson and her family.

From Local to Imperial War

At the beginning of the war, the advantage was with the French. That nation's population was three times larger than Britain's, and its Army was ten times the size. Even more important, the French state was more centralized and hence better prepared to coordinate the massive effort that an international war required. The

British government knew that lack of coordination among its North American colonies could cripple the war effort. Hence, as early as the summer of 1754, it instructed all the colonies north of Virginia to plan for a collective defense and to shore up the alliance with the Six (Iroquois) Nations. Pennsylvania's Benjamin Franklin offered the delegates, who met in Albany, a plan, known as the Albany Plan of Union, which every colony rejected.

The characteristic localism of the American colonies made cooperation difficult if not impossible. This localism was a deeply ingrained value, one that was profoundly suspicious of the centralized European state and its army of professionals.

Britain was now engaged in its fourth war with the French in less than a century. The British government had authorized Virginia's foray into the Ohio River Valley and sent two regiments, under the command of General Edward Braddock, to Virginia in late 1754, hoping that the colonists could fight the war with only a little British assistance. But the disarray at Albany continued: Colonial soldiers were reluctant to obey an officer from another colony, let alone one from the British Army.

The French, with four times as many troops as the British had in North America, superior leadership, and the lack of intercolonial rivalries, dominated the first phase of the war, from 1754 through 1757. The British and colonial governments, with armies made up of British regulars and colonials, planned to besiege four French forts: Fort Duquesne (Pittsburgh), Fort Niagara (Niagara Falls), Fort St. Frédéric (Crown Point, at the southern end of Lake Champlain), and Fort Beauséjour (Nova Scotia).

Braddock was to lead the attack on Fort Duquesne, with a combined force of British regulars and colonial troops. No Indians, however, accompanied the expedition. Braddock had alienated the regional Indians, who moved back into the French alliance. After a grueling two-month march in which they built their own roads ahead of them, on July 9, 1755, Braddock's forces were surprised just a few miles from their objective by a French and Indian force. Almost 1,000 British and colonial troops were killed or wounded, including Braddock himself. One of the survivors was George Washington, who had been serving as an unsalaried adjutant to Braddock to learn the art of war.

Two of the other three planned assaults ended in disappointment as well. William Shirley, who became commander in chief of the British forces, decided to lead the attack on Fort Niagara himself, and he assigned leadership of the attack on Fort St. Frédéric to William Johnson, a Mohawk Valley Indian trader. Johnson was well suited for leading Iroquois forays against the French. Shirley, however, sent Johnson to besiege Fort St. Frédéric, a four-story stone tower surrounded by thick limestone walls. Johnson led a force of about 3,500, including 300 Iroquois, building their road ahead of them. Their advance was stopped by an ambush from the French and their Native American allies. But with equal casualties on both sides and the capture of the French commander, the British declared it a victory . The British settled in for the winter of 1755–1756 to build Fort William Henry, and the French, Fort Carillon (which the British renamed Ticonderoga).

Hampered by a rough terrain and intercolonial political wrangling, Shirley's force never made it to Fort Niagara. The only outright success was at Fort Beauséjour, across an isthmus from the British colony at Nova Scotia, the only one of the four campaigns that did not require an arduous wilderness march. A British-financed expedition of New England volunteers easily seized the fort, and the British evicted 10,000 Acadians (French residents of Nova Scotia) who would not take an oath of loyalty. War was officially declared in May 1756. Like the British, the French had reluctantly increased their expenditures on the war, but both nations still expected their colonists to carry most of the load. The British defeats and continued intercolonial rivalries left the British vulnerable and the frontier exposed. The French began a cautious but highly successful offensive. First, they encouraged Indian raids along the frontier from Maine to South Carolina. Indians swung back to the French because the French appeared less dangerous than the land-hungry British. The price for French friendship, however, was participation in the war against the British. Indians attacked all along the frontier. By the fall of 1756, some 3,000 settlers had been killed, and the line of settlement had been pushed back 150 miles in some places.

In the more conventional part of their offensive, the French and their Indian allies seized Fort Bull in March 1756 and Fort Oswego several months later. A little over a year later, the French assembled a massive force to attack Fort William Henry. This loosely organized army of 8,000 included 1,000 Indian warriors from as far as 1,500 miles away and another 800 converted Algonquians accompanied by their Catholic priests.

After a seven-day siege and heavy bombardment, the British commander surrendered on August 9, 1757. Montcalm, the French commander, offered them European-style terms: The British were to return their French and Indian prisoners, keep their personal weapons, and march back to Fort Edward, on the lower Hudson River, promising not to fight the French for 18 months. Historians still debate whether Montcalm knew what was about to take place. The Indians had expected, as was their custom, to be allowed to take plunder and captives. Denied this opportunity by Montcalm, they fell on the British, including the sick, women, and children, as they were evacuating the fort the next morning. Montcalm later commented that "what would be an infraction in Europe, cannot be so regarded in America."

The massacre at Fort William Henry had significant repercussions. Still angry at being denied the spoils of war, Montcalm's Indian allies returned home, taking smallpox with them. The French would never again have the assistance of such a significant number of Indian allies; the British were outraged. The new British commander, Lord Jeffrey Amherst, declared the surrender terms null and void. Later, under his order, Delaware Indians who had been invited to a peace talk were given, ostensibly as presents, blankets that had been infected with smallpox.

Problems with British-Colonial Cooperation

The British blamed the colonists and the colonists blamed the British for their collective defeats. There was some truth in each side's accusations: unwillingness to sacrifice and disastrous infighting among the colonists, and arrogance among the British. These recriminations, more than any failing on either side, created problems. The colonists and the British had different expectations about how each should contribute to the war effort, grounded in diverging political economies. The colonists were not prepared for the high taxes or sacrifice of liberty that waging an international war required. The two chief areas of conflict between the British and the colonists were raising money and troops and discipline and direction in the Army.

The British were dismayed by what they perceived as the colonists' selfishness. Colonists engaged in profiteering and trading with the enemy. In Albany, colonists were selling boards to the army at prices inflated 66 percent. Colonial governments were no more generous. Braddock's expedition to Fort Duquesne was delayed by the colonies' unwillingness to provision his Army.

After Braddock's defeat, it was not only supplies the Army needed; it was troops, too, as colonials deserted en masse. The British began recruiting servants and apprentices, angering their masters. Another serious problem was that of quartering soldiers. Under English law, which did not extend specifically to the colonies, troops in England could call on local communities for shelter, wood, and candles. Also, they were lodged in public buildings rather than private homes. In the colonies, however, there weren't enough buildings in which to house soldiers without resorting to private homes. The residents of Albany took in soldiers only under threat of force. Philadelphians faced the same threats but were rescued by the ever-resourceful Franklin, who opened a newly built hospital to the troops. In Charleston, soldiers had to camp outdoors, where they fell victim to disease.

A second set of problems arose from joint operations. The British Army was a trained and disciplined professional fighting force, led by members of the upper classes; service in it was a career. In contrast, colonial soldiers were primarily civilian amateurs, led by members of the middle class from their hometowns. Colonial soldiers believed that they were fighting under contracts, limiting them to service under a particular officer, for a set period of time, for a specific objective, and a set rate of pay. If any of the terms were violated, the soldier considered himself free to go home.

The British, however, expected the same adherence to military discipline from the colonists as they did from their professional army. All colonial soldiers operating with regular forces were subject to British martial law, which was cruel and uncompromising. One regular soldier, for example, was sentenced to 1,000 lashes for stealing a keg of beer, which a merciful officer reduced to a mere 900! The British officers neither understood nor forgave the colonists' different expectations and were almost unanimous in their condemnation of the colonial soldiers. According to Brigadier General James Wolfe, "The Americans are in general the dirtiest most contemptible cowardly dogs that you can conceive."

Yet the colonists certainly believed that they were doing their share. Taxes were raised dramatically. In Virginia, the tax rate tripled in three years, while in Massachusetts it went up to about £20 per adult man, a considerable sum when the average wealth was £38 per capita. The human contribution was even more impressive. At the height of the war, Massachusetts was raising 7,000 soldiers a year, out of a colony with only 50,000 men. Perhaps as many as three out of ten adult men served in the military at some point during the war, and only the Civil War and the Revolution had higher casualty rates.

The British Gain the Advantage

Montcalm's victory at Fort William Henry marked the French high-water mark. With a change of British government in 1757 came a new resolve to win the war, as William Pitt became head of the cabinet. His rise to power represented the triumph of the commercial classes and their vision of the empire. Pitt was the first British leader who was as committed to a victory in the Americas as in Europe, believing that the future of the British Empire lay in the extended empire and its trade. Consequently, Britain's aim in North America shifted from simply regaining territory to seizing New France itself. Pitt sent 2,000 additional troops, promised 6,000 more, and asked the colonies to raise 20,000 of their own. To support so large an army, Pitt raised taxes on the already heavily taxed British and he borrowed heavily, doubling the size of the British debt. He won the cooperation of the colonies by promising their legislatures that Britain would pay up to half of their costs for fighting the war. As all of this money poured into the colonies, it improved their economies dramatically.

Now the British were prepared to take the offensive (see Map 6–2). In a series of great victories, they won Louisbourg on Cape Breton Island in July 1758; then Fort Frontenac in August; and finally, in November, Fort Duquesne, which the British renamed Fort Pitt. The only defeat was at Fort Carillon (called Ticonderoga

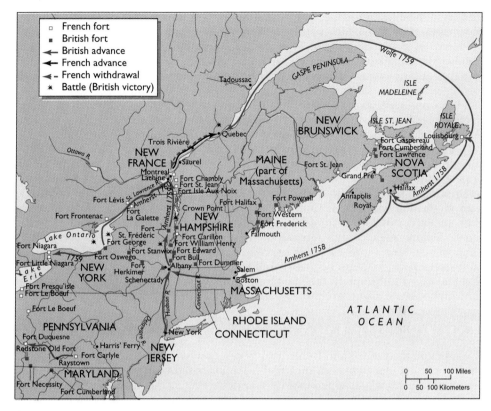

Map 6–2   The Second Phase of the French and Indian War, 1758–1763
This map shows British advances in Pennsylvania, New York, and Canada.

by the British). Once the British seized Fort Frontenac, disrupting the supply lines from the French to the Ohio Valley Indians, those Indians shifted their allegiance. At the same time, the British moved from a policy of confrontation to one of accommodation. In the Treaty of Easton (1758), more than 500 representatives of 13 Ohio Valley tribes agreed to remain neutral in return for a promise to keep the territory west of the Alleghenies free of settlers. At the same time, gifts to the Iroquois brought them back into the fold.

The British were now ready for the final offensive. Historians always argue about when and why a war is "lost": Unless an army has been annihilated and the population entirely subjugated, which is rare, when to surrender is always a subjective decision. Those who wield political and military power must decide when the loss in lives and resources can no longer be justified, and the population must agree that further fighting is pointless. By 1759, some of the French believed that the war was essentially over. Casualties were extremely high, food was in short supply, and inflation was rampant. Most of the Indian allies had deserted the cause, and the French government was unable to match Pitt's spending on the war. The army in North America was still large, however, and it would take two more years of fighting and the loss of thousands more lives before the French surrendered.

In the summer of 1759, General James Wolfe took the struggle for North America into the heart of Canada, laying siege to Quebec. French defenses made the city almost impregnable, so for months Wolfe bombarded the city and tried to wear down its citizens, terrorizing those who lived on its outskirts by burning crops and houses. In mid-September, Wolfe ordered an assault up the 175-foot cliff below the city. Hauling two cannons up with them, Wolfe's well-trained soldiers reached the top, and in a battle that lasted only half an hour, claimed victory on the Plains of Abraham. Each side suffered casualties of 15 percent, and both Wolfe and his French opponent, Montcalm, were killed. Four days later, New France's oldest permanent settlement surrendered to the British. By the time the British reached Montréal, the French Army numbered fewer than 3,000 men.

The Treaty of Paris, which concluded the war, was signed in 1763. By that time, Britain had also seized the French sugar islands in the Caribbean, and, after Spain entered the war on the French side, Havana and the Philippines. Pitt would have continued to fight, but the British public was unwilling to pay more to increase the size of the Empire. The French too, thoroughly tired of war, surrendered all of Canada except for two small fishing islands in return for the right to hold onto the most valuable sugar islands. France even gave New Orleans and all of its territory west of the Mississippi to Spain as compensation for losing Florida, which the British claimed (see Map 6–3). (Britain let Spain keep Havana and the Philippines.) Britain staked its future on the mainland of North America, believing correctly that it would ultimately be more valuable than the sugar islands of the Caribbean.

ENFORCING THE EMPIRE

Even before the French and Indian War began, some members of the British government believed that tighter control had to be exercised over the American colonies. What British officials stationed in the colonies saw during the war only reinforced that

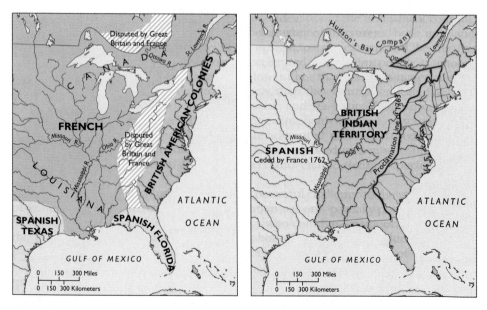

Map 6–3   The North American Colonies Before and After the French and Indian War
In the Treaty of Paris in 1763, more American territory was transferred than at any time before or since.
Source: Helen Hornbeck Tanner, Atlas of Great Lakes Indian History (Norman: University of Oklahoma Press, 1987), p. 54.

view. Colonists smuggled and even traded with the enemy throughout the war, while the colonial assemblies sometimes impeded the war effort. Pitt had increased Britain's national debt to pay for the war, rather than waiting for the colonial assemblies. Now, with the war over, Britain faced a staggering debt of £122,603,336. Moreover, there was a huge new territory to govern, a territory that was coveted by speculators and settlers and inhabited by Indian tribes determined to resist encroachment.

The American Revolution grew out of Britain's attempts to draw its American colonies more closely into the imperial system. Although from time to time various master plans for reorganizing the empire had been circulated, there was never an overarching design or a clear set of guidelines. What was new in 1763 was both financial stress and a new resolve to enforce a set of assumptions about how an empire should function and what the role of colonies in it should be. In 1760 a new king, the 22-year-old George III, ascended to the throne upon the death of his grandfather. Reasonably well-educated, although lacking in genius, the young king was determined to play a role in government. He changed ministers frequently, which made the British government chaotic. Some historians suggest that this turnover was one of the sources of the Revolution. It is not clear, however, that more enlightened leadership would have prevented the war, for George's ministers pursued a consistent, if imperfectly executed, policy toward the colonies. In resisting that policy, the American colonists developed a new and different idea of the purpose of government, one that propelled them to revolution.

Pontiac's Rebellion and Its Aftermath

Because the British had defeated the French in war and had entered into alliances with the Iroquois and the Ohio Valley Indians, peace in the West should have been easy to secure. The British, however, soon made the same mistake that the French had made when they discontinued presents to their Indian allies 15 years earlier. Thinking that they could impose their will on the Indians, the British instead found themselves embroiled in another war.

At the conclusion of the French and Indian War, the western Algonquian tribes hoped that the British would follow the practices of the middle ground by mediating their disputes, trading with them at advantageous prices, and giving them presents. Lord Jeffrey Amherst, who commanded the British forces in North America, cut off the presents, believing them too expensive. He thought that threats of an Indian revolt were exaggerated, and he was willing to take the risk of war.

The war that resulted in 1763 is commonly known as Pontiac's Rebellion, named after the Ottawa chieftain who played a prominent role. It was the first battle in a long, and ultimately unsuccessful, attempt by Indians to keep the region between the Mississippi River and the Alleghenies free of European settlers. The war spawned violence all along the frontier. Casualties were high, about 2,000 civilians, 400 soldiers, and an unknown number of Indians. Tortures by both sides were horrific. For their part, American colonists took out their aggressions on peaceful or defenseless Indians living in their midst. Although colonial leaders decried acts of violence, they did little to prevent or punish them. British officials saw the inability of the colonists to maintain order on the frontier and protect innocent Indians from violence as further evidence of the fecklessness of colonial governments. King George himself ordered the colonial governors "to remedy and prevent those Evils, which are as contrary to the Rules of good Policy as of Justice and Equity."

Even before Pontiac's Rebellion ended in a draw, the British had decided that peace with the western Indians could be preserved only by keeping colonial settlers and speculators away. The Proclamation of 1763 confined the colonists to the east of an imaginary line running down the spine of the Alleghenies. George Washington called the proclamation "a temporary expedient to quiet the minds of the Indians" and, like other speculators, ignored it. Washington instructed his surveyor to "secure some of the most valuable lands. . . . under the pretense of hunting [game]." Speculators tried a number of pretexts to claim territory by force, such as dubious land treaties with Indians and border skirmishes, but Britain was not ready to permit speculators or settlers to claim the land.

Paying for the Empire: Sugar and Stamps

On the edge of the British Empire, the colonies were important, but not nearly as important as Britain's domestic concerns. One of George III's highest priorities was to maintain the size of the army. During the French and Indian War, the size of the British army had doubled, and it was filled with officers who were loyal to the king. Responding to the king's wishes, Parliament in 1763 voted to maintain a huge peacetime army; 20 regiments (typically 1,000 men each) would be stationed in the colonies and West Indies. Colonists feared that the British intended to use the army to enforce customs regulations rather than to police the Indians.

This large army, of course, was going to strain the British budget, already burdened by a huge war debt. George Grenville, the new prime minister, believed that the colonists should pay a portion of the £225,000 a year that the standing army would cost.

Under Grenville's leadership, Parliament passed four pieces of legislation to force the colonies to contribute to their own upkeep. The Molasses Act of 1733 had established a duty of 6 cents per gallon, but smugglers paid off customs officials at the rate of 1 1/2 cents a gallon. At Grenville's urging, Parliament passed the Sugar Act (1764), which dropped the duty to 3 cents but established procedures to make certain it was collected. To discourage smuggling, all shippers were required to file elaborate papers each time an item was loaded onto a ship. In addition, accused violators were to be tried in admiralty courts, where the burden of proof would be on the defendant, and the judgment would be rendered by judges rather than a jury.

To regulate the colonial economies so that they served the interest of British creditors, the Currency Act (1764) forbade the issuing of any colonial currency. The immediate cause was the complaint of British merchants that colonists were discharging their debts in depreciated paper money. Moreover, the Sugar Act and the Stamp Act (passed the following year) required that duties and taxes both be paid in specie, that is, hard money. The colonists complained, however, that there simply was not enough specie to go around.

The third and most important piece of imperial legislation enacted in this flurry was the Stamp Act (1765). Its objective was to raise revenue. Unarguably the first direct tax on the American people, the Stamp Act placed a tax on documents used in court proceedings; papers used in clearing ships from harbors; college diplomas; appointments to public office; bonds, grants, and deeds for land mortgages; indentures, leases, contracts, and bills of sale; articles of apprenticeship and liquor licenses; playing cards and dice; and pamphlets, newspapers (and the ads in them), and almanacs.

The final piece of legislation, the Quartering Act (1765), required the colonies to provide housing for troops in public buildings and to provide them with firewood, candles, and drink. New York was the first colony to confront the implications of this act when it called on British troops to put down uprisings of tenants on Hudson River estates in 1766 but refused to pay to provision the troops.

Although the colonists objected to all of these pieces of legislation, the Stamp Act was the most troubling. By taxing newspapers and pamphlets, it angered printers and editors. This was a foolish group to alienate at a time when newspapers were taking the lead in criticizing the government and were perhaps the most significant public institution in the colonies. In addition, by taxing legal documents, the Stamp Act angered lawyers, for every time a lawyer performed the simplest task of his trade, he would have to buy a stamp. Collectively, these laws fell hardest on the most affluent and politically active colonists, the merchants, lawyers, and printers. In contrast, when Parliament wanted to raise money in Britain to pay for the army and the national debt, it levied a tax on cider, the drink of the common man. All of these pieces of legislation were an extension of the British government and its political economy, an attempt to tie the colonies into a modern, centralized state. As the colonists framed their response to the new laws, they struggled with a question that has been central to American history: Could the people share in the benefits of the modern state, in particular a trade protected by its navy and borders secured by its army, without the state itself?

REJECTING THE EMPIRE

Colonial resistance to the imperial legislation of 1763 to 1765, especially the Stamp Act, was swift and forceful. A coalition of elite leaders and common people, primarily in the cities, worked to overturn the most objectionable aspects of the new regulations. In 1765, there was no thought of revolution, nor would there be for almost ten years. Instead, the colonists rested their case on the British Constitution. All they wanted, they claimed, were the rights of Englishmen. Although in theory the colonists, as British subjects, were entitled to all of those rights, precisely how the British Constitution applied to colonists had never been clarified. The first phase of opposition, then, took the form of a debate about the British Constitution, with the colonists insisting on their rights and the British government focusing on the colonists' obligations.

An Argument About Rights and Obligations

All along, Britain had maintained its right to regulate the colonies. Precisely what this meant became a matter of dispute after 1763. Did it mean regulation of trade? Taxation? Legislation? When Parliament passed these pieces of legislation, it represented a change in British practices, not in how Britons thought about the colonies or the empire. The empire was a whole, the parts existed for the benefit of the whole, and Parliament had the authority to govern for the whole.

Britons were justifiably proud of their Parliament, which was one of the premier institutions of self-government in the world at the time. In principle Parliament represented all the elements in society: the king, the aristocrats (in the House of Lords), and the common people (in the House of Commons). Applying the terms used by the Greek philosopher Aristotle, this was a mixed or balanced form of government. It mixed and balanced these three elements of society, which also represented the three possible forms of government—monarchy, rule by the king; aristocracy, rule by the hereditary aristocrats; and democracy, rule by the people—thus preventing both tyranny and anarchy and preserving liberty.

The British believed, and American colonists agreed, that their superb government was the product of centuries of struggle. First the aristocrats struggled with the king for more freedom for themselves, gaining it in the Magna Carta of 1215, and then the people struggled and won liberty, most recently in the Glorious

Revolution of 1688. In this view, liberty was a collective right held by the people against the rulers. A chief example of public or civil liberty was the right to be taxed only by one's own representatives. After the Glorious Revolution, this principle was firmly established. Taxes were a free gift of the people that they might yield up but that no monarch could demand.

These ideas about the British government can be described as constitutionalism. Constitutionalism comprised two elements: the rule of law and the principle of consent, that one could not be subjected to laws or taxation except by duly elected representatives. Both were rights that had been won through struggle with the monarch.

In the decade between 1765 and the outbreak of the American Revolution, the colonists worked out their own theory of the place of the colonies in the empire. A consensus formed on two major points: the importance of the rule of law and the principle of consent. Those colonists who became revolutionaries never wavered on these two points. What the colonists debated in the decade between the Stamp Act and the beginning of the American Revolution was whether particular pieces of legislation violated these principles and how far the colonists should go in resisting those that did.

British officials never denied that the colonists should enjoy the rights of Englishmen. They merely asserted that the colonists were as well represented in Parliament as the majority of Britons. In fact, only one out of ten British men could vote, compared to about 70 percent of American white men. Yet British officials said that all Britons were represented in Parliament, if not "actually," by choosing their own representatives, then by virtual representation, because each member of Parliament was supposed to act on behalf of the entire empire, not only his constituents. In Britons' minds, Parliament was supreme, and it had full authority over the colonists. In the decade between the Stamp Act and the beginning of the American Revolution, the controversy turned on only two questions: How forcefully would the British government insist on the supremacy of Parliament? And could colonial radicals put together a broad enough coalition to resist Britain's force when it came?

The Imperial Crisis in Local Context

While colonial political thinkers were filling newspapers and pamphlets with denunciations of the new imperial legislation, Americans in every colony were taking their protests to the streets and to the colonial legislatures. Everywhere, a remarkable cross-class alliance of prosperous merchants and planters who had been the chief beneficiaries of the consumer revolution, and poor people who had not yet enjoyed its benefits, joined to protect what they perceived as their rights from encroachment by British officials.

By the day that the Stamp Act was to go into effect, November 1, 1765, every colony except Georgia had taken steps to ensure that the tax could not be collected. In Virginia, the House of Burgesses took the lead. A young and barely literate lawyer, Patrick Henry, played a key role in the debate on the Virginia Resolves, the four resolutions protesting the Stamp Act that were passed by the Burgesses. They asserted that the inhabitants of Virginia brought with them from England the rights of Englishmen, that Virginia's royal charters confirmed these rights, that taxation by one's own representatives was the only constitutional policy, and that the people of Virginia had never given up their rights, including the right to be taxed only by their own representatives. In Boston, as in the other colonies, the protest united the elite with poorer colonists, building on long-standing tensions between colonists and royal officials. Massachusetts was still reeling from the loss of life and extraordinary expense of the French and Indian War. Now that the war was over, imperialists such as Lieutenant Governor Thomas Hutchinson wanted to tie Massachusetts more tightly to the empire. He advocated a consolidation of power, a diminution of popular government (e.g., by reducing the power of the town meeting), making offices that were elective appointive instead, and limiting the freedom of the press.

Boston's public was ready for a much stronger response to the Stamp Act than the Massachusetts House of Representatives seemed prepared to make. The *Boston Gazette* criticized the House's resolution as a "tame, pusillanimous, daubed, insipid thing." Once word of the more radical Virginia Resolves arrived, the *Gazette* rebuked the weak political leaders of Massachusetts. A group of artisans and printers who called themselves the Loyal Nine and later changed their name to the Sons of Liberty began organizing the opposition, probably in concert with more prominent men who would emerge as leaders of the revolutionary movement such as James Otis, John Adams, and his cousin Samuel Adams, the Harvard-educated son of a brewer.

In a carefully orchestrated series of mob actions, Bostonians made certain that the Stamp Act would not be enforced. When the militia refused to protect royal officials including Andrew Oliver, the collector of the stamp tax, the officials took refuge in Castle William in the harbor. Over a period of several days, the mob slowly and systematically vandalized the homes of several wealthy government loyalists. Although the mob consisted mostly of artisans and poor people, it had the support of Boston's merchant elite, for no one was ever punished. The protest succeeded, and the Stamp Act was never enforced.

Not only did each colony mount its own protest against the Stamp Act, but a majority of the colonies were now ready to act together. In October 1765, delegates from nine colonies met in New York in the Stamp Act Congress to ratify a series of 14 resolutions protesting the Stamp Act on constitutional grounds. The congress asserted, for example, "that it is inseparably essential to the freedom of a people,

Stamp Act riots. A crowd in New Hampshire stones an effigy of a stamp distributor.

and the undoubted rights of Englishmen, that no taxes should be imposed on them, but with their own consent, given personally, or by their representatives." Activists shut down colonial courts so that no stamps could be used, and merchants agreed not to import any British goods until the act was repealed. With 37 percent of British exports going to the colonies at this time, this was no idle threat.

In the face of this opposition, the British partly backed down. George Grenville had been replaced by the 35-year-old Marquess of Rockingham, who preferred race-horses to politics. He remained in office just long enough for Parliament to repeal the Stamp Act. Parliament was not prepared to concede the constitutional point, however, and in the Declaratory Act of 1766 asserted ominously that Parliament "had, hath, and of right ought to have, full power and authority to make laws and statutes . . . to bind the colonies and people of America, subjects of the crown of Great Britain, in all cases whatsoever."

Contesting the Townshend Duties

Britain gave up on trying to tax the colonies directly, for even some prominent Britons such as William Pitt sided with the colonists on that point. But between 1767 and 1774, those in power still tried to tighten the bonds of empire by forcing their vision of empire on the colonies. In response, radical activists and thinkers coa-lesced into a national opposition. Together these radicals took constitutionalism in new directions. By the time of the American Revolution, they had turned it into a new theory of government to support a new political economy.

This cartoon shows the repeal of the Stamp Act, with George Grenville and other British officials carrying a coffin containing the Act. In the background, languishing on the dock, is cargo that could not be shipped to America during the colonial boycott.

After a brief return to power by William Pitt, Charles Townshend became the third prime minister in as many years. His first act was to punish New York's assembly, which intentionally violated the Quartering Act. The assembly, denied the right to pass any legislation until it complied with the Quartering Act, quickly backed down.

The colonies refused, however, to comply with Parliament's next piece of legislation, the Townshend Revenue Act of 1767, which levied import duties on lead, paint, glass, paper, and tea. Townshend believed that the colonists objected only to taxes within the colonies, "internal taxes," but that they would accept an "external tax," such as an import duty. The revenue would be used to support colonial officials, making them independent of the colonial assemblies that had paid their salaries.

Resistance to the Townshend Act built slowly. Even though standard constitutional arguments were used, it was hard for colonists to make a case against all duties. Merchants were now complying with the new Revenue Act of 1766, which reduced the duty on molasses to 1 cent per gallon. Those colonists who had been most troubled by the first round of imperial legislation, however, were convinced that the Townshend Duties were part of a pattern of British oppression that would lead to tyranny.

A body of thought known as republicanism helped the colonists make sense of British actions. Republicanism was a set of doctrines rooted in the Renaissance that held that power is always dangerous, for "it is natural for Power to be striving to enlarge itself, and to be encroaching upon those that have none." Republicanism supplied constitutionalism with a motive. It explained how a balanced constitution could be transformed into tyranny. Would-be tyrants had at their disposal a variety of tools, one of which was a standing army, whose ultimate purpose was not the protection of the people but their subjection. Tyrants also engaged in corruption, in particular by dispensing patronage positions. So inexorable was the course of power that it took extraordinary virtue for an individual to resist its corruption. Consequently, republican citizens, it was thought, had to be economically independent. The poor were dangerous because they could easily be bought off by would-be tyrants. A secular theory with connections to Puritanism, republicanism asserted that people were naturally weak and that exceptional human effort was required to protect both liberty and virtue.

Not only did people have to keep a close eye on power-hungry tyrants, they also had to look inside themselves. According to republican thought, history demonstrated that republics fell from within, when their citizens lost their virtue. The greatest threat to virtue was luxury, an excessive attachment to the fruits of the consumer revolution. When colonists worried that they saw luxury and corruption everywhere, they were criticizing the world that the consumer revolution had created. Although it is understandable why poor people, who saw others getting rich while they were squeezed, embraced republicanism, it might seem perplexing that wealthy merchants and planters were among the most vocal in their denunciations of "malice, covetousness, and other lusts of man." Yet the legacy of Puritanism was powerful, and even those who were profiting most from the new order felt ambivalent about the direction of change in their society. Joining with poorer people in criticizing British officials, and accusing them of attempting to undermine colonial liberties, helped forge a cross-class alliance.

The colonial legislatures slowly began to protest the duties. Massachusetts's House of Representatives, led by Sam Adams, sent a circular letter to each of the other lower houses in the colonies, asking them to join in resisting "infringements of their natural & constitutional Rights because they are not represented in the British Parliament . . ." When Lord Hillsborough, a hard-liner recently appointed to the new post of secretary of state for the colonies, received the letter, he instructed the colonial governors to dissolve any colonial assembly that received the petition from Massachusetts. Massachusetts refused to rescind its letter, so Governor Francis Bernard dissolved the legislature. With representative government threatened, those colonial legislatures that had not already approved the Massachusetts circular letter did so now, and were then dissolved. In response, many legislatures met on their own, as extralegal representative bodies.

Not only did legislators assert their own authority, but ordinary people did so as well. In each colony, the radicals who called themselves Sons of Liberty organized a nonimportation movement, using both coercion and patriotic appeal to the entire community. Women were actively recruited into the movement, both to encourage household manufacture (an economic activity redefined as a political one) and to refuse British imports. In 1769 women in little Middletown, Massachusetts, wove 20,522 yards of cloth, and in towns and cities throughout the colonies women added their names to the nonimportation agreements. Although there were pockets of defiance, the movement succeeded in cutting imports dramatically. By the time that the Townshend Duties were repealed in 1770, Britain had collected only £21,000, and lost £786,000 in trade.

A REVOLUTION IN THE EMPIRE

The resistance to the Townshend Duties established a pattern that would be repeated again and again in the years before the Revolution. Each attempt to enforce the empire met with organized colonial opposition, to which the British government responded with a punitive measure. Ostensibly economic regulations such as the Sugar Act, the Townshend Duties, and the subsequent Tea Act, when rejected by the colonies, led to clearly political responses from Britain. Economics and politics became inseparable, as two visions of political economy came into conflict. Britain saw the colonies as a small but integral part of a large empire held together by an increasingly centralized and powerful government. The goal of the empire was to enhance its collective wealth and power, albeit under a system of constitutional government. While not rejecting the notion of a larger empire outright, increasingly the colonists equated representative government with prosperity, not just for the empire as a whole, but for its citizens in the colonies as well. Each round of colonial protest mobilized a larger segment of the population, eventually reaching out into the countryside and even to women.

"Massacre" in Boston

Years of conflict with royal officials, combined with a growing population of poor and underemployed, had made Boston the most radical and united spot in the colonies. The popular political leadership had learned how to win popular favor in their ongoing strife with the governor and those who were loyal to him. The repeated attempts of the British government to enforce its legislation, exerting increasing pressure on Boston, led finally to revolution.

In an attempt to tighten up the collection of customs duties, the British government, now led by Lord North, decided to make an example of John Hancock, Boston's wealthiest merchant. Hancock valued popularity more than wealth, and he sacrificed much of his fortune in the quest for popularity in the revolutionary movement. In June 1768, Boston's customs commissioners seized Hancock's sloop, the *Liberty*, on a technical violation of the Sugar Act. Hancock and several associates were threatened with fines totaling £54,000 (most of which would go into the pockets of the governor and the informer). All charges were dropped, however, after a riot of 2,000 "sturdy boys and men" sent the customs officials once again scuttling off to Castle William for protection.

In the wake of the *Liberty* riot, Governor Bernard called for troops to support the customs commissioners. Rather than restoring order, the arrival of the troops led to further conflict. British soldiers scoured the city, searching people's homes for deserters. For a year and a half there was tension, as might be expected with so many soldiers stationed in a city of 15,000. Because of an economic depression, liquor was cheap, and off-duty soldiers regularly became drunk and offensive. Prostitution increased, women were assaulted, and every citizen had to be prepared to stop and identify himself or herself, at the point of a bayonet. Most important, moonlighting soldiers were willing to work cheaper than Bostonians. The Boston Massacre grew out of these tensions.

What angry colonists called a "massacre" was the culmination of several months of scuffling between young men and adolescents and soldiers, perhaps inevitable in a town with so many men competing for work. Most of the participants knew one another from previous conflicts. On March 5, 1770, a fracas between a young apprentice and an Army officer escalated as a crowd surrounded the officer, insulting him and pelting him with snowballs. Someone shouted "Fire," and the crowd grew. Seven soldiers came to rescue their terrified colleague, and they too were hit with snowballs and taunts of "Kill them." When one was knocked down, he screamed, "Damn you, fire!" and the soldiers fired on the crowd. Eleven men were wounded, and five were killed. One victim was Crispus Attucks, a free black sailor. Subsequently the soldiers were tried, but the only two who were convicted were later pardoned. The British withdrew their troops from Boston.

As long as the British were willing to back down, more serious conflicts could be avoided. The Boston Massacre was followed by a three-year period of peace. The Townshend Duties had been repealed, except the one on tea, which the colonists could not manufacture themselves, and the nonimportation movement had collapsed. Colonial trade resumed its previous pace, and in 1772, imports from England and Scotland doubled. Colonists were not prepared to deny themselves consumer goods for long. The Quartering Act had expired and the Currency Act was repealed. As long as Britain allowed the colonists to trade relatively unimpeded, permitted them to govern themselves, and kept the Army out of their cities, all could be, if not forgotten, at least silenced by the clink of coins in the shopkeeper's till.

The Empire Comes Apart

Although the British government was under the control of conservatives who believed that sooner or later the colonists would need to acknowledge Parliament's supremacy, the move that led directly to revolution was more accidental than calculated. The North American colonies were only part of Britain's extended empire. There were powerful British interests in India, where the British East India Company was on the verge of bankruptcy. Parliament decided to bail out the company, both to rescue its empire in India and also to help out the influential stockholders. They canceled the duty for importing tea into Britain, but kept the one for tea to America. Moreover, Parliament allowed the company to sell directly to Americans through a small number of agents, cutting out all the middlemen. As a result, the price of tea would drop below that of smuggled Dutch tea. Also, in all of Massachusetts, only five men would be allowed to sell British tea—two sons, a nephew, and two friends of the much-despised Governor Thomas Hutchinson. The agents in the other colonies were also loyalists who gained their appointments by their connections.

Radicals faced a real challenge, for they realized that once the tea was unloaded and the duty paid, colonists would be unable to resist the cheap tea. In each port city, activists warned their fellow colonists that the Tea Act (1773) was a trick intended to con them into accepting the principle of taxation without representation. According to the New York Sons of Liberty, the purpose of the Tea Act was "to make an important trial of our virtue. If they succeed in the sale of that tea, we shall have no property that we can call our own, and then we may bid adieu to American liberty." In Philadelphia, a mass meeting pronounced anyone who imported the tea "an enemy to his country."

As might be expected, the most spirited resistance came in Boston, where Hutchinson refused to let the first ship coming into port return without paying the duty. Sam Adams led extralegal town meetings attended by 5,000 people each (almost one-third of the population of Boston) to pressure Hutchinson to let the ship return. When Hutchinson refused, Adams reported back to the town meeting, on December 16, 1773, "This meeting can do nothing more to save the country!" (see Table 6–1). Almost as if it were a prearranged signal, the crowd let out a whoop and poured out of the meetinghouse for the wharf. There, about 50 men, their faces darkened and wearing Indian blankets, boarded three tea-bearing ships, escorted the customs officials ashore, opened 340 chests of tea, and dumped their contents into Boston Harbor, 90,000 pounds, worth £9,000. Perhaps as many as 8,000 Bostonians observed the "tea party." John Adams, never much for riots, was in awe. "There is," he said, "a Dignity, a Majesty, a Sublimity in this last Effort of the Patriots that I greatly admire."

Where radicals saw dignity and patriotism, the British government saw defiance of the law and wanton destruction of property. Parliament passed five bills in the spring of 1774 to punish Boston and Massachusetts collectively for their misdeeds. First, the Boston Port Bill closed the port of Boston to all trade until the East India Company was repaid for the dumped tea. Second, the Massachusetts Government Act changed the Charter of 1691 in several important ways. From then on, the Council (upper house) would be appointed by the king, rather than elected by the House, town meetings were forbidden without approval of the governor, the governor would appoint all the provincial judges and sheriffs, and the sheriffs would select juries, who until then had been elected by the freeholders. Third, the Administration of Justice Act empowered the governor to send to Britain or another colony for trial any official or soldier accused of a capital crime who appeared unlikely to get a fair trial in Massachusetts. Fourth, a new Quartering Act permitted the quartering of troops in private homes. Fifth, not directly related, but also odious to Protestant colonists, was the Quebec Act, for the administration of Quebec. It assigned to Quebec the Ohio River region, which the colonists coveted. Moreover, in Quebec, there was to be no representative government, civil cases would be tried without juries, and the Roman Catholic religion would be tolerated. Together, these acts were known in Britain as the Coercive Acts and in the colonies as the Intolerable Acts.

At the same time, General Thomas Gage was appointed governor of Massachusetts and authorized to bring as many troops to Boston as he needed. As regiment after regiment arrived, Boston became an armed camp. The Port Act was easily

TABLE 6–1

Major Events Leading to the Revolutionary War, 1763–1774		
1763	Proclamation of 1763	Confines colonists to the east of an imaginary line running down the spine of the Allegheny Mountains.
1764	Sugar Act	Drops duty on molasses to 3 cents/gallon, but institutes procedures to make sure it is collected, such as trial at Admiralty Court (closest is in Nova Scotia), where burden of proof is on defendant and verdict is rendered by judge rather than jury.
1764	Currency Act	Forbids issuing of any colonial currency.
1765	Stamp Act	Places a tax on 15 classes of documents, including newspapers and legal documents; clear objective is to raise revenue.
1765	Quartering Act	Requires colonies to provide housing in public buildings and certain provisions for troops.
1766	Declaratory Act	Repeals Stamp Act, but insists that Parliament retains the right to legislate for the colonies "in all cases whatsoever."
1767	Townshend Revenue Act	Places import duty on lead, paint, glass, paper, and tea; objective is to raise money from the colonies.
1770	Boston Massacre	Several citizens killed by British soldiers whom they had pelted with snowballs; grew out of tensions caused by quartering of four army regiments in Boston to enforce customs regulations.
1773	Tea Act	After Townshend Duties on all items other than tea are removed, British East India Company is given a monopoly on the sale of tea, enabling it to drop price—and cut out middlemen.
1773	Boston Tea Party	To protest Tea Act, Bostonians dump 90,000 pounds of tea into Boston Harbor.
1774	Intolerable Acts	To punish Massachusetts in general and Boston in particular for the "Tea Party": 1. Port of Boston closed until East India Company repaid for dumped tea. 2. King to appoint Massachusetts's Council; town meetings to require written permission of governor; governor will appoint judges and sheriffs, and sheriffs will now select juries. 3. Governor can send officials and soldiers accused of capital crimes out of Massachusetts for their trials. 4. Troops may be quartered in private homes.
1774	Quebec Act	Gives Ohio River valley to Quebec; Britain allows Quebec to be governed by French tradition and tolerates Catholic religion there.
1774	First Continental Congress	Representatives of 12 colonies meet in Philadelphia and call for a boycott of trade with Britain, adopt a Declaration of Rights, and agree to meet again in a year.

CHRONOLOGY

1715–1716	Yamasee War
1717	French build Fort Toulouse
1718	French build New Orleans
1720	French build Louisbourg and Fort Niagara
1731	French build Fort St. Frédéric
1733	Molasses Act
1739–1744	War of Jenkins's Ear
1741	Attack on Cartagena fails
1744–1748	King George's War
1748	Village of Pickawillany established by La Demoiselle and his band of Miamis
1749	French military expedition fails to win back dissident Indians in Ohio River valley
1752	Tanacharison cedes huge chunk of Ohio River valley to Virginia
1753	French build small forts near forks of Ohio River
1754	Albany Plan of Union
1754–1763	French and Indian War
1755	Braddock's forces defeated
1757	British defeated at Fort William Henry, survivors massacred William Pitt accedes to power in Britain

enforced as Gage deployed troops to close the ports of Boston and Charlestown. The Government Act was another matter. Citizens who were summoned by the sheriff simply refused to serve on juries, and some judges even refused to preside. When Gage called for an election to the legislature, only some towns elected delegates, and a shadow Massachusetts Provincial Congress met in Concord in October 1774. The citizens of Massachusetts had taken government into their own hands.

The British had thought that Massachusetts could be isolated. Their chief miscalculation was in underestimating the colonists' attachment to their liberties. The threat to representative government presented by the Intolerable Acts was so clear that the other colonies soon rallied around Massachusetts. In June 1774, the Virginia Burgesses sent out a circular letter suggesting a meeting of all the colonies.

1758	Treaty of Easton secures neutrality of Ohio Valley tribes in return for territory west of Alleghenies
1759	British seize Quebec
1761	Writs of Assistance Case
1763	Treaty of Paris, ending French and Indian War, signed Pontiac's Rebellion Proclamation of 1763 Parliament increases size of peacetime army to 20 regiments
1764	Sugar Act Currency Act
1765	Stamp Act Quartering Act Stamp Act Congress
1766	Declaratory Act
1767	Townshend Revenue Act
1768	Lord Hillsborough's circular letter John Hancock's sloop *Liberty* seized Treaty of Fort Stanwix
1770	Boston Massacre
1773	Tea Act Boston Tea Party
1774	Intolerable Acts (known as Coercive Acts in Britain) Lord Dunmore's War First Continental Congress

At about the same time, Massachusetts had issued a similar call for a meeting in Philadelphia. Spurred by the two most radical colonies, the others agreed to meet in early September.

The First Continental Congress

Every colony except Georgia sent delegates to the First Continental Congress, which convened on September 5, 1774. Only a few of the delegates had ever met any of their counterparts from the other colonies, an indication of just how provincial the colonies were. First impressions, however, were positive. Everyone admired the Virginians. "More sensible, fine fellows you never saw," according to Delaware's Caesar

Rodney. For seven weeks these strangers met in formal sessions and social occasions. Together they laid the foundation for the first national government.

With Massachusetts and Virginia almost ready to take up arms, and the middle colonies still favoring conciliation, the greatest challenge was how to achieve unity. Massachusetts needed the support of the other colonies, and hence it was prepared to abandon any discussion of offensive measures against the British. In return, the Congress ratified the Suffolk Resolves, a set of resolutions adopted by Massachusetts's Suffolk County that recommended passive resistance to the Intolerable Acts.

Having addressed Massachusetts's problem, the delegates could now consider national action. Hoping to exert economic pressure on Britain, Congress issued a call for a boycott of all trade, both imports and exports, between the colonies and Britain and the West Indies. Then the delegates adopted a Declaration of Rights that reiterated, refined, and for the first time expressed as the collective determination of every colony (except Georgia) their standard constitutional arguments. The colonists were entitled to all the "rights, liberties, and immunities of free and natural-born subjects" of England. Parliament could regulate trade for the colonies only by the "consent" of the colonies. Parliament could neither tax nor legislate for the colonies. Again and again, the Declaration reiterated the twin principles on which resistance had been based: consent and the rule of law.

Finally, Congress agreed to reconvene in half a year, on March 10, 1775, unless the Intolerable Acts were repealed. Although the Congress was less radical than John Adams and Patrick Henry might have wished, the delegates had achieved consensus on the principles that would shortly form the basis for a new and independent national government.

CONCLUSION

Within a decade, the British empire had come apart on its westernmost edge. The ground had been prepared decades earlier when Britain unintentionally allowed the colonies to develop in ways that assured more self-government and personal freedom than in Britain itself, without requiring them to pay a proportionate share of the costs of empire. As a result, the colonies developed their own political economy that linked self-government and limited government with prosperity. Once Britain decided to knit the colonies more tightly into the empire and impose on them the controls of the centralized state and its political economy, conflict was inevitable. At the same time, both Britons and Americans revered the same Constitution, and Americans' protests invoked the values and protections of that political system. That those protests would culminate in revolution was by no means a foregone conclusion. Revolution would require two key elements: Britain's unwillingness to compromise on issues of governance, and the ability of colonial radicals to convince moderates that there was no other way. By the end of 1774 that point had almost been reached.

FURTHER READINGS

Fred Anderson, *Crucible of War: The Seven Years' War and the Fate of Empire in British North America, 1754–1766* (2000). An engaging narrative that argues that the Seven Years' War was a critical episode in itself and not simply the prelude to the Revolution.

John Brewer, *The Sinews of Power: War, Money and the English State, 1688–1783* (1990). Brewer's book demonstrates how important war and its financing were in shaping the British state in the eighteenth century.

John Demos, *The Unredeemed Captive: A Family Story From Early America* (1994). A beautifully written and deeply moving narrative about what happened to the Williams family when they were captured in an Abenaki raid on their Deerfield, Massachusetts home in 1704.

Jack P. Greene, *Colonies to Nation, 1763–1789: A Documentary History of the American Revolution* (1975). A superb collection of political documents through which the development of an American political ideology can be traced.

Douglas Edward Leach, *Arms for Empire: A Military History of the British Colonies in North America* (1973). A comprehensive and readable account of colonial military history.

Ian K. Steele, *Betrayals: Fort William Henry and the "Massacre"* (1990). A brief but gripping account of the siege at Fort William Henry in 1757, later fictionalized in James Fenimore Cooper's *The Last of the Mohicans.*

Richard White, *The Middle Ground: Indians, Empires, and Republics in the Great Lakes Region, 1650–1815* (1991). A brilliant analysis of the conflict among the French, British, and Great Lakes Indian tribes for control of that region.

Please refer to the document CD-ROM for primary sources related to this chapter.

7

Creating a New Nation

1775–1788

James Madison Helps Make a Nation • **The War Begins**
Winning the Revolution • **The Challenge of the Revolution**
A New Policy in the West • **Creating a New National**
Government • **Conclusion**

JAMES MADISON HELPS MAKE A NATION

*W*hy do some people achieve greatness? Perhaps it is not as much a matter of personal qualities as a match between the person and the times, an ability to understand and respond to the needs of the age. There was nothing in James Madison's childhood to suggest that he would become a leader of a revolutionary nation in a revolutionary age.

Madison grew up on the plantation his grandfather and his slaves had cleared out of the Virginia Piedmont forest in 1732. He went north to college, attending Princeton in New Jersey. After his graduation in 1771 at the age of 20, he suffered some sort of breakdown. Back in Virginia, Madison described himself as "too dull and infirm now to look out for any extraordinary things in this world . . ." Short and slight of build, Madison was convinced that his poor health would lead to an early death. The event that drew this sickly, nervous young man out of his shell was the American Revolution. He became a leader in the nation that he helped create and whose Constitution he helped write. James Madison committed himself to the principles of liberty and order, and he devoted his life to establishing a government that would ensure both. Perhaps more than any other leader at the time, Madison understood how difficult reconciling these two principles would be.

Madison believed that strife and violence were deeply embedded in human nature, and he spent his adult life trying to create a government that would ensure peace without destroying liberty. He helped write the Constitution and worked for the adoption of the Bill of Rights. His first political battle in Virginia had been on behalf of the Baptists, a dissenting Protestant denomination that demanded religious liberty. Madison was convinced that freedom of conscience was fundamental and that religion must be kept absolutely free from governmental interference. As a political thinker and leader, Madison came to advocate the great liberal principles of his age: the rights of conscience, consent, and property. Believing fervently in both the rights of property and human liberty, he could never reconcile himself either to slavery or its abolition. He put his faith in the new government, hoping that just as he had learned to live with his own mental and physical disabilities, so the nation would rise above its internal conflicts and inconsistencies.

Of the generation that created the new government, no one better understood the American political economy than Madison. Others more fully grasped the contradiction presented by slavery. But Madison understood Americans' twin commitments to liberty and to property, and he saw how they fit together in a system that rested on the principle of consent.

THE WAR BEGINS

By the end of 1774, conflict between the colonists and Britain seemed unavoidable. The British government, under the leadership of Lord North and King George III, seemed unwilling to make significant concessions. In the colonies, the radical opponents of British rule dominated politics. Despite these signs of impending conflict, no one anticipated eight years of warfare that would make the colonies a single nation under a centralized government.

The First Battles

Before he became governor of Massachusetts in 1774, General Thomas Gage had a long record of advocating force. He had called for the stationing of troops in Boston in 1768, leading to the Boston Massacre. Even before the Boston Tea Party and Britain's retaliation with the Coercive Acts, he recommended limiting democratic government in Massachusetts. He believed that the merchants and lawyers of Boston were instigating the poor; hence, his objective always was to isolate the colonial revolutionary elite, by force if necessary.

In the spring of 1775, Gage received orders from England to take decisive action against the colonists. He was determined to seize the colonists' military supplies, stored at Concord, but the alert Bostonians worked out a system to signal the patriot leaders once British troops began to march. On the night of April 18, the silversmith Paul Revere and the tanner William Dawes slipped out of Boston on horseback to carry the message that British troops were on the move. Militiamen from several towns began to gather.

The British soldiers arrived at Lexington at daybreak and ordered the militia to surrender, which they refused to do. Exactly what happened next remains unclear. The colonists swore that British soldiers opened fire, saying, "Ye villans, ye Rebels, disperse; Damn you, disperse." The British major insisted that the first shot came from behind a tree. British soldiers then lost control and fired all about, and the colonists returned fire. When order was restored, eight Americans were dead, most killed while attempting to flee.

At the same time that the militia in Lexington was gathering, the Concord militia assembled. When the British marched up the road toward the North Bridge, the militia pulled back about a mile, allowing the British to enter an almost-deserted town. Fighting broke out when a fire that the British troops had set spread to the courthouse. Determined to protect their town, the militia began marching on the British. When the Americans drew near, the British fired. In the ensuing exchange, three British soldiers were killed and several more were injured. The British were forced back across the bridge. The entire battle took two or three minutes.

Once news of the fighting at Lexington and Concord spread, militias converged on Boston to evict Gage and his troops. More than 20,000 men were encamped in Boston, ready to fight. Gage declared that all the inhabitants of Massachusetts who bore arms were rebels and traitors, although he was willing to pardon everyone but John Hancock and Sam Adams, two leaders of the defiant Provincial Congress. Rather than backing down, the colonists fortified Breed's Hill (next to the more famous Bunker Hill) in Charlestown, overlooking Boston. On June 17, Gage sent out 2,400 soldiers to take the hill. A thousand soldiers and 92 officers were casualties (compared to 370 casualties among the colonists). The British learned an important lesson: not to make frontal assaults against fortified positions.

At about the same time, other New Englanders were taking matters into their own hands. A group of New Englanders under the leadership of Benedict Arnold, an ambitious, 34-year-old New Haven merchant, and Ethan Allen, the leader of the Vermont Green Mountain Boys, seized the crumbling fort at Ticonderoga on Lake Champlain as well as several other small posts. In these heady days early in the Revolution, many colonists thought that this would be a quick and painless war.

Congress Takes the Lead

When the Second Continental Congress convened in Philadelphia on May 10, its greatest challenge was to maintain consensus. The most radical leaders, such as Sam and John Adams from Massachusetts and Richard Henry Lee from Virginia, were ready for war. However, many leaders, especially in the middle colonies, still hoped that war could be avoided.

Because Congress was an extralegal body, the duly elected colonial assemblies might easily have rejected its authority. But one after another, they transferred their allegiance from the British government to Congress. Although some moderates in Congress hoped for a negotiated settlement with Britain, they were caught between a public and a British government that both anticipated war. The British ministry refused even to acknowledge the petition sent by the First Continental Congress. That refusal, combined with Gage's attack on Breed's Hill, convinced the moderates that military preparations were necessary. Congress voted to create a Continental Army and put it under the leadership of Virginia's George Washington. Not only was Washington experienced in military matters and widely respected, but his selection helped solidify the alliance between New England and the South. Congress decided to attack Canada in the hope that a significant defeat would force the British to accede to American demands. To justify all of these actions, Congress also adopted the Declaration of the Causes and Necessities of Taking up Arms, a rousing indictment of British "despotism," "perfidy," and "cruel aggression" drafted by Virginia's Thomas Jefferson.

At the same time, to preserve unity with the moderates, the radicals agreed to petition the king one more time. While not making any concessions, the Olive Branch Petition appealed to George's "magnanimity and benevolence." Nevertheless, on August 23, 1775, the king declared the colonists to be in "an open and avowed Rebellion." Although Congress had neither declared war nor asserted independence, the American Revolution had begun.

Military Ardor

Military ardor in the colonies reached its high point in the fall of 1775 and the spring of 1776. Colonists expected war, and they thought it would be quick and glorious. As a consequence, the first enlistments were for a term of only a year. Even if the war was not over by then, revolutionaries were fearful of creating a permanent standing army.

In the summer of 1775, with military fervor at its height, the Continental Army marched on Canada. Victory would have either forced the British to the bargaining table or at least protected New York and New England from assault from the north. The contingent of the Continental Army under General Benedict Arnold's command sailed from Newburyport, Massachusetts, to Maine and then marched 350 miles to Quebec. In early November, after a grueling march, Arnold's forces prepared to assault Quebec, joined by troops under the leadership of General Richard Montgomery, who had just seized Montréal. The battle was a disaster. Half of the 900 soldiers were killed, captured, or wounded, including Montgomery. By the time the expedition retreated to New York in the spring, 5,000 men had been lost. The suffering was extraordinary, but it only increased American resolve.

Declaring Independence

By the beginning of 1776, moderates in Congress who still hoped for a peaceful settlement found themselves squeezed from both directions. The king and Parliament were unyielding, and popular opinion increasingly favored independence. Word arrived from Britain that all American commerce was to be cut off and the British Navy was to seize American ships and their cargoes. Britain also began hiring German mercenaries known as Hessians, and Virginia's Governor Dunmore shelled Norfolk from warships offshore. He had already offered freedom to any slaves who would fight for the British. It seemed that every frightening prediction that the radicals had made was coming true.

Public opinion also pushed Congress toward a declaration of independence. In January 1776, Thomas Paine, an expatriate English radical, electrified the public with his pamphlet *Common Sense,* which sold more than 100,000 copies in a few weeks. In it, Paine liberated Americans from their ties to the British past so that they could start their government fresh. The idea of a balanced constitution that combined king, nobles, and the common people in one government, was "farcical," and monarchy was "exceedingly ridiculous." Paine had a message for Congress, too: "The period of debate is closed."

Most members of Congress either desired a declaration of independence or thought it inevitable. Most delegates also agreed that unanimity was more important than speed, so they waited through the spring of 1776 as one by one, the state delegations received instructions in favor of independence. Then, under instructions from his colony, on June 7, 1776, Virginia's Richard Henry Lee asked Congress to vote on the resolution that "these United Colonies are, and of right ought to be, free and independent States." A committee of five, including Thomas Jefferson, Benjamin Franklin, and John Adams, was appointed to draft a declaration of independence. Adams asked Jefferson, a 33-year-old Virginia radical who had already demonstrated his ability to write stirring prose, to write the first draft. For four days, the delegates debated Jefferson's draft and took preliminary votes. A clause that accused King George of forcing African slaves on the colonies was deleted. On July 2, the delegates voted unanimously to declare independence.

Many years later Thomas Jefferson insisted that there was nothing original about the Declaration of Independence, and he was not entirely wrong. The long list of accusations against King George, which formed the bulk of the Declaration, contained little that was new, and even some of the stirring words in the preamble had been used by the radicals time and again. Moreover, the revolutionaries borrowed ideas from a number of British and European sources, including constitutionalism, republicanism, Enlightenment thought (see Chapter 6, "Conflict on the Edge of Empire"), and millennial Christian thought. The millennial strain in evangelical Protestantism suggested that the 1,000-year reign of Christ might begin soon in America if Americans would repent their sins, seek a spiritual rebirth, and defend their liberties.

However, in a different sense the Declaration of Independence was truly original. Nowhere else, except in Paine's *Common Sense,* had any American set out so clearly a vision of society. Jefferson's achievement was to reformulate familiar principles in a way that made them simple, clear, and applicable to the American situation.

The most important of these principles was human equality, that all people were born with certain fundamental rights. Second, and closely related, was the belief in a universal, common human nature. If all people were the same and had the same rights, then the purpose of government was to protect those rights. Just as people created government to protect their rights, they could abolish any government that became despotic. Third, government should represent the people.

It was many years, however, before the radical implications of the Declaration became fully evident to the American people. At the moment more attention was focused on immediate political struggles. The Revolution succeeded because moderates and radicals were able to create effective alliances, reversing the pre-Revolutionary trend toward class and political conflict. To maintain their positions as leaders of the opposition to Britain, elite revolutionaries like John Hancock continually appealed to their poorer and often more radical countrymen and women and looked out for these people's interests as well as their own.

The result was a revolution that was more moderate than it might otherwise have been, not to mention a revolution that succeeded. But it also meant ongoing struggles between radicals and moderates over the meaning of the Revolution. Just as military fervor reached its high point in the spring of 1776, so did political unity.

Creating a National Government

Although both the public and the state governments acted as if Congress were a legitimate national government, it actually had no more authority over the states than they were willing to give it, and it had none whatsoever over the people. At the same time that Richard Henry Lee presented Congress with his proposal for independence, he also suggested that Congress create a permanent national government, a confederation of the states with a written constitution. John Dickinson, a moderate, was assigned to draft the Articles of Confederation. He sketched out a weak central government with the authority to make treaties, carry on military and foreign affairs, request the states to pay its expenses, and very little else. There was no chief executive, only a Congress in which each state would have one vote. Any act of Congress would require nine votes (of 13), and the Articles would not go into effect until all 13 states had approved them.

With Congress functioning adequately and state jealousies strong, it took Congress more than a year to revise and accept a watered-down version of the Articles of Confederation. Not until March 1781, with the end of the war only a few months away, did the final state ratify the Articles of Confederation, thereby putting them into effect. By then, the weaknesses in a national government with no means of enforcing its regulations were becoming evident.

Creating State Governments

In 1776, all attention was focused on state governments, where the new ideas about liberty, equality, and government were put into practice. Americans were exhilarated by the prospect of creating their own governments. Between 1775 and 1780, each of the 13 states adopted a new written constitution.

The new state governments were the products of both theory and experience. Because the revolutionaries feared concentrations of power, the powers of governors were sharply limited. In two states, Pennsylvania and Georgia, the position of governor was abolished and replaced with a council. Governors were given term limits or required to run for re-election every year. Because the colonists had seen royal governors appoint their cronies to powerful positions, governors also were stripped of their power of appointment.

The new state constitutions made the legislatures more democratic. The number of representatives was doubled in South Carolina and New Hampshire and more than tripled in Massachusetts, to a ratio of about one representative for every 1,000 people. As with governors, many constitutions imposed either term limits or frequent elections for representatives. As the property qualifications for holding office were lowered, poorer men came to sit in legislatures alongside richer ones. The admission of more ordinary men into government was one of the greatest changes brought about by the Revolution. Now the elite had to learn to share power and to win the votes of men they had once scorned.

WINNING THE REVOLUTION

The British entered the war with clear advantages in population, wealth, and power, but with a flawed premise about how the war could be won. Britain, arguably the most powerful nation in the world, had the mistaken idea that the colonists could be made to submit by a swift and effective use of force. It also assumed that Americans loyal to the Crown would rally around the British troops. The actions of Britain's troops, however, alienated Americans. Probably no more than one-fifth of the population remained loyal to Britain, but many more shifted loyalties depending on local circumstances. The war ultimately became a struggle for the support of this unpoliticized, local-minded population.

Competing Strategies

British political objectives shifted during the war. The first goal, based on the belief that resistance was being led by a handful of radical New Englanders, was to punish and isolate Boston. This was the strategy of 1774 and 1775, with the Intolerable Acts, and the battles of Lexington, Concord, and Breed's (Bunker) Hill. This strategy failed miserably. The early failures derived from the faulty assumption that well-trained British regular soldiers were necessarily superior to untrained colonial rustics. However, if the British had a misplaced faith in their invincibility, the Americans had a misplaced faith in their moral superiority. Over the course of the war, most people realized that neither British professionalism nor American moral superiority could guarantee victory. The result was a long war, as both sides tried to avoid decisive engagements that might prove fatal.

For seven years, the two armies chased each other across the eastern seaboard. Neither side had masses of men to pour onto the battlefield. Moreover, there was no consensus in Britain about the strategic or economic value of the colonies, and hence there was always opposition to the war and a limit to the investment that the British were prepared to commit to the war effort. Consequently, every battle presented a significant risk that troops who were lost could not be replaced.

Manpower was also a serious problem for the Americans. It was difficult to recruit enough soldiers into the Continental Army. After a defeat in battle or near the end of the year when terms of enlistment were up, men left the Army to return home. Militia strength rose and fell depending on the prospects for success. Hence, one of the goals of the American war effort was to avoid demoralizing the colonists. In other words, there was limited incentive to risk all in battle.

Early in the war, however, both sides hoped for a decisive victory. The Americans failed in their assault on Quebec. The British pursued the Americans back to Ticonderoga on Lake Champlain, but Benedict Arnold's leadership prevented the British from pushing the Americans any farther. The theater of action then shifted to southern New York and the middle colonies. Having given up hopes of crushing New England directly, the British planned to isolate the region and defeat the Continental Army under George Washington's leadership.

The British also aimed at seizing all the major American cities. Indeed, at one point or another during the war, the British captured Boston, Newport, New York, Philadelphia, Charleston, and Savannah. The capture of American cities, however, did not bring about an American surrender. With 90 percent of the American population living in the countryside, the British found that the seizure of a major city did not strike the hoped-for psychological or economic blow.

The British on the Offensive: 1776

In preparation for a British offensive in 1776, the new commander, General William Howe, assembled a huge force on Staten Island: 32,000 soldiers and 13,000 seamen, carried by 73 warships and several hundred transports.

In anticipation of battle and hoping to protect New York, Washington moved his army south to New York (see Map 7–1). He had about 19,000 soldiers, too few to hold up to the British in a pitched battle. Washington kept about half his troops in Manhattan and sent the other half to Brooklyn Heights, where they dug in, in hopes of protecting Long Island. The British sneaked up behind the Americans, inflicting heavy casualties, and on August 27, 1776, Washington pulled the remainder of his Brooklyn forces back into Manhattan. Had the British pursued rapidly,

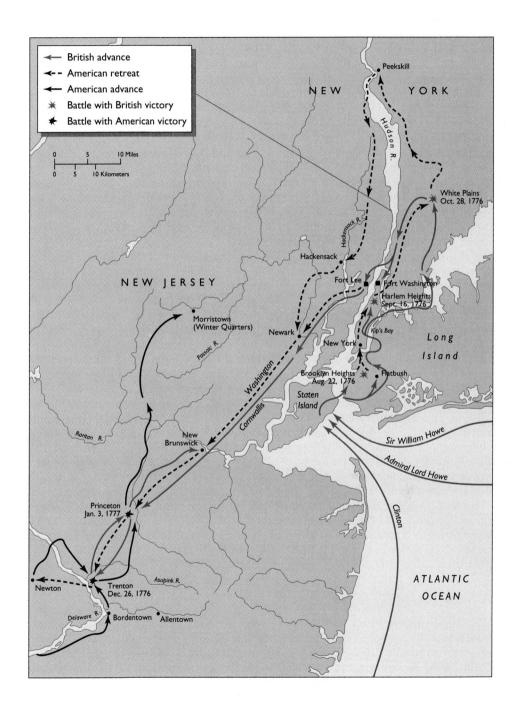

Map 7–1   New York and New Jersey Campaigns, 1776–1777
In the second half of 1776, British troops chased Washington out of New York and across New Jersey. As he would for the remainder of the war, Washington took care never to let the British capture him and his troops, leaving him free to attack at Trenton and Princeton.

they probably could have crushed Washington's army, but Howe may have been more concerned with winning a peace than a war. After Washington retreated, Howe invited members of the Continental Congress to meet with him privately on Staten Island. He was unable to recognize American independence, which was what the representatives insisted on, so his peace strategy failed.

Still hoping for peace, Howe then began pushing Washington back, first out of lower Manhattan, then out of the northern part of the island. Simultaneously, he offered peace to any colonists in the region who would declare their loyalty, and thousands accepted the offer. On November 16, the British succeeded in forcing the Americans out of Manhattan. Howe pursued them to White Plains and then through New Jersey to New Brunswick. The British almost caught Washington twice in New Jersey, but on December 8 the Americans crossed the Delaware at Trenton, taking every boat in the area with them to prevent pursuit. By Christmas Eve, Washington had only 3,000 soldiers, and General Charles Lee, the commander of the other half of the Continental Army, had been captured. As Thomas Paine wrote, "These are the times that try men's souls."

Howe had captured New York, had taken possession of New Jersey, and was poised to seize Philadelphia (which fell in September 1777). At the end of 1776, the British were close to achieving their objective. Then, on Christmas night, with morale in the Continental Army dangerously low, Washington took his army across the ice-clogged Delaware and surprised the British garrison at Trenton at dawn, capturing a 1,000 Hessian soldiers. About a week later, Washington evaded a British trap and sneaked behind the lines to capture an outpost at Princeton.

These American successes were enough to bring another 1,000 troops into the army. Even more significant, the British decided to concentrate their troops near New Brunswick, fearing the loss of any more garrisons, which were necessary for defending the Loyalists. This strategic decision revealed the weakness in the British position and demonstrated why, at the moment when victory seemed closest, it was very far away. Never able to raise enough troops to overcome the Americans' home advantage, the British needed to make certain that civilians did not aid the Revolutionary War effort. However, the British were seizing the civilians' goods and property for the war effort. Once the garrisons were withdrawn, those who had declared loyalty to the British were vulnerable to the reprisals of the patriots.

The British could control the American countryside only by maintaining troops there, but once the troops were withdrawn, civil warfare would break out. Thus, even though Washington's victories at Trenton and Princeton were small, they exposed the incapacity of the British to defeat the revolutionaries unless they settled an army of occupation on the Americans, something they were not prepared to do.

A Slow War: 1777–1781

With the British held off and a major defeat avoided, Washington settled in for a long war, enlisting soldiers for an extended period. He never had enough soldiers to confront the British head-on, so he mostly led the British on chases across the countryside. As a result, the war dragged on for five more years. Maintaining such an army year after year was expensive, but the American population was unwilling to be taxed at high rates. Soldiers in the Continental Army, who were from the bottom tier of society, suffered grievously; at Jockey Hollow, New Jersey, in the winter of 1779–1780, men roasted their own shoes to eat and even devoured their pet dogs.

In 1777, the British political objective was still the same: to isolate New England by seizing the middle colonies after taking the capital at Philadelphia. American troops had the advantage in upstate New York by three to one, however, and they defeated the British under General John Burgoyne at Saratoga, stopping the British advance.

The victory at Saratoga convinced the French to enter into a formal alliance, negotiated by Benjamin Franklin, the American envoy. Winning French support was perhaps the major accomplishment of the middle phase of the war. Not only did the entry of the French tie down the British in other parts of the world, but it also brought America more than $8 million in aid.

The British strategy of isolating New England had failed, and it proved impossible to pacify the countryside of the middle colonies. As a result, the focus shifted away from the least loyal section of America, New England, to the most loyal area, the South. Stated British war aims shifted, too, in response to political realities at home. The new justification was to protect the Loyalists from vengeful patriots.

Seeking to capitalize on internal conflicts and to rally southern Loyalists, the British invaded Georgia in 1778 and South Carolina in 1780. After seizing Charleston and trapping the American commander and thousands of troops, the British ranged out into the countryside, trying to rally the Loyalists and live off the land—the same contradictory strategy that had failed in New Jersey.

In the meantime, the Continental Army and the militia worked together to wear down the British. The Continental Army in the lower South was never large enough to risk a major battle. However, as the British marched through South Carolina and North Carolina, they were harassed by bands of irregulars and militia. Each hit depleted the British forces, and each small victory brought more men into the American ranks. This, in fact, became the American strategy as the Continental forces, now commanded in the South by Nathanael Greene, drew the British, led by Lord Cornwallis, on a wild chase (see Map 7–2).

Finally, with the British near exhaustion, Greene met the British at Guilford Court House in March 1781, inflicting heavy losses on them. Although the battle was a draw, Cornwallis, his forces depleted, retreated to Virginia.

The British had been seriously weakened by the war of attrition. George Washington, working closely with the French, drew most of his forces to Virginia and laid siege. Trapped, Cornwallis surrendered on October 19, 1781.

Securing a Place in the World

The United States revolted to escape from the British Empire and turn its back on European power politics. However, to win the war, the new nation had to strike bargains with those same European powers. These alliances and treaties set the stage for national and international struggle as Americans tried to establish a place for themselves in the new world political and economic order. Successful diplomatic relations were critical to the success of the American political economy, for they would make possible the new nation's survival and prosperity.

Early in the war the United States called on Britain's continental enemies— France, Spain, and Holland— for support, and it played these new allies off against Britain with as much intrigue and cunning as any Old World diplomat. Benjamin Franklin, Congress's envoy to France, now 70, arrived at court in 1776 dressed like a country rustic instead of wearing the expected silks and powdered wig. His unfashionable appearance was a ruse, intended to make the French think that he was innocent and uncalculating. France entered the war in the hope of breaking up the British Empire and re-establishing itself as the world's most powerful nation. France and Spain both wanted the United States to be independent but small and weak.

Map 7–2   The War in the South, 1779–1781
In 1779, the theater of action shifted to the South. Washington's objective was to wear the British down, avoiding decisive battles in which his outmanned troops might be defeated. With the help of the French, his strategy succeeded, leading to the British surrender at Yorktown in October 1781.

The United States wanted to secure its own independence, first and foremost, but it had no intention of remaining small or feeble. Americans hoped to obtain the territory between the Appalachians and the Mississippi River and a sizable chunk of Canada, as well as the right to navigate the Mississippi. In return for French and Spanish assistance, the United States at first offered only the right to trade, vastly overrating the value of the American trade to European heads of state.

Because America wanted France and Spain to fight for expanded American territory, while those two nations wanted instead to keep the new nation small, it took three years, until 1778, to negotiate formal treaties. Franklin pushed the French along by holding secret truce discussions with a British agent late in 1777 and then leaking reports to well-placed French friends. Although the alliance was an impressive accomplishment for the new nation, it involved several concessions. The Americans promised not to negotiate separately with Britain and to remain France's ally "forever."

The United States broke both promises. In April 1782, after Cornwallis's surrender at Yorktown but before France and Spain had gained their military objectives, Franklin began peace negotiations with a British representative. By November, a draft of the treaty had been completed, although Franklin assured the French that nothing would be signed without their consent. It was clear, however, that the agreement primarily served British and American interests. Under the terms of the Treaty of Paris, signed in 1783, Britain recognized American independence, and the United States acquired the territory between the Appalachians and the Mississippi River and south of the Great Lakes (see Map 7–3).

In the long run Britain probably struck the shrewder bargain. The land it ceded was of little use. By the mid-1780s, the British had forbidden the Americans to trade directly with either Britain or the West Indies, and these restrictions seriously damaged the new nation's economy. Neither France nor Spain gained much from the war. Although Spain won Florida, neither country achieved its other territorial objectives, and as was always the case after international wars, France was left with a large debt.

If America's allies were relative losers, so also were Britain's allies, the American Loyalists and Indian tribes that fought with them. The best the British could do for the Loyalists was to secure a commitment of no further reprisals against them and Congress's promise to get the states to consider making restitution. Rather than attempting to protect their Indian allies, the British sold them out by transferring their land (the territory between the Appalachians and the Mississippi) to the United States. Although in many ways a stunning achievement, the Treaty of Paris also set the stage for future conflicts.

THE CHALLENGE OF THE REVOLUTION

During the Revolution and in the years that immediately followed, Americans experienced all the upheavals of war: death, profiteering, and inflation followed by economic depression. There were other challenges as well, those presented by the ideology of the Revolution, based on novel ideas about liberty and equality.

Radicals and moderates had compromised to begin and win the Revolution, yet there were significant disagreements between them that resurfaced once the fighting ended. One of the greatest challenges that Americans faced was endeavoring to design political structures that could contain these conflicts. The other great challenge came from the philosophy of revolution itself. Equality implied a transformed political economy. Followed to its natural conclusion, not only would the transformation lead to widespread prosperity, it would necessarily challenge slavery and the subordination of women.

The Departure of the Loyalists

About 15 to 20 percent of the white population had remained loyal to the Crown during the Revolution, along with a majority of the Indians and a minority of slaves.

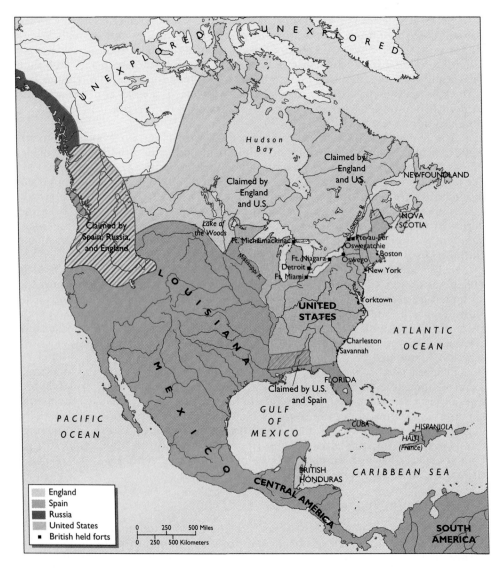

Map 7–3 The Treaty of Paris
The Treaty of Paris confirmed the boundaries of the new United States, north to the Great Lakes, south to Spanish Florida, and west to the Mississippi River. But it left the British in several forts west of the Appalachians, which they did not abandon until 1797.
Source: Walter LaFeber, The American Age, 2nd ed. (1994), p. 29.

Although this was a sizable number of people (almost half a million whites), the Loyalists were never well-organized enough to present a real danger to the success of the Revolution.

During the war, partisan fighting was fierce in those regions where neither side could maintain control, such as the Carolinas and New Jersey, but there was relatively little retribution after the war. There were no trials for treason, mass executions, or significant mob actions directed against whites. Nor was there any significant resistance from the Loyalists. Perhaps as many as 80,000 left the country for Canada, Great Britain, or the West Indies.

The exiles came disproportionately from the top tier of society, and their departure left a void that less prominent Americans scrambled to fill. Confiscated Loyalist property represented a great deal of wealth to be redistributed. Most often, it was people just below the top rung of society who took the Loyalists' places. The departure of the Loyalists enhanced the democratizing tendencies of the Revolution by removing the most conservative element in American society and creating an opportunity for many Americans to rise to power.

The Challenge of the Economy

Wars disrupt the economy in two ways. First, they interfere with production and exchange, hurting some people and creating opportunity for others. Second, because wars are expensive, they require some combination of increased taxation and deficit spending.

Those who suffered the greatest economic hardships and enjoyed the greatest opportunities from the Revolution were those most deeply involved in the market. During the war, trade with Britain and the British West Indies was cut off, and the British Navy seized American ships and destroyed the New England fishing industry. After the war, Britain continued to exclude American ships from the West Indies. Congress, operating under the Articles of Confederation, was too weak to negotiate a more advantageous trade relationship, and merchants who had depended on trade with Britain and the West Indies were ruined.

At the same time, other opportunities opened up. Merchants who were willing to risk seizure of their ships continued the trade with Europe and sold the goods they imported at astronomical prices. Provisioning the Continental Army offered another avenue for profit. In 1779 alone, the Army spent $109 million on provisions, fueling a wartime economic boom. In addition, the Army's demand for supplies drove prices up. Prices for grain increased 200 to 600 percent in some regions, while those for wheat in Maryland skyrocketed 5,000 percent. Enterprising Americans with a little capital to invest could rise quickly.

Not everyone could take advantage of the dislocations of the revolutionary economy. In fact, although the Revolution eliminated a portion of the ruling elite, it did not level the social classes. Those who could not profit from the war economy had to work harder and struggle with rising prices. To meet the Army's demand for cloth and make up for the lack of imports, women increased the pace of home production. Because cities and states set prices for cloth, however, women were unable to reap exorbitant profits for their work. Skyrocketing prices fell hardest on those with limited incomes.

Even before the war ended, America's growing population was clamoring for land. Between 1776 and 1790, America's population grew by almost 70 percent, from 2.3 million to 3.9 million, almost all from natural increase. Since before the Revolution, colonists had been pushing against the Indians to the west. By 1783, the Wilderness Road had taken thousands of settlers into Kentucky; seven years later, 100,000 people were living in Kentucky and Tennessee.

All along the western frontier, farmers rushed in to take up new lands. Speculators grew rich as they sold land at extraordinary profits. This rush into newly opened farming regions reversed the trend that was taking place before the Revolution, when the growing population had sought employment in the cities.

With the opening of new regions to the west, America would remain a farming nation for decades more, rather than industrializing rapidly and displaying the rigid class stratifications of European industrial economies. At the same time, slavery expanded into new territories in the South, ensuring the persistence of racial inequalities.

Even more than the dislocations of the revolutionary economy, the financing of the Revolution challenged the American economy. Taxing the population was out of the question, not only because Americans had begun the Revolution precisely to avoid high taxes, but also because Congress had no authority to tax. Instead it simply printed more money. There was no increase in underlying wealth to back up this currency, and the more Congress printed, the less it was worth. By 1780, Congress had printed more than $241 million. In addition it paid for supplies and soldiers' wages with certificates that circulated like money. These certificates put another $95 million into circulation.

The plan was for each state to raise taxes to buy up the Continental currency and remove it from circulation. However, the states were either unable or unwilling to buy up enough currency to maintain its value. Moreover, the states issued their own paper money. Eventually, the states had to tax their inhabitants at rates far higher than had ever been seen before. Levying taxes was one thing; collecting them was another: People could not pay in hard money, and the Continental currency depreciated so rapidly that it was almost worthless.

By April 1777, Continental currency was worth only half its face value and by April 1781, only half a percent of its face value. By the end of the war, some creditors were refusing to accept paper money for the debts owed to them, insisting on hard money instead. Then, when the war ended and trade with Britain resumed, imports increased sharply (because of pent-up demand for consumer goods), while exports fell (because trade restrictions kept American goods out of British markets). The result was severe *deflation*, or falling prices and wages.

The weak central government was almost powerless to address these economic upheavals. In 1780 it stopped paying the army, which almost led to a mutiny. Congress looked to the states, which addressed their economic problems in different ways. Each state had to decide what to do about its debt and which element of its population to serve. In states where taxes rose to pay off the state debts (at just the time when the postwar depression hit), hard-pressed debtors clamored for tax relief. In western Massachusetts, a group of farmers led by Revolutionary War captain Daniel Shays shut down the courts to prevent them from collecting debts. This is known as Shays' Rebellion.

Contesting the New Political Economy

Economic upheaval and popular uprisings against state governments led many Americans to question whether democratic government could survive. The rebellion that began in 1765 seemed to be beginning again, this time directed against the new republican state governments. Americans now had to face the same issue that had led to conflict with Britain: Were they willing to pay the costs of waging a huge war? Could they avoid the perils of tyranny, on the one hand, and anarchy, on the other?

Shays' Rebellion, an extreme form of the protest that occurred in many states against high taxes in a deflationary economy, was an attempt by debtors from western Massachusetts to force the government to alleviate their economic distress. By 1786, many western Massachusetts farmers had become accustomed to the absence of government. Courts had been shut down in the region since 1774, and this area often

This picture of Col. Daniel Shays and his associate Job Shattuck is from a 1787 almanac. Shays and Shattuck are depicted wearing the clothing appropriate to their rank in the insurrection, with both wearing the clothing of gentlemen and carrying swords.

declined to send representatives to any provincial bodies. Those who put down Shays' Rebellion did so in republican terms, faulting the Shaysites for inadequate virtue. How could the gains of the Revolution be preserved in the face of hostility to all government?

Every state that faced such uprisings learned that peace could best be preserved by going easy on the rebels. After Shays' Rebellion was put down, John Hancock was elected governor with the support of the Shaysites on a platform of amnesty for the rebels and relief for debtors. As a rule, popular uprisings by economically independent men (as distinguished from those by dependent laborers or slaves) have been punished very lightly in America, which might be a source of political stability.

Although the relatively light punishments meted out to debtor insurgents and the generally inflationary policies of state governments quelled popular unrest, the postwar depression and the inability of Congress to negotiate trade agreements with Britain devastated commerce. The huge national debt went unpaid, leaving numerous creditors holding worthless pieces of paper. Popular unrest in the states had helped debtors but hurt those to whom they owed money. The nationalists, a group of commercial-minded political leaders centered in Congress and including James Madison, Gouverneur Morris, Robert Morris, and Alexander Hamilton, began to make a case for a strong national government that would actively advance commerce and protect private property. These nationalists were, in general, the moderates of the revolutionary era. Radicals envisioned a political economy based on a weaker central government, a more localized democracy, and a hands-off approach to the economy. Whether these two visions of the American political economy could be reconciled was one of the greatest challenges presented by the Revolution.

Can Women Be Citizens?

The American Revolution raised questions that threatened and in some cases changed the social order. A revolution based on beliefs in human equality and a common human nature brought into question all social relations, including the role of women.

Women had been actively recruited into the boycott movements of the 1760s and 1770s, and they had eagerly participated both in boycotts and in increased home production. Many women identified with the goals of the Revolution and participated actively in one of its engines of enforcement: riots against merchants suspected of unfair dealings. Women could turn their efforts against the revolutionary governments, as well, when they perceived interference with their rights as consumers and duties as homemakers. Early in the war, the women of Kingston, New York, mobbed the town's revolutionary committee and threatened that unless the committee turned over the tea it held, "their husbands and sons shall fight no more."

If it was generally agreed that women could extend their traditional economic roles as producers and consumers to support the war effort, there was no consensus on how greatly women's political roles should be expanded. Some women pointed out that the right to be taxed only by one's own representatives should apply to them, too. Married women were generally denied the right to own property, but what was the basis for denying the vote to unmarried women who owned property? In 1776, New Jersey extended the vote to unmarried women who met the property qualification (although this right was rescinded in 1807). Few revolutionaries were willing to go this far.

Although American revolutionaries were not prepared to let women vote, except in New Jersey, they began to expand their views about women's intellectual and political capabilities in other ways. The state laws that confiscated Loyalists' property, for example, often presumed that married women were capable of making their own political choices. This notion was a radical break with the past, which had always asserted that married women had no political will separate from their husbands.

The Revolution challenged the idea that women lacked independent minds and could not think for themselves. The Enlightenment belief that all human beings were endowed with the capacity to reason led to significant improvements in women's education after the war. Reformers, many of them women, argued that if women appeared ignorant or incapable, it was only because of their inferior education. Enlightenment ideas about women's intellectual abilities meshed neatly with republican ideas about the need for virtue and liberal ideas about the necessity of consent. If the fate of the nation depended on the character of its citizens, both men and women should be able to choose intelligent, upright, patriotic partners. Likewise, the Revolution's rejection of arbitrary power accelerated a trend for people to choose their own marriage partners and marry for love rather than for crass material interest. If women were to make such choices wisely, then they must be educated well.

Yet once again the revolutionary impulse had its limits. Discussions about women's citizenship and intellectual capacities implicitly applied only to prosperous white women. Moreover, almost no one advocated professional education or even knowledge for its own sake for women. Women's education was supposed to make them better wives and better mothers and enable them to perform their domestic roles better.

The ideas of the Revolution presented a powerful challenge to the subordination of women, one that the revolutionary generation was only partially prepared to meet. Women were recognized as intelligent beings who could make important choices in the market, about their families, and even about their political loyalties. They were partial citizens, and this revealed the limits of revolutionary doctrines of equality.

The Challenge of Slavery

No institution in America received a greater challenge from the egalitarian ideals of the Revolution than slavery. The world's first antislavery movement began before the

Liberty Displaying the Arts and Sciences. So powerful was the revolutionary idea of human equality that many came to believe in the liberating potential of education for both women and blacks.

Revolution with the Pennsylvania Quaker John Woolman, who in 1754 condemned slavery in humanitarian and religious terms. Within a few years, radicals in both the North and the South recognized that the institution was inconsistent with their ideals of freedom.

African-American slaves immediately saw that the Revolution offered opportunities for freedom. The combination of egalitarian ideas and wartime disruption enabled thousands of slaves to claim their freedom. Some used a combination of Christian and revolutionary principles of liberty to petition for "the natural rights and privileges of freeborn men." Others fought for their liberty by joining the revolutionary forces or, more commonly, by taking advantage of British offers of freedom to slaves who deserted their masters. Even more slaves ran away, especially in areas occupied by the British or torn by war.

This combination of revolutionary ideals of freedom and African-American activism presented a significant challenge to white Americans, and they were able to meet it in part. Every state north of Delaware eliminated slavery, either in their constitutions or through gradual emancipation laws. In addition, the Northwest Ordinance of 1787 prohibited slavery in the Northwest Territory (the future states of Ohio, Indiana, Illinois, Michigan, and Wisconsin). In the states of the upper South (Virginia, Maryland, and Delaware) legislatures passed laws making it easier to emancipate slaves.

If slavery was eliminated in the North and questioned in the upper South, it still survived in every state south of New Jersey. Revolutionary ideals made slaveholders uncomfortable with the institution. Unwilling to eliminate it, they offered excuses, protesting that abolishing slavery was too difficult or inconvenient. Historians still debate whether the inroads revolutionary thought made against slavery were one of the Revolution's greatest successes—or whether its inability to curtail the institution was its greatest failure.

A New Policy in the West

The new nation faced a major challenge in the West. It had to devise a policy that would be consistent with its political economy, rejecting the old colonial models of Britain, France, and Spain. But how would the United States organize the new territory acquired through the war? There was at the time no useful model that would enable new territories and their citizens to become equal members of an expanding, democratic nation.

The Indians' Revolution

At the beginning of the American Revolution, most Indians regarded it as a fight among Englishmen that did not concern them. At the end of the war, all Indians were losers, as land-hungry Americans poured into the region beyond the Appalachians.

By 1776, both the British and the Americans were recruiting Indians for their causes. Within a few years Indians all along the frontier had been drawn into the struggle, most often on the British side. These Indians were fearful of American encroachments onto their land; also, only the British could provide the customary "presents" that cemented alliances. Indians struck at American communities all along the frontier.

In retaliation, Washington ordered General John Sullivan to accomplish "the total destruction and devastation" of Iroquois settlements in New York and western Pennsylvania and the capture of "as many prisoners of every age and sex as possible." In the fall of 1778, Sullivan's expedition burned forty Iroquois towns, 160,000 bushels of corn, and all the crops that were ready for harvest. Such brutality understandably undermined American efforts to keep Indian allies.

The End of the Middle Ground

The end of the Revolution brought neither peace nor order. The Indians who had won victories on the frontier were amazed when word came that the British had surrendered and turned over all of the Indians' land to the Americans. Needing land for settlers more than it needed diplomatic allies, the United States soon abandoned the middle ground (see Chapter 2, "Colonial Outposts"). No longer able to play one group of Europeans against another, Indian tribes had little leverage.

Western Indians soon found themselves in the midst of a competition among whites for their land. Congress wanted to establish a national claim to Native American lands so it could sell them to pay off the war debt, while New York, Pennsylvania, North Carolina, and Virginia all attempted to seize land that lay within their borders. Speculators moved in, knowing that they could sell land at an immense profit. At the end of the Revolution, one-third of the men in western Pennsylvania were landless and they believed that the Revolution's promise of equality entitled them to cheap land. Some of the poorest settlers poured across the Appalachians into Kentucky and Ohio, even as the Revolution was being fought, squatting on Indian-owned lands.

Those who had already lived on the frontier and both suffered from and inflicted frontier violence maintained a visceral hatred of Indians, sometimes advocating their extermination. These settlers expected government to secure frontier land for them and to protect them from the Indians who still claimed it. Both Congress and the states moved quickly to force Indians, some of whom had no authority to speak for their tribes, to sign treaties ceding their land.

Such treaties (15 were signed between 1784 and 1796) were almost meaningless. Native Americans refused to honor agreements made under duress that did not include the customary exchange of gifts and wampum belts, while the states would not recognize another state's claims or those of the national government. Indian leaders who attempted to rally their communities were encouraged by the British and the Spanish. Years of struggle ensued, and not until well into the nineteenth century were American claims to Indian land east of the Mississippi secured and Indian resistance put down.

Settling the West

Establishing effective government in the West was one of the biggest problems the new nation faced. Many frontier regions (in particular Kentucky and the area north of the Ohio River, as well as portions of Vermont and Maine) were claimed by competing groups of speculators from different states. The Articles of Confederation gave Congress limited powers of government in the West, and it soon became clear that a national policy was necessary. In the years just after the Revolution, groups of dissident settlers in New York, Pennsylvania, Kentucky (then part of Virginia), and Tennessee (then part of North Carolina) all hatched plans to create their own states.

Both state governments and nationalists in Congress believed that the union was in peril. Yet it was difficult to reach a compromise among the competing interests. States with significant western claims wanted Congress to recognize their claims, while states without any western lands wanted all of the western lands to be turned over to Congress. In several regions, groups of speculators with dubious claims to the land—secured, for instance, by plying cooperative Indians with liquor—were selling it to settlers at bargain prices.

The Northwest Ordinance, ratified by Congress on July 13, 1787, was a compromise among these competing interests. Finally realizing that they could not manage vast areas of territory, the large states yielded their claims to Congress. Congress, however, was willing to tolerate respectable speculators, gentlemen who bought directly from Congress. The Northwest Ordinance set out a model of government for the western territories that reflected the liberal political philosophy of nationalists in Congress, and established a process for the admission of new states into the nation. In a clear rejection of Britain's colonial model of territorial expansion, territories would be eligible to apply for statehood once they had 60,000 free inhabitants. There were other important breaks with the past as well. Slavery was now forbidden north of the Ohio River, the first time that a line was drawn barring slaves from a particular region. There was also a provision forbidding any laws that impaired contracts. Trial by jury and habeas corpus were guaranteed, as well as the right to bail and freedom of religion. Cruel and unusual punishments were barred. These were important principles that, except for the provision excluding slavery, would all appear again in the Constitution and Bill of Rights.

The Northwest Ordinance was designed to create an orderly world of middle-class farmers who obeyed the law, paid their debts, worshiped as they pleased, and were protected from despotic government and the unruly poor. The ordinance represented the triumph of the moderate revolutionaries' vision of government.

CREATING A NEW NATIONAL GOVERNMENT

At the beginning of the Revolution, radicals and moderates had been able to work together to accomplish their common goals. The years of war, however, slowly pulled the radicals and moderates apart. During this period, many moderates, particularly those who served in Congress or as officers in the Continental Army, became nationalists. They worked with men from other states on national projects, and they came to think of the states as a threat to the success of the Revolution. Many of the radicals, meanwhile, retained a local perspective. Still influenced by republican political thought, they continued to dread a centralized government, and they feared that the Continental Army would become a standing army that might take away their liberties.

This split between moderate nationalists and radical localists culminated in the battle over the Constitution. This conflict was not simply about political beliefs; it also represented a profound disagreement about the future of the American political economy. The nationalists were deeply involved in the market economy as merchants, financiers, farmers, and planters who wished to sell abroad or to regional markets. The localists, as a rule, were much less involved in the market and suspicious of those who were. As long as taxes were low and their creditors did not harass them, they were satisfied. From their perspective, the Articles of Confederation provided all the national government and economy that was needed.

A Crippled Congress

It soon became evident to nationalists in Congress that the national government was powerless to address the most pressing economic questions. By 1779 Congress had printed $200 million worth of paper money that was dropping in value by the day, and it had shut down its printing presses. It then told the states that it was their responsibility to provision the Army. State legislatures dithered while the Army went unclothed and unfed, and the unpaid Army threatened mutiny. Congress gave up trying to pay its war debt and passed that back to the states as well. Some states refused. States such as Massachusetts that raised taxes to pay off their portion faced armed upheavals such as Shays' Rebellion.

Congress was powerless to alleviate the economic distress. At the end of the war, British goods flooded into a nation that had been starved for them, and consumer demand seemed insatiable. However, there was no comparable British demand for American exports; in fact, Britain closed its ports to American trade. America could not retaliate by closing its ports to British ships, because the Articles of Confederation denied Congress the authority to regulate commerce. Additional foreign loans, which had kept the nation afloat during the Revolution, were out of the question. Congress could not pay back the loans it had already taken out from France, Spain, and Holland.

Even western policy, the area of Congress's greatest triumph, presented problems. The states had ceded western territory to Congress. Yet once those lands came under Congress's jurisdiction (leading to the passage of the Northwest Ordinance), Congress discovered what the British government had learned at the end of the French and Indian War: It takes an army and a great deal of money to police a territory inhabited by Indians and coveted by land-hungry settlers. Congress did not have that money, and it could not even pay the army that it had.

By the early 1780s, nationalists were attempting to strengthen Congress, but these attempts failed without the approval of the states. By the middle of the decade, several of the boldest nationalists had decided that reform was not only impossible but undesirable. They were convinced that a new and stronger form of government should be created. When James Madison returned to Virginia at the end of 1783 (a victim of term limits, having served the maximum of three consecutive years in Congress), he began a study of history to learn the principles of effective government. Other nationalists began talking about calling a constitutional convention. But the challenge they faced was how to effect changes against the will of the states.

The road that led to the Constitutional Convention in Philadelphia in 1787 ran through two earlier meetings. First, in 1785, at Madison's suggestion, commissioners from Virginia and Maryland met at George Washington's home, Mount Vernon, to resolve disputes about navigating the Potomac River. Madison suggested a further meeting of representatives from all the states in Annapolis, Maryland, to build on the accomplishments from Mount Vernon. When only 12 men, representing five states, arrived, they issued a call for another meeting, in Philadelphia, nine months later. In those nine months, Shays' Rebellion and the continued stalemate in Congress persuaded nationalists that strengthening the government should be considered. So, over the summer of 1787, 55 men from 12 states met in Philadelphia to write one of the most influential documents in the history of the world.

Writing a New Constitution

The men who assembled in Philadelphia were primarily moderate nationalists. It is a measure of their commitment to the goals of the Revolution that they sought, in James Madison's words, "republican remedies" for the problems of republican government. The 55 delegates met for almost four months during the summer of 1787, finally ratifying the Constitution on September 17. They conducted their deliberations in secret, enabling them to talk freely and achieve compromises. Hence, the shutters to the room were closed and nailed shut, and precautions were taken to ensure that the talkative Benjamin Franklin did not spill any secrets. The heat and stench of sweat in the room must have been almost unbearable.

Although there were sharp differences of opinion on specific issues, there were wide areas of agreement. Most of the delegates had considerable experience in state and national government. George Washington, a member of Virginia's delegation, was the most widely respected man in the nation. He was elected the presiding officer of the convention.

Collectively the delegates were young, with most in their 30s and 40s. No one played a more important role in the convention than James Madison, who had just turned 36. Madison came to the Constitutional Convention with a design for the new government already worked out. Known as the Virginia Plan, it was presented by Edmund Randolph of Virginia, and it became the outline for the Constitution.

The Virginia Plan was a blueprint for substantial change: a strong central government divided into three branches, executive, legislative (itself with two branches), and judicial, that would check and balance one another; a system of federalism that guaranteed every state a republican government; and proposals for admitting new states and amending the Constitution. The only alternative, the New Jersey Plan, offered on June 15, was rejected three days later. It proposed a single-house legislature, with all states having an equal vote, and also a plural executive, chosen by the legislature (see Table 7–1).

The delegates were in basic agreement that the new national government would have to be much stronger: Congress would now have the power to collect taxes and duties, to pay the country's debts, to regulate foreign commerce, and to raise armies and pay for them. Once the delegates compromised on a method for choosing the president (by electors chosen in each state) and the length of his term (four years, eligible for re-election), they readily agreed to grant him considerable power to propose legislation, veto bills of Congress (subject to congressional override), conduct diplomacy, and command the armed forces.

TABLE 7–1

Key Provisions of the Articles of Confederation, the Virginia Plan, the New Jersey Plan, and the Constitution

	Articles of Confederation	Virginia Plan	New Jersey Plan	Constitution
Executive	None	Chosen by Congress	Plural; chosen by Congress	President chosen by electoral college
Congress	One house; one vote per state	Two houses	One house	Two houses
Judiciary	None	Yes	Yes	Yes
Federalism	Limited; each state retains full sovereignty	Yes; Congress can veto state laws	Yes; acts of Congress the "supreme law of the states"	Yes; Constitution the "supreme law of the land"; states guaranteed a republican form of government; Supreme Court to adjudicate disputes between states
Powers of Congress	Conduct diplomacy and wage war; cannot levy taxes or raise army	All powers of Articles of Confederation, plus power to make laws for nation	All powers of Articles of Confederation, plus power to regulate commerce and make states pay taxes	Numerous powers, such as levy taxes, declare war, raise army, regulate commerce, and "make all laws which shall be necessary and proper" for carrying out those powers

The delegates vested judicial authority in the Supreme Court and inferior federal courts and granted them authority over the state constitutions as well. Although the delegates were able to reach agreement rather easily on the structure and powers of the new government, they argued bitterly any time the interests of their states seemed in jeopardy. The most difficult issues related to representation: Would the numbers of senators and representatives be based on population or wealth, or would each state have equal numbers? If based on population or wealth, would slaves be counted? Large states generally wanted representation to be based on either population or wealth (they had more of both), while northern states did not want slaves to be counted, either as population or wealth. The conflict between the large and small states was resolved by Roger Sherman's Connecticut (or Great) Compromise: Each state would have an equal number of senators, satisfying the small states. The number of representatives would be based upon either population or wealth, satisfying the large states.

The Connecticut Compromise solved the conflict between small and large states, but only by creating another between slave and free states. The South Carolinians were adamant: Whether slavery was called population or wealth, the institution must be protected. The argument was fierce, with several delegates threatening to walk out. Finally the convention compromised. Representation in the House would be based on the entire free population (including women and children, but not Indians) plus three-fifths of the slaves, thus increasing the South's representation. The delegates recognized that the Three-Fifths Compromise was fundamentally illogical, but only when it had been accepted could the delegates agree to the Connecticut Compromise. The Three-Fifths Clause made the Connecticut Compromise possible.

The Three-Fifths Clause became the most notorious provision in the Constitution. Although the delegates were careful not to use the word "slave" (instead using bland phrases such as "other persons"), clearly they were establishing a racial line. The Convention made two other concessions to slavery. First, it agreed that Congress could not ban the slave trade until 1808 at the earliest. In addition, the Constitution included a fugitive slave clause, which required states to return runaway slaves.

The nationalists were determined not to leave Philadelphia until they had a constitution and were willing to enter into whatever compromises seemed necessary. Despite occasional impasses and heated debates, those compromises were achieved, and the convention adjourned on September 17. The delegates' work was not over, however. Now the Constitution had to be ratified.

Ratifying the Constitution: Politics

There was nothing inevitable about the nation, the Constitution, or the particular form either took; that the Constitution would be ratified was by no means a given. The Constitution was the creation of a small group of men who thought nationally, the Federalists. They then had the difficult task of getting the Constitution ratified by a nation that still thought about government in almost wholly local terms.

The Philadelphia Convention decided that the Constitution would go into effect once nine states had ratified it. They could not bind any states that had not ratified, but the nine signatories could go ahead. Ironically, after all the small states/big states debate in the Convention, small states were the first to ratify, because they were the ones that most needed the union. For example, Georgia, the fourth state to ratify, was still in many ways a frontier region, vulnerable to Indian assault, its capital at Augusta an armed camp. The most serious opposition came from the large, powerful states of Massachusetts, New York, and Virginia.

The convention had concluded on September 17, and by December 7, Delaware had already ratified the Constitution. By January 9, 1788, New Jersey, Georgia, and Connecticut followed, with barely any dispute. The Federalists in Pennsylvania forced ratification by using strong-arm tactics. The Federalists in other states learned from these mistakes and more willingly made concessions to their Antifederalist opponents.

In Massachusetts, as in Pennsylvania, there was considerable opposition from the western part of the state among those sympathetic to Shays' Rebellion. In an inspired move that would be used also in Virginia, the Federalists made certain that the Constitution was debated section by section, enabling them to win point by point. And in another critical strategic decision, the Federalists agreed that the convention in Massachusetts should propose amendments. Equally important was the form that these amendments would take, not as a condition for ratification, but as part of a package that recommended ratification. This concession, which ultimately made the Constitution both stronger and more democratic, was critical in winning ratification.

Only three more states were necessary for the Constitution to go into effect. The more politically adept Federalists postponed or stalled the debate until states that were most favorable to the Constitution had ratified it. The Virginia ratifying convention was one of the most dramatic, with leaders of the Revolution divided over the issue. Patrick Henry spoke in opposition. Each of Henry's impassioned speeches was rebutted by James Madison's careful and knowledgeable remarks. Having worn down the Antifederalists (as the opponents of the Constitution were called) with logic, the Federalists carried the day, and the Constitution was ratified. As in Massachusetts, the Antifederalists agreed to abide by the result, even though there had been threats of armed rebellion. The decision of Antifederalists to accept the Constitution and to participate in the government it created was one of the most important choices made in this era.

In New York, the Federalists stalled the debate until news of Virginia's ratification. Then they posed the inevitable question: The Constitution had been ratified; would New York join in or not? Once nine states ratified the Constitution, it went into effect. Eventually it was ratified by all the states. As a condition for ratification, several states had insisted that the first Congress consider a number of amendments. These amendments became the Bill of Rights.

Ratifying the Constitution: Ideas

The Constitution was the product of many compromises, and it did not precisely fit anyone's previous ideas. As the Federalists explained the benefits of the Constitution in terms that would make sense to skeptical Americans, and as the Antifederalists tried to explain what they thought was wrong with it, a new understanding of what American government should be evolved. Although there were still significant disagreements, particularly about the shape of the American political economy, this new understanding (which incorporated the Bill of Rights) was sufficiently broad that Antifederalists could join the new government.

Nonetheless, the differences between the Federalists and Antifederalists were profound. As a rule, the Antifederalists were more rural and less involved in the market, came from the western or backwoods regions, and were more likely to be veterans of the militia than of the Continental Army. The Antifederalists were, above all, old-line republicans, who continued to use the language of corruption, tyranny, and enslavement, although now it was the Federalists, not the British government, who represented the danger to liberty.

The Antifederalists believed passionately in the local community. They asserted that republics could survive only in homogeneous communities, where all people had the same interests and values. They believed that too much diversity, whether economic, cultural, ethnic, or religious, destroyed a republic. Although Antifederalists generally, like Federalists, supported freedom of religion, they also favored the spread of Protestantism as a means for assuring morality.

At the same time, the Antifederalists were committed to individual rights, and it is to them that the nation is indebted for the Bill of Rights. They retained the republican fear of power; they did not trust the person they could not see. If government were remote, then it would become oppressive, it would deprive the people of their liberties, and it would tax them. One of the most consistent complaints of the Antifederalists was not so much that taxation would be enacted without rep-resentation as that it would be enacted at all. If the national government needed money, let it ask the states for it (although this system had been tried and had failed under the Articles of Confederation). The Antifederalists turned against the new government out of the same fear of centralized government and hatred of taxation that had led them to revolt against Britain. The Antifederalist contribution to American political thought was a continuing critique of government itself.

Federalists shared many of the beliefs of the Antifederalists. They were firmly committed to the rights of individuals, which was why they so readily accepted the Antifederalist proposal to list and protect those rights as amendments to the Constitution. The second area of overlap was a suspicion of government. Most Federalists agreed with Thomas Paine that "government even in its best state is but a necessary evil." The separation of powers and elaborate series of checks and bal-ances that the Constitution created, as well as the system of federalism itself, reflects this fear. The Federalists divided power; unlike the Antifederalists, they did not deny it.

Their experience in the market economy, as officers in the Continental Army, and as members of the national government provided the Federalists with a differ-ent perspective on political economy. They had come to believe that all people were motivated by self-interest. While the Antifederalists hoped to reform people out of their self-interest, the Federalists were willing to accept self-interest and build a gov-ernment around it.

The experience of the 1780s had convinced the Federalists that no government could rest entirely on the virtue of its people. The challenge was to construct a gov-ernment out of imperfect human materials that would preserve liberty instead of destroying it. In *The Federalist* No. 10 (one of a series of 85 essays written by Madison, Hamilton, and John Jay and published anonymously to influence the ratification debate), Madison explained that the causes of conflict "are sown into the nature of man." The only way of eliminating them would be either by "giving to every citizen the same opinions, the same passions, and the same interests" (the Antifederalist solution) or by destroying liberty itself. But "as long as the reason of man continues fallible, and he is at liberty to exercise it, different opinions will be formed." Toleration was the price of liberty and the necessary result of human imperfection.

In the Philadelphia Convention, the Federalists had been so intent on working out compromises and reconciling their own states' competing interests that they had not had time to develop a philosophy to explain the profound changes they were proposing. That philosophy emerged from the ratification debates, where it was met by the alternative philosophy of the Antifederalists. Both these bodies of thought, sometimes in harmony, sometimes in disagreement, constitute the legacy of the Revolution. This dialogue has continued to frame American government from their day until ours.

CONCLUSION

In rejecting the increasingly centralized British state, the revolutionaries were clear about what they did not want. Over the course of the Revolution, they began to envi-sion the kind of society and nation that they hoped to create. It would ensure individ-ual liberty and economic opportunity. But this was a vague vision for the future. As the first modern nation created by revolution, the United States was entering uncharted territory. Winning independence from the world's most powerful nation, ratifying the

CHRONOLOGY

1775	Battles of Lexington and Concord Fort Ticonderoga seized Battle of Breed's Hill Second Continental Congress convenes Continental Army created, with George Washington in charge Congress adopts "Declaration of the Causes and Necessities of Taking up Arms" George III declares colonists in rebellion Governor Dunmore offers freedom to Virginia slaves who fight for the British Continental Army attacks Canada
1776	Thomas Paine writes *Common Sense* Declaration of Independence Articles of Confederation drafted British capture Manhattan Washington captures Trenton and Princeton New Jersey Constitution allows unmarried, property-owning women to vote Washington captures Princeton
1777	British capture Philadelphia American victory at Saratoga
1778	French enter into treaty with United States British conquer Georgia Sullivan expedition into New York and Pennsylvania
1779	Continental troops winter at Jockey Hollow
1780	British conquer South Carolina
1781	Articles of Confederation ratified Battle of Guilford Court House Cornwallis surrenders
1782	Franklin begins peace discussions with British
1783	Newburgh Conspiracy Treaty of Paris
1785	Land Ordinance of 1785 Virginia and Maryland commissioners meet at Mount Vernon
1786–1787	Shays' Rebellion Meeting at Annapolis
1787	Northwest Ordinance Constitutional Convention
1787–1788	Federalist Papers published Constitution ratified

federal Constitution, and planning for the admission of new territories into the federal union were all extraordinary accomplishments, unique in world history.

Yet there were many problems left unresolved. Although the United States had more than doubled its size, much of the new territory could not be settled because it was inhabited by Indians who refused to recognize America's sovereignty. There were disagreements among Americans themselves, particularly about political economy. How could a nation founded on the principle of liberty practice slavery? How would individual rights be reconciled with the general welfare? Whose economic interests would be served? The American people had embarked on a great experiment whose outcome was far from assured.

FURTHER READINGS

David Brion Davis, *The Problem of Slavery in the Age of Revolution, 1770–1823* (1975). A brilliant analysis that places the first debates about slavery in America in the context of the first worldwide abolition movement.

Linda K. Kerber, *Women of the Republic: Intellect and Ideology in Revolutionary America* (1980). Demonstrates the centrality of gender to revolutionary ideology and the importance of revolutionary ideology in thinking about gender.

Adrienne Koch, ed., *Notes of Debates in the Federal Convention of 1787 Reported by James Madison* (1987). A remarkable record, which shows history being created as a roomful of men attempted to reconcile principal and interest in the writing of the Constitution.

Jack N. Rakove, *Original Meanings: Politics and Ideas in the Making of the Constitution* (1996). A new and compelling account of the writing of the Constitution.

Charles Royster, *A Revolutionary People at War: The Continental Army and American Character, 1775–1783* (1979). A dazzling and beautifully written analysis of conflict between ideology and military necessity in the winning of the Revolution.

John Shy, *A People Numerous and Armed: Reflections on the Military Struggle for American Independence* (1990). A provocative series of essays that places the war for American independence in the wider context of military history.

Gordon S. Wood, *The Creation of the American Republic, 1776–1787* (1969). One of the most important books ever written on the American Revolution, it makes a powerful case for a profound change in the way some Americans thought about the nature and purpose of government over the course of the Revolution.

Please refer to the document CD-ROM for primary sources related to this chapter.

CHAPTER

The Experiment Undertaken

1789–1800

Washington's Inauguration • Conceptions of Political Economy in
the New Republic • Factions and Order in the New Government
A State and Its Boundaries • America in the Transatlantic
Community • Conclusion

WASHINGTON'S INAUGURATION

The procession assembled just after noon on April 30, 1789 and wound slowly through lower New York City. At the head of the file came the military guard, including an entire company of Scottish Highland bagpipers. The escort committees of the new Senate and the new House of Representatives came next, followed by local officials, merchants, wealthy artisans, and other "gentlemen of distinction." At their heels pressed an eager crowd of onlookers.

In the middle of it all, dressed in a simple brown cloth suit and (according to some) markedly ill at ease, was the man they had come to see: the President-Elect of the United States of America, George Washington.

As the procession approached its destination, the military escort divided into two columns, forming a corridor through which Washington, the official committees of Congress, and a small group of special guests entered Federal Hall. After a few moments, Washington stepped out onto the gallery overlooking Broad Street. There, in the presence of Congress and a now-hushed "multitude of citizens," he took the oath of office prescribed by the Constitution of the United States.

The silence was abruptly shattered. "Long Live George Washington!" someone shouted. As 13 cannons boomed a salute, the entire crowd took up the cry. "LONG

LIVE GEORGE WASHINGTON!" they chanted, over and over. For George Washington, April 30, 1789, was a day of sober reflection. At every stop along his journey to New York, he had been feted with banquets, toasts, parades, pageants, and military reviews. Nevertheless, every step of the way he had felt like a culprit skulking to his punishment. Quieting the crowd, his first words after taking the oath of office were to confess that "Among all the vicissitudes incident to life, no event could have filled me with greater anxieties" than the news that he had been elected president of the United States.

Washington's anxiety was well-founded. Even as he took office, the new nation was beset with problems. The requisite nine states had ratified the Constitution, but not without serious reservations. Farmers complained that rich eastern elites sought to dominate the new government. In the territories, would-be settlers and large proprietors fought with each other over rights to the land, even as both groups occupied Native American homelands. On the edges of the nation, France, Spain, and especially Great Britain bided their time until the republic faltered.

These immediate problems implied larger, long-term challenges: Who were the American people? Were "the people" only the nation's partisans, or did they include political critics, newcomers, disfranchised inhabitants, slaves, and Native Americans? In his inaugural address, Washington asserted that an "indissoluble" correspondence existed between the ends of an orderly government and the "characteristic rights of freemen" in a republic. But what were those rights? Did they extend to women? What types of institutions were necessary to protect those rights, and what type of society could produce citizens able to insist on such a government? The new Constitution structured a government and recognized the importance of certain social and economic values, but it left most of these larger questions unresolved. For good and for ill, in the turmoil of time Americans would answer those questions and constantly revise their answers.

In the meantime, Washington was equipped with a handful of advisors, the ragtag remnants of an army, no judiciary system, a Congress that was still straggling into town, a staggering war debt, and his personal reputation. Before the end of Washington's first term, the backcountry careened near civil war, and competing philosophies of government and political economy gelled into bitterly antagonistic political parties. By the end of his second term, one foreign war had been narrowly averted and another loomed on the horizon.

CONCEPTIONS OF POLITICAL ECONOMY IN THE NEW REPUBLIC

Most free Americans believed that the success of the republic depended ultimately on the political virtue of its citizens. By political virtue, they meant the essential characteristics of good republican citizens, characteristics they associated with economic life. When people grew too wealthy and accustomed to luxury, many Americans believed, they grew lazy and were willing to support corrupt governments for their own selfish purposes. Poverty, on the other hand, led to desperation, riots, and anarchy. What kind of economic life supported a middle course, encouraging both personal ambition and an abiding interest in the common good? What kinds of work and property, and what levels of commerce expressed the correct balance of interests?

Labor, Property, and Independence

The answers that individual Americans gave to these questions reflected the circumstances and aspirations of their own lives. In 1790, 97 percent of free Americans lived in nuclear households (parents and children) on farms or in rural villages, where they produced their own food, clothes, tools, and furnishings. Only three percent of the free population lived in cities (see Table 8–1), renting their dwellings and dependent on wages for their living. A tiny fraction made up the merchant families and landed proprietors whose livelihoods depended on extensive commercial transactions.

For most citizens, then, republican virtue was rooted in the land, and particularly in the working farm. This rural way of life emphasized private ownership of property, personal labor, and self-reliance. In *Letters From an American Farmer* (1782), J. Hector St. John de Crevecoeur had identified the new nation as "a people of cultivators scattered over an immense territory . . . animated with the spirit of an industry that is unfettered and unrestrained, because each person works for himself." Jefferson had echoed this view in his *Notes on the State of Virginia* (1785): "Those who labor in the earth are the chosen people of God, if ever he had a chosen people, whose breasts He has made His peculiar deposit for substantial and genuine virtue."

The ideal of self-sufficiency resided not simply in farming, but more specifically in owning the property one farmed. The ownership of land enabled people to achieve self-sufficiency in the present, and also opened the prospect of self-sufficiency for future generations.

This emphasis on labor and the private ownership of land did not mean that rural Americans disparaged all forms of manufacturing and trade. Most rural households were tied to villages where farming families bought, sold, and bartered with independent craftspeople for what they could not produce. Even in the backcountry village of Hallowell (in the later state of Maine), for example, neighbors depended on midwife Martha Ballard to birth their children and on her husband

TABLE 8–1

Americans in 1790: Population 3,929,000					
Northeast		**North Central**		**South**	
Whites	1,901,000	Whites	50,000	Whites	1,271,000
African Americans	67,000	African Americans	1,000	African Americans	690,000
Urban	160,000	Urban	0	Urban	42,000
Rural	1,807,000	Rural	51,000	Rural	1,919,000
				Free African Americans	58,000
				African-American Slaves	700,000

*In 1789, most Americans lived in the countryside and considered farming the activity most likely to pro-
duce political virtue in the new republic. As this illustration suggests, by "farming" Americans meant not
simple subsistence, but a division of the land into cultivated, privately owned (and at least partly commercial) property.*

to survey their land and saw their trees into lumber. Even Jefferson, far to the south,
who loathed the "workshops" of Europe, conceded that "carpenters, masons,
smiths" were essential to an agrarian way of life.

American citizens embraced international as well as local commerce as a component of republican political economy. Jefferson considered overseas trade essential to rural virtue, because it gave Americans access to manufactured goods
without the scourge of industrialization. As trade with Britain improved and
European demand for American agricultural products climbed, rural Americans
grew convinced that the success of the new nation required a booming free international commerce (see Table 8–2).

Even though most farmers viewed commerce as part of a good republican economy, they were suspicious of the vast revenues enjoyed by large merchants and landowners. This suspicion had many origins. Many of the great landed proprietors and large
merchants had laid the foundations of their fortunes before the Revolution, with the
help of the Crown. In Boston, the wealthy merchant families who made up 10 percent
of the population controlled 65 percent of the wealth of the city, while the poorest
one-third of the population owned less than one percent of the wealth.

Now, at the birth of the republic, urban elites continued to dominate the rural
economy. Great proprietors controlled the most precious commodity of the countryside, land. They hired surveyors to stake their claims, refused to sell homesteads in
favor of charging high rents, and threw squatters off the land. Both large landowners
and merchants tended to support strong governments, which meant higher taxes.

Farmers, small shopkeepers, landless settlers, and craftworkers saw these
sources of income ("rents, money at interest, salaries, and fees") as the moral equivalent of theft; in contrast, they viewed labor as the central act of independence and
the only authentic claim to the ownership of physical property. "[N]o person can
possess property without laboring," farmer and tavernkeeper William Manning
emphasized, "unless he get it by force or craft, fraud or fortune, out of the earnings
of others." Manning viewed this distinction between "those that labor for a living

TABLE 8–2

Sources of Federal Revenue, 1790–1799		
	Tariffs	Internal Taxes	Other (Including Sale of Public Lands)
1790–1791	$4,399,000	—	$ 10,000
1792	3,443,000	$209,000	17,000
1793	4,255,000	338,000	59,000
1794	4,801,000	274,000	356,000
1795	5,588,000	338,000	188,000
1796	6,568,000	475,000	1,334,000
1797	7,550,000	575,000	563,000
1798	7,106,000	644,000	150,000
1799	6,610,000	779,000	157,000

Source: Curtis P. Nettels, The Emergence of a National Economy, 1775–1815 (White Plains, NY: Holt, Rinehart, and Winston, 1962), p. 221.

and those who get one without laboring—or, as they are generally termed, the Few and the Many"—as "the great dividing line" of society.

Unsurprisingly, the "independent Lords" saw matters differently. Merchants and landed proprietors agreed that republican virtue resided in labor, but they meant commercial labor, which opened markets and expanded trade. Commerce, they believed, especially large-scale commerce, nurtured ambition and daring, taught discipline, and contributed new wealth to the community as a whole. Alexander Hamilton, the first Secretary of the Treasury of the new nation, was a chief proponent of this view. Born in the West Indies, he was raised by his mother, Rachel, a shopkeeper, who died when he was 13. Hamilton then entered the merchant firm of Beekman and Cruger as a clerk, eventually proving himself so valuable that Cruger paid for his college education. These experiences taught Hamilton that the merchant class (traders, investors, and financiers who risked their private means to generate new wealth, new markets, and new ideas) best embodied the qualities needed in republican citizens.

Just as farmers viewed merchants and financiers with distrust, so wealthy merchants and proprietors often regarded Americans of the middling and laboring ranks as their inferiors. The mass of the people were undisciplined and gullible, Hamilton believed. Vulnerable to the deceptions of fanatics and demagogues, they required proper leadership.

Large merchants and great proprietors were contemptuous of their back-country compatriots, whom they tagged "yahoos" and "clodpoles." In the eyes of more affluent citizens, the rude huts of homesteaders, their barefoot children, and their diets of beans, potatoes, and coarse bread all signaled not the hardships of settlement, but rather the laziness of the settlers. The merchants and proprietors also disliked the casualness with which country people treated debt. Rural people conducted trade in a combination of barter, cash, and promissory notes, with payments constantly renegotiated in terms of the goods, services, or whatever paper money might be at hand. As their creditors, merchants and proprietors needed timely payment, preferably in hard currency, to pay off their own debts, make new investments, or arrange long-distance transactions.

The Status of Slaves, Women, and Native Americans

Thomas Jefferson observed that "Dependence begets subservience and venality, suffocates the germ of virtue, and prepares fit tools for the design of ambition." At the republic's founding, nevertheless, most of its inhabitants (slaves, married free women, and children) were legal "dependents" who owned neither their own labor nor its products. Moreover, most citizens viewed Native Americans as incapable of the industry required for republican citizenship.

Slavery was a thriving institution in the United States in 1789. Of a population of 3.9 million, an estimated 700,000 (or roughly 18 percent) were enslaved. In large areas of Virginia and South Carolina, slaves made up at least half of the population. Moreover, although slavery was a predominantly southern institution, it was not yet unique to the South. In 1789 northerners still owned more than 30,000 slaves and northern merchants remained active in the slave trade. Most white Americans denied that hard work produced republican virtue in slaves. They argued that because slaves could not own the property they produced, slaves' labor could never lead to self-reliance or the stake in the public order essential to citizenship. This view was rife with contradictions. As Thomas Jefferson, himself a slaveowner, pointed out in *Notes on the State of Virginia*, slavery undermined the ambition of slaveowners. "[I]n a warm climate, no man will labor for himself who can make another labor for him," Jefferson wrote. Even more fundamentally, if slaves were incapable of virtue simply because of their status as slaves, then surely the institution of slavery was itself unrepublican.

By 1789, many northerners had come to oppose the institution of slavery. Vermont banned it in its 1777 state constitution, and the Massachusetts Supreme Court ruled in the early 1780s that slavery was contrary to its state constitution. In the 1780s, Pennsylvania, Connecticut, and Rhode Island all instituted measures for gradual abolition. Free property-owning African-American males enjoyed the right to vote in some northern states in the first years of the republic.

Even in the North, however, slavery died slowly. New York passed an emancipation act in 1799, and New Jersey did so in 1804. Meanwhile, regional opposition to slavery did not prevent northern states from ratifying a national constitution that permitted slavery and protected the international slave trade until 1808. In 1793, Congress passed a national Fugitive Slave Act, requiring that Americans everywhere return escaped slaves to their owners.

For most white northerners, moreover, opposition to slavery did not amount to a belief in the equality of African Americans. All across the northern states, white craftsmen refused to work in shops that employed free African Americans, white passengers refused to ride in stagecoaches alongside them, and landlords refused to rent them any but the worst housing. Scattered early antislavery societies challenged these attitudes and behaviors. A 1789 petition signed by Benjamin Franklin, president of the Pennsylvania Society for the Abolition of Slavery, called on Philadelphians to oppose slavery and to join to help free African Americans obtain employment and education. Still, even many white opponents of slavery doubted that emancipated slaves could survive in American society. The anonymous author of the antislavery tract *Tyrannical Libertymen: A Discourse on Negro-Slavery in the United States* (published in New Hampshire in 1795) argued that during the transition to freedom, younger slaves should be held in "a state of dependence and discipline," after which they should be resettled in the territories. Older slaves should be shipped to Africa.

Although most Americans believed free white women to be citizens in some general sense, women labored under severe legal disabilities and social prejudices. Under the English common law principle of *coverture*, a married woman subsumed her separate legal identity under that of her husband. Although some individual women (usually wealthy women who had access to special legal measures) did own property in their own names, as a category married women could not own property or wages, could not enter into contracts, and were not the legal guardians of their own children. The abolition of primogeniture and the practice of giving eldest sons a double portion did improve daughters' inheritance prospects, and reformed divorce laws enabled women to obtain legal separations more easily. Still, most women lost control of their property when they married and took little property other than their own clothing in divorce.

Social prejudice also made it difficult for most women to earn a living. Women had always provided an important part of the livelihood of their households, and that contribution was even more essential in the hard economic years after the war. But the more lucrative male crafts and professions were closed to them, and most working women struggled to make ends meet.

Women also faced a broad social bias against the idea of female autonomy. As the *Apollo Magazine* put it in 1795, the exemplary woman married and asked no more than that "Her good man [was] happy and her Infants clean." Many Americans viewed women as incapable of "substantial and genuine virtue" and given to timid and irrational behavior. "Male and female," Thomas Paine had written in *Common Sense* in 1776, "are the distinctions of nature."

Somewhat contradictorily, American authors of the late eighteenth century were fond of claiming that societies could be evaluated based on the status of (white) women, which reflected the progress of "civilization." This belief helped provoke a lively discussion of whether the new nation could really consider itself free if women were excluded from the polity. The debate was punctuated in 1792 by the publication of Englishwoman Mary Wollstonecraft's controversial *Vindication of the Rights of Woman*, which insisted that women were educated to be vain and frivolous. Their inability to function as good citizens, she argued, was thus a construction of society, not an expression of their natures.

Although slaves (and, by extension, African Americans generally) and most free women were viewed as incapable of fulfilling the demands of republican citizenship, they were nonetheless perceived as a part of society and participants in the economy. In contrast, most white Americans viewed Native Americans as outsiders who occupied land white settlers wanted for themselves and embodied a way of life seen as the opposite of the political economy required for a republic. White Americans

The frontispiece of the September 1792, Philadelphia Lady's Magazine reflected the importance of Wollstonecraft's Vindication of the Rights of Women in the United States. Here, "The Genius of the Ladies Magazine, accompanied by the Genius of Emulation [Ambition] ... approaches Liberty, and ... presents her with a copy of the Rights of Woman."

saw Indians as "spontaneous products of nature" who survived (as Thomas Jefferson wrote to James Madison in 1787) altogether "without government" and subsisted instinctively through simple hunting and gathering. White Americans pronounced Native Americans wasteful, "lazy," and hostile to "civilization." In fact, Indians did improve the land and engage in commerce. The fur trade with Native Americans had provided Europeans with their first economic foothold in eastern North America, and most eastern Indians lived in fairly settled agricultural communities. The town of Kekionga ("Miami Town") illustrated the vibrancy of Indian economies in the late eighteenth century. Kekionga was strategically located east of Lake Erie on the portage of the Maumee and Wabash Rivers, near a British fort. The village was surrounded by huge cornfields and vegetable gardens, supported large herds of cattle, and accommodated guests of all backgrounds and purposes. Residents and visitors bargained furs, tools, quills, beads, animals, food, and services.

Native Americans did live under systematic forms of governance, although those systems were less centralized than the new government of the United States. Most Indian communities identified their leaders through consensus rather than formal balloting. Councils met as needed and policy was implemented through the personal authority of leaders and the willingness of others to follow them. Over the years, Native Americans had shared land and resources, reconciled differences, sustained elaborate and long-distance trade relations, and supported powerful intertribal confederacies. Where native people differed from Americans of European descent was in the political economy that supported and constituted civilization. Eastern Woodland and Great Lakes Indians did not share Euro-American views on the importance of privately owned property. Few Indian societies valued material accumulation for its own sake. Instead, they encouraged gift giving as a mark of rank. White American society seemed to native people to be driven by an "insatiable avarice" that clouded the heart and distorted the mind.

Native Americans were especially offended at the European idea that the land itself could constitute property, to be bought, sold, and possessed by individuals. In 1799, American agent Benjamin Hawkins reported that the mere mention of selling land to settle a debt "excites very disagreeable emotions" among the Creeks. Indians

This 1790 drawing suggests the complex economic arrangement of the Maumee River Indian towns and the diverse groups that occupied the towns.

understood that their way of life depended on preserving the land uncolonized. As the Hallowing King of the Lower Creek village Cowetas put it in 1789, " . . . they [white settlers] never mean to let their foot rest; our lands are our life and breath; if we part with them, we part with our blood. We must fight for them."

FACTIONS AND ORDER IN THE NEW GOVERNMENT

Concerns about the political economy of the new nation focused not only on the character of citizens, but also on the character and operation of government. Here, too, questions of property loomed large. In *The Federalist* No. 10, James Madison had argued that the most common cause of internal conflict in a nation was "the various and unequal distribution of property," arising from selfish interests on the state and local level. He felt that an important benefit of the new central government would be its capacity "to break and control" provincial interests. Most state ratifying conventions had expressed just the opposite worry, however: that a strong central government would become the tool of the wealthy for personal gain.

The States and the Bill of Rights

Although they had ratified the Constitution, the state conventions had formally suggested more than 200 changes in the document, possibly to be added as a bill of rights. Many Federalists opposed the idea of a bill of rights: If the Constitution itself did not protect liberty and property, no appended list of rights would help. Originally James Madison had agreed with this view but by the time he ran for the House of Representatives, he pledged that his first priority would be to secure additional safeguards.

Within a month of Washington's inauguration, Madison set about making good on his promise. By no means did all of the state proposals deal directly with questions of property. For example, the ratifying conventions were adamant about the need for freedom of religion and freedom of the press. The state proposals betrayed a fear that the new federal government would seek to amass power against the interests and freedom of individual citizens. To prevent this, states proposed amendments to limit the power of Congress to levy taxes and to protect the right to bear arms, the right to trial by a jury, and the right against unreasonable search and seizure.

Madison never expected to incorporate all 200 of the state proposals in a bill of rights, and he never imagined that he could placate all of the groups critical of the Constitution. But he did believe that, with a few minor changes, moderate Antifederalists could be brought into sympathy with the new order. This goal of broadening moderate support for the Constitution guided Madison's selection of proposed amendments. He tended to reject proposals that altered the structure of the central government or strengthened the powers of the states at the expense of the federal government. Instead, Madison favored amendments that affirmed human rights in broad and abstract terms. The First Amendment protected citizens against congressional interference with freedom of religion, speech, the press, the right of assembly, and the right of petition. The Fourth Amendment protected the rights of citizens "to be secure in their persons, houses, papers, and effects, against unreasonable [government] searches and seizures." The Fifth, Sixth, Seventh, and Eighth Amendments laid down the rights of citizens accused of crimes. The Ninth and Tenth Amendments addressed rights not specifically enumerated in the Constitution. The Ninth affirmed that the Constitution's silence on a specific right of the people "shall not be construed" as a denial of that right, and the Tenth ambiguously reserved all rights not delegated to the new government "to the States respectively, or to the people."

Congress eventually sent 12 amendments to the states for ratification. Of these, two were rejected: one addressing the process for changing the compensation of Congress (finally adopted in 1992 as the Twenty-Seventh Amendment) and one covering representation. The remaining ten amendments were declared in force on December 15, 1791.

Congress Begins Its Work

Although George Washington did not take the oath of office until April 30, his term began on March 4, 1789. By the time Washington was inaugurated, then, Congress was already in session. It had not made a promising start: Only 13 members of the House of Representatives and eight senators were on hand when the first Congress convened.

Among Congress's first task was deciding what the president should be called, a purely symbolic matter that revealed the sensibilities of the new republic. Some members of the Senate thought the executive officers of the republic should have impressive titles to demonstrate that the new nation was "civilized." A Senate committee recommended, "His Highness the President of the United States of America, and Protector of the Liberties." But the House argued that the Senate's suggestion smacked of aristocratic pretension. In the end, the House insisted simply on "The President of the United States."

Meanwhile, the Congress approved a series of official advisors to the president (the cabinet). Washington's first administration reflected both his own close circle of friends and the political clout of the large states. The president was from Virginia, the most populous state, as were his Secretary of State, Thomas Jefferson, and his Attorney General, Edmund Randolph. For his Secretary of the Treasury he chose former aide-de-camp Alexander Hamilton of New York. Washington's Vice President (John Adams), his Secretary of War (Henry Knox), and his Postmaster General (Samuel Osgood) were from Massachusetts. The Constitution had specified the existence of a third branch of government, a judiciary, but had not offered much of a blueprint for its structure. The Constitution also gave to the federal court systematic power over "all cases, in law and equity, arising under this Constitution, the laws of the United States, and treaties made." Given such a wide compass, Congress might have created a federal system that dominated state courts. Recalling the high-handedness of British courts, however, Congress was loath to place great power in the least representative branch of government. In September, Congress passed the Judiciary Act of 1789, which created a federal court system with limited power. Under its first chief justice, John Jay, the Supreme Court remained a minor branch of government.

Political Economy and Political Parties

As Congress deliberated the structure of government, Secretary of the Treasury Alexander Hamilton turned to the problem of financial solvency. His recommendations to Congress concerning the fiscal operation of the new nation soon polarized views on the political economy.

The first challenge was to raise money for the current expenses of the government. Hamilton proposed that Congress place a tariff on imported goods and the foreign ships carrying them. The Tariff Act of 1789 passed easily. In the coming years the federal government would depend on tariffs for the vast majority of its funds (see Table 8–2).

Hamilton was also eager for the United States to pay off the enormous debt left over from the American Revolution. He advised that the federal government should guarantee the payment of all remaining state and national debts incurred in the Revolution. Those debts existed in the form of script and paper money the states and Continental Congress had used to purchase goods and services during the war. Hamilton suggested that the national government replace all of these obligations dollar-for-dollar with new federal bonds. To fund the plan, he proposed that the government sell additional bonds, the interest from which could be used only to pay off the interest and principal on the debt.

Madison and Jefferson were alarmed. Most southern states had paid their debts by 1790. Federal assumption would force them to help pay northern debts as well, in effect rewarding northern states for being slow to meet their financial obligations. Although many members of Congress disliked Hamilton's proposal, other issues eventually led to its passage. Southerners were also unhappy about the possibility that the nation's capital (temporarily located in New York) might be moved permanently to Philadelphia, preferring a site on the Potomac River in Virginia. At last representatives struck a compromise: Hamilton got his debt plan, and southerners got the nation's capital. The following December, Hamilton asked for a series of new taxes, including one on spirits, to generate revenue. This excise tax became law in March 1791.

Hamilton next recommended the creation of a national bank to manage fiscal functions. He saw the bank as ensuring a stable currency and enabling the government to mobilize large amounts of capital for development, two activities he considered essential to an expanding commercial economy. The bank would be chartered by Congress to collect, hold, and pay out government receipts; would hold the new federal bonds and oversee their payment; would issue currency; and would be backed up by government bonds.

The bank proposal passed Congress against the opposition of Madison, Jefferson, and other Virginians, who viewed the bank as an extralegal structure to support the interests of merchants and financiers against "the republican interest." When Washington asked his cabinet for guidance, Jefferson advised the president to veto the bill on the grounds that the Constitution gave the federal government no expressed authority to create such an institution, a position known as strict constructionism. Hamilton countered that every specified power in the Constitution implied "a right to employ all the means requisite . . . to the attainment" of that power. In granting the federal government the responsibility to coin and regulate money, pass and collect taxes, pay debts, and "make all laws which shall be necessary and proper" to these ends, the Constitution implied the power to create a bank. In the end, Washington accepted Hamilton's position and signed the bank bill.

Hamilton's final major recommendation to Congress was that the federal government subsidize domestic manufacturing. Jefferson and Madison were now convinced that the republic was being sold out to the interests of speculators and financiers. Hamilton had been using a Philadelphia newspaper, John Fenno's *Gazette of the United States* (founded in 1789), to promote his views. In October 1791, Jefferson and Madison prevailed on their friend Philip Freneau to come to Philadelphia to establish a newspaper favorable to their position, and Madison began to use Freneau's *National Gazette* to publish a series of essays in which he framed the rationale for the permanent necessity of political parties in a republic. There would always be schemers who placed self-interest above the good of the whole, and true republicans would always be forced to organize against them. Parties, according to Madison, arose in a struggle of the true "republican interest" against dangerous conspirators, a struggle of "good" against "evil." He identified the two groups as "Republicans" and "Anti-Republicans."

In late 1792 and early 1793, sympathizers with Jefferson and Madison became known as Democratic Republicans, after the Democratic Republican Societies, which opposed a strong central government and vowed to maintain vigilance against the "monied interests" who threatened "liberty and equality." The societies included some common people, but most of the known members were from middling and even prosperous families. Washington blamed the societies for stirring up trouble in the backcountry and labeled their members irresponsible men who "disseminated, from an ignorance or perversion of facts, suspicions, jealousies and accusations of the whole government."

Hamilton and his supporters were no more tolerant of disagreement than were the Democratic Republicans. In the election of 1792, allies of Hamilton identified themselves as supporters of Washington's administration, advocates of the policies of the secretary of the treasury, or, increasingly, as Federalists, using the name to suggest their abiding commitment to union and the new government. As late as the election of 1794 most candidates resisted formal party alignment, and congressional voting patterns showed little sense of "party" discipline. There were several reasons for this, including the tendency of most citizens (including many of the partisans themselves) to associate political parties with corruption and a loss of independence. By 1796, however, the lines had become clearly drawn. The jumble of labels had sorted itself out to Democratic Republicans and Federalists, and congressional voting patterns revealed a distinct tendency to vote on one side or the other.

Making a Civic Culture

Through the young parties, Americans formed and debated their views of republican government and organized their political identities as citizens of a new nation. But the process of forming a civic culture was not restricted to overtly political settings. The process occurred simultaneously in numerous other social institutions, many of which had existed, in some form, before the Revolution.

America's mushrooming press not only communicated information from place to place but also bridged some differences in outlook between different parts of the new nation. By 1790 the new republic had 106 newspapers; by 1800, more than 200. Much of the content of these newspapers was strictly local, but editors published official government documents and reprinted articles from other papers. In the process, they created a reading experience of the nation as a coherent whole. The addition of numerous articles reprinted from European papers implied a corresponding American national identity.

In addition to newspapers, Americans purchased printed sermons and tracts, magazines, and novels. The magazines carried essays, poems, dramas, anecdotes, and articles on travel and the sciences. Many of these were reprinted from European sources, but some, like Judith Sargent Murray's "The Gleaner" series (first published in *Massachusetts Magazine* in 1792–1794), were original attempts to envision an ideal American society. The 1790s also saw the beginnings of an indigenous fictional literature. In 1789, William Hill Brown published *The Power of Sympathy*, often considered the first genuinely American novel because some of its content was based on contemporary events in Boston. Susannah Rowson's historical novel *Rachel and Reuben* (1798) imagined the lives of the fictional heirs of Columbus, and Charles Brockden Brown chose the countryside outside of Philadelphia as the setting for *Weiland* (1798), a tale of religious zealotry and the fallibility of human reason. In Connecticut, a group of poets known collectively as the Hartford Wits (Federalist in sympathy) produced political satires that celebrated New England as the model for national order and self-discipline.

Regional and national news was easiest to come by in the cities, but a variety of information sources linked city to backcountry and region to region. Newspapers and periodicals found their way out into the countryside and comparatively high literacy rates produced a reading audience that went beyond urban elites. Rural political philosopher William Manning, who had less than six months of formal education, described himself as "a constant reader of public newspapers." Where papers did not reach, travelers, itinerant peddlers, and preachers served as conduits of information and opinion. In Virginia, peddlers organized mercantile fairs that brought together large groups of people to swap news as well as make deals. The early republic was also an era of school building, primarily academies to prepare sons for professions or university training and daughters to participate in the discussions (if not the formal electoral politics) of republican society. More than 350 academies for females opened between 1790 and 1830, most of them directed by women.

Citizens also formed societies intended to provide relief to the needy in their communities. A group of prosperous Philadelphians established an almshouse to improve the care and housing of the poor and to teach them the values of industry and a penitentiary to reform criminals by isolating them from one another's influence. African-American citizens in Philadelphia organized The Free African Society to assist destitute members of their community. Jewish organizations founded in New York in the late eighteenth century provided aid for medical care, food, shelter, and burial costs for the city's small Jewish community.

To these associations were added a variety of occupational and manufacturing societies. Masters and journeymen formed craft associations to promote their interests. In 1791, to promote his economic plans, Alexander Hamilton and his assistant secretary, Tench Coxe, formed the Society for Establishing Useful Manufacturers, a joint-stock corporation intended to demonstrate the economic virtues of investment cooperation between the private sector and the government.

In the early years of the republic, masters (presumably acting on behalf of their workers) organized associations intended to share information, lobby for favorable government policies, and protect the integrity of the craft. The members of this shop belonged to the Society of Master Sailmakers (1797).

A State and Its Boundaries

By transferring to the Confederation almost all of the area west of the Appalachians to the Mississippi River and south to the Gulf of Mexico, the Treaty of Paris had created an empire with vast subject territories. The Northwest Territory was already organized for national settlement (see Chapter 7, "Creating a New Nation"). South of the Ohio River valley lay territories where the western land claims of individual states had not yet been fully ceded and where Spain still claimed territories. Most white Americans viewed these areas as an inexhaustible reservoir of land that would ensure propertied independence for future generations, preventing the great disparities of wealth and power that characterized European society.

The Problem of Authority in the Backcountry

For all of its symbolic importance as the reservoir of republican order, the backcountry had so far been a setting for constant conflict among owners and settlers and between Indians and Americans.

Americans fought over land prices and rights of ownership. Seeking quick revenue, the government sold large tracts of land to speculators and large proprietors, some of whom were federal officials. For example, Alexander Hamilton and Secretary of War Henry Knox were both silent partners in the huge Macomb Purchase in New York. Proprietors subdivided their tracts for sale, but the resulting prices were often too high for average settlers, who squatted on lands and claimed the rights of possession and improvement, much to the annoyance of the legal owners.

Despite their differences, squatters, proprietors, and governments shared the assumption that the land was theirs to fight over. The Treaty of Paris had contained no acknowledgment of Indian claims, and treaty promises that Indians would be left in peace in exchange for land cessions proved illusory. By the time Washington took office in 1789, the backcountries were in an uproar. Undisciplined federal troops and freebooting state militias criss-crossed western lands in search of a fight, often attacking neutral or sympathetic Indian villages. Betrayed and angry, Indians banded together in loose confederations, retaliating against settlers and striking alliances with the British and Spanish.

By 1789, the lives and cultures of Eastern Woodland and Great Lakes nations had been deeply altered by the westward pressure of white settlement. In the North, a group of Iroquoian villages, the battered remnants of a once-powerful confederation, traded large tracts of land for promises of security and called on the tribes of the Northwest Territory to do the same. However, these peoples refused to compromise with the whites and effectively shut down settlement north of the Ohio River valley. In the South, the Creeks, trapped between oncoming white settlement and the Native American nations of the Mississippi River valley, allied with militant Cherokees to keep the Georgia, Tennessee, and Kentucky frontiers ablaze with war parties.

There were additional reasons for Washington to worry about order in the western territories. By 1789, Spain was actively luring United States settlers into New Spain at the foot of the Mississippi River. It was a strategy designed to weaken the loyalty of the West to the new United States government. In the Great Lakes region, meanwhile, Great Britain hung onto the string of forts it had promised to give up as a part of the Treaty of Paris. Many Americans believed that Britain was biding its time to regain control of the lands south of the Great Lakes.

All of this turmoil took its toll in the East. The inability of the national government to control Native Americans angered states, would-be settlers, and the small business people who expected to profit from settlement. Landowners complained that their property rights were not being protected, and small settlers complained of favoritism in land distribution. Understanding that not only external relations, but also the domestic authority of the federal government was at stake, Washington turned immediately to the problem of the backcountry. His policy was twofold. On the one hand, working with Secretary of War Henry Knox, Washington sought to bring consistency and a greater degree of fairness to Indian policy. On the other hand, he used the territories to demonstrate the power of the federal government.

Taking the Land: Washington's Indian Policy

Less than a month after assuming office, Washington submitted to Congress a report on Indian affairs authored by Henry Knox. Knox argued that the United States should acknowledge a residual Indian "right in the soil" not affected by a treaty between Britain and the United States. That right could be extinguished, Knox insisted, only by some separate dealing with the Indians, and he recommended that the United States purchase Indian claims to disputed lands. At Knox's suggestion, in 1789, Congress appropriated $20,000 for negotiations.

In part, Knox and Washington saw this policy shift as required by justice, but they were also trying to avoid the costs of having to take the Northwest Territory by war. A change in tactics did not constitute a change in ultimate goals, however. Although Knox undertook to keep white settlers outside treaty boundaries, his policy did not recognize the Native Americans' right to refuse to negotiate. Seeking to bolster the authority of the national government, Knox argued that Indian bands were not communities within state borders, but rather foreign entities, on the level of nations. Indian relations were therefore properly the business of the federal government. Knox in effect declared Indians aliens on their own lands, lending the weight of federal policy to American inclinations to see the Indians as the ultimate outsiders.

By 1790 continuing troubles in the Northwest Territory convinced Washington that the federal government had to project a military presence into that region. His first two efforts were dismal failures. In 1790 a combined Native American force led by the Miami war leader Little Turtle routed the United States Army, led by General Josiah Harmar. The next year a much smaller party crushed the troops of territorial Governor General Arthur St. Clair. To stem the resulting crisis of confidence in the new government, in 1792 Washington sought and received congressional authorization to build a "strong coercive force" (bigger, better paid, and better trained) in the Northwest Territory.

To lead the army, Washington turned to a 47-year-old infantry officer noted for his aggressive tactics, Pennsylvanian Major General Anthony Wayne. By the time Wayne found the Indians in 1794 at Fallen Timbers, near the west end of Lake Erie, his army numbered more than 3,000. Facing a force of only 400 warriors, Wayne claimed a decisive victory.

According to the Treaty of Greenville, signed August 3, 1795, Indians ceded two-thirds of the later state of Ohio and a piece of present-day Indiana. In return, they received annual federal payments ranging from $1,000 to $500 per band. The annuities bought the United States influence within Indian communities and rendered the Indians more economically dependent. In addition, the treaty tried to convert the Indians to white ideas of work and economy by offering to pay the annuities in the form of farm equipment, cows, and pigs.

Indian efforts at confederacy proved less successful in the South, where deep fractures existed within the Cherokee and Creek nations. At the Treaty of New York in 1790, Creek leaders agreed to exchange lands belonging to the entire Creek nation for annual payments from the federal government and promises of U.S. protection for their remaining lands. A faction of the Cherokee nation entered into a similar pact at Holston in 1791.

These internal disputes weakened Indian military efforts. When the government proved unable to stem the tides of settlers flowing into the future state of Tennessee, younger Creeks, Chickamaugas, Cherokees, and Shawnees repudiated the treaties and attacked the American community at Buchanan's Station, near Nashville, Tennessee, planning to proceed south to Nashville itself. Older Cherokee leaders, fearing reprisals, betrayed the plan, and the assault was thrown back. United States Indian commissioners used a series of military victories to coerce new land cessions from the southeastern nations and to insinuate white customs more deeply into Indian cultures, especially that of the Cherokees.

Resistance continued, in both the North and the South, but dreams of a pan-Indian confederation were temporarily stymied. They would be resurrected at the turn of the century by two Shawnees, already young men by the time of Wayne's victory. One, Tenskwatawa, would later become an important prophet. The other, his half-brother, was named Tecumseh.

Western Lands and Eastern Politics: The Whiskey Rebellion

The West posed a domestic, as well as an external, threat to the federal government. By 1791 western settlers were disenchanted with the seeming inability of the government to protect their interests and had fallen into the practice of disregarding federal policy. They trespassed onto Indian lands, dispatched unorganized militias to enforce their claims, and traded illegally with Indians. In 1791, western Pennsylvanians took the step of repudiating the authority of the federal government explicitly, setting the stage for a direct confrontation.

The trouble began with the passage of Hamilton's excise tax. Living in an area perfectly situated to function as a gateway to the Northwest Territory, residents of western Pennsylvania anticipated an economic bonanza from free-flowing westward migration and were frustrated with the failure of the government to secure safe passage into the Ohio River valley. Hamilton's tax on spirits gave their simmering anger another focus, the question of republican fairness. Many Americans regarded excise taxes (internal taxes on specific goods) as unfair in principle. This particular tax seemed targeted specifically at western farmers, who found it easier to transport their grain in liquid than in bushel form.

Popular protests had begun within months of the tax's passage, and they intensified at each new report of the Army's failure in the Northwest Territory (efforts the tax was supposed to fund). Western Pennsylvanians dug in their heels, vowing that they would not pay the tax and calling on citizens to treat the collectors with "contempt." Washington took the challenge seriously, and in August 1794 he sent 13,000 troops into western Pennsylvania. In the face of this show of force, the rebellion fizzled, but the government drove its point (and power) home. Remaining protestors were roughly rounded up and held in open pens; 20 men were returned to Philadelphia to face treason charges, and two were sentenced to death. Washington eventually pardoned both, but he had proven the authority of federal law in the new republic.

The citizens of western Pennsylvania were not without sympathizers, however. The congressional elections of 1792 were fought as contests between the policies of Alexander Hamilton and those of the self-named "republican interest," many of whom identified the settlers as defenders of republican virtue.

AMERICA IN THE TRANSATLANTIC COMMUNITY

Still reeling from internal conflicts, the United States was soon confronted by external challenges as well. On February 1, 1793, France (the sister republic of the new United States) and Spain declared war on Great Britain and Holland. Americans were divided over their proper response. Many Democratic Republicans (among them Jefferson and Madison) had been avid supporters of the French Revolution and viewed with horror the possibility that America might join with its former colonial master against a fellow republic. Hamiltonians, meanwhile, looked with disdain on the social and political chaos of France and believed that friendly relations with Great Britain best served American interests. Searching for a middle ground, President Washington endorsed neutrality. Then, on May 16, Edmond Charles Genêt, citizen of France, arrived in Philadelphia, now the nation's temporary capital.

Between France and England

Genêt came to America as the minister of a French republic that saw its destiny as inextricably joined to that of the United States. Not only was the United States still formally allied with France, but the American Revolution had served as the model for the French.

France had several hopes for the Genêt mission. The revolutionary government believed that it was the destiny of the French republic to free the oppressed people of Europe from their tyrannous monarchs. As a part of this undertaking, Genêt was to incite the European colonies in the Americas to revolution. Genêt was also to press the United States for a new commercial treaty allowing French naval forces and privateers to rearm and provision themselves in American ports as they battled Great Britain on the seas. These hopes were not entirely fanciful. Impoverished as it was, the Washington administration had advanced money to help the new French government, and Washington had instructed the U.S. ambassador to France, Gouverneur Morris, to recognize the republic as the legitimate government of France. Also, many Americans would have been only too happy to see colonial rebellions throw Spain and England out of North America.

The French overestimated the lengths to which the American government would go to achieve that goal. Preferential treatment for French ships, either warships or commercial ships, could only strain relations between America and England. Barely able to muster a force to the northwest, President Washington was not about to risk a foreign war or to have tensions further inflamed on the nation's western borders. Washington considered Genêt's proposals reckless.

Many Americans, especially Jefferson, had welcomed Genêt warmly, and he might have believed that Washington's views did not represent the sentiments of Americans generally. Undeterred, he put into motion a series of actions that assumed essential American support for French goals. He authorized the refitting of a captured English ship, anchored in Philadelphia, which was intended for duty as a French privateer, and he encouraged efforts to organize American settlers in Kentucky to attack the Spanish.

Washington was furious. "Is the Minister of the French Republic to set the Acts of this Government at defiance, with impunity?" he fumed. Issuing a formal Proclamation of Neutrality, Washington disavowed Genêt and in August 1793 demanded that he be recalled. Disappointed by Washington's growing support of Federalist policies, Jefferson resigned as Secretary of State in December.

To the Brink of War

Even without Genêt's provocations, by 1794 tensions with Great Britain were high. To the old issues of unsettled Revolutionary War reparations and the British forts in the Northwest had been added new charges that the British Navy was harassing U.S. merchant ships.

Still, Washington sought to avoid confrontation. In spite of restrictions on British ports, U.S. shipping had been steadily expanding. Under these conditions, it was hard to argue that British policies were so injurious as to warrant the risk of a trade war. Washington dispatched Chief Justice of the Supreme Court John Jay as a special emissary to England to resolve outstanding issues between the two nations.

Although Great Britain at first had little interest in the mission, the heating up of French–British animosities enabled Jay to negotiate a treaty that reduced tensions between Britain and the United States. Britain agreed to open West Indies ports to some U.S. ships, and both countries agreed that (except for tonnage restrictions) their ships would receive equal treatment in each other's ports. They also agreed to establish boards of arbitration to set the boundary between Canada and the United States, and Britain promised to evacuate its forts in the Northwest by June 1, 1796.

Most Americans knew nothing about the provisions of Jay's Treaty until after it was approved, for the Senate debated it in secret. When Democratic Republicans learned of its contents and its ratification, they protested the concealed character of the deliberations and objected that the treaty would benefit the merchant class while taxing everyone to pay for its provisions. But public protest soon fizzled. News of Anthony Wayne's victory against the Great Lakes tribes cast the treaty's provisions for the evacuation of the British forts in a more positive light. Word followed that Thomas Pinckney had also concluded a treaty with Spain (see Map 8–1), opening the Mississippi River to U.S. navigation and permitting Americans to store goods duty-free in New Orleans. (Pinckney's Treaty also set the boundary between the United States and Florida at the 31st Parallel.) The treaty was a sign of Spanish weakness. Seeing the United States make peace with Britain, and fearful of an Anglo-American alliance, Spain resigned itself to the possibility of increased American encroachment across the river and sought peace with the new republic.

Taken together, Wayne's victory and Jay's and Pinckney's negotiations seemed at last to open the territories to settlement. Western land prices soared and the U.S. export trade boomed. By the time opponents in the House of Representatives tried to scuttle Jay's Treaty by denying the funds necessary to enforce it, popular sentiment had shifted to strong support for the treaty as an element of returning prosperity.

The Administration of John Adams

George Washington had been reluctant to serve a second term in office and had been convinced to do so when Jefferson and Hamilton argued that no one else could bring the young republic's fractious politics together. But Washington refused to run for a third term, and in 1796 the nation faced its first contested presidential election.

In his farewell address, published on September 19, 1796, Washington made clear his own essentially Federalist concern with social order and personal discipline. Having acknowledged the right of the people to alter their Constitution, he stressed the "duty of every individual to obey the established Government," until it

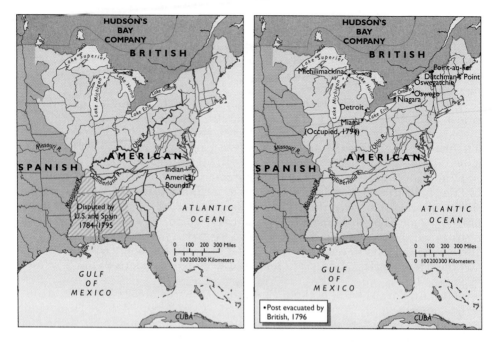

Map 8–1   Extension of United States National Territories, 1783 and 1795
The Treaty of Paris with Great Britain (1783) left the United States's borders with Spain (much of the western and southern boundaries) ambiguous. Those borders were clarified in the Pinckney Treaty with Spain (1795).

was changed "by an explicit and authentic act of the whole people." Sounding themes that would echo through the first half-century of the republic, he warned against unlawful "combinations and associations" with designs on the rightful "power of the people," an image that, 30 years later, would drive the emergence of Jacksonian democracy.

Led by Hamilton, Federalists put forward Vice President John Adams as their candidate. Adams had served in the Continental Congress, been a part of the committee to draft the Declaration of Independence, served as representative to France during the American Revolution, helped negotiate the peace treaty, and served two terms as vice president. Thomas Pinckney of South Carolina was their vice presidential choice. For president, Democratic Republicans supported former Secretary of State Thomas Jefferson, along with Madison, the most visible opponent of Hamilton. New Yorker Aaron Burr was intended as vice president.

The election of 1796 was not decided by popular majority. State legislatures chose two-fifths of the members of the Electoral College. Moreover, procedures in the Electoral College did not permit a distinction between votes for the office of president and vice president. The person who received the most electoral votes became president. The person who received the second highest number of electoral votes became vice president.

This procedure proved dangerously volatile and yielded unexpected results. While the Federalist Adams received a majority of electoral votes (71) and became president, but the Democratic Republican Jefferson received the second highest count (68 to Pinckney's 59) and became vice president.

As the view of Philadelphia's busy Market Street shows, social, commercial and political—"public" and "private"—life all commingled on the streets of the early republic's cities.

Benjamin Franklin once said of John Adams that he was "always an honest man, often a wise one, but sometimes, and in some things, absolutely out of his senses." Wise he might have been, and honest, but he was also cranky, defensive, and plagued by self-doubt. He was not the man to negotiate growing party rifts successfully. Many Federalists looked to Hamilton, rather than Adams, for direction, but any possibility for alliance between those two was dashed when Adams learned that Hamilton had considered supporting Pinckney for the presidency.

These party resentments formed the background against which Adams confronted an increasingly hostile relationship with France. Unsurprisingly, Franco-American relations had been harmed by the signing of Jay's Treaty, which seemed to France to ally America with England, and by the French practice of plundering American ships. Even before his inauguration on March 4, 1797, Adams began to entertain the possibility of sending a special envoy to France to resolve these issues. When Adams's cabinet objected, the president temporarily abandoned the plan. At the end of March, he learned that newly arrived American ambassador Charles Pinckney had been unceremoniously kicked out of France. The French foreign minister had informed Pinckney that the French government would "no longer recognize or receive" an ambassador from the United States. In this context, Adams returned to the idea of sending a mission to France. In the end, he appointed Elbridge Gerry, John Marshall, and Pinckney, who was still in Europe.

When the American mission arrived, French Foreign Minister Talleyrand let it be known that he expected a bribe for his willingness to talk. Arrangements of this sort were not uncommon in eighteenth-century European politics, but to the starched and circumspect Adams, the idea was abhorrent. He turned over the entire documentation of the affair to Congress, altering the papers only to the extent that he identified Talleyrand's agents by letters: W, X, Y, and Z.

The news of the so-called XYZ Affair came to a largely Federalist Congress, which immediately suspended commercial ties to France, empowered American ships to seize armed French vessels, and embarked on an expansion of the nation's military. But the Federalists also used the scandal to attack their political opponents. Insisting that pro-French influence was endangering the nation, in 1798 Congress passed the Alien and Sedition Acts, measures aimed at gagging the Democratic Republican opposition and preventing it from using the war issue to win the 1800 election. The acts required a 14-year naturalization period, empowered the president to deport any "suspicious" aliens, and established a broad definition of sedition, intended to stop all Democratic Republican criticism of the administration's policies.

The Alien and Sedition Acts backfired against the Federalists. The acts were so transparently partisan that individuals convicted under them became martyrs to the Democratic Republican cause. A Vermont congressman who published criticisms of administration policies was re-elected even as he served out his four-month jail term.

Although Democratic Republicans insisted that the acts were unconstitutional, they hesitated to challenge them in the Supreme Court, both because the court was dominated by Federalists and because Democratic Republicans did not want to set a precedent for giving the Supreme Court the power to rule on constitutionality. Instead, Madison and Jefferson encouraged the states to pass resolutions denouncing the Alien and Sedition Acts. Madison, who had since retired from Congress, authored a set of resolutions in Virginia affirming the rights of states to judge the constitutionality of federal laws. Jefferson, who was Vice President of the United States, framed a more militant set of resolutions for the Kentucky legislature, stating that states might declare federal laws they deemed unconstitutional to be "without force" within their state boundaries.

Jefferson and Madison likely expected that other states would rally to the support of the Virginia and Kentucky Resolves, but they did not. Rather, voters simply returned the Democratic Republicans to power in the election of 1800, and the acts expired in 1801.

Before retiring, the Federalist Congress got off one more shot at the Democratic Republicans. In January 1801, just as the session expired, Congress passed the Judiciary Act of 1801, which gave John Adams the power to expand the federal judiciary by appointing new judges, justices of the peace, attorneys, clerks, and marshals. Needless to say, he filled these positions with good Federalists, and then he left office.

CONCLUSION

George Washington died at Mount Vernon on December 14, 1799. In his retirement, as during his presidency, he had continued to worry that Americans lacked the judgment, restraint, and generosity of spirit to "act the part of good citizens."

Indeed, the first decade of the federal government's existence demonstrated that the love of liberty and the love of order sometimes gave rise to very different visions of what constituted "good" citizenship. Democratic Republicans fumed at what they saw as the liberties Federalists had taken with the Constitution. Federalists were convinced that Democratic Republicanism was tantamount to lawlessness. The 1790s had witnessed a steady escalation of suspicion and distrust, of which the Whiskey Rebellion, the Alien and Sedition Acts, and the Virginia and Kentucky Resolves had been striking illustrations. The political parties organized that fractious spirit but did little to defuse it. As Americans struggled to give shape to a republican political economy, Madison's deepest concerns about factionalism seemed justified. Liberty seemed to give rise to lawlessness and prosperity to greed.

CHRONOLOGY

1785	Thomas Jefferson's Notes on the State of Virginia is published
1789	George Washington inaugurated Congress approves the first cabinet Judiciary Act of 1789 Tariff Act of 1789 Henry Knox recommends new Indian policy ("rights in the soil") John Fenno founds Gazette of the United States William Hill Brown publishes The Power of Sympathy
1790	Alexander Hamilton's two-part Report on the Public Credit recommends federal assumption of debts and creation of national bank Assumption Act passes
1791	Excise Tax (including tax on whiskey) passes Washington signs bill creating first Bank of the United States Philip Freneau establishes National Gazette Hamilton's Report on the Encouragement of Manufactures recommends federal subsidies to manufacturing Bill of Rights ratified
1792	Whiskey Rebellion begins Judith Sargent Murray begins publication of "The Gleaner" essays in Massachusetts Magazine (published as book, 1798)
1793	Fugitive Slave Act Edmond Genêt arrives in the United States
1794	Battle of Fallen Timbers Washington sends 13,000 troops to end Whiskey Rebellion
1795	Jay's Treaty approved by Senate Treaty of Greenville Pinckney's Treaty
1796	John Adams elected president in the first contested election
1798	XYZ Affair Charles Brockden Brown publishes Alcuin Alien and Sedition Acts
1798–1799	Virginia and Kentucky Resolves
1800	Jefferson elected president
1801	Judiciary Act of 1801

Even in its quieter, less dramatic manifestations, the expanding presumption of liberty was changing the republic. As they experimented with the mechanisms of elections, gathered in taverns and shops to read the latest news, and pondered the seemingly endless wars in Europe, Americans were learning to embrace the possibilities of personal freedom and choice. In this spirit, voters elected Virginian Thomas Jefferson as the third president of the United States in 1800. Also in this spirit, another Virginian, a slave by the name of Gabriel, plotted his own road to freedom.

FURTHER READINGS

Harriet B. Applewhite and Darlene G. Levy, eds., *Women and Politics in the Age of the Democratic Revolution* (1993). This collection of essays by noted women's historians evaluates the impact of the eighteenth-century democratic revolutions on the political lives of women in Europe and North America.

Richard R. Beeman, *The Evolution of a Southern Backcountry: A Case Study of Lunenburg County, Virginia, 1746–1832* (1984). This history of a single county in Virginia offers a window into the ongoing social, economic, and political conflicts between wealthy planters and common farmers in revolutionary and postrevolutionary America, with a particular emphasis on the importance of religion in shaping ideas of authority and legitimacy in the South.

Michael Merrill and Sean Wilentz, eds., *The Key of Liberty: The Life and Democratic Writings of William Manning, "A Laborer," 1747–1814* (1993). This volume reprints writings of Massachusetts farmer, tavern owner, and political philosopher William Manning, along with a detailed and accessible introduction to Manning's life and the political culture of the early republic.

James Roger Sharp, *American Politics in the Early Republic: The New Nation in Crisis* (1993). An overview of the first decade of American politics, this study pays particular attention to the sharp conflicts that divided Republicans from Federalists and includes an especially insightful discussion of the election of 1800.

Wiley Sword, *President Washington's Indian War: The Struggle for the Old Northwest* (1985). Wiley traces the evolution of Washington and Knox's Indian policy in the Old Northwest from its origins in Confederation policies and practices to its eventual reliance on armed warfare.

Alan Taylor, *Liberty Men and Great Proprietors: The Revolutionary Settlement on the Maine Frontier, 1760–1820* (1990). Using the Maine frontier as a microcosm of continuing conflicts over the meaning of liberty in the early republic (especially the tensions between individual freedom and social stability), Taylor describes the militant and often violent resistance of land-poor white settlers to the legal claims of wealthy proprietors.

Please refer to the document CD-ROM for primary sources related to this chapter.

CHAPTER

9
Liberty and Empire
1800–1815

Gabriel's Conspiracy for Freedom • Voluntary Communities in the
Age of Jefferson • Jeffersonian Republicanism: Politics of
Transition • Liberty and an Expanding Commerce • The Political
Economy of an "Empire of Liberty" • The Second War with
England • Conclusion

GABRIEL'S CONSPIRACY FOR FREEDOM

On the morning of October 10, 1800, Gabriel, a tall man, 24 years of age, with a bearing of "courage and intelligence," mounted the gallows in the town center of Richmond, Virginia. Gabriel, a slave, was about to pay with his life for leading a dangerous conspiracy for freedom.

The plot had been a bold one. Inspired by a recent slave revolt in Saint Domingue, the rebels planned to take control of Richmond and free slaves throughout the countryside. The conspiracy was discovered, but not before hundreds of slaves had been recruited to the cause. Twenty-seven African Americans, including Gabriel, were eventually executed. According to white witnesses, all went to their deaths with "a sense of their rights and a contempt of danger." It was a determination, Congressman John Randolph later recorded grimly, "which, if it becomes general, must deluge the Southern country in blood."

It is impossible to know when Gabriel first dreamed of rebellion. Surely he was angry that the American Revolution had left slavery intact. Perhaps he heard stories of the successful slave revolution in Saint Domingue beginning in 1791. Perhaps as he went about the daily business of hiring out his own labor in town (when he was not needed on the plantation), negotiating his own hours, handling his own pay, and working side by side with free men, he raged against the society that kept him enslaved.

In some ways, Gabriel's yearnings for freedom reflected larger patterns in American society in 1800. The Revolution had promised greater liberty, yet most Americans still lived and worked in some form of legally sanctioned paternalistic relation (wife-to-husband, worker-to-master, slave-to-owner) that curtailed both their economic freedom and legal rights. By 1800, many of those Americans, enslaved as well as free, were pushing at old assumptions about order, subordination, and hierarchy. Some left home in search of new economic opportunities. Some challenged the authority of their masters and mistresses by forming new trade guilds or self-help societies. Some came together in philanthropic efforts, and many joined (or formed) new religious organizations. In family life, religious life, and economic life, they were trying out a new, more democratic political economy based on opportunity rather than restraint and on liberty rather than deference. In 1800, in what Thomas Jefferson would later call "as real a revolution in the principles of our government as that of 1776 was in its form," voters extended their experiment to the national government, throwing out the Federalists, and choosing instead Jefferson's Democratic Republican Party.

In some ways, the election of 1800 marked a revolution. The Federalists never regained the presidency, and their pleas for a society based on rank and deference were soon drowned in a sea of democratic yearnings. And yet the ultimate meaning of the rising republican spirit in the United States was complex. Liberty expanded unevenly. New freedoms for some spelled deepened bondage for others. The Democratic Republican political economy did not always lead where Americans had intended. Most free Americans still associated personal liberty with property, and property with the kind of agrarian ideal propounded by Jefferson. Joining liberty to property, they thought, they could realize the full promise of the republic. But in their pell-mell rush for western lands, they brought catastrophe to the Native Americans living there, planted slavery deep in the soil of the new nation, and laid the foundations for a political economy that would ultimately give rise to the very dependencies they sought to avoid.

VOLUNTARY COMMUNITIES IN THE AGE OF JEFFERSON

From the Revolution on, free Americans had differed about the potential of individuals to conduct their own affairs. Federalists pointed to the French Revolution, the Whiskey Rebellion, and Gabriel's Conspiracy as examples of the dangers of too much liberty. By 1800, however, free Americans were taking a growing amount of personal liberty for granted.

Communities of Faith

One of the earliest ways in which Americans began to act on their changing conceptions of liberty was by forming new communities of faith.

With political independence had come a demand for freedom from the state-supported Anglican and Congregational churches. Anglicanism had been disestablished in the South in the 1780s, replaced by the Protestant Episcopal Church. That change encouraged the growth of new evangelical faiths, especially the Methodists (who had seceded from the Anglican Church in 1784) and Baptists (who had migrated into the South from New England). These sects stressed the personal, emotional nature of religion and the ability of individuals to struggle for their own redemption. Methodists, for example, rejected what they deemed artificial differences among Christians, pronouncing "[o]ne condition, and only one" required for salvation: "a real desire." Emphasizing inner truth, a plain style, and congregational independence, the evangelical denominations offered a more egalitarian vision of the community of believers. This proved attractive to the poor and disfranchised, including both enslaved and free African Americans and white women. Some congregations went so far as to question the morality of owning slaves.

This religious turmoil led to a series of turn-of-the-century revivals, beginning in Virginia and western New England. The revivals first spread west, fed perhaps by the isolation of backcountry life. In 1800, religious pressure in Kentucky and Tennessee exploded, sending out a tidal wave that raced back through the Carolinas and Virginia, up through Pennsylvania, into New York, and by 1802, to that bastion of Congregationalism, Connecticut. The most famous of these revivals occurred in 1801 in Cane Ridge, Kentucky, attracting thousands of people. Eventually, the awakening spread to all parts of the country and to virtually all faiths.

Many members of older denominations (especially Congregationalists and Presbyterians) were unhappy that revivals were led by unschooled preachers and encouraged unconventional beliefs and extravagant emotionalism. Between 1803 and 1805 these misgivings led to schism, as the "Old Light" members of the Kentucky Synod purged "New Light" revivalists.

Where Congregationalists and Presbyterians saw confusion, Methodists and Baptists saw possibility. In the first years of the nineteenth century, the number of Baptist congregations increased more than sixfold and membership in Methodist churches more than doubled.

Some observers thought religion and politics were directly linked. For example, Thomas Robbins, Congregational minister of Danbury, Connecticut, assumed that all evangelicals were Democratic Republicans. The linkages were seldom so simple. Neither Jefferson nor Madison, the founding lights of the Democratic Republican Party, embraced evangelical faiths. Yet religion and politics did reflect one another. Americans tended to formulate visions of the ideal political community in religious and specifically Christian images and to suspect those who disagreed with them not only of bad politics, but of moral weakness.

African Americans in the Early Republic

For no group of Americans had the promises of the Revolution proved emptier, or the dangers of the new society more palpable, than for African Americans. For no group were new communities of freedom more vital.

The failure to abolish slavery was not the only sign that life in the new nation might become harder for African Americans. Although some slaves had escaped during the war and some had been freed afterward, the struggle for national independence also harmed slave communities. The rhetoric of revolution had alarmed southern whites, who feared slave insurrection. News of the Saint Domingue rebellion, followed by the arrival of large numbers of refugees and reports of conspiracies, reawakened these fears. Southern legislatures moved to limit emancipations and to tighten legal surveillance over slaves. Slaveowner efforts to capitalize on new economic opportunities after the war often proved devastating to slave communities and families. When owners faltered, slaves paid the price with less food, poorer housing, and longer hours of work. When planters failed, slaves became the liquid capital through which they settled their debts. In some parts of the South, the sale of slaves as a result of death or insolvency in the 1780s and 1790s substantially increased the incidence of slave owning among whites, giving a larger part of the white community a personal stake in the institution. All of these changes fostered a reluctance to tolerate even minor criticism of the institution of slavery.

A small, fragile free African-American community took shape, made up of individuals and families who had escaped during the war or been freed after it. Most free African Americans migrated to the cities in search of jobs and opportunity. By 1800, New York and Baltimore claimed free African-American communities of 3,500 and 2,700, respectively. Philadelphia, the gateway to the North, had the largest free African-American population, almost 6,400.

In Philadelphia, as in other cities, African Americans created a range of institutions to ensure survival, foster growth, and project their presence into the larger community. By 1814, Philadelphia's African-American community had organized 11 mutual aid societies and four Masonic lodges. Led by teachers, in 1800 African-American Philadelphians took control of the education of their children. In 1807, Cyrus Bustill founded an organization to guarantee the financial autonomy of the schools.

This early-nineteenth-century drawing of an African-American scrubwoman is interesting both because it individualizes the subject and because the subject, a worker, is presented in a style of almost classic reflection.

No institution was more important to the survival of these fragile communities than the church. African Americans responded warmly to the new evangelical religions, especially to Methodism, drawn by the communal character of revivals, their ecstatic tone (which echoed African religious practice), and the immediacy with which preachers dramatized the cataclysmic triumph of good over evil. Yet in many white-dominated congregations, African Americans were restricted to segregated seating and excluded from offices. By 1814, Philadelphia's black community had organized an African Episcopal church, an African Presbyterian church, an African Baptist church, and two Methodist churches.

A few members of Philadelphia's free African-American community achieved spectacular prosperity, but for most, daily life remained a struggle. African-American women worked as tavern-keepers, bakers, seamstresses, chimney sweeps, street vendors, cooks, washerwomen, and gardeners. They set up small groceries in their homes. They fished along the wharves and sold their catch in market stalls, or dug roots or oysters for sale on the city streets. African-American men worked as carpenters, shipbuilders, shopkeepers, blacksmiths, silversmiths, sailors, day laborers, brewers, and in a variety of personal service jobs.

The obstacles free African Americans faced increased after the turn of the century, as the attitudes of white Americans hardened into racial prejudice. Cities, states, and even the federal government began to restrict African Americans from certain occupations. As early as 1798 the Secretary of War and the Secretary of the Navy had each tried to bar African Americans from the military. In 1810, the federal government excluded African Americans from delivering mail. Meanwhile, northern states moved one by one to deny free black men the right to vote. In 1816, whites formed the American Colonization Society, dedicated to removing free African Americans from their native land to Liberia, in Africa. That year, in response to repeated attacks on African-American churches and churchgoers, African-American Methodists from Baltimore and Philadelphia founded the African Methodist Episcopal Church.

Communities of Masters and Journeymen

That the destruction of older, hierarchial institutions did not always result in increased equality was also suggested by the breakdown of the craft shop in these years. In the late eighteenth century, most American manufacturing occurred either in individual households or in small craft shops where a master presided over one or more journeymen and an apprentice or a helper or two. By custom the master paid at least part of workers' wages in food and lodging and supervised them almost like a father.

By the mid-1790s these paternalistic relationships were disappearing. The shift was apparent in many crafts. Eager to increase sales to cotton planters in the South and rich sugar planters in the West Indies, for example, furniture makers sought to cut costs and improve efficiency. They achieved these ends by subdividing the tasks of production, which allowed them to employ cheap, inexperienced workers whom they paid in cash and to whom they had a lessened sense of obligation. Master tailors and shoemakers also sought ways to cut costs and increase production for burgeoning markets for low-cost goods. Meanwhile, many large merchants and retailers branched out into production, creating new competition. Prosperous masters were able to keep up and sometimes expand their business. Smaller shops often went under.

Workers paid for these changes in falling wages. Pressed to the edge of destitution, journeymen in Philadelphia, New York, and Baltimore began to organize secretly into trade associations. In 1805, in the first strike in United States history, Philadelphia journeyman shoemakers tried to demand higher wages. In the eyes of the law, this amounted to a conspiracy against the rights of trade. The shoemakers were arrested, tried, convicted, and required to pay stiff fines.

Among workers, this conflict assumed an increasingly ethnic cast. On Christmas 1806, for example, gangs of native-born and Irish workers, many employed as laborers or in occupations undergoing sharp reorganization, battled in the streets of New York. The cause of the riot was deep occupational insecurities and growing competition for jobs and for decent wages.

By 1800 manufacturers were beginning to assert a new authority in the economy by lobbying for protective tariffs, arguing that investment in manufacturing would "tend to assimilate and strengthen the union." The petitioners included craft masters who had ascended through the ranks as well as merchants. Initially, the traditional craft masters refused to associate with these new entrepreneurs. By the early 1800s, however, societies of masters began slowly to admit the newcomers and, reluctantly, to turn a blind eye to their hiring practices.

JEFFERSONIAN REPUBLICANISM: POLITICS OF TRANSITION

A quiet revolution in Americans' ideas of personal freedom underlay the national political revolution of 1800. A government dominated by old elites and committed to federal activism was replaced by one devoted, as Jefferson's Secretary of the Treasury Albert Gallatin put it, to "principles of limitation of power and public economy." In his inaugural address, Jefferson promised "a wise and frugal government" devoted to the "encouragement of agriculture and of commerce as its handmaid." Both he and other Democratic Republicans set about reforming the policies of the Federalists, laying the groundwork for national economic independence through agriculture at home and unimpeded free trade abroad.

A New Capital, A New President

The character of Jefferson's presidency was captured concretely in the new national capital where he was inaugurated on March 4, 1801. The city (named Washington, District of Columbia, after the nation's first president, and designed by French engineer Major Pierre Charles L'Enfant) had been in the planning since 1790.

President and Abigail Adams moved into the new executive mansion in the fall of 1800. Abigail Adams found the city dirty, its inhabitants disreputable, and the executive mansion damp and cold. Like the executive mansion, the Capitol was not complete. Congress took up its duties under an unfinished roof, and the Supreme Court set to work in temporary chambers in the basement. It was in the unfinished Capitol that Thomas Jefferson took the oath of office. Few people better embodied the transitional state of the republic than the new president himself. Jefferson was born in 1743 and lived until July 4, 1826 (the 50th anniversary of the Declaration of Independence), a span that witnessed the flowering and decline of the European Age of Reason and the birth of the American market revolution. Jefferson belonged to both eras.

Jefferson's economic worldview was shaped by eighteenth-century mercantilism. He was a planter, producing raw materials for European markets and reliant on those markets for the production of manufactured goods. This relation produced friction with wealthy European merchants, who extended credit to planters and held their debts. As a man who lived most of his adult life in debt, Jefferson distrusted paper money and banks, which he saw as tools that privileged merchants used to subjugate vulnerable producers. The influence of merchants over transatlantic politics convinced Jefferson of the importance of national commercial independence.

But Jefferson also associated liberty with self-sufficient agriculture and with commerce unfettered by state-imposed restrictions. He was unreservedly optimistic about the future of the United States and unabashedly certain of the right of Americans to claim and exploit the continent's vast natural resources. Like many Americans, he was a "mechanic," always seeking pragmatic uses of abstract principles. Among his inventions were a ventilating system, a device for copying documents, and a moldboard plow. He was equally willing to experiment with social structures. In 1789, he suggested to Madison that the laws and constitutions of states should be renewed every 19 years to ensure that future generations would not be saddled with the ideas and institutions of earlier ones.

No issue of his personal or political life revealed these two worlds in conflict more dramatically than Jefferson's views on slavery. Like many other members of the eighteenth-century planter class, Jefferson was deeply dependent for his own comfort on slavery. But Jefferson was also the single person most directly responsible for the exclusion of slavery from the Northwest Territory, and as president he signed the bill outlawing the foreign slave trade. The wholesale executions that followed the discovery of Gabriel's Conspiracy sickened and frightened him.

Jeffersonian Republicans in Power

After gaining control of the national government, Democratic Republicans closed a loophole in the Constitution that had almost cost them the election. With 53 percent of the popular vote, Jefferson had clearly defeated Adams. But in the Electoral College, the practice of balloting by party allegiance (rather than by office) had spelled disaster. Both Jefferson and Aaron Burr, the Democratic Republican vice-presidential candidate, received 73 votes. In the House of Representatives, Federalists threatened to support Burr to block Jefferson. Only after 34 ballots was Jefferson elected. Stunned Democratic Republicans rushed to pass the legislation that became the Twelfth Amendment (1804), providing for party tickets in national elections.

Democratic Republicans turned next to the judiciary, where they attempted to eliminate a Federalist justice by impeaching Associate Supreme Court Justice Samuel Chase. Chase was notorious for his open partisanship during the Sedition Act prosecutions, but it was unclear whether his behavior met the constitutional standard of "Treason, Bribery, and high Crimes and Misdemeanors." Although Democratic Republicans were suddenly content with a loose reading of the Constitution, Federalists took up strict constructionism, arguing that the power to impeach had been narrowly drawn and should be used only in cases of clear criminal behavior. In the final vote, Chase was acquitted. The Supreme Court remained Federalist, 5 to 1. Jefferson's desire for a Democratic Republican court had to wait for unforced vacancies in 1804 and 1807 and the creation of a new western circuit in 1807.

In a move that ultimately produced a landmark Supreme Court decision, Jefferson went after John Adams's last-minute judicial appointments, authorized by the Judiciary Act of 1801. While Secretary of State James Madison refused to issue the necessary commissions for new justices, Congress repealed the Judiciary Act of 1801, reinstating the Judiciary Act of 1789, with its smaller court system. The 1789 act had given the Supreme Court oversight over the delivery of new judicial commissions. Its reinstatement had the effect of making the Supreme Court (with its new chief justice, Federalist John Marshall) the judge of Madison's actions. One of the rebuffed Adams appointees, William Marbury, sued. Marshall's decision focused on the question of whether the Supreme Court had a right to hear Marbury's case. The Marshall Court ruled that it did not. In granting the court jurisdiction over the delivery of judicial commissions, Marshall reasoned, Congress had exceeded the Constitution, which gave the court no such authority. *Marbury* v. *Madison* established the principle of judicial review. The decision identified the Supreme Court as the final arbiter of constitutional intent and, thus, as the highest embodiment of "the people's will." Marbury's petition was denied, and Democratic Republicans carried the day, but federalism (as invoked by Justice Marshall) left a lasting imprint on the structure of power in the republic.

Protecting Commerce

Jefferson entered his presidency determined to reduce the size of the federal government. Working with Secretary of the Treasury Albert Gallatin, he slashed the Army budget by half and the Navy budget by more than two-thirds. He also supported congressional efforts to reduce the $80 million national debt and to repeal internal taxes. By 1807 the Democratic Republicans had paid off all the debts they could legally call in.

These efforts at thrift were soon derailed by the politics of overseas commerce. The monarchs of the North African nations of Tunis, Algeria, Morocco, and Tripoli had long sought to dominate shipping on the Mediterranean, exacting tribute as the price of permitting ships to travel the Barbary Coast. As soon as the United States became a separate nation, it became liable for such payments. In 1794 the United States created the Navy to protect American shipping in the Mediterranean, the very Navy whose budget Jefferson cut.

Renewed demands for tribute in May 1801 brought the crisis to a head. Democratic Republicans opposed war as expensive and tending to enlarge the powers of the federal government. Yet to pay tribute was to abandon the principle of free trade. Concluding that his only hope lay in a small, contained war, Jefferson supported a Congressional appropriation for warships and gunboats "to protect our commerce and chastise their insolence—by sinking, burning or destroying their ships and vessels wherever you shall find them."

Results were mixed. Democratic Republicans did manage to avoid new internal taxes, but only by financing the war from the large surplus inherited from the Federalists and from tariff increases. The consequence was a spectacular rise in the tariff, which ultimately nurtured a boom in domestic manufacturing. America's military intervention in the Mediterranean was not particularly successful, however. The warship *Philadelphia* ran aground off Tripoli and would have become loot of war had a raiding party led by Lieutenant Stephen Decatur not burned it before it could be taken.

LIBERTY AND AN EXPANDING COMMERCE

These military frustrations paled in the light of economic prosperity. Wars in Europe and new traffic to the Indian Ocean produced new and expanded markets for United States products. Bolstered by the rise of cotton as an export crop, overseas commerce financed the import of manufactured items. The promise of agricultural profits drove up land prices. Farmers hired extra workers, teamsters hurried goods to port, shipbuilders turned out new ships at an astonishing rate, and captains hired crews to sail around the world. Jefferson's advocacy of a political economy based on free international commerce seemed vindicated.

The Political Economy of Cotton

The most significant boost to American commercial agriculture arose from the late-eighteenth-century mechanization of the English textile mills and the resulting increased demand for cotton. The colonies had not been an important source of raw cotton, because the only variety that grew well in most parts of North America was laborious to clean. Spurred by the new English markets, in 1793 Eli Whitney invented a mechanism that reduced the cleaning time of this short-staple cotton from a pound a day to 50 pounds a day. Almost at a stroke, Whitney's gin made cotton a viable cash crop for much of the South.

The invention occurred at a critical moment. American indigo was losing English market share to indigo from the East Indies. Sales and prices of tobacco were in decline. The market for rice was still strong, but rice cultivation required such large investments of land and labor as to exclude most farmers from production. Meanwhile, the mechanization of British textile mills increased demand for raw cotton. Between 1790 and 1810, American cotton production increased from 3,000 bales to 178,000 bales a year. After 1800, cotton was the largest single U.S. export commodity.

The profits available in cotton set off an explosion of migration into southern North Carolina, South Carolina, Georgia, and later, Alabama, Mississippi, Louisiana, Arkansas, and Texas. Most of this land had become available to the United States as a result of diplomacy. The Pinckney Treaty (1795) had clarified United States claims to present-day Alabama and Mississippi. The Louisiana Purchase (1803) added present-day Louisiana and part of Mississippi. In 1814, Andrew Jackson would claim remaining lands in Mississippi, Alabama, and western Georgia in his war against the Creeks.

The cotton boom fatefully reinvigorated the institution of slavery. Planters scrambled to beat the 1807 constitutional deadline on the foreign slave trade, when Congress would first be able to limit the sale of slaves into the country. In the two decades between ratification of the Constitution and 1807, the United States imported more slaves than in any other 20-year period, perhaps as many as 200,000 people.

The Golden Age of Shipping

American maritime prosperity seemed to affirm Jefferson's vision of a republic based on agriculture and international commerce. American shipping was of three types: export (wheat, rice, indigo, tobacco, some sugar, and especially cotton), re-export (the shipping of goods between two foreign ports with an intermediate stop in the United States), and some simple carrying trade between two foreign ports. Overall, American shipping tonnage tripled, reaching almost 11 million tons annually by 1807. American ships increased their share of the traffic between England and the United States from 50 percent in 1790 to 95 percent by 1800, and American-owned vessels sailed on virtually every known ocean. They carried goods from the West Indies to the United States and then to Europe, between ports in Europe, and from Europe and the United States to Asia.

This commercial prosperity rested in part on cotton and in part on the efficiency of the American shipping industry. But it was also due to the U.S. success in steering clear of, and profiting from, the European wars that raged almost continuously during this period. War created demand in Europe and also hindered the ability of European shippers to meet that demand. Although American shipping was not entirely free from harassment (notably the British seizure of American

From the late eighteenth to the early nineteenth century, America's tall-masted oceangoing ships, like the ones shown here, dominated global trade.

sailors to serve on British ships), the value of the re-export carrying trade increased from about $500,000 a year in the 1790s to about $60 million a year in 1807.

Ironically, this flourishing commerce, so desired by Jefferson to safeguard against industrialization, strengthened the attitudes and the institutions on which industrialization would eventually be based. High commercial profits encouraged the development of business services, especially in the middle and northern states. Banks, credit houses, retail stores, warehouses, and insurance companies prospered, creating the infrastructure and the personal fortunes that would later underwrite early industrialization.

Shipping also produced catalysts for more democratic change. While settlers in the West expressed their new autonomy in religious revival, young adults on the East Coast (mostly men, but a few women) tried out the republic of the sea. Sailing was dangerous and low paid, but aboard ship, status, ethnicity, and nativity mattered less than skill and hard work. In the first years of the nineteenth century, as many as one-fifth of American seamen were foreign born, and another fifth were African American.

Invention and Exploration

The invention of the cotton gin illustrated the relationship between expanding economic opportunity and advances in science and technology. By the late 1790s, one northerner claimed that "every neighborhood had its mechanical genius, as local inventors experimented with everything from textile-making devices to water-powered sawmills to horse-drawn rollers for squeezing the juice from sugar cane." In 1803, Philadelphian Oliver Evans nearly succeeded in mechanizing the process of milling flour. Evans's mill weighed, cleaned, ground, and partly packaged flour. Workers were needed only to dump the grain down a chute at the beginning of the process and to close the barrels at the end.

In 1793, Samuel Slater established a mechanized spinning factory in Pawtucket, Rhode Island. The firm employed children in the mill itself and their parents to weave yarn in their homes. Both the economic and the political circumstances of the late 1790s boded well for mills like Slater's. The expansion of cotton production in the South provided raw fiber for the mills. The expansion of slavery in the South and the federal military buildup during the Adams administration created a demand for cotton yarn. By 1800 Slater's first mill employed more than 100 workers, and a second mill was underway. In 1804, there were four cotton mills in New England. By 1809, there were 87.

The needs of the United States government provided other spurs to invention. The war fever that accompanied the XYZ Affair encouraged an aggressive search for new technologies in arms production. Two proposals seemed promising— one from Simeon North of Berlin, Connecticut, and one from Eli Whitney, in Hamden, Connecticut. Both men proposed more efficient production through the use of water power and the subdivision of labor. Both also espoused the principle of interchangeable parts, so that "the component parts" of each weapon "may be fitted to any other." The principle of interchangeability promised enormously increased efficiency in both production and use. The military not only promoted technological change, but also became an important reservoir of scientific knowledge. In 1802, the federal government founded the U.S. Military Academy at West Point, New York, with an initial curriculum that emphasized science and technology. This focus reflected the actual day-to-day deployments of the U.S. Army. Mustered out to escort settlers, protect surveyors, punish Indians, and enforce treaties, the Army was the government's arm of continental discovery. It was an Army officer, Meriwether Lewis, whom Jefferson sent to explore the Louisiana Purchase in 1804. Military men led many of the subsequent early scientific expeditions into the Trans-Mississippi West: Zebulon Pike in the

Samuel Slater's water-powered Pawtucket Mill, shown here in the early nineteenth century, lacked a power loom but showed that textile manufacturing could be a successful industry in the United States.

Mississippi Valley and along the Arkansas River in 1805–1806 and 1806–1807, Stephen Long across the Great Plains in 1819, and John C. Frémont in the Pacific Northwest in 1843–1844.

The Rule of Law and Lawyers

Americans had long emphasized the importance of the written law to the preservation of the republic. By the turn of the century, however, it was apparent that the law lay only partly in written statutes. In a world of increasingly complex commercial contracts, patents, and land claims, law also existed in the skill of lawyers to argue cases and in the authority of judges to interpret them.

For workers, the social power of judicial interpretation became alarmingly clear in March 1806, when the striking Philadelphia journeyman bootmakers and shoemakers were found guilty of common law conspiracy to restrain trade. Conservative Philadelphia newspapers applauded the verdict, but the Jeffersonian *Aurora* protested that there was nothing in the (written) Pennsylvania or U.S. Constitution to support such a decision. The unwritten common law, the *Aurora* insisted, would soon "reduce the laboring whites to a condition still more despicable and abject" than "the unfortunate Africans."

New statutes echoed the common law bias against workers. All but four of the states passed laws that reinforced the power of masters over apprentices. Such laws hinted at a growing restlessness of young workers and at keen competition among employers for workers.

When the common law tradition clashed with economic development, judges tended to side with the entrepreneurs. For example, English common law assumed the owners and users of waterways had a right to enjoy those waterways undisturbed by alterations upstream. As households and businesses experimented with the use of water power in manufacturing, they sought to erect dams and millraces that altered the flow of streams. In 1805, in *Palmer* v. *Mulligan*, a New York court ruled in favor of the right of development, against customary common law rights. This bias toward economic development would later be reflected in national judicial decisions.

The composition of Congress began to mirror the growing status and importance of lawyers. About one-third of the members of the first Congress were lawyers. By 1815 that proportion was more than half. The power of the legal profession made itself felt even in the territories—as Daniel Boone learned to his chagrin. Well into the 1790s, Boone had been able to turn his knowledge of Kentucky into a thriving business as a land hunter, earning commissions from speculators and accumulating a large land holding of his own. But by the turn of the century, the skills of the backwoodsman were giving way to the skills of the lawyer, as new arrivals hired lawyers to contest Boone's land titles.

THE POLITICAL ECONOMY OF AN "EMPIRE OF LIBERTY"

For Jefferson, the right of empire, like the right of free trade, was fundamental to the political economy of the republic. "By enlarging the empire of liberty," President Jefferson once observed, "we multiply its auxiliaries, and provide new sources of renovation, should its principles, at any time, degenerate, in those positions of our country which gave them birth." When Jefferson purchased the Louisiana Territory in 1803, he doubled the size of the United States. For many Americans, this enlarged opportunities for freedom. For others, it had the opposite effect. The cotton boom had cemented slavery in the political economy of the South. The Louisiana Pur-

TABLE 9–1

Population of the Western States and Territories			
State	1790	1800	1810
Kentucky	73,677	220,955	406,511
Tennessee	35,691	105,602	261,727
Ohio		45,365	230,760
Indiana		5,641	24,520
Illinois			12,282
Mississippi		8,850	40,352
Louisiana (Missouri)			20,845
Territory of Orleans (Louisiana)			76,556
Michigan			4,762

Source: E. R. Johnson and collaborators, History of Domestic and Foreign Commerce of the United States (New York: B. Franklin, 1915) Table 12.

chase supplied new territories for slavery's march west. In both the North and the South, the Louisiana Purchase ensured that the American assault on Native American lands would be projected across the Mississippi River (see Table 9–1).

The Louisiana Purchase

Many citizens of the republic, including Jefferson himself, had long presumed that white Americans would eventually settle west of the Mississippi River but Pinckney's Treaty of 1795 (which had improved American access to the Mississippi) had removed any need for immediate action.

Napoleon Bonaparte changed all that. By the turn of the century, American–French relations had chilled. Ambitious to establish his own empire in the Americas and determined to prevent further United States expansion, in 1800 Napoleon acquired Louisiana from Spain. Jefferson worried that France would eventually send troops to occupy New Orleans. Hoping to block Napoleon, and perhaps to win West Florida (ownership of which had been left unclear in the sale), Jefferson dispatched Robert Livingston to France.

Bonaparte had indeed intended to fortify New Orleans, but he first diverted his troops to Saint Domingue in an attempt to reverse the revolution there. Some 30,000 French troops died in the failed attempt. When a frustrated Bonaparte grew weary of his American enterprise, Livingston saw his chance. Perhaps, he hinted, if West Florida were offered as a gift, the United States would take Louisiana off France's hands by purchase. On April 12, 1803, the deal was struck. The United States paid France $11.25 million and agreed to satisfy American claims against France (from the Revolution) up to a value of an additional $3.75 million. For $15 million, or roughly 3.5 cents an acre, the United States obtained the Louisiana Territory (see Map 9–1).

Jefferson's own "strict" reading of the Constitution indicated that the purchase required a constitutional amendment. But this Democratic Republican belief in explicit powers ran counter to his Democratic Republican belief that the nation required land for expansion. Congress granted citizenship to French and Spanish

Map 9–1   Exploring the Trans-Mississippi West
Although Lewis and Clark made the first exploration of the Louisiana Purchase, other explorers quickly fol-
lowed. Among the most important were Zebulon Pike, who explored the Arkansas and Red Rivers, and Steven
Long, who explored the Arkansas and Platte Rivers. Long described the plains as the "Great American Desert."

inhabitants of the territory, ignored the status of Indians living there, rebuffed an
effort to outlaw slavery, and authorized the purchase without further ado. Jefferson
rationalized "that the good sense of our country will correct the evil of [loose] construction when it shall produce ill effects."

Surveying Louisiana

When the United States had requested a statement of the exact boundaries of its purchase, French Minister Talleyrand had declined: "You have made a noble bargain for
yourselves, and I suppose you will make the most of it." Indeed, long before Louisiana
was in the hands of the United States, Jefferson began to plan its exploration.

To lead the expedition, Jefferson appointed his trusted secretary, Captain
Meriwether Lewis, and another officer, William Clark. Lewis was an ambitious soldier with some experience in the old Northwest, and he enjoyed Jefferson's complete confidence. Clark, who had commanded troops on the Mississippi, was a
skilled surveyor and mapmaker. Their mission was "to explore the Missouri River,
& such principal streams of it, as, by its course and communication with the waters
of the Pacific Ocean, whether the Columbia, Oregon, Colorado or any other river
may offer the most direct & practicable water communication across this continent
for the purposes of commerce." The commerce Jefferson sought was not across the
Pacific, but rather with the Indians along the northern Missouri River and its tributaries who traded chiefly with the British.

The expedition set out from St. Louis on May 14, 1804. It included three boats containing 45 men and a dog, firearms, medicines, scientific instruments, tools, flour, and salt. The party traveled first up the Missouri River, closely observed by the Mandans and the Minnetarees and later the Hidatsas, who visited their camps at night and sent ahead stories of these curious people. In early November, the white men made their winter camp. When the expedition broke camp the following spring, a Shoshone woman, Sacagawea, her French-Canadian trapper husband, and their newly born child left with them.

As a young girl, Sacagawea had been captured and adopted by the Minnetarees. Now, traveling with Lewis and Clark, she would return home. En route, her foraging and fishing skills supplemented the party's diet and she became an invaluable guide and interpreter.

Some of the expedition's encounters with Native Americans were less friendly. Far more dangerous than the Indians, however, were waterfalls and rapids, freezing temperatures and paralyzing snows, accidents, diseases (especially dysentery), and dead-end trails. The final portage across the Rocky Mountains in the fall of 1805 proved longer and more difficult than anticipated. Snow and hail brought the expedition to a standstill. Exhausted and underfed animals wandered off. Supplies ran out. On the verge of slaughtering their pack animals, the expedition at last cleared the worst of the mountains and came to Indian villages where they were fed and sheltered. On November 7, 1805, Lewis and Clark reached the Pacific Ocean.

Throughout their journey, Lewis and Clark had represented themselves as the envoys of a great nation with whom the Native Americans should now trade. To cement relations, they presented medals of friendship to Indian leaders. But they also kept an eye out for the prospects of future settlement. What they found, according to Lewis, was "a most delightfull country . . . fertile in the extreem . . . covered with lofty and excellent timber." After their return, in 1806, parts of their journals and letters, including detailed maps and drawings, slowly found their way into print, advertising to the settlers who would soon follow the full extent of America's new "empire of liberty."

The Burr Conspiracy

If any man was born to prominence, it was Aaron Burr. The scion of an old New England family (his grandfather was minister Jonathan Edwards), Burr had been elected to the Senate from New York at a young age and had been a presidential candidate in the 1796 election. By 1804, as vice president, he seemed destined for greatness.

There had always been nagging reservations about Burr's character. Alexander Hamilton was particularly severe, declaring Burr a man of "extreme and irregular ambitions . . . far more cunning than wise, far more dextrous than able." When he heard of Hamilton's remarks in 1804, Burr challenged him to a duel. Hamilton was mortally wounded, and Burr's public career was ruined.

Burr refocused his ambitions on the West. In 1805, after leaving office, he made his way to New Orleans. He might have intended to foment rebellion in Louisiana or to assemble a corps of mercenaries to invade Mexico or Florida. By 1806 he had raised a force of several thousand men. Convinced that Burr intended treason, Jefferson ordered his arrest. Burr was captured and brought back to Richmond to stand trial before John Marshall, who happened to be presiding over the federal circuit. Prosecution proved difficult. Marshall interpreted treason in the narrowest sense possible, as requiring two witnesses to an overt act of war against the United States. No witnesses were forthcoming. Acquitted, Burr lived to a ripe old age in New York.

Indian Resistance to Republican Empire

In the world of the slave Gabriel, the political economy of national expansion had heightened the agonies of slavery. In the world of the Eastern Woodlands, the same political economy collided violently with Native American practices.

In 1800, large areas of land remained under dispute in the trans-Appalachian region. As settlers occupied new lands, Indians lost their villages and fields. Thrown back on the fur trade, they overhunted dwindling grounds. By the turn of the century, many of the pelts and skins brought to traders in the Northwest Territory had been hunted west of the Mississippi River, and the deer were all but gone in the Southeast. Protestant missionaries urged the Indians to adopt Euro-American religious and social practices, including male-headed households and private ownership of property. Unscrupulous agents coaxed and bullied Indian nations into signing away their land. When the Indians resisted, the agents made deals with leaders they knew to be of doubtful legitimacy, promising bounties and annuities for territory. This crisis of cultural and economic survival virtually ensured armed confrontation.

Although he expressed benevolence toward Indians, President Jefferson believed that they must give way to American settlement. Not only did the territories represent the supply of land necessary to nurture republican virtues and stabilize republican institutions; they also provided a buffer against Britain, France, and Spain on the western borders. Preferring that American westward expansion occur peacefully, Jefferson fostered a cycle of growing dependency through which Indians would eventually turn to settled agriculture and sell off their lands (see Map 9–2).

Native Americans resisted these assaults on their autonomy. Seneca communities accepted missionary aid but refused to abandon their community holdings, gender division of labor, and matrilineal households. The southern nations declined Jefferson's promise of new lands in the West and focused on constructing internal institutions that Americans might recognize as "civilized." For example, the Cherokees adopted a series of laws that functioned as a constitution, established a congress, and executed individual land titles. Resistance to Euro-American culture also took the form of a broad movement for spiritual revitalization. Ganioda'yo (Handsome Lake), who rose to influence among the Senecas after 1799, preached revival through a synthesis of traditional beliefs and Christianity, but among other groups revitalization centered on cleansing themselves of Euro-American practices. In the South, Cherokees revived the Green Corn Ceremony, which celebrated the importance of personal bonds and repudiated material wealth. The rejection of Euro-American culture was not purely symbolic, however. As early as 1807, William Henry Harrison, governor of Indiana Territory, heard rumors of "a general combination of the Indians for a war against the United States." Two Shawnee leaders, Tecumseh and his half-brother, Tenskwatawa (known as The Prophet), coalesced the diffuse anger into organized resistance. Tecumseh fought against whites both in the Northwest and in the South, experiences that helped him build a pan-Indian alliance. Tenskwatawa became influential after 1805 as the leader of a movement that rejected white culture. About 1808, Tecumseh and Tenskwatawa founded a village in present-day Indiana on the banks of the Tippecanoe River. The Prophet remained there while Tecumseh traveled widely, encouraging organized resistance to white settlement.

By 1811, Tecumseh's widespread success alarmed Harrison. That fall, Harrison marched an army toward Tecumseh's village on the Tippecanoe River. Although cautioned by Tecumseh not to be drawn into battle in his absence, on November 7, 1811, The Prophet engaged Harrison's troops and was defeated. The Prophet was discredited, but when war broke out between Britain and the United States the following

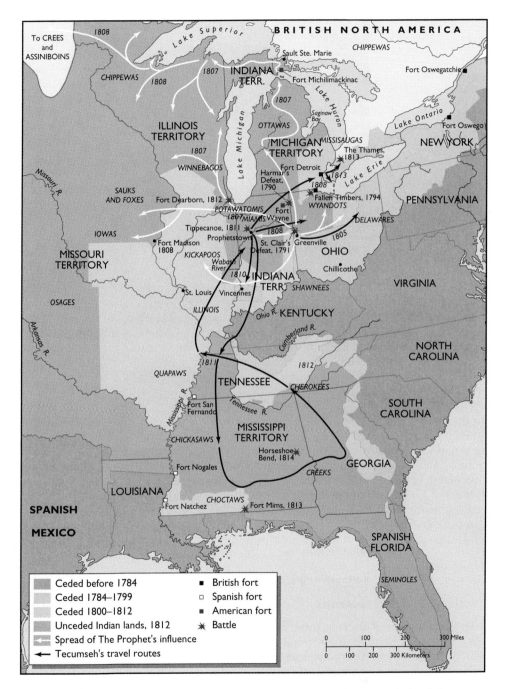

Map 9–2 *Mounting Land Pressure, 1784–1812, and the Rise of Tecumseh's Confederation*
The pan-Indian movement led by Tecumseh and The Prophet was the culmination of years of United States incursions into Indian lands and pressure, official and unofficial, on Indians to cede territories to the United States. As this map suggests, the influence of Tecumseh and The Prophet was greatest in the regions most recently ceded or where ongoing pressure was greatest between 1800 and 1810.

Tecumseh, a sagacious Shawnee leader and skilled warrior, organized the last concerted resistance to white settlement east of the Mississippi River.

year, Tecumseh retained sufficient influence to amass a huge force on the side of the British. He played a decisive role in the British victory over United States troops at Detroit but was killed in battle in October 1813. His death marked the end of organized Indian resistance east of the Mississippi.

THE SECOND WAR WITH ENGLAND

In the fall of 1804, Jefferson's popularity was soaring. Internal taxes had been abolished, the national debt was falling, the United States had (seemingly) stood up to international coercion, and, most amazing, America had acquired a huge western empire. Choosing George Clinton of New York as his running mate, Jefferson won re-election handily, and the Democratic Republicans took control of both houses of Congress. Faced with the prospect of federal surpluses, Jefferson again abandoned strict constitutionalism and began to contemplate a future role for the federal government encouraging "the great objects of public education, roads, rivers, canals, and such other objects of public improvement as may be thought proper." But Jefferson's second term had barely begun when his attention was riveted to developments in Europe.

Neutrality and Isolation

In his first inaugural address, Jefferson had counseled "peace, commerce, and honest friendship with all nations, entangling alliances with none." He remained committed to American neutrality, but by 1805 Napoleon's growing power in France and his expansionistic designs on Europe had considerably complicated this policy. On the one hand, Jefferson knew he might need Napoleon's help to settle the unresolved question of West Florida, still claimed by Spain. On the other hand, France's increasing indifference toward American shipping rights raised the possibility that the United States might need Britain as an ally. Napoleon's victory over Austria in 1805 made France the undisputed master of Western Europe. At the same time, English victories over the fleets of France and Spain had made England the undisputed master of the seas. The stalemate had dire consequences for American shipping.

Jefferson's early hopes that Britain might respect the neutrality of American ships were dashed in 1805 when Britain reasserted an old policy to seize ships traveling between enemy ports. The revived practice was announced with the seizure of more than 200 American ships in that year alone. Not to be outdone, Napoleon declared a blockade of England and also began confiscating American ships. In June 1807 the British ship *Leopold* stopped the American frigate *Chesapeake* just as it left the port of Norfolk, Virginia. Insisting that the *Chesapeake* had recruited British deserters for its crew, the captain of the *Leopold* demanded the right to search the American ship. When he was denied, he fired on the ship, boarded it, and took four men prisoner, leaving the *Chesapeake* to limp home.

Jefferson immediately ordered all British ships out of American waters and demanded reparation for the *Chesapeake*. In secret sessions, Congress passed an act that permitted only those American ships with the president's express approval to sail into foreign ports and prohibiting foreign ships from the American export trade. In effect, the United States had embargoed itself.

It was the most disastrous policy of Jefferson's career. Because enforcement was impossible, wealthy merchants who could bear the risks enjoyed the large profits of smuggling. At the same time, small merchants, sailors, and shopkeepers who depended on steady maritime trade were thrown into crisis, and farmers in the South and West, who needed regular markets, had trouble finding overseas trading outlets. As the economy settled into depression in 1808, the remaining Federalists charged that the embargo was helping Napoleon, whose weaker navy was free to concentrate on the British. Adding to American frustration, Napoleon then slyly claimed the right to attack U.S. ships in any continental port, because by Jefferson's own order they could not be legal carriers.

The ironies of the embargo did not end there. As violations mounted, Congress passed, and the president signed, ever more repressive versions of the embargo. The final, fifth Embargo Act (signed January 9, 1809) swept away protections against self-incrimination and the right to due process and trampled on the right to trial by jury. By comparison, even the Alien and Sedition Acts looked tame.

As he himself acknowledged, the Embargo Acts represented the final failure of Jefferson's agrarian political economy. His dream of a republic of farmers was dead, the victim of the principles of territorial expansion and free trade on which he had based it. Pinning America's need for manufactured goods solely on "this exuberant commerce," as Jefferson admitted in 1809, "brings us into collision with other powers in every sea, and will force us into every war of the European powers. The converting of this great agricultural country into a . . . mere headquarters for carrying on the commerce of all nations, is too absurd."

With American prestige turned into a joke, commerce deteriorating, and agriculture crying out for relief, on March 1, 1809, Jefferson signed a bill repealing the Embargo Act. Three days later, Jefferson left the office that he now described as a "splendid misery."

Democratic Republican Power and Disunity

Jefferson's was not the only misery. The embargo inflicted hardship on most average Americans. Sailors were stranded in port, artisans saw their sales dwindle, and farmers had no markets for their export crops. The anguish caused by the Embargo Acts brought into the open long-simmering dissension within Democratic Republican ranks.

The most serious rupture came in the aftermath of the Louisiana Purchase. Although Jefferson insisted that he had obtained West Florida as a part of the Louisiana Purchase, Spain claimed that it had never ceded that land to France in the first place. Napoleon hedged, but his ministers let it be known that the right price might convince them to lobby the American cause with Spain. Jefferson approached Congress for the money.

To his critics, Jefferson's willingness to bribe France was the last straw. Loosely organized, Jefferson's Congressional critics dubbed themselves the *Tertium Quid* (the "third something") to distinguish themselves from both the Federalists and the Democratic Republicans. Their most vocal spokesperson, John Randolph, broke publicly with the administration. But the renegade Quids were outnumbered. When he publicly sided with Randolph, Speaker of the House Nathaniel Macon lost the speakership.

By 1808, the Quids were threatening open rebellion. Although Secretary of State James Madison seemed the logical heir to Jefferson's presidency, Quids talked of throwing their support to James Monroe of Virginia or even Vice President George Clinton of New York. To avoid the risk of public party brawling, in 1808 party loyalists met in closed caucus to select Jefferson's successor. They chose James Madison. In the election, Madison captured 122 electoral votes to Federalist Charles C. Pinckney's 47. Clinton, who ended up on the ballot, won only 6 electoral votes. The Democratic Republicans again won both houses of Congress.

From 1801 until 1829, the federal government would remain under the control of a single party. In and of itself, that did not challenge Democratic Republican principles. Neither Madison nor Jefferson considered a two-party system a necessary feature of American political life. Both, however, warned against the day when a small cadre of like-minded men would meet together in secret to choose the nation's ruler. Democratic Republican ascendancy itself had now come to rest upon just such a closed institution.

The War of 1812

James Madison had stood side by side with Thomas Jefferson on virtually every important political and ideological issue since the founding of the nation. In 1809 Madison inherited his friend's presidential woes.

In 1809, with Madison's approval, Congress replaced the embargo with the Non-Intercourse Act, reopening trade with all of Europe except England and France, but authorizing the president to resume commercial ties with whichever of these countries dropped its restrictions and attacks on American shipping. The act set off a series of diplomatic feints on the part of England and France, both pretending to alter their policies without making actual concessions.

France eventually won the game. In the summer of 1810, Napoleon's ministers officially communicated to Madison that, as of November of that year, France would stop seizing American ships on the condition that Britain would do likewise. Probably correctly, Britain did not believe France would follow through on this policy. But Madison accepted the French declarations, and he altered American Non-Intercourse Act policy to apply to Britain alone.

Still, war might have been averted. A quarter of a century of European wars and Napoleon's continental policy, which closed continental markets to English goods, had taken its toll on Britain's economy. Although far more powerful militarily than the United States, Britain would have been happy to avoid the cost of an additional war. On June 1, 1812, in light of continuing British attacks on American shipping,

Madison requested that Congress declare war on Great Britain. On June 4, the House voted to pass a war bill. On June 18, the Senate concurred. Ironically, unaware of events in the United States, England announced that it was revoking its maritime policy against United States ships.

The war vote in Congress went largely along party and regional lines. New England shippers remained firmly opposed, protesting that shipping was just beginning to recover and that American prosperity was dependent on Britain. Farmers and planters in the West and South were ready to fight to open up the seas. They suspected that the war might prove useful in other ways, too. Western migrants were convinced that Creek and Shawnee resistance was the work of the British, still hanging onto their forts along the Great Lakes. War with England could provide the excuse for an American invasion of Canada, which could both grab more land and wipe out the Indians. Even the Democratic Republicans were not fully unified, however. Led by Henry Clay of Kentucky and John C. Calhoun of South Carolina, the War Hawks (a group of fiercely nationalistic and resolutely expansionist young men who had come of age since the Revolution) were eager to respond to British insults. Moderate Democratic Republicans were more hesitant. They dreaded the cost of the war and doubted that the nation could gear up to take on such a formidable foe.

All of these tensions were reflected in the election of 1812. Maverick Republican De Witt Clinton rallied the support of Federalists and ran as Madison's opposition. He did not win, but his 89 electoral votes (to Madison's 128) constituted a higher proportion than the Federalists had enjoyed since the election of 1800.

Doubts about America's war readiness were soon justified. An attempt in the summer of 1812 to invade Canada foundered in confusion and indecision. Two thousand American troops surrendered at Detroit, and two overland advances failed when state militiamen insisted that their military obligations did not include leaving the country to fight. Only Commodore Perry's dramatic victory on Lake Erie saved American honor in the north. On September 10, 1813, Perry forced the surrender of the entire British Great Lakes squadron. "We have met the enemy," he relayed to a relieved General William Henry Harrison, "and they are ours—two ships, two brigs, one schooner, and a sloop."

The War of 1812 was primarily a naval war, and a comparable victory eluded Americans in the Atlantic. After a few initial successes at sea, the tiny American Navy was easily overwhelmed by superior British sea power. Americans turned to private schooners and sloops and by the war's end managed to capture more than 1,300 British vessels. Nevertheless, by 1813 the British Navy had succeeded in blockading the American coast from the Chesapeake Bay south through the Gulf of Mexico to New Orleans. The following year the blockade was extended to New England. The British fleet pummeled the cities and villages along the U.S. coast. On August 24, 1814, the British troops invaded Washington, burned the Capitol, the White House, the Treasury Building, and the Naval Yard, and terrorized the civilian population. The entire cabinet, including President James Madison, fled in confusion to a quickly devised hideout.

While Washington lay smoldering, the British turned their attention to Baltimore. Through the night of September 13 and 14 the ships fired on Fort McHenry, the island citadel that guarded Baltimore's harbor. Among the anguished observers in the harbor was a Washington lawyer by the name of Francis Scott Key. Elated when the rising sun revealed the United States flag still flying over the fort, Key quickly scribbled the words that would in 1931 be adopted as the lyrics of the national anthem, "The Star-Spangled Banner."

In the South, Andrew Jackson used the war to suppress Indian resistance to U.S. settlement. When news reached Nashville that the militant Creek faction known as the Red Sticks had attacked a U.S. fort and settlers in Mississippi Territory, Jackson assembled a volunteer militia, including free African Americans and Indians, and went in pursuit. In March 1814, Jackson defeated the insurgents at Horseshoe Bend, forcing them to sign a treaty ceding two-thirds of remaining Creek lands to the United States.

The Making of Heroes and Knaves

For a time the war worked in favor of the Federalists. Although they did not win the presidency in 1812, they doubled their numbers in Congress. Perhaps misled by those results, some Federalists grew rash. Angry at declining profits and frustrated by Virginia's domination of the presidency, in October 1814, Massachusetts Federalists called for a convention of the New England states "to lay the foundation for a radical reform in the National compact." They planned to meet on December 15 in Hartford, Connecticut.

The Federalists who convened in Hartford were divided. Extreme Federalists, arguing that the union could no longer be saved, lobbied for a separate New England confederacy that could immediately seek an end to the war. More moderate voices prevailed, and in the end, the convention sought amendments to the Constitution. They demanded restrictions on the power of Congress to declare war, an end to the Three-Fifths Compromise that allowed slaves to be counted for purposes of representation, exclusion of naturalized citizens from elective federal office, and restrictions on the admission of new states. The Federalists also sought to limit the number of terms a president could serve and the frequency with which the candidate for president could be chosen from a given state. The resolutions expressed a developing identification of the Democratic Republicans as the party of the South.

Federalists misjudged their strength and mistimed their efforts. By 1814, weary of war, Great Britain was ready to end the skirmish with its former colonies. Emerging as the dominant power in Europe, Britain had little incentive to offer the Americans more than simple peace. Signed in Ghent, Belgium, on December 24, 1814, the treaty that ended the War of 1812 was silent on the issues of free trade and impressment that had triggered the war. The Treaty of Ghent also sidestepped boundary disputes between Canada and the United States. On one point the British negotiators gave ground: They agreed to remove British troops from the Northwest, in effect acknowledging the failure of Indian resistance to white settlement.

Only Andrew Jackson's ragtag militia saved Americans from outright humiliation in the war. After the victory at Horseshoe Bend, Jackson's troops moved south to Pensacola and west to New Orleans, where a British fleet prepared to attack the city and take control of the mouth of the Mississippi River. Unaware that a peace treaty had been signed, on January 8, 1815, a force of 7,500 British regulars stormed Jackson's position. In 30 minutes the battle was over, and miraculously, the Americans won. Establishing Jackson as a national hero, the Battle of New Orleans signaled the rise of a new star, a rise that would eventually spell the end of Democratic Republican domination of American national politics.

But that day was still a decade away. In 1815, the chief political importance of Jackson's victory was the lift it gave to American nationalism and the light it cast on the Federalist Hartford Convention, still meeting in Connecticut. Threatening secession was one thing in the context of a failing war, but quite another in a moment of national triumph. Suddenly, the proceedings at Hartford seemed downright traitorous.

CHRONOLOGY

1800	Gabriel's Conspiracy Thomas Jefferson elected president American ships carry 95 percent of U.S.–British trade Samuel Slater's Pawtucket Spinning Mill employs 100 people
1801	Federalists pass Judiciary Act of 1801 Cane Ridge (Kentucky) Revival Barbary War
1803	Louisiana Purchase *Marbury* v. *Madison* establishes principle of judicial review
1804	Jefferson re-elected Lewis and Clark begin exploration of Louisiana
1805	*Palmer* v. *Mulligan* (New York) Essex Decision (British Admiralty Court)
1806	Philadelphia journeyman shoemakers convicted of conspiracy
1807	First Embargo Act
1808	External slave trade becomes illegal (by 1807 act of Congress) Democratic Republicans nominate James Madison in closed Congressional caucus Madison elected president
1809	Non-Intercourse Act
1810	American cotton production reaches 178,000 bales a year
1811	Tecumseh at peak of influence Battle of Tippecanoe River
1812	Congress declares war on Great Britain James Madison re-elected
1814	Federalists convene Hartford Convention Treaty of Ghent ends War of 1812
1815	Battle of New Orleans
1816	American Colonization Society founded African Methodist Episcopal Church founded

CONCLUSION

It was more than the turn of a century that made the Age of Jefferson an age of transition. Between 1800 and 1815, both the people and the political leaders built upon the institutions that had characterized the beginnings of their republican experiment (liberty of belief, voluntary citizenship, economic freedom). They also changed those institutions, gradually laying the foundation for the industrial political economy of nineteenth-century America. They embraced the continuing development of a market economy and free labor that relied on the institution of slavery. American settlers humbled themselves before their God, but the renewal of grace did not deter their proud march across the continent. Buoyed by the end of the War of 1812, the market expanded and further loosened bonds of deference and rank. But many Americans worried what kinds of communities would be fostered in the new democracy.

FURTHER READINGS

Gregory Evans Dowd, *A Spirited Resistance: The North American Indian Struggle for Unity, 1745–1815* (1992). Dowd argues for the emergence, in Jeffersonian America, of a coordinated and militant resistance, led by prophets like Tenskwatawa and his half-brother, Tecumseh, and expressed through a pan-Indian spiritual revival.

Douglas R. Egerton, *Gabriel's Rebellion: The Virginia Slave Conspiracies* (1993). The source of much of the discussion of Gabriel in this chapter, Egerton's book locates Gabriel's rebellion within both the political ferment between Republicans and Federalists in late-eighteenth-century Virginia and the history of slave resistance in the Americas.

Gary B. Nash, *Forging Freedom: The Formation of Philadelphia's Black Community, 1720–1840* (1988). This study of the struggles of Philadelphia's African-American population (both enslaved and free) to build a community in the early republic includes discussions of work, religion, class, and the responses of the African-American community to growing white hostility.

Curtis P. Nettels, *The Emergence of a National Economy, 1775–1815* (1962). Although almost 50 years old, this remains one of the clearest and most comprehensive overviews of shipping, farming, business, and manufacturing in Jefferson's America and of the inventors, workers, and settlers who made those changes possible.

Howard B. Rock, *Artisans of the New Republic: The Tradesmen of New York City in the Age of Jefferson* (1984). Rock traces the experience of the craftworkers of New York City from 1800 to 1815, examining the legacy of pride and independence that mechanics and tradesmen carried with them from the Revolution and the dislocations and loss of status threatened by the changing marketplace and the expanding commercial economy.

Robert W. Tucker and David C. Hendrickson, *Empire of Liberty: The Statecraft of Thomas Jefferson* (1990). This exploration of Jefferson's political philosophy and foreign policy is an especially useful guide to the circumstances surrounding the Louisiana Purchase and the War of 1812.

Laurel Thatcher Ulrich, *A Midwife's Tale: The Life of Martha Ballard, Based on Her Diary, 1785–1812* (1990). A 20-year-long diary provided the primary source for this careful examination of the work, family events, and daily social interactions of a midwife in rural Maine in the early republic.

 Please refer to the document CD-ROM for primary sources related to this chapter.

10

The Market Revolution

1815–1824

Cincinnati: *Queen of the West* • **New Lands, New Markets
A New Nationalism** • **Firebells in the Night** • **The Political
Economy of Regionalism** • **Conclusion**

CINCINNATI: QUEEN OF THE WEST

O**n February 13, 1815, the Cincinnati newspaper** *The Western Spy* **rushed to
print a special edition on Jackson's victory at New Orleans. Ten days later
the paper was elated to announce "Peace Between England & America."
By April the celebration of victory was giving way to jubilation at the return of
business. The April 1 issue touted a long list of "New Goods, at Peace Prices."
Subsequent issues of the *Spy* testified to Cincinnati's steadily expanding economy.
Borrowing against their collateral, shopkeepers stocked groceries, drugs, and farming
equipment. Merchant Robert Best offered eight-day clocks and mounted silver
swords, and Rachel Gulick and her sisters opened a new dressmaking shop. The
Cove Ferry added flatboats and skiffs to accommodate traffic across the Ohio River.
Best of all, there were new jobs. Richard Allen "Wanted Immediately" an experienced brickmaker for his brickyard. William Baley needed "5 or 6 coopers, to whom
constant employment will be given." Like other settlements on the Ohio and Mississippi Rivers, Cincinnati's location positioned the town to become a thriving trade
center, shipping wheat, corn, rye, and livestock overland to Pittsburgh and downriver
to New Orleans, and selling goods and services to local farmers. Even before the
War of 1812, Cincinnatians had begun to reorient their trade from overland routes
across Pennsylvania to water routes down the Mississippi. The outcome of the war**

guaranteed the United States access to those routes all the way to the Gulf of Mexico and opened the way for the newly invented steamboat to carry goods upriver as well. By 1819, when it incorporated as a city, Cincinnati had 10,000 residents and had earned the title "Queen of the West."

Like many other cities, in 1819 Cincinnati plunged abruptly from prosperity into economic and political turmoil. Runaway speculation led to a collapse of credit and panic in 1819. At the same moment, Missouri's controversial application to enter the union as a slave state exposed wrenching contradictions between Cincinnati's economy (increasingly dependent on southern states downriver) and its political identity in a free state. Reflecting the ambivalence felt by many of their readers, the editors of *The Western Spy* assumed a hands-off, states' rights position, and heaved a sigh of relief when Congress struck a compromise. By 1825, business was improving, and construction was about to begin on a canal linking Cincinnati to Lake Erie. Meanwhile, city leaders upheld a draconian "Black Code" to discourage the immigration of free African Americans or runaway slaves.

The history of Cincinnati between 1815 and 1830 reflected the history of the republic. The end of the War of 1812 ushered in an era of expansion, based increasingly on the interdependency of farmers and manufacturers, linked by new internal cash markets. The new political economy captured the qualities the citizens of the republic had long sought: national self-sufficiency and the promise of personal opportunity. The growth of internal markets reinforced a pattern of regional economic specialization and interdependency and gave rise to a robust nationalism based on westward expansion. These developments also heightened regional differences in political economy, especially distinctions between a North increasingly identified with wage labor and a South based on enslaved labor. In every region, moreover, the market economy was a roller-coaster ride, bringing bust as often as boom.

NEW LANDS, NEW MARKETS

From the time of the earliest colonies, Americans had relied on goods manufactured in Europe as well as goods and services produced and exchanged locally. This pattern of economic activity seemed to vindicate Jefferson's faith in the power of international free trade to protect average Americans from deeper market dependence. Ironically, the War of 1812, the war fought to protect that political economy, altered it forever. With Britain out of the picture, American settlement in the trans-Appalachian territories swelled. The communities they settled, the goods they produced, and the demands they created all fostered domestic markets for eastern goods. Merchants and local entrepreneurs alike were eager to meet these new demands. The foundation was laid for America's market revolution.

Westward to the Mississippi

The biggest market of all was the market in land. The Treaty of Paris ending the American Revolution had officially awarded the new nation the territory beyond the Allegheny Mountains north to the Great Lakes, west to the Mississippi River, and south almost to the Gulf of Mexico. But the War of 1812 secured practical control of this dominion.

The Treaty of Ghent called for the restoration of Indian lands taken in battle, but the federal government had little will to oppose the land hunger of its citizens and good reason to support it. Land sales promised revenue. For a time, the federal government tried to control the encroachment of white Americans into the territories. First, the federal government moved to shore up its control of trade with the Indian nations. But eager private traders opposed government control of commerce, and in 1822 the government trading houses were closed, throwing the frontier open to settlers. As a result the business of obtaining Indian lands and selling them to settlers became the paramount issue of American policy.

Of course, the land first had to be acquired from its inhabitants. The use of treaties to force land cessions had begun in the first years of the republic, but this practice was now pursued on an unprecedented scale and with growing assertiveness.

In the South, years of forced cessions had left the Cherokees with only a fraction of their homelands in the Smoky Mountains. Struggling to avoid further cessions, in 1817 eastern Cherokees at last affirmed their willingness to "follow the pursuits of agriculture and civilization" (in other words, to live like Euro-Americans) if they could keep their remaining lands. When the federal government threatened nevertheless to terminate all payments and federal protections, however, the Cherokee National Council signed treaties in 1817 and 1819 ceding 4 million acres of land in Georgia, Tennessee, and the Carolinas. In signing the treaties, the Cherokees believed they had retained the right to remain on the remnants of their eastern lands. They soon discovered that the United States had no intention of honoring that option. In the actual sale of the lands, the federal government had conflicting interests. On the one hand, making the land accessible to settlers of modest means would speed settlement and benefit the economy by increasing agricultural production. On the other hand, selling the land at high prices to wealthy investors would yield greater revenues.

Specific policies changed over time, tracing a compromise between the two goals. The Land Act of 1800 had reduced the size of the minimum parcel from 640 acres to 320 acres and for the first time permitted buyers to spread their payments over time. In 1804, the minimum size was decreased to 160 acres, and the price was reduced from $2.00 to $1.64 an acre. The cost of land and supplies was still beyond the reach of the poorest Americans, but lower minimums and the ability to buy on credit opened the West to tens of thousands of new settlers. The Treaty of Ghent set off an unprecedented fury of migration into the territories (see Map 10–1). The populations of the older western states swelled. Kentucky grew from 407,000 inhabitants in 1810 to 688,000 in 1830, and Tennessee grew from 262,000 inhabitants to 682,000. Even Ohio, admitted to statehood in 1803, increased its population from 231,000 to 938,000 inhabitants. Equally important, settlement led to the organization of new states. After Ohio in 1803, nine years passed before the next new state, Louisiana, entered in 1812. But then Indiana became a state in 1816, Mississippi in 1817, Illinois in 1818, and Alabama in 1819. By then both Missouri and Maine were also eager to join the union.

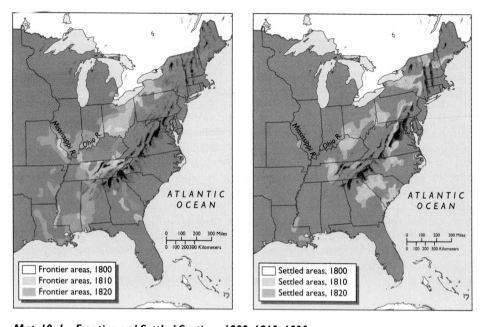

Map 10–1   Frontier and Settled Sections 1800–1810–1820
Although by 1820 Americans were beginning to project a presence across the Mississippi River, settlement was still thin in much of the region between the Appalachians and the Mississippi.

The old Northwest Territory lacked the lure of cotton profits, but it offered rich farming lands and (as settlers in Cincinnati had foreseen) favorable possibilities for transportation economies. Speculators were eager to seize the chance for huge returns on land investment, and migrants were eager to escape debt, taxes, oppressive jobs, and overworked soil.

As a result, American westward migration was a remarkably heterogeneous parade. The earliest arrivals were hunters, fur traders, explorers, and surveyors. Wealthy speculators (European as well as American) sometimes traveled to the backcountry to buy up the best parcels of land, then scurried home to sell them to other investors and would-be migrants. Single men picked their more humble ways along dusty roads, sometimes on horseback, often on foot. Families soon followed. Experienced and well-off families packed food and seed, household items, an ax, and perhaps a gun into a small wagon and herded a cow or a few pigs alongside.

However they traveled, the trek cross-country was seldom easy. Harriet Noble described her family's migration from Geneva, New York, to Michigan as consisting of three stages. First came a wagon trip over "bad roads" to Buffalo, followed by a "tedious" boat trip over Lake Erie to Detroit, concluded by a four-day hike through mud and over "fallen timber, brush, &c." to Ann Arbor. For the Nobles, as for other families, the first attempt at homesteading proved a failure, and the family moved again a year after their arrival in Ann Arbor.

Forced land cessions created homelessness for many Native Americans. Some individual and coordinated resistance continued, but most white migrants encountered Native Americans not as war parties, but as transients entering settlements in search of trade goods or food. In the South, the migrants included slaves, for whom westward settlement often meant forced separation from friends and family. Twenty-year-old Elizabeth Ramsey and her infant daughter, Louisa, were sold from South Carolina to a Georgia cotton planter by the name of Cook. When high living landed Cook in bankruptcy, he fled to Mobile, Alabama, where he hired out both Elizabeth and Louisa as domestic servants. His fortunes still failing, he eventually sold Elizabeth to a new owner in Texas and her daughter to a man in New Orleans.

Before 1808 most enslaved people were taken south and west as part of planter migrations. But by the 1820s, as many as one-third of all migrating slaves (about 15,000 people a year) went west as the property of traders. The internal slave trade was a highly organized business. Some slaves were shipped south on boats, but they were often driven overland. It was a "singular spectacle," one English visitor to Tennessee remembered: "In the early gray of the morning, [coming upon] a camp of negro slave drivers, just packing up to start. They had about three hundred slaves with them, who had bivouacked the preceding night in chains in the woods."

Former slave Frederick Douglass, born in Maryland, later described the terror that the threat of being "sold South" struck in the hearts of enslaved African Americans. His owner died when Douglass was eight or nine years old: "I have no language to express the high excitement and deep anxiety which were felt among us poor slaves during this time," Douglass wrote. "Our fate for life was now to be decided. . . . A single word from the white men was enough—against all our wishes, prayers, and entreaties—to sunder forever the dearest friends, dearest kindred, and strongest ties known to human beings."

Not all westward migration was voluntary. By the 1820s, the internal slave trade was a highly developed business. Traders purchased slaves in the upper South, drove them in large groups into the West and Southwest, and sold them off as labor for the new plantations there.

The Transportation Revolution

Westward migration created vastly enlarged domestic markets. Settlers were eager to get their farm products to coastal and European customers, and merchants and manufacturers were impatient to get their manufactured goods to rural stores. Making that connection was a backbreaking task.

The first efforts at improving transportation came in a spate of locally sponsored toll roads. Most of the capital came from investors in the immediate neighborhood who expected to benefit from tolls. In an effort to bolster the trade from cities like Cincinnati, Pennsylvania extended an older highway that ran from Philadelphia to Lancaster all the way to Pittsburgh. But the toll roads proved a poor investment. In the end, the most important consequence of road building was the encouragement it gave to bridge building. Bridges made a dramatic difference in the time and cost of transport and usually turned a good profit.

Far more important, however, was the use of the steam engine. By the postwar era, the steam engine had reached a sufficient level of development to attract investors. A few hardy souls experimented with steam-powered overland rail carriers, but these lines remained fragmentary until the 1850s. The use of steam engines to power boats proved more successful. In August 1807, Robert Fulton and his patron Robert Livingston announced the Hudson River trial run of the North River Steamboat of Clermont, a 140-foot-long vessel with two steam-driven paddle wheels. "The distance from New York to Albany is one hundred and fifty miles," Fulton explained. "I ran it up in thirty-two hours, and down in thirty. I overtook many sloops and schooners beating to windward, and parted with them as if they had been at anchor."

Although he did not invent the steamboat, Fulton demonstrated its practicality for the transportation of people and goods. By 1817 steamboats were common in the East and Great Lakes, but their most telling impact occurred on the western rivers: the Ohio, the Wabash, the Monongahela, the Cumberland, and especially the Mississippi. In 1809 Livingston and Fulton hired Nicholas Roosevelt to survey the rivers from Pittsburgh to New Orleans, and in 1811 they sent the steamboat *New Orleans* downriver from Pittsburgh. In 1815 steamboats began to ply regular private routes upriver on the Mississippi.

The steamboat bolstered the market development of the Mississippi River Valley by knitting together its northern and southern regions. Able to move goods downstream and to carry passengers and goods upstream, the steamboat spread the cotton boom to the southern Mississippi River Valley. In 1811 the Mississippi River Valley produced some 5 million pounds of cotton. Within two decades it produced 40 times that much, virtually all of it carried to market on steamboats. The steamboat also opened the Ohio River Valley to economic development. In 1817 the overland route from Cincinnati through Pittsburgh to Philadelphia or New York took nearly two months. On steamboats, freight sent downriver from Cincinnati through New Orleans and on by packet to Philadelphia took about half that time.

Even steamboats were limited by the existing waterways. Since the turn of the century, various investors and inventors had sought ways to link those water routes through canals. By 1815, only about 100 miles of canals existed in the United States. None earned much money. Thus, when, at the end of the war, New York City Mayor De Witt Clinton proposed building a canal to connect Albany and Buffalo, many people thought he had taken leave of his senses. The canal would run 364 miles, making it the longest in the world. It would require an elaborate system of aqueducts and locks to negotiate a 571-foot rise in elevation and would cost $7 million. Opponents derided the idea as "Clinton's Big Ditch."

Clinton was not deterred. He insisted that the canal would tie the "most fertile and extensive regions of America" to the city of New York, making that city "the granary of the world, the emporium of commerce, the seat of manufactures, the focus of great moneyed operation." In 1817 he convinced the state legislature not only to authorize the project, but also to pay for it, a gamble that amounted to a $5 per capita levy for the entire population of New York state.

Begun on July 4, 1817, the Erie Canal was completed in 1823 and opened two years later. Clinton's gamble paid off spectacularly. Passenger boats and transport barges crowded each section as quickly as it was opened, producing revenues so high that the state was able to pay for later stages of construction from the profits of earlier ones. Transportation costs from Buffalo to New York City fell from $100 a ton to about $10 a ton and dropped even lower later on.

The Waltham System of Manufacturing

Westward migration created large new markets for manufactured goods. In cities and in the countryside, laborers needed cheap clothing and shoes. Settlers needed seed, building materials, and equipment. By 1814, mechanics and investors had laid the foundations for industrial manufacturing in America.

Americans had been experimenting with industrial technologies since 1790, starting with Samuel Slater's water-powered carding and spinning machines. Industrialization was advanced by Eli Whitney's invention of the cotton gin, by Whitney's and Simeon North's attempts to manufacture weapons with inter-changeable parts, and by ongoing experiments with steam-powered engines.

The first full applications of these advances to manufacturing came to fruition through the efforts of a wealthy Boston merchant named Francis Cabot Lowell. Along the northern Atlantic coast, the War of 1812 disrupted profits from overseas trade and accelerated a shift in investment to internal commerce. Some eastern merchants put money in transportation projects; others speculated in land.

Lowell had his eye on textile manufacturing. The success of Slater's mills had demonstrated the feasibility of developing a domestic textile industry. However, because Slater lacked the power loom (its design was a jealously guarded secret in England), the Rhode Island mills were unable to turn yarn into finished cloth. A grad-uate of Harvard with a knack for machine design, Lowell traveled to England to see the loom and to memorize its design. At home, he worked with mechanic Paul Moody to duplicate the English model. Armed with a special charter from the Massachusetts legislature, in 1814 Lowell and his associates (organized as the Boston Manufacturing Company) opened the first fully mechanized textile mill in the United States, in Waltham, Massachusetts. Within three years the mill had expanded to two buildings, was paying 20 percent dividends, and was using all available water power.

Lowell died in 1817, but under Nathan Appleton's leadership the company (now the Merrimack Manufacturing Corporation) financed a second group of mills in East Chelmsford, Massachusetts. A sleepy rural village of 200 in 1820, by 1826 East Chelmsford had grown to 2,600 residents, had become the site of a second set of mills, and had incorporated as the city of Lowell, America's first industrial town.

The Waltham system, as the process was called, differed from earlier American manufacturing enterprises in several ways. First, it was the largest industrial under-taking ever attempted in America. Waltham also represented a new approach to business organization. Detaching ownership from supervision, the Boston Manufacturing Company hired a manager to oversee the daily operation of the mill. Finally, employees lived in subsidized and supervised housing at the mill site.

Slater's early Rhode Island mills had lacked the power loom. Frances Cabot Lowell stole the design from England and replicated it first in Waltham and later in the Lowell Mills.

For their work force, the owners turned to young women in the surrounding area. The decision to hire women was not altogether remarkable. Textiles were traditionally women's work. Because most observers assumed that water- or steam-powered equipment would make that work easier, there was no reason to associate machinery with men. Female workers were also cheaper than men.

At least in the early years, parents and daughters both saw benefits in mill work for unmarried young women. Going into the mills before marriage could help the family by reducing the number of mouths to be fed. The residential system put to rest any fears that a young woman was compromising her respectability. Matrons supervised company-owned boarding houses. Strict rules of behavior guided the workers' leisure time, and factory bells started and ended the workday and announced lunch breaks. Meanwhile, the young women themselves enjoyed a financial and social independence unknown under the parental roof. They lived, ate, and played together and looked for much of their guidance to a female head of household. Many kept all or most of their pay, enjoying (perhaps for the only time in their lives) a separate disposable income. Later, after employers cut pay and intensified production, the Lowell operatives viewed their experiences in the mills far less favorably. But in the early years, the mills of Waltham and Lowell, like the new territories of the West, seemed to herald a new age of independence and opportunity.

A NEW NATIONALISM

Democratic Republicans remained in power after the War of 1812. In 1817, James Monroe, the third Virginian in a row to hold the office of president, succeeded James Madison. Monroe thoroughly defeated New Yorker Rufus King, the last Federalist to run for the presidency. When Monroe ran for re-election in 1820, he was opposed not by a Federalist, but by a member of his own party, John Quincy Adams, who garnered a single electoral vote. Beneath this apparent calm, however, the Democratic Republican Party was continuing along a path of transformation. Democratic Republicans continued to clarify the boundaries of the nation, extending its territory and influence whenever they could. They gave up the hope that the republic could survive based on a political economy of limited government, free international trade, and agrarianism. Under the influence of a new generation of leaders, the Democratic Republican Party embraced principles of governmental activism, entrepreneurialism, and the development of large-scale domestic manufacturing.

A New Republican Political Economy

In the early nineteenth century the Democratic Republican Party fell increasingly under the influence of younger politicians. Having come of age during the troubled years of the Confederacy, and having witnessed the effects of poor transportation and a weak federal military in the War of 1812, these men did not fear a strong national government. To the contrary, they believed that an activist national government might well be the nation's best protection against localism and dangerous fragmentation. By the election of 1824, they would identify themselves as National Republicans.

This new brand of Republicanism was epitomized by four men: Henry Clay of Kentucky, John C. Calhoun of South Carolina, and Daniel Webster and John Quincy Adams of Massachusetts. Although they preached nationalism, these Republicans bore the imprint of regional politics. Henry Clay (1777–1852) entered national politics as the champion of the large planters and merchants of Kentucky. Putting aside possible differences of interest among them, the Kentucky elites had turned to the federal government for support for projects (especially transportation improvements) they could not win at home. John C. Calhoun (1782–1850) was first a representative and later senator and vice president. Although both Calhoun and South Carolina later became symbols of states' rights sentiment, in the postwar years South Carolinians believed that their export economy (based on rice, indigo, and cotton) was best served by a strong federal government able to ensure access to international markets.

Adams and Webster, both New Englanders, illustrated the compatibility of National Republicanism with the old Federalist views. Webster steadfastly promoted the interests of New England's banking classes. He was a strong supporter of protective tariffs after the War of 1812, as Massachusetts merchants shifted from importing to manufacturing. Born in 1767, John Quincy Adams was influenced by his father's Federalist views, and he was first elected to the Senate in 1800 by the Federalist Massachusetts legislature. Adams broke rank with his party when it opposed the Louisiana Purchase, however. Led by Clay, the new nationalists fashioned a vision of a Republican political economy based on individual entrepreneurial and market development (including domestic manufacturing), guided by the active involvement of the federal government. Calhoun promised his colleagues that the private virtues of ambitious, self-promoting men would lead to the public virtue of the entire nation. He called on Americans to endorse a policy of "prosperity and greatness," but these broad principles concealed a number of differences among Republicans. Some emphasized geographic expansion; some stressed the importance of developing manufactures and business infrastructure. Like the old Federalists, some Republicans felt that "ambitious, self-promoting men" required the guidance of wiser men on the federal level. Others advocated a strong central government as the way to control the excesses of an expanding capitalist economy. Some viewed a strong central government as the best protection against northeastern financial elites, for whom they still harbored a Jeffersonian distrust.

Not surprisingly, their platform, the American System, was a patchwork devised to appeal to local interests and identities. In the West and South, that meant promoting a national subsidy to improve transportation. For the Northeast, National Republicans called for a protective tariff and a new national bank. (The 20-year charter of the First Bank of the United States had expired in 1811.)

The various elements of the American System came before Congress as separate bills, each of which commanded a different coalition of supporters. The bills to create the Second Bank of the United States and to increase the national tariffs passed with relative ease and were signed by President Madison. Authorized in 1816, the Second Bank of the United States was chartered for 20 years and located in Philadelphia, with the federal government providing one-fifth of its $35 million capitalization and appointing one-fifth of its directors. The tariff bill (passed soon after) was less aggressively protective than some nationalists wished. A particular beneficiary of the new tariff was the young Massachusetts textile industry.

Transportation subsidies fared less well. Madison was skeptical about the constitutionality of this form of federal intervention. In his annual messages of both 1815 and 1816 he urged Congress to initiate a constitutional amendment to clarify federal power in this area. Although deeply torn, Congress eventually passed a bill creating a federal fund for internal improvements. On his last day in office, Madison vetoed it. His successor, James Monroe, made clear in his inaugural address that he could support such legislation only "with a constitutional sanction." In 1818, the federal government opened a section of the National Road, a highway that connected Baltimore to Wheeling, Virginia (later West Virginia). Otherwise, federal transportation initiatives fell victim to questions of constitutionality and regional jealousies.

The United States in the Americas

In the eyes of most Americans, national "greatness" included achieving an undisputed stature in transatlantic diplomacy and politics. The Treaty of Ghent, which had wrested control of the old Northwest Territory and the lower Mississippi Valley from Great Britain, had marked an important step toward this goal. By 1819 the United States would assert territorial claims that stretched all the way to the Pacific. By 1823 it would claim a diplomatic sovereignty over the entire hemisphere.

The first initiatives in this direction were a series of agreements clarifying details of the country's relations with British colonies in North America. In 1817 acting Secretary of State Richard Rush and British Minister Charles Bagot agreed to limit British and American forces on the Great Lakes, establishing the precedent of an unmilitarized border. The next year, the Convention of 1818 extended that border along the 49th parallel to the Rocky Mountains, establishing the longest unfortified national boundary in the world. It also formally acknowledged American fishing rights off the Labrador and Newfoundland coasts.

In 1819, the United States at last negotiated clear southern and western boundaries for the Louisiana Purchase. After the purchase, Jefferson had attempted unsuccessfully to buy Florida from Spain. His successor, Madison, had simply declared that West Florida had been a part of the Louisiana Purchase all along. Taking the Florida peninsula itself had been left for James Monroe. With Spain too weak to prevent Seminole raids into Georgia and South Carolina, Monroe authorized war hero Andrew Jackson to lead a raid into Florida, ostensibly to frighten the Seminoles into leaving white settlers alone. But Jackson wanted more. Without clear authorization, in 1818 Jackson's troops entered Florida, destroying Seminole settlements, capturing a Spanish fort (contrary to explicit orders), and executing two British citizens whom Jackson held responsible for supporting Indian resistance. Jackson did not conquer all of Florida; there was no need. By May 1818 it was plain that the United States could take the territory whenever it chose.

A year later, in the Transcontinental Treaty of 1819, Spain ceded all of Florida to the United States in return for the U.S. government's agreement to assume private American claims against Spain in the amount of about $5 million. The Transcontinental Treaty also clarified the border between the United States and Spanish Mexico. The United States gave up claims not only to California (which few people considered part of the original purchase), but also to Texas (which many people did). In return, the United States gained a boundary that ran in a series of ascending steps from Louisiana to the Pacific (see Map 10–2). This treaty defined the United States as a nation that spanned the continent. In the 1820s, under Monroe, the United States began to view itself as American, not quasi-European, and as protector of the Americas against Europe. By 1815 a number of former Spanish colonies, including Argentina, Chile, and Venezuela, had revolted, and an independence movement was underway in Mexico. As these new republics won their independence, they turned to the United States for recognition and support. Against this tide, the absolute monarchies in Europe sought to preserve and extend their territorial empires. France supported the Spanish monarchy against an internal revolt and offered to help Spain regain its colonies in South America. Russia reasserted and strengthened its long-standing claims in the Pacific Northwest.

Great Britain offered to make a joint declaration with the United States, disavowing future territorial ambitions in the Americas and warning other nations against intruding into the internal affairs of Western Hemisphere countries. An alliance with Britain would have enhanced U.S. diplomatic credibility, but many Americans suspected that once it established a right to have its Navy in the area, Britain would squeeze the United States out of South American markets.

Secretary of State John Quincy Adams saw an additional problem. Adams was getting ready to run for the presidency. He needed a strategy for enlarging his support beyond New England and for distinguishing himself from other potential candidates, including both Clay and Calhoun. Adams convinced Monroe to refuse the British offer and, instead, to issue a unilateral statement of support for the new republics. It would be far better, he argued, to act independently than to seem "to come in as a cockboat in the wake of the British man-of-war." Adams hoped that being identified with this policy would help him shed the pro-British tag that was associated with many New Englanders.

In his annual message to Congress in 1823, Monroe enunciated the policy that has since become known as the Monroe Doctrine. Monroe asserted a special United States relationship with all parts of North and South America, with which, he insisted, "we are of necessity more immediately connected." "We owe it . . . to candor and to the amicable relations existing between the United States and those [European] powers," he continued "to declare that we should consider any attempt on their part to extend their system to any portion of this hemisphere as dangerous to our peace and safety." The Monroe Doctrine marked an important milestone in the development of American nationalism and internationalism. The United States not only asserted a new relation (as peer) to the European nations, but a new relation to the Americas as well. Surveillance over the nations of North and South America would be the domestic right of the United States.

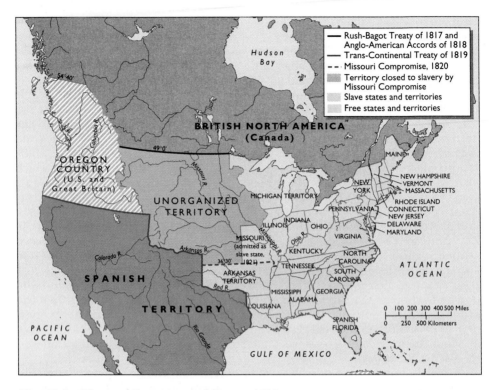

Map 10–2   Westward Expansion and Slavery, 1820
As treaties signed with Great Britain and Spain in 1817, 1818, and 1819 began to outline a United
States that would stretch from the Atlantic Ocean to the Pacific Ocean, Americans worried about the division of that territory into areas open to slavery and areas closed to slavery. Although in 1820 more acres
were closed to slavery than not, the Missouri Compromise permitted slavery in territories where it had
not existed before, reinforcing northerners' fears that planter interests dominated in national policy.

Judicial Nationalism

In the years immediately after the War of 1812, the new, nationally oriented Republicans found important support in the Supreme Court. The court was still guided by
Jefferson's old nemesis, John Marshall. But between 1819 and 1824, in a type of
judicial nationalism, the Marshall court delivered three landmark decisions that
strengthened the power of the federal government and legitimated the new Republican vision of an America of expansive economic growth.

   The earliest of the three, *Dartmouth* v. *Woodward* (1819), reinforced the principle that the rights of people were best protected through the rights of contract. The
case concerned an attempt by the state legislature of New Hampshire to alter the
original charter of Dartmouth College, given to the college by King George III in
1769. New Hampshire argued that the original charter was not binding on the current state government, but Dartmouth insisted that the charter was covered under
Article VI of the Constitution, which protected contracts entered into before the
Revolution. Acting to ensure the stability of contract in the broadest sense, the
court ruled in Dartmouth's favor.

The case of *McCulloch* v. *Maryland*, also decided in 1819, centered on the Second Bank of the United States. Since its establishment, the Second Bank had created a number of branches, one of which was in Baltimore. Viewing the presence of the federal institution within its borders as a potential threat to its sovereignty, Maryland attempted to assert its authority over the Baltimore branch by taxing it. Acting on behalf of the bank, James W. McCulloch, chief clerk of the branch, refused. Maryland appealed to the Supreme Court, arguing that because the federal government was a creation of the states, its branch institutions could be taxed in the states. Marshall's court unanimously rejected this position, finding instead that the federal government was the direct creation of the people acting through the special conventions that ratified the Constitution and was thus superior to the states.

Gibbons v. *Ogden* (1824) concerned a disputed ferryboat monopoly in New York. Having been awarded exclusive rights to operate steamboats in the state's waters, Robert Fulton and Robert Livingston had, in turn, "contracted" a part of this right, giving Aaron Ogden a ferry monopoly across the Hudson River from New York to New Jersey. At the same time, however, a man by the name of Thomas Gibbons had obtained a federal license to operate a boat line along a coastal route that came into conflict with Ogden's line. The question was who controlled these waters and had the right to grant licenses, New York or the federal government. Consistent with its national view of development, the Marshall court found in favor of the federal power.

FIREBELLS IN THE NIGHT

Visitors to the new nation often praised the freedom of its citizens and marveled at its robust economy. Yet they noted discrepancies in the expanding democracy: the survival of slavery, the treatment of Native Americans, the deterioration of some city neighborhoods, and the reckless mania for speculation. In 1819, the bubble of speculation suddenly burst, casting the nation into the worst financial crisis of its young history. Also in 1819, Missouri applied for statehood, forcing the issue of slavery onto the national political agenda. Referring to Missouri, Thomas Jefferson wrote, "This momentous question, like a firebell in the night, awakened and filled me with terror." Both events awakened such anxieties.

The Panic of 1819

In 1819 Americans learned that the market revolution could produce dream-shattering plunges as well as exhilarating rises. Having signed the bill chartering the Second Bank of the United States in 1816, James Madison had appointed an old political ally, Captain William Jones, as its director. Jones speculated in bank stock and accepted bribes to overlook reckless local practices. By the time Jones was replaced, bank stock was at an all-time low, and the state banks had glutted the economy with unsecured paper money.

Jones's successor, Langdon Cheves, moved quickly to cut the supply of paper money, calling in loans and redeeming the bank's holdings of currency issued by state banks. The state banks were forced in turn to retrench. As credit dried up and the value of paper money plummeted, the nation was thrown into depression. Without credit or sufficient circulating money, commodity prices crashed throughout the Atlantic region. For three long years, the economy stalled. When people could not pay their mortgages, farms and businesses failed, and tens of thousands of workers lost their jobs. Because the branches of the Second Bank of the United

States reached far beyond the East Coast, so did the panic. When the branch in Cincinnati, Ohio, suddenly called in the debts it held from local banks, those local banks scurried to collect their loans.

Cheves had saved the monetary system of the United States, but he had not made many friends for the Second Bank. State legislators, who saw the national bank (not runaway speculation or wildcat state banks) as the villain, scrambled to reduce its power. After opening 18 branches in 1817 (including the one in Cincinnati), the Second Bank opened no additional new branches until 1826.

The Panic of 1819 underscored persistent weaknesses and inequities in the market economy. Although some people realized huge returns from investments and speculations, even in the best of times it took money to make money. The original investors in the Boston Manufacturing Company enjoyed average annual dividends of 20 percent, but on an initial investment of $400,000. On a smaller scale, the E. I. du Pont de Nemours gunpowder works, established in 1802 near Wilmington, Delaware, was capitalized at 18 shares of stock worth $2,000 each. Even $2,000 was several times more than the annual income of most professionals in America at the turn of the century and more money than most workers saw in a decade.

It was not only in the new manufacturing sector that it took money to make money. Although the federal government had been modifying its land sales policies, in 1820 the minimum parcel was still 80 acres at $1.25 an acre. The $100 cash needed to purchase an 80-acre plot was more than half a year's wages for many journeymen in 1820, and for most female workers it represented an entire year's income. Land dealing was still an occupation of the rich and well connected.

The Missouri Compromise

By 1819, land had come to represent national as well as individual prosperity for many Americans. Only in 1819, when Missouri applied for permission to organize as a state, did Americans begin to perceive that settlement of the West had the power, paradoxically, to tear the nation apart (see Map 10–2).

The question of Missouri was principally a question of political power on the federal level, but it was inextricably tied to the question of slavery. Northerners had long been unhappy with what they saw as the unfair advantage awarded to southern states by the Constitution's Three-Fifths Compromise, which allowed states to count slaves (on a three-fifths basis) toward representation in Congress. Admission of Missouri would extend that unfair pattern of representation in the House and create a new imbalance in the Senate. In 1819 there were 22 states in the Union, 11 free and 11 slave. Admission of Missouri would give the slave states domination in any purely sectional dispute.

There were other issues. Northerners feared that Missouri, the first wholly new state to be organized from the Louisiana Purchase, would set a precedent for extending slavery into additional new states. Moreover, by 1819 many northerners no longer believed that slavery would simply die out of its own accord, as it seemed to be making some headway even in free states. When Illinois had entered the union in 1818, for example, it had entered as a free state, but with a Black Code that limited the economic and civil rights of free African Americans and permitted the continuation of slavery in the southern parts of the state.

The trouble over Missouri began almost at once. In the course of the House debate, New York Representative James Tallmadge proposed that Missouri be admitted under two conditions: First, no more slaves were to be brought into the state, and second, slavery was to be gradually abolished after the state was admitted to the union. Southerners lined up unanimously against the amendment, while northerners voted unanimously in favor of it. The amendment cleared the House but was rejected in the Senate, where it died in committee.

By the time Congress reconvened, positions on both sides had hardened. Northern congressmen insisted that Congress had the power to prohibit slavery from the Louisiana Territory and should do so. Southern congressmen responded that the Constitution provided no such power. In addition, they argued that in guaranteeing that no citizen could be deprived of life, liberty, or property without due process of law, the Fifth Amendment protected the right of slaveowners to carry slaves into new states.

Both in its general outlines and in its specific arguments, the struggle over Missouri foreshadowed subsequent congressional debates over slavery. It also foreshadowed the reluctance of the North to press the confrontation. Arguing for the continuation of slavery, Senator Nathaniel Macon of North Carolina cautioned his northern colleagues that in no place in the United States were free people of color truly welcome. No one rose to dispute him. Indeed, racism was codified in many northern state constitutions.

The firestorm over Missouri was resolved when Maine applied for statehood as a free state. Under Speaker of the House Henry Clay's guidance, the two bills were linked, preserving the balance in the Senate. The compromise, which also contained a provision that slavery would be permitted in Arkansas Territory but excluded from the rest of the Louisiana Purchase, passed narrowly in March 1820.

THE POLITICAL ECONOMY OF REGIONALISM

The economic expansion of the postwar years rested on a rough regional specialization: a South built on plantation-style export agriculture, a North built on business and trade, and a raw backcountry in the West. No region was completely uniform, and none was autonomous. Southerners relied on the North for shipping and business services, agricultural products, and manufactured goods. Northern merchants and bankers depended on southern customers. Both areas looked to the West for new lands and markets. As the Missouri controversy foreshadowed, however, the economic systems of the regions were fostering distinctive social and political systems that would, in time, prove incompatible.

Cities, Markets, and Commercial Farms in the Northeast

In the Northeast, port cities had developed in tandem with the agricultural hinterlands that surrounded them. By 1820, the region radiated from the northern Atlantic seaports through a web of interior cities, towns, villages, and farms all the way to western New York and Pennsylvania. It was united by the density of cash markets, the growing importance of wage labor, and the steady spread of urban institutions.

The Northeast remained anchored in the cities of the northern Atlantic coast. By 1820, New York claimed a population of 152,056, Philadelphia of 63,802, Boston of 43,738, and Baltimore (at the northern tip of the Chesapeake) of 62,738. By the 1820s the swelling populations in these cities had encouraged the growth of substantial urban manufacturing sectors. Old craft shops competed with larger retail manufacturers to produce boots, shoes, furniture, clothing, coaches, tools, ships, and other goods, some intended for the local trade, some shipped south, west, or overseas.

Early nineteenth-century cities were churning cauldrons of human activity. This depiction of the Procession of Victuallers in Philadelphia suggests the swarms of people, the mingling of purposes, the crowded living conditions, and the crush of shops that characterized urban life in 1819.

After 1820 this urban growth was fed by waves of immigration. The end of the Napoleonic Wars and crop failures in Germany, Scandinavia, and Ireland forced hundreds of thousands of peasants off the land. New immigrants who were able (especially Germans and Scandinavians) joined the trek west. Poorer immigrants tended to remain in the Northeast, where they took jobs as laborers and factory workers.

Even beyond its largest cities, the Northeast was far more urban than either the South or the West—the result of an intricate pattern of interdependent markets that tied farms to villages to towns to interior cities to the eastern ports. Through these intermediate layers, commercial markets penetrated the countryside to an extent that sometimes surprised recent immigrants. "'The whole world is set upon money &c.' Why do you say so?" Mary Ann Archbald wrote to her cousin in Scotland in 1816. "You ought to have left this observation for me to make on the west side of the Atlantic. It applies exactly to the people here!"

Most households made the transition to greater cash dependency without much conscious thought. City wage workers had little choice. Fewer and fewer employers were willing to hire individuals "found" (i.e., with room and board as part of their pay). In the countryside, farmers responded to improved transportation by growing food for more distant markets. Some farmers continued to carry their own produce to market, but the need to ship longer distances promoted the rise of intermediate agents, attached to merchants or buyers who did not have direct contact with the farmers. These conditions favored the rise of formal systems of payment and credit over personal systems of barter and trust.

After 1810, in response to the demand in cities and in the South for manufactured goods, rural workers oriented work they had previously done for their own families—making brooms, cheese, yarn, and, later, straw hats—toward the commercial market. At first, local stores functioned as collecting points, paying farm people in store credits while building up inventories to be shipped east to wholesalers. By the 1830s, family members worked directly for contractors who provided raw materials and paid them by the piece for items they made at home.

Urbanization and the growing reliance on cash exchange and wages altered the foundations of family and community life in several ways. With family holdings too small to provide land to all the male children, young men took to the roads as peddlers, hired out as agricultural wage workers, moved to cities, or struck out for the West. Daughters took jobs in the mills or as schoolteachers or left for the city to find employment in shops or as domestic workers. These changes diminished the importance of patriarchy and eroded older notions of republican virtue based on community obligation. Increasingly, civic virtue consisted of individual achievement, especially as measured in cash terms.

In cities, family size decreased, beginning a century-long decline among native-born white families. The decrease was most marked in families in which the women were educated. Perhaps these women were better informed about their own health, more attentive to prescriptive writing about childrearing, and more able to assert their own preferences about family size.

By bringing more people into closer proximity, urban life encouraged the growth of organizations of all kinds, from libraries and reform associations to charity groups. Elite women had long been involved in such groups, but in the early decades of the nineteenth century, middle-class urban women also began joining in growing numbers, especially in response to what they perceived as the breakdown of old family bonds. These extrafamilial organizations would eventually draw northeastern middle-class women into much more extensive involvement in public life.

The cities offered opportunity. For Mrs. J. Cantelo, a New York seamstress, the 1820s were flush years. Her dressmaking establishment did so well that she moved to a new location, hired "a fashionable dressmaker" and a milliner, and scheduled a lavish grand opening for May 1, 1826. Cantelo's timing was perfect. Having recovered from the slump of 1819, New York's economy was booming. Southern families were resuming their shopping trips north, and middling and wealthy urban families once again had disposable income for new wardrobes. But there were troubling signs in the new political economy. Small manufacturing shops relied increasingly on workers trained in only one aspect of a craft, employees who could be easily replaced and could not command high wages. Also, good housing was hard to find because builders focused on the needs of prosperous families. By 1826 two third-floor rooms in a house in lower Manhattan cost double the wages of most workers.

Planters, Yeomen, and Slaves in the South

In contrast to the network of towns and cities that criss-crossed the Northeast, the South remained largely agricultural, preserved in that way of life by overseas and northern markets, a temperate climate, and slavery. By 1820 the cotton boom had extended the political economy of slavery into virtually all of the territory south of Pennsylvania and the Ohio River Valley and east of the Mississippi River, as well as into Missouri and Louisiana.

The symbol of the South was the plantation, a large farm owned and operated by a single white family and worked under the supervision of hired employees by 20 or more enslaved laborers. Cotton plantations proliferated in the new western lands. Meanwhile, the reopening of international markets gave new life to tobacco plantations in Virginia and North Carolina, rice plantations in South Carolina and Georgia, and sugar plantations in Louisiana.

Some plantations were complex economic concerns, with dispersed fields, multiple barns and outbuildings, batteries of craft workers, a village of slave cabins, and an elegantly furnished "big house." Many were somewhat less noble, however. Northerner Emily Burke described the big house of a Georgia plantation as a mere husk of a building with unplastered walls, a plank floor she could see through, and a roof like a sieve.

Of the 1.5 million enslaved inhabitants of the South in 1820, probably three-quarters lived on plantations. The number of slaves on a given plantation varied widely. Sugar plantations averaged 30 or more workers, and the wealthiest families of the South owned hundreds of slaves. On plantations, most men and women worked in the fields, their days determined by the crop and the season. Tobacco workers were especially busy in the spring, carefully transplanting young plants and pruning off extra shoots. At harvest, cotton workers dragged their load as they pulled the sticky cotton fibers from their bolls, continuing by the light of torches long after sunset. Masters on sugar plantations reputedly drove their workers hardest, but it was rice cultivation, where workers stood ankle-deep in mud under the blazing sun in snake-infested, swamp-land fields, that was "by far the most unhealthy work in which slaves are employed." The crop also influenced the organization of labor. Skilled rice cultivators commonly worked by the "task" system, under which workers were assigned a specific objective for the day's work (e.g., repairing a drainage ditch) and were able to exercise some autonomy over their labor. On large cotton plantations, slaves were more likely to be organized in "gangs," set at repetitive tasks (like hoeing or picking) with close supervision.

On big plantations and on plantations in the older states, where soil was exhausted and planters made part of their income by selling and renting out slaves, as much as one-quarter of the work force was assigned to domestic service or to crafts intended to make the plantation self-sufficient. Although white observers tended to view household servants as fortunate, the lot of house servants was not necessarily better than that of field workers. Constantly on call, their workday could last even longer than that of field workers. They were also especially vulnerable to the caprices and violent outbursts of owners.

Cultivating rice, considered by many to be the most dangerous type of plantation labor.

More independent were the 5 to 8 percent of the work force trained for craft work. Men became carpenters, iron workers, and boatmen. A smaller number of women became spinners, weavers, seamstresses, and dairy maids. Because their work was housed in separate shops, craft workers often enjoyed a degree of autonomy rare for most slaves.

Neither slave-owning nor plantation farming typified the experiences of southern whites, most of whom lived on small holdings of several hundred acres or less. These "yeoman" households typically owned no slaves, although they sometimes hired slaves from nearby planters. Living in rough and isolated dwellings, they produced as much of their own food as they could; planted small amounts of cash-crop tobacco, cotton, or grain; and often relied on nearby planters as agents in selling their crops or purchasing new equipment. Beneath the yeoman households, economically and socially, was a white underclass of tenant farmers and day laborers and a precarious free black population.

Although most white people did not own slaves, the institution of slavery influenced their material lives and personal values. Siphoning private investment away from transportation and manufacturing, slavery and plantation agriculture prevented the development of an internal market network comparable to that in the Northeast. Small farmers could hire field slaves from larger planters at rates cheaper than they could hire free labor, and planters could put a slave to craft work for less money than it would cost to hire a free artisan. These circumstances discouraged the development of a free labor-wage market in the South. By 1820 the South did have mills and factories, but most of the workers were slaves. Some white southerners supported transportation improvements and improved communication. But the South was favored with navigable rivers and a long coastline. Because enslaved labor could be employed in off-seasons to transport commodities, improved speed had little effect on the ultimate cost of production.

Plantation slavery also stunted the growth of cities and of an urban working or middle class. Even in the older seacoast states, less than 3 percent of southerners lived in cities. This number included planters taking refuge during the malaria season, slaves hired out to domestic service for the urban professional class, and the South's free African-American population. In a long-standing practice, southern planters looked to Philadelphia and New York for services and luxury goods. When planters sought alternatives to this pattern of external dependence, they looked not to local villages or towns but to their own plantations, reassigning field workers to produce the butter, cheese, and tools they might otherwise have purchased locally. With a few exceptions, the economies of southern cities were based narrowly on the commerce of slaves and cotton.

Most white southerners continued to live in rural settings under the authority of fathers. In this environment, white southerners clung to an older understanding of republican virtue still based on the interdependencies of rural life, increasingly romanticized to obscure the fact that most of those dependencies were coerced. In this version of republicanism, the good citizen was the patriarchal father who protected his family, wisely stewarded his human and nonhuman resources, and was generous to his neighbors. The dearth of formal cash networks preserved the centrality of personal reputation in both economic and social relations, heightening the emphasis on personal integrity as an aspect of southern republican manhood.

Depicting slaves merely as a type of dependent to be guided with wisdom and compassion, this version of republicanism obscured both the violence of the institution itself and the violent influence it had on the culture of the South. Slavery required a legal system honed over time to the purpose of condoning violence, an extralegal system of vigilante groups ready to step in should the law falter, and a society of individuals (especially men) ready to react to even the smallest insubordination. Violence was potential in every interaction; when it occurred it was often both publicly witnessed and publicly approved.

In all its forms, slavery constituted a steady assault on the selfhood and the family and community life of slaves. The killing of a slave was the most extreme example of this aggression. More common were the casual humiliations and interference with daily life. The early life of Elizabeth Keckley (who later purchased her freedom and founded the Contraband Relief Organization to support freed slaves during the Civil War) illustrated common patterns of dislocation. Born in 1818, Keckley scarcely knew her father, who belonged to a different Virginia planter. When she was 18, Keckley was hired out to a man in North Carolina, by whom, cut off from the protection of family and friends, she conceived a child. She later returned to Virginia, where she lived with her mother, but was then forcibly taken west to St. Louis. There, faced with the threat of having her aging mother hired out for service, Keckley worked for wages as a seamstress, "ke[eping] bread in the mouths of seventeen persons."

It was not unusual for enslaved women to bear children whose fathers were free and white. Undoubtedly, some intimate relations between enslaved women and free men were consensual, but most were not. In *Incidents in the Life of a Slave Girl*, Harriet Jacobs described the limited choices available to female slaves. Jacobs's master began making sexual advances when she was only 15: "[S]hudder[ing] to think of being the mother of children who should be owned by my old tyrant," and hoping to make him so mad that he would sell her, Jacobs entered a sexual relationship with another white man, with whom she eventually bore two children.

Nevertheless, slaves constructed rich familial and community bonds. Whites denied legal recognition to slave marriages, but slaves sanctioned their own relationships, combining African ceremonies with European wedding rituals, and struggled to provide stability in their children's lives. White owners flattered themselves that they were the masters of all their chattel, but African-American parents made certain their children understood, as Jacobs remembered her father's words, "You are my child, and when I call you, you should come immediately, if you have to pass through fire and water."

Enslaved workers also found camaraderie and strength in labor. Field workers carved out implicit understandings with their masters about at least some of the terms of their labor. Task groups who finished early expected to be rewarded with free time. Individuals with particular expertise expected deference from drivers, overseers, and even owners. Throughout much of the South, a two-hour lunch break in the hottest part of the summer day was customary, and slaves had Sunday for their own work and families.

The power of whites over African Americans was never absolute. While whites used violence, sexual assault, and vigilante terrorism to intimidate slaves, slaves fought back with arson, poison, feigned illness, work slowdowns, and the threat of violence. Harriet Jacobs remembered that her grandmother delivered "scorching rebukes" to her master.

As slaves built the economy of the South, they also left a lasting imprint on southern culture. Enslaved African Americans began converting to Christianity in the late eighteenth century, and many embraced the religious revivals of the early nineteenth century. Yet as they accepted Christianity, they made it their own. Slave preachers made selective use of Christian themes, emphasizing the story of Moses and the escape from bondage over homilies on human depravity and the importance of absolute obedience. Newly arrived Africans provided a constant infusion of African religious forms, such as dancing, spiritual singing, chanting, and clapping. They also introduced distinctly African and Afro-Caribbean religions, such as voodoo. Slave religious practice became both the embodiment and the instrument of self-assertion. The call to "cross over Jordan" that constituted the refrain of many slave songs symbolized the harshness of slave life, but it might also signal the singer's intention to escape.

The River and the West

The trans-Appalachian West was not a uniform region with a single culture or perfectly homogeneous interests. Indeed, even more than the other regions, the West was as much an idea as a place and its borders were constantly shifting. Although the Mississippi River offered a rough western border for the region, soon after the War of 1812 settlers were pouring into Arkansas Territory beyond the river.

The West overlapped both the South and the Northeast and reflected the economies and cultures of both. Settled largely by northeasterners, the Northwest (Ohio, Indiana, northern Illinois, and Michigan Territory) was characterized by family farming, small manufacturing, and wage labor. In contrast, the Southwest (western Georgia, Alabama, Mississippi, Louisiana, southern Illinois, Florida and Arkansas Territories, Kentucky, and Tennessee), settled by southerners, depended on slavery and was oriented toward export farming.

These two regions were bound together by the Ohio and Mississippi Rivers, flowing from the western border of Pennsylvania to the Gulf of Mexico. For years this had been a one-way system. Indians, trappers, and fur traders had used the Mississippi to float hides downstream. Farmers and merchants followed suit, building large flatboats to carry salted or dried pork, corn, and wheat downriver for sale or export. So long as goods could only move downstream, however, settlers in the Northwest used the river to ship cargo downstream to New Orleans for sale, but they did their buying in the East, carrying purchases home overland. The development of the steamboat, which enabled goods to be moved efficiently upriver as well as downriver, drew transplanted New Englanders and transplanted Virginians and Carolinians into a web of common interests.

Western settlers were also knit together by the politics of land. Most migrants to the West were farm families looking for affordable land and access to eastern and foreign markets. They favored generous federal land policies and easy credit, but the land boom, and the ways that Congress structured land sales, encouraged corruption. The Act of 1804 required that lands be bought at auction and required an immediate downpayment, features that benefited wealthy speculators. Land office agents, who controlled the auction calendars, exacted bribes for setting auction dates favorable to particular bidders and used their inside information to buy up cheap lands in danger of repossession. Unregulated state banks offered sweetheart deals to wealthy patrons.

Settlers fought back for fair access to the new lands. They lobbied Congress to allow settlers to claim land before it came up for auction, and for a guaranteed fair price for improvements on repossessed property. When the federal government resisted these remedies as endangering overall receipts, settlers took measures into their own hands. Some new arrivals simply "squatted" on the land they wanted and defied federal agents to push them off. Organized in loose vigilance associations, neighbors attended land auctions, using the threat of their presence and sometimes their fists to intimidate speculators and profiteers.

The population of the West doubled during these years. In Ohio the number of people per square mile increased from about 4 in 1810 to about 24 in 1830, and in Indiana it increased from less than 1 to almost 10. By 1825 the West had developed a discernible regional political economy based on commercial agriculture and trade and oriented toward the western rivers. Farmers produced corn, wheat, and livestock in the North and cotton, sugar cane, and some grain in the South. Villages and small towns functioned as collection points for crops. Larger cities on the waterways collected the inland produce, processed it, and channeled goods north or south to market. With New Orleans, gateway to the Gulf, at one end and Pittsburgh, gateway to the East, at the other, the Ohio–Mississippi system included Cincinnati, Louisville, St. Louis, and Memphis. Functioning initially as shipping hubs, the western cities soon developed into regional manufacturing centers as well. By 1820, Cincinnati offered tailors, seamstresses, milliners, cabinet makers, saddlers, chandlers, iron manufacturers, a tannery, tin and copper workers, brick-makers and papermakers, a steam mill, and a gunpowder maker.

The Northwest's relatively dense pattern of settlement permitted the development of societies and civic groups reminiscent of the Northeast. Cincinnati supported a circulating library, a seminary for young ladies, a medical society, a saving society, a literary magazine, a chapter of the Bible and Tract Society, and a society for rescuing people who fell into the river. Still, the western cities had a rough-and-ready character that distinguished them from their eastern counterparts: gamblers looking for an easy mark, land agents looking for buyers, dispirited newcomers looking for supplies, Indians looking for food, and aging frontiersmen looking for a fight.

Settlement remained sparse in most places, and migrants could find themselves isolated for the first several years. Creating a new home called on all the resources that settlers could muster. In Dexter, Michigan, their second stop, Harriet Noble's family found the shell of a cabin already built, but it lacked a roof, a door, and a chimney. Noble described it as a "square log pen." By late November the cabin still lacked a chimney. "I said to my husband, 'I think I can drive the oxen and draw the stones, while you dig them from the ground and load them'," she remembered. "He . . . loaded them on a kind of sled; I drove to the house, rolled them off, and drove back for another load. I succeeded so well that we got enough in this way to build our chimney." "I was not at all particular what kind of labor I performed," she reflected, "so we were only comfortable and provided with the necessaries of life."

Most new arrivals settled for caves or huts, or (like the young Abraham Lincoln, whose family migrated to Indiana from Kentucky in 1816) lived in "half-faced camps" (three-sided cabins with trees for corner posts and branches for a roof) and turned their immediate attention to getting a crop in. Settlers often staked their claims in isolated, wooded areas, where the family cleared four or five acres to start: a small patch each for a kitchen garden and for flax, larger plots for wheat and corn. Men felled trees; women and children dragged them away for use building barns or cabins or as firewood. Women worked alongside men in planting and hoeing, and later in harvesting the crop.

CONCLUSION

In many respects, the years between 1815 and 1824 were years of political consolidation, diplomatic success, and heady economic growth. As the United States asserted breathtaking new national and international claims, it transformed itself in-

CHRONOLOGY

1807	First trip of Robert Fulton's North River Steamboat of Clermont
1814	Treaty of Ghent Waltham mills open
1815	Steamboats begin regular two-way trips on the Mississippi
1816	Second Bank of the United States is created Tariff is passed James Monroe elected president
1817	Madison vetoes Federal Transportation Subsidies Bill New York begins construction of Erie Canal (opened 1825)
1818	United States and Great Britain negotiate Convention of 1818
1819	*Dartmouth v. Woodward* and *McCulloch v. Maryland* Missouri applies for statehood United States and Spain negotiate Transcontinental Treaty Panic of 1819
1820	Maine becomes a state
1821	Missouri becomes a state
1823	Monroe Doctrine Merrimack Manufacturing Company mills produce first finished cloth
1824	*Gibbons v. Ogden* John Quincy Adams elected president
1825	Erie Canal opens

ternally into a land of expanding interdependent regional markets and well-oiled political institutions.

And yet there were firebells enough, for those who chose to hear them. The American System had to be carefully negotiated in Congress, and it authorized a bank that helped bring about economic pandemonium. In some cases, nationalism and expansionism seemed to heighten fragmentation, suggesting that the national political economy was in fact a series of discrete political economies, with different ways of organizing material life and promoting different personal values and national politics. Most citizens decided that the lesson of Missouri was simply to avoid the issue of slavery altogether. Few took notice, in January 1821, when, in the wake of the Missouri controversy, a newspaper writer by the name of Benjamin Lundy founded the first openly antislavery newspaper, the *Genius of Universal Emancipation*.

FURTHER READINGS

Frederic Bancroft, *Slave Trading in the Old South* (1931). This classic study of the internal slave trade (the first major examination of slavery to attack the mythology of slavery as a benevolent institution) details both the interregional movement of enslaved workers in the antebellum South and the institutions that facilitated the diaspora.

George Dangerfield, *The Awakening of American Nationalism, 1815–1828* (1965). Dangerfield's book remains one of the most readable overviews of United States life and politics in the wake of the enormous expansion of markets that followed the conclusion of the War of 1812.

Thomas Dublin, *Women at Work: The Transformation of Work and Community in Lowell, Massachusetts, 1826–1860* (1979). *Women at Work* traces the founding and early years of the textile industry in Lowell, Massachusetts, with particular attention to the family and economic backgrounds of the female operatives, the social relations of their work in the mills, early organizing as conditions of labor began to deteriorate in the 1830s, and the growth of an Irish work force.

John Mack Faragher, *Sugar Creek: Life on the Illinois Frontier* (1986). Faragher uses the history of a single Illinois community to examine the motivations that led early settlers west; the day-to-day hardships they faced in obtaining land, getting in a crop, and settling a family; and the circumstances that led some settlers to remain permanently in Sugar Creek while others soon moved on to other frontiers.

William G. McLoughlin, *Cherokee Renascence in the New Republic* (1986). McLoughlin examines the history of the Cherokees, 1789–1833, with emphasis on the destructive impact of United States Indian policy and the various military, diplomatic, and cultural strategies through which Cherokees sought to preserve their lands and autonomous society.

 Please refer to the document CD-ROM for primary sources related to this chapter.

11
Securing Democracy
1820–1832

Jackson's Election • **Perfectionism and the Theology of Human Striving** • **The Common Man and the Political Economy of Democracy** • **The Democratic Impulse in Presidential Politics President Jackson: Vindicating the Common Man** • **Conclusion**

JACKSON'S ELECTION

"If vigilance and exertion be the conditions upon which we hold our rights," the *United States Gazette* warned early in 1828, "there never was a moment when they were more imperiously called for than the present." Although the tone suggested that foreign invasion was imminent, the object of the *Gazette*'s fears was none other than General Andrew Jackson. For two years the editors of the *Gazette* had watched with growing apprehension as Jackson's men had moved across America, lobbying local politicians, flattering voters, funding newspapers, and silently converting the electoral system into a network of pro-Jackson forces. To Jackson's opponents, the mere idea of a Jacksonian presidency was abhorrent. The man was an infidel and a would-be "despot," they charged.

Eight months later, the *Gazette*'s worst fears were realized. On March 4, 1829, Andrew Jackson became the seventh president of the United States.

For Jackson supporters, the general's election represented not cataclysm, but something far closer to national salvation. At long last, according to some observers, "the people in all their majesty" had defeated the last vestiges of European-style "Aristocracy." Like ecstatic believers in the throes of conversion, Jackson supporters swarmed the nation's capital, jamming the halls of Congress and mobbing the White

House. "I never saw such a crowd here before," Daniel Webster declared, ". . . and they really seem to think that the country is rescued from some dreadful danger!"

In truth, the election of 1828 was not Armageddon, and the conditions that led to it did not constitute a stark drama of good and evil. By the mid-1820s the United States had shed its earlier, deferential republican character. Revivalists called on Americans to assume responsibility for their own destinies, and the robust economy and geographical expansion offered opportunity to free men of modest means.

Still, prosperity had come at the price of deepened commercial and industrial dependencies, single-party rule, an activist government, and the beginnings of economic consolidation. By 1828 disaffection ran through the ranks of small farmers and working people, who believed that evil conspirators were arrayed against them.

Jackson did not create this paradox of surging optimism and brooding distrust, but he captured it perfectly in his life history and in temperament. The archetypical individual of the Age of Jackson was the white, male westward migrant, ingenious, self-reliant, and scrappy. Especially after the Panic of 1819, many Americans feared this "common man" was being sacrificed to the interests of eastern banks, merchants, and speculators. Jackson himself had left the East Coast a penniless boy and fought his way to wealth and fame in Tennessee. As president he attacked privileged eastern elites, corporations that gave special advantages to the wealthy, and political parties that trampled on the needs of common folk.

However triumphal the rhetoric, Jacksonian democracy was limited. Not only did the political economy of the Jacksonian era exclude African Americans and women from economic, political, and social liberty, but it also failed to address the growing plight of wage-earning men. White male suffrage became virtually universal in these years, but Jackson himself had little use for the crowds of angry workers who filled city streets, as he had no patience for evangelicals, reforming women, or opponents of slavery. These internal contradictions were the fault lines along which the new political economy would eventually fracture.

PERFECTIONISM AND THE THEOLOGY OF HUMAN STRIVING

American religious life in the 1820s reflected the paradoxes of the age. Some Americans looked at the changes of the preceding decades and saw a nation on the verge of losing its moral compass. Convinced that the day of final reckoning grew near, they preached doom and withdrew from society into covenanted communities to prepare themselves for the end of time. Others remained hopeful that the nation could yet be redeemed. These reformers believed that it was the responsibility of each individual to work actively to perfect American society. Where the reformers agreed with separatists, however, was in their conviction that social life should be modeled on the principles of Protestant Christianity. This broad belief in the Christianizing of society bound together a national culture in the first 25 years of the nineteenth century.

Millennialism and Communitarians

Separatist communities were not new to the American spiritual landscape in these years, and they never accounted for more than a minority of the American people. Nevertheless, they enjoyed renewed success in the 1820s. As a group, these religious communitarians sought to create more perfect societies on earth, an effort they undertook by withdrawing from daily contact with their neighbors and instituting tightly controlled spiritual, social, and economic regimens.

One of the earliest of these religious communities was the United Society of Believers in Christ's Second Appearing, a radical branch of Quakerism. This group was soon dubbed "Shakers" by its critics, for the "[d]ancing, singing, leaping, clapping . . . , groans and sighs" that characterized its services. Shakerism was rooted in the experiences of Ann Lee, a late-eighteenth-century English factory worker and lay preacher who believed that she was the second, female embodiment of the Messiah. Lee preached that believers should return to the simplicity and purity of the early Christian Church, pooling their worldly resources, withdrawing from the vanities of the society, and observing celibacy. The Shakers migrated to North America in 1774 and established their first community near Watervliet, New York. "Mother" Ann died in 1784, but by the turn of the century the Shakers had established a dozen communities in New England. Soon after they began to move west, establishing four settlements in Ohio and Kentucky. By the 1830s membership approached 4,000.

Shaker beliefs required the establishment of a community on the basis of a "union of faith, of motives, and of interest" of all members. To ensure this perfect unity, Shakers organized their communities into "families" of 30 to 100 members, each of which was supervised by a panel of eight people (two women and two men to oversee spiritual matters, and two men and two women to oversee temporal concerns). The

Outsiders labeled members of the United Society of Believers in Christ's Second Appearing "Shakers" after the active twirling and shaking movements that accompanied their services. Here Shakers engage in a ritual dance called "The Whirling Gift."

"families" within a community were guided by a ministry (also composed equally of men and women), and the individual communities submitted to the authority of a head ministry at New Lebanon, New York.

Their search for perfection led the Shakers to repudiate the values of the increasingly market-driven American economy. Although Shakers sold goods to outsiders, they rejected materialism and competitive individualism, allocating individual labor according to the needs of the community. This alternative political economy resulted in prosperity and a high level of invention. Shaker gardeners developed the first American seed industry, and Shaker farmers produced bumper crops of grain and bred large and healthy herds of dairy cattle.

Women appear to have been especially drawn to Shakerism, probably because of the separation of the sexes and formal equality between men and women. Labor was strictly organized by gender. Shakers believed in the spiritual equality of men and women. This was reflected in the authority structure of the communities, with "sisters" and "female elders" supervising the women's lives and "brothers" and "male elders" supervising the men's. The Shaker practice of celibacy afforded women freedom from the dangers of childbirth.

Like the Shakers, the followers of German farmer George Rapp rejected the private ownership of property and practiced celibacy. Believing that "the kingdom of Jesus Christ is approaching near," they considered it the responsibility of the truly devout to amass great material wealth to put at the disposal of Jesus Christ upon his return to earth.

Rapp and several hundred followers arrived in North America in 1803 and migrated to western Pennsylvania, where they established the town of Harmony. They moved in 1815 to the banks of the Wabash River in Indiana Territory. By 1824 their membership numbered 800, and their holdings had grown to more than 20,000 acres. There they grew fruit, grain, and cotton; grazed sheep; and erected a cotton and woolen mill and a distillery. Unfortunately, the climate that made the Wabash hospitable to agriculture also made it hospitable to malaria. Weary of yearly scourges, in 1824 the Rappites sold New Harmony to the English social reformer Robert Owen and moved back to western Pennsylvania.

In terms of numbers and longevity, the most important of the millennial communities of the early nineteenth century was the Church of Jesus Christ of Latter-day Saints, also known as the Mormons. Founder Joseph Smith, Jr., was born in upstate New York in 1805. In 1820, Smith was informed in a vision that God was soon to establish his true church on earth. Three years later, Smith had a second vision in which an angel disclosed to him the existence and location of golden tablets that described God's intentions for the "latter days" of creation, now approaching. In 1830 Smith published the plates as the *Book of Mormon* and formally founded the Church of Christ.

Smith's preaching gradually attracted a body of rural followers, most of them people who had been displaced by the changes affecting the antebellum North. To these listeners, Smith preached that it was God's will that they go forth into the wilderness to found the city of Zion, where they would reign over the coming millennium.

The opposition of their neighbors, who considered Mormon beliefs blasphemous, soon forced the Mormons to leave New York. Smith first moved his followers to Ohio, where they organized a communal economy run by the church, and then to Missouri. In 1839 a large group of Mormons moved on to Illinois, where they founded the city of Nauvoo. By the early 1840s, Smith had begun to preach the doctrine of plural marriage. The Mormon community split and anti-Mormon outrage flared anew. Smith was arrested and thrown in jail in Carthage, Illinois, where, on

June 27, 1844, he was murdered by a mob (allegedly with the help of a jail guard and the support of leading citizens). In 1847, under the guidance of Brigham Young, the Mormons uprooted once more, this time reaching the Great Salt Lake in the West. By 1850, hard work, irrigation, and careful cultivation had turned the desert into a garden paradise inhabited by more than 11,000 people.

Urban Revivals

Separatist millennialists represented a relatively minor stream in the floods of religious organizing that characterized the 1820s. Far more numerous were the Americans who sought to perfect society by carrying the spirit of reform into their own communities. This massive evangelizing of America took many forms. Itinerant Methodists and Baptists continued to minister to newly settled churches in the backcountry. By the 1820s, however, the revivals had also assumed an urban character. Soon even the great metropolises like Boston, Philadelphia, and New York became hothouses of evangelism.

The career of Presbyterian minister Ezra Stiles Ely reflects this shift in mainstream American religious life. From 1811 to 1813, Ely was a chaplain for the Society for Supporting the Gospel, working with men and women who lived in public shelters. He led religious services, distributed Bibles, and prayed at the bedsides of the sick and dying, observing firsthand the growing poverty of American cities. After the War of 1812, he extended his work into the shanties and tenements of New York's poor neighborhoods. He increasingly understood his mission to be not merely providing solace but also converting souls. Ely and other city missionaries did not believe that they could save people who were not chosen by God, but they did believe that the elect could be found even among the poor.

The new urban-based missionary societies soon turned their attention to the boomtowns of the West. The New York Evangelical Missionary Society of Young Men raised money to send missionaries to new settlements of western Pennsylvania, upstate New York, and Georgia. Of these missionaries, none was more successful or controversial than Charles Grandison Finney, who became an influential advocate for a dynamic Protestantism based on personal responsibility.

Finney had originally trained in the law, but in 1821 he experienced a calling to the ministry. Although Finney's rejection of the Presbyterian belief in original sin worried his teachers, he soon developed into a charismatic preacher, and in March 1824, he was ordained as a minister and moved to upstate New York to begin his work.

By the 1820s construction of the Erie Canal was well advanced, drawing even the most remote farmers closer to the markets of the East Coast and enmeshing them in relations of cash and commerce. Inhabitants of towns and small cities were at the center of the rapidly developing market economy. Some of those people were troubled by the swirl of development around them. Others were more alert to the possibilities for success and were attracted to the way the new economy appeared to reward industry, hard work, and personal ambition.

To this latter audience, Finney preached a message of the power of human spiritual striving. In the place of the stern God of Calvinism, he offered a God of Justice, who laid his case before a humankind "just as free as a jury" to accept salvation or not. This theology gave great latitude to human effort, but it also placed a new burden on the sinner. If "a man that was praying week after week for the Holy Spirit . . . could get no answer," Finney insisted, it must be that the man "was praying from false motives," not that an indifferent God had abandoned him.

Finney enjoyed immediate success in the Genesee Valley of New York. Especially drawn to his preaching were those most directly benefiting from the economic boom: the families of merchants and bankers, grain dealers and mill owners, and young, ambitious employees in such businesses. Finneyite Presbyterianism set individual ambition in a new context as part of the process of salvation, a sign of the human potential for good. Eventually, Finney repudiated the older Calvinism, claiming for America a new and optimistic religion based on the power of the individual.

Finney's preaching alarmed the Presbyterian establishment in the East, which feared the emotional style and unorthodoxy of the revivals and Finney's influence in the new western areas. Among the eastern leaders was Lyman Beecher, pastor of the prestigious Hanover Street Presbyterian Church in Boston. Like many New Englanders of his generation, Beecher was convinced that the future greatness of the United States lay in transferring New England culture, and especially New England orthodoxy, westward. Finney represented a dangerous threat to that orthodoxy. In 1832, Beecher moved his family to the new boomtown of the West, Cincinnati, where he wrote *A Plea for the West*, in which he predicted that the final battle of the Christ and the Antichrist would take place in the American West.

Social Reform in the Benevolent Empire

"Every truly converted man turns from selfishness to benevolence," Charles Finney said, "and benevolence surely leads him to do all he can to save the souls of his fellow man." The new evangelical emphasis on personal agency soon assumed the character of a broad impulse for social reform, expressed in religious terms and organized through a loose network of charities and associations, often referred to as the Benevolent Empire.

The Benevolent Empire was grounded in Americans' love of organizing, a tendency observed by Frenchman Alexis de Tocqueville when he visited the United States in 1831–1832. Americans, Tocqueville wrote, "combine to . . . found seminaries, build churches, distribute books, and send missionaries to the antipodes. . . . [I]f they want to proclaim a truth or propagate some feeling by the encouragement of a great example, they form an association."

Local societies linked up into national umbrella groups. Among the largest of these were the American Bible Society (which distributed Bibles in cities and new settlements), the Female Moral Reform Society (devoted to reclaiming women from prostitution), and the American Board of Commissioners for Foreign Missions (which promoted missions in the West). In addition, every major city fostered Bible groups, asylums to help the poor, houses of industry, orphanages, and humane societies, among others. By 1830 evangelical benevolence had also given rise to a Sunday school movement and a movement to prohibit the delivery of mail on the Christian Sabbath.

Benevolent societies represented a curious combination of emotional and rational approaches to reform. The method of the Benevolent Empire was moral suasion. Reformers believed that social change came about not from external rules but rather through the gradual internal awakening of individual moral purpose through personal contact, testimony, and (where needed) exhortation. Yet increasingly, the structure of benevolence became that of the bureaucratic corporation.

Founded in 1816 in New York by a group of wealthy Christian men, the American Bible Society illustrates this paradox. The society consisted initially of a volunteer board of managers who hired out the printing and binding of Bibles. By 1818, however, the board hired a full-time salaried manager to oversee its business affairs, and before 1832, the society added four more professional staff members and built its own building in Manhattan. However, the society still depended on idealistic young ministers as its traveling agents and local volunteer organizations as its community contacts.

As they pursued their good deeds, whether distributing Bibles, praying with the sick, or handing out religious tracts, evangelicals came into intimate contact with the poor and began to minister to their material needs. They arranged fuel deliveries and medical care, helped homeless families find lodging, and organized soup kitchens to feed the poor.

Both men and women were engaged in the charitable associations of the early nineteenth century, but voluntary reform offered special opportunities for women. Women had already been active in organizing maternal societies to discuss and scrutinize their parenting habits and Bible societies to discuss their own moral failings. By the second decade of the nineteenth century, women were founding orphan asylums, becoming involved in the Sunday school movement, starting homes for wayward girls, and establishing asylums for "respectable" homeless adults. By the 1820s women had become the acknowledged volunteer backbone of the Benevolent Empire.

THE COMMON MAN AND THE POLITICAL ECONOMY OF DEMOCRACY

Americans had long associated republican virtue with labor, particularly with labor that afforded economic independence. In the early years of the republic, that virtue-producing labor was most often represented in the figure of the farmer. Nineteenth-century Americans continued to praise the self-sufficient and industrious common citizen as the mainstay of the nation's political economy, but the celebration of labor became more democratic and the figures through which Americans evoked the virtues of work became more varied. Paradoxically, the ideal embodiment of that virtue became more gendered and racialized.

The Political Economy of Free Labor

This shift toward a more democratic idiom of work mirrored changes in the American economy, especially the growing political and economic importance of westward migration, commerce, and manufacturing. The farmer was now likely to be depicted as a scrappy backwoods pioneer. But more people were taking up nonfarm occupations, and the ways in which Americans talked about labor reflected that shift. Writers broadened the concept of the virtuous worker to include the mass of "honest and industrious citizens who earn their daily bread by the sweat of their brow": the self-made shopkeeper, clerk, and craft worker. It was the fact of gainful employment, not the specific occupation, that conferred dignity.

Some Americans expressed a lurking uneasiness that individual opportunity was under assault. Economic hard times before and during the War of 1812 gave rise to a protest literature that focused on the dignity and importance of labor. In 1817 Cornelius Blatchly, a Quaker physician from New Jersey, published a pamphlet titled *Some Causes of Popular Poverty,* arguing that property owners had become tyrants, enabled by law to steal from laborers the value that they produced and that rightfully belonged to them. The Panic of 1819 reawakened that skepticism. The sudden collapse of credit and agricultural prices and the consequent widespread business failures and unemployment showed how precarious the new economy was. The harshest lessons were dealt to small farmers and wage workers, who began to suspect that their interests were not being well served by Republican policies. Even in the improving economic climate of the 1820s, workers became more assertive about the value and dignity of their labor.

The concept of the dignity of labor stood in contrast to both the parasitism of wealthy elites and the degradation of slavery. Many free workers saw slavery as antirepublican and viewed slaves as the embodiment of a state of dependence against which free workers struggled. As one man noted, free hired workers refused to be referred to as servants, because of the habit of "confounding the term servant with that of slave" in white southern culture. No white male worker feared actually being enslaved, but the declining standard of living of many white workers in the aftermath of 1819 and the fact that some slaves were hired out for wages blurred the distinctions between free workers and slaves. White workers began to describe their employment not simply as labor, but rather as "free labor." When they described their worsening condition, they portrayed bosses bent on reducing them to "a degrading vassalage" and rendering them "abject slaves."

Suffrage Reform

At the founding of the nation, suffrage was restricted not only by gender and race, but even more on the basis of property ownership and tax payment. Urban mechanics, who often owned little more than their tools and clothing, had objected to this state of affairs, demanding the vote on the basis of their military service, loyalty, and economic importance to the nation. Most of all, they had demanded the vote as the emblem of liberty. As white working men felt their status eroding in the early nineteenth century, they returned to the issue of the vote as the battleground on which to establish their credentials as free men.

The new political economy sharpened their demand for suffrage. Improvements in transportation, the growth of manufacturing and banking, and westward expansion highlighted the regional and national economic importance of nonfarm waged occupations, from hauling to dredging to figuring accounts. The geographical extension of the market and the interdependencies of its parts meant that few communities were insulated from decisions made at the federal level. When Jefferson declared an embargo against England and France, not only workers on the East Coast but also those who were far from the seaboard felt the repercussions. Exposed to the consequences of government policies, wage workers demanded the right to help select the policymakers.

The new, less settled states led the way in expanding white male suffrage. Vermont entered the union in 1791 (the first new state after the original 13) with virtually universal white manhood suffrage. The following year, neighboring New Hampshire dropped its last effective qualification, and Kentucky entered the union without restrictions on adult white males. Tennessee, which became a state in 1796, required that voters own property but did not set a minimum value. Ohio became a state in 1803 without property requirements for voting, and every one of the six states admitted between 1812 and 1821 entered with universal white male suffrage (see Map 11–1).

In 1817 Connecticut became the first of the older states to abolish all property qualifications for white men. By 1821 the demand for suffrage reform had reached the proportions of a "passion . . . pervading the union." Three years later, when

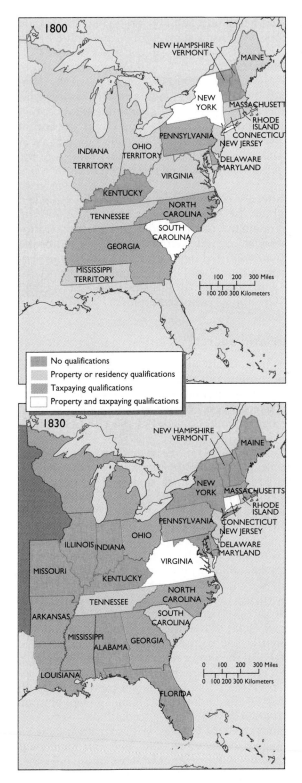

Map 11–1   Toward Universal White Male Suffrage

As the western territories organized and entered the union, they formed a band of states in which there were no property qualifications on white male suffrage, and often minimal taxpaying qualifications. By 1830, Virginia and Connecticut were unusual in the nation for restricting white male suffrage based on both property and tax payment. At the same time, free black males and women lost the vote where they had enjoyed it.

Jackson made his first run for the presidency, only Virginia, Louisiana, and Rhode Island retained any significant restrictions on white male suffrage and only 6 of the 24 states retained indirect selection of the delegates to the Electoral College.

The struggle for an expanded male suffrage was fought openly on the landscape of race. Opponents of suffrage reform offered lurid visions of politically energized African Americans taking advantage of loosened property restrictions. Already defensive about the possible association of waged labor with enslaved labor, in state after state workers and suffrage advocates quickly abandoned any aim of universal male suffrage and argued instead for universal white male suffrage. Every new state admitted from 1819 on specifically excluded African Americans from the vote, and older states that had once permitted propertied black men to vote revised suffrage laws to exclude them.

The partial exception to this pattern was Rhode Island, where elites blocked universal white male suffrage throughout the 1830s. When, in 1841, white working men called a People's Convention to demand universal white male suffrage, they rejected pleas to include African-American men in their demands. Spurned by the white working men, African Americans supported the conservative opposition, creating a situation in which the state militia was mobilized against white workers. When Rhode Island conservatives later broadened the franchise, they repaid African-American men for their earlier support by including them.

Opposition to Special Privilege and Secret Societies

Since the nation's founding, one strain of American political rhetoric had focused on corrupt insiders who enjoyed opportunities not available to other citizens. In the early nineteenth century, the religious and economic emphasis on personal striving combined with the growing political assertiveness of white working men to reinvigorate those older fears. Politics became a symbolic battle of the virtuous "many" against the corrupt "few."

Early in the century, specially chartered corporations became visible symbols of affluence and the target of these suspicions. Created by special acts of state legislatures, these corporations were, theoretically, open to all Americans. However, the charters were granted on a highly personal basis to people known to individual legislators, people of wealth, power, and reputation.

The movement to use charters to promote development accelerated after the War of 1812. States chartered companies to build roads, provide transportation, and establish banks. Local reactions to specially chartered projects were mixed. Many ambitious persons of modest means shared journalist William Leggett's bitterness that "Not a road can be opened, not a bridge can be built, not a canal can be dug, but a charter of exclusive privileges must be granted for the purpose." Yet some of the specially chartered initiatives, especially banks, seemed to aid local farmers and workers by providing easy credit. When the Panic of 1819 ended that bubble of easy local credit, devastated by the contraction, shopkeepers, farmers, and urban workers focused their anger on the power of eastern bankers, especially the Second Bank of the United States, and grew suspicious that the new Republican leadership was bent on increasing preferential rules. By 1820 John C. Calhoun noticed the appearance, in "every part of the Union," of "a general mass of disaffection to the Government . . . looking out anywhere for a leader."

Corporations were not the only focus of hard feelings. With so many people on the move, social relations were characterized by a fear that American society was riddled with passers of bad notes, vendors of nonexistent western lands, and other schemers. In western New York, where the opening of the Erie Canal had ushered in an economic boom and widespread social instability, tensions exploded in a virulent fear of Masons in the late 1820s.

The Masonic movement had originated as an organization to counter aristocratic power and protect craft masons against encroachments on their trade. But in the eighteenth century a new Order of Freemasons emerged, made up of urban businessmen, shopkeepers, merchants, professionals, and politicians who pledged their political and economic support to one another. By the 1820s the Masons seemed to many working people to embody a dangerous antidemocratic spirit. This vague distrust was galvanized into popular opposition in 1826 by the mysterious disappearance (and presumed murder) of New Yorker William Morgan, who had authored an exposé of the order's purported secret designs on public power. Morgan vanished when he was released from jail after being arrested on a small debt charge. The story spread that Morgan had been ferreted away to Niagara Falls, held for three days, and then drowned. The seriousness of this subversion of justice was magnified, in the popular outcry, by the fact that public officials, including both Andrew Jackson and Henry Clay, were also Masons. By 1827 New Yorkers who opposed the Masons had organized a separate political party and pledged never again to vote for a Mason and to work for the defeat of any Masons already in office.

The Antimason Party spread from New York into other states, doing especially well in local elections in Massachusetts, Pennsylvania, and Vermont. In 1831 Antimasons held the first open presidential nominating convention, choosing William Wirt of Maryland as their candidate. Wirt carried only one state, and the party remained a minor player in national politics. Nevertheless, the battle against secret cabals illustrated the belief that American party politics amounted to a struggle of common people against the monied aristocracy. This would become a staple of Jacksonian political rhetoric.

Workingmen's Parties

Suffrage reform was a step toward political empowerment, but many working men wanted to do more than vote. They wanted to set the political agenda through the formation of their own political parties.

As the labor newspaper *The Working Men's Advocate* complained in 1830, candidates for office did not reflect the interests of workers. No one talked about unemployment and underemployment, proposed reforms of debt and eviction laws, or argued for better and cheaper housing, safer working conditions, or education for the children of workers.

By the late 1820s workers had begun to mobilize to make their votes more effective. In 1827 a group of workers in Philadelphia formed the Mechanics' Union of Trade Associations. Within a year they had dissolved that group into the Philadelphia Working Men's Party, a new political party dedicated to promoting "the interests and enlightenment of the working classes." Over the next five years, under various names, the movement spread through most of the nation, becoming strongest in the cities from Philadelphia northward.

That such parties came into existence at all suggests that workers were at a crossroads. On the one hand, the formation of the Working Men's Party implied that workers still remained optimistic that change was possible. That optimism was reflected in the party's demands, which stopped short of indicting the entire system. Instead, they argued that the greed of the commercial classes was made possible by the policies of a government grown too large and distant. Moreover, working men thought of themselves as citizens with the right and power to affect the entire social and cultural makeup of the republic. This was evident in the variety of issues they advocated, including public education, broadened incorporation laws, an end to imprisonment for debt, and banking reform.

On the other hand, the organization of a separate political party indicated that workers remained deeply skeptical that the existing parties would be responsive to their concerns and that workers were moving toward a distinct identity within the new political economy.

The Democratic Impulse in Presidential Politics

Americans' homage to the principles of personal responsibility and the dignity of the common man revealed the paradox of national culture in the 1820s. Both concepts expressed faith in human nature and social life, a belief that citizens would conduct their affairs responsibly and deserved to live free from restraint. Yet the energy with which Americans insisted on these principles also suggested a suspicion that the republic was not living up to its highest purposes. That combination of confidence and mistrust described exactly the man who was elected to office in 1828, Andrew Jackson.

Jackson's Rise to National Prominence

In his person and his life, Andrew Jackson embodied the volatile mixture of confidence and defensiveness that characterized the United States in the years following the War of 1812. After the war, Jackson studied law in North Carolina, but his restlessness carried him west to search for property and prosperity in the territories. Jackson purchased land and settled near the future city of Nashville, Tennessee. He was soon called on to serve as a district attorney and a judge. By the time he first ran for the presidency in 1824, he had served briefly in the House of Representatives and the Senate.

Jackson became a national figure during the War of 1812, first as commander of the devastating campaign against the Creek Nation and then, at war's end, as the hero of the Battle of New Orleans. His controversial but effective campaign against the Seminoles in 1818 and 1819 and his subsequent brief career as governor of the Territory of Florida completed his credentials as an unyielding champion of the western settler.

The Election of 1824 and the "Corrupt Bargain"

When the Tennessee legislature nominated Jackson for the presidency in 1822, few politicians took the candidacy seriously. Jackson was running against some of the nation's most experienced and respected leaders: John Quincy Adams (Monroe's Secretary of State), John C. Calhoun (Monroe's Secretary of War), Henry Clay (Speaker of the House), and William H. Crawford of Georgia (Monroe's Secretary of the Treasury). Jackson's detractors underestimated his popularity as a war hero and the attractiveness of his humble background to an electorate inching its way toward a more democratic political culture. As an orphan and a westerner, Jackson was temperamentally the outsider, a position with which many voters identified.

An early indication of the importance of this changing political sensibility came with the Republican nomination. Because James Monroe had not designated a successor, the selection was thrown to the Republican Congressional caucus, a circumstance expected to benefit Crawford. But this time, unlike earlier nominations, the other candidates pulled out, loudly disowning the caucus as a corrupt and irregular institution. So effective was the repudiation that only 66 of a possible 216 Republican members of Congress attended the caucus. As expected, Crawford got the nod, while the other potential candidates relied on their own networks of supporters to organize their campaigns.

When the election was held, no candidate claimed a majority either of the popular vote or of the Electoral College. Jackson finished first, with 43 percent of the popular vote and 99 electoral votes (see Map 11–2). Next was Adams, who tallied 31 percent of the popular vote and 84 electoral votes. Crawford managed only 41 electoral votes. Clay came in last with 37 electoral votes.

The election was thus thrown to the House of Representatives, where members had to select from among the three candidates with the highest electoral count. Initially, Jackson was confident, but by late December 1824 he began to hear rumors "that deep intrigue is on foot." Those rumors were correct. Although Adams did not receive a single popular vote in Kentucky, and although the Kentucky state legislature had directed its delegation to vote for Jackson, Clay used his prestige to override those instructions and to marshal additional support for Adams in other states. With Clay behind him, Adams received the votes of 13 of the 24 state delegations. Jackson received 7 and Crawford received 4.

Jackson later charged that Adams had bought Clay's support with the promise of the post of Secretary of State. In fact, Adams did give Clay that job. Even without a reward, however, Clay had good reasons for allying himself with Adams. Clay and Adams shared

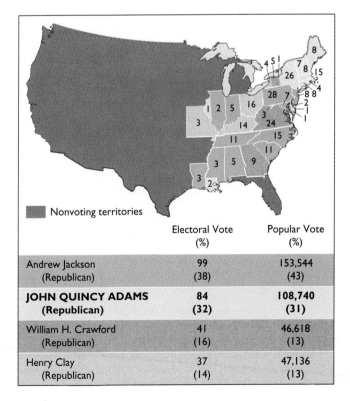

Map 11–2 The Election of 1824

No candidate won a majority of either the popular or electoral vote, and the election was thrown to the House of Representatives, resulting in charges of intrigue and corruption.

■ Nonvoting territories

	Electoral Vote (%)	Popular Vote (%)
Andrew Jackson (Republican)	99 (38)	153,544 (43)
JOHN QUINCY ADAMS (**Republican**)	84 (32)	108,740 (31)
William H. Crawford (Republican)	41 (16)	46,618 (13)
Henry Clay (Republican)	37 (14)	47,136 (13)

similar political philosophies. In addition, Jackson and Clay vied for the same regional vote. Supporting Jackson in 1824 would have helped the Tennessean build a stronger western base for 1828.

Jackson was furious. "Intrigue, corruption, and sale of public office is the rumor of the day," he roared. His supporters charged that the election had been stolen in a "corrupt bargain" brokered by insiders who debased the virtue of the republic and flagrantly disregarded the clear will of the electorate.

The Adams Presidency and the Gathering Forces of Democracy

John Quincy Adams was a wise and principled statesman, but he was unable to set an independent agenda for his presidency. Defensive and prickly in public, he was not good at creating strong political alliances. Not a particularly canny politician, he underestimated the gulf developing within the American electorate.

Adams's first mistake was to offer Clay the position of Secretary of State. Although Adams might have assumed that the election produced a mandate for National Republicanism, the selection of Clay not only looked like a payoff but also sent Vice President Calhoun's supporters into the Jackson camp. Opposition to Clay and Adams grew strong in Congress.

Adams also provoked fiscal conservatives and even some moderates by using his first annual message to Congress in 1825 to lay out a grand vision for federal involvement in the nation's political economy. He called not only for economic projects, like transportation improvements, but also for the creation of a national university, a national observatory, and a naval academy, as well as an elaborate system of roads and canals supported by federal expenditures. In a particularly ill-chosen phrase, Adams urged Congress not to be "palsied by the will of our con-stituents." His opponents objected that this was clear evidence of his intention to benefit the wealthy at the expense of the common people.

Jackson's supporters attempted to discredit Adams further on the issue of the tariff. The tariff was unpopular in the South and much of the West but increasing-ly popular in the manufacturing Northeast. Jackson supporters in the North wished to associate themselves with the tariff without implicating Jacksonians elsewhere in the country, thus increasing support for Jackson in the mid-Atlantic, Northwest, and Northeast. The plan was to propose a tariff so outrageously high on raw mate-rials that the East and West would eventually join with the South to defeat it.

In their eagerness to force New Englanders to oppose the bill, southerners insisted that every outrageous provision be preserved. In the end, New Englanders did win a few modifications and concluded that bad protectionism was better than none at all. Representatives from New York and New England abandoned their ear-lier free trade positions and were willing to absorb higher prices for raw materials. The Northeast swallowed the bitter pill and voted "yes," and the Tariff of 1828 became law.

The Election of 1828

The Congressional fight over the tariff provided the stage on which the early phases of the election of 1828 were fought, but the underlying issue was the deep conflict over the power of the federal government. This was not a simple question of na-tionalism versus localism. Jackson was a nationalist who was willing to support some level of protective tariff and had even conceded in the 1824 campaign that "It is time we became a little more Americanized." The difference between Adams and Jackson was the question of the basis of federal legitimacy. In what actions could the federal government claim the authority of the American people? And in what actions did it overstep that authority? That conflict was now infused with the energy of a rising democratic spirit.

Both camps sought to manipulate the heightened religious sensibilities of the age. Adams's supporters tarred Jackson as a liar and a blasphemer incapable of self-restraint. They accused Jackson of having "prevailed upon the wife of Lewis Robards of Mercer County, Kentucky, to desert her husband, and live with himself, in the character of a wife."

Jackson supporters retorted that Adams was a Sabbath breaker, a closet Federalist, and an unprincipled hypocrite whose long residence in Europe had taught him disdain for popular government. To make the point, Jacksonians began to refer to themselves as Jacksonian Democrats.

The Democratic campaign of 1828 ushered in a new era of national political campaigning. Whereas earlier campaigns had been fought primarily on the local level and among a far smaller group of potential voters, in 1828 Martin Van Buren coordinated a Democratic national campaign designed to appeal to a mass electorate. Van Buren oversaw the creation of a highly controlled party hierarchy structured like the Benevolent Empire, with local societies linked to state societies linked to the national organization. Van Buren pioneered the use of carefully choreographed demonstrations and converted nonpartisan occasions (like Fourth of July celebrations) into Democratic rallies by sending out armies of Jackson supporters armed with American flags and placards. Van Buren also engineered the use of political imagery to evoke campaign themes. Taking advantage of Jackson's nickname, "Old Hickory" (for the hardest wood in the United States), campaign workers handed out hickory canes to crowds at political events. At the same time, supporters used editorials and campaign tracts to describe Jackson as the embodiment of the common man. Turning Jackson's obstinacy and lack of formal education into strengths, they argued that he was nature's product, with a "native strength of mind" and "practical common sense."

When the votes were counted in 1828, Jackson had won a clear majority: 56 percent of the popular vote and 178 electoral votes to Adams's 83 electoral votes. Although Adams had retained New England, New Jersey, Delaware, and northern Maryland, Jackson had solidly taken the South and the West, as well as Pennsylvania, most of New York, and even northern Maine.

Jackson was elected by a strong cross-section of voters who identified with his stance as an outsider to, and victim of, eastern elites. He was the candidate of westerners, migrants, settlers, and landowners who opposed eastern banks and Congressional land policies, but Jackson also drew support from urban professionals, shopkeepers, laborers, and craftsmen who believed that special privilege was denying them their chance of prosperity. A planter and a southerner, Jackson could claim the mantle of Jeffersonian Republicanism. Reflecting that older political economy, he favored limited government, feared concentrations of economic and political power, and seemed to share Jefferson's emphasis on the individual.

PRESIDENT JACKSON: VINDICATING THE COMMON MAN

Even in the pandemonium of the inauguration, the message of the new presidency was clear: "As the instrument of the Federal Constitution," Jackson declared in his inaugural address, "I shall keep steadily in view the limitations as well as the extent of the Executive power." He advocated fiscal restraint, an end to government patronage, and a constitutional amendment to remove "all intermediary agency in the election of President and Vice-President." The task of his administration, Jackson announced, must be "the task of reform."

Jacksonian Democrats in Office

The Jacksonians were vague about exactly where political virtue resided. Structurally, they believed that it evolved from the states. This endorsement of federal restraint was confused, however, by Jackson's equally strong conviction that he was the people and his will was indistinguishable from theirs. The ironic result was a continuous migration of power from the states to the executive during the presidency of the man elected to protect the common man.

A tendency to personalize political struggle characterized Jackson's presidency. He never forgave the National Republicans for publicly questioning the legitimacy of his marriage. Later, he viewed his battle against the Second Bank of the United States in the same highly personal terms: "The Bank," he informed Van Buren, "is trying to kill me, but I will kill it."

If Jackson understood himself as the embodiment of the people's will, he understood the new Democratic Party as its direct instrument. After personal loyalty to Jackson, party loyalty became the avenue to appointment and the justification for an unprecedented turnover in appointees. Unfortunately, party loyalty did not guarantee competence or honesty. Jackson's choice for New York customs collector, Samuel Swartwout, used his position to embezzle more than $1 million.

The overall results were mixed. Invigorated by his confidence that he spoke for the nation, Jackson expanded the powers of the presidency, but his conviction that he alone embodied the true virtue of the republic also led to personal pettiness, widespread patronage, and turmoil within his cabinet. His efforts to abolish the Second Bank of the United States wreaked serious material hardship for average Americans, and his hostility to Native Americans resulted in widespread death and impoverishment.

A Policy of Indian Removal

For Andrew Jackson, the quintessential "common man" was the western settler, struggling to bring new lands under cultivation and new institutions to life. Pioneers confronted various obstacles, but none loomed larger than the resistance of Indian peoples. The War of 1812 had brought an end to intertribal resistance east of the Mississippi River. By 1828, most of the Great Lakes nations had been pushed out of Ohio, southern Indiana, and Illinois, but the Ojibwa, Winnebago, Sauk, Mesquakie, Kickapoo, and Menominee retained sizable homelands in the Northwest. In the South, in spite of repeated forced cessions, the Chickasaws, Choctaws, Creeks, Cherokees, and Seminoles retained ancestral territories.

Jackson's views concerning Native Americans had been formed in the crucible of the Indian wars of the 1790s. "Does not experience teach us that treaties answer no other Purpose than opening an Easy door for the Indians to pass [through to] Butcher our citizens?" he wrote in 1794.

Despite recurrent wars and federal treaties, western settlers were no happier with federal initiatives in the 1820s than they had been in the 1790s. Tension ran especially high in Georgia. There officials complained that the federal government had not kept its promise to remove all Indians from the state, a condition of Georgia's agreement to cede its western land claims to the federal government in 1802. A few Creeks and most of the Cherokee nation remained. In 1826 the federal government pressured the Creeks to give up all but a small strip of their remaining lands in Georgia, but white Georgians were not satisfied. Georgia Governor George Michael Troup sent surveyors onto that last piece of Creek land. When President Adams objected to this encroachment on federal treaty powers, Troup threatened to call up the state militia.

The election of Andrew Jackson emboldened the Georgians to go after Cherokee land. They invalidated the constitution of the Cherokee nation within Georgia and proclaimed that the Cherokees were subject to the authority of the state of Georgia. When discoveries of gold sent white prospectors surging onto Cherokee land, Georgia refused either to stop the trespassers or to protect the Indians. Jackson quickly made his position clear, notifying the Cherokee that it was his duty, as president, to "sustain the States in the exercise of their rights."

In fact, the states were not exercising their rights. In 1831, in *Cherokee Nation v. Georgia,* Justice Marshall ruled that the Cherokees were a "domestic dependent nation" with valid claims arising from treaties with the federal government. The following year, in *Worcester v. Georgia*, the Supreme Court ruled that the Cherokees came under the direct protection of the federal government, and Georgia had acted unconstitutionally. Jackson refused to enforce this decision. He had long believed that the best policy, "not only liberal, but generous," would be to remove the Indians entirely from lands sought by settlers. The place he had in mind was across the Mississippi River. Because full-scale removal of the Indians involved shifting populations across state lines and into federal territories, however, it required Congressional consent. In Congress the Native Americans found unexpected allies. To the old Adams men, now led by Henry Clay, "removal" was the policy of states, forced on the federal government. For Congress to pass an act authorizing the policy would mean encouraging states to trample on federal powers. Clay was supported by numerous foot soldiers of the Benevolent Empire. Led by the American Board of Commissioners for Foreign Missions, reformers (women as well as men) lobbied hard against the bill. Van Buren responded by forming a counterlobby, the Board for the Emigration, Preservation, and Improvement of the Aborigines of America, which argued that Indians were ill equipped for contact with white civilization and that removing them was humane.

Passed in 1830 by a margin of five votes, the Removal Act empowered the president to purchase Indian homelands in the East in exchange for lands west of the Mississippi. In one sense, the act only made official a policy that Americans had pursued since the founding of the nation, but official approval accelerated the process. In 1830 the Choctaws were forced from their lands in Mississippi to a location in present-day Oklahoma. The Chickasaws and the Creeks followed in 1832.

Three years later, after their unsuccessful appeals to the Supreme Court and after several years of continued resistance, the Cherokees were removed from their eastern lands (see Map 11–3). In a forced march that became known as the Trail of Tears, they were driven off their homelands to Indian Territory in what is now eastern Oklahoma. Most people had delayed leaving until the last moment and had made few preparations for the journey. Many died of disease, malnutrition, dehydration, and exhaustion along the way.

Indians did not accept removal willingly. The Sauk and Fox resorted to arms. In 1831, the Sauk and Fox (a population descended from Native Americans who had earlier been pushed across the Great Lakes region) were forced to relocate once again. No sooner did they reach their new lands, however, than they began to hear rumors that whites were desecrating their former burying grounds. When Indians recrossed the Mississippi to rebury their dead and harvest produce from their old fields, white farmers and Illinois militia attacked them.

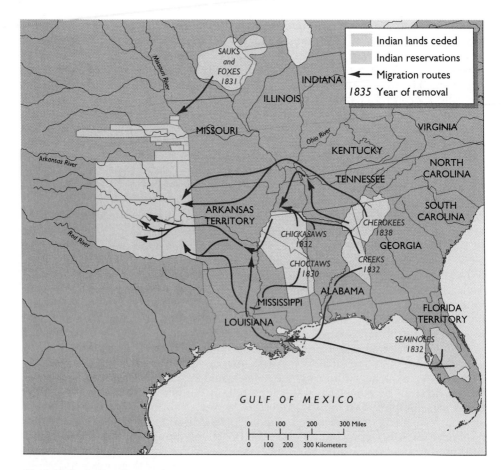

Map 11-3 Indian Removals
Jackson's policy of Indian removal required Native American peoples to leave their homelands east of the Mississippi River for government-designated lands west of the Mississippi. Some Indian groups signed treaties ceding their lands, but these groups often lacked authority to do so. Some groups (like the Cherokee) fought removal in court. Others (like the Seminoles, Sauk, and Fox) fought the policy in open combat.

The Sauk and Fox turned for leadership to a revered old fighter, Black Hawk, who raised a band of 500 warriors. Attacked by state militiamen, they spent the summer fighting a series of skirmishes called Black Hawk's War. Finally, on August 2, 1832, low on food and exhausted, the remnants of Black Hawk's band were cornered and massacred by the Army.

More successful were the Florida Seminoles, also a diverse community including militant Creek warriors, known as Red Sticks, and runaway slaves. When federal troops arrived to remove the Seminoles in 1832, the Indians resisted with skill and determination. Unfamiliar with the terrain and vulnerable to malaria, the American troops were picked off by both disease and snipers. The war dragged on for seven years. Not until 1842 could President John Tyler proclaim victory.

The Trail of Tears, depicted here by Brummett Echohawk, shows Cherokees being forced from their home-lands in eastern states to Indian territory in what is now Oklahoma.

The Bank War

Jacksonians saw the Indians as the western barrier to their progress, but when they looked eastward, they saw a different obstacle: the special privileges and unfair advantages available to the rich and well-connected. In his career, Jackson had associated this obstacle with Henry Clay, John Adams, John Calhoun, and the Republican caucus. By 1828 Jackson focused his anger on the Second Bank of the United States.

Jackson hated the bank for all the reasons common among southerners and westerners: It was powerful and privileged, and its private stock was held by wealthy easterners and foreign investors.

Soon after his first election, Jackson heard rumors that the Second Bank of the United States had used its power to buy votes for Adams in 1828. Declaring that the bank threatened "the purity of the right of suffrage," Jackson vowed to oppose it.

Nicholas Biddle, the bank's president, refused to take Jackson's criticisms seriously. Confident that the bank enjoyed the support of most Americans (which it probably did), Biddle decided to force the issue before the next presidential election. Although the bank's authorization ran until 1836, on January 6, 1832, Biddle requested Congress to take up renewal. Jackson might have felt Biddle's behavior to be a personal challenge, because when the act reached him in July 1832, he vetoed it.

The Democrats carried the bank veto proudly into the 1832 election. It was, they insisted, a contest of "the Democracy and the people, against a corrupt and abandoned aristocracy." The Republicans responded that Jackson's veto showed his tendency toward despotism. The Supreme Court had ruled the national bank constitutional, and Congress had voted to recharter it. Jackson had trammeled the authority of both of the other branches of government, taking upon himself the sole right to determine the future of the bank.

Jackson won re-election in 1832, although by a smaller majority than he had won with in 1828. By 1833 he was ready to move ahead with his plans to disassemble the Second Bank of the United States. He asked Secretary of the Treasury Louis McLane to select other banks into which the federal government could move its deposits. McLane balked, worried that the selection would be compromised by politics and that the state banks would lose all fiscal restraint. Impatient, Jackson replaced McLane with William J. Duane, and then replaced Duane with Attorney General Roger Taney. On October 1, 1833, the federal government began to distribute its deposits to 22 state banks. By the close of the year, the government deposits had been largely removed.

The deposits in question had been used to make loans to individuals and corporations around the country. To make the funds available, the Second Bank set furiously about calling in loans and foreclosing on debts. In effect, and no doubt with a certain grim relish, Biddle was repeating the process that triggered the Panic of 1819. In six months he took more than $15 million worth of credit out of the economy.

As recession gripped the nation, the Senate passed an unprecedented resolution censuring Jackson for assuming "authority and power not conferred by the constitution and laws." Jackson's response underscored the new "democratic" politics of the times: "The President," he maintained (and no other branch of government), "is the direct representative of the American people." The expansion of white male suffrage (and the spreading practice of electing members of the Electoral College directly) made Jackson the first president who could claim to be elected directly by the voters. Congress, on the other hand, would soon become the symbolic repository of "republicanism" and the power base of transregional elites.

The first recession passed quickly as state banks that received the federal deposits began to churn out loans and wildcat banks sprang up to take advantage of the glut of paper money. Much of the borrowing went for land sales.

Correctly, Jackson believed that the excess of paper money in circulation had caused the recession. As soon as conditions began to improve, he implemented a hard money policy. Late in 1833 he had announced that the federal government would no longer accept drafts on the Second Bank in payment of taxes, a move that reduced the value of the bank's notes. In 1834 Jackson declared that the "deposit" banks receiving federal monies could not issue paper drafts for amounts under $5 (later raised to $20), an act that reduced the small-denomination paper in circulation. In July 1836 he had the Treasury Department issue the Specie Circular, which directed land offices to accept only specie in payment for western lands. This effectively shut out actual settlers, who could not get together enough gold or silver for their purchases. Meanwhile, the Deposit Act, passed in June 1836, expanded the number of "pet banks" to nearly 100 and provided for the distribution of a federal surplus of more than $5 million to the states. This money was on top of the more than $22 million already deposited in the state banks from the Second Bank of the United States. Underregulated and susceptible to local pressure, the state banks were incapable of absorbing this flood of funds. They issued loans and printed money that vastly exceeded their assets. When the bubble burst in 1837, the nation was thrown into the worst financial disaster of its young history.

CONCLUSION

The political economy of the Jacksonian consensus was forged from belief in the efficacy of the individual, a distrust of unfair privilege, and a commitment to geographic expansionism. Few of these elements were new to the American political economy, but their meanings had undergone important shifts since 1776. The republic was becoming a democracy.

CHRONOLOGY

1816	American Bible Society founded
1824	John Quincy Adams elected president (the "Corrupt Bargain")
	Rappites sell New Harmony to Robert Owen and return to Pennsylvania, establishing third community, Economy
	Charles Grandison Finney begins preaching in upstate New York
1825	Owen establishes New Harmony labor reform community
1827	Antimason Party organized
1828	Andrew Jackson elected president
	Virtually universal white male suffrage
	Philadelphia workers organize the Philadelphia Working Men's Party
	Protective Tariff of 1828 passes
1830	Shakers support 60 communities
	Removal Act passes
	Joseph Smith organizes the Church of Jesus Christ of Latter-day Saints
1831	Antimason Party holds first open presidential nominating convention
	Cherokee Nation v. Georgia
1831–1832	Alexis de Tocqueville visits United States
1832	*Worcester v. Georgia*
	Black Hawk's War
	Jackson vetoes act rechartering Second Bank of the United States
	Jackson re-elected
1834	Female Moral Reform Society formed
1836	Deposit Act expands number of Jackson's "pet banks" and provides for distribution of federal surplus

The harmony that seemed to be expressed in the Jacksonian celebration of democracy and individualism was misleading. Consensus was always partial and contingent, and conflict was always present and growing. African-American men were excluded from suffrage, workers were excluded from opportunity, and Indians were excluded from their homelands. If Jackson the southerner, the settler, and the son of common parents was able to draw support from across a wide variety of constituencies, he was not without his detractors. These included southerners who hated the tariff, reformers who opposed his policies, and merchants and entrepreneurs who wanted a more stable currency. Within 25 years of Jackson's election, workers were in the streets, hundreds of thousands of Americans were petitioning to end slavery, the political parties had dissolved into chaos, and the nation stood on the brink of civil war.

FURTHER READINGS

Donald Jackson, ed., *Black Hawk: An Autobiography* (1955). This volume reprints an 1833 publication alleged to be the autobiography of the influential Sauk leader Black Hawk, along with a critical introduction examining the authenticity of the document (which was written down by a French interpreter and edited and published by an American journalist) and raising important questions about how students and historians should read and use such evidence.

Paul E. Johnson and Sean Wilentz, *The Kingdom of Matthias: The Story of Sex and Salvation in Nineteenth-Century America* (1994). Focusing on the role of urbanization, gender, and class in nineteenth-century popular religious movements, this study of lay preacher and cult leader Matthias the Prophet captures the drama of the urban religious revivals of the 1820s and 1830s and touches on the careers of a number of other famous reformers of the era, including Isabella Van Wagenen (later Sojourner Truth) and Joseph Smith, founder of the Church of Jesus Christ of Latter-day Saints.

Mary P. Ryan, *Cradle of the Middle Class: The Family in Oneida County, New York, 1790–1865* (1981). Ryan examines the impact of the market revolution on household structure and patterns of family authority in upstate New York, arguing that the breakdown of older community structures encouraged the enlarged participation of women in social affairs, especially through the mechanism of the Finneyite revivals.

John William Ward, *Andrew Jackson—Symbol for an Age* (1953). Half a century old, Ward's study remains highly provocative in suggesting the qualities of background and personality that underlay Jackson's popularity and his ability to embody the broad democratic movement impulses of his times.

Harry L. Watson, *Liberty and Power: The Politics of Jacksonian America* (1990). Although its primary focus is on politics and parties, *Liberty and Power* grounds the party politics of the Jacksonian era securely in broad social and economic currents of the age, including slavery, westward expansion, and Indian removal.

Deborah Gray White, *Ar'n't I a Woman? Female Slaves in the Plantation South* (1985). This path-breaking study of the experiences of enslaved women examines the work that female slaves performed in the plantation economy, the experiences of female slaves as family members, the important community roles that enslaved African-American women played, and the networks of friendships that female slaves constructed with each other.

 Please refer to the document CD-ROM for primary sources related to this chapter.

CHAPTER

12

Reform and Conflict

1828–1836

Free Labor Under Attack • The Growth of Sectional Tension
The Political Economy of Early Industrial Society • Self-Reform
and Social Regulation • Conclusion

Free Labor Under Attack

In the summer of 1832, months before Andrew Jackson was re-elected as president, former Rhode Island carpenter Seth Luther traveled across New England denouncing the political economy of Jacksonian America. Luther condemned the "tyranny," "avarice," and "exclusive privilege" that drove "AMERICAN MANUFACTURE" and laid before his sympathetic audiences a chilling catalogue of the havoc wrought in the lives of the "producing classes." He reminded his listeners of the 15-hour days, driven by the despotism of the clock and "the well seasoned strap" of the boss—all for a mere 75 cents a day. He described adults exhausted and brutalized and children made "pale, sickly, haggard . . . from the worse than slavish confinement of the cotton mill." Early industrialization was turning out vast quantities of cottons and woolens, but it created a social order in which "the poor must work or starve" while "the rich . . . take care of themselves."

In some respects, Luther's harangue was simply the labor counterpart of a standard Jacksonian political stump speech. It denounced wealth and special privilege, praised the worth and dignity of common people, demanded reform, and flamed with images of the impending Armageddon. However, Luther was addressing a nation in which the common man had presumably reigned triumphant for four years. Luther's closing exhortation that workers were free men in name only hinted at deep failures in Jacksonian democracy.

271

In some respects, Luther's indictment seems unaccountable. By 1832, Jackson had done a good deal to reward the expectations of the voters. He had cleaned house of National Republican appointees. He had supported white claims to Indian lands in the West, opening hundreds of thousands of acres to new settlement. He was preparing to take on that behemoth of elite privilege, the Second Bank of the United States.

But Jackson's first four years in office had also revealed unreconciled tensions within the new democratic political economy. The expansion of personal liberties created a society in which inequities were all the more obvious, their persistence underscored by Americans' commitment to perfectibility. Slavery was the glaring exception to democracy. Continuing slave resistance served as a constant reminder that the institution was neither benign nor stable. White southerners began to fight back the tides of democratic discourse by asserting the distinctive character of the South and claiming a unique kinship to the more hierarchical republicanism of the founding generation. The disappearance from the North of slavery and indentured servitude led even northerners who did not care about slaves to view the South as a region of peculiar, even alien, customs.

Economic expansion and the widening rhetoric of democracy also exposed problems in the political economy of free labor. Of all groups in the United States, white working men had experienced the most dramatic expansion of their political rights in the early nineteenth century. Yet, as Luther's criticisms made clear, many American workers felt threatened by the new industrial order. Worker protests had become common in cities and manufacturing centers, and working men's parties had begun to assume an oppositional stance toward the major political parties.

Americans of middling means responded to the volatility of industrial society by attempting to withdraw from it and to distance themselves from the struggles of workers. They elaborated a distinctive style of living, based on a belief in the individual household as the last sanctuary of morality in an increasingly dangerous world. If workers were poor, this new middle class suggested, perhaps they lacked ambition, were negligent, drank too much, or were irreligious. Criticisms of workers focused on Irish immigrants, whose growing numbers brought to the surface the virulent anti-Catholicism of many native-born Americans.

In this atmosphere of dislocation and division, reform itself became an object of controversy. The increasingly vocal struggle against slavery aroused deep hostility. The visibility of women in abolition and other radical reform movements was especially offensive to the new middle-class domestic sensibility. Most reform women and men shunned controversy and focused their efforts on the need for control in a democratic society. Some extolled the importance of self-control through education and temperate personal habits. Others called for new laws and institutions to save those who would not save themselves. Ironically, as the common social ground slipped away, the rhetoric of democracy grew more shrill, and political leaders denounced their enemies as the foes of a democratic political economy itself.

THE GROWTH OF SECTIONAL TENSION

The strains in Jacksonian America became apparent almost immediately after Jackson's first inauguration in the form of growing sectional conflict. Americans had not always viewed the differences in the political economies of the North and South as bad, but economic growth eventually matured old differences into open conflict.

The Political Economy of Southern Discontent

Many white southerners had felt betrayed by northern criticisms of slavery during the Missouri controversy. A series of economic and political frustrations in the 1820s nurtured that sense of mistreatment, causing the planter class to see itself as the victim of dishonorable conspiracies in the nation's capital.

Most important was the economy. By 1828 cotton prices were about one-third of their 1815 levels. Many planters and farmers tried to compensate for declining profits by planting more acres, but worn-out fields kept production low. Large eastern planters rode out the hard times by selling off slaves, lands, and city houses. Small farmers, dependent on cotton as their cash crop, were forced to sell out. Conditions were not much better in the cities, where small businesses failed, property values plummeted, and beggars became numerous.

Probably most important in framing the way southerners saw the North was the impact of the Missouri debates in coalescing antislavery sentiment in northern states. In 1824 Ohio asked Congress to consider a plan for the gradual abolition of slavery throughout the United States. On July 4, 1827, New York completed its process of gradual emancipation, an occasion celebrated by free African Americans as far south as Virginia. Peddlers and manufacturers' agents from the North were blunt about their "great aversion to the . . . Slaveholding States," even as they made their living there, and northern farmers migrating into the upper South were outspoken in their criticisms of slavery, suffrage restrictions, and the political power of planters.

The Tariff of 1828 helped give focus to southern insecurities. The new tariff hurt the South in two ways. First, although some southern products benefited from protection, as an export-oriented economy the South as a whole needed open markets with other nations. But these nations reacted to reduced American sales with reduced purchases from America. In addition, by raising the costs of imported goods, the tariff further concentrated southern buying in the North while allowing northern prices to rise.

Among the slaveholding states, South Carolina was particularly sensitive to perceived interference from beyond its borders. White South Carolinians were faced with a growing African-American majority (the result of white migration west), a demographic condition that heightened their fears of slave insurrection. Those fears were triggered in 1822, when white authorities claimed they had exposed a plot to launch a statewide slave rebellion, allegedly devised by free carpenter Denmark Vesey. Although Vesey and 34 others were executed, the white regime of South Carolina was deeply shaken.

These events helped revive interest among white South Carolinians in theories of nullification (the right of states to disregard laws they considered repugnant). In response to rumors that free African-American sailors encouraged rebellion, the state legislature mandated that free black sailors arriving in Charleston be held in jail until their ships left port. Under pressure from an organization of planters known as the South Carolina Association, the sheriff of Charleston imprisoned free

Jamaican sailor Harry Elkinson. When Elkinson's case came to court, lawyers argued that any treaty that interfered with the power of the state to guard against internal revolution must be unconstitutional. The court rejected this position (agreeing with Secretary of State Adams that the law violated international treaties), but South Carolina continued to enforce the act.

Passage of the Tariff of 1828, the "tariff of abominations," again revived nullification talk in South Carolina and gave the position a new defender, John C. Calhoun. Calhoun had been disenchanted by the experiences of the 1820s and was a far less enthusiastic nationalist than he had once been. Yet he retained enough faith in the Democratic Party to believe that Democrats would lower the tariff and could be made to see the injury that such national laws were inflicting on southern states. Hoping to encourage both results, in 1828 Calhoun wrote the *South Carolina Exposition and Protest*, in which he laid out the historical, legal, and social justification for the theory of nullification. Calhoun argued that the federal government was the creation of the states, not of "the people" as a whole. In agreeing to create a federal government, Calhoun argued, the states had ceded some of their powers, but only conditionally. They had always reserved whatever powers were necessary for their survival as distinct entities. Should federal policies threaten a state, that state had the right to assert its reserved sovereignty. It was at such a juncture, Calhoun argued, that the states of the South had arrived in 1828.

There was much in America's history to support Calhoun's view. The states had existed before the federal constitution. Representation at the Constitutional Convention and ratification of the Constitution had been by state, and representation in the federal government continued to be on the basis of states.

On the other hand, the Constitution's status as the supreme law of the land rested on the fact that it had been ratified by the people, acting through special conventions, not by the state governments. Moreover, the Hartford Convention (see Chapter 10, "The Market Revolution") had associated states' rights arguments with a lack of patriotism. The *Exposition* went a good deal farther than the convention resolutions: Calhoun argued explicitly that if all else failed, states always retained the right to withdraw from the compact.

By 1828, however, many Americans viewed the federal government as the creation of "the people," not the states. Among these was President Jackson.

The Nullification Crisis

Other southern states did not rush to endorse the *Exposition*. Late in the year, however, the question of slavery once again intruded into the houses of Congress. As with so many issues of antebellum American life, the immediate subject was western migration.

Eager to attract population, the territories and western states had long lobbied for a reduction in the price of federal lands. Southern representatives now offered to support such a measure provided that the western states would join in opposing the tariff. For New Englanders, western migration continued to create a labor shortage and to strengthen fears of becoming a political backwater. In December 1829 Senator Samuel A. Foot of Connecticut advocated limiting land sales in the West. Seeking a South–West alliance, Senator Robert Y. Hayne of South Carolina charged that the idea was a conspiracy to pool cheap labor in the East. He insinuated that the government was keeping land prices high to build a slush fund "for corruption—fatal to the sovereignty and independence of the states."

When Massachusetts Senator Daniel Webster rose to defend his region, Hayne made the serious tactical error of bringing up the Hartford Convention. Webster responded that it was South Carolina, not the Northeast, that posed a threat to national unity, and he pointed for evidence to the South Carolina *Exposition*. Hayne protested that the *Exposition* was in the honored tradition of American political protest, but Webster was contemptuous. The Revolution had been fought by the American people, and the American people had created the federal government. What Webster said next was prescient of later events: "When my eyes shall be turned to behold, for the last time, the sun in heaven, may I not see him shining on the broken and dishonored fragments of a once glorious union . . . on a land rent with civil feuds . . ." No, he insisted: "Let their last feeble and lingering glance rather behold the gorgeous ensign of the republic . . . , not a stripe erased or polluted, not a single star obscured." And let that ensign not bear that motto of southern malcontents, "'Liberty first and Union afterwards'; but . . . that other sentiment, dear to every true American heart—Liberty and Union, now and forever, one and inseparable."

Although Webster's address was enthusiastically received in the North, Calhoun and the South Carolinians remained convinced that all true Americans, certainly all true southerners, must agree with them. The following April, at a banquet commemorating Jefferson's birthday, they put that assumption to the test. With President Jackson, the entire cabinet, more than 100 congressmen, and various other federal officials present, southern congressmen rolled through a series of prepared toasts celebrating the principle of state sovereignty. A mortified Jackson reputedly stared hard at John Calhoun and lifted his glass: "Our Federal Union," he declared. "It must be preserved."

Although he supported the federal union, Jackson sympathized with southern complaints that tariff levels were too high and advocated tariff reform. The Tariff of 1832 lowered duties on many goods, but not on textiles and iron. In this continued protection for the largest northern industries, South Carolinians saw a reaffirmation of a special relationship between northern interests and the federal government.

By the time South Carolina responded, the South had been the scene of another slave insurrection. In the summer of 1831 an African-American preacher by the name of Nat Turner launched a slave rebellion in Virginia. Inspired by a millennialist fervor, for two days Turner and his followers had controlled parts of southern Virginia, recruiting allies as they executed whites and freed slaves. Before the uprising was put down 57 whites had died. Southern whites instituted a month-long reign of vigilantism in which many African Americans who had no part in the revolt were summarily executed.

The insurrection left its mark. Southern whites remained in a state of apprehension and felt certain that northerners and southern slaves were conspiring against them. In November 1832 South Carolina Radicals called a statewide convention whose delegates nullified the tariffs of both 1828 and 1832 and forbade the collection of the tariffs within South Carolina.

For Jackson, the act of nullification transformed the crisis into a question of national union. In December he issued a proclamation asserting his conviction that the union was a creation of the people, not the states. "The laws of the United States must be executed," he declared, "I have no discretionary power on the subject; my duty is emphatically pronounced in the Constitution." Jackson asked Congress for a law affirming his responsibility to compel the collection of the tax in South Carolina, by force of arms if necessary.

Congress rushed to find a compromise. In early 1833 it passed a tariff that gradually reduced duties over the next decade, but it also passed the law Jackson had requested, known as the Force Bill. On March 2, 1833, Jackson signed both the new tariff law and the Force Bill.

In 1832 South Carolina stood virtually alone even among southern states. The supporters of nullification withdrew their ordinance, but they also voted to nullify the Force Bill within South Carolina. Jackson let the gesture pass, and at least for the time being, the constitutional crisis was over.

Antislavery Becomes Abolition

By 1832, the growing sectional crisis was no longer a question exclusively for politicians to debate. By the time Jackson left office, a small but dynamic social movement against slavery had taken shape in the North, and slavery had become a nationally divisive issue.

By the late 1820s, the movement for African-American self-sufficiency had yielded a rich harvest of mutual aid and benevolent associations. Organizing was most lively in Philadelphia, where free African Americans established more than 40 new societies between 1820 and 1835, but the self-help impulse extended south to Baltimore and Charleston and north to New York and Boston. Although some societies were limited in membership to the prosperous, organizing was vigorous across economic lines: coachmen, porters, barbers, brickmakers, sailors, cooks, and washerwomen all formed associations.

In the 1820s, in the wake of the Missouri debates and the steady erosion of African-American male suffrage, African-American organizing became more political and antislavery. At first, African-American associations protested the efforts of the American Colonization Society to deport emancipated slaves. By 1826, with the formation of the first all-African-American antislavery organization, the General Colored Association of Massachusetts, African Americans were targeting the institution of slavery itself. In New York in 1827 John Russwurm and Samuel E. Cornish founded the first African-American newspaper, *Freedom's Journal*, devoted to exposing the evils of slavery.

African-American protests of the late 1820s reflected the expectation that African Americans could not and should not count on white allies. In 1829 David Walker, a secondhand clothes dealer in Boston, published a pamphlet titled *An Appeal to the Colored Citizens of the World*, calling on African Americans to resist slavery by armed insurrection, if necessary. In 1832 Maria Stewart, a free black woman in Boston, urged African Americans gathered at Boston's Franklin Hall to take their destinies into their own hands. "If they kill us," she said simply, "we shall but die."

These entreaties found responsive audiences. From 1830 until 1835 (and less regularly thereafter), free African Americans met in annual conventions intended to coordinate antislavery efforts and secure to free African-American men "a voice in the disposition of those public resources which we ourselves have helped to earn." This National Negro Convention movement consistently framed its goals in the idiom of "manhood," calling for "the speedy elevation of ourselves and brethren to the scale and standing of men." Nevertheless, African-American women worked to raise funds for the antislavery press and to raise awareness by inviting antislavery speakers to address their societies. In 1832 African-American women formed female antislavery societies in Salem, Massachusetts and Rochester, New York.

Although many whites in the North disliked the institution of slavery, most were reluctant to confront an issue that had such power to ignite violence and political division. Few white northerners thought of African Americans as their equals. Many based their livelihoods directly or indirectly on the southern economy. For all of these reasons, white antislavery activism took root slowly. In 1821 Ohio newspaperman Benjamin Lundy began publication of *The Genius of Universal Emancipation*, the first white abolitionist paper. In the years that followed, a few northern states passed laws making it more difficult for masters to recapture runaway slaves. Nevertheless, in the mid-1820s the American Colonization Society (see Chapter 9, "Liberty and Empire") was the primary focus of northern efforts at improving the conditions of slaves.

It took the growth of the perfectionist impulse to begin to dislodge northern complacency. The most dramatic break came in the person of William Lloyd Garrison, Lundy's co-editor, whose commitment to perfectionism led him to found his own abolitionist newspaper, the *Liberator*, in Boston in 1831. In the first issue Garrison announced his absolute break with all forms of antislavery sentiment that compromised with the institution: "I will not equivocate—I will not excuse—I will not retreat a single inch—and I will be heard." Garrison's approach, known as immediatism, called on antislavery reformers not only to work for the immediate abolition of slavery but also to confront all forms of compromise with slavery, public or personal, wherever they encountered them.

Immediatist antislavery activism centered in Boston and tended to attract individuals, like Garrison, who had been only peripherally linked to the mainstream Benevolent Empire. Most were urban professionals from liberal Protestant backgrounds, such as the author Lydia Maria Child, wealthy lawyer Samuel Sewall, Wendell Phillips (scion of an old Massachusetts family), and Henry and Maria Weston Chapman (he a merchant, she the principal of a young ladies' high school before her marriage). In 1831, under Garrison's leadership, they formed the New England Anti-Slavery Society.

AMERICAN SLAVERY.

Through drawings like this one, published in Garrison's Liberator *on May 3, 1834, abolitionists in the United States tried to convince Americans to put aside their complacency about slavery by emphasizing the brutality of the owner or overseer and the helplessness of the enslaved worker.*

Other antislavery workers were more willing than the Garrisonians to risk contact with the imperfect world. One of these was Theodore Dwight Weld. Born in Connecticut, Weld was an early supporter of the Colonization Society. After his conversion in the Finneyite revivals of 1825 and 1826, however, he began to doubt that the society would ever risk alienating its southern constituency. By the 1830s Weld was a committed abolitionist. As a student at Lane Seminary in Cincinnati, Ohio, he organized 18 days of antislavery discussions and led a group of students out of Lane to Oberlin College when Lane President Lyman Beecher moved to squelch their activities. In 1834, Weld became a full-time antislavery organizer.

There were some quick converts to the new, energized antislavery movement, especially in urban areas of the Northeast, upstate New York, and Pennsylvania, and in western states heavily settled by New Englanders, especially Ohio. Quakers and liberal Congregationalists were particularly active. Local antislavery societies formed throughout New England by 1832. Although Garrison envisioned a gender and racially integrated abolition movement, local societies were generally sex-segregated and racially segregated. By the end of 1833, local and state organizations had grown strong enough to support a national society, the American Anti-Slavery Society, which included six African Americans on its original board.

Abolitionism and Antiabolition Violence

The American Anti-Slavery Society dedicated itself to the abolition of slavery without compensation for owners and to the admission of African Americans to full citizenship. Society members pledged to pursue their goals through nonviolent moral suasion, by exhorting individuals to undertake voluntary self-reform and the reform of society.

Although nonviolent, moral suasion was not nonconfrontational. In 1835 the Society flooded the United States mails with abolitionist literature. The campaign was intended to support recruitment and organizing in the North and to take the antislavery fight directly into the South.

Abolitionists had relied on the press to spread their views since the early 1820s. Yet in the early 1830s even Garrison's *Liberator* remained largely unknown. In 1835 the Society dramatically increased its publication of antislavery pamphlets from approximately 100,000 pieces to 1 million pieces. Roughly 20,000 tracts, fliers, and periodicals were mailed to southern destinations. Meanwhile, agents and lecturers spread out across the North.

The response, in the North as well as the South, was immediate and fierce (see Map 12–1). In the South, anger and panic turned violent. With the memory of Nat Turner still fresh, slaveowners denounced the campaign as incendiary. Southern communities offered rewards for prominent abolition leaders, dead or alive. Local authorities appointed vigilante committees to police free African-American neighborhoods, to patrol coastal boats for runaway slaves, and to search post offices for offending materials. In Charleston, South Carolina, a mob broke into the post office, ransacked the mail, stole abolitionist literature, and burned it publicly.

Even before the 1835 campaign, northerners had begun to express their disapproval of abolitionists. In 1833, whites had boycotted a Connecticut school for young women when its principal, Prudence Crandall, admitted two African-American scholars. When Crandall admitted an entirely African-American student body, white citizens lobbied for laws to bar black students from the state, threatened Crandall, and burned the school to the ground.

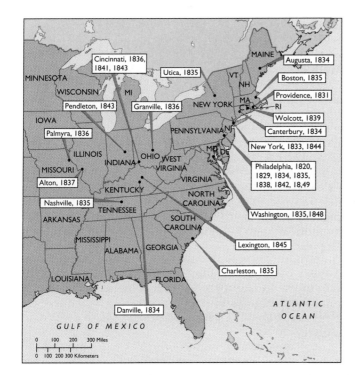

Map 12–1   Primary Sites of Antiabolition Violence

The postal campaign unleashed a new fury in the North. Anti-African-American and antiabolitionist riots tore through St. Louis, Pittsburgh, Cincinnati, and Philadelphia. From Boston to Utica, New York, to Granville, Ohio, abolitionist meetings were broken up by mobs. In Boston in 1835, a crowd captured William Lloyd Garrison and dragged him through the streets on a rope.

Responding to the abolitionists' use of the press, antiabolitionist mobs targeted newspapers. In 1836, an antiabolitionist mob in Cincinnati made "the destruction of their Press on the night of the 12th instant," the symbolic warning of greater violence to come. Rioters in Alton, Illinois, destroyed abolitionist newspaper editor Elija Lovejoy's press four times in 1837. In the last attack, they murdered Lovejoy himself.

Many white northerners who opposed slavery were nonetheless distressed by the violence. A few northern state legislatures admonished radical abolitionists for their extreme measures, although none passed laws restricting abolitionist activity. Many antislavery activists chastised what they saw as the extreme fringe of their own movement, criticizing them for a too-zealous approach. Writers for the *Boston Courier* worried that the abolitionists would dangerously "inflame the passions of the multitude, including the women and children."

Abolitionists were undeterred and even began to find a wider range of converts. Antiabolition violence suggested to some moderates that proslavery forces would stop at nothing—even the flagrant violation of civil rights, the destruction of property, and murder. They were alarmed when, in his annual address to Congress in 1835, President Jackson asked for measures curtailing antislavery organizing, including closing the mails to abolitionist literature. Congress refused, but northerners were shocked by the idea that the president would propose to restrict freedom of the mails to protect southern interests.

If antislavery advocates took heart from Congress's refusal to interfere with the mails, they were less happy with other decisions. Opponents of slavery had long petitioned Congress to end slavery in the nation's capital. Seeking to mollify southerners, in June 1836 the House of Representatives resolved that antislavery petitions to Congress be automatically tabled. The resolution, known as the "gag rule," was renewed by succeeding Congresses until 1844.

The American Anti-Slavery Society was quick to capitalize on the passage of the gag rule. In July the society published *An Appeal to the People of the United States*, charging that the gag rule was a flagrant violation of the right of petition. That same summer, female antislavery leaders from across the North began organizing a systematic, widespread drive to obtain signatures on antislavery petitions. Female abolitionists traveled across the North, speaking in private parlors and in public halls. Within two years, they collected some 2 million signatures, more than two-thirds of which were women's.

The petition campaign called attention to the gag rule, to Congressional support of slavery, and to the ability of proslavery forces to abridge the rights of all Americans. It also provided moderate northerners with a nonconfrontational avenue of protest. Benefiting from a growing public discussion of slavery, the American Anti-Slavery Society grew from 225 local auxiliaries in 1835 to more than 1,500 by the end of the decade.

Immediatist sentiment often contained a critique of the North as well as of the South. The critique expressed disillusionment with northern reformers who were willing to compromise with slavery. Perhaps, "besotted by the influence of the institution of slavery," as Garrisonian Samuel J. May would later put it, the North had already lost its moral bearing in the headlong rush to industrial prosperity.

THE POLITICAL ECONOMY OF EARLY INDUSTRIAL SOCIETY

Abolitionists were not the only Americans to criticize the political economy of the industrializing North. Seth Luther's indictment of the "American system of manufacturing" focused on the cotton and woolen mills across the 12 nonslave states of the union, but by 1832 the wage dependency Luther deplored extended far beyond the textile mills. Shoemaking, the nation's second-largest industry, employed tens of thousands of men and women. Another 10,000 women in Boston, New York, Philadelphia, and Baltimore labored in the garment industry. In Luther's eyes, artisans and craft workers were being crushed in "a cruel system of exaction" that destroyed their bodies and minds. Luther had a name for what they had become: "the Working Classes."

Wage Dependency

By 1830, in response to growing regional and local markets, master craftsmen had subdivided the production process into smaller discrete tasks. When possible, they distributed aspects of the production to outworkers, who worked part of the shoe, or hat, or shirt, returning it to the manufacturer (or a subcontractor) for piece wages. In house, employers relied more and more on the labor of apprentices or poorly trained helpers, whose labor came cheaper than that of journeymen. As work was subdivided, workers became more interchangeable, and their wages dropped.

The Panic of 1819 had thrown thousands of people out of work, driving wages down and prices up. The reviving economy of the 1820s did not reverse those trends, which were deepened by depressions in 1829 and 1837. Seth Luther was not alone in his indictment of the American system of manufacturing. In an 1833 appeal, workers in Manayunk, Pennsylvania, protested fourteen-and-a-half-hour days in "overheated" rooms "thick with the dust and small particles of cotton, which we are constantly inhaling to the destruction of our health, our appetite, and strength." "Our wages," they declared, "are barely sufficient to supply us with the necessaries of life." They cited the larger system of market relations that gripped them in its vice: "It requires the wages of all the family who are able to work," they explained.

The lives of outwork seamstresses, of whom there were tens of thousands in the eastern cities, were even more harrowing. Philadelphia philanthropist Mathew Carey estimated the wages of Philadelphia seamstresses at $1.25 a week. As it turned out, Carey was overly optimistic. A committee of seamstresses quickly informed him that they were lucky to earn $1.12 1/2 a week. After rent, they were left with a little more than a nickel a day for food, clothing, heat, and anything else they needed.

By 1830 the urban Northeast was bearing witness to the damages of wage dependency and the subdivision of labor. In the largest cities, neighborhoods had become stratified by class. The New York neighborhood of Five Points had once been a thriving community of master craftsmen and trade shops. By 1829, it was the home of prostitutes, beggars, public drunks, thieves, and confidence men. In working-class neighborhoods, high rents crowded whole families into single unventilated rooms. Many people went homeless or threw up makeshift shanties.

New York was not unique. In New Haven in the 1820s and 1830s, many poor whites lived in tenement houses erected specifically for the working class, and African Americans and immigrants occupied housing that reminded one observer

Seamstresses were among the most exploited and impoverished workers of the early industrial Northeast. In this picture, exhausted women sew by bad lighting in an overcrowded central shop under the tyranny of the clock. Seamstresses were generally paid by the piece.

By 1827 Five Points in New York City, once the site of a thriving community of craft shops and small retailers, had become one of New York City's poorest neighborhoods and, as this drawing suggests, a symbol of urban poverty, immorality, and crime.

of "barracks." Increasingly dependent on the market for their most basic subsistence needs, workers were able to afford only the bare minimum, the cheapest, and the poorest quality goods.

Labor Organizing and Protest

By the mid-1820s, poor working and living conditions produced a clamor of protest, as workers formed unions and took to both the press and the streets to air their grievances. In 1826 New Yorker Langton Byllesby published *Observations on the Sources and Effects of Unequal Wealth.* Byllesby called for producers' cooperatives to return to workers some control of the products of their labor.

Workers turned out in huge numbers to hear social critics denounce the growing inequities of American life. Scotswoman Frances Wright, one of the most popular of these speakers, focused on education and religion, charging that the clergy conspired to keep workers shackled to superstition. Wright also inveighed against slavery and advocated for women's rights.

In addition to using these older forms of protest and redress, workers turned to labor unions. The unions of the 1820s and 1830s came into existence chiefly to oppose the overwhelming power of employers to control wages and hours. The unions' weapon was the strike.

Among the earliest of the new trade unions was one formed by New Orleans printers in 1823. Weavers, carpenters, tailors, cabinet makers, masons, stevedores, and workers in other crafts turned out on strike throughout the major cities of the nation. In 1825 Boston carpenters struck for a ten-hour workday. Strikers argued that the shorter day was essential if they were to have time to refresh themselves, to spend with their families, and to obtain the education necessary for newly enfranchised voters.

Cross-trade demands for the ten-hour day and the repeated failures of individual strikes helped bring about the formation of the citywide and regional labor organizations. The first, the Mechanics' Union, was established in Philadelphia in 1827. Pledged to the ten-hour day, the Union protested the mental and spiritual exhaustion associated with industrialization and the "desolating evils which . . . arise from a depreciation of the intrinsic value of human labor."

When the Philadelphia Mechanics' Union dissolved, leadership passed to the New England Association of Farmers, Mechanics, and Other Workingmen, founded in 1831 by, among others, Seth Luther. The New England Association invited "every citizen whose daily exertions . . . are his means of subsistence" to participate in its efforts. The association also used its newspaper, the *New England Artisan*, for worker self-education and organizing and published Luther's *Address to the Workingmen*.

Strikes multiplied throughout the 1830s. In February 1831, with wages in sharp decline, more than 1,800 women who worked in the tailoring craft struck the New York garment industry. The women drew up a constitution, elected officers, and stayed out on strike for five months.

Deteriorating labor conditions led to protest even in that industrial paradise, Lowell (see Chapter 10). After a decade of rapid expansion, the market stalled in 1834. In response to falling prices, the owners cut wages by 12.5 percent. In response, some 800 female operatives walked off their jobs. The protest failed (owners used the break in production to lower their inventories), but two years later, when the owners tried to increase the price of company housing, 2,000 operatives went out on strike, forcing the owners to rescind the increases. The 1836 victory was fleeting, however. Business was booming, and the owners had a vested interest in keeping the mills open. When business was slow or inventories high, workers would have far less power to assert their interests.

Workers attempted to strengthen their position by forming regional and national associations, now a possibility thanks to improved transportation and interdependence of markets. The most successful national association was the National Trades' Union (NTU), formed in 1834. The NTU survived for a number of years, but it was unable to effect the type of statewide coordinated actions its organizers envisioned. In the end, much of the energy of the national union went into lobbying for currency reform, worker access to education, free land for workers, and the ten-hour day.

A New Urban Middle Class

Seth Luther framed his criticisms of American industrial society in terms of a struggle between "the producing classes" and the "rich." However, this bipartite division did not adequately describe American industrial society. The concept of the "producing classes" was ambiguous, encompassing Americans of many different standards of living and levels of wealth. When Luther used the term he meant primarily urban-based households dependent on wage labor. Luther sometimes fell into a more complex way of analyzing American society, distinguishing among the "poor," the "rich," and the "middling classes." Americans had long taken pride in their great "middling" ranks of solid farmers and artisans. But the composition of the category had changed by the 1830s, as had its relation to the group Luther now called the "working classes."

These new middling classes were difficult to define exactly. Like the new working classes, the middling classes were primarily urban based. Middle-class households tended to receive their income in the form of fees and salaries, rather than wages, and their paid workers were employed in jobs that required mental, rather than physical, labor. These included doctors, lawyers, ministers, middle managers, agents, supervisors, tellers, clerks, shopkeepers, editors, writers, and schoolteachers.

The relationship of these urban households of moderate means to the new industrial economy was complicated. On the one hand, they were not immune to catastrophic economic reversal, in the form of sudden unemployment, business failure, or bad speculation. Popular essayist Lydia Maria Child underscored this point in her 1829 *The American Frugal Housewife*. Addressing "persons of moderate fortune," Child nevertheless concluded the book with a sobering chapter titled "How to Endure Poverty."

At the same time, the new middle class was created by and benefited from the industrial transformation. The paid occupations on which middle-class families depended had expanded enormously as a result of the growth of commerce and industrialization. These jobs brought annual salaries ranging roughly from $1,000 to $1,500, compared to the $300 to $400 an average working man might earn. In addition, middle-class families tended to have access to a variety of other resources, through family, friends, and business connections.

The middle class celebrated the new political economy, commended the expansion of democracy, praised the growth of individual opportunity, and deplored lingering evidence of the special privilege of the wealthy. As a group they were profoundly religiously oriented. Embracing the doctrines of personal agency, they were churchgoers who both donated to and participated in the causes of the Benevolent Empire.

Individuals who aspired to urban middle-class status took far greater pains to distinguish themselves from the urban poor than from the rich. This was especially evident in their understanding of personal responsibility and material success. In sermons and tracts, children's books and novels, members of the new middle class described the industrial economy as a test of personal character. Success demonstrated superior individual industriousness and self-discipline; failure signified the opposite. These beliefs took their toll on the middle class itself, because middle-class families did fail, bringing on themselves social and psychological censure. Nevertheless, middle-class writers continued to hone the broad idiom of the "common man" into the more class-based language of the "self-made man" of business. From this point of view, the middle class saw itself as the repository of moderation in the changing political economy, the heir of Jefferson's idealized "husbandmen."

Meanwhile, middle-class families struggled to distinguish themselves from the working class. Middle-class parents recoiled from the "ungentility" of manual labor and urged their sons to become "a rich merchant, or a popular lawyer, or a broker." They expressed a new value for education, even for their daughters. While workers crowded into smaller and smaller living areas, the emerging middle class expressed itself in terms of increasingly elaborate residential space. The ideal home of the emerging middle class, the "cottage," offered a private sitting room for the family and a separate "public" parlor for receiving guests. The parlor also provided a stage where the family could present tangible evidence of their success through display of costly furnishings and decorations.

To emphasize their desired distance from the industrial world, the new urban middle class insisted on a "natural" division of temperament and capability between men and women. Although men were required to expose themselves to the degradations of labor, women were of a gentler disposition, intended by nature to remain at home to revive the hardened sensibilities of husbands and raise children protected from the ravages of industrialization.

This view of women as the primary influence on children represented a dramatic change from colonial opinions. Moreover, it was largely inaccurate, because many middle-class women pursued paid labor. They took in boarders, did fancy sewing, opened schools, and worked in family-owned businesses. All women of the new middle classes worked unpaid at the daily labor of cooking, cleaning, washing, ironing, preserving food, sewing, and caring for children. Nevertheless, domestic womanhood became the primary symbol of middle-class respectability and a bulwark against the many contradictions of the new industrial political economy.

Immigration and Nativism

Swept up in enormous changes, even those Americans who seemed to be benefiting from early industrial society were alert for sources of potential danger. Many labor leaders and utopianists felt that industrialists were posing that danger. More common, however, was the tendency to focus anxieties on the poor, who were deemed incapable of achieving republican virtue. The targets of such nativism were the immigrants, and especially the Catholic Irish.

In spite of the difficulties encountered by wage workers, the robust economy of the United States drew increasing numbers of immigrants from Europe. Ninety percent of the immigrants came from England, Germany, or Ireland. The largest group by far was Irish. Plagued by recurrent poverty and harsh British rule, almost 60,000 Irish citizens migrated to the United States in the 1820s, 235,000 in the 1830s, and 845,000 during the potato famines of the 1840s. Through most of the period, Irish immigrants accounted for more than one-third of all immigrants.

Their customs and their poverty made Irish immigrants conspicuous. Unable to afford land, they remained crowded in the seaports where they arrived. Unfamiliar with urban life, they were the prey of con artists. Desperate, they often had to accept jobs and conditions that native-born workers scorned. Because they had no other place to go, one boss observed, the Irish could "be relied on at the mill all year round."

Not all of the Irish went into mills. Many built roadways, dredged river bottoms, and built canals. Irish women cooked and did laundry for the camps or hired out as domestic workers in middle-class households.

Most of all, the Irish were distinguished by their Catholic religion. By 1830, immigration had virtually doubled the number of Catholics in the country. Not all Catholics were Irish, but many were, leaving the Irish particularly visible as targets of long-standing American anti-Catholic prejudices. Anti-Irish sentiment often took the form of stereotypes that represented Catholics as given to superstition and unthinking obedience. Funded by members of the new middle class and supported by Protestant ministers, anti-Catholic newspapers charged the Catholic hierarchy with "tyrannical and unchristian" acts "repugnant to our republican institutions."

By the early 1830s, anti-Catholicism spilled over into street violence. Organizations such as the New York Protestant Association, founded in 1831, sponsored "public discussions" on the immorality of monks, the greed of priests, and the Pope's alleged designs on the American West. The debates soon deteriorated into small riots, which Protestant newspaper editors described as Papist attacks on "the liberty of free discussion." Anti-Catholicism took an especially dangerous turn in Massachusetts. In 1834, the associated Congregational Clergy of Massachusetts issued a frantic challenge to all Protestants to rescue the republic from "the degrading influence of Popery." Sermons and editorials whipped up a frenzy of anti-Catholic fear. The hysteria was aimed especially at an Ursuline Convent in Charleston, in which, purportedly, nuns were brainwashing their innocent Protestant students. On the night of August 11, 1834, a mob torched the convent, cheering as it burned to the ground. Anti-Catholicism was beginning to serve as a bond among Americans who otherwise had less and less in common with one another.

Internal Migration

The constant stream of internal migrants also heightened the sense of antebellum America as a society in turmoil. The swirl of internal migration was evidence of growth and opportunity, but it also produced a constant stream of individuals who seemed to have no settled stake in American society.

Many of these travelers were westward settlers, but many were rural folks losing out in the industrial revolution and migrating to the cities in search of employment. They were mainly unmarried young adult men. There was both a push and a pull to this internal movement. Children were pushed out from farming families whose land could no longer support them. They were pulled to the cities by the same conditions that spelled disaster for the artisan tradition: the breakdown of the apprentice system and the subdivision of skills.

In the cities, these young people often lived in rented rooms, apart from adult guidance. Young men joined neighborhood fire companies that served as gathering places for fun and sport. Young women navigated the city unescorted. Young men and women used their earnings to buy the things unavailable in the countryside: new shoes, clothing of the latest cut, hats, and canes. Perhaps most unsettling of all, these young people moved almost too fast to be counted.

Migrants did not usually move very far in any single trek, traveling the fairly short distances to the nearest large towns and cities. Nonetheless, they swelled the populations of the midsized cities in which most American manufacturing took place. About 50 miles up the Schuylkill River from Philadelphia, Reading, Pennsylvania, was a hub for regional manufacturing, transportation, and trading. In the 1840s, Reading's population doubled to 15,000 people. Nearly half of the unskilled laborers in Reading had come from within 25 miles, mainly from areas with poor land and big families.

The constant, restless migration of Americans westward provoked alarm among the eastern, urban middle class. Moralistic observers worried that this migration was sapping ambitious, upright citizens away from the East Coast, exposing them to the dangers of the wilderness, and leaving the dregs of society behind. Most westward migrants, however, were not irresponsible and rootless young adults but rather married couples beginning families. They were not people without other options; the expense of outfitting a trip westward ensured that most settlers were not from the poorest classes.

Observers like Lyman Beecher (author of *A Plea for the West*) worried about the influence of the West on future American citizens. The West lacked all those institutions that easterners associated with civilization and civic responsibility. There were few schools and churches and too many unattached young men, saloons, and brothels. Moreover, in some respects westward migration canonized the materialism and greed that easterners were beginning to worry about. The desire for money drove some families on and on in an almost endless migration. One family, the Shelbys, had made four moves by 1850, when they ended up in Oregon. The father had been born in Kentucky, the mother in Tennessee, three children in Illinois, three in Iowa, and the youngest in Oregon.

Into this land of apparently unsteady habits were being born more and more of the nation's young. Once the frontier had passed the stage of initial exploration and families had begun to pour in, fertility rates in the newly settled areas became far higher than they were in the older, coastal regions. Easterners were alarmed by the specter of a generation of children growing up in the wilderness, without the proper social constraints. The values of self-reliance, industry, and civic virtues, values that only a decade before had seemed to capture the essence of American nationalism, appeared to be in danger of disappearing. By the 1820s, these observers had begun to focus their fears on the growing waves of European immigrants.

SELF-REFORM AND SOCIAL REGULATION

In his address to working men in 1832, Seth Luther explained that he would uncover "principles and practices which will, if not immediately eradicated and forsaken, destroy all the rights, benefits, and privileges intended for our enjoyment, as a free people." Earlier reformers had adopted a far more optimistic tone. Faced with deep divisions and seemingly insurmountable obstacles to perfecting industrial society, American reformers began to refocus their efforts away from broad programs of social perfection, to endeavors that centered on self-control and external restraint.

A Culture of Self-Improvement

Answering criticisms from fellow senators that only the rich and well-connected enjoyed the benefits of the new American industrial order, in 1832 Henry Clay rose to the defense of the entrepreneurial class. "In Kentucky," he asserted, "almost every manufactory known to me is in the hands of enterprising and self-made men, who have acquired whatever wealth they possess by patient and diligent labor." Clay's emphasis on personal enterprise captured a perspective that was increasingly common among ambitious Americans by the 1830s. Success or failure was less a matter of external injustice and constraint than of individual striving. Those who truly worked hard—who were industrious and clever and frugal—would succeed.

The new emphasis on self-improvement was not limited to the privileged. Poor Americans, African American and white, were quick to perceive the importance of self-reliance. Much of the popularity of radical labor lecturers like Fanny Wright resided in their attacks on the cultural controls of "professional aristocrats." Wright decried workers' dependence on wealthy individuals for everything workers knew about their bodies and their world. Wright founded a "Hall of Science" in New York where workers could educate themselves about a variety of subjects (including health).

Yet, as Clay's words had implied, the culture of self-improvement enjoyed a particular popularity among members of the new middle class. The emphasis on self-creation helped to resolve middle-class ambivalence about industrial society: Middle-class families had escaped the worst ravages of wage labor not because they were lucky or had some special advantage, but because they worked harder.

The culture of self-improvement was not limited to lessons for the mind and spirit, however. It embraced the body as well. From the 1820s to the 1840s, health reform became a national obsession, as Americans experimented with new diets, clothing, exercise programs, abstinence in various forms, and hydropathy, the cleansing of the body through frequent bathing and drinking water. Particularly influential among the health reformers was Sylvester Graham, who came to prominence in 1832 as Americans braced themselves for a return of cholera. In a series of lectures, Graham argued that Americans were susceptible to illness because they ate too much meat and spicy food and drank too much alcohol, coffee, and tea. Graham recommended a diet of fruits, vegetables, and coarsely ground wheat (the origin of the graham cracker), combined with regular bathing and loose clothing. By 1834, Graham had extended his regimen of self-discipline to warn that sexual excess (masturbation, but also too frequent sexual relations between spouses) "cannot fail to produce the most terrible effects."

Men and women of the new middle class crowded lectures and devoured written materials that espoused the philosophy of self-culture. By 1831 the lyceum movement claimed several thousand local organizations and a national umbrella association and sponsored such speakers as the writer Ralph Waldo Emerson, Daniel Webster, and later Abraham Lincoln himself. Meanwhile, middle-class readers supported a publishing bonanza in novels, periodicals, and tracts devoted to self-improvement.

These publications promoted a variety of images of the self-made American. In his *Leatherstocking Tales*, James Fenimore Cooper celebrated the pioneer. Novels like Catharine Sedgwick's *Rich Man, Poor Man* romanticized urban poverty and suggested that "true wealth" (virtue) lay within the reach of even the most humble family, if only they worked hard.

Although in most of its manifestations, the myth of the self-made American was decidedly male, it also implied a new emphasis on childrearing and therefore on women. The primary audience of prescriptive writers was mothers. Periodicals like

Americans' enormous interest in self-improvement in the antebellum years was reflected in their enthusiasm for public lectures, known as the lyceum movement. This cartoon gently spoofed a lecture by James Pollard Espy, a meteorologist. As the drawing suggests, women were prominent in lyceum audiences.

the *Ladies Magazine* and *Godey's Lady's Book* (both edited by popular author Sarah Josepha Hale) and advice books like Lydia Maria Child's *The Mother at Home* and William Alcott's *The Young Mother* instructed women on the development of proper mental and moral habits in the young.

A generation of female novelists appropriated the themes of self-culture (especially as they applied to women) for their fiction. Catharine Maria Sedgwick, in her 1827 novel *A New-England Tale*, told the story of a young orphan, left penniless by an improvident wealthy father and a pampered mother. Jane, the protagonist of the tale, learns that hard work builds both economic independence and strength of character and is appropriately rewarded with a prosperous husband, children, and a safe middle-class home.

Some writers mounted a determined assault on the new American political economy. American Transcendentalists like Ralph Waldo Emerson, Margaret Fuller, and William Ellery Channing believed in the power of the independent mind not only to understand the material environment but also to achieve a spiritual wholeness with the world. They saw that in contemporary America self-improvement was often cultivated only for immediate material gain. In his essay "Self-Reliance" (1841), Emerson tried to distinguish true independence of mind from slavish rushing after preferment and celebrity. Although Emerson was a professional man, not a laborer, in many respects his attack on the political economy of antebellum America echoed the themes of Seth Luther.

Temperance

Of the many movements for regulating the body, the largest by far—and the longest lived—was the temperance movement. By the 1840s hundreds of thousands of Americans had taken the pledge to swear off demon rum.

Prior to the nineteenth century, liquor played a central role in the work and social lives of Americans. The Puritans (even ministers) had insisted on having their good supply of wine, beer, and hard cider. In craft shops, workers took rum breaks from their labor. Well into the 1840s, advice-manual writers felt they needed to convince mothers that it was safe to forego the occasional dollop of hard spirits to the children.

Some religious groups, especially the Quakers and the Methodists, had opposed the drinking of hard liquor in the eighteenth century, but it was only in the early nineteenth century, in Saratoga, New York, in 1808, that the first temperance society was formed. Within the next five years, at least four more temperance societies were established in New England.

In the 1820s, the temperance movement was taken over by evangelicals who understood demon rum as the enemy not just of piety, but of that self-control so central to the broad perfecting of society. Evangelists began to depict drinking as one of the signs of social disorder in democratic America. Propounding this new view, in a series of six sermons preached in 1825, Lyman Beecher effectively changed the debate over alcohol. He did not call for absolute abstinence from hard liquor, and he inveighed on his followers to form voluntary associations to drive the demon rum from American society. The following February saw the formation of the American Society for the Promotion of Temperance (ASPT). Using the structure of the Benevolent Empire, the ASPT quickly set about organizing local chapters across the country. By 1834 there were at least 5,000 state and local temperance societies.

THE
TEMPERANCE
FAMILY ALMANAC
FOR THE YEAR OF OUR LORD
1835:
Containing, besides the usual Astronomical Calculations, many
Valuable Suggestions and Important Statements on
THE SUBJECT OF TEMPERANCE.

THE PILLARS OF A GROG-SHOP.
BOSTON:
RUSSELL, ODIORNE & METCALF, School Booksellers,
LEMUEL GULLIVER, and FORD & DAMRELL.

The cover of this almanac revealed the association of alcohol with the working classes and with sin. Notice the devil figure lurking in the background, tending the still, and the neglected children in the foreground.

The Common School Movement

By the 1830s workers, members of the new middle class, and elite philanthropists all identified education as a critical arena for reform. In this as in other reform movements, however, the motives of different groups varied widely.

Since the founding of the nation, educational opportunities for the sons and daughters of prosperous parents had steadily increased. Children from wealthy urban families had private tutors, followed (for boys) by formal training in private seminaries and academies. By the 1820s young women from prosperous northern families could choose from a growing number of formal seminaries. Meanwhile, subscription schools offered basic education to rural children.

These schools were out of reach for working-class children. Labor reformers linked this lack of schooling directly to the larger process of industrial oppression. In their 1831 constitution, the Working Men's Association of New York placed the demand for "a system of equal, republican education" above every other goal, convinced, as they explained, that education "secures and perpetuates every political right we possess." Seth Luther elaborated on the theme, blasting industrialization as "a cruel system of exaction on the bodies and the minds of the producing classes," preventing them "from a participation in the fountains of knowledge." Benevolent reformers had founded charity schools in many eastern cities, but workers saw these as inferior. Only free public education, workers argued, could defy "the siege of aristocracy."

Many middle-class parents were also unable to afford the costs of private academies. In 1830, worried fathers in Utica, New York, called for a public school system that would permit children to "keep pace with the age in its improvements" and "calculate their own profits in the world."

Middle-class parents were anxious about daughters as well as sons. They worried that traditional housewifery skills would be of little use to daughters who faced increasingly complex market relations and new domestic technologies. Most of all, they worried that their daughters might not marry or might marry into families that would face financial ruin. These conditions suggested that daughters, as well as sons, should be educated.

Reformers often also supported expanded public education out of anxieties that the expanded suffrage would introduce volatility into the American electoral process. "The great bulwark of republican government is the cultivation of education," Governor Clinton urged the New York legislature in 1827. If white working men and their sons were to vote, it was important that they first be educated.

This convergence of interests led to a growing demand for expanded common schools. Nevertheless, broad segments of the American public resisted the idea. In Cincinnati, wealthy property owners opposed paying taxes to send poor children to school. Other skeptics considered the whole idea an invasion of their rights as free citizens. States were often reduced to passing simple enabling legislation, like Pennsylvania's 1834 act, that made public schools a local option.

In 1837 the Massachusetts legislature at last ventured further, creating a state Board of Education and appointing long-time educational reformer Horace Mann as its first secretary. Mann framed the common school debate in language that reflected the anxieties of more prosperous Americans. On the one hand, he reassured middle-class parents that relying on an extrafamilial institution was both right and natural, given the vast changes in society. On the other hand, he assured them that nothing else need change about the industrial society on which they depended. Poverty, he later wrote, was not decreed by God or required by American society. Only the lack of education barred the poor from prosperity. "When we have spread competence through all the abodes of poverty," Mann reassured his fellow citizens, then America would realize its long-deferred potential as the treasury of human virtue. Mann provided a comforting vision of a world in which benevolence and education would "disarm the poor of their hostility toward the rich."

Whites were less concerned about the potential hostility of the small free African-American community. Until the 1850s, free African-American children were excluded from public common schools, and public school tax monies were not used to establish schools for them. Education for free black children came almost entirely from the work of the free African-American community. In the North, the efforts bore fruit, but in the South opposition to the education of slaves hardened. In fact, many enslaved and free African-American southerners did learn to read and write, but usually surreptitiously.

Penal Reform

In the first years of the republic, when memories of British injustice were still fresh, Americans tended to think of crime as a problem of bad laws, not flawed individual character. Fair laws would nurture good republican character, and good republican citizens would respect laws they had a hand in passing.

Yet by the 1820s eastern cities were incarcerating thousands of citizens—some for debt (which a growing number of people considered inappropriate in a republican government) but many for robbery, larceny, fraud, vagrancy, and disorderly conduct. To many Americans—especially members of the middle class—it seemed that good laws were not sufficient to create a good citizenry. Like salvation, law-abiding behavior was a function of individual effort. Where individuals failed to obey the law, the community must devise some mechanism for its own protection.

The solution that enjoyed the greatest popularity from the 1820s on was the establishment of state prison systems, where deviant individuals could be kept apart from the striving community but where inmates might also be rehabilitated. State and city prisons soon began to replace older charity institutions. The two primary models, devised by New York and Pennsylvania, were variants on a single principle: The first step in making prisons places of genuine reform was to prevent inmates from influencing one another.

The New York version became most widely associated with the penitentiary at Ossining, New York, known as Sing-Sing. At Sing-Sing, prisoners worked side by side all day but were prevented from talking or even looking at one another. They slept in separate cells. The Pennsylvania model, put into practice in the late 1820s, called for absolute isolation of the prisoners.

Visitors to the United States often toured these prisons and frequently applauded them, but they also commented on the exaggerated hopes that Americans seemed to invest in them. Famous French visitor Alexis de Tocqueville observed of American reformers: "Philanthropy has become for them a kind of profession, and they have caught the monomanie of the penitentiary system, which to them seems to remedy for all the evils of society."

CONCLUSION

By the time Andrew Jackson left office in 1837, the coalition that had elected him was deeply divided. In the wake of increasing social and economic differentiation in the American political economy, it was hard to say just who the American "common man" was. Jackson himself always associated the image with tough-minded western settlers, but angry urban wage workers pointed out that their labor was fueling the new industrial system, and anxious members of the new middle class insisted that they best embodied republican industriousness and virtue. As the decade wore on, these differences produced sharper and sharper conflicts.

In this context, the impulse for reform, once the source of optimism, now became the tool of division. Middle-class reformers took refuge in new mechanisms of control—of themselves and of others—and a growing number of Americans, weary of compromise, began to demand that the first item of reform be to purify the nation of the moral stain of slavery. In the nation's short history, the West had always functioned as the republic's social and cultural release. Soon that symbol of reconciliation and prosperity would become the site of America's insoluble conflicts.

FURTHER READINGS

Lawrence J. Friedman, *Gregarious Saints: Self and Community in American Abolitionism, 1830–1870* (1982). Friedman provides a compelling overview of the immediatist wing of the United States abolition movement, from its origins in early nineteenth-century millennialism to victory in the Civil War, and offers detailed discussions of such leaders as Garrison, Arthur and Lewis Tappan, Marie Weston Chapman, Gerrit Smith, and Lucretia Mott.

CHRONOLOGY

1822	Denmark Vesey conspiracy
1826	General Colored Association of Massachusetts formed American Society for the Promotion of Temperance formed
1827	Russwurm and Cornish found *Freedom's Journal*
1828	Andrew Jackson elected president Tariff of 1828 Calhoun writes *South Carolina Exposition and Protest*
1829	David Walker publishes *An Appeal to the Colored Citizens of the World*
1830	National Negro Convention Movement begins
1831	Nat Turner leads rebellion in Virginia William Lloyd Garrison begins publication of *The Liberator* New England Anti-Slavery Society founded New England Association of Farmers, Mechanics, and Other Workingmen founded New York Protestant Association founded Lyceum movement begins
1832	Tariff of 1832 Jackson re-elected South Carolina passes Nullification Resolution Maria Stewart lectures in Boston
1833	Congress passes Force Bill American Anti-Slavery Society founded
1834	Anti-African American riots in major cities Anti-Catholic mob burns Ursuline Convent in Charleston, Massachusetts Lowell operatives go on strike National Trades' Union formed
1835	American Anti-Slavery Society begins postal campaign Lyman Beecher publishes *A Plea for the West*
1836	Congress passes Gag Rule
1837	Abolitionist editor Elija Lovejoy murdered in Alton, Illinois Bread riots in New York City Massachusetts creates first State Board of Education; Horace Mann appointed secretary

Carl F. Kaestle, *Pillars of the Republic: Common Schools and American Society, 1780–1860* (1983). This fine survey traces Americans' views of education and education policy from the founding of the nation to the eve of the Civil War, grounding the common school movement in the broad social and cultural currents of the early republic.

Leon F. Litwack, *North of Slavery: The Negro in the Free States, 1790–1860* (1961). Litwack provides a thorough and illuminating depiction of the restrictions on African Americans' civil, legal, and economic rights in the "free" antebellum North.

David R. Roediger, *The Wages of Whiteness: Race and the Making of the American Working Class* (1991). This collection of essays explores the importance of racialized thinking in the emergence of the wage system in the North, with particular attention to the importance of the institution of slavery in shaping Northern "free labor" ideology.

Christine Stansell, *City of Women: Sex and Class in New York, 1789–1860* (1986). In one of the very few studies of the impact of urbanization, the industrial reorganization of labor, and early class formation on laboring women, Stansell explores the ways in which working-class women's experiences differed both from those of men in their class and from more prosperous women.

David Walker, *David Walker's Appeal to the Coloured Citizens of the World* (1995). Calling on Africans in all nations to unite against racial injustice and urging African Americans in the United States to take control of their own destinies by whatever means were available, including armed rebellion, Walker's 1829 Appeal illuminates the growing assertiveness of free African Americans organizing in the 1820s.

 Please refer to the document CD-ROM for primary sources related to this chapter.

13
Manifest Destiny
1836–1848

Mah-i-ti-wo-nee-ni Remembers Life on the Great Plains
**The Setting of the Jacksonian Sun • The Political Economy of the
Trans-Mississippi West • Slavery and the Political Economy of
Expansion • Conclusion**

MAH-I-TI-WO-NEE-NI REMEMBERS LIFE
ON THE GREAT PLAINS

Mah-i-ti-wo-nee-ni was born in the mid-1830s in the Black Hills. Her father was Cheyenne, and her mother was Lakota (or Sioux). Her homelands had been a part of Jefferson's 1803 Louisiana Purchase and would later become the states of South Dakota and Wyoming. In the 1830s, however, the Great Plains remained Indian country.

By the time Mah-i-ti-wo-nee-ni was born, nevertheless, contact with whites had been reshaping the life of Great Plains Indians for more than two centuries. The Cheyenne had once been a semiagricultural people who "planted corn every year . . . then went hunting all summer," returning in the fall to gather the crops. The reintroduction of the horse by the Spanish in the sixteenth century had enabled Plains Indians to become faster and more efficient hunters, and more effective raiders. Over time, the Cheyenne had given up farming and had organized their economic life around the hunt, foraging other food as they went. Now whole villages migrated to seasonal hunting grounds. Competing for game, they sent out raiding parties to steal horses or take captives for exchange. Individuals and small groups criss-crossed the landscape in search of trade. Mah-i-ti-wo-nee-ni recalled a time in her childhood (probably in 1840) when the Cheyennes and the Arapahoes traveled south to meet in a great peace council with their traditional enemies, the Kiowas, Comanches, and Apaches.

By the 1830s, the proximity of white Americans was beginning to affect the Cheyenne in direct ways. Although Mah-i-ti-wo-nee-ni did not remember much contact with white people during her early childhood, at the time of the great southern peace council, massive U.S. overland migration to the Pacific was already underway. For these settlers, migration was part of a personal search for liberty, opportunity, and the political process of nation building. In the West, many Americans believed, the nation renewed its virtues and purified the republican model of government. In the mid-1840s, Americans coined a lasting phrase for this association of land and liberty. Taking the continent was their "manifest destiny".

American settlement of the West implied a different destiny for Mah-i-ti-wo-nee-ni and her people, however. First came missionaries, exhorting Indians to convert to Christianity. The settlers soon followed, trampling Indian plantings, destroying villages, spreading disease, and decimating the buffalo. At first the U.S. agents who appeared among the Cheyenne wished merely to trade gifts of kettles, coffeepots, knives, and blankets for Indian promises to permit settlers to cross Cheyenne lands. Soon, the U.S. government wanted the land itself. Although the nomadic Cheyenne long resisted removal, in 1877, after years of struggle and compromise, Mah-i-ti-wo-nee-ni and her people were forcibly displaced from their homelands to the Black Hills and conveyed south into Indian Territory.

Because much of the land Americans sought for settlement lay within the boundaries of the nation of Mexico: The trans-Mississippi manifest destiny of white Americans also implied a distinct destiny for Mexicans. Claiming mistreatment by the Mexican government, white American settlers in the Mexican province of Coahuila y Tejas formed the Republic of Texas and sought entry into the United States. In 1846 the United States provoked a war with Mexico to claim large portions of that nation's northern territories.

That war gained the United States secure access to the Pacific Ocean. But Americans also paid the costs of the manifest destiny. Each stage of geographical expansion reignited controversies over the institution of slavery. While many white Southerners claimed a fundamental constitutional right to own slaves, and felt betrayed by growing Northern opposition, Northern reformers inveighed against the immorality of the institution and flooded the mails with abolitionist tracts, and Congress with anti-slavery petitions. This collision of interests and ideals flared within a national political system ill equipped to respond to it effectively. American politicians continued to try to forge compromises between slave-owning and non-slave-owning interests, but the party structure was in disarray, and no strong leader arose to hold it together. By 1848, some Americans were prepared to give up on their government altogether.

The Setting of the Jacksonian Sun

By 1837, both the material and the moral costs of America's expansionist political economy and the flaws in Jackson's policies were becoming dramatically apparent. Jackson had undermined the old Republican dynasty, but his Democratic Party contained too many diverging interests to remain stable. Democrats were torn apart by the nation's competing systems of political economy, one based on slavery and the other on wage labor. These party troubles were heightened by the fiscal consequences of the bank war. Elected in 1836, Democrat Martin Van Buren would lose re-election by a landslide in 1840 and fail again when he ran on a third-party ticket in 1848.

Political Parties in Crisis

The expansion of white male suffrage and the translation of moral reform agendas into electoral politics energized American politics in the 1830s and 1840s. In 1840, 66 percent of the electorate voted in Massachusetts, 75 percent in Connecticut, and 77 percent in Pennsylvania. Yet the capacity of major political parties to accommodate a wide range of conflicting interests and beliefs was limited.

Increasingly fractured since the election of 1824, the Republican Party struggled to reorganize on the basis of hatred of Andrew Jackson. Jackson's war on the national bank offered the immediate occasion. Although unable to save the bank, Henry Clay and the anti-Jacksonians narrowly passed a Senate resolution censuring Jackson for assuming "authority and power not conferred by the Constitution and the laws." In that debate Clay identified his anti-Jackson position as "Whiggish" (opposed to executive tyranny, like the Whigs of eighteenth-century England), a label that would stick to the new Whig Party.

Former National Republicans in the urban Northeast and upper West made up the bulk of the new party. Some of these were beginning to doubt the wisdom of uncontrolled geographic expansion, which seemed to promote political corruption, sectional conflict, and the extension of slavery. Nevertheless, they continued to embrace market expansion and the American Plan: a new national bank, a strong protective tariff, and aggressive internal improvements. Fearing the power of wildcat settlers, wage workers, the urban poor, and immigrants to subvert orderly economic relations, former National Republicans redoubled their commitment to a strong, interventionist government.

By 1834, some former Democrats were also disenchanted with the party of Jackson. Prospering shopkeepers and middling merchants began to understand their own interests as distinct from those of the urban laboring classes. They were attracted by the Whig emphasis on personal and political discipline and order. Some southerners were still angry over the tariff and the Nullification Crisis. Some small farmers and shopkeepers who had been wiped out by the Depression of 1837 blamed Jackson for their hard times. Workers, who had little trust for the merchant classes that made up the core of the new Whig Party, tended to form splinter parties or to stay with the Democrats.

Through the 1830s the Whigs remained an amorphous and disorganized opposition. Unable to decide on a single candidate, in 1836 the Whigs ran four regional challengers, hoping to deny Van Buren a majority in the Electoral College. The Whig field included William Henry Harrison (Indiana, but nominated by an Antimason convention in Pennsylvania), Senator Hugh Lawson White (nominated by unhappy Democrats in Tennessee), Daniel Webster (nominated by the Massachusetts legislature), and Willie P. Mangum (a protest candidate of the South Carolina Nullifiers).

Jackson's Vice President, Martin Van Buren, seemed the candidate to withstand the Whig onslaught. To Van Buren went much of the credit for creating a successful Democratic coalition. Van Buren had been constantly at Jackson's side, first as Secretary of State and then as Vice President. Van Buren's power in New York gave him a sufficient base in the North to risk publicly declaring himself "the inflexible and uncompromising opponent of any attempt on the part of Congress to abolish slavery in the District of Columbia" or to interfere with slavery "in the states where it exists." Van Buren was hopeful that this position would solidify southern support and make him a national choice.

The results of the election of 1836 suggested otherwise. Not only was Van Buren unable to draw the nation together, but he almost lost. Van Buren did well in New York, New England (except Massachusetts), and the mid-Atlantic states, but he lost Ohio and Indiana and almost lost Pennsylvania. Unable to convince southerners that a northerner could head "the party of Jefferson," he lost Georgia (Crawford country), Tennessee, and South Carolina and barely captured Mississippi and Louisiana. A shift of fewer than 2,000 votes in Pennsylvania would have deprived Van Buren of an Electoral College majority and thrown the election to the House of Representatives.

Van Buren and the Legacy of Jackson

The signs of hard economic times were already visible when Van Buren was inaugurated in March 1837. His first legacy from his mentor was the Panic of 1837.

The Panic was the result of the politics of the bank war, in combination with economic troubles in Europe. Jackson's hard money measures, culminating in the Specie Circular (see Chapter 11, "Securing Democracy"), had effectively drained the nation of specie, leaving American prosperity to float on the bubble of credit flowing from European financiers and the largely unregulated "pet banks." When conditions in England suddenly produced a demand for hard currency, strapped European capitalists called in their American loans.

As credit evaporated, interest rates rose, paper money depreciated, and debt mounted. The credit-dependent cotton market began to collapse, taking with it several large import–export firms in New York and New Orleans. In the context of years of high inflation, the failures ignited a run on the overextended banks, as depositors tried to hoard their savings before the hard currency was paid out for mercantile debts. Perhaps a strong federal hand could have stemmed the damage, but Van Buren shared Jackson's view that the federal government should not manage currency. Van Buren's announcement on May 4 that he intended to maintain the Specie Circular in force ensured that the pressure on banks would continue. On May 10, 1837, frightened depositors drained $650,000 from their reserves and New York City banks closed. Only a show of force by the military prevented a riot.

Coinciding with large waves of German and Irish immigration, the depression fell with special severity on the East Coast. Wages declined faster than prices. Unemployment was widespread, and losses touched even the prosperous middle classes. Hard times remained until 1843. While Democrats scrambled to avoid political responsibility and bombarded Van Buren with contradictory advice, the new Whig Party began to look ahead optimistically to 1840.

Although an additional distribution of federal funds to state banks in 1837 might only have fed the frenzy, Van Buren's decision to delay the distribution (on the grounds that the windfalls had amounted to a federal influence over banking practice) added a new confusion. In an effort to return stability to the nation's monetary system, Van Buren proposed that the Treasury Department establish its own financial institutions to receive, hold, and pay out government funds. The institutions would exist for the sole purpose of managing government accounts. They would not issue paper currency and would not make loans to business.

The proposal for an independent treasury met with substantial opposition. Predictably, Whigs objected that removing government holdings from circulation in the economy would reduce credit. But many Democrats also opposed the independent treasury for the brake it would put on growth. The independent treasury did not pass until 1840, when it was enacted as an entirely separate, specie-based system, empowered neither to receive nor to pay out paper currency.

Disputes on the Canadian border underscored the volatile mood of the American electorate in the late 1830s. In northern Maine, by 1838 Americans and Canadians were ready to fight over who owned the rich timber reserves of the Aroostook Valley. Believing that Canadian lumberjacks had been setting up new camps in the region, Maine Democrats demanded federal protection. Van Buren sent in the Army under General Winfield Scott. Aware that the economy was in no condition to support a war, however, he also instructed Scott to offer terms for a truce. If Canada would acknowledge Maine's predominant interest in the valley, the United States would respect existing Canadian settlements pending final disposition of the area.

Electoral Politics and Moral Reform

As reformers grew frustrated with the seeming resistance of social problems to moral suasion, they turned increasingly to electoral politics for solutions. The effect was to fragment and weaken party organization rather than to consolidate it. The political landscape became littered with specialized and often largely local parties, demonstrating the inability of the major parties to address fundamental areas of social conflict.

Nowhere did possession of the vote assume a more central role than among newly enfranchised white male workers. During the struggles of the 1820s and 1830s, laboring people had concluded that many of their problems would be remedied only through electoral action. As long as the economic power of employers was backed up by laws that oppressed workers (debt laws that imprisoned them, bankruptcy laws that took their property, conspiracy laws that made union organizing illegal), strikes and petitions would never be enough.

In the winter of 1835–1836 anger at the legal system came to a head. With inflation and unemployment running high, New York City journeymen tailors went out on strike. The leaders of the union were arrested, tried, convicted on conspiracy charges, and fined. The labor press denounced the courts as "the tool of the aristocracy, against the people!" Nearly 30,000 people (the largest crowd in American history to that date) turned out to protest the convictions. The protesters resolved to meet the following fall in Utica, New York, to organize a "separate and distinct" political party to represent workers' interests. The 93 "workers, farmers, and mechanics" who met in Utica six months later voted to form the Equal Rights Party.

Labor movements in other states also began to focus their efforts on legislative reform. The ten-hour day, a long-standing demand, re-emerged in the late 1840s as a central point of labor organizing. Throughout New England workers supported candidates friendly to the ten-hour day, petitioned legislatures for state laws setting work hours, and testified before legislative committees. Much to the shock of their middle-class detractors, female workers sometimes testified as well, using their life stories to create sympathy for the cause. It was male workers, however, who had the power to vote representatives out of office.

A Voice from the People!
—
Great Meeting in the Park!!

The General Trades' Union of New York used this symbol on signs encouraging workers to participate in the 1836 meeting to protest the conviction and fines of striking journeymen tailors; 30,000 supporters turned out for the rally. Note the distinctly masculine (and white) portrayal of workers in the image.

Other reform movements also began to focus their energies on electoral strategies, although their motives for doing so varied. The Female Moral Reform Society, which had long worked to redeem prostitutes from their sins, shifted strategies and began advocating and lobbying for the passage of rent laws and property protections for women. This growing emphasis on legal reform grew out of an enhanced sense of connection between the reformer and the recipient of her aid.

Throughout the 1840s temperance workers focused their efforts increasingly toward state legislators and the passing of laws. Among some temperance advocates (especially females) the shift was motivated by concern for legal protections for the wives and families of alcoholic men. But an increasing emphasis on legal strategies also expressed a growing belief on the part of middle-class, native-born reformers that alcoholism was a problem of the unruly immigrant working classes. As they identified drinkers as fundamentally different from themselves, temperance workers grew less interested in working directly with drinkers and more willing to take recourse to legal controls.

The new interest in electoral politics created major divisions in some reform movements, most notably in abolitionism. Among moderate abolitionists, the passage of the Congressional Gag Rule had raised questions about the effectiveness of Garrison's antipolitical stance (see Chapter 12, "Reform and Conflict"). They also flinched at the increasingly aggressive tactics of the Garrisonian-led movement and at the visible participation of women and African Americans.

These tensions were palpable in 1840 as the American Anti-Slavery Society met for its national convention. Participants quickly divided over whether women should participate in deliberations and whether the organization should work to elect abolitionist candidates to office. The Garrisonian branch took control of the convention. When Abby Kelley was elected to the previously all-male business committee of the association, anti-Garrisonians walked out. The exodus freed the renegades, led by philanthropists Arthur and Lewis Tappan, to launch an abolitionist political party. By the end of the year, the new Liberty Party, formed on the platform that the Constitution barred the federal government from creating slavery in any new states or territories, had nominated abolitionist James Birney for the presidency.

By definition, recourse to electoral reform excluded females. Nevertheless, some women were among the earliest advocates of the new electoral strategies. Laboring women worked for bankruptcy reform, ten-hour laws, and an end to conspiracy trials. Middle-class women advocated temperance laws and supported antislavery candidates for office. In the 1830s few of those women intended to claim electoral rights for themselves.

An Independent Woman's Rights Movement

Reform work permitted women to participate actively in shaping the new democratic order and to perfect skills useful in civic culture. They ran meetings, kept track of money, took notes, maintained records, and honed their skills at public speaking.

Reform women soon learned that there were limits to the authority that religion or domesticity could confer, however. Even those women who were involved in the mildest of reform activities (e.g., as members of the American Bible Society) were rebuked for "acting out of their appropriate sphere." Women engaged in more controversial activities like labor reform or abolition work were often heckled and sometimes hounded by mobs.

In 1837, in her *Essay on Slavery and Abolitionism,* Catharine Beecher attacked female abolitionists for violating the bounds of "rectitude and propriety" and accused them of being motivated by unwomanly "ambition." The same year, the Massachusetts clergy issued a pastoral letter attacking Sarah and Angelina Grimké (members of the southern planter class who were touring the North in the abolitionist cause) for daring to take "the place and tone of man as public reformer."

By the late 1830s women involved in abolition work were subjected to growing criticism from within their own ranks. Although Garrison remained a staunch ally, other leaders like the Tappan brothers believed that outspoken, assertive women were embarrassing the movement. For women who had given years of their labor and had endangered their lives in the cause of abolition, these attacks were galling. Disappointing, too, was the willingness of such men to abandon the old moral reform strategies. In moral reform, women were men's peers. The central act of moral suasion, personal conversion, was not limited to either gender. But the turn toward electoral reform reduced women to second-class status in reform. They could still raise money, lobby, and speak, but they could not perform the new essential act of reform, voting.

After the 1840 split of the American Anti-Slavery Society, in which controversies over political strategies and women's rights figured centrally, abolitionist women spearheaded a drive for an organized woman's rights movement. Early efforts came to fruition in Seneca Falls, New York, in July 1848. On July 14, five women (including the seasoned Quaker abolitionist Lucretia Mott, and the much younger Elizabeth Cady Stanton) placed an advertisement in the *Seneca County Courier* stating, "A convention to discuss the social, civil and religious condition and rights of woman will be held in the Wesleyan Chapel, Seneca Falls, New York, on Wednesday and Thursday, the 19th and 20th of July current, commencing at 10 a.m."

This image shows Elizabeth Cady Stanton (1815–1902) in the 1840s, when she helped launch the woman's rights movement. At that time, Stanton was a young mother, new to reform causes. She would end up devoting her life to social change.

The response was overwhelming. On July 19, 300 people (including perhaps 40 men, among them the famous abolitionist Frederick Douglass) showed up. By the end of the second day, the group had debated, voted on, and passed a Declaration of Sentiments (modeled after the Declaration of Independence) and a list of resolutions. They demanded specific social and legal changes, including a role in lawmaking, improved property rights, equity in divorce, and access to education and the professions. All of the resolutions passed unanimously but one: a demand for the vote. Even as American reform became ever more deeply embedded in electoral strategies, some of the assembled reformers considered suffrage too radical for women.

THE POLITICAL ECONOMY OF THE TRANS-MISSISSIPPI WEST

As their political interests fragmented, Americans sought reconciliation of geographical expansion. Manifest destiny, the belief that white Americans had a providential right to as much of North America as they wanted, had been part of the beliefs of citizens and of U.S. policy since the founding of the republic. It was implicit in the Northwest Ordinance, in scores of Indian treaties, in the Louisiana Purchase, in the Transcontinental Treaty, in the 1824 Monroe Doctrine, and in the Removal Act of 1830. But only in 1845 did the phrase enter the American vocabulary, when journalist John O'Sullivan proclaimed grandiosely that it is "Our manifest destiny . . . to overspread the continent allotted by Providence for the free development of our yearly multiplying millions." As the United States' treatment of Native Americans had long made clear, according to many Americans the manifest destiny of the nation was racial as well as territorial.

Texas

By the terms of the 1819 Transcontinental Treaty the United States had given up claims to Spanish lands south of the 42nd parallel. Nevertheless, within a few years Americans began to enter the region.

Many of these immigrants were specifically invited; some were not. The Spanish had conceived of their northern region as a buffer zone against the Lipan Apaches and Comanche Indians, on the one hand, and between New Spain and the United States, on the other. After independence, the Mexican government expanded those policies by offering land grants to Americans in return for the promise to bring settlers. The first American to take full advantage of the invitation was Stephen F. Austin, who began settling a colony on the banks of the Brazos and Colorado Rivers in 1821. By 1830 there were more than 20,000 Americans (including 1,000 slaves) living in the northeastern province of Mexico, adjacent to Louisiana.

Conflict between immigrant Americans and resident Tejanos was inevitable. Tejano residents in the region resented the influx of Americans. The national government often awarded to Americans lands that already belonged to Tejanos or that included Tejano communities. Tejanos complained that the *empresarios* (American landholders) had no respect for existing claims and made little attempt to control their settlers or illegal squatters who used the American colonies to hide stolen livestock.

In fact, although they were happy to take advantage of the cheap prices Mexico offered, many Americans had never fully acknowledged the right of Mexico to these lands. Viewing the region as the natural next frontier for American plantation agriculture, southerners had denounced the 1819 treaty and lobbied first John Quincy Adams and then Andrew Jackson to purchase the tract free and clear. By 1839 some Americans were convinced that Texas was destined to become the "land of refuge for the American slaveholders." The immigrants framed their criticisms of the Mexican government in the standard language of republicanism. They objected to high taxes and they protested efforts to get them to convert to Catholicism and adopt the Spanish language.

Beneath the Americans' objections to policies of the Mexican government were two more fundamental issues: slavery and the immigrants' disdain for Mexican culture. There had been African-American slaves in the region for at least 300 years, but very few. The number of slaves increased after 1800, when slave traders began to use Texas as an entry to the U.S. market. Mexicans condemned the trade as anti-republican. Ironically, the central government encouraged slave-owning immigrants from the southern United States to settle in the region.

The new Mexican government faced much the same dilemma the new U.S. government had faced 30 years earlier: Should they strengthen the economy by protecting property rights (including the right to own slaves), or should they enforce the republican ideal of liberty by banning slavery? By the mid-1820s, however, the immigrants had developed a cotton economy dependent on slave labor and were determined to preserve the institution. They regarded Mexican inconsistency and resistance as evidence of betrayal. By 1824 Stephen Austin, never a devoted supporter of slavery, devised a set of regulations for his colony that included harsh provisions for slaves who tried to escape or free people who abetted runaways. By 1830 Austin had come to the conclusion that "Texas must be a slave country. Circumstances and unavoidable necessity compels it. It is the wish of the people there. . . ." "The people," in Austin's view, included only white U.S. immigrants and others who agreed with their goals.

The immigrants who defended slavery claimed a cultural superiority over their Mexican hosts. The Americans associated "civilization" with a particularly aggressive and entrepreneurial notion of manhood. Mexicans were lazy and unmanly, the immigrants declared, a "mixed race" in which European descent had been diluted by intermarriage with Indians and African Americans. Mexicans were incapable of taking advantage of the lands they owned. Mexicans were Catholic, while the U.S. immigrants were predominantly Protestant. Reflecting the growing anti-Catholicism of the United States, the immigrants identified Mexican Catholicism with superstition, dependence, and antirepublican attitudes.

Tension between the immigrants and the Mexican government increased. After 1830 the government took steps to stem immigration and located troops on the United States–Mexican border. Immigrants interpreted these measures as obstructions to their rightful claims. In 1832 the Anglos demanded the right to organize a separate state within Mexico.

The rise of General Antonio Lopez de Santa Anna provided the occasion for acting on that ambition. When Santa Anna dissolved the Mexican Congress and made himself dictator in 1834, Anglo-Texans sharpened their criticisms of Mexican government. Casting themselves as the quintessential republicans, they vowed to fight for the old Mexican constitution, and they drew up a new state constitution. Their clear goal was complete independence, however, not reformation, and on March 2, 1836, Texas declared itself a sovereign republic.

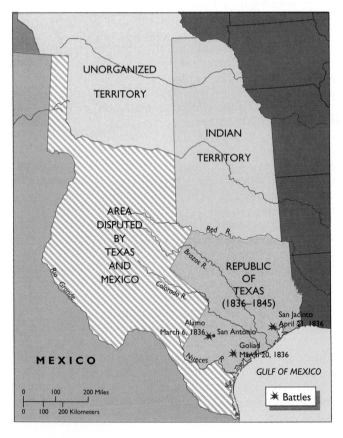

Map 13–1   Republic of Texas

After the decisive American victory at San Jacinto that resulted in the independence of Texas, the border dispute between Texas and Mexico continued until it was resolved by the Mexican War a decade later.

Armed conflict broke out on March 6, 1836, when the huge Mexican Army, led by Santa Anna, wiped out 187 Texas patriots barricaded in a mission called the Alamo. It was a costly and fleeting victory. Santa Anna's Army suffered 1,544 casualties and created martyrs for the rebels' cause. Under the leadership of Sam Houston, the rebels retreated east, gathering recruits as they went. On April 21 they surprised an encampment of Mexican troops on the San Jacinto River and scored a huge victory, crowned by the capture of Santa Anna himself. Bargaining to save his life and purchase his freedom, Santa Anna declared Texas a free nation. Ecstatic Texans drew up a constitution, made Sam Houston their first president, and called for annexation to the United States (see Map 13–1). With the nation in economic crisis and his own party already bickering over who was responsible, the last thing Van Buren wanted as president was a bitter battle over Texas and slavery. He doubted that the Constitution permitted annexation, and he feared that annexation would be construed as meddling in Mexico's internal affairs. Anticipating Texas's application for admission, abolitionists had made opposition to annexation a central issue in their massive petition campaign of 1837–1838, giving the controversy a wide popular foundation in the North. John Quincy Adams had delivered a stirring speech against annexation in the House, and some senators were publicly denouncing slavery in general and especially in Texas. Southerners had responded with their own states' rights petitions. In the end, Van Buren did not submit Texas's request for statehood to Congress.

Pacific Bound

The question of Texas was in many ways the question of the West and of manifest destiny. That larger question could not be indefinitely tabled. By the early 1840s the lands beyond the Mississippi had become the scene of a massive migration of settlers, bent on making new homes across the Great Plains.

The migration began modestly enough, as a trickle of missionaries in the 1830s. In 1831 rumors reached the East Coast of four young Indians who had appeared in St. Louis, exhausted and sick, imploring the white clergy there to carry Christianity to their people. Whether true or not, such stories enabled missionaries to claim that they had been invited into Indian communities. In 1834 the Methodist Missionary Society sent the Reverend Jason Lee west to found a mission in the Willamette Valley of Oregon Territory. Two years later, in January 1836, the American Board of Commissioners for Foreign Missions voted to send six people (including two women) to settle permanent missions in Oregon.

For their first mission, the board selected Marcus and Narcissa Prentiss Whitman, a doctor and a Sunday school teacher. In September 1836, after a three-month-long trip west, the Whitmans established their mission among the Cayuse Indians near Fort Walla Walla on the Columbia River. Their fellow missionaries Henry and Eliza Hart Spalding founded a mission 125 miles away among the Nez Percés.

At first, the Whitmans seemed to thrive. Marcus Whitman preached and doctored among the Cayuse and taught the men agriculture, and Narcissa taught school and oversaw the domestic operation of the large mission. Over the following decade, however, as white immigration into the region swelled, the Cayuse came to view the missionaries as the cause of the constant influx of white people and new diseases. In 1847, in response to a deadly measles epidemic, a Cayuse band attacked the mission, killing Marcus and Narcissa Prentiss Whitman and a number of other white people.

By then, overland migrants to the West Coast were so numerous that the roads of Iowa "were literally lined with long blue wagons . . . slowly wending their way over the broad prairies," leaving deep, rutted tracks. In the years of heaviest migration, watering holes were so overused and sanitary conditions so poor that the road west became a breeding ground for typhoid, malaria, dysentery, and cholera (see Map 13–2).

Most of the migrants were farming families of moderate means, pushed out of the Midwest by the hard times of 1837. Preparations for the trip took up to half a

Map 13-2 Major Overland Trails
The overland trails to the West started at the Missouri River. The Santa Fe Trail was a conduit for traders and goods to Mexico. The Oregon Trail traveled through Wyoming and then branched off to California and Oregon.

year. Men arranged to sell the land and farm equipment and whatever stock was not to go with them, repaired harnesses and traces, and purchased wagons. Women prepared the clothing, bedding, soap, food, containers, medicine, and utensils the family would need. As Kit Belknap recorded in her diary in October 1848, "Now, I will begin to work and plan to make everything with an eye to starting out on a six month trip" the following April.

Not everyone cherished those dreams with equal pleasure. Women appear often to have felt more keenly than men the wrenching separation from family, church, and community and the hardship of the trail. Nevertheless, the excitement of moving west was not limited to men and the sorrow of leaving family and friends was not limited to women. Narcissa Whitman pronounced herself healthier and in better spirits than ever as she faced the Overland Trail. Migrants kept their spirits up by singing, telling stories, playing games, and picking wildflowers.

Travelers funneled through St. Louis (where they bought supplies), crossed Missouri to rendezvous with wagon trains near St. Joseph or Independence, Missouri, and then followed one of two main routes west. The northern route, known as the Oregon Trail, zigzagged northwest at roughly the 42nd parallel to the Rocky Mountains. At that point, the trail split. The northern branch followed the Snake River up into the Willamette Valley near the Columbia River. The southern branch veered into the Mexican province of California. Another line of settlers journeyed southwest out of Independence on the Santa Fe Trail, which led along the Arkansas River through the future state of Kansas before heading into Mexican lands. At Santa Fe, the trail divided, feeding immigrants west along the Old Spanish Trail (mapped by Franciscan missionaries) or south to Chihuahua, Mexico.

The overland migrants traveled in families, in groups of families from the same neighborhood, and occasionally in entire communities. If they did not have team animals, families pulled their possessions in two-wheeled handcarts. Wagons and team animals did not ensure an easy trip. Wagons carried supplies, so most migrants walked west. Wagons broke down, were washed away in river crossings, or had to be emptied to ease the burden on the animals. After they left the plains, wagon trains sometimes went days without finding water or game. Women as well as men drove the wagons and herded the cattle, collected firewood, and caught small animals for food. When broken equipment or sickness slowed individual families, the trains were often forced to leave them behind, lest the others not clear the Rocky Mountains before winter. The harrowing dangers of that possibility were immortalized in the ill-fated Donner Party, caught by an early winter trying to clear the Sierra Nevada. For four months the party was trapped by snow in the mountains, without sufficient fuel, blankets, or food, slowly starving. When relief finally arrived in mid-February 1847, "the dead were lying about on the snow, some even unburied, since the living had not strength to bury their dead," according to one survivor. Of the 87 persons snowed in, 42 died.

For migrants who survived the journey west, the rewards were not always immediately apparent. "My most vivid recollection of that first winter in Oregon," one woman recalled, "is of the weeping skies and of Mother and me also weeping." As soon as their homes were built and their fields plowed, though, many of the newcomers were ready to declare Oregon "this best country in the world." The climate was hospitable to crops of wheat, flax, and corn and to apple and pear orchards. Lumber was plentiful, and the streams ran full of fish. Farther south was the "mild and delightful climate of California," an even greater attraction after 1848, when rumors of "inexhaustible" gold strikes began to filter north and east.

Nations of the Trans-Mississippi West

American settlers considered themselves journeying through national territories. Indigenous communities, like Mah-i-ti-wo-nee-ni's friends and family, viewed the settlers as trespassers in Indian country. Most wagon trains departed from Missouri, which meant that settlers first crossed Indian Territory, where Native Americans had been guaranteed refuge from white intrusion. Between Independence, Missouri, and the Rocky Mountains lay the Indian nations of the prairies and Great Plains: the Blackfoot and Crow to the northwest; the Sioux, Pawnee, Arapaho, and two great nations from which Mah-i-ti-wo-nee-ni claimed heritage, the Shoshone and the Cheyenne, through the northern and central Plains; and the Kiowa, Apache, Comanche, and Navajo in the Southwest. Along the Pacific were the Yakima, Chinook, Cayuse, and Nez Percés, and to the south, in California, Pomo, Chumash, Yuma, and many other groups. Most of this vast territory was part of Mexico, and Great Britain laid claim to Oregon. Crossing to utopia meant transgressing the boundaries of all of these nations.

American penny novelists would depict this contact of peoples as a violent confrontation, in which cunning and bellicose Indians swooped down to massacre naïve and well-meaning migrants. In fact, of the more than 250,000 settlers who crossed the plains between 1840 and 1860, fewer than 400 were killed by Native Americans, about the same number of deaths as those inflicted by white migrants on the Indians.

Prior to the massive migration of the 1840s, official U.S. policy toward the Indians had been one of removal, by force or by pressured sale of lands and physical relocation. Even in the 1830s observers saw no evidence that Americans recognized a boundary short of the Pacific Ocean. Alexis de Tocqueville noted that "when it promises these unlucky people a permanent asylum in the West," the U.S. government "is well aware of its inability to guarantee this." The trans-Mississippi migrations of the middle of the nineteenth century proved the wisdom of Tocqueville's observation.

By the late 1830s, as the last of the eastern "removals" were completed, federal policy toward Indians began to shift. Removal and resettlement continued to be the primary stated goal, and many western tribes were confined to reservations or moved to Indian Territory. But later removals aimed more overtly at relocation culminating in individual ownership of reservation lands rather than tribal ownership. Such interference with the land customs of Indians was, of course, what many Americans had sought for decades, believing that Native Americans should be brought into the "civilized" political economy of the United States through individual ownership of property. Allotment became the official U.S. policy toward all Indians by the end of the century.

By the mid-1830s, when white Americans started crossing the Mississippi River in huge numbers, most of these nations had already tasted the effects of expansionism. The Comanches (the largest of the southwestern nations) and the Apaches had been at war with Euro-Americans for several centuries. They had fought the Spanish, then the Mexicans, and since the 1820s both the Mexicans and the U.S. settlers in Texas. All of the Plains Indians, especially the Sioux, the Kiowa, and the Comanches, had felt the impact of eastern Indians who had been displaced or officially relocated west. The Sioux, for example, had been at war for decades with the Indians of the old Northwest Territory, who were being pushed across the Mississippi River by white settlers, the militias, and the U.S. Army.

For the western Indians, the effects of the migration of the 1840s were social, cultural, and economic. Although the number of deaths from warfare was low, deaths from disease were far higher. Epidemics took especially high tolls on the children and the old, wiping out both the elders who carried a community's history and collective wisdom and the young people who represented its future. Under demographic stress, Native communities confronted missionaries, new forms of medicine, new codes of behavior, new forms of knowledge, and new goods such as guns and alcohol.

Contact gradually altered the Indians' social organization and gender division of labor. As it became harder to claim and protect planting grounds, tribes shifted from semiagricultural to more nomadic ways of life. The relative importance of women's foraging and planting diminished, and the relative importance of men's skills as hunters and warriors increased.

By 1840, the northern grasslands and southern plains supported a complex economy of hunting and foraging. The Indians consumed corn, melons, berries, wild sweet potatoes, turnips, and fowl and small game, harvested in a seminomadic way of life and traded through networks that ran north to south. At the center of this economy stood the bison, supplying not only food but also material for clothing, shelter, and trade.

This way of life was threatened as the bison declined in number. Settlers' need for food had only a minor impact on the buffalo. More deadly was their fascination with hunting and killing such a huge creature, regardless of whether they needed its meat and hides. Recreational hunting parties, as well as bands of hunters intent on wiping out the Indian communities' means of support, took their toll. By 1848, Thomas A. Harvey, western superintendent of Indian Affairs, was warning of the inevitable effects of "the immense traveling of emigrant companies over the prairies, and the consequent increased destruction of buffalo."

As early as 1842 and 1843 the Teton Sioux had complained to federal Indian agents that the heavy migrations were harming their hunting grounds. By 1846 the Sioux were demanding that the U.S. government stem the migrations and prevent the migrants from killing animals indiscriminately. When the government ignored the complaints, the Sioux prevented wagon trains from passing until migrants had paid a toll in money, tobacco, or supplies. Indignant overland

In 1834–1835, western artist George Catlin observed the importance of the buffalo to Plains Indians. Here he depicted Comanche women dressing buffalo robes and drying buffalo meat. Notice the presence of horses in the village, a sign of European influence on western Indian life.

travelers criticized the federal government for coddling the Indians and demanded that the trails be reopened.

In the mid-1840s the energies of the federal government were primarily engaged in Texas, where American nationalists were demanding action against Mexico. In the northern plains, the government constructed a chain of forts across the West. These forts were intended as quarters for armed rifle units called dragoons, who would, theoretically, drive the Indians back from intimidating the overland migrants. The strategy was not very effective. During the late 1840s, the Indians continued to exert control over white migration through northern Indian country.

SLAVERY AND THE POLITICAL ECONOMY OF EXPANSION

Even as individual Americans poured west, expansion became a source of controversy within the collective politics of the nation. The problem was not the principle of manifest destiny, a principle that few politicians questioned. By the late 1830s, expansion was linked in the public debate with the extension of slavery. That subject, controversial in itself, raised other problems. Southerners viewed northerners as unfaithful to a 50-year-old compromise ratified in the Constitution. Northerners looked with envy on the wealth of the new Southwest (Louisiana, Mississippi, Alabama, and Arkansas) and worried about the political leverage of a new slave state the size of Texas.

Log Cabins and Hard Cider: The Election of 1840

As they approached the election of 1840, the major parties were engaged in a balancing act. Both hoped to exploit certain aspects of regional difference, but without raising the most divisive issues associated with slavery. Whigs considered Van Buren vulnerable, both because the nation still languished under the effects of the Depression of 1837, and because he was a northerner who seemed to be blocking the annexation of Texas. Henry Clay, leader of the Whigs, opposed the annexation of Texas, but he calculated that southern Democrats would choose a Kentuckian over a New Yorker. Aware of Van Buren's liabilities in the South, Democrats were eager to keep slavery out of the debates, although Van Buren was willing to have northerners see him as the alternative to a southern president. A number of northern Whigs were suspicious of Clay's ties to the South.

There were ominous signs that slavery would haunt the election. In June 1839 the *U.S.S. Washington* had intercepted the ship *Amistad* in American coastal waters. Although the ship was Spanish-owned, it was under the control of its cargo of kidnapped Africans, who were attempting to sail it home to Sierra Leone. Tricked by the ship's pilot, they had sailed instead into Long Island Sound. Almost immediately the case became the center of heated controversy, as pro- and antislavery forces argued over whether the Africans should be returned to slavery. Ultimately the case reached the U.S. Supreme Court, where John Quincy Adams argued successfully that because the international slave trade was illegal in the United States, the Africans must be returned to their homes. The *Amistad* quickly became a cause célèbre among abolitionists, but the impact of the case went beyond activist circles. Heavy newspaper coverage aroused the sympathy even of moderate opponents of slavery, again broadening the antislavery debate and increasing interest in the new Liberty Party.

As anticipated, Van Buren received the Democratic nomination, but in an effort to skirt the explosive sectional issues, the Whigs turned to William Henry Harrison, an outspoken advocate of cheap western land and the hero of the battle of Tippecanoe (see Chapter 9, "Liberty and Empire").

Harrison was the candidate, out of the crowded 1836 Whig field, who had run strongest against Van Buren. To bolster the broad appeal of their slate, for their vice presidential candidate the Whigs chose a former Democrat, John Tyler of Virginia, a strong advocate of states' rights, and (at the time) a Clay supporter.

Harrison was a "sentimental" candidate. Through him, the Whigs hoped to evoke feelings of military glory and westward expansion. Studiously avoiding tough issues, they threw their energy instead into crafting a Jackson-like campaign for "Tippecanoe and Tyler, too." When a newspaper editor derided Harrison as a country bumpkin whose highest aspiration in life consisted of sitting on his porch drinking cider, the Whigs took up the image with gusto. In what came to be known as the "Log Cabin and Hard Cider Campaign," the Whigs celebrated Harrison as a simple man of the people (like Jackson). In point of fact, Harrison was from a wealthy old Virginia family. But he could be linked to the West, and, as Daniel Webster observed, Harrison's main appeal was the vague "hope of a better time."

The turnout was large and the popular results were close, but the Electoral College was a different story. Harrison, who had taken every large state but Virginia, triumphed with 234 electoral votes to Van Buren's 60. The anti-Harrison vote was suggestive, however. The Democrats held New Hampshire, Illinois, Missouri, Arkansas, Alabama, Virginia, and South Carolina. Except for New Hampshire, they were all states with deeply proslavery sentiments.

And Tyler, Too

Whig jubilation was short lived. Harrison became ill shortly after his inauguration and died on April 4, 1841, the first president to die in office. Harrison was followed in office by his vice president, John Tyler. Most observers assumed that Tyler would function as a caretaker president until the next general election. He soon proved them wrong, setting the precedent for vice presidents to succeed to the full stature and authority of the presidency.

Tyler's ascendancy threw the Whig Party into chaos, for once in office he reverted to his Democrat roots. There was much about Tyler that was reminiscent of Jackson. Not only did Tyler oppose the American System (see Chapter 10, "The Market Revolution") and favor slavery and the annexation of Texas, but also like Jackson, Tyler was willing to use the full power of the executive to enforce those views. Unlike Jackson in office, Tyler was an enthusiastic advocate of southern states' rights positions.

Tyler's attention was first drawn to diplomatic troubles with Britain. In 1841 the slave crew of the U.S. ship *Creole,* en route from Virginia to New Orleans, had seized control of the vessel and forced it into the port of Nassau where, by British law, the crew was freed. To no avail, white southerners demanded the return of the crew. Meanwhile, northern anti-British feeling flared over the question of the Oregon Territory, a vaguely defined expanse between northern California and Alaska that Britain and the United States had agreed in 1818 to occupy jointly. By 1842, reports of the North American Pacific Coast as a veritable "storehouse of wealth in all its forests, furs, and fisheries" had stimulated immigration and stirred American desire to claim the Oregon Territory.

In 1842 U.S. Secretary of State Webster and British emissary Ashburton concluded negotiations on the Webster–Ashburton Treaty, which drew a northern boundary between the United States and Canada from Maine to the Rocky Mountains (Oregon was left undivided), established terms of extradition between the two nations, and created a joint effort to restrict the international slave trade. Great Britain also agreed not to interfere with foreign vessels.

Tyler's success in foreign relations was overshadowed by his 1841 break with his own party. Led by Henry Clay, Whigs in Congress succeeded in passing legislation that embodied the Whig platform, including various tariff bills, a national bank bill, and a bill to distribute federal surpluses to states. Tyler vetoed almost every initiative. He denounced federal distribution as inappropriate when the federal government was in deficit. At last, in 1842, Congressional Whigs offered lower tariff increases than Clay wished and detached the tariff from the question of distribution. Citing the need for federal funds, Tyler signed the bill. Tyler supported the repeal of the independent treasury, a Whig goal, but this, too, proved a bitter victory for Clay and the Whig Party, because Tyler vetoed the national bank with which the Whigs wanted to replace the independent treasury.

Tyler soon found himself a president without a party. As early as January 1843, there were calls in the House of Representatives for his impeachment. That year, when Tyler vetoed the bill rechartering the national bank, his entire cabinet resigned, except Webster.

"His Accidency" proved more resilient than Clay anticipated. Tyler interpreted Democratic gains in the 1842 elections as support for his positions, particularly on the national bank. Urged on by extreme states' rights advocates in Virginia and South Carolina, Tyler took up the cause of the annexation of Texas. After Daniel Webster resigned from the cabinet in the spring of 1843 Tyler fell almost entirely under the influence of southerners who were committed to Texas.

Texas did everything in its power to make annexation an urgent issue. It allowed Great Britain to serve as an intermediary in Texas's efforts to win official recognition from Mexico and hinted that, as an independent republic, Texas might abolish slavery. The idea of an alliance between Texas and Great Britain reawakened old anti-British sentiments in the United States. In addition, the prospect of a nonslave republic so close to their borders filled southerners with dread.

Seeking to capitalize on these anxieties, in 1843 President Tyler secretly opened negotiations with Texas for admission to the union, expecting to justify the completed treaty as necessary to protect the United States against British influence. In 1844, Tyler submitted a treaty of annexation to Congress. He hoped that the potential for controversy would be buried in American expansionist interests. He was wrong. Even before the treaty was submitted, John Quincy Adams and 12 other Whigs denounced it as constitutionally unauthorized and warned that it would bring the nation to "dissolution." Abolitionists labeled the move a naked power grab by slaveowners. Even moderate northerners worried that annexing Texas would cause war with Mexico, consuming taxes and killing soldiers without yielding the North any tangible gains. Some southerners worried that Texas would compete with the depleted lands of the South, harming cotton and sugar profits.

By then, other election-year dramas were afoot. John Calhoun still longed for the presidency. He believed that he had a reasonable chance against Tyler, another southerner, if he could deny Van Buren the Democratic nomination. To that end, Calhoun wrote a note to the British minister that the U.S. goal in Texas was to protect slavery against British abolitionists. As Calhoun hoped, the note became public. The explicit association of Texas and slavery drove Van Buren away from endorsing the treaty, an act that might have made him a stronger candidate in the South. An overwhelmingly sectional vote defeated the treaty in Congress, but Calhoun believed a Democratic victory in 1844 would revive it.

Occupy Oregon, Annex Texas

By the fall of 1844 the American political party system was in disarray. Harrison's impressive victory in 1840 had not signaled a broad endorsement of Clay or the American System, any more than Van Buren's victory in 1836 had signaled a strong hard money, antibank sentiment. To the contrary, between 1836 and 1844 the party system seemed most successful at polarizing American interests.

Nowhere was that state of affairs more evident than in the 1844 Democratic convention in Baltimore. Van Buren's supporters believed that the party owed him the nomination, yet his liabilities were legion. In the South, proslavery, proannexation Democrats led by Calhoun were vowing to make "a slaveholder for President next time regardless of the man." Andrew Jackson was disappointed with Van Buren's refusal to endorse annexation and encouraged former Tennessee governor James K. Polk to run. In the North, workers and entrepreneurs who had been hard hit by years of deflation were disenchanted with the "Little Magician." Van Burenites were unable to block a convention rule requiring a candidate to receive a two-thirds vote to secure the nomination. Van Buren could not marshal that level of support, but neither could Tyler, Calhoun, or Lewis Cass, a compromise candidate. Finally, on the eighth ballot the convention fell back on Jackson's choice, James Polk. Tyler accepted renomination by a renegade group of supporters, also meeting in Baltimore, who styled themselves Democratic Republicans.

The 1844 Democratic Party ran on the platform of manifest destiny, calling for "the reoccupation of Oregon and the reannexation of Texas." It was an odd formulation, given that the United States had several times officially denied possession of Texas and had yet to occupy Oregon fully. The platform went even further on Oregon. Although the U.S. claim to Oregon had never extended beyond the 49th parallel, the Democrats now declared their willingness to go to war to gain the entire region ("Fifty-four forty or fight!"). Their bellicose strategy incorporated war fears over Texas into a broader assertion of national destiny.

Meanwhile, in 1844 Henry Clay at long last secured the Whig nomination. Clay was certain that opposition to the extension of slavery was too strong to tolerate a Texas–Oregon compromise and that Americans would not support a war with Mexico. Clay ran primarily as a supporter of the American System as the necessary means for stabilizing economic growth.

The election results suggested a nation teetering on the edge of political division. Polk, annexation, and manifest destiny won, but by only 38,000 of more than 2.5 million votes cast. More striking, James G. Birney of Ohio, the candidate of the new, explicitly antislavery Liberty Party, drew 62,000 votes, most of them from Clay. Had Birney not run, the election might have been a dead heat (see Table 13–1).

TABLE 13–1

The Liberty Party Swings an Election					
Candidate	Party	Actual Vote in New York	National Electoral Vote	If Liberty Voters Had Voted Whig	Projected Electoral Vote
Polk	Democratic	237,588	170	237,588	134
Clay	Whig	232,482	105	248,294	141
Birney	Liberty	15,812	0	—	—

Nevertheless, both Tyler and Congress read the election as a referendum on the Democratic platform and specifically on Texas. Early in 1845, with Tyler still in office, a bill approving annexation passed the House. To move it through the Whig-dominated Senate, Senator Robert Walker of Mississippi suggested the Senate version include the option of negotiating a whole new treaty. Only days away from the presidency, Polk was said to favor this approach, and Whigs thought a revised treaty might better address their objections and get them out of a politically costly position. With the appended option, the Senate approved the treaty. The Whigs expected Tyler to concede the decision to the incoming president, but in the last hours of his presidency he sent notice to Texas that (contingent on its own agreement) the republic was annexed to the United States of America. Mexico immediately severed relations with the United States.

War with Mexico

The annexation of Texas was the ostensible cause of the outbreak of war with Mexico in April 1846, but Texas was only a partial explanation for the war. In Polk's eyes, the annexation of Texas was a piece of a larger acquisition: not only Oregon but also present-day New Mexico, Arizona, and California. Certainly, Polk would have been happy to make these acquisitions peacefully, but he was willing to go to war.

Polk's two-track approach to foreign relations soon became evident. In December 1845 he announced his decision to withdraw from negotiations over Oregon, and he called on Congress to terminate the United States–Great Britain Convention of Joint Occupancy. Compromise would constitute an abandonment of American "territorial rights . . . and the national honour," he insisted, and could never be entertained. Polk's rhetoric was more threatening than his intentions: He simultaneously informed his advisors that he was prepared to hear a compromise offer from England. When one came, proposing a boundary at the 49th parallel, Polk submitted it to Congress. By June 1846 the deal had been struck.

In Oregon, Polk threatened war but quickly accepted peace. Thomas Hart Benton later suggested that appearance and intent were reversed in the Mexican borderlands. What Polk really wanted there, Benton claimed, was "a little war," big enough to justify grabbing the Southwest but not so big as to break the budget. Texas provided the excuse.

As a condition of his surrender and release, the Mexican General Santa Anna had agreed to the Rio Grande as the boundary between Texas and Mexico, a boundary that would have run northward to include present-day New Mexico as well as western Texas. The Mexican government had instead drawn the border at the Nueces River, recognizing only about half the territory claimed by Texans. Polk intended to set the boundary at the Rio Grande, and he might have intended to secure not only the disputed Texas territory but also large portions of northern Mexico.

To achieve these aims, he once again played a double game. As late as September, Polk appealed for a peaceful resolution. That month, he dispatched former Louisiana Congressman John Slidell to Mexico to offer to purchase New Mexico and Texas for $30 million. The Mexican government refused to receive Slidell.

Meanwhile, Polk prepared for war. In the spring of 1845 he had sent 1,500 soldiers under the command of General Zachary Taylor allegedly to protect Texas against a possible invasion by Mexico. When Texas approved union with the United States, Polk reinforced Taylor's troops and ordered them to approach the Rio Grande, while also sending an army under General Stephen Kearny into the northern part of the disputed territory. In August 1846, Kearny occupied Santa Fe. At the same time, Polk ordered the U.S. squadron in the Pacific closer to the California coast and directed the U.S. consul in California, Thomas Larkin, to encourage local disaffection with the Mexican government. When American settlers in the Sonoma Valley staged a rebellion in June and July, the representatives of the United States claimed California. Kearny later crossed into California to solidify the claim.

By that time, Polk's brinkmanship on the Rio Grande had produced results. Mexican troops had crossed the river to drive out Taylor's force, and American soldiers had been killed and wounded. In May 1846, Congress declared that "by the act of the Republic of Mexico, a state of war exists" between the two nations (see Map 13–3).

The United States entered the war unprepared. Although 100,000 volunteers signed up, at the outbreak of hostilities the United States Army had only 7,500 troops. Perhaps Polk shared the widely held expansionist view that Mexico was a "miserable, inefficient" nation. Mexico (and New Spain before it) had always been less interested in its northern provinces than in other parts of the nation. Moreover, the Mexican government had recently undergone a coup and remained unstable. With California guarded by Frémont and the naval squadron, the United States could bring its military power to bear on Mexico City.

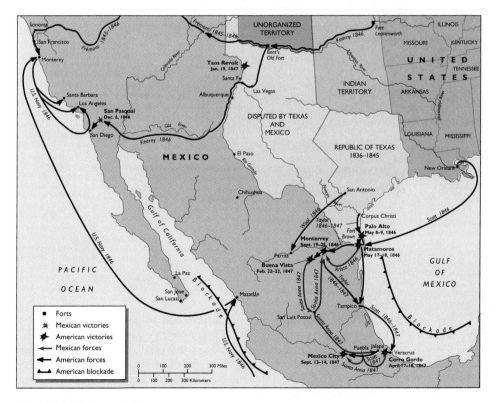

Map 13–3 Mexican War
General Zachary Taylor's victories in northern Mexico established the Rio Grande as the boundary between Texas and Mexico. Colonel Stephen Kearny's expedition secured control of New Mexico. General Winfield Scott's invasion by sea at Veracruz and his occupation of Mexico City ended the war.

CHRONOLOGY

1834	First missionaries arrive in Oregon Territory
1836	Martin Van Buren elected president Equal Rights Party formed Whig Party runs candidates for president Texas declares independence
1837	Sarah and Angelina Grimké tour North opposing slavery Pastoral Letter of Massachusetts Clergy
1838	"Aroostook" War Anti-Slavery Petition campaign at height
1839	*Amistad* Mutiny
1840	Independent Treasury Bill Anti-Slavery Society splits Liberty Party nominates James Birney for the presidency Large-scale overland migration to West Coast begins Whig candidate William Henry Harrison elected president
1841	John Tyler succeeds Harrison in office Creole Mutiny
1842	Webster–Ashburton Treaty
1844	James Polk is elected president
1845	The United States annexes Texas
1846	The United States declares war on Mexico
1848	Independent woman's rights movement begins at Seneca Falls, New York Treaty of Guadalupe Hidalgo Teton Sioux tax white settlers passing through their lands

Finding the right leader for such a campaign proved tricky. Taylor, the obvious choice, was a Whig of growing popularity. Polk finally settled on Winfield Scott, who also harbored Whig political ambitions. In the late winter of 1847, a naval squadron of 200 ships conveyed Scott's army through the Gulf of Mexico to Veracruz, where his army of 10,000 soldiers forced that city to surrender in April. Scott's troops fought their way to the outskirts of Mexico City. Scott began his final assault on September 8, and on September 14 Mexico City fell.

For all the military brilliance of the American campaign, support for the war steadily eroded. From the beginning, the war raised the question of slavery. Northern Democrats saw the war with Mexico as a transparent ploy to extend slavery. Northern antislavery activists spoke out against the war, and opposition grew as stories of U.S. military atrocities filtered back east.

In spite of the unpopularity of the war, the end of hostilities found Mexico so weak that Polk and his advisors thought of extracting greater concessions. His minister in Mexico, Nicholas P. Trist, opposed this proposal, however. In 1848 Trist negotiated the Treaty of Guadalupe Hidalgo, recognizing the Rio Grande as the border of Texas and granting the United States the territory encompassed in the present states of New Mexico, Arizona, Colorado, Utah, and Wyoming, as well as California. In return, the United States paid Mexico $15 million and assumed war claims of American citizens against Mexico. The Senate approved the treaty on March 10, 1848. The following May 25, Mexico concurred. Although Polk's presidency was dominated by the war with Mexico, the tariff and the independent treasury continued to haunt domestic politics. In each case, Polk was victorious. Like Jackson, Polk opposed protective tariffs, which he saw as benefiting industrialists at the expense of farmers and republican values. Although Whigs in Congress pushed for higher tariffs to support domestic man-ufacturing, the 1846 tariff eliminated flat duties and revised overall levels down-ward. Also like Jackson, Polk opposed the national bank. In 1846 he persuaded Congress to reinstate Van Buren's independent treasury to handle the federal government's financial transactions. Meanwhile, he vetoed Whig attempts to enact legislation supporting internal improvements.

The similarities between Jackson and Polk extended to their broader under-standing of politics and to the way in which they used the political machinery. Like Jackson, Polk framed policy battles as battles between good and evil, between indi-vidual opportunity and elite finance and capital. At the same time, also like Jackson, Polk exercised executive power as the tool of the people's will. He was convinced that the president, not the legislature (Whig controlled by his final years in office) represented the people's will. Before he left office, virtually every important item on his political agenda had been accomplished. Lost for the moment in that flush of victory was the steady erosion of popular support for the Democratic Party.

Conclusion

In 1820, Fanny Wright noted that many observers worried about the differences be-tween the American North and South, but Wright was buoyantly optimistic. If all else failed, she declared, the western states, settled by migrants from both North and South, would always be "powerful cementers of the Union."

By the end of the 1840s, it was clear that Wright's confidence had been mis-placed. The war with Mexico revealed just how far apart the North and South had grown. By 1848, the northern tier of states was deeply implicated in a political econ-omy of free labor. The southern states, meanwhile, had grown ever more committed to the political economy of slavery. The Mexican War signaled the beginning of an era in which differences between the North and South would seem undeniable and intractable—and symbolized in the West.

In 1848, Henry David Thoreau mounted a lecture platform in Concord, Massachusetts to explain his refusal to pay poll taxes, which he considered money paid to support the institution of slavery and its expansion in the war with Mexico. Thoreau declared himself ready to separate from his government—indeed, to see the union itself destroyed—rather than support the United States in the West. Thoreau's words were fateful: "How does it become a man to behave toward this

American government today?" he asked. "I answer, that he cannot without disgrace be associated with it. I cannot for an instant recognize that political organization as my government which is the slave's government also."

FURTHER READINGS

John Mack Faragher, *Women and Men on the Overland Trail* (1979). Faragher describes the migration of white Americans into Oregon Territory in the 1840s through the 1860s, including discussions of motivations that prompted families to undertake the trek, the preparations required for the journey, the routes taken, the obstacles faced, and the ways in which the experience of westering differed for women and men.

Lacy K. Ford, Jr., *Origins of Southern Radicalism: The South Carolina Upcountry, 1800–1860* (1988). Ford offers an examination of society and economy in South Carolina as a case study in the rise of white secessionist thought in the South, from the Nullification Crisis through the regional politics that characterized South Carolina in the late 1830s, the 1840s, and the 1850s.

Reginald Horsman, *Race and Manifest Destiny: The Origins of American Racial Anglo-Saxonism* (1981). Horsman traces the ascendancy of ideas of racial superiority throughout the antebellum years, examining both the presence of racial thinking in broad currents of American culture and the ways in which those intellectual perspectives shaped the politics of westward expansion.

Gerda Lerner, "The Political Activities of Antislavery Women," in *The Majority Finds Its Past: Placing Women in History* (1979). Lerner traces the process through which antislavery activities in general (including the petition campaigns) and the antislavery work of the Grimké sisters in particular created new forms of public power for women, creating one of the avenues through which women came to the demand for the vote.

James M. McCaffrey, *Army of Manifest Destiny: The American Soldier in the Mexican War, 1846–1848* (1992). This brief study of the largely volunteer American Army of the Mexican War furnishes useful insights into the high politics, the broad military strategies, and the daily experience of common soldiers in Polk's war of expansion against Mexico in 1846.

Please refer to the document CD-ROM for primary sources related to this chapter.

CHAPTER

14

The Politics of Slavery

1848–1860

Frederick Douglass • **The Political Economy of Freedom and Slavery**
Slavery Becomes a Political Issue • **Nativism and the Origins
of the Republican Party** • **A New Political Party Takes Shape**
An "Irrepressible" Conflict? • **The Retreat from Union**
Conclusion

FREDERICK DOUGLASS

Frederick Douglass denounced the war with Mexico as "disgraceful, cruel, and iniquitous." Northern support for what he saw as a slaveholders' war reinforced Douglass's conviction that the U.S. Constitution had created an unholy union of liberty and slavery. The only solution was for New England to secede. "The Union must be dissolved," Douglass wrote, "or New England is lost and swallowed up by the slave-power of the country."

Douglass had been urging disunion for several years, ever since he became the most compelling antislavery voice in America. His authority derived from his extraordinary intelligence, his exceptional skill as a public speaker, and above all from his personal experience. Frederick Douglass was not simply an abolitionist, he was also the most famous runaway slave in America.

He was born Frederick Augustus Washington Bailey, in Talbot County, Maryland, in 1818. At the age of seven he was sent to Baltimore, where he became a skilled caulker working in the shipyards. He learned to hire out his labor, paying his master three dollars each week and keeping the rest himself. And there, in Baltimore,

319

he grew to resent the arrangement. For the rest of his life he would associate freedom with the right to earn a living. When Frederick's master revoked their arrangement and demanded that the slave hand over all his earnings, Frederick planned his escape.

On May 3, 1838, Frederick Bailey dressed up as a sailor and boarded a north-bound train using a friend's borrowed papers. By September, Frederick Douglass was living and working in New Bedford, Massachusetts, where he began attending anti-slavery meetings. He subscribed to William Lloyd Garrison's fiery abolitionist newspaper, the *Liberator*. In 1841 he was invited to speak during an abolitionist convention, where he stunned his listeners with an eloquent recital of his experience as a slave. Garrison himself was in the audience, and he invited Douglass to speak for the American Anti-Slavery Society. For the next several years Douglass was a leading spokesman for the Garrisonian wing of the abolitionist movement.

The Garrisonians believed that the Constitution was hopelessly corrupted by its compromises with slavery. They saw no point in pursuing political reforms; instead they advocated the separation of the North from the South. The Garrisonians rejected all violent efforts to overthrow slavery, including slave rebellion. Their preferred solution was moral persuasion of their opponents. Frederick Douglass initially believed all of these things.

The Mexican War was a turning point in Douglass's thinking. By the late 1840s, he saw growing numbers of northerners join the Free Soil Party dedicated to halting the expansion of slavery, and he wondered why this could not become a political coalition against slavery itself. During the 1850s Douglass moved further from the Garrisonians: He openly supported slave rebellion, came to believe that political action was necessary to eliminate slavery, and began to doubt the wisdom of dismissing the Constitution as a proslavery document.

Douglass moved closer to the mainstream of northern politics because anti-slavery sentiment had suddenly entered the mainstream. For more than half a century the major parties had studiously avoided slavery. At the center of American politics was an unspoken agreement not to discuss the issue. However, after the war with Mexico the slavery issue pushed all others aside and a third "party system" emerged in American politics. The Whig Party collapsed entirely, and in its place emerged the new Republican Party, openly hostile to slavery and sworn to restricting its expansion. Shortly thereafter the Democratic Party was captured by proslavery extremists. For the first time in American history the political mainstream could accommodate a radical abolitionist like Frederick Douglass, so Douglass moved to the mainstream. By 1861 he was urging the president to uphold the Constitution by suppressing the South's attempt to secede.

THE POLITICAL ECONOMY OF FREEDOM AND SLAVERY

The politics of slavery erupted at a moment of tremendous economic growth. As the depression of the 1840s lifted, the American zeal for internal improvements revived. The canals that had been constructed between 1800 and 1830 were systematically widened during the 1840s and 1850s to accommodate the new steamboats. Railroad construction, which had collapsed during the depressed 1840s, came back stronger than ever in the 1850s. On the eve of the Civil War, the United States boasted more miles of railroad track than the rest of the world combined. No less spectacular was the rapid adoption of the telegraph. Invented by Samuel F. B. Morse in 1844, the telegraph made it possible for two human beings separated by oceans and continents to sustain virtually instantaneous communication. By 1860, there were 50,000 miles of telegraph wire in America. The first transcontinental line was completed in 1861.

These developments tied all Americans together and so might have inhibited the growth of sectionalism. An efficient transportation and communication network helped integrate the United States into a single national market. But market integration only tied together two different political economies based on two very different systems of labor. By the 1850s the differences between North and South overwhelmed the connections that bound them together.

A Changing Economy in the North

The 1850s were booming years for northern farmers. Few farm communities in the North were untouched by the national market. It took less than a week to transport meat and grains from midwestern cities to the East Coast. Because of the dramatic reduction in the price of commodities, Northern farmers could devote more time and effort to producing crops for sale rather than for consumption at home. Inventions like the steel plow, seed drills, and the McCormick reaper allowed northern farmers to increase their production of goods for market. Between 1820 and 1860 northern farmers quadrupled their productivity.

Farmers could grow more crops for sale because more Americans were living in cities and working for wages. Wage earners produced little of their own food, clothing, or shelter. Yet so productive was American agriculture that the proportion of farmers declined. In 1820, 75 percent of the labor force was devoted to agriculture. By 1860 the figure had dropped to 57 percent. The growth of wage labor in the North was so rapid that native-born workers could not fill the demand for labor in the cities and factories. In the mid-1840s the number of Europeans coming to the United States jumped sharply, and 3 million arrived in the single decade between 1845 and 1854. More than two-thirds were Irish or German, a substantial proportion of whom were Roman Catholic. By 1855 a larger proportion of Americans was foreign born than at any other time in the nation's history.

Many immigrants, especially the Irish, came to America impoverished. Arriving penniless at East Coast ports, they congregated in the growing cities and factory towns of the North. By 1860 immigrants made up more than one-third of the residents in northern cities with populations of at least 10,000.

Impoverished immigrants became wage laborers in numbers that far outstripped their proportions in the population. In New York City, for example, immigrants accounted for 48 percent of the 1860 population but 69 percent of the city's labor force. Men worked in unskilled jobs on the docks, at construction sites, or on railroads and canals. They were conspicuous in the coal mines and iron foundries of Pennsylvania. Women worked as seamstresses, laundresses, or domestic servants. In the textile mills and shoe factories of New England, Irish families worked together, husbands and wives alongside sons and daughters.

Industrialization was not the only reason for the growth of wage labor. By the 1850s a growing middle class of white-collar employees also worked for wages. White-collar employees kept the increasingly complex accounting records, maintained the expanding files, and kept track of the growing volume of sales. As the scale of industrial production increased, individual businesses opened large downtown stores to sell their goods. Between 1859 and 1862, for example, A. T. Stewart built a huge dry goods store covering a full square block in lower Manhattan. The financial needs of these large-scale enterprises were met by an expanding number of banks, insurance companies, and accounting firms that employed armies of white-collar workers.

Thus, economic growth in the North during the 1850s rested on important social changes. A rural society became more urban. Industry was replacing agriculture as the driving economic force. Wage labor was replacing independent labor. A Protestant nation encountered the first great wave of Catholic immigrants. Machines made it possible for one person to cultivate more acres than ever before. All of this signaled the birth of a political economy based on new sources of wealth and new forms of work.

Strengths and Weaknesses of the Southern Economy

"You dare not make war on cotton," James Henry Hammond warned his fellow senators in 1858. "Cotton is king." This was a plausible argument for a South Carolinian to make in the prosperous 1850s, when the price of cotton (and of slaves) rose steadily. Recovering from the economic doldrums of the 1840s, southern states threw themselves into the business of railroad construction with unprecedented vigor. By 1860 the South had a fairly large railroad network, smaller than the North's but impressive by world standards. Steamboats plied the South's rivers. Telegraph wires sped news of inland cotton prices to the Atlantic coast. Southerners boasted of their region's commitment to progress and prosperity. In this context, Senator Hammond, one of the wealthiest cotton planters in the South, could openly defy slavery's critics.

But slavery could not transform the South as wage labor was transforming the North. The South had changed in many ways during the previous century. It had expanded across half the continent. Cotton had become the region's most profitable crop. The Atlantic slave trade was closed off, and a native-born, largely Christian slave population had grown up. And yet, the social structure that was in place by 1750 was largely unchanged a century later.

Even in prosperous times slavery's critics pointed to what they saw as weaknesses in the southern economy. Under King Cotton's reign, urban life stagnated while the rural economy boomed. In the North, prosperity rested on a growing number of wage earners in business and industry. In the South, especially the lower South, good times reinforced the wealth of the long-established slave-owning class.

To be sure, there were important signs of social change, especially in the upper South. The immigrant workers Frederick Douglass met on the Baltimore docks were caught up in the same process of economic development as the dock workers of New England. The steady sale of slaves from the upper to the lower South reduced the political influence of slaveholders in states like Maryland and even

Virginia. Indeed, among whites across the entire South the proportion of slave-holders had been declining for decades. In 1830 one-third of southern white families held slaves. By 1860 the proportion had dropped to one in four.

The Importance of the West

Both the North and the South coveted western lands. By 1850 many northerners believed that slavery, if allowed to expand into the West, would deprive free laborers of an important source of prosperity and independence. But slaveholders had come to believe that their prosperity depended on the diffusion, or extension, of the slave economy into the West. The disposition of the land acquired in the War with Mexico therefore forced Americans into a sustained public debate over the future of slavery.

Slavery had expanded more than halfway across the continent of North America in about half a century, from the eastern seaboard to the mines of New Mexico and the plains of Kansas, and white southerners grew accustomed to viewing territorial expansion as a sign of progress. The westward movement of the southern frontier demonstrated the continued strength of the political economy of slavery. To call a halt to that movement was to dam up the wellsprings of southern prosperity. It was an insult to the moral decency of white southerners, an obstacle to their economic vitality, and an unconstitutional infringement on their right to carry their property with them wherever they saw fit. So argued slavery's defenders with increasing vehemence in the 1850s.

But the economic growth of the North created equally strong ties between the East and the West. Mountains and rivers generally ran north and south, but turnpikes, canals, and especially railroads tended to run east and west. Of the approximately 20,000 miles of railroads built in the 1850s, few crossed the Mason-Dixon line to link the northern and southern economies (see Map 14–1). The transportation revolution thus strengthened the ties between northeastern cities and the western frontier.

Northerners came to view the West as essential to their prosperity. The public lands of the West "are the great regulator of the relations of Labor and Capital," Horace Greeley explained, "the safety valve of our industrial and social engine." This safety valve theory was repeated over and over again in the North, even though there was not much truth in it. To move west, buy land, and establish a farm required resources far beyond the means of many, perhaps most, wage laborers at the time. Nevertheless, in the eyes of many northerners, westward expansion was critical to the stability and prosperity of their entire social order. It was no wonder that the westward expansion of slavery caused so much anxiety in the North.

SLAVERY BECOMES A POLITICAL ISSUE

Westward expansion forced the issue of slavery into the political mainstream. For the next 15 years national politics would focus on one crucial question: Should Congress restrict the movement of slavery into the West?

Wilmot Introduces His Proviso

On August 8, 1846, David Wilmot, a Democratic congressman from Pennsylvania, attached to an appropriations bill an amendment banning slavery from all the territories acquired in the war with Mexico. The aim of the famous Wilmot Proviso was to preserve western lands for white settlement. "I plead the cause and rights of the free white man," Wilmot insisted.

Map 14–1 Railroad Expansion
This map shows that there were two distinct patterns of railroad development in the United States. In the
North, rail lines connected the western states to the eastern seaboard. In the South, railroads tied the
inland plantation districts to the coastal ports. Few lines connected the North to the South.

Initially, northern Whigs and Democrats joined in support of the proviso, while their southern counterparts opposed it. When it was reintroduced in the next session of Congress, however, the proviso went down to defeat. Nevertheless, it paralyzed Congress for several years in the late 1840s, a time when conditions in the West demanded federal legislation. Mormon settlers had been pouring into the basin of the Great Salt Lake, and they required some form of government. The discovery of gold in California brought a rush of settlers and a good deal of disorder to the mining camps of the Sierra foothills and the boomtown of San Francisco. Territorial governments required Congressional action, but Congress was frozen by sectional differences.

By 1850 four positions had hardened into place. At one extreme were northern congressmen who favored a Wilmot-like solution that would ban slavery in all the territories. At the other extreme were the southern followers of John C. Calhoun, who argued that Congress had no right to regulate slavery in the territories. In between there were two different positions. Some wanted to extend the Missouri Compromise line, which would have pushed the North–South division all the way

WELL! LET EM COME ON . WE'RE ARM'D.

THE LITTLE GIANT IN THE CHARACTER OF THE GLADIATOR.

Senator Stephen A. Douglas, the "Little Giant" from Illinois, became the leading advocate of "popular sovereignty" as a solution to the crisis over slavery in the 1850s.

to the Pacific Ocean. Finally there was popular sovereignty, the position later supported by Stephen A. Douglas of Illinois. Popular sovereignty gave settlers the right to decide for themselves whether they would have slavery in their territory.

The four conflicting positions disrupted the major parties. In the presidential election of 1848 antislavery men bolted both the Democrats and the Whigs and threw their support to the Free Soil Party. With the Wilmot Proviso as their platform, the Free Soilers won 14 percent of the northern vote. Meanwhile, proslavery fire-eaters threatened to walk out of the Democratic convention. The Whigs survived this turmoil to elect President Zachary Taylor, a hero of the war with Mexico. The Whig triumph was short lived, however. In 1849 President Taylor urged New Mexico and California to apply directly for admission to the Union without going through the usual territorial stage. California's application for statehood arrived with a constitution that prohibited slavery, provoking a fight over whether new slave states should be admitted to the Union. The House of Representatives, with a strong northern majority, reaffirmed the Wilmot Proviso, condemned the slave trade in Washington, DC, and almost abolished slavery in the District of Columbia. The Senate, which had a strong southern wing, blocked all such measures.

This was no ordinary Congressional stalemate. Fistfights broke out in the halls of Congress. Elected representatives challenged each other to duels. Threatening secession, proslavery partisans called for a southern rights convention to meet at Nashville in June 1850. The stage was set for one of the most dramatic debates in Congressional history.

A Compromise Without Compromises

Into this stalemate marched the "great triumvirate" of distinguished old senators, Henry Clay of Kentucky, Daniel Webster of Massachusetts, and John C. Calhoun of South Carolina. Clay, who had been instrumental in securing the Missouri Compromise of 1820, tried one last time to save the Union. He devised a series of eight resolutions designed to balance the conflicting interests of North and South. Under the first pair of measures, California would be admitted as a free state, but the rest of the Mexican territories would have no conditions regarding slavery attached to their applications for statehood. The second pair limited the number of slave states that could be carved out of Texas Territory, but in return required the federal government to assume Texas's debt. The third pair abolished the slave trade in Washington, DC, but protected slavery itself from federal interference. The compromise package included two more provisions that were partial to the South: a formal promise not to interfere in the interstate slave trade and a new fugitive slave law.

Clay gathered all eight provisions of his compromise into a single package dubbed the Omnibus Bill. The senator's goal was simple: to gain enough support from centrists in each party to override both southern fire-eaters and northern Free Soilers.

The Congressional debate over Clay's package in the spring and summer of 1850 included a series of extraordinary speeches. Daniel Webster eloquently supported the compromise measures. Appealing for sectional harmony, Webster claimed to speak "not as a Massachusetts man, nor as a Northern man, but as an American." Calhoun, by contrast, spoke very much as a southern man. He warned that the bonds tying the sections together had been snapped by the North's continued agitation of the slavery question. If constitutional protection of slavery were not enforced, the union would be severed. In response, New York's William H. Seward argued that the Constitution gave Congress every right to restrict slavery in the territories.

The sectional hostilities exposed in the debate suggest why Clay's Omnibus Bill was doomed. Antislavery senators voted against the bill for its various provisions protecting slavery. Proslavery senators opposed it for its restrictions on slavery. On July 31, after months of wrangling, the Senate killed the package. Exhausted and angry, Clay gave up and left Washington. The old generation had failed to resolve the crisis.

From that moment on national politics would be dominated by a new generation of Congressional leaders. One of them was William Seward. Another was Senator Stephen A. Douglas, the "Little Giant" from Illinois who used his adroit parliamentary skills to rescue the compromise. He broke the omnibus package up into five separate bills, each designed to win different majorities. Antislavery and moderate congressmen joined to secure the admission of California as a free state. Proslavery congressmen voted with moderates to pass a fugitive slave law. By similar means, Congress settled the Texas border, determined that New Mexico and Utah would apply for statehood under the principle of popular sovereignty, and abolished the slave trade in the District of Columbia. Although proslavery and antislavery forces never compromised on a single issue, the five bills that Douglas and his allies steered through Congress came to be known as the Compromise of 1850.

Douglas's efforts were aided by the untimely death of the president. Zachary Taylor's replacement, Millard Fillmore, was more sympathetic to sectional reconciliation. Fillmore pronounced the Compromise of 1850 the "final settlement" of the slavery question. For the next few years moderate politicians across the country avoided all discussion of slavery. In the short run, the compromise apparently worked. The southern rights convention at Nashville fizzled, and the radical edge of the southern rights movement was blunted. But fire-eaters in the South and Free Soilers in the North insisted that the day of reckoning had only been postponed. And in the North, opposition to one feature of the compromise, the fugitive slave law, came with unanticipated intensity.

The Fugitive Slave Act Provokes a Crisis

The Fugitive Slave Act of 1850 was one of the least debated features of the compromise. The Constitution had a fugitive slave clause, and a law enforcing the clause had been in place since 1793. Why, then, did the new Fugitive Slave Act provoke such an uproar? Many northern states had passed laws to restrain fugitive slave catchers by guaranteeing the rights of due process to accused runaways. The 1850 statute took jurisdiction over fugitive slave cases away from northern courts and gave it to federal commissioners who were paid $10 if they ruled that a black captive should be returned to slavery but only $5 if they ruled that the captive was legitimately free. Abolitionists naturally charged that this amounted to a bribe to send captives into slavery.

The Fugitive Slave Act sent waves of terror through northern African-American communities. Slaves who had run away decades earlier now faced the prospect of being captured and sent back to the South. Even free-born blacks feared being kidnapped into slavery, unable to prove their freedom in a court of law. Across the North, vulnerable African Americans moved to the far West, the upper North, or Canada. A convention of blacks denounced the Fugitive Slave Act as "the most cruel, unconstitutional, and scandalous outrage of modern times."

White abolitionists were no less vehement. The Reverend Charles Beecher denounced the Fugitive Slave Act as "the vilest monument of infamy of the nineteenth century." Even white northerners who cared little about the fate of blacks were upset. The South seemed to be imposing its laws and institutions on the North. Appalled by the act, Harriet Beecher Stowe published *Uncle Tom's Cabin* in

The tremendous popularity of Harriet Beecher Stowe's novel, Uncle Tom's Cabin, *reflected the surprisingly intense northern concern about the Fugitive Slave Act of 1850. This illustration from an early edition of Stowe's novel shows one of the book's most dramatic scenes, in which Eliza the slave clings to her daughter as she leaps across the ice-clogged Ohio River while being pursued by howling dogs.*

1852. The astonishing success of Stowe's novel was one measure of northern anxiety about the Fugitive Slave Act. In vivid, melodramatic prose, Stowe drew a sentimental portrait of a slave mother and her infant child as they fled from a master who had contracted to sell them apart. Few readers missed the point. Anyone who helped Eliza save her child stood in violation of the Fugitive Slave Act of 1850.

A surprising number of northerners tolerated violations of the Fugitive Slave Act. President Fillmore vowed to enforce the law with federal marshals if necessary, but Frederick Douglass, revealing how far he had moved from his earlier pacifism, advocated violent resistance. "A half dozen or more dead kidnappers carried down South," he suggested, "would cool the ardor of Southern gentlemen, and keep their rapacity in check."

The Election of 1852 and the Decline of the Whig Party

White southerners were outraged by the North's unwillingness to obey the Fugitive Slave Act. The Democratic Party made enforcement of the Compromise of 1850 its rallying cry in 1852. The Democrats, torn by sectional divisions, nominated Franklin Pierce, a northerner thought to be sympathetic to southern interests. Pierce and the Democrats ran on a platform pledged to silencing discussion of slavery by strict federal enforcement of the Compromise of 1850, "the act for reclaiming fugitives included."

The Whigs found no such unifying principle. White southerners abandoned the party because it harbored antislavery advocates, and northern voters punished the Whigs for their association with the Compromise of 1850. Henry Clay wrote the Fugitive Slave Act. Daniel Webster supported it. Millard Fillmore signed and aggressively enforced it as well. All were Whigs. The Whig Party convention met in Baltimore a month after the Democrats, but it produced no comparable show of unity. After 52 ballots, the convention nominated Winfield Scott of Virginia, despite nearly unanimous southern opposition. The southern delegates secured a platform that reaffirmed the party's commitment to the Compromise of 1850, but this only meant that the Whigs would run a candidate who was objectionable in the South on a platform that was objectionable in the North.

Southern defections all but assured a major Whig defeat in the November election. Pierce won 254 electoral votes and Scott won only 42. The Democratic candidate won 27 out of 31 states. Severely weakened by the 1852 election results, the Whigs found themselves unable to meet another challenge that burst into American politics in the early 1850s, hostility to immigrants, otherwise known as nativism.

NATIVISM AND THE ORIGINS OF THE REPUBLICAN PARTY

The politics of nativism destroyed a Whig Party already weakened by sectionalism. From 1852 through 1854 the nativist American Party gained surprising strength. Hostility to immigrants, however, was not enough to rally northerners concerned about slavery. What, then, would replace the Whig Party in the North? A new and powerful political force, the Republican Party, was dedicated to halting slavery's westward expansion.

The Nativist Attack on Immigration

The arrival of large numbers of Catholic immigrants stirred nearly as much animosity among Yankee Protestants as did slavery. In the early 1850s the Catholic Church was widely known for its conservatism. The Pope expressed an abiding contempt for "progress," and the Vatican condemned the liberal revolutions that swept across Europe in 1848, revolutions that were widely supported by Americans.

Anti-Catholicism had about it a strong odor of middle-class condescension. Nativism appealed to shopkeepers, independent craftsmen, and white-collar clerks, people for whom the Protestant ethic of steadiness and sobriety amounted to a scriptural injunction. They looked with disdain on a working class of Irish and German immigrants who drank heavily, lived in squalor, and lacked economic independence. But it was immigrant voting, particularly among Irish Catholics, that most unsettled the nativist soul: the Irish voted Democratic.

The Democrats' appeal to Irish Catholics was double-edged. On the one hand, the party's populist rhetoric attracted working-class immigrants who were stung by the snobbery of Yankee Whigs. At the same time, as Democrats stepped up their racist invective, Irish Americans heaped contempt on African Americans with whom they competed for jobs and housing. Democrats cultivated this sentiment, using racism to assimilate Irish working-class voters into American politics at a time when many Americans were organizing to keep immigrants out. The consequences for sectional politics were significant. The Democrats argued that abolition would force white workers into economic competition with an inferior race. With the critical support of the Irish voting bloc, the Democratic Party sponsored new restrictions on the civil rights of free African Americans in many northern states.

In the elections of 1854, voters who believed that immigration was the greatest threat to the American way of life cast their ballots for the American Party. (They were often called "Know-Nothings" because of their origins in a secret organization whose members insisted, when questioned, that they "know nothing" about it.) Voters who cared more about the threat of slavery voted for the Free Soil Party. American Party candidates won 25 percent of the vote in New York and 40 percent in Pennsylvania; in Massachusetts, they took control of the state legislature.

In 1854 it seemed as though nativism would eclipse slavery as the great issue of American politics. But slavery and nativism were never entirely separate issues. Middle-class Yankees often viewed the struggle against Catholicism as inseparable from the struggle against slavery. Both were said to represent authoritarianism, ignorance, and a rejection of the "modern" values of individualism and progress. Given the close ties between nativism and antislavery sentiments, it was unclear which issue would eventually prevail. The question was decided on the sparsely settled plains of Kansas and Nebraska (see Map 14–2).

The Kansas-Nebraska Act Revives the Slavery Issue

In 1853, the House of Representatives passed a bill banning slavery in Nebraska Territory on the grounds that it fell north of the Missouri Compromise line. Southerners killed the Nebraska Bill in the Senate. The following year Stephen Douglas reintroduced it, this time organizing the territory on the principle of popular sovereignty.

Map 14–2   The Kansas–Nebraska Act of 1854
Stephen Douglas's Kansas–Nebraska Act carved the Kansas Territory out of the larger Nebraska Territory. Because Missouri was already a slave state, the map indicates that slaveholders could move west and settle in Kansas. But because Kansas lay north of the 1820 Missouri Compromise line, many northerners wanted slavery restricted from the territory.

No one was satisfied with Douglas's proposal. Northerners were outraged that the 1850 agreement to extend the Missouri Compromise line was so quickly scuttled. Militant southerners, suspicious of Congressional attempts to regulate slavery in the territories, now rejected popular sovereignty in principle. Douglas withdrew the bill and reintroduced it in January 1854, but with a new twist. He split Nebraska Territory in two, Kansas to the west of the slave state of Missouri and Nebraska to the north of Kansas. Both were to be organized on the principle of popular sovereignty, but everyone expected that Kansas would become a slave state and Nebraska a free state. To win the support of southern congressmen, the final version of Douglas's bill explicitly repealed the Missouri Compromise of 1820.

Debate over the bill was ferocious: Southerners denied that Congress had the right to regulate slavery in the territories, through popular sovereignty or any other means. Northerners pointed out that the federal government had been regulating slavery in the territories since the 1780s.

In the end, Douglas succeeded in winning passage of the Kansas–Nebraska Act. Yet as with other southern victories, the Act increased support for antislavery politicians in the North. It persuaded many northerners that popular sovereignty was a proslavery swindle, even though Douglas believed that it would produce mostly free states. Yet for that very reason southerners no longer trusted popular sovereignty either. Douglas had paid a heavy price for his victory. In the 1854 elections the number of northern Democrats in Congress fell from 91 to 25. The Kansas–Nebraska Act split the Democratic Party in two, destroyed the credibility of popular sovereignty, and damaged expansionism as a political program.

The Expansion of Slavery as a Foreign Policy

The Pierce administration's disastrous support for the Kansas–Nebraska Act undermined its ability to pursue the expansionist policies of its Democratic predecessors. To be sure, Pierce packed his presidential addresses with bluster about America's right to more Mexican territory and to various parts of the Caribbean, particularly Cuba. But all of Pierce's expansionist efforts were southward, and that meant they all promised the expansion of slavery. This was hardly an accident. Pierce filled his cabinet with southerners and appointed slaveholders to crucial diplomatic posts.

Pierce sent a South Carolinian, James Gadsden, to Mexico with instructions to spend up to $50 million to acquire a substantial portion of northern Mexico. Mexico's leader resisted Gadsden's extravagant offer. The American returned to Washington, DC, with a treaty giving the United States just enough territory to build a transcontinental railroad across the southern tier of the nation. But even this was too much for most northern senators. For the first time in American history, Congress rejected land ceded to the United States. The Gadsden Purchase ended up securing only a small piece of land for $10 million to even out the southern border of the United States.

Pierce's expansionist designs fared even worse in Cuba. The president appointed Pierre Soulé, a Louisianan, as minister to Spain. Soulé was instructed to negotiate the purchase of Cuba, with the understanding that if Spain refused to sell he should encourage the Cubans to rise in rebellion. To Soulé's presumptuous behavior the Spanish government offered an extraordinary response. It proposed to free millions of Cuban slaves and arm them for the defense of the island against a possible American invasion.

The United States responded with the Ostend Manifesto, which declared that Cuba was "naturally" a part of the United States and urged Spain to accept an offer of $120 million for the island. If Spain refused, the United States would use all of its power to "wrest" the island of Cuba by force.

The Ostend Manifesto, promulgated in 1854, at the height of northern reaction against the Kansas–Nebraska Act,was immediately denounced as yet another example of slavery's insatiable hunger for expansion. Expansionism was now hopelessly tainted by its association with slavery. As Pierce's Secretary of State, William L. Marcy, admitted, "the Nebraska question" had shattered the Democratic Party in the North "and deprived it of that strength which was needed and could have been more profitably used for the acquisition of Cuba."

Kansas Begins to Bleed

Under the terms of the Kansas–Nebraska Act, the people in Kansas would determine whether their territory would enter the Union as a slave or free state. Elections for the territorial legislature were set for March 1855. Hoping to secure victory for the antislavery forces, the New England Emigrant Aid Company sent settlers opposed to slavery. By election day, however, proslavery settlers probably would have won a fair fight, but on the day the polls opened proslavery partisans from neighboring Missouri crossed the border and cast thousands of phony ballots. This cast doubt on the legitimacy of the newly elected proslavery legislature. To make matters worse, the new legislature made it a crime to question slavery in Kansas, made it a capital crime to protect fugitive slaves, and expelled the few antislavery members who had been elected.

Free-state settlers responded by repudiating the proslavery government. In January 1856 free-staters elected a governor and legislature of their own. By the spring of 1856 Kansas found itself with two competing governments, a proslavery one in Lecompton and an antislavery one in Topeka. By then free-state settlers were in the majority. Nevertheless, local sheriffs and federal marshals, backed up by more "border ruffians" from Missouri, tried several times to enter the town of Lawrence to arrest free-staters. They tried again May 21, 1856, only to discover that most of the free-staters had fled. The frustrated Missourians promptly destroyed two printing presses and burned the Free State Hotel to the ground. Although little blood was shed, the eastern press blasted this latest example of proslavery violence. Kansas, they said, was bleeding.

Three days after the sack of Lawrence, Kansas really did begin to bleed when John Brown launched his famous raid on proslavery settlers at Pottawatomie Creek. Brown was an awesome and in many ways a frightening man, a fierce Calvinist who saw human degradation everywhere he looked. The wrath of God, not moral persuasion or political organization, was Brown's preferred solution to the problem of slavery.

The day after he learned of the sack of Lawrence, Brown organized a small band of men to take revenge. Among his seven-man legion were four of his own sons and a son-in-law. Armed with finely honed swords and even sharper zeal, Brown's troops went into battle late in the evening on May 24. At their first stop they shot James Doyle in the head, split open the skulls of two of his sons, and then hacked up the bodies. They committed similar atrocities at two other settlers' cabins. Then they went back to their camp, having stolen several horses along the way. Brown never admitted his involvement in the so-called Pottawatomie Massacre, but the evidence against him was overwhelming.

As blood flowed in the western territories, another battle erupted on the floor of Congress. Prompted by the sack of Lawrence, abolitionist Senator Charles Sumner of Massachusetts delivered a two-day harangue exposing the "Crime Against Kansas." The speech was filled with overheated sexual metaphors: Proslavery forces, Sumner declared, had set out to "rape" the virgin territory of Kansas. He accused Senator

Andrew Butler of South Carolina of consorting with a "polluted . . . harlot, Slavery." Two days later Congressman Preston S. Brooks, a nephew of Butler's, walked into a nearly empty Senate chamber and brutally attacked Sumner with his cane.

Across the South, Brooks was hailed as a hero. Southern congressmen prevented his expulsion from the House. Northerners, shocked by the South's reaction to the Sumner–Brooks affair, responded by casting their ballots for a new Republican Party dedicated to halting the expansion of the slave power.

A New Political Party Takes Shape

The election of 1856 presented Americans with a clear choice. A candidate's position on the Kansas–Nebraska Act betrayed his convictions about slavery. And slavery, in turn, raised questions about the relative value of wage labor and slave labor. What was at stake, in other words, was the fundamental conflict between the political economy of slavery and of freedom. In the past the Whigs and Democrats had avoided sectional issues by running candidates who appealed to both the North and the South. In 1856 a new major party, the Republicans, appealed exclusively to northern voters.

The First Sectional Election

In 1856 antislavery became the umbrella under which the Democratic Party's opponents in the North could gather. That new umbrella was the Republican Party, and its first presidential candidate was John C. Frémont.

The Republican Party platform called for a prohibition on the expansion of slavery into any western territories, but Frémont was pledged to a larger vision of political economy as well. The Republicans presented themselves as the party of active government on behalf of economic progress. They wanted the federal government to sponsor the construction of a transcontinental railroad and to set high tariffs to protect industries. They proposed a homestead act to encourage small farmers to settle the West and supported the creation of land grant colleges to encourage technological innovation in agriculture. For Republicans, government activism on behalf of free labor went hand in hand with the withdrawal of government support for slavery.

The Republicans were unified because they did not have to appeal to the South. In contrast, the Democrats faced the difficult task of finding a candidate acceptable to both the northern and southern wings of the party. They turned to James Buchanan of Pennsylvania, "a northern man with southern principles."

Where the Republicans promised to interfere with slavery in the territories, the Democrats pledged "non-interference by Congress with slavery." This wording kept the principle of popular sovereignty alive without actually endorsing it. Northern and southern Democrats could thus unite around a candidate committed, above all else, to ending to public discussion of slavery.

The Democratic candidate could thus claim to be the only national candidate, the only one who could prevent the breakup of the Union. Southern leaders repeatedly warned that if Frémont and the Republicans won the presidency, the South would secede. The Democrats played on widespread fear of disunion. The "grand and appalling issue" of the campaign, Buchanan wrote, is "Union or Disunion."

For the first time in their history, Americans were asked to decide in a presidential election whether the Union was worth preserving. That decision had become terribly complicated. The worth of the Union now depended on the kind of society that Union would embrace in the future. Would it be a society whose wealth was based on the labor of slaves or one that staked its prosperity on the progress of free labor?

The Labor Problem and the Politics of Slavery

Northern Democrats warned that a Republican victory would flood the North with emancipated slaves, placing them "side by side in competition with white men." The interest of northern workers therefore required the preservation of southern slavery within the Union. The most articulate spokesman for this view was Stephen Douglas.

Southern Democrats argued that white men who worked hard to get ahead had earned the right to accumulate slaves. Slavery, in this view, was the reward for free labor. The southern labor system provided a poor white man with the opportunity to rise up the social ladder by acquiring slaves "as soon as his savings will admit." Thus, southern Democrats claimed, slavery solved the labor problem by preserving the independence of free whites.

By contrast, Republicans insisted that slavery degraded all labor, black and white, and that the expansion of slavery threatened the economic well-being of free labor in the North. Slavery destroyed the work ethic by depriving slaves of any incentive to get ahead. Among the masters, slavery allegedly bred a haughty disdain for hard work and self-discipline. And by stifling the economic progress of the South, slavery denied poor whites opportunities for advancement. Hobbled by an inefficient work force and an aristocratic ruling class, the South was said to be doomed to economic backwardness. In contrast, Republicans depicted the North as a society in which labor was free and hard work was rewarded. The Protestant virtues of thrift, sobriety, and diligence were cultivated, opportunities for upward mobility were abundant, and progress was manifest.

The fact that the southern economy was booming presented a theoretical problem for Republicans. To explain slavery's strength they asserted the existence of an increasingly aggressive slave power that had taken control of the federal government and used its position to keep a backward system alive. To compensate for slavery's intrinsic weaknesses the slave power grew ever more arrogant, and it was prepared to undermine the freedom of northern whites to perpetuate slavery.

The slave power theory captured the imagination of a growing number of northern voters. It allowed whites to feel threatened by slavery without having to sympathize with the plight of the slaves. The greater evil was not the oppression of the slave but the power of the slaveholder. "With the negroes I have nothing to do," one Massachusetts Republican explained, "but with their masters I propose to try conclusions as to our respective political rights."

The Republicans did not succeed in the short run. Buchanan won five northern states and all but one of the slave states, winning 45 percent of the popular vote and 174 electoral votes. Frémont swept the upper North and Ohio, winning 114 electoral votes. No one was surprised that Frémont lost; what startled observers was that he did so well. All the Republicans needed to win four years later was Pennsylvania and either Illinois or Indiana. Never before had a clearly sectional party made so strong a showing in a presidential election. The slavery issue would not disappear until slavery itself did.

AN "IRREPRESSIBLE" CONFLICT?

In 1857 Democrat James Buchanan was inaugurated as president. His efforts to silence the slavery issue proved a disastrous failure. By the end of 1858 the most prominent Republican politician in America, William Seward, had declared that the sectional conflict between North and South was "irrepressible." When Buchanan left office in 1861 his party was in disarray, a Republican had been elected his successor, and the Union had collapsed.

The Slavery Issue Persists

Within days of Buchanan's inauguration, the Supreme Court, dominated by southern Democrats, issued one of the most controversial decisions in American history. The case stretched all the way back to 1833, when John Emerson, an Army surgeon from Missouri, was assigned to duty at Fort Armstrong, Illinois, and took a slave named Dred Scott with him. Emerson spent two years in Illinois and two more years at Fort Snelling in Wisconsin Territory (now Minnesota). Slavery was illegal in Illinois and Wisconsin Territory. In 1846, after Scott had been brought back to Missouri, he sued his owners, claiming that several years of residence on free soil made him legally free. Having lost his suit in 1854, Scott appealed to the U.S. Supreme Court. By then two questions stood out: First, was Dred Scott a citizen, such that his suit had standing in a court of law? Second, did the laws of the free state of Illinois or the free territory of Wisconsin prevail over the master's property right?

The justices could have issued a narrow ruling that merely upheld the lower court's decision against Scott. But instead the majority decided, with some inappropriate coaxing from President-Elect Buchanan, to render a sweeping decision covering some of the most explosive issues of the day.

It was not the majority decision against Scott that created the uproar. The problem was Chief Justice Taney's provocative and highly partisan opinion. Taney argued, first, that Dred Scott was not a citizen because he was black. Since before the republic had been founded, the Chief Justice reasoned, African Americans had "been regarded as beings of an inferior order . . . so far inferior that they had no rights which the white man was bound to respect." If this was true in 1776, Taney reasoned, it was true in 1857. The problem is that it was clearly not true in 1857 or in 1776: Free blacks were discriminated against throughout America, but nowhere were they denied all the rights of citizenship. They held property, entered into contracts, brought suits in court, and exercised the rights of speech, press, and assembly.

Second, Taney argued that Dred Scott's residence in Wisconsin Territory did not make him a free man, because the Missouri Compromise, by which Congress excluded slavery from the territory, was unconstitutional. This ruling gave legal sanction to the most extreme prosouthern position. In effect, Taney declared, Congress had no power to regulate slavery in the territories. Finally, Taney declared that two years' residence in Illinois constituted only a temporary "sojourn" and did not, therefore, invalidate a master's right to travel with his slave property in a free state. But if a master could hold a slave in a free state for two years, abolitionists asked, why not five, 10, or 20 years? By defining slave ownership as a constitutional right, Taney's decision threatened to restrict even the power of states to abolish slavery within their borders.

Republicans were infuriated by the decision, but they were put in an awkward position. If they questioned the legitimacy of a Supreme Court decision, they skirted dangerously close to Calhoun's old argument for the right of the states to nullify federal law. But the Dred Scott decision also hurt the Democrats because Taney's decision implicitly undermined the doctrine of popular sovereignty, the position advocated by most northern Democrats. Thus while Republicans fumed, Democrats in the North were left scrambling to salvage what they could from the Dred Scott decision.

The Lecompton Constitution Splits the Democratic Party

The cause of the final Democratic rupture was, once again, Kansas. In 1858 Congress had to choose between two different constitutions accompanying the territory's petition for admission to the Union. The so-called Lecompton Constitution was drawn up by proslavery partisans, who represented a minority of Kansas residents. Free-staters, knowing they were in the majority, submitted their own constitution to a popular referendum, whereas supporters of the Lecompton Constitution sent their document directly to Congress. President Buchanan supported the proslavery minority. But the leading Democrat in the Senate, Stephen Douglas, had no choice but to reject the Lecompton Constitution, because it clearly violated his principle of popular sovereignty.

Douglas was in a difficult position. Southern Democrats assailed popular sovereignty as an antislavery ruse. Northern critics pointed out that the Dred Scott decision had rendered popular sovereignty meaningless. But Douglas stood his ground: He insisted that if the people of a territory refused to pass the laws necessary to protect slavery, no master would dare go there with his human property. Douglas's logic infuriated southern Democrats, who demanded a federal slave code enforcing the rights of slave ownership in all the territories. Once again Douglas had no choice but to oppose them, aware that in doing so the Democratic Party would split irrevocably along sectional lines.

Lincoln and Douglas Debate

Campaigning for re-election to the Senate in 1858, Douglas was forced to state his position in a series of extraordinary debates with a little-known Republican adversary named Abraham Lincoln. Even at the time, observers recognized the significance of these seven debates, which spelled out clearly, and at times brilliantly, the fundamental differences between Democrats and Republicans on the issue of slavery.

Lincoln's argument was a familiar one in antislavery circles. The Founding Fathers recognized that slavery was inconsistent with the principles of the Declaration of Independence, Lincoln argued. They provided for the nation's withdrawal from the Atlantic slave trade, abolished slavery in every northern state, and restricted the expansion of slavery into western territories. In short, Lincoln argued, the Founders had put slavery on the "course of ultimate extinction." But now, the Democrats had repudiated the Founders' intentions. They invented a constitutional right to slave ownership that the Founders had never dreamed of. A Democratic Supreme Court had declared that a majority of voters in any territory could not prohibit the importation of slaves. By these means, Lincoln charged, the Democratic Party had repudiated the intentions of those who brought the nation into existence.

This situation could not continue much longer, Lincoln concluded. In a controversial speech just prior to his debates with Douglas, Lincoln warned that "A house divided against itself cannot stand." The government could not continue to survive "half slave and half free." Lincoln could see only two alternatives. "Either the opponents of slavery will arrest the further spread of it, and place it . . . in the course of ultimate extinction; or its advocates will push it forward, till it shall become alike lawful in all the States, old as well as new—North as well as South."

Douglas dismissed Lincoln's "House Divided" speech as absurd. The Union had survived for generations "half slave and half free," and there was no reason it should not continue to do so. The Founders had recognized that slavery was a local institution, Douglas argued. By allowing each state to decide on slavery for itself, the Founders implicitly endorsed popular sovereignty.

Douglas's most consistent tactic was to confuse the question of slavery with the question of race relations. He claimed that there was little difference between northern discrimination against blacks and southern slavery. And he argued that by opposing slavery Lincoln was claiming that blacks and whites should be politically and socially equal.

Lincoln answered that his not wanting an African-American woman as his slave did not mean that he wanted her as his wife. "I am not, nor ever have been in favor of bringing about in any way the social and political equality of the white and black races," Lincoln protested. He was not in favor of granting blacks the right to vote, to sit on juries, to hold public office, or to intermarry with whites.

Although upsetting to modern ears, Lincoln's views on blacks were moderate for his time. Unlike Douglas, who took every opportunity to parade his virulent racism, Lincoln was uncomfortable with the subject. In later years he would invite leading blacks to the White House and support a limited suffrage for blacks. Even in 1858, in the face of Douglas's relentless race-baiting, Lincoln grew firmer in his insistence that blacks were fully entitled to the basic rights of life, liberty, and the pursuit of happiness. Here was the fundamental difference between Lincoln and Douglas in their famous debates. Douglas was openly indifferent to slavery and was prepared to see it expand wherever whites wanted it. Lincoln believed slavery was fundamentally wrong and should be put on a course of ultimate extinction.

Lincoln narrowly lost the 1858 Senate election, but his epic battle with the Little Giant (as Douglas was known) made him a leading spokesman for the Republican Party. Elsewhere in the North, the Republicans were victorious. The southern demand for a federal slave code had proved a disaster for northern Democrats. Their problems persisted even after the elections. Southern Democrats formed an obstructionist block in Congress, successfully thwarting the passage of several bills dear to the hearts of many northerners, including a homestead law designed to encourage the settlement of the West by small farmers and a bill to facilitate the construction of a transcontinental railway. As in the late 1840s, Congress was paralyzed by entrenched sectional animosities, and once again a Congressional stalemate transformed every vote into a test of sectional loyalty.

THE RETREAT FROM UNION

Between 1858 and 1860 both the North and the South rejected the sanctity of the Union. In the South the retreat from unionism was a reaction to John Brown's raid on Harpers Ferry. Brown's death was greeted as a martyr's execution throughout much of the North, leading many southerners to conclude that a union of the North and the South was no longer viable. In 1860, with the election of Abraham Lincoln, the North abandoned a long-standing pattern of compromising with slavery for the sake of maintaining the Union.

John Brown's War Against Slavery

In the fall of 1858 the mysterious John Brown re-emerged to launch another battle in his private war against slavery. Since the massacre at Pottawatomie Creek, Brown's movements had been obscure. He traveled between Canada and Kansas, New England, and Ohio. By the late 1850s he had concocted a plan to invade Virginia and free the slaves. Friends told Brown his plan was unworkable; Frederick Douglass advised him to give it up. But Brown found support from a group of well-connected Bostonians who were dazzled by his appeal to action rather than words. While they promised more money than they delivered, they delivered enough.

Brown rented a farm in Maryland, about five miles from the town of Harpers Ferry in Virginia, where a small federal arsenal was located. He apparently planned to capture the arsenal and distribute the guns to slaves from the surrounding area, inciting a slave rebellion. On the evening of October 16, 1859, Brown and 18 followers crossed the Potomac River with a wagonload of guns, cut the telegraph wires leading into Harpers Ferry, overwhelmed a guard, and seized the armory. Brown ordered his men to scour the surrounding countryside to liberate slaves and take slaveholders prisoner. They found Colonel Lewis Washington, a member of the first president's family, and carried him back to Harpers Ferry as a hostage. Brown's mission was accomplished. He sat back and waited for the slaves to rise.

The slaves did not rise, but the armed forces did. Marines were sent from Washington, DC, led by Lieutenant Colonel Robert E. Lee and his assistant, Lieutenant J. E. B. Stuart, both of whom would become leading Confederate generals. On the morning after Brown took control of Harpers Ferry, the militia surrounded the arsenal. The next day Stuart ordered Brown to surrender, and when Brown refused, 12 Marines charged the room with bayonets. Two of Brown's men and one Marine were killed, and Brown himself was wounded. The rebellion was over in less than two days.

The entire raid was "absurd," Abraham Lincoln later said. "It was not a slave insurrection," he added. "It was an attempt by white men to get up a revolt among slaves, in which the slaves refused to participate." The condemnation of Brown by responsible northerners and the embarrassment of Brown's supporters initially calmed southern outrage over the invasion. Over the next several weeks, however, northern opinion changed from contempt to admiration for Brown. It was not the raid itself that caused this shift of opinion. It was Brown's calm and dignified behavior in prison, at his trial,

Artist John Curry's painting of John Brown brilliantly captures Brown's larger-than-life personality. The biblical imagery is reminiscent of Moses and suggests Brown's charismatic capacity to attract followers.

and at his own hanging. Brown's eloquent statements to the court and on the gallows moved northerners in vast numbers to extraordinary demonstrations of sympathy. On December 2, the day Brown was hanged, northern churches tolled their bells. Militia companies fired salutes. Public buildings across the North were draped in black. Although mainstream politicians disavowed Brown and his raid, white southerners saw that John Brown had become a hero among northerners.

Northern sympathy for John Brown shocked the white South even more than the actual raid. Across the South, newspapers and politicians responded to Harpers Ferry by questioning the value of the Union itself. The *Baltimore Sun* announced that the South could not "live under a government, the majority of whose subjects or citizens regard John Brown as a martyr and a Christian hero, rather than a murderer and robber."

At a critical moment in the nation's history, Brown's trial and execution galvanized northern public opinion against slavery and southern opinion against the Union. His spirit hovered over the 1860 presidential election, long after his body was laid to rest at an abolitionist community in upstate New York.

Northerners Elect a President

In the space of a decade the entire party structure of American politics had undergone a revolution. In 1860, no major party candidate could appeal to both the North and the South. For all practical purposes there were two different presidential elections that year. In the slave states a southern Democrat ran against a Constitutional Unionist. In the free states a northern Democrat ran against a Republican. On the surface slavery in the territories remained the dominant issue. Below the surface, the future of the Union was about to be determined.

The Democratic Party met in April in Charleston, South Carolina, the center of extreme secessionist sentiment. Southern fire-eaters demanded federal recognition of slavery in all the territories as part of the Democratic Party platform. But Stephen Douglas, the leading candidate for the party's nomination, insisted on a reaffirmation of popular sovereignty. Douglas had a bare majority of the delegates supporting him, enough to push his platform through but not enough to win the party's nomination. When Douglas's plank was passed, 49 delegates from eight southern states walked out. The convention was deadlocked. After 57 ballots, the Democrats adjourned, agreeing to reconvene in Baltimore a month and a half later.

But the delay only made matters worse. In Baltimore, 110 southerners nominated their own candidate. Thus the Democrats put up two presidential aspirants in 1860. Stephen Douglas ran in the North advocating popular sovereignty and insisting that the Union itself hung in the balance of the election. John Breckinridge, the southern Democratic candidate, ran on a platform calling for federal recognition of slavery in all the territories. Another candidate, John Bell of Tennessee, tried unsuccessfully to revive the Whig Party by running on a Constitutional Unionist ticket. Neither Douglas, Breckinridge, nor Bell had much chance of winning.

The Republicans were far more united. With the scent of victory in their nostrils, tens of thousands of Republicans poured into Chicago. The leading candidate for the Republican nomination was William H. Seward of New York. But Seward's strength was limited to the uppermost states in the North. In the border states such as Pennsylvania, Indiana, and Illinois, Seward's antislavery politics were seen as too radical. What the party needed was a candidate whose antislavery credentials were unquestioned, but whose moderation could carry the critical states of the lower

North. That candidate was Abraham Lincoln. Not only was Lincoln from Illinois, he was also a moderate. Unlike conservative Republicans, Lincoln did not race-bait very much, and he opposed nativist restrictions on immigration. Unlike the party's radicals, Lincoln had supported the enforcement of the Fugitive Slave Act, denounced John Brown's raid on Harpers Ferry, and insisted that the federal government not interfere in states where slavery already existed. Still, Lincoln made clear his view that slavery was immoral, that Congress had the right to restrict slavery's expansion into the territories, and that the entire slave system should be placed "in the course of ultimate extinction." No major party had ever run a candidate dedicated to such a proposition.

Throughout the campaign Lincoln and the Republicans scoffed at secessionist threats coming from the South. Breckinridge the Democrat and Bell the Constitutional Unionist also played down the possibility of disunion. But Stephen Douglas was so convinced that the election of Lincoln would result in secession and war that he actively campaigned as the only candidate who could hold the Union together. When it became clear that Lincoln was going to win, Douglas rearranged his campaign schedule to make a series of speeches in the slave states. He went South "not to ask for your votes for the Presidency," he told his audiences, "but to make an appeal to you on behalf of the Union."

Lincoln won every free state except New Jersey, where he took the majority of electoral votes. Douglas got the second largest number of votes but took only one

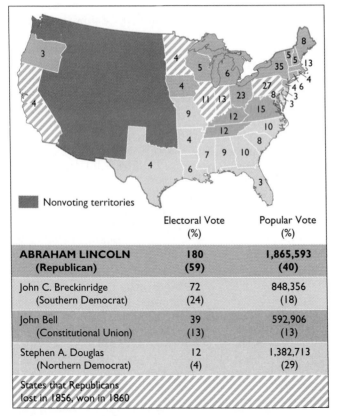

Map 14–3   The Election of 1860

By 1860, no presidential candidate could appeal to voters in both the North and the South. By then the northern population had grown so rapidly that a united North could elect Lincoln to the presidency without any southern support.

■ Nonvoting territories

	Electoral Vote (%)	Popular Vote (%)
ABRAHAM LINCOLN (Republican)	**180** **(59)**	**1,865,593** **(40)**
John C. Breckinridge (Southern Democrat)	72 (24)	848,356 (18)
John Bell (Constitutional Union)	39 (13)	592,906 (13)
Stephen A. Douglas (Northern Democrat)	12 (4)	1,382,713 (29)

States that Republicans lost in 1856, won in 1860

CHRONOLOGY

1838	Frederick Douglass escapes from slavery
1844	Samuel F. B. Morse invents the telegraph
1846	David Wilmot introduces his "proviso"
1847	Treaty of Guadalupe Hidalgo
1848	Zachary Taylor elected president
1850	Taylor dies; Millard Fillmore becomes president Compromise of 1850
1852	*Uncle Tom's Cabin* published in book form Franklin Pierce elected president
1854	Gadsden Purchase Ratified Kansas–Nebraska Act Ostend Manifesto
1856	"Bleeding Kansas" Sumner–Brooks affair James Buchanan elected president
1857	Dred Scott decision
1858	Lincoln–Douglas debates
1859	John Brown's raid on Harpers Ferry
1860	Abraham Lincoln elected first Republican president
1861	First transcontinental telegraph completed

state, Missouri. Breckinridge, the southern Democrat, took 11 slave states, although his support within those states was concentrated in the districts with the lowest proportions of slaves. The slaveholders continued to vote their traditional Whig sympathies, supporting John Bell's Constitutional Unionist candidacy.

Lincoln did not campaign in the South. His name was not even on the ballot in most of the slave states. Nevertheless, he was able to win by appealing exclusively to voters in the North (see Map 14–3). This in turn allowed Lincoln to run on a platform dedicated to bringing slavery to an end. Here was a double vindication for antislavery forces in the North: Not only did the Republican victory show wide appeal for an antislavery platform, it also suggested that a dynamic political economy based on free labor was bound to grow faster than a slave society. In their own way, white southerners agreed. They concluded that no matter what assurances Lincoln gave them, the future of slavery in the Union was doomed.

CONCLUSION

Frederick Douglass personally hoped that Abraham Lincoln would win the election. "Slavery is the issue—the single bone of contention between all parties and sections," he insisted. The political economies of slavery and freedom had guided the nation onto two different historical pathways. The North was developing an urban, industrial economy based on the productive energy of wage labor. In the South, a prosperous slave economy fastened in place an agricultural way of life and an older social order. The political tensions that arose from these differences finally pushed the nation into civil war. And as the war progressed, the same differences in political economy would shape the destiny of the Union and Confederate forces.

FURTHER READINGS

Tyler Anbinder, *Nativism and Slavery: The Northern Know-Nothings and the Politics of the 1850s* (1992). Anbinder demonstrates the close ties between opposition to immigration and opposition to slavery in the North.

Don E. Fehrenbacher, *The Dred Scott Case: Its Significance in American Law and Politics* (1978). This is a lucid, exhaustive account. There is an abbreviated paperback edition titled *Slavery, Law, and Politics*.

Eric Foner, *Free Soil, Free Labor, Free Men: The Ideology of the Republican Party Before the Civil War* (1970). The standard interpretation emphasizing the centrality of the labor issue and the fundamental conflict over slavery.

William W. Freehling, *The Road to Disunion: Secessionists at Bay, 1776–1854* (1990). The best treatment of the southern road to secession.

William E. Gienapp, *The Origins of the Republican Party, 1852–1856* (1987). This book is the definitive study, encompassing local as well as national issues.

Michael Holt, *The Political Crisis of the 1850s* (1978). The most astute alternative to Foner. Holt stresses the way politicians made calculated use of the slavery issue, but he doubts that the issue itself was fundamental.

Bruce Levine, *Half Slave, Half Free: The Roots of the Civil War* (1992). A good brief overview emphasizing social differences between the North and the South.

William McFeely, *Frederick Douglass* (1991). McFeely's book is the best biography of the most important black abolitionist.

Stephen B. Oates, *To Purge This Land With Blood: A Biography of John Brown* (1970). This is an outstanding account of the life of a highly controversial figure.

David Potter, *The Impending Crisis, 1848–1861* (1976). A masterpiece; perhaps the most profound one-volume examination of the political crisis of the 1850s.

 Please refer to the document CD-ROM for primary sources related to this chapter.

CHAPTER

15

A War for Union and Emancipation

1861–1865

Edmund Ruffin • From Union to Emancipation • Mobilizing for War • The Civil War Becomes a Social Revolution • The War at Home • The War Comes to a Bloody End • Conclusion

EDMUND RUFFIN

*E*dmund Ruffin was born in 1794 into one of the wealthiest planter families in eastern Virginia, by the age of 20 Ruffin was the master of a substantial plantation on the James River. Yet from his youth Edmund Ruffin was discontented and angry. He coveted a political career but his contempt for democracy thwarted him. In 1823 he won election to a four-year term in the Virginia state senate, but he was unwilling to forge the alliances and make the compromises that would bring him political influence. Before his term expired, Ruffin resigned his seat, "tired and disgusted with being a servant of the people." He never held public office again.

During the 1830s and 1840s Ruffin retreated to his plantations, publishing the results of his experiments in crop rotation, drainage techniques, and various new fertilizers. His work paid off in improved productivity, higher profits, and growing public esteem. But Ruffin, more interested in politics than farming, used his fame as an agricultural reformer to spread his proslavery message. By 1850 Ruffin was urging his fellow Virginians to secede from the Union to preserve slavery.

Ruffin made his leap from agricultural reformer to secessionist through the logic of political economy. A more productive slave economy, he reasoned, would protect the South from the growing power of the industrializing North. As Ruffin read the writings of other proslavery authors, he ended up placing all the world's peoples on a sliding scale that rose from the most savage to the most civilized. Savages, Ruffin asserted, were concerned only with meeting their bare physical needs. By contrast, civilized peoples sought to raise the standard of living by cultivating the mind as well as the body. The only way for barbaric peoples to rise above savagery, Ruffin claimed, was for the powerful and industrious to force shiftless and lazy people to work, usually by enslaving them. Slavery thus spurred both civilization and prosperity.

But Ruffin's general defense of slavery left several important questions unanswered: Who, for example, should be enslaved? Equals could not enslave equals, for that was both morally objectionable and socially disruptive. Southern slavery escaped this problem, Ruffin believed, because whites only enslaved racially inferior blacks. And what of the abolitionist claim that slavery was less efficient than wage labor? Ruffin agreed that in principle slaves lacked the motive of self-interest that made wage laborers more efficient, but he pointed to the exceptional conditions that tipped the balance in the United States. As long as western lands were available to absorb the surplus labor of the North, free laborers would work on their own farms at their own pace. But slaves were compelled to labor on precious cash crops that could be produced in climates where, Ruffin believed, only African Americans could work. As long as these exceptional conditions prevailed, slavery would be as efficient as free labor.

Over time the West was sure to fill up, and when that happened, Ruffin argued, free men and women would have no choice but to sell their labor at miserably low wages. Eventually the cost of free labor would sink so low that it could outperform slavery, but at that point, the misery of free laborers would give rise to socialism and anarchy. Thus northerners would pay the price of perpetual social unrest for their wealth and prosperity. Southern whites, by contrast, had struck the perfect balance between material well-being and social peace. By enslaving an "inferior" race, they could raise the general level of civilization without the disruptions associated with wage labor.

Edmund Ruffin had always believed that slavery was the issue dividing the North from the South. Ironically, as the two sections approached war, it was the northerners who clung to the belief that the Union could be held together with slavery intact. Most northerners started out thinking that the war could be fought only to restore the Union. Over time, they came to see it as a struggle to rid the nation of slavery as well. Edmund Ruffin was not surprised that the northern crusade to preserve the Union eventually became a crusade for the abolition of slavery.

FROM UNION TO EMANCIPATION

Southerners made it clear that they were going to war to preserve the political economy of slavery. In 1861 Confederate President Jefferson Davis justified secession on the grounds that northern Republican rule would make "property in slaves so insecure as to be comparatively worthless." Southerners talked in general about defending "states' rights" or "property rights," but they were referring specifically to the right of the states to maintain slavery and the right of individuals to hold property in slaves.

Northerners made it equally clear that they were not going to war to destroy slavery. Many northerners thought slavery was wrong, and many more believed that a slave power had caused the war, but few cared enough about the plight of African Americans to support a war to secure their freedom. In his 1858 debates with Stephen Douglas, Abraham Lincoln had insisted that the Republican Party had no intention of interfering with slavery where it already existed. In his inaugural address of March 1861, Lincoln reasserted this promise. He claimed to be fighting for nothing more than the restoration of the Union. Within the next few years, under the pressures of war, Lincoln's position would change dramatically.

The South Secedes

As the news of Lincoln's presidential election flashed across the telegraph wires, the South Carolina state legislature called a secession convention. On December 20, 1860, the state withdrew from the Union on the grounds that northerners had denied their "rights of property" in slaves. "They have encouraged and assisted thousands of slaves to leave their homes," South Carolina declared, "and those who remain have been incited . . . to servile insurrection." Within weeks Mississippi, Florida, Alabama, Georgia, Louisiana, and Texas followed suit (see Map 15–1). Then the secession movement came to a halt. The slave states of the upper South refused to leave the Union simply because Lincoln was elected. Ardent secessionists began to suspect that the South was not unified in its opposition to the North.

When Lincoln took office in early March 1861, the upper South was dominated by cooperationists rather than secessionists. Cooperationists were committed to remaining in the Union, provided the Lincoln administration "cooperated" with southern demands. Thus even after Lincoln's inauguration Virginia, Arkansas, and Missouri would not secede. The state legislatures of Kentucky and Delaware refused to convene secession conventions, and in Tennessee and North Carolina the voters refused. Lincoln and many Republicans hoped that if they moved cautiously they could keep the upper South in the Union and thereby derail the secession movement. But cooperationism in the upper South turned out to be a weak foundation on which to rebuild the Union. Cooperationists pledged their loyalty to the Union only if the federal government met certain demands for the protection of slavery.

Cooperationist demands formed the basis of several last-minute attempts at sectional compromise. The most famous was a series of constitutional amendments proposed by Senator John J. Crittenden of Kentucky. The Crittenden Compromise would have restored the Missouri Compromise line and guaranteed federal protection of slavery south of that line in all territories currently held or thereafter acquired by the United States. It would have virtually prohibited Congress from abolishing slavery in Washington, DC, and from regulating the interstate slave trade. Finally, it required the federal government to compensate masters who were unable to recover fugitive slaves from the North.

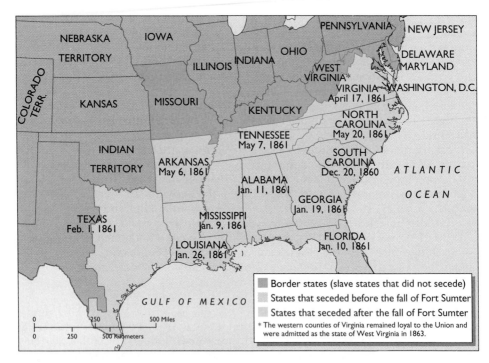

Map 15–1   The Secession of the Southern States

The South seceded in two stages. During the "secession winter" of 1860–1861, the lower South states seceded in reaction to the election of Abraham Lincoln. The following spring the upper South seceded in response to Lincoln's attempt to resupply Fort Sumter. The border slave states of Maryland, Delaware, Kentucky, and Missouri never left the Union.

Each of these concessions was unacceptable to the Republicans, especially the one protecting slavery in all territories acquired in the future. This struck Republicans as an open invitation for southerners to expand the slave power into Central America, South America, and the Caribbean. In any case, once the lower South seceded, the sanctity of the Union replaced the expansion of slavery as the chief concern of most northerners. By early 1861 northern Democrats who cared little about slavery were nevertheless unwilling to compromise with southern states that had left the Union. For this reason the Crittenden proposals fell on deaf ears throughout the North.

Furthermore, by the spring of 1861 most southerners agreed with Edmund Ruffin that there should be no more compromise with the North. Out of respect for his long years of service to the cause, southern fire-eaters invited Ruffin to South Carolina where he was given the privilege of firing one of the first shots of the Civil War. At 4:30 in the morning on April 12, 1861, Ruffin aimed a rifle at Fort Sumter and began shooting. For 33 hours Confederates bombarded the fort, located on an island in Charleston harbor, to prevent the U.S. government from fortifying its troops with nonmilitary supplies. With no alternative, the Union commander raised the white flag of surrender. Fort Sumter fell to the Confederates, and the Civil War began.

Lincoln probably understood that his attempt to resupply Fort Sumter would provoke an armed assault. By announcing that he would send no weapons on the resupply mission to Fort Sumter, Lincoln had skillfully maneuvered the South into firing the first shot. The next day he issued a call to the states for 75,000 militiamen to report for duty within 90 days. The governors of Tennessee, Virginia, North Carolina, Arkansas, Kentucky, and Missouri refused to comply with Lincoln's request. Two days later Virginia seceded, and within a month Arkansas, Tennessee, and North Carolina did the same. Northern hopes of holding on to the upper South had vanished.

But the South remained divided. Four slave states (Kentucky, Maryland, Delaware, and Missouri) never joined the Confederacy. In the mountains of western North Carolina and eastern Tennessee, Unionist sentiment remained strong throughout the war years. Virginia was literally torn apart: The western third of the state voted overwhelmingly against secession; when the eastern slaveholders decided to leave the Union, western counties formed their own state government. (In 1863 the state of West Virginia was admitted to the Union.) These were among the earliest indications that southern whites were not united. Where slavery was weak, support for secession was weak also. Where slavery thrived, so did the sentiment for secession. Yet despite these internal divisions, white southerners put up a long, hard fight to sustain the independence of the Confederacy.

Civilians Demand a Total War

Most Americans expected the war to last only a few months. Lincoln's first call for troops asked volunteers to enlist for 90 days. Confederate soldiers initially enlisted for 12 months. A year later Union troops were signing up for three years, and Confederates were required to serve "for the duration" of the war. Although both sides began with relatively limited military and political goals, the conflict steadily descended into a "hard" war, one that could end only in unconditional surrender, demolition of the enemy's army, and destruction of the enemy's capacity to fight. This in turn meant bringing the war to civilians. In the end it would mean the destruction of slavery.

In the weeks following the Fort Sumter crisis enthusiasm for war overflowed in both the Union and the Confederacy. Mere military victory was not enough. In the spring of 1861 one southern woman prayed that "God may be with us to give us strength to conquer them, to exterminate them, to lay waste to every Northern city, town and village, to destroy them utterly." The following year southern troops burned the town of Chambersburg, Pennsylvania, to the ground, and in 1864 Jefferson Davis sent Confederate agents to New York City, where they set fire to ten hotels, hoping to send the city up in flames.

Northerners felt no differently toward southerners. Even before the fighting began, in December 1860, Ohio Senator Benjamin Wade talked of "making the south a desert." In the wake of Fort Sumter, one northern judge argued that if the war persisted, the North should "restore New Orleans to its native marshes, then march across the country, burn Montgomery to ashes, and serve Charleston in the same way. . . . We must starve, drown, burn, shoot the traitors." The war had barely begun and the civilians in the North and the South were already pressuring their political leaders to get on with the destruction of the enemy.

The military was more hesitant. For several months both the Union and Confederate commanders concentrated on building up their armies. Neither side was prepared for battle and neither sought it. Under the direction of aged war hero General Winfield Scott, Union military strategy was initially designed to take advantage of the North's naval superiority by blockading the entire South. Confederate strategists hoped to maintain a defensive posture. The North would have to attack, but the South needed only to hold its ground.

As spring became summer, however, civilians in both the North and the South demanded something more dramatic. "Forward to Richmond!" cried Horace Greeley, echoing northern sentiment for a swift capture of the new Confederate capital.

Slaves Take Advantage of the War

In the South the enthusiasm for battle was compounded by fantasies of a race war between African Americans and whites. The lower South seceded while still in the grip of the insurrection panics that followed John Brown's raid on Harpers Ferry. Few slaves actually joined with Brown, but that did little to calm the fears of southern whites. Such fears were usually exaggerated. In 1861 this was no longer the case.

Shortly after Lincoln was inaugurated, several slaves in Florida escaped to Fort Pickens, claiming their freedom. In Virginia, scarcely a month after Fort Sumter, Union commander Benjamin F. Butler refused to return three runaway slaves on the grounds that they would have been put to work on Confederate military fortifications. Butler called the runaways "contrabands" of war, and the label stuck. As the number of contrabands mounted, Butler demanded that his superiors clarify Union policy. "As a military question it would seem to be a measure of necessity to deprive their masters of their services," he wrote on May 27, 1861. A week later, Secretary of War Simon Cameron approved Butler's policy of refusing to return contraband slaves to their masters.

These were not random actions on the part of a tiny handful of slaves. As soon as the war began, slaves made strenuous efforts to collect war news. House servants listened in on conversations at the masters' residences and reported the news to field hands in the slave quarters. Every neighborhood had one or two literate slaves who got hold of a newspaper. News of the war's progress spread along what the slaves called the "grapevine telegraph."

Northern officials were forced to take official notice of the slaves' disruptive behavior, and Butler's contraband policy was the first tangible result. Nevertheless, the Republicans were still pledged to leave slavery undisturbed. In July 1861 Congress passed a resolution reaffirming that the war was aimed at nothing more than the restoration of the Union. Even radical Republicans held their tongues, despite their growing conviction that the war could not be prosecuted without an attack on slavery. After the first major battle of the war in the summer of 1861, the radicals broke their silence.

First Bull Run and the Shift in War Aims

On July 21, inadequately trained Union and Confederate forces fought by a creek called Bull Run at the town of Manassas Junction, Virginia, 25 miles from Washington. Everyone knew the battle was coming. Spectators with picnic baskets followed the Union Army out of Washington to watch from the surrounding hillsides. Among the southerners who came to watch was Edmund Ruffin.

The Confederates took up a defensive line stretching eight miles along Bull Run and waited for the enemy to attack. Union troops had failed to keep Confederate reinforcements bottled up in the Shenandoah Valley. A flanking maneuver by Union commander Irvin McDowell nearly succeeded in dislodging the Confederate forces, but southern officer Thomas J. Jackson, perched on his horse "like a stone wall," inspired his men to drive back the Union advance. (It would not be the last time "Stonewall" Jackson would give the Union Army grief.) The green Union troops, unaccustomed to the confusion of the battlefield, turned back in retreat. As they headed east toward Washington, frightened spectators clogged the road in panic and the retreat turned into a rout.

Most southerners were ecstatic, and perhaps somewhat overconfident, as a result of their victory. By contrast, the chaos in the Union ranks shocked the North into the realization that this would be no 90-day war. To discipline the Union troops, Lincoln put George B. McClellan in command of the Army of the Potomac. The defeat also prompted northerners to rethink their war aims. Radicals broke their silence and began arguing that emancipation was a "military necessity." Signaling this shift, the Republican-dominated Congress passed a Confiscation Act within weeks of the battle of Bull Run. For the first time, the federal government committed itself to confiscating any property, including slaves, used to prosecute the war against the United States. Benjamin Butler's contraband policy now had the status of law.

Senator Crittenden denounced the Confiscation Act as "revolutionary," but Lincoln signed it anyway. Some northern military commanders began enforcing the law somewhat liberally. By the fall of 1861 the Union Army was relying on the labor of fugitive slaves to support the northern military effort, thus stretching the definition of "military necessity." By the end of 1861 the nature of the Civil War was already changing.

Also prodding the shift in war aims was the North's determination to keep England and France from recognizing the Confederate government. The Confederacy hoped to keep Europeans from respecting the Union blockade of southern ports. A diplomatic crisis loomed in late 1861 when a Union Navy captain intercepted a British ship, the *Trent*, in Havana. He forced two Confederate commissioners to disembark before allowing the *Trent* to sail on. The commissioners had slipped through the Union blockade and were headed for Europe, hoping to secure diplomatic recognition of the Confederacy. When the British protested, the Lincoln administration wisely backed down and released them. "One war at a time," Lincoln said.

MOBILIZING FOR WAR

By the end of the first summer, both sides realized that the conflict would last for more than a few months and would demand all the resources the North and South could command. But, in 1860, neither side had many military resources to command. When Lincoln was elected president, the U.S. Army had 16,000 men. By the end of the war approximately 2.1 million men had served in the Union armed forces. Another 900,000 served the Confederacy. To raise and sustain such numbers was an immense political and social problem. To feed, clothe, and arm such numbers of fighters was an equally immense technological problem. To pay for such armed forces was an immense economic problem. As the Civil War progressed, it therefore became a test of the competing political economies of the North and the South (see Figure 15–1).

Southern Political Weaknesses

By the spring of 1861 the secessionists had persuaded 11 states to leave the Union. They had convened a constitutional convention in Montgomery, Alabama, and drafted a basic charter for their new government, the Confederate States of America. They had proclaimed Richmond, Virginia, their nation's capital, and they had selected as president an experienced politician and Mississippi planter, Jefferson Davis.

The Confederate constitution varied in only minor ways from the U.S. Constitution. True to the South's Jacksonian tradition, the Confederacy banned protective tariffs and Congressional appropriations for internal improvements. The

Figure 15–1   The Productive Capacities of the Union and Confederacy

Confederate president served a single, six-year term and had a line-item veto. The Confederate constitution explicitly protected slavery, whereas the U.S. Constitution did so implicitly.

But these minor constitutional differences masked larger political differences that eventually favored the northern war effort. The most important was the absence of a two-party system in the South. The Whig Party had collapsed in the North during the early 1850s, and the Republican Party took its place. Throughout the war, the northern Democrats represented a strong but loyal opposition to the Lincoln administration. In the South, by contrast, the Democratic Party ruled without opposition after the Whigs collapsed. As a result, internal dissent within the Confederacy had no legitimate institutional base. Furthermore, the white South's commitment to states' rights conflicted with the Confederacy's need to mount a concerted defense of the new nation. Political opposition therefore bred bitter personal feuds, often provoked by the competing wishes of state and national officials.

Union Naval Supremacy

From the outset northern strategists hoped to use their superior naval forces to prevent the Confederacy from selling its cotton abroad. Ironically, the Confederacy initially complied with northern strategy. Much of the industrial world depended on slave-produced cotton, and southern leaders sought to withhold cotton from the market, thus crippling northern industry while forcing England into diplomatic recognition of the Confederacy. This was the first test of the political economy of slavery.

By the closing months of 1861, the Union Navy controlled vast stretches of the Atlantic and Gulf coasts. By early 1862 Union forces were in a position to enforce their blockade, except for a magnificent new weapon designed to thwart Union naval supremacy. The South refitted an old Union ship, the *Merrimac*, with thick iron plates that rendered it all but impervious to conventional weapons. Rechristened the *Virginia*, the ironclad ship sailed into Union-controlled waters at Hampton Roads, Virginia, on March 8, 1862, and proceeded to wreak havoc on helpless northern ships. But that night the Union's ironclad, the *Monitor*, arrived from New York. For most of the following day the "battle of the ironclads" raged on, with neither vessel dominating. The *Virginia* slipped up the James River to assist in the defense of Richmond, but in May the Confederates destroyed the vessel rather than allow it to be captured by Union forces. A standoff between the *Monitor* and the *Virginia* left the Union Navy in control of the coast and better able to enforce its blockade.

Southern Military Advantages

On land, however, the southern military probably had an important edge. More southerners went to military academies than did northerners. In the early years of the war these graduates brought skill and discipline to the Confederate Army that the Union could not match. The South's greatest advantage, however, was that it was defending its own territory. It did not have to invade the North, destroy the Union Army, or wipe out the North's industrial capacity. Closer to their sources of supply, the southern armies operated in the midst of a friendly civilian population, except for the slaves.

By contrast, the North had to fight an offensive war. It had to invade the South, destroy the Confederate armies, capture and retain a huge Confederate territory, and wipe out the South's capacity to fight. Northern soldiers fought on unfamiliar ground surrounded by a hostile civilian population, not counting the slaves.

The Union required longer lines of supply and much larger supply provisions. An invading northern army of 100,000 men had to carry with it 2,500 wagons and 35,000 animals. It consumed 600 tons of supplies a day. The further it penetrated into southern territory, the more its ranks were thinned by the need to maintain increasingly tenuous supply lines. The more territory the Union troops conquered, the more they were shifted from battle duty to occupation forces. As a result, many major battles were fought by roughly even numbers of Union and Confederate troops.

Even in battle the defensive posture of the Confederate Army was an advantage. Forts and cities on high ground (like Vicksburg and Fredericksburg) could maintain themselves against large numbers of invading troops. In the Union invasion of northern Virginia in 1864, Confederate General Robert E. Lee repeatedly held off much larger Union forces.

The Political Economy of Slavery Inhibits the Confederacy

Secessionists argued that slavery gave the South several clear military assets. The industrial world's dependence on cotton, they believed, would soon cripple northern textile mills and bring diplomatic recognition from England. In addition, a very high proportion of white men were able to serve in the southern military because slaves stayed home and performed productive labor. This helped balance out the North's advantage in the number of military-age men.

In certain ways, the relative backwardness of the slave economy had military advantages. Because of slavery the South had remained a largely rural society. Southern men therefore knew how to shoot guns and how to ride and treat horses. Hence the Confederate cavalry during the first years of the war was far superior to that of the North. Over time this advantage disappeared, as the Union cavalry improved and the development of the rifle made traditional cavalry charges deadly. When the war started, many white southerners assumed that the average Confederate could easily whip two Yankees.

But the southerners assumed incorrectly. They overestimated England's dependence on American cotton and underestimated the strength of Britain's economic ties to the North. The English refused to break the Union blockade of the South or grant diplomatic recognition to the Confederacy. King Cotton diplomacy failed, as did the political economy of slavery. If slavery freed 60 percent of southern men for military service, it eliminated from military service the 40 percent of the population that was enslaved. Leaving slaves at home while white men went off to war only made it easier for thousands of southern blacks to run to Union lines.

Above all, slavery diminished the South's industrial strength. Ninety percent of the nation's factories were in the North. Furthermore, the bulk of the Confederacy's industrial capacity was located in the upper South, which was overrun by Union forces early in the war. The South's ability to arm and supply its military was therefore severely restricted. Nevertheless, the South did manage to find enough rifles. The Confederacy also did a remarkable job of producing gunpowder and ammunition. As a result, the Confederate soldier was generally well armed. But he was not well fed or well clothed. The South simply could not provide its Army with food enough to keep its soldiers adequately nourished. Confederates often fought in rags and barefoot.

Slavery also crippled the South's ability to finance its war. The cotton crop was systematically embargoed. Because slaves earned no money, they could not be tapped for income taxes as northern workers were. In any case white southerners remained true to the Jacksonian tradition of resistance to taxation. To finance its military campaign, the South began to print money in huge quantities. By 1865 a Confederate dollar had the purchasing power that one Confederate cent had in 1861.

In the North, prospering farms and growing factories generated substantial taxable income. In addition to the $600 million generated by taxes on incomes and personal property, the Union government eventually raised $1.5 billion from the sale of government bonds. The North also supplemented its tax revenues by printing money, the famous "greenbacks," which became legally acceptable as currency everywhere in the country. The Union government also floated war bonds. To ease the flow of so many dollars, the Republicans passed the National Bank Act in 1863. This law rationalized the monetary system, making the federal government what it remains today, the only printer of money and the arbiter of the rules governing the nation's banking structure.

What Were Soldiers Fighting For?

Political, military, and economic differences are the tangible reasons that armies win or lose wars, but there are also important psychological reasons. Southern soldiers fought from a variety of motives. Many were simply caught up in the initial outburst of enthusiasm. Most took for granted that they were fighting to keep African Americans enslaved, but because they took slavery for granted, southern soldiers emphasized other motives, especially patriotism.

Among southerners the "spirit of 1776" loomed large. In letters and diaries, Confederate soldiers declared that they were struggling to preserve the liberty that their forefathers had won from Great Britain. Confederate soldiers often warned that northern power was threatening southern freedom. Besides the patriotic struggle to preserve their liberty and independence, southern soldiers were motivated by the defense of their homes and families. The protection of southern womanhood was a particularly potent theme in the soldiers' letters. Because most of the fighting was done on southern soil, confederate troops were, quite literally, defending their homes against a northern invasion.

Nevertheless, class distinctions affected the levels of patriotism in the Confederate armed forces. Slaveholders and their sons were far more likely to express patriotic sentiments than were soldiers from yeoman families. Troops from states where slavery was relatively unimportant, such as North Carolina, were markedly less enthusiastic about the war than were troops from states like South Carolina, where slavery was strong.

Class divisions were less severe in the Union Army. Impoverished immigrants sometimes joined the military to secure a steady source of income and, in later years, a substantial bounty. But Catholic immigrants were less likely to fight than native-born Protestants. As with their southern counterparts, the most common motivation among northern soldiers was patriotism. They, too, thought of themselves as the proud protectors of America's revolutionary heritage, but where southern soldiers emphasized independence and the eternal struggle between liberty and tyranny, northern troops equated freedom with the preservation of the Union. The Union as a "beacon of liberty" throughout the world was a common theme in the letters and diaries of northern soldiers.

A few northern soldiers were motivated by antislavery principles, but many more were offended by the idea that they were risking their lives to free slaves. As the war aims changed, however, so did the sentiments expressed by Union soldiers. By the end of the conflict most had accepted that emancipation was a legitimate goal of the war.

THE CIVIL WAR BECOMES A SOCIAL REVOLUTION

By 1862 the North and the South had built up powerful military machines. At the same time, the North's war aims were shifting to include the abolition of slavery, which meant the destruction of the southern social system. In the summer of 1862 the Lincoln administration adopted the radical Republican position that emancipation was a military necessity. Within a year Lincoln himself would be pointing to the abolition of slavery to justify the increasingly bloody war. Throughout the South the moment of truth had arrived: Would the slaves remain loyal, as their masters had so often proclaimed, or would they seek their freedom by running to Union lines, as the Lincoln administration hoped? The answers to these questions depended on the fate of the two armies on the field of battle.

Union Victories in the West

In early February 1862, the Union Army and Navy joined in an aggressive strike deep into Confederate Tennessee. Led by Ulysses S. Grant, the Union Army captured Fort Henry on the Tennessee River and, shortly thereafter, Fort Donelson on the Cumberland River (see Map 15–2). To the shock of Confederate officers at Fort Donelson, Grant insisted on "unconditional and immediate surrender." The Tennessee campaign also showed some Union commanders that they could free up their armies by supplying them from the goods owned by local civilians.

The war's growing ferocity became clear eight weeks later, at the battle of Shiloh. Southern General P. G. T. Beauregard, the hero of Manassas, caught Grant's troops off guard at a peach orchard in southern Tennessee. The Confederate's surprise attack on April 6 forced the Union lines steadily backward, although the line did not break. By the end of the day Beauregard was telegraphing Richmond with news of his victory. But on the morning of April 7, Confederate troops were stunned by a counterattack from Union forces. Grant's troops pushed Beauregard's army back over the ground it had taken the day before. When the Confederates finally retreated from Shiloh, the two armies had suffered an astounding 23,741 casualties. The Civil War was quickly becoming a fight for the total destruction of the enemy's forces.

With Confederate forces busy at Shiloh, New Orleans had few defenses beyond two forts on the Mississippi River 75 miles south of the city. But they were impressive forts. It took six days of Yankee bombardment before Union commander David

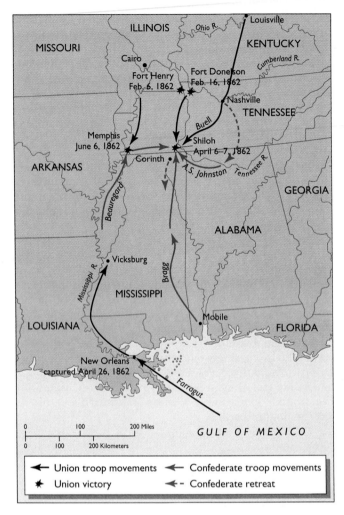

Map 15–2   The War in the West in 1862

As Union armies floundered in the East, northern troops in the West won a decisive series of battles. Here the nature of the war changed. First, General Ulysses S. Grant demanded "unconditional surrender" of the southern troops at Forts Henry and Donelson. Then a bloody battle at Shiloh foreshadowed the increasing brutality of the war. Finally, the western theater produced two of the Union's most effective generals, Grant and William Tecumseh Sherman.

Glasgow Farragut attempted to break through. In the middle of the night of April 24, Farragut forced his Union fleet upriver through a blaze of burning rafts and Confederate gunfire that lit up the sky. Within a few days the Confederates evacuated both forts, and New Orleans fell to Union forces.

Union victories in the West gave rise to northern optimism that war would be over by summer. Republicans took advantage of the mood to enact a bold legislative agenda. During the first half of 1862 Congress and President Lincoln virtually reorganized the structure of national government in the North. Early in the year Lincoln appointed the ruthlessly efficient Edwin M. Stanton as Secretary of War. Stanton built a powerful war-making bureaucracy. Congress was even more aggressive. For years Democratic majorities had blocked passage of laws that Republicans considered essential to their vision of the American political economy. Now the Republicans had the votes and the popular support to push their agenda through Congress.

They began with a critical financial reform. To sustain the integrity of the currency, the Republicans passed a Legal Tender Act protecting northern greenbacks from inflationary pressure. To maintain the manpower of the armed forces, the

Republicans instituted the first military draft in United States history. In addition, in 1862 they established a system of land-grant colleges designed to promote the scientific development of American agriculture and passed a Homestead Act that promised land to free settlers in the West. Finally, the Republicans financed the construction of the nation's first transcontinental railroad. Together these laws reflected the Republican Party's commitment to the active use of the central government to preserve the Union and promote capitalist development.

The Confederate government also moved to reform its bureaucracy to sustain its military struggle. Southern leaders realized that they had made a mistake by withholding the region's cotton from the world market. The Confederate economy was already showing signs of the weakness that would lead to its financial collapse. To remedy the situation, the Confederate Congress passed a comprehensive tax code that produced only disappointing revenues. In April 1862 the Confederacy established a national military draft. By centralizing taxation and conscription, however, Jefferson Davis's government at Richmond faced powerful resistance from advocates of states' rights, particularly in Georgia and North Carolina. Thus while military victories in the West allowed northern Republicans to enact an expansive legislative agenda, the Confederate government had trouble winning popular support for its own centralizing measures, despite the success of its troops turned against a massive northern offensive in Virginia.

Southern Military Strength in the East

The Peninsula Campaign of 1862 crushed the North's earlier optimism. The goal of the Union Army had been to capture the Confederate capital, Richmond, and that was what Lincoln expected George B. McClellan to do as commander of the Army of the Potomac. McClellan's great strength was his ability to administer and train a huge army. He instituted systematic drills and careful discipline and, after their defeat at Bull Run, successfully restored his soldiers' morale. Unfortunately, McClellan was reluctant to fight. He was forever exaggerating the size of his opponents' forces and demanding more troops before he would take the offensive. Throughout the fall and winter of 1861 and 1862, McClellan stubbornly resisted Lincoln's suggestions to attack. McClellan held all politicians in contempt, and none more than the president. He sent insulting dispatches to his superiors and wrote pompous letters to his wife declaring himself the savior of the republic.

Only under intense pressure, and not until his own reputation was at stake, did McClellan devise an elaborate strategy to capture Richmond. McClellan very slowly moved his huge army of 112,000 men up the peninsula between the York and James Rivers. Instead of directly attacking Richmond, however, McClellan dug in at Yorktown, thinking that he faced a more formidable enemy than he actually did. The Confederates quickly became skilled at manipulating McClellan's weaknesses. They moved small numbers of soldiers back and forth to make him think there were more enemy troops than there really were and planted fake cannons along their lines. Then, during the night of May 4, 1862, the outnumbered Confederates withdrew toward Richmond. When McClellan discovered their escape, he declared it a Union victory.

The Army of the Potomac inched its way up the peninsula toward Richmond, but it never took the offensive. Instead, Union troops were forced into battle by Confederates fighting under Robert E. Lee. Confederate General Joseph E. Johnston attacked the divided Union forces at Seven Pines on May 31, and both sides took heavy losses. Far more serious were the brutal battles of the Seven Days beginning in late June. Notwithstanding heavy Confederate losses, Lee repulsed McClellan's larger army, saving Richmond and sending the Army of the Potomac lumbering back to its fortifications around Washington, DC. There McClellan did what he did best: He revived his soldiers' sagging morale and whipped the Army of the Potomac back into fighting shape. But he still would not do the fighting. McClellan let Union General John Pope take the offensive alone, but Pope led his troops to a disastrous defeat at the Second Battle of Bull Run (August 29–30), while McClellan's huge army stood by.

By the fall of 1862, the Union and Confederate forces had reached a military stalemate. The North had scored tremendous victories in the West. In the East, however, Robert E. Lee turned out to be one of the most skillful and daring commanders of the war. Stonewall Jackson, Lee's "right arm," had likewise proven himself brilliantly aggressive.

With his victory at Second Bull Run, Lee launched his first invasion of the North. He hoped the Confederacy could win the war in the East before losing it in the West. Lee therefore marched his confident troops across the Potomac into Maryland. Before Lee reached Pennsylvania, however, Union forces discovered his plan. McClellan at last met Lee's army at Sharpsburg, Maryland, beside Antietam Creek, on September 17.

By launching his forces in three consecutive assaults rather than a single simultaneous maneuver, McClellan nearly lost Antietam. His tactics allowed the Confederates to shift their men around the battlefield whenever the fighting moved to a different location. By failing to deploy his reinforcements, McClellan missed a chance to break the center of the Confederate line. By delaying, McClellan gave Confederate reinforcements time to arrive on the scene and turn back an attack on Lee's right. Nevertheless, Lee's men suffered staggering casualties and were unable to maintain their invasion of the North. It might have been even worse for the South, but despite intense pressure from Washington, McClellan refused to pursue the disoriented southern army as it retreated across the Potomac. A total of 4,800 soldiers died and 18,000 more were wounded at Antietam, the single bloodiest day of the war. Nevertheless, Antietam was a Union victory, and Lincoln took advantage of it to announce an important shift in northern war aims.

Emancipation as a Military Necessity

By the summer of 1862, Lincoln, searching for a dramatic gesture that would break the military stalemate and convince European powers to side with the Union, decided to issue the Emancipation Proclamation. Northern public opinion was shifting in favor of such a move. Union military advances in the plantation South in early 1862 had produced a flood of runaway slaves pouring across northern lines. As slaves took advantage of the opportunity to escape from their masters, Union commanders responded in a variety of ways. Some put the contrabands to work behind Union lines. Others sent the runaways back into slavery, to the horror of African Americans and the dismay of northern radicals. To clarify the situation, in March 1862 Congress prohibited the use of Union troops to return fugitives to the South.

In April Congress moved further by abolishing slavery in Washington, DC. For the first time, the federal government exercised the power to emancipate slaves. Swept along by the surging tide, General David Hunter, commander of Union forces in low-country South Carolina and Georgia, abolished slavery in the entire area. Lincoln revoked the order because he did not think Hunter had the legal authority to issue it. But Lincoln himself was moving quickly in the direction of emancipation, and Congress was moving even faster. In June 1862 Congress prohibited slavery in the western territories. The following month a second Confiscation Act was passed, this one declaring "forever free" the slaves of any "traitors" engaged in rebellion against the United States. Congress also passed a militia act making it possible for "persons of African descent" to join the Union Army.

By mid-July 1862, Lincoln had decided to issue an Emancipation Proclamation and announced his intentions to his cabinet. For Lincoln, emancipation had become an inescapable reality, and even conservative Republicans had come to support it. Like the radicals who had first made the argument, Lincoln justified his move as a "military necessity." In fact "military necessity" was Lincoln's pretext more than his motive for proclaiming emancipation. On the advice of his cabinet, however, the president waited for a battlefield victory to make his proclamation public.

Antietam provided Lincoln with that victory. On September 22, five days after Lee was turned back, Lincoln vowed to declare "free" all slaves held in areas still in rebellion against the Union on January 1, 1863. One month before the proclamation took effect, Lincoln proposed a plan of gradual emancipation in all areas under Union control. When the new year arrived, Lincoln's final proclamation also sanctioned the enlistment of African Americans in the Union Army. Critics sniffed that the proclamation did not free a single slave, because it emancipated only those in areas controlled by Confederates. In fact, the proclamation transformed Union soldiers into an army of liberation and was an open invitation for slaves to run away to Union lines, disrupting the Confederacy still further.

In the North the proclamation provoked intense criticism from the increasingly vocal peace wing of the Democratic Party. Many northern whites were enraged by the idea that the war was being fought to free the slaves, and many northern soldiers were embittered by the Emancipation Proclamation. "I came out to fight for the restoration of the Union . . . ," one northern soldier wrote, "not to free the niggers." But most Union troops had reached the conclusion that for the war to end the South had to be destroyed, and that meant the destruction of slavery.

The Moment of Truth

The effectiveness of the Emancipation Proclamation depended on the willingness of slaves to take matters into their own hands. "How do we get the slaves to run away?" the president asked Frederick Douglass. But slaves across the South had long been running to their freedom. Now, with emancipation as a war aim, slaves pushed still further beyond the limits of official policy. In low-country South Carolina and New Orleans, slaves celebrated their freedom on January 1, 1863, even though those areas were under Union occupation and were therefore technically unaffected by the proclamation.

On plantations across the South this was the moment of truth: Would the slaves prove as faithful as their masters hoped, or as faithless as many masters feared? As the war progressed, more and more openings for the slaves to act were created. In many cases the master and his sons were away in the army. Edmund Ruffin frequently left his plantation to aid the Confederate defense of Virginia. He returned from one such expedition in July 1862 to find his plantation ransacked, his fields destroyed, and all of his "faithful" slaves gone. The master's fears were vindicated.

White southerners were astonished by how quickly the slaves learned about the Emancipation Proclamation and other war news. The Union Army was now an army of liberation. Its mere approach, or even the mere rumor of its approach, sent terror through the white community. Sometimes slaves left without warning. It made no difference whether a master had been kind or cruel; the slaves left anyway. "We were all laboring under a delusion," one South Carolina planter confessed. "I believed that these people were content, happy, and attached to their masters." Nothing, however, so angered southern whites as the appearance of blacks in uniform.

African-American Union troops were conclusive evidence that the Civil War had become a social revolution. Although they had fought in the American Revolution and the War of 1812, blacks had never been allowed in the regular Army. The Militia Act of 1862 finally allowed black troops, but Lincoln remained reluctant to enlist them. In the summer of 1862, he was still trying to persuade the border states to accept compensated emancipation, and he feared that African-American troops would provoke a backlash in those areas. By the end of the year Lincoln had given up on the border states, and he soon became an active supporter of black enlistment. "The bare sight of 50,000 armed and drilled black soldiers upon the banks of the Mississippi," he said in March 1863, "would end the rebellion at once."

By the war's end 186,000 African Americans had enlisted, 134,111 of them recruited in the South. Although they made up nearly ten percent of the Union Army, black soldiers were never treated as the equals of white soldiers. Few African-American officers were commissioned, and black soldiers were paid less than whites. They were often held back from combat for fear that Confederates would kill such men if captured. But when they went into combat blacks performed respectably, and in so doing they changed the minds of many northern whites.

For African Americans themselves, especially for former slaves, the experience of fighting a war for emancipation was exhilarating. In a society that drew increasingly sharp distinctions between men and women, slaves who became soldiers often

African Americans serving in the Union Army symbolized the revolutionary turn the Civil War took once emancipation became the policy of the North. This scene depicts the nearly suicidal attack by the Massachusetts 54th regiment on Fort Wagner on the South Carolina coast in July 1863. Despite overwhelming loss of life among the African-American troops, their bravery impressed many northerners and helped change white attitudes about the goals of the Civil War.

felt as though they were, in the process, becoming men. "Now we sogers are men," one black sergeant explained, "men the first time in our lives."

Black Union troops were an exhilarating spectacle for those still enslaved, but to white southerners, this was the "world turned upside down." As African-American troops marched through the streets of southern cities, whites shrieked in horror. They shook their fists at them, spat at them from behind windows, and found it all but impossible to control their rage and indignation. But southern whites were not alone in their opposition to the revolutionary turn the Civil War had taken.

THE WAR AT HOME

African-American troops could not end the rebellion "at once," as Lincoln hoped. Instead the war persisted for two more years. As body counts rose and the economic hardships mounted, civilians in both the North and South began to register their discontent.

The Care of Casualties

At Shiloh, 24,000 men had fallen. More than that fell during a single day of fighting at Antietam. The following year 50,000 men would die or suffer wounds at Gettysburg. At the battles of Chickamauga and Franklin, Tennessee, Confederate troops would suffer appalling losses. And in Grant's struggle against Lee in the spring of 1864, both sides would lose 100,000 men in seven weeks. Casualties, partly the consequence of inept leadership and inadequately prepared troops, were mostly caused by the fact that military technology had outpaced battlefield tactics. Generals continued to order traditional assaults on enemy lines even though newly developed rifles and repeating carbines made such assaults almost suicidal.

If advances in military technology multiplied the casualties, primitive medical practices did even more damage. Of the 620,000 soldiers who died, two out of three were felled by disease. Thousands of soldiers were killed by contaminated water, spoiled food, inadequate clothing and shelter, mosquitoes, and vermin. Crowded military camps were breeding grounds for dysentery, diarrhea, malaria, and typhoid fever. Doctors had never heard of "germs" and so had no idea that sterilization made any difference. No one knew what caused typhoid fever or malaria. There were no antibiotics, and liquor was often the only anesthesia available. Nobody knew how to prevent gangrene, so field hospitals were littered with piles of amputated arms and legs.

In one area, nursing, the Civil War advanced the practice of medicine. The Civil War overturned long-standing prejudices against the presence of women in military hospitals. The Confederacy lagged behind in institutional developments, but hundreds of southern women volunteered their services to the southern forces. Even in the North the thousands of women who volunteered their services to the Union Army had to overcome institutional barriers against them. In mid-1861, however, northern reformers persuaded Lincoln to establish the United States Sanitary Commission. Led by men but staffed by thousands of women, the "Sanitary" became a potent force for reform of the Army Medical Bureau. It established the first ambulance corps for the swift removal of wounded soldiers from the battlefield, pioneered the use of ships and railroad cars as mobile hospital units, and made nursing a respectable profession for women after the war ended.

But the heroic efforts of the Sanitary Commission could not undo the fact that the Civil War had caused unprecedented bloodshed. As the war dragged on, and as the aims of the war shifted, Americans raised their voices in opposition to the policies of the Lincoln and Davis administrations.

Northern Reverses and Antiwar Sentiment

Lincoln struggled for years to find a commander who could stand up to great southern generals like Robert E. Lee and Stonewall Jackson. For failing to crush Lee's army after Antietam, Lincoln at last fired McClellan and gave command of the Army of the Potomac to a reluctant Ambrose Burnside. But Burnside could not hope to match Lee's brilliant, unorthodox strategy. At Fredericksburg, Virginia, on December 13, 1862, Lee's army subjected Burnside's men to a calamitous slaughter. Lincoln quickly replaced Burnside with "Fighting Joe" Hooker, a swaggering braggart who was no better at fighting than Burnside had been. At Chancellorsville, Virginia, in May 1863, Lee overwhelmed Hooker's forces. It was one of the bloodiest Union defeats of the war. Every commander Lincoln had put in charge in Virginia proved more disastrous than the last.

Northern military reverses sustained a wave of political opposition to emancipation. Northern Democrats had always favored compromise with the South on slavery and continued to argue that the only legitimate aim of the war was the restoration of the Union. In the elections of 1862 Peace Democrats (known as Copperheads) took control of the legislatures in Illinois and Indiana and threatened to withhold troops from the war effort. Troops from southern Illinois deserted in droves in early 1863, after the Emancipation Proclamation was issued. Democrats were scandalized when the War Department authorized the formation of African-American regiments in early 1863.

With the beginning of military conscription in March 1863, northern Democrats added the draft to their list of Republican atrocities. Because northern draftees could escape conscription by paying a $300 commutation fee, many working-class men, especially Irish immigrants, complained that the rich could buy their way out of combat. In fact, the Irish were underrepresented in the Union Army, and there were means by which working men could pay the commutation fee. But the taint of inequity remained so strong that Congress later abolished commutation.

Drafting white men to fight for black emancipation provoked anger. Dissent became so widespread that Lincoln claimed the constitutional authority to suspend habeas corpus. The Peace Democrats' leading spokesman, Clement L. Vallandigham, repeatedly attacked the president's "despotic" measures. If forced to choose between loss of freedom for whites and continued enslavement of African Americans, he said, "I shall not hesitate one moment to choose the latter alternative."

In 1862 whites protesting the drift toward emancipation rioted in several northern cities. In New York City, Irish Democrats responded to the opening of a draft office by rioting in the streets. Working-class immigrants had suffered most from wartime inflation, and were most susceptible to economic competition from African Americans. Their frustration exploded into the great New York City draft riots, which began on July 13, 1863, and continued for several days.

Rioters attacked the homes of leading Republicans and assaulted well-dressed men on the streets, but they mostly attacked blacks. White mobs lynched a dozen African Americans and set fire to the Colored Orphan Asylum. More than 100 people died, most of them rioters killed by police and soldiers. Thereafter violent northern opposition to the war subsided, partly because the draft riots had discredited the Copperheads, but also because of the improving military fortunes of the Union Army.

Gettysburg and the Justification of the War

As criticism of the Lincoln administration swelled in the summer of 1863, Lee sensed an opportunity to launch a second invasion of the North. On July 1 the opposing armies converged on the small town of Gettysburg, Pennsylvania. For three days they fought the most decisive battle of the war. On the first day it looked as though the South was on its way to another victory. Confederate troops pushed the Union enemy steadily backward through the streets of Gettysburg and onto the hills south of the town. But as evening fell the Union Army commanded the heights. Through the night Union General George Gordon Meade secured a two-mile line of high ground. On the second day, Lee ordered two flanking attacks and a third assault on the Union center, but the Union line held. On the third day, against the strong advice of his trusted General James Longstreet, Lee ordered a direct attack by George Pickett's troops on the strongly fortified Union center. Pickett's Charge was a devastating loss for the southern troops. On July 4 the Confederates began their retreat back toward the Potomac River.

As northerners were celebrating Lee's defeat, news came of another Union victory in the West. For months the Mississippi River town of Vicksburg, Mississippi, had proved invincible, to the endless frustration of General Grant. After a succession of failed strategies, Grant laid siege to the town. He cut Vicksburg off from all supplies and waited until the soldiers and civilians in the town were starved into submission. For six weeks the people of Vicksburg lived in caves, bombarded by sharpshooters during the day and by cannon fire at night. They subsisted on mules and rats. On June 28, the Confederate soldiers threatened mutiny, and less than a week later, Vicksburg surrendered. The Confederate commander at Port Hudson surrendered as well. The Mississippi River was now opened to Union navigation, and the Confederacy was split in two. Vicksburg and Gettysburg, together, were the greatest Union victories of the war.

Lincoln seemed to think so. In November, the president went to Gettysburg to speak at the dedication of a military cemetery at the battlefield. There he articulated a profound justification of the Union war effort. The Civil War, Lincoln said, had become a great test of democracy and of the principle of human equality. The soldiers who died at Gettysburg had dedicated their lives to those principles, the president noted. It remained only "for us the living" to similarly "resolve that these dead shall not have died in vain—that this nation, under God, shall have a new birth of freedom—and that government of the people, by the people, for the people, shall not perish from the earth."

With the Gettysburg Address Lincoln took brilliant advantage of the North's improving military fortunes to elevate the meaning of the war beyond the simple restoration of the Union. After 1863 antiwar sentiment in the North diminished substantially. In the South it exploded.

Discontent in the Confederacy

Southerners, both military and civilian, suffered proportionally far more casualties than did northerners. Day-to-day deprivation and physical destruction were common experiences in the Civil War South. This alone provoked resistance to Confederate war measures. But the slave states were divided over secession from the very beginning, and as the war became more relentless the divisions grew more disruptive.

Although most whites in the seceded states remained loyal to the Confederacy, many attacked the government of Jefferson Davis. After Lee's defeat at Gettysburg, Edmund Ruffin littered his diary with vituperative assaults on the Confederate president. Although formed in the name of states' rights, the Confederate government became a huge centralized bureaucracy that taxed white southerners far beyond anything in their prewar experience.

As the Confederate economy collapsed, severe wartime shortages provoked bread riots by desperate women in many southern cities. Most of these women remained loyal to the Confederate cause, but their protests revealed severe strains in southern society.

Early in the war the government in Richmond took control of the military draft. The South relied much more heavily on draftees than did the North. A "planter's exemption" allowed the sons of wealthy slaveholders to purchase replacements, which generated tremendous hostility. Ordinary southerners complained of a "rich man's war but a poor man's fight." The most important resistance came from Georgia, where a trio of powerful politicians (Governor Joseph Brown, Vice President Alexander Stephens, and Senator Robert Toombs) launched a vitriolic assault on the Confederate government. Faced with swelling internal opposition, Davis followed Lincoln's course and suspended habeas corpus in many parts of the Confederacy.

Bread riots erupted in a dozen southern cities in 1863. On April 2, about 1,000 hungry citizens, mostly women, rampaged through the streets of Richmond, Virginia, looting stores for food and clothing. By then life for millions of southerners had become miserable and desperate. Confederate money was becoming worthless, and the army swallowed up much of the precious food supply.

The failure of the southern political economy and the wholesale destruction of southern property sent Edmund Ruffin into a profound depression. All of his money was invested in worthless Confederate war bonds. He could not understand why northerners had not risen in rebellion. Yet Ruffin himself was shocked by the disloyalty of ordinary whites, and he called for a dictator to take control of the Confederacy. In May 1864 Ruffin's son was killed in battle and his plantation was occupied by Union troops, yet neither Ruffin nor his fellow Confederates abandoned their commitment to a separate nation.

THE WAR COMES TO A BLOODY END

In the face of civilian bread riots, war weariness, and disloyal slaves, a crippled Confederacy nonetheless sought desperately to maintain itself. At the same time, northern society seemed stronger than ever. Amidst the most ferocious fighting ever witnessed on North American soil, the commander in chief submitted himself for re-election to the presidency and won.

Grant Takes Command

During the summer of 1863 Union forces under the command of William S. Rosecrans succeeded in pushing Braxton Bragg's Confederate troops out of central Tennessee. Bragg retreated all the way to Chattanooga, a critical rail terminal. After some prodding from Washington, Rosecrans began moving his army toward Chattanooga in mid-August; by early September he was joined by Ambrose Burnside. Outnumbered and almost surrounded, Bragg abandoned Chattanooga and retreated into Georgia. Jefferson Davis sent reinforcements to Georgia and ordered Bragg to return to the offensive. At the same time, Union General George Thomas reinforced Rosecrans and Burnside. On September 19 the two armies discovered each other at Chickamauga Creek in eastern Tennessee. The bloodiest battle of the western theater was about to begin. It lasted two days and ended in the Union troops' retreat and almost total rout.

Weeks after their defeat at Chickamauga, Union armies were still stuck in Chattanooga unable to feed themselves. A frustrated President Lincoln swiftly reorganized the military structure of the western theater, putting General Grant in charge of all Union military activities between the Mississippi River and the Appalachian Mountains. In November 1863 Grant and William Tecumseh Sherman rescued the Union troops trapped at Chattanooga. Together with General Thomas, they dislodged the Confederates from the railroad terminal in eastern Tennessee. Two days later Union forces routed the enemy at Lookout Mountain, driving Confederate troops into Georgia. The war in the West was nearly over.

Lincoln at last had a general who would fight. In March 1864 he put Grant in charge of the entire Union Army. Grant decided on a simple two-pronged strategy: He would take control of the Army of the Potomac and confront Lee's Army of Northern Virginia while Sherman would hunt down and destroy Joseph E. Johnston's troops in Georgia. In these two engagements the Civil War reached its destructive heights. "From the summer of 1862, the war became a war of wholesale devastation," John Esten Cooke explained. "From the spring of 1864, it seems to have become nearly a war of extermination."

The Theory and Practice of Hard War

McClellan, Burnside, and Hooker had all withered under Lee's assaults. Grant did not. The two generals—Lee and Grant—hurled their men into battle, often directly into the lines of enemy fire. Rebuffed at one spot, they turned and tried again somewhere else. The immediate result was a month-long series of unspeakably bloody encounters beginning in the spring of 1864. The first battle took place on May 5 and 6, in a largely uninhabited stretch of woods, thick with underbrush and criss-crossed with streams. Appropriately called the Wilderness, the terrain made it difficult to see for any distance and impossible for armies to maintain strict lines. Soldiers and commanders alike were confused by the woods and smoke, by the deafening roar of gunfire, and by the wailing of thousands of wounded. Entire brigades got lost. In two days of fighting the Union Army suffered 17,000 casualties, the Confederates 11,000, and there was more to come.

Grant's goal was to break through Lee's defensive line and capture Richmond. Despite Grant's aggressive maneuvering, though, Lee always managed to take the defensive position. With the smoke still billowing in the Wilderness, Grant marched his army south hoping to outflank Lee at Spottsylvania Court House. As usual Lee kept one step ahead, and from May 10 to May 12 the bloodbath was repeated. There were another 18,000 Union casualties; another 12,000 Confederates were lost. Still Grant pushed his men further south. Determined to break through Lee's defenses, Grant waged a series of deadly skirmishes culminating in a frightful assault at Cold Harbor on June 3. Bodies piled on top of bodies until finally Grant realized the hopelessness of the exercise and called a halt. Seven thousand Union men were killed or wounded at Cold Harbor, most of them in the first 60 minutes of fighting. The armies moved south yet again, but when Lee secured the rail link at Petersburg (a link that was critical to the defense of Richmond), Grant settled in for a prolonged siege. The brutal Virginia campaign had not ended the war. More than 50,000 Union men were killed or wounded, but Grant had not destroyed Lee's army or taken Richmond. The war was at a standoff, and Lincoln was up for re-election in November.

Two other military achievements saved the election of 1864 for the Republicans. The first was General Philip Sheridan's Union cavalry raid through the Shenandoah Valley in the summer of 1864 and his defeat of the Confederate cavalry's raid into Maryland. Ordered by Grant to wipe out the source of supplies for Lee's army, Sheridan's men swept through the Shenandoah valley, burning barns and killing animals. Sheridan's Valley Campaign demonstrated that the Union Army now had a cavalry that could defeat the Confederacy.

Meanwhile General Sherman provided Lincoln with a second piece of good news by taking Atlanta. On September 1, as the election campaign was heating up in the North, Sherman telegraphed Lincoln: "Atlanta is ours, and fairly won."

After Atlanta Sherman came to believe that southern civilians had to be subdued as well as armies. Sherman stopped short of "total" war, however. He never attacked civilians themselves. Instead, Sherman destroyed the homes and farms, indeed the towns and cities, on which southern civilians depended. The white South had sustained the rebellion, Sherman concluded, and it would remain rebellious until forced to taste the bitter reality of civil war. "War is cruelty," he told the citizens of Atlanta who petitioned him for mercy. The "terrible hardships of war" are inevitable, "and the only way the people of Atlanta can hope once more to live in peace and quiet at home, is to stop the war." Sherman had become a theorist of "hard" war.

Northern Democrats were horrified by the destructive turn the war had taken. In 1864 they nominated George McClellan, the general Lincoln had fired, for president on a platform advocating compromise, a swift end to the war, and a negotiated settlement with the South. Inevitably, Lincoln's policy of hard war became the major issue of the campaign. The fact that McClellan won 45 percent of the votes suggested that a substantial portion of the northern electorate disapproved of the administration's aggressive policy. But by election day Sheridan had laid waste to the Shenandoah valley, and Sherman had taken Atlanta. The majority of northern voters could smell a Union victory and Lincoln won convincingly. All Confederate attempts to offer anything less than unconditional surrender were rejected. Lee's hopes were dashed, and the siege of Petersburg continued.

Sherman Marches and Lee Surrenders

A week after Lincoln's re-election, Sherman's men burned half of Atlanta to the ground, turned east, and marched toward the sea. Hood tried to distract Sherman by moving west toward Alabama and then up into Tennessee, but half of Sherman's army outnumbered Hood's entire force, and half is what Sherman sent to chase

Hood down. In two devastating battles, at Franklin and Nashville, Tennessee, Union troops led by George Thomas destroyed Hood's army.

Meanwhile Sherman's troops were unleashing their destructive energies through hundreds of miles of Georgia countryside. In late December, Sherman telegraphed Lincoln and offered him Savannah as a Christmas present. From Savannah Sherman's men marched northward. As they crossed into South Carolina, the birthplace of secession, Union soldiers brought the practice of hard war to its ferocious climax. They torched homes and barns, destroyed crops, and slaughtered livestock. With Charleston in Union hands and the state capital of Columbia up in flames, Sherman continued his movement northward. Once they left South Carolina, however, Union soldiers were better behaved.

By then events in Virginia were bringing the war to a conclusion. Lee's army was fatally weakened when Union forces closed off Petersburg's last line of supply. On April 2, 1865, the Army of the Potomac broke through the Confederate defenses and forced Lee to abandon Petersburg. The next day the Confederate leaders fled from Richmond. Lee moved his tired and hungry troops westward in one last attempt to elude Grant's force, but when he reached Appomattox Court House, Lee surrendered and the war was over.

The Meaning of the Civil War

The Civil War was a vindication of the northern political economy based on free labor. Despite the draft riots, Copperheads, wartime inflation, and the terrible loss of life, the Civil War years had been good for the North's economy. Mechanization allowed northern farmers to increase wheat production, despite the fact that the army drained off one-third of the farm labor force. Huge orders for military rations propelled the growth of the canned food industry. The railroad boom of the 1850s persisted through the war. By contrast, the political economy of slavery was convincingly defeated. Much of the South lay in ruins. Thousands of miles of railroad track had been destroyed. One-third of the livestock had been killed; one-fourth of the young white men were dead. The southern social order, grounded on slavery, had been destroyed.

Northern prosperity and southern devastation implied a dramatic reconfiguring of the national political economy. In 1860 the North and the South had identical per-capita incomes and nearly identical per-capita wealth. By 1870, however, the North was 50 percent wealthier than the South. The redistribution of political power was equally dramatic. Until 1860 slaveholders and their allies had controlled the Supreme Court, dominated the presidency, and exercised disproportionate influence in Congress, but the Civil War destroyed the slaveholding class and with it the slaveholders' political power. In 1861 Republicans took control of the national government, and emancipation made that transfer of power permanent. For the rest of the century the North and the West would dominate national politics.

Union victory strengthened the advocates of a stronger, more centralized national government. The growth of this "nationalist" sentiment can be traced in the speeches of Abraham Lincoln. When the Civil War began he emphasized the restoration of the "Union." By the end of the war Lincoln was more likely to talk of saving the "nation." An influential new magazine entitled, significantly, *The Nation* was founded in 1865 on the principle that the Civil War had established the supremacy and indivisibility of the nation-state.

The war itself propelled the growth of the central government, beginning with unprecedented control of the economy. Both the Union and Confederate

CHRONOLOGY

1860	South Carolina secedes
1861	Lower South secedes
	Abraham Lincoln inaugurated
	First shots fired at Fort Sumter
	Upper South secedes
	North declares runaway slaves "contraband"
	First Battle of Bull Run
	McClellan takes command of Army of the Potomac
	First Confiscation Act
	Trent affair
1862	Battles of Fort Henry and Fort Donelson
	"Battle of the ironclads"
	Battle of Shiloh
	Union capture of New Orleans
	Slavery abolished in Washington, DC
	Homestead Act
	Confederacy establishes military draft
	Peninsula Campaign
	Slavery prohibited in western territories
	Second Confiscation Act, Militia Act, Morrill Land Grant College Act, and Internal Revenue Act all passed by northern Congress
	Second Battle of Bull Run
	Battle of Antietam
	Preliminary Emancipation Proclamation
	Battle of Fredericksburg

governments ordered the construction of railroads and regulated their operation. Both the North and the South instituted new taxes on income, property, and consumption. The North and the South issued paper money on a scale previously unimaginable; both went deeply into debt by issuing massive numbers of government bonds. Driven by wartime demands for military mobilization, most of these centralized activities disappeared when the fighting stopped.

But some of the changes were permanent. By implementing a homestead policy, establishing land-grant colleges, and subsidizing the transcontinental railroad, Congress intervened directly to facilitate national economic development. Financial reforms designed to assist the Union war effort became a permanent part of the nation's regulatory system. The commissioner of internal revenue, a position created during the war, became a fixed institution in the federal bureaucracy, and greenbacks became "legal tender." The National Banking Act set rules for state and local banks that created a standardized national system. By the time the war was over, anyone who relied on a private bank, who traded in

1863	Emancipation Proclamation
	Union establishes military draft
	Battle of Chancellorsville
	Battle of Gettysburg
	Vicksburg surrenders
	New York City draft riots
	Battle of Chickamauga
	Gettysburg Address
	Battle of Lookout Mountain
1864	Wilderness Campaign
	Battle of Cold Harbor
	Siege of Petersburg begins
	Sherman captures Atlanta
	Philip Sheridan raids Shenandoah Valley
	Lincoln re-elected
	Sherman burns Atlanta and marches to the sea
	Battles of Franklin and Nashville
1864–1865	Sherman's march through the Carolinas
1865	House of Representatives approves Thirteenth Amendment
	Lincoln's second inauguration
	Lee surrenders to Grant at Appomattox
	Lincoln assassinated

greenbacks, or who held government bonds had a stake in the security of the United States Treasury.

The most dramatic consequence of the war was the emancipation of more than 4 million slaves and the destruction of southern slave society. Was it worth 600,000 lives to destroy what Republicans called the slave power? No one was more tortured by the question than Abraham Lincoln. By 1865 he was firmly committed to the permanent abolition of slavery. To ensure that emancipation would not be overturned when peace was restored, he and his cabinet lobbied furiously for passage of the Thirteenth Amendment abolishing slavery in the United States. On January 31, 1865, the House of Representatives approved it with only two votes to spare.

Yet even Lincoln was stunned by the price the nation had paid for emancipation. He wondered whether the bloodshed was a form of divine retribution for the unpardonable sin of slavery. In his Second Inaugural Address, in March 1865, he prayed that the "mighty scourge of war may speedily pass away." But, Lincoln added, "if God wills that it continue, until all the wealth piled up by the bond-man's two hundred and fifty years of unrequited toil shall be sunk, and until every drop of blood drawn with the lash, shall be paid by another drawn with the sword, as was said three thousand years ago, so still it must be said, 'the judgments of the Lord, are true and righteous altogether.'"

The bloody war had ended, but there was more blood to be shed. On the evening of April 14, 1865, a disgruntled southern actor named John Wilkes Booth assassinated Abraham Lincoln at Ford's Theatre in Washington, DC.

CONCLUSION

The president who had led the nation through the Civil War would not oversee the nation's reconstruction. Lincoln had given some thought to the question of how to incorporate the defeated southern states into the Union, but when he died neither he nor his fellow Republicans in Congress had agreed on any particular plan. Would the Union simply be restored as swiftly as possible? Or would the South be reconstructed, continuing the revolution begun during the Civil War? At the moment Lincoln died, nobody was sure of the answer to these questions. They would emerge over the next several months and years, as the freed people in the South pressed to expand the meaning of their freedom.

FURTHER READINGS

Ira Berlin, et al., *Slaves No More: Three Essays on Emancipation and the Civil War* (1992). This collection gives a well-researched account of the process of emancipation.

David Herbert Donald, *Lincoln* (1995). This is the best modern biography by a master of the genre.

Gary W. Gallagher, *The Confederate War* (1997). A pugnacious study arguing that southern whites were overwhelmingly loyal to the Confederacy.

Mark Grimsley, *The Hard Hand of War: Union Military Policy Toward Southern Civilians, 1861–1865* (1995). This text argues persuasively that Union military policy stopped significantly short of "total" war, an unusually thoughtful study.

Leon Litwack, *Been in the Storm So Long* (1979). An evocative account of the end of slavery as the slaves themselves experienced it.

James McPherson, *The Battle Cry of Freedom: The Civil War Era* (1988). A superb one-volume history of the war.

Philip Shaw Paludan, *A People's Contest: The Union and the Civil War, 1861–1865* (1988). *A People's Contest* covers the northern home front.

Emory Thomas, *The Confederate Nation, 1861–1865* (1979). A fine modern treatment of the Confederacy.

 Please refer to the document CD-ROM for primary sources related to this chapter.

16

Reconstructing a Nation

1865–1877

John Dennett Visits a Freedmen's Bureau Court
Wartime Reconstruction • Presidential Reconstruction, 1865–1867
Congressional Reconstruction • The Retreat from Republican
Radicalism • Reconstruction in the North
The End of Reconstruction
Conclusion

JOHN DENNETT VISITS A FREEDMEN'S BUREAU COURT

Ohn Richard Dennett arrived in Liberty, Virginia, on August 17, 1865, on a tour of the South during which he sent back weekly reports for publication in *The Nation*. The editors wanted accurate accounts of conditions in the recently defeated Confederate states and Dennett was the kind of man they could trust. He graduated from Harvard, was a firm believer in the sanctity of the Union, and belonged to the class of elite Yankees who thought of themselves as the "best men" the country had to offer.

At Liberty, Dennett was accompanied by a Freedmen's Bureau agent. The Freedmen's Bureau was a branch of the U.S. Army established by Congress to assist the freed people. Dennett and the agent went to the courthouse because one of the Freedmen's Bureau's functions was to adjudicate disputes between the freed people and southern whites.

The first case to arrive was that of an old white farmer who complained that two blacks who worked on his farm were "roamin' about and refusin' to work." He wanted the agent to help find the men and bring them back. Both men had wives and children living on his farm and eating his corn, the old man complained. "Have you been paying any wages?" the Freedmen's Bureau agent asked. "Well, they get what the other niggers get," the farmer answered. "I a'n't payin' great wages this year." There was not much the agent could do. He had no horses and few men, but one of his soldiers volunteered to go back to the farm and tell the blacks that "they ought to be at home supporting their wives and children."

A well-to-do planter came in to see if he could fire the blacks who had been working on his plantation since the beginning of the year. The planter complained that his workers were unmanageable now that he could no longer punish them. The sergeant warned the planter that he could not beat his workers as if they were still slaves. In that case, the planter responded, "Will the Government take them off our hands?" The Freedmen's Bureau agent suspected that the planter was looking for an excuse to discharge his laborers at the end of the growing season, after they had finished the work but before they had been paid. "If they've worked on your crops all the year so far," the agent told the planter, "I guess they've got a claim on you to keep them a while longer."

Next came a "good-looking mulatto man" representing a number of African Americans. They were worried by rumors that they would be forced to sign five-year contracts with their employers. "No, it a'n't true," the agent said. They also wanted to know if they could rent or buy land so that they could work for themselves. "Yes, rent or buy," the agent said. But the former slaves had no horses, mules, or ploughs to work the land. So they wanted to know "if the Government would help us out after we get the land." But the agent had no help to offer. "The Government hasn't any ploughs or mules to give you," he said. In the end the blacks settled for a piece of paper from the Freedmen's Bureau authorizing them to rent or buy their own farms.

The last case involved a field hand who came to the agent to complain that his master was beating him with a stick. The agent told the field hand to go back to work. "Don't be sassy, don't be lazy when you've got work to do; and I guess he won't trouble you." The field hand left "very reluctantly," but came back a minute later and asked for a letter to his master "enjoining him to keep the peace, as he feared the man would shoot him, he having on two or three occasions threatened to do so."

Most of the cases Dennett witnessed centered around labor relations. The southern economy had been devastated by the war, and successful rebuilding depended on the creation of a political economy based on free labor. There was, however, little agreement about what kind of free labor system should replace slavery. The cases John Dennett saw showed how difficult the labor problem was. The freed people preferred to work their own land, but they lacked the resources to rent or buy farms. Black workers and white owners who negotiated wage contracts had trouble figuring out the limits of each other's rights and responsibilities. The former masters wanted to retain as much of their old authority as possible, while the former slaves wanted as much autonomy as possible.

The Freedmen's Bureau was placed in the middle of these conflicts. Most agents tried to ensure that the freed people were paid for their labor and that they were not brutalized as they had been as slaves. Southern whites resented this intrusion, and their resentment filtered up to sympathetic politicians in Washington, DC. As a result, the Freedmen's Bureau became a lightning rod for the political conflicts of the Reconstruction period.

Reconstruction raised challenging questions for Americans: What conditions should the federal government impose on the southern states before they could be readmitted to the Union? Should these conditions be set by the president or by Congress? How far should the federal government go to protect the economic well-being and civil rights of the freed people? Politicians in Washington disagreed violently on these questions. At one extreme was Andrew Johnson who, as president, believed in small government and a speedy readmission of the southern states and looked on the Freedmen's Bureau with suspicion. At the other extreme were radical Republicans, who believed that the federal government should redistribute confiscated land to the former slaves, guarantee their civil rights, and give African-American men the vote. They viewed the Freedmen's Bureau as too small and weak to do the necessary job. Between the radicals and the president's supporters were moderate Republicans who at first tried to work with the president but later shifted toward the radical position.

Regardless of where they fell on the political spectrum, policymakers in the nation's capital responded to what went on in the South. Events in the South were shaped in turn by the policies emanating from Washington. What John Dennett saw in Liberty, Virginia, was a good example of this. The Freedmen's Bureau agent listened to the urgent requests of former masters and slaves, his responses shaped by the policies established in Washington. But those policies were, in turn, shaped by reports on conditions in the South sent back by Freedmen's Bureau agents like him and by journalists like John Dennett. From this interaction the political economy of the "New South" slowly emerged.

WARTIME RECONSTRUCTION

Long before the Civil War was over, Republicans in Congress and the White House had considered the reconstruction of the southern states. What system of free labor would replace slavery? Under what political conditions should the southern states be readmitted to the Union? What civil and political rights should the freed people receive? As Congress and the Lincoln administration responded piecemeal to developments in regions of the South under Union control, a variety of approaches to Reconstruction emerged. Some approaches, notably those developed in Louisiana, established precedents that shaped Reconstruction for many years.

Experiments with Free Labor in the Lower Mississippi Valley

Southern Louisiana came under Union control early in the war. The sugar and cotton plantations around New Orleans therefore provided the first major experiments in the transition from slave to free labor. The Union commander of the area, General Nathaniel Banks, hoped to stem the flow of black refugees to Union lines. Unsympathetic to the former slaves, Banks issued harsh labor regulations designed to put the freed people back to work quickly. The Banks Plan required freed people to sign year-long contracts to work on their former plantations, often for their former owners. Workers would be paid either five percent of the proceeds of the crop or three dollars per month. The former masters would provide food and shelter. African-American workers were forbidden to leave the plantations without permission. So stringent were these regulations that to many critics Banks had simply replaced one form of slavery with another. Nevertheless, the Banks Plan was implemented throughout the lower Mississippi Valley, especially after the fall of Vicksburg in 1863.

The Banks Plan touched off a political controversy. Established planters had the most to gain from the plan, which allowed them to preserve much of the prewar labor system. Louisiana Unionists, who had remained loyal to the government in Washington, formed a Free State Association to press for more substantial changes. Lincoln publicly supported the Free State movement and issued a Proclamation of Amnesty and Reconstruction to undermine the Confederacy by cultivating the support of southern Unionists. The Proclamation contained the outline of the so-called Ten-Percent Plan, which turned out to be not much of a plan at all.

Lincoln's Ten-Percent Plan versus the Wade–Davis Bill

The Ten-Percent Plan promised full pardons and the restoration of civil rights to all those who swore loyalty to the Union, excluding only a few high-ranking Confederate military and political leaders. When the number of loyal whites in a former Confederate state reached ten percent of the 1860 voting population, they could organize a new state constitution and government. The only stipulation was that they recognize the abolition of slavery. Abiding by these conditions, Free State whites met in Louisiana in 1864 and produced a new state constitution. It provided for free public education, a minimum wage, a nine-hour day on public works projects, and a graduated income tax. However, although it abolished slavery, it also denied blacks the right to vote.

By the spring of 1864 such denials were no longer acceptable to radical Republicans, a small but vocal wing of the Republican Party. They were active in many parts of the South immediately after the war, and they developed strong ties to leading radicals in Congress, such as Thaddeus Stevens of Pennsylvania and Charles Sumner of Massachusetts. Despite their differences, most radicals favored distributing land to the former slaves and federal guarantees of the civil rights of former slaves, including the right to vote. Radicals were prepared to use the full force of the federal government to enforce Congressional policy in the South. Although the radicals never formed a majority in Congress, they gradually won over the moderates to many of their positions. As a result, when Congress took control of Reconstruction after the elections in 1866, the process became known as radical Reconstruction.

The radicals were particularly strong in New Orleans, thanks to the city's large and articulate community of free blacks. In the spring of 1864 they sent a delegation to Washington to meet with President Lincoln and press the case for voting rights. The next day Lincoln wrote to the acting governor of Louisiana suggesting a limited suffrage for the most intelligent blacks and for those who had served in the Union Army. The delegates to Louisiana's constitutional convention ignored Lincoln's suggestion. Shortly thereafter free blacks in New Orleans and former slaves together demanded civil and political rights and the abolition of the Banks labor regulations. Radicals complained that Lincoln's Ten-Percent Plan was too kind to former Confederates and that the Banks Plan was too harsh on former slaves.

Moved largely by events in Louisiana, congressional radicals rejected the Ten-Percent Plan. In July 1864 Congressmen Benjamin F. Wade and Henry Winter Davis proposed a different Reconstruction plan. Under the Wade–Davis Bill, Reconstruction could not begin until a majority of a state's white men swore an oath of allegiance to the Union. In addition, the Wade–Davis Bill guaranteed full legal and civil rights to African Americans, but not the right to vote. Lincoln pocket vetoed the bill because he was still interested in cultivating southern Unionists. By the spring of 1865, however, Lincoln had shifted toward the radical position. In his last speech Lincoln publicly supported voting rights for some freedmen.

The Louisiana experience made several things clear. The radical Republicans were determined to press for more civil and political rights for blacks than moderates initially supported; however, the moderates showed a willingness to move in a radical direction. Equally important, any Reconstruction policy would have to consider the wishes of southern blacks.

The Freed People's Dream of Owning Land

Freedom meant many things to the former slaves. It meant they could move about their neighborhoods without passes, that they did not have to step aside to let whites pass them on the street, and that their marriages would be secured by the law. Following emancipation, southern blacks withdrew from white churches and established their own congregations, and during Reconstruction the church emerged as a central institution in the southern black community. Freedom also meant literacy. Even before the war ended northern teachers poured into the South to set up schools. The American Missionary Association organized hundreds of such northern teachers. When the fighting stopped, the U.S. Army helped recruit and organize thousands more northern women teachers. The graduates of the missionary schools sometimes became teachers themselves. As a result, hundreds of thousands of southern blacks became literate within a few years.

But even more than churches and schools, the freed people wanted land. Without land, the former slaves saw no choice but to work for their old masters on

Charlotte Forten, born to a prominent African-American family in Philadelphia, was one of many northern women who went to the South to become a teacher of the freed slaves. Forten helped found the Penn School on St. Helena's Island in South Carolina.

their farms and plantations. As the war ended many African Americans had reason to believe that the government would assist them in their quest for independent land ownership.

Marching through the Carolinas in early 1865, Union General William Tecumseh Sherman discovered how important land was to the freed people on the Sea Islands. "The way we can best take care of ourselves is to have land," they declared, "and turn it out and till it by our own labor." Persuaded by their arguments, Sherman issued Special Field Order No. 15 granting captured land to the freed people. By June 1865, 400,000 acres had been distributed to 40,000 former slaves.

Congress seemed to be moving in a similar direction. In March 1865, the Republicans established the Bureau of Refugees, Freedmen and Abandoned Lands, commonly known as the Freedmen's Bureau, which quickly became involved in the politics of land redistribution. The Freedmen's Bureau controlled the disposition of 850,000 acres of confiscated and abandoned Confederate lands. In July 1865, General Oliver Otis Howard, the head of the Bureau, issued Circular 13, directing his agents to rent the land to the freed people in 40-acre plots that they could eventually purchase. Many Bureau agents believed that to re-educate them in the values of thrift and hard work, the freed people should be encouraged to save money and buy land for themselves. From the Bureau's perspective, redistributing land was like giving it away to people who had not paid for it.

From the perspective of the former slaves, however, black workers had more than earned a right to the land. "The labor of these people had for two hundred years cleared away the forests and produced crops that brought millions of dollars annually," H. C. Bruce explained. "It does seem to me that a Christian Nation

Before the Civil War it was illegal in most southern states to teach a slave how to read. With emancipation, the freed people clamored for schools and teachers, such as the one pictured here. Within a few years, hundreds of thousands of former slaves became literate.

would, at least, have given them one year's support, 40 acres of land and a mule each." Even Abraham Lincoln seemed to agree. But in April 1865 Lincoln was dead and Andrew Johnson became president of the United States.

PRESIDENTIAL RECONSTRUCTION, 1865–1867

When Andrew Johnson took office in April 1865, it was still unclear whether Congress or the president would control Reconstruction policy, and whether that policy would be lenient or harsh. Like so many Democrats, Johnson's sympathy for the common man did not extend to African Americans. Determined to reconstruct the South in his own way and blind to the interests of the freed people, Johnson grew increasingly bitter and resentful of the Republicans who controlled Congress. As a result, presidential Reconstruction was a monumental failure.

The Political Economy of Contract Labor

In the mid-nineteenth century, Congress was normally out of session from March until December. Having assumed the presidency in April 1865, Johnson hoped to take advantage of the recess to complete the Reconstruction process and present the finished product to lawmakers in December. At the end of May the president offered amnesty and the restoration of property to white southerners who swore an oath of loyalty to the Union, excluding only high-ranking Confederate military and political leaders and very rich planters. He named provisional governors to the seceded states and instructed them to organize constitutional conventions. To earn readmission to the Union, the seceded states were required to nullify their secession ordinances, repudiate their Confederate war debts, and ratify the Thirteenth Amendment abolishing slavery, terms far more lenient than those Lincoln and the

Congressional Republicans had contemplated. They did nothing to protect the civil rights of the former slaves.

Johnson's leniency encouraged defiance among white southerners. Secessionists had been barred from participating in the states' constitutional conventions, but they participated openly in the first elections held late in the year because Johnson issued thousands of pardons. Leading Confederates thus assumed public office in the southern states. Restored to power, white southerners demanded the restoration of all properties confiscated or abandoned during the war. In September 1865 Johnson ordered the Freedmen's Bureau to return all confiscated and abandoned lands to their former owners.

In late 1865 thousands of black families were ordered to give up their land. On Edisto Island off South Carolina, for example, the freed people had carved farms out of the former plantations. But in January 1866 General Rufus Saxton restored the farms to their previous owners and encouraged the freed people to sign wage contracts with their old masters. The blacks unanimously rejected his offer, whereupon the general ordered them to evacuate their farms within two weeks. By the end of 1865 former slaves were being forcibly evicted from the 40-acre plots they had been given by the Union Army or the Freedmen's Bureau.

The Johnsonian state governments enacted a series of "Black Codes" severely restricting the civil rights of freed people. Vagrancy statutes, for example, allowed local police to arrest and fine virtually any black man. If he could not pay the fine, the "vagrant" was put to work on a farm, often the one owned and operated by his former master. Even more disturbing to the former slaves were apprenticeship clauses that allowed white officials to remove children from their parents' homes and put them to work as "apprentices" on nearby farms.

Presidential Reconstruction left the freed people with no choice but to sign labor contracts with white landlords. The contracts restricted the personal as well as the working lives of the freed people. In one case, a South Carolina planter

Slaves in parts of coastal South Carolina were freed early in the Civil War. Here the freed people in Edisto Island in 1862 are shown planting sweet potatoes rather than cotton. In other parts of the South, the former slaves returned to the cultivation of cash crops.

contractually obliged his black workers to "go by his direction the same as in slavery time." Contracts required blacks to work for wages as low as one-tenth of the crop, and cotton prices were steadily falling. It is no wonder that contract labor struck the freed people as little different from slavery.

Resistance to Presidential Reconstruction

In September 1865 blacks in Virginia issued a public appeal for assistance. They declared that they lacked the means to make and enforce legal contracts, because the Black Codes denied African Americans the right to testify in court in any case involving a white person. In many areas planters blocked the development of a free labor market by agreeing among themselves to hire only their former slaves and by fixing wages at a low level. Finally, there were numerous incidents in which black workers who had faithfully obeyed the terms of their contracts were "met by a contemptuous refusal of the stipulated compensation."

Across the South whites reported a growing number of freed people who would not abide by the humiliating conditions of the contract labor system. Some blacks refused to perform specific tasks while others were accused of being "disrespectful" to their employers or to whites in general. Most important, thousands of freedmen declined to renew their contracts for another year.

As black defiance spread, reports of a violent white backlash flooded into Washington. A former slave named Henry Adams claimed that "over two thousand colored people" were murdered around Shreveport, Louisiana, in 1865. Near Pine

In this satirical cartoon, Andrew Johnson and Congress square off against one another. The political struggle over who should control Reconstruction policy led to Congress's impeachment and trial of the president.

Bluff, Arkansas, in 1866 a visitor arrived at a black community the morning after whites had burned it to the ground. Blacks were assaulted for not speaking to whites with the proper tone of submission, for disputing the terms of labor contracts, or for failing to work up to the standards white employers expected. Through relentless intimidation, whites prevented blacks from buying their own land or attending political meetings to press for civil rights.

Northerners read these reports as evidence that "rebel" sentiment was reviving in the South. When Congress came back into session in December 1865, moderate Republicans were already suspicious of presidential Reconstruction. Radicals argued that the contract system made a mockery of their party's commitment to free labor and insisted that the only way to protect the interests of the freed people was to grant them the right to vote.

Congress Clashes with the President

Increasingly distressed by events in the South, Republican moderates in Congress moved toward the Radical position of active government in the South and voting rights for black men. President Johnson, meanwhile, became obsessed with fears of "negro rule" in the South. When he insisted on the swift readmission of southern states that were clearly controlled by unrepentant Confederates, Congress refused. Instead, the Republicans formed a Joint Committee on Reconstruction to propose the terms for readmission. Established in December 1865, the Joint Committee reflected Congress's determination to follow its own course on Reconstruction.

In February 1866 Congress voted to extend the life of the Freedmen's Bureau and empowered the Bureau to set up its own courts, which would supersede local jurisdictions. The Bureau's record during its first year had been mixed. It provided immediate relief to thousands of individual freed people, and it assisted in the creation of schools. But in the crucial area of labor relations, the Bureau too often sided with the landowners and against the interests of the freed people.

Nevertheless the understaffed and overworked Bureau agents often acted under difficult circumstances to protect the freed people from racist violence, unfair employers, and biased law enforcement officials. For this reason, thousands of freedmen and freedwomen looked to the Bureau as their only hope for justice. For the same reason, however, thousands of southern whites resented the Bureau, and they let Andrew Johnson know it.

To the amazement of moderate Republicans, Johnson vetoed the Freedmen's Bureau Bill, complaining that the legislation would increase the power of the central government at the expense of the states. He invoked the Jacksonian political economy of the free market, insisting that the "laws that regulate supply and demand" were the best way to resolve the labor problem. Republicans fell just short of the two-thirds vote they needed to override the veto. Johnson reacted to his narrow victory with a speech attacking the Republicans in Congress and questioning the legitimacy of the Joint Committee on Reconstruction.

Origins of the Fourteenth Amendment

In March 1866 Congress passed a landmark Civil Rights Act. It overturned the Dred Scott decision by granting United States citizenship to Americans regardless of race. This marked the first time that the federal government intervened in the states to guarantee due process and basic civil rights. But President Johnson vetoed the Civil Rights Act of 1866. In addition to the usual Jacksonian rhetoric

Led by President Andrew Johnson, attacks on the Freedmen's Bureau became more and more openly racist in late 1865 and 1866. This Democratic Party broadside was circulated during the 1866 election.

about limited government, Johnson made an overtly racist argument to justify his veto. He doubted that blacks "possess the requisite qualifications to entitle them to all the privileges and immunities of citizens of the United States."

Johnson's actions and rhetoric forced the moderate Republicans to confront the president. The Republican Congress overrode Johnson's veto of the Civil Rights Act and passed another Freedmen's Bureau Bill. Once again Johnson vetoed it, but this time Congress overrode his veto.

To ensure the civil rights of the freed people, the Joint Committee on Reconstruction proposed a Fourteenth Amendment to the Constitution. The most powerful and controversial of all the Constitution's amendments, it guaranteed citizenship to all males born in the United States, regardless of color (see Table 16–1). Although the amendment did not guarantee blacks the right to vote, it based representation in Congress on a state's voting population. This punished southern states by reducing their representation if they did not allow blacks to vote.

By mid-1866, Congress had refused to recognize the state governments established under Johnson's plan, and it had authorized the Freedmen's Bureau to create a military justice system to override the local courts. Congress thereby guaranteed the former slaves basic rights of due process. Finally, it made ratification of the Fourteenth Amendment by the former Confederate states a requirement for their readmission to the Union. Congress and the president were now at war, and Andrew Johnson went on a rampage.

Race Riots and the Election of 1866

A few weeks after Congress passed the Civil Rights Act, white mobs in Memphis rioted for three days. They burned hundreds of homes, destroyed churches, and attacked black schools. Five women were raped and 46 blacks died. Three months later, white mobs in New Orleans rioted as well. They focused their fury on a convention of radical leaders who were demanding constitutional changes that would give black men in Louisiana the right to vote. Disciplined squads of white police and firemen marched to the convention site and proceeded to slaughter the delegates. Thirty-four blacks and three whites were killed.

TABLE 16-1

Reconstruction Amendments, 1865–1870			
Amendment	Main Provisions	Congressional Passage (2/3 majority in each house required)	Ratification Process (3/4 of all states including ex-Confederate states required)
13	Slavery prohibited in United States	January 1865	December 1865 (twenty-seven states, including eight southern states)
14	1. National citizenship	June 1866	Rejected by twelve southern and border states, February 1867
	2. State representation in Congress reduced proportionally to number of voters disfranchised		Radicals make readmission of southern states hinge on ratification
	3. Former Confederates denied right to hold office		Ratified July 1868
	4. Confederate debt repudiated		
15	Denial of franchise because of race, color, or past servitude explicitly prohibited	February 1869	Ratification required for readmission of Virginia, Texas, Mississippi, Georgia Ratified March 1870

The Memphis and New Orleans massacres quickly became political issues in the North, thanks in large part to Andrew Johnson's reaction to them. In late August the president undertook an unprecedented campaign tour designed to stir up voters' hostility to Congress, but his trip backfired. The president blasted Congressional Republicans, blaming them for the riots. At one point he suggested that Radical Congressman Thaddeus Stevens should be hanged. Republicans charged in turn that Johnson's own policies had revived the rebellious sentiments in the South that led to the massacres.

The elections of 1866 became a referendum on presidential Reconstruction. The results were "overwhelmingly against the President," the *New York Times* noted, "clearly, unmistakably, decisively in favor of Congress and its policy." The Republicans gained a veto-proof hold on Congress, and Republican moderates moved further to the radical position. Congressional Reconstruction was about to begin.

CONGRESSIONAL RECONSTRUCTION

Johnson's outrageous behavior during the 1866 campaign, capped by a Republican sweep of the elections, ended presidential Reconstruction. Congressional Reconstruction would be far different. It was an extraordinary series of events, second only to emancipation in its impact on the history of the United States.

Origins of the African-American Vote

The Congress that convened in December 1866 was far more radical than the previous one. Nothing demonstrated this as clearly as the emerging consensus among moderate Republicans that southern blacks should be allowed to vote. Radical Republicans and black leaders had been calling for such a policy for two years, but moderate Republicans initially resisted the idea. At most, moderates like Abraham Lincoln contemplated granting the vote to veterans and to educated blacks who had been free before the war. Not until early 1867 did moderates conclude that the way to avoid a lengthy military occupation of the South was to put political power into the hands of all male freedmen.

Andrew Johnson finally pushed the moderate Republicans over the line. Ignoring the results of the 1866 elections, Johnson urged the southern states to reject the Fourteenth Amendment. Frustrated moderates thereupon joined with radicals and repudiated presidential Reconstruction. On March 2, 1867, Congress assumed control of the process by passing the First Reconstruction Act. It reduced the southern states to the status of territories and divided the South into five military districts directly controlled by the army (see Map 16–1). Before the southern states could be readmitted to the Union they had to draw up new "republican" constitutions, ratify the Fourteenth Amendment, and allow African-American men

Map 16–1   Reconstruction and Redemption
By 1870 Congress readmitted every southern state to the Union. In most cases the Republican Party retained control of the "reconstructed" state governments for only a few years.

to vote. The Second Reconstruction Act, passed a few weeks later, established the procedures to enforce African-American suffrage by placing the military in charge of voter registration. Johnson vetoed both acts, and in both cases Congress immediately overrode the president. This was Congressional Reconstruction at its most radical, and for this reason it is often referred to as radical Reconstruction.

Radical Reconstruction in the South

Beginning in 1867, the constitutions of the southern states were rewritten, thousands of African Americans began to vote, and hundreds of them assumed public office. Within six months 735,000 blacks and 635,000 whites had registered to vote across the South. African Americans formed electoral majorities in South Carolina, Florida, Mississippi, Alabama, and Louisiana. In the fall these new voters elected delegates to conventions that drew up progressive state constitutions that guaranteed universal manhood suffrage, mandated public education systems, and established progressive tax structures.

The Republican governments elected under Congressional authority were based on an unstable political coalition. Northern whites occupied a prominent place in the southern Republican Party. Stereotyped as greedy carpetbaggers, they included Union veterans who stayed in the South when the war ended, idealistic reformers, well-meaning capitalists, and opportunistic Americans on the make. More important to the Republican coalition were southern whites, or scalawags. Some of them lived in upcountry regions where resistance to secession and the Confederacy had been strongest. Others had been Whigs before the war and hoped to regain some of their former influence. But new black voters were

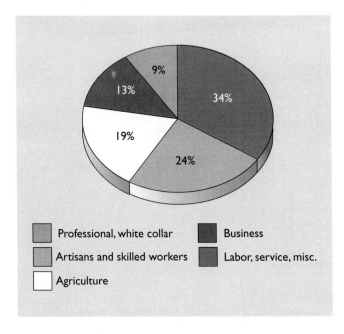

Figure 16–1   Occupations of African-American Officeholders During Reconstruction
Source: Eric Foner, Freedom's Lawmakers: A Directory of Black Officeholders during Reconstruction, 2d. ed. (Baton Rouge, LA), p. xxi

the Republican Party's core constituency in the South. Like the carpetbaggers and scalawags, black voters were a varied lot. Elite black artisans and professionals did not always share the interests of poor black farmers and farm laborers. Nevertheless, most African Americans were drawn together by a shared interest in securing civil rights.

In the long run the class and race divisions within the southern Republican coalition weakened the party, but in the late 1860s and early 1870s the southern Republicans launched an impressive experiment in interracial democracy in the South. Racist legend paints these years as a dark period of "negro rule" and military domination, but military rule rarely lasted more than a year or two, and in only one state, South Carolina, did blacks ever control a majority of seats in the legislature. Blacks who held office came largely from the ranks of the prewar free African-American elite. Teachers, ministers, and small businessmen were far more common among black elected officials than were field hands and farmers. Nevertheless, these Reconstruction legislatures were more representative of their constituents than most legislatures in nineteenth-century America (see Figure 16–1).

Achievements and Failures of Radical Government

Once in office, southern Republicans had to cultivate a white constituency and at the same time serve the interests of their black constituents. To strengthen this biracial coalition, white Republican leaders emphasized active government support for economic development. Republican legislatures granted tax abatements for corporations and spent vast sums to encourage the construction of railroads. They preached a "gospel of prosperity" that promised to bring the benefits of economic development to ordinary white southerners.

In the long run, the gospel of prosperity did not hold the Republican coalition together. Outside investors were unwilling to risk their capital on a region marked by political instability. By the early 1870s, black politicians questioned the diversion of scarce revenues to railroads and tax breaks for corporations. Instead, they demanded public services, especially universal education. But more government services meant higher property taxes at a time of severe economic hardship. Small white farmers had been devastated by the Civil War. Unaccustomed to paying high taxes and strong believers in limited government, they grew increasingly receptive to Democratic appeals for restoration of "white man's government." Thus southern Republicans failed to develop a program that could unite the diverse interests of their party's constituents.

Despite powerful opposition at home and lukewarm support from Washington, DC, radical governments in the South boasted several important achievements. They funded the construction of hospitals, insane asylums, prisons, and roads. They introduced homestead exemptions that protected the property of poor farmers. One of their top priorities was the establishment of universal public education. Republican legislatures established public school systems that were a major improvement over their antebellum counterparts. The literacy rate among southern blacks rose steadily.

Nevertheless, public schools for African Americans remained inadequately funded and sharply segregated. In Savannah, Georgia, for example, the school board allocated less than five percent of its 1873 budget to black schools, although white children were in the minority in the district. In South Carolina, fewer than one in three school-age children were being educated in 1872.

RADICAL MEMBERS
OF THE So. CA. LEGISLATURE.

One of the greatest achievements of Congressional Reconstruction was the election of a significant number of African Americans to public office. Only in South Carolina, however, did African Americans ever form a legislative majority.

The Political Economy of Sharecropping

Congressional Reconstruction made it easier for the former slaves to negotiate the terms of their labor contracts. Republican state legislatures abolished the Black Codes and passed "lien" laws, statutes giving black workers more control over the crops they grew. Workers with grievances had a better chance of securing justice, as southern Republicans became sheriffs, justices of the peace, and county clerks, and as southern courts allowed blacks to serve as witnesses and sit on juries.

The strongest card in the hands of the freed people was a shortage of agricultural workers throughout the South. After emancipation thousands of blacks sought better opportunities in towns and cities or in the North. And even though most blacks remained as farmers, they reduced their working hours in several ways: Black women withdrew from field work in significant numbers, and children attended school. The resulting labor shortage forced white landlords to renegotiate their labor arrangements with the freed people.

The contract labor system that had developed during the war and under presidential Reconstruction was replaced with a variety of arrangements in different regions. On the sugar plantations of southern Louisiana, the freed people became wage laborers. In low-country South Carolina, former slaves became independent farmers. But in tobacco and cotton regions, where the vast majority of freed people lived, a new system of labor called *sharecropping* developed. Under the sharecropping system, an agricultural worker and his family typically agreed to work for one year on a particular plot of land, the landowner providing the tools, seed, and work animals. At the end of the year the sharecropper and the landlord split the crop, perhaps one-third going to the sharecropper and two-thirds to the owner.

Sharecropping shaped the political economy of the postwar South by transforming the way cash crops were produced and marketed. Most dramatically, it required landowners to break up their plantations into family-sized plots, where sharecroppers worked in family units with no direct supervision. Each sharecropping family established its own relationship with local merchants to sell crops and buy supplies. Merchants became crucial to the southern credit system because during the Civil War, Congress had established nationwide banking standards that most southern banks could not meet. Therefore storekeepers were usually the only people who could extend credit to sharecroppers. They provided sharecroppers with food, fertilizer, animal feed, and other provisions over the course of the year, until the crop was harvested.

These developments had important consequences for small white farmers. As the number of merchants grew, they fanned out into upcountry areas inhabited mostly by ordinary whites. Reconstruction legislatures meanwhile sponsored the construction of railroads in those districts. The combination of merchants offering credit and railroads offering transportation made it easier for small farmers to produce cash crops. Thus Reconstruction accelerated the process by which the southern yeomen abandoned self-sufficient farming in favor of cash crops.

Sharecropping spread quickly among black farmers in the cotton South. By 1880, 80 percent of cotton farms had fewer than 50 acres, the majority of which were operated by sharecroppers (see Map 16–2). Sharecropping had several advantages for landlords. It reduced their risk when cotton prices were low and encouraged workers to increase production without costly supervision. Further, if sharecroppers changed jobs before the crop was harvested, they lost a whole year's pay. But the system also had advantages for the workers. For freed people who had no hope of owning their own farms, sharecropping at least rewarded those who worked hard. The bigger the crop, the more they earned. It gave the former slaves more independence than contract labor.

Sharecropping also allowed the freed people to work in families rather than in gangs. Freedom alone had rearranged the powers of men, women, and children within the families of former slaves. Parents gained newfound control over the lives of their children. They could send sons and daughters to school; they could put them to work. Successful parents could give their children an important head start in life. Similarly, African-American husbands gained new powers.

The laws of marriage in the mid-nineteenth century defined the husband as the head of the household. Once married, women often found that their property belonged to their husbands. The sharecropping system assumed that the husband was the head of the household and that he made the economic decisions for the

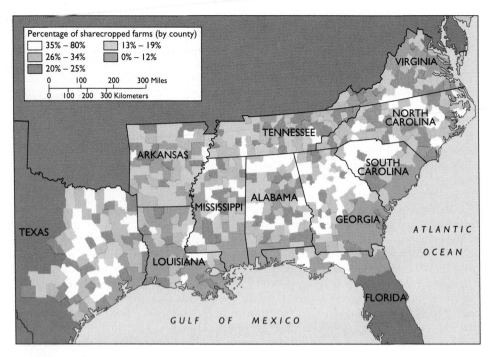

Map 16–2   Sharecropping
By 1880 the sharecropping system had spread across the South. It was most common in the inland areas where cotton and tobacco plantations were most common before the Civil War.

entire family. Men signed most labor contracts, and most landlords assumed that the husband would take his family to work with him.

Sharecropping thereby shaped the political economy of the postwar South: It influenced the balance of power between men and women; it established the balance of power between landowners and sharecroppers; and it tied the southern economy to agriculture, in particular to cotton production, seriously impeding the region's overall economic development. Yet even as this new way of life was taking shape, the Republican Party was retreating from its commitment to the freed people.

THE RETREAT FROM REPUBLICAN RADICALISM

By the late 1860s the Republican coalition was splintering in ways that weakened the party's continued commitment to radical Reconstruction. By 1868 the Republicans were presenting themselves to voters as the party of moderation. The success of this appeal brought in its wake the last major achievements of Reconstruction.

The Impeachment and Trial of Andrew Johnson

Throughout 1866 and much of 1867, President Johnson waged a relentless campaign against Congress and the radicals. Inevitably, this conflict led to a struggle over control of the military in the South. The First Reconstruction Act placed the entire South under direct military power. The Freedmen's Bureau itself was a branch of the

Court proceedings were held in the Senate chambers during the impeachment trial of President Andrew Johnson. It was an extraordinary thing to put a president on trial.

U.S. Army. Judicial authority was vested in the provost marshals. The military also oversaw voter registration. But the president was the commander in chief of the military, and exercising his authority over the military, Andrew Johnson removed dozens of Freedmen's Bureau officials who enforced the Civil Rights Act of 1866. He replaced Republican provost marshals with men who were hostile to Congress and contemptuous of the former slaves. In short, Johnson went out of his way to undermine the law.

Radicals called for Johnson's impeachment, but moderates and conservatives resisted. Instead, Congress hoped to restrain the president by refining the Reconstruction Acts and by using the Tenure of Office Act of March 2, 1867. This act prohibited the president from removing officials whose appointments required Congressional approval. One purpose of the law was to prevent Johnson from firing Secretary of War Edwin M. Stanton, who was sympathetic to the Republicans. A related statute required that all presidential orders to the military pass through General Ulysses S. Grant. Republicans hoped that this would prevent the president from removing military officials who enforced the Reconstruction Acts.

Congress's actions only provoked the president. In his veto messages and public pronouncements Johnson indulged in blatant racist pandering. He played on fears of "amalgamation," "miscegenation," and racial "degeneration." He expressed fear for the safety of white womanhood. In the off-year elections of 1867, northern Democrats played the race card relentlessly and successfully. Democratic victories erased many of the huge Republican gains of 1866 and inspired the president to defy Congressional restraints. As a deliberate provocation, Johnson asked Secretary of War Stanton to resign on August 5, 1867. Stanton refused, and the president appointed General Grant as interim Secretary of War. Still Stanton would not budge, so in February 1868 Johnson fired him. For this the House of

Representatives voted to impeach the president and put him on trial in the Senate. Yet for all the Congressional animosity that Johnson had aroused by his obnoxious behavior, the Senators trying him took their job seriously. Many were concerned that the Tenure of Office Act, which Johnson was accused of violating, was in fact unconstitutional. Others wondered whether his technical breach of the law was serious enough to warrant his removal from office. These and other doubts, along with Johnson's promise of good behavior in the future, led the Senate to acquit the president by a single vote.

Republicans Become the Party of Moderation

While Andrew Johnson was on trial in the Senate, voters in Michigan went to the polls and overwhelmingly rejected a new state constitution that granted blacks the right to vote. Coming on the heels of Democratic victories in 1867, Republicans read the Michigan results as a rejection of radical Reconstruction.

During the 1868 elections Republicans repudiated the radicals' demand for nationwide black suffrage, arguing that the black vote was a uniquely southern solution to a uniquely southern problem. The northern states should be free to decide for themselves whether to grant African-American men the vote. Congress

The Ku Klux Klan was one of a number of racist vigilante groups trying to restore the Democratic Party to power in the postwar South.

readmitted six southern states to the Union, thereby demonstrating that Republican policies had successfully restored law and order to the South. By nominating General Ulysses Grant as their presidential candidate, the Republicans confirmed their retreat from radicalism. "Let Us Have Peace" was Grant's campaign slogan.

In sharp contrast, the Democrats nominated Horatio Seymour, who ran a vicious campaign of race baiting. The Democratic platform denounced the Reconstruction Acts and promised to restore white rule to the South. Seymour suggested that a Democratic president might nullify the governments organized under Congressional Reconstruction. Where the Republicans promised order and stability, the Democrats seemed to promise continued disruption. Northern fears were confirmed by the violence that swept the South during the election, incited by Southern Democrats to keep black voters from the polls.

The Ku Klux Klan, which systematically intimidated potential black voters, was one of several secretive organizations dedicated to the violent overthrow of radical Reconstruction and the restoration of white supremacy. They included the Knights of the White Camelia, Red Shirts, and Night Riders. Some tried to force blacks to go back to work for white landlords. Some attacked African Americans who refused to abide by traditional codes of racial etiquette. But in the main, such organizations worked to restore the political power of the Democratic Party in the South. They intimidated white Republicans, burned homes of black families, and lynched African Americans who showed signs of political activism. It is fair to say that in 1868 the Ku Klux Klan served as the paramilitary arm of the southern Democratic Party.

As a means of restoring white supremacy, the Klan's strategy of violence backfired. A wave of disgust swept across the North, and the Republicans regained control of the White House, along with 25 of the 33 state legislatures. The victorious Republicans quickly seized the opportunity to preserve the achievements of the Reconstruction.

The Grant Administration and Moderate Republicanism

The Republicans reinforced their moderate image by attempting to restore law and order in the South. Congressional hearings produced vivid evidence of the Klan's violent efforts to suppress the black vote. Congress responded with a series of Enforcement Acts, designed to "enforce" the recently enacted Fifteenth Amendment (see the following section). After some initial hesitation, the Grant administration used the new laws to initiate anti-Klan prosecutions that effectively diminished political violence throughout the South. As a result the 1872 presidential elections were relatively free of disruption.

In this period the Republicans shifted to an aggressive foreign policy. Before the Civil War, Republicans associated expansionism with the slave power and the Democratic Party. But with the triumph of nationalism, the Republicans equated American overseas expansion with the spread of liberty. They went on the offensive: In 1867 Secretary of State William Seward successfully negotiated the purchase of Alaska from Russia. The administration was equally adroit in its negotiations with Great Britain over the settlement of the so-called *Alabama* claims. In 1872 the English accepted responsibility for having helped equip the Confederate Navy during the Civil War and agreed to pay over $15 million for damage to American shipping by the *Alabama* and other southern warships built in England.

But Grant's aggressive foreign policy did not go uncontested. In 1869 the president set his sights on Santo Domingo (now the Dominican Republic), but the administration bungled the deal. Grant's private secretary negotiated a treaty without informing the cabinet. Grant tried to bulldoze the treaty through Congress, but succeeded only in alienating members of his own party. The Senate rejected the annexation of Santo Domingo, and the Republicans were weakened by the debacle.

RECONSTRUCTION IN THE NORTH

Although Reconstruction was aimed primarily at the South, the North was affected as well. The struggle over the black vote spilled beyond the borders of the defeated Confederacy. Although not as dramatic as developments in the South, the transformation of the North was still an important chapter in the history of Reconstruction.

The Fifteenth Amendment and Nationwide African-American Suffrage

Before the Civil War African Americans in the North were segregated in theaters, restaurants, cemeteries, hotels, streetcars, ferries, and schools. Most states denied them the vote. The Civil War galvanized the northern black community to launch an assault on racial discrimination, with some success. In 1863 California removed the ban on black testimony in criminal courts. Two years later Illinois did the same. During the war, many northern cities abolished streetcar segregation. But when they considered black voting, northern whites retained their traditional racial prejudices. In 1865 voters in three northern states (Connecticut, Wisconsin, and Minnesota) rejected constitutional amendments to enfranchise African-American men. In 1867, even as the Republican Congress was imposing the black vote on the South, black suffrage was defeated by voters in Ohio, Minnesota, and Kansas.

The shocking electoral violence of 1868 persuaded many northerners that, given the chance, southern whites would quickly strip blacks of the right to vote. In Iowa and Minnesota, voters finally approved black suffrage. Emboldened by their victory in the 1868 elections, the following year Republicans passed the Fifteenth Amendment to the Constitution. It prohibited the use of "race, color, or previous condition of servitude" to disqualify voters anywhere in the United States. By outlawing voter discrimination on the basis of race, the Fifteenth Amendment protected the most radical achievement of Congressional Reconstruction.

The Fifteenth Amendment brought Reconstruction directly into the North by overturning the state laws that discriminated against black voters. In addition, Congress required ratification of the amendment in those southern states still to be readmitted to the Union. Virginia, Mississippi, and Texas did so and were restored to the Union in early 1870. On March 30, 1870, the Fifteenth Amendment became part of the Constitution. For the first time, racial criteria for voting were banned everywhere in the United States, North as well as South.

Women and Suffrage

The issue of black voting divided northern radicals, especially feminists and abolitionists, who had long been allies in the struggle for emancipation. Signs of trouble appeared as early as May 1863 when a dispute broke out at the convention of the Woman's

Elizabeth Cady Stanton, a leading advocate of women's rights, was angered when Congress gave African-American men the vote without also giving it to women.

National Loyal League in New York City. One of the convention's resolutions declared that "there never can be a true peace in this Republic until the civil and political rights of all citizens of African descent and all women are practically established." For some of the delegates, this went too far. The Loyal League had been organized to assist in defeating the slave South. Some delegates argued that it was inappropriate to inject the issue of women's rights into the struggle to restore the Union.

By the end of the war, radicals were pressing for black suffrage in addition to emancipation. This precipitated an increasingly rancorous debate among reformers. Abolitionists argued that while they supported women's suffrage, the critical issue was the protection of the freed people of the South. This, abolitionist Wendell Phillips argued, was "the Negro's Hour." Phillips's position sparked a sense of betrayal among women's rights activists. For 20 years they had pressed their claims for the right to vote. They were loyal allies of the Republican Party, and now the Republicans abandoned them. It would be better, Elizabeth Cady Stanton argued, to press for "a vote based on intelligence and education for black and white, man and woman." Voting rights based on "intelligence and education" would have excluded virtually all the freed slaves as well as the working-class Irish, Germans, and Chinese. Thus, Stanton's remarks revealed a strain of elitism that further alienated abolitionists.

Not all feminists agreed with Stanton, and as racist violence erupted in the South, abolitionists argued that black suffrage was more urgent than women's suffrage. The black vote "is with us a matter of life and death," Frederick Douglass argued. "I have always championed women's right to vote; but it will be seen that the present claim for the negro is one of the most urgent necessity."

Stanton was unmoved by such arguments. For her the Fifteenth Amendment barring racial qualifications for voting was the last straw. Supporters of women's suffrage opposed the Fifteenth Amendment on the ground that it subjected elite, educated women to the rule of base and illiterate males, especially immigrants and blacks. Abolitionists were shocked by such opinions. They favored universal suffrage, not the "educated" suffrage that Stanton was calling for. The breach among reformers weakened the coalition of radicals pushing to maintain a vigorous Reconstruction policy in the South.

The Rise and Fall of the National Labor Union

Inspired by the radicalism of the Civil War and Reconstruction, industrial workers across the North organized dozens of craft unions, Eight-Hour Leagues, and working men's associations. The general goal of these associations was to protect northern workers who were overworked and underpaid. They called strikes, initiated consumer boycotts, and formed consumer cooperatives. In 1867 and 1868 workers in New York and Massachusetts launched campaigns to enact laws restricting the workday to eight hours. Shortly thereafter workers began electing their own candidates to state legislatures.

The National Labor Union (NLU) was the first significant postwar effort to organize all "working people" into a national union. William Sylvis, an iron molder, founded the NLU and became its president in 1868. Like most worker organizations of the time, the NLU subscribed to a "producers ideology." It sought to unify all those who produced wealth through their own labor and skill. The NLU targeted bankers, financiers, and stockbrokers as the enemies of the producing classes.

Under Sylvis's direction the NLU advocated a wide range of political reforms, not just bread-and-butter issues. Nevertheless, the NLU was thwarted by the limits of producer ideology. Sylvis believed that through successful organization American workers could take the "first step toward competence and independence." Thus Sylvis's NLU clung to the Jeffersonian vision of a society of independent petty producers. By the 1860s this vision was an outdated relic of an earlier age, because wage labor rather than economic independence had become the rule for the majority of American workers. Sylvis showed little interest in organizing women, blacks, rural workers, or unskilled wage laborers. After a miserable showing in the elections of 1872, the NLU fell apart. By then Reconstruction in the South was also ending.

THE END OF RECONSTRUCTION

National events had as much to do with the end of Reconstruction as did events in the South. A nationwide outbreak of political corruption in the late 1860s and 1870s provoked a sharp reaction. Influential northern Liberals, previously known for their support for Reconstruction, abandoned the Republican Party in disgust in 1872. The end of Reconstruction finally came after electoral violence corrupted the 1876 elections. Republican politicians in Washington, DC, responded with a sordid political bargain that came to symbolize the end of an era.

Corruption as a National Problem

Postwar Americans witnessed an extraordinary display of public dishonesty. Democrats were as prone to thievery as Republicans. Northern swindlers looted the public treasuries from Boston to San Francisco. In the South, both black and white legislators took bribes. Corruption, it seemed, was endemic to postwar American politics.

If corruption was everywhere in the late 1860s and 1870s, it was largely because there were more opportunities for it than ever before. The Civil War and Reconstruction had swollen government budgets. Never before was government so active in collecting taxes and disbursing vast sums for the public good. Under the circumstances, many government officials accepted bribes for votes, embezzled public funds, or used insider knowledge to defraud taxpayers.

The federal government set the tone. In the most notorious case, the directors of the Union Pacific Railroad set up a dummy corporation called the Credit Mobilier, awarded it phony contracts, and protected it from inquiry by bribing influential congressmen. The Grant administration was eventually smeared with scandal as well. Although personally honest, the president surrounded himself with rich nobodies and army buddies rather than respected statesmen. Grant's own private secretary was exposed as a member of the "Whiskey Ring," a cabal of distillers and revenue agents who cheated the government out of millions of tax dollars every year.

State and city governments in the North were no less corrupt. Wealthy businessmen curried favor with politicians whose votes would determine where a railroad would be built, which land would be allocated for rights of way, and how many government bonds had to be floated to pay for such projects. State officials regularly accepted gifts, received salaries, and sat on the boards of corporations directly affected by their votes. Municipalities awarded lucrative contracts for the construction of schools, parks, libraries, water and sewer systems, and mass-transportation networks, creating temptations for corruption. The Tweed Ring alone bilked New York City out of tens of millions of dollars. By these standards the corruption of the southern Reconstruction legislatures was relatively small.

William Marcy Tweed, the boss of New York's notoriously corrupt, "Tweed Ring" was parodied by the great cartoonist, William Nast. Nast's portrayal of the bloated public official became an enduring symbol of governmental corruption.

But corruption in the South was real enough, and it had particular significance for Reconstruction. Southern Republicans of modest means depended heavily on the money they earned as public officials. These same men found themselves responsible for the collection of unusually high taxes and for economic development projects. As elsewhere in industrializing America, the lure of corruption proved overwhelming. The Republican governor of Louisiana grew rich while in office by "exacting tribute" from railroads seeking state favors. Corruption on a vast scale implied petty corruption as well. Individual legislators sold their votes for as little as $200.

In many cases opponents of Reconstruction used attacks on corruption to mask their contempt for Republican policies. Their strategy helped galvanize opposition, destroying Republican hopes of attracting white voters. Finally, corruption in the South helped provoke a backlash against active government nationwide, weakening northern support for Reconstruction. The intellectual substance of this backlash was provided by influential liberal Republicans, many of whom had once been ardent supporters of radical Reconstruction.

Liberal Republicans Revolt

The label "liberal Republicans" embraced a loosely knit group of intellectuals, politicians, publishers, and businessmen from the northern elite who were discouraged by the failure of radical Reconstruction to bring peace to the southern states and disgusted by the corruption of postwar politics. Although small in number, liberals exercised important influence in northern politics.

At the heart of liberal philosophy was a deep suspicion of democracy. Liberals argued that any government beholden to the interests of the ignorant masses was doomed to corruption. They believed that public servants should be chosen on the basis of intelligence, as measured by civil-service examinations, rather than by patronage appointments that sustained corrupt party machines. Indeed, to liberals, party politics was the enemy of good government.

Liberals therefore grew increasingly alienated from the Republican Party and from President Grant. Above all they resented the fact that the Republican Party had changed as its idealistic commitment to free labor waned and its radical vanguard disappeared. To the rising generation of Republican leaders, getting and holding office had become an end in itself.

As Republicans lost their identity as moral crusaders, liberal reformers proposed a new vision of their own. In 1872 they supported Horace Greeley as the Democratic presidential candidate. The liberal plank in the Democratic platform proclaimed the party's commitment to universal equality before the law, the integrity of the Union, and support for the Thirteenth, Fourteenth, and Fifteenth Amendments. At the same time, liberals demanded "the immediate and absolute removal of all disabilities" imposed on the South as well as a "universal amnesty" for ex-Confederates. Finally, the liberals declared their belief that "local self-government" would "guard the rights of all citizens more securely than any centralized power." In effect, the liberals were demanding the end of federal efforts to protect the former slaves.

In the long run, the liberal view would prevail, but in 1872 it did not go over well with the voters. The liberals' biggest liability was their presidential candidate. Horace Greeley's erratic reputation and Republican background were too much, and Democrats refused to vote for him. Grant was easily re-elected, but he and his fellow Republicans saw the returns as evidence that Reconstruction was becoming a political liability.

The 1874 elections confirmed the lesson. Democrats made sweeping gains all across the North, and an ideological stalemate developed. For a generation, neither party would clearly dominate American politics. The Republicans would take no more risks in support of Reconstruction.

During his second term, therefore, Grant did little to protect black voters from violence in the South. Not even the Civil Rights Act of 1875 undid the impression of waning Republican zeal. Ostensibly designed to prohibit racial discrimination in public places, the Civil Rights Act lacked enforcement provisions. The bill's most important clause, prohibiting segregated schools, was eliminated from the final version. Southern states ignored even this watered-down statute, and in 1883 the Supreme Court declared it unconstitutional. Thus the last significant piece of Reconstruction legislation was an ironic testament to the Republican Party's declining commitment to equal rights.

A Depression and a Deal "Redeem" the South

Angered by corruption and high taxes, white Republicans across the South succumbed to the Democratic Party's appeal for restoration of white supremacy. As the number of white Republicans fell, the number of black Republicans holding office in the South increased, even as the Grant administration backed away from civil rights. But the persistence of black officeholders only reinforced the Democrats' determination to "redeem" their states from Republican rule. Democrats had taken control of Virginia in 1869. North Carolina was redeemed in 1870, Georgia in 1871, and Texas in 1873. Then depression struck.

The severe depression that followed the financial panic of 1873 drew the attention away from the problems of Reconstruction.

In September 1873 America's premier financial institution, Jay Cooke, went bankrupt after overextending itself on investments in the Northern Pacific Railroad. Within weeks hundreds of banks and thousands of businesses went bankrupt as well. The country sank into a depression that lasted five years. Unemployment rose to 14 percent as corporations slashed wages. To protect their incomes, railroad workers tried to organize a nationwide union and attempted to strike several times. Their employers, however, repeatedly thwarted such efforts, and the strikes failed.

As the nation turned its attention to labor unrest and economic depression, the Republican Party's commitment to Reconstruction all but disappeared. Democrats regained control of the governments of Alabama and Arkansas in 1874. In the few southern states where black Republicans clung to political power, white "redeemers" used violence to overthrow the last remnants of Reconstruction.

Mississippi established the model in 1875. Confident that authorities in Washington, DC, would no longer interfere in the South, Democrats launched an all-out campaign to regain control of the state government. The Democratic campaign was double edged. Crude appeals to white supremacy further reduced the dwindling number of scalawags. To defeat black Republicans, White Leagues organized a campaign of violence and intimidation to keep blacks away from the polls. Republicans were beaten, forced to flee the state, and in several cases murdered. Washington turned a deaf ear to African-American pleas for protection. In the end

By the mid-1870s the Republican Party lost its zeal to sustain Reconstruction. In many parts of the South, violent repression left African Americans feeling abandoned by the Republican Party to which they had been so loyal.

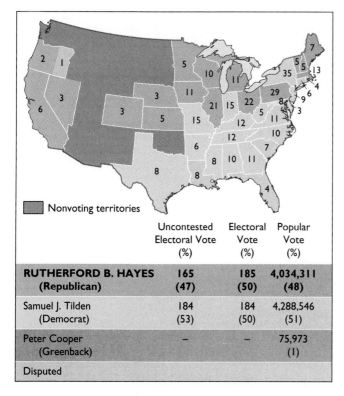

	Uncontested Electoral Vote (%)	Electoral Vote (%)	Popular Vote (%)
RUTHERFORD B. HAYES (Republican)	**165** **(47)**	**185** **(50)**	**4,034,311** **(48)**
Samuel J. Tilden (Democrat)	184 (53)	184 (50)	4,288,546 (51)
Peter Cooper (Greenback)	–	–	75,973 (1)
Disputed			

Legend: ▨ Nonvoting territories

Map 16–3   The Presidential Election, 1876
In 1876 the Democratic presidential candidate, Samuel Tilden, won the popular vote but was denied the presidency because the Republicans who controlled Congress chose to interpret voting irregularities in Louisiana, South Carolina, Oregon, and Florida in a way that gave their candidate, Rutherford B. Hayes, all of the disputed electoral votes.

enough blacks were kept from the polls and enough scalawags voted their racial prejudices to put the Democrats in power. Mississippi was redeemed.

The tactics used in Mississippi were repeated elsewhere the following year, with dramatic consequences for the presidential election of 1876. Amidst a serious economic depression, and with an electorate tired of Reconstruction, the Democrats stood a good chance of winning the presidency. In fact, the Democratic candidate, Samuel J. Tilden, won 250,000 more votes than the Republican, Rutherford B. Hayes (see Map 16–3). But electoral fraud in South Carolina, Louisiana, Florida, and Oregon threw the results into doubt.

If all of the electoral votes from those states had gone to Hayes, he would win, but if even a single electoral vote went to Tilden, he would have won, the first Democrat to win the presidency in 20 years. The outcome was determined by an electoral commission with a Republican majority, and the commission awarded every disputed electoral vote to the Republican candidate. When Hayes was inaugurated on March 4, 1877, the legitimacy of his presidency was already in doubt. But what he did shortly after taking office made it appear as though he had won thanks to a sordid "compromise" with the Democrats to end Reconstruction in the South. There is no solid evidence that such a deal was ever

CHRONOLOGY

1863	Lincoln's Proclamation of Amnesty and Reconstruction
1864	Wade–Davis Bill
1865	General Sherman's Special Field Order No. 15
	Freedmen's Bureau established
	Lincoln's second inaugural
	Lincoln assassinated; Andrew Johnson becomes president
	General Howard's Circular 13
	President Johnson orders the Freedmen's Bureau to return confiscated lands to former owners
	Joint Committee on Reconstruction established by Congress
1866	Congress renews Freedmen's Bureau; Johnson vetoes renewal bill
	Civil Rights Act vetoed by Johnson
	Congress overrides presidential veto of Civil Rights Act
	Congress passes Fourteenth Amendment
	Congress passes another Freedmen's Bureau Bill over Johnson's veto
	Johnson begins "swing around the circle"
	Republicans sweep midterm elections
1867	First and Second Reconstruction Acts
	Tenure of Office Act
1868	Johnson fires Secretary of War Stanton
	House of Representatives impeaches Johnson
	Senate trial of Johnson begins
	Acquittal of Johnson
	Fourteenth Amendment ratified
	Ulysses S. Grant wins presidential election
1869	Congress passes Fifteenth Amendment
1870	Fifteenth Amendment ratified
1872	"Liberal Republicans" leave their party
	Grant re-elected
1873	Financial "panic" sets off depression
1875	"Mississippi Plan" succeeds
	Civil Rights Act of 1875 enacted
1876	Disputed presidential election
1877	Electoral commission awards presidency to Rutherford B. Hayes

actually made. Nevertheless, Hayes ordered the federal troops guarding the Republican statehouses in South Carolina and Louisiana to leave. This order marked the formal end of military occupation of the South and the symbolic end of Reconstruction. By late 1877, every southern state had been redeemed by the Democrats.

The following year the Supreme Court began to issue rulings that further undermined the achievements of Reconstruction. In *Hall v. DeCuir* (1878) the Supreme Court invalidated a Louisiana law that prohibited racial segregation on public transportation. In 1882, the justices declared unconstitutional a federal law that protected southern African Americans against racially motivated murders and assaults. More important, in the Civil Rights Cases of 1883, the Supreme Court declared that the Fourteenth Amendment did not pertain to discriminatory practices by private persons. The Supreme Court thus put the finishing touches on the national retreat from Reconstruction.

CONCLUSION

Inspired by an idealized vision of a political economy based on free labor, Republicans expected emancipation to bring about a dramatic transformation of the South. Freed from the shackles of the slave power, the entire region would soon become a shining example of democracy and prosperity. If the results were less than Republicans expected, the achievements of Reconstruction were nonetheless impressive. Across the South, African-American men and women carved out a space in which their families could live more freely than before. Black men by the tens of thousands elected to office some of the most democratic state legislatures of the nineteenth century. Thousands more black workers repudiated an objectionable contract labor system in favor of an innovative compromise known as sharecropping. Furthermore, Reconstruction added three important amendments to the Constitution that transformed civil rights and electoral laws throughout the nation.

Nevertheless, the Republicans washed their hands of Reconstruction with unseemly haste. The Republicans left the former slaves unprotected in a hostile world. Sharecropping offered them a degree of personal autonomy but little hope of real economic independence. Democratic redeemers excluded blacks from the substance of power. Tired of Reconstruction, Americans turned their attention to the new and difficult problems of urban and industrial America.

FURTHER READINGS

Michael Les Benedict, *The Impeachment and Trial of Andrew Johnson* (1973). Especially strong on the constitutional issues and highly critical of Andrew Johnson.

Dan T. Carter, *When the War Was Over: The Failure of Self-Reconstruction in the West* (1985). Reveals the weaknesses of presidential Reconstruction.

W. E. B. DuBois, *Black Reconstruction in America, 1860–1880* (1935). This classic is one of the greatest American history books ever written.

Eric Foner, *Reconstruction: America's Unfinished Revolution, 1863–1877.* (1988). The best one-volume treatment of the period.

John Hope Franklin, *Reconstruction: After the Civil War* (1961). The first modern treatment of African-American politics in the South.

Jacqueline Jones, *Labor of Love, Labor of Sorrow: Black Women, Work, and the Family from Slavery to the Present* (1985). This text includes a pioneering treatment of women's experience of Reconstruction.

Leon Litwack, *Been in the Storm So Long* (1979). This is a detailed and poignant treatment of the former slaves' first experience of freedom.

Roger Ransom and Richard Sutch, *One Kind of Freedom* (1977). The authors provide a clear picture of the breakup of the plantation system and the emergence of sharecropping.

Kenneth M. Stampp, *The Era of Reconstruction* (1965). Stampp gives a lucid overview of events in Washington, DC.

Mark W. Summers, *The Era of Good Stealings* (1993). *Good Stealings* is a lively treatment of the corruption issue.

 Please refer to the document CD-ROM for primary sources related to this chapter.

17
The Triumph of Industrial Capitalism
1850–1890

Rosa Cassettari • The Political Economy of Global Capitalism
The Rise of Big Business • A New Social Order • Clearing the West
for Capitalism • The Economic Transformation of the West
Conclusion

ROSA CASSETTARI

In 1884 Rosa Cassettari left the Italian village of Cugiono, near Milan, to marry a man named Santino, a miner in Union, Missouri. Rosa was reluctant to go, especially because she had to leave behind her infant son. "It is wonderful to go to America even if you don't want to go to Santino," Rosa's friends told her at the train station in Milan. "You will get smart in America. And in America you will not be so poor." Along with millions of others, Rosa entered a stream of migrants coming from the far corners of Europe. At Le Havre, France, she embarked on a ship for America. "All us poor people had to go down through a hole to the bottom of the ship," she remembered. But she was going to "America! The country where everyone would find work! Where wages were so high that no one had to go hungry! Where all men were free and equal and where even the poor could own land!"

Rosa's first taste of America did not live up to such dreams. In New York she was cheated and forced to make the long trip to Missouri with nothing to eat. When she arrived at the town of Union she found a shabby collection of tents and shacks. Life in the mining camp lived up to her fears rather than her hopes. With no doctors or midwives available, Rosa gave birth to a premature child alone on the floor of her cabin. Santino was an abusive husband and a cruel father. Rosa had to supplement his earnings by cooking for 12 additional miners.

Yet Rosa was impressed by many things about America. Poor people did not behave humbly in the presence of the rich, for example, and even in the difficult circumstances of the mining camp Rosa became accustomed to wearing decent clothing and eating meat every day, things she could never do back in Europe.

When Rosa discovered that her husband planned to spend all their savings to open a house of prostitution, she separated from Santino. With the help of her immigrant friends from Missouri, Rosa moved to Chicago with her two children. She took a job at a place called Hull House where the social workers were so impressed by her life story that they wrote it down and published it *as Rosa Cassettari's Autobiography.*

Rosa was one of millions of men and women who were moving around the world in the late nineteenth century. They moved from the countryside to the city or from town to town. They moved from less developed regions to places where industrialization was well underway. The nerve center for all of the movement was a powerful core of industrial capitalist societies, and at the center of the core was the United States. Migrants were on a worldwide trek, but more of them came to the United States than any other nation.

Perpetual human migration, global in its extent, had become a hallmark of the political economy of industrial capitalism. Common laborers moved from place to place because jobs were unsteady. Railroads hired construction workers who moved as the track was laid and had to find other work when the line was finished. African-American sharecroppers in the South moved at year's end. Over time they moved into cotton-growing districts, into towns and cities, or out of the South. White tenant farmers moved into mill towns. Native Americans were pushed off their lands throughout the trans-Mississippi West, making room for a flood of white settlers. And all across America the children of farmers abandoned the rural life: They went to mill villages and to huge cities like New York, Chicago, and Philadelphia.

They went looking for work, and for most migrants that meant working in a bureaucracy under professional managers who controlled the work process. It meant working with new and complicated machines. It meant working with polluted air, dirty rivers, or spoiled land. Most of all, industrial capitalism meant wage labor. Working people had been freed from the things that tied them to the land in other places and earlier times, such as feudal dues, slavery, and even independent farming. But wage labor released men and women to move about from community to community, from country to country, and finally from continent to continent. To watch Rosa Cassettari as she traveled from Cugiono to Missouri and Chicago is to witness one small part of a global process set in motion by the triumph of wage labor.

THE POLITICAL ECONOMY OF GLOBAL CAPITALISM

The economic history of the late nineteenth century was sandwiched between two great financial panics in 1873 and 1893. Both were followed by prolonged periods of high unemployment and led directly to tremendous labor unrest. The years between the two panics were marked by a general decline in prices that placed a terrible burden on producers. Farmers found that their crops were worth less at harvest time than they had been during planting season. Manufacturers increased production to maintain profits, but the more they produced, the lower prices for their products fell. In search of an inexpensive work force that could produce more for less, industrialists turned to an international labor market. Amidst financial panics and nationwide strikes, depressions and deflation, Americans experienced a dramatic economic transformation. When it was over, the United States had become the leading capitalist nation on earth.

The "Great Depression" of the Late Nineteenth Century

On July 16, 1877, workers for the Baltimore and Ohio Railroad struck at Martinsburg, West Virginia. Within days the strike spread to the Pennsylvania Railroad, the New York Central, the Great Western, and the Texas Pacific. Governors issued orders for the strikers to disperse and asked for federal assistance. Federal troops were sent to major cities, but confrontations between workers and armed forces only fanned the flames of insurrection. "Other workingmen followed the example of the railroad employees," explained Henry Demarest Lloyd, a prominent social critic. "At Zanesville, Ohio, fifty manufactories stopped work. Baltimore ceased to export petroleum. The rolling mills, foundries, and refineries of Cleveland were closed. . . . Merchants could not sell, manufacturers could not work, banks could not lend. The country went to the verge of a panic." A strike in one key industry now threatened the entire nation.

The railroad strike of 1877 was fueled by an economic depression that began with the Panic of 1873 (see Chapter 16, "Reconstructing A Nation") and spread throughout the developed world. The number of immigrants who had arrived in New York—200,000 every year between 1865 and 1873—fell to less than 65,000 in 1877. Although employment recovered in the 1880s, prices and wages continued to fall. Then in 1893 another panic struck. Once again several major railroads went bankrupt and more than 500 banks and 15,000 businesses shut down. From 1873 to 1896 a "Great Depression" blighted much of the globe.

The world was shrinking, and most Americans knew it. In 1866 a telegraph cable was laid across the Atlantic Ocean. From that moment, Americans could read about events in Europe in the next morning's newspaper. Railroads slashed the distances that separated Eastern from Western Europe and the East Coast from the West Coast of the United States. Steamships brought distant ports into regular contact. Midwestern farmers sold their wheat in Russia. Chinese workers laid the tracks of the Union-Pacific Railroad. Eastern Europeans worked the steel mills of Pittsburgh. The political economy of capitalism was tying the world's nations together.

The clearest sign of this linkage was the emergence of an international labor market. As economic change swept through the less developed parts of the world, men and women were freed from their traditional ties to the land and hurled into a global stream of wage laborers. Irish women went to work as domestic servants. African Americans took jobs as railroad porters. Wage laborers built and maintained the transportation network, the steel mills, and the petroleum refineries; slaughtered beef in Chicago; sewed ready-made clothing in factories; and staffed department store sales counters.

The Political Economy of Immigration

Nineteenth-century migrants tended to leave areas already in the grip of social and economic change. Rosa Cassettari, for example, had worked in a silk-weaving factory in Italy. At first, the largest numbers emigrated from the most developed nations, such as Great Britain and Germany. Later in the century, as industrial or agricultural revolution spread, growing numbers of immigrants came from Scandinavia, Russia, Italy, and Hungary (see Map 17–1). As capitalism developed in

Map 17–1   Patterns of Global Migration, 1840–1900
Emigration was a global process by the late nineteenth century, but more immigrants went to the United States than to every other nation combined.
Source: London Times Atlas.

these areas, small farmers were forced to produce for a highly competitive international market. The resulting upheaval sent millions of rural folk into the worldwide migratory stream.

Improvements in transportation and communication were a sign that capitalism was spreading; they also made migration easier. In 1856, more than 95 percent of immigrants came to America aboard sailing vessels. By the end of the century, more than 95 percent came in steamships. The Atlantic crossing took one to three months on a sailing ship, but only 10 days on a steamship. Beginning in the 1880s fierce competition among steamship lines dramatically lowered the cost of a trans-Atlantic ticket, making two-way movement easier. Many immigrants went back and forth across the Atlantic, particularly workers in seasonal trades like construction.

But the great migrations of the late nineteenth century were also related to political upheaval. In China, for example, the Taiping Rebellion of 1848 was accompanied by an economic disaster rivaling the Irish potato famine of the same decade. This combination of economic and political disruption sent some 300,000 Chinese to the Pacific Coast of North America between 1850 and 1882. They labored in mines and panned for gold, and large numbers of Chinese workers helped build the transcontinental railroad. Desperate for employment and willing to work for low wages, the Chinese soon confronted racist hostility from American and European workers. Union organizers in San Francisco argued that the Chinese threatened the "labor interests" of white workers. In 1882 Congress responded by passing the Chinese Exclusion Act, banning further immigration from China.

A similar combination of economic and political forces lay beneath European immigration. The revival of employment in the 1880s brought with it a revival of movement. After 1890 immigration from Northern and Western Europe fell off sharply, as capitalist development made labor scarce in those areas. But by then agrarian crisis and political disruption had set off a wave of emigration from Eastern and Southern Europe. In Austria-Hungary, for example, the revolution of 1848 brought with it economic and political changes that resulted, by the 1880s, in a profound agrarian crisis. In southern Italy, citrus fruits from Florida and California arrived on the market, and protective tariffs thwarted the sale of Italian wines abroad. Desperate farmers from southern Italy started coming to the United States.

Jewish immigration was propelled by a different combination of politics and economics. The assassination of Czar Alexander II in 1881 was followed by a surge of Russian nationalism. Anti-Jewish riots (called pogroms) erupted in 1881–1882, 1891, and 1905–1906, during which countless Jews were massacred. Anti-Semitic laws forced Russian Jews to live within the so-called Pale of Settlement along Russia's western and southern borders, and the May Laws of 1882 severely restricted Russian Jews' religious and economic life. In the 1880s, Russian Jews began moving to America in significant numbers.

Most immigrants came to America looking for work. Some came with education and skills; some were illiterate. Most came with little more than their ability to work, and they usually found their jobs through families, friends, and fellow immigrants. Letters from America told of high wages and steady employment. Communities of immigrant workers provided the information and the connections that newcomers needed. Large Scandinavian communities settled the upper Midwest; the Chinese were concentrated on the West Coast. Some immigrants settled directly on farms, but the overwhelming number lived in cities.

America Moves to the City

Between 1850 and 1900 the map of the United States was redrawn thanks to the appearance of dozens of new cities (see Figure 17–1). Of the 150 largest cities in the United States in the late twentieth century, 85 were founded in the second half of the nineteenth century. In 1850 the largest city in the United States was New York, with a population of just over half a million. By 1900 New York, Philadelphia, and Chicago each had more than a million residents.

The industrial city was different from its predecessors. By the middle of the nineteenth century the modern "downtown" was born, a place where people shopped and worked but did not necessarily live. Residential neighborhoods separated city dwellers from the downtown districts and separated the classes from one another. Streetcars and commuter railroads brought middle-class clerks and professionals from their homes to their jobs and back, but the fares were beyond the means of the working class. The rich built their mansions uptown, but workers had no choice but to remain within walking distance of their jobs.

As cities became more crowded they became unsanitary and unsafe. Yellow fever and cholera epidemics, were among the scourges of urban life in the nineteenth century. Fires periodically wiped out entire neighborhoods. In October 1871 much of Chicago went up in flames. Along with fires and epidemics, urban life was marred by poverty and crime. Beginning in New York in the 1880s, immigrants lived in a new kind of apartment building—the "dumb bell" tenement, five- or six-story walkups housing huge concentrations of people. Immigrant slums appeared in most major cities of America, as well as mill towns and mining camps. In 1890 Jacob Riis published *How the Other Half Lives*, his famous exposé of life in the immigrant slums of New York. He described a dark three-room apartment inhabited by six people. The two bedrooms were tiny, the beds nothing more than boxes filled with "foul straw." Such conditions were a common feature of urban poverty in the late nineteenth century.

Yet during these same years urban reformers set about to make city life less dangerous and more comfortable. Professional fire departments were formed in most big cities by the 1860s. Professional police departments appeared around the

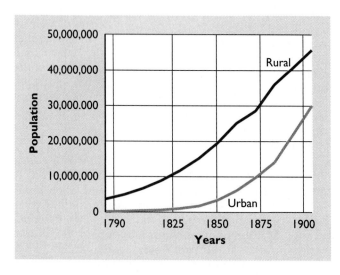

Figure 17–1   Proportion of Population Living in Cities, 1790–1900

A growing proportion of Americans lived in cities, but not until the twentieth century did city dwellers outnumber rural Americans.

same time, greatly reducing urban violence. In 1866 New York City set up the first board of health.

In the second half of the nineteenth century American cities undertook the colossal task of making urban life decent and safe. To a large degree they succeeded: Cities provided clean drinking water, efficient transportation, and great museums, public libraries, and parks. And so the city, which the Jeffersonian tradition had long associated with corruption and decay, was increasingly defended as an oasis of diversity and excitement.

Annie Aitken, who moved from Scotland to Pittsburgh, Pennsylvania, in 1840, would have agreed. Aitken was prospering in the United States while her sister Margaret's family back in Scotland was sinking fast. Margaret's husband, Will, had been a traditional handloom weaver whose livelihood was destroyed by the rise of textile mills. With Aitken's encouragement, in 1848 Will and Margaret Carnegie and their two sons, Tom and Andrew, left Scotland and moved to Pittsburgh. Annie Aitken let her sister's family live rent-free in a small house she owned. Her nephew, Andrew, took a job in a textile mill for $1.20 a week. Fifty years later, Andrew Carnegie sold his steel mills to J. Pierpont Morgan for $480 million.

THE RISE OF BIG BUSINESS

Before the Civil War the only enterprises in the United States that could be called "big businesses" were the railroads. Indeed, railroads became the model for a new kind of business—big business—that emerged during the 1880s. Big businesses had massive bureaucracies that were managed by professionals rather than owners and were financed through a national banking system centered on Wall Street. They marketed their goods and services across the nation and around the world and generated wealth in staggering concentrations, giving rise to a class of men whose names—Carnegie, Rockefeller, Morgan, and Vanderbilt—became synonymous with American capitalism.

The Rise of Andrew Carnegie

Andrew Carnegie was an immigrant, whereas most businessmen were native born. His childhood in Scotland was marked by poverty, whereas most of America's leading men of business were raised in relative prosperity. Certainly few working families in the late nineteenth century could hope to match Carnegie's spectacular climb from rags to riches. Nevertheless, Andrew Carnegie was the perfect reflection of the rise of big business. In the course of his career, Carnegie mastered the telegraph, railroad, petroleum, iron, and steel industries and introduced modern management techniques and strict accounting procedures to American manufacturing. Other great industrialists and financiers made their mark in the last half of the nineteenth century—Henry Clay Frick, Collis P. Huntington, George M. Pullman, John D. Rockefeller, and Cornelius Vanderbilt—but none of their lives took on the mythic proportions of the Scottish lad who came to America at the age of 12 and ended up the richest man in the world.

"I have made millions since," Carnegie once wrote, "but none of these gave me so much happiness as my first week's earnings." Young Andrew might have been happy to earn a wage, but he was not content with his job in a mill. He enrolled in a night course to study accounting, and a year later got a job as a messenger boy in a telegraph office. So astute and hard working was Andrew that by

1851 he was promoted to telegraph operator. In his dealings with the other operators, Carnegie soon displayed the leadership ability that served him throughout his career. He recruited talented, hard-working men and organized them with stunning efficiency.

The most successful businessmen in Pittsburgh, such as Tom Scott, a superintendent for the Pennsylvania Railroad, noticed Carnegie's talents. In 1853, Scott offered Carnegie a job as his secretary and personal telegrapher. Carnegie stayed with the Pennsylvania Railroad for 12 years during a time when railroad construction soared. Railroads stood at the center of the booming industrial economy. They would become the steel industry's biggest customer. Petroleum refiners shipped their kerosene by rail. Mining corporations needed railroads to ship their coal and iron. Ranchers shipped their cattle by rail to the slaughterhouses of Chicago, and meat packers distributed butchered carcasses in refrigerated railroad cars. Thus his position at the Pennsylvania Railroad gave Carnegie an unrivaled familiarity with the workings of big business.

By the mid-1850s, the largest factory in the country, the Pepperell Mills in Biddeford, Maine, employed 800 workers, while the Pennsylvania Railroad had more than 4,000 employees. If the men who maintained the track fell down on the job, if an engineer arrived late, or if a fireman came to work drunk, trains were wrecked, lives were lost, and business failed. The railroads thus borrowed the disciplinary methods and bureaucratic structure of the military to ensure that the trains ran safely and on time.

The man who introduced this organizational discipline to the Pennsylvania Railroad was Tom Scott, the man who hired Andrew Carnegie. J. Edgar Thomson, the Pennsylvania's president, was a pioneer of a different sort. He established an elaborate bookkeeping system that provided detailed knowledge of every aspect of the Pennsylvania's operations. Scott used the statistics Thomson collected to reward managers who improved the company's profits and eliminate those who failed.

Carnegie succeeded. After Scott was promoted to vice president in 1859, Carnegie took Scott's place as superintendent of the western division, where he helped make the Pennsylvania Railroad into a model of industrial efficiency. By 1865 the Pennsylvania had 30,000 employees and had expanded its line east into New York City and west to Chicago. It was the largest private company in the world.

Carnegie's experience at the Pennsylvania Railroad gave him a keen understanding of the modern financial system. Railroads dwarfed all previous business enterprises in the amount of investment capital they required and in the complexity of their financial arrangements. Railroads were the first corporations to issue stocks through sophisticated trading mechanisms that attracted investors from around the world. To organize the market in such vast numbers of securities the modern investment house was developed. J. Pierpont Morgan grew rich selling railroad stocks. The House of Morgan prospered greatly from its association with Andrew Carnegie, for there was no shrewder investor in all of America.

Carnegie Becomes a Financier

Carnegie began making money from money in 1856. On Tom Scott's advice Carnegie borrowed $600 and invested it in Adams Express Company stock, which soon began paying handsome dividends. Carnegie had become a successful capitalist, and for the next 15 years he made a series of financial moves that earned him several more fortunes.

Carnegie invested in the Woodruff Sleeping Car Company in the late 1850s and, a decade later, used his shares and influence to help win George Pullman near-monopoly control of the industry—and make millions in the bargain. Carnegie brokered a similar deal that created the Western Union monopoly of the telegraph industry. He invested in an oil company in western Pennsylvania and demonstrated that strict management would produce steady profits. He made shady deals on the international financial markets; he made millions selling worthless bonds to naïve German investors. More substantially, he created the Keystone Bridge Company, which built the first steel arch bridge over the Mississippi River and provided the infrastructure for the Brooklyn Bridge over New York's East River. With Keystone, Carnegie perfected a model of managerial organization that was the envy of the industrial world.

By 1872 Carnegie was tired of financial speculation and ready for something new. He was 37 years old and had proven himself a master of the railroad industry, a brilliant manager, and a shrewd financial manipulator. Now Carnegie wanted to create an industry of his own. "My preference was always for manufacturing," he explained. "I wished to make something tangible." He would make iron and steel.

Carnegie Dominates the Steel Industry

In 1865 Carnegie acquired a controlling interest in the Union Iron Company. Carnegie's first goal was to speed the flow of materials to his Keystone Bridge Company. This was an important innovation. Iron manufacturing in America had always been decentralized, with each stage of production handled by a different manufacturer. But Carnegie forced Union Iron and Keystone Bridge to coordinate their operations, thereby eliminating middlemen and making production more efficient.

Andrew Carnegie won the bid to provide much of the steel for the construction of the Union-Pacific railroad. Here Chinese workers are pictured laying the tracks at Promontory Point, Utah, in 1869.

Carnegie also forced Union Iron to adopt the managerial techniques and accounting practices he had learned at the Pennsylvania Railroad. By keeping a strict account of all costs, Carnegie could locate the most wasteful points in the production process and reward the most efficient workers. Because he knew exactly what his costs were, Carnegie figured out that his iron mill would be more profitable if he invested in expensive new equipment. He ran his furnaces at full blast, wearing them out after only a few years and replacing them with still more modern machines. Carnegie's great achievement was his introduction of modern management techniques to American industry, but it was in steel rather than iron that Carnegie would prove the worth of those techniques.

As with so many industries, the development of steel was driven by the development of railroads. Traditional iron rails deteriorated rapidly, and as trains grew larger and heavier, iron withered under the load. J. Edgar Thomson, head of the Pennsylvania Railroad, began experimenting with steel rails in 1862. Steel was also a better material for locomotives, boilers, and railroad cars themselves. In the 1860s two developments cleared the path for the transition from iron to steel. First, Henry Bessemer's patented process for turning iron into steel became available to American manufacturers. Second, iron ore began flowing freely onto the American market from deposits in northern Michigan.

Andrew Carnegie was uniquely situated to take advantage of these developments. His experience with Union Iron taught him how to run a mill efficiently, and he had access to investment capital. In 1872 Carnegie built a steel mill, the Thompson Works. Despite a worldwide depression, the steel mill was profitable from the start.

Big Business Consolidates

In the late nineteenth century the names of a handful of wealthy capitalists became closely associated with different industries: Gustavus Swift in meat packing, John D. Rockefeller in oil refining, Collis P. Huntington in railroads, J. P. Morgan in financing, and Andrew Carnegie in steel (see Map 17–2). These powerful individuals, sometimes called "robber barons," represented a passing phase in the history of American enterprise. Most big businesses were so big that no single individual or family could own them. They were run by professionally trained managers, and the highest profits went to companies with the most efficient bureaucracies. Because the businesses were so big and their equipment was so expensive, they had to be kept in operation continuously. An average factory could respond to an economic slowdown by closing its doors for a while, but big businesses could not afford to do that.

Beginning in the 1880s big businesses developed strategies designed to shield them from the effects of ruinous competition. The most common strategy was vertical integration, the attempt to control as many aspects of a business as possible, from the production of raw materials to the sale of the finished product. Carnegie integrated the steel industry from the point of production forward to the distribution of steel but also backward to the extraction of iron ore. He bought iron mines to produce his own ore and railroads to ship the ore to his mills and the finished product to market. His Keystone Bridge Company then purchased the steel.

In 1882 John D. Rockefeller devised a new solution to the problem of ruinous competition by forming the Standard Oil Trust. Rockefeller had founded Standard Oil in 1867 in Cleveland, Ohio. Like Carnegie, Rockefeller surrounded himself with the best managers and financiers to build and run the most efficient modern refineries, but he was more willing than Carnegie to use ruthless tactics to wipe out

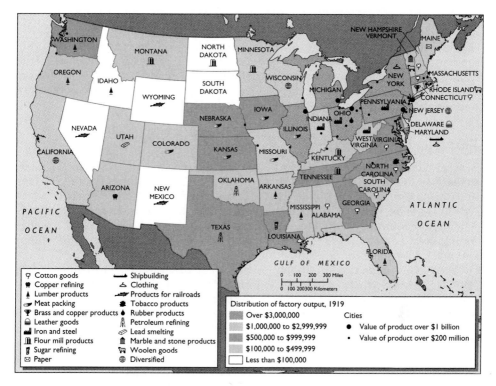

Map 17–2   Major American Industries c. 1890
An industrial map of late nineteenth century America shows regions increasingly defined not by their crops but by their major industries.

his competitors. Rockefeller extracted preferential shipping rates from the railroads, giving him a critical advantage in the savagely competitive oil business. In 1872 Rockefeller began imposing on the national oil refining industry the same control that he had already achieved in Ohio. As president of the National Refiner's Association he formed cartels with the major operators in other states. But the cartels were too weak to eliminate independent refiners.

Rockefeller therefore set out to control the entire oil industry by merging all of the major companies together under Standard Oil. By 1879 the Standard Oil monopoly was largely in place, but not until 1882 was it formalized as a "trust," an elaborate legal device by which different producers came together under the umbrella of a single company that could police competition internally. In 1889 the New Jersey legislature passed a law that allowed corporations based in that state to form "holding companies" that controlled companies in other states. Thus the trust gave way to the holding company, with Standard Oil of New Jersey as its most prominent example. Within a decade many of the largest industries in America were dominated by massive holding companies.

Rockefeller's Standard Oil monopoly was a notorious example of how big business had changed the American economy. Rockefeller himself came to represent a powerful new class of extraordinarily wealthy businessmen. Their names—Carnegie, Rockefeller, Morgan, Harriman, and others—soon became associated with the upper class of the new social order of industrial America.

A New Social Order

Classes were not supposed to exist in the United States the way they existed in Europe, as many Americans continued to believe in the late nineteenth century. Yet the reality of class divisions was so obvious that it had become part of public discussion. It was hard not to notice the conspicuous gap between the astonishing wealth of Andrew Carnegie and the daily struggles of Rosa Cassettari.

Lifestyles of the Very Rich

Between 1850 and 1890 the proportion of the nation's wealth owned by the 4,000 richest families nearly tripled. At the top of the social pyramid rested some 200 families worth more than $20 million each. Concentrated in the Northeast, especially in New York, these families were known throughout the world for their astonishing wealth. Spread more evenly across America were the several thousand millionaires whose investments in cattle ranching, agricultural equipment, mining, commerce, and real estate made them wealthy capitalists.

As a group America's millionaires had a lot in common. Most traced their ancestry to Great Britain. Most were Protestant, usually Episcopalians, Presbyterians, or Congregationalists. By the standards of their day they were unusually well educated. Except in the South, America's upper class voted Republican.

The upper classes lived in spectacular houses in neighborhoods that became famous for their wealth: Fifth Avenue in Manhattan, Nob Hill in San Francisco, Rittenhouse Square in Philadelphia, and Boston's Back Bay. Wealthy suburbs (Brooklyn Heights, Philadelphia's Main Line, and Brookline, Massachusetts) acquired similar reputations as privileged retreats. The richest families also built rural estates that rivaled the country homes of England and the chateaus of France. In the late nineteenth century the richest families built a string of spectacular summer homes along the Newport, Rhode Island, shoreline.

The leading figures in New York's high society competed with one another to stage the most lavish balls and dinner parties. The competition reached a climax on March 26, 1883, when Mrs. William Vanderbilt staged a stupendous costume ball that challenged Mrs. William Astor's long-standing position as the queen of New York's upper class. The ball was a great success. All of New York society turned out at the magnificent Vanderbilt mansion where the hostess made a grand entrance dressed as a Venetian princess.

It was left to the new middle class to preserve the traditional virtues of thrift and self-denial.

The Consolidation of the New Middle Class

In 1889 *The Century Dictionary* introduced the phrase "middle class" in the United States. The new term reflected a novel awareness that American society had become permanently divided in a way that earlier generations had stoutly denied.

Professionals were the backbone of the new middle class that emerged in the nineteenth century. All professions defined what it meant to be a member of their tribe, organized themselves into professional associations, and set educational standards for admission. By these means professionals could command high salaries and enjoy both prestige and a comfortable standard of living. Between 1870 and 1890 some 200 societies were formed to establish the educational requirements and maintain the credentials of their members. Even the management of corporations became a professional occupation, as business schools appeared to train professionals in the science of accounting and the art of management. Some professionals succeeded in having their standards written into law. In most states, by 1900 doctors and lawyers could practice legally only when licensed under the auspices of professional associations.

Behind the new professional managers marched an expanding white-collar army of cashiers, clerks, and government employees. They were overwhelmingly men, and they earned annual incomes far beyond those of independent craftsmen and factory workers. They also enjoyed much better opportunities for upward mobility. A beginning clerk might make only $100 a year, but within five years his salary could be closer to $1,000. At a time when the average annual income of a skilled factory worker in Philadelphia was less than $600, over 80 percent of the male clerks in the Treasury Department earned over $1,200 a year.

As it developed, the middle class withdrew from the messy uncertainties of the central city. Improved roads and mass-transit systems allowed middle-class families to escape the urban extremes of great wealth and miserable poverty. Middle-class residents idealized the physical advantages of trees, lawns, and gardens, as well as the comfortable domestic life that suburbs afforded.

Only the most successful craftsmen matched the incomes and suburban lifestyles of white-collar clerks. Butchers might earn more than $1,600 annually, for example, but shoemakers averaged little more than $500. A shoemaker who owned his own tools and ran a small shop maintained the kind of independence that was long cherished among middle-class Americans, yet his income scarcely distinguished him from skilled factory workers. The manual crafts were therefore a bridge between the remnants of the independent middle class and the growing industrial working class made up of men and women like Rosa Cassettari.

The Industrial Working Class Comes of Age

"When I first went to learn the trade," John Morrison told a Congressional committee in 1883, "a machinist considered himself more than the average workingman; in fact he did not like to be called a workingman. He liked to be called a mechanic." Morrison put his finger on one of the great changes in the political economy of nineteenth-century America. Before the Civil War, urban workingmen were skilled laborers who were referred to as artisans and mechanics. "Today," Morrison explained, the mechanic "is simply a laborer." Big businesses replaced mechanics with semiskilled or unskilled factory laborers. For traditional mechanics, this felt like downward mobility.

But most factory operatives and common laborers were migrants (or children of migrants) from small towns and farms. Few, therefore, experienced factory work as a degradation of their traditional skills, as John Morrison did. But most migrants did experience industrial labor as a harsh existence. Factory operatives worked long hours in difficult conditions performing repetitious tasks with little job security.

The clothing industry is a good example of the lives of urban workers. The introduction of the sewing machine in the 1850s gave rise to sweatshops where work was subdivided into simple, repetitive tasks. One group produced collars for men's shirts, another produced cuffs, and another stitched the parts together.

Jobs were defined to ensure that workers could be easily replaced. Factory operatives learned this lesson quickly. They were young; often they were women or children who moved into and out of different factory jobs with astonishing frequency. But even among men, factory work was at best unsteady. The business cycle swung hard and often, leaving few factory operatives with secure, long-term employment.

At the bottom of the hierarchy of wage earners were the common laborers, whose trademark was physical exertion. Their numbers grew throughout the century until by 1900 common laborers accounted for a third of the industrial work force. Hundreds of thousands of common laborers worked for railroads and steel companies. Before Andrew Carnegie and his competitors revolutionized their industry, for example, no more than 20 percent of iron and steel workers were common laborers. By the 1890s 40 percent of steel workers were common laborers.

Common laborers were difficult to organize into effective unions. A large proportion were immigrants and African Americans, and ethnic differences and language barriers often frustrated the development of workers' alliances. Even the kind of work common laborers performed inhibited the growth of effective unions. It was rarely steady work. Men who laid railroad tracks or dug canals and subway tunnels generally moved on when they finished. Common labor was often seasonal; as a result unskilled workers changed jobs frequently. Common laborers were unusually mobile and easily replaceable, and they increasingly came from parts of the world where the idea of organized labor was unknown. Even when they did organize, common laborers faced the biggest, most powerful, most effectively organized corporations in the country.

A great deal of the wage work done by women fell into the category of common labor. In 1900 women accounted for nearly one of every five gainfully employed Americans. They stood behind the counters of department stores and young Irish women worked as domestics in northern middle-class homes. In the South, African-American women worked as domestics. A smaller proportion of women held white-collar jobs, as teachers, nurses, or low-paid clerical workers and sales clerks.

The same hierarchy that favored men in the white-collar and professional labor force existed in the factories and sweatshops. In the clothing industry, for example, units dominated by male workers were higher up the chain of command than those dominated by women. Indeed, as the textile industry became a big business, the proportion of women working in textile mills steadily declined. The reverse trend appeared among white-collar workers. As department stores expanded in the 1870s and 1880s, they hired low-paid women, often Irish immigrants, with none of the prospects for promotion still available to men. White-collar work was not a signal of middle-class status for women as it was for most men in the late nineteenth century.

The story was somewhat different for married women and their children. As few as one in 50 working-class wives and mothers took jobs outside the home. Women supplemented the family income by taking in boarders or doing laundry. Most often, however, working-class families survived by sending their children to work. Even in the families of the highest paid industrial workers, 50 percent of the children worked. Among the poorest working-class families, three out of four children worked. Child labor was a clear sign of class distinction. The rich sent their daughters to finishing schools and their sons to elite boarding schools, middle-class parents sent their children to public schools, and working-class families sent their children to work. This was especially true in the South, where sharecropping was becoming a form of wage labor.

Sharecropping Becomes Wage Labor

As the southern economy recovered from the devastation of the Civil War many observers predicted a bright future for the region. Optimists saw a wealth of untapped natural and human resources, a South freed from the constraints of an inefficient slave labor system ripe for investment, brimming with opportunities, and ready to go.

In an age when Americans were building railroads at an exuberant clip, southerners built them faster. By 1890 nine out of ten southerners lived in a county with a railroad. By then impressive steel mills were coming to life in Birmingham, Alabama. The Piedmont plateau (running along the eastern foothills of the Appalachian Mountains from Virginia to Georgia) was dotted with textile mills bigger and more efficient than those in New England. Southerners were migrating from the countryside to the towns, expanding the production of cotton into new areas, bringing the rich soil of the Mississippi Delta under cultivation. For ordinary southerners, however, especially African Americans, there was no great prosperity in the New South.

After the war most blacks returned to work on land they did not own (see Chapter 16). In place of the master–slave relationship emerged a new labor relationship between landlords and sharecroppers. Between the landlords and croppers, supplying the credit that kept the system alive, arose a powerful class of merchants. At the beginning it was unclear how much power the landlords, the merchants, and the sharecroppers each had. The most important question was who owned the cotton crop at the end of the year: the sharecropper who produced it, the landlord who owned the farm, or the merchant who loaned the supplies needed until the crop came in. The answer would be decided in the state legislatures and courts where the credit laws were written and interpreted.

The resolution was legally complete by the middle of the 1880s. First the courts defined a sharecropper as a wage laborer. The landlord owned the crop and paid his workers a wage in the form of a share of what was produced. Landlords also won a stronger claim on the crop than the merchant creditors. The struggle among landlords, sharecroppers, and merchants was therefore settled in favor of the landlord.

Under the circumstances, merchants were reluctant to loan money to sharecroppers. Many left the plantation districts and moved to the upcountry where they established commercial relations with white yeomen farmers. Trapped in a cycle of debt, white farmers in the 1880s began losing their land and falling into tenancy. Meanwhile in the "black belt" (where most African Americans lived and most of the cotton was produced), successful landlords became merchants while successful merchants purchased land and hired sharecroppers of their own. By the mid-1880s, black sharecroppers worked as wage laborers for the landlord-merchant class across much of the South.

Sharecropping differed in two critical ways from the wage work of industrial America. First, sharecropping was family labor, depending on a husband and father who signed the contract and delivered the labor of his wife and children to the landlord. Second, because sharecropping contracts were year long, the labor market was restricted to a few weeks at the end of each year. If croppers left before the end of the year, they risked losing everything.

The political economy of sharecropping impoverished the South by binding the region to a single crop—cotton—that steadily depleted the soil even as prices fell. Yet for most southern blacks there were few alternatives. Over time a small percentage of black farmers purchased their own land, but their farms were generally tiny and the soil poor. The skilled black artisans who had worked on plantations before the Civil War moved to southern cities where they took unskilled, low-paying jobs. Industrialization was not much help for African Americans. Northern factories were segregated, as were the steel mills of Birmingham, Alabama, and the Piedmont textile mills. Black women worked as domestic servants to supplement their husbands' meager incomes. Wage labor transformed the lives of southern blacks, but it did not bring prosperity.

Hoping to escape the poverty and discrimination of southern life, a number of former slaves moved west. One group, the Exodusters, began moving to the Kansas prairie during the mid-1870s. By 1880 more than 6,000 blacks had joined them, searching for cheap land on which to build independent farms. The Exodusters became locked in the same battles with cattlemen that troubled white farmers, and blacks who settled in cowtowns like Dodge City and Topeka found the same pattern of discrimination they had known in the South. Nevertheless, some of the Exodusters did manage to buy land and build farms. In this respect, the black exodus was similar to the movement of Americans headed west for relief from the constraints of urban and industrial America.

CLEARING THE WEST FOR CAPITALISM

The Homestead Act, passed by Congress during the Civil War, was designed to ensure that the West would be settled by hard-working, independent small farmers. And millions of farmers actually did settle in the West during the second half of the nineteenth century. Their movement has become the stuff of legend.

But these hardy individuals did not settle an empty prairie. Waiting for them in the West were native peoples, some helpful and many hostile. And far from escaping the hierarchy of industrial capitalism, the settlers brought it with them. By the time the director of the U.S. Census declared the frontier "closed" in 1890, the political economy of the American West was composed of railroad tycoons and immigrant workers, commercial farmers and impoverished Native Americans.

The Overland Trail

"Left home this morning," Jane Gould wrote in her diary on April 27, 1862. Along with her husband, Albert, and their two sons, Jane loaded a covered wagon in Mitchell, Iowa, and joined a group of migrants on the Overland Trail to California (see Map 17–3). It would be a long and difficult journey. Albert got sick shortly after they left, and Jane had to nurse him, drive the wagon, and care for the children. The farther they traveled the more distressed Jane became. The Overland Trail was littered with the remnants of wagon trains that had gone before, including discarded furniture, dried bones, and lonely graves. In early October the Goulds reached their new home in the San Joaquin Valley. Five months later, Jane's husband died.

A popular image pictures the West as a haven for rugged men who struck out on their own, but most migrants went in family groups, and the families were mostly middle class. Few poor people could afford the expense of the journey and still hope to buy land and set up a farm in the West.

Map 17–3 The Overland Trail
There was no transcontinental railroad until the late 1860s. Before then, and even thereafter, most settlers moved west on a series of well-developed overland trails.

The journey across the Overland Trail became safer over the years. In the late 1840s the U.S. government began building forts along the overland routes. Besides protecting migrants from Indians, the forts became resting points for wagon trains. By the 1850s Mormon settlers in Utah had built Salt Lake City into a major stopping point. Migrants came to rely on the facilities there to ease the journey. Also during the 1850s the government began to pursue a long-term solution to the growing problem of Native American–white relations in the West.

The Origins of Indian Reservations

In 1851 more than 10,000 Native Americans from across the Great Plains converged on Fort Laramie in Wyoming Territory. All the major Indian peoples were represented: Sioux, Cheyenne, Arapaho, Crow, and many others. They came to meet with government officials who hoped to develop a long-term solution to the growing problem of Indian–white relations. Since the discovery of gold a few years earlier, white migrants had been crossing through Indian territory on their way to California, most of them already prejudiced against the Indians. U.S. officials wanted to prevent hostility between whites and Indians from breaking out into violence and to restrain the conflicts among Indians themselves. They proposed the creation of a separate territory for each Indian tribe, with government subsidies to entice the Indians to stay within their territories. This was the beginning of the reservation system, and for the rest of the century the U.S. government struggled to force the Indians to accept it.

From the start the reservation system was corrupt and difficult to enforce. Agents for the Bureau of Indian Affairs cheated Indians and the government alike, sometimes reaping huge profits. But primarily, the reservations failed because not all Indians agreed to restrict themselves to their designated territories, leading to armed confrontations and reprisals.

By the late 1860s the tensions between Indians and whites were at a fever pitch, as Senator James R. Doolittle of Wisconsin discovered on a fact-finding mission through the West. In Denver he asked an audience of whites whether they preferred outright extermination of the Indians to a policy of restricting Indians to reservations. The crowd roared its approval for extermination. Army officers agreed. The government "must act with vindictive earnestness against the Sioux," General William Tecumseh Sherman declared.

Senator Doolittle and his colleagues resisted the calls for extermination, opting instead for a more comprehensive reservation policy. The government pursued this approach by means of two important treaties that divided the Great Plains into two huge Indian territories. The Medicine Lodge Treaty, signed in Kansas in October 1867, organized thousands of Indians across the Southern Plains. In return for government supplies, most of the Southern Plains peoples agreed to restrict themselves to the reservation. The Northern Plains Indians did not sign onto the reservation so readily. A treaty was drafted, but a band of holdouts demanded further government concessions. Inspired by their leader Red Cloud, the Indians insisted that U.S. forces abandon their forts along the Bozeman Trail. When the government agreed, Red Cloud signed the Fort Laramie Treaty in November 1868.

Red Cloud respected the treaties for the rest of his life, but they nevertheless failed. Most white settlers still preferred extermination to reservations, and not all the Plains Indians approved of the treaties. Nor did the U.S. Army abide by the reservation policy. Within weeks of Red Cloud's signature on the Fort Laramie Treaty, for example, the Seventh Cavalry led by Colonel George Armstrong Custer massacred Cheyenne at Washita, Oklahoma, on November 27, 1868. As long as the U.S. Army sustained the settlers' hunger for extermination, Indian "policy" was made on the battlefield rather than in government offices.

By 1870 it was clear that western Indians would not voluntarily retire to reservations and that the military could not force them into surrender. If any further evidence of the Indian resistance was needed, it came in South Dakota, where, after discovery of gold in the Black Hills, thousands of whites poured onto Indian territory. When the Lakota Sioux rejected demands that they cede their lands to the miners, the government sent in the Army led by General Custer. Custer was an arrogant man, and he made two critical mistakes. First he divided his army in two, and then he failed to keep them in communication with each other. Custer and hundreds of his men were slaughtered at Little Bighorn, Montana, in 1876 by 2,000 Indian warriors led by Sitting Bull and Crazy Horse.

The Destruction of Indian Subsistence

Custer's Last Stand did not signal any change of fortunes for the Plains Indians. By the 1870s whites had learned that they could undermine Native American society most effectively by depriving Indians of their sources of subsistence, especially the bison. "Kill every buffalo you can," a U.S. Army colonel urged one hunter, "Every buffalo dead is an Indian gone." Federal authorities did not actually sponsor the mass killing of the bison; they merely turned a blind eye. Railroads joined the process, sponsoring mass kills from slow-moving trains as they crossed the prairies. Some 13 million bison in 1850 were reduced, by 1880, to only a few hundred.

With their subsistence destroyed, Chief Sitting Bull and his starving men finally gave up in 1881. The Sioux war ended in 1890 with a shocking massacre of 200 Native American men, women, and children at Wounded Knee, South Dakota.

In the Northwest in 1877 the Nez Percé, fleeing from Union troops, set out on a dramatic trek across the mountains into Yellowstone in an attempt to reach Canada. The Nez Percé eluded government troops and nearly made it over the Canadian border. However, hunger and the elements did what the Union Army had failed to do. Chief Joseph and his exhausted people agreed to go to their reservations.

Reformers who advocated reservations over extermination always believed that the Indians should be absorbed into the political economy of capitalism. By "confining the Indians to reservations," explained William P. Dole, Lincoln's Commissioner of Indian Affairs, "they are gradually taught and become accustomed to the idea of individual property." Most white settlers considered Native Americans an inferior race worthy of destruction. By contrast, Dole believed that "Indians are capable of attaining a high degree of civilization." But reformers like Dole equated civilization with the cultivation of "individual property." Accordingly, reformers set out to destroy Native American society. They introduced government schools on Indian reservations to teach children the virtues of private property, individual achievement, and social mobility.

The reformers' influence peaked in 1887 when Congress passed the Dawes Severalty Act, the most important piece of Indian legislation of the century. Under the terms of the Dawes Act, land within the reservations was broken up into separate plots and distributed among individual families. The goal was to force Indians to live like stereotypical white farmers. But the lands allotted were generally so poor, and the plots so small, that their owners sold them as soon as they were allowed. By the early twentieth century there were virtually no reservations left, except for a few parcels in the desert Southwest. With the Indians subdued, the path was cleared for the capitalist transformation of the West.

THE ECONOMIC TRANSFORMATION OF THE WEST

A few hundred civilians died in Indian attacks during the late nineteenth century. More than 5,000 died building the railroads. Lawless violence and wild speculation were very much a part of the western experience, as were struggling families, temperance reformers, and hard-working immigrants. By 1900 the West provided Americans with the meat and bread for their dinner tables, the wood that built their homes, and the gold and silver that backed up their currency. The West was being drawn into the political economy of global capitalism.

Cattlemen: From Drovers to Ranchers

The cowboy is the great mythic figure of the American West: a rugged individual, a silent loner who scorned society for the independence of the trail. Like many myths, this one has elements of truth. Cowboys were usually unattached men. They worked hard, but when their work was over they played just as hard, spending their earnings on a shave, a new suit of clothes, and a few good nights in town. Driving cattle was hard work, often dangerous, and even more often boring. Civil War veterans, emancipated slaves, displaced Indians, and Mexican *vaqueros* all became cowboys at various times. Cowboys were poorly paid, their work was unsteady, and their chances of reaching real independence were slim.

Longhorn cattle were as much a part of western legend as the cowboys who drove them. With the destruction of the bison and the westward spread of the railroads, it became possible to drive huge herds of Texas longhorns north onto the Great Plains. With relatively little capital, cattle herders could make substantial profits. Cowboys drove gigantic herds, sometimes numbering half a million, to a town with a railroad connection from which the cattle could be shipped, such as Abilene, Wichita, or Dodge City, Kansas. Cattlemen sold half of their stock to eastern markets and the other half in the West, to Californians, or to the government, which purchased beef to feed soldiers and Indians on reservations.

But the Texas longhorn had several drawbacks that eventually led to its replacement. Most seriously, it carried a tick that devastated many of the grazing animals that came into contact with it. In addition, the longhorn took a long time to fatten up and never produced good beef. Wealthy investors began to experiment with hybrid cattle that did not carry the deadly tick, fattened up quickly, and produced higher quality meat. By the early 1880s investors were pouring capital into mammoth cattle-herding companies. At the same time it was becoming clear that the Great Plains were seriously overstocked. The grazing lands were depleted, leaving the cattle weak from malnutrition. In the late 1880s several severe winters devastated the sickly herds.

Open-range herding became so environmentally destructive that it was no longer economically feasible. In addition, long drives became increasingly difficult as farmers settled the plains and fenced in their lands. By the 1890s huge cattle companies were giving way to smaller ranches that raised hybrid cattle. The western railroad network was by then so extensive that it was no longer necessary to drive herds hundreds of miles to reach a railhead. Cowboys became ranch hands who worked for regular wages, like miners and factory workers.

In the mid-1880s, more than 7 million head of cattle roamed the Great Plains, but their numbers declined rapidly, and in their place came sheep. Sheep fed on the growths that cattle would not eat. In fact, the sheep ate so many grasses that they proved even more ecologically destructive than cattle. Nevertheless, by 1900 sheep herding had largely replaced the cattle industry in Wyoming and Montana and was spreading to Nevada. Sheep herding had one other crucial advantage: It did not interfere with small farmers as much as cattle driving did.

Commercial Farmers Subdue the Plains

Between 1860 and 1900, the number of farms in America nearly tripled, thanks largely to the economic development of the West. On the Great Plains and in the desert Southwest, farmers took up former Indian lands. From San Francisco to Los Angeles, white settlers poached on the estates of Spanish-speaking landlords, stripping them of their natural resources and undermining their profitability. Over time Hispanic ranchers gave way to Euro-American farmers. The Hispanic population of Los Angeles fell from 82 percent in 1850 to 19 percent in 1880. A similar pattern displaced the Mexican-American landowners in New Mexico and Texas.

This ethnic shift signaled profound changes in the ecology and political economy of the West, driven by the exploding global demand for western products. Cattle ranchers were feeding eastern cities. Lumber from the Pacific

Northwest found its way to Asia and South America. By 1890 western farmers produced half of the wheat grown in the United States, and they shipped it across the globe.

But farming in the arid West was different from farming in the East. To begin with, the 160-acre homesteads envisioned by eastern lawmakers were unrealistic: Farms of that size were too small for the economic and ecological conditions of western agriculture. From the beginning, western farmers were businessmen. To produce wheat and corn for the international market they needed steel plows, costly mechanical equipment, and extensive irrigation. To make these capital investments, western farmers mortgaged their lands. For mechanized, commercial agriculture to succeed on mortgaged land, western farms had to be much bigger than 160 acres.

Most western agricultural settlement took place not on government-sponsored homesteads but through the private land market. By some estimates land speculators bought up nearly 350 million acres of western lands from state or federal governments or Indian reservations. Railroads were granted another 200 million acres by the federal government. The more farmers who settled in the West, the more agricultural produce they could regularly ship back East. Therefore, railroads set up immigration bureaus and advertised for settlers, offering cheap transportation, credit, and agricultural assistance, filling up the Great Plains with settlers from the East Coast and from Ireland, Germany, and Scandinavia. In 1890 the director of the Bureau of the Census reported that the frontier had at last been filled.

Changes in the Land

The trans-Mississippi West was no Garden of Eden waiting for lucky farmers to move in and reap the land's abundant riches. The climate, particularly in the Great Plains and the desert Southwest, was too dry for most kinds of farming. The sod on the plains was so thick and hard that traditional plows ripped like paper; only steel would do the job. With little wood or stone to build houses, farmers lived first in dugouts or sodhouses. Fierce winter blizzards gave way to blistering summers, each rocked by harsh winds. Yet settlers seemed determined to overcome, and to overwhelm, nature itself. To build fences where wood was scarce, manufacturers invented barbed wire. Windmills dotted the prairie to pump water from hundreds of feet below ground. Powerful agricultural machinery tore through the earth, and new strains of wheat from Europe and China were cultivated to withstand the brutal climate.

The western environment was transformed. Wolves, elk, and bear were exterminated as farmers brought in pigs, cattle, and sheep. Tulare Lake, covering hundreds of square miles of California's central valley, was sucked dry by 1900. Hydraulic mining sent tons of earth and rock cascading down the rivers flowing out of the Sierra Nevada, raising water levels to the point where entire cities became vulnerable to flooding. The skies above Butte, Montana, turned grey from the pollutants released by the copper smelting plants. Sheep herding destroyed the vegetation on the eastern slopes of the Rocky Mountains and the Sierra Nevada.

By the turn of the century, the bison had all but disappeared, and the Indians had been confined to reservations. Industrial mining corporations, profitable cattle ranches, and mechanized farms now dominated the West. The frontier was gone, and in its place were commercial farmers whose lives were shaped by European weather, eastern mortgage companies, commodity brokers, and railroad conglomerates. Cowboys sold their labor to cattle companies owned by investors in

CHRONOLOGY

1848	Taiping Rebellion spurs Chinese emigration to U.S. Revolution in Austria-Hungary Andrew Carnegie emigrates to U.S.
1851	Fort Laramie Treaty establishes Indian reservations
1856	St. Paul's boarding school opens
1857	Henry Bessemer develops process for making steel
1862	Pacific Railroad Act Homestead Act Rebellion of Dakota Sioux in Minnesota
1864	Sand Creek Massacre
1865	First trans-Atlantic telegraph cable begins operation
1866	Battle of One Hundred Slain
1867	Medicine Lodge Treaty
1868	Second Fort Laramie Treaty Washita Massacre
1871	October: Great Chicago fire
1872	Edgar Thompson Steel Works open near Pittsburgh
1873	Financial panic, followed by depression
1876	Custer's Last Stand at Little Bighorn
1877	"Great Strike" of railroad workers begins
1878	American Bar Association founded
1881	Czar Alexander II of Russia assassinated
1882	Chinese Exclusion Act John D. Rockefeller forms Standard Oil "Trust" Edison Electric Company lights up New York buildings
1887	Dawes Severalty Act
1890	Jacob Riis publishes *How the Other Half Lives* Massacre at Wounded Knee, South Dakota Director of U.S. Census declares frontier "closed"
1893	Financial panic, followed by depression

Boston and Glasgow. Mining and lumber corporations employed tens of thousands of wage laborers.

Big cities sprang up almost overnight. San Francisco had 5,000 inhabitants in 1850, but by the time the Gold Rush was over, in 1870, there were 150,000 people living there. Denver was incorporated in 1861 but its population hovered at just below 5,000 until the railroad came in 1870. Twenty years later Denver had more than 100,000 inhabitants.

CONCLUSION

Rosa Cassettari and Andrew Carnegie never met, but together their lives suggest the spectrum of possibilities in industrializing America. Both were immigrants who, caught up in the political economy of industrial capitalism, made their way to the United States. Yet the same grand forces touched the two immigrants in different ways. Cassettari moved to a mining camp west of the Mississippi River before making her way to Chicago—the city that opened the west to the dynamism of industrial capitalism. Carnegie migrated, almost overnight, from the preindustrial world of Scotland to the heart of the industrial revolution in America—Pittsburgh, with its railroads, oil refineries, and steel mills. Cassettari struggled all her life and achieved a modest level of comfort for herself and her children. She did as well as most immigrants could hope for, and in that sense her biography reflects the realities of working-class life in industrial America. Cassettari's experience with failure—the harsh life of the mining camp and a bad marriage—impelled her to move on in search of something better. It was success, however, that made Carnegie itch for something different. By 1890, having made his millions, he remade himself by becoming a patron of culture. He moved to New York and traveled the world, befriending the leading intellectuals of his day. He built libraries and endowed universities. He had helped create an industrial nation. Now he set out to re-create American culture.

FURTHER READINGS

Alfred D. Chandler, *The Visible Hand: The Managerial Revolution in American Business* (1977). The standard account of the rise of corporate bureaucracy.

William Cronon, *Nature's Metropolis: Chicago and the Great West* (1991). Meticulously charts the way Chicago's influence stretched across much of the West.

Eric Hobsbawm, *The Age of Empire: 1875–1914* (1987). Establishes the global context for the industrial transformation of the United States.

Maldwyn Jones, *American Immigration*, 2nd ed. (1992). Unusually sensitive to the political and economic background to global migration.

Harold Livesay, *Andrew Carnegie and the Rise of Big Business* (1975). Does an unusually fine job of placing Carnegie in historical context.

David Montgomery, *The Fall of the House of Labor: The Workplace, the State and American Labor Activism, 1865–1925* (1987). Shows how the rise of big business changed the daily labor of the American working class.

Gregory Nobles, *American Frontiers: Cultural Encounters and Continental Conquest* (1997). A brief survey reflecting the latest scholarship in western history.

Henry Nash Smith, *Virgin Land: The American West as Symbol and Myth* (1950). The premier example of the much-maligned "myth and symbol" approach to American studies, this is a classic account of the "image" of the West in the nineteenth century.

C. Vann Woodward, *Origins of the New South, 1877–1913* (1951) is one of the great works of American historical literature.

Richard White, *'It's Your Misfortune and None of My Own': A History of the American West* (1991) is a comprehensive survey by a leading historian of the West.

Please refer to the document CD-ROM for primary sources related to this chapter.

18

Cultural Struggles of Industrial America

1850–1895

Anthony Comstock's Crusade Against Vice • The Varieties of Urban Culture • The Elusive Boundaries of Male and Female Immigration as a Cultural Problem • The Creation of High Culture • Artistic Realism Embraces Urban and Industrial America • Conclusion

ANTHONY COMSTOCK'S CRUSADE AGAINST VICE

Anthony Comstock devoted most of his adult life to putting the owners of brothels, gambling dens, abortion clinics, and dance halls out of business. "You must hunt these men as you hunt rats," Comstock declared, "without mercy." There was little in his background to foreshadow such zeal. While still a young man, Comstock had moved from rural Connecticut to New York City, where he worked as a clerk in a dry goods store. White-collar careers of this sort were a familiar path for native-born Protestant men in the middle of the nineteenth century. Fame came to him in 1873 when the United States Congress enacted a statute that bore his name. The Comstock Law banned the production, distribution, and public display of obscenity. Thereafter, Comstock spent much of his life chasing down and prosecuting pornographers, prostitutes, and strippers.

Comstock and like-minded citizens were disturbed by the municipal corruption that kept police departments from enforcing obscenity laws. To overcome this obstacle, reformers established private organizations with quasi-official authority. Among the most influential was Anthony Comstock's New York Society for the Suppression of Vice, commonly known as the SSV. Founded in 1873, the SSV was dedicated to "the enforcement of laws for the suppression of the trade in, and circulation of, obscene literature and illustrations, advertisements, and articles of indecent or immoral use."

As head of the SSV, Comstock was appointed a special agent of the U.S. Post Office. Along with other SSV leaders Comstock disregarded the rights of due process by entrapping his victims. But they always defended their actions by claiming that the established legal procedures of the police and the judiciary were ineffective in preventing the sale of smut.

Comstock maintained that his chief concern was the protection of children. In his most famous book, *Traps for the Young* (1883), he warned that obscenity was enticing American youngsters into deviant ways by artificially nourishing youthful appetites and passions until they exerted "a well-nigh irresistible mastery over their victim." The evils that trapped America's children were thought to be concentrated in the cities that, in the late nineteenth century, attracted millions of young people. Urban life was relatively anonymous and it was also driven by vast amounts of cash. In the last third of the nineteenth century the income of nonfarm employees in America rose steadily, while prices declined. Except for the very poorest workers, urban Americans had more money to spend and more time to spend it than ever before. And if industrial workers enjoyed more leisure time, white-collar employees enjoyed even more. The big city offered Americans new entertainments that frequently provoked the ire of those determined to defend traditional standards of respectability.

For Comstock urban culture was a cesspool of vice and corruption. For modern historians, a great deal of urban culture resided in its immigrant neighborhoods, with their distinctive family structures and religious practices. But at the time, many Americans looked at immigrant slums as utterly devoid of culture. To them, culture referred only to the great works of Western art, literature, and music. High culture, in this sense, was seen as an alternative to the sordid realities of urban and industrial America. Ironically, the best artists and writers of the late nineteenth century were "realists." While Anthony Comstock tried to suppress the vices of the city, realists embraced them, translating them into compelling fiction and dramatic canvases.

In the second half of the nineteenth century, cultural clashes were as much a part of the political economy of industrial capitalism as were class conflict and political upheaval. Rural America reacted defensively to the culture of the city. Native-born Protestants struggled against the cultures of immigrants. Defenders of high culture fought against the rise of popular culture. Amateur sportsmen sniffed at the emergence of spectator sports. Victorian moralists were shocked by the apparent collapse of traditional gender distinctions. Yet these struggles reflected the efforts of Americans to absorb the dramatic social transformations that accompanied the rise of industrial capitalism.

THE VARIETIES OF URBAN CULTURE

In 1850 nonfarm workers comprised just over 35 percent of all workers; by 1890 the figure was almost 60 percent. Americans moved to the city in vast numbers during these years, and they both loved and hated the cities in which they lived. Their mixed feelings showed up in the varieties of entertainment they embraced during the second half of the nineteenth century. In unprecedented numbers Americans went to theaters, music halls, concert saloons, baseball stadiums, and sports arenas. City life, long associated with poverty and crime, now came to mean fun and excitement as well.

Minstrel Shows as Cultural Nostalgia

In the late nineteenth century the western frontier became one of the most popular themes in American show business. As rugged pioneers gave way to wage earners, commercial farmers, and industrialists, the mythology of the West grew. The most spectacular example of this was Buffalo Bill Cody's hugely successful Wild West Show, which toured the country parading live Indians before delighted urban spectators. Audiences watched displays of horsemanship and highly stylized reenactments of the Plains wars. America's fascination with a romanticized frontier was one example of a popular nostalgia for ways of life that were thought to have been simpler than the life of the city. Nowhere was this nostalgia more obvious than in the minstrel shows.

Minstrel shows were the most significant form of public entertainment for most of the nineteenth century. During the 1830s and 1840s minstrel shows were dominated by white performers in blackface. Although the minstrels stereotyped plantation slaves as happy and carefree, the earliest performances were not as viciously racist as they became later. In the mid-1850s, however, the tone of blackface minstrel shows changed. As the slavery controversy forced white northerners to take sides on a divisive issue, popular troupes like New York's Christy Minstrels took the side of the slaveholders. During the Civil War and Reconstruction, minstrel shows attacked white reformers in the North who supported emancipation and black rights. They portrayed blacks with gross racial stereotypes and subjected abolitionists to ridicule. Minstrel troupes staged corrupted versions of *Uncle Tom's Cabin*, stripped the novel of its abolitionist theme, and reduced the plot to a simplistic story of beleaguered southern whites. Yet throughout the period, minstrel shows continued to poke fun at the aristocratic pretensions of cultural elites. Indeed, minstrel shows commonly combined racism with populism, lampooning elites by playing them in blackface wearing fancy clothes and putting on airs.

In the 1870s minstrel shows grew larger and more elaborate. J. H. Haverly led the way: He hired the most players, dressed them in the gaudiest costumes, placed them in the most spectacular sets, and had them perform the widest variety of numbers. He toned down the emphasis on blackface singers and plantation themes and added scantily clad women and off-color routines. Haverly expanded his audiences with extensive advertising. By 1881 he had theaters in New York, Brooklyn, Chicago, and San Francisco; three national minstrel troupes; and four touring comedy theaters. Of Haverly's three companies, two were white and one was black. There were other black companies as well. As national minstrel shows abandoned their commitment to authentic representations of southern life, blacks often took to the stage and kept the plantation theme alive, operating within the racial stereotypes established by prewar whites in blackface. The most famous black minstrel of the nineteenth century, Billy Kersands, drew huge audiences with his portrayals of ignorant and comical characters. Yet as the plantation theme became the preserve of black players, some of the early criticism of slavery crept back into the productions. When black minstrels romanticized the Old South, their nostalgia was reserved for slaves. Meanwhile, the largest and most successful minstrel shows retained their exclusively white casts and their heavy-handed racism.

As productions grew more ornate and expensive, show business entrepreneurs put smaller local troupes out of business or swallowed them up into national companies. From more than 60 troupes in the late 1860s, the number of minstrel troupes fell to just 13 by the early 1880s. Differences from one company to the next diminished as minstrel shows became uniform and somewhat bland. Yet, more popular than ever, they expanded their audiences into the far West and the deep South. By 1890 a handful of huge entertainment moguls controlled the minstrel shows.

Minstrel shows never lost their nostalgic appeal to rural America. However, by the late nineteenth century they looked more and more like vaudeville, an art form that was born and bred in the big city.

The Origins of Vaudeville

Unlike the minstrels, vaudeville shows did not rely on nostalgia. Rather, vaudeville and its cheaper cousins (concert saloons and dollar theaters) flourished in American cities after elites succeeded in distinguishing serious theater from variety shows. As the cost of a ticket to a Shakespeare production rose beyond the means of most working people, urban audiences turned to inexpensive houses that offered music, singing, sketches, and variety acts. At first the audiences in such theaters were rowdy and exclusively male. Yet these concert saloons and variety theaters attracted patrons from up and down the social scale. In 1883 a Chicago guidebook claimed that the city's variety theaters were patronized not only by "the lower class of society, but [by] journalists, professional men, bankers, railroad officials, politicians, and men of rank in society." Even so, there were no blacks.

Increasingly, however, there were women. Beginning in the 1880s, a handful of show business entrepreneurs tried to develop variety theaters that appealed to audiences with both men and women. The respectability of a mixed audience was one of the distinguishing signs of vaudeville. Vaudeville producers booked a variety of acts to appeal to a broad audience. They also developed continuous performances, which allowed patrons to come to a vaudeville show any time of the day or evening.

Continuous performances kept the prices down, thereby increasing the size of the potential audience. Locating downtown in the heart of the city had the same effect. Theater owners also regulated smoking and, over time, banned alcohol consumption, thus promoting the image of family entertainment. Finally, they booked great opera singers or distinguished musicians for brief appearances, in a conscious effort to enhance vaudeville's reputation for respectability.

Growing audiences made it possible for vaudeville producers to construct huge and ornate theatrical "palaces" that housed ever more elaborate productions. The high cost of such theaters kept the number of competitors down. As a result, a handful of companies came to dominate the vaudeville theater industry, much as minstrel companies had become concentrated in the hands of a few owners. By the turn of the century, vaudeville was one of the most popular forms of public entertainment in American cities. But minstrel shows and vaudeville theaters were not the only places Americans went during their leisure time.

Sports Become Professional

As growing numbers of Americans went to the theater to be entertained, still more went to the baseball park or sports arena. For a significant segment of the urban population, sports was becoming something to watch rather than something to do.

As the number of spectators increased, baseball and prizefighting became professionalized. Prizefighting had long been a disreputable amusement of shady bars and lower class streets, but during the 1880s, it became an organized sport attracting a huge national audience. Richard Kyle Fox, owner of the *National Police Gazette*, used his popular magazine and his considerable financial resources to transform boxing. Because Fox put up the prize money, he had the power to reform the sport. He made it both more profitable and more respectable and introduced standardized rules.

As the sport grew in popularity, entrepreneurs sponsored fights at indoor rings where they could control unruly audiences with police and security guards. Thereafter, as prizefighter John L. Sullivan explained in 1892, "the price of admission is put purposely high so as to exclude the rowdy element, and a gentleman can see the contest, feeling sure that he will not be robbed . . . or in any way be interfered with." Although prizefighting never completely lost its aura of disrepute, by the 1890s it was one of the most popular spectator sports in America, second only to baseball.

Like prizefighting, baseball was professionalized in the last half of the nineteenth century. By the 1860s baseball had become tremendously popular among city dwellers, particularly immigrants and their children. They formed leagues in urban neighborhoods all across the country. But not until 1869, when the Cincinnati Red Stockings went on tour and charged admission, did baseball become a professional spectator sport. Soon thereafter standardized rules appeared for the first time.

Within a decade the owners of eight baseball clubs had formed a National League that had all the earmarks of a corporate cartel. It restrained the power of players, restricted the number of teams to one per city, prohibited Sunday games, banned the sale of alcohol at ballparks, hired umpires, and set schedules and admission prices. Chafing under these restrictions, many players jumped to a new American Association that formed in 1882. The owners regrouped, however, and within a year the two leagues merged and quickly reinstated the restrictions on players. In reaction the players formed a league of their own but were unable to match the wealth and power of the owners. By the mid-1890s the National League controlled professional baseball.

Baseball idealized the principle of success based purely on merit. Objective statistics identified the best players without respect to their personal background. A model of ordered competition, the baseball meritocracy provided a useful lesson in the way capitalist society was supposed to work. Professional players became working-class heroes, many of them having risen from factories and slums. But professional baseball reflected the realities as well as the ideals of American capitalism. The owners' cartel prevented professional athletes from taking advantage of the market. In addition, baseball's meritocracy had no place for the merits of black players, who were excluded from the professional sport. Even the seating arrangements in ballparks reflected America's social divisions. Working-class fans sat in the bleachers, the middle class occupied the stands, and elites took the box seats.

The popularity of sports was reflected in the growing numbers of participants as well as spectators. As daily work became more sedentary, especially for white-collar workers, Americans spent more time in physical recreation. During the late nineteenth century, "the sporting life" became an American pastime. The popularity of bicycling exploded, for example, particularly after the invention of the modern "safety bike" in 1888. Within a decade there were 10 million bicycles in the United States. Men joined the YMCA or organized local baseball teams. At Harvard, Yale, and Princeton young men took up football, basketball, and rowing. At Smith, Vassar, and Berkeley young women played baseball, basketball, and tennis. In urban neighborhoods ethnic groups organized Irish, Italian, and German baseball teams. Women began riding bicycles, swimming, and playing golf and croquet.

But appearances were deceptive. The sports craze mirrored the inequalities and anxieties of industrial America. Men who believed that independence was a sign of masculinity became concerned that wage labor would make them soft and "feminine." A vocal segment of the American elite turned to athletic activities as an antidote to the supposedly feminizing tendencies of industrial capitalism. Theodore Roosevelt, the product of an old and wealthy New York family, who became president of the United States, believed that "commercial civilization" placed too little stress on "the more virile virtues." There was, Roosevelt argued, "no better way of counteracting this tendency than by encouraging bodily exercise and especially the sports which develop such qualities as courage, resolution and endurance."

As baseball and prizefighting became both popular and professional, elites reacted by glorifying the amateur ideal, embracing vigorous athletic activity for its own sake rather than for monetary reward. In the late nineteenth century wealthy Americans pursued the sporting life at elite colleges, exclusive race tracks, and private athletic clubs, country clubs, and yacht clubs. By the turn of the century, the most exclusive colleges in the Northeast had formed football's Ivy League, a designation that became synonymous with elite private universities.

The rigors of sport taught elite men how to face the rigors of business competition, weeded out the weak, and prepared society's leaders for the contest of daily life. Thus the elite's attraction to rugged sports reinforced a self-serving view of American society: In the political economy of competitive capitalism the best nations, like the best men, would rise to the top.

The most significant attempt to spread such values more widely was the founding of the Young Men's Christian Association (YMCA) in 1851. By 1894 there were 261 YMCAs across the nation. A strong reform impulse sustained the YMCA movement. Its founders hoped that organized recreational activity would distract workers from labor radicalism and that classes and games would assimilate immigrants to the laws, customs, and language of the United States. In many ways the YMCA was an extension of Anthony Comstock's movement to suppress vice: It hoped to provide wholesome amusements to young men who might otherwise succumb to the temptations of city life.

World's Fairs: The Celebration of the City

To celebrate the accomplishments of urban and industrial society, the city of London hosted a spectacular world's fair at the Crystal Palace in 1851. Over the next 50 years the cities of the Western world became showcases for the technological and cultural achievements of industrial capitalism. By 1900 there had been expositions in Paris, Vienna, Brussels, Antwerp, Florence, Amsterdam, Dublin, and even Sydney, Australia. Most celebrated the achievements of the host countries and the civic pride of their sponsoring cities, as well as the triumph of technology and the progress of humanity. American fairs were no exception. A dozen major American cities sponsored world expositions in the late nineteenth and early twentieth centuries.

The first major world's fair in the United States took place in Philadelphia in 1876, timed to commemorate the centennial of American independence. In keeping with the theme of global interaction, the fair's sponsors asked the nations of the world to build pavilions of their own. The pavilions were arranged to reflect not the harmony of nations, but the differences among the world's "races." Americans were only beginning to develop such ideas in 1876, but the broad outlines of the racial categories were already evident. France and its colonies, "representing the Latin races," were grouped together, as were England and its colonies, "representing the Anglo-Saxon races," and "the Teutonic races," represented by Germany, Austria, and Hungary. Within 20 years, these racial categories would harden into an elaborate hierarchy that embraced all the peoples of the world.

The World Columbian Exposition in Chicago was the largest of the world's fairs that became popular in the late nineteenth century. Among other things, they were celebrations of the technology and city life that were becoming the characteristics of modern, industrial civilization.

Nowhere was this hierarchy more visible than at the greatest fair of the century, the World's Columbian Exposition in Chicago in 1893. Built on Lake Michigan several miles south of downtown, the Chicago fair had twice as many foreign buildings as its Philadelphia predecessor, covered 686 acres, and attracted 25 million visitors. The exposition was divided between the White City and the Midway Plaisance. The White City showcased American industrial might with immense steam engines and the latest consumer goods. But the Midway Plaisance featured carnivals, the first ferris wheel, games, and sideshows. It also featured an ethnographic exhibit providing a popular rendition of principles of scientific racism. The exhibit portrayed the "races" of the world in a hierarchy from the most civilized (Europeans) to the least civilized (Asians and Africans).

Where earlier forms of popular entertainment had romanticized preindustrial society and the rural life, the world's fairs celebrated the new political economy of cities and industry. The White City, the heart of the World's Columbian Exposition in Chicago, was an idealized vision of urban life. Rural simplicity had given way to the majestic city as the model for civilization.

THE ELUSIVE BOUNDARIES OF MALE AND FEMALE

Anthony Comstock saw the city as a place where traditional morality broke down, particularly standards of sexual propriety. In fact, the political economy of industrial capitalism and the triumph of wage labor compelled men and women to rethink traditional conceptions of masculinity and femininity. As they did so, spectacular new cities and newfound leisure time offered Americans unprecedented opportunities to test the conventional boundaries of sexual identity.

The Victorian Construction of Male and Female

Until the mid-1700s most European doctors believed that there was only one sex: Females were simply inferior, insufficiently developed males. Sometime after 1750, however, scientists and intellectuals began to argue that males and females were fundamentally different, that they were "opposite" sexes. For the first time it was possible to argue that women were naturally less interested in sex than men or that men were "active" while women were "passive." Nature itself seemed to justify the infamous double standard that condoned sexual activity by men but punished women for the same thing.

In the nineteenth century Victorians drew even more extreme differences between men and women. Victorian boys were reared on moralistic stories of heroes who overcame their fears. In this way boys were prepared for the competitive worlds of business and politics, worlds from which women were largely excluded. To be a "man" in industrial America was to work in the rough-and-tumble world of the capitalist market. Men proved themselves by their success at making a living and therefore at taking care of a wife and children.

Victorian men defined themselves as rational creatures whose reason was threatened by their overwhelming sexual drives. Physical exertion was an important device for controlling a man's powerful sexual urges. Because in Victorian America masturbation was an unacceptable outlet for these drives, men were urged to channel their sexual energies into strenuous activities such as sports and, conveniently enough, wage labor. Masculinity was defined as the ability to leave the confines of the home and compete successfully in the capitalist labor market.

Where masculinity became a more rigid concept, femininity became less certain. Women's schools established their own sports programs. Thousands of women took up bicycling, tennis, and other physical activities. Yet at the same time the stereotype persisted that women were too frail to engage in the hurly-burly of business and enterprise. Lacking the competitive instinct of the male, the female was destined to become a wife and mother within the protective confines of the home. Just as men congregated in social clubs and sports teams, a "female world of love and ritual" developed. Middle-class women often displayed among themselves a passionate affection that was often expressed in nearly erotic terms. But genuinely passionate female sexuality was deeply disturbing to the Victorians. Evidence of sexual passion among women was increasingly diagnosed, mostly by male doctors, as a symptom of a new disorder called "neurasthenia."

Over time the differences between men and women were defined in increasingly medical terms. Victorian doctors redefined homosexuality as a medical abnormality, a perversion, and urged the passage of laws outlawing homosexual relations. The new science of gynecology powerfully reinforced popular assumptions about the differences between men and women. Distinguished male physicians argued that the energy women expended in reproduction left them unable to withstand the rigors of higher education. In extreme cases physicians would excise a woman's clitoris to thwart masturbation or remove her ovaries to cure neurasthenia.

On the assumption that motherhood was a female's natural destiny, doctors pressed to restrict women's access to contraception and to prohibit abortion. Before the Civil War abortion in the first three months of pregnancy was tolerated, although not necessarily approved. This began to change as the medical profession seized control over the regulation of female reproduction. The American Medical Association (AMA, founded in 1847) campaigned to restrict the activities not only of quacks and incompetents but also of female midwives and abortionists. Doctors, most of whom were males, accepted prevailing assumptions about the maternal destiny of women. Hence doctors opposed attempts by women to interfere with pregnancy. The AMA supported passage of the Comstock Law, which outlawed the sale of contraception. Doctors also pushed successfully to criminalize abortion.

Victorians Who Questioned Traditional Sexual Boundaries

In a new political economy based on wage labor, large numbers of Americans, especially young men, now found themselves with cash and leisure time. The anonymity of huge cities gave them the opportunity to defy established standards of sexual behavior. Freed from the constraints of parents and the scrutiny of small-town life, wage earners frequented prostitutes in unprecedented numbers, attended shows that featured sexually provocative entertainers, read erotic novels, and purchased pornographic prints. Many Americans began to explore unconventional sexual practices.

The major venues of popular entertainment increasingly displayed a looser, more relaxed attitude toward sex. Can-can girls, off-color jokes, and comedy skits focusing on the war of the sexes all contradicted Victorian propriety. Even the styles of clothing that consumers purchased in mass quantities were a rejection of the stifling conventions of the Victorian middle class. Trousers got looser, starched collars disappeared, and women's dresses were simplified and rendered considerably more comfortable. The sensuous human body became an object of fascination in much of the popular culture. Minstrels, musical variety shows, and the vaudeville theater all glorified female sexuality. For the first time male sports heroes were openly admired for their physiques. Much of the literature of the day was infused with the theme of homosexual relations. Walt Whitman's poems celebrated sexual attraction among men, and some scholars see elements of homoeroticism in Huckleberry Finn's relationship with Jim in Mark Twain's famous novel. A more obvious case is Horatio Alger. In the late nineteenth century he wrote a series of books about young boys who lived on the streets of New York and made their way out of poverty. Alger's heroes thus embody the American dream of upward mobility. Alger began his own career as a Unitarian minister in Brewster, Massachusetts, but he was expelled from his pulpit for "the revolting crime of unnatural familiarity with boys." Alger left New England in disgrace and moved to New York, where he developed a keen interest in the problems of young boys who roamed loose on the city streets.

Alger's charity work became the basis of his fiction. In most of his novels, the young heroes shared the same physical attributes. They were dirty but handsome. In most cases it was the boy's good looks that attracted the attention of the wealthy male patron. Alger's novels depicted the relationships between men and boys in terms reminiscent of a seduction. Once rescued from rags and gainfully employed, Alger's hero typically set up house with a roommate. These households were fastidiously neat, and their inhabitants were thrifty and sober. The only difference from an ideal middle-class household was that both inhabitants were male. In one case, two male roommates, having both been saved and made respectable, actually "adopted" a little boy, a street urchin named "Mark the Matchboy."

Few readers saw Horatio Alger's novels as experiments in unconventional sexuality, but their homoeroticism was consistent with the increased sexual frankness of urban life in the late nineteenth century. It was not surprising that reformers like Anthony Comstock looked at the city and saw an explosion of vice. Others, however, were struck less by urban sexuality than by the profusion of immigrants who were transforming the culture of the city.

IMMIGRATION AS A CULTURAL PROBLEM

When novelist Henry James returned to the United States in 1907 after a quarter of a century in Europe, he was stunned and disgusted by the pervasive presence of immigrants in New York City. On the streetcars he confronted "a row of faces, up and down, testifying, without exception, to alienism unmistakable, alienism undisguised and unashamed." James was one of the many native-born Americans who assumed that their culture was Protestant, democratic, and English-speaking. They were deeply disturbed, therefore, by the arrival of vast numbers of immigrants who were none of those things and by the way ethnic subcultures seemed to flourish in United States cities. Yet among immigrants and their children, an ethnic identity was often a sign of assimilation into a broader American culture.

Josiah Strong Attacks Immigration

"Every race which has deeply impressed itself on the human family has been the representative of some great idea," Josiah Strong wrote in *Our Country*. Greek civilization was famed for its beauty, he explained, the Romans for their law, and the Hebrews for their purity. The Anglo-Saxon race had two great ideas to its credit, Strong argued. The first was the love of liberty, and the second was "pure spiritual Christianity." Published in 1885, Strong's bestselling book was revised and reprinted in 1891 and serialized in newspapers across America. Strong spoke to the concerns of vast numbers of native-born Americans who saw themselves as the defenders of Anglo-Saxon culture. Strong was optimistic that as representatives of "the largest liberty, the purest Christianity, the highest civilization," the powerful Anglo-Saxon race would "spread itself over the earth."

But there was a problem. To Strong and his readers, the Anglo-Saxon in America was threatened by the arrival of vast numbers of immigrants. The typical immigrant, he warned, was not a freedom-loving Anglo-Saxon Protestant but a "European peasant." Narrow-minded men and women "whose moral and religious training has been meager or false," immigrants brought crime to America's cities and undermined the nation's politics. Immigrants voted in blocks, and their influence was enhanced by the fact that they were concentrated in big cities. "[T]here is no more serious menace to our civilization," Strong warned, "than our rabble-ruled cities."

At the core of the problem was the fact that immigrants could not be assimilated into the American way of life. "Our safety demands the assimilation of these strange populations," Strong wrote. But they were coming in such huge numbers that assimilation was becoming impossible (see Map 18–1). Worst of all, the Catholic Church held millions of immigrants in its grip, filling their heads with superstition rather than "pure Christianity." It did not help that immigrants had large numbers of children. Through its elaborate network of parochial schools, the Catholic Church was training new generations to love tyranny rather than liberty.

Strong and his readers need not have worried. The millions of immigrants who came to the United States adapted quickly to American society. Indeed, Strong misread much of his own evidence. By cultivating the German vote or the Irish vote,

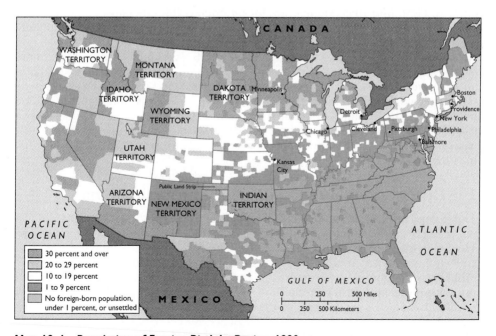

Map 18–1   Population of Foreign Birth by Region, 1880

Source: Clifford L. Lord and Elizabeth H. Lord, Lord & Lord Historical Atlas of the United States (New York: Holt, 1953).

for example, politicians went far toward assimilating immigrants into American political culture. Nor were immigrants as slavishly subservient to the Catholic Church as Strong thought. In the end, the Church played an ambiguous role in the cultural history of American immigrants.

From Immigrants to Ethnic Americans

Critics like Strong scarcely noticed the regional and class differences that immigrants brought with them. In the middle of the nineteenth century, most immigrants came with loyalties to their regions and villages, but not to their nationality. In New York City German-speaking immigrants thought of themselves primarily as Bavarian or Prussian rather than as German. Irish immigrants identified with their home counties more than their native country. Immigrant churches across America were torn by such regional conflicts.

After immigrants arrived in the United States, however, regional differences began to decline. One reason was the growth of secular fraternal organizations. Fraternal organizations often began as mutual aid societies designed to help newcomers find jobs and housing. In 1893 mineworkers formed the Pennsylvania Slovak Catholic Union to help cover burial expenses for those killed in the mines. Most often, however, middle-class immigrants took the lead in forming fraternal organizations; in other cases local priests played prominent roles. Regardless of their leadership, about half of all immigrants eventually joined ethnic fraternal societies.

As they grew, fraternal organizations became national in their scope, as immigrants constructed a new "ethnic" identity that united all members under a single national rubric. In some cases immigrant businessmen led the drive toward the development of a unified ethnic identity. Marco Fontana, who ran the Del Monte company in California, encouraged the growth of an "Italian" identity among his workers. He found that regional loyalties hindered the efficient operation of his enterprises. Eventually, immigrants began to think of themselves as members of ethnic groups that shared the same national ancestry.

It was not merely coincidental that immigrants developed "national" identities in the United States. Nationalism was spreading throughout the Western world during the nineteenth century. While immigrants in America were coming to see themselves as Irish or Italian, the same thing was happening back home in Ireland and Italy. In the United States the Civil War had unleashed a wave of nationalistic fervor, and a series of liberal revolutions did the same thing in Europe. As the decades passed immigrants brought to America an increasingly powerful sense of their ethnic identities.

The Catholic Church and Its Limits in Immigrant Culture

The Roman Catholic Church played a complicated role in the development of ethnic cultures among immigrants. In some cases churches were established to preserve Old World traditions. In 1841, for example, the Reverend Johann Raffeiner collected the money to build Holy Trinity, a German-speaking Catholic church. In other ways the church smoothed the transition into American life by serving as a mutual aid society. Polish churches in Chicago and German parishes in Milwaukee used their women's groups and youth clubs as mutual aid societies for their local immigrants.

The church sometimes unintentionally sped the development of ethnic identities. The Irish became more devout in America as they came to rely on the church to assist them in resisting an overwhelmingly Protestant culture. Germans also gravitated toward the church and in the process overcame their regional differences. But the more they came to equate their German identity with Catholicism, the more they resented Irish domination of the church hierarchy. Thus German Catholics worked to establish their own churches and parish schools or to have sermons preached in German. By contrast, the Italians were largely alienated from the official church, the hierarchy of which was largely Irish. By the late nineteenth century North American bishops were trying to standardize Catholicism in America. They published uniform catechisms, established powerful bureaucratic structures, and tried to suppress the folk rituals of Italian Catholicism. Thus Italians were ironically united in their suspicion of the church.

The church's power was reinforced by the struggle for control over the education of immigrant children. Throughout the nineteenth century public schools were heavily Protestant. Josiah Strong and other native-born reformers tried to use public education to "Americanize" immigrant children. They taught the Protestant Bible. They shifted the focus in the classroom away from the classics and toward "practical" education and language training, with the goal of turning immigrants into reliable workers and patriotic citizens. But immigrants fiercely resisted such efforts, and the bulwark of their resistance was the church.

During the second half of the nineteenth century both the Catholic and Lutheran Churches established parochial school systems to protect immigrant children from the biases of public education. So comprehensive was the Catholic Church's effort that by 1883 all but two parishes in the city of Chicago had their own parochial schools.

Ironically, parochial education contributed to assimilation among immigrants. Catholic or Lutheran schools in Irish or German parishes reinforced the growth of distinctively American ethnic identities and bound ethnicity to an increasingly standardized and Americanized Catholicism or Lutheranism.

The Political Economy of Immigrant Culture

Despite assimilation, the ethnic identities that immigrants developed in America remained distinctive. Irish Americans, for example, fused together songs from various parts of Ireland and added piano accompaniment. Similarly, Polish immigrant bands expanded beyond the traditional violin of their homelands by adding accordions, clarinets, and trumpets. But the results were still distinctively Polish-American or Irish-American music. Hundreds of immigrant theaters sprang up offering productions that adjusted traditional plot lines to the New World. Jewish plays told of humble peddlers who outwitted their prosperous patrons. Italian folk tales emphasized the importance of the family. In these ways distinctive ethnic identities, adapted to urban and industrial America, developed.

One of the most distinctive features of immigrant culture was family size. At a time when middle-class families had only two or three children, immigrant families remained large. There were sound economic reasons for this. There were no child-labor laws restricting the employment of minors and few compulsory-education laws requiring children to attend school. Working-class families relied heavily on the incomes of their children, particularly teenagers. Children in the immigrant working class were expected to contribute to the economic well-being of their families.

At the turn of the century, Italian mothers in Buffalo, New York, had an average of 11 children. Among Polish wives the average was closer to eight. In

Pennsylvania's coal-mining district, working-class immigrant women had 45 percent more children than native-born women. But the death rate among immigrant children was also high. In 1900, one out of three Polish and Italian mothers had seen one of their children die before his or her first birthday.

As ethnicity developed in the late nineteenth century, class divisions were increasingly difficult to isolate from cultural distinctions. The middle class, for example, was overwhelmingly native born, white, Anglo-Saxon, and Protestant. The working class was, by contrast, African American, foreign born, Catholic, or Jewish. By 1900, 75 percent of the manufacturing workers in the United States were immigrants or the children of immigrants. In large cities, five out of six new manufacturing jobs were filled by immigrants and their children. In the South, wage laborers were overwhelmingly black sharecroppers. It was in this context that educated elites constructed a definition of high culture that would distinguish the middle classes from the allegedly uncultivated and uncultured working classes.

THE CREATION OF HIGH CULTURE

During the second half of the nineteenth century many leading intellectuals sought to isolate and define a tradition, *high culture*, that stretched through Western history from ancient Greece and Rome to the present. By the 1890s high culture embodied principles of social, cultural, and political hierarchy that were firmly installed in museums, libraries, and universities across the United States. A high culture had been created.

High Culture Becomes Sacred

The leading advocate of high culture was an Englishman, Matthew Arnold. In *Culture and Anarchy*, published in 1869, Arnold promoted the study of "the best which has been thought and said in the world" as an antidote to the "anarchy" of capitalist society. Similar views about high culture spread on both sides of the Atlantic. "Certain things are not disputable," *Harper's Magazine* declared in 1867; authors such as Homer, Shakespeare, and Dante "are towering facts like the Alps or the Himalayas. . . . It is not conceivable that the judgment of mankind upon those names will ever be reversed." American elites looking for firm moral guidelines were turning to a canon of great cultural achievements the way earlier generations had looked to holy scripture, and secular culture therefore assumed sacred qualities.

Lurking beneath the sacred view of culture was the fear that the modern world had undermined traditional values, especially religious values. "Organizations are splitting asunder, institutions are falling into decay, customs are becoming uncustomary," one observer complained in 1865. Particularly troubling was the apparent decline in religious fervor. Middle-class men and women often confessed to a loss of their own faith.

The middle class never lost its faith entirely. On the contrary, Victorians retained their overwhelmingly Protestant orientation and their deep suspicion of Roman Catholicism. What they lost was a strong theology and missionary zeal. Victorians moved restlessly from one denomination to another, but few found the spiritual satisfaction or moral guidance they sought. As religious fervor waned, the Victorian middle class looked for comfort in more secular pursuits.

Jacob Riis, who included this photo in his classic study of immigrant slums, How the Other Half Lives, *believed that immigrant neighborhoods were plagued by the absence of culture.*

Thomas Wentworth Higginson typified this shift. Nurtured in the reform movements of antebellum New England, Higginson had been an abolitionist and supporter of women's rights and during the Civil War commanded a regiment of African-American troops. Fully engaged in the politics of his day, Higginson was equally at home in the literary culture of his native New England, turning to culture for relief from the sordid realities of capitalist political economy.

In 1871, two years after Matthew Arnold published *Culture and Anarchy*, Higginson made a strikingly similar case. Culture, he explained, "pursues" art and science for their intrinsic worth. It "places the fine arts above the useful arts." It sacrifices "material comforts" for the sake of a "nobler" life. At its best, Higginson believed, culture "supplies that counterpoise to mere wealth which Europe vainly seeks to secure by aristocracies of birth." Like Matthew Arnold, Higginson saw culture as a defense against materialism.

Despite his contempt for the European aristocracy, Higginson could write just as condescendingly about ordinary people. He thus shared the Victorian conviction that culture was an attribute of the middle classes. At the top of the social order stood an increasingly dissolute and unrestrained capitalist class. At the bottom, poor working men and women lived lives utterly devoid of gentility and refinement. To many progressive intellectuals, therefore, saving America from barbarism required an infusion of culture into the lives of ordinary city folk.

Yet these very classes, the greedy capitalists at the top and the ignorant masses below, seemed to grow in influence as cities grew in size. To counteract this threat, American elites worked to transform American cities into centers of high art and cultural distinction.

The Creation of a Cultural Establishment

In the early nineteenth century Shakespeare was the most popular playwright in America. Traveling through the country in the 1830s, Alexis de Tocqueville encountered Shakespeare even in "the recesses of the forests of the New World. There is hardly a pioneer's hut that does not contain a few odd volumes of Shakespeare." In established theaters, Shakespearean plays were performed more than any others, and the repertoire was not limited to a few classics. American audiences were familiar with a substantial body of Shakespeare's work.

A Shakespearean play was usually performed as the centerpiece of an entire evening's entertainment that included music, dancing, acrobats, magicians, and comedians. The show generally ended with a short humorous skit, or farce. Audiences attending these shows came from all walks of life, and they often made a noisy crowd.

Americans preferred highly melodramatic renditions of Shakespeare. It was best if the moral ambiguities were smoothed out, the lessons made sharp and clear. Ideally the ending was always satisfying. Good always triumphed over evil. Instead of committing suicide, Romeo and Juliet lived happily ever after. By 1850 Americans were so familiar with Shakespeare that politicians could safely make allusions to his plays without fear of losing an audience.

All of this changed in the second half of the nineteenth century. Shakespeare was redefined as high culture, anwd performances of his plays were separated from popular entertainment. This shift was evident as early as the 1850s, when a San Francisco theater announced that its production of *A Midsummer Night's Dream* would be performed by itself, with "NO FARCE." The entertainments that had once accompanied Shakespearean performances became the basis of the vaudeville theater, and theater audiences became segregated by class. The respectable classes retreated from the boisterous houses into quieter theaters, where the prices rose beyond the means of ordinary working people.

The same thing happened to opera and to orchestral music. Opera changed from an eclectic and highly popular art form to an elite entertainment. Opera became associated with high fashion and elite culture, and the opening of the opera season became synonymous with the opening of the "social season" among the very rich.

In the first half of the nineteenth century, local bands sprang up in thousands of communities across America (3,000 of them by 1860) with a repertoire that included popular and classical pieces. Beginning in the 1840s, classical music became the preserve of elite symphony orchestras in large cities.

To sound their best, orchestras like the New York Philharmonic and the Chicago Symphony needed expensive new halls. Opera companies needed endowments. Serious theater needed generous patrons. Thus great infusions of private wealth were necessary to support lavish arts programs. In the late nineteenth century, the rich formed an alliance with leading performers and intellectuals to create a cultural establishment that endures to this day. Opera houses and symphony halls were built with and sustained by the patronage of the wealthy. They were the architectural embodiment of high culture.

Great cities required great museums as well. Americans built a stunning array of secular temples devoted to the world's great art. Major museums were founded in New York, Boston, Philadelphia, and Chicago in the 1870s. Spectacular new public libraries appeared at the same time. By 1900 many Americans had come to associate culture with impressive institutions lodged in major cities. By this reasoning, for example, the cultural life of Chicago was embodied not in the immigrant neighborhoods or the popular theaters, but in the Art Institute, Symphony Hall, and the Chicago Public Library.

Orchestra Hall in Chicago was one of many stately auditoriums built to house America's major symphony orchestras in the second half of the nineteenth century.

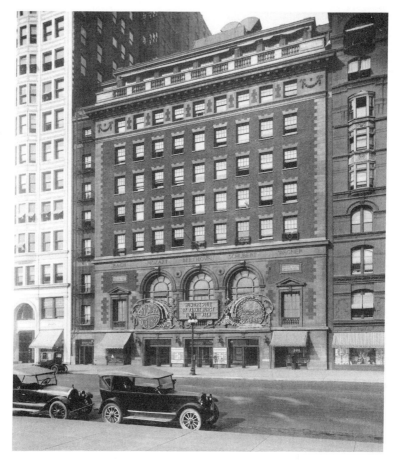

The Emergence of the Modern University

At the same time that American elites were endowing museums and libraries they stepped up their commitment to the establishment of distinguished private universities. Cornell, Johns Hopkins, Vanderbilt, Stanford, and the University of Chicago all appeared between the late 1860s and the 1890s. Wealthy businessmen had good reason to endow great universities. The political economy of industrial capitalism rested on technological developments, which in turn depended on up-to-date scientific learning. Research universities played a central role in such developments and provided the training for the new business and engineering elite. And finally, corporate philanthropists agreed with many Americans that a great Western nation required great universities.

   The new colleges reflected a new conception of how universities should be organized. Daniel Coit Gilman, the first president of the Johns Hopkins University in Baltimore, created specialized departments of history, English, and the various sciences that were responsible for recommending appointments and promotions and for developing courses. He encouraged the publication of academic journals and established the first university press in 1878. Gilman had created the modern university with a faculty of specialists dedicated to research and the training of other scholars. His innovations spread quickly and led to the undergraduate major, the system of numbered courses, unit requirements, electives, and PhD programs with research seminars and dissertations based on original research.

In this new setting, the study of modern literature entered the college curriculum for the first time. Some professors, influenced by German scholarship, emphasized sentence structures, word roots, and forms of publication. This approach appealed to those who sought to make the study of literature into a science. But beneath the surface was a set of assumptions about the intrinsic superiority of Western European languages. A leading Oxford scholar, Friedrich Max Muller, saw "an unbroken chain between us and Cicero and Aristotle." Muller and his American followers created a canon of great works that they believed defined culture of the "West." They also defined the study of literature as the preserve of specialists.

Leading scholars in the new "social sciences" of sociology, anthropology, and political science also divided the world into great and inferior nations. Best of all were the so-called Teutonic nations of western Europe and North America. Anthropologists, sociologists, and professional economists also claimed that the human hierarchies they constructed were grounded in the objective methods of pure science. Science was becoming the model for the production of all human knowledge.

Social Darwinism and the Growth of Scientific Racism

In 1859 Charles Darwin published his masterpiece of evolutionary theory, *On the Origin of Species*. Several scientists had already suggested that life had evolved over a long period of time, but Darwin offered the first persuasive theory of how this might have taken place. He argued that a process of "natural selection" favored those biological changes that were most suited to the surrounding environment. In Darwinian theory, natural selection was the single most important explanation for the vast array of life forms on earth. American scientists were remarkably receptive to Darwinism. Asa Gray at Harvard and Joseph LeConte at the University of California spread the evolutionary word in their influential textbooks on botany and geology. By 1900 virtually all the science textbooks used in American high schools embraced evolution.

Darwin's remarkable influence did not stop with the natural sciences. Social scientists applied the theory of natural selection to social evolution. This combination of social theory with evolutionary science was known as social Darwinism. Social Darwinists argued that human inequality was the outcome of a struggle for survival in which the fittest rose to the top of the social ladder. This theory made the rich seem more fit than the poor; it made blacks seem less fit than whites. To social Darwinists, inequality was the natural order of things. In this way Darwinism was put to use in defense of the political economy of industrial capitalism.

From the moment he published *On the Origin of Species* in 1859 Darwin's theory of natural selection was used to support a theory of African racial inferiority. Racists had argued that emancipation would force blacks to compete with their white superiors and that this competition would end in the disappearance of the African race. When the 1890 census seemed to show that blacks were withering under the strain of competition with whites, racial theorists unleashed a volley of influential studies.

In 1892 biologist Joseph LeConte weighed in with an article on "The Race Problem in the South." In conditions of free competition with whites, LeConte argued, blacks faced either "extinction" or permanent subordination. Only the protection of whites could shield blacks from their natural fate.

Far more influential than the LeConte article was Frederick L. Hoffman's full-length treatise, *Race Traits and Tendencies of the American Negro*, published in 1896. Hoffman's book quickly established itself as one of the most important studies of race relations written in the nineteenth century. Hoffman himself was a statistician, and the tables and figures scattered throughout his book gave it the authoritative air of the new social sciences. Yet from beginning to end the book was an ideological rant. Ever since they had left the protective cover of slavery, Hoffman argued, blacks had shown clear signs of moral degeneration and were doomed to poverty and social inferiority.

Social scientists like Hoffman prided themselves on their commitment to the truth as it was revealed in facts and statistics. Like advocates of high culture, sociologists and anthropologists claimed to have isolated the definitive truths of human society. But not all "realists" sought solace in the past or justified the inequalities of the present. The best American artists of the late nineteenth century openly embraced the realities of urban and industrial America.

ARTISTIC REALISM EMBRACES URBAN AND INDUSTRIAL AMERICA

"This is the age of cities," writer Hamlin Garland declared. "We are now predominantly urban and the problem of our artistic life is practically one of city life." In the second half of the nineteenth century, artists and writers embraced the world that Anthony Comstock wanted to suppress and that Matthew Arnold wanted to escape. They called themselves realists and saw themselves as part of the first major artistic movement that was grounded in urban and industrial America. As writer Fanny Bates put it, the people of the cities "live more in realities than imagination."

The Triumph of Literary Realism

In April 1861 the *Atlantic Monthly* published a powerful story called "Life in the Iron Mills" by a writer named Rebecca Harding. Her story created a sensation. Rarely had the dreary lives of ordinary workers been presented in such relentless detail. In the decades to come, the best writers in America joined in the crusade to make fiction realistic. "The public demands realism," Willa Cather explained, "and they will have it." The leading spokesperson for realistic fiction was William Dean Howells, the author of one of the best realist novels, *The Rise of Silas Lapham*, and editor of the *Atlantic Monthly*, one of a handful of influential magazines that championed literary realism.

Realists tried to bridge the gap between "high" and "popular" culture by making great literature out of the details of everyday life. To "enjoy the every-day life," Sarah Orne Jewett explained in *Deephaven*, one must "find pleasure in thought and observation of simple things, and have an instinctive, delicious interest in what to other eyes is unflavored dullness." By writing about failed businessmen or runaway slaves, writers like Howells and Mark Twain hoped to reveal both courage and cowardice in the lives of ordinary men and women. This was the great achievement of Twain's *Huckleberry Finn*.

The characters in realistic novels were flawed men and women who struggled with the moral dilemmas they encountered in their daily lives. In Howells's greatest novel, Silas Lapham had to decide whether to mislead the men who wanted to buy his failing paint company. Huck Finn had to decide whether to turn in a runaway slave. Yet neither Lapham nor Finn was "heroic" in the way that earlier heroes were. Lapham was an ill-educated social climber who drank and talked too much. Huck Finn was a barely literate seeker of adventure who played hooky, spoke improper English, and spun absurd fantasies. In the end both Silas Lapham and Huck Finn made the right moral decisions, but neither found his decision easy to make, and Lapham suffered for having done so.

The realist movement was greeted with shock by the defenders of the genteel tradition of American letters. In March 1885 the public library committee of Concord, Massachusetts, banned *Huckleberry Finn* from its shelves, denouncing it as "the veriest trash." Members of the committee characterized Twain's masterpiece as "rough, coarse and inelegant, dealing with a series of experiences not elevating, the whole book being more suited to the slums than to intelligent, respectable people."

Realists dismissed such criticism as evidence of the "feminine" taste that prevailed in American letters and saw realism as a "masculine" alternative to sentimental writing that appealed to women novel readers. In their commitment to the unvarnished truth, realists thought of themselves as "virile and strong." But female realists such as Kate Chopin also rejected the assumption, common to sentimental fiction, that women's lives should be bounded exclusively by the needs of their husbands and children. Louisa May Alcott wanted her female characters to be "strong-minded, strong-hearted, strong-souled, and strong-bodied." Realistic writers thus challenged the sentimental depiction of women as nervous, frail, and destined only for the domestic life.

Other authors, most notably Walt Whitman, pushed the radical possibilities of realism even further. Like most realists, Whitman aspired to "manly" writing. Through his poems he hoped "to exalt the present and the real, to teach the average man the glory of his daily walk and trade." He was the poet of the city who filled his verse with vivid details of urban life. For Whitman that meant he would embrace the "goodness" as well as the "wickedness" of modern America. Just as vaudeville flirted more and more openly with sexual titillation, Whitman wrote more and more openly about eroticism. Thus Whitman, like so many realists, fused the themes of popular culture with the forms of "high" art.

Painting Reality

In 1878 New York artist John Ferguson Weir declared that "art, in common with literature, is now seeking to get nearer the reality, to 'see the thing as it really is.'" Like the best writers of the post-Civil War era, the finest painters rejected romanticism in favor of realism. Winslow Homer and Thomas Eakins shifted the emphasis of American painting from sentiment to realism, from unspoiled nature to the facts of social life in urban and industrial America. Realists did not always paint the city, but even when they depicted rural life, or in Winslow Homer's case the life of the seafarer, realists generally avoided romanticism.

Homer was, in the words of one critic, a "flaming realist—a burning devotee of the actual." He left several important bodies of work, all realistic in different ways. A series of Civil War studies, notably *Prisoners From the Front* (1866), presented ordinary soldiers with ragged uniforms and worn, tired expressions. This was a sharp departure from a tradition of painting military men in heroic poses. As an illustrator for *Harper's Weekly*, the first successful mass-circulation magazine in America, Homer also drew realistic scenes of factories, railroad workers, and other aspects of industrial life.

Two of Homer's most enduring contributions were his sensitive depictions of African Americans and his remarkable portrayals of seafaring men struggling against nature. At a time when intellectuals were perfecting theories of black racial inferiority and minstrel shows presented blacks in the grossest stereotypes, Winslow Homer represented blacks as varied men and women who worked hard and struggled with dignity against the difficulties of everyday life. In the process, Homer produced some of his finest paintings.

Thomas Eakins was an even more thoroughgoing realist, determined to drain his paintings of all romantic sentiment. He wielded his paintbrush with the precision of a scientist in a laboratory. Indeed, in his effort to represent the human body with perfect accuracy, Eakins attended medical school. After studying for several years in Europe, Eakins returned to his native Philadelphia in 1870 and was soon shocking viewers with warts-and-all portraits of his own sisters. Eakins, one critic sniffed, "cares little for what the world of taste considers beautiful."

Eakins established his reputation with a series of lifelike paintings of rowers. Even at the beginning of his career, Eakins could render scenes with startlingly three-dimensional effects. In 1875, he shocked the art world once again with *The Gross Clinic*, a large canvas depicting the gruesome details of a surgical procedure. The selection committee for the 1876 Philadelphia Centennial Exposition rejected *The Gross Clinic* on the grounds that "the sense of actuality about it was . . . oppressive."

Eakins was fascinated by the human form. He photographed dozens of naked men and women and used some of them as the basis for full-scale paintings. *The Swimming Hole* (ca. 1884) was based on a photograph Eakins had taken. By 1886 the directors of the Academy had had enough. Eakins was fired after he pulled the loincloth from a male model posing before a group of female students.

Thomas Eakins was a pioneer in the artistic use of photography. By using photography as the basis for painting, and by using scenes of ordinary life as the basis of high art, Eakins demonstrated his commitment to artistic realism in paintings such as The Agnew Clinic.

Critics complained that Eakins was obsessed with nudity, but for Eakins himself the exact details of the human body were merely the entryway into a deeper exploration of the characters and personalities of his subjects. In the late 1880s and 1890s Eakins produced a number of portraits that were stunning both for their physiological accuracy and their psychological penetration. Like Winslow Homer's portrayals of blacks, Eakins's women were thoughtful and dignified. *Miss Amelia C. van Buren* (1891) conveys its subject's intelligence and complexity with no sacrifice of accuracy. Eakins thereby did for painting what Henry James did for literature. Both demonstrated that distinguished works of art could be impressively realistic and at the same time deeply insightful.

Is Photography Art?

As city life became the subject matter of painters and writers, a major technological development—photography—created a new medium of artistic expression. In the fall of 1862 Mathew Brady mounted an exhibit of Civil War photographs in his New York gallery. This was the first time a large viewing public was able to see realistic pictures of the most gruesome facts of war. The camera had been invented scarcely a generation earlier, in 1839, by a Frenchman named Louis Daguerre. By the early 1860s photographic technology had improved dramatically, and Mathew Brady knew how to take advantage of it. His 1862 exhibition had electrifying effects.

By the 1880s journalists used photographs to heighten the reality, the sense of "truth," conveyed by their stories. The effect of Jacob Riis's *How the Other Half Lives*, published in 1890, was enhanced by the fact that he included a series of dramatic photographs documenting the misery of the urban poor. Photography had become part of the body of factual evidence.

The camera's eye inevitably fascinated realistic writers and artists. In the second half of the nineteenth century photography set the standard for accurate representation to which many artists aspired. Thomas Eakins, for example, used the camera to freeze images that he intended to paint on canvas. He photographed horses in motion to guide him as he painted. Eakins soon became a skilled photographer, producing hundreds of portraits of his subjects. He took numerous photos of the naked human form, and not always as a basis for later paintings. Eakins was thus one of the first artists to recognize the artistic element of photography itself. His work thereby raised questions that remain unanswered: Is a painting based on a photograph a work of art? Is photography art?

Civil War photography, pioneered by Mathew Brady's New York studio, was part of a larger artistic movement toward realism. The photos were not simply graphic; the best of them were works of art.

Some writers applauded the camera's capacity to capture the "truth." Writers as varied as Walt Whitman and Harriet Beecher Stowe used photographic metaphors to describe the effects they hoped to achieve with their words. But others were not persuaded that the photograph could ever be a genuine work of art. The camera captures only "the external facts," *The Galaxy* magazine declared, it "does not tell the whole truth."

Anthony Comstock worried a great deal about the difference between art and photography. Millions of copies of great and not-very-great works of art flooded the market in the late nineteenth century. Photographs of naked men and women suddenly became a new form of readily accessible pornography. "Is a photograph of an obscene figure or picture a work of art?" Comstock asked. "My answer is emphatically, No." Artists who paint nude portraits use lines, shadings, and colors in ways that "seem to clothe the figures"; their artistry diverts the viewers' attention from the nudity. Photographers have no such artistic devices at their disposal, Comstock explained. "A photograph of a nude woman in a lewd posture, with a lascivious look on her face," was to Comstock no work of art, for it lacked "the skill and talent of the artist."

CONCLUSION

When Comstock questioned whether photography could be art he was participating in a larger debate about what counted as culture in the new political economy of industrial capitalism. Did it include the popular culture of the city, or was American culture restricted to the nation's great libraries, universities, museums, and opera houses? And what was culture supposed to do for people? Americans argued over whether culture should maintain traditional values or boldly face up to the realities of the new political economy.

These cultural struggles easily spilled over into politics. Urban reformers proposed public policies to elevate the cultural level of slum dwellers. Elites convinced politicians to subsidize the construction of huge public libraries. Nevertheless, American politics in the late nineteenth century had not yet become cultural politics. The issues that brought Americans into the streets and into the voting booths remained, for the most part, economic issues. Just as American culture was transformed by the rise of cities and industry, the problems of the capitalist political economy became the focus of American politics in the late nineteenth century.

FURTHER READINGS

John D'Emilio and Estelle Freedman, *Intimate Matters: A History of Sexuality in America* (1988). This text is an innovative overview with important chapters on the late nineteenth century.

Elliot J. Gorn and Warren Goldstein, *A Brief History of American Sports* (1993). True to its title, this provides a brief but intelligent introduction to the subject.

John Higham, *Strangers in the Land: Patterns of American Nativism, 1860–1925* (1955). Higham has prepared a classic study of the response of native-born Americans to immigrants.

CHRONOLOGY

1851	YMCA is founded First world's fair is held at Crystal Palace in London
1859	Charles Darwin publishes *On the Origin of Species*
1861	Rebecca Harding publishes "Life in the Iron Mills"
1862	Mathew Brady exhibits Civil War photos at his New York studio
1866	New York Athletic Club opens Horatio Alger expelled from his pulpit in Brewster, Massachusetts Winslow Homer paints *Prisoners From the Front* and *Near Andersonville*
1869	Cincinnati Red Stockings charge admission to watch baseball games Matthew Arnold publishes *Culture and Anarchy*
1870	Metropolitan Museum of Art and Boston Museum of Fine Arts are founded
1870s	National League is formed; baseball becomes professional
1871	Walt Whitman publishes *Democratic Vistas* Thomas Eakins paints *Max Schmitt in a Single Scull*
1873	New York Society for the Suppression of Vice (SSV) founded Congress enacts the Comstock Law
1875	First Harvard-Yale football game is played Thomas Eakins paints *The Gross Clinic*
1876	World's Fair held in Philadelphia Philadelphia Museum of Art founded

Lawrence Levine, *Highbrow/Lowbrow: The Emergence of Cultural Hierarchy in America* (1988). Levine, a leading cultural historian, has effected a masterful study.

Roy Rosenzweig, *Eight Hours for What We Will: Workers and Leisure in an Industrial City, 1870–1920* (1983). Rosenzweig demonstrates the importance of leisure time to industrial workers.

David Shi, *Facing Facts: Realism in American Thought and Culture, 1850–1920* (1995). Refer to this for a broad introduction to the topic.

	Daniel Coit Gilman becomes first president of Johns Hopkins University
1878	Johns Hopkins establishes the first university press
1879	Art Institute of Chicago founded
1880s	Richard Kyle Fox professionalizes boxing
1883	Anthony Comstock publishes *Traps for the Young*
1884	Mark Twain publishes *The Adventures of Huckleberry Finn* Winslow Homer paints *The Life Line* Thomas Eakins paints *The Swimming Hole*
1885	William Dean Howells publishes *The Rise of Silas Lapham* Josiah Strong publishes *Our Country*
1888	Modern "safety" bike invented
1890	Jacob Riis publishes *How the Other Half Lives*
1891	Thomas Eakins paints *Miss Amelia C. van Buren*
1893	World's Columbian Exposition held in Chicago
1894	Vaudeville producer B. F. Keith opens the New Theatre in Boston
1896	Frederick L. Hoffman publishes *Race Traits and Tendencies of the American Negro*
1899	Winslow Homer paints *The Gulf Stream*

Robert Toll, *Blacking Up: The Minstrel Show in Nineteenth-Century America* (1974). *Blacking Up* is very good at tracing changes over time.

Alan Trachtenberg, *The Incorporation of America: Culture and Society in the Gilded Age* (1982). Trachtenberg gives a brief, spirited overview of the topic.

 Please refer to the document CD-ROM for primary sources related to this chapter.

19
The Politics of Industrial America

1870–1892

The "Crusade" Against Alcohol • Two Political Styles • Economic
Issues Dominate National Politics • Government Activism and Its
Limits • Middle-Class Radicalism • Discontent Among Workers
Conclusion

THE "CRUSADE" AGAINST ALCOHOL

*A*A few days before Christmas in 1873, Dr. Diocletian Lewis arrived in
Hillsboro, Ohio, to speak on the evils of alcohol. He had given the speech
many times before, but on this occasion the women who came proved
unusually responsive. Lewis told them how, when he was a boy, his mother saved his
father from drink by persuading a local saloonkeeper to stop selling liquor. The next
morning a group of Hillsboro women met for prayer and then marched through the
town urging local merchants to stop selling liquor. Inspired by their success, the women
kept up the pressure through the winter of 1873–1874.

The Crusade, as it came to be called, quickly spread to more than 900 towns and
cities in 31 states and territories. The women closed down thousands of liquor stores
and saloons and secured written pledges from hundreds of druggists and hotel-
keepers not to sell alcohol. With the dramatic success of the Crusade of 1873–1874,
temperance was reborn as a movement dominated by women. The Woman's
Christian Temperance Union (WCTU), organized in late 1874, would eventually
bring tens of thousands of women directly into the political arena.

The WCTU dwarfed all other women's political organizations in the late nineteenth century. By the early 1890s, for example, the National American Woman Suffrage Association had 13,000 members; the less-radical General Federation of Women's Clubs had 20,000. The WCTU had 150,000 adult members and 50,000 in its young women's auxiliary.

Much of this success could be attributed to the WCTU's powerful and charismatic president, Frances Willard. The child of well-educated parents, she attended college in Milwaukee and completed further studies in Rome, Berlin, and Paris. While in Europe, she settled on the question that would guide her life: "What can be done to make the world a wider place for women?" In her early 30s, Willard attended the founding convention of the WCTU and was appointed corresponding secretary. At first "conservatives" who wanted to restrict its activity to the suppression of liquor dominated the organization. But Willard had grander visions, and so, apparently, did the WCTU's members. In 1879 they elected Willard their national president, a position she held until her death in 1898.

The temperance movement broadened its interests and grew steadily more radical and more popular. It embraced women's suffrage, workers' rights, and finally "Christian socialism." Nevertheless, the WCTU's appeal and its radicalism were restricted by its predominantly prosperous membership. The middle-class Protestant bias of the WCTU was consistent with its disdain for most forms of party politics.

To be sure, the WCTU convened huge rallies, but Willard contrasted them to party conventions. WCTU gatherings were depicted as clean, well-disciplined affairs with oratory that was substantive rather than bombastic. Unlike the major parties, the WCTU combined education with interest-group pressure. Willard and her associates gave speeches, wrote articles, published books and newspaper columns on the evils of drink, organized petition campaigns, and lobbied officeholders. The crusade against alcohol grew into a broad-ranging political campaign to alleviate the problems of a new industrial society. In this sense the WCTU was typical of American politics in the late nineteenth century.

The political economy of industrial capitalism had thrown into doubt long-standing beliefs about the limited role of government in the regulation of the economy. The spectacular growth of big business worried voters, so politicians responded with the first tentative steps toward government regulation of commerce. But a growing number of Americans, though, stepped outside the two-party system to propose more radical solutions to social problems. Dissatisfied with party politics itself, many activists turned to wholesale political reforms. The WCTU tried all of these approaches, imitating the tactics of party politics while positioning itself outside the political mainstream. The effect of these competing styles was a dramatic increase in the number of politically active Americans, most of them demanding that their government actively confront the problems of industrial society.

Two Political Styles

There were two distinct political styles in late nineteenth-century America. One was partisan, the other was voluntary. Partisan politics included all the eligible voters who counted themselves as Democrats or Republicans, attended party parades and electioneering spectacles, and cast their ballots in record numbers. This was largely a world of men. The second political style, voluntarism, embraced a vast network of organizations, including women's assemblies, reform clubs, labor unions, and farmers' groups.

The Triumph of Party Politics

In the late nineteenth century American men voted along very strict party lines. Political parties printed and distributed their own ballots, and loyal Republicans and Democrats simply dropped a party ballot in the appropriate box. Party allegiances and discipline were strict, and campaigns were carefully organized. At no other time in American history did voters ally themselves so tightly to the two major parties.

And never again would so large a proportion of American men participate in presidential elections. From the 1840s through the 1860s an average of 69 percent of those eligible voted in presidential elections. During the final quarter of the century, the average rose to 77 percent. The figures were less impressive in the South, although they followed the same general pattern. Between 1876 and 1892, nearly two out of three southern men cast ballots in presidential elections. In the North 82 percent of men went to the polls every four years between 1876 and 1892. In the presidential elections of 1896 and 1900, northern voter turnout peaked at 84 percent.

Newspapers played a critical role in maintaining this level of political participation. Most editors were strong party advocates. Papers survived with the help of official advertisements and contracts to print ballots and campaign documents. Strong-willed editors such as Horace Greeley of the *New York Tribune* and William Cullen Bryant of the *New York Evening Post* became influential party leaders. Papers editorialized relentlessly in favor of their candidates and their party and slanted stories to show their party in the most favorable light. Some papers printed logos boasting of their partisan affiliation. "Republican in everything, independent in nothing," the *Chicago Inter Ocean* declared. Newspapers thus presented to their readers a starkly partisan world in which the difference between parties was the same as the difference between good and evil.

Spectacular political campaigns reinforced the partisan attachments promoted by newspapers. The parties organized political clubs to drum up enthusiasm for elections. Military marching companies organized the party foot soldiers as well. The clubs and marching groups in turn organized an endless series of competing party parades. Marchers rang bells, set off cannons, raised banners, and unfurled flags. Millions of American men, perhaps a fifth of all registered voters, participated in these huge spectacles.

Conspicuously absent from these events were the candidates themselves, particularly in presidential contests. Throughout the nineteenth century it was considered unseemly for presidential candidates to stump for votes. Those who did campaign—for example, Stephen Douglas in 1860, Horace Greeley in 1872, or James G. Blaine in 1884—were notoriously prone to losing the election. As the *Philadelphia Inquirer* explained in 1884, "It is better that the country should make its choice between the two candidates from what they know of their public records rather than from what they may learn of their personal appearance."

Masculine Partisanship and Feminine Voluntarism

Party politics was a largely masculine activity in the late nineteenth century. Both major parties functioned like fraternal organizations, and voting was increasingly referred to as a "manly" or a "manhood" right. Denying a man his right to vote was like denying his masculinity.

If the electoral sphere of campaigns and voting was a man's world, the private sphere of home and family was widely understood as a woman's world. In practice, women always participated in the background of popular politics. They sewed the banners, decorated the meeting halls, prepared the food for rallies and picnics, and joined the parades dressed as symbolic representations of the Goddess of Liberty or some similarly feminine icon. Nevertheless, politically active women opted for a different style of politics.

The stereotypes of the public man and the private woman rested on the assumption that women were destined to remain at home as protectors of the family's virtue. By the middle of the century, increasing numbers of women used that female stereotype to develop their own form of political activism. Female virtue justified women's support for moral reform movements such as abolitionism and temperance. Thus many women entered the public sphere to protect the private sphere. By defining "the family" in broad terms, women expanded the horizons of political activity beyond the confines of the two-party system. Thus a stereotype that initially restricted feminine political activity became a justification for women's increasing participation in public crusades.

Women pursued politics as representatives of voluntary associations that were dedicated to specific reforms, such as Sabbatarian laws that would prohibit working and drinking alcohol on the Sabbath or the struggles against slavery, prostitution, and poverty. Because it grew out of voluntary associations rather than political parties, this style of political activity is known as voluntarism.

Most of those who joined voluntary associations came from the educated middle class, and voluntary associations inevitably reflected the class biases of their members. By upholding the home as the special preserve of feminine authority, for example, reformers ignored the fact that working-class families depended heavily on the labor of children.

Sometimes women's associations copied the style of partisan politics. The WCTU staged mass marches and rallies. But because many politically active women were critical of the emotional style of mass politics, voluntary associations concentrated less on rousing voters than on educating them and lobbying elected officials.

Although men also joined voluntary associations, they were dismissed by mainstream politicians as "namby-pamby, goody-goody gentlemen." In the late nineteenth century, voluntarism was associated with feminine politics and party politics was associated with masculinity.

The Critics of Popular Politics

The combination of partisanship and voluntarism made American politics more "popular" than ever before. Women and men, blacks and whites, immigrants and the native born, working class and middle class all found places in the popular politics of the late nineteenth century. But not all Americans appreciated popular politics. After the Civil War a small but influential group of conservatives reacted with disgust to the American rage for politics. Contemptuous of partisanship, they advocated a new style of nonpartisan politics and questioned the

A satirical cartoon from 1869 belittled the campaign for women's suffrage. Entitled "Women on Top," the image reflected the common assumption that electoral politics was a strictly masculine activity.

principle of universal suffrage. Because they laid the groundwork for a new style of politics that would prevail in the twentieth century, the critics were ahead of their time.

"Universal suffrage can only mean in plain English the government of ignorance and vice," Charles Francis Adams complained in 1869. Adams spoke for a traditional American elite that saw popular politics as a degradation of public life. To such men, economic independence was the precondition for political virtue, among voters and public officials alike. The fact that the American working class was made up largely of blacks, Asians, and Catholic immigrants only made matters worse.

But blatantly antidemocratic rhetoric was a losing proposition in the late nineteenth century. Elites who hoped to maintain political influence learned to avoid direct assaults on the principle of universal suffrage. Instead they became advocates of good government, government run by professionals rather than party bosses and staffed by civil servants rather than party favorites. They became, in short, advocates of *nonpartisan* politics.

Nonpartisan politics was a reaction against the upheavals of the political economy of industrial capitalism. Many elites were haunted by what they saw as the twin evils of radicalism and immigration. In the wake of the nationwide strikes of 1877, *The Nation* magazine, a reliable barometer of elite opinion, asked whether an "alien" proletariat had transformed universal suffrage from a democratic blessing into a nightmare for the "well-to-do and intelligent" classes. In 1881, supporters of good government organized the National Civil Service Reform League to prevent political parties from filling government positions with their supporters. Victory came two years later with the establishment of a Civil Service Commission that would assign federal jobs on the basis of merit rather than patronage.

But civil service reform would not stop the phenomenal growth of a working-class electorate made up largely of recent immigrants. Political opposition to immigration, known as nativism, had enjoyed some success in the 1850s, and in 1882 nativists had secured a Congressional ban on the further immigration of Chinese. Anti-Catholicism spread across the country, especially in the Midwest in the late 1880s. Immigrants were Catholic and working class, so Yankee Protestants often saw working-class radicalism as a double threat. One nativist pointed to the "two lines" of foreign influence that were threatening the American republic. One line led to the radical politics of "agrarianism" and "anarchy." The second line tended toward Catholic "superstition." Both led "by different roads to one ultimate end, despotism!"

By the mid-1890s, as the number of immigrants from Eastern and Southern Europe increased, nativist rhetoric grew more racist. It was no longer merely radicals and Catholics who were swarming into the United States, but darker skinned peoples from Italy, Russia, and Eastern Europe. Social scientists wrote treatises on the inherent intellectual inferiority of such peoples, giving the imprimatur of science to the most vicious stereotypes. Italians were said to be genetically predisposed to organized violence, Jews to thievery and manipulation. Anti-immigrant parties and nativist societies appeared across America.

Throughout most of the nineteenth century, however, the critics of popular politics remained a vocal minority. Most Americans entered the political arena with deep concerns over the problems of a society that was rapidly becoming more urban and industrial. The political economy of industrial capitalism generated the issues that dominated American public life in the late nineteenth century.

As the number of immigrants to America swelled, so did opposition to them. This 1891 cartoon blames immigration for causing a host of social and political evils.

ECONOMIC ISSUES DOMINATE NATIONAL POLITICS

By the late nineteenth century Americans were accustomed to the idea that government should oversee the distribution of the nation's natural resources. After the Civil War federal officials distributed public lands to homesteaders and railroads and granted rights to mining, ranching, and timber companies. By the late nineteenth century, the rise of big business led growing numbers of Americans to believe that the government should regulate the currency and also protect American commerce and workers from ruinous foreign competition. To undertake these new responsibilities fairly and professionally, government employees had to be freed from the hold of political parties. These issues, all of them touching on the government's role in the regulation of the economy, dominated party politics in the late nineteenth century.

Weak Presidents Oversee a Stronger Federal Government

Starting in the mid-1870s, the Democrats and Republicans had nearly equal electoral strength, and from 1876 through 1896, not a single president enjoyed a full term during which his own party controlled both houses of Congress, nor did any president during these years take office with an overwhelming electoral mandate. After Grant's re-election in 1872, no president was re-elected to two consecutive terms until 1900.

In some cases, a president took office already tainted by the process that put him there, as was certainly true of Rutherford B. Hayes's election in 1876. Hayes's fellow Republicans were annoyed by his efforts to conciliate the southern Democrats who were conducting Congressional investigations of his election and frustrated by the president's contradictory position on civil service reform. Hayes forbade his party from raising money by assessing Republican officeholders, and he wrestled with the mighty Roscoe Conkling, Republican boss of New York City, for control of the New York Customs House—the most lucrative source of patronage in America. But although Hayes spoke for civil service reform, he acted the role of the party patron by lavishly rewarding his own supporters. Civil service reformers soon turned away from Hayes.

In 1877 Hayes took one important step toward strengthening the presidency. When railroad workers went on strike, Hayes dispatched federal troops to suppress them. This was an important precedent. Later presidents would often exercise their authority to intervene directly in disputes between workers and employers. But except for calling out the troops, Hayes's policy was to do nothing whatsoever to relieve the distress caused by the depression of the 1870s. Millions of Americans were suffering from the sharp fall in wages and prices, yet Hayes vetoed a bill that would have modestly inflated the currency. By 1880 the president was so unpopular that his fellow Republicans happily took him up on his offer not to run for re-election.

The results of the 1880 election were typical of the era. Republican James A. Garfield won the presidency by a tiny margin. He received 48.5 percent of the votes, and Democrat Winfield Hancock received 48.1 percent. As usual, the Republicans did best in New England, the upper Midwest, and the West. The Democrats swept the South but also took New Jersey, Nevada, and California. As a general rule, the Republicans appealed to southern blacks and to a northern middle class that was native born and overwhelmingly Protestant. The Democrats could count on strong support from working-class immigrants and southern whites.

As usual, economic issues dominated the 1880 campaign. But this did not mean that the Democrats and Republicans differed on economic policy. Both parties were addicted to the patronage system, so neither pressed for civil service reform. In theory the Democrats favored lower tariffs than the Republicans. In practice, neither party advocated free trade, and both parties had strong "protectionist" blocks (those who supported high tariffs to protect American business) as well as significant numbers who favored lower tariff rates. Neither party wanted to reverse the prevailing deflationary policies. Finally, while Republicans made periodic gestures in support of southern blacks, they had abandoned the freed people of the South. Thus Garfield's victory for the Republicans in 1880 did not foreshadow any major shifts in government policy.

On July 2, 1881, the president was shot by a lunatic who claimed to be a disappointed office-seeker. Garfield died two months later, and Chester A. Arthur, the product of a powerful patronage machine, became president. The assassination that put him in office made it dangerous for the president to resist the swell of popular support for civil service reform. The Republicans in control of Congress did resist, however, and Democrats swept into office on a tide of resentment against Republican corruption and patronage. The following year Congress passed, and President Arthur signed, the landmark Pendleton Civil Service Act.

The Pendleton Act prohibited patronage officeholders from contributing to the party machine that gave them their jobs. More important, the law authorized the president to establish a Civil Service Commission to administer competitive examinations for federal jobs. Before the century ended, the majority of federal jobs were removed from the reach of the patronage machines. The Pendleton Act was a major turning point in the creation of a stable and professional government bureaucracy.

Although Arthur signed the Pendleton Act, he squandered his chance of gaining popular credit as a reformer by distributing lavish patronage to his supporters in a shameless bid for re-election in 1884. He likewise threw away an opportunity to lead the way on tariff reform. With the return of prosperity in the late 1870s and early 1880s, government coffers bulged with surplus revenues from import taxes. Cries for lower tariffs grew louder, but the president succumbed to the political manipulations of the high-tariff forces in Congress. The so-called Mongrel Tariff he signed in 1883 did nothing. Arthur was no more successful in his attempts to strengthen the Navy or carry out an aggressive foreign policy. To make matters worse, the economy began to slow down again. Arthur approached the 1884 elections a tainted president. His fellow Republicans would not even renominate him.

The Democrats nominated Grover Cleveland. In his brief career as mayor of Buffalo and governor of New York, Cleveland had developed a reputation as an honest man and a moderate. Cleveland, the first Democrat elected to the presidency in nearly 30 years, made reconciliation between the North and the South a theme of his administration.

Cleveland's conviction that the federal government should defer to southern whites derived in part from his commitment to local government. Accordingly, Cleveland was not an activist president. During his first two years in office he initiated no new programs, but neither did he thwart Congressional moves to strengthen the authority of the central government. Cleveland approved legislation that raised the Agriculture Department to the status of a cabinet office and signed the Dawes Severalty Act of 1887, which placed the federal government in direct control over most Native Americans (see Chapter 17, "The Triumph of Industrial Capitalism"). In the same year, Cleveland signed the Interstate Commerce Act, the first federal legislation designed to regulate big business. It empowered a five-member Interstate Commerce Commission to curb monopolistic and discriminatory practices by railroads.

Cleveland earned few points for merely signing laws passed by Congress, so when his fellow Democrats lost control of the House of Representatives in 1886, he decided to take the lead on some important issue. The issue he chose was the tariff. In December 1887, shortly before his re-election campaign was to begin, Cleveland devoted his annual message to Congress almost entirely to sharp reductions in the tariff. He insisted that he was not an advocate of free trade; he simply thought that the tariff was too high.

But having staked so much on tariff reduction, the president merely watched passively as Congress produced a doomed bill that was biased in favor of southern interests. When his own party included only a weak endorsement of tariff reform in the 1888 platform, Cleveland did nothing. Throughout his campaign for re-election, he spoke not one word on the subject. Cleveland went before the voters with no tariff reform, and little else, to show for his four years in office.

Running a skillful campaign on an overtly protectionist platform, the Republicans won back the White House in 1888. A Republican president, Benjamin Harrison, at last presided over a Republican majority in Congress. Making good on their campaign promises, Republicans enacted high tariff rates. The Harrison–McKinley Tariff of 1890 also gave the president the authority to raise or lower tariffs with nations that opened their markets to American businesses. Thus the legislation gave the president important new authority in the conduct of foreign affairs. Also in 1890 the Republicans passed the Sherman Anti-Trust Act, declaring it illegal for "combinations" to enter into arrangements that would restrain competition. By failing to define precisely what constituted a "restraint of trade," the Sherman Act left it to the probusiness courts to decide. Still, the Sherman Anti-Trust Act was yet another indication of the federal government's increasing involvement in the regulation of the economy.

The Republicans received little credit for their efforts, and part of the problem was the president himself. Nicknamed "the human iceberg," Harrison was too stiff and pompous to rally the people. But the larger problem was the rising discontent among voters. In 1890 they put the Democrats back in control of the House of Representatives, and in 1892 they re-elected Grover Cleveland president. Once again, however, a president took office without a popular majority. Cleveland was the last of a string of relatively weak presidents (see Table 19–1).

TABLE 19–1

Electoral Margins in the Gilded Age			
Year	Popular Vote	% of Popular Vote	Electoral Vote
1876	4,036,572	48.0	185
	4,284,020	51.0	184
1880	4,453,295	48.5	214
	4,414,082	48.1	155
	308,578	3.4	—
1884	4,879,507	48.5	219
	4,850,293	48.2	182
1888	5,477,129	47.9	233
	5,537,857	48.6	168

But the weakness of the executive did not indicate an inactive central government. In addition to the Pendleton Act, the Interstate Commerce Act, and the Sherman Anti-Trust Act, the government tried to inflate the currency by modestly increasing the amount of silver in circulation. By maintaining high tariffs politicians effectively protected the wage rates of workers and the economic security of businesses. Nevertheless, the weakness of the federal government left growing numbers of Americans with the impression that the political system could not solve the problems associated with the political economy of industrial capitalism.

GOVERNMENT ACTIVISM AND ITS LIMITS

There are two standard themes in the political history of the late nineteenth century. The first theme stresses that government in this era was replete with corruption and bribery. The second theme emphasizes that the late nineteenth century was the great age of limited government and unregulated markets. After the retreat from Reconstruction, the government stepped back and allowed the new industrial economy to grow at its own rapid pace. There is a kernel of truth in each of these themes. Corruption was a real problem in late-nineteenth-century politics, and the government's regulatory powers were trivial compared to what would come later. Nevertheless, government in the late nineteenth century did become more centralized and somewhat more involved in the regulation of the economy. The conflicting impulses toward limited and active government can be seen most clearly in one of the most disruptive issues of late-nineteenth-century American politics, the regulation of the currency.

Greenbacks and Greenbackers

People have always disagreed over how much money governments should produce and how they should produce it. During the eighteenth century, American colonists complained that there was not enough money in circulation to sustain their economic needs. In the first half of the nineteenth century Americans fought over how much power the government should give to banks to regulate the amount of money in circulation. After the Civil War, capitalist development sparked another political debate over the role of government in the organization of the economy.

During the Civil War, the U.S. government printed $450 million worth of *greenbacks* to support the Union effort. Greenbacks were paper bills that were backed by the government's word, but not by the traditional reserves of gold or silver. When the war ended most Americans agreed that the greenbacks should be withdrawn from circulation. But after the depression of the 1870s a growing number of Americans demanded that the government keep the greenbacks in circulation. Those who wanted to return to the gold standard by making greenbacks convertible for "specie"—gold or silver—were called *resumptionists*, that is, they wanted the government to resume specie payments. Those who wanted the government to keep greenbacks in circulation to help inflate the currency were called greenbackers.

The supporters of the gold standard associated sound money with sound religion. In 1878, for example, the *Christian Advocate* compared greenbackers to atheists. And in fact, greenbackers were often radical critics of the new political economy. They formed a Greenback-Labor Party, which garnered more than 1 million votes in the 1878 Congressional elections and elected 14 members of

This cartoon belittles those who advocated a more inflationary policy by using silver as well as gold as the basis of the money supply. The implication of the image is that "bimetallism"—the use of both gold and silver—would create economic instability.

Congress. But the sound money forces won out, and in 1879 the $300 million in greenbacks that were still in circulation were made convertible into gold.

Supporters of inflation next took up the issue of "free silver." To counteract the deflationary trend, they argued, the government should add to the amount of money in circulation by allowing the unlimited coinage of silver. In 1878 the inflationists and sound money forces in Congress passed the Bland–Allison Act authorizing the Treasury to purchase silver and mint it in amounts tied to the amount of gold being minted. With the return of prosperity in the 1880s the currency question died down, to be revived with the arrival of another severe depression in the 1890s.

Foreign Policy and Commercial Expansion

Capitalist development reshaped American foreign policy just as it dominated domestic politics. In the 1860s William Henry Seward shifted the emphasis of American foreign policy from the acquisition of territory to the expansion of American commerce. As the Secretary of State for Abraham Lincoln and Andrew Johnson, Seward argued for foreign and domestic policies that promoted industrial expansion. Prewar southern expansionism had dampened Seward's enthusiasm for the acquisition of more land: He came to believe that "political supremacy follows commercial supremacy," and so he shifted his attention to the opening of American markets in Latin America, Canada, and the Pacific region, including Asia.

In the late 1860s, as Congressional Republicans struggled with President Johnson over Reconstruction, many of Seward's plans got caught in the crossfire. His biggest success came on April 9, 1867, when the Senate ratified the treaty purchasing Alaska for $7.2 million (see Map 19–1). A few months later, however, the Senate blocked a treaty with Denmark for the purchase of the Virgin Islands. Seward likewise failed to win approval for a naval base in Santo Domingo and a treaty with Colombia giving the U.S. exclusive rights to build a canal across the isthmus of Panama. Nevertheless, Seward established the principle that commercial interests would drive American foreign policy.

Those commercial interests were increasingly global. Between 1860 and 1897 American exports tripled, surpassing $1 billion per year. After 300 years of trade deficits, in 1874 America's exports began to surpass its imports. Nearly 85 percent of those exports were agricultural commodities, but the growth of industrial exports was even more spectacular. Iron and steel exports jumped by 230 percent between 1888 and 1898. John D. Rockefeller's Standard Oil corporation shipped three-quarters of its kerosene overseas between the 1860s and the 1880s. In the 1880s, U.S. multinational corporations became a fixture of international commerce.

This expansion of overseas commercial interests did not mean that the U.S. had abandoned its territorial ambitions. President Grant and Senator Charles Sumner revived long-standing American hopes of annexing Canada, but the Canadians seemed intent on cementing their ties to Great Britain. Nevertheless, until the twentieth century many Americans cherished the dream of absorbing Canada into the United States.

European powers similarly thwarted U.S. territorial ambitions in Latin America, but so did racist concerns about bringing large numbers of nonwhites into the United States. A rebellion in Cuba in 1868 heightened American interest in annexing the island. But Secretary of State Hamilton Fish had long resisted the idea of

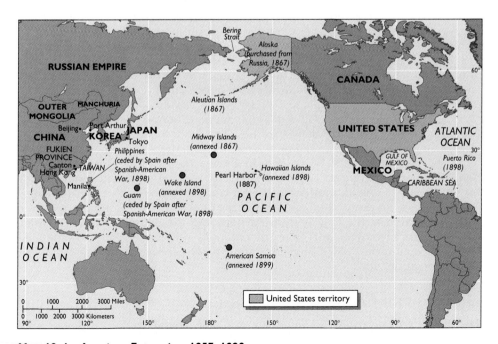

Map 19–1   American Expansion, 1857–1898
By the 1860s, Secretary of State William Henry Seward established the principle that American foreign policy would be driven by commercial interests.

absorbing half a million Cubans of "every shade and mixture of color." Similar inhibitions led the Senate to reject President Grant's 1869 treaty with Santo Domingo.

Despite the territorial restraints imposed by European power and racial ideology, aggressive secretaries of state reaffirmed Seward's commitment to commercial expansion. In 1886, for example, James G. Blaine worried openly that rapidly industrializing European nations were diverting Latin American commerce away from the United States. Concern for access to foreign markets pushed successive administrations to assert America's exclusive right to build a canal across Central America. The canal, President Harrison argued in 1891, "is the most important subject now connected with the commercial growth and progress of the United States." Hoping to thwart European commercial expansion by forging ties of friendship with Latin America, the United States convened the first Pan-American Conference in 1889.

Mexico provided the most vivid demonstration of U.S. commercial expansion. Although Americans had been buying up property in Mexico since before the Civil War, political instability limited Mexico's attractiveness as an investment. In 1876, however, Porfirio Díaz seized power in Mexico and began a reign of 35 years that proved a boon to American commercial interests. American investors quickly swarmed into Mexico, building railroads, selling life insurance, and digging oil wells. By 1910 Americans owned 43 percent of all the property in Mexico, more than Mexicans themselves owned.

United States attention also turned toward Asia and the South Pacific. In the 1880s the United States nearly went to war with England and Germany over disputed claims to Samoa. An 1876 reciprocity treaty gave Hawaiian sugar favored treatment on the American market, prompting a huge influx of Hawaiian sugar into the U.S. market (along with a backlash against the treaty by sugar producers on the mainland). By 1886, however, two-thirds of Hawaiian sugar was produced on American-owned plantations. Consequently, President Cleveland supported the treaty's renewal by referring to "our close and manifest interest in the commerce of the Pacific Ocean." By the 1890s American power in Hawaii had grown so great that it provoked among native Hawaiians a backlash that culminated in Queen Liliuokalani's ascension to the throne in January 1891. Two years later Hawaiians favorable to the United States dethroned the queen and President Harrison sent a treaty of annexation to the Senate.

The United States treaded somewhat more cautiously in East Asia, where European powers had long-established ties. The United States negotiated treaties with Japan and Korea that substantially increased American access to Asian markets.

From 1865 to 1890 the Senate repeatedly rejected treaties negotiated by presidential emissaries, but a succession of powerful secretaries of state compensated for a succession of weak presidents. By the late 1880s America's extensive global interests began to shape the nation's military policy. In 1890 Congress approved the construction of the first modern warships and the Supreme Court extended the president's control over "our international relations." The growing links between commercial and diplomatic interests were reviving the powers of the American presidency.

Growth of the Central Government

Despite its archaic rules and outdated structure, the central government grew steadily after 1860. Even after the inevitable retrenchment that followed the Civil War, the government continued to grow as new bureaucracies were created: Congress consolidated the United States Geological Survey in 1879, established the

Interstate Commerce Commission in 1887, and created the Department of Justice in 1870 and the Department of Agriculture in 1889.

The number of civilian federal employees rose from 53,000 in 1871 to 256,000 in 1901. The growth of the civil service provides the clearest evidence of the emergence of a permanent government bureaucracy. In 1883, when Congress passed the first civil service law, 13,780 federal jobs were "classified," meaning that applicants had to pass an exam to qualify. Fifteen years later, 89,306 federal positions were classified, amounting to nearly half of the jobs in the national government. This expansion of the number of civil service jobs substantially weakened the power of the Democratic and Republican Parties. As the proportion of "classified" federal jobs swelled, the patronage well dried up.

By the turn of the century the rudiments of a permanent federal bureaucracy were in place. The Interstate Commerce Commission lacked the power to enforce its own rulings, so it was forced to rely on the courts, which were dominated by supporters of big business. The Sherman Anti-Trust Act was even weaker. Few monopolies were broken up, much less threatened, by it. Finally, only about 15 percent of the wage labor force was actually protected by the high tariffs. By 1900 the federal government had developed in important ways, yet it remained small and weak by later standards. Indeed, it was not the federal, but rather the state and municipal governments that responded most aggressively to the problems of the new political economy.

States Regulate; Municipalities Reform

Even as Americans called on their government to do more and more, politicians proclaimed their opposition to the taxes and bureaucracies that active government required. The result was a jarring contradiction. At the state level, politicians enacted policies of retrenchment. In contrast to the federal government, for example, late-nineteenth-century state legislatures passed fewer laws, lowered their taxes, and balanced their budgets.

State politicians also established new regulatory bodies to govern the exploding municipalities of urban and industrial America. During the late nineteenth century state officials often transferred municipal power from elected officials and party politicians to experts and specialists on unelected boards. Mayors, city council members, and aldermen lost much of their authority over budgets, schools, police, and parks. For example, reformers handed control of the police to commissions staffed by middle-class citizens rather than by working-class immigrants. Parks commissions, sanitation commissions, public health commissions, and transportation commissions were generally staffed by middle-class professionals who were appointed to their posts and who prided themselves on their "nonpartisan" approach to government. The quality and professionalism of police and fire services increased dramatically over the course of the nineteenth century.

At least as important for the proper functioning of city government was the willingness of municipalities to raise taxes. As states retrenched, cities increased their property taxes to pay for streets, sewers, reservoirs, and public transportation. In the late nineteenth century city governments produced some of the great urban achievements of American history. Huge public parks, such as Central Park in New York and Golden Gate Park in San Francisco, sprang up across the country. At the same time cities sponsored spectacular feats of engineering and architecture. New Yorkers built the Brooklyn Bridge; Chicagoans literally reversed the flow of the Chicago River. Municipal governments went a long way toward enhancing the civility and decency of urban life in America.

San Francisco's Golden Gate Park, designed by Frederick Law Olmsted, was one of the most impressive of the great municipal parks built in cities across America in the late nineteenth century.

Yet Americans grew dissatisfied with their governments. Some were disgusted by corruption and inefficiency; others were offended by the hoopla of popular politics. To a significant number, government policies seemed inadequate to the demands of a new political economy. The powers of government grew slowly, but they were dwarfed by the private power of huge new corporations. Frustrated by piecemeal reforms, middle-class Americans turned to radical campaigns for social and economic transformation.

MIDDLE-CLASS RADICALISM

In the late nineteenth century a number of middle-class radicals argued that the political economy of industrial capitalism had undermined individual liberty and equality. Yet while their attacks on capitalism were severe, their assumptions were surprisingly traditional. They were usually frightened, not motivated, by socialism. They often worried that if substantial reforms were not undertaken, a discontented working class would overthrow the reign of private property. Their radical critiques of industrial society exposed deep wells of discontent among Americans.

Henry George and the Limits of Producers' Ideology

Henry George was born in Philadelphia in 1839, the son of middle-class parents. Although his formal education was limited, George traveled extensively and read widely. Like many middle-class Americans of his generation, he was shocked by the fact that as the United States grew richer the number of poor people grew as well. He studied the problem for many years and in 1879 published his conclusions in a bestselling book called *Progress and Poverty*.

George's explanation rested on what historians have called producers' ideology. It started from the assumption that only human labor could create legitimate wealth. Anything of value, such as food, clothing, or steel rails, came from the world's producing classes. By contrast, stockbrokers, bankers, and speculators made money from money rather than from the goods they produced. Producers' ideology therefore deemed their wealth illegitimate. Starting from these premises, Henry George divided the world into two classes: producers and predators.

The harmony of capital and labor was a central theme of producers' ideology. Henry George dreamed of a world in which working people owned their own farms and shops, making them both capitalists and laborers. His critique of industrial capitalism thus harkened back to Thomas Jefferson's vision of a society of small farmers and independent shopkeepers. America used to be that way, George believed, but as society "progressed," the land was monopolized by a wealthy few. Producers were forced to go to work for wealthy landholders. Employers then invested in technology that increased the productivity of their workers, but they kept the added wealth for themselves. Technology thus multiplied the wealth of the predators at the expense of the producers.

George's solution for the inequities of industrial society was a so-called Single Tax on rents. Because all wealth derived from labor applied to land, he reasoned, rents amounted to an unnatural transfer of wealth from the producers to the landlords. To thwart that transfer, George suggested taxing rents and improvements on land at prohibitive levels. This would discourage the accumulation of land by the landowning class. All other taxes would be abolished, including the tariffs that protected big business.

George presented his Single Tax as an alternative to the dangerous socialist doctrines that he thought were spreading among the working class. George attacked as "faulty" the socialist idea that there was an inherent conflict between labor and capital. He opposed government regulation of the economy, and he was a fiscal conservative, suspicious of proposals to counteract deflation by putting more money in circulation. Despite his apparent radicalism, George's popularity testified to the strength of middle-class concerns about the political power of the working class.

John F. Weir's 1877 painting, Forging the Shaft: A Welding Heat, *graphically depicts the forms of industrial wage labor that Henry George feared. His response was to propose the restoration of a Jeffersonian economy of small, independent producers.*

Edward Bellamy and the Nationalist Clubs

In 1888 Edward Bellamy, a 38-year-old Massachusetts editor, published a bestseller with a critique of capitalism even more powerful than Henry George's. Bellamy's *Looking Backward* was a utopian novel set in the future. The plot revolves around Julian West, who goes to sleep in Boston in 1887 and wakes up in the year 2000. His host, Doctor Leete, introduces West to the miraculous changes that have taken place. Technological marvels have raised everyone's standard of living. Boston has become a clean and orderly city. The great problems of industrial civilization have been solved. This was possible, Doctor Leete explains, because Americans had overcome the "excessive individualism" of the late nineteenth century, which "was inconsistent with much public spirit."

What about "the labor question?" Julian West asks. It had been "threatening to devour society" in 1887 when West fell asleep. Bellamy's critique of capitalism is contained in Doctor Leete's answer to West's question. In the early years of the American republic, the doctor explains, workers and employers lived in harmony. Upward mobility was common. This changed when "great aggregations of capital" arose. Like Henry George's, Bellamy's criticism of capitalism was grounded in traditional Jeffersonian ideals. For both authors the triumph of wage labor led to concentrations of wealth that undermined the harmony of capital and labor.

But where *Progress and Poverty* proposed the restoration of the simple virtues of Jeffersonian society, *Looking Backward* imagined a high-tech future in which consumer goods were provided in abundance. Henry George reasserted the values of hard work and self-restraint, whereas Edward Bellamy embraced the modern cult of leisure. For Henry George technology led to misery and inequality, but for Edward Bellamy machines would free mankind from the burdens and inequities of the modern world.

In spite of these differences, Bellamy and George were both motivated by a profound fear of militant workers. *Looking Backward* catered to a middle class craving for order amidst the chaos of industrial society. Superficially, Bellamy's futuristic Boston appeared to be a socialist utopia. Decisions about what to produce were made collectively, and society as a whole owned the means of production. Yet Bellamy was contemptuous of socialism and called his vision "nationalism." Under nationalism, the restoration of social peace was so complete that there was little or no need for government. This vision inspired thousands of middle-class Americans to form "Bellamy Clubs" or "Nationalist Clubs," particularly in New England.

The Woman's Christian Temperance Union

"Edward Bellamy's wonderful book" likewise inspired Frances Willard, president of the WCTU. She called nationalism "the fulfillment of man's highest earthly dream." Fifteen years earlier such support would have been impossible. The temperance movement that had revived in the early 1870s had initially restricted itself exclusively to the suppression of alcohol.

Even under Frances Willard's direction the WCTU never lost sight of its central goal. All across America, new laws established prohibitive license fees for the sale of liquor. Others banned the sale of liquor on Sunday. States passed "local option" laws giving communities the power to regulate the sale of alcohol. But to temperance purists such victories presented a problem. Liquor licenses implied the government's endorsement of alcohol; local option meant that towns were free to permit the consumption of liquor. Thus the ultimate goal of the WCTU became prohibition of the manufacture and sale of alcohol throughout the United States.

Under Willard's direction, temperance became the springboard to a wide range of political and social reforms. The WCTU endorsed women's suffrage and formed an alliance with the country's largest labor union. She supported laws restricting the workday to eight hours and prohibiting child labor. Even the WCTU's attitude toward alcohol changed. By the 1890s Willard viewed drunkenness as a public health problem rather than a personal sin, a problem of political economy rather than individual failure. Accordingly, temperance advocates supported reforms designed to relieve poverty, improve public health, raise literacy, alleviate the conditions of workers, reform prisons, suppress public immorality, and preserve peace. In the end, Willard attributed the evils of liquor to the inequities of corporate capitalism.

Three factors explain the WCTU's success. The first was Frances Willard's paradoxically conservative approach to radical reform. Her justification for female political activism always came back to women's distinctive calling as protectors of the home. The second reason for the WCTU's success was its decentralized structure. Willard left the local chapters of the Union free to adjust their activities to suit their particular needs. In the southern unions there was little talk of women's suffrage. Willard called this the "Do Everything" policy. Finally, the WCTU appealed to middle-class women who felt isolated by a culture that restricted them to the home. Women found in the WCTU a source of camaraderie as well as political activism.

For all its success, however, temperance remained a middle-class reform movement. The organization rested on a constituency that was concentrated in cities, especially in the North.

The WCTU did not attract many immigrants, for example. The official policy of toleration was undermined by the prejudices of middle-class members. For many temperance advocates immigrants were the Union's targets rather than its constituents, and the strong Protestant identity of the WCTU limited its appeal among working-class Catholics. One of its first major campaigns in the 1870s was aimed at replacing altar wine with grape juice in Christian services, a switch that Catholics and Lutherans were unwilling to make. As radical as it was, the WCTU would never reflect the interests of black sharecroppers, white tenant farmers, or immigrant workers. Nevertheless, like the Single-Taxers and the Bellamy Clubs, WCTU reformers reflected a growing sense that the American political system was unable to solve the problems of an industrial political economy.

DISCONTENT AMONG WORKERS

Radicalized workers shared the conviction that mainstream politics could not confront the problems of industrial capitalism. Workers turned to violence, and employers demanded that government use its police powers to put down strikes. Labor radicals began to question one of the premises of producers' ideology: that American democracy was secured by a unique harmony between capital and labor. But if the harmony of capital and labor had been destroyed, advocates of the producers' ideology continued to search for a political solution to the labor problem.

The Knights of Labor and the Haymarket Disaster

Between 1860 and 1890 wages overall grew by 50 percent, but the bulk of the growth was confined to elite skilled and semiskilled workers in a handful of industries, such as printing and metalworking. The vast majority of workers suffered directly from the deflation and economic instability of the late nineteenth century. By 1880, 40 percent of industrial workers lived at or below the poverty line, and the average worker was unemployed for 15 to 20 percent of the year. To relieve their plight, American workers sought political solutions to economic problems.

The most important labor organization to emerge from the crisis of the 1870s was the Noble and Holy Order of the Knights of Labor. Founded in 1869, the Knights of Labor was inspired by the producers' ideology and admitted everyone from self-employed farmers to unskilled factory workers. It appealed to a nostalgic vision of a world dominated by ordinary working people. Nevertheless the Knights of Labor advocated a host of progressive reforms, including the eight-hour day, equal pay for men and women, the abolition of child and prison labor, inflation of the currency to counteract the deflationary spiral, and a national income tax.

By the late 1870s leaders realized that the union needed a strong national organization to hold various locals together. A new constitution, drawn up in 1878, required all members to pay dues and allowed the national organization to support local boycotts and thereby boost its credibility among workers. Thereafter the Knights grew rapidly, from 19,000 members in 1881 to 111,000 in 1885. True to the producers' tradition, leader Terence Powderly favored the consumer boycott over the strike. His approach proved most successful during the sharp recession of 1884, when trade union strikes were being broken. By 1886 membership in the Knights skyrocketed to more than 700,000.

But the more the Knights of Labor grew, the more the strains among its members showed. The interests of shopkeepers and small factory owners were very different from those of wage laborers. The critical issue dividing self-employed producers from wage-earning producers was the use of the strike as a weapon of organized labor. Self-employed producers preferred the consumer boycott, and so did the leadership of the Knights of Labor. By contrast, wage laborers saw the strike as their most powerful weapon.

With the return of prosperity, trade unions called for a nationwide strike for the eight-hour day. On May 1, 1886, workers across the country walked off their jobs in one of the largest and most successful labor walkouts in American history. In Chicago 80,000 workers went out on strike. The Chicago job action was largely peaceful until May 4, when at an Anarchist rally at Haymarket Square near downtown, someone from the crowd tossed a bomb into a line of police. One policeman was killed instantly, and seven more died within days. The number of civilian casualties was never determined. Although the bomb thrower was never identified, eight anarchists were tried for inciting violence, and four were put to death.

Anarchists—who questioned the legitimacy of all government power—had been active in Chicago for several years. Although they had little influence on the labor movement, their fiery rhetoric advocating the use of violence made them conspicuous. At the Haymarket rally on the evening of May 4 anarchist speakers used the same violent rhetoric. Samuel Fielden, for example, urged his listeners to "throttle" and "kill" the legal system or else, he warned, "it will kill you." This remark provoked Captain James Bonfield to rush 170 policemen to the dwindling rally, and into this crowd of policemen someone threw a bomb.

Haymarket was a turning point in American labor politics. With the support of its president, Terence Powderly, the Knights of Labor had tried to prevent its locals from supporting the May Day walkouts. Powderly had put himself into a bind. Members resented his failure to support the strikes, while outside the union a wave of revulsion against labor agitation swept the country. The Knights of Labor never recovered from the Haymarket disaster. Thereafter worker agitation split dramatically into two competing wings. Small farmers formed their own organizations, and wage laborers organized separately into industrial trade unions.

Agrarian Revolt

The late nineteenth century was a desperate time for American farmers, especially in the West and South. To compete they had to buy expensive agricultural equipment, often from manufacturers who benefited from tariff protections. Then they had to ship their goods to market on railroads that charged higher rates to small farmers than to big industrialists. When their goods reached a market, they faced steadily declining prices.

As the economy became global, southern cotton had to compete against cotton from India and the Near East. Western wheat competed with Russian and Eastern European wheat. To keep up, farmers increasingly went into debt, and in a deflationary spiral the money they borrowed to plant their crops was worth more when it came time to pay it back, while their crops were worth less. Farmers mortgaged their homes and land. The proportion of owner-occupied farms declined while the number of tenants rose.

Farmers were traditionally opposed to active government, but they began to press for government action, beginning with inflation of the currency. Inflation lowered the value of the money farmers borrowed while it raised the value of the crops they produced. Farmers also sought railroad regulations to end rate discrimination. They sought to reform a tariff system that protected manufacturers but left them exposed to the insecurities of an international market. Eventually, militant farmers began to press for antitrust legislation to break up concentrations of wealth in the steel, oil, and railroad industries.

But farmers were notoriously hard to organize. They were scattered over large sections of the country, they were committed to an ideology of economic independence, and they were traditionally hostile to government intervention. If American farmers were to pursue their political agenda effectively, they needed to overcome these and many other obstacles.

One of the first attempts to organize farmers was the Patrons of Husbandry, generally called the Grange. The Grange began to attract large numbers of farmers during the depression of the 1870s and claimed 1.5 million members by 1874. Consistent with producers' ideology, the Grange organized cooperatives designed to eliminate the role of merchants and creditors. By storing grain collectively, farmers held their products back from the market in the hope of gaining control over commodity prices. But inexperience made the Grange cooperatives difficult to organize and sustain. After 1875 their membership dwindled.

The National Farmers' Alliance and Industrial Union, known simply as the Farmers' Alliance, was much more effective than the Grange. Founded in Texas in 1877, the Farmers' Alliance spread rapidly across the South. Its potency was demonstrated at a huge meeting at Ocala, Florida, in 1890. The Ocala Platform supported a host of reforms, many of which had been staples of radical politics for a generation: currency inflation through the free coinage of silver, lower tariffs, and a constitutional amendment providing for direct election of senators. The Ocala Platform also demanded that the government establish a system of "subtreasuries," or public warehouses in which farmers could store their crops until they could get the best prices. Finally, the Alliance called for strict government regulation, and if necessary direct government ownership, of the nation's railroad and telegraph industries.

The Farmers' Alliance steered clear of politics and instead judged political candidates by the degree to which they supported the reforms advocated in the Ocala Platform. But very little such support was forthcoming from either of the major parties. Farmers' Alliance members therefore formed their own third parties, with

CHRONOLOGY

1867	U.S. purchases Alaska from Russia Patrons of Husbandry (the Grange) founded
1869	Noble and Holy Order of the Knights of Labor founded Suez Canal opened
1870	Department of Justice created
1872	Grant re-elected
1873	"Crusade" against alcohol begins in Hillsboro, Ohio
1874	WCTU is formed
1876	Rutherford B. Hayes elected president Porfirio Díaz seizes power in Mexico
1877	Farmers' Alliance founded
1878	Bland-Allison Act
1879	Frances Willard becomes president of the WCTU Henry George publishes *Progress and Poverty*
1880	James Garfield elected president
1881	Garfield assassinated; Chester Arthur becomes president WCTU endorses women's suffrage
1883	Pendleton Civil Service Act "Mongrel Tariff"

some success on the Great Plains in the election of 1890. Out of these initial forays into politics came the most significant third party of the late nineteenth century, the People's Party, otherwise known as the Populists.

The Rise of the Populists

On February 22, 1892, a huge coalition of reform organizations met in St. Louis, including Single Tax advocates inspired by Henry George, greenbackers who wanted an inflationary currency policy, representatives of the Knights of Labor, and members of the Farmers' Alliance. Together they founded the People's Party and called for a presidential nominating convention to meet in Omaha, Nebraska, on July 4. There they nominated General James B. Weaver of Iowa for president and drew up the famous Omaha Platform.

Inspired by the producers' ideology, the People's Party called for the unity of all working people and for harmony of interests between small property holders and wage earners. The Populist platform was a vigorous restatement of the

1884	Grover Cleveland elected president
1886	Nationwide strike for eight-hour day Riot at Haymarket Square in Chicago
1887	Interstate Commerce Act Four Haymarket anarchists executed Dawes Severalty Act
1888	Benjamin Harrison elected president Edward Bellamy publishes *Looking Backward*
1889	U.S. convenes first Pan-American Conference Department of Agriculture created
1890	Harrison–McKinley Tariff Sherman Anti-Trust Act Ocala Platform
1891	Queen Liliuokalani assumes the Hawaiian throne
1892	Omaha Platform of the People's Party Grover Cleveland re-elected
1893	Queen Liliuokalani overthrown
1898	Frances Willard dies

proposals laid out two years earlier by the Farmers' Alliance. Like the Ocala Platform, the Omaha Platform demanded an inflationary currency policy and subtreasuries. The Populists called for a graduated income tax, direct government ownership of the railroad and telegraph industries, and the redistribution of lands owned by the railroads.

In the 1892 elections the Populist presidential candidate won about 1 million votes and elected several senators, representatives, governors, and state legislators. But there was no support among wage earners outside the South and West. The producers' ideology, for all its talk of the unity of working people, was frankly incompatible with the interests of industrial workers, who had little reason to oppose protective tariffs that shielded the industrial economy. Inflation would only undermine the value of their wages and raise the price of commodities, and income taxes would shift the tax burden from landowners and importers to wage laborers. Conversely, farmers had every reason to oppose the eight-hour day and laws restricting child labor. In short, Populism was grounded in a rural society of independent farmers and craftsmen, a world that was rapidly disappearing.

CONCLUSION

After the Civil War the problems of industrial capitalism placed increasing strain on the political system. The two major parties were so closely matched in electoral strength that neither could risk bold new programs to meet the needs of a new political economy. So restless workers, desperate farmers, and an anxious middle class turned in increasing numbers to voluntary organizations, labor unions, and farmers' alliances.

The politics of industrial society reached a dramatic turning point in the 1890s. During that decade American voters went to the polls in record numbers. Organized farmers made their most radical demands; labor agitation reached a violent climax. And as night follows day, a conservative reaction set in. Movements to restrict the number of voters emerged, particularly in the South. Opponents of immigration made significant strides. The Supreme Court declared constitutional one of history's greatest social experiments, systematic racial segregation. In short, radicalism and reaction reached their peak in the 1890s. During the closing decade of the nineteenth century, a recognizably modern America was born.

FURTHER READINGS

Paul Avrich, *The Haymarket Tragedy* (1984). This is an exhaustive account by the leading historian of American anarchism.

Ruth Bordin, *Woman and Temperance: The Quest for Power and Liberty, 1873–1900* (1981). *Women and Temperance* is the best single volume available on the subject.

Leon Fink, *Workingmen's Democracy: The Knights of Labor and American Politics* (1983). This case study, with broad implications, shows the connections between political mobilization and labor organization.

Lawrence Goodwyn, *Democratic Promise: The Populist Moment in America* (1976). Goodwyn traces the roots of populism to the Farmers' Alliance.

Walter LaFeber, *The New Empire: An Interpretation of American Expansion, 1860–1898* (1963). LaFeber ties American foreign policy to commercial expansion.

Michael McGerr, *The Decline of Popular Politics: The American North, 1865–1928* (1986). This text is particularly strong on the culture of popular politics in the late nineteenth century.

John L. Thomas, *Alternative America: Henry George, Edward Bellamy, Henry Demarest Lloyd, and the Adversary Tradition* (1983). Thomas's work is a sensitive examination of middle-class radicalism and its limits.

 Please refer to the document CD-ROM for primary sources related to this chapter.

20

Industry and Empire

1890–1900

Dealmaking in the White House • The Crisis of the 1890s
A Modern Political Economy • The Retreat From Politics
American Diplomacy Enters the Modern World • Conclusion

DEALMAKING IN THE WHITE HOUSE

O n an icy February morning, J. Pierpont Morgan walked the short distance from his hotel to the White House. He pulled his scarf up around a scowling face known to millions of newspaper readers. He had not wanted to come to Washington. The commander in chief of the nation's bankers was going to meet the president to keep the United States from going bankrupt.

The events leading up to this urgent meeting stretched back five years, to 1890, when business failures in Argentina toppled London's venerable Baring Brothers investment house and triggered a collapse in European stock prices. As depression spread, European investors sold off their American holdings, and in early 1893 the panic reached the United States. Fourteen thousand businesses soon folded, along with more than 600 banks.

Wall Street went into a tailspin. In New York 55,000 men, women, and girls in the clothing industry were thrown out of work. Banks refused to cash checks, and coins vanished from circulation. The governor of Nebraska instructed the police to deal leniently with the thousands of homeless people on the roads. Breadlines formed.

The anger of workers and farmers, which had been simmering for decades, was about to boil over. President Grover Cleveland called Congress into special session and pledged to keep the dollar on the gold standard, but it was not enough. A wave of strikes swept the country. Unemployed workers battled police on the Capitol grounds. By January 1895, as panicky investors cashed government bonds, the Treasury's gold reserve was half gone. Reluctantly, President Cleveland opened negotiations with Morgan.

Admired and reviled, Morgan was the preeminent financial manipulator of the late nineteenth century. Like his contemporaries, steelmaker Andrew Carnegie and oil magnate John D. Rockefeller, Morgan's skill lay in organization. He restructured railroads, rooting out waste and competition and driving down wages. Cleveland was about to place the Treasury in this man's hands.

The president opened the meeting by suggesting that a new bond issue might stabilize the Treasury. No, Morgan replied flatly, the run on gold would continue until European investors regained confidence. If the president agreed, Morgan would arrange a private loan and personally guarantee the solvency of the U.S. Treasury. After a stunned silence, the two men shook hands. News of the deal instantly calmed the bond markets. The crisis was over.

Culminating two decades of economic turbulence, the Panic of 1893 and the depression that followed permanently transformed the American political economy. Businessmen like Morgan created enormous corporate combinations and placed them under the control of professional managers. They used technology and "scientific management" to control the workplace and push laborers to work faster and harder. Workers resisted, and the 1890s witnessed brutal clashes between capital and labor.

The 1890s were also a turning point in American politics. After the 1896 election, many Americans withdrew from the electoral process. African-American leaders and union organizers urged their followers to turn away from politics in favor of "bread and butter" economic issues. Patriotism, once synonymous with partisanship, now became identified with the United States' global military and economic ambitions. As Americans became more conscious of their military power, they watched the horizon, fearing that well-being at home could hinge on far-away events.

Americans began to feel that their economy's links to the world—and the changes manufacturing and rapid communications brought to politics and daily life—had transformed society fundamentally. Morgan's rescue required simultaneous transactions on two continents. The speed of industry, trade, and information, and the ability of machines and technology to span distance and time created a sense that the environment and the future could be controlled.

Between 1890 and 1900 Americans made their country recognizably modern. Financiers and giant corporations assumed control of a vast portion of the American economy. The significance of voting declined, and a decade that opened with a global economic catastrophe ended with a dramatic display of the global reach of U.S. power.

THE CRISIS OF THE 1890S

Financial convulsions, strikes, and the powerlessness of government against wealth rudely reminded Americans of how much their country had changed since the Civil War. When Illinois sent Abraham Lincoln to Congress, Chicago's population was less than 5,000; in 1890 it exceeded 1 million. Gone was the America of myth and memory, where class tensions were slight and upward (or at least westward) mobility seemed easy. Many Americans, one British diplomat noted, predicted the imminent collapse of civilization: "They all begin with the Roman Empire and point out resemblances." Others, however, felt that the United States was passing into a new phase of history that would lead to still greater trials and achievements.

Hard Times

Chicago in 1893 captured the hopes and fears of the new age. To celebrate the 400th anniversary of Columbus's discovery of America, the city staged the World's Columbian Exposition, transforming a lakefront bog into a gleaming vision of the past and the future, but just outside the exposition's gates lay the city of the present. In December 1893 Chicago had 75,000 unemployed, and the head of a local relief committee declared that "famine is in our midst." In the nation's second largest metropolis, thousands lived in shacks or shared rooms in high-rise tenements in which each floor had only a single bathroom. Jobs were hard to find, and when groups of men gathered at the exposition's gates to beg for work, the police drove them away.

As the depression deepened, the Cleveland administration ordered troops to guard Treasury branches in New York and Chicago. Jobless people began banding together, forming "industrial armies," many with decidedly revolutionary aims. Hundreds heeded the call of Jacob Coxey, a prosperous Ohio landowner and Populist. Coxey appealed in 1894 to the unemployed to march on Washington and demand free silver and a public road-building program that would hire a half-million workers. When Coxey set out with 100 followers, reporters predicted the ragged band would disintegrate as soon as the food ran out, but well-wishers turned out by the thousands to greet the Coxeyites and offer supplies for the trip.

Industrial armies set out from Boston, St. Louis, Chicago, Portland, Seattle, and Los Angeles. When Coxey arrived in Washington on May 1 with 500 marchers, Cleveland put the U.S. Army on alert. The march ended ignominiously. In front of the Capitol, police wrestled Coxey into a paddy wagon, and his disillusioned army dispersed. Still, after the march no one could deny that something was seriously wrong. Ray Stannard Baker, a reporter for the *Chicago Record*, acknowledged that "the public would not be cheering the army and feeding it voluntarily without a recognition, however vague, that the conditions in the country warranted some such explosion."

The Overseas Frontier

At noon on September 16, 1893, thousands of settlers amassed along the borders of the Cherokee Strip, a 6-million-acre tract in northwestern Oklahoma. In the next six hours, the last great land rush came to an end. The line of settlement that had been marked on census maps throughout the nineteenth century had ceased to exist.

Frederick Jackson Turner, a historian at the University of Wisconsin, explained the implications of this event. Steady westward movement had placed Americans in "touch with the simplicity of primitive life," he explained, and allowed the nation to renew the process of social development continuously. The frontier furnished "the forces dominating the American character," and without its rejuvenating influence, democracy itself might be in danger. Turner's thesis resonated with Americans' fears that modernity had robbed their country of its unique strengths. For the previous ten years, Populists and financiers had worried that the end of free lands would signal trials for free institutions. "There is no unexplored part of the world left suitable for men to inhabit," Populist writer William "Coin" Harvey claimed, "and now justice stands at bay."

That assertion turned out to be premature. More homesteaders claimed more western lands after 1890 than before, and well into the twentieth century new "resource frontiers"—oil fields, timber ranges, Alaskan ore strikes—were explored. Irrigation technology and markets for new crops created a bonanza for dry-land farmers. Nonetheless, the economic and social upheavals of the 1890s seemed to confirm Turner's contention that new frontiers would have to be found overseas.

While farmers had always needed to sell a large portion of their output abroad, until the 1890s manufactured goods had sold almost exclusively through domestic distribution networks. As the total volume of manufactured goods increased, the composition of exports changed. Oil, steel, textiles, typewriters, and sewing machines made up a larger portion of overseas trade. American consumers still bought nine-tenths of the output of domestic factories, but by 1898 the extra tenth was worth more than $1 billion (see Figure 20–1).

As American firms entered foreign markets they discovered that other nations and empires guarded their markets with restrictive tariffs just as the United States did, to promote domestic manufacturing. Government and business leaders acknowledged that to gain a larger share of world trade, the United States might have to use political or military leverage to pry open foreign markets. Their social Darwinist view of the world—as a jungle in which only the fittest nations would survive—justified engaging in global competition for trade and economic survival.

Recognizing that naval power could extend economic influence, and wanting to find a use for surplus steel, Congress authorized the construction of three large battleships in 1890. In 1894, Congress sent a commission to Nicaragua to study the feasibility of a canal across Central America. In 1895 industrialists organized the National Association of Manufacturers to urge the government to help open for-

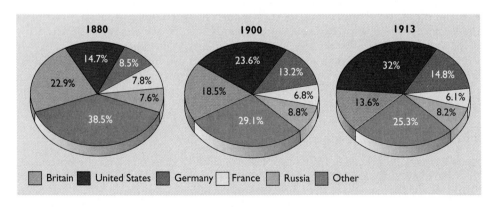

Figure 20–1   Relative Shares of World Manufacturing
The United States was a significant industrial power by 1880, but by the turn of the century it moved into a position of dominance.

eign markets. The administration created a Bureau of Foreign Commerce and urged U.S. consuls abroad to seize opportunities to extend sales of American industrial products.

Congress also knew that tariff rates could influence the expansion of trade. Before 1890 taxes on imports had been set high to raise revenue and to help domestic manufacturers by making foreign goods unaffordable. The Harrison–McKinley Tariff of 1890 did something different. It allowed the president to use the tariff to punish countries that closed their markets to U.S. goods or reward them for lifting customs barriers. This "bargaining tariff" put the full weight of the U.S. economy behind the drive to open markets around the world.

The United States began to reorganize itself to compete in a global marketplace. The struggle required the executive branch to enlarge the military and take on additional authority. It also meant that domestic industries had to produce higher quality goods at less cost to match those being turned out in Germany or Japan. Employers and workers had to gear up for the global contest for profits.

The Drive for Efficiency

In mines, factories, and mills production depended on the knowledge of skilled workers. Laborers used their knowledge to rationalize their work, to set work routines, and to bargain with managers who wanted to change the pace or conditions of work. As profits stagnated and competition intensified, managers tried to prevent labor from sharing control over production. In the struggle for control in the workplace, employers relied on three allies: technology, scientific management, and federal power. Workers resisted, organizing themselves and enlisting the support of their communities.

Advances in management techniques enabled employers to break routines favored by laborers and to dictate new methods. Frederick Winslow Taylor, the first "efficiency expert," reduced each occupation to a series of simple, precise movements that could be easily taught and endlessly repeated. To manage time and motion scientifically, Taylor explained, employers should collect "all of the traditional knowledge which in the past has been possessed by workingmen" and reduce "this knowledge to rules, laws, and formulae."

Taylor's stopwatch studies determined the optimal load of a hand shovel (21.5 pounds), how much pig iron a man could load into a boxcar in a day (75 tons), and the amount the man ought to be paid (3.75 cents per ton). Even office work could be separated into simple, unvaried tasks. Taylorism created a new layer of college-educated "middle managers" who supervised production in offices and factories.

Although Taylorism accelerated production, it boosted absenteeism and job turnover. Telephone operators had a 100 percent yearly turnover rate. Another new technique, "personnel management," promised to solve this problem with tests to select suitable employees, team sports to ward off boredom, and social workers to regulate the activities of workers at home.

As the nineteenth century ended, management was establishing a monopoly on expertise and using it to set the rhythms of work and play, but workers did not easily relinquish control. In the 1890s, the labor struggle entered a new phase. New unions confronted corporations in bloody struggles that forced the federal government to decide whether communities or property had more rights. Skilled workers asserted leadership over the labor movement, and they rallied to the cause of retaining control of the conditions of work.

A TAYLOR SYSTEM MACHINIST "UP-TO-DATE"

An argument without words

Corporations used stop-watches and social workers to stretch each machine and worker to full capacity. The method was called Taylorism.

Progress and Force

To accelerate production, employers aimed to seize full control over the workplace. They had private detective agencies at their disposal, the courts on their side, and federal troops ready to act. In Pennsylvania and Chicago this antagonism led to bloody confrontations.

In 1892 Andrew Carnegie's mill at Homestead, Pennsylvania, the most modern steel works in the world, turned out armor plating for American warships and steel rails for shipment abroad. In June Carnegie's partner, Henry Clay Frick, broke off talks with the plant's American Federation of Labor affiliated union and announced that the plant would close on July 2 and reopen a week later with a nonunion work force. The union contended that Frick's actions constituted an assault on the community, and the town agreed. On the morning of July 6, as 300 armed detectives tried to land from barges, they were raked by gunfire. Townspeople forced the detectives to surrender.

The victory was short-lived. A week later the governor of Pennsylvania sent in the state militia, and under martial law strikebreakers reignited the furnaces. Homestead became one of labor's most celebrated battles, but it broke the union and showed that corporations, backed by government, would defend their prerogatives at any cost.

The Pullman strike, centered in Chicago, paralyzed the nation's railroads for two weeks in the summer of 1894. It pitted the American Railway Union (ARU) against 24 railroads and the powerful Pullman Company over the company's decision to cut pay by 30 percent. The calm at the center of the strike was Eugene V. Debs, charismatic president of the ARU, who urged strikers to obey the law, avoid violence, and respect strikebreakers. When Cleveland sent in the Army over the governor's protests, enraged crowds blocked tracks and burned railroad cars. Police arrested hundreds of strikers. Debs went to jail for six months and came out a Socialist. Pullman and Homestead showed that the law was now on the side of the proprietors.

Newspapers, magazines, and novels portrayed Pullman and Homestead as two more battles in an unending war against the savage opponents of progress. Frederic Remington, famous for his reporting on wars against the Navajo and Apache Indians, covered the Pullman strike for *Harper's Weekly*. In his account, rough-hewn cavalrymen, having defeated the Sioux, now came to rescue civilization from the unions.

The business elite's influence over cultural expression (see Chapter 18, "Cultural Struggles of Industrial America") allowed it to define the terms of this contest, to label its enemies as enemies of progress. Workers did not object to efficiency or modernization, but they wanted a share of its benefits and some control over the process of change. With state and corporate power stacked against them, these goals appeared beyond reach.

Just as the massacre at Wounded Knee in 1890 had ended the armed resistance of Native Americans, the violence at Homestead and Chicago signified that the struggle of industrial workers had entered a new phase.

Corporate Consolidation

In a wave of mergers between 1897 and 1904, investment bankers consolidated leading industries under the control of a few corporate giants, and J. P. Morgan led the movement. His goal was to take industry away from the industrialists and give it to the bankers. Bankers, he felt, had better information about the true worth of an industry, and they could make better decisions about its future. Financiers could create the larger and leaner firms needed to take on foreign competitors.

Morgan's greatest triumph was the merger of eight huge steel companies, their ore ranges, rolling mills, railroads, and shipping lines into the colossal U.S. Steel. Announced in March 1901, the merger created the world's largest corporation. Its capital amounted to 7 percent of the total wealth of the United States (by comparison, Microsoft's total assets in 1998 amounted to less than one-third of 1 percent of the gross national product). U.S. Steel's investors (Morgan especially) earned profits "greatly in excess of reasonable compensation," according to one government report.

Bankers outnumbered steelmakers on U.S. Steel's board, and they controlled the company. *McClure's* magazine reported that the new company was "planning the first really systematic effort ever made by Americans to capture the foreign steel trade." Morgan's son wrote to his stepmother that "Father is in the same category with Queen Victoria." He did not say what category U.S. Steel's employees and customers fell into.

A Modern Political Economy

Grover Cleveland's bargain with Morgan revived the industrial economy, but farm prices, wages, and the president's popularity remained flat. The escalating cycle of economic and political crises, farmer and labor insurgencies, middle-class radicalism, and upper class conservatism fractured political parties. Democrats, Republicans, and Populists all called for stronger government action, but each party split over what action to take. In 1896 the "currency question" dominated a watershed election that transformed the two major parties and destroyed the third.

Currency and the Tariff

The soundness of the dollar, which Morgan and Cleveland worked so hard to preserve, was a mixed blessing for Americans. Based on gold, the dollar helped sell American goods in foreign markets, especially in Europe, where currencies were also based on gold. The United States traded on a much smaller scale with countries—

like Mexico or China—that used silver. "Without exception," Cleveland's Secretary of Commerce explained, "prices are fixed in the markets of countries having a gold standard." Gold, however, was valuable because it was scarce, and many Americans suffered from that scarcity. The low prices and high interest rates Populists complained of were a result of the gold standard.

Increasing the money supply would reduce interest rates and make credit more available. There were two ways to put more money in circulation: The government could print paper greenbacks, or it could coin silver (see Chapter 19, "The Politics of Industrial America"). "Free silver" advocates generally favored coining a ratio of 16 ounces of silver for each ounce of gold. Populists initially wanted greenbacks but later found silver an agreeable compromise. Western mining interests pushed silver as well. To Americans in the 1890s, the crucial political issues—jobs, foreign trade, the survival of small farms, and the prosperity of big corporations—boiled down to one question: Would the dollar be backed by gold or silver? The election of 1896 was "the battle of the standards."

The Cross of Gold

A dark mood hung over Chicago as delegates arrived at the Democratic Convention in July 1896. They had come to bury Cleveland and the party's commitment to the gold standard along with him. The draft platform denounced Cleveland for imposing "government by injunction" during the Pullman strike. When the platform came before the full convention, delegates had to decide whether the party would stand for silver or gold and who would replace Cleveland as the candidate for president.

Both questions were decided when a former congressman from Nebraska, William Jennings Bryan, mounted the stage. Handsome and only 36 years old, he was an electrifying speaker. "You come and tell us that the great cities are in favor of the gold standard," he said. "Destroy our farms, and the grass will grow in the streets of every city in the country!" Bryan delivered his lines in the rhythmic cadence of a camp preacher. "We will answer their demand for a gold standard by saying to them"—he paused stretching out his arms in an attitude of crucifixion—"You shall not press down upon the brow of labor this crown of thorns. You shall not crucify mankind upon a cross of gold!" The hall exploded with cheers. Bryan won the nomination handily.

Two weeks later the Populists, meeting in St. Louis, also nominated Bryan. The Ocala and Omaha platforms, which imagined comprehensive changes in the money system and American institutions, had been reduced to a single panacea: silver. Republicans overwhelmingly adopted a progold plank drafted with the approval of J. P. Morgan and nominated William McKinley, the governor of Ohio, a supporter of industry. The parties could hardly have offered two more different candidates or two more different visions of the future.

The Battle of the Standards

In one of the most exciting contests since the Civil War, the candidates employed new techniques in radically different ways. McKinley ran like an incumbent: He never left his home. Instead, delegations came to him. Some 750,000 people from 30 states trampled McKinley's grass and listened to speeches affirming the candidate's commitment to high tariffs and sound money. The speeches were set in type and distributed as newspaper columns, fliers, and pamphlets throughout the country. The campaign used public relations techniques to educate the electorate on the virtues of the gold standard. Posters reduced the campaign's themes to pithy slogans like "Prosperity or Poverty," or "Vote for Free Silver and be Prosperous Like Guatemala."

The genius behind the campaign was a Cleveland coal-and-oil millionaire named Marcus Hanna who bankrolled his publicity blitz with between $3 million and $7 million raised from industrialists. He assessed a share of the campaign's expenses from corporations and banks based on calculations of the profitability and net worth of each. The combination of big money and advertising revolutionized presidential politics.

With only $300,000 to spend, Bryan ran like a challenger even though his party occupied the White House. He logged 29,000 miles by rail and buggy and made more than 500 speeches in 29 states. Oratorical ability had won Bryan the nomination, but audiences were unaccustomed to hearing a candidate speak for himself, and many considered it undignified. "The Boy Orator has one speech," wrote an unsympathetic Republican, John Hay. "He simply reiterates the unquestioned truths that . . . gold is vile, that silver is lovely and holy."

Industrialists genuinely feared the prospect of a Bryan presidency. Factory owners threatened to close shop if Bryan won. Just before election day, crop failures abroad doubled the price of wheat in the Midwest. In the final tally, Bryan won the South and West decisively, but McKinley won the populous states of the industrial Northeast, as well as several farm states in the upper Midwest, capturing the electoral college by a majority of 271 to 176.

The election of 1896 changed the style of campaigns and shifted the political positions of both major parties. By pushing currency policies, Bryan's Democrats abandoned their traditional commitment to minimal government. The Republicans recognized that the electorate would judge the president on his ability to bring prosperity to the country. As president, McKinley asserted his leadership over economic policy, calling Congress into special session to pass the Dingley Tariff Act, which levied the highest taxes on imports in American history.

In the election of 1896 fundamental economic questions—Who is the economy supposed to serve? What is the nature of money?—were at stake in a closely matched campaign. No wonder voter turnout hit an all-time high, and Americans long remembered that raucous campaign when the nation's economic future was up for grabs.

THE RETREAT FROM POLITICS

The economy improved steadily after 1895 but this latest business panic and its aftermath left lasting marks on corporate and political culture. Industrial workers made a tactical retreat in the face of a new political and legal climate. In the South, depression, urbanization, and the modernizing influence of railroads accelerated the spread of legalized racial segregation and disfranchisement. What was happening in the South was part of nationwide decline of participatory politics. With the slackening of agrarian unrest and the exhaustion of resistance to corporate capitalism, politics lost some of its value. Voter participation declined, and Americans felt less of a personal stake in election campaigns. Disaffected groups—such as labor and African Americans—had to devise new ways to build community and express resistance.

The Lure of the Cities

In the South as in the North people left the countryside and moved to towns and cities. By 1900 one out of six southerners lived in town. With the lone exception of Birmingham, Alabama, southern cities were not devoted to manufacturing but to commerce and services. Doctors' offices, haberdasheries, dry goods stores, and groceries could be found near warehouses where cotton was stored, ginned, and pressed and near the railway station where it was shipped to textile mills.

The growth of villages and towns in the South was the product of rural decay. Crop liens, which gave bankers ownership of a crop before it was planted, and debt drove people from the countryside. The young and the ambitious left first, while older and poorer residents stayed behind.

While white newcomers settled on the outskirts of towns, African Americans moved into industrial districts along the railroad tracks. Cities became more segregated as they grew, and by 1890 most blocks in the larger cities were either all black or all white. Still, towns offered things that were missing in the country, such as schools. A Little Rock, Arkansas, resident noted that newly arrived African-American parents were "very anxious to send their children to school." Jobs were often available, too, although more frequently for women than for men. Men looked for seasonal labor at farms or lumber camps some distance from town. This meant families faced a tough choice between poverty and separation.

Despite setbacks, the newcomers gained a place for themselves in urban life. By 1890 every southern city had an African-American business district with churches, insurance companies, lawyers, doctors, undertakers, and usually a weekly newspaper. Benevolent and reform organizations, sewing circles, and book clubs enriched community life. There were limits to how high educated African Americans could ascend. Professionals like lawyers, doctors, and nurses had to work within their community. Jobs on the bottom rung of the corporate ladder—clerk, salesman, telephone operator, stenographer, railroad conductor—were reserved for whites.

Inventing Jim Crow

In June 1892 Homer Plessy boarded the East Louisiana Railway in New Orleans for a trip to Covington, Louisiana. Having purchased a first-class ticket, he attempted to board the whites-only car and was arrested under a Louisiana law that required African Americans and whites to ride in "equal but separate accommodations." Before Judge John H. Ferguson could try the case, Plessy's lawyer appealed on the grounds that the separate car law violated the Constitution's Fourteenth Amendment.

When *Plessy* v. *Ferguson* came before the Supreme Court in April 1896, lawyers for the state of Louisiana argued that the law was necessary to avoid the "danger of friction from too intimate contact" between the races. In separate cars, all citizens enjoyed equal privileges. Plessy's lawyer, Albion Tourgée, replied that the question was not "the equality of the privileges enjoyed, but the right of the state to label one citizen as white and another as colored." In doing so, the government gave unearned advantages to some citizens and not to others. The issue for Tourgée was not racial conflict or even prejudice, but whether the government should be allowed to divide people arbitrarily. The court upheld the "separate but equal" doctrine. The Plessy decision provided legal justification for the system of official inequality that expanded in the twentieth century. Informal segregation had existed since the Civil War. People associated with members of their own race when they could, and when they could not—at work, in business, or when traveling—unwritten local customs usually governed their interaction. By the 1890s those informal customs were being codified in law. Railroads, as symbols of progress, were a chief point of contention.

The political and economic tensions created by the depression helped turn racist customs into a rigid caste division. Competition for jobs fed racial antagonisms, as did the migration into cities and towns of a new generation of African Americans, born since the war, who showed less deference to whites. New notions of "scientific" racism led intellectuals and churchmen to regard racial hostility as natural. Angry voters in many southern states deposed the coalitions of landowners and New South industrialists that had governed since Reconstruction and replaced them with Populist "demagogues."

Between 1887 and 1891 nine states in the South passed railroad segregation laws. Trains began pulling separate cars for African Americans, called "Jim Crow" cars after the name of a character in a minstrel show. Soon Jim Crow laws were extended to waiting rooms, drinking fountains, and other places where African Americans and whites might meet.

Segregation was also enforced by terror. The threat of lynching poisoned all relations between the races, and African Americans learned that they could be tortured and killed for committing a crime, talking back, or simply looking the wrong way at a white woman. Lynchings occurred most frequently in areas thinly populated by whites, but killings and mob violence also occurred in the largest cities. Between 1882 and 1903, nearly 2,000 African-American southerners were killed by mobs. Victims were routinely tortured, flayed, castrated, gouged, and burned alive, and members of the mob often took home grisly souvenirs like a piece of bone or a severed thumb.

Many African-American southerners fought segregation with boycotts, lawsuits, and disobedience. Ida Wells-Barnett, a Nashville journalist, organized an international antilynching campaign (see Chapter 21, "A United Body of Action"). Segregation was constantly negotiated and challenged, but after 1896 it was backed by the U.S. Supreme Court.

The Atlanta Compromise

When Atlanta invited African-American educator Booker T. Washington, to address the Cotton States Exposition in 1895, northern newspapers concluded that a new era of racial progress had begun. The speech made Washington the most recognized African American in the United States. Starting with 40 students and an abandoned shack, Washington had built Tuskegee Institute into a nationally known institution, the preeminent technical school for African Americans. Washington was a guest in the stately homes of Newport and at Andrew Carnegie's castle in Scotland. When Atlanta staged an exposition to showcase the region's industrial and social progress, the organizers asked Washington to speak.

Washington's address stressed racial accommodation. It had been a mistake, he argued, to try to attain equality by asserting civil and political rights. "The wisest among my race understand that agitation of questions of social equality is the extremest folly," he said, "and that progress in the enjoyment of all the privileges that will come to us must be the result of severe and constant struggle rather than artificial forcing." He urged white businessmen to employ African-American southerners "who have, without strikes and labor wars, tilled your fields, cleared your forests, built your railroads and cities." Raising his hand above his head, stretching out

Lynchings were public spectacles. When 17-year-old Jesse Washington was killed in Waco, Texas in 1916, a crowd of several thousand, including the mayor, police chief, and students from Waco High, attended the event on the lawn of city hall. Afterwards, the murderers posed for a photograph and sold their victim's teeth for $5 apiece.

his fingers and then closing them into a fist, he summarized his approach to race relations: "In all things that are purely social, we can be as separate as the fingers, yet one as the hand in all things essential to mutual progress." The largely white audience erupted into applause.

Washington's "Atlanta Compromise" stressed the mutual obligations of African Americans and whites. African Americans would give up the vote and stop insisting on social equality if white leaders would keep violence in check and allow African Americans to succeed in agriculture and business. White industrialists welcomed this arrangement, and African-American leaders felt that for the moment it might be the best that could be achieved.

Disfranchisement and the Decline of Popular Politics

After the feverish campaign of 1896, elections began to lose some of their appeal. Attendance fell off at the polls. Some 79 percent of voters cast ballots in the battle of the standards; eight years later the figure was down to 65 percent. More visibly, the public events surrounding campaigns drew thinner crowds. Organizers fretted about apathy, which seemed to have become a national epidemic.

In the South, the disappearance of voters was easy to explain. As Jim Crow laws multiplied, southern states disfranchised African Americans (and one out of four whites) by requiring voters to demonstrate literacy, property ownership, or knowledge of the Constitution before they could register. Louisiana added the notorious grandfather clause, which denied the vote to men whose grandfathers were prohibited from voting (see Table 20–1).

Whites saw disfranchisement and segregation as modern, managed race relations. Demonizing African Americans enforced solidarity among white voters, who might otherwise have voted on local or class interests.

No new legal restrictions hampered voting in the North and West, but participation fell there, too. This withdrawal from politics reflected the decline of political pageantry as an element of cultural and social life, but it also reflected the disappearance of intense partisanship. For American men, the cliffhanger contests of the late nineteenth century provided a sense of identity that matched and strengthened ethnic, religious, and neighborhood identities.

A developing economy with new patterns of recreation, class relations, and community participation undermined the habits of partisanship, but so did the new style of campaigns. The emphasis on advertising, education, and fundraising reduced the personal stakes for voters. Educated middle- and upper-class voters liked the new style, feeling that raucous campaigns were no way to decide important issues. They sought to influence policy more directly, through interest groups rather than parties. Unintentionally, they discarded traditions that unified communities and made voters feel connected to their country and its leaders.

TABLE 20–1

The Spread of Disfranchisement		
	State	**Strategies**
1889	Florida	Poll tax
	Tennessee	Poll tax
1890	Mississippi	Poll tax, literacy test, understanding clause
1891	Arkansas	Poll tax
1893, 1901	Alabama	Poll tax, literacy test, grandfather clause
1894, 1895	South Carolina	Poll tax, literacy test, understanding clause
1894, 1902	Virginia	Poll tax, literacy test, understanding clause
1897, 1898	Louisiana	Poll tax, literacy test, grandfather clause
1899, 1900	North Carolina	Poll tax, literacy test, grandfather clause
1902	Texas	Poll tax
1908	Georgia	Poll tax, literacy test, understanding clause, grandfather clause

Organized Labor Retreats From Politics

Workers also withdrew from politics as organized labor turned away from political means and goals and redefined objectives in economic terms. As traditional crafts came under attack, skilled workers created new organizations that addressed immediate issues: wages, hours, and the conditions of work. The American Federation of Labor (AFL), founded in 1886, built a base around skilled trades, and grew from 150,000 members to more than 2 million by 1904. The AFL focused on immediate goals that would improve the working lives of its members. Its founder, Samuel Gompers, was born in London's East End and apprenticed as a cigar maker at the age of ten. Three years later his family moved to New York, where Gompers joined the International Cigar Makers Union.

Although affiliated with the Knights of Labor, the cigar makers were more interested in getting higher wages than in remaking the economy. They concentrated on shortening work hours and increasing pay. High dues and centralized control allowed the union to offer insurance and death benefits to members while maintaining a strike fund. Gompers applied the same practices to the AFL. His "pure and simple unionism" made modest demands, but it still encountered fierce resistance from corporations, which were backed by the courts.

In the 1895 case of *In re Debs*, the Supreme Court allowed the use of injunctions to criminalize strikes. The court then disarmed one of the few weapons left in labor's arsenal, the boycott. In the 1908 case of *Loewe* v. *Lawlor*, popularly known as the Danbury Hatters case, the court ruled that advertising a consumer boycott was illegal under the Sherman Anti-Trust Act.

Gompers believed that *industrial unions*, associations that drew members from all occupations within an industry, lacked the discipline and shared values needed to face down corporations and government, and that unions organized around a single trade or craft would break less easily. However, because the AFL was organized by skill, it often ignored unskilled workers, such as women or recent immigrants. Because employers used unskilled newcomers to break strikes or to run machinery that replaced expert hands, Gompers excluded a large part of the labor force. Organizers recruited Irish and German workers through their fraternal lodges and saloons while ignoring Italian, African-American, Jewish, and Slavic workers. The union attacked female workers for stealing jobs that rightfully belonged to men.

Even leaders who rejected Gompers's philosophy and strategy built unions that represented the immediate interests of their members. Under the leadership of Eugene V. Debs, railroad workers merged the old railroad brotherhoods into the ARU in 1893. The United Mine Workers (UMW), founded in 1890, unionized the bituminous (soft coal) mines of Pennsylvania, Ohio, Indiana, and Michigan. The ARU and the UMW were industrial unions that tried to organize all of the workers in an industry. These new unions faced determined opposition from business and its allies in government.

AMERICAN DIPLOMACY ENTERS THE MODERN WORLD

The Republican victory in 1896 encouraged proponents of foreign trade. Before the turn of the century, the new president announced, the United States would control the markets of the globe. Many in McKinley's party wanted both war and colonies. Called "jingoes," they included Assistant Secretary of the Navy Theodore Roosevelt; John Hay, the ambassador to London; and Senators Albert Beveridge and Henry

Cabot Lodge. Britain, France, and Germany were seizing territory around the world, and jingoes believed the United States needed to do the same. McKinley, at first reluctantly but later enthusiastically, pushed for the creation of an American empire that stretched to the far shores of the Pacific.

Sea Power and the Imperial Urge

Few men better exemplified the jingoes' combination of religiosity and martial spirit than Alfred Thayer Mahan. A naval officer and strategist, Mahan connected naval expansion and empire to the problem of overproduction in the United States. A great industrial country needed trade, trade required a merchant fleet, and merchant shipping needed naval protection and overseas bases. Colonies could provide markets for goods and congregations for Christian missionaries, and naval forces could protect sea lanes and project United States power abroad.

World leadership, Mahan argued, belonged to the nation that controlled the sea. He urged the United States to build a canal across Central America, allowing manufacturers on the Atlantic coast to "compete with Europe . . . for the markets of eastern Asia." He felt that naval bases should be established along routes connecting the United States with markets in Latin America and the Far East. Congress and the Navy Department began implementing these recommendations even before McKinley took office.

If subduing continents with cross, Constitution, and gatling gun appealed to anyone, it was Theodore Roosevelt. Imperialism seemed to him the essential characteristic of modernizing countries. Roosevelt was acutely conscious of how modern forces—globalized trade, instant communications, the reach of modern navies, and imperialism—had altered domestic and international politics. He sought to position the United States at the center of these modernizing currents, a place that would have to be earned, he felt, both on foreign battlefields and at home, where the material and technological gains of the nineteenth century had not yet been translated into the social and moral advancement that marked a true civilization. Sharing the social Darwinist belief (see Chapter 18) that nations and races were locked in a savage struggle for survival, Mahan and Roosevelt expected the United States to prevail and benefit from the approaching conflict.

The Scramble for Empire

For jingoes, China was the ultimate prize in the global contest for trade and mastery. It had more people than any other country, hence more customers and more souls to be brought to Christ: The number of American missionaries in China doubled in the 1890s. Even though no more than 1 or 2 percent of U.S. exports went to Chinese ports, manufacturers believed that China could absorb the output of America's overproductive factories. In 1890 Standard Oil began selling kerosene in Shanghai. Fifteen years later, China was the largest overseas market for American oil.

In 1894 Japan declared war on China, and within months it occupied Korea, Manchuria, and China's coastal cities. When the fighting was over, Western powers seized slices of Chinese territory. In November 1897, German troops captured the port of Qingdao on the Shandong Peninsula. An industrial area on the northeast coast, Shandong was the center of American missionary activity, investment, and trade. To Americans, the invasion of Shandong presaged the beginning of an

Thanks to the work of missionaries in China, Mark Twain observed, "the people who sit in darkness . . . have become suspicious of the blessings of civilization."

imperial grab for territory and influence. The McKinley administration watched the events unfolding in China carefully, but in the winter of 1897–1898 the Departments of State and War had more pressing concerns closer to home.

War With Spain

While other European powers were expanding their empires, Spain was barely hanging on. Since the 1860s its two largest colonies, Cuba and the Philippines, had been torn by revolution. Between 1868 and 1878 Cuban nationalists fought a prolonged war of independence. Spain ended the war by promising reforms but U.S. tariffs ruined the island's chief export industry, sugar, and plunged the colony into debt. When rebellion resumed in 1895, the rebels practiced a "scorched earth" policy, dynamiting trains and burning plantations to force Spain to withdraw or the United States to intervene.

Spain retaliated with a brutal campaign of pacification. General Valeriano Weyler herded civilians into reconcentration camps enclosed by barbed wire. Nearly 100,000 died, many of them women and children. William Randolph Hearst's *New York Journal* and other newspapers provided readers with lurid details that fixed the public's attention on Cuba.

Cleveland had tried to minimize U.S. involvement in Cuba, but McKinley moved quickly toward confrontation. In July 1897 he demanded that Spain withdraw from Cuba. The government in Madrid retreated, and McKinley breathed a sigh of relief. Despite his bluster, he realized that he could pay for a war only by coining silver. However, events in Havana were soon outracing policy. Riots erupted, and American expatriates demanded protection. The president asked the Navy to send a warship to Havana, and Theodore Roosevelt selected the *Maine*, one of the new battleships that had been built at Mahan's urging (see Map 20–1).

The arrival of the *Maine* reduced tensions for a while, but on February 15 an explosion ripped through the ship. Almost the entire crew of 266 perished. Navy investigators later concluded that the explosion had been internal, probably in the new oil-fired boilers, but the newspapers had already blamed Spanish treachery.

McKinley hesitated, mindful of the budget and the unfolding events in China, but Roosevelt ordered Commodore George Dewey's Asiatic Squadron to Hong Kong to prepare for an attack on Spain's colony in the Philippines. Congress appropriated $50 million for arms.

In March the economic picture took a turn for the better, and McKinley sent Spain an ultimatum demanding independence for Cuba. On April 11 he asked Congress for authorization to use force, and Congress passed a declaration of war. Expansionists such as Roosevelt, Mahan, and Adams would not have had their way if war had been less popular. Corporate interests favored it, immigrants and southerners saw it as a way to assert their patriotism, and newspapers found it made good copy. "We are all jingoes now," declared the *New York Sun*.

The war opened with a cliffhanger that even Hearst could not have invented. On May 1 news arrived that Dewey's Asiatic Squadron was battling the Spanish fleet in Manila Bay in the Philippines. The war had begun half a world away on the far edge of the Pacific Ocean. The telegraph cable connecting Manila to the outside world was cut, and for six anxious days the American public awaited word from the Far East.

It arrived in the early morning of May 7, interrupting a poker game in the newsroom at the *New York Herald*. The paper's Hong Kong correspondent reported that Dewey had destroyed Spain's entire fleet of 12 warships. The country went wild with relief and triumph. McKinley consulted a map to see where the Philippines were, and Roosevelt quit his job and ordered Brooks Brothers to make him a uniform.

The war in Cuba unfolded less spectacularly. The Navy bottled up Spain's Atlantic fleet in the Bay of Santiago de Cuba. A bit of drama was provided by the voyage of the U.S.S. *Oregon*, which left its West Coast base and traveled around the southern tip of South America in 68 days to join the Atlantic fleet too late for the fighting. Its journey dramatized the need for a canal connecting the Atlantic and the Pacific.

In the years before the war, Congress had poured money into the Navy but not the Army, and it took some time before soldiers could be trained and equipped. Recruits were herded into camps in Florida without tents, proper clothing, or latrines. Soldiers in woolen uniforms died of dysentery and malaria, a scandal that forced the government to elevate the status of the surgeon general and to regard disease prevention as important to national defense.

The Army landed on the Cuban coast and marched inland to engage Spanish defenders. Roosevelt came ashore with the First Volunteer Cavalry, known as the Rough Riders. He recruited, trained, and publicized the regiment, and afterwards he wrote its history, all with an eye to symbolism. The regiment traveled with its own film crew and a correspondent from the *New York Herald*.

Spanish forces stubbornly resisted around the city of Santiago. At San Juan Hill, 500 defenders forced a regiment of the New York National Guard to retreat. The all-African-American 9th and 10th Cavalry took their place along with the Rough Riders, with Roosevelt cautiously waiting until artillery could be brought up from the rear. The capture of Santiago effectively ended Spanish resistance. When fighting

Map 20–1   The Spanish–American War in the Caribbean.
The Spanish–American War in the Pacific

ended, U.S. troops occupied Cuba, Guam, Puerto Rico, and the city of Manila. The war had lasted only four months.

As American and Spanish diplomats concluded a peace treaty, McKinley had to decide which occupied territories to keep as colonies. Congress, not wanting to inherit the island's $400 million debt, had already resolved not to annex Cuba. McKinley decided that Guam and Puerto Rico would make ideal naval bases.

The president also seized the opportunity to annex the island nation of Hawaii. In 1893 American sugar planters, led by Sanford Dole, overthrew the islands' last queen, Liliuokalani, and petitioned for annexation (see Chapter 19). They had a powerful ally in the U.S. Navy: Mahan had identified the deep-water port at Pearl Harbor, on Oahu, as a vital base. McKinley now decided to take up Dole's annexation offer.

The Philippines presented more of a problem. Its 7,000 islands were far from the United States and had a population of several million. What the United States needed was a naval base and a fuel station close to the China coast, but holding just one island would be impossible: Shortly after Dewey's victory, British and German warships anchored in Manila Bay, intending to divide up whatever territory the United States did not claim. McKinley felt that he could not let go.

However, the United States did not actually control the Philippines, and in Manila it was increasingly clear that it would take a war to do so. Rebels led by Emilio Aguinaldo had seized most of the country outside of the capital. Rather than surrender to the Filipinos, the Spanish surrendered to the Americans on August 13, 1898. At Malolos, 25 miles north of Manila, Aguinaldo proclaimed himself president of the independent Philippines and issued a constitution modeled on that of the United States. When the U.S. Army finally arrived, American troops filled Spanish trenches opposite the Philippine lines. At the end of 1898, the two armies still faced each other across a no-man's land.

Spanish negotiators recognized Cuban independence and surrendered most of the Spanish empire to the United States for free, but they gave up the Philippines only after the United States agreed to pay $20 million. The treaty was signed December 10, 1898.

The Anti-Imperialists

Many prominent Americans opposed both the annexation of new colonies and the approaching war with the Philippines. The movement included ex-presidents Grover Cleveland and Benjamin Harrison, William Jennings Bryan, labor and business leaders including Samuel Gompers, Eugene Debs, and Andrew Carnegie, and writers such as Mark Twain and Ambrose Bierce. The anti-imperialists advanced an array of moral, economic, and strategic arguments. Filipinos and Hawaiians, they said, had sought American help in good faith and were capable of governing themselves. The islands could not be defended. Imperialism distracted attention from domestic problems and took tax money that could be spent at home. White supremacists asked whether Filipinos would become citizens or be allowed to vote and emigrate to the mainland.

The most moving objections came from those who believed imperialism betrayed America's fundamental principles. "Could there be a more damning indictment of the whole bloated ideal termed 'modern civilization' than this amounts to?" William James asked. To Mark Twain imperialism was the modern form of greed. Opponents of annexation organized an Anti-Imperialist League and lobbied for the rejection of the Paris Treaty.

Congress whittled away at anti-imperialist objections, banning Philippine immigration, placing the colonies outside the tariff walls, and promising eventual self-government. Jingoes had military victory and public acclaim on their side. Anti-imperialists could not offer a vision comparable to naval supremacy, the evangelization of the world, or the fabled China market. On February 6, 1899, the Senate ratified the Paris Treaty and annexed the Philippines. A day earlier, on the other side of the world, the Philippine–American War began.

The Philippine–American War

McKinley believed he had annexed islands full of near savages "unfit for self-rule," but the Philippines by 1899 had an old civilization with a long tradition of resistance to colonialism. When Magellan discovered the islands in 1521, he found a literate population linked by trade to India, Japan, and China. By 1898 much of the upper class, the *illustrados*, had been educated in Europe. Aguinaldo convened a national assembly comprised of doctors, lawyers, professors, and writers.

Dewey had given Aguinaldo his word that America desired no colonies. Aguinaldo continued to have faith in that word long after the occupation of Manila made it clear that the United States intended to stay. On February 4 an argument between American and Filipino sentries ended in gunfire.

By midsummer the Filipino armies fell back into the mountains and abandoned conventional warfare for guerilla tactics. Some 4,000 Americans were killed and another 3,000 wounded out of a total force of 70,000. Frustrated by guerilla conflict, American soldiers executed and tortured prisoners, looted villages, and raped Filipino women. An American general on the island of Samar ordered his soldiers to kill everyone over the age of ten.

Newspaper accounts of torture and massacres fueled opposition to the war, but just as the anti-imperialist movement gained steam, U.S. forces scored some victories. Recognizing that they were fighting a political war, U.S. officers took pains to win over dissidents and ethnic minorities. In early 1901 this strategy paid off when Brigadier General Frederick Funston, leading a band of Filipino fighters working for the U.S., entered Aguinaldo's camp and kidnapped the president.

After three weeks in a Manila prison, Aguinaldo surrendered. "Enough of blood, enough of tears and desolation," he pleaded. Resistance continued for another year. The U.S. Army increased the pressure by imposing the same reconcentration policies the United States had condemned in Cuba, and produced the same result. On July 4, 1902, President Theodore Roosevelt declared the war over.

The Open Door

As Americans celebrated their victories, European powers continued to divide China into quasi-colonial "concessions." An alarmed imperial court in Beijing began a crash program of modernization, but reactionaries within the government overthrew the emperor and installed the conservative "dowager empress" Ci Xi. In the countryside, Western missionaries and traders came under attack from local residents led by street-corner martial artists known as Boxers. Americans feared that the approaching disintegration of China would mean the exclusion of U.S. trade.

To keep China's markets open, Secretary of State John Hay drafted an official letter known as the Open Door Note. Sent to each of the imperial powers, it acknowledged the partitioning of China into spheres, and urged that each of the powers keep its areas open to the trade of other countries.

The Open Door was mostly bluff. The United States had no authority to ask for such a pledge and no military power to enforce one. The foreign ministers of Germany, Japan, Russia, Britain, and France replied cautiously, agreeing to issue a declaration when the others had done so, but Hay adroitly played one power off another. Once Britain and Japan, the two strongest powers in China had agreed, France reluctantly acquiesced, as did Russia and Germany. Hay proclaimed the Open Door as a diplomatic watershed on the order of the Monroe Doctrine. The United States had secured access to China without war or partition, but the limits of Hay's success soon became apparent.

In early 1900, the antiforeign Boxer movement swept through Shandong province, attacking missions and foreign businesses, destroying railroads, and massacring Chinese Christians. Empress Ci Xi recruited 30,000 Boxers into her army and declared war on all foreign countries. The Western powers rushed troops to China, but before they arrived, Chinese armies laid siege to Western embassies in Beijing. An international force of British, Russian, Japanese, and French troops gathered at Tianjin to capture the Chinese capital.

Without consulting Congress, McKinley ordered American troops from Manila to Tianjin. John Hay issued a second Open Door Note, asking the allied countries to pledge to protect China's independence. Again, the imperial powers reluctantly agreed. On August 15, 1900, U.S. cavalry units under General Adna Chaffee reached Beijing along with Russian, French, British-Indian, German, and Japanese troops. After freeing the captive diplomats, the armies looted the city. The United States was unable to maintain the Open Door in China, because Russia and Japan established separate military zones in northeast China in defiance of the Beijing government and American protests. However, the principle of the Open Door, of encouraging free trade and open markets, guided American foreign policy throughout the twentieth century. It rested on the assumption that, in an equal contest, American firms would prevail, spreading manufactured goods around the world, and American influence with them. Just one year after the Spanish–American War, Hay's notes rejected imperial expansion in favor of trade expansion. This bold new strategy placed the United States on a collision course with the great empires of the world.

CONCLUSION

In the turbulent 1890s the social and economic divisions among Americans widened. The hope that a solution to these divisions could be found outside the United States was short-lived. Imperialism promised new markets and an end to the wrenching cycle of depression and labor strife. The United States conquered an overseas empire and challenged other empires to open their ports to free trade, but the goal of prosperity and peace at home proved elusive.

In many ways social Darwinism became a self-fulfilling prophecy, as competition rather than compromise prevailed. Workers and businessmen, farmers and bankers, middle-class radicals and conservatives, whites and African Americans saw each other as enemies. Racial segregation showed that middle ground, where whites and African Americans could meet on equal terms, had disappeared. Workers, farmers, African Americans, radicals, and reformers had to decide what was politically possible and devise new bargaining strategies.

Economic recovery and victory in global conflict closed the decade on an optimistic note. Prosperity, power, and technology seemed to have rewritten the rules of human affairs to America's advantage. Henry Adams, standing in the American

CHRONOLOGY

1890	Global depression begins United Mine Workers founded Battle of Wounded Knee ends Indian wars Harrison–McKinley Tariff passed Standard Oil markets kerosene in China
1892	Homestead strike
1893	Financial crisis leads to business failures and mass unemployment World's Columbian Exposition in Chicago Cherokee Strip land rush American sugar planters overthrow Queen Liliuokalani of Hawaii
1894	Coxey's Army marches on Washington Pullman strike U.S. commission charts canal route across Nicaragua
1895	Morgan agrees to Treasury bailout Booker T. Washington gives "Atlanta Compromise" address Revolution begins in Cuba Japan annexes Korea and Taiwan
1896	*Plessy* v. *Ferguson* declares "separate but equal" facilities constitutional William McKinley elected president
1897	Germany captures Qingdao, on China's Shandong Peninsula
1898	Maine explodes in Havana's harbor U.S. declares war on Spain Dewey defeats Spanish fleet at Manila Bay In the Treaty of Paris, Spain grants Cuba independence, cedes Guam, Puerto Rico, and the Philippines to the United States Aguinaldo proclaims Philippine independence
1899	Senate votes to annex Puerto Rico, Hawaii, and the Philippines Philippine–American War begins Hay issues first Open Door Note
1900	Hay issues second Open Door Note U.S. Army joins British, French, Russian, German, and Japanese forces in capture of Beijing Great Exposition of Paris showcases American technology William McKinley re-elected
1901	Aguinaldo captured McKinley assassinated; Theodore Roosevelt becomes president
1902	Roosevelt declares Philippine–American war over

exhibit at the Paris Exposition of 1900 contemplated a 40-foot dynamo—a "huge wheel, revolving within arm's-length at some vertiginous speed, and barely murmuring"—and felt as if he had crossed a "historical chasm." The machine's immense force, scarcely understood or controlled and emanating from "a dirty engine-house carefully kept out of sight," seemed a metaphor for the power of the modern age.

FURTHER READINGS

Edward L. Ayers, *The Promise of the New South: Life After Reconstruction* (1992). A study of daily life, work, and politics in the turn-of-the-century South.

H. W. Brands, *The Reckless Decade: America in the 1890s* (1995). A lively look at some of the decade's noteworthy events and characters.

Ron Chernow, *The House of Morgan: An American Banking Dynasty and the Rise of Modern Finance* (1990). The life and business of J. P. Morgan and his heirs, the lions of Wall Street for more than a century.

James B. Gilbert, *Perfect Cities: Chicago's Utopias of 1893* (1991). The fears and dreams that led Chicago's elite to create the World's Columbian Exposition.

Robert Kanigel, *The One Best Way: Frederick Winslow Taylor and the Enigma of Efficiency* (1997). The most famous efficiency expert and how his system changed the world.

Stanley Karnow, *In Our Image: America's Empire in the Philippines* (1989). America's colonial venture in the Philippines from 1898 to 1986.

David L. Lewis, *W. E. B. Du Bois: Biography of a Race, 1868–1919* (1993). The story of the man who "pleaded with a headstrong, careless people to despise not Justice," and the era that produced him.

Ivan Musicant, *Empire by Default: The Spanish American War and the Dawn of the American Century* (1998). A misnamed but thorough account of the war and its meaning.

Nick Salvatore, *Eugene V. Debs: Citizen and Socialist* (1982). From the railroad yards to federal prison, the story of one of America's great labor leaders.

Please refer to the document CD-ROM for primary sources related to this chapter.

21

A United Body of Action

1900–1916

Alice Hamilton • **Toward a New Politics** • **The Progressives**
Progressives in State and Local Politics • **The Presidency Becomes**
"The Administration" • **Rival Visions of the Industrial Future**
Conclusion

ALICE HAMILTON

On an October morning in 1902, three friends, Maude Gernon of the Chicago Board of Charities, Gertrude Howe, director of the kindergarten at Hull House, and Dr. Alice Hamilton, a professor of pathology at Northwestern University, stood over two open sewer drains catching flies. Hamilton had organized the hunting expedition to prove a point. Chicago was in the grip of a typhoid epidemic. The disease had ravaged the city's 19th Ward, a working-class neighborhood. To find out why, Hamilton "prowled about the streets and the ramshackle wooden tenement houses," which often had illegal outdoor privies because landlords refused to install plumbing. It was then that she noticed the flies. Army doctors in the Spanish–American War had found a link between flies, poor sanitation, and the spread of typhoid. Hamilton incubated her test tubes for several days, examined the contents under a microscope, and confirmed that Chicago's flies carried the typhoid bacillus.

When her findings appeared in the *Journal of the American Medical Association*, they touched off a furor. Hull House attacked the Board of Health for failing to enforce sanitary codes, and an inquiry discovered that landlords bribed sanitation inspectors to overlook the outdoor privies. Further investigations found that tap water was pumped straight from Lake Michigan and that broken pumping equipment channeled raw sewage into the water mains. Chicago's city government was directly responsible for an epidemic that killed hundreds of people.

Hamilton chose to become a doctor because "I could go anywhere I pleased . . . and be quite sure that I could be of use anywhere." She attended the Fort Wayne College of Medicine and in 1892 entered the University of Michigan, later doing advanced work in bacteriology and pathology at Leipzig and Munich. Despite her training, she was not able to find work anywhere she pleased, but in Chicago she found a university position and a supportive environment in Hull House, a "settlement house" founded by women who wanted to live among the poor and avoid patronizing forms of charity. Hamilton lived there for 22 years while conducting research on tuberculosis among Jewish garment workers in the neighborhoods nearby. Hamilton pushed for state laws on occupational disease, and in 1911 Illinois became the first state to pass legislation giving workers compensation for job-related disability. By the 1930s, all major industrial states had similar laws.

Alice Hamilton was among the thousands of "progressives" who reshaped government and business by intervening in politics in new ways. Responding to the challenges of immigration, industrialization, and urbanization, Americans agitated for change on a broad variety of issues. Women, who did not have the vote, took the lead and created a new style of political activism.

Some reformers feared the uncontrolled wealth and power of corporations, while others feared losing wealth and power to the uncontrolled political passions of the poor. Although they disagreed on many of their goals and methods, progressives saw politics and economics, according to W. E. B. Du Bois, as "but two aspects of a united body of action and effort." They were pessimistic about the ability of people, particularly nonwhite people, to improve themselves. Science and evangelical Protestantism, as progressives understood them, justified the supervision of human affairs by qualified experts and the state.

Although reformers accepted capitalism and industry as fixtures of a modern political economy, they were outraged by the disease, waste, and corruption the factory system left behind. They sought a middle ground between revolutionary socialism and uncontrolled corporate capitalism. Progressivism, as it came to be called, was the first and perhaps the only reform movement experienced by all Americans.

TOWARD A NEW POLITICS

The political and economic crises of the 1890s contributed to the strength of progressivism. Politics became less participatory, and millions of Americans lost the strong loyalties they once had to traditional parties. Egged on by a national press, progressives organized at the local, state, and national levels to solve the problems of the new industrial world. Progressives recognized that large-scale industrial capitalism was here to stay and worked to make an erratic and brutal system more predictable, efficient, and humane. In pushing for reform, however, they were willing to use state power to tell people what was good for them and then make them do it. The movement rewrote the Democratic and Republican platforms and gave politics a new purpose.

The Insecurity of Modern Life

Most people who lived in cities at the turn of the century had grown up in the country or in smaller towns. They remembered living in communities where people knew each other, where many of the foods they ate and clothes they wore were made locally. In contrast, life in a modern metropolis, connected by rail, telephone, and telegraph to other cities and the world beyond meant depending on strangers. Meat and bread came not from a familiar butcher or baker, but from distant packinghouses and producers. Tap water, gas for heating and lighting, and transportation were all supplied by large, anonymous corporations. City dwellers felt more sophisticated than their parents but also less secure.

City living carried risks. In Chicago marketplaces journalist Upton Sinclair found milk preserved with formaldehyde, peas colored green with copper salts, and smoked sausage doctored with toxic chemicals. Druggists sold fraudulent cures for imaginary diseases. Cures available over the counter included wood alcohol, cocaine, heroin, and other dangerous substances.

Simply finding a place to live could involve hazards. Tenement blocks housing hundreds of people often had no fire escapes or plumbing. Unscrupulous bankers and real estate brokers could hoodwink families out of their savings. Consumers were at the mercy of unrestrained monopolies and hucksters.

Tragedy reminded New Yorkers of these dangers on March 25, 1911, when fire engulfed the Triangle Shirtwaist Company. On the top three floors of a ten-story building, 500 Jewish and Italian women manufactured blouses. When fire broke out, they raced for the exits, which had been locked to discourage employees from taking breaks. Desperate to escape the flames, many women jumped from ledges in groups, holding hands. Others dove into empty elevator shafts. In all, 146 died. Such episodes demonstrated to many Americans that although the political economy was enormously productive, it was also deadly.

Government not only failed to address these problems, it contributed to them. Regulation by legislature or elected city officials often supplied a pretext for kickbacks and bribery. City and state machines were riddled with graft. In 1904 and 1905, journalists and investigators uncovered corruption in state after state. Trials in San Francisco disclosed that Boss Abraham Ruef ruled the city with a slush fund donated by public utilities. The Minneapolis police, with the connivance of the mayor's office, protected brothels and gambling dens in return for bribes. By creating a demand for campaign contributions and jobs for loyal party officials, elections became invitations to graft. Politics, journalist Lincoln Steffens complained, merely amplified the power of big corporations.

Around many urban centers a ring of "street car suburbs" grew in the latter years of the nineteenth century, filled with Victorian homes belonging to business managers, accountants, engineers, lawyers, doctors, and highly skilled workers. These citizens became conscious of themselves as a class, with common interests and common ideas on how cities should run. Modern corporations had to have clear lines of authority, an emphasis on efficiency, and reliable sources

Employers had locked the emergency exits when fire broke out at the Triangle Shirtwaist Factory. The death toll provoked state and federal investigations and a public clamor for regulation.

of information. Yet these virtues were frustratingly absent from civic life. Government needed to become more responsive, accountable, and vigilant against dangers to the public.

The Decline of Partisan Politics

In the early twentieth century many Americans, particularly the middle and upper classes, began seeking new ways to compel government to deal with the problems of industrial, urban society. They demanded civil service reform, the regulation of monopolies, and an end to the rule of party machines. They voted not as members of a party but as independents.

As the new activism increased, popular party politics declined. Participation in national and state elections dropped off sharply (see Figure 21–1). Literacy tests accounted for much of the decline in the South, but in all regions the old spectacular style of electioneering gave way to campaigns that were more educational and less participatory. "Listless" was how one observer described the 1904 turnout. Worse from the parties' point of view, more voters split their tickets. The ethnic and sectional loyalties that led people to vote a straight party ballot in the late nineteenth century were weakening.

Increasingly, Americans participated in politics through voluntary associations. Pressure groups took over important functions that formerly belonged to the parties: educating and socializing voters and even making policy. Some voluntary organizations were concerned with public morals, others with urban corruption, restraining monopolies, or caring for the poor. A few functioned almost as parties did, even running candidates for local office, but most worked outside the system to gather support for a particular cause or proposal. Built on the idea that reform was a continuous process, they strove for permanence. Some, like the National Association for the Advancement of Colored People (NAACP), the Salvation Army, and the Sierra Club, remain prominent today.

Figure 21–1   Voter Participation, 1896–1920
After the intense partisanship and high-stakes elections of the 1890s, campaigns became more "educational" and voters lost interest.
Source: Michael E. McGerr, The Decline of Popular Politics (New York: Oxford University Press, 1986), pp. 185–186.

Social Housekeeping

The growing clamor for social change aroused latent political strength in unexpected places. Women's social clubs had been nonpolitical before the turn of the century. Club women, generally white and upper or middle class, enjoyed sufficient freedom from housework to attend meetings dedicated to art, speaking, reading, and conversation. They met "without some work of benevolence or reform in view," but were nonetheless highly organized, with local, state, and national chapters. The urgency of social problems led many clubs to launch campaigns on behalf of free kindergartens, civil service reform, and public health.

Club women explained that activism was a natural outgrowth of their domestic responsibilities as wives and mothers. One could hardly keep a safe, comfortable home in the midst of a dangerous and corrupt community. Club membership grew alongside activism. The 50,000 members of the General Federation of Women's Clubs in 1898 expanded by 1914 to well over a million, and the organization became a powerful lobby. In some communities the women's club was the only organized voice for civic improvement.

By the turn of the century, the first generation of graduates from the new women's colleges had reached adulthood—and some, like Alice Hamilton, had attained advanced professional degrees—at a time when few men had a college education. These "new women," as historians have called them, had different ambitions and values from women of their mothers' generation. About half of the female college graduates did not marry. Because the career paths their male classmates followed were closed to them, educated women served in voluntary organizations. Reform politics allowed them to use their talents for a larger purpose.

Educated women found careers by finding problems that needed solving. Florence Kelley, trained as a lawyer, became Illinois' first state factory inspector and later directed the National Consumers' League. Margaret Sanger, a New York public health nurse, distributed literature on birth control and sex education when it was illegal to do so. Female activists "discovered" problems, publicized them, lobbied for new laws, and then staffed the bureaus and agencies created to administer solutions.

Middle-class women remained concerned with the welfare of women and children and with issues related to their homes and neighborhoods. By uniting with others around the country, however, they changed the political culture. Activities that had once been considered charity or volunteer work became political. Through national networks, activists learned that the problems of their neighborhoods arose elsewhere and could not be solved at the local level. Ultimately, to maintain decent and safe homes, women needed the help of the state.

The logic of social housekeeping called for enlarging state powers and increasing women's influence over the state. The experiences of women's clubs and associations taught political activists the importance of cooperation, organization, and expertise. When women's clubs built a playground and donated it to the city or urged lawmakers to address an issue, they increased their own stake in the political system. They gave themselves new reasons to demand full citizenship.

The women's suffrage movement quietly built momentum in the early years of the century. Women had gained the vote in four states—Colorado, Wyoming, Utah, and Idaho—early on, but between 1896 and 1910 no other states adopted a women's suffrage amendment.

Competing suffrage organizations joined forces under the National American Women's Suffrage Association (NAWSA), which developed a strategy based on professional lobbying and publicity. Suffragists appealed to club women and middle-class reformers by linking suffrage to moderate social causes, such as temperance and education. This strategy paid off: After 1910, five states adopted suffrage amendments in rapid succession, but the opposition rallied and defeated referendums in three eastern states.

Frustrated with the glacial pace of progress, Alice Paul's National Woman's Party adopted more radical tactics, picketing the White House and staging hunger strikes. Despite setbacks, women led the transformation of politics through voluntary organizations and interest groups and were on the threshold of even greater gains.

Evolution or Revolution?

No group was more buoyantly optimistic about the prospects for revolutionary change than the Socialists. The Socialist Party of America (SPA) met in Indianapolis in the summer of 1901 and declared its confidence in the inevitability of capitalism's downfall. By 1912, Eugene V. Debs, the party's candidate for president, garnered almost 1 million votes, some 6 percent of the total. Socialists elected two members of Congress, 56 mayors, and 33 state legislators.

Even more impressive was their influence within the labor movement. A third of the delegates to the AFL's 1912 convention had party cards. Jewish workers in New York and Germans in Milwaukee formed powerful urban voting blocs. "Gas and water" Socialists, who demanded public ownership of utilities, captured municipal offices in smaller cities across the country. In the plains states, socialism drew strength from primitive Baptist and Holiness churches and held revival-style tent meetings.

Debs's party dreamed of a peaceful evolution to an economy that rewarded cooperation and valued human labor. Although tinged with religion, Socialists' analysis of modern problems was economic. They maintained that the profit motive distorted human behavior, forcing people to compete instead of joining together to promote the common good. Driven by the need for profits, corporations could not be trusted to look after the welfare of their customers or workers. Socialists demanded the collective ownership of industries, starting with railroads and city utilities. They were sure socialism was coming "like a prairie fire," a socialist newspaperman told his readers, "You can see it in the papers. You can taste it in the price of beef."

When the Industrial Workers of the World (IWW), known as the Wobblies, talked about revolution they meant a war, not an election. Founded in 1905, the IWW unionized some of the most rugged individuals in the West: miners, loggers, and even rodeo cowboys. Wobblies organized unskilled workers, challenging both the AFL's elite unionism and the Socialists' gradualism. Membership remained small, fewer than 100,000, but the union frightened people with its calls for sabotage and a general strike. At IWW strikes in Lawrence, Massachusetts, and Paterson, New Jersey, strikers clashed with police and paraded with red flags. To sensationalist newspapermen and anxious middle-class readers, these activities were signs of approaching class warfare.

Socialism's greatest influence might have been the push it gave conservatives to support moderate reform. Theodore Roosevelt worried that unless something was done the United States might split into two parties, one representing workers, the other capital.

The failure of the two parties to deal with urgent social problems created a chance to redefine politics and citizenship. Precisely because they had been outside the system, women—particularly middle-class, educated, Protestant women— gained a moral authority that enabled them to transform humanitarian concerns and voluntary activities into a new kind of politics. The specter of revolution aided their efforts. As the new century began, Americans were scrapping their old political rules and getting ready to fashion new institutions to deal with the challenges of modern society.

THE PROGRESSIVES

As the old politics declined, a new politics of associations and activists took its place. Historians have found it difficult to define the progressives. Progressives addressed a wide variety of social problems with many different tactics, but for people of the time the connectedness was apparent. A rally to end child labor, for instance, might draw out young lawyers, teachers, labor unionists, woman suffragists, professors, and politicians. A series of overlapping movements, campaigns, and crusades defined the era from 1890 to 1920.

Progressivism was not a unified movement with a platform or set of goals. It was more like a political style, a way of approaching problems. Progressives had no illusions that wage labor or industrialism could be eliminated or that it was possible to re-create a rural commonwealth, but they shared an optimistic conviction that modern institutions could be made humane, responsive, and moral.

In choosing solutions, progressives relied on scientific expertise. Rival points of view could be reconciled more easily by impartial authority. Like the salaried managers many of them were, progressives valued efficiency and organization. No problem could be solved in a single stroke. Instead, remedies could be enforced only by repeated actions by institutions dedicated to reform. Instead of organizing a reform party, progressives formed interest groups to lobby government and raise public awareness.

Convinced that science and God were on their side, progressives often imposed their views on others. Such measures as identifying "born criminals" who could be put on probation for life without ever having committed a crime would be described as "progressive." To southern progressives "scientific" principles of race justified segregation and paternalism. Reforms could be unpopular—as the drive to ban alcoholic beverages was—but this posed a strategic rather than a philosophical problem. Progressives demanded more democracy when it led to "good government," but if, in their view, the majority was wrong progressives readily handed power to unelected managers.

Progressives shared the conviction that social problems required urgent action. "There are two kinds of people," Alice Hamilton learned from her mother, "the ones who say 'Someone ought to do something about it but why should it be I?' and the ones who say, 'Somebody must do something about it, then why not I?'" Hamilton and other progressives were the second kind.

Social Workers and Muckrakers

Among the first to hear the call to service were the young women and men who volunteered to live among the urban poor in "settlement houses." Stanton Coit established the first on New York's lower east side in 1886, but the most famous was Hull House, which opened in Chicago three years later. Its founders, Jane Addams and Ellen Starr, bought a run-down mansion, formerly a country estate, that now stood among sweatshops, factories, and overcrowded tenements. Poverty, back-breaking labor, and disease blighted life for residents of the 19th Ward. The women of Hull House attacked these problems by opening a kindergarten and a clinic, taking sweatshop bosses to court, investigating corrupt landlords, criticizing the ward's powerful alderman, and building the first public playground in Chicago.

Addams drew together a remarkable group of women with similar backgrounds. Florence Kelley pushed some of the nation's first occupational safety laws through the Illinois legislature. Julia Lathrop headed the state's Children's Bureau. All three women were raised in affluent Quaker homes, and their parents were all abolitionists. Like Alice Hamilton, all three attended college and afterward traveled or studied in Europe.

As the fame of Hull House spread, women (and some men) organized settlement houses in other cities. By 1910 there were more than 400. Reformers often began by using social science techniques to survey the surrounding neighborhoods, gathering information on the inhabitants' national origins, income, housing conditions, and occupations. One of the most ambitious research projects was the Pittsburgh Survey, a six-volume study of conditions in the steel city published between 1909 and 1914. By relying on survey data, progressives acknowledged that the causes of poverty were social, not personal. Because economic conditions, not laziness or immorality, caused poverty, progressives did not offer charity; they were social workers.

This outlook motivated settlement workers to attack urban problems across a broad front. Social workers labored to improve the urban environment by making food safe, repairing housing, and sponsoring festivals and pageants. Working conditions, especially for women and children, drew special attention, but the "young enthusiasts" attacked with equal indignation working-class vices—gambling dens, saloons, and brothels.

Settlements touched many lives. Harry Hopkins, Eleanor Roosevelt, and Frances Perkins, who would each attain political prominence in the 1930s, acquired a taste for activism in settlement houses. Others participated vicariously by reading popular books written by settlement workers. Newspaper accounts and memoirs awakened readers to the suffering of the urban poor and carried the hopeful message that action and intelligence could change things for the better.

The loudest voice of progressivism came from a new type of journalism introduced on the pages of *McClure's* magazine in 1902. *McClure's* published Lincoln Steffens's investigation of graft in St. Louis, "The Shame of the Cities," and Ida Tarbell's "History of the Standard Oil Company," two sensational exposés that disclosed crimes of the nation's political and economic elite. As cities grew and periodicals competed for a mass readership, newspapers and magazines enticed readers with promotional stunts, crusades, celebrity correspondents, and "sob sister" features. The new ten-cent magazines, like *Everybody's, Cosmopolitan,* and *McClure's,* had national audiences and budgets big enough to pay for in-depth investigations. The result was a type of reporting Theodore Roosevelt disdainfully called "muckraking." An article exposing some new corporate or public villainy could easily sell half a million copies.

Upton Sinclair described the grisly business of canning beef. Ray Stannard Baker investigated railroads and segregation. Samuel Hopkins Adams cataloged the damage done by narcotics in popular medicines. Tarbell's articles in *McClure's* exposed John D. Rockefeller's methods: camouflaged companies, espionage, sweetheart deals, and predatory pricing. The series shattered the notion that industrial giants competed in a free market. Amid a national outcry, the Justice Department sued Standard Oil in 1906 for conspiracy to restrain trade.

The ten-cent magazines reached subscribers across the country and projected local problems onto a national canvas. Newspapers had covered municipal corruption before, but Steffens's series revealed that bribery, influence peddling, and protection rackets operated in nearly every major city. Magazines also carried news of progressive victories, allowing solutions adopted in one city to spread to others. Muckraking translated the outrage of millions of readers into "public opinion," a force that could shake politicians and powerful corporations.

Dictatorship of the Experts

For doctors, lawyers, engineers, and members of other licensed occupations, progressive reforms offered a chance to apply their special skills to urgent problems. Experts like Alice Hamilton led crusades and adorned the boards of reform leagues. Much of the reformers' optimism came from their faith in the powers of science and expertise to solve modern problems. Rapid advances seemed to justify this faith. In just a generation, antiseptic techniques and a new understanding of disease transformed medicine from a collection of folk beliefs into a science. Advances in engineering, architecture, chemistry, and agriculture confirmed science's ability to shape the future.

Crime, education, labor relations, and other problems came under attack from social engineers using scientific or pseudoscientific methods. Social workers copied doctors, diagnosing each case with clinical impartiality and relying on tests and individual histories. Dietitians descended on school cafeterias, banishing pierogies and souvlaki and replacing them with bland but nutritionally balanced meals.

Trust in science sometimes led to extremes. One was the practice of eugenics, an attempt to rid society of crime, insanity, and other defects through selective breeding. In 1907 Indiana passed a law authorizing the forced sterilization of "criminals, idiots, rapists, and imbeciles." Seven other states followed suit.

Behind progressives' emphasis on expertise lay a thinly veiled distrust of democracy. Education reform was one example. Professional educators took control of the schools, certified teachers, and classified students based on "scientific" intelligence tests. Reformers wanted to consolidate schools and extend education beyond the eighth grade. The new "high schools" had courses that prepared students to become experts themselves. To reformers, education was far too important to be left to amateurs, like teachers, parents, or voters.

Progressivism created new social sciences, such as sociology, changed the agendas of others, and made universities into centers of advocacy. The study of government became political science, and "scientific" historians searched the past for answers to modern problems. John R. Commons, Richard Ely, and Thorstein Veblen used economics to study modern institutions. Legal scholars like Louis Brandeis and Roscoe Pound called for revising the law to reflect social realities.

This stress on expertise made progressive-era reforms different from earlier ones. Instead of trying to gain success at a single stroke—by passing a law or trouncing a corrupt politician—progressives believed reform had to be a process. When they could, progressives set up permanent organizations and procedures that would keep the pressure on and make progress a habit.

Progressives on the Color Line

In her international crusade against lynching, Ida B. Wells-Barnett pioneered some of the progressive tactics of research, exposure, and organization. She documented mob violence against African Americans and mobilized opinion in the United States and Britain. As her Afro-American Council took on national and then international scope, she joined forces with white suffragists, social workers, and journalists, but her cause fell outside of the progressive mainstream. Theodore Roosevelt's Progressive Party refused to seat African-American delegates to its convention or even to hear a resolution that called for equal rights.

Wells-Barnett referred to lynch mobs and their supporters as "barbarians," inverting the progressives' code word for peoples eligible for patronizing. Reformers debated how much progress Native Americans, African Americans and other non-Anglo-Saxons were capable of, but they were inclined to be pessimistic. Following educated opinion, public policy incorporated assumptions about the diminished capabilities of various races. Trade schools, not universities, were deemed appropriate for educating Filipinos and Hawaiians. Progressives took Indian children from their families and placed them in boarding schools. The "scientific" racism of the day classified nonwhites as subjects to control rather than citizens.

Wells-Barnett was not alone in finding doors through this stone wall of racial ideology. William Edward Burghardt Du Bois documented the costs of racism in *The Philadelphia Negro* (1898). Sponsored by settlement workers, the survey spoke the progressives' language, insisting that discrimination was not just morally wrong but inefficient, because it took away steady work and encouraged alcoholism and crime. Du Bois soon transformed the politics of race in America as profoundly as Addams had transformed the politics of the cities.

Raised in Massachusetts in a large family that had been free citizens for three generations, Du Bois learned Latin and Greek in public schools. At 17, he received a scholarship to Fisk University in Tennessee, where he "came in contact for the first time with a sort of violence that I had never realized in New England." He also had his first encounter with African-American religion and gospel music, which stirred him deeply. Du Bois later studied at Harvard and the University of Berlin.

Du Bois and Booker T. Washington (see Chapter 20, "Industry and Empire") espoused opposing visions of African Americans' place in the political economy of the United States. Both emphasized the importance of advancement through thrift and hard work. Du Bois, however, rejected Washington's willingness to accept legal inequality. Gradually, Du Bois believed that the Atlanta Compromise led to disfranchisement and segregation and disliked the way Washington's influence with the national press and his standing with white philanthropists silenced other voices.

In *The Souls of Black Folk* (1903), Du Bois argued that the strategy of accommodation contained a "triple paradox": Washington had urged African Americans to seek industrial training, build self-respect, and become successful in business, but to stop striving for higher education, civil rights, or political power. How could a people train themselves without higher education or gain self-respect without having any of the rights of citizens? Economic, political, and educational progress had to move together. African Americans could not stop demanding the right to vote, civic equality, or education at all levels.

In July 1905, Du Bois and 28 prominent African-American leaders met on the Canadian side of Niagara Falls (hotels on the United States side would not accept African-American lodgers) to declare that "the voice of protest of ten million Americans must never cease to assail the ears of their fellows, so long as America is unjust." The Niagara Movement was one of several organizations formed to lobby against racial violence, segregation, and disfranchisement. In 1909, Ida Wells-Barnett,

Editor of The Crisis *(circulation 103,000), William Edward Burghardt Du Bois was the voice of African-American progressives. "We expect revolutionary changes to come mainly through reason, human sympathy, and the education of children,"* he wrote.

Lillian Wald, Jane Addams, and other reformers formed the NAACP and named Du Bois as editor of its newspaper, *The Crisis.* The NAACP attacked segregation and disfranchisement in print and the courts. In 1915 it won a Supreme Court decision outlawing the grandfather clause, which denied the vote to descendants of slaves.

In the towns and modern cities of the South, whites struggled to maintain their system of social and legal supremacy, while African Americans fought to fulfill the promise of freedom. By challenging the laws and customs that supported injustice, Du Bois anticipated the struggle against segregation and disfranchisement that would take the next 60 years to complete. "The problem of the Twentieth Century," he predicted, "is the problem of the color line."

PROGRESSIVES IN STATE AND LOCAL POLITICS

Progressives were of two minds about the public. Walter Lippmann, a journalist and reformer, wrote fondly of "the voiceless multitudes," but contemptuously of the "great dull mass of people who just don't care." As reformers engaged in politics, their tactics betrayed this split vision. To bring the cities and states under control, they made changes that enlarged the influence of the small-town and urban-middle-class reform constituency while reducing that of immigrants and the working class.

Redesigning the City

The political insiders who ran American cities proved remarkably adaptable to the changing political environment. To immigrants and factory workers, the local boss was one of the few people looking out for the interests of the average person. He rushed to fire scenes to offer help to victims. He distributed turkeys at Christmas. When a family member was jailed or out of work, he was ready to help. Jane Addams acknowledged that as a benefactor to the city's disinherited, Hull House had nothing on Johnny Powers, boss of Chicago's 19th Ward, "a stalking survival of village kindness."

Yet Powers and other aldermen also sheltered the brothels, saloons, gambling dens, and petty "boodlers" who, in Addams's view, exploited honest workers. Big corporations could do what they liked, so long as they padded the right wallets. As city budgets and tax burdens grew, voters turned to reform candidates. Decrying the faults and ignoring the merits of machine politics, progressives set out to replace the fatherly generosity of the ward boss with efficient, scientific administration.

After the depression of 1893, scores of city improvement leagues and good government associations sprang up. The structure of many cities resembled the federal government in miniature. A mayor, elected by the whole city, presided over a council comprised of representatives from each neighborhood, or ward. This system diluted the influence of the "better classes," reformers argued, and allowed the chiefs of a few powerful wards to rule the city. In 1899 Louisville's Conference for Good City Government proposed a new model, the "strong mayor" system. It abolished wards, gave more power to the mayor, and required that the council be chosen in citywide elections. Two years later, Galveston, Texas, experimented with an even bolder plan, placing power in the hands of a nonpartisan commission of five officials, each of whom managed a city department. Des Moines, Iowa, copied and improved on Galveston's design, and by 1911 some 160 cities had commission governments.

The city commission plan imitated features of the modern corporation. The commission was comparable to a board of directors. The honesty and skills that made for business success, reformers argued, could improve a city, too. This philosophy led Detroit voters to elect Ford Motor Company's chief efficiency expert, James Couzens, as mayor. Other cities, led by Dayton, Ohio, placed government in the hands of an unelected "city manager."

Middle- and upper-class professionals led this revolution in city government, and they gained the most from it. The new city officials could explain where tax money was spent, and they responded to criticisms from leading citizens and newspapers, but there were no turkeys at Christmas. Reform administrations targeted urban "vice," which included prostitution and drugs, but also working-class recreations like drinking and gambling. Businesslike efficiency did not lower taxes: Budgets continued to grow along with the public's demand for services.

Reform Mayors and City Services

A new breed of reform mayors gained heroic reputations by cleaning up and humanizing their cities. Samuel "Golden Rule" Jones won election three times as the independent mayor of Toledo. He enacted the eight-hour day for city employees, pushed for public ownership of city utilities, built kindergartens and public playgrounds, and staged free concerts in the parks. "Everyone was against him," one of his aides remembered, "except the workers." Reform mayors worried less about inefficiency and saloons and more about thieving public utility magnates. Vice raids and blue laws, they agreed, paled next to the larceny of public contracts, tax breaks, and exclusive franchises for favored businesses. Milwaukee, Schenectady, and other cities bought or regulated the private monopolies that supplied street lighting, garbage removal, water, and streetcars.

Architects, engineers, and planners also endeavored to improve urban life through the reform of public space. Voluntary art and planning commissions formed a City Beautiful movement that sought to soften the urban landscape with vistas, open spaces, and greenery. New York enacted zoning laws in 1916, and planning became a permanent feature of city administration.

Progressivism and the States

Reform at the state level displayed a regional character. In the East it mimicked the tactics and agenda of urban reform. New York's progressive governor, Charles Evans Hughes, passed laws prohibiting gambling and creating a state commission to regulate public utilities. In southern states, progressivism often meant refining the techniques of segregation and disfranchisement. White leaders justified segregation and disfranchisement using the same terms that justified urban reform in the North: The "better classes" had an obligation to prevent the disorder and corruption that came from too much democracy.

States in the West and Midwest produced the boldest experiments in governmental reform. In Oregon the drive was led by William S. U'Ren, an itinerant farmer who went into politics after reading Henry George's *Progress and Poverty* (see Chapter 19, "The Politics of Industrial America"). Under U'Ren's guidance, Oregon adopted the secret ballot and voter registration to protect the polls from manipulation and passed three Populist measures: the initiative, recall, and referendum. The initiative allowed voters to place legislation on the ballot by petition; the referendum let the legislature put proposals before the voters for approval; and

"Annual Parade of the Cable Trolley Cripple Club," from The Verdict, *March 20, 1899. Injuries attributed to private firms that ran city transportation, water, and sewage monopolies led to demands for public supervision or control of essential services.*

the recall gave voters the chance to remove officials from office. Other states soon adopted all or part of the "Oregon system."

The best known of the progressive governors was Robert M. "Fighting Bob" La Follette. La Follette claimed that as a young congressman the offer of a bribe had awakened in him a resolve to break the power of "corrupt influence." More probably, La Follette responded to his constituents' demands for state action against corporate interests.

Elected governor in 1900, La Follette pushed through a comprehensive program of social legislation. Powerful railway and public utility commissions placed some of the state's largest corporations under public control. A tax commission designed a "scientific" distribution of the tax burden, including a state income tax. Other commissions regulated hours and working conditions and protected the environment. Wisconsin also implemented the direct primary, which allowed party nominees to be chosen directly by the voters. Defying laissez-faire prescriptions, the state's economy prospered under regulation.

By shaking up city halls and statehouses, progressives made government more responsive, but they knew that social problems did not respect city and state boundaries. National corporations and nationwide problems had to be attacked at the federal level, and that meant capturing the White House.

THE PRESIDENCY BECOMES "THE ADMINISTRATION"

If Theodore Roosevelt stood at the center of the two great movements of his age, imperialism and progressivism, it was because he prepared himself for the part. The Roosevelt family was one of the oldest and wealthiest in New York, but Theodore embarked instead on a series of pursuits that were unusual for a man of his class. After graduating from Harvard in 1880, he married, started law school, wrote a history of the War of 1812, bought a cattle ranch in the Dakota Territory, and most surprisingly, ran for the state legislature.

Roosevelt's political bid stunned his family and friends, who believed that government was no place for gentlemen. Roosevelt felt avoiding the "rough and tumble" only conceded high offices to those less fit to lead. Roosevelt's flair for publicity got him noticed, and in 1886 the Republican Party nominated him for mayor of New York. He finished a poor third, lagging behind the Tammany nominee and the United Labor Party candidate. Losing to a Socialist gave him a conviction, shared by many progressives, that reform was necessary to keep voters from turning to more radical, or even violent, alternatives.

A turn as head of New York's board of police commissioners from 1895 to 1897 deepened Roosevelt's commitment to reform. While supervising 38,000 policemen, Roosevelt made friends with two muckraking journalists, Lincoln Steffens and Jacob Riis, with whom he stalked the dark streets looking for officers on the take. Roosevelt's crackdown on saloons and corruption in the police department earned him a reputation as a man who would not be intimidated, even by his own party's bosses, and when McKinley captured the presidency he named Roosevelt Assistant Secretary of the Navy. The Spanish–American War catapulted him to national fame (see Chapter 20), and in quick succession he became governor of New York, vice president, and then president of the United States.

The Executive Branch Against the Trusts

Roosevelt approached politics the way Jane Addams approached poverty, studying it, living in its midst, and carefully choosing his battles. His fear that economic desperation could lead to political violence was borne out in September 1901 when President William McKinley was assassinated by Leon Czolgosz, who came from the slums of Cleveland. Czolgosz claimed to have done it on behalf of the poor.

Roosevelt entered the White House at the age of 42. With characteristic vigor, he moved to increase the power of the presidency and bring order and efficiency to governmental administration. The first president to call himself a progressive, Roosevelt set out to remake the executive as the preeminent branch of government, the initiator of legislation, molder of public opinion, and guardian of the national interest at home and abroad. Instead of asking Congress for legislation, he drafted bills and lobbied for them personally. He believed federal administrators should intervene in the economy to protect citizens or to save business from its own shortsightedness. McKinley had already decided that action against the trusts was necessary, but his plans were not as bold as his successor's.

Challenging the megacorporations would be no easy task. Roosevelt took office less than a decade after J. P. Morgan saved the federal Treasury. In an 1895 decision, the Supreme Court gutted the Sherman Anti-Trust Act, one of the few laws that allowed federal action against monopolies. The underfunded Interstate Commerce Commission (ICC) possessed only theoretical powers. In 1903 Roosevelt established a Department of Commerce and Labor with a Bureau of Corporations to penetrate the shroud of secrecy surrounding mergers and corporate activities and to put business information before the public.

The Justice Department revitalized the Sherman Act with vigorous prosecutions. Selecting cases for maximum publicity, Attorney General Philander Knox filed suit against J. P. Morgan's holding company, Northern Securities. Morgan expected that the matter could be settled in the usual way, and his attorney asked how they might "fix it up." "We don't want to fix it up," Knox replied. "We want to stop it." When the court handed Roosevelt a victory in 1904, Americans cheered.

With this case, Roosevelt gained an undeserved reputation as a "trust buster." Although he opposed serious abuses, he distinguished between good and bad trusts and believed government should restrain the bad and encourage the good. His thinking mirrored that of progressives who imagined a professionalized central government staffed by nonpartisan experts who would monitor the activities of big corporations to ensure efficiency and head off destructive actions.

Progressives had different ideas of what the ideal corporation should look like. Brandeis and Woodrow Wilson envisioned a political economy of small, highly competitive firms kept in line by regular applications of the Sherman Act. To Roosevelt, large combinations were necessary, even desirable, fixtures of modern life. It was government's obligation not to break them up but to force them to serve the public interest.

To this end, Roosevelt revitalized the ICC. He secured passage of the Hepburn Act (1906), which allowed the commission to set freight rates, and banned special deals between carriers and favored clients. The Elkins Act (1910) gave the ICC authority over telephone, telegraph, and cable communications and allowed the commission to act without waiting for an injured party to file a complaint. The Pure Food and Drug Act (1906) made it a crime to ship or sell contaminated or fraudulently labeled food and drugs. Under Roosevelt, the federal government gained authority and tools to counterbalance the power of business, and the number of federal employees almost doubled between 1900 and 1916.

The Square Deal

Roosevelt's exasperation with big business reached a peak during the anthracite strike of 1902. The UMW represented 150,000 miners in the coal fields of eastern Pennsylvania. The miners, mostly Polish, Hungarian, and Italian immigrants, earned less than $6 a week in a dirty, hazardous line of work. More than 400 died underground yearly. Seventy percent of the mines were owned by six railroads, which in turn fell under the control of Morgan, Rockefeller, and other financiers. The owners refused to deal with the UMW, declaring it a band of outlaws. When the miners struck in May 1902, they had the public's sympathy; newspapers urged the president to take the mines away from the owners.

The "gross blindness of the operators" infuriated Roosevelt. A coal shortage might kill hundreds in the cities and lead to class warfare. Rumors spread of a general strike in support of the miners. Roosevelt exhausted the options his office allowed, publicly and privately urging the two sides to settle. In early October, as schools in New England closed for lack of heat, he invited UMW officials and the

Nearly one of every five American children worked full time in 1900. This Pennsylvania coal mine started its workers at age eight.

operators to Washington for arbitration. John Mitchell, head of the mineworkers, eagerly accepted, but the owners refused to deal with "criminals" and "anarchists."

Roosevelt drew up plans for the Army to place the mines under government control. The Secretary of War warned Morgan of the impending move, and the owners agreed to submit the dispute to a federal commission. The commission produced a compromise: Miners received a 10 percent pay increase and a nine-hour workday, but owners did not have to recognize the union.

Roosevelt's direct action set precedents that made the federal government a third force in labor disputes. For the first time a strike was settled by federal arbitration and a union struck against a strategic industry without being denounced as revolutionary. The government would no longer automatically side with the corporations. Instead, Roosevelt acknowledged the legitimacy of labor, farm, and consumer groups who would work to make a corporate economy more congenial to wage earners and families.

Conserving Water, Land, and Forests

Roosevelt enraged Congress by stretching the definitions of presidential power, nowhere more so than in the area of conservation. When Congress sent him a bill to halt the creation of new national forests in the West, Roosevelt created or enlarged 32 national forests, then signed the bill. To stop private companies from damming rivers, he set aside 2,500 of the best hydropower sites as "ranger stations." The energy behind his program came from Gifford Pinchot, the chief forester of the United States, who saw conservation as a new frontier. Unsettled, undeveloped lands were growing scarce, and Pinchot convinced the president that hope for the future lay in using the available resources more efficiently. Preserving nature for its own sake had no place in his plans. Forests, deserts, and ore ranges were to be used, but wisely, scientifically, and in the national interest.

One of the first victories for the new policy of resource management was the Newlands Reclamation Act (1902), which gave the Agriculture Department authority to build reservoirs and irrigation systems in the West. To prevent waste, Roosevelt put tighter controls on prospecting, grazing, and logging. Big lumber and mining companies had few complaints about rationalized resource administration, but small-scale prospectors and ranchers were shut out of federal lands. Naturalists, like John Muir, also resisted, pointing out that nature was to be appreciated, not used.

By 1909, conservation had become a national issue. Hikers, sightseers, and tourism entrepreneurs drawn to the new parks and forest reserves were forming a powerful antidevelopment constituency. By quadrupling the acreage in federal reserves, professionalizing the forest service, and using his "bully pulpit" to build support for conservation, Roosevelt helped create the modern environmental movement.

Roosevelt and Big Stick Diplomacy

The expansion of U.S. overseas investment and new threats to American security placed greater demands on foreign and military policy. American investors wanted assurances that Washington would protect their overseas factories and railroads. The diplomatic and military budgets grew to meet these demands, and the United States staffed permanent embassies in many Latin American capitals, staffed with trained, professionalized Foreign Service officers. Conducting foreign relations was no longer a matter of weathering "incidents" but of making policy.

Roosevelt's view of world affairs flowed from his understanding of both history and the future. Global trade and communications, he believed, separated civilized nations from savage and barbarian peoples. His foreign policy aimed to keep the United States at the center of global trends such as commerce, imperialism, and military (particularly naval) modernization. The United States had a moral duty, he felt, to interfere with "barbarian" governments in Asia, Latin America, or Africa that blocked progress.

Building an interoceanic canal topped Roosevelt's list of foreign policy priorities. A canal would be a hub of world trade and naval power in the Atlantic and Pacific. He pressed Britain to drop its claim to joint control over a canal, urged Congress to choose the Colombian province of Panama as the site, and bought out a failed French canal venture. He manipulated the Colombian government to agree to the canal, and when that failed, encouraged Panama to secede from Colombia. Congress launched an investigation of his behavior, but while that went on, so did the building of the canal.

Engineers, led by George W. Goethals, removed a mountain to let water into the isthmus and built another to shore up an artificial lake (see Map 21–1). Colonel William C. Gorgas defeated malaria and yellow fever, reducing the death rate in Panama to below that of an average American city. The canal, a 50-mile cut built at a cost of $352 million and more than 5,600 lives, opened in 1914.

Once construction was underway, Roosevelt protected the canal from other imperial powers. Poverty and unrest in the Caribbean states created opportunities for European navies to establish bases on Panama's doorstep. Neighboring nations owed millions to European investors, and imperial practice allowed creditor nations to seize the ports and customs houses of debtors. In 1904 a civil war caused the Dominican Republic to renege on its loans.

As four European nations laid plans for a debt-collecting expedition, Roosevelt went before Congress in December 1904 and announced a policy later known as the Roosevelt Corollary. It stipulated that when chronic "wrongdoing or impotence" in a Latin American country required "intervention by some civilized nation" the United States would do the intervening. Its language captured the president's worldview. White "civilized" nations acted; nonwhite "impotent" nations were acted on.

By enforcing order and administrative efficiency in the Caribbean, Roosevelt extended progressivism beyond the borders of the United States; the movement gained footholds in the Far East, too. Governor General William H. Taft took municipal reform to Manila. In 1906 the U.S. federal courts created a court outside the United States, in Shanghai, China, to control prostitution in the American community.

Roosevelt extended American stewardship to conflicts in Asia and Africa. He won the Nobel Peace Prize for mediating the end of the Russo–Japanese War in 1905, and he proposed a compromise settlement to the British–French–German dispute over Morocco. In each case, the solution involved extending open door trade.

Taft and Dollar Diplomacy

Enormously popular at the end of his second term, Roosevelt chose his friend, William H. Taft, to succeed him. Taft easily defeated William Jennings Bryan in the 1908 election, and as president he began consolidating Roosevelt's programs with the help of a more progressive Congress. He sent to the states constitutional amendments for the

COLORADO NEBRASKA IOWA NEW YORK MASSACHUSETTS
RHODE ISLAND
INDIANA PENNSYLVANIA CONNECTICUT
KANSAS ILLINOIS OHIO NEW JERSEY
MISSOURI WEST DELAWARE
NEW **UNITED STATES** VIRGINIA MARYLAND
MEXICO KENTUCKY VIRGINIA
Columbus OKLAHOMA TENNESSEE NORTH
ARKANSAS CAROLINA
U.S. Expeditionary SOUTH
Force, 1916–1917 MISSISSIPPI CAROLINA
Santa TEXAS GEORGIA
Ysabel ALABAMA
CHIHUAHUA Houston LOUISIANA
Parral New Orleans

0   200   400 Miles
0   200 400 Kilometers

ATLANTIC
OCEAN

FLORIDA

GULF OF MEXICO
U.S. troops, 1898–1902, 1906–1909;
1912, 1917–1922
Platt Amendment, 1903–1934

Miami BAHAMAS
(Br.)

U.S. troops, 1915–1934
Financial supervision, 1916–1941

U.S. takes control of customs house, 1905
U.S. troops, 1916–1924
Financial supervision, 1905–1941

MEXICO Tampico

Mexico City U.S. seizure, 1914
Veracruz

Havana

CUBA Guantánamo

U.S. Naval
Base, 1903

U.S. possession
after 1898

VIRGIN ISLANDS
(purchased from
Denmark, 1917)

JAMAICA HAITI
BRITISH (Br.) DOMINICAN PUERTO GUADELOUPE
HONDURAS U.S. troops, 1907, REPUBLIC RICO (Fr.)
1924–1925 MARTINIQUE
GUATEMALA HONDURAS U.S. troops, 1909–1910, 1912–1925, 1926–1933 (Fr.)
EL SALVADOR Financial supervision, 1911–1924 CARIBBEAN BARBADOS
NICARAGUA (Br.)
U.S. leased SEA
PACIFIC Corn Islands, 1914 Caracas TRINIDAD
Canal option, 1916 Inset PANAMA (Br.)
OCEAN COSTA Venezuela debt crisis, 1903–1904
RICA VENEZUELA
U.S. acquired Canal Zone, 1904 COLOMBIA GUYANA
Canal completed, 1914
Bogota BRAZIL

0   2   4 Miles
0   2   4 Kilometers

CARIBBEAN
SEA Colón

Limon PANAMA
Bay

Locks
Chagres
Dam Gatun

Panama Canal Zone Madden
follows the Dam Madden
100' contour around Lake
Gatun Lake
Panama Canal Zone
follows the
260' contour around
Darien Madden Lake

Gamboa

Gatun Lake PANAMA
CANAL
Las ZONE
Las Cascadas

Gaillard
Cut
Paraíso Pedro Miguel
Homedeo

Locks

Lake Miraflores

Panama City
Miraflores
PANAMA Locks

Panama Canal
Locks
Dam
Railroad

GULF OF PANAMA

**Map 21–1
The United
States in the
Caribbean**
U.S. troops inter-
vened repeatedly
in the Caribbean
and Central
America to
protect invest-
ments and guard
against perceived
threats to order.
Panama,
Nicaragua, Haiti,
and the
Dominican
Republic were
under nearly con-
tinuous U.S. occu-
pation until the
mid-1920s.

Source: Thomas Patterson, American Foreign Relations, Vol. II (Boston: D.C. Heath, 1995), pp. 55, 40.

direct election of senators and the income tax. His administration increased antitrust enforcement and levied the first tax on corporations.

In the Caribbean, Taft put the Roosevelt Corollary into action. The United States bought up the debts of Honduras and Nicaragua to prevent another incident like the one in the Dominican Republic. Taft persuaded four New York banks to refinance Haiti's debt to prevent German intervention. For Caribbean nations, American financial protection meant allowing the Americans to impose high import taxes, and a revolt usually followed. Marines went into Honduras and Nicaragua in 1912.

Dollar diplomacy also aimed to harness corporate investment power to foreign policy. Shortly after his inauguration, Taft mobilized a consortium of financiers to invest in China's planned Chinchow-Aigun railway. With one railroad Taft felt he could drive a wedge between the imperial powers—Britain, Russia, and Japan—and compel them to resume open door trade. Instead, they joined forces and signed a protocol opposing U.S. interference in China. Roosevelt criticized the China venture, but Taft believed that he was only taking his mentor's vision of modern diplomacy seriously. Military force was outmoded, he felt, and soon economic power would be the only kind that mattered.

Taft disappointed both conservatives and progressives in his party. He urged Congress to reduce the tariff, but when protectionists in the Senate put up a fight he retreated and signed the Payne–Aldrich Tariff in 1909, lowering rates for some goods but raising rates on steel, cotton, silk, and other important imports. Taft's flip-flop disgusted La Follette and other midwestern progressives.

Taft's Secretary of the Interior, Richard Ballinger, siding with ranchers and miners who opposed resource management, opened a million acres of public land to private development. When Pinchot publicly accused Ballinger of catering to corporate interests, the party's divisions over conservation came into the open.

Taft maintained but did not extend Roosevelt's reforms. To the former Rough Rider, that was not enough. Enlarging the president's powers did no good unless the president was willing to use them. Roosevelt began to believe his country needed him back.

RIVAL VISIONS OF THE INDUSTRIAL FUTURE

After Roosevelt returned from a safari in Africa in 1910, Pinchot, La Follette, Croly, and others trooped to his home at Sagamore Hill to complain about Taft. Roosevelt re-entered politics because his views had evolved, and because politics was what he knew best. Just 54 years old, his energy was undiminished. He took more radical positions on corporations, public welfare, and labor than he had during his presidency. The election of 1912 defined the future of industrial America.

The New Nationalism

At a sunbaked railroad stop in Osawatomie, Kansas, in August 1910, Roosevelt declared that "the essence of any struggle for liberty . . . is to destroy privilege, and give the life of every individual the highest possible value." He laid out a political program he called the New Nationalism. It included the elimination of corporate campaign contributions, regulation of industrial combinations, an expert commission to set tariffs, a graduated income tax, banking reorganization, and a national workers' compensation program. The message drew cheers from some, but to the *New York Times*, the speech crossed "the ultimate boundary line of radicalism."

From the beginning, Roosevelt had the newspapers while Taft had the delegates. The nomination fight tested the new system of direct primaries. Taft's control of the party machinery gave him an advantage in states that chose delegates by convention, but in a number of key states Roosevelt could take his campaign to the voters. When the convention met in Chicago in June 1912, Taft's slim but decisive majority allowed him to control the platform and win over undecided delegates. Grumbling that he had been robbed, Roosevelt walked out.

Roosevelt returned to Chicago in August to accept the nomination of the newly formed Progressive Party. The party platform endorsed the New Nationalism, along with popular election of senators, popular review of judicial decisions (which would allow the voters to second-guess the courts), and women's suffrage. Women served as delegates, and Jane Addams gave the speech seconding Roosevelt's nomination. The gathering had an evangelical spirit. "We stand at Armageddon," Roosevelt declared, "and we battle for the Lord."

The 1912 Election

Meanwhile in Baltimore the Democratic convention nominated a former college professor and governor of New Jersey. Woodrow Wilson entered politics by an unusual route, the university. Obtaining a doctorate in government from Johns Hopkins University in 1886, he published his first book, *Congressional Government*, at age 28. It advocated reforming the federal structure by enlarging the power of the executive branch. As a professor and later president of Princeton University, he became a well-known lecturer and commentator for national political magazines. In 1910 he won election as governor of New Jersey and enacted a sweeping program of progressive reforms. For Democrats, Wilson offered a new image and the ability to unite the South and the East under a progressive program.

With Roosevelt in the race, Wilson had to stake his own claim to the progressive constituency. To compete with the New Nationalism, Wilson devised a program called the New Freedom that challenged Roosevelt's fundamental approaches to the economy and politics. Simply regulating the trusts, Wilson argued, would not make the economy friendly to consumers, workers, or small entrepreneurs. He wanted antitrust laws that would allow a lean but powerful government to return competition and economic mobility to the marketplace. While Roosevelt appealed to a collective, national interest, Wilson stressed the needs of individual consumers and investors. In contrast to the New Nationalism's evangelical style, Wilson appealed to reason and self-interest.

On election day, the split in the Republican Party gave Wilson a plurality. He won 42 percent of the popular vote, compared to 27 for Roosevelt, 23 for Taft, and 6 for Debs, the Socialist candidate. Although his margin was thin, Wilson could interpret the large combined vote for the progressive candidates as a mandate for change.

The New Freedom

Within a year and a half of his inauguration, Wilson produced one of the most coherent and far-reaching legislative programs ever devised by a president. The New Freedom advocated lower tariffs, increased competition, and vigorous antitrust enforcement. Three monumental bills passed through Congress in rapid succession.

The first bill was the Underwood–Simmons Tariff, which made the first deep cuts in tariff rates since before the Civil War. The bill overturned the protectionist tariff and it helped farmers and consumers by lowering prices and increasing competition, but Wilson argued that its real beneficiaries would be manufacturers. Lower tariffs would help persuade other countries to reduce taxes on imports from the United States, he reasoned. The Singer, Ford, and Camel brand names began appearing in bazaars, souks, and godowns from Caracas to Mandalay. The Underwood–Simmons Tariff (1913) also permanently shifted the revenue base of the federal government from tariffs to income taxes.

Wilson's next target was the banking system. The Federal Reserve Act of 1913 set up a national board to supervise the banking system and created 12 regional reserve banks. Banks were now watched to ensure that their reserves matched their deposits. The system's real advantage was the flexibility it gave the currency. The Federal Reserve Board could put more dollars into circulation when demand was high and retire them when it subsided. Regional banks could adjust the money supply to meet the needs of different parts of the country. The system broke Wall Street's stranglehold on credit and opened new opportunities for entrepreneurship and competition.

Finally, Wilson attacked the trusts. He established the Federal Trade Commission (FTC) to enforce free and fair competition. It had the right to subpoena corporate records and issue cease-and-desist orders. The Clayton Antitrust Act (1914) prohibited price fixing, outlawed interlocking directorates, and made it illegal for a company to own stock in its competitor. In 1916 Wilson produced another crop of reform legislation, including the first national workers' compensation and child-labor laws, the eight-hour day for railroad workers, and the Warehouse Act, which extended credit to cash-strapped farmers.

These programs furthered Wilson's goal of "releasing the energies" of consumers and entrepreneurs, but they also helped business. Businessmen headed many of the regulatory boards, and the FTC and Federal Reserve Board brought predictability to unruly markets. The New Freedom linked liberal reform to individual initiative and the free play of markets.

CONCLUSION

By 1900 America's political economy had outgrown the social relationships and laws that served the earlier rural republic. Squeezed between the indifference of corporate elites and the large, transient immigrant communities that controlled urban politics, middle-class reformers experimented with the structure of decision making at the municipal and state levels and vested the state with responsibility for the quality of life of its citizens. Progressives challenged but never upset the system. Above all, they wanted managed, orderly change. Science and the pressure of informed opinion, they believed, could overcome resistance without open conflict.

The progressive presidents continued this movement on the national stage. Roosevelt and Wilson helped position the federal government as a broker among business, consumer, and labor interests. In less than two decades, the federal government overcame its reputation for corruption and impotence and adapted to a new role at the center of economic and social life. The concept of a "national interest" that superseded individual and property rights was now firmly ingrained. The president's leadership now extended beyond the administration to Congress and public opinion. These achievements created a modern central government just at the time when military, diplomatic, and economic victories made the United States a global power. The consensus favoring a strong central government and the strength of American influence abroad would both be tested by events unfolding in Europe.

CHRONOLOGY

1889	Hull House founded
1890	General Federation of Women's Clubs founded
1893	Illinois passes eight-hour day for women
1895	National Association of Manufacturers organized
1900	Robert La Follette elected governor of Wisconsin
1901	Socialist Party of America founded
	Galveston introduces commission government
	McKinley assassinated; Theodore Roosevelt inaugurated president
1902	Newlands Reclamation Act funds construction of dams and irrigation systems
	Alice Hamilton investigates Chicago's typhoid epidemic
	McClure's publishes first episodes of Ida Tarbell's "History of the Standard Oil Company" and Lincoln Steffens's "The Shame of the Cities"
	Roosevelt settles anthracite strike
1903	Roosevelt establishes Department of Commerce and Labor
	Panama declares independence from Colombia
	W. E. B. Du Bois publishes *The Souls of Black Folk*
1904	Justice Department sues Standard Oil under the Sherman Anti-Trust Act
	U.S. Supreme Court orders Northern Securities Company dissolved as an illegal combination
	Roosevelt elected president
	The Roosevelt Corollary announced
1905	U.S. takes over Dominican customs
	Industrial Workers of the World founded
	Roosevelt mediates end to Russo–Japanese War

FURTHER READINGS

Jane Addams, *Twenty Years at Hull House* (1910). In her autobiography, Addams urges respect for the traditions of immigrants and action against the causes of crime and poverty.

John Milton Cooper, Jr., *The Warrior and the Priest: Theodore Roosevelt and Woodrow Wilson in American Politics* (1983). A dual biography of the progressive presidents compares their backgrounds, philosophies, and political styles.

J. Anthony Lukas, *Big Trouble: A Murder in a Small Western Town Sets off a Struggle for the Soul of America* (1997). The anxiety and tension of the progressive-era West comes to the surface in the trial of three labor leaders for the murder of a former governor of Idaho.

1906	Hepburn Act passed, allowing the Interstate Commerce Commission to set freight rates
	Pure Food and Drug Act requires accurate labeling
1907	Indiana passes forcible sterilization law
1908	William H. Taft elected president
	Supreme Court upholds maximum-hours laws for women in *Muller* v. *Oregon*
1909	Payne–Aldrich Tariff goes into effect
	NAACP founded
1910	Taft fires chief forester Gifford Pinchot
	Elkins Act authorizes Interstate Commerce Commission to regulate electronic communications
	Roosevelt announces the New Nationalism
1911	Triangle Shirtwaist Company fire
1912	U.S. troops occupy Nicaragua
	Woodrow Wilson elected president
1913	Federal Reserve Act reorganizes banking system
	Underwood–Simmons Tariff
1914	Panama Canal completed
	Clayton Act strengthens antitrust enforcement
1916	New York City enacts zoning laws
	Federal workers' compensation, child labor, and eight-hour-day laws passed

Kevin Starr, *Inventing the Dream: California Through the Progressive Era* (1985). The century's first decade in a state that was defining a distinct local identity through planning, art, and reform.

David Thelen, *Robert M. La Follette and the Insurgent Spirit* (1976). The life and philosophy of the progressive governor and senator from Wisconsin.

Robert H. Wiebe, *The Search for Order, 1877–1920* (1967). This classic study of progressivism traces the movement's origins to the middle class's yearning for a lost Eden of small towns and personal relationships.

 Please refer to the document CD-ROM for primary sources related to this chapter.

CHAPTER

22

A Global Power

1914–1919

Walter Lippmann • **The Challenges of Revolution and Neutrality**
The Drift to War • **Mobilizing the Nation and the Economy**
Over There • **The Black Cloud in the East** • **Conclusion**

WALTER LIPPMANN

"**W**ar in Europe is impending," Walter Lippmann wrote in his diary on July 29, 1914. Vacationing in Belgium, the 24-year-old journalist witnessed the aftershocks of a crisis in the Balkans. Four weeks earlier, the heir to the throne of Austria-Hungary, Archduke Ferdinand, had been shot as he drove through the Serbian city of Sarajevo, plunging Europe into war. As stock markets tumbled and refugees crowded train stations, Lippmann found himself caught up in a conflict between the world's most powerful states: Austria and Germany on one side, and Russia, France, and Britain on the other.

In the twilight of August 4, Britain's foreign minister, Sir Edward Grey, asked Parliament for a war resolution. Two hours later, in Berlin, the Reichstag declared war on France. "We sit and stare at each other and make idiotically cheerful remarks," Lippmann wrote, "and in the meantime, . . . nothing can stop the awful disintegration now."

Lippmann had come of age in the progressive era. As a student at Harvard, he came to believe that reason and science would allow his generation to "treat life not as something given but as something to be shaped." He worshiped Theodore Roosevelt, and after graduation he set out to become a political journalist. "It was a happy time, those last few years before the First World War," he remembered many years later; " . . . it was easy for a young man to believe in the inevitability of progress, in the perfectibility of man and of society, and in the sublimation of evil."

The European war crushed those hopes. Just days after Lippmann left Belgium, German armies sliced through the neutral nation in a maneuver that aimed to encircle the French Army, but reserve troops from Paris struck the German flank and stopped the advance at the Marne River in northeastern France. By November, the western front had stabilized into the bloody stalemate that would prevail for four years, absorbing between 5,000 and 50,000 lives a day.

The carnage horrified Americans. German soldiers used terror against Belgian civilians, killing more than 5,000 hostages. Two weeks after the invasion began, German troops burned the picturesque medieval city of Louvain in retaliation for a Belgian attack.

"We Americans have been witnessing supreme drama, clenching our fists, talking, yet unable to fasten any reaction to realities," Lippmann told his readers. For three years, Americans watched as a civilization they had admired sank into barbarism. They recoiled from the war's violence and the motives behind it, and they debated what, if anything, they could do to stop it.

When the United States entered the fight in 1917, it mobilized its economy and society. The war both interrupted and culminated the progressive movement. In the name of efficiency, government stepped in to manage the economy as never before. The war transformed many of the most controversial items on the progressive social agenda—women's suffrage, prohibition of alcohol, restrictions on prostitution—into matters of national urgency. On the battlefield, American forces brought swift triumph, but victory failed to impose a stable peace. The experience of war brought home the dangers of a modern, interdependent world, but it also revealed the United States' power to shape the global future.

THE CHALLENGES OF REVOLUTION AND NEUTRALITY

The Great War disturbed the American president's sense that order could be imposed on foreign relations. Like other progressives, Wilson saw similar evils assailing the United States from within and without. Wilson opposed revolutionary radicalism, and he tried to fashion "organic" institutions and processes to mediate disputes and foster orderly change. However, Wilson believed order had to be forced on those who resisted. Opponents of reform "who will not be convinced," he wrote, deserved to be "crushed."

Imposing order, the president believed, was both a political duty and an economic opportunity for the United States. Imperialism and revolution endangered the free trade that was necessary for world peace and the economic health of the United States. It was the government's duty to ensure the safety of foreign travel, investments, and markets to secure American prosperity and its benefits for the world.

This combination of idealism and self-interest, humanitarianism and force, produced a foreign policy that seemed contradictory. Wilson renounced "dollar diplomacy" but used Taft's tactics when the open door was threatened in China. He atoned for the imperialism of prior administrations but intervened repeatedly in Central America. He believed the United States had a mission to promote democracy, yet he considered many peoples unready to govern themselves.

These contradictions are explained by Wilson's view of history. As he saw it, the modernizing forces of commerce and communications were creating a global society with new rules of international conduct. With Europe aflame, the United States remained the sole voice of reason, the hope for the future, and therefore had to remain out of the war. He was also preoccupied with matters closer at hand. In April 1914 American troops had invaded Mexico in an attempt to overthrow its revolutionary government.

The Mexican Revolution

In May 1911, Francisco Madero's rebels overthrew Mexican dictator of Porfirio Díaz, ending more than three decades of enforced order and rapid industrialization. Díaz and a clique of intellectuals and planners known as *científicos* had spanned the country with railroads, built up Mexican industry, and turned Mexico into one of the world's leading exporters of petroleum. Foreign investment poured in, and by 1911 Americans owned 40 percent of the property in the country (see Chapter 19,"The Politics of Industrial America"). Mexicans grew to resent the privileged colonies of foreign businessmen and the heavy taxes needed to keep industrialization going. When Madero's revolt broke out, the army folded, Díaz fled to Spain, and power changed hands in a nearly bloodless coup.

The fall of Díaz gave the United States little cause for concern: Madero left foreign investments undisturbed and held an election to confirm his presidency, but in February 1913, just two weeks before Wilson's inauguration, General Victoriano Huerta seized power and had Madero shot. Outraged Mexican states raised armies and revolted against Huerta's regime, beginning a long and bloody civil war. In the mountains south of Mexico City, Emiliano Zapata led a guerrilla resistance; along Mexico's northern border, Venustiano Carranza organized a constitutionalist army and bought weapons in Texas and New Mexico.

Wilson denounced Huerta, warning that he would "teach the South American republics to elect good men." He gave arms to Carranza's soldiers and sent 7,000 U.S. Marines to occupy Mexico's largest port city, Veracruz, in April 1914. The invasion radicalized the revolution, unifying all sides against the United States. When Carranza deposed Huerta a few months later, he promised to nationalize oilfields owned by Americans.

Still determined to "put Mexico on a moral basis," Wilson pressured Carranza to resign while providing arms to his enemy, Francisco "Pancho" Villa. Joining forces with Zapata, Villa briefly seized the capital at the end of 1914, but Carranza counterattacked, reducing Villa's army to outlaw bands. Reluctantly, Wilson recognized the Carranza government and cut off supplies to Villa; stung by Wilson's betrayal, Villa attacked the U.S. Thirteenth Cavalry outpost at Columbus, New Mexico.

Wilson responded with a "punitive expedition" of 10,000 troops under General John J. Pershing who pursued Villa 400 miles into Mexico and clashed with Carranza's army. Like the Veracruz adventure, Pershing's invasion unified Mexicans against the United States. Facing a choice between declaring war on Mexico and

In April 1914, Wilson ordered the capture of Mexico's largest port, Veracruz. The Mexican population resisted, and American warships shelled the city before Veracruz was taken in bitter street fighting.

giving up the hunt for Pancho Villa, Wilson ordered Pershing home with nothing to show for his efforts. Villa was still at large, Carranza was seeking German arms, the civil war still raged, and American lives and property were still in danger.

Bringing Order to the Caribbean

In principle, Wilson opposed imperialism and gunboat diplomacy, but his desire to impose order on neighboring countries led him to use force. He sent Marines into more countries in Latin America than any other president. United States troops quashed a revolution in Haiti in 1915 and landed in the Dominican Republic the following year, where they stayed until 1924. Wilson kept in place the Marines that Taft had sent to occupy Honduras, Panama, and Nicaragua, and briefly sent troops into Cuba. From each of these countries Wilson obtained the right to intervene if necessary to restore order. These agreements reassured American business that the United States would maintain what Wilson called "orderly processes" in foreign markets.

Congress had less enthusiasm for treaties that promised to embroil American soldiers in one crisis after another. Senator Robert La Follette explained that corporations were in the business of exploitation, whether in Wisconsin or Mexico. La Follette and Senator George W. Norris argued that in some countries revolutions might be necessary to protect the rights of the many against the power of the few.

Opponents of Wilson's policies in Mexico and the Caribbean also urged the United States to stay out of the Great War in Europe. In April 1916, progressive writers and social workers met at New York's Henry Street Settlement House to organize the American Union Against Militarism and protest against intervention in Mexico. Jane Addams and Carrie Chapman Catt founded the Woman's Peace Party, whose 25,000 members supported a mediated settlement to the European conflict. Peace advocates supported Wilson's policy of neutrality but saw signs that the United States was being drawn into war.

A One-Sided Neutrality

As German armies crossed Belgium in August 1914, Woodrow Wilson declared a policy of strict neutrality. The war took him by surprise, and like Addams he found it "incredible" that civilized nations could display such savagery. His first worry was that America's immigrant communities, filled with people newly arrived from the warring countries, would split into "camps of hostile opinion, hot against each other."

With 32 million Americans either born abroad or having at least one parent from overseas, and more than 10 million with family ties to Germany and Austria-Hungary, Wilson's concern was understandable. The Allies (Britain, France, Italy, and Russia) and the Central Powers (Germany, Austria-Hungary, and Turkey) did their best to sway opinion. Britain cut the telegraph cable between Germany and the United States to ensure that news had to pass through censors in London. In 1915 a New York City subway policeman found a German secret plan to fund peace groups in the United States. Both the president and the press worried that propaganda could push the electorate to demand American intervention.

Wilson did his best to appear completely neutral. He told Americans that this was a war "whose causes cannot touch us," but privately he believed that a German victory would be a catastrophe. With Europe and possibly Asia controlled by a single power, the United States would be vulnerable and alone.

Modern warfare and commerce made true neutrality difficult, and Wilson's bias soon became clear. The belligerent powers desperately needed United States exports: food, textiles, steel, chemicals, and fuel. The economy rose on a tide of war orders, mainly from the Allies. American trade with the Allies grew to more than $3 billion by 1916, while trade with the Central Powers sank from $170 million to less than $1 million. U.S. loans to the Allies grew to $2.5 billion by 1917, but the Central Powers received only $127 million in credit. The American economy was already in the war on the side of the Allies.

Wilson's reaction to the British and German naval blockades helped the Allies capture American trade. The British fleet closed European ports and laid mines across the North Sea, preventing American ships from reaching Germany. London's actions violated the "freedom of the seas," but the Wilson administration never strenuously protested or used force to break the blockade. Wilson reacted differently to Germany's violations. On February 4, 1915, Berlin announced a policy of "unrestricted submarine warfare" against ships entering a "war zone" around the British Isles. A German *Unterseeboot* or U-boat, a small, fragile submarine with a crew of only 32 men, could not stop, board, and escort ships into port, as required by law, without giving up the stealth and surprise that were its only weapons, but while Wilson was willing to excuse the British blockade, he insisted that German U-boats observe the letter of international law.

The *Lusitania's* Last Voyage

Germany posted advertisements in American newspapers warning passengers not to travel on ships bound for the war zone; Americans were horrified by the targeting of ships carrying civilian men, women, and children. Wilson declared that Germany would be held to "strict accountability" for American lives or property destroyed by U-boats.

On the afternoon of May 7, 1915, submarine U-20 sighted the luxury liner *Lusitania* off the coast of Ireland. A torpedo struck the starboard side behind the bridge, and the massive ship broke apart and sank. Of almost 2,000 passengers aboard, 1,198 drowned, including 94 children. Of these, 124 were Americans. Newspaper headlines accused Germany of savagery. A German in Berlin remarked that although the Americans she knew "had always professed to be neutral . . . a sudden change now took place. . . . Their rage and horror at the idea that Americans had been killed knew no bounds."

Wilson demanded that Germany pay reparations and stop attacking ships without warning. He hinted that unless these demands were met, the United States would break relations. Accusing Wilson of pushing the country into war, Secretary of State William Jennings Bryan resigned.

Public opinion was also divided. Newspapers called for war, but as Lippmann wrote to a friend in England, "the feeling against war in this country is a great deal deeper than you would imagine by reading editorials." When Germany promised not to attack passenger liners without warning, this guarantee, known as the Sussex Pledge, restored calm. However, official and public opinion had turned against Germany. American involvement no longer seemed impossible.

THE DRIFT TO WAR

The *Lusitania* disaster opened an unbridgeable gap among progressives on the issue of the war. Peace advocates like Addams, Bryan, and La Follette urged a stricter neutrality to prevent another tragedy that might require retaliation. Others believed war, or preparations for war, were justified. The *Lusitania* incident "united Englishmen and Americans in a common grief and a common indignation" and might "unite them in a common war," Lippmann predicted. Thousands of preparedness supporters marched down New York's Fifth Avenue under an electric sign declaring "Absolute and Unqualified Loyalty to our Country."

The preparedness leagues, headed by businessmen and conservative political figures, called attention to the pathetic state of the armed forces. When Pancho Villa attacked the 13th Cavalry at Columbus, New Mexico, every one of the Americans' machine guns jammed. Pershing's punitive expedition suffered from chronic shortages of trucks, planes, and supplies. The preparedness campaign adopted patriotic rituals once reserved for elections. Wilson himself led the parade in Washington in 1916, wearing a red tie, white trousers, and a blue blazer.

The Election of 1916

In campaigning for re-election, Wilson had to reconcile the public's overwhelming desire for peace with his own feeling that the United States could not remain uninvolved. Nonetheless he campaigned under the slogan "He kept us out of war." It was a sure vote-getter.

The preparedness issue reunited Theodore Roosevelt with the Republicans. Bringing the Progressive Party with him, he endorsed Supreme Court Justice Charles Evans Hughes, the Republican candidate. The party organizations took a back seat to modern advertising campaigns waged by poster and press release. Democrats charged Hughes with sympathy to Germany, while Republicans accused Wilson of "leniency with the British Empire." Woman suffragists campaigned against Wilson. They picketed the White House with signs asking "Mr. President? How long must women wait for liberty?"

Although the country remained strongly Republican, Hughes proved an inept campaigner. He won pivotal states in the North and East but lost in the South and West. Wilson won narrowly; a shift of a few thousand votes in California would have cost him the election. Republicans gained seats in the House and the Senate. Still, re-election freed Wilson to pursue a more vigorous foreign policy. As Lippmann realized, "What we're electing is a war president—not the man who kept us out of war."

The Last Attempts at Peace

After the election, Wilson launched a new peace initiative. Looking for an opening for compromise, he asked each of the belligerent powers to state its war aims. The results were disappointing. Each side insisted on punishing the other and enlarging its own territories. Going before Congress in January 1917, the president called for a "peace without victory," based on self-determination of all nations and the creation of an international organization to enforce peace.

Germany toyed with accepting Wilson's proposals and decided to wait. Having subdued the Balkans and pushed deep into Russia by February 1917, it could begin shifting armies from the Eastern front to France. It seemed that the summer of 1917 might bring a German victory. To accelerate that outcome, Germany resumed unrestricted submarine warfare. U-boats torpedoed British passenger liners and American merchant ships. In late February, British intelligence officers showed the U.S. ambassador in London an intercepted telegram from the German foreign minister, Arthur Zimmermann, to his ambassador in Mexico City. It instructed the ambassador that if the United States joined the war on the Allied side he should invite Carranza to ally with Germany. Together, Germany and Mexico would fight to regain "lost territories" in Arizona, California, and New Mexico. The Zimmermann Telegram confirmed Americans' darkest fears about the implications of a German victory, and it provoked alarm in the West, where antiwar feeling had been strongest.

Americans disagreed then, as historians do today, on why the United States went to war. Economic and strategic issues were at stake, as was national honor and the ability to shape the peace. Critics pointed to the influence of munitions makers and banks that stood to gain from war. Publicly and in private, Wilson stressed two considerations that led to his decision: First, attacks on American ships had forced him to retaliate. Second, joining the war was necessary for the United States to influence the peace settlement. Unless it took part in the conflict, Wilson told Jane Addams, the United States would have to shout "through a crack in the door."

Wilson's War Aims

On the evening of April 2, 1917, Wilson asked Congress for a declaration of war. The conflict, he told his audience, was in its last stages and American armies could bring it to a quick, merciful end. Neutrality had provided no safety for American travelers or American trade. The only hope for avoiding future wars that might pose even graver dangers was to place the United States in a position to dictate the peace. This would be a war to end all wars, to make the world safe for democracy.

In urging Congress to vote for war, the president explicitly rejected the war aims of the Allies. "We have no quarrel with the German people," he said. "We have no feeling towards them but one of sympathy and friendship." His argument was with the Kaiser and all other emperors and autocrats who stood in the way of his plan to rebuild the world on "American principles."

Allied diplomacy contradicted Wilson's sense of what a progressive foreign policy should be. He wanted to prevent the kind of peace that would lead to more imperialism, absolutism, and war, and he believed the conclusion of the war would allow only a momentary chance to establish institutions that could enforce a durable peace.

A national preparedness movement campaigned for compulsory military training and modernization of the U.S. Army, which ranked 17th in the world. Campaigners used parades, such as this one in Mobile, Alabama, to overcome public doubts. Some residents of Mobile could remember greeting the U.S. Army on different terms.

Wilson's trusted advisor, Edward House, assembled a secret committee, known as the Inquiry, to draft a peace proposal, based on "American principles," that would be both generous enough to show "sympathy and friendship" to the German people and harsh enough to punish their leaders. Made up of economists, historians, geographers, and legal experts, it met in New York, with Lippmann as secretary. The Inquiry produced a set of 14 recommendations that redrew the boundaries of Europe, created a league of nations, and based peace on the principles of freedom of the seas, open door trade, and ethnic self-determination.

The Fight in Congress

After Wilson's war message to Congress, Robert La Follette told his colleagues that if this was a war for democracy, it should be declared democratically. He asked for a national referendum on the war. The country had voted only five months earlier for the peace candidate for president, and there were strong reasons to suspect a declaration would fail a national vote.

Prowar representatives blocked the referendum and brought the declaration to a vote on April 6, when it passed by a margin of 82 to 6 in the Senate and 373 to 50 in the House. As debate turned to questions of how to pay for the war and who would fight in it, the divisions resurfaced. Wilson wanted universal conscription, the first draft since the Civil War. The 1917 draft law created a selective service system comprised of 4,000 local boards manned by volunteers. Men between the ages of 18 and 45 were required to register. The draft would be a "melting pot," said one representative, that would "break down distinctions of race and class and mold us into a new nation."

Congressman Claude Kitchin argued that if young men were to be drafted, profits should be drafted too. He proposed to pay for the war with increased taxes on incomes, corporations, and war profits. Business interests wanted to finance the war instead with sales taxes and bonds, passing the cost on to consumers and future generations. Senator Porter J. McCumber (R–ND) worried that if the rich were taxed heavily it would "dampen their ardor and destroy their war spirit."

In the end, antiwar progressives had too few votes to stop conscription, but they managed to make an exemption for conscientious objectors and to reduce some of the taxes on sugar, bread, and coffee used to pay for the war. Voices of opposition were soon silenced by patriotic calls for unity at all costs.

MOBILIZING THE NATION AND THE ECONOMY

News of the war declaration, carried in banner headlines on Easter Sunday, 1917, set the nation astir with activity. William Percy, a college student from Mississippi, rushed home to Greenville and found women "knitting and beginning to take one lump of sugar instead of two, men within draft age were discussing which branch of the service they had best to enter, men above draft age were heading innumerable patriotic committees and making speeches." Businesses converted to war production. Hull House started a bond drive, eventually raising $50,000 from its neighbors in the 19th Ward.

Wilson recognized that he was asking the nation to undertake an unprecedented effort. Raising an army of more than 3 million men, supplying it, and transporting it across submarine-infested waters to France were Herculean feats. Americans would spare from their dinner plates and send to Europe 1.8 million tons of meat, 8.8 million tons of cereals, and 1.5 million tons of sugar. Factories that produced sewing machines, automobiles, and textiles would retool to make howitzers, tanks, and explosives.

Wilson and others feared that the strain of war could widen political divisions and destroy the achievements progressives had made in the previous 15 years, but some felt that sharing sacrifices would consolidate the progressives' gains. Lippmann hoped the war would open Americans to new ideas. "We are living and shall live all our lives now," he predicted, "in a revolutionary world."

Enforcing Patriotism

The summons to a war to end all wars allowed many progressive pacifists to put aside their opposition and join in the task at hand. Still, some resistance remained. The Socialist Party, whose presidential candidate polled more than half a million votes in 1916, maintained its opposition. Midwestern farmers continued to grumble about the draft and taxes on consumption, but expressing dissent openly soon came to be seen as dangerous.

Since 1914, mysterious explosions had disrupted American munitions factories and ports. On July 30, 1916, across the river from New York City, the largest arms storage facility in the country, known as Black Tom, exploded. Thousands of pounds of shells and guns bound for Russia were destroyed. Four days after Wilson declared war, saboteurs blew up a munitions factory outside of Philadelphia and killed 112 workers, mostly women and girls. Federal agents rounded up large numbers of aliens, but the fear of internal enemies persisted.

Congress gave the president sweeping powers to suppress dissent. The Espionage Act (1917) and the Sedition Act (1918) effectively outlawed opposition to the war and used the postal service and the Justice Department to catch offenders. The Justice Department raided the Chicago offices of the Industrial Workers of the World and imprisoned 96 of the union's leaders on charges of sedition. Eugene V. Debs, leader of the Socialist Party, received ten years for telling a Cincinnati audience that "You need to know that you are fit for something better than slavery and cannon fodder."

The Justice Department organized a volunteer auxiliary, the American Protective League (APL), with a quarter of a million members who opened mail, wiretapped phones, and conducted searches. In September 1918, the APL conducted a "slacker raid" in downtown Manhattan, arresting suspected draft dodgers in offices, subways, and shops. The dragnet pulled in more than 50,000 people. States also passed laws criminalizing opposition to the war and deputizing volunteer enforcers.

Towns, schools, and clubs with German-sounding names changed them. East Germantown, Indiana, became Pershing. Hamburgers became "liberty sandwiches." Americans who had once proudly displayed their ethnicity now took pains to disguise it.

Mennonites, Jehovah's Witnesses, and other pacifist faiths faced their own ordeals. Some sects had come to America to avoid conscription in Germany or Russia. Many could not comply even with the conscientious objector statute, which required submission to military control. Fifteen hundred Mennonites and Hutterites fled to Canada to avoid being placed in camps, while others obeyed their consciences by going to prison.

Advertising the War

Josephus Daniels, the Secretary of the Navy, enlisted the new art of mass advertising to overcome the public's indifference and mold the American people into a "white-hot mass." He turned to former muckraker George Creel, who had helped to mastermind Wilson's publicity campaign in 1916. Creel's propaganda bureau, the Committee on Public Information (CPI), made films, staged pageants, dispatched public speakers, and churned out display ads, billboards, posters, leaflets, and press releases. The CPI sold the war by telling Americans they were fighting to save their own homes. In a famous poster, a fleet of German bombers pass over a shattered, headless Statue of Liberty while New York burns in the background.

Propaganda images represented Germany as menacing and bestial. Following Wilson's example, propaganda distinguished between Germany and the German people, especially Germans who had emigrated to the United States. The CPI distributed leaflets in German offering "Friendly Words to the Foreign Born." Billboards encouraged the foreign born to think of themselves as Americans.

Creel cast women as symbols of progress and patriotism, depicting them as mothers, nurses, and patriotic consumers. The National Woman's Party seized on this theme and began highly publicized pickets outside the White House. Wilson endorsed the suffrage amendment in January 1918 in words that might have been lifted from a CPI poster: "We have made partners of the women in this war. Shall we admit them only to a partnership of suffering and sacrifice and toil and not to a partnership of privilege and right?" Advertising mobilized Americans for war while advancing progressive agendas like assimilation of immigrants, women's suffrage, and reconciliation between labor and management.

Regimenting the Economy

The first prolonged conflict between industrial nations, World War I introduced the public to the term "total war." It was a struggle to protect not just territory or state interests but fundamental values and ways of life. It subordinated all human efforts,

THE NAVY NEEDS YOU! DON'T READ AMERICAN HISTORY — MAKE IT!

U·S·NAVY RECRUITING STATION
34 EAST 23rd ST., NEW YORK

The new business of commercial advertising came to the aid of the war effort, producing memorable images and slogans for mass-circulation magazines.

ideas, and institutions to the needs of the nation. When the War Department laid plans to place a million-man American Expeditionary Force in Europe by the spring of 1918, it became clear that the economy would have to be reorganized, planned, and centralized. The government began issuing contracts, enlisting men, and building camps on a gigantic scale.

To build ships to carry an army across the Atlantic, the United States commissioned the construction of a vast shipyard on Hog Island, outside Philadelphia. It was to have 250 buildings and 80 miles of railroad track, employ 34,000 workers, and have facilities to build 50 ships simultaneously. Wilson asked steelmaker Charles M. Schwab to build the facility, and Schwab signed contracts for the delivery of machinery, cement, steel, and timber. Manufacturers loaded goods on trains headed for Hog Island. The result was the Great Pile Up, the biggest traffic jam in railroad history. Within weeks railroad cars could get no closer than Pittsburgh or Buffalo. Schwab begged the railroads to cooperate, to no avail. The voluntary system for mobilizing the nation's resources had failed, and on January 1, 1918, Wilson nationalized the railroads.

The Hog Island fiasco demonstrated the need for national supervision of the economy. Wilson created a War Industries Board (WIB) to set prices, regulate manufacturing, and control transportation. Wilson found the overseer he needed in Bernard Baruch, a Wall Street financier, who believed in central control of the economy by "socially responsible" businessmen. He drafted corporate executives to fill the top positions and paid them a salary of a dollar a year.

The dollar-a-year men regimented the economy and put business at the service of government, but they also guaranteed profits and looked after manufacturers' long-term interests. One of their innovations was the "cost-plus" contract, which assured contractors the recovery of costs plus a percentage for profit. Under these arrangements, the Black and Decker Company used its factories to make gun sights, and Evinrude stopped making outboard motors and turned out grenades instead. The contract allowed companies to build up revenues to reconvert or to launch new product lines after the war.

Not all businesses submitted willingly to "war socialism." The Ford Motor Company, unwilling to scrap its network of dealerships, refused to completely stop making cars. When other automakers followed suit, the board threatened to cut off the industry's supply of coal and steel. After months of negotiations, the auto manufacturers agreed to cut production by three-fourths. The delay hurt. When American troops went into battle, they had only two tanks.

The war economy was a culmination of two movements: Wall Street's drive for corporate consolidation and the progressives' push for federal regulation. Businessmen recognized that the WIB could rationalize the economy. These "New Capitalists" wanted to end cutthroat competition and bring central organization and "scientific management" to the economy, and they saw the war as their chance. They established the National Foreign Trade Council and other trade associations to represent them in government. They worked to control price fluctuations, share technology, make business predictable, and make workers identify with the company through stock sharing and bonus plans.

The WIB prevented economic chaos, held down inflation, standardized products, and forced manufacturers to pay attention to quality. It changed fashion, removing metal stays from corsets and saving enough metal to build two battleships. Above all, it demonstrated how a corporate economy could work for the national interest.

The Great Migration

The war economy gave Americans new choices and opportunities. As factories geared up for war production, corporate managers, facing a shortage of labor, found a ready supply in the South. In small towns and rural junctions, labor recruiters offered free rides to the North and well-paid employment on arrival. Large manufacturers came to rely on the labor of former sharecroppers. In some northern cities, African-American migrants arrived at the rate of 1000 a week. The massive movement of African Americans from the rural South to the urban North and West that began during World War I came to be called the Great Migration.

Almost half a million people came north during the war years, emptying out some counties in the South and creating panic among the whites left behind. Mississippi lost 75,000 African-American workers, leaving farms without tenants and delivery wagons without drivers. Southern states passed laws banning recruiters and free passes on the railroads. In some places, migrants were discouraged by violence, and the number of lynchings increased, provoking still more migration.

Memories of discrimination and brutality made the decision to move an easy one for many African Americans, but encouragement also came from the *Chicago Defender*, an African-American newspaper available in any county that had a railroad. The paper estimated the war would create 1.5 million jobs for African Americans in northern cities. Classified ads promised jobs in factories. For the price of a $20 ticket, a sharecropper could be at a factory in St. Louis or Cleveland in six hours.

African-American workers moved into low-paying jobs as janitors, domestics, and common laborers in stockyards, steel mills, and factories. The work was back-breaking and often dangerous, and the migrants faced hostility from employers and unionized white workers. Prices were substantially higher in the cities. Still, African-American workers could earn wages 70 percent higher than in the South. Almost no one went back.

The new arrivals found apartments and boarding houses in ghetto neighbor-hoods and adapted to the rhythms of city life. "South State Street was in its glory then, a teeming Negro street with crowded theaters, restaurants, and cabarets," Langston Hughes wrote of Chicago in 1918. "Midnight was like day. The street was full of workers and gamblers, prostitutes and pimps, church folks and sinners."

With new construction stopped by the war, housing was in short supply, and African-American renters found their options limited to overcrowded districts wedged between industrial zones and unfriendly white neighborhoods. Ghetto neighborhoods were both expensive and decrepit. On Chicago's South Side, rents were 15 to 20 percent higher than in white neighborhoods, and the death rate was comparable to that of Bombay, India.

White property owners and real estate agents worked hard to create the ghettos and define their boundaries. In Chicago's South Side, the Hyde Park-Kenwood Property Owners Association organized to "Make Hyde Park White." When discrimination failed to deter "undesirables" from owning homes, the neighbors used dynamite. From 1917 to 1919 there were 26 bombings of African-American residences in Chicago. On July 2, 1917, in East St. Louis, Illinois, rumors that Republicans were "colonizing" the county with African Americans led a mob of white workers to attack a black neighborhood, killing 47 people and leaving 6,000 homeless.

Three years later, in Washington, DC, when a mob invaded the ghetto, residents fought back and retaliated against white neighborhoods. "This new spirit is but a reflex of the great war," an African-American newspaper explained. The "New Negro," urban, defiant, demanding rather than asking for rights, became the subject of admiring and apprehensive reports. Editorials in African-American newspapers urged readers to recognize their own beauty and prowess: "The black man is a power of great potentiality upon whom consciousness of his own strength is about to dawn."

Reforms Become "War Measures"

"Why not make America safe for democracy?" asked the signs carried by marchers protesting racism in New York. The NAACP, in response to the East St. Louis riots, urged Congress to outlaw lynching as a "war measure." African Americans were not alone in using the war emergency to justify immediate reform. Carrie Chapman Catt told Wilson that he could enact women's suffrage "as a 'war measure' and enable our women to throw, more fully and wholeheartedly, their entire energy into work for their country." On a variety of issues, reformers used the war to advance the pro-gressive agenda.

Catt's National American Woman Suffrage Association (NAWSA) worked to identify women with the war effort. NAWSA members sold liberty bonds and knitted socks for the Red Cross, making clear to the president and Congress that they expected to be rewarded with suffrage. Alice Paul's National Woman's Party (NWP) contrasted the nobility of the administration's war aims with its treatment of American women. Pickets at the White House carried signs insisting, in Wilson's own words, on "the right of those who submit to authority to have a voice in their own governments." When Wilson announced his support for suffrage in 1918, he cited women's war service as the reason. The Nineteenth Amendment was finally ratified in 1920, "so soon after the war," according to Jane Addams, "that it must be accounted as the direct result of war psychology."

As it had for African Americans, the wartime shortage of labor increased opportunities for women. Women replaced men as bank tellers, streetcar operators, mail carriers, and laborers in factories. Women in low-skilled and low-paid occupations found room for upward movement. Cashiers became sales clerks, file clerks became stenographers, and line workers became supervisors. Most of these opportunities vanished when the war ended, but in rapidly expanding sectors like finance, communications, and office work women made permanent gains. By 1920, more than 25 percent of working women labored in offices or as telephone operators, and 13 percent were in the professions. The new opportunities made work a source of

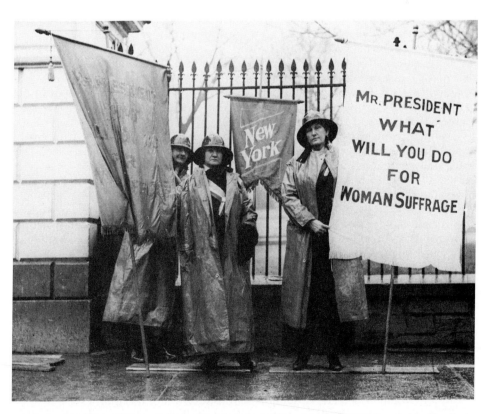

Members of the National Woman's Party picket outside the White House in 1917. Founded by Alice Paul, the NWP campaigned for suffrage through civil disobedience.

prestige and enjoyment for women. War propaganda enhanced the glamour, portraying working women as "our second line of defense."

The general appreciation for women's sacrifices afforded a chance to revisit the issue of special protection for female workers. Sociologist Mary Van Kleeck and Mary Anderson of the Women's Trade Union League persuaded the Army Ordnance Department to recommend uniform standards for women's work, including an eight-hour day, prohibitions on working at night or in dangerous conditions, and provisions for rest periods, lunchrooms, and bathrooms. For military contractors the standards were mandatory, but a number of other firms voluntarily followed them, and several states enacted them into law.

The shortage of labor and high turnover in industrial jobs, combined with strikes in critical industries and an increase in the number of labor disputes, threatened to slow the war effort. Union leaders recognized that the war affected labor relations. Samuel Gompers believed it would lead to a "general reorganization" of the economy that could either help or hurt labor. Workers were prepared to make "any sacrifice which may be necessary to make our triumph sure," he told mineworkers, "but we are not going to make sacrifices that shall fill the coffers of the rich." Conservative unions like the AFL supported the war and backed the administration's repression of more radical unions.

In return, Wilson went further than any previous president had in recognizing the interests of labor. He authorized a National War Labor Board to intervene in critical industries. The board set an unofficial minimum wage based on the cost of living. For the first time the federal government recognized workers' rights to organize, bargain collectively, and join unions. Wilson ordered a wage hike for railroad workers after nationalization.

Beer, wine, and spirits were early casualties of war. The Anti-Saloon League and the Woman's Christian Temperance Union had assembled a powerful antiliquor coalition by 1916. Congress would have passed prohibition without war, but in the rush to mobilize, temperance became a patriotic crusade. Temperance groups touted the liquor ban as the cure for slums, insanity, poverty, high taxes, and inefficiency.

Military regulations prohibited the sale of liquor in the vicinity of Army camps and outlawed selling or giving alcohol to men in uniform. Food conservation laws made it illegal to use grain to make liquor. Finally, on December 22, 1917, Congress passed the Eighteenth Amendment, banning the "manufacture, sale, or transportation of intoxicating liquors." The amendment was ratified in 1919, and Congress passed a "bone dry" enforcement act, sponsored by Congressman Andrew J. Volstead, that defined liquor as any beverage containing half a percent of alcohol or more. Wilson opposed the Volstead Act, favoring restrictions on hard liquor only, but Congress overrode his veto. At midnight on January 28, 1920, the Anti-Saloon League celebrated the dawn of "an era of clear thinking and clean living." Bootleggers, smugglers, and organized crime continued to slake American thirsts, but liquor prices rose and consumption declined.

The war also lent patriotic zeal to antivice crusaders. During the progressive era, vice commissions attacked gambling dens, brothels, and dime-a-dance parlors, while muckrakers exposed the police-protection rackets that allowed them to thrive. Within days of the declaration of war, reformers identified prostitutes as domestic enemies who sabotaged the health of American troops. Gonorrhea reportedly afflicted a quarter of the Allied forces in France, and proper middle-class Americans worried what might become of soldiers sent to such a moral wilderness.

The administration mobilized against venereal disease. The president formed an Interdepartmental Board of Social Hygiene, which implemented severe restrictions known as the "American Plan." Military police could arrest any woman found within five miles of a military cantonment in the United States and force her to submit to medical tests. If infected, she could be sentenced to a "detention home" until cured. Authorities confined 15,520 afflicted women during the war and closed vice districts in port cities. Cities and states followed the Army's lead and mounted their own attacks on prostitution and disease. The war permanently changed the crusade for public morals. Before 1917, reformers targeted commercial vice as a source of political and social corruption, but afterward they directed their efforts at women as carriers of disease.

The Army acted against liquor and prostitution, but it shrank from challenging racial injustice. At training camps in the South, clashes between uniformed African-American soldiers and white local officials easily turned violent. A riot in Houston in August 1917 began when soldiers from nearby Camp Logan rushed to the aid of an African-American woman being beaten by police. Twenty policemen and soldiers died and 54 soldiers received life sentences.

After the Houston riot, African-American units were dispersed to camps across the country. Training was continually interrupted by menial assignments like road building or freight handling. The Army remained segregated, and southern communities used military discipline to strengthen Jim Crow laws. Encouraged by the Army's "work or fight" order, which required draft-age men to either enlist or get a job, states and localities passed compulsory work laws that were intended to keep laborers in the fields and servants in the kitchens at prewar wages.

Over There

When the U.S. Senate took up the enormous war budget the president submitted in April 1917, the finance committee questioned Major Palmer E. Pierce about what would be done with all of that money. "Clothing, cots, camps, food, pay," he replied, "and we may have to have an army in France." "Good Lord!" exclaimed Senator Thomas Martin of Virginia, "You're not going to send soldiers over there, are you?" After the horrors of the Somme and Verdun, where men died by the tens of thousands, it seemed mad to send Americans to such a place. "One would think that, after almost four years of war, . . . it would have been all but impossible to get anyone to serve," one veteran later recalled. "But . . . we and many thousands of others volunteered."

Americans went to France believing they could change the war and the peace. Trench warfare was not for them. They planned to sweep in formations across open fields, as Americans had at Antietam and Gettysburg. To a remarkable degree, they got the war they wanted. Europeans watched their civilization destroy itself in the Great War, but Americans saw theirs rising.

Citizens Into Soldiers

The job of enlisting, training, and transporting soldiers began with a rush of excitement. Camps housing 400,000 recruits went up in 30 days. A Wisconsin man found that Fort Sheridan had "an atmosphere somewhat like that of a college campus on the eve of a big game." Conscription went smoothly, and soon 32 camps were in operation, housing 1.3 million men. Commander John J. Pershing arrived in France in June with 40,000 men and the first of 16,000 women who would serve in the American Expeditionary Force (AEF).

Once Wilson was firmly committed to war, the British government revealed how financially desperate it was. London had barely enough dollar reserves to last another two weeks. Wilson advanced $200 million immediately, and loans to the Allies eventually amounted to $10 billion.

The Allies agreed that funds, food, and ammunition were needed more urgently than men, but that changed in October 1917, when German and Austrian forces smashed through the Italian lines at Caporetto, finishing the war on that front. When the Bolshevik Revolution curtailed Russian resistance in the east in November, Britain and France saw that by the next spring Germany would be able to break through to Paris. The war became a race between the United States and Germany to see who could place the most men on the western front in 1918.

To get troops to the war the United States needed ships, but for a time the United States had to cut back draft calls because it had scarcely a dozen ships for carrying men. The War Department confiscated 16 German passenger ships docked in U.S. ports, and the British converted freighters to use as transports. The Navy, meanwhile, cured the U-boat problem. The addition of the American destroyer fleet allowed the Allies to convoy effectively for the first time, cutting losses dramatically. When a torpedo was sighted, destroyers would sprint to the far end of its wake and deploy depth charges in a circle around the U-boat. By July 18, some 10,000 troops a day boarded the "Atlantic Ferry" for the ride to France.

The Fourteen Points

Meanwhile the Inquiry completed its work, sending the president a memorandum titled "The War Aims and the Peace Terms It Suggests" on Christmas Day, 1917. Consulting with Colonel Edward House, Wilson redrafted the report and presented it in an address to Congress on January 8, 1918. The Fourteen Points outlined U.S. objectives and suggested a new basis for peace. Unlike nineteenth-century wars waged for limited territorial or political objectives, the Great War was a total war, fought for unlimited aims. The principal belligerents—Britain, France, Russia, Germany, and Austria-Hungary—were global empires whose trade and law spanned continents and oceans. Each side wanted to destroy the other's future as a great power, economically and militarily. Wilson replaced these imperial visions of total victory with a peace based on limited gains and struck among nations, instead of empires.

The Fourteen Points were grouped around four themes: national self-determination; freedom of the seas; enforcement of peace by a league of nations; and open, instead of secret, diplomacy. The Inquiry's memorandum included maps marked with new European boundaries based on national, ethnic identities. The new state of Poland, for instance, should govern only territories with "indisputably Polish populations." Point III restated the Open Door, urging free trade. Wilson thus hoped to eliminate what he saw as the two leading causes of war, imperial and commercial rivalry. By calling for open diplomacy and national rights, he appealed directly to the people of Europe, over the heads of their governments. Creel printed 60 million copies of the Fourteen Points and had them distributed around the world. Planes dropped copies over Germany and Austria.

Wilson hoped the Fourteen Points would dispel not only the old dream of empire but also the new one of world socialist revolution. On November 7, Russian workers overthrew the Provisional Government of Alexander Kerensky. The one-party regime of the Bolsheviks, led by Vladimir Lenin, took its place and summoned workers everywhere to rise against their governments and to make peace. "The crimes of the ruling, exploiting classes in this war have been countless. These crimes cry out for revolutionary revenge." In December, Lenin sued for peace based on the principle of self-determination. The Council of People's Commissars allocated 2 million rubles to encourage revolutions around the world.

Two world leaders—Lenin and Wilson—now offered radically different visions of the new world order, and Lenin was putting his into effect. Wilson continued to hope that the revolution would move in a more liberal direction and that Russia would stay in the war. Those hopes ended with the Treaty of Brest-Litovsk, signed by Russia and Germany in March 1918. The treaty showed the fearful price of defeat in modern war. Russia lost the Ukraine, Poland, and Finland, three-quarters of its iron and steel, one-quarter of its population, and most of its best farmland. With its eastern front secure, Germany began transferring ten divisions a month to the west.

Wilson was the first, but not the last, American president to be haunted by the specter of a German–Russian alliance, uniting the immense war-making resources of Europe and Asia. He refused to recognize the Bolshevik government, and he sent 7,000 American troops to Russia to support anti-Bolshevik forces and to restart the war on the eastern front. U.S. troops joined Japanese forces invading Siberia from the east. Meanwhile, the battle for the control of Europe was about to begin.

The Final Offensive

The German high command knew the spring offensive would be the last. Risking everything, the German commander Erich Ludendorff launched his offensive on March 21, 1918. Specially trained shock troops hurled the British Fifth Army back to Amiens (see Map 22–1). In May they penetrated French lines as far as Soissons, 37 miles from Paris. As gaps opened in the lines, French General Ferdinand Foch and British General Douglas Haig appealed to Pershing to allow American troops to reinforce trenches under British and French command. Pershing opposed the idea. He wanted the American Army to play "a distinct and definite part" in the war to strengthen the United States' negotiating position and use his own strategy for defeating the Germans.

Pershing criticized European commanders for remaining on the defensive when the war could be won only by "driving the enemy out into the open and engaging him in a war of movement." He saw trenches not as protection against the murderous efficiency of modern weaponry but as symbols of inertia. Pershing favored overwhelming the main German force with massed assaults. Infantry commanders, he decided, "must oppose machine guns by fire from rifles." Pershing saw Europe's war as a replay of the American Civil War, revealing a habit of mind that would typify American geopolitical thinking for the next century: the belief that as the most advanced industrial nation, the United States was historically "ahead" of other countries, an advantage that allowed Americans to understand the world through the prism of their own experience.

The German onslaught interfered with Pershing's plans. On May 27, German divisions pierced French lines at Château-Thierry and advanced on Paris at a rate of 10 miles a day. Bowing to urgent requests, Pershing threw the AEF into the breach. Column after column of fresh American troops filled the roads from Paris to the front. Photographs show doughboys marching to meet the enemy across fields of wildflowers. Ahead of them lay five German divisions, poison gas, minefields, rolling artillery barrages, and machine guns. The Americans stopped the Germans, but at a fearful cost. The Marine brigade that took Belleau Wood lost half its men. Without artillery or tanks, they assaulted machine gun nests head on with rifles. The Americans, with help from a global influenza epidemic, stopped the German drive.

By mid-July, the initiative passed to the Allies. On September 12, Pershing tried his tactics against the Saint Mihiel salient, a bulge in the French lines. The doughboys

Map 22–1   Western Front, 1918

On the western front, the opposing armies fought from trenches fortified with earthworks and barbed wire. The parallel trench lines stretched thousands of miles from the North Sea to Switzerland.

raced behind the retreating enemy past their planned objectives, even outdistancing their own supply wagons. Saint Mihiel vindicated Pershing's strategy, and he yearned for another chance. It came two weeks later, at the battle of the Meuse-Argonne.

The Argonne Forest contained some of the most formidable natural and man-made defenses on the western front. Atop parallel ridges lay three fortified trench lines, or *stellung*, consisting of concrete pillboxes, barbed wire, artillery, and observation posts. Half a million German troops had defended these fortifications for four years. Against this force, Pershing arrayed the American First Army, 1,031,000 men. Pershing's battle plan called for overwhelming the German defenses with speed and numbers, breaching the first trench line and reaching the second, 10 miles inside the German front, the first day.

Breaking through the first line of German trenches after a day and a half, the battle turned into a deadly crawl up the Romagne heights into the teeth of the second *stellung*. In two weeks of fighting, 26,277 Americans died. French soldiers reported seeing the American dead lying in rows, cut down by machine guns as they marched in formation. Finally, on November 10, American troops reached their objective and dynamited the rail line connecting the cities of Metz and Sedan. Meanwhile, Germany announced that it would accept the Fourteen Points as the basis for an armistice and negotiations. At 11:00 a.m. on November 11, 1918, the guns fell silent.

African-American troops advance toward the sound of gunfire in northern France, 1918. "Our boys went on the battlefield last night singing," one wrote home.

American intervention had been decisive. The American economy lent its immense industrial and agricultural productivity to the Allies at a crucial moment. Pershing failed to transform strategy, but by striking the final blow, Americans had the illusion that their way of war had been triumphant.

Although they fought on the same battlefields, Americans and Europeans fought two vastly different wars. The Americans' war was swift and victorious; the Europeans' was a prolonged catastrophe that consumed an entire generation. For Europeans, the mental world of the prewar era, with its faith in modernity, science, and democracy, vanished forever. War validated Americans' confidence in the virtues of their own civilization, while reinforcing their suspicions of foreign systems and ideas. Confidence in the inevitability of progress became a distinctive feature of U.S. culture. In much of the world "American" became almost synonymous with "modern," but not everywhere. In the East another political and economic system shouted its claim to the future.

THE BLACK CLOUD IN THE EAST

Americans celebrated the armistice with bonfires, automobile horns, church bells, and uplifted voices. Outside the White House a choir from Howard University sang "The Spirit of Victory," a cantata written for the occasion, as army biplanes flew overhead. Wilson told Congress that "everything for which America fought has been accomplished," but he observed that the situation in Russia cast doubt on the durability of peace. Over the next months, revolutions broke out throughout Eastern Europe. Just as diplomats prepared to make peace in Europe, journalist Ray Stannard Baker wrote, there arose a "black cloud of the east, threatening to overwhelm and swallow up the world."

Wilson in Paris

For Wilson, the moment he had planned for in 1917 had arrived: The United States, he believed, would help set the terms of peace. Sure that the public would view the nation's victory as his victory, he made mistakes that undermined his support at home. First, he tried to turn the victory to political advantage. Republicans in the House and Senate had supported the president during the war, and the bipartisanship might have lasted had Wilson not dispelled it with an advertisement in the *New York Times*. "If you have approved my leadership," it read, "I earnestly beg that you will express yourself unmistakably to that effect by returning a Democratic majority to both the Senate and the House." Republicans attacked the ad as an insult to their patriotism. When the ballots were counted in the 1918 midterm elections, Republican majorities took power in both houses.

He next decided to go to Paris to negotiate himself, and passed up an opportunity to produce a bipartisan treaty by including a prominent Republican in the delegation. The chances for ratification would rest largely on Wilson's prestige and popularity.

In December 1918, Walter Lippmann, now an Army captain, stood on the balcony of the Crillon Hotel witnessing Wilson's triumphal entry into Paris. Huge crowds lined the streets, and as the procession entered the center of the city, a great cheer went up. For the next month, Wilson toured France, Italy, and Britain with cries of "Viva Veelson" ringing in his ears.

By the time he arrived for the treaty talks at the Palace of Versailles, two of the Fourteen Points had already been compromised, and Wilson's popularity provided little help at the negotiating table. Britain's David Lloyd George refused to accept the point on freedom of the seas, which would thwart the use of the Royal Navy in a future conflict. Wilson's own actions undercut his position on point six, respect for Russia's sovereignty, because American troops were occupying Russian territory in Siberia. Wilson was unable to prevent Britain, France, and Japan from dividing Germany's colonies among themselves and imposing harsh peace terms. Germany had to sign a humiliating "war guilt" clause and pay $33 billion in reparations, enough to cripple its economy for decades.

Wilson "growing grimmer and graver, day by day" concentrated his efforts on creating the League of Nations. He took the lead in drafting the League Covenant, which committed each member to submit disputes to arbitration and pledged them to take action against "any war or threat of war." Wilson presented the covenant to the peace delegations and declared, "A living thing is born."

The Senate Rejects the League

To many observers in the United States the Treaty of Versailles' imperial land grabs and severe treatment of the vanquished nations betrayed the goals Americans had fought to attain. Few in Congress and the press shared Wilson's confidence that the League of Nations would prevent future wars. They felt instead that it might only guarantee that the United States would be involved in the next conflict. To Republican leaders, like

Henry Cabot Lodge, the United States' best bet was to look to its own security and work out international relations independently rather than as part of a league.

In early March 1919, before the treaty was concluded, Lodge and 38 other senators—more than enough to defeat the treaty—signed a petition opposing the League of Nations. James A. Reed of Missouri said the covenant would turn American foreign policy over to foreigners. Senator William Borah called it "the greatest triumph for English diplomacy in three centuries of English diplomatic life." Wilson knew he would have to fight, but he believed that in the end the Senate would not reject the treaty.

In September, Wilson went "over the heads" of Congress and stumped for the treaty on a nationwide tour. Traveling more than 8,000 miles and speaking before large audiences without loudspeakers took a toll on the president's health. After a speech in Pueblo, Colorado, he became so ill that he was rushed back to Washington, where he suffered a stroke that left him paralyzed on his left side and unable to concentrate for more than a few minutes a day. Mrs. Wilson and the president's physician kept his condition secret and refused to allow anyone to see him.

With the League of Nations' champion secluded in the White House, the Senate defeated the treaty. Down to the end, Wilson refused to allow Senate Democrats to accept any modifications. Lodge and the Republicans were not ready to retreat into isolation, but they preferred diplomatic strategies that employed the United States' overwhelming economic power rather than its relatively weak military forces. They also saw Latin America as more critical than Europe to U.S. security.

Meanwhile, European governments organized the League of Nations without the United States or the Soviet Union. Over the next decade, U.S. influence abroad grew enormously. American automobiles, radios, and movies could be seen in far corners of the globe. However, the United States was cautious in its diplomatic dealings in Europe and Asia, to avoid being drawn into what the *New York Tribune* called the "vast seething mass of anarchy extending from the Rhine to the Siberian wastes."

Red Scare

On May 1, 1919, a dozen or more mail bombs were sent to prominent Americans, including J. P. Morgan, John D. Rockefeller, and Supreme Court Justice Oliver Wendell Holmes. None of the packages reached its intended target, but one blew up in the hands of a maid in the home of Senator Thomas Hardwick. A month later a bomb exploded outside the residence of Attorney General A. Mitchell Palmer in Washington. Investigations showed that the bombings were the work of lone lunatics, but many people concluded that communists were trying to overthrow the government. Since the Russian Revolution, newspapers, evangelists, and government officials had fed fears of Bolshevism.

The Communist risings in Europe terrified conservatives in the United States and led them to look for Soviet accomplices, particularly among immigrants and unionized workers. They drew no distinctions among Socialists, anarchists, Communists, and labor unionists; they were all "red." When steelworkers in Gary, Indiana, struck for higher wages and shorter hours in September 1919, Judge Elbert Gary, president of U.S. Steel, denounced them as Bolsheviks. Enlisting the help of local loyalty leagues, Judge Gary broke the strike.

Using the patriotic rhetoric of the war, industry leaders labeled strikers as dangerous aliens. They persuaded the courts to take action, and a series of Supreme Court decisions made union activity virtually illegal. In 1919 the court allowed antitrust suits under the Sherman Act to be filed against unions, and it later declared boycotts illegal and limited strikers' freedom to picket. In January 1920 a series of

CHRONOLOGY

1911	Mexican Revolution begins
1914	U.S. troops occupy Veracruz, Mexico World War I begins
1915	U.S. troops occupy Haiti (until 1934) *Lusitania* sunk
1916	U.S. forces invade Mexico in search of Pancho Villa U.S. forces enter the Dominican Repubic Woodrow Wilson re-elected
1917	Russian czar abdicates; parliamentary regime takes power U.S. declares war on Germany East St. Louis riot Houston riot October Revolution overthrows Russian government; Lenin takes power
1918	Wilson announces U.S. war aims: the Fourteen Points Wilson nationalizes railroads Sedition Act outlaws criticism of the U.S. government Armistice ends fighting on the western front
1919	Eighteenth Amendment outlaws manufacture, sale, and transport of alcoholic beverages Versailles Treaty signed in Paris Mail bombs target prominent government and business figures Gary, Indiana, steel strike U.S. Senate rejects Versailles Treaty
1920	Nineteenth Amendment secures the vote for women Palmer raids arrest thousands of suspected Communists Sacco and Vanzetti arrested on charges of robbery and murder

crackdowns known as the Palmer raids began. Some 250 members of the Union of Russian Workers were arrested and deported to Russia on an Army transport. In one night, 4,000 suspected Communists were arrested in raids across the country.

The most notorious case associated with the "Red Scare" began in May 1920 when Nicola Sacco and Bartolomeo Vanzetti, a shoemaker and a fish peddler, were arrested for robbing a shoe company in South Braintree, Massachusetts. Two men were killed during the robbery, and ballistics experts claimed that the bullets came from Sacco's gun. The trial, however, focused on the fact that the defendants were Italian and anarchists. The state doctored evidence and witnesses changed testimony, but the judge favored the prosecution. Despite Sacco's corroborated testimony that he was in Boston at the time of the robbery and the sworn confession of another man, Judge Webster Thayer sentenced Sacco and Vanzetti to death.

The appeals lasted six years, and protests for their release mounted. As the day of the execution approached, Europeans and Latin Americans organized boycotts of American products. Riots in Paris took 20 lives. Governments called on the president to intervene, but on August 23, 1927, Sacco and Vanzetti died in the electric chair.

Americans who had talked in 1917 about making the world safe for democracy now seemed ready to throw their freedoms away out of fear of anarchy. By the end of 1920, the original terror subsided, but labor unions and radicals would have to fend off the charge of communism for decades to come.

CONCLUSION

Wilson tried to lead America toward what he called a new world order, a world where nations and international law would count more than empires and where the United States could light the way toward progress, stability, and peace. He failed to recognize that for many Americans this future was filled with terrors as well as promise. The strains of war introduced new divisions in American society. Progressivism, which had given coherence and direction to social change, was a spent force. The growth of federal administration, the new powers of big business, internal migrations, and new social movements and values added up to what Lippmann called a "revolutionary world." Americans entered the 1920s with a sense of uneasiness. They knew that their nation was the world's strongest, but they were unsure about what that might mean for their lives.

FURTHER READINGS

Nancy K. Bristow, *Making Men Moral: Social Engineering During the Great War* (1996). How government and women's groups attempted to use military training to mold men into model citizens.

John Eisenhower, *Intervention! The United States and the Mexican Revolution, 1913–1917* (1993). The story of the U.S. occupation of Veracruz and Pershing's search for Pancho Villa.

Meirion Harries, *The Last Days of Innocence: America at War, 1917–1918* (1997). A lively anecdotal history of the war years.

David M. Kennedy, *Over Here: The First World War and American Society* (1980). The best study of the home front during World War I.

N. Gordon Levin, Jr., *Woodrow Wilson and World Politics* (1968). The progressive president's response to the disorder of world politics. Levin analyzes the idealism and realism of Wilsonian foreign policy.

H. C. Peterson and Gilbert C. Fite, *Opponents of War, 1917–1918* (1957). Still the best study on wartime peace movements and the Wilson administration's attempts to suppress dissent.

Ronald Steel, *Walter Lippmann and the American Century* (1980). More than any other journalist, Lippmann shaped American foreign policy in the twentieth century.

 Please refer to the document CD-ROM for primary sources related to this chapter.

CHAPTER

23
The 1920s

"The Queen of Swimmers" • A Dynamic Economy • A Modern
Culture • The Limits of the Modern Culture • A "New Era" in
Politics and Government • Conclusion

"THE QUEEN OF SWIMMERS"

On August 6, 1926, Gertrude Ederle walked across the beach at Cape Gris-
Nez on the French coastline. Her body and her bright red swimsuit were
heavily greased. At 7:00 a.m., the 19-year-old from New York City plunged
into the water and began to swim toward the coast of England.

"Trudy," the daughter of a German immigrant butcher, was a champion distance
swimmer who had won medals at the 1924 Olympics, but no woman had ever
completed the long, hazardous swim across the English Channel. In fact, only five
men had accomplished the feat. Ederle herself had tried and failed the year before.

This time was different. Despite the tides, the chill water, and the threat of sharks,
Ederle persevered, spurred on by her competitive instincts, her eagerness to please her
mother, and her father's promise to buy her a new car, a roadster, if she succeeded.

Inspired by thoughts of that roadster, Ederle fought the choppy waves and
hunted for a favorable tide. Finally, after 14 hours and 31 minutes in the water, she
came ashore at Kingsdown, England, at 9:40 p.m. Ederle had become the first
woman to swim the channel and had made the crossing faster than any of the men
before her. Back in the United States, newspapers trumpeted Ederle's stunning
achievement in page-one headlines and analyzed it in editorials. Ederle came home
to a tumultuous ticker-tape parade in New York. "No President or king, soldier or
statesman," reported the *New York Times*, "has ever enjoyed such an enthusiastic and
affectionate outburst of acclaim by the metropolis as was offered to . . . the 'Queen of

Swimmers.'" She was overwhelmed with offers to endorse products and to appear on stage and in the movies.

Gertrude Ederle's enormous reception said a great deal about the United States in the 1920s. Once again at peace, America could afford to indulge an interest in the exploits of a long-distance swimmer. The nation's dynamic industrial economy seemed effortlessly to produce plenty of roadsters, movies, and prosperity.

Ederle herself exemplified a new national culture, rooted in the booming economy. Emphasizing the importance of pleasure, this modern culture celebrated leisure activities. The new culture glorified the purchase and consumption of material goods such as the roadster Ederle wanted and the merchandise she advertised. The teenage swimmer embodied still other aspects of the new culture—its fascination with youth, its endorsement of a child-centered family life, and its infatuation with pleasure-seeking, independent women.

In the euphoria of the ticker-tape parade, it was easy to conclude that Americans welcomed the emerging cultural and political order as much as they welcomed Trudy Ederle. In fact, many people were troubled by the changes of the 1920s. The new order did not speak to the social and economic inequalities that plagued national life. As a result, the new cultural and political order faced a powerful backlash, just as Ederle faced a hostile tide in the English Channel. Nevertheless, like the swimmer, the new culture and politics seemed to overcome all opposition as the decade moved to a close.

A DYNAMIC ECONOMY

By and large, the 1920s were a prosperous time for America. After a recession during 1920 and 1921, the economy stabilized and then grew. Consumer prices remained steady throughout the decade, and jobs were plentiful; the unemployment rate went as low as 1.8 percent in 1926. Wages jumped: The nation's net income—the value of its earnings from labor and property—leapt from $64.0 billion in 1921 to $86.8 billion in 1929. This prosperity was driven by the dynamism of the evolving industrial economy. New technologies, increased efficiency, a maturing automobile industry, and new businesses all contributed to the economic gains.

Despite the general prosperity, the transformation of the economy involved defeats for organized labor and decline for many farmers. The relative weakness of agriculture and the strength of industry helped to turn the United States into a predominantly urban nation. In the prosperous 1920s, as always, industrial capitalism was a transforming force.

The Development of Industry

Several long-term factors shaped the development of American industry in the 1920s. In their continuing quest for more efficient production, businessmen made use of new technologies and other innovations during the decade.

The switch from coal to electricity, underway since the 1910s, was an important innovation in factories. By the end of the 1920s, electricity powered more than two-thirds of American manufacturing plants.

Henry Ford's car company pioneered another critical innovation, the system that became known as mass production. By the 1910s, Ford, like other American manufacturers, used interchangeable parts, simple and accurate machine tools, and electric power to speed output at its Highland Park factory complex in Detroit, Michigan. However, auto production was slowed by a traditional manufacturing practice. Frames, transmissions, and other key subassemblies remained in place on stands while teams of workers moved from one stand to another to work.

Eager to meet the rising demand for the popular Model T car, Ford's managers reversed the process by "moving the work to the men." Beginning in 1913, the Ford plant used conveyor belts and chains to send subassemblies past groups of stationary workers. Instead of making an entire engine or subassembly, a worker might tighten a few bolts or install a single part. This led to an astonishing increase in output. In 1914, Ford produced 300,000 Model Ts. In 1923, the company produced more than 2 million. By that time, other manufacturers were racing to copy Ford's techniques.

Mass production, electrification, and other innovations spurred an extraordinary increase in productivity for American industry. Output per worker skyrocketed 72 percent from 1919 to 1929.

Along with increased productivity, the rise of several industries drove the economy. Auto production now dominated as textiles, railroads, iron, and steel had earlier. In 1921, there were 9.3 million cars on American roads. By 1929, the figure had reached 23 million. By producing all those cars, auto manufacturers stimulated demand for plate glass, oil, gasoline, and rubber.

Other sectors of the industrial economy also grew rapidly. The demand for processed foods, household appliances, office machinery, and chemicals increased dramatically. Emerging industries such as aircraft demonstrated their potential economic importance.

Arguably the first powered, fixed-wing flight had occurred in December 1903, when Wilbur and Orville Wright brought their "Flyer" to the beach at Kitty Hawk, North Carolina. With Orville lying at the controls, the fragile plane flew 120 feet in 12 seconds. But, the civilian airplane industry did not take off until the 1920s. Aircraft production rose from less than 300 in 1922 to more than 6,000 in 1929. By then, fledgling airlines were flying passengers on scheduled flights.

The Trend Toward Large-Scale Organization

The development of industry reinforced the trend toward large-scale organization that was basic to U.S. capitalism. Only big businesses had the financial resources to pay for mass production. By 1929, corporations produced 92 percent of the nation's manufactured goods.

The largest firms also benefited from more efficient organizational structures. When the recession of 1920 and 1921 left big corporations with too many unsold goods, companies reorganized. Now top managers, aided by financial, legal, and other experts, oversaw the work of semiautonomous divisions that supplied different markets. At General Motors, for example, the Chevrolet division produced huge numbers of relatively inexpensive cars, while the Cadillac division turned out a smaller number of expensive cars. The new organizational system made corporations more flexible, efficient, and responsive to changes in consumer demand.

Corporate growth was not confined to industry. Chains such as A & P grocers and F. W. Woolworth's variety stores increased their share of the nation's retail sales from 4 percent to 20 percent. One percent of the nation's banks managed nearly half of the country's financial assets.

Giant firms and their leaders had often been the targets of suspicion, hostility, and reform during the Progressive era, but many Americans softened their attitude toward business in the prosperous 1920s. Basking in the glow of public approval, big business confidently forecast a central role for itself in the nation's destiny.

The Transformation of Work and the Work Force

The modern corporation changed the nature of work and the work force in the 1920s. Industrial efficiency was not just a matter of electricity and machines. To speed up production, the managers at Ford and other factories had to speed up the labor process.

Accordingly, the spirit of scientific management continued to sweep through American industry. Laboring under ever tighter supervision, workers were pushed to work faster and harder. Ford's system of mass production shared Frederick Winslow Taylor's determination to simplify and regiment labor. The result was less satisfying work. Instead of making a whole engine, a Ford assembly-line worker might spend his day turning a few nuts on one engine after another.

The development of industry contributed to the transformation of occupational structure. As the economy became increasingly efficient, the nation experienced a net loss of about a million jobs in manufacturing, coal mining, and railroading. The growth of other kinds of employment more than compensated for this decrease, however. The ranks of white-collar workers increased 80 percent from 1910 to 1930, when nearly one worker in three did white-collar work rather than manual labor. The nation had already begun a long-term evolution from an industrial economy based on manual labor to a postindustrial economy based on white-collar work.

The development of the economy also encouraged the continuing, gradual movement of women into the paid work force. By the end of the 1920s, women made up a majority of clerical workers. Married women were more likely than ever to work outside the home.

Despite these changes, women still faced discrimination in the workplace. They were paid less than men who did comparable work. Hardly any women held high-level managerial jobs. Moreover, there was still resistance to the idea that women should work outside the home. Most people continued to believe that a woman's place was in the home, especially if she had children. Only economic necessities—families' need for income and employers' need for workers—reconciled American society to women's employment in the 1920s.

The Defeat of Organized Labor

The American labor movement did not respond effectively to the transformation of work and the work force. In an age of increasing economic organization, workers became less organized. In 1920 nearly one nonagricultural worker in five belonged to a union. By 1929, little more than one in 10 was a union member. The labor movement was especially weak in the developing mass-production industries such as automobiles and steel and barely addressed the growing ranks of clerks and other white-collar workers.

The weak state of organized labor partly resulted from prosperity. Earning relatively good wages, many workers were less interested in joining unions. To convince them that unions were unnecessary, corporations promoted *welfare capitalism,* a set of highly publicized programs ranging from lunch-hour movies to sports teams to profit-sharing plans.

While some firms tried to win over their workers with baseball teams and company unions, many employers used tougher tactics to battle the labor movement. Management crusaded for the "open shop"—a workplace free of labor organization—and found an ally in the judicial system. During the 1920s, rulings by the U.S. Supreme Court made it easier for lower courts to grant injunctions against union activities. State and federal courts issued injunctions to stop unions from striking and exercising their rights and allowed businesses to sue unions for damages.

The labor movement also hurt its own cause. The leadership of the major national organization, the AFL, was increasingly conservative and timid. The heads of the AFL, white males with Western European roots who represented skilled crafts, had little interest in organizing women workers and wanted nothing to do with socialists, radical unionists, or African-American workers. The AFL was slow to admit or even pay attention to the Brotherhood of Sleeping Car Porters, the assertive union of African-American workers organized in 1925 under socialist A. Philip Randolph. Despite pleas from Randolph and others, the AFL failed to organize unskilled workers, many of whom were African Americans or white immigrants from Eastern and Southern Europe.

Weakened by internal divisions, welfare capitalism, the open-shop crusade, and the courts, the labor movement did not challenge the ongoing transformation of industrial labor. Nationwide, the number of strikes and lockouts dropped from 3,411 in 1920 to 604 in 1928. All too often, these labor actions ended in defeat for workers.

The Decline of Agriculture

Against the backdrop of national prosperity, American agriculture continued its long decline. Prices for basic crops such as cotton and wheat fell, and the number of farms dropped.

The larger story of decline obscured important signs of growth and health. Some agricultural sectors were as dynamic as industry, and for the same reasons—increased efficiency promoted by new technologies and large-scale organization. Mechanization made farm labor more efficient, as did the increasing development of irrigation systems since the turn of the century. By the 1920s, the irrigated farms of the Southwest were producing bumper crops of cotton, fruits, and vegetables. The Southwest also witnessed the rise of huge farms with owners who could afford mechanization and irrigation. These innovative "factories in the fields" depended on the old-fashioned exploitation of farm labor, as well as on size and technology. In California's Imperial Valley and elsewhere, migrant workers labored in harsh conditions for low pay.

Ironically, the dynamism of the agricultural economy created a problem for many American farmers. Midsize farms could not compete with the "factories in the fields." Increased efficiency, meanwhile, led to bumper crops that did not always find a market at a good price. Farmers were hurt by changes in Americans' diet, such as declining consumption of bread and potatoes, as well as by the rise of competitors overseas. The resulting glut reduced the price of farm products. As their incomes lagged behind those of urban workers, farmers yearned for *parity*—the return of high pre-World War I agricultural prices.

Farmers' purchasing power did improve as nonagricultural prices dropped and farm prices rose toward the end of the decade, but the basic reality did not change. As a Georgia farmer observed, "The hand that is feeding the world is being spit upon."

The Urban Nation

The woes of agriculture contributed to a long-term shift in the geographical distribution of the American population. For the first time, according to the federal census of 1920, a majority of Americans—54 million out of 105 million—lived in urban territory. This did not mean the United States had become a nation of big cities. The census defined "urban territory" as places with as few as 2,500 people. Nevertheless, the United States was no longer predominantly rural.

The decline of farming spurred this transformation. As agricultural prices fell, millions of Americans fled the nation's farms, and the growth of the industrial economy swelled the population of towns and cities. In the 1920s, factory production was still centered in urban areas. Manufacturing gave many cities their identity. Detroit was becoming the "motor city." Pittsburgh, Pennsylvania, and Birmingham, Alabama, symbolized the steel industry. Most of the new white-collar jobs were located in cities.

The rise of the automobile also contributed to the emergence of the urban nation. The car made it practical for Americans to live in suburbs. In the 1920s, the suburban lifestyle was still mostly for the well-to-do. Elite suburbs, such as Grosse Pointe outside Detroit, and Glendale and Inglewood outside Los Angeles, grew explosively. The transformation of the countryside into suburbs was a powerful symbol of the new urban nation.

A Modern Culture

The 1920s saw the full emergence of a modern culture. So perfectly symbolized by Gertrude Ederle, the new culture extolled the virtues of modernity, pleasure, leisure, and consumption. It reflected the needs of an industrial economy that had to sell the goods rolling off the assembly lines. Supported by advertising and installment buying, the culture of leisure and consumption offered spectator sports, movies, popular music, radio, and sex. The new culture entailed new views of gender, family life, and youth and placed renewed emphasis on the old values of individualism in an increasingly organized society.

The Spread of Consumerism

By the 1920s, many Americans, encouraged by big business, increasingly defined life as the pursuit of pleasure. People were invited to seek gratification through the consumption of goods and services. This philosophy of consumerism saturated American society by the end of the decade.

In addition to higher wages, many workers had more free time. For salaried, middle-class workers, the annual vacation had become a tradition by the 1910s. Although blue-collar workers seldom enjoyed a vacation, they spent less time on the job. Some employers, including Henry Ford, instituted a five-day work week during the 1920s. More commonly, businesses shortened their workday.

A change in attitude accompanied these changes in wages and workdays. The work ethic seemed less necessary in a prospering economy. Thanks to Fordism and Taylorism, work was less satisfying, too. In these circumstances, people justified pleasure as an essential antidote to labor.

The advertising industry encouraged the new attitude toward pleasure. During the 1920s, ads appeared everywhere—in newspapers and magazines, on billboards and big electric signs, and, by the end of the decade, on radio. Impressed by successful ad campaigns for such products as Listerine antiseptic and mouthwash and Fleischmann's yeast, big businesses increasingly turned to advertising agencies to sell goods and services. Expenditures for advertising leaped from $682 million in 1914 to nearly $3 billion by 1929.

Advertising, like the new culture, optimistically embraced change and innovation. According to advertisements, purchasing the right products would solve people's problems and thereby bring them fulfillment.

Selling mouthwash and consumerism. An elegant and rather restrained ad was part of the successful campaign to market Listerine to Americans.

When an antiseptic is needed use Listerine, the *safe* antiseptic

LAMBERT PHARMACAL COMPANY, SAINT LOUIS, U.S.A.
TORONTO   LONDON   MELBOURNE   PARIS   MADRID   MEXICO CITY

Along with advertising, business used installment plans to encourage Americans to buy goods and services. The booming sales of such consumer goods as automobiles, radios, pianos, and washing machines depended on allowing customers to buy "on time." Credit buying spread so rapidly that the nation's total consumer debt more than doubled from 1922 to 1929.

New Pleasures

The culture of the 1920s offered many pleasures, especially spectator sports, movies, popular music, and radio. Gertrude Ederle was part of a golden age for spectator sports. Tennis, boxing, and auto racing flourished during the decade. The American Professional Football Association, which became the National Football League, played its first season in 1920. Baseball remained the most popular American sport, thanks in part to the exploits of the New York Yankees' home-run-hitting outfielder, Babe Ruth.

While spectator sports enthralled millions, another passive pleasure, the movies, was undeniably the most popular consumer attraction of the 1920s. Movies had matured into a big business commanding the loyalty of millions of Americans. Spreading through the cities and into the suburbs, theaters became larger and more elegant. By the 1920s, lavish movie "palaces," such as the Roxy in New York and the Tivoli in Chicago, were designed to evoke the Orient and other exotic faraway places.

Movie attendance doubled from 40 million a week in 1922 to 80 million a week in 1929. That attendance fueled the development of the handful of film companies that dominated the industry. By the 1920s, the center of movie production had shifted from New York to Hollywood, California. Technological innovation promised that this big business would grow still bigger. In 1927, Warner Brothers successfully released the first sound movie, *The Jazz Singer.*

It was fitting that the first sound movie was about the impact of jazz. Popular music in general and jazz in particular played an important role in the new consumer culture. Created by African Americans in the 1910s, jazz was a rhythmically and harmonically innovative music. The new music emerged in New Orleans, home to the first major jazz composer, Jelly Roll Morton, and to the first jazz superstar, trumpeter and singer Louis Armstrong. As jazz became nationally popular, its focus moved to Chicago and New York, as did so many African Americans.

For young white people, jazz was the music of outsiders, of African Americans. Soon white musicians were contributing to the evolution of the music. For many whites, jazz summed up a period seemingly dominated by the pursuit of liberating pleasures. The 1920s became known as the "Jazz Age."

The great popularity of jazz and other musical genres was made possible by the phonograph, originated by Thomas Edison in the 1870s and modified by other inventors. In the 1920s, the electrical recording microphone dramatically improved the sound quality of records and made the new music accessible to millions of Americans.

A newer technological innovation, the radio, also allowed Americans to hear popular music. After Italian inventor Guglielmo Marconi transmitted the first radio waves through the air in 1895, a series of innovations made possible the inauguration of commercial radio broadcasting in the United States by 1920. The federal government began licensing radio stations the next year.

Jazz pioneers: The Washingtonians, led by pianist, composer, and arranger Edward Kennedy "Duke" Ellington (seated at right). By the end of the 1920s jazz had swept across the nation, and Ellington had become one of the new music's great stars.

Like the movies, radio quickly became big business. By 1923, there were more than 500 stations. Americans tuned in to hear broadcasts of live music, news, sports, and soap operas. To meet the demand for radios, manufacturers turned out more than 2 million sets a year by 1925. Radio, like the movies, played a key role in disseminating the values of consumerism, as corporations rushed to advertise their products by sponsoring radio programs.

A Sexual Revolution

Along with such new pleasures as radio and movies, modern culture offered a new attitude toward an old pleasure, sex. By the 1920s, Americans' sexual attitudes and behavior were changing. During the progressive era, reformers forced the public discussion of such sexual issues as prostitution and venereal disease. The popular amusements of the 1910s and 1920s inundated Americans with sexual images.

The increased openness about sex reflected the growing belief that sexual pleasure was necessary and desirable, particularly within marriage. Married couples increasingly considered intercourse as an opportunity for pleasure as well as procreation.

The new view of marital sexuality helped to change attitudes toward contraception. By the 1910s, an emerging grassroots movement, led by socialists and other radicals, promoted sex education and contraceptives, which were largely illegal. The crusade's best known figure was the fiery former nurse and socialist organizer, Margaret Sanger. In 1915, Sanger coined the term "birth control." Birth control gradually became respectable—and widely practiced—in the 1920s.

Although most Americans still insisted publicly that sexual intercourse should be confined to marriage, and they still condemned homosexuality, a sexual revolution was underway. The emergent modern culture insisted that sexual pleasure was an integral aspect of life.

Changing Gender Ideals

The shifting attitude toward sex was closely tied to new gender ideals. By the 1920s, Americans' sense of what it meant to be female was changing. Since the late nineteenth century, Americans had been talking about the "New Woman," who claimed the right to attend school, vote, and have a career. The "New Woman" of the 1920s was now a sexual being, too. An object of male desire, she was also a fun-loving individual with desires of her own.

The most popular image of the American woman of the 1920s was the vivacious young "flapper," with her short skirt, bound breasts, and bobbed hair. The flapper was likely to wear cosmetics and to smoke cigarettes—practices once associated only with prostitutes.

Symbols of the fun-loving culture of the "Jazz Age": a flapper and two jazz musicians on the cover of McClure's Magazine.

Notions of masculinity were also changing. With the growing emphasis on female needs and desires, men were urged to be attentive and responsive and to focus on the home. As the world of work became less satisfying, experts told men to look for fulfillment in family life. The family man of the 1920s, unlike the stereo-typical Victorian man, was not supposed to be a distant, stern patriarch. Instead, he was a companion to his wife and a doting friend to his children.

In practice, many men still defined themselves in terms of their work, rather than their domestic life. Moreover, American society still regarded women as the primary caretaker of children. Despite the clear change in domestic values, many men were still relative outsiders in the home.

The Family and Youth

Changing gender ideals were directly related to a reconsideration of family life and youth. In the 1920s, the American family no longer played a direct role in economic production. To most Americans, the family was no longer a group of productive workers. Child labor laws increasingly made sure that boys and girls spent their time in school rather than in the workplace. The family became primarily a unit of leisure and consumption. The home was the place where men, women, and children found pleasure and fulfillment, where they congregated around the radio and used their Fleischmann's yeast and Listerine mouthwash.

Reflecting the values of the modern culture, parents became more likely to indulge their children, who enjoyed more toys, possessions, spending money, and pleasures than had earlier generations. The automobile gave young people more mobility, too. With their new freedom, they could begin to create their own sepa-rate culture.

Most adults accepted this situation partly because they admired and envied youthfulness. The modern culture, unhappy with work and anxious for fun, glori-fied youth. "Flaming Youth" became a symbol of the culture of the 1920s.

The Celebration of the Individual

The emphasis on the individual, so evident in changing views of sex, gender, family, and youth, was a fundamental aspect of the modern culture. In addition to Gertrude Ederle and Babe Ruth, Americans admired a host of sports heroes and heroines, in-cluding tennis player Helen Wills Moody, boxer Jack Dempsey, golfer Bobby Jones, and football running back Red Grange. In the 1920s, the movie industry increasingly focused public attention on the distinctive personalities of stars. Individualism was basic to the "New Woman," too.

The resurgence of individualism was not surprising. The belief in the impor-tance of the individual was deeply engrained in the American political economy. Paradoxically, the development of industrial capitalism intensified the importance of both individuals and organizations. As corporations grew larger and produced more, these giant firms needed to stimulate consumerism. Consumerism depend-ed on a willingness to define life in terms of gratifying individual needs and desires.

There were serious obstacles to true individualism in the 1920s. Powerful organizations, including corporations, controlled individual life. Even the most famous individual exploit of the decade depended on organization. On May 20–21, 1927, Charles A. Lindbergh flew his monoplane, *The Spirit of St. Louis*, from New York City to Paris. This first nonstop solo crossing of the Atlantic made Lindbergh an international symbol of what an individual could accomplish, but Lindbergh's feat relied on a group of businessmen who put up the money and a corporation that built the plane. Organization and individualism, the new and the old, were interdependent in the 1920s.

THE LIMITS OF THE MODERN CULTURE

The modern culture had clear limits in the 1920s. For millions of Americans, much of the consumer lifestyle was out of reach. Despite general prosperity, low incomes and poverty persisted. As late as 1928, six out of ten American families made less than the $2,000 a year required for the "basic needs of life."

The spread of the new values was as limited as the spread of prosperity. Many Americans, among them artists and intellectuals, were unwilling to define their lives by the pursuit of pleasure, leisure, and consumption. For them the modern culture represented an unwelcome abandonment of old values. In different ways, fundamentalist Christians, immigration restrictionists, and the Ku Klux Klan demanded a return to an earlier United States. Others, such as Chicanos and African Americans, found that the new culture did not address their needs or had in reality changed very little.

The "Lost Generation" of Intellectuals

Many artists and intellectuals felt alienated from the United States of the 1920s. For white, mostly male writers and artists who came of age during World War I, the conflict represented a failure of Western civilization, a brutal and pointless exercise in destruction. Its aftermath left these Americans angry, alienated, and rootless. In a nation supposedly devoted to individualism, they did not feel free. They were, as the writer Gertrude Stein described them, a "Lost Generation."

However prosperous and peaceful, the postwar years did not reassure the Lost Generation about the course of American life. Artists and intellectuals argued that the nation had not changed much at all. In such works as *Winesburg, Ohio* (1919), novelist Sherwood Anderson portrayed a still-repressive society that denied people real freedom and individuality. The acid-tongued critic H. L. Mencken, editor of the magazine *The American Mercury*, excoriated a provincial and parochial culture.

At the same time, other American artists and intellectuals feared that their country had changed too much. Although excited by the potential of the machine, they noted the toll that industrialization exacted in increasingly routinized work and a culture devoted to the pursuit of superficial pleasures. In his 1922 novel, *Babbitt*, Sinclair Lewis satirized the life of a midwestern Republican businessman obsessed with consumerism. F. Scott Fitzgerald, in such fiction as *This Side of Paradise* (1920) and *The Great Gatsby* (1925), conveyed the sense of loss and emptiness in the lives of fashionable "Flaming Youth."

From a different angle, 12 southern intellectuals, including Allen Tate, Robert Penn Warren, Donald Davidson, and John Crowe Ransom, attacked the modern culture in *I'll Take My Stand: The South and the Agrarian Tradition* (1930). Their essays offered a spirited defense of the rural, traditional culture and lamented an industrial consumer society that demeaned work and exalted individualism.

The artists and intellectuals of the decade did not set off a mass rebellion against modern culture, but they did articulate the ambivalence and uneasiness many people felt. In different and contradictory ways, artists and intellectuals laid out an agenda for Americans as they came to terms with modern, consumer society in the decades to come.

Fundamentalist Christians and "Old-Time Religion"

For many Americans of faith, the rapid growth of the modern culture promoted a sense of profound and unsettling change. The new culture was troubling because it was so secular. American society seemed to define life in terms of material satisfaction rather than spiritual commitment. Many Protestants, feeling that their own churches had betrayed them, resented the influence of liberal Protestants who had tried to accommodate their faith to the methods and discoveries of science and scholarship.

Fundamentalists, or opponents of liberalism, took their name from *The Fundamentals*, a series of essays by conservative Protestant theologians that appeared in 1909. By the end of World War I, fundamentalists dominated the Southern Baptist Convention and were fighting liberals for control of the northern churches.

Fundamentalists rejected liberalism above all for its willingness to question the historical truth of the Bible. The fundamentalist movement urged people to return to biblical, patriarchal, and denominational authority, to what came to be called "old-time" religion.

The high point in the fundamentalist–liberal battle came in a courtroom in Tennessee in 1925. That year, a high school biology teacher, John Scopes, tested a new state law banning the teaching of "any theory that denies the story of the divine creation of man as taught in the Bible, and that teaches instead that man has descended from a lower order of animals." Scopes's trial became a national media event. The chief lawyer for the prosecution was William Jennings Bryan, the former Democratic presidential candidate and Secretary of State who had become a leading crusader for fundamentalism. While Bryan was a long-time champion of rural America, Scopes's attorneys—Clarence Darrow and Dudley Field Malone—represented the city and modern culture. (Malone had helped to finance Gertrude Ederle's swim across the English Channel.) In a dramatic confrontation, Darrow called Bryan to the stand and forced him to concede that the Bible might not be literally accurate. Although Scopes was convicted and fined, Bryan and the fundamentalists lost credibility.

Nativists and Immigration Restriction

While fundamentalist Christianity sought a return to old-time religion, a resurgent nativist movement wanted to go back to an earlier, supposedly more homogenous America. As mass migration from Europe to the United States resumed after World War I, nativist feeling revived among Americans from Western European backgrounds. Thanks to the Russian Revolution and the domestic Red Scare, they associated immigrants with anarchism and radicalism and called for a return to a simpler, less ethnically diverse nation.

This view decisively shaped public policy. In 1921, Congress overwhelmingly passed a law temporarily limiting the annual immigration from any European country to 3 percent of the number of its immigrants who had been living in the United States in 1910. This quota sharply reduced the number of new immigrants from Southern and Eastern Europe, but nativists wanted even tougher action. Congress responded with the National Origins Act of 1924. This limited the annual intake from a European country to 2 percent of the number of its immigrants living in the United States in 1890—a time when there were few Southern and Eastern Europeans in America. The Act also excluded Japanese immigrants altogether. The legislation had the desired effect: Immigration fell from 805,000 arrivals in 1921 to 280,000 in 1929 (see Table 23–1).

TABLE 23–1

The Impact of Nativism: Immigration, 1921–1929			
	(Arrivals in Thousands)		
Origin	1921	1925	1929
Eastern Europe & Poland	138	10	14
Southern Europe	299	8	22
Asia	25	4	4
Mexico	31	33	40
Total	805	294	280

Source: Historical Statistics of the United States, I, 401. (Note: Itemized groups do not add up to totals.)

The Rebirth of the Ku Klux Klan

Nativism and fundamentalism helped spur another challenge to the new cultural order of the 1920s. In 1915, the Ku Klux Klan, the vigilante group that had terrorized African Americans in the South during Reconstruction, was reborn and enjoyed explosive growth after World War I. The "Invisible Empire" borrowed the rituals of the nineteenth-century Klan, including its costume of white robes and hoods and its symbol of a burning cross. Like the old Klan, the twentieth-century version was driven by a racist hatred of African Americans, but the new Klan took on new targets, including Jews, Roman Catholics, immigrants, religious liberalism, and change in general.

The reborn Klan had extremist views but a mainstream, national membership, flourishing in every region, in cities as well as the countryside. The Klan was an extremist group with surprisingly strong roots in "respectable" America.

The Invisible Empire condemned modern culture, charging that the nation now valued "money above manhood." Klan rallies rang with denunciations of big business. Above all, the Klan condemned the new culture of leisure and pleasure. The Klan was hostile to the new gender ideals, to birth control and freer sexuality, and to the independence of youth. In essence, the Ku Klux Klan lamented the transformations of the twentieth century and yearned for an earlier America in which white Protestant males had power over women, youth, and other groups and had nothing to fear from big business.

For several years, the Klan proved extraordinarily successful. At its peak, the organization enrolled perhaps 3 to 5 million secret members. Because so many politicians sympathized with the Klan or feared its power, the organization had considerable political influence. Working with both major parties, the order helped to elect governors, senators, and other officials.

At the height of its power, however, the Invisible Empire collapsed under the weight of scandal. One former imperial wizard was revealed to have drunk alcohol, read pornography, and consorted with prostitutes. Assistants to the current imperial wizard were caught, drunk and nude, in an adulterous tryst. Incidents such as these, along with financial scandals, revealed the lawlessness and hypocrisy of the Klan's leadership. It had also become obvious that most Americans, however uneasy about the new culture, had no desire to support prejudice, lawbreaking, and violence. The Klan's membership dropped precipitously in the late 1920s.

White-robed men, women, and children of the Ku Klux Klan arriving in Cincinnati, Ohio, to celebrate the organization and its defense of "traditional" values.

Mexican Americans

Despite the activities of immigration restrictionists and the Klan, the United States remained a diverse nation at the end of the 1920s, in some ways, more diverse than ever. The struggle of Chicanos, ethnic Mexicans, to make a life in the United States revealed both the opportunities created by the dynamic economy and the limits of the new culture.

In the 1890s the migration of Mexicans began a dramatic, long-term increase. Perhaps a million to a million and a half Mexicans entered the United States legally or surreptitiously between 1890 and 1929. They left primarily to escape the transformation of Mexican agriculture that made it impossible for the rural poor to make a living off the land, and to avoid the upheaval of the Mexican Revolution of 1910 (see Chapter 22, "A Global Power"). Ironically, the restrictionist immigration legislation of the 1920s helped ensure that Mexicans would find work in the United States: Unable to get enough European or Asian workers, employers turned eagerly to Mexico as a source of cheap and often temporary seasonal labor. In particular the Southwest's rapidly developing economy needed workers for mines, railroads, construction gangs, and above all, farms. By the end of the 1920s, Chicanos dominated low-wage labor in the Southwest.

Like a large number of immigrants from Europe, many Mexican migrants did not plan to stay in the United States. They traveled back and forth to their homeland, or returned permanently. Gradually, however, many chose to stay as they developed economic and family ties in the United States. The National Origins Act, which made it costly, time-consuming, and often humiliating for Mexicans to cross the border, also encouraged migrants to remain in the United States. As a result, the Mexican population of the United States rose from 103,000 in 1900 to 478,000 by 1920. At the turn of the century, the majority of immigrants lived in Texas and Arizona, but California, with its booming agricultural economy, rapidly became the center of the Mexican population. The city of Los Angeles, growing phenomenally in the early twentieth century, particularly attracted Mexican migrants. The city's Mexican population, less than 5,000 in 1900, grew to perhaps 190,000 by 1930.

Chicanos, like so many other ethnic groups in the United States, wrestled with complex questions about their national identity. Were they still Mexicans or had they become Americans or some unique combination of the two nationalities? Those questions were more complicated because Mexican immigrants had left one rapidly changing country for another. The meaning of "Mexican" and the meaning of "American" were both fluid. In the United States, moreover, ethnic Mexicans received a mixed reception: While employers were eager for labor, they and many other native-born whites thought that Mexican workers should return to Mexico rather than live permanently in the United States. Many white Americans stereo-typed Mexicans as a lazy and shiftless race who would take jobs from native-born workers and who could not be assimilated into American life and culture. Still other white Americans, drawing on the reform techniques of the progressive era, wanted to "Americanize" Chicanos by teaching them English and the middle-class values of thrift and time discipline.

The economy also presented Chicanos with a mixed message. Limited education and persistent discrimination prevented most from earning the larger incomes needed to enjoy American-style consumerism. In many towns and cities, they were effectively segregated in certain neighborhoods—*barrios*—in poor conditions.

Mexican immigrant workers, posed on the tracks of a railroad in Texas in the 1900s. It was the railroad that helped disrupt life in Mexico and offered the promise of jobs in the United States.

In the face of this ambivalent and often hostile reception, ethnic Mexicans forged their unique identities. In varying degrees, Chicanos clung to their old national identities and adapted to their new home. Mexican Americans, eager to hold onto the advantages they had won by birth and long-time residence in the United States, feared that the immigrants would compete for jobs and cause native-born whites to denigrate all Mexicans alike. The immigrants, in turn, often derided Mexican Americans as *pochos*—bleached or faded people—who had lost their true Mexican identity.

Nevertheless, ethnic Mexicans created a distinctive culture in the United States. For all their differences, Chicanos shared a sense of common cultural origins and common challenges. In a white-dominated society, they saw themselves as *La Raza*—the race—set apart by heritage and skin color.

Mexicans' response to the consumer culture helped create a common identity. Like other American workers, Mexicans went into debt to buy consumer goods. Largely ignored by corporations marketing goods nationwide, the Chicanos supported their own businesses, listened to their own Spanish-language radio programs, and bought records made by Mexican-American musicians. Among the most popular forms of Mexican-American music were *corridos*, the traditional folk ballads from rural Mexico adapted to life in the United States. Singing of things that Mexicans were often reluctant to say, *corridos* testified both to the distinctiveness of Chicanos' culture and to their uneasiness in American culture.

Nevertheless, hundreds of thousands of Mexicans came to the United States and struggled for equal rights and economic progress. In 1928, a farm workers' strike in the Imperial Valley led to the creation of the Federation of Mexican Workers Unions. A year later, Chicano businessmen and professionals in Texas formed the League of United Latin American Citizens (LULAC) in Texas.

African Americans and the "New Negro"

Like Chicanos, African Americans found the new cultural terrain of the United States appealing but unsatisfying. They enjoyed and helped to create the new culture, but modern culture did little to alter discrimination against blacks. Everywhere, African Americans lived with economic inequality.

While discrimination had not changed, many African Americans insisted that they had. The decade that saw the "New Woman" also witnessed the appearance of the "New Negro." This new ideal was partly the product of a fresh sense of freedom as African Americans left the southern countryside for the cities. It was also the product of frustration as African Americans encountered inequality along with opportunity in urban areas. The "New Negro" was militant and assertive in the face of mistreatment by whites.

The "New Negro" was also defined by a profound sense of racial difference. In the 1920s, African Americans applauded the distinctiveness of their life and culture. The Harlem Renaissance was a result of this effort. Harlem, the section of upper Manhattan in New York City where many African Americans had moved since the turn of the century, became a center of artistic and intellectual creativity. Novelists such as Zora Neale Hurston, Jessie Fauset, Claude McKay, Jean Toomer, and Dorothy West; poets such as Langston Hughes and Countee Cullen; and artists such as Aaron Douglas and Augusta Savage produced a new birth of African-American creativity.

The militance of the "New Negro" was reflected in the development of the NAACP, which turned increasingly to African-American leadership. The organization's key figure, W. E. B. Du Bois, became more critical of whites and more deter-mined that white-dominated nations should return Africa to African control. The NAACP also pushed the cause of African-American civil rights more aggressively and attacked the white primary system that denied African Americans any say in the dominant Democratic Party organizations of the South. The NAACP continued a long-time antilynching campaign, which bore fruit in the 1920s, as southern whites were increasingly embarrassed by vigilante justice. In 1921, for example, white min-isters in Athens, Georgia, condemned the burning of John Eberhardt, an African American accused of murder, as "barbarism."

For a time, the NAACP's efforts were overshadowed by the crusades of Marcus Garvey. A Jamaican immigrant to New York City, Garvey founded the Universal Negro Improvement Association (UNIA), which became the largest African-American political organization of the 1920s. Garvey focused on African-American self-help and on Africa. Garvey wanted African Americans to develop their own businesses and thus become economically self-sufficient. Like Du Bois, he insisted that the imperial powers give up their colonial control of the African continent. Sure that blacks could never find equality in a white-dominated nation, Garvey believed African Americans should return to Africa.

While the NAACP attracted mostly middle-class members, UNIA developed a vast following among the African-American working class. In 1919, Garvey launched an economic self-help project, the Black Star Line, which, he promised, would buy ships and transport passengers and cargo. Many of his followers invest-ed in the Black Star Line, but it collapsed due to mismanagement. Garvey himself was indicted for mail fraud in connection with the project. By the end of the decade, federal authorities had deported him to Jamaica, and the UNIA had lost its mass following.

As the fate of the UNIA suggested, militance could be costly for African Americans. The NAACP also saw its membership drop dramatically during the decade. Nevertheless, African Americans' struggles during the 1920s laid the groundwork for more successful struggles in the future.

A "NEW ERA" IN POLITICS AND GOVERNMENT

Uneasiness with modern culture had only a limited impact on American politics and government. Other factors—the resurgence of individualism, the power of organi-zations, and the spread of consumerism—shaped public life more decisively in the 1920s. The decade witnessed the emergence of the modern political system charac-terized by advertising, weak parties, and low voter turnout. A succession of Republi-can presidents monopolized the White House during the decade. The Republican ascendancy brought the return of a political economic vision centered on minimal-ist government and a less internationalist foreign policy.

The Modern Political System

The 1920s marked the emergence of a political system that had been taking shape since the late nineteenth century. The major political parties grew weaker as their control over political culture loosened with the emergence of new media. Unlike newspapers, radio stations and movie theaters had no political affiliations. As a re-sult, partisanship no longer engulfed Americans, and the number of independent voters probably increased.

As the parties weakened, a new, educational political style flourished, emphasizing the objective, nonpartisan presentation of facts. Pressure groups and other organizations used the educational style to lobby voters and legislators about public policies. In Washington, Congress was besieged by lobbyists from corporations, business groups, professional organizations, and single-issue pressure groups such as the Anti-Saloon League.

The other dominant political style of the 1920s drew its inspiration from consumerism. Copying big business, politicians used ads to appeal to voters. Because of the decline of intense partisanship, political advertising campaigns reflected the individualist focus of modern culture, selling the personality of individual candidates.

Nationwide, voter turnout fell from 79 percent for the presidential election of 1896 to just 49 percent in 1920 and 1924. A number of factors accounted for this drop-off: African Americans in the South had been effectively disfranchised, and newly enfranchised women were less likely to vote than men, but white male turnout dropped dramatically, too. The new political styles simply did not engage and motivate voters the way the old-style partisanship had.

The Republican Ascendancy

The chief beneficiaries of the new politics were the Republicans. Determined to win back the White House in 1920, the Republican Party chose an uncontroversial, conservative ticket. Handsome and charismatic, presidential nominee Warren G. Harding of Ohio had accomplished little during a term in the Senate. His running mate, Governor Calvin Coolidge of Massachusetts, was best known for his firm stance against a strike by the Boston police the year before.

The Republican ticket was not imposing, but neither was the opposition. The Democratic presidential nominee, Governor James M. Cox of Ohio, was saddled with the unpopularity of the Woodrow Wilson administration. His running mate, Franklin Roosevelt of New York, was a little-known cousin of former President Theodore Roosevelt who had served as Assistant Secretary of the Navy.

While the Democrats ran an ineffective campaign, the Republicans made excellent use of advertising. And Harding neatly appealed to the reaction against Wilson's activist government, offering a return to normal after the progressive innovations that had disrupted American society during and after the war.

Harding won a huge victory with 60.3 percent of the popular vote, a new record; he won 37 states for a total of 404 electoral votes. Cox carried only 11 southern and border states. The Republican Party substantially increased its majorities in the House and the Senate.

The Harding administration was plagued by revelations of fraud and corruption, some involving the so-called "Ohio Gang," political cronies from Harding's home state. The director of the Veterans' Bureau, caught making fraudulent deals with federal property, went to prison. One of the Ohio Gang, fearing exposure of the group's influence-peddling schemes, committed suicide in 1923.

Harding died suddenly of a misdiagnosed heart attack in August 1923, but the scandals continued. Congressional hearings revealed that former Secretary of the Interior Albert B. Fall had apparently accepted bribes in return for leasing U.S. Navy oil reserves at Teapot Dome, Wyoming, and Elk Hills, California. Teapot Dome, as the scandal came to be called, eventually earned Fall a fine and a jail term. In 1924, another member of Harding's cabinet, Attorney General Harry Daugherty, resigned because of his role in the Ohio Gang.

The parade of scandals damaged the reputation of the dead president, but they did not seriously harm his party or his successor, Calvin Coolidge. The former vice president proved well-suited to the political moment. The picture of rectitude, Coolidge restored public confidence in the presidency after the Harding scandals.

In 1924, Coolidge easily won the presidency in his own right against the Democrat John W. Davis, a colorless, conservative corporate lawyer from West Virginia, and the standard-bearer of the new Progressive Party, Senator Robert M. La Follette of Wisconsin. The choice, insisted Republicans, was either "Coolidge or Chaos." Holding onto the White House and to their majorities in Congress, the Republicans continued their ascendancy.

The Politics of Individualism

The Republicans practiced the politics of individualism. Eager to serve big business, they wanted a political economy driven by individualist values and minimalist government. They denounced the activist, progressive state and called instead for less government and more individual freedom. Coolidge declared that "the chief business of the American people is business."

Despite such slogans, Republicans sometimes used government power to spur economic development. The Federal Highway Act of 1921 provided federal matching grants to improve the nation's roads, and the Fordney–McCumber Tariff of 1922 restored high taxes on imports to shelter American producers from foreign competition.

These measures were exceptions, however. Above all, the Harding and Coolidge administrations called for reduced spending and lower taxes. The Republicans also condemned budget deficits and pledged to reduce the national debt; they succeeded on all counts. Federal expenditures dropped from $6.4 billion in 1920 to $3.1 billion in 1929 (see Figure 23–1). Congress repeatedly cut income and other taxes, but the federal government produced annual budget surpluses and reduced its debt.

Figure 23–1   Shrinking Federal Spending, 1919–1929
Source: Historical Statistics of the United States, II, 1104.

Republicans' commitment to minimal government was obvious in their lax enforcement of progressive-era legislation. During the Harding and Coolidge administrations, the federal government made only weak attempts to enforce prohibition. Congress failed to commit enough money and manpower to stop the production and sale of illegal "bootleg" liquor.

Harding and Coolidge allowed the regulatory commissions of the Gilded Age and the progressive era to atrophy. The Interstate Commerce Commission (ICC) and the Federal Trade Commission (FTC) were effectively controlled by the businesses they were supposed to regulate.

Herbert Hoover, the Secretary of Commerce in both the Harding and Coolidge administrations, had a more activist view of the government's role in the economy than either of his bosses. Trained as an engineer, Hoover had become a national hero by supervising the government's effort to relieve famine in Europe during and after World War I. He aggressively sought ways to enlarge the size and power of the Commerce Department. Sensitive to business interests, Hoover promoted "associationalism"—organized cooperation among business trade groups. However, businessmen did not trust one another enough to make voluntary cooperation effective, and Hoover did not advocate federal action to force them to cooperate. Hoover believed above all in what he called "American individualism."

Republican Foreign Policy

After America's intense involvement in international affairs during World War I, the 1920s were a period of relative withdrawal. No crisis thrust foreign policy to the center of American life. Nevertheless, the United States, the world's greatest power, played an active role around the globe. In the aftermath of World War I, a surging international peace movement developed, supported in the United States by a broad range of women's groups and religious organizations. Their push for disarmament influenced the Harding administration to organize the Washington Naval Conference in 1921. The world's leading naval powers produced the first international arms-reduction agreement. The United States, Great Britain, and Japan agreed to scrap some of their largest ships and, along with France and Italy, to limit the tonnage of their existing large ships, abandon gas warfare, and restrict submarine warfare.

The peace movement was less successful in achieving its second goal, the outlawing of war. In 1928, the United States and 14 other countries signed the Kellogg–Briand Pact foreswearing war as an instrument of national policy. Enthusiastically received in the United States and elsewhere, the measure nevertheless contained no effective mechanism to stop a nation from going to war. U.S. membership in a World Court, the third major goal of the peace movement, was not achieved in the 1920s. Too many Americans believed that the court, like the League of Nations, would undermine U.S. sovereignty.

While Americans debated membership in the court, the U.S. economy became increasingly bound up in the world economy. American investment grew substantially overseas during the 1920s, American bankers made major loans around the world, and American companies exported their products around the world.

The growth of American economic activity abroad complicated the foreign policy priorities of the Harding and Coolidge administrations. In the 1920s, the United States had more interests than ever to protect overseas, but the American people were wary of government action that might lead to war. Many Americans were also uneasy about the nation's continuing military role in its own possessions and in supposedly sovereign nations.

In these circumstances, the Harding and Coolidge administrations tried to pull back from some imperial commitments. Marines withdrew from the Dominican Republic in 1924. American Marines also left Nicaragua in 1925 but returned the next year when the country became politically unstable.

The Harding and Coolidge administrations also attempted to promote a stable world in which American business would thrive. During the 1920s, the United States was involved in negotiations to increase Chinese sovereignty and thereby reduce the chances of conflict in Asia. The United States also tried to stabilize Europe in the years after World War I. With the quiet approval of Republican presidents, American businessmen intervened twice to help resolve the controversial issue of how much Germany should be expected to pay in reparation to the Allies.

Extending the "New Era"

The Republicans' cautious foreign and domestic policies proved popular. There was no serious challenge to the Republican ascendancy as the decade came to a close.

The backlash against modern culture hurt the Democrats more than the Republicans. The Democratic Party depended on support not only from nativists, fundamentalists, and Klansmen, but also from their frequent targets—urban Catholics and Jews. By the mid-1920s, these constituencies had split the party. The antagonism helped doom the Democrats' chances in the 1924 and 1928 elections.

In 1928, the Democrats nominated Al Smith, the governor of New York, for president. The first Irish Catholic presidential nominee of a major party, Smith displeased fundamentalists and nativists. Smith represented a new generation of urban, ethnic Democrats who were ready to use activist government to deal with social and economic problems. Their brand of urban liberalism would be influential in later years, but in 1928, Smith's politics and background could not galvanize a majority of voters.

Meanwhile, Herbert Hoover, the Republican nominee, polled 58.2 percent of the popular vote and carried 40 states for a total of 444 electoral votes—the Republicans' largest electoral triumph of the decade. Moreover, the Republicans increased their majorities in both the House and the Senate. The "New Era" would continue.

CONCLUSION

The Republicans' victory in 1928 underscored the limits of the resistance to modern culture. Like the tides that confronted Gertrude Ederle in the English Channel, nativists, fundamentalists, and Klansmen could not beat back the many changes of the "New Era." As Hoover prepared to take over the White House, the triumph of the new culture and politics seemed assured. The modern culture offered a renewed sense of individual worth and possibility, promised new freedom to women and youth, and held out an alluring vision of material pleasures.

Nevertheless, the modern culture and its Republican defenders were vulnerable. Perhaps more than ever before, the nation's dominant value system equated human happiness with the capacity to pay for pleasures. What would happen if Americans lost their jobs and their purchasing power? The new culture and the "New Era" had survived the dissent of alienated and excluded Americans, but it would not survive the sudden end of prosperity.

CHRONOLOGY

1913	Introduction of assembly line at Ford Motor Company
1919	Black Star Line founded by Marcus Garvey
1920	Beginning of recession
	Beginning of commercial radio broadcasting
	First season of the American Professional Football Association
	Warren G. Harding elected president
1921	Sheppard–Towner Maternity Act
1922	Fordney–McCumber Tariff
	Sinclair Lewis, *Babbitt*
1923	Death of Harding
	Calvin Coolidge succeeds as president
1924	Teapot Dome scandal
	Dawes Plan for German war reparations
	National Origins Act
	Calvin Coolidge elected president
1925	Founding of the Brotherhood of Sleeping Car Porters
	Scopes trial
1926	Gertrude Ederle's swim across the English Channel
1927	Charles Lindbergh's flight across the Atlantic Ocean
	First "talking picture," *The Jazz Singer*
1928	Kellogg–Briand Pact
	Herbert Hoover elected president

FURTHER READINGS

Nancy F. Cott, *The Grounding of Modern Feminism* (1987). Cott's book is a perceptive exploration of feminist ideas and activism.

Lynn Dumenil, *The Modern Temper: American Culture and Society in the 1920s* (1995). Dumenil surveys key elements of the modern culture, including consumerism and changing gender roles, and emphasizes the importance of large-scale organization in American life.

Paula S. Fass, *The Damned and the Beautiful: American Youth in the 1920s* (1977). This monograph details the emergence of a distinctive youth culture during the decade.

Robert H. Ferrell, *The Presidency of Calvin Coolidge* (1998). Ferrell's book offers a balanced examination of the Republicans' use of power in the 1920s.

Robert S. Lynd and Helen Merrell Lynd, *Middletown: A Study in Contemporary American Culture* (1929). This pioneering sociological study of Muncie, Indiana, charts the spread of modern culture in an American community.

Nancy MacLean, *Ku Klux Klan: The Making of the Second Ku Klux Klan* (1994). This study of Klan activity in a Georgia county stresses the importance of the Klansmen's hostility to the modern culture.

Roland Marchand, *Advertising the American Dream: Making Way for Modernity, 1920–1940* (1985). This study shows how the pioneering advertising men defined their profession and tried to shape popular tastes after World War I.

Michael E. McGerr, *The Decline of Popular Politics: The American North, 1865–1928* (1986). This monograph traces the cause of declining voter turnout to changes in political styles.

David Nasaw, *Going Out: The Rise and Fall of Public Amusements* (1993). Nasaw's book engagingly describes the evolution of movies, sports, and other amusements that helped to constitute the consumer culture of the 1920s.

George Sánchez, *Becoming Mexican American: Ethnicity, Culture, and Identity in Chicano Los Angeles, 1900–1945* (1993). A sensitive exploration of the Mexican encounter with life in the United States as the new consumer culture flourished.

 Please refer to the document CD-ROM for primary sources related to this chapter.

24

A Great Depression and a New Deal

1929–1939

Sidney Hillman and the Search for Security • The Great Depression • The First New Deal • The Second New Deal Crisis of the New Deal • Conclusion

SIDNEY HILLMAN AND THE SEARCH FOR SECURITY

"The ideals of the labor movement" Sidney Hillman told his union in 1935, "must be security for every man and woman in the country." Hillman, leader of the Amalgamated Clothing Workers of America (ACWA), argued that the goal must be a fairer, government-moderated capitalism. Throughout the 1930s he worked tirelessly with President Franklin Delano Roosevelt's New Deal to create this new political economy that would, he hoped, provide a greater measure of security to working people.

Born in 1887 in Lithuania, Hillman grew up in a small Jewish village. He was supposed to become a rabbi, but instead embraced socialism and became involved in the revolutionary movements challenging the Russian czar. In 1907 he emigrated to the United States and found work in the clothing industry, where he recognized the insecurity faced by most working people and resolved to fight it.

In 1910 a massive strike in Chicago shaped Hillman's destiny. Begun by a few seamstresses angry at a wage cut, it quickly expanded to more than 40,000 workers and shut down clothing manufacture in the city for months. Hillman emerged as a practical leader who convinced his employer to recognize the union and to arbitrate the dispute.

In 1914 Hillman was offered the presidency of the ACWA, and the union grew rapidly. During World War I Hillman enlisted the help of the government to compel manufacturers of military clothing to accept the union. This move, and the over-heated economy of wartime, expanded the ACWA's membership to nearly 140,000, making it the fourth largest union in the nation.

With the advent of the Great Depression in 1929, as the American economy tumbled, Hillman struggled to keep his union together. After the election of Franklin Roosevelt in 1932, Hillman took a prominent role in the National Recovery Administration and used its provisions for business, government, and labor cooperation to stabilize the clothing industry. This endeavor failed for a variety of reasons, including the fact that workers in most industries remained unorganized.

Hillman and others formed the Committee (later "Congress") on Industrial Organizations (CIO), which quickly organized hundreds of thousands of workers in the steel, auto, electric, and rubber industries. At the same time, Hillman formed Labor's Non-Partisan League to support the re-election of FDR. Roosevelt's triumph in 1936 cemented a decades-long marriage of organized labor and the Democratic Party.

The New Deal pushed America's political economy in the direction Hillman had struggled for all of his life. Government regulation of the financial system prevented the kind of collapse that took place after 1929. Federal officials no longer fought organized labor. The elderly and disabled were protected by Social Security. Unemployment insurance was available to millions of workers, and there was a minimum wage in many jobs. In line with Hillman's dreams, this was capitalism made more stable and more socially responsible.

THE GREAT DEPRESSION

In mid-October 1929 confidence in the continued growth of the stock market suddenly failed, sending tremors throughout the economy. On October 29, "Black Tuesday," stock values lost more than $14 billion, and within the month the market stood at only half its precrash worth. Although the stock market crash did not cause the ensuing depression, it did expose the underlying weakness of the economy.

Causes of the Great Depression

No single factor explains the onset and persistence of the Great Depression. Among the politicians, bureaucrats, and business leaders responsible for addressing the problem, nobody had a clear idea of why things had gone wrong. Today most scholars believe that numerous flaws in the national and international economic structure,

TABLE 24–1

Labor Force and Unemployment, 1929–1941 (Numbers in Millions)			
		Unemployment	
Year	Labor Force	Number	% of Labor Force
1929	49.2	1.6	3.2
1930	49.8	4.3	8.7
1931	50.4	8.0	15.9
1932	51.0	12.1	23.6
1933	51.6	12.8	24.9
1934	52.2	11.3	21.7
1935	52.9	10.6	20.1
1936	53.4	9.0	16.9
1937	54.0	7.7	14.3
1938	54.6	10.4	19.0
1939	55.2	9.5	17.2
1940	55.6	8.1	14.6
1941	55.9	5.6	9.9

Source: United States Department of Commerce, Historical Statistics of the United States (1960), p. 70.

along with ill-conceived government policies, bear a large degree of responsibility for the catastrophe (see Table 24–1).

In the 1920s the base of the economy had begun to shift. New industries that sold complex consumer goods like automobiles, radios, clothing, and processed foods became the driving force. This shift toward a consumer-oriented economy was fueled by favorable business conditions, high rates of employment, and a new willingness to buy on credit. The limits of this market had, however, been reached even before the Great Crash. When the stock market fell, the sudden collapse of purchasing power slowed the transition to the new economy.

A rickety credit and financial system added to the problems of the late 1920s. Even in the boom times banks failed by the hundreds. For rural banks these failures could be traced directly to the crisis in the farm economy. But all over America, financial institutions suffered from inept and criminal management. Banks were free from regulation, and in the boom of the 1920s many invested their depositors' money in the shaky stock market or made risky loans. These practices magnified the impact of the crash by causing banks to fail.

Like the banks, the investment industry was free from regulation and given to misrepresentation, manipulation of stock prices, and corrupt inside deals. The corruption became apparent after the crash and inhibited the ability of legitimate companies to raise money.

Misguided government policies also played a role. The Republican administrations of the 1920s were committed to reducing the interference of government in the economy, lowering taxes on the wealthy, and reducing government spending. As a result, little was done to counter the chaotic state of banks, address the problems of farmers, or redistribute wealth. The Federal Reserve might have dampened speculation in stocks and forced banks to adopt sounder policies or, after the Depression had begun, expanded the currency to promote growth. Instead, the

Harding and Coolidge administrations and the Federal Reserve Board only made matters worse. Moreover, government lacked the data needed to understand and resolve the economic crisis.

The Great Depression was magnified by an international economic system still reeling from World War I. Unable to repay their war debts, Britain, France, and other allies had demanded large reparations from Germany and Austria. The United States had helped to reduce these reparations payments in the mid-1920s but refused to forgive the debts. While the American economy boomed, capital from the U.S. poured into Germany and Austria, flowed back through the Allied nations, and on to American vaults. This cycle was broken with the onset of depression in the United States. The European nations attempted to protect themselves by devaluing their currencies and raising trade barriers. The result was steady economic decline that made reparations and loan repayments impossible. In 1931, the international financial system crashed, bringing with it more American banks and deepening the economic crisis.

The United States Descends into Depression

The Great Depression was a year old when an unemployed worker in Pottstown, Pennsylvania, wrote a harsh letter to President Hoover. "I am one of the men out of work," he explained, "but the rich don't care so long as they have full and plenty." He pleaded with Hoover to speed up aid to "the struggling starving working class [of] under nourished men, women, and children."

Between 1929 and 1933 every index of economic activity showed a slide into depression. Gross national product shrank from $104.4 billion in 1929 to $74.2 billion in 1933. The combined incomes of American workers fell by more than 40 percent. Bank failures increased from 640 in 1928 to 2,294 in 1931. Both exports and imports fell by more than two-thirds.

As business activity collapsed, joblessness skyrocketed. Periodic bouts of unemployment had always been a feature of capitalist economies; what distinguished the Great Depression was the extent and duration of unemployment. At the lowest point of the slump in the early 1930s, between 20 and 30 percent of wage earners were out of work. In 1933 more than 12,600,000 Americans were unemployed.

Behind the grim statistics lay terrible human costs. In the spring of 1930, bread lines appeared in major cities. In the fall apple peddlers crowded street corners hoping to earn a few nickels. Unemployed men and women stood in lines at factory gates desperately seeking work, at soup kitchens hoping for a meal, and at overflowing homeless shelters.

The basic necessities were suddenly hard to get. Schoolteachers reported growing numbers of students listless from hunger. Big city hospitals began receiving children suffering from rickets, a disease caused by a deficiency of vitamin D and niacin. Inadequate protein caused another disease, pellagra, to reappear in many parts of the South. More and more tenants were evicted; more and more banks foreclosed on mortgages. Apartments stood vacant and homes went unsold, yet by 1932 more than 1 million homeless people occupied shanty towns on the outskirts of cities or slept in doorways and alleys. Hoboes traveled railroads and highways in search of something to eat, somewhere to live, and someplace to work.

Farmers faced both economic and environmental disaster. Grain and cattle farmers in the plains states and the West aggressively increased production in the 1920s and then watched the markets for corn, wheat, beef, and pork collapse after the Great Crash. Between 1929 and 1932, farmers' income dropped by two-thirds.

As the Depression deepened, bread lines appeared on the streets of cities all across America.

Then the drought struck. Between 1930 and 1936, the rains stopped in large parts of the South, Southwest, and Great Plains. Exposed by decades of wasteful farming practices, the earth dried up and blew away. Dust storms carried topsoil hundreds of miles, giving a new name—the Dust Bowl—to a large swath of the southern plains. Dust and depression ripped thousands of farm families from the land, sending them to California in search of work.

The Great Depression affected nearly everyone in America, but it was most severe for those already disadvantaged. While the environmental shock of the Dust Bowl affected many poor white farmers, the agricultural depression was more devastating for black and white sharecroppers, workers in the wheat fields of the Midwest, and the migrant labor pools that traveled the East and West Coasts picking fruits and vegetables. In cities, African Americans, who held the least secure jobs, found themselves pushed from unskilled work by desperate white workers.

By 1932 private charities, the major social safety net, failed to meet the needs of desperate citizens. Economic losses reduced the resources of charities and the ability of the better-off to give. Summing up the state of charities, Arthur T. Burns, the president of the Association of Community Chests and Councils, said, "The funds we have are altogether inadequate to meet the situation."

Public moneys were just as scarce. Only eight states provided unemployment insurance, most of it meager. State welfare agencies were poorly funded and stretched beyond their limits. Frustrated politicians and citizens looked to the federal government, but beyond pensions for veterans, little existed in the way of social welfare: no Social Security, no federal unemployment insurance, no food stamps.

The federal government thus found itself under unprecedented pressure to do something to relieve the Depression. Labor leaders and farmers' spokesmen, even bankers and businessmen, abandoned their traditional resistance to a strong cen-

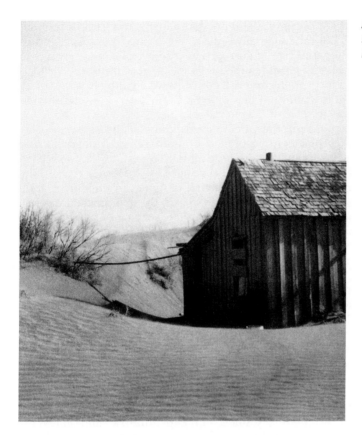

A dust storm threatens to swallow up this prairie home.

tral government. The president of Columbia University suggested that a European-style dictatorship might provide more effective leadership. Others warned of social revolution if the government did not act swiftly.

Hoover Responds to the Depression

In 1928 Herbert Hoover was widely considered the most qualified man in the country to be president. Trained as an engineer at Stanford University, Hoover had roamed the world to build and manage mining operations and had become a millionaire by his mid-20s. Like many other young progressives, Hoover sought to apply business skills to social problems. He won fame as the brilliant administrator who saved Europe from starvation after World War I and then as the powerful Secretary of Commerce during the booming 1920s.

Hoover believed that a complex, modern political economy required accurate economic information, careful planning, and large-scale coordination. At the same time, he rejected the idea that only a large and overbearing government could provide these services. His political philosophy, termed associationalism, envisioned a federal government empowered to collect and disseminate information and structured to encourage voluntary cooperation among businesses but forbidden to intervene further.

Hoover easily won the presidency in 1928. Once in office, he quickly implemented his ideas. One of the first achievements of his administration was the Agricultural Marketing Act of 1929, enacted before the crash. The bill established a Federal Farm Board, which brought together representatives of various farming interests to establish agricultural cooperatives designed to purchase surplus crops and to make the distribution and sale of farm products more efficient.

When the market crashed, Hoover's initial goal was to get business to cooperate to maintain wages and investment. In 1931, as banks were failing at a rate of 25 a week, he encouraged the formation of the National Credit Corporation, in which banks could pool resources to stave off a general collapse.

Hoover approached relief for the unemployed in much the same way. He opposed government unemployment insurance or poor relief. Instead he first organized the President's Emergency Committee on Employment, which sought to convince companies not to lay off workers and cut wages. Next Hoover created the President's Organization on Unemployment Relief, designed to encourage individuals and corporations to contribute to charities to help the unemployed. But the breadth and depth of the Depression overwhelmed these schemes. Crop prices fell so low that the Farm Board could not afford to buy staple crops above the market price. Instead the cooperatives began to dump their surpluses onto the market, further depressing prices and aggravating the plight of farmers.

In September 1931, U.S. Steel cut wages across the board, and countless other companies followed suit. Moreover, parts of Hoover's own administration refused to cooperate with his programs. In November, Treasury Secretary Andrew Mellon, a former banker, refused to support the National Credit Corporation's effort to save the Bank of Pittsburgh from going under. By the beginning of 1932, Hoover's approach to the Depression had come to nothing, and he conceded the need for more aggressive government programs. Recognizing that the National Credit Corporation could not save the banks, he proposed that Congress create the Reconstruction Finance Corporation (RFC). The RFC was authorized to loan $2 billion to corporations and financial institutions to stimulate investment. Other measures to increase government revenues, cut expenditures, and allow the Federal Farm Board to distribute surpluses to the needy were also enacted, but it was too little too late.

Republican policies not only failed to relieve the Depression; they increased its severity. Unable to control his own party, Hoover watched helplessly as Congress passed the Hawley–Smoot Tariff in 1930, raising import duties to their highest level in history, stifling hope that international trade might help the economy, and causing damage to the weak nations of Europe. Despite the president's misgivings about the tariff, he signed the bill into law. At the same time Hoover vetoed massive public works bills sponsored by Congressional Democrats. Finally, Hoover's commitment to the gold standard, like his belief in a balanced budget, stifled economic growth and aggravated the effects of the Depression.

Hoover reinforced his reputation as a cold and aloof protector of the privileged classes by his response to the Bonus Marchers in 1932. In 1924 Congress had promised the veterans of World War I a "bonus" to be paid in 1945. But as the Depression threw millions out of work, veterans asked for their bonuses early. When the government declined, some veterans refused to take no for an answer.

In the summer of 1932 the veterans formed a "Bonus Expeditionary Force" to march on Washington. Riding freight cars and buses, more than 20,000 Bonus Marchers encamped on the Capitol grounds and the swamplands across the Anacostia River. "Families were there galore, just couples and families with strings of kids," one marcher remembered. Hoover ordered the Army to remove the marchers from downtown Washington; General Douglas MacArthur exceeded his orders and attacked the marchers' encampment with tanks and mounted cavalry.

The Bonus Expeditionary Force, or Bonus Marchers, arrived in Washington, DC, in the summer of 1932, the height of the Depression, asking that the government pay veteran's bonuses earlier than scheduled.

Major George S. Patton, with sabre drawn, galloped through the encampment, setting fire to the tents and shacks. Hoover's silent support of MacArthur solidified the president's reputation for callousness.

As Congress struggled to relieve unemployment and suffering, Hoover flatly dismissed the "futile attempt to cure poverty by the enactment of law." By the end of his presidency the "Great Humanitarian" had become sullen and withdrawn. It was a dispirited Republican convention that nominated Hoover for re-election in 1932.

THE FIRST NEW DEAL

When the Democratic convention chose its candidate for president in 1932, Franklin Delano Roosevelt flew to Chicago to accept the nomination in person, a dramatic gesture in an age new to air travel and personal politics. "I pledge myself," he told the enthusiastic crowd, "to a new deal for the American people." Ever since, the reforms enacted between 1933 and 1938 have been known as the New Deal. The programs came in two great waves commonly referred to as the "first" and "second" New Deals. The first commenced with the Hundred Days, a burst of executive and legislative activity following FDR's inauguration.

The Election of 1932

The Depression reached its lowest depths as the 1932 election approached, and the Republicans seemed headed for disaster. Hoover was a symbol of the government's failure. The Democrats had to overcome serious internal divisions if they were to take advantage of the situation.

Throughout the 1920s the Democratic Party had been split along cultural lines between the ethnically diverse, wet (i.e., anti-Prohibition), urban wing concentrated in the North and the East and the Anglo-Saxon Protestant rural southern and western wings. Many ideological divisions separated different constituencies within the party.

The leading candidate for the Democratic nomination, New York's governor Franklin D. Roosevelt, had the background to overcome these divisions. Because FDR came from an upstate rural district he was not associated with the machine politics of New York City. His interest in conservation endeared him to westerners. He had built strong ties to the southern Democrats while serving as Woodrow Wilson's Assistant Secretary of the Navy. As governor of New York Roosevelt had built a strong record of support for progressive social reforms that appealed to urban liberals.

FDR also had immense personal charm. Despite having been crippled by polio since 1921 he proved a tireless campaigner. He was a patrician, raised in wealth and educated at Groton and Harvard. Yet he spoke in clear, direct language that ordinary Americans found persuasive and reassuring.

During the campaign, Roosevelt simultaneously embraced old orthodoxies and enticed reformers with hints of change. He campaigned on a promise to cut government spending, balance the federal budget, and support the gold standard. Yet he also promised government relief for the poor. How he would finance such relief while also balancing the budget, FDR declined to say, but it hardly mattered. In November 1932, the Republicans were swept out of office, and FDR and the Democrats promised "a new deal" for the American people.

Behind the scenes during the campaign, Roosevelt worked to develop a program to fight the Depression. While governor of New York, FDR had surrounded himself with a group of intellectuals, the "Brains Trust," who attempted to convince him that the Depression was caused by the maldistribution of wealth within the United States. Because the rich held onto too large a share of the profits of American industry, the economy was producing much more than Americans could consume. Despite the influence of the Brains Trust, however, Roosevelt never fully bought their ideas and never allowed any one group to dominate his thinking.

It was FDR's comfort with experimentation and chaos that would allow his administration to confront the Depression. Where Hoover had retreated into dogmatism, FDR endorsed "bold, persistent experimentation." Above all, he ordered his officials, "try something." And rather than trying to unite his followers behind a single idea or policy, Roosevelt seemed to enjoy watching his advisers feud while he arranged the final bargains and compromises. FDR's goal, as one adviser put it, was "to put at the head of the nation someone whose interests are not special but general, someone who can understand and treat with the country as a whole."

Roosevelt Takes Command

In the weeks before the inauguration the ailing American banking system took a sharp turn for the worse. In mid-February the governor of Michigan declared an eight-day bank holiday. Stock prices dropped, and banks saw funds fly out of the tellers' windows at an alarming rate. On the morning of the inauguration, New York and Illinois, the two great centers of American finance, joined most of the other states in calling a bank holiday. The New York Stock Exchange and Illinois Board of Trade also closed. To many it seemed like the end of the American economy that had so recently been the envy of the world.

The nation turned expectantly to the new president: Roosevelt did not disappoint. "First of all," he declared, "let me assert my firm belief that the only thing we have to fear is—fear itself, nameless, unreasoning, unjustified terror." In the midst of a frightening financial collapse, FDR's speech, delivered with verve and determination, transformed the mood of the nation almost overnight.

Roosevelt knew that reassuring words alone would not end the banking crisis. He also declared a national bank holiday to last through the end of the week, instructed his Secretary of the Treasury to draft emergency legislation, and called Congress into special session. When Congress convened on March 9 the drafting team had barely finished a bill, but Congress was ready to act. Breaking all precedent, the House unanimously shouted its approval of the bill after less than one-half hour of debate; that evening the Senate did the same with only seven dissents. That night the president signed into law the Emergency Banking Act, a conservative bill aimed at shoring up the existing banking system. It gave the Treasury Secretary the power to determine which banks could safely reopen and which had to be reorganized. It also enabled the RFC to shore up sound banks by buying their stocks. The act legitimized Roosevelt's national bank holiday and extended it through the weekend to give the Treasury time to decide which banks could open the following Monday.

On Sunday night, one week after taking office, FDR went on national radio to deliver the first of his many "fireside chats." Sixty million people tuned their radios to hear Roosevelt explain, in his resonant, fatherly voice, his measures to address the banking crisis. He assured Americans that their money would be "safer in a reopened bank than under the mattress." This was a tremendous gamble because the government was not completely sure how solid most banks truly were, but it worked. The next day, 12,756 banks reopened. The run stopped and deposits began flowing back into the system. The immediate crisis was over.

To ensure that the financial system would remain sound in the long run, the administration next sponsored bills to implement more enduring reforms. The Glass–Steagall Banking Act of 1933 imposed conservative banking practices nationwide. Speculative loans, investments in the stock market, and shady business practices were outlawed. In addition, the newly created Federal Deposit Insurance Corporation protected the savings of individual depositors. Two years later, the Banking Act of 1935 reorganized the Federal Reserve, bringing the entire system under centralized and democratic control.

One reason the banking system had become so vulnerable was its ties to the unregulated securities markets. The banking reforms prohibited such ties, but they left the stock market unregulated. So the administration sponsored a Truth in Securities Act that required all companies issuing stock to file detailed financial reports with the FTC and to disclose accurate information to prospective buyers. The following year Congress passed the Securities and Exchange Act to regulate the markets that sold stocks. It prohibited inside trading and other forms of stock manipulation, gave the Federal Reserve Board the power to control how much credit was available for stock purchases, and established the Securities and Exchange Commission (SEC).

Federal Relief

Roosevelt's unemployment relief programs more sharply distinguished him from Hoover than had the banking measures passed in his first days in office. In May, Congress passed a bill providing a half-billion dollars for relief and creating the Federal Emergency Relief Administration (FERA) to oversee it. Headed by Harry Hopkins, a shrewd social worker and Roosevelt confidant, FERA distributed money at a terrific rate. As winter came on, however, Hopkins convinced Roosevelt that only a massive new federal program could avert disaster. At FDR's request Congress created the Civil Works Administration (CWA), which employed more than 4 million men and women. During the winter, the CWA built roads, schools, and other public buildings and paid teachers' salaries. When spring came the CWA was eliminated—Roosevelt did not want the nation to get used to a federal welfare program—but FERA continued to run programs on a smaller scale.

Roosevelt generally used relief only out of necessity, but he was enthusiastic about one program, the Civilian Conservation Corps (CCC). FDR believed that life in the countryside and service to the nation would have a positive moral impact on the young men of the cities. The CCC employed these young men building roads and trails in the national parks. By 1942 the program had transformed America's public lands and employed more than 3 million teenagers and young adults.

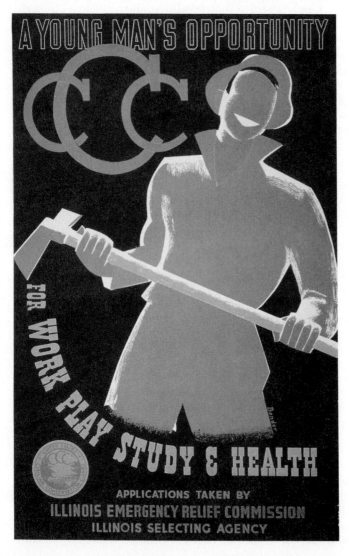

This poster advertises the Civilian Conservation Corps, which put thousands of unemployed Americans to work on conservation projects across the country in the 1930s.

The New Deal Confronts the Farm Crisis

By the spring of 1933, prices of basic commodities like corn, cotton, wheat, and to-bacco had fallen so low that it was not even worth the cost of harvesting them. The banking crisis left farmers without access to the necessary credit to continue, and millions faced foreclosure and homelessness. On the southern plains the Dust Bowl was destroying millions of acres of land. In the Midwest the Farmers' Holiday Asso-ciation was calling for a nationwide strike if Washington did not take immediate ac-tion. New Deal efforts to reform the agricultural economy fell into three broad categories: land-use planning and soil conservation, modernization of rural life, and the effort to eradicate rural poverty. The program that came closest to fulfilling each of these goals was Tennessee Valley Authority (TVA). The TVA was a "corporation clothed with the power of government but possessed of the flexibility and initiative of a private enterprise." According to its administrator, it aimed to change the envi-ronment, the economy, the way of life, and the "habits, social, economic, and per-sonal" of a region that spanned nine states.

One of the most ambitious projects of the entire New Deal, the TVA was also astonishingly successful. The dams it built served many purposes. They controlled flooding in the Tennessee Valley, created reservoirs for irrigation, and provided cheap hydroelectric power to new factory complexes. The TVA took responsibility for soil conservation, reforestation, improved navigation, and even the manufacture of fertil-izer. The poor, mountainous region along the Tennessee–North Carolina border went from growing cotton to manufacturing. The average income of the area's residents increased tenfold. As a comprehensive, centrally planned development scheme, the TVA came closest to the brains trusters' vision. But it was an exception among New Deal programs, which tended to be more fragmented and improvisational.

Inspired by the success of the TVA, the Roosevelt administration established the Rural Electrification Administration (REA) in 1935; by 1945, 40 percent of America's farms had electricity, up from only 10 percent when the REA was found-ed. Electricity made life more comfortable for millions of farm families and allowed industry to move into new areas, bringing jobs to some of the poorest parts of the country.

In many other respects, however, the New Deal did little for the rural poor. Price supports, production controls, soil conservation, irrigation, rural electrifica-tion, and various long-term reforms tended to benefit independent commercial farmers. The landless poor—Mexican migrant workers in the Far West, and tenants and sharecroppers, black and white, in the cotton South—did not benefit from New Deal programs.

Native Americans suffered especially severe rural poverty. Shunted onto reser-vations in the late nineteenth century, by 1930 the majority of American Indians were landless, miserably poor, and subject to the corrupt paternalism of the Bureau of Indian Affairs. Alcoholism, crime, and infant mortality were all more common on reservations than among the poorest whites. John Collier, FDR's Commissioner of Indian Affairs, was determined to correct the situation, and the Indian Reorganization Act of 1934 gave him the power to try. Under the New Deal, forced land sales were ended and the reservations were enlarged. Tribal democracy replaced bureaucratic authority. In an effort to preserve Indian cultures, Collier used the agencies of the New Deal to build progressive schools on the reservations. The same agencies built hospitals and implemented soil conservation programs.

But the problems of Native Americans were too great even for someone as sym-pathetic and powerful as Collier. Congressional opponents remained committed to

Homeless share-croppers shortly after being evicted from their farms by the landowners.

the principle of forced assimilation. Even on its own terms Collier's plan could be only partially successful. What worked for the Pueblo Indians might not work for the Navajos, for example. And Indians themselves were divided over policies and goals. As a result, while the New Deal relieved some poverty among Native Americans, it did not solve the long-term problem.

The Flight of the Blue Eagle

Reviving manufacturing was the key to ending the Depression. However, FDR had no fixed plan for industrial recovery and preferred to wait until business interests could agree on one before acting. Congress, however, moved independently to pass a bill aimed at spreading employment by limiting the work week to 30 hours. Heading off what he thought an ill-conceived plan, Roosevelt put forward the National Industrial Recovery Act. It created a National Recovery Administration (NRA) and mandated that business, labor, and government officials negotiate a code of business conduct for each industry that would regulate trade practices, wages, hours, and production quotas. The hope was to raise prices by limiting production, simultaneously protecting the purchasing power of workers. Big businesses were granted exemptions from the antitrust laws if they signed onto the codes. Organized labor was guaranteed the right of collective bargaining. Finally, $3.3 billion was earmarked for job creation.

The NRA suffered from many of the same problems as Hoover's earlier schemes. It brought together representatives from hundreds of industries to draw up their respective codes, but the process tended to be dominated by business. Few strong unions existed, and the government lacked personnel trained in industrial management. Smaller businesses were shut out, leaving America's largest corporations to write the codes in their interest. For a time in 1933 and 1934 the NRA's

Blue Eagle, the symbol of compliance with the codes, flew proudly over the American economy. Soon, however, dissatisfaction dampened enthusiasm, and by 1935 the eagle had come to roost atop a shaky and unpopular agency.

THE SECOND NEW DEAL

The first Hundred Days had been extraordinary by any standard. Congress had given the president unprecedented power to regulate the economy. The financial system had been saved from collapse. Federal relief had been extended to the unemployed. The agricultural economy was given direct federal support. Almost everyone was dazzled by what had happened, but not everyone was pleased. If Hoover had been too rigid, FDR struck even his admirers as hopelessly flexible. By 1935 the New Deal was besieged by critics from all directions. But rather than becoming demoralized, Roosevelt responded to criticism by keeping Congress in session throughout the hot summer of 1935. The result was another dramatic wave of reforms, the second New Deal.

Critics Attack from All Sides

In May 1935 one of William Randolph Hearst's emissaries traveled to Washington to warn Roosevelt that the New Deal was becoming too radical. Hearst had long been one of the most powerful newspaper publishers in America, and like many businessmen he had "no confidence" in many of Roosevelt's advisers. Saving capitalism had always been one of Roosevelt's goals, but shortsighted businessmen and financiers never appreciated his efforts. The rising hostility of the business and financial communities was of concern to FDR's re-election campaign in 1936. These wealthy Americans rejected virtually all of the president's overtures. And after some initial gestures of cooperation, most industrialists became critics of the NIRA. In the long run they proved more potent critics than all of Roosevelt's radical opponents combined.

The fate of the Communist Party illustrates the difficulties radicals faced during the New Deal. On the one hand, the 1930s were "the heyday of American Communism." Jolted by the apparent collapse of the capitalist system, perhaps a quarter of a million Americans joined the Communist Party. The Communists had proved themselves skillful grassroots organizers at a critical moment in the history of American labor unions. The Communist Party also took the lead in defending the Scottsboro Boys, a group of nine young African-American men falsely accused of raping two white women in Alabama. Yet the party's appeal was greatest after 1935 when it adopted a "popular front" strategy of support for the New Deal. Thus the Communists were most popular when they were pragmatic rather than revolutionary. While Americans joined the Communist Party by the tens of thousands, they also left it by the tens of thousands.

The Socialists fared even worse. Notwithstanding the appeal of its lively and intelligent standard-bearer, Norman Thomas, the Socialist Party lost ground during the 1930s, polling 900,000 votes in the presidential election of 1932 but only 200,000 in 1936. The reason was simple: Roosevelt had stolen the socialists' thunder. Although FDR was committed to saving the capitalist system, he also believed that it was deeply flawed and needed fundamental reforms. Socialists were skeptical as to just how much reform Roosevelt wanted.

More troublesome to Roosevelt were Coughlinism, Townsendism, and Huey Longism. Father Charles Coughlin was a Catholic priest in Detroit who attracted listeners to his weekly radio show by blaming the Depression on international bankers and Wall Street as well as Communist and Jewish influence in Washington. His solution was to nationalize the banking system and inflate the currency. FDR was careful not to anger Coughlin, and at first the radio priest attacked the New Deal while defending Roosevelt personally. But by 1935 Coughlin was openly critical of the president. He formed the National Union for Social Justice to pressure Congress to enact further reforms.

In California, Dr. Francis Townsend offered a reform program that was especially popular among older Americans. Through a transaction tax of 2 percent, the government would fund generous retirement pensions. By requiring the elderly retirees to spend all of their pensions each month, the program would pump money into the economy and stimulate a recovery. Townsend's figures did not add up, but his following multiplied dramatically. Townsend clubs appeared across the country, and several dozen congressmen pledged their support.

Huey Long's "Share Our Wealth" program was more comprehensive than Townsend's and more popular than Father Coughlin's. As governor of Louisiana, Long had amassed nearly dictatorial powers, which he used to build roads, hospitals, and schools; his programs reduced adult illiteracy, enhanced the quality of Louisiana State University, improved conditions in prisons and mental asylums, and established more rigorous training for doctors and nurses. After moving from the governorship to the Senate, Long broke with the president and by 1934 was proposing his own alternative to the New Deal.

Because Long believed that the Depression was caused by the maldistribution of income, his program called for the redistribution of wealth through confiscatory taxes on the rich and a guaranteed minimum income of $2,500 per year. Like Townsend's and Coughlin's proposals, Long's "Share Our Wealth" program rested on a kernel of truth about the American economy. Elderly Americans were indeed desperate, the currency did need to be inflated, and wealth was unequally distributed in the United States. Hence the reforms proposed by Townsend, Coughlin, and especially Long seemed plausible to millions of Americans.

As criticism of the New Deal grew, the conservative-dominated U.S. Supreme Court struck down many of the key laws of the first Hundred Days. On May 27, 1935, the Court handed down a decision in *Schechter Poultry Corporation* v. *United States* that invalidated the NIRA. The justices ruled that the NIRA was unconstitutional and did so in a way that made it difficult for Congress to regulate the economy to any significant degree. Then, in January 1936, the Supreme Court overturned the Agricultural Adjustment Act. By the spring it seemed that the federal government was powerless to address the economic emergency.

Roosevelt Launches the Second Hundred Days

FDR loved a good fight. After 1935 the rhetoric flowing from the New Dealers became noticeably more radical. When the Supreme Court invalidated the NIRA, Roosevelt kept Congress in session through the sweltering Washington summer and forced through a raft of legislation in a "second Hundred Days," which marked the beginning of the second New Deal.

A few of the new proposals were designed to salvage important pieces of the NIRA. The Works Progress Administration (WPA), for example, revived the popular jobs program. Similarly, the Wagner Act recovered and strengthened Section 7(a) of the NIRA, which had guaranteed workers the right to bargain collectively.

Other reforms of the second Hundred Days were designed to silence radical critics. Hoping to undermine Huey Long, Roosevelt proposed a Revenue Act that would encourage a "wider distribution of the wealth" by raising estate and corporate taxes and raising personal income taxes in the top bracket to 79 percent.

Despite the political motives behind the bill, it made certain economic sense. Before the 1935 Revenue Act most New Deal programs had been financed by regressive sales and excise taxes. Thereafter programs were funded with progressive income taxes that fell most heavily on the rich.

The Wheeler–Rayburn Act was another major achievement of the second New Deal. The law grew out of Roosevelt's concern about the concentrated power of holding companies in the nation's utility industry. It gave the SEC the power to break up utilities that made no geographic sense. It took many years for the SEC to rationalize the nation's power industry, but forcing power companies to focus on specific regions actually made them more profitable.

The first New Deal had been preoccupied with the dire emergency of 1933. The second New Deal left a more enduring legacy. The administration put in place a Social Security system that became the centerpiece of the American welfare state for the remainder of the century, and it allied itself with organized labor, thereby creating a new and powerful Democratic Party coalition. By late August 1935, the most important achievements of the New Deal were in place.

Social Security for Some

Bolstered by big Democratic gains in the 1934 elections, FDR pursued a massive effort to fund work relief by sponsoring the Emergency Relief Appropriations Bill. Providing nearly $5 billion, more than the entire 1932 federal budget, it breathed new life into the relief programs of the first New Deal and created a new WPA, headed by Harry Hopkins. The WPA lasted for eight years, employing as many as 3.3 million Americans at one time. Two-thirds of WPA workers were unskilled, but the WPA also commissioned artists to decorate post offices and write plays, and WPA historians collected the stories of mill workers and former slaves. The program was hugely popular.

Critics complained with some justice that the WPA put people to work on meaningless "make-work" jobs or that the workers were incompetent. Political corruption was a more serious problem. WPA officials, especially at the local level, often used the agency as a patronage machine. Corruption was not rampant, but there was enough to provide ammunition to the WPA's opponents. Because the WPA paid its workers the "prevailing" local wage, its effectiveness differed from one locale to another. In many states, particularly in the South, local officials openly discriminated against poor African Americans. Finally, the WPA was never funded adequately, and its funds were doled out unpredictably, making it difficult to plan public-works projects rationally.

In the face of these obstacles, however, the WPA did a remarkable job. New York City used WPA employees to transform its public parks into a model for recreational facilities nationwide. In Georgia the WPA built 145 libraries, especially in isolated rural counties. The WPA Women's and Professional Division hired hundreds of thousands of women, and youth programs put hundreds of thousands of young men and women through high school and college. The WPA was never able to employ all those who needed work, but for millions of Americans it provided immediate relief from hunger and misery.

In addition to short-term relief, the New Deal created a permanent system of long-term economic security. In 1932 there were no national programs of unemployment insurance, workers' compensation, old-age pensions, or aid to needy children. As a result, most Americans had little or no protection from economic calamity.

The Social Security Act of 1935 took a critical first step toward providing such protection. It established matching grants to states that set up their own systems of workers' compensation, unemployment insurance, and aid to families with dependent children. Even more important, the federal government created a huge new Social Security system that guaranteed pensions to millions of elderly Americans. FDR insisted that it be funded as an insurance plan with payroll taxes paid by employees and employers to protect the system from the political attacks that welfare programs commonly encountered.

Most New Dealers had hoped to go further. Secretary of Labor Frances Perkins wanted to include agricultural laborers and domestic servants, mostly women and blacks, in the new Social Security system, but that would have provoked enough opposition from southern conservatives to kill the program.

Powerful conservative opposition thus limited the extent of the New Deal's plans for social welfare and economic security. As a result, welfare and insurance programs were weaker in the South than in the North and weaker for women and blacks than for white men. Despite such strong opposition, the New Deal actually accomplished a great deal. By 1939 every state had established a program of unemployment insurance and assistance to the elderly. More Americans than ever before were thereby protected from the ravages of unemployment, disability, poverty, and old age.

Labor and the New Deal

The 1930s saw unions take a new role in America's political economy. The number of Americans organized in unions leaped by the millions, and by 1940 nearly one in four nonfarm workers was unionized. Unions also became key players in the Democratic Party.

During the 1930s FDR moved from grudging acceptance to open support for organized labor. Section 7(a) of the NIRA, which had guaranteed workers the right to bargain collectively, was the first indication of this shift. Across the country workers sensed the change and responded with a spontaneous wave of strikes. At the same time, a talented group of national leaders, including John L. Lewis of the United Mine Workers, Sidney Hillman of the Amalgamated Clothing Workers, and David Dubinsky of the International Ladies' Garment Workers, all took advantage of Section 7(a) to launch huge organizing drives.

Employers fought back, using methods to intimidate workers—espionage, blacklisting, and armed assault—that had worked in earlier decades. But when it became clear that the federal government would now protect workers seeking to organize and bargain collectively, employers formed company unions to thwart independent action by workers. By 1935 the employers seemed to be winning, particularly when the Supreme Court declared the NIRA, including Section 7(a), unconstitutional. But the hopes of organized labor were kept alive by an influential and imaginative liberal senator from New York, Robert Wagner.

Wagner took the lead in expanding the limited protections of Section 7(a) into the National Labor Relations Act, also known as the Wagner Act. Wagner believed that workers had a basic right to join unions and hoped that effective unions would stimulate the economy by raising workers' wages. Like Section 7(a), the Wagner Act guaranteed workers the right to bargain collectively, but it also outlawed company unions, prohibited employers from firing workers after a strike, and restricted many traditional tactics companies used to inhibit the formation of unions. Most important, the Wagner Act created the National Labor Relations Board (NLRB) to enforce these provisions.

While Wagner and his colleagues moved in Congress, John L. Lewis and Sidney Hillman pressed the conservative leadership of the AFL to accept the principle of industrial unions, which would organize workers in an entire sector of the economy, such as steel manufacturing. The traditionalists of the AFL held fast to the notion that workers should instead be organized by crafts. Thwarted by the AFL leadership, Lewis, Hillman, and their allies formed a rival organization that eventually became the CIO.

The CIO organized some of the most powerful and prosperous industries in the country. The government's new attitude toward organized labor played an important role. For example, when the United Automobile Workers initiated a series of "sitdown strikes" against General Motors, neither FDR nor the Democratic governor of Michigan sent in troops to remove workers from the factories they were occupying. In addition, the NLRB protected the new unions from an employer counterattack during the recession of 1937.

Thus by the late 1930s a crucial political alliance had been formed. A newly vigorous labor movement had become closely associated with a reinvigorated Democratic Party. Having won the ability to organize, industrial workers used their power to increase their wages, enhance their job security, improve their working conditions, and secure their retirements. Organized labor now had a new stake in preserving the system from economic collapse. The successful unionization of industrial workers helped stabilize American capitalism.

The New Deal Coalition and the Triumph of 1936

Franklin Roosevelt believed that to overcome his varied opposition and win re-election he had to create a Democratic coalition far broader than that of 1932. Roosevelt was not interested in building a cult of personality but in rebuilding the party system. By 1936, under Roosevelt's charismatic leadership, the Democratic Party was transformed. For the first time since the Civil War, a majority of voters identified themselves as Democrats, and the Democrats retained majority status for decades. FDR achieved this feat by forging a coalition between the competing wings of the party. In the end, however, the coalition that made the New Deal possible also limited its progressivism.

The rural South had been overwhelmingly Democratic for a century, and it remained a crucial part of the party's coalition. But Democrats became the majority because the New Deal increased the party's appeal to urban voters in the North. This shift was well underway during the 1920s, but hard times and the New Deal confirmed the loyalty of ethnic blue-collar voters to the Democratic Party.

Both symbolism and substance attracted the urban working class to the New Deal. Jews and Catholics (Italian as well as Irish) served Roosevelt as advisers and cabinet officers. Many more accepted appointments to the federal judiciary. More important, thousands of working-class city dwellers found relief from the Depression through New Deal jobs programs. Those same programs generated patronage appointments that endeared Roosevelt to local Democratic machines. Finally, FDR's backing of the Wagner Act and his growing support for organized labor were reciprocated by the unions. The CIO poured $600,000 into Roosevelt's 1936 campaign, and its members helped get out the vote.

The New Deal's programs for the poor and unemployed help to explain the dramatic shift of allegiance among African-American voters. As they migrated to the urban North, blacks became a significant voting bloc, bringing with them their traditional allegiance to the Republicans, the party of Abraham Lincoln. But the Depression and the New Deal broke this pattern, and by 1936 northern blacks voted overwhelmingly for FDR and the Democrats. This was not because the

Democrats had suddenly become the party of civil rights: The New Deal sponsored no legislation against discrimination, and FDR sat silently as Congress rejected anti-lynching laws.

Nevertheless, New Deal agencies offered more assistance to poor, unemployed blacks than any previous federal programs, and some New Dealers were determined to run their agencies without discrimination. Mary McLeod Bethune, a prominent black educator and close friend of Eleanor Roosevelt, served as director of the National Youth Administration's Office of Negro Affairs, which gave jobs and training to 300,000 young African Americans. Bethune successfully pressured other New Deal administrators to open their programs to blacks. With perhaps a million black families depending on the WPA by 1939, black voters had solid economic reasons for joining the New Deal coalition.

A similar logic explains why prominent women reformers threw their support to the Democrats. FDR had no feminist civil rights agenda, and New Deal programs discriminated against women by offering them lower pay, restricting them to stereotypical "female" jobs, and terminating women's programs before all others. But as with blacks, women benefited in unprecedented numbers from New Deal programs. Through the first lady, Eleanor Roosevelt, a small but influential group of women suddenly assumed a prominent place in national politics. For the first time in American history a woman, Frances Perkins, was appointed to the cabinet.

The most prominent female reformer associated with the New Deal was Eleanor Roosevelt. She was the last representative of a woman's reform tradition of the late nineteenth and early twentieth centuries. She had worked in a settlement house and campaigned for suffrage and progressive causes. She became for many Americans the conscience of the New Deal, the person closest to the president who

New York Governor Herbert Lehman, Eleanor Roosevelt, and FDR after a speech in which the president rejected charges that his administration promoted communism. In fact, FDR was committed to saving capitalism by reforming it.

spoke most forcefully for the downtrodden. Her reputation for compassion protected her husband in at least two ways. Liberals who might have been more critical of the New Deal relied on Eleanor Roosevelt to push the president toward more progressive reform. At the same time, conservatives who were charmed by FDR's personality blamed all the faults of the New Deal on his wife.

Although four years of the New Deal had not lifted the Depression, the economy was steadily improving. Jobs programs had put millions of Americans to work. The banking crisis was over. The rural economy had stabilized. Based on this record and the backing of his powerful coalition of southern whites, northern urban voters, the labor movement, and blacks, FDR won re-election by a landslide in 1936. He captured over 60 percent of the popular vote and, in the electoral college, defeated his Republican opponent Alf Landon in every state but Maine and Vermont. The new Democratic coalition also won sweeping command of the Congress. Seventy-six Democratic senators faced a mere 16 Republicans; in the House, the Democratic majority was 333 to 89. Roosevelt now stood at the peak of his power.

CRISIS OF THE NEW DEAL

When the members of the new Congress took their seats in 1937 it seemed as if Roosevelt was unbeatable, but within a year the New Deal was all but paralyzed. A politically costly fight to "pack" the Supreme Court and a sharp recession encouraged the New Deal's enemies and provoked an intellectual crisis within the administration. In 1938, when the Republicans regained much of their Congressional strength, the reform energies of the New Deal were largely spent.

Conservatives Launch a Counterattack

With conservative opponents seemingly vanquished, progressives like Frances Perkins hoped that the legislation hastily passed in the rush of the first Hundred Days, or in compromises with Congressional conservatives, could now be strengthened.

FDR himself appeared to be poised to launch the next great wave of New Deal reforms, but one barrier stood in the way: the Supreme Court. The court had already struck down the NIRA and the AAA, and recent rulings made it seem that not much of the second Hundred Days would survive. Before he went on, Roosevelt wanted to change the court. Having had no opportunity to appoint any new justices, FDR instead launched a reckless and unpopular effort to "reform" the Court. He proposed legislation that would allow the president to appoint a new justice for every sitting member of the court over 70 years of age. This "court packing" plan, as Roosevelt's opponents labeled it, would have given the president as many as six new appointments.

Conservatives smelled their chance. Ever since the first Hundred Days they had complained that Congress had given the president "dictatorial" powers to meet the economic crisis. The court reform seemed to confirm their warnings. Conservatives formed the National Committee to Uphold Constitutional Government. They skillfully cultivated Congressional allies, allowing Democrats to take the lead in opposing court reform. Even the New Deal's allies refused to campaign for the president's bill. By the end of the summer of 1937, it was all over and the bill defeated.

Ironically, Roosevelt eventually won his point: The Supreme Court backed away from its narrow conception of the role of the federal government, and several of the justices soon retired, giving FDR the critical appointments he needed. As a result, New Deal legislation was protected from judicial assault.Nevertheless, FDR's court reform plan proved a costly political mistake. Its defeat emboldened the president's opponents. Critics who had remained silent for fear of presidential retribution now joined the opposition.

In November 1937 the administration's opponents gathered their forces and produced a Conservative Manifesto. In its call for balanced budgets, states' rights, lower taxes, and the defense of private property and the capitalist system, the manifesto heralded the themes around which conservatives would rally for the remainder of the century. Behind the Manifesto lay some hard political realities that drove the conservatives into opposition.

Southern congressmen were motivated by special regional concerns. Federal programs that offered an alternative to the bare subsistence wages of black and white agricultural workers compromised the ruling political economy of the South. Southern conservatives began to complain and to blame the New Deal.

In the South and West there were growing fears that the New Deal was too closely tied to the urban working class in the Northeast. To counteract this trend, conservatives appealed to the deeply rooted American suspicions of the central government. Still, the conservatives were not strong enough to block all New Deal legislation, because farm-state representatives needed Roosevelt's support. In late 1937 the administration succeeded in passing a Housing Act and a new Farm Tenancy bill. In 1938 Congress passed the Fair Labor Standards Act, the last of the major laws of the New Deal. It required the payment of overtime after 40 hours of work in a week, established a minimum wage, and eliminated child labor.

However, the 1938 Congressional elections gave the conservatives the strength they needed to bring New Deal reform to an end. Republicans gained 75 seats in the House and were now strong enough in the Senate to organize an effective anti-New Deal coalition with southern Democrats. By then, a jolting recession had created a crisis of confidence within the New Deal itself.

The "Roosevelt Recession" and the Liberal Crisis of Confidence

During the 1936 campaign Roosevelt was stung by conservative criticism of his failure to balance the budget. He had leveled the same charge against Hoover four years earlier, but the demands of the Depression made it dangerous to reduce spending. Furthermore, deficit spending seemed to be reviving the economy.

Hoping to silence his conservative critics after his re-election, Roosevelt ordered a sharp cutback in relief expenditures in 1937. On top of a contraction of the money supply ordered by the Federal Reserve and the removal of $2 billion from the economy by the new Social Security taxes, Roosevelt's economy measure was disastrous. Once again, the stock market crashed and industrial production plummeted. Even the relatively healthy automobile, rubber, and electrical industries were hurt. Opponents now carped about the "Roosevelt recession" and accused the administration of destroying business confidence.

This was an important turning point in the intellectual history of the New Deal, as well as twentieth-century American politics. Until 1938 the association between economic health and balanced budgets was firmly entrenched in government and the business community. Experience with the recession of 1937–1938 converted most young New Dealers to the newer economic theories of English economist John Maynard Keynes. During periods of economic stagnation, Keynes argued, the government needs to stimulate recovery through deficit spending. The goal of fiscal policy was no longer to encourage production, but to increase purchasing

CHRONOLOGY

1928	Herbert Hoover elected president
1929	Stock market crash
1931	National Credit Corporation authorized
1932	Franklin Roosevelt elected president
1933	FDR declares a bank holiday
	First Hundred Days
	Emergency Banking Act passed
	Economy Act passed
	Civilian Conservation Corps (CCC)
	U.S. goes off the gold standard
	Agricultural Adjustment Act (AAA)
	Emergency Farm Mortgage Act
	Tennessee Valley Authority (TVA)
	Truth in Securities Act
	Home Owners' Loan Act
	National Industrial Recovery Act (NIRA)
	Glass–Steagall Banking Act
	Farm Credit Act
1935	Second Hundred Days
	NIRA declared unconstitutional
	National Labor Relations Act
	Social Security Act
1936	AAA overturned
	Gone With the Wind published
	FDR re-elected
1937	FDR announces "court packing" plan
	Economy goes into recession
1938	Second Agricultural Adjustment Act
	Fair Labor Standards Act
	New Deal opponents win big in Congress
1939	Administrative Reorganization Act

power among ordinary consumers. Roosevelt himself never fully embraced these theories, but members of his administration found them attractive. Moreover, the massive inflow of government funds during World War II brought breathtaking economic revival and seemed to confirm the wisdom of Keynesian economics. Until the 1980s, presidents of both parties subscribed to Keynesian theory.

CONCLUSION

The New Deal did not bring an end to the Great Depression. Nevertheless, Franklin Roosevelt achieved other important goals. "I want to save our system," he told a White House visitor in 1935, "the capitalistic system." By this standard, the New Deal was a smashing success. Still more impressive, the New Deal allowed Americans to survive the worst collapse in the history of capitalism while preserving the democratic political system. Perhaps most important, the New Deal created a system of security for the majority of Americans. National systems of unemployment compensation, old-age pensions, and welfare programs grew from the stout sapling planted during the 1930s. Farm owners received new protections, as did the very soil of the nation. Workers won the right to organize, work hours were limited, child labor was ended, and a minimum wage was enacted. Moreover, the financial system was made more secure to the benefit of investors, depositors, and the economy as a whole.

America was a safer place at the end of the 1930s, but the world had become more dangerous. After 1938 the Roosevelt administration was increasingly preoccupied with the threatening behavior of nations that had responded poorly to the challenge of the Great Depression.

FURTHER READINGS

Alan Brinkley, *The End of Reform* (1995). An intellectual history of the "internal crisis" of the New Deal.

Lizabeth Cohen, *Making a New Deal: Industrial Workers in Chicago, 1919–1939* (1990). This work successfully combines labor history with the history of popular culture.

James Goodman, *Stories of Scottsboro* (1994). A highly readable retelling of the Scottsboro incident through the eyes of various participants.

Ellis W. Hawley, *The New Deal and the Problem of Monopoly: A Study in Economic Ambivalence* (1966). One of the first scholarly critiques of the New Deal.

Eric Hobsbawm, *The Age of Extremes: A History of the World, 1914–1991* (1994). This text puts the Depression into a global context.

Richard Hofstadter, *The American Political Tradition* (1948). The highly critical chapter on FDR is a classic that anticipated most later critiques.

David M. Kennedy, *Freedom From Fear: The American People in Depression and War* (1999). A strong recent synthesis of the period from 1933 to 1945.

William E. Leuchtenberg, *Franklin D. Roosevelt and the New Deal* (1963). Still the best short survey of the New Deal and the president who made it.

Arthur Schlesinger, Jr., *The Age of Roosevelt*, 3 vols. (1957–1960). A literary and scholarly masterpiece of heroic history.

 Please refer to the document CD-ROM for primary sources related to this chapter.

CHAPTER

25

The Second World War

1941–1945

A. Philip Randolph • Island in a Totalitarian Sea • Turning the Tide
Organizing for Production • Between Idealism and Fear
Closing with the Enemy • Conclusion

A. PHILIP RANDOLPH

"Who is this guy Randolph?" Joseph Rauh asked. "What the hell has he got on the President of the U.S.?" It was June 1941 and Rauh, a government attorney, had just been instructed to draft a presidential order prohibiting discrimination on grounds of "race, color, creed, or national origin" in defense industries. Reversing decades of official support for legalized racism, it would use the economic muscle of the federal government to overturn job segregation nationwide. The president was bending to pressure, Rauh learned, from African Americans led by a labor organizer named A. Philip Randolph.

Randolph had founded the largest African-American labor union, the Brotherhood of Sleeping Car Porters, in 1925. Porters traveled the railroads as baggage handlers and valets, and during the Depression years Randolph's influence extended into every big-city station and small-town depot. According to the Federal Bureau of Investigation, which kept a secret file on Randolph's activities, he was a socialist. "Randolph believes race discrimination stems from the economic abuses of capitalism," a Bureau informant reported, "he joined the Socialist Party because it advocates unconditional social, political, and economic equality for Negroes."

In 1941, it looked to Randolph like only a matter of months before the United States would enter the war in Europe and Asia. President Franklin Roosevelt was sustaining Britain's struggle against Nazi Germany with weapons, food, and fuel, and Japan's drive into Southeast Asia threatened the U.S. colony in the Philippines. Randolph believed "that Negroes make most fundamental gains in periods of great social upheaval." War would create an opportunity to achieve equality, but only if African Americans demanded it.

In January 1941, Randolph called for African Americans to march to Washington to demand an end to job discrimination. The March on Washington Movement (MOWM) was largely a bluff. No buses were chartered, and there were no plans for where the thousands would sleep and eat, but Roosevelt and the FBI worried.

Roosevelt also had the power to accede to Randolph's demands. Using his leverage over thousands of manufacturers who had federal contracts in preparation for war, the president could single-handedly desegregate a large portion of the economy. The organizers agreed to cancel the march in return for a presidential directive—Executive Order 8802—establishing a Fair Employment Practices Committee to ensure fairness in hiring.

It was a victory for civil rights and for Randolph personally. Within a year, thousands of African Americans would be working at high-tech jobs in aircraft factories and arms plants. Randolph had recognized that war created an opening for changing the economic and political rules of the game. The social upheaval of war touched all Americans. The armed forces sent millions to serve and fight. Millions of others worked in plants producing war materiel. Government stepped in to run the economy, and corporations and labor fashioned new relationships to the federal government. War stimulated revolutionary advances in science, industry, and agriculture. The United States became the foremost military and economic power in the world.

These changes enlarged the discretionary powers of the federal government, particularly the presidency. As the MOWM proved, the president's enhanced powers could enlarge the freedoms and opportunities enjoyed by Americans, but they could also restrict individual liberties. FDR also ordered thousands of Japanese Americans to be "relocated " to internment camps and the FBI placed Randolph's name on a list of persons to be placed in "custodial detention" in the event of a national emergency. The war unsettled the economy and society, enlisting all Americans in a global crusade, and arousing both idealism and fear.

ISLAND IN A TOTALITARIAN SEA

Randolph's movement capitalized on a world crisis that reached back to the end of World War I. Global depression heightened international tensions, turning regional conflicts in Africa, Europe, and Asia into tests of ideology and power. In 1937 Japan attacked China. Two years later when Germany invaded Poland, France and Britain declared war, beginning World War II in Europe.

Americans were divided on how their country should respond to the growing threat. Isolationists believed the United States should stay out of war, marshaling its defenses to secure the Western Hemisphere against attack. In contrast, Roosevelt and other internationalists believed the United States should support the nations fighting Germany and Japan while the war was still far from America's frontiers.

In 1940, most Americans opposed aid to the enemies of fascism, fearing that such aid would involve the United States in the fighting. When France's defeat left Britain to fight alone, more Americans saw aid to Britain as an alternative to U.S. involvement. Japan's attack on Pearl Harbor in December 1941 ended a debate that divided the nation.

A World of Hostile Blocs

In most of the world, economic growth in the 1920s had been less vigorous than in the United States. Europe stagnated under the burdens imposed by the Versailles Treaty. Germany had to pay $33 billion in war reparations to France and Britain, who in turn owed billions to the United States. The United States then loaned money back to Germany. Funds that could have created jobs, homes, and new industries went instead into this financial merry-go-round. One of the worst hit economies was in Italy, where unemployment contributed to the rise of Benito Mussolini's fascist government in 1922.

Like Italy, Japan was on the winning side of World War I, but its economy gained little from victory. Chinese consumers boycotted Japan to protest land grabs during the war. In 1923, an earthquake, fires, and a tidal wave leveled Tokyo and Yokohama, killing 150,000 people. Financial panics toppled companies and prime ministers. The one bright spot was in the foreign market for silk. Ninety percent of Japan's silk went into stockings worn by American women, and until 1930, that market seemed safe.

When the Depression hit, countries tied to a single commodity or to the American market suffered the most. After the crash, Americans stopped buying stockings, and the price of silk dropped by three-quarters. By the end of 1932, Japanese silk farmers were starving. International prices for Australian wool, Cuban sugar, Canadian wheat, Egyptian cotton, and Brazilian coffee plummeted. Everywhere the environment and the economy joined forces to destroy farmers. Those who survived bankruptcy succumbed to drought, floods, or famine.

In the industrial countries, jobless people stood in bread lines. More than 2 million workers were unemployed in Britain. American loans to Germany dried up in 1930, and by the end of the year more than 6 million Germans, 44 percent of the labor force, were out of work. This catastrophe, together with a hyperinflation that wiped out the savings of most of central Europe's middle class, silenced political moderates. In the worst economic crisis in memory, voters demanded extreme action.

The Depression destroyed the liberal international order based on free trade. For a century, governments around the world had favored policies that increased the movement of goods, people, and investment across borders. Movement toward an open-door world slowed during World War I and the 1920s and stopped completely with the Depression. World trade shrank from almost $3 billion a year in 1929 to less than $1 billion in 1933. Empires and nations restricted immigration, rationed the flow of capital, and imposed tariffs. The gold standard, the symbol of free trade, had once allowed dollars, pesos, and francs to be exchanged freely, but by 1936 Britain, the United States, and France had all abandoned it. Free trade had been replaced by autarky, the pursuit of national self-sufficiency.

Each country now looked out for itself, hoarding its scarce resources. Japan merged its colonies in Taiwan, Korea, and Manchuria into the Greater East Asia Co-Prosperity Sphere. The 1932 Ottawa Accords organized Britain, its empire, Canada, and Australia into a self-contained Sterling Bloc. To succeed, each bloc needed to have within its borders the ingredients of industrial growth—fuel, metals, skilled manpower, food—or it needed to take them from someone else.

In Germany, this policy was called *Grossraumwirtschaft*, the economics of large areas. It was the program of the National Socialist (Nazi) Party led by Adolf Hitler, who became chancellor in 1933. Hitler rose to power by playing on fears of economic chaos and resentment toward the Versailles Treaty. The harsh peace terms had been inflicted on Germany, he said, by a conspiracy of socialists and Jews. He promised to restore German greatness and carve out a German economic sphere in Eastern Europe and the Ukraine.

Autarky exacted heavy demands on citizens, requiring them to sacrifice prosperity, liberty, and lives for the nation. Efficiency was more important than democracy, and regimes around the world became more ruthless and less free. In Japan, secret groups within the army stalked and assassinated dissenting politicians. In Italy, Mussolini regimented the economy and outlawed opposition parties. Nazi ideology, in Hitler's words, placed "the good of the State before the good of the individual." Americans began to use a new word, *totalitarian*, to describe fascist and Communist regimes that demanded complete loyalty and obedience.

Even to Americans, dictatorships had a high-tech, modern sheen. Sleekly streamlined Italian trains and warships were the most beautiful in the world. Japan built a glistening new capital atop Tokyo's ruins and rationalized its economy with Frederick Taylor's time and motion techniques. Fascist economies pulled quickly out of the Depression, cutting unemployment and earning admirers in the United States.

Dictators enticed their followers with visions of imperial conquests and racial supremacy. Japanese schoolchildren learned that they belonged to a "Yamato race," purer and more virtuous than the inferior peoples they would rule. In Germany, Hitler built a state based on racism and brutality. Urging Germans to defend themselves against the *Untermenschen*, subhumans, in their midst—Jews, Gypsies, homosexuals—he suspended civil rights, purged non-Aryans from government and the professions, and compelled art, literature, and science to reflect the Nazi party's racial conception of the world.

Jews were the main target of Nazi terror. In 1935, the Nuremberg Laws stripped Jews of citizenship and outlawed intermarriage with Germans. On the night of November 9, 1938, Nazi stormtroopers and ordinary citizens rampaged throughout Germany, burning synagogues, destroying Jewish shops, homes, and hospitals, killing 100 Jews and arresting 30,000 more. Until *Kristallnacht*, the "night of the broken glass," Franklin Roosevelt had believed international opinion would restrain Hitler. Now he was no longer sure.

Germany, Italy, and Japan, known as the Axis powers, sought to solve their economic problems through military conquest. Italy invaded Ethiopia in 1935. In July 1937, Japan attacked China. The following year, Hitler's troops marched into Austria. American leaders feared that in a world of rival economic blocs, totalitarianism would outcompete democracy. Free markets and free labor might be no match for the ruthless, modern efficiency of the fascist states. "If Hitler destroys freedom everywhere else, it will perish here," *Fortune* magazine predicted. The United States would be "forced to become a great military power," to enlist industry, labor, and agriculture into a "state system, which, in its own defense, would have to take on the character of Hitler's system."

The Good Neighbor

Some Americans believed the United States ought to retreat into its own self-contained "dollar bloc," and in the early 1930s policy had briefly taken that direction. Industries and agriculture clamored for tariff protection. Free trade had been a hallmark of American foreign policy since John Hay proclaimed the open door policy in 1899, but Congress set the Smoot–Hawley Tariff of 1930 high enough to block most imports. Then, in April 1933, Roosevelt devalued the dollar. The move might have saved the banking system from collapse, but Roosevelt's own budget director called it "the end of Western civilization." One month after Roosevelt took office, the United States appeared to be moving toward autarky.

Within a year, Roosevelt reversed course and began pushing foreign trade as the answer to America's economic problems. He reacted partly to the failure of early New Deal programs but mainly to the vision of his single-minded Secretary of State, Cordell Hull, who believed the open door was the answer to the problems of dictatorship and depression. The best way to ensure peace, he argued, was to give all countries equal access to the world's markets.

Using loans and the lure of the vast American market, Roosevelt and Hull began to reopen markets in Latin America. The "Good Neighbor" policy meant encouraging trade ties and renouncing the use of force. Hull surprised the Pan American Conference at Montevideo, Uruguay, in 1933 by voting in favor of a declaration that no nation had the right to intervene in the affairs of another. Roosevelt tried to extend good neighborly policies to the rest of the world, urging peace-loving nations to "quarantine" aggressors, but the democracies were reluctant to join forces against the Axis powers.

In 1938, after absorbing Austria, Hitler demanded that Czechoslovakia cede part of its territory to Germany. Czechoslovakia's allies, Britain and France, agreed to negotiations, and in a meeting at Munich they yielded to Hitler's demands. The victors of World War I feared that a small war over Czechoslovakia would escalate into a larger one. After World War II, the term "Munich" came to symbolize the failure of attempts to appease aggressors, but in 1938 Americans were unsure how best to guard their freedoms in a hostile world.

America First?

Disillusioned by the results of the last war and anxious to concentrate on problems at home, Americans earnestly wanted to stay out of the conflicts in Europe and Asia. In 1935 and 1936, Congress passed temporary Neutrality Acts that prohibited loans and credits to nations engaged in war. In 1937 the act became permanent. A constitutional amendment requiring a national referendum to declare war narrowly missed getting a two-thirds majority in the House. Congress deliberated against the backdrop of the Spanish Civil War in which fascist forces, aided by Germany and Italy, fought against democratic, loyalist forces aided by the Soviet Union. Congress decided to stay out of the conflict, and the Neutrality Acts restricted the president's ability to aid the enemies of fascism just as Munich made the danger clear.

Between August 1939 and May 1940, Roosevelt watched as the United States became an island in a world dominated by force. The Soviet Union signed a nonaggression treaty with Germany. In September 1939, German armies struck Poland, using tanks and dive-bombers to slice deep into the interior. Hitler and Soviet leader Josef Stalin split Poland between them. Britain and France declared war on Germany.

The following April, Nazi armies invaded Denmark and Norway. On May 10, German tank columns pierced French lines in the Ardennes Forest and turned right toward the English Channel. France folded along with Belgium and the Netherlands. Britain stood alone against the German onslaught.

Roosevelt now had to face the possibility that Britain might collapse or surrender, placing the British fleet, control of the Atlantic, and possibly even Canada in Hitler's hands. Already the German air force, the *Luftwaffe*, was dueling for control of the skies over southern England. Determined to shore up this last line of defense, Roosevelt used his powers as commander in chief to bypass the Neutrality Acts. In June 1940, he submitted a bill to create the first peacetime draft in American history. He declared army weapons and supplies "surplus" so they could be sold to Britain. In September 1940, he traded Britain 50 old destroyers for leases to eight naval bases in Newfoundland, Bermuda, and the Caribbean.

Congress grumbled, but the isolationists now found themselves isolated. Sympathy for Britain grew as radio audiences heard the sounds of air attacks on London. Two-thirds of the public favored the draft, but isolationists were not ready to give up. In September 1940, the America First Committee launched a new campaign that urged Americans to distance themselves from Europe and prepare for their own defense.

Roosevelt worried that the 1940 election would become a referendum on intervention. Isolationist Senator Robert Taft was a leading contender for the Republican nomination. But the party's convention chose Wendell L. Willkie, a Wall Street lawyer with internationalist views. In his acceptance speech, Willkie endorsed the draft and expressed sympathy for Britain's struggle. Willkie stood by his principles, but it was a tactical error. With defense and foreign policy issues off the table, the only thing Willkie had to offer was a younger, fresher face. Roosevelt won an unprecedented third term by a 5-million-vote margin.

Means Short of War

British Prime Minister Winston Churchill waited until after election day to broach the urgent issue of war finances. Britain had been buying American arms on a "cash and carry" basis, but the Exchequer had run out of funds. Britain had defaulted on its World War I loans, and the Neutrality Act prohibited new loans. Churchill knew the chances of securing credits from Congress were slim, but without funds the war would stop. FDR produced a solution: Instead of loaning money, the United States would lend arms and equipment. Lend-Lease, as the program came to be called, put the U.S. "arsenal of democracy" on Britain's side and granted FDR unprecedented powers to extend aid in the nation's defense and to accept repayment "as the president deems satisfactory." The Lend-Lease bill passed the Senate by a two to one margin in 1941.

Repayment took the form of economic concessions. Hull insisted that in return for Lend-Lease aid, Britain discard the Sterling Bloc and open its markets to American trade. Churchill's economic adviser, John Maynard Keynes, reluctantly agreed. Britain was now, at least formally, committed to the open door. Later that year Churchill and Roosevelt met aboard cruisers off Newfoundland to issue a declaration of war aims, the Atlantic Charter. It assured all nations, "victor and vanquished," equal access to trade and raw materials.

In June 1941, Hitler stunned the world by launching a lightning invasion of the Soviet Union. Three million men backed by 3,000 tanks slashed through the Soviet defenses and rolled toward Moscow and Leningrad. Soviet involvement took pressure off Britain and gave the Allies a real chance to defeat Hitler. Roosevelt extended Lend-Lease aid to Moscow. The Germans advanced without interruption, but to the dismay of Hitler's officers, the Soviets did not collapse under the *Blitzkrieg* as France and Poland had.

The German Navy concentrated on severing Britain's trans-Atlantic lifelines, sinking half a million tons of shipping a month. To ease the burden on the British Navy, Roosevelt fought an undeclared naval war against Germany in the western Atlantic. The U.S. Navy convoyed merchant ships as far as Iceland, where British destroyers took over. Sparring between the American and German navies became common, and in September a German U-boat fired two torpedoes at the USS *Greer*, and the destroyer threw back depth charges. Roosevelt ordered aggressive patrols to expel German and Italian vessels from the western Atlantic. He had moved from neutrality to belligerency, and he appeared to be seeking an incident that would make it official.

Japan, meanwhile, probed into Southeast Asia in an effort to encircle China. In 1939, Japanese militarists had adopted a "go south" strategy, planning to capture oilfields in the Netherlands East Indies and cut China's lifelines through French Indochina and Burma. Because the Philippines, a U.S. territory, lay across the invasion route, the question for the Japanese was not whether to declare war on the United States, but when. In July 1941, Japanese troops established bases in French Indochina. Roosevelt saw this as a clear threat and opened talks with Japan while Marshall, the Army Chief of Staff, mobilized the Philippine Army. When Japanese

Japan's attack on the U.S. Navy's principal Pacific base at Pearl Harbor brought the United States into World War II. For Japan, it was the opening phase of a campaign to capture European and American colonies in Southeast Asia.

troop convoys moved into the South China Sea, Hull broke off negotiations and cut off Japan's only source of oil. On November 27, Marshall warned Army and Navy commands in Hawaii and the Philippines to expect "an aggressive move by Japan" in the next few days.

On Sunday afternoon, December 7, Americans listening to the radio heard that aircraft "believed to be from Japan" had attacked U.S. naval and air bases at Pearl Harbor in Hawaii. At 7:40 a.m. Hawaii time, 181 planes had bombed and strafed the airfields on Oahu, destroying or damaging more than 200 planes on the ground. Bombers then attacked the 96 ships of the U.S. Pacific Fleet anchored next to each other. The battleships *Oklahoma, Maryland,* and *Arizona* were lost, along with more than 2,000 men. Hours later, Japanese bombers caught American planes on the ground in the Philippines. The following day, President Roosevelt asked Congress for a declaration of war against Japan. On December 11, Germany honored its alliance with Japan and declared war on the United States.

Some historians have argued that Roosevelt knew of the approaching attack but withheld warnings to draw the United States into war. In fact, naval authorities at Pearl Harbor anticipated an attack, but they expected it to come in the form of sabotage or harassing raids. They doubted that Japan had the ability or audacity to project air and sea power across the Pacific in secrecy. Such preconceptions blinded commanders to the warning signs and reinforced their assumption that the Japanese would strike elsewhere.

TURNING THE TIDE

For the Allies there was only bad news in the first half of 1942. In January, a German U-boat sank the tanker *Coimbra* off Long Island. Japan's Combined Fleet commanded the waters between Hawaii and India, striking at will. General Douglas MacArthur declared Manila an open city and braced for an Alamo-style defense of the Bataan peninsula and the fortress island of Corregidor. Bataan held out until April 9; Corregidor until May 6 (see Map 25–1).

Few could see it, but the tide was beginning to turn. The Soviets stopped the German advance in front of Moscow and held the line through the summer of 1942. On April 18, U.S. Colonel James Doolittle's B-25 bombers raided Tokyo, inflicting little damage but lifting American spirits. In Washington, leaders were trying to figure out how to build an overwhelming force and then how to use it. Roosevelt wanted to hold the line in the Pacific while coming to the aid of Britain and the Soviet Union as soon as possible. This meant stopping Japan's Combined Fleet, creating an American army, arming it, and putting it into action on the other side of the Atlantic. None of those jobs would prove to be easy.

Midway and Coral Sea

After Pearl Harbor, panic-stricken Americans imagined enemy landings on the California coast, but Japan's strategy was never so ambitious. It called for expelling the United States and Britain from the western Pacific and fortifying a defensive screen of islands to hold the Allies at bay until they sued for peace. After Pearl Harbor, the fleet turned west and south, raiding the coast of Australia and British bases in Ceylon, sinking thousands of tons of commercial shipping. "The fact that the Japanese did not return to Pearl Harbor and complete the job was the greatest help for us," Chester Nimitz, the U.S. Pacific commander, later

Map 25–1   World War II in the Pacific, 1942–1945
Japan established a barrier of fortified islands across the western Pacific. U.S. forces penetrated it westward from Hawaii and from Australia northward through the Solomon Islands to the Philippines.

remembered, "for they left their principal enemy with time to . . . rebuild his forces."

After the Doolittle raid, the Japanese realized their error and laid plans to lure the U.S. Pacific Fleet into battle. The increase in Japanese radio traffic helped Commander Joseph Rochefort, who had already partly succeeded in breaking the Japanese naval codes. In late April, he was confident enough to tell Nimitz that Japan was planning an attack on Port Moresby on the island of New Guinea. Nimitz dispatched two carriers, *Lexington* and *Yorktown*, to intercept the convoy. The Japanese expected American interference, but not from two flattops. The Battle of Coral Sea was the first engagement between carrier task forces in naval history. Sailors in the two fleets never saw the other's ships. Aircraft carried the battle to the enemy with devastating speed. The two sides withdrew after fighting to a draw. Port Moresby was saved.

Yamamoto next chose to attack the American fleet directly. Sending a small force north to mount a diversionary attack on the Aleutian Islands, he assembled a massive armada led by four carriers to assault Midway Island. Both targets were vital to the Americans, and Yamamoto gambled that Nimitz would divide his forces, allowing the Combined Fleet to crush the remnant guarding Hawaii. Trusting Rochefort's codebreakers, Nimitz knew the real target was Midway. He also learned from Coral Sea that aircraft, not battleships, were the winning weapons. He assembled task forces around the carriers *Hornet* and *Enterprise* and reinforced airfields on Midway and Oahu. Crews worked night and day to repair the *Yorktown*, damaged at Coral Sea, for the battle. The American fleet was still outnumbered, but this time surprise was on its side.

When Japanese aircraft encountered unexpectedly stiff resistance from Midway's flak gunners on the morning of June 4, they returned to their carriers and prepared for an unplanned second attack. With bombers, bombs, and aviation fuel littering their decks, the Japanese carriers were vulnerable. Japanese Zero fighters had been drawn down to the water by a U.S. attack. At that moment dive bombers from *Yorktown* and *Enterprise* burst out of the clouds, destroying three carriers in a matter of minutes. Before being sunk by American bombs, the remaining carrier launched an attack against the *Yorktown*. The mighty Combined Fleet ceased to exist. Midway put Japan on the defensive and allowed the United States to concentrate on building an army and winning the war in Europe.

Gone with the Draft

Long after the tank became the dominant land weapon, the U.S. Army continued to use horse cavalry. The German Army that overran France in May 1940 consisted of 136 divisions at a time when the United States could field only five. "Against Europe's total war," *Time* observed, "the U.S. Army looked like a few nice boys with BB guns."

Recognizing their weakness, U.S. officials drew up plans for the creation of a 10-million-man force that would invade Europe in July 1943. As in World War I, the United States had to house, equip, and transport the Army, but this time it would be five times larger. After the Selective Service Act passed in September 1940, 16 million men registered for the draft and those selected moved into hastily constructed camps. By December 1941, 2 million men and 80,000 women had enlisted. A year later the total exceeded 5 million. The draft revealed what a decade of Depression had done to the health and education of the country. Half of the recruits were rejected in 1941, mostly for bad teeth and eyes, signs of malnutrition. One-fifth were illiterate.

Buses rolled into the new camps and unloaded recruits in front of drill instructors who barked incomprehensible orders. Boot camp aimed to erase the civilian personality and replace it with an instinct for obedience and action. Selectees, as they were called, learned that there were three ways of doing things: the right way, the wrong way, and the Army way.

The new camps disrupted life in the towns and cities where they were located. Distinctions of apparel and race acted as stimuli for violence between recruits and locals. Southerners lynched African-American soldiers for wearing their uniforms. In 1943, sailors idled in Los Angeles attacked Mexican-American youths who wore fashionable "zoot suits." Aided by the Los Angeles police, the riot lasted for over a week, whereupon the city council passed an ordinance outlawing zoot suits. The problem for the council and for white southerners was what the clothes signified: the disintegration of the established social order, a process accelerated by the war.

The Army leadership struggled to preserve its racial traditions against the pressures of wartime expansion. Like the multiethnic imperial armies of Britain and France, the U.S. Army consisted of racially segregated units. African Americans served in the Army in segregated units, and until 1942 they were excluded from the Navy altogether. Roosevelt ordered the services to admit African Americans and appointed an African-American brigadier general, Benjamin O. Davis, but injustices remained. Even blood plasma was segregated in military hospitals.

Two issues aroused the most anger: treatment of African-American soldiers on and around southern bases and exclusion from combat. In a letter to *Yank* magazine in 1944, Corporal Rapiered Trimmingham described how he and five other GIs in uniform had been refused service in a Texas lunchroom where German prisoners of war were being served. Mutinies and race riots erupted at bases in Florida, Alabama, and Louisiana. The Army responded by moving African-American GIs to the war theaters.

Although desperately short of infantrymen, the Army kept African Americans out of front-line units, assigning them to menial chores. Combat symbolized full citizenship to both blacks and whites, and the NAACP pressed Roosevelt to create African-American fighting units. An African-American infantry division, the 92nd, went into battle in Italy; three air units—among them the 99th Pursuit Squadron, known as the Tuskegee Airmen—flew against the Luftwaffe; and one mechanized battalion, the 761st Tanks, received a commendation for action in the Ardennes. However, most African Americans went into the line as replacements when manpower was critically low. NAACP head Walter White observed that racially mixed units aroused few complaints in the field; resistance to desegregation came mainly from Washington.

With manpower in short supply, the armed forces hesitantly enlisted women to perform service roles. Eventually more than 100,000 women served as mechanics, typists, pilots, cooks, and nurses, but the unusual feature of women's service in the U.S. forces was not how many served, but how few. In nearly every other warring country women were fully mobilized for industry and combat, and the state stepped in to perform traditional female jobs, particularly caring for children, the sick, and the elderly, functions it continued to perform after the war. This "welfare state" came to be accepted and appreciated by the public in Europe, Canada, and Australia but not in the United States.

The *99th Pursuit Squadron, known as the Black Eagles, trained at* Tuskegee *Institute and engaged the Luftwaffe in the skies over North Africa.*

The Winning Weapons

During World War II weapons technology advanced with blinding speed. Entering the war late, the United States gained a technological edge. American factories tooled up to produce models using the latest innovations, but many of these would not reach the fighting fronts until 1943 or later.

Until then, troops had to make do with weapons that were outclassed by their Axis counterparts. Marines went into action on Guadalcanal wearing World War I-era helmets and carrying the 1903 Springfield rifle. Japan's Zero was substantially faster and lighter than American fighter planes.

After 1943, the advantage began to pass to the Americans. Artillery was precise and lethal, and American crews became skilled at the devastating "time-on-target" technique, which delivered shells onto a target from several directions simultaneously. In the air, the elegant P-51 Mustang, a high-speed ultra-long-range fighter, dominated the French skies after D-Day. American four-engine bombers—the B-17 Flying Fortress and the B-24 Liberator—were superior in range and capacity to German or Japanese air weapons. In 1944, the B-29 Superfortress, with its 10-ton bomb load and awesome 4,200-mile range, took to the skies over the Pacific. Superforts incinerated Japanese cities one after another. American tanks, however, remained inferior to their German counterparts throughout the war, owing to the U.S. Army's failure to recognize the importance of this weapon.

American designers sometimes cut corners to make a product that could be mass produced. The results were impressive. When Allied troops landed in France in 1944, they enjoyed a superiority of 20 to 1 in tanks and 25 to 1 in aircraft. When Roosevelt set a production target of 50,000 aircraft in 1940, the Germans considered it a bluff, but American factories turned out almost 300,000 planes during the war. Often, abundance resulted in "attrition" tactics that pitted American numbers against Axis skill.

The War Department funded defense laboratories at Johns Hopkins, MIT, Harvard, and other universities, forging a permanent link between science and military research. American and British scientists invented one of the first "smart" bombs, the proximity fuse, which set its own range by bouncing a radio signal off its target. Collaboration between American and British scientists produced improvements in sonar and radar, penicillin, and the atomic bomb.

The Manhattan Project that produced the atomic bomb was the war's largest military-scientific-industrial enterprise. In 1939, three scientists who had fled Nazi Europe—Leo Szilard, Eugene Wigner, and Edward Teller—urged the famous physicist Albert Einstein to warn Roosevelt that the Germans might invent a nuclear weapon. General Leslie R. Groves was put in charge of the project, which eventually employed 600,000 people, cost $2 billion, and transformed the way science was done. Afterward, scientists would work in teams at government-funded laboratories on problems assigned by Washington.

The Second Front

To reassure Britain and the Soviet Union, FDR adopted a "Europe First" strategy, holding the line against Japan while directing the main effort at defeating Nazi Germany. The Allies had little in common except that Hitler had chosen them as enemies. Roosevelt needed to keep this shaky coalition together long enough to defeat Hitler. His greatest fear was that one or both of the Allies would make a separate peace or be defeated before the American economy could be fully mobilized.

As the Nazis closed in on the Soviet oilfields during the 1942 summer offensive, Stalin pleaded with Britain and the United States to launch a cross-channel invasion of France. Roosevelt and Marshall also wanted a second front to relieve pressure on the Soviets. To the British, however, the idea of a western front evoked the horrors of the trench warfare of World War I. Instead, Churchill wanted to encircle the Nazi empire, encourage insurrections, and finally invade when the enemy was weakened. He proposed attacking the Axis from the Mediterranean (see Map 25–2).

Concerned about the safety of the North Atlantic sea lanes—still prowled by U-boats—and about the inexperience of American troops, FDR reluctantly accepted Churchill's plan. A month after Pearl Harbor he promised Stalin a second front "this year." Finally, in June 1943, he told Stalin it would not take place until 1944.

Map 25–2   World War II in Europe and North Africa, 1942–1945
While the Soviets reduced the main German force along the eastern front, the British and American allies advanced through Italy and France.

The delays reinforced Stalin's suspicions that the capitalist powers were waiting for the USSR's defeat.

Instead of invading Europe, the British and Americans chose a softer target, North Africa, and American troops commanded by Lt. General Dwight Eisenhower landed in Algeria and Morocco on November 8, 1942, moving east to link up with British forces. As Americans advanced on the mountainous Tunisian border in February 1943, General Erwin Rommel burst through the Kasserine Pass, trapping American columns in the high, rocky terrain. Panicky troops surrendered or fled, blowing up their ammunition stores. Rommel briefly had the chance to encircle and defeat the Allied forces, but his commanders ordered him to advance in another direction. Kasserine revealed fatal flaws in American organization and training.

Eisenhower sacked the corps commander responsible for defending the Kasserine and replaced him with Major General George S. Patton. The Army increased basic training from 13 to 17 weeks and reviewed its doctrine and weapons, discovering that American tanks were too small and artillery too weak. For Patton, Kasserine showed that firepower, delivered by air, tanks, and artillery, was more reliable than infantry. His preference for technology over bravery became ingrained in American strategy after the war.

Allied forces captured Tunis and Bizerte on May 7, bagging 238,000 German and Italian prisoners. Rommel fought the Americans again in France a year later. At that time he would encounter a larger, more experienced, and better equipped American Army. As it mobilized to fight, the United States was changing, too. Government took on new functions, and industry shifted into high gear.

ORGANIZING FOR PRODUCTION

To defeat regimented, totalitarian enemies, Americans had to gear their political economy for war. They willingly, even gladly, concentrated power in business, government, and labor. Big was beautiful because it made possible the "miracle of production" that both won the war and raised living standards on the home front. War contracts created 17 million new jobs and doubled industrial production. The employment dial reached "full" in 1942 and stayed there until Japan surrendered. People had money to save or spend. "People are crazy with money," a Philadelphia jeweler explained. "They purchase things . . . just for the fun of spending."

A Mixed Economy

Government planners were so enthusiastic about the potential for war production that military leaders felt a need to warn them against trying to beat Germany "by out-producing her." The Roosevelt administration created war mobilization agencies to control prices, assign labor, and gear up industry. It dusted off the tried-and-true methods from World War I—dollar-a-year-men and "cost plus" contracts—and added new incentives, such as tax breaks for retooling and federal loans and subsidies.

Output soared. At Willow Run, near Detroit, Ford turned out a fleet of B-24s larger than the Luftwaffe. Cargo ships, which took longer than a year to build in 1941, came out of the Kaiser Shipyards in an average of 56 days. Entirely new industries such as synthetic rubber (to replace natural rubber, grown in Japanese-controlled Southeast Asia) appeared overnight. Industrial techniques applied to agriculture—mechanization and chemical herbicides and pesticides—raised output by one-third while the number of farmers fell by 17 percent.

Business leaders regained the prestige they had lost during the Depression. Big business was now government's partner in the war effort. Major corporations were even running parts of the supersecret Manhattan Project. "The Government supplies most, if not all, of the capital, buys the goods produced, and generally controls operations, but with management in private hands," Edwin Witte, a member of the National War Labor Board explained. This produced "a mixed economy, which is not accurately described as either capitalism or socialism, as these terms have been used by the theorists."

Industry Moves South and West

Although Detroit got its share, the bulk of war contracts went to states in the South and Southwest and on the Pacific Coast, shifting industry's center of gravity. The B-29 Superfortress was manufactured in Seattle, Omaha, Wichita, and Marietta, Georgia. Three of the Manhattan Project's largest facilities—the gaseous diffusion plant in Oak Ridge, Tennessee, DuPont's plutonium factory in Hanford, Washington, and the bomb design laboratory at Los Alamos, New Mexico—likewise broke the historic pattern that had concentrated high-tech industry in the Northeast and Midwest.

There were several reasons for this shift. Industries that needed power gravitated to the huge hydroelectric grids created by the New Deal. The federal government also encouraged construction in the middle of the country to lessen the danger from enemy bombers. Corporations moved south and west to find low-wage nonunion workers. Southern and western senators, who controlled military appropriations, steered new factory development into their states.

The results were visible. The population of the West increased by 40 percent. Towns became cities overnight. Los Angeles, Houston, Denver, Portland, Seattle, and Washington, DC became wartime boomtowns. While "old" industries such as automobiles and steel remained the mainstay of the economy above the Mason-Dixon line, the South and West became the home of the gleaming industries of the future: plastics, aluminum, aircraft, and nuclear power.

Few people objected to government direction of the economy when it meant new jobs and industry in regions that had been poor. The war effort was so popular that the administration did not worry much about propaganda. Americans recognized that running a war was a complex business that required supervision from a large bureaucracy. Roosevelt and other war managers—many of them former progressives—had learned a lesson from World War I: In gaining public support, inducements worked better than coercion.

New Jobs in New Places

The following advertisement appeared in a Chattanooga, Tennessee, newspaper in September 1942: "Wanted: Registered druggist; young or old, deaf or dumb. Must have license and walk without crutches. Apply Cloverleaf Drug Store." Labor was in such short supply that prisoners were considered model employees. The need for workers pushed up wages, brought new employees into the work force, and set people on the move in search of better opportunities. It also swelled the ranks of organized labor from 10 million to almost 15 million between 1941 and 1945.

As it had with business, the federal government enlisted labor as a partner in the war effort. Wartime inflation and resistance from management created tremendous pressure to strike, even in plants producing vital war supplies. Through the National Defense Mediation Board (NDMB), the Roosevelt administration encouraged cooperative bargaining between unions and Washington. When United Auto Workers struck North American Aviation (NAA) plants in Los Angeles in 1941, the NDMB first called on union leadership to mediate. When that failed, the government sent the Army to break the strike, but the NDMB then forced NAA's management to accept the union's wage demands. Through a combination of carrots and sticks, federal administrators encouraged a more collaborative, managerial style of union leadership. Unions did not have to struggle as much for membership or recognition; in return, they curbed militant locals and accepted federal oversight.

Some 4 million workers, taking with them another 5 million family members, migrated as war mobilization redrew the map of economic opportunity. Some 200,000 Mexican farm workers, known as *braceros*, crossed the border to harvest crops. As they had during World War I, African Americans from the South proved especially willing to move. By leaving Mississippi to take a factory job in Los Angeles, a sharecropper could multiply his salary six- or sevenfold. In war plants, workers were protected by antidiscrimination clauses, and wages were federally set. Salaries of African Americans rose twice as fast during the war as those of whites.

Workers were generally happy with higher wages, but many would have been glad to have a decent place to live. War Manpower Commissioner Paul V. McNutt complained that all the new factories were going to places with no housing to spare. Frustrations over the housing shortage sometimes boiled over into racial conflict. In 1943, when the federal government constructed a housing project with 1,000 units in Detroit along the border between Polish and African-American neighborhoods, mob violence erupted over who would take possession of the dwellings.

Women in Industry

"Rosie the Riveter," the image of the glamorous industrial worker laboring to bring her man home sooner, was largely a creation of the Office of War Information. Some 36 percent of the wartime labor force was female, slightly more than in peacetime. Few women left housework for war work solely for patriotic reasons. Instead, the war economy shifted women workers into new roles, allowing women with factory jobs to take better paid and more highly skilled positions.

The number of manufacturing jobs for women grew from 12 million to 16.5 million, with many women moving into heavy industry as metalworkers, shipwrights, and assemblers of tanks and aircraft, jobs that had been off limits before. Women worked coke ovens in the hottest parts of steel plants; they operated blast furnaces and rolling mills. For many women, the war offered the first real chance for occupational mobility.

Even so, employers did not offer women pay equal to that of men. Unions either refused women membership or expelled them when the war ended. Despite government encouragement, neither employers nor federal agencies offered much help for women trying to juggle job and family. Under the Lanham Act, which provided the first federal support for day care, the government constructed 2,800 centers, but it was not nearly enough. Government experts and social scientists saw female labor as necessary for the war effort but dangerous in the long run. After the war, women were expected to yield their jobs to returning servicemen. They were blamed for neglecting their duties and encouraging juvenile delinquency, a backlash that began to build even before the war ended.

BETWEEN IDEALISM AND FEAR

In the movies Americans marched to war (and war plants) singing patriotic tunes, but in real life this war was noticeably free of high-minded idealism. A sentimental nationalism filled soldiers' letters in the Civil War and World War I, but GIs seldom wrote home to praise their leaders or their cause. Americans had already fought once to end all wars and keep the world safe for democracy. They were not ready to buy that bill of goods again quite yet. On the home front, to writer Dwight Macdonald the war seemed to represent "the maximum of physical devastation accompanied by the minimum of human meaning."

To fill this moral vacuum, wartime leaders took idealistic hyperbole to new heights. Churchill spoke of the triumph of the "English-speaking peoples." Roosevelt said Americans were fighting for the Four Freedoms: freedom of speech, freedom of worship, freedom from want, and freedom from fear.

Americans did know what they were fighting against: totalitarianism, Gestapos, and master races. Totalitarianism provided a powerful symbol of what America and Americans ought to oppose. "You don't wanna be like Hitler, do ya?" Frank Sinatra asked in a wartime ad. Nobody did, but while some groups found they could shame the government into living up to its own rhetoric, others found that in the face of wartime fears, the ideals voiced by leaders offered little protection.

Double V

African Americans improved their economic status in an atmosphere of seething racial hostility. In Maryland, Michigan, New York, and Ohio white workers engaged in "hate strikes" to prevent the hiring of African Americans. White employees of a naval shipyard burned black neighborhoods in Beaumont, Texas, in June 1943 when rumors circulated that their jobs would be given to African Americans. Curfews, rumors of riots, and white citizen's committees kept many other cities on edge.

African Americans responded by linking their struggle for equal rights in the United States to the global war against fascism. Thurgood Marshall, chief counsel for the NAACP, compared the Detroit rioters to "the Nazi Gestapo."

The nationwide African-American press and the blocs of black voters in northern cities made African Americans a more potent political force than they had been during World War I. In 1942, the *Pittsburgh Courier* launched the "Double V" campaign to join the struggles against racism and fascism. "Defeat Hitler, Mussolini, and Hirohito" it urged, "by Enforcing the Constitution and Abolishing Jim Crow." Membership in the NAACP grew tenfold during the war, and new groups that became household names during the civil rights movement of the 1960s began their work. In Chicago, activists inspired by the nonviolent tactics of Indian nationalist Mohandas Gandhi organized the Congress of Racial Equality (CORE), which desegregated restaurants and public facilities in the North. The NAACP won a legal victory in the Supreme Court case of *Smith* v. *Allwright* (1944), which invalidated all-white primary elections.

Along with other veterans, African-American soldiers received the benefits of the GI Bill. Many returned from the war determined not to accept discrimination any longer. The war prepared a generation of African Americans for the struggle ahead.

Japanese Internment

Idealism was no match for fear, and in the days after Pearl Harbor, journalists, politicians, and military authorities perpetrated an injustice on American citizens of Japanese descent. Ominous signs reading "Civilian Exclusion Order" went up in California and the Pacific Northwest in February 1942. They instructed "Japanese aliens and non-aliens" to report to relocation centers for removal from the Pacific coast "war zone." FBI investigators found no suspicious plots and told the president so, but the press continued to print rumors of Japanese saboteurs. Responding to the press, the military, and the California Congressional delegation, FDR ordered the relocation.

At assembly centers, armed soldiers met the families, inspected the few belongings they were allowed to bring, and herded them onto trains. Some 112,000 Japanese Americans were moved to 10 barbed-wire enclosures in remote regions of the West and Arkansas. Rows of wooden barracks were surrounded by guard towers, high fences, and sentry posts with machine guns facing inward. The internees reacted differently to their imprisonment. Some wanted to show loyalty by cooperating, while others were unwilling to repudiate Japanese culture or refrain from protest.

Internees and civil liberties lawyers challenged the legality of confining American citizens without charge or trial. Fred Korematsu, a welder from San Leandro, California, took a new name and had his face surgically altered in a futile attempt to stay out of the camps. When he was arrested, the American Civil Liberties Union used his case to challenge the exclusion order. Supreme Court Justice Hugo Black upheld the evacuation policy as justified by "military necessity."

No Shelter From the Holocaust

The United States might have saved more victims of Hitler's "final solution" had it chosen to do so. A combination of fear and anti-Semitism led American leaders to dismiss the Holocaust as someone else's problem. Between 1938 and 1941 the United States could have provided a haven for the millions of Jews trying to flee Europe. Instead, the State Department erected a paper wall of bureaucratic restrictions that kept the flow of immigrants to a trickle.

Nazi Germany's systematic extermination of the Jews made news in the United States. Stories in the *New York Times* as early as 1942 described the deportations and concluded that "the greatest mass slaughter in history" was underway. At Auschwitz, Poland, in the most efficient, high-tech death camp, 2,000 people an hour could be killed with Zyklon-B gas. Jewish leaders begged War Department officials to bomb the camp or the rail lines leading to it. The factory areas of Auschwitz were bombed twice in 1944, but John J. McCloy, the Assistant Secretary of War, refused to target the camp, dismissing it as a humanitarian matter of no concern to the Army. Roosevelt, who also knew of the Holocaust, might have rallied public support for Hitler's victims and made rescue a military priority. His inaction, according to historian David Wyman, was "the worst failure of his presidency."

When American soldiers penetrated Germany in 1945, they gained a new understanding of what they were fighting for and against. On April 15, Patton's Third Army liberated the Buchenwald death camp. Eisenhower ordered photographs and films to be taken, and he brought German civilians to witness the mass burial, by bulldozer, of the corpses. Many GIs doubted that the things they had witnessed would be believed.

Americans went into the First World War flushed with idealism and became disillusioned in victory's aftermath. The Second World War followed the reverse trajectory. Americans slowly came to see that their shopworn ideals offered what little protection there was against the hatred and bigotry that afflicted all nations, including their own.

CLOSING WITH THE ENEMY

The American Army was small—only 5 million compared to Germany's 9 million—but it was amply supplied and agile. Tactics emphasized speed and firepower. In 1944 and 1945 the United States carried the war to Japan and into the heart of Europe with a destructiveness never before witnessed.

Taking the War to Europe

Using North Africa as a base, the Anglo-American Allies attacked northward into Italy, knocking one of the Axis powers out of the war. In Sicily, where the Allies landed in July 1943, Patton applied the mobile, aggressive tactics he had advocated since 1940. Slicing the island in half and trapping a large part of the Italian Army, he swung east to Messina but arrived too late to block the Germans' escape. The defeat shook Italy. Strikes paralyzed the major cities, and Parliament deposed Mussolini and ordered his arrest. German troops took control and fiercely resisted the Allied landings at Salerno in September. Winter rains stopped the Anglo-American offensive south of Rome.

To break the deadlock, Churchill ordered an amphibious assault behind German lines at Anzio in January. Catching the Germans by surprise, three Anglo-American divisions came ashore unopposed, but the Germans quickly surrounded the small beachhead, pinning down the Allies in a siege that lasted until May. The Germans sent glider bombs and remote-controlled tanks filled with explosives into the Allied lines. American troops finally broke through to Rome on June 5, 1944.

The assault on France's Normandy coast the next day, D-Day, finally created the second front the Soviets had asked for in 1942. Early on the morning of June 6, 1944, the Allied invasion armada, thousands of supply and troop ships and hundreds of warships, assembled off England's channel coast and began the run into beaches designated Juno, Gold, Sword, Utah, and Omaha. Hitler had fortified the beaches with an "Atlantic Wall" of mines, underwater obstacles, heavy guns, and cement forts. On Omaha Beach the small boats headed straight into concentrated fire from shore batteries. The boats unloaded too soon, and men with full packs plunged into deep water. Floating tanks overturned and sank with crews inside. Commanders briefly considered calling off the attack, but soldiers in small groups began moving inland to outflank German firing positions. By the end of the day, they held the beach.

Eisenhower's greatest fear was another Anzio. The hedgerow country behind the beaches contained the most defensible terrain between the Channel and Germany. Each field and pasture was protected by earthen mounds topped with shrubs, natural walls that isolated troops. However, just as had happened on Omaha Beach, the defects of the generals' strategy were compensated by the initiative of GIs. On their own, tankers experimented with metal tusks to gouge holes through the hedgerows. By the end of the month the U.S. advance, led by "rhino tanks," broke through the German defenses and captured the critical port city of Cherbourg.

Once in the open country, highly mobile American infantry chased the retreating enemy across France to the fortifications along the German border. There, in the Ardennes Forest, Hitler's armies rallied for a final desperate counterattack.

Thirty divisions, supported by 1,000 aircraft, hit a lightly held sector of the American lines, broke through, and opened a "bulge" 40 miles wide and 60 miles deep in the Allied front. Two whole regiments were surrounded and forced to surrender, but the 101st Airborne held onto a critical road junction, slowing the German advance and allowing the Allies to bring in reinforcements. The Battle of the Bulge lasted a month and resulted in more than 10,000 American dead and 47,000 wounded, but the German Army had lost the ability to resist.

Island Hopping in the Pacific

To get close enough to aim a knockout blow at Japan, the United States had to pierce the barrier of fortified islands stretching from Alaska to Australia using only a fraction of the resources going to fight the war in Europe. The Army and the Navy bickered over supplies and the shortest route to Tokyo. MacArthur favored a thrust northward from Australia through the Solomon Islands and New Guinea to retake the Philippines. Nimitz preferred a thrust across the central Pacific to seize islands as staging areas for an air and land assault on Japan.

By November 1943, MacArthur's forces had advanced to Bougainville, the largest of the Solomon Islands and the nearest to the Japanese air and naval complex at Rabaul. Jungle fighting on these islands was especially vicious. Atrocity stories became self-fulfilling, as each side treated the other without mercy, killing prisoners and mutilating the dead. Air attacks pulverized Rabaul's airfields and harbor in early 1944, opening the way for an advance into the southern Philippines.

Meanwhile, Nimitz launched a naval attack on Japan's island bases. With 11 new aircraft carriers, each holding 50 to 100 planes, the Fifth Fleet attacked Tarawa, a tiny atoll that contained 4,500 Japanese troops protected by log bunkers and hidden naval guns. Tarawa, captured at a cost of more than 3,000 casualties, provided a base for an invasion of the Marshall Islands, which in turn, allowed an advance into the Marianas. Following a strategy called "island hopping," American forces bypassed strongly held enemy islands and moved the battle lines closer to Japan.

The Allied capture of Saipan, Tinian, and Guam in July 1944 brought Japan within range of B-29 bombers. General Curtis LeMay brought his 21st Bomber Command to Saipan in January 1945 and launched a new kind of air offensive against Japanese cities. LeMay experimented with low-level attacks using a mix of high explosives (to shatter houses and buildings) and incendiary bombs (to set fire to the debris). On the night of March 9, 1945, LeMay sent 334 bombers to Tokyo to light a fire that destroyed 267,000 buildings. The heat was so intense that the canals boiled, oxygen was burned from the air, and 83,000 people died from flames and suffocation. In the following months LeMay burned more than 60 percent of Japan's urban area.

Building a New World

As the war progressed across Europe and the Pacific, officials in Washington planned for the postwar future, and Allied leaders met to discuss their visions of the world after victory. Meeting in Casablanca in 1943, Roosevelt and Churchill agreed to demand the unconditional surrender of the Axis powers, to give the Allies a free hand to set the terms of peace. The U.S. State, War, and Navy departments undertook a comprehensive survey of the world, examining each country and territory to determine its importance to the United States. The planners believed that American security would depend on having a functioning international organization, a global system of free trade, and a worldwide network of American military bases.

Roosevelt envisioned a strong international organization led by the world's principal powers, who would act as "policemen" within designated spheres of influence. The new organization would work to disband empires, placing "trusteeships" over colonial territories preparing for self-government. The world after victory would be a world of nations, not empires or blocs. In September 1944, delegates from 39 nations met at Dumbarton Oaks and sketched out a plan for a United Nations comprised of a general assembly, in which all nations would be represented, and an executive council made up of the United States, China, the Soviet Union, Britain, and France.

To American leaders, the lesson of the 1930s had been that without prosperity there could be no peace. They wanted to create an open-door world, in which goods and money could move freely, eliminating the need for conquest. In July 1944, 44 nations attended a conference at Bretton Woods, New Hampshire, to create a system to manage and stabilize the international movement of money. The U.S. dollar would become an international currency, fixed against gold at the rate of $32 an ounce. Other countries would fix or "peg" the value of their currencies against the dollar, making it easy to set prices on the world market. To rescue unstable currencies, the delegates created an International Monetary Fund along with an International Bank for Reconstruction and Development (generally known as the World Bank). The "Bretton Woods system" gave rise to the network of regional development banks and international aid agencies that govern international finance today.

Military planners were not ready to stake America's future security on trade or international organizations. Pearl Harbor had shown that the Atlantic and Pacific Oceans offered no protection against aggression. Beginning in 1943, military leaders laid plans for a global system of military bases encircling the vast Eurasian land mass. Planners could not say who the next enemy would be, but with such an extensive base network, the United States could act preemptively against any challenger. Britain and the Soviet Union looked on this base system warily, suspecting they might be its targets, but American leaders were willing to take diplomatic risks to attain security.

The Fruits of Victory

Despite rumors of the president's failing health, Americans elected Franklin Roosevelt to a fourth term in 1944 by a margin of 53.5 percent to 46 percent for the challenger Thomas E. Dewey. On April 12, 1945, less than three months after his inauguration, Roosevelt died suddenly of a cerebral hemorrhage at Warm Springs, Georgia, days before Allied troops in Europe achieved the great victory for which Roosevelt had struggled and planned. On April 25, American and Soviet troops shook hands at Torgau in eastern Germany. On May 8, all German forces surrendered unconditionally.

Harry S Truman, the new vice president, was now commander in chief. Shortly after he took office, aides informed him that the Manhattan Project would soon test a weapon that might end the war in Asia. The first atomic explosion took place in the desert near Alamogordo, New Mexico, on July 16, 1945. Truman, meeting with Churchill and Stalin at Potsdam, Germany, was elated by the news. He informed Stalin while Churchill looked on, watching the expression of the Soviet leader. The bomb had been developed to be used against the Axis enemy, but by the time

Residents walk amid the ruins of Nagasaki, August 1945.

Truman learned about it, American leaders already saw it as a powerful instrument of postwar diplomacy. Stalin urged Truman to put the weapon to good use. Through intermediaries, Japanese diplomats had suggested an armistice on the condition that the emperor's life be spared, but Truman held out for unconditional surrender.

As American forces neared the Japanese home islands, defenders fought with suicidal ferocity. On Okinawa, soldiers and civilians retreated into caves and battled to the death. GIs feared the invasion of Japan's home islands, where resistance could only be worse. Then on August 6, a B-29 dropped an atomic bomb on Hiroshima. Two days later the Soviet Union declared war on Japan, and Soviet armies attacked deep into Japanese-controlled Manchuria. On August 9, the United States dropped a second atomic bomb, this time on Nagasaki. A few days later a French Red Cross worker saw the ruins of Hiroshima. "On what remained of the station facade the hands of the clock had been stopped by the fire at 8:15. It was perhaps the first time in the history of humanity that the birth of a new era was recorded on the face of a clock."

Conclusion

Emperor Hirohito announced Japan's unconditional surrender on August 14. In New York, crowds celebrated, but in most of the world there was silence and reflection. Thirty million people had been killed; great cities lay in ruins. At the end of the war, the United States' economic, scientific, and military mastery reached a pinnacle never attained by any of the great empires of history. America's air armada dominated the skies; its naval fleet had more ships than the navies of all its enemies and allies combined. Senator Claude Pepper asked Navy Secretary James Forrestal where he intended to put all of the 1,200 warships at his disposal. "Wherever there's a sea," Forrestal replied. Then there was the atomic bomb. The rest of the world looked for signs of how the United States would use its formidable wealth and power.

CHRONOLOGY

1930	Smoot–Hawley Tariff passed
1933	Hitler becomes chancellor of Germany President Roosevelt devalues the dollar The United States recognizes the Soviet Union
1934	Reciprocal Trade Act passed Export-Import Bank created
1935	Congress passes first Neutrality Act
1937	War begins in Asia
1938	Mexico nationalizes oil fields Munich agreement gives Hitler Sudetenland
1939	War begins in Europe
1940	Germany defeats France, Netherlands, Belgium Destroyers-for-bases deal between the U.S. and Britain
1941	Lend-Lease passed Executive Order 8802 ends discrimination in defense industries Roosevelt and Churchill sign Atlantic Charter Germany invades the Soviet Union Japan attacks the United States at Pearl Harbor U.S. declares war on Axis powers
1942	Philippines fall to Japan Internment of Japanese Americans begins Battles of Coral Sea and Midway turn the tide in the Pacific Allies land in North Africa
1943	Allies land in Sicily Churchill and Roosevelt meet at Casablanca U.S. troops advance to Bougainville Marines capture Tarawa
1944	U.S. troops capture Rome Allied landings in Normandy U.S. troops capture Saipan Bretton Woods Conference Roosevelt re-elected for fourth term
1945	Roosevelt dies Harry S Truman becomes president Germany surrenders Truman meets Churchill and Stalin at Potsdam Atomic bombs dropped on Hiroshima and Nagasaki Japan surrenders

FURTHER READINGS

Thomas Childers, *Wings of Morning* (1995). A historian reconstructs the lives and war experiences of the last B-24 crew shot down over Germany.

I. C. B. Dear, *The Oxford Companion to World War II* (1995). Easily the best single-volume reference work on the war. Contains full descriptions of battles and campaigns, biographies of leading figures, chronologies, maps, and as many statistics as you could want.

Michael D. Doubler, *Closing With the Enemy: How GIs Fought the War in Europe, 1944–1945* (1994). World War II has been seen as a "general's war," but Doubler explains how the tactics that beat the Nazis came from the bottom up. The U.S. Army's ability to listen to the lowliest GIs was its best asset.

Doris Kearns Goodwin, *No Ordinary Time: Franklin and Eleanor Roosevelt: The Home Front in World War II* (1994). The story of the nation at war through the eyes of the family that led it.

E. B. Sledge, *With the Old Breed at Peleliu and Okinawa* (1990). A classic memoir, the story of a Marine infantryman's war in the Pacific told with candor and feeling.

Ronald H. Spector, *Eagle Against the Sun: The American War With Japan* (1985). A comprehensive history of the Pacific War from a leading military historian.

 Please refer to the document CD-ROM for primary sources related to this chapter.

The Cold War

1945–1952

The Fall of Esther and Stephen Brunauer • The Origins of the Cold War • Fighting the Cold War Abroad • The Reconversion of American Society • The Frustrations of Liberalism • Fighting the Cold War at Home • Conclusion

THE FALL OF ESTHER AND STEPHEN BRUNAUER

*E*sther Caukin and Stephen Brunauer were an American success story. Born in California in 1901, Esther graduated from Mills College, earned a doctorate from Stanford University, and became an administrator for the American Association of University Women. In 1931, she married Stephen Brunauer, a successful chemist who had come to the United States from Hungary.

The Brunauers hated fascism. In the 1930s, Esther tried to educate Americans about the threat from Adolf Hitler's Germany. When World War II came, she went to work in the State Department. Stephen also worked for the government as a Navy explosives expert. After the war, he traveled to Hungary to gather intelligence for the government and help Hungarian scientists emigrate.

With fascism defeated and their careers well launched, the Brunauers should have looked forward to a happy, prosperous future. But in 1947 a U.S. congressman accused Esther of being one of the "pro-Communist fellow travelers and muddle heads" in the State Department, and a federal agency refused to let Stephen attend a meeting about atomic energy because in the 1920s he had belonged to a group with Communist ties.

Then things got worse. On March 13, 1950, Senator Joseph R. McCarthy of Wisconsin suggested that Esther and Stephen were supporting Communism. Esther, McCarthy testified, had engaged in "Communist-front activities"; Stephen, purportedly a member of the Communist Party, had access "to some of the topmost secrets" of the U.S. military. McCarthy demanded that the Senate subcommittee subpoena federal records to find out whether the Brunauers had betrayed their country.

Two weeks later Esther took the witness stand to defend herself and her husband before the subcommittee. She accused McCarthy of betraying American values. Esther revealed how much McCarthy's accusations had already hurt her family. They had received "anonymous telephone calls at all hours of the day and night, accompanied by threats and profanity. All of you who have families . . . how would you feel if it were happening in your home?"

The subcommittee's report concluded that McCarthy's charges against the Brunauers were "contemptible," and "a fraud and a hoax." But the damage had been done. The Brunauers' employers, the State Department and the Navy, were unwilling to keep such controversial people on the job. In 1951 both were suspended. Stephen quit his job; Esther tried to fight her suspension but found herself charged with "close and habitual association" with her husband. In 1952, the State Department fired her as a "security risk."

How had it happened? At the end of World War II, things had seemed so promising. Americans lived in a country and a world that had been saved from ruin. At home, the economic boom of World War II had swept away the Great Depression. Abroad, the United States had helped to destroy the threat of fascism. Understandably, Americans expected the postwar world to be stable and safe.

Before two years had passed, however, the cold war disrupted American life. Convinced that the Soviets intended to expand their power and spread Communism across Europe, U.S. leaders challenged their former allies. The confrontation with Communism was deeply rooted in the long-standing values and the new conditions of the American political economy at the close of World War II. Partly the product of the political economy, the cold war in turn deeply affected it. To contain Soviet expansion, the U.S. government took unprecedented peacetime actions—massive foreign aid, new alliances, and a military buildup—that helped to transform the political economy.

The new American policies did not prevent the cold war from widening and intensifying. By 1950, the nation was fighting a hot war in Korea, and the Soviet Union had nuclear weapons that could conceivably devastate the United States. In response, the Truman administration stepped up military spending and developed more powerful nuclear weapons. As the cold war seemed to spiral out of control, fear gripped American society. In one way or another, the cold war unsettled the lives of all Americans for years to come.

THE ORIGINS OF THE COLD WAR

In just two years, the United States and the Soviet Union went from a wartime alliance to the strained relations known as the cold war. From the outset, the United States and the Soviet Union tried to blame the cold war on each other. For a long time, Americans wanted to believe that the Soviet Union, authoritarian and expansionist, was solely responsible. However, historians generally agree that both countries helped to start the cold war.

Ideological, political, military, and economic factors all played a role in the conflict. Ever since the founding of the Soviet Union toward the end of World War I, Soviets and Americans were ideological adversaries. Despite their differences, the two countries were allies in World War II, but in peacetime, the Soviet Union and the United States were the only countries strong enough to threaten each other. Moreover, they had quite different political, military, and economic interests which, by 1947, produced open antagonism.

Ideological Adversaries

The Russian Revolution of 1917 created the Soviet Union and committed the new nation to Communism. The Bolshevik revolutionaries installed a government dominated by the Communist Party. They also installed a socialist economy in which the state—the government—owned all property. At home, the Soviet Union limited individual rights, including freedom of speech and religion. Abroad, the new nation endorsed the revolutionary overthrow of capitalism.

The Soviets' Communist ideology set them at odds with the political economy of the United States. The vast majority of Americans favored a capitalist economy, individualism, freedom of speech, freedom of religion, and democratic government based on free elections. Although the United States did not always live up to these values, most Americans were sure that the "Red" Soviet Union never would.

Nevertheless, open conflict between the two countries was not inevitable. The Soviet Union posed no military threat to the United States in the 1920s and 1930s. President Franklin Roosevelt, eager to promote U.S. trade and restrain Japanese expansion, officially recognized the Soviet Union in 1933.

Uneasy Allies

World War II demonstrated that the United States and the Soviet Union could become allies. Still, the wartime alliance also laid the groundwork for trouble. For many Americans, the lesson of the war was that no new dictator should ever take over other European countries unopposed, as Adolf Hitler had in the 1930s. It was easy to view authoritarian Soviet Communism as another kind of fascism and the brutal Soviet leader Josef Stalin as another Hitler.

Wartime decisions also promoted tensions between the United States and the Soviet Union. The delay of the Allied invasion of France until 1944 embittered the Soviets, who were desperately resisting the Germans at the cost of millions of lives. The American government further strained relations by sharing news of its atomic bomb project with the British but not with the Soviets.

Decisions about the postwar world led to trouble as well. At a conference in Yalta in the Soviet Union during February 1945, Franklin Roosevelt, Josef Stalin, and British Prime Minister Winston Churchill promoted conflicting visions of the postwar world.

On the one hand, the "Big Three" supported the self-determination of nations, and in a Declaration of Liberated Europe, stated that nations would be free and democratic. The three leaders also laid plans for the United Nations, an organization that would encourage states to cooperate in keeping the world free, safe, and secure.

On the other hand, the Big Three believed that powerful nations such as theirs were entitled to spheres of influence in which they would exercise power independently and limit the self-determination of smaller states. Clearly, spheres of influence and unilateral action conflicted with democracy, self-determination, and collective action.

The conflict was made apparent when the three leaders dealt with the future of Poland, the Soviet Union's neighbor to the west. Stalin wanted to install a Polish government loyal to the Soviet Union. He could not risk an independent Poland that might become the staging area for another invasion of the USSR. Churchill and Roosevelt, however, favored a self-governing Poland. Stalin agreed to elections, but seemingly felt that Roosevelt promised him a free hand in postwar Poland. This lack of clarity set the stage for future misunderstandings.

So did differences over the future of Germany. The United States wanted Germany, safely controlled by the Allies, to become a healthy part of the world economy. Stalin, determined never to be attacked by Germany again, wanted the country formally divided and weakened. In the end, the Big Three agreed that Germany would be temporarily divided into four separate zones of occupation, administered by the United States, the USSR, Great Britain, and France. Although Berlin, the German capital, lay within the Soviet zone, the four conquering powers would each control a section of the city.

Coldwar leaders at Potsdam in July 1945. The determined expressions of British Prime Minister Winston Churchill, U.S. President Harry Truman, and Soviet Premier Josef Stalin reveal the tensions that would produce confrontation after World War II.

The uncertainties and contradictions of the Yalta meeting quickly led to Soviet–American disagreements. When Vice President Harry Truman succeeded Roosevelt in April 1945, he objected to the Soviets' attempt to control Poland. Promising to "stand up to the Russians," Truman held a tense meeting in Washington with the Soviet foreign minister.

When Truman met with Stalin and the British prime minister at the German city of Potsdam in July, relations were more cordial, and Truman reluctantly accepted the realities of power. Because Soviet troops occupied most of Eastern Europe and much of Germany, Truman had to go along with Stalin's demand that some German territory be given to Poland. There was no progress on planning the future reunification of Germany.

From Allies to Antagonists

After the war, the relationship between the United States and the Soviet Union eroded rapidly. With vastly different political economies and visions of the postwar world, the two nations defined their national security interests in conflicting ways (Map 26–1).

Stalin and the Soviet leadership took a cautious approach. Although they were committed to the overthrow of capitalism, their immediate concern was to protect

Map 26–1 Cold War in Europe, 1950
Five years after World War II, the cold war had divided Europe into hostile camps, with NATO members allied to the United States and Warsaw Pact signers tied to the Soviet Union.

the Soviet Union from invasion. In addition to establishing a pro-Soviet Eastern Europe, Stalin wanted to make sure he could not be attacked from the south, through Turkey and Iran, and that Germany and Japan never menaced his country again. Trying to rebuild the war-torn USSR, Stalin promoted national economic independence and had little interest in encouraging speedy rebuilding and easy trade relations for other nations.

The leaders of the United States looked at the postwar world differently. Truman did not have to worry about the immediate security of U.S. borders or fear any other military power. But American leaders feared that some other power might seize control of parts of Europe and Asia, making the United States isolated and susceptible to attack.

To avoid this dismaying scenario, American leaders took nearly the opposite of the Soviet approach to the postwar world. Truman favored the quick reconstruction of nations, including Germany and Japan, that would participate in a world economy based on free trade. The United States needed healthy trading partners to maintain prosperity at home. America also needed contented allies who would accept U.S. military bases on their soil.

The different needs and interests of the Soviet and U.S. political economies soon translated into combative rhetoric. In February 1946 Stalin declared that capitalism and Communism were incompatible. A month later, Winston Churchill, no longer prime minister of Great Britain, ominously declared that "an Iron Curtain has descended across the Continent" of Europe.

American leaders thought that Stalin wanted more than just safety from invasion. The Soviet Union, they concluded, aimed to expand abroad. George Kennan, an American diplomat in Moscow, sent to the State Department a long telegram that shaped the thinking of American policymakers. The Soviet leadership, explained Kennan, believed "there can be no permanent peaceful coexistence" between capitalism and socialism. Stalin and his regime were sure that capitalist nations would attack socialist nations and one another. Acting on this unfounded fear, the USSR would try to destabilize capitalist nations, especially the United States. The Soviet "problem," Kennan concluded, could be resolved without war, but the solution was "undoubtedly the greatest task our diplomacy has ever faced and probably . . . will ever have to face."

Truman's words and actions reflected Kennan's analysis. In 1946 the president tried to counter the apparent expansionism of the USSR, warning the Soviets against trying to increase their influence over Iran and Turkey. When the Soviets kept troops in Iran past the agreed-on deadline for their withdrawal, Truman sent a battleship to the eastern Mediterranean and successfully pressed Moscow to withdraw.

Relations between the United States and the Soviet Union deteriorated further in 1947, as Truman took aggressive steps to counter apparent Soviet expansionism in Turkey and Greece. The USSR had been pressing for a role in Turkey for some time. In Greece, the monarchist regime was under attack from Communist guerrillas, seemingly aided by pro-Soviet Eastern European nations. Great Britain had played the key role in supporting the Greek and Turkish governments, but by 1947 the British could no longer afford this aid. For Truman and his advisors, British withdrawal was disastrous. Control of Turkey would have given the Soviets access to the Indian Ocean and to the oil fields of the Middle East. Worse, successes in Greece and Turkey could have helped Communism everywhere in Europe and the Middle East.

To prevent this disaster, the Truman administration wanted to provide $400 million in aid to the Greek and Turkish governments. To persuade Congress to appropriate the money, Truman told a joint session of Congress on March 12, 1947, that the world once again faced a choice between freedom and totalitarianism. The president announced what became known as the Truman Doctrine. "I believe," he said, "that it must be the policy of the United States to support free peoples who are resisting attempted subjugation by armed minorities or by outside pressures." Congress voted overwhelmingly to provide the aid to Greece and Turkey.

The crisis marked the turning point in the U.S.–Soviet relationship. By 1947 the term *cold war* was being used to describe the American–Soviet confrontation. Dividing the world into good and evil, the United States was ready to support "free peoples" and oppose Communism. Former allies were now bitter antagonists.

Was the confrontation inevitable? It is difficult to see how the United States and the Soviet Union could have avoided antagonism. They had a history of tension and hostility, and they both possessed great military power. Most important, the two nations' political economies had produced clashing ideologies and needs.

It is much harder to say that the precise form of that confrontation was inevitable. The cold war was the product of human choices, such as Truman's decision to "scare hell out of the American people," and of human mistakes, such as Kennan's erroneous conclusion that the Soviets were bent on territorial expansion. Those choices and mistakes were certainly not inevitable. With good reason, Americans would wonder for decades whether the cold war could have been different.

FIGHTING THE COLD WAR ABROAD

The cold war intensified almost as soon as it started. In the late 1940s the United States implemented a strategy of containment to combat Soviet expansion. Moreover, the cold war quickly widened beyond Europe to include the entire world and, at the same time, became more dangerous. When the Soviets exploded their own atomic bomb, the United States dramatically stepped up military spending and built the hydrogen bomb. As the arms race spiraled, the cold war seemed frighteningly out of control.

The Strategy of Containment

Committed to opposing Soviet and Communist expansion, the Truman administration had to figure out how to fight the cold war. Once again, diplomat George Kennan helped give expression to American thinking. In 1947 Kennan argued "that the main element of any United States policy toward the Soviet Union must be that of a long-term, patient but firm and vigilant containment of Russian expansive tendencies."

The term containment aptly described American policy for the next 40 years, but it was a broad, rather vague concept. Truman and his successors had to decide just where and when to contain the Soviet Union as well as what combination of diplomatic, economic, and military programs to use.

To implement containment, Truman and his advisors revolutionized American policies on foreign aid, overseas alliances, and national defense. Soon after the decision to help Greece and Turkey, the United States had to confront the slow recovery of war-ravaged Europe. Given their fears that an impoverished Europe would hurt the U.S. economy and embrace Communism, Truman and his advisors were determined to help the continent rebuild. In a speech at Harvard University in June 1947, Truman's new Secretary of State, General George C. Marshall, proposed a European Recovery Plan to promote "political and social conditions in which free institutions can exist." Sixteen nations eagerly supported what became known as the Marshall Plan, and in 1948 Congress approved the plan with bipartisan support.

The Marshall Plan, the largest aid program ever initiated by any nation, served its purposes remarkably well. From 1948 to 1952, $13 billion went to restore agricultural production, boost industrial output, increase exports, and promote economic cooperation. Politically, the return of prosperity helped stabilize Western European governments and weaken the region's Communist parties. In the process, Western European nations were bound more tightly to the United States. Because of the Marshall Plan, Communism seemed much less likely to spread into Western Europe.

In addition to aid programs, containment demanded the kind of peacetime alliances that the United States had historically avoided because of fears that such agreements might drag the nation into war. Facing the unique challenge of the cold war, American leaders saw alliances as a way of preventing armed conflict. By promising to defend other countries if they were attacked, the United States could make the Soviet Union think twice about pushing further into Europe.

This thinking led the Truman administration to forge the first peacetime military alliance with Europe. In 1949, the United States joined ten Western European nations and Canada to form the North Atlantic Treaty Organization (NATO). Under the NATO agreement, an attack on any member nation would be treated as an attack on every member nation. Congress appropriated $1.3 billion in military aid for NATO countries, and Truman ordered American troops to Europe under the command of General Dwight D. Eisenhower.

As these actions suggested, containment also depended on a strong military establishment. The Truman administration pushed for the reorganization of the military. In 1947 Congress passed the National Security Act, which put the Army, Navy, and Air Force under a single cabinet secretary, the Secretary of Defense. This act also created both the Central Intelligence Agency (CIA) to gather information on national security and the National Security Council (NSC) to advise the president on security matters.

To build up the military, Congress passed a new Selective Service Act in 1948, allowing the government to draft men between ages 19 and 25 in peacetime. Finally, in 1949, Congress adopted another National Security Act, which brought together the Joint Chiefs of Staff, the heads of each of the armed services, to advise the president on military matters.

The Dangers of Containment

Containment exposed the United States to dangers. Confrontation with the Soviets had the potential to get out of hand and become a war. The dangers became clear in 1948 during a showdown over access to Berlin. That spring, the Americans, British, and French began to unify their zones of occupation in Germany into a single administrative unit. Faced with the prospect of a wealthy, unified, anti-Communist Western Germany, Stalin threw a blockade around Berlin, the German capital, located within the Soviet zone but jointly occupied by all four former allies. The 2.5 million people in the American, British, and French sections of Berlin were at risk of running out of food and coal. If the U.S. military tried to bring in supplies over land across the Soviet zone of Germany, there might have been war.

Instead, the Truman administration sent relief to Berlin by air. American transport planes carried 2,500 tons of food and fuel a day to the people of Berlin. In May

1949 the Soviets ended the blockade. Put to the test, the strategy of containment had worked, but the risks were obvious.

The dangers of containment became even greater for the United States later that year, when American reconnaissance planes over the Pacific collected evidence that the Soviet Union had exploded an atomic bomb. The U.S. monopoly on nuclear weapons was over, and confrontation with the Soviets now had potentially lethal consequences for the American people.

The Globalization of the Cold War

While the dangers of the cold war became frighteningly clear, the scope of the conflict widened. Events in China played a key role in this globalization of the cold war.

At the end of World War II, the Chinese nationalist government of Jiang Jieshi, America's ally, faced a revolution led by the Communist Party of Mao Zedong. The Truman administration, concluding that the nationalist regime could not be saved, agreed to $2 billion in aid for the nationalists but refused to send American troops. In December 1949 the defeated nationalists fled the Chinese mainland for the island of Formosa, also known as Taiwan.

The Chinese Revolution widened the cold war. Although Stalin did not direct the Chinese Communists, Americans saw Jiang's defeat as a victory for the Soviet Union. The Truman administration refused to recognize the new mainland Chinese regime, the People's Republic of China.

By this time American policymakers believed that Communism was a potential threat in almost every part of the world. The United States moved to make sure that Communism did not spread to Latin America. At a conference in the Brazilian city of Rio de Janeiro in August 1947, the United States and 20 Latin American republics agreed to the Inter-American Treaty of Reciprocal Assistance. Under the terms of the Rio Pact, the United States promised to train Latin American military leaders, regulate the flow of military supplies, and coordinate the defense of the region. In 1948 the United States joined with Latin American nations to create the Organization of American States (OAS). This body promoted hemispheric solidarity and economic development and enforced the Rio Pact.

Even Africa, which was not critical to the defense of the United States, became a battlefield of the cold war. In 1948 Truman improved diplomatic relations with the white supremacist government of South Africa, partly because of its opposition to Communism and Soviet expansionism.

The Cold War Turns Hot in Korea

With the United States working to hold off Communism around the world, it was not surprising that the nation was drawn into war. Americans were startled when their soldiers went into battle in South Korea in 1950 (see Map 26–2), but the Korean War was firmly rooted in the logic of the cold war.

Korea had been liberated from the Japanese in 1945. American troops occupied the territory south of the 38th Parallel while Soviet troops occupied the territory to the north. Despite American policymakers' professed support for self-determination, they opposed a left-wing movement of Koreans who wanted their nation to become an independent "people's republic." The Truman administration aided the anti-Communist government of Syngman Rhee in the South, while the Soviet Union promoted the regime of the Communist Kim Il Sung in the North. In 1948 the United States went along with the permanent division of Korea at the 38th

← North Korean offensive, June–Sept. 1950

← U.N. offensive, Sept.–Nov. 1950

◄ - Communist Chinese offensive, Nov. 1950–Jan.1951

Map 26–2   The Korean War, 1950–1953
The shifting lines of advance mark the back-and-forth struggle that would end with stalemate and the permanent division of Korea.

Parallel. Then, in June 1950, after a series of incidents along the border, North Korea invaded South Korea.

The Korean invasion was the greatest crisis of Truman's presidency. The president and his advisors clearly believed that the Soviet Union was responsible for the North Korean attack. After the "loss" of China, the Truman administration could not afford to allow Communism to advance further in Asia and secured approval from the United Nations for international action in Korea. Although troops from 15 countries eventually fought for the United Nations, nine out of ten soldiers came from the United States. America was at war then, or was it? Claiming that the conflict was only a "police action," Truman never asked Congress for a declaration of war.

At first, the fighting did not go well. U.S. troops had to fall back before the North Korean army. But in the summer, U.N. forces under the leadership of American general Douglas MacArthur halted the North Koreans' advance. In September, American troops stormed ashore at Inchon on the west coast of South Korea. Within weeks, the South was reclaimed.

Then Truman and his advisers made a fateful decision. Truman gave the order to invade North Korea and push for the reunification of the Korean peninsula. MacArthur, who privately thirsted for war with the Chinese Communists, pushed quickly northward, ever closer to China. Fearing an American invasion, the Chinese unleashed a broad attack on U.N. troops. As MacArthur's army fled back south to the 38th Parallel, the general admitted it was an "entirely new war."

The Korean "police action" settled into a troubling stalemate. MacArthur wanted to expand the war effort and fight back aggressively, but the Truman administration, giving up on Korean reunification, was prepared to accept the division at the 38th Parallel. When MacArthur broke the U.S. military's unwritten rule against public criticism of its civilian leadership, Truman fired his popular general. Meanwhile, the war dragged on.

The Korean stalemate underscored some difficult realities of the cold war. The confrontation with Communism had the potential to sacrifice American lives in seemingly insignificant countries far away from the United States. American soldiers had to go into battle without a declaration of war and accept a less-than-total victory. Moreover, the American people had to acknowledge that the fighting could easily spread into a wider war, perhaps even a nuclear war with the Soviet Union.

Escalating the U.S. Effort

The "loss" of China, the Soviet atomic bomb, and the Korean War had important consequences for American policy. The Truman administration increased its support for anti-Communist causes, such as the French war in Southeast Asia.

Vietnam, along with Laos and Cambodia, made up Indochina, a southeast Asian colony of France. After losing Indochina to Japan during World War II, the French were ready to take over again in 1945. By then, however, many Vietnamese wanted their land to be independent. Led by the Communist and nationalist Ho Chi Minh, the Viet Minh freedom fighters declared Vietnamese independence and appealed to the Truman administration for support in 1945 and 1946. However, the United States refused to oppose the interests of a valued European ally. Truman did not even answer Ho's letters.

With help from the Soviets and the Chinese Communists, the Viet Minh frustrated the French Army. By 1950, France needed help from the United States, and the Truman administration gave military equipment and direct financial aid to the French war effort in Vietnam.

Another consequence of the events of 1949 and 1950 was the escalation of the arms race. To deploy troops around the world and counter Soviet nuclear weapons, the United States had to strengthen its forces. In April 1950 the NSC approved a secret guideline for American policy, NSC 68, which warned that America, vulnerable to Soviet attack, must develop "clearly superior overall power." Increased defense spending was an absolute necessity.

In September 1950, at the president's urging, Congress passed the Defense Production Act, which nearly doubled defense spending in a single year. By 1952, defense expenditures had nearly doubled again, to $44 billion, and the armed forces grew from 1.5 million before the Korean War to 3.6 million in 1952 (see Figure 26–1).

The president had already made perhaps the most momentous decision of all. Early in 1950, Truman ordered the building of "the so-called hydrogen or super-bomb." Successfully tested in November 1952, the hydrogen bomb had far more explosive power than the earlier atomic bomb. Less than a year later, the USSR had its own H-bomb.

The confrontation with Communism was transforming the American political economy. To fight the cold war, Americans accepted things they had long feared in peacetime: alliances, foreign aid, and a massive standing army. These innovations magnified the role of the federal government in the economy and society. The president held more power than ever before. The federal government, its budget swollen by military expenditures, had new power to shape the economy.

THE RECONVERSION OF AMERICAN SOCIETY

While the cold war escalated, the United States confronted domestic challenges that tested the political economic arrangements of the Depression and World War II. With the end of the war, Americans focused on reconversion, the restoration of the economy and society to a peacetime footing. Reconversion was a welcome process, but also a cause for worry. Americans feared a return to the bleak economic conditions of the 1930s; labor, women, and African Americans feared losing their wartime gains.

The Postwar Economy

As World War II ended, economists and policymakers worried that the end of the federal government's massive spending for the war effort would force businesses to lay off workers and cut investment. Americans questioned whether the economy could provide enough jobs for the returning servicemen.

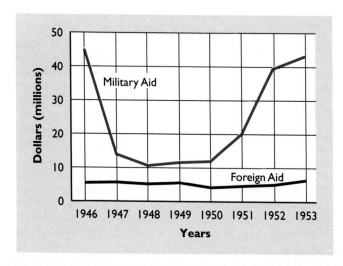

Figure 26–1   The Cost of the Cold War: U.S. Military and Foreign Aid Expenditures

Source: Statistical Abstract of the United States, 1952, p. 199; 1953, pp. 225, 886; 1957, p. 879; Historical Statistics of the United States, II, p. 1124.

The economic disaster never came. Unemployment rose to almost 4 percent in the first few years after the war, but never approached the double-digit rates of the 1930s. Despite brief downturns, the economy remained healthy.

This strong performance reflected several factors. Returning servicemen and women did not put excessive strain on the economy, partly because so many of them went back to school rather than look for work. Thanks to the generous provisions of the GI Bill of 1944, half of the nation's 15.4 million returning veterans went to school or received technical training.

Spending by the federal government also helped to prevent a return to the economic conditions of the 1930s. The GI Bill illustrated how that spending stimulated the economy. Pumping nearly $14.5 billion into the educational system, the bill encouraged colleges and universities to expand and to hire new faculty. Entire new educational systems, such as the State University of New York, were created.

Reconversion also went well because of the gradual transformation of the economy. In the late 1940s, the United States was still an industrial nation, with production centered in the Northeast and Midwest, but during and after the war, economic activity shifted toward the South and West, and the nature of the economy changed. In 1945, coal provided more than half the nation's energy. Five years later oil and natural gas provided the majority of energy. New technologies and industries, such as plastics and aviation, grew rapidly. This economic dynamism eased the process of reconversion.

Finally, the dominant role of the United States in the world economy facilitated reconversion. At the end of World War II, America was the only major industrial nation whose economy was undamaged. As late as 1950, America, with only 6 percent of the world's population, accounted for 40 percent of the value of all the goods and services produced around the globe. Demand for American exports helped to provide jobs for returning veterans and to sustain the economy.

Although the economy did not suffer from unemployment, it did confront inflation. The strong job market contributed to a rise in prices. With steady paychecks, Americans were eager to buy the appliances, cars, and houses that had been unavailable during the war. Driven by shortages of houses and other goods, the consumer price index rose 14.4 percent in 1946. By the late 1940s production caught up with demand, inflation decreased, and an economic boom continued.

The Challenge of Organized Labor

Reconversion posed special challenges for workers and the labor movement. After pledging not to strike during World War II, organized labor was eager to test and expand its power in peacetime. The unions wanted wage increases; some also wanted more control over the way corporations did business. Not surprisingly, corporate executives were reluctant to give up their power or profits.

The result was a huge wave of strikes as soon as the war ended in August 1945. At the start of 1946, 2 million workers were on strike. Machinists in San Francisco, longshoremen in New York City, and other workers across the country called a record 4,985 strikes that year.

Late in 1945, the United Auto Workers (UAW) struck General Motors (GM) for a 30 percent raise in hourly wages, access to the company's account books, and more of a say in the company's decisions. UAW vice president Walter Reuther insisted that higher wages would stimulate consumption without forcing the prosperous car company to raise prices; however, GM refused access to its books and rejected union interference in management decisions. When the strike finally ended after

113 days, the UAW won only some of its wage demands. The GM strike marked a turning point. Unions never again made such bold demands to participate in management, focusing instead on questions of pay and benefits.

The coal and railroad strikes were even more contentious than the GM work stoppage. The United Mine Workers (UMW) and the railway unions refused to accept federal arbitration. As the coal supply dwindled, power systems suffered and railroad passengers were stranded. The situation tested the strong relationship between the liberal Democratic Party and organized labor as an angry President Truman ordered federal takeovers of both the mines and the railroads. The strikes came to an end in May. When the UMW struck again in November, Truman took the union to court for violating a federal injunction. Forced to pay heavy fines, the union ended its walkout. Although angry unionists condemned Truman, much of the public applauded the president's action, believing that union leaders had become too powerful for the good of the country.

Counting on the public's unhappiness with unions, Congress soon moved to limit the power of organized labor. In 1947, Republicans and conservative Democrats passed the Taft–Hartley Act, which made it easier for employers to hire nonunion workers and to oppose the formation of unions. The bill also limited unions' right to organize supervisors, boycott employers, and engage in political activity. Most humiliating of all, it compelled union leaders to swear that they did not belong to the Communist Party. To angry unionists and their Democratic allies, the measure was the "Tuff–Heartless Act." Truman vetoed it, but Congress overrode him in June 1947.

The passage of the Taft–Hartley Act was not the end of organized labor's problems. A drive to unionize the low-wage industries of the South went poorly, in part because of divisions between white and African-American workers. Labor's attempts to force the repeal of Taft–Hartley failed.

Despite these setbacks, workers and unions prospered. In 1948 the UAW won guaranteed cost-of-living adjustments (COLAs) and an annual wage increase tied to rises in worker productivity. In 1950 the UAW obtained other increases and a pension plan. In return for pensions and protection against inflation, the auto workers gave management stable, predictable labor relations over the long term.

Opportunities for Women

Reconversion also posed special challenges to the status of American women. During World War II, the shortage of male civilian labor had expanded women's employment opportunities. At the end of the war, most working women did not want to give up those opportunities. But there was a widespread belief that women should surrender jobs to returning servicemen. American culture still assumed that women's ideal place was in the home.

Employers gave away women's jobs—high-paying industrial positions, in particular—to male veterans. The number of women in the labor force dropped 13 percent from 1945 to 1946, but three-quarters of the women who wanted to stay at work managed to find jobs.

Women's role in the postwar workplace was the product of both their desire and financial necessity. By 1953 the number of women in the work force matched the level of 1945. A higher percentage of women was employed than before World War II. The number of women in nontraditional jobs increased, too. More women than ever before were skilled craftspersons, forepersons, physicians, and surgeons.

The number of married women in the postwar labor force was especially notable. Traditionally, married women were expected to devote themselves to husbands and children, not jobs and careers. However, in the late 1940s there was a shortage of single female workers, so employers needed married women workers. By 1947 there were already more married women than single women in the wage labor force.

Reconversion did not cause a return to the prewar days when women had almost no place in the military. In 1947 Congress passed the Army–Navy Nurse Act, which granted women permanent status in the armed forces. The next year Congress merged the separate women's military organizations, such as the Women's Army Corps, into the regular armed services.

Despite these gains, women continued to face discrimination in the workplace. The vast majority of female workers had to settle for traditionally female, low-paying jobs. Women's hourly pay rose only half as much as men's in the first years after the war. In the military, women were largely confined to traditionally female roles such as nursing.

Women faced discrimination in the larger society as well. There was little interest in women's rights. After a meeting with female activists, Truman dismissed a constitutional amendment guaranteeing equal rights for women as a "lot of hooey." Nevertheless, women's opportunities gradually expanded after World War II as the combination of women's desires and the economy's needs slowly promoted the feminization of the labor force.

Civil Rights for African Americans

Like women, African Americans made significant gains during World War II. They played new roles in the military, filled higher paying jobs in the civilian economy, and pushed their demand for civil rights. Like women, African Americans wanted to preserve and extend their rights and opportunities in the postwar period but faced substantial resistance.

Several factors, including economic change, legal rulings, and wartime experiences, stimulated African Americans' drive for equal rights and opportunities. By the end of the war, the transformation of the southern economy was undermining the old system of segregation and denial of voting rights. African Americans continued to leave farms for the region's growing cities and for the North and West. One of the fundamental rationales for segregation—the need for an inexpensive and submissive labor force to work the fields—was gradually disappearing. Meanwhile, the African-American migrants to northern and western cities increased black votes and political influence in the nation.

During the 1940s, a series of Supreme Court decisions struck at racial discrimination. In *Smith* v. *Allwright* in 1944, the court banned whites-only primary elections. In *Morgan* v. *Virginia* in 1946, the court ruled that interstate bus companies could not segregate passengers. In *Shelley* v. *Kraemer* in 1948, the court banned restrictive covenants, private agreements between property owners not to sell houses to African Americans and other minorities. These and other court decisions made long-established forms of discrimination seem vulnerable and showed that African Americans might have a judicial ally in their struggle for justice.

African Americans' own wartime experiences also encouraged them to demand more from the United States. African-American veterans, having fought for their country, now expected justice. "Our people are not coming back with the idea of just taking up where they left off," an African-American private wrote.

That kind of determination spurred civil rights activism. In the South, African Americans increasingly demanded the right to vote after *Smith* v. *Allwright*. The National Association for the Advancement of Colored People (NAACP) set up citizenship schools in southern communities to show African Americans how to register to vote. Across the South, local organizations challenged the disfranchisement of African Americans. The voting campaign was driven, too, by grassroots, often spontaneous action. In July 1946 Medgar Evers, a combat veteran, tried to vote in the Democratic Party primary in Decatur, Mississippi. Such activism met resistance from many southern whites. A white mob kept Medgar Evers from voting. In Georgia, whites killed an African-American voter. More often, whites manipulated registration laws to disqualify would-be black voters. An African-American voter might have to answer such questions as "How many bubbles are there in a bar of soap?" African-American voter registration in the South, only 2 percent in 1940, rose to 12 percent by 1947. With that increasing percentage came the election of a few black officials and better service from local government.

While the campaign for voting rights went forward in the South, civil rights activists fought segregation in all parts of the country. To test the Supreme Court's decision in *Morgan* v. *Virginia*, the Congress of Racial Equality (CORE) sent an integrated team of activists on a bus trip through the upper South in 1947. The activists' attempt to desegregate buses and bus terminals met with violence and arrests. That year, an interracial CORE group forced the integration of an amusement park in New Jersey. Civil rights activists had more success promoting antidiscrimination laws in the North than in ending legal segregation in the South. By 1953 fair-employment laws had been adopted in 30 cities and 12 states.

Activists also pressured President Truman to support civil rights. In the spring and summer of 1946, picketers marched outside the White House with signs that read, "SPEAK, SPEAK, MR. PRESIDENT." Racial discrimination was an embarrassment for a nation claiming to represent freedom and democracy around the world, but support for civil rights was a political risk. Nevertheless, Truman took significant steps to fight discrimination.

In the fall of 1946, the president set up a Committee on Civil Rights. The committee's report, *To Secure These Rights*, called for strong federal action, including suppression of lynching, protection of African-American voters, enforcement of civil rights laws, desegregation of the armed forces, and promotion of equal employment opportunities. Admitting that "there is a serious gap between our ideals and some of our practices," Truman insisted "this gap must be closed."

African Americans, meanwhile, kept the heat on. To protest continuing discrimination in the military, A. Philip Randolph, the head of the Brotherhood of Sleeping Car Porters, proposed an African-American boycott of the draft. In July 1948 Truman responded with Executive Order 9981, which created the Committee on Equality of Treatment and Opportunity in the Armed Services. The committee moved vigorously to end discrimination in the military. At the same time, Truman established the Fair Employment Board, which moved more slowly against discrimination in federal hiring.

During the Truman years, the most publicized blow to racial inequality landed not in the White House or the courts, but rather on the baseball diamond. When the Brooklyn Dodgers called up infielder Jackie Robinson from the minor leagues in 1947, he became the first black man in decades to play in the majors. Fast, powerful, and exciting, Robinson finished the season as the National League's Rookie of the Year, and his success paved the way for increasing numbers of African-American players in the major leagues over the next several years.

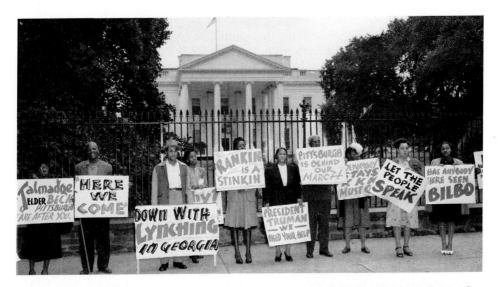

"President Truman, We Need Your Help." African Americans picket the White House to demand justice for the black victim of a lynching in Georgia. The placards condemning powerful white southern Democrats—Senator Eugene Talmadge, Senator Theodore Bilbo, and Representative John Rankin—are a reminder that Truman risked alienating white support if he responded to black demands for civil rights.

On the whole, African Americans preserved and sometimes expanded their wartime gains. Nevertheless, they still encountered injustice and inequality in most aspects of daily life. Legalized segregation and disfranchisement remained in the South. Although improving, the median income of African-American families was little more than half that of white families at the end of the 1940s. Moreover, most whites were not eager to redress these inequalities.

For African Americans, women, and organized labor, reconversion turned out to be better than feared and worse than hoped. All struggled to preserve and expand their rights and opportunities in the political economy of the late 1940s and confronted the limits of their power to change society.

Instead of falling back into economic depression, America generally prospered. The political economic arrangements that had emerged from the Depression and World War II seemed to work well enough, but the difficulties of African Americans, women, and organized labor were unfinished business that the United States grappled with for the next half-century.

THE FRUSTRATIONS OF LIBERALISM

During the Great Depression, liberalism, in the form of Franklin Roosevelt's New Deal, had reshaped the American political economy. The liberal Democratic agenda had stalled during World War II, and after the war liberalism met with frustration.

The Democrats' Troubles

An accidental president, Harry Truman faced skepticism from many Americans. They wondered whether this unassuming, plain-spoken man could take the place of Franklin Roosevelt. Liberals wondered, too, whether Truman really shared their ideas.

At the same time, the president was handicapped by skepticism about the Democrats' liberal approach to the political economy. During the Great Depression, Americans had been willing to endorse the liberals' faith in an activist government, but in a fairly prosperous peacetime, people felt less need for government and more need for individual freedom.

The president embraced more of liberalism than the liberals expected. Shortly after he took office in 1945, Truman presented a 21-point legislative program that included liberal proposals on education, employment, insurance, social security, and civil rights. Yet a Full Employment Bill met overwhelming conservative and moderate opposition. Watered down by Congress, the resulting Employment Act of 1946 did nothing to increase the role of the federal government in promoting employment.

Truman and the liberals suffered an even sharper defeat over the president's proposal for a compulsory health insurance system that would guarantee medical care to all Americans. Conservatives and the medical profession condemned Truman's proposal as "the kind of regimentation that led to totalitarianism in Germany." The bill failed to pass Congress, and so did the rest of Truman's proposals.

Nevertheless, the federal government's role in national life continued to grow. For example, even though national health insurance was defeated, federal intervention in the health-care system increased. The Veterans Administration established a vast network of federal hospitals. The Hill–Burton Act appropriated federal money for hospital construction, and Congress created the Communicable Disease Center (later called the Centers for Disease Control) to monitor infectious diseases, reorganized the National Institutes of Health, and established the National Institute of Mental Health.

While Truman struggled with domestic and foreign policy, he became increasingly unpopular. The president looked weak and ineffective to some Americans and tyrannical and overbearing to others. In the 1946 Congressional elections, voters gave the Republican Party a majority in both the House and the Senate for the first time in 16 years.

Truman's Comeback

The 1946 elections seemed to point toward Truman's certain defeat in the presidential contest two years later, but the president managed a stunning comeback. The turnaround began with the victorious Republican majority of the Eightieth Congress that convened in 1947. Led by Senator Robert Taft of Ohio, the Congressional Republicans hoped to beat back New Deal liberalism. Taft, the son of former president William Howard Taft, believed in limited government and wanted "free Americans freely working out their destiny."

The Republicans did win passage of the Taft–Hartley Act, which was a blow to labor, liberals, and the president, but Taft and the Republicans found themselves hamstrung by Americans' ambivalence about liberalism. People did not want bold new liberal programs such as national health insurance, but Americans clearly wanted to hold on to the government benefits they had won in the Depression and World War II. Besides the Taft–Hartley Act, the Eightieth Congress did not accomplish much of the Republican agenda.

Nevertheless, things looked bleak for Harry Truman. By March 1948 only 35 percent of the people approved of his performance in office. Moreover, his party was splitting apart. On the left, his former Secretary of Commerce Henry Wallace was running for president as a Progressive appealing to liberals. On the right, Democratic Governor Strom Thurmond of South Carolina was running as a "Dixiecrat," appealing to white supporters of segregation.

Truman's Republican opponent, Governor Thomas E. Dewey of New York, thought Truman was certain to lose. Dewey believed he could get away with a mild, uncontroversial campaign. But Truman worked hard to pull the Democratic New Deal majority back together. Climbing aboard his railway car, Truman visited more than half the states on an old-fashioned "whistle-stop" campaign, reaching out to African Americans, labor, farmers, senior citizens, and other beneficiaries of New Deal liberalism. "Give 'em hell, Harry," the crowds shouted, and he did, deriding the "do-nothing" Republican Congress. "The Democratic Party puts human rights and human welfare first," he declared. "These Republican gluttons of privilege . . . want a return of the Wall Street economic dictatorship."

On election day Dewey attracted fewer votes than he had four years before. Holding together the New Deal coalition, Truman won the presidency in his own right with only 49.5 percent of the vote. Moreover, the Democrats recaptured the House and the Senate.

Truman soon discovered that an election victory did not mean a mandate for his ideas. In his State of the Union address in January 1949, Truman declared that "every individual has a right to expect from our Government a fair deal." But the president's Fair Deal legislation made little headway in Congress. The liberal vision of the political economy could not command the politics of cold war America.

"Give 'em hell, Harry!" President Harry Truman speaks to a crowd from the back of his railroad car during the 1948 election campaign.

FIGHTING THE COLD WAR AT HOME

While conservatives and liberals battled over domestic policy, the cold war increasingly affected life in the United States. Billions of dollars in defense expenditures eventually stimulated economic growth, but in the short run, the main domestic byproduct of the cold war was a largely irrational fear of Communist subversives. By the 1950s, this fear was a powerful force capable of destroying the lives of thousands of Americans, including Esther and Stephen Brunauer.

Doubts and Fears in the Atomic Age

Despite the U.S. triumph in World War II, American culture was surprisingly dark and pessimistic in the late 1940s. The rise of fascism, the Holocaust, and the bombings of Hiroshima and Nagasaki raised troubling questions. The cold war did nothing to calm those concerns. People felt small and powerless in an age of giant corporations, big unions, big government, and super bombs.

Nuclear weapons were perhaps the greatest source of fear. The unprecedented power of the atomic bomb dominated the popular imagination. For many Americans, this was the Atomic Age. They dealt with their anxiety in a variety of ways. Some people tried humor. Americans drank "atomic cocktails" and danced to the "Atomic Polka." But the Soviets' development of the atomic bomb and the hydrogen bomb was impossible to laugh away.

Americans' fear was also reflected in the hardening of attitudes toward foreigners who wanted to live in the United States. The Immigration and Nationality Act of 1952 continued tight restrictions on immigration, particularly from Asia. It also kept out Communists and homosexuals and allowed the deportation of American citizens suspected of disloyalty.

The Anti-Communist Crusade Begins

Americans might have feared disloyalty most of all. The search for traitors quickly became a panicky "Red Scare," much like the one that followed World War I.

Historians debate the origins of the second Red Scare. Anti-Communism was already deeply rooted in American culture, but the powerful politicians of both major parties gave domestic anti-Communism its particularly dangerous form.

The crusaders had to search hard for Communism at home. The Communist Party of the United States of America (CPUSA), a legal political party, never received more than 0.3 percent of the popular vote in any presidential election. Nevertheless, the party became the target of persecution. In June 1948 the Truman administration charged 12 American Communist leaders with violations of the 1940 Smith Act, which had criminalized membership in "a group advocating . . . the overthrow of the government by force." Eleven were convicted and jailed.

With so little open Communism, some Americans searched for secret Communists. The hunt was led by the House of Representatives' Committee on Un-American Activities, known as the House Un-American Activities Committee (HUAC). In 1947 the HUAC held hearings to lay bare a supposed Communist plot in Hollywood. Much of the film industry cooperated with the HUAC, but eight screenwriters, a producer, and a director, who were Communists, cited their First Amendment rights and declined to testify about their political beliefs and activities.

The "Hollywood Ten" were convicted of contempt of Congress and sent to jail for up to a year, with the eventual concurrence of the Supreme Court.

Hollywood got the message. Film studios refused to hire writers, directors, and actors even remotely suspected of Communist ties. The studios put out over-wrought anti-Communist movies such as *The Red Menace.*

Afraid of looking "soft" on Communism, the Truman administration helped promote the Red Scare by encouraging the idea that there was a real problem with domestic Communism. "Communists," declared Truman's Attorney General, Tom Clark, "are everywhere . . . and each carries with him the germs of death for society."

In 1947 the president created a permanent Federal Employee Loyalty Program. Any civil servant could lose his or her job by belonging to any of the "totalitarian, Fascist, Communist or subversive" groups listed by the attorney general. People accused of disloyalty were denied due process and had to prove their own innocence. Although only about 300 employees were actually discharged for disloyalty, the program helped create the impression that there was a serious problem with Communism in Washington.

The Hunt for Soviet Spies

There was, in fact, spying going on inside the federal government. The Soviet Union, like the United States, carried out espionage abroad. In 1945 an illegal raid by the Office of Strategic Services, the predecessor of the CIA, turned up secret U.S. government documents in the offices of *Amerasia,* a magazine that favored the Chinese Communists. The Canadian government found evidence of a spy ring that had passed American atomic secrets to the Soviets during World War II.

Thanks to information from the Canadian case, the FBI began to suspect that Alger Hiss, an aide to the secretary of state, was a Soviet agent. Hiss was quietly eased out of his job. Then, in 1948, the HUAC took testimony from Whittaker Chambers, an editor of *Time* magazine, who accused Hiss of being a Communist. Hiss denied the charge against him, said he had never even met Chambers, and sued the magazine editor for libel.

The suave Hiss appeared far more credible than the rumpled Chambers, who was an admitted perjurer, but Republican Congressman Richard Nixon of California forced Hiss to admit that he had known Chambers under an alias. Chambers charged that Hiss had given him secret information in the 1930s. In front of reporters at his farm in Maryland, Chambers pulled rolls of microfilm out of a hollowed-out pumpkin. The film contained photographs of secret documents, some of which had apparently been typed on a typewriter belonging to Hiss's family. Under the statute of limitations, it was too late to try Hiss for spying, but it was not too late to indict him for lying to Congress. Hiss was convicted in January 1950. While Hiss sat in prison for almost four years, Chambers wrote a bestseller and Nixon became a senator. The case was a triumph for Republicans and conservatives and a blow to Democrats and liberals.

As the Hiss case ended, another scandal stimulated Americans' fears. In early 1950, British authorities arrested Klaus Fuchs, a physicist who had worked at the nuclear research facility in Los Alamos, New Mexico. The investigation led to David Greenglass, who had worked on the atomic bomb project during World War II. Greenglass admitted that he had passed information about the bomb to his brother-in-law, Julius Rosenberg. Rosenberg, a former member of the Communist Party, and his wife Ethel were convicted in a controversial trial on charges of conspiracy to commit espionage and sentenced to death in April 1951. The Supreme Court refused to review the case. Ignoring appeals for clemency from around the world, the federal government finally electrocuted the Rosenbergs in June 1953. The controversy over their guilt has continued to the present day.

There now seems little disagreement over the reality of Soviet spying in the early years of the cold war. The USSR obtained some American nuclear secrets, but the impact was not as great as conservatives feared or as minimal as liberals insisted. Most likely, espionage sped up the Soviets' work on an atomic bomb that they would have developed anyway.

The Rise of McCarthyism

Two weeks after Hiss's conviction, one week after Truman's announcement of the decision to build the hydrogen bomb, and days after the arrest of Klaus Fuchs, Senator Joseph McCarthy of Wisconsin took command of the anti-Communist crusade.The previously obscure senator claimed to have the names of 205 Communists working for the State Department. In fact, McCarthy had no names of State Department Communists at all. Instead, he named other people as subversives, including Esther and Stephen Brunauer. A Democratic-controlled Senate subcommittee dismissed McCarthy's charges.

Nevertheless, frightened by the developments of the last five years, many people believed McCarthy. Some Americans shared McCarthy's resentment of New Dealers and other privileged elites—the powerful figures he derided as "egg-sucking phony liberals."

Many Democrats hated McCarthyism, but they were afraid to challenge such a powerful political force. Frightened Democratic legislators even helped Congress pass the Internal Security Act of 1950, which forced the registration of Communist and Communist-front groups, allowed the internment of suspicious persons in national emergencies, provided for the deportation of allegedly subversive aliens, and barred Communists from defense jobs. Truman vetoed the bill, but Congress overrode his veto.

Eventually, McCarthy went too far. Angry that one of his aides, David Schine, had not received a draft deferment, the senator launched an investigation of the Army. The Secretary of the Army, Robert T. Stevens, claimed that McCarthy had pressured the service to take care of Schine. In April 1954, before a television audience of 20 million people, McCarthy failed to come up with evidence of treason in the Army. When he tried unjustifiably to smear one of the Army's young lawyers as a Communist, McCarthy was suddenly exposed. "Have you no sense of decency, sir, at long last?" asked the Army's Chief Counsel, Joseph Welch. It was an electric moment. McCarthy's popularity ratings dropped sharply, and the Senate condemned him for "unbecoming conduct." Three years later he was dead.

The fall of McCarthy did not end McCarthyism, however. Americans were looking everywhere for Communists in the 1950s. At several universities, faculty members lost their jobs. Communism had become a useful charge to hurl at labor unions, civil rights, and even modern art. Politicians and communities attacked nonrepresentational, abstract expressionist artists as "tools of the Kremlin" and "our enemies." The Cincinnati Reds renamed their team the "Redlegs." Across the country, Americans became more careful about what they said out loud. Containment abroad seemed to have produced an uncontainable fear at home.

CHRONOLOGY

1945	Yalta conference
	Harry S Truman's succession to the presidency
	Potsdam conference
	Beginning of postwar strike wave
1946	Winston Churchill's "Iron Curtain" speech
	George Kennan's "long telegram" on Soviet expansionism
	Employment Act of 1946
	Morgan v. *Virginia*
	Election of Republican majorities in the House and Senate
1947	Announcement of Truman Doctrine
	Beginning of Federal Employee Loyalty Program
	CORE's Journey of Reconciliation
	Integration of Major League baseball by Jackie Robinson
	HUAC Hollywood hearings
	Rio Pact
	Taft–Hartley Act
	National Security Act of 1947
	Report by Presidential Committee on Civil Rights, *To Secure These Rights*
1948	*Shelley* v. *Kraemer*
	Congressional approval of Marshall Plan
	Truman's Executive Order 9981
	Beginning of Berlin crisis
	Selective Service Act
	Truman elected president
1949	Formation of North Atlantic Treaty Organization
	Communist takeover of mainland China
1950	NSC 68
	Alger Hiss's conviction for perjury
	Joe McCarthy's speech in Wheeling, West Virginia
	Treaty of Detroit
	Beginning of Korean War
	Internal Security Act of 1950
1951	Truman fires General Douglas MacArthur
1952	Immigration and Nationality Act
	Test of hydrogen bomb
1953	Execution of Ethel and Julius Rosenberg
1954	Army–McCarthy Hearings

CONCLUSION

By the time Esther Brunauer lost her job in 1952, the cold war had deeply disrupted American life. To contain Communism, the United States had made unprecedented peacetime commitments that transformed the nation's political economy. Despite these changes, the cold war had widened and intensified. Just seven years after dropping the first atomic bomb on the Japanese, Americans lived with the threat of nuclear annihilation. They lived, too, with the frenzied search for domestic Communists.

As Esther and Stephen Brunauer moved back to Illinois to find peace and rebuild their lives, other Americans needed peace as well. They wanted the fighting in Korea to end. Anxious to avoid a nuclear holocaust, they wanted the cold war confrontation with the Soviets to stabilize. Meanwhile, American society needed to focus on the unfinished business of reconversion, including the rights of labor, women, and African Americans. However, it would be impossible to avoid the consequences of the cold war.

FURTHER READINGS

Richard M. Fried, *Nightmare in Red: The McCarthy Era in Perspective* (1990). Provides a concise overview of the anti-Communist crusade.

William Graebner, *The Age of Doubt: American Thought and Culture in the 1940s* (1991). Probes the fears and insecurities that shaped American society during the cold war.

Alonzo L. Hamby, *Man of the People: A Life of Harry S. Truman* (1995). A full biography of the first cold war president.

Melvyn P. Leffler, *A Preponderance of Power: National Security, the Truman Administration, and the Cold War* (1992). One of several important conflicting accounts of the origins of the cold war.

Nelson Lichtenstein, *The Most Dangerous Man in Detroit: Walter Reuther and the Fate of American Labor* (1995). Examines the hopes and frustrations of the labor movement after World War II.

David M. Oshinsky, *A Conspiracy So Immense: The World of Joe McCarthy* (1983). An engaging, even-handed biography of the most famous anti-Communist crusader.

Arnold Rampersad, *Jackie Robinson: A Biography* (1997). Explores the complicated man who integrated Major League Baseball.

Richard Rhodes, *Dark Sun: The Making of the Hydrogen Bomb* (1995). An engaging narrative account of a key development in the nuclear arms race.

Allen Weinstein, *Perjury: The Hiss–Chambers Case* (1978). Provides a thorough, controversial study of one of the most controversial episodes of the cold war.

Please refer to the document CD-ROM for primary sources related to this chapter.

CHAPTER

27

The Consumer Society

1950–1960

E. J. Korvettes • Living the Good Life • A Homogeneous Society?
The Eisenhower Era at Home and Abroad • Challenges to the
Consumer Society • Conclusion

E. J. KORVETTES

At the end of World War II, Harry Ferkauf owned two luggage stores in midtown Manhattan in New York City. An immigrant Jewish man from Eastern Europe, he haggled with customers over prices in the old way and made a decent living. He did not want or expect much more.

Harry's son, Eugene, was unwilling to accept the old limits. After the war, Gene began offering discounts on luggage, watches, and other goods. Other neighborhood storeowners resented this low-priced competition. Father and son argued frequently. In 1948, Gene quit the business and put all his savings into his own discount store that would compete with the full-priced stores of the other merchants.

Gene envisioned a new kind of store, where customers could buy appliances and other goods without haggling, at low, fixed prices. Discounting his merchandise by a quarter and even a third, Gene could not make much money from a single sale. But if he sold enough televisions and refrigerators, he would earn more than his father ever had. Gene and his wife distributed thousands of cards announcing the new store on East 46th Street. On opening day, crowds filled the small shop and spent $3,000. Harry, who usually took in about $50 a day, was impressed.

In a few years, Gene had five successful discount stores in and around New York City. The business was called "E. J. Korvettes"—E for Eugene, J for his partner Joe

Zwillenberg, and Korvettes after the small, quick Canadian warships of World War II. Korvettes appealed to a new generation, young men and women eager to buy televisions and other appliances and unafraid to go into debt. Prosperous, they were leaving their parents' neighborhoods in the city for new suburbs. Gene Ferkauf understood these people; he was one of them.

In December 1953 Gene opened a vast new department store in Westbury, Long Island, where farmland was giving way to new suburban housing developments. The crowds were so big that salesmen could not get back into the store after their lunch hours. The suburban store pulled in $28 million in a year.

Riding the suburban wave, Gene Ferkauf had made it big. Gene closed the stores in New York City and kept expanding into the suburbs. He had left his father's world behind.

Gene Ferkauf's success reflected one of the central developments that shaped American society after World War II. Along with the cold war, economic prosperity transformed the nation in a host of ways. Just as Gene left his father's world behind, American society left behind the sense of economic limits and constraints that marked the Great Depression and the war. The 1950s marked the culmination of the nation's long transformation into a full-fledged consumer society. Gene Ferkauf profited because mainstream culture celebrated consumption and pleasure instead of work and self-restraint and because televisions and suburbs defined the consumer lifestyle.

The emergence of the consumer society strongly affected the American political economy, producing a more homogeneous, seemingly more harmonious society, characterized by decreasing class differences, changing gender relations, and a baby boom. In later years, American culture would look back nostalgically at the 1950s, but the consumer society had its conflicts, failures, and limits. In different ways, teenagers and some other Americans rebelled against the conformity and constraints of the 1950s. The benefits of the consumer society did not reach every group; consumerism did not solve the problem of racial inequality or end the cold war. By the close of the decade, many Americans worried about the inadequacies of the consumer society, even as they enjoyed its benefits.

LIVING THE GOOD LIFE

Consumerism was not a new development, but it was only in the 1950s that consumer values and habits finally dominated the American economy and culture. Never before had so many Americans had the chance to live the good life.

They tended to define that "good life" in economic terms. A dynamic, evolving economy provided more leisure and income. Sure of prosperity, Americans had the confidence to spend more of their time and money in the pursuit of pleasure. Millions of people lived the dream of homeownership in new suburbs, bought flashy automobiles, purchased their first televisions, and enjoyed a new openness about sex.

Economic Prosperity

Consumerism could not have flourished without prosperity. Despite three short recessions, the 1950s were a period of economic boom. The economy grew solidly, and the gross national product—the value of all the country's output of goods and services—grew at an average of 3.2 percent a year.

Several major factors spurred this economic growth. The shortage of consumer goods during and just after World War II had left Americans with money to spend. Because of the cold war, the federal government was also ready to spend money. Washington's expenditures for the defense buildup and foreign aid helped to stimulate the demand for American goods and services. At the same time, the industrial economy was evolving. Traditional heavy manufacturing—the production of steel and automobiles—was still crucial to national prosperity, but newer industries—electronics, chemicals, plastics, aviation, and computers—became increasingly important.

The emergence of the computer business was especially significant for the long-term transformation of the economy. In 1946, two engineers at the University of Pennsylvania, J. Presper Eckert, Jr., and John William Mauchly, completed the first fully electronic digital computer, loaded with hot bulky vacuum tubes. The Electronic Numerical Integrator and Computer (ENIAC) weighed more than 30 tons and filled a large room. Then Eckert and Mauchly produced the UNIVAC 1 (Universal Automatic Computer), a more advanced machine that was used to count census data in 1951 and presidential election returns in 1952.

As tiny solid-state transistors replaced vacuum tubes, computers became smaller, more powerful, and more common. By 1958, American companies were producing $1 billion worth of computers a year. Because computers were still so large and expensive, they were used mostly by universities, corporations, the Department of Defense, and other federal agencies. By 1961, there were about 10,000 computers in use, and the nation was on the brink of the computer age.

As American industry continued to evolve, the nation's distribution and service sectors played a larger economic role than ever before. While the number of manufacturing jobs barely changed, employment in retail stores like E. J. Korvettes increased 19 percent. Jobs in the service sector, such as restaurants, hotels, repair shops, hospitals, and universities, jumped 32 percent. The United States had begun to develop a post-industrial economy, less dependent on production and more dependent on service and consumption.

The prosperity of the 1950s also rested on relative labor peace. After the instability of the late 1940s, relations between workers and employers settled down. Unionized workers, their wages and benefits rising, seldom challenged employers.

Economic prosperity greatly benefited big business. In the 1950s, corporations loomed larger than ever before. New firms such as E. J. Korvettes emerged and grew. Established corporations became still larger. By 1960, corporations earned 18 times as much income as the rest of the nation's businesses combined.

Corporations enjoyed public approval as well as economic prosperity. Business executives now seemed to be leading the nation into an economic golden age. As a result, the popular suspicion of big business, so strong during the Depression, evaporated. Even liberals, once critical of corporate power, now celebrated the benefits of large-scale business enterprise.

American workers also benefited from the prosperity of the 1950s, enjoying high employment, low inflation, and rising incomes. Typically, less than 5 percent of the work force was out of a job at one time. Wages rose dramatically. Factory workers' average hourly pay more than doubled between 1945 and 1960. Moreover, consumer prices rose less than 2 percent per year. The percentage of people living in poverty declined.

The economy also gave Americans more leisure time. By the 1950s, the 40-hour work week was commonplace in American factories. Many workers now looked forward to two- or three-week paid annual vacations. As life expectancy increased and the economy boomed, more and more Americans could expect to retire at age 65 and then live comfortably off their pensions and Social Security.

The impact of World War II and the cold war, the development of the industrial and service sectors, and stable labor relations fostered a comfortable sense of economic well-being. Corporations and consumers alike had the means to live the good life.

The Suburban Dream

For growing numbers of people, the good life lay outside the city. In the 1950s, many urban and rural Americans dreamed of living in a house in the suburbs. American culture had long idealized homeownership, and suburbs, developing since the nineteenth century, were nothing new. Yet the suburbs had been mainly for the well-to-do. Most Americans had never owned their own homes. But entrepreneurship, efficient construction methods, inexpensive land, and generous federal aid made possible a host of affordable housing developments outside the nation's cities. Along with Gene Ferkauf and his family, much of America moved to the suburbs in the 1950s.

William J. Levitt's pioneering development, Levittown, illustrated how entrepreneurship, low-priced land, and new construction techniques fueled a suburban housing boom. Levitt came back from military service in World War II with an optimistic vision of the future. He wanted to make houses affordable for middle-class and working-class people. Drawing on the assembly-line techniques of automaker Henry Ford, he intended to build houses so efficiently that they could be sold at remarkably low prices. Levitt bought 1,000 acres of cheap farmland on New York's Long Island. He put up simple houses, with prefabricated parts, no basements, and low price tags. The original Cape Cod-style house cost $7,990, an appealing price for young couples buying their first homes.

Like Korvettes, Levittown quickly became a huge success. Buyers signed 1,400 contracts for houses on a single day in 1949. The development grew to 17,500 dwellings housing 82,000 people. Levitt soon built more Levittowns, as did imitators all around the country.

The Pursuit of Pleasure

The consumer society depended on Americans' eagerness to pursue pleasure. Businesses made sure that nothing would prevent Americans from buying goods and services. If their wages and salaries were not enough, consumers could borrow. Along with federally guaranteed mortgage loans, people could now get credit cards. In 1950, the Diner's Club introduced the credit card for well-to-do New Yorkers. By the end of the decade, Sears Roebuck credit cards allowed more than 10 million Americans to spend borrowed money. In 1945, Americans owed only $5.7 billion for consumer goods other than houses. By 1960, they owed $56.1 billion.

In the 1950s, discount stores such as Korvettes made shopping seem simpler and more attractive, and so did another new creation, the shopping mall. In 1956, Southdale, the nation's first enclosed suburban shopping mall, opened outside

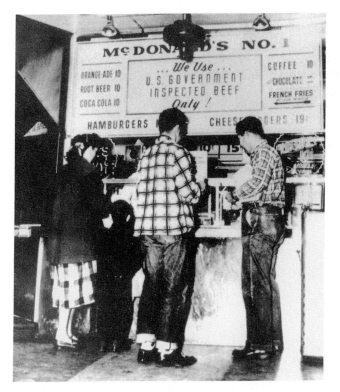

Symbol of the consumer society: The first McDonald's fast food restaurant, opened by the McDonald brothers in San Bernadino, California, in 1948.

Minneapolis, Minnesota. Consumers bought meals more easily, too. The first McDonald's fast-food restaurant opened in San Bernardino, California, in 1948. Taken over by businessman Ray Kroc, McDonald's began to grow into a national chain in the mid-1950s.

To get to McDonald's, the Southdale Mall, Korvettes, and Levittown, Americans needed cars. In the 1950s, cars reflected Americans' new sense of affluence and self-indulgence. Big, high-compression engines burning high-octane gasoline powered ever bigger cars. Unlike the drab autos of the Great Depression, the new models had "Passion Pink" and "Horizon Blue" interiors and two-tone and even three-tone exteriors studded with shiny chrome.

Automakers used that chrome to solve one of the main problems of a consumer society—getting people who already had plenty to want to buy even more. How could Detroit persuade Americans to trade in old cars that were running just fine and purchase new ones? The answer was to make the new models look different from the old ones. The result was what General Motors's chief designer called "dynamic obsolescence," the feeling that the old model with last year's styling was somehow inadequate (see Table 27–1).

More than ever, automakers offered cars as a reflection of a driver's identity. The car of the 1950s clearly announced its owner's affluence. General Motors's line of cars rose up the socioeconomic ladder, from the ordinary Chevrolet, to the more prosperous Pontiac, Oldsmobile, and Buick, all the way up to the sumptuous Cadillac.

Automobiles also spoke to sexual identity. Detroit designed the interior of cars to appeal to women. Inside, the autos of the 1950s had to seem like comfortable or

TABLE 27–1

Automobiles and Highways, 1945–1960			
Year	Factory Sales (in 1,000s)	Registrations (in 1,000s)	Miles of Highway (in 1,000s)
1945	69.5	25,796.9	3,035
1946	2,148.6	28,217.0	5,057
1947	3,558.1	30,849.3	15,473
1948	3,909.2	33,355.2	21,725
1949	5,119.4	36,457.9	19,876
1950	6,665.8	40,339.0	19,876
1951	5,338.4	42,688.3	17,060
1952	4,320.7	43,823.0	22,147
1953	6,116.9	46,429.2	21,136
1954	5,558.8	48,468.4	20,548
1955	7,920.1	52,144.7	22,571
1956	5,816.1	54,210.9	23,609
1957	6,113.3	55,917.8	22,424
1958	4,257.8	56,890.5	28,137
1959*	5,591.2	59,453.9	32,633
1960	6,674.7	61,682.3	20,969

*Denotes first year for which figures include Alaska and Hawaii.

Source: Historical Statistics of the United States, 1976, Vol. 2, pp. 711, 716.

luxurious living rooms. The exterior offered men a combination of power and sexuality. Automakers tried to make men feel like they were flying supersonic jets. While the back of a 1950s car looked like the winking afterburners of a jet, the front spoke to something else. The chrome protrusions on 1950s Cadillacs were known as "Dagmars" after the name of a large-breasted female television star. A car, as a Buick ad promised, "makes you feel like the man you are."

It was not remarkable that the chrome on a Cadillac would make Americans think of a television star. In the 1950s, television became a central part of American life. Technological advances made TV sets less expensive. As sales boomed, there were new opportunities for broadcasters. By 1950, the Federal Communications Commission (FCC) had licensed 104 TV stations, mostly in cities. By 1960, 90 percent of the nation's households had a television (see Table 27–2). In 15 years, TV had become a part of everyday life.

From its early days, television reinforced the values of consumer society. Advertisements for consumer products paid for programming that focused mainly on pleasure and diversion. Nightly national news broadcasts lasted only 15 minutes. There were operas, documentaries, and live, original dramas in what some critics consider television's "golden age," but most of the broadcast schedule was filled with variety shows, sports, westerns, and situation comedies.

One of the hallmarks of American culture in the 1950s was a new openness about sexuality. To his surprise, Dr. Alfred C. Kinsey of Indiana University commanded enormous public attention with two pioneering academic studies—*Sexual*

TABLE 27–2

Year	Television Stations	Television, 1941–1960 Households With Television Sets (in 1,000s)
1941	2	—
1945	9	—
1950	104	3,875
1955	458	30,700
1960	579	45,750

Source: George Thomas Kurian, Datapedia *(Lanham, MD: Bernan Press, 1994), pp. 299–300.*

Behavior in the Human Male (1948) and *Sexual Behavior in the Human Female* (1953). To his readers' surprise, Kinsey reported that Americans were more sexually active outside of marriage than had been thought.

The new candor about sexuality was probably best represented by *Playboy* magazine, first published by Hugh Hefner in December 1953. Hefner presented sex as one part of a hedonistic, consumer lifestyle complete with flashy cars, expensive stereos, and fine liquor.

The different tall tail fins of two late-1950s Cadillacs epitomized the gaudy "dynamic obsolescence" of the consumer society.

The success of *Playboy*, along with the popularity of TV and tail fins, underscored how much American attitudes had changed since the Great Depression. Armed with money, leisure, and confidence, many Americans devoted more of life to enjoyment. Business encouraged them with credit cards, shopping malls, fast-food restaurants, and dynamic obsolescence. Before long, it became clear that many Americans could not afford consumerism, but for a while at least, the nation seemed to be living the good life.

A HOMOGENEOUS SOCIETY?

The spread of consumerism reinforced a sense of sameness in America during the 1950s. Declining class differences strengthened the feeling that people were becoming more alike, as did a rush to attend church and have children. Along with the renewed emphasis on religion and family, Americans faced pressure to conform to gender roles.

Nevertheless, the United States remained a heterogeneous society. While ethnic differences among whites decreased, race remained a powerful divider. Despite fears of conformity, the nation still encouraged difference and individuality.

The Discovery of Conformity

In the years after World War II, sociologists and other writers noticed a disturbing uniformity across American society. People were becoming increasingly alike, partly because they shared more and more experiences, such as consumerism and suburban lifestyles. Some commentators and social critics feared the loss of the personal freedom and individuality that seemed so basic to American life.

A variety of factors promoted homogeneity. During the frenzied search for domestic Communists, people did not want to risk accusations by appearing different or unusual. Moreover, as corporations merged and small businesses disappeared, Americans worked for the same giant companies. The new suburbs intensified the sense of homogeneity.

To some observers, this similarity was more than a matter of shared experience. Americans, they believed, wanted to be like one another. In *The Lonely Crowd* (1950), sociologist David Riesman suggested that instead of following their own internalized set of values, Americans adjusted their behavior to meet the expectations of the people around them. In *The Organization Man* (1956), William H. Whyte, Jr., described the conformist style of white-collar workers in big corporations. In the office or at home in the suburbs, the "organization man" was all too willing to go along with others.

The Decline of Class Differences

The homogeneity of American society was reinforced by the apparent decline of class differences. By the 1950s, the old upper class—the families of the Gilded Age industrialists and financiers—had lost much wealth and power thanks to the Great Depression, income and inheritance taxes, and sheer waste and mismanagement. In his book *The Power Elite* (1956), sociologist C. Wright Mills argued that an interlocking military, political, and economic elite ran the country. However, this rather drab group did not have the bold, public swagger of the old, opulent upper class.

American farmers had also been disappearing for a long time. Since the late nineteenth century, the increasing efficiency of American agriculture, along with overseas competition, had meant the nation needed fewer farmers. The number of American farms fell from more than 6 million in 1944 to just 3.7 million 15 years later.

In contrast, the working class remained large and apparently healthy. Manual and service workers, some 33 million strong, were still the nation's largest occupational group in 1960. About one-third of workers belonged to unions. The labor movement's size and power were underscored in 1955 when the AFL and the CIO merged to become the gigantic AFL-CIO.

Well-paid blue-collar workers appeared content with American society and their role within it. Labor leaders endorsed consumerism and anti-Communism. Some observers argued that American workers had become essentially middle class in their buying habits and social values.

This apparent transformation, along with the decline of farmers and the upper class, made it easier to think of the United States as a classless society. Different social groups were evidently becoming more middle class in their values and outlook. The middle class itself was burgeoning. By 1960, the white-collar sector made up 40 percent of the work force.

Even the ethnic differences no longer seemed significant. Whites from different ethnic backgrounds mixed together in the new suburbs. The rate of intermarriage between ethnic groups increased. Anxious to prove their loyalty during the cold war, newer Americans were reluctant to emphasize their origins. Ethnicity had apparently disappeared in the national melting pot of the consumer society.

Many Americans, especially powerful ones, had long wanted to believe that the United States was a unified society devoted to middle-class values. In the 1950s, there was probably more basis for this belief than ever before. Nevertheless, prosperous Americans were ignoring some troublesome realities. The very poor remained concentrated in inner cities and remote rural areas. Social classes still differed significantly. The completely unified, classless society was an illusion, but many people preferred this illusion to reality.

The Resurgence of Religion and Family

Americans went back to church in the 1950s. Church membership doubled to 114 million between 1945 and 1960. The surge in attendance mostly benefited Christian denominations. By 1960, there were 64 million Protestants, 42 million Roman Catholics, and fewer than 6 million Jews (see Table 27–3).

Denominations encouraged the attendance boom by adapting religion to the consumer society. Naturally, they made use of television. Charismatic preachers such as Roman Catholic Bishop Fulton J. Sheen and evangelist Billy Graham became TV stars. The nation's political leaders encouraged the religious revival, too. Freedom of religion, they insisted, differentiated the United States from allegedly godless Communist nations. To underscore the national commitment to religion, the federal government put the words "In God We Trust" on all its currency.

American culture celebrated the family along with religion in the 1950s. Detroit presented its big automobiles as "family" cars. Manufacturers promoted television as a way of holding families together. American society venerated what *McCall's* magazine christened family "togetherness."

This "togetherness" meant the nuclear family, with a mother, a father, and plenty of children. After decades of decline, the birth rate rose during and after World War II. Beginning in 1954, Americans had more than 4 million babies a year. Thanks to new drugs, more of these babies survived. Antibiotics reduced the risk of diphtheria, typhoid fever, influenza, and other infections. The Salk and Sabin vaccines virtually wiped out polio. The average number of children per family went from 2.4 in 1945 up to 3.2 in 1957, and the population grew by a record 29 million people to reach 179 million.

TABLE 27–3

Religious Revival and Baby Boom, 1945–1960		
Year	Membership of Religious Bodies (in 1,000s)	Live Births (in 1,000s)
1945[1]	71,700	2,858
1946[1]	73,673	3,411
1947	77,386	3,817
1948	79,436	3,637
1949	81,862	3,649
1950	86,830	3,632
1951	88,673	3,823
1952	92,277	3,913
1953	94,843	3,965
1954	97,483	4,078
1955	100,163	4,104
1956	103,225	4,218
1957	104,190	4,308
1958[2]	109,558	4,255
1959*	112,227	4,245
1960	114,449	4,258

*Denotes first year for which figures include Alaska and Hawaii.
[1]Based on 50 percent sample for 1951–1954, 1956–1960.
[2]Includes Alaska

Source: George Thomas Kurian, Datapedia (Lanham, MD: Bernan Press, 1994), pp. 37, 146.

Like the religious revival, the "baby boom" of the 1940s and 1950s is somewhat difficult to explain. For more than 100 years, Americans had reduced the size of their families. The economic prosperity of the cold war era may have persuaded couples that they could afford to have more children. But prosperity alone did not explain why American culture became so much more child-centered during these years.

Maintaining Gender Roles

In the 1950s, American culture strongly emphasized differences between the sexes: Women were expected to be homemakers and men, providers. The reality was more complicated. Women's roles, in particular, changed. Both sexes, meanwhile, were warned against deviating from gender stereotypes.

American culture underscored the differences between genders in a variety of ways. Standards of beauty highlighted the physiological differences between women and men. Popular movie actresses such as Marilyn Monroe and Jayne Mansfield were large-hipped, large-breasted women. During the baby boom, women were expected to be helpful wives and devoted mothers. Men were encouraged to define themselves primarily as family providers.

However, traditional gender roles evolved during the 1950s. Society stressed a man's domestic role more than before. Experts urged husbands to do some of the housework and to spend more time nurturing their children, although few men lived up to the new ideal.

Female roles evolved more dramatically. Women were not simply confined to the domestic sphere. To help pay for the consumer lifestyle, many wives went to work outside the home. Gene Ferkauf's wife, while taking care of their child, helped publicize the first Korvettes store. By 1960, almost one married woman in three held a job, and women made up more than one-third of the labor force.

To a degree, American culture supported the expanding role of women outside the home. In the cold war competition with the Soviets, Americans celebrated the supposedly greater freedom and opportunity for women in the United States. Television featured situation comedies with feisty women who stood up to their men.

Nevertheless, women faced a difficult situation with relatively little help. Congress voted an income tax deduction for child-care costs in 1954, but little first-class child care was available. At work, women were expected to watch men get ahead of them. Women's income was only 60 percent of men's in 1960.

American culture strongly condemned women and men who strayed outside conventional gender norms. *Modern Woman: The Lost Sex*, a 1947 bestseller by Marynia Farnham and Ferdinand Lundberg, censured feminism as the "deep illness" of "neurotically disturbed women" with "penis envy." Psychologists and other experts demonized lesbians, who had become a more visible subculture during the 1940s.

Like women, men faced condemnation if they failed to play conventional social roles. In the 1950s, unmarried men risked accusations of homosexuality. Along with lesbian women, gay men became targets of abuse during the cold war. Police cracked down on gay bars. The message was clear: Men were supposed to be heterosexual; they were supposed to be husbands and fathers. Those roles, in turn, forced men to conform to social expectations.

Persisting Racial Differences

In spite of the many pressures toward conformity, American society was still heterogeneous. Society continued to segregate and discriminate against African Americans and Native Americans. The rapid growth of the Hispanic population helped to ensure that the United States would remain a multiracial nation.

Although suburbanization broke down ethnic differences among whites, it intensified the racial divide between those whites and African Americans. The nation's suburbs were 95 percent white in 1950. As whites moved into Levittown and other suburbs, African Americans took their place in cities. By 1960, more than half of the black population lived in cities. By custom in the North and law in the South, African Americans were clearly set apart from white Americans.

Native Americans, living on their reservations, were also set apart. In 1953, Congress did try to "Americanize" the Indians by approving the termination of Indians' special legal status. Termination meant the end of federal aid to tribes and the end of many reservations. The new policy was intended to turn Indians into full members of the consumer society.

It did not turn out that way. As reservations became counties, Indians had to sell valuable mineral rights and lands to pay taxes. Despite short-term profits, tribes faced poverty, unemployment, and social problems. Encouraged by the federal government's new Voluntary Relocation Program, about one in five Native Americans moved to cities. But whether they lived on reservations or crowded city blocks, the nation's quarter of a million Indians remained largely separate and ignored.

The increasing migration of Puerto Ricans also reinforced the multiracial character of American society. Beginning in the 1940s, a large number of Puerto Ricans, who were U.S. citizens, left their island hoping for more economic opportunity on the mainland. By 1960, the Puerto Rican population in the mainland United States had reached 887,000, two-thirds of it concentrated in the East Harlem section of New York City. These new migrants found opportunities in the United States, but they also found separation and discrimination.

Mexican immigration further contributed to racial diversity. After 1945, increasing numbers of Mexicans left their impoverished homeland for the United States, particularly the booming Southwest. Congress, bowing to the needs of southwestern employers, continued the Bracero Program, the supposedly temporary wartime agreement that had brought hundreds of thousands of laborers, or *braceros,* to the United States. Meanwhile, illegal Mexican migration increased dramatically.

Like other Mexican migrants before them, the newly arrived Chicanos met with ambivalence. As in the years before World War II, Mexicans already living in the United States worried that the new arrivals would compete for jobs, drive down wages, and feed American prejudice. Mexican Americans feared that the federal government would use the provisions of the Internal Security Act of 1950 and the Immigration and Nationality Act of 1952 to deport Mexicans and thereby break up families. The government's intention became clear in 1954 with the launching of Operation Wetback, which sent more than 1 million immigrants back to Mexico in that year alone.

About 3.5 million Chicanos were living in the United States by 1960. The great majority worked for low wages in the cities and on the farms of the Southwest. Many Chicanos continued to live in *barrios* apart from whites. Because of Operation Wetback and other instances of prejudice, some Mexican Americans became more vocal about their circumstances and their rights. The League of United Latin American Citizens denounced the impact of the Immigration and Nationality Act. More outspoken was the American GI Forum, an organization of Mexican-American veterans. Ernesto Galarza, an official of the National Agricultural Workers' Union, also spoke out about the plight of Mexicans.

The experiences of Hispanics, Native Americans, and African Americans underscored the continuing importance of race in the United States. Mostly living apart, whites and nonwhites faced different conditions and different futures. Prosperity and consumerism did not change that reality. As long as race was such a potent factor in national life, the United States would never be a homogeneous society.

The Survival of Diversity

Along with race, a variety of forces ensured the survival of diversity. Despite the appearance of suburbs all over the country, the states continued to differ from each other. As in the past, internal migration and the expansion of national boundaries promoted diversity. During the 1950s, more than 1.6 million people, many of them retired, moved to Florida. As a result, the state increasingly played a distinctive national role as a center for retirement and entertainment.

Meanwhile, Americans moved westward. During the 1950s, California gained more than 3 million new residents. California earned a reputation as the pioneer state of the consumer society, the home of the first Disneyland amusement park and the first McDonald's.

The admission of two new states highlighted the continuing diversity of the United States. In 1959, Alaska and Hawaii became, respectively, the 49th and 50th states in the union. Racially and culturally diverse, climatically and topographically distinctive, they helped make certain that America was not simply a land of corporations and Levittowns.

Popular music also exemplified the continuing diversity of the United States. Swing bands gave way rapidly to such popular singers as Frank Sinatra and Patti Page. Jazz split into different camps—traditional, mainstream, and modern. Country music, rooted in white rural culture, included cowboy songs, Western swing, honky-tonk, and bluegrass. A range of African-American musical forms, including blues, jazz, and vocal groups, became known as "rhythm and blues" (R & B).Gospel music thrilled white and African-American audiences. Mexican Americans made Tejano music in Texas, and Cajuns played Cajun music in Louisiana.

R & B collided with country music to create rock and roll. By 1952, white disc jockey Alan Freed was playing R & B on his radio show, "Moondog's Rock 'n' Roll Party," out of Cleveland. By 1954, a white country group, Bill Haley and the Comets, had recorded the first rock-and-roll hit, "Rock Around the Clock." Rock and roll produced both African-American and white heroes in its first years.

The biggest rock-and-roll sensation of all was a young white singer and guitar player, Elvis Presley. Born in Mississippi and raised in near poverty in Memphis, Tennessee, Presley grew up hearing a wide range of music. Beginning with his first commercial record, "That's All Right, Mama," in 1954, Presley sang in a distinctive style that listeners could never quite pigeonhole.

Because of Presley and other musicians, the sound of American popular music was anything but homogeneous. Because of the distinctiveness of Florida, California, Alaska, Hawaii, and other states, the United States was hardly monolithic. In these ways, at least, American society remained diverse after World War II.

THE EISENHOWER ERA AT HOME AND ABROAD

Prosperity encouraged Americans to demand less from government in the 1950s. In a period of rapid social change and continuing international tensions, most people wanted reassurance rather than boldness from Washington. The politics of the decade were dominated by President Dwight D. Eisenhower, a moderate leader well-suited to the times. His middle-of-the-road domestic program, "Modern Republicanism," appealed to a prosperous electorate wary of government innovation. But Eisenhower's anti-Communist foreign policy did little to diminish popular anxieties about the cold war.

"Ike" and 1950s America

Dwight Eisenhower, a charismatic military hero with a bright, infectious grin, would have been an ideal public figure in almost any era of American history, but the man known affectionately as "Ike" was especially suited to the 1950s. Throughout his life, Eisenhower managed to reconcile the old and the new. Raised on the individualistic values of the Midwest, Eisenhower adopted the bureaucratic style of modern organizations. He succeeded in the military after World War I, not because he was a great fighter or strategist, but because he was a great manager. A believer in teamwork, Eisenhower was the quintessential "organization man." As a commander in World War II, Eisenhower worked to keep sometimes fractious allies together. After the war, he deepened his organizational experience as president of Columbia University and then as the first commander of the armed forces of NATO.

Just as he accommodated the rise of big organizations, Eisenhower accommodated the extension of the nation's commitment abroad. Ike had grown up in the isolationist Midwest, among people who feared American involvement in the world's problems. But his military career rested on his acceptance of an activist role for the United States around the world.

Eisenhower easily fit the dominant culture of the 1950s. He was an involved, loving husband and father. In a society zealously pursuing pleasures, he was famous for his many hours on the golf course. His wife, Mamie, eagerly wore the "New Look" fashions inspired by designer Christian Dior and avidly watched television soap operas.

Nominated for president by the Republicans in 1952, Eisenhower ran against Adlai Stevenson, the liberal Democratic governor of Illinois. Stevenson, witty and eloquent, was no match for Eisenhower. Running a moderate, conciliatory campaign, the former general avoided attacks on the New Deal and promised to work for an end to the Korean War. Meanwhile, his running mate, Senator Richard Nixon of California, accused Stevenson of being soft on Communism. The Republican ticket won 55 percent of the popular vote and 442 electoral votes. The Republican Party took control of the White House and both houses of Congress for the first time in 20 years.

Modern Republicanism

Eisenhower advocated Modern Republicanism for the American political economy. This philosophy attempted to steer a middle course between traditional Republican conservatism and Democratic liberalism. With a conservative's faith in individual freedom, the president favored limited government and balanced budgets, but Eisenhower the organization man believed that Washington had an important role to play in protecting individuals. Eisenhower also recognized that most Americans did not want to give up such liberal programs as Social Security and farm subsidies.

Accordingly, the president took some steps to limit governmental control over the economy, such as tax cuts for the wealthy and decreased federal regulation of business. With the Submerged Lands Act of 1953, the federal government turned over offshore oil resources to the states for private exploitation. With the Atomic Energy Act of 1954, Washington allowed private firms to sell power produced by nuclear reactors.

Nevertheless, the Eisenhower administration did little to undermine the legacy of the New Deal and the Fair Deal. Eisenhower went along with increases in Social Security benefits and farm subsidies. Despite his belief in balanced budgets, his administration produced several budget deficits. Federal spending, including the highway program, helped fuel the consumer economy.

Modern Republicanism frustrated liberals as well as conservative "old-guard" Republicans, but many Americans appreciated the president's moderation. "The public loves Ike," a journalist observed. "The less he does the more they love him."

Eisenhower's popularity was confirmed at the polls in 1956. The president once again headed the Republican ticket with Richard Nixon, and the Democrats nominated Adlai Stevenson. This time Eisenhower won an even bigger victory, with 58 percent of the popular vote and 457 electoral votes.

An Aggressive Approach to the Cold War

Like President Harry Truman before him, Eisenhower was committed to opposing Communism at home and around the world. The president helped the crusade against alleged Communist subversives and tolerated its excesses. He refused to criticize the tactics of Senator Joseph R. McCarthy in public and declined to stop the execution of the convicted atomic spies, Julius and Ethel Rosenberg, in 1953. Eisenhower denied the security clearance that J. Robert Oppenheimer, the former director of the Manhattan Project, needed to continue work on the government's nuclear projects. Thousands of other alleged security risks also lost their federal jobs during the Eisenhower era.

Campaigning in 1952, Eisenhower and his advisers talked of rolling back Soviet power in Europe. Moving beyond containment, Eisenhower spoke of the need to free already "captive peoples" from Communism. Presumably, that would mean contesting Soviet control of Eastern Europe. This assertive approach seemed more likely to lead to armed confrontation with the Soviets.

In office, Eisenhower and Secretary of State John Foster Dulles coupled their rhetoric with a new national security policy. Dulles threatened "instant, massive retaliation" with nuclear weapons in response to Soviet aggression. To support this threat, the U.S. military adopted the "New Look," a strategy that de-emphasized costly conventional armies and increased the nuclear arsenal with long-range bombers, missiles, and the first nuclear-powered submarines. Not surprisingly, massive retaliation and the New Look stirred fears of nuclear war.

The president also used the CIA to counter Communism by stealthier means. At the president's direction, the CIA carried out secret activities: As a presidential commission observed, the cold war was "a game" with "no rules." At home, the agency explored the possible uses of lysergic acid diethylamide—the dangerous hallucinogenic drug known as LSD—by using it on hundreds of unwitting Americans. Abroad, the agency gave secret aid to pro-American regimes and ran secret programs against hostile governments.

In August 1953 a covert CIA operation, code-named Ajax, orchestrated a coup that removed Mohammed Mossadeq, the nationalist prime minister of oil-rich Iran. Eisenhower and Dulles feared that this "madman," who had nationalized oil fields, would open the way for Communism and the Soviet Union. He was replaced by the young Shah Mohammed Reza Pahlavi, who gratefully accepted $45 million in U.S. aid, turned his back on the Soviets, and made low-priced oil available to American companies.

The next year, Pbsuccess, a secret CIA operation modeled on Ajax, overthrew another foreign leader. Eisenhower and Dulles worried that a "Communist infection" in the Central American nation of Guatemala could spread to the United States-controlled Panama Canal and further north to Mexico. In fact, the Soviet Union had made no effort to help Guatemala's new president, Jacob Arbenz Gúzman, who supported the redistribution of land and threatened the interests of a powerful American corporation, United Fruit. In June, Pbsuccess used misleading "disinformation," a small force of Guatemalan exiles, and CIA-piloted bombing raids to persuade Arbenz Gúzman to resign.

Avoiding War with the Communist Powers

Despite the tough talk, the Eisenhower administration tried to avoid direct confrontation with the two major Communist powers, the People's Republic of China and the Soviet Union. Eisenhower knew he had to end the Korean conflict. As he promised in his 1952 campaign, Eisenhower traveled to Korea to observe conditions firsthand before his inauguration. Once in office, he pushed to end the military stalemate that ultimately killed 33,629 Americans. A cease-fire agreement in July 1953 left the United States without a victory. Although North and South Korea remained divided, the agreement ended a costly, difficult war. It was, Eisenhower declared, "an acceptable solution."

Ending an old war with one Communist power, the Eisenhower administration avoided a new conflict with the other. In October 1956, Hungarians rose up against their pro-Soviet government. The Soviet Union sent troops to break the rebellion. Despite all its tough talk, the Eisenhower administration did not intervene to help the Hungarian rebels. The United States would not contest Soviet control of Eastern Europe after all.

More broadly, Eisenhower was cautious about military confrontation with the Soviets and the Chinese. Eisenhower declined to unleash nuclear weapons that would "destroy civilization." Although he sent out CIA agents to conduct covert operations, the president was more reluctant than Truman to send American soldiers into open battle.

At the same time Eisenhower, like Truman, knew the cold war was an economic and political fight. The Eisenhower administration maintained foreign-aid programs and fought a propaganda war with the Soviets. In front of a model American kitchen in Moscow in 1959, Vice President Richard Nixon and Soviet leader Nikita Khrushchev argued the merits of the their two systems. Not surprisingly, Nixon turned this "Kitchen Debate" into a celebration of the prosperity and freedom of the consumer society.

The Eisenhower administration took some modest steps to improve relations with the Soviets. After the death of Soviet leader Josef Stalin in 1953, his successors signaled their desire for "peaceful coexistence" with the United States and the West. Responding cautiously, Eisenhower told the United Nations that he wanted to pursue disarmament and the peaceful use of atomic power with the Soviets. The president proposed an "Atoms for Peace" plan in which an international agency would experiment with nonmilitary uses for nuclear materials. The Soviets, however, dragged their feet. Although the International Atomic Energy Agency was formed in 1957, the United States and the Soviet Union did not cooperate significantly to control the nuclear arms race during the Eisenhower years.

The president made another attempt at improving relations with the Soviets. In July 1955, Eisenhower joined Soviet leader Nikita Khrushchev in Geneva, Switzerland, for the first meeting between an American president and Soviet rulers since World War II. The relatively amicable Geneva talks sparked some optimism about American–Soviet relations. That optimism ended by May 1960, when the Soviets shot down an American U-2 spy plane flying high over the USSR.

The U-2 incident underscored the continuing rivalry between the United States and the major Communist powers. The Eisenhower administration refused even to recognize the Communist Chinese regime officially.

Crises in the Third World

Although Eisenhower worried most about the fate of Western Europe, his administration increasingly focused on the threat of Communist expansion in Africa, Asia, Latin America, and the Middle East. These regions, which made up the industrializing third world, were enmeshed in the confrontation between the first world of industrial, non-Communist nations and the second world of industrial, Communist countries. Often plagued by poverty, violence, and civil war, many third-world societies struggled to break free from imperial domination.

Under Khrushchev, the Soviet Union tried to exploit third-world discontent and conflict. Anxious to preserve America's influence and access to natural resources, the Eisenhower administration stood ready to counter Soviet moves with the techniques of containment—aid, trade, and alliances. Eisenhower offered increased foreign aid to third-world countries and tried to stimulate trade with them. He also encouraged closer military ties: The United States signed individual defense pacts with the Philippines, South Korea, and Taiwan.

Eisenhower's approach to the third world was sorely tested in Southeast Asia. When he took office in 1953, the United States continued to support France's war to hold onto Vietnam and its other Southeast Asian colonies. The president feared that a Communist victory in Vietnam would deprive the West of raw materials and encourage the triumph of Communism elsewhere. Comparing the nations of Asia and the Pacific to "a row of dominoes," Eisenhower explained that the fall of the first domino—Vietnam—would lead to the fall of the rest.

Despite vast American aid, the French could not defeat the nationalist forces of the Viet Minh, led by the Communist Ho Chi Minh and helped by the mainland Chinese. By 1954, the Viet Minh had surrounded French troops at Dienbienphu in northern Vietnam. Unwilling to fight another land war in Asia, Eisenhower refused to send American troops. The president also rejected the use of atomic bombs. Without further help from the United States, France surrendered Dienbienphu in May.

In 1954, peace talks at Geneva produced an agreement to cut Vietnam, like Korea, in half. Ho Chi Minh's forces would stay north of the 17th Parallel; his pro-French Vietnamese enemies would stay to the south of that line. The peace agreement stipulated that a popular election would unite the two halves of Vietnam in 1956. Certain that Ho Chi Minh and the Communists would win the election, the United States refused to sign the agreement.

Instead, the Eisenhower administration worked to create an anti-Communist nation south of the 17th Parallel. To protect South Vietnam, the United States created the South East Asian Treaty Organization (SEATO) in 1954 (see Map 27–1). To ensure South Vietnam's loyalty, the Eisenhower administration backed Ngo Dinh Diem, an anti-Communist who established a corrupt, repressive government. The United States sent military advisers and hundreds of millions of dollars to Diem.

By thwarting the Geneva Accords and establishing an unpopular regime in the South, Eisenhower ensured that Vietnam would be torn by civil war in the years to come. In the short run, however, Eisenhower had avoided war and seemingly stopped the Asian dominoes from falling.

Eisenhower soon confronted another crisis in the Middle East. Gamal Abdel Nasser, who had seized power in Egypt in 1954, emerged as a forceful spokesman for Arab nationalism and Middle Eastern unity. Fearing that Nasser would open the way for Soviet power in the Middle East, John Foster Dulles withdrew an offer to aid the Egyptians. Nasser struck back by taking over the British- and French-owned Suez Canal in 1956. In retaliation, Britain and France, with Israel's cooperation, moved against Nasser. As Israeli troops fought their way into Egypt in October, Britain and France stood ready to take back the Suez Canal. Eisenhower feared the invasion could give the Soviets an excuse to move into the Middle East and threatened economic sanctions. Khrushchev threatened to launch Soviet rockets in defense of the Egyptians. The British, French, and Israelis soon withdrew.

After the Suez crisis, in January 1957, the president announced what became known as the Eisenhower Doctrine. The United States, he promised, would intervene to help any Middle Eastern nation threatened by Communist armed aggression. The next year, in an illustration of his doctrine, Eisenhower sent troops to Lebanon. The soldiers were not really needed, but they did send a message about American power and resolve. The president underscored that message in 1959, when the United States encouraged the formation of another regional defense organization patterned after NATO. The new group, which included Turkey and

Map 27–1   America's Cold War Alliances in Asia
Members of SEATO (the South East Asian Treaty Organization) and signers of other treaties with the United States. Through these pacts, the Eisenhower administration hoped to hold back the threat posed by Communist mainland China.

Iran, was known as the Central Treaty Organization (CENTO) for its geographical position between NATO and SEATO.

Eisenhower had helped to stabilize the Middle East for a time, but as in Vietnam, his policy had intensified local divisions. The two third-world crises had been resolved temporarily, but Eisenhower's actions had increased the odds of future trouble. During the 1960s and 1970s, the United States would have to deal with Eisenhower's legacy in the third world.

CHALLENGES TO THE CONSUMER SOCIETY

While the Eisenhower administration managed crises abroad, American society confronted challenges at home. In different ways, a rebellious youth culture, the alienated beat movement, and the divisive civil rights struggle upset the stability of the Eisenhower era. They demonstrated that consumerism had not solved all the nation's problems or won over all of its citizens.

Rebellious Youth

In the 1950s, the emergence of a distinct youth culture, built around rock and roll, customized cars, comic books, and premarital sexual exploration, troubled many adults. The youth culture was the culmination of a trend apparent since the 1920s and 1930s. As more and more teenagers attended high school, they were segregated in their own world. Within that world, they developed their own values and practices. In the 1950s, young people claimed rock and roll as their own music. They wore blue jeans; they read comic books and teen magazines. Expressing their individuality, boys modified standard Detroit cars into customized "hot rods." Teens were attracted to alienated and rebellious movie characters such as the troubled son played by James Dean in *Rebel Without a Cause* (1955). A wave of juvenile delinquency appeared to be sweeping the country.

Many young people were rebellious, but not nearly as much as adults feared. Despite all the publicity, juvenile delinquency did not actually increase after World War II and neither did rates of sexual intercourse among teenagers. Most young people never questioned the political system. On the whole, youth culture exaggerated rather than rejected the values of adult, consumer society.

The early career of Elvis Presley illustrated the boundaries of youthful rebellion. Presley's appeal rested on an unsettling combination of rock-and-roll music and open sexuality. Presley's style—his sensual mouth, disheveled "duck's ass" haircut, and gyrating hips—powerfully amplified the music's sexuality.

Despite his appeal to teenagers, Presley remained relentlessly polite and soft-spoken, devoted to his parents and deferential to interviewers. Buying a pink Cadillac and other luxury cars, he was caught up in the consumer culture. Like Gene Ferkauf and millions of other Americans, Presley joined the suburban migration when he bought his house, Graceland, on the outskirts of Memphis, Tennessee. Presley was a new version of the old American dream of upward mobility.

Still, many adults blamed Presley, rock and roll, and mass media for the spread of dishonesty, violence, lust, and degeneration among young Americans. One popular television program showed Presley only from the waist up. To get rid of blue jeans and other teenage fashions, high schools imposed dress codes on their students. There was a crusade against comic books, teen magazines, and movies that were supposedly "brainwashing" teenagers. In well-publicized hearings, the Senate's Subcommittee to Investigate Juvenile Delinquency focused attention on the corrupting power of the mass media. However, the campaign against youth culture had little impact in a society devoted to free speech and consumerism.

The Beat Movement

A second group of rebels was smaller in numbers but a bit older and much more critical of American society. The beat movement, which emerged in New York City in the 1940s, expressed a sense of both alienation and hope. Worn down by contemporary culture, the beats searched hopefully for a way to get beyond it.

Elvis Presley delights a crowd–particularly its female members–in Long Beach, California, in June 1956.

Uptown at Columbia University and downtown in Greenwich Village, Allen Ginsberg, Jack Kerouac, John Clellon Holmes, William Burroughs, and others wanted, as one of them put it, "to emote, to soak up the world." Beats explored their sexuality, sampled mind-altering drugs, and investigated the spirituality of Eastern religions.

The beats had a dark vision of American society and were fascinated by outsiders and outcasts. Like the teen culture, the beats were drawn to the culture of African Americans. But while teenagers danced to the relatively simple and upbeat sounds of African-American R & B, the beats embraced the rhythmically and harmonically challenging bop music of black jazz musicians. Moreover, the beats were not nearly as positive about the consumer culture. In a society captivated by bright colors, "beatniks" declared their alienation from consumerism by wearing black.

Few in number, the beats sometimes seemed absurd, but the media's attention suggested just how important they were. The beat movement was a clear sign of budding dissatisfaction with consumer society, conventional sexual mores, and politics as usual.

The Struggle for Civil Rights

The African-American struggle for civil rights also challenged the political moderation of the Eisenhower era. By the 1950s, segregation was under increasingly effective attack in the courts and on the streets.

As in the 1940s, the NAACP fought segregation in the courts. Focusing on public schools, the organization directly assaulted the discriminatory legacy of the

Supreme Court's *Plessy* v. *Ferguson* ruling of 1896. In 1951 the NAACP's special counsel, Thurgood Marshall, combined five different lawsuits aimed at segregation in the public schools. In one of these lawsuits, an African-American welder, Oliver Brown, challenged the constitutionality of a Kansas state law that allowed cities to segregate their schools. When the Brown case reached the Supreme Court in December 1952, Thurgood Marshall attacked the *Plessy* argument that justified "separate but equal" facilities for whites and African Americans. As a result of segregation, Marshall maintained, African Americans received both an inferior education and a sense of their own inferiority. He concluded that segregation violated the citizenship rights guaranteed by the Fourteenth Amendment.

In May 1954, the court, led by new Chief Justice Earl Warren, handed down its ruling in *Brown* v. *Board of Education, Topeka, Kansas.* Overturning the *Plessy* decision, the justices ruled unanimously that public school segregation was unconstitutional under the Fourteenth Amendment. Warren's tenure as chief justice was one of the most important in the history of the court; no ruling of the Warren Court would prove more significant than the decision in the Brown case. African Americans and white liberals were jubilant. Marshall foresaw the dismantling of school segregation before the end of the decade.

It did not work out that way. When the Supreme Court ruled on the enforcement of school desegregation in May 1955, the justices turned to local school boards, dominated by whites, to carry out the integration of the schools. Federal district courts were to oversee the process of desegregation, which should occur with "all deliberate speed." In other words, school segregation had to end, but not right away.

Taking heart from this ruling, many whites refused to give up Jim Crow. For some white southerners, as one put it, a "reasonable time" for the end of segregation would be "one or two hundred years." Amid calls for massive resistance to desegregation, White Citizens' Councils formed to prevent schools from integrating. Some states passed laws intended to stop school integration. There was violence, too. In 1955, white Mississippians killed Emmett Till, a 14-year-old black boy from Chicago.

African Americans, encouraged by the court's action, were ready to fight even harder against segregation. On December 1, 1955, Rosa Parks, a 42-year-old African-American tailor's assistant in Montgomery, Alabama, boarded a bus to go home from work. State law dictated segregation on city buses. Local custom required an African American to give up her seat to a white passenger and then move to the back of the bus, but when the bus driver told her to move, Parks would not get up. The angry driver had Parks arrested.

Local African-American leaders, who had encouraged her to test the law, seized on the arrest of this respectable woman to challenge segregation. African-American men and women began to boycott the city's bus system. Twenty-six-year-old Martin Luther King, Jr., pastor of the Dexter Avenue Baptist Church, agreed to lead the boycott. The son of a noted Atlanta preacher, King was already developing a brilliant oratorical style and a philosophy of nonviolent protest against segregation.

The boycott met immediate resistance. The city outlawed carpools and indicted the leaders; African-American homes and churches were bombed. In November 1956, however, the U.S. Supreme Court ruled Alabama's bus segregation law unconstitutional. By then, the boycott had cost the bus company and downtown storeowners dearly, and the white community had lost the will to resist. The city settled with the boycotters and agreed to integrate the buses.

Montgomery showed that a combination of local activism and federal intervention could overcome Jim Crow in southern communities. It established a charismatic new leader with a powerful message, and it soon brought forward a new civil rights

A white student heckles an African-American student trying to integrate Central High School in Little Rock, Arkansas, in September 1957.

organization, the Southern Christian Leadership Conference. For one journalist, Montgomery "was the beginning of a flame that would go across America."

The flame did not travel easily. In 1957, the school board of Little Rock, Arkansas, accepted a federal court order to integrate the city's Central High School, but in September the state's segregationist governor, Orval Faubus, called out National Guard troops to stop black students from enrolling. Even after meeting with President Eisenhower, Faubus would not order the troops away from the school. When he finally did remove the soldiers, an angry mob of whites made it impossible for the African-American students to stay.

Little Rock created a dilemma for the president. Not a believer in racial equality, Eisenhower wanted to avoid the divisive issue of civil rights. The president knew, however, that his government was being defied in Little Rock and humiliated around the world. So Eisenhower sent in troops of the crack 101st Airborne of the U.S. Army. With that protection, nine African-American students went to Central High.

Like the Montgomery bus boycott, Little Rock demonstrated that a combination of federal action, however reluctant, and African-American courage could triumph. The Central High crisis showed, too, how the cold war helped tip the balance against segregation. Competing with the Soviets for support from the multiracial third world, no president could afford the embarrassment of racial inequality at home. Segregation and discrimination would continue to upset the stability of Eisenhower's America. It was, the president concluded, "troublesome beyond imagination."

An Uneasy Mood

Youth culture, the beat movement, and the civil rights struggle contributed to an uneasy mood in America by the end of the 1950s. Even people who did not share the beats' values worried that the consumer society was flawed. Consumerism itself could seem like a trap. In his bestseller *The Hidden Persuaders* (1957), Vance Packard played on the fears that advertisers were manipulating American consumers.

Americans were troubled, too, by signs of corruption in the consumer society. In 1958, they learned that record companies had paid Alan Freed and other disc jockeys to play particular records on the radio. The same year, Americans were shocked by revelations that contestants on popular TV quiz shows had secretly been given the answers to questions in advance.

While Americans worried about whether the consumer society was corrupt, they wondered whether it could meet the challenge of the cold war. In October 1957, the Soviet Union sent Sputnik, the world's first satellite, into orbit, setting off a wave of fear in the United States. If the Soviets could send up a satellite, they could be ahead in nuclear weapons and economic growth too.

Sputnik intensified concerns about the quality of American education. A diverse and growing student population, along with rising parental demands, had strained the nation's schools. Now Americans worried that the schools were not preparing children to compete with the Soviets in science and technology. In 1958, Congress, previously reluctant to provide aid to schools, passed the National Defense Education Act. This wide-ranging measure promoted instruction in science, math, and foreign languages, supported construction of new schools, and offered loans and fellowships to students.

Sputnik forced Washington to accelerate the space program. The first U.S. satellite launch collapsed in flames. In January 1958 the government successfully launched its first satellite, Explorer I. Later that year, Congress created the National Aeronautics and Space Administration (NASA) to coordinate space exploration. These initiatives did not wipe away fears about the fate of a society caught up in consumerism and the cold war, however.

Eisenhower did little to change the national mood. Slowed by poor health, the president now seemed old and out of ideas. A few days before the end of his presidency in January 1961, Eisenhower fed the uncertain mood with a warning about the political economy in his farewell address. Noting that cold war spending had built up the military and the defense industry, he warned against allowing this "military-industrial complex" to gain too much power. It was a stunning admission that the cold war's transformation of the political economy might destroy rather than save democracy in America.

Eisenhower's difficulties were a sign of new stresses on American society. The great majority of Americans were not about to give up the benefits of the prosperous consumer economy, but many people worried whether consumerism and Modern Republicanism were enough to meet the challenges of the cold war world.

CONCLUSION

Along with the cold war, the triumph of consumerism dramatically affected the United States in the 1950s. The booming consumer economy gave Gene Ferkauf and other Americans a new sense of security and affluence during the unsettling confrontation with Communism. Breaking with the past, they moved to the suburbs, had record numbers of children, bought televisions at E. J. Korvettes, and defined life as the pursuit of material pleasures. Consumerism helped promote homogeneity and conformity in American society and spurred the victory of Dwight Eisenhower and his moderate approach to the political economy.

CHRONOLOGY

1947	Opening of Levittown suburban development
1948	Opening of first McDonald's fast-food restaurant Alfred Kinsey, *Sexual Behavior in the Human Male*
1950	Introduction of Diner's Club credit card
1951	UNIVAC 1 computer
1952	Dwight D. Eisenhower elected president
1953	Opening of first suburban E. J. Korvettes store First issue of *Playboy* magazine Beginning of Federal Termination policy for Native American reservations CIA Operation Ajax in Iran Cease-fire in Korea Eisenhower Atoms for Peace proposal
1954	Atomic Energy Act "Baby boom" birth rate over 4 million per year Bill Haley and the Comets, "Rock Around the Clock" Supreme Court school desegregation decision, *Brown* v. *Board of Education, Topeka, Kansas* Federal Operation Wetback Army–McCarthy Senate hearings CIA Operation Pbsuccess in Guatemala Creation of divided Vietnam in Geneva peace talks Beginning of Senate hearings on juvenile delinquency

For a moment, perhaps, it seemed as if America had achieved stability and harmony in a dangerous cold war world, but that feeling did not last. At the end of the 1950s, many Americans questioned whether the consumer society could provide prosperity, equality, and security for all its citizens. The next decade, a tumultuous time, would give them an unsettling answer.

FURTHER READINGS

Stephen E. Ambrose, *Eisenhower*, 2 vols. (1983–1984). Evenhandedly chronicles the life of the general and president.

David L. Anderson, *Trapped by Success: The Eisenhower Administration and Vietnam, 1953–1961* (1993). Examines the American decision to support South Vietnam after the French withdrawal.

Taylor Branch, *Parting the Waters: America in the King Years, 1954–1963* (1988). A lively narrative focusing on the role of Martin Luther King, Jr., in the civil rights struggle.

1955	Formation of AFL-CIO
	Eisenhower Open Skies proposal
	Beginning of bus boycott in Montgomery, Alabama
1956	National System of Defense Highways Act
	William H. Whyte, Jr., *The Organization Man*
	Opening of Southdale suburban shopping mall
	Suez crisis
	C. Wright Mills, *The Power Elite*
	Re-election of President Eisenhower
1957	Announcement of Eisenhower Doctrine
	Confrontation over school desegregation in Little Rock, Arkansas
	Jack Kerouac, *On the Road*
	Soviet Sputnik satellite launch
1958	National Defense Education Act
	Rock-and-roll "payola" scandals
	TV quiz show scandals
1959	Alaska and Hawaii statehood
	Nixon–Khrushchev "Kitchen Debate" in Moscow
1960	President Eisenhower's Commission on National Goals
	Soviet downing of U.S. U-2 spy plane
1961	Eisenhower's farewell address on "military-industrial complex"

John P. Diggins, *The Proud Decades: America in War and in Peace, 1941–1960* (1988). Gives a broad overview of the postwar period.

Barbara M. Kelly, *Expanding the American Dream: Building and Rebuilding Levittown* (1993). Details the evolution of the quintessential suburban development.

Karal Ann Marling, *As Seen on TV: The Visual Culture of Everyday Life in the 1950s* (1994). Engagingly explores the emerging consumer culture.

Joanne Meyerowitz, ed., *Not June Cleaver: Women and Gender in Postwar America, 1945–1960* (1994). An important set of essays that collectively change our understanding of women in the postwar period.

Grace Palladino, *Teenagers: An American History* (1996). Persuasively describes the development of youth culture in the 1950s.

 Please refer to the document CD-ROM for primary sources related to this chapter.

28

The Rise and Fall of the New Liberalism

1960–1968

"We Would Never Be Beaten": Vietnam, 1968 • The Liberal
Opportunity • Implementing the Liberal Agenda • Winning Civil
Rights • Fighting the Cold War • The American War in Vietnam
The Great Society Comes Apart • Conclusion

"WE WOULD NEVER BE BEATEN": VIETNAM, 1968

O n the night of January 10, 1968, Second Lieutenant Fred Downs of the
U.S. Army looked up at the stars over the coast of South Vietnam. Only
23, he was thousands of miles from the Indiana farm where he had grown
up. Why was he so far from home?

Downs's presence in South Vietnam reflected two factors that shaped American
life after 1945: the cold war and prosperity. Downs was in South Vietnam because of
the ongoing U.S. opposition to the spread of Communism. His job was to protect
South Vietnam's government from forces loyal to the North Vietnamese Communists. Downs was there, too, because of his country's wealth. Only a prosperous
society could afford to send several hundred thousand military personnel to fight
halfway around the world.

Downs's presence in South Vietnam also emphasized a critical change in the
United States from the 1950s to the 1960s. During the 1950s, the U.S. government
had a cautious sense of the limits of American power, but leaders in the 1960s,

buoyed by the prosperous economy, were more daring. Faced with the likely collapse of South Vietnam, the U.S. government had sent its troops to battle in 1965.

Fred Downs shared his leaders' confidence. "I knew we would never be beaten," he declared. Still, the months in Vietnam had tested his confidence. He worried about stepping on land mines and booby traps. He worried whether he could trust the South Vietnamese. He worried whether his country was fighting the war the right way.

Downs was wounded four times, but the Army rewarded him with medals for bravery and he put aside his worries. "My men thought I was invulnerable," he reported. "I did too." On the night of January 10 he saw "no clouds on my horizon." "Nothing would happen to me," he believed.

The next morning, his platoon moved out. At 7:45, he went through a gate at the top of a hill and stepped on a mine. The explosion threw Downs into the air, ripped through his ear drums, tore away pieces of his legs and hips, mutilated his right hand, laid bare the bones of his right arm, and blew off his left arm at the elbow. Horrified, Downs looked at his wounds. "I felt," he recalled, "the total defeat of my life."

Fred Downs's story mirrored the experience of his country in the 1960s. With growing confidence in its wealth, power, and wisdom, the United States tried bold projects. Americans turned to a vigorous liberalism that took an activist approach to the political economy. The nation's leaders pledged to fight Communism abroad and to reform life at home. By the mid-1960s, the federal government had gone to war in Vietnam and had begun to create a "Great Society" in the United States. The country tried to wipe out poverty, heal race relations, protect consumers and the environment, and improve education and health care. Fred Downs's fate reflected the fate of his nation. By 1968 the United States had to confront the limits of its power, just as Fred Downs had to confront the new limits of his life without an arm.

THE LIBERAL OPPORTUNITY

Americans' uneasiness about their society, rather unfocused in the 1950s, became increasingly focused in the 1960s. During the new decade, people realized that the prosperous consumer economy had left millions in poverty and damaged the environment. Meanwhile, the grassroots protests of African Americans dramatized the persistence of racial inequality.

These popular discontents created an opportunity for new ideas and new leaders in the 1960s. A fresh brand of liberalism promised a new approach to the political economy. Confident that the federal government could keep the economy growing, liberals wanted to use more of the nation's wealth to improve life at home and to confront the Communist challenge abroad.

Discontent in the Consumer Society

Despite the economic boom after World War II, the percentage of Americans living in poverty had hardly budged by 1960. Millions of people lived the consumerist good life, but millions of others did not. By the standards of the day, about one in five people were poor, and the majority of the poor were white.

By the 1960s the rest of country found it harder and harder to ignore the poor or to blame poverty on the failings of poor people. In his influential book *The Other America* (1962), Michael Harrington stressed that the poor remained poor because of racism and a lack of opportunity, not because of personal shortcomings. Thanks in part to Harrington, more Americans began to ask why their affluent consumer society failed to provide decent housing, education, and jobs for all citizens.

At the same time, people were asking why the economy had to do so much ecological damage. Americans could no longer ignore the fact that their large, flashy automobiles, the symbol of the consumer society, were polluting the air. They began to criticize society's cavalier attitude toward the natural world. In the mid-1950s, environmentalists had blocked the construction of the Echo Park Dam in the upper basin of the Colorado River that would have inundated the Dinosaur National Monument. A new environmental movement, determined to protect wilderness lands from development, emerged from that battle. Americans became further sensitized to the threat that the consumer economy posed to the countryside because of the bestselling book *Silent Spring* (1962), which emphasized the dangerous power that human beings held over the natural world. The author, marine biologist Rachel Carson, warned that environmental contamination, like nuclear weapons, threatened human survival.

In the 1960s, some Americans recognized that pollution was not the only threat to consumers. The uncritical approval of corporations in the 1950s gave way to a more skeptical view of big business. In 1965, Ralph Nader, an intense young lawyer, published a disturbing book, *Unsafe at Any Speed*, charging that car manufacturers cared more about style and sales than about safety. American cars lacked safety features, such as seat belts, that could save lives. Moreover, Nader reported, executives at General Motors had ignored safety defects in the Chevrolet Corvair. Faced with these revelations, General Motors seemed to confirm its arrogance by trying to discredit Nader rather than promising immediately to improve the Corvair.

The End of Deliberate Speed

In the early 1960s, Americans expressed their growing discontent with consumer culture largely through bestsellers and polite speeches. In contrast, the civil rights movement increasingly protested racial inequality with bold grassroots action. A new generation of African Americans was impatient with the slow "deliberate speed" of integration that the Supreme Court had mandated in *Brown* v. *Board of Education* and was prepared to confront segregation in the South. In 1960, the spirit of grassroots activism inspired a wave of sit-ins and the formation of a new civil rights organization.

The sit-ins began in Greensboro, North Carolina. On February 1, 1960, four black male students from North Carolina Agricultural and Technical College politely insisted on being served at a whites-only lunch counter. When the white waitress refused their order, the students, who would become known as the Greensboro Four, stayed all afternoon. Returning the next day with 30 colleagues, the Greensboro Four were again denied service. Soon hundreds of African-American students from North Carolina A & T and other campuses, along with some white students, were besieging lunch counters.

The sit-in resembled the protests of the 1940s, but it had a far greater impact. Sit-ins spread across Greensboro and North Carolina, and then to other states. The demonstrations forced reluctant whites to open up lunch counters and other facilities to black patrons. The demonstrations also helped produce a new civil rights organization, the Student Nonviolent Coordinating Committee (SNCC). The SNCC (pronounced "Snick") brought together white and African-American young people, influenced by "Judaic-Christian traditions" and eager to create "a social order permeated by love."

The Emergence of the New Liberalism

By the 1960s, liberals were offering a fresh agenda that responded to the discontents of the consumer society, to the civil rights movement, and to the continuing cold war confrontation with Communism. The key to this new liberalism was faith in American economic growth. To meet its domestic and international challenges, the United States needed to expand its economy. As one liberal economist observed, growth would provide "the resources needed to achieve great societies at home and grand designs abroad." The liberals charged that the Eisenhower administration had failed to expand the economy enough in the prosperous 1950s, and they were confident that greater growth could be achieved in the 1960s. By manipulating its budget, they reasoned, the federal government could keep the economy growing. The right amount of taxes and expenditures would ensure full employment, strong consumer demand, and a rising gross national product.

Growth alone would not make America great, the liberals cautioned. Economic growth had to be used to create a better, more satisfying life for all Americans. Because the private sector could not solve pressing national problems, the federal government had to step in to deal actively with poverty, racial inequality, pollution, housing, education, world Communism, and other problems.

Like the liberals of the 1930s and 1940s, liberals at the start of the 1960s believed in using government to correct problems created or ignored by the private sector. They also remained staunchly anti-Communist. Nevertheless, the new liberalism differed from the old in important ways. New Dealers had worried most of all about restoring and maintaining prosperity; the new liberals almost took prosperity for granted. They were sure that the economy could pay for a host of reforms. The old liberals had feared that big business and class conflict posed dangers for the United States. Their successors generally saw racial divisions as the country's greatest domestic problem. Most of all, the new liberalism rested on a powerful feeling of confidence in America's prosperity and power.

The Presidential Election of 1960

The presidential election of 1960 seemed to offer a clear choice between a vaguely liberal future and the status quo. The Democratic nominee, Senator John F. Kennedy of Massachusetts, was open to the liberals' agenda and shared their optimism. Kennedy was youthful, energetic, and charismatic. Although he had compiled an undistinguished record in Congress, he promoted a sense of expectation. The candidate exuded, said one of his speechwriters, "the promise, almost limitless in dimensions, of enormous possibilities yet to come."

Kennedy gave voice to that promise during the campaign. Americans, he explained, stood "on the edge of a New Frontier—the frontier of the 1960s—a frontier of unknown opportunities and paths, a frontier of unfulfilled hopes and threats." The

United States needed to foster economic growth, rebuild slums, end poverty, improve education for the young, and enhance retirement for the old.

In contrast, Kennedy's Republican opponent, Vice President Richard Nixon of California, represented the cautious Eisenhower administration that favored balanced budgets and limited government. As a result, the campaign presented an apparent choice between maintaining the stability of the 1950s and exploring an exciting but unclear liberal future.

Kennedy's stirring rhetoric did not produce a great victory; in fact the election was the closest in history. Kennedy polled 49.7 percent of the vote to Nixon's 49.5 percent (see Map 28–1). Kennedy managed to keep much of the Democratic New Deal coalition of liberals, workers, and African Americans together, but he won by less than 120,000 votes. However narrowly, the voters had turned to a Democrat, influenced by liberal ideas, who was eager to explore the New Frontier.

Kennedy's Unfulfilled Promise

From the first moments of his presidency, Kennedy voiced the confident liberal faith in America's unlimited power and responsibility. "Let every nation know," he declared in his inaugural address in January 1961, "that we shall pay any price, bear any burden, meet any hardship, support any friend, oppose any foe to assure the survival and the success of liberty." Kennedy's extravagant promise perfectly captured the optimistic spirit of the early 1960s. So did the dramatic escalation of the space race.

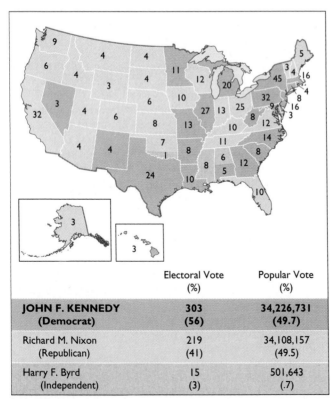

Map 28–1   The Presidential Election, 1960

Democrat John F. Kennedy's clear margin in the electoral vote belies just how narrowly he outpolled Republican Richard M. Nixon in the popular vote.

	Electoral Vote (%)	Popular Vote (%)
JOHN F. KENNEDY **(Democrat)**	**303** **(56)**	**34,226,731** **(49.7)**
Richard M. Nixon (Republican)	219 (41)	34,108,157 (49.5)
Harry F. Byrd (Independent)	15 (3)	501,643 (.7)

The exploration of space seemed like an ideal occupation for confident Americans in the 1960s. Moreover, the space race allowed Kennedy to reject the cautious Eisenhower policies of the 1950s and to confront the Soviet challenge. In April 1961 the Soviet Union sent up the first astronaut to orbit Earth. The next month, NASA managed only to launch astronaut Alan Shepard for a brief, suborbital flight. Once again Americans feared "that the wave of the future is Russian."

The Kennedy administration responded with dramatic rhetoric and the abundant resources of the growth economy. The president boldly pledged to land "a man on the moon . . . before the decade is out." With 60,000 workers and billions of dollars, the Apollo program began. In February 1962 astronaut John Glenn became the first American to orbit Earth. That year the United States launched Telstar, a sophisticated communications satellite. In all, the space program mixed practical achievements such as Telstar with less practical, more symbolic gestures such as manned space flights.

That mixture of style and substance reflected the Kennedy administration as a whole. The president maintained a dynamic, energetic image, but his administration, hampered by a weak electoral mandate, did not venture too far out onto the liberal New Frontier.

How much Kennedy might have accomplished would never be known. On a trip to Dallas, Texas, on November 22, 1963, the president was shot while riding in an open limousine at 12:33 P.M. Two bullets tore through Kennedy's throat and skull, and doctors pronounced him dead half an hour later. That afternoon, police arrested Lee Harvey Oswald for the shooting. A quiet former Marine, Oswald had spent

The Kennedy assassination, November 22, 1963. Jacqueline Kennedy tries to help her mortally wounded husband, John F. Kennedy, as his motorcade drives through Dallas.

time in the Soviet Union. Two days later, as police transferred him from one jail to another, he was shot and killed by Jack Ruby, the troubled owner of a local nightclub.

Americans were shocked and numbed by the assassination and its aftermath. Some could only believe the assassination was the product of a dark conspiracy, but there was never any proof of such a plot. The presidency of John Kennedy, little more than 1,000 days long, left a sad sense of unfulfilled promise. Kennedy gave voice to the new liberalism, but he seldom translated liberal ideas into action.

Lyndon Johnson's Mandate

In background and personality, the new president, Lyndon Johnson, seemed far different from his slain predecessor. Johnson was never an eloquent public speaker or a charismatic figure. He lacked Kennedy's polish and glamour. He himself was often blunt and crude, rather than cool and suave, but he was an especially effective legislator who knew better than Kennedy how to bully and cajole Senate colleagues into making a deal.

Despite the obvious differences in style and background, there were more fundamental similarities between Johnson and Kennedy. Both were members of the Democratic Party that engineered the New Deal, won World War II, and fought the cold war. Both shared the liberals' sense of limitless possibility for the United States. "We're the richest country in the world, the most powerful," Johnson declared. "We can do it all."

Johnson seemed to feel he could do it all after his landslide victory in the presidential election of 1964. The contest gave voters an unusually clear choice between competing visions of the political economy. Johnson stood for activist government, growth economics, and the new liberalism. His Republican opponent, Senator Barry Goldwater of Arizona, just as plainly stood for an emerging brand of conservatism. Goldwater flatly opposed liberal domestic policy, including civil rights and activist government.

It was not much of a contest. Goldwater was too outspoken for many voters. The Johnson campaign portrayed him as a dangerous radical who would gut liberal programs and perhaps start a war. Johnson, in contrast, was supposed to be a statesman and a man of peace. He won 61.1 percent of the popular vote, 44 states, and 486 electoral votes. Moreover, the Democrats increased their majorities in the House and Senate. Goldwater represented the wave of the future; by 1980 his views would not seem extreme. But in 1964 Johnson spoke for the mass of Americans.

IMPLEMENTING THE LIBERAL AGENDA

In the 1960s the federal government attempted to create what Lyndon Johnson called the Great Society, "a society of success without squalor, beauty without barrenness, works of genius without the wretchedness of poverty." The Democratic-controlled Congress passed a wave of new laws, the most important body of legislation since the New Deal, that aimed to wipe out poverty and enhance the quality of life for all Americans. At the same time, the Supreme Court afforded new protections for individual rights. By 1967 the principles of the new liberalism, turned into law, were transforming American government and society.

Declaring War on Poverty

For liberals, the persistence of poverty amid prosperity stood as a chief failure of the consumer society and an embarrassment for the United States around the world. Liberals argued that the poor needed help from the federal government to become productive workers and contribute to economic growth. Increasing the productivity of the poor was not a simple matter, however. Liberals contended that the battle against poverty should include improved housing, education, health, and job opportunities, as well as job training.

Kennedy supported some modest antipoverty measures. In 1961 he signed into law the Area Redevelopment Act to help revive depressed areas. He also signed the Omnibus Housing Act to clear slum housing and bring urban renewal to inner cities. But these measures were not enough to wipe out poverty.

Declaring its "unconditional war on poverty," the Johnson administration embraced a much broader range of liberal programs. In 1964 Congress created an independent federal agency, the Office of Economic Opportunity (OEO), to spend nearly $1 billion on antipoverty programs. The OEO managed Volunteers in Service to America (VISTA), whose workers taught literacy and other skills in impoverished areas. It ran the Job Corps, which taught necessary job skills to poor youth, and implemented Community Action Programs (CAPs), which encouraged the poor to organize themselves in American cities.

In 1965 and 1966 Congress continued the war on several fronts. It established an expanded food stamp program and created Head Start, which provided early schooling, meals, and medical exams for impoverished preschool-aged children. To protect the rights of the poor, the Legal Services Program brought lawyers into slums. To improve urban life, the Model Cities Program targeted 63 cities for slum clearance and redevelopment. The War on Poverty was at least a partial success. Mainly because of the ongoing economic boom, the percentage of people living in poverty decreased to 13 percent by 1970. But that meant that 25 million Americans were still poor. Moreover, poverty was unevenly distributed. About a third of African Americans and a quarter of Americans of Spanish origin were impoverished as the 1970s began. Still, the liberal War on Poverty made a significant, enduring difference in American life.

Improving the Quality of Life

Johnson wanted the Great Society to improve the quality of life for all Americans. Beginning in 1964, Congress enacted measures affecting health care, consumer protection, education, and culture, using the fruits of economic growth to furnish security, opportunity, and cultural enrichment.

One of the fundamental commitments of New Deal liberalism was to provide greater economic security for Americans. Federally subsidized health insurance was part of that goal. The Great Society took a major step toward national health insurance when Congress created Medicare in 1965. This program provided the elderly with insurance coverage for doctors' bills, surgery, and hospitalization. At the same time Congress created Medicaid, a program that helped the states provide medical care to the nonworking poor. The Johnson administration also dealt with the issue of consumer protection. Congress passed the National Traffic and Motor Vehicle Safety Act of 1966, which set the first federal safety standards for automobiles, and the Highway Safety Act, which required states to establish highway safety programs.

The president and Congress adopted the new liberals' belief in using the federal government to support education at all levels. The Elementary and Secondary School Act of 1965 channeled $1.3 billion into school districts around the country. The Higher Education Act of 1965 encouraged youth to attend college by offering federally insured educational loans.

TABLE 28–1

Expanding the Federal Government, 1955–1970					
Year	Civilian Employees (thous.)	Total Spending (millions)	Defense (millions)	Space (millions)	Health (millions)	Education & Manpower (millions)
1955	2,397	$ 68,509	$40,245	$ 74	$ 271	$ 573
1960	2,399	$ 92,223	$45,908	$ 401	$ 756	$1,060
1965	2,528	$118,430	$49,578	$5,091	$ 1,704	$2,284
1970	2,982	$196,588	$80,295	$3,749	$12,907	$7,289

Source: Historical Statistics of the United States (1976), II, pp. 1102, 1116.

The Great Society included programs for cultural enrichment. In 1965 Congress established the National Endowment for the Arts to fund the visual and performing arts and the National Endowment for the Humanities to support scholarly research. The Public Broadcasting Act of 1967 established a nonprofit corporation to support educational and cultural programming. Before long, the Corporation for Public Broadcasting would be giving money for such commercial-free television shows as *Sesame Street*.

The Great Society's programs added up to a major change in the American political economy. Government claimed more authority than ever to manage many Americans' daily lives. The Great Society brought a massive expansion of the size, cost, and power of the federal government (see Table 28–1).

That expansion would be controversial for years to come. Some Great Society measures—Medicare in particular—proved to be enormously expensive. Conservatives did not welcome an enlarged federal government, and some corporations resented the government's regulation of business in the name of consumer protection. Despite these concerns, the various attempts to improve the quality of life represented some of the greatest successes of the new liberalism.

Protecting the Environment

Protection of the environment was a natural issue for liberals to address. Here was a problem, created by the booming consumer economy, that government could solve. During Johnson's presidency, more than 300 pieces of legislation led to the expenditure of more than $12 billion on environmental programs. In 1963 the Clean Air Act encouraged state and local governments to set up pollution control programs. Two years later, amendments established the first pollution emission standards for automobiles. The Air Quality Act of 1967 further strengthened federal authority to deal with air pollution. Meanwhile, the Water Quality Act of 1965 and the Clean Waters Restoration Act of 1966 enabled states and the federal government to fight water pollution. The Wilderness Act of 1964 responded to environmentalists' calls for a system of wilderness lands protected from development.

Preserving Personal Freedom

The new liberalism contained a paradox: Liberals wanted to enhance the power of the federal government and to expand individual rights. Their concern for individual rights was apparent in their support for civil rights for African Americans and in a series of decisions by the Supreme Court, led by Chief Justice Earl Warren.

In *New York Times* v. *Sullivan* in 1964, the justices encouraged free speech by making it more difficult for public figures to sue news media for libel. In addition, two important decisions protected the rights of people accused of crimes. In 1963 the court ruled in *Gideon* v. *Wainwright* that governments had to provide lawyers to poor felony defendants. Three years later, *Miranda* v. *Arizona* required police to inform individuals of their rights when they were arrested, including the right to remain silent and the right to an attorney.

The Warren Court also protected sexual and religious freedom. In 1965 in *Griswold* v. *Connecticut* the court threw out a state law that banned the use of contraceptives. In 1963 the court acted to prohibit mandatory prayer in the nation's public schools. *School District of Abington Township* v. *Schempp* prohibited state and local governments from requiring public school students to say the Lord's Prayer or read the Bible.

The Supreme Court's rulings were controversial. Some people charged that the court was "driving God out" of the classroom. Others believed that the court had gone too far to protect the rights of alleged criminals. Through its rulings, the liberal majority on the court substantially increased individual freedom, but few people had yet thought much about the tension between expanding both individual rights and government power.

Much of the liberal agenda had been accomplished by 1967. The Great Society dealt with the key issues of the political economy, such as poverty, health care, and consumer protection. The most significant body of legislation since the New Deal, Johnson's program vastly expanded the reach of the federal government and changed the lives of Americans for decades to come.

WINNING CIVIL RIGHTS

Of all the domestic challenges confronting the Great Society, none was more difficult than civil rights. The fervor of the grassroots civil rights movement helped spur the new liberalism in the 1960s, yet many whites were still determined to preserve the old racial order. Civil rights activists needed allies in the federal government, and the Great Society produced major legislation outlawing segregation and restoring black voting rights in the South—at least on paper.

White Resistance and Federal Reluctance

The civil rights movement did not win any easy victories in the South during the early 1960s. In one location after another, attempts to break down segregation and promote African-American voting met with resistance. The character of white resistance became evident in the spring of 1961. After the Supreme Court outlawed the segregation of interstate bus terminals, a small group of African-American and white "Freedom Riders" traveled south on buses to test the decision. The Freedom Riders met with beatings from white citizens and harassment from local authorities. Only then did the Kennedy administration send federal marshals to protect them.

White resistance could prove effective, especially if there were no federal marshals around. In 1961, when SNCC started a voter-registration drive in Mississippi, white people struck back. SNCC workers were beaten and shot. When SNCC tried to register black voters in the small city of Albany, Georgia, members of the Albany Movement, as it was called, were beaten and arrested. Martin Luther King, Jr.,

The price of civil rights: Freedom Riders outside their burning bus, which was set on fire by a white mob determined to stop the desegregation of southern bus terminals in May 1961.

leader of the Southern Christian Leadership Conference (SCLC) and veteran of the Montgomery bus boycott of 1955–1956, came to Albany and got arrested, too, but segregation still ruled in the city.

SNCC activists resented the lack of presidential support for their work, and the defiance of southern whites gradually pushed Kennedy toward action. In 1962 the governor of Mississippi, Ross Barnett, disregarded a federal court order by preventing a black student from enrolling at the University of Mississippi. When federal marshals escorted the student, James Meredith, to school, white students pelted them with rocks and Molotov cocktails. After the rioting killed two people and wounded more than 100 marshals, Kennedy called in federal troops to stop the violence and allow Meredith to enroll.

Two confrontations in Alabama forced the president's hand in 1963. In April, Martin Luther King, Jr., and the SCLC tried to end segregation in the Southern steel-making center, Birmingham, perhaps the most segregated city in America. The city's Public Safety Commissioner, Eugene "Bull" Connor, was a stereotypical racist white southern law enforcement officer. To win a badly needed victory, King and local allies planned to boycott department stores and overwhelm the jails with arrested protesters. Calling for the end of segregation, King laid down the gauntlet to Connor and the white community. In the next days, Connor's officers arrested demonstrators by the hundreds. King ignored a judge's injunction against further protests and ended up in solitary confinement. In a powerful statement, *Letter From Birmingham Jail*, King responded to critics of the demonstrations. "We know through painful experience," he wrote, "that freedom is never voluntarily given by the oppressor; it must be demanded by the oppressed." King rejected further patience: "We must come to see . . . that 'justice too long delayed is justice denied.'" Out on bail, King and the SCLC pushed harder for justice with demonstrations by thousands of young African-American students.

Goaded by the new protests, "Bull" Connor turned fire hoses on young demonstrators, set dogs on them, and hit them with clubs. Shocking pictures of the scenes, shown around the world, increased the pressure on the white leadership of Birmingham and on President Kennedy. Mediators from Kennedy's Justice Department arranged for a deal in which the SCLC gave up the demonstrations and local businesses gave up segregation and promised to hire African Americans. However, soon thereafter the Ku Klux Klan marched outside the city and bombs went off at the home of King's brother and at SCLC headquarters. In response, African Americans rioted in the streets of Birmingham. Kennedy was forced to send federal troops to keep the peace.

A second confrontation in Alabama drew the president still deeper into the civil rights struggle. The state's segregationist governor, George Wallace, defied federal officials and tried to stop two black students from enrolling at the University of Alabama. Only then did President Kennedy take an open stand on civil rights in an eloquent televised address and propose sweeping civil rights legislation.

Two months later, on August 28, a march on Washington brought together a crowd of nearly 200,000 people, including 50,000 whites, at the Lincoln Memorial to commemorate the 100th anniversary of the Emancipation Proclamation and to

Martin Luther King, Jr., and his wife, Coretta Scott King, at the front of the civil rights march from Selma, Alabama, on March 30, 1965. Male and female, old and young, black and white, the marchers illustrate the diversity of the coalition that walked with linked arms and determined faces to demand the right to vote for African Americans.

demand "jobs and freedom." Whites and African Americans, workers and students, singers and preachers joined hands to sing the stirring civil rights anthem, "We Shall Overcome." Martin Luther King, Jr., moved the nation with his vision of racial harmony. "I have a dream," he said, "that one day . . . little black boys and black girls will be able to join with little white boys and white girls as sisters and brothers." King looked forward to "that day when . . . black men and white men, Jews and Gentiles, Protestants and Catholics, will be able to join hands and sing . . . 'Free at last! Free at last! Thank God Almighty, we are free at last!'"

Kennedy's address and the March on Washington marked a turning point. The surging grassroots movement for racial equality had created broad-based support for civil rights and finally forced the federal government to act.

The Death of Jim Crow

In the 10 weeks after the Birmingham confrontation, 758 demonstrations led to 14,733 arrests across the United States. When a bomb killed four African-American girls in a Baptist church in Birmingham in September, African-American rioters burned stores and destroyed cars, and the police killed two more children.

The violence continued the following year: CORE, SNCC, SCLC, and the NAACP had created the Council of Federated Organizations (COFO) to press for African-American voting rights in Mississippi. Robert Moses, an African-American schoolteacher, led the COFO crusade that united young African-American and white activists to register black voters and start "Freedom Schools" for African-American children. The effort, known as Freedom Summer, met hostility from whites. In June 1964 two white activists, Michael Schwerner and Andrew Goodman, and one African-American activist, James Chaney, disappeared near Philadelphia, Mississippi. They were found a month later, shot to death. Eventually a white deputy sheriff, a local Klan leader, and five other whites were convicted of "violating the rights" of Chaney, Goodman, and Schwerner.

The violence continued in Mississippi throughout the Freedom Summer of 1964. Homes and churches were burned, and three more COFO workers were killed.

Lyndon Johnson could not escape the events in Mississippi. In the summer of 1964, the Mississippi Freedom Democratic Party (MFDP) sent a full delegation to the Democratic National Convention in Atlantic City, New Jersey. The MFDP delegates, including the eloquent Fannie Lou Hamer, hoped at least to share Mississippi's convention seats with the whites-only Democratic Party delegation. Hamer, the daughter of sharecroppers, told the national Democratic Party's Credentials Committee how she had been jailed and beaten for trying to register African-American voters. Afraid of alienating white southern voters, Johnson tried to stop the publicity and offered the delegates two seats in the convention. "We didn't come all this way for no two seats," Hamer retorted. The MFDP delegation went away empty-handed.

Johnson and the Democratic Party were clearly not ready to share power with African-American activists, but they were ready to end legalized segregation. In July, with Johnson's prodding, Congress adopted the Civil Rights Act, which outlawed racial discrimination in public places. The measure also set up an Equal Employment Opportunity Commission (EEOC) to stop discrimination in hiring and promotion. Even the schools gradually became integrated. In 1964 hardly any African-American students attended integrated schools; by 1972 nearly half of African-American children attended integrated schools.

However, across the South, most African Americans still could not vote. In January 1965 the SCLC and SNCC tried to force the voting rights issue with protests in Selma, Alabama. Predictably, the demonstrations produced violent opposition and helpful publicity. The sight of state troopers using tear gas, cattle prods, and clubs on peaceful marchers built support for voting rights.

Seizing the moment, Johnson called for the end of disfranchisement, and Congress passed the Voting Rights Act of 1965. This powerful measure forced southern states to give up literacy tests used to disfranchise black voters and empowered federal officials to make sure that African Americans could register to vote. In three years, Mississippi saw African-American registration increase from 6 percent to 44 percent of eligible voters.

Together with the Civil Rights Act of 1964, the Voting Rights Act transformed the South. These twin achievements of the civil rights movement effectively doomed Jim Crow and laid a foundation for African-American political power. However, the struggle for racial equality was far from over.

FIGHTING THE COLD WAR

The new liberalism was staunchly anti-Communist, but the New Frontier and the Great Society modified the defense and foreign policies of the 1950s. More confident about American power and wisdom, the Kennedy administration increased the nation's defense spending and international commitments and confronted Communism throughout the third world. Meanwhile, Kennedy and Johnson maintained the core American commitment to containing the Soviet Union that helped to produce dangerous crises in the early 1960s.

Flexible Response and the Third World

Although Kennedy shared President Eisenhower's commitment to containing Communism, Kennedy believed the nation could afford to spend more money on the military. He also abandoned the doctrine of massive retaliation, Eisenhower's threat to use nuclear weapons against any Soviet aggression. Kennedy and his advisers preferred flexible response, a strategy that allowed the president to choose different military options, not just nuclear weapons, in dealing with the Soviets. While spending generously on nuclear weapons, the Kennedy administration built up the country's conventional ground forces and special forces—the highly trained troops, known as Green Berets, who could fight in guerilla wars. Flexible response better prepared the United States for challenges around the world.

Kennedy was more willing than Eisenhower to intervene in the affairs of the third world. This was partly a reflection of Kennedy's characteristic confidence about American power and partly a response to Soviet actions. In January 1961 Nikita Khrushchev announced Soviet support for "wars of national liberation" against established governments in Asia, Africa, and Latin America. In reply, Kennedy used different, even contradictory strategies to keep Communism out of the third world in the 1960s. His administration encouraged democracy and prosperity in developing countries. However, the United States also helped to thwart third-world independence and democracy in the name of anti-Communism.

To stop the spread of Communism, Kennedy supported modernization in Africa, Asia, and Latin America; that is, policymakers wanted these continents to develop capitalist, democratic, independent, and anti-Communist regimes along the lines of the American political economy. To encourage modernization, the

Kennedy administration created the Peace Corps in 1961, sending thousands of young volunteers around the world to promote literacy, public health, and agriculture. The Peace Corps reflected both the idealism and anti-Communism of the Kennedy years as well as many Americans' arrogant sense of superiority.

To promote the modernization of Latin America, Kennedy announced the formation of the Alliance for Progress in 1961. Over the next eight years, this venture provided $20 billion for housing, health, education, and economic development for poorer countries in the Western Hemisphere. The Kennedy administration did not always support independence and democracy. In some cases, the United States intervened in the domestic affairs of supposedly independent countries. In the Belgian Congo (now the Democratic Republic of Congo), which later became known as Zaire, the CIA engineered the election of an anti-Communist leader. The United States also backed antidemocratic, but anti-Communist, regimes and went along with the military overthrow of legitimate governments.

In Cuba, Kennedy inherited a plan from the Eisenhower administration for a CIA-directed invasion by anti-Communist Cuban exiles. The president wanted to bring down Fidel Castro, whose successful revolution was an example for the rest of Latin America. To conceal U.S. responsibility for the invasion, Kennedy canceled U.S. flights that would have protected the invaders. As a result, nearly all 1,500 exiles who landed at the Bay of Pigs in April 1961 were killed or captured by Castro's troops. Embarrassed, Kennedy turned to the CIA, which launched an unsuccessful secret campaign to kill or depose Castro. The Cuban leader, aware of the American plot, declared himself a Communist and turned to the Soviets for help.

Kennedy's assassination made little difference for American defense and foreign policies. Johnson too was a committed cold warrior with an optimistic view of American power. He kept flexible response in place and was equally willing to undermine the independence of third-world countries. In 1965, Johnson sent 22,000 American troops to the Dominican Republic to stop an increasingly violent struggle for political power. The president acted without obtaining evidence of a Communist threat and without consulting Latin American countries as required by treaty.

The U.S. intervention in the Dominican Republic and Cuba underscored the increased importance of the third world for American policymakers. Anxious to stop the Soviets, Kennedy and Johnson were willing to ignore the sovereignty of Latin American, African, and Asian countries as well as the idealistic commitment to democracy reflected in the Peace Corps and the Alliance for Progress. As would become clear in Vietnam, the costs of the U.S. preoccupation with the third world could be enormous.

Two Confrontations With the Soviets

Kennedy faced two direct confrontations with the Soviet Union. In 1961, Khrushchev threatened to stop Western traffic into West Berlin, which was surrounded by Soviet-dominated East Germany. In response, Kennedy called up reserve troops, asked Congress to increase defense spending, and hinted at a pre-emptive nuclear strike against the Soviets. Khrushchev backed down, but the East German government built a barbed-wire and concrete fence between East Berlin and West Berlin. By halting the embarrassing flight of East Germans to freedom in West Berlin, the so-called Berlin Wall defused the crisis and became a symbol of cold war Europe, a visible "iron curtain" that separated Communists and non-Communists.

In 1962 Kennedy entered a more dangerous confrontation with the Soviet Union. On October 15 photos from an American spy plane showed that the Soviets were building launch sites in Cuba for nuclear missiles that could strike the United States. To force the Soviet Union to withdraw the missiles, the president put ships in place on October 22 to intercept Soviet vessels bound for Cuba. That night, a somber Kennedy told a television audience about the Russian missiles and demanded their removal. Khrushchev backed down and withdrew the missiles in exchange for the removal of obsolete American missiles from Turkey.

The Cuban Missile Crisis both eased and intensified the cold war. The close call with nuclear war gave both sides a chance to think carefully about a nuclear conflict; neither found the prospect appealing, and both sought to ease tensions. A teletype "hotline" was installed between the White House and the Kremlin so that Soviet and American leaders could communicate quickly during a crisis. In 1963 the two powers also approved a Limited Test Ban Treaty halting above-ground tests of nuclear weapons. On the other hand, the crisis made both the Soviets and the Americans more determined to stand firm against each other.

The Berlin and Cuban crises were reminders that the heart of the cold war was the confrontation between the United States and the Soviet Union. The Test Ban Treaty might have marked the beginning of the end of the cold war, but that confrontation was still far from over.

THE AMERICAN WAR IN VIETNAM

The war in Vietnam was a decisive episode for the new liberalism and the nation in the 1960s. American participation in the conflict reflected the liberals' determined anti-Communism and their boundless sense of power and responsibility. Driven by these beliefs, Kennedy deepened the U.S. commitment to protect South Vietnam in the early 1960s, and Johnson made the fateful decision to send American troops into battle in 1965. As the fighting stretched on, Americans divided passionately over the conflict, and the economy faltered. By the end of 1967 the war was beginning to destroy the Great Society.

Kennedy's Deepening Commitment

Kennedy inherited a deteriorating situation in South Vietnam in 1961. Ngo Dinh Diem's non-Communist government faced increasing attacks from the Viet Cong, guerrillas determined to overthrow his regime. Diem also faced a new political organization, the National Liberation Front, that was trying to mobilize his Communist and non-Communist opponents. In addition, he faced the continuing hostility of Ho Chi Minh's Communist government in North Vietnam, which was secretly sending soldiers and supplies into South Vietnam.

Like Eisenhower, Kennedy tried to shore up the Diem government, providing advice and financial aid. Further, Kennedy sent American advisers, including the Special Forces, to teach the South Vietnamese Army how to stop the Viet Cong insurgency. Before Kennedy took office, there were 900 American troops filling noncombat roles in South Vietnam. At his death, there were more than 16,000.

Despite all this support, Diem's regime spiraled downward. His army could not stop the Viet Cong. A cold, unpopular ruler, he alienated his own people. Losing confidence in Diem, the Kennedy administration did nothing to stop a military coup that resulted in the murder of the South Vietnamese leader at the beginning of November.

Kennedy's interventions made South Vietnam weaker, not stronger. After the assassination, some Americans wanted to believe that the president would have kept the United States out of the Vietnam War if he had lived. Yet there was no compelling evidence that Kennedy intended to withdraw American troops. Instead, Kennedy's commitment had only made it more difficult for his successor to pull the United States out of Vietnam.

Johnson's Decision for War

At first, Johnson followed Kennedy's policy. The new president believed in the domino theory, the idea that the fall of one country to Communism would lead to the fall of others. Like many Americans who witnessed the rise of Adolf Hitler in the 1930s, Johnson thought it was a mistake to tolerate any aggression. Finally, the president felt he could not turn his back on commitments made by Kennedy, Eisenhower, and Truman. Johnson sent more aid and advisers to South Vietnam and stepped up covert action against the North.

This covert action helped Johnson get Congressional approval to act more aggressively. On August 2, 1964, a U.S. destroyer, the *Maddox*, was cruising a few miles off the coast of North Vietnam in the Gulf of Tonkin. When three North Vietnamese patrol boats unsuccessfully attacked the *Maddox*, the American ship sank two of the boats and damaged a third. Two days later the *Maddox*, along with a second U.S. destroyer, fired mistakenly at a nonexistent North Vietnamese attack. Johnson ordered retaliatory strikes from U.S. aircraft carriers and asked Congress for the power to protect American military personnel. Congress approved what became known as the Tonkin Gulf Resolution, which gave the president the authority, without a declaration of war, to use military force to safeguard South Vietnam. After American soldiers were killed in a Viet Cong attack on a U.S. base in February 1965, Johnson authorized air strikes against North Vietnam itself. In March the U.S. began Operation Rolling Thunder, a series of bombing raids on military targets in North Vietnam.

When the raids failed to deter the North Vietnamese and Viet Cong, Johnson had a disagreeable but clear choice. If he wanted to save both South Vietnam and his reputation, he had to commit American ground troops to battle; otherwise, he would be blamed for the loss of South Vietnam to Communism. In July 1965, Johnson gave the order to send 180,000 soldiers to fight in South Vietnam.

Johnson's decision was the ultimate expression of the new liberalism. The president went to war not only because he opposed Communism, but also because he had faith in American wealth and wisdom. Johnson believed that the United States could transform a weak, divided South Vietnam into a strong, united, modern nation. Even though he was cautious about going to war, Johnson could not accept that the United States might lose. Moreover, he believed that the United States could afford to fight a war abroad and build a Great Society at home.

Fighting a Limited War

Johnson and his advisers believed the United States did not need all its power to save South Vietnam (see Map 28–2). Vietnam was to be a limited war in which American forces, led by General William Westmoreland, would use conventional weapons against military targets. The goal was to kill enough enemy soldiers to persuade the North Vietnamese and the Viet Cong to give up. The measure of American success would be the number of dead North Vietnamese and Viet Cong. Relying on America's superior technology, Westmoreland expected the United States to prevail by the end of 1967.

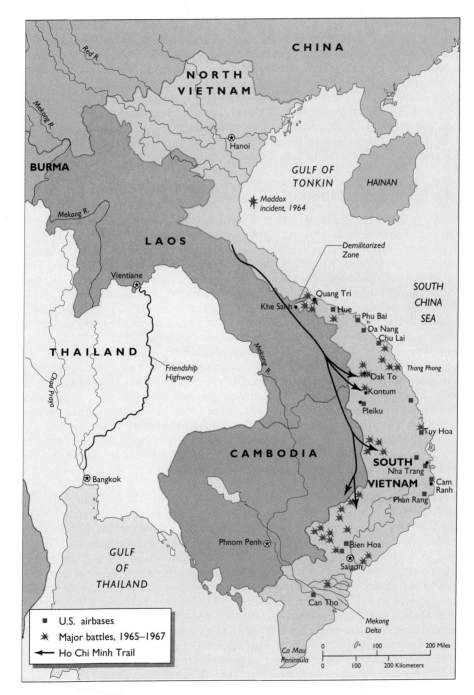

Map 28–2   America's War in Vietnam, 1965–1968
The many military bases suggest how much power the United States had to commit to South Vietnam; the many major battles show how hard American troops had to fight to protect the South Vietnamese regime from the Viet Cong and from the North Vietnamese soldiers who traveled the Ho Chi Minh Trail.

Westmoreland's strategy turned out to be poorly suited to the realities of Vietnam. As Fred Downs discovered, the North Vietnamese and the Viet Cong usually escaped by hiding in tunnels, fleeing through the jungle, fighting mainly at night, or retreating into Cambodia, Laos, and North Vietnam. Their strategy was to live long enough for a frustrated U.S. military to leave South Vietnam.

At the close of 1967, when the war should have been ending, too many North Vietnamese and Viet Cong were still alive and committed to the overthrow of South Vietnam. Even though there were now half a million troops in Westmoreland's command, he had not won the war. He had not lost the war, either; the United States had just run out of time to fight (see Table 28–2).

The War's Impact at Home

The war in Vietnam had a major impact back home. An impassioned antiwar movement emerged to condemn American policy.

To antiwar protesters, mostly students on college and university campuses, the Vietnam War epitomized the failings of the Great Society. The war revealed how undemocratic America had become. Johnson, the radicals pointed out, had ignored the Constitution by sending troops into battle without a declaration of war. In addition, the selective service law was forcing a repugnant choice on young men: They could either fight this illegal war or obtain student deferments to stay in school and prepare for empty lives in the consumer society.

Forced to rethink their basic assumptions about the United States and the cold war, a growing number of liberals and Democrats shared at least some of the radicals' analysis. These "doves" acknowledged that the United States was backing an antidemocratic government in a brutal and apparently unnecessary war. The conflict appeared to be a civil war among Vietnamese rather than some plot to expand Soviet or Chinese influence. Meanwhile, the war had shattered many liberals' and Democrats' overconfident view of the Great Society. The United States, confessed Senator J. William Fulbright of Arkansas in 1966, was a "sick society" suffering from an "arrogance of power." The nation apparently could not solve major problems as readily as the liberals had believed a few years earlier.

Some African Americans viewed the conflict as a painful illustration of American racism. A disproportionate number of poor African Americans, unable to go to college and avoid the draft, were being sent to kill nonwhites abroad on behalf of a racist United States. First SNCC and then Martin Luther King, Jr., condemned the war. Refusing to be drafted, boxer Muhammad Ali was sentenced to jail and stripped of his championship in 1967. The growing opposition to the war produced large and angry demonstrations. In 1965 students and faculty staged "teach-ins" at college campuses to explore and question American policy in Vietnam. In April, 20,000 people gathered at the Washington Monument to protest the war. Some young men risked jail by returning or burning their draft cards. On campuses, students protested the presence of recruiters trying to hire workers for defense contractors. Radicals in Oakland, California, tried to shut down an Army draft induction center. Meanwhile, nearly 100,000 people rallied in Washington, DC, to protest the war.

Yet most Americans supported the war. To many people, the demonstrators were unpatriotic. "America—Love It or Leave It," read a popular bumper sticker. "Hawks," mostly conservative Republicans and Democrats, wanted Johnson to fight harder. Nevertheless, by October 1967 support for the war in one public opinion poll had fallen to 58 percent, and only 28 percent of the people approved of Johnson's conduct of the war.

TABLE 28–2

The Escalating War in Vietnam, 1960–1968			
Year	U. S. Troops	U.S. Battle Deaths	S. Vietnamese Battle Deaths	N. Vietnamese & Viet Cong Battle Deaths (estimated)

Year	U. S. Troops	U.S. Battle Deaths	S. Vietnamese Battle Deaths	N. Vietnamese & Viet Cong Battle Deaths (estimated)
1961	3,164	11	(three-year	12,000
1962	11,326	31	total =	21,000
1963	16,263	78	13,985)	21,000
1964	23,310	147	7,457	17,000
1965	184,000	1,369	11,403	35,382
1966	385,000	5,008	11,953	55,524
1967	486,000	9,378	12,716	88,104
1968	536,000	14,589	27,915	181,149

Sources: Michael Clodfelter, Vietnam in Military Statistics, pp. 46, 57, 209, 258; Fox Butterfield, ed., Vietnam War Almanac, pp. 50, 54, 57, 64, 102, 132, 158, 192; Shelby Stanton, ed., Vietnam Order of Battle, p. 333.

Bad economic news contributed to the public mood. Massive government spending for the war and the Great Society had overstimulated the economy. With jobs plentiful, strong consumer demand drove up prices, which in turn put upward pressure on wages. Anxious about inflation, the Federal Reserve contracted the money supply, making it harder for businesses to get loans. When interest rates reached their highest levels since the 1920s, there were fears of a financial panic. Despite liberal economic policies, the United States had not created perpetual prosperity after all.

By the end of 1967 the war had put enormous stress on the Great Society. It undermined liberals' commitment to anti-Communism and their confidence in American power and wisdom. By dividing the nation, the conflict also undermined support for the Great Society. By weakening the economy, furthermore, the Vietnam War made it harder to pay for the Great Society. The United States could not, as Johnson believed, "do it all." The new liberalism had reached its crisis.

THE GREAT SOCIETY COMES APART

Liberals attained power in the early 1960s because their agenda responded to popular discontent with the consumer society, but even as Congress enacted that agenda, many Americans were expressing new dissatisfactions that liberalism could not accommodate. The Black Power movement, the youth rebellion, and a reborn women's movement exposed the limits of the liberal vision. In 1968 the strain of new demands, the Vietnam War, and economic realities tore apart the Great Society, destroyed the fortunes of Lyndon Johnson, and badly wounded the Democratic Party and the new liberalism.

The Emergence of Black Power

For many African Americans, the Great Society's response to racial inequality was too slow and too weak. As the controversy over the MFDP delegation suggested, Johnson and many white Democrats were unwilling to share power with African

Americans. Meanwhile, other events dramatized the gap between the promise of the Great Society and the reality of life in black America. Even as the civil rights movement reached its climax in the mid-1960s, a wave of race riots spread across the United States. When a white policeman shot a 15-year-old African American in New York in July 1964, angry African Americans burned and looted buildings. In August 1965 friction between white police and African-American citizens touched off a riot in Los Angeles. In five days more than 1,000 fires burned, and 34 people died. The wave of riots peaked in Detroit in July 1967 when 43 people died. There were more than 300 race riots from 1964 to 1969 in all parts of the country, not just the South.

The disturbances flowed from the real frustrations of African Americans. Despite the civil rights movement's successful challenge to legalized segregation in the South, African Americans still lived with poverty and discrimination all across the country. The riots signaled that the civil rights movement and the new liberalism had not addressed some of the most difficult problems of racial inequality.

For years King and other activists had relied on nonviolent demonstrations and ties to white liberals to achieve integration, but that approach proved ineffective in the North. In 1965, King went north to confront "the Negro's repellent slum life" in Chicago and join marches protesting the de facto segregation of the city's educational system. King faced the determined opposition of the city's Democratic political boss, Mayor Richard Daley. Reluctant to challenge the powerful mayor, the Johnson administration would not give King real support. In 1966, King returned to lead the "Chicago Movement" to wipe out slums and win access to better housing in white neighborhoods. Daley accepted a compromise on fair housing but repudiated it as soon as King left town. Under the leadership of 24-year-old Jesse Jackson, Operation Breadbasket threatened demonstrations and boycotts against businesses that refused to hire African Americans. The project produced few results; King's nonviolent tactics had failed.

African Americans already had the example of a different approach to the problem of black/white relations. The Nation of Islam believed that whites were devils and African Americans were God's chosen people. The Black Muslims, as they were known, preached separation of the races and the self-reliance of African Americans. One of the Muslims' most powerful preachers was Malcolm X, who angrily rejected integration and nonviolence. He moderated his view of whites before being gunned down, apparently by Muslims, in 1965, but Malcolm X was best known for his militant call "for the freedom of the 22 million Afro-Americans by any means necessary."

By the mid-1960s, many African Americans were willing to follow at least some of Malcolm X's example. Rejecting the longtime goal of integration, they now emphasized maintaining and celebrating a separate African-American identity, declaring that "black is beautiful." In asserting their distinctive identity, some African Americans accentuated their African heritage. They wore African robes and dashikis, explored African language and art, and observed the seven-day holiday Kwanzaa, based on an African harvest festival.

In rejecting nonviolence and integration, a number of African-American activists adopted a more militant stance that was encapsulated in the new slogan "Black Power." The new slogan had different meanings for different people. The most radical interpretation came from the Black Panthers, who were first organized in Oakland, California, by Huey P. Newton and Bobby Seale. Dressed in black clothes and black berets, the Panthers armed themselves to protect their neighborhoods from white police. The Panthers also founded schools and promoted peaceful community activism, but they were best known in the media for their aura of violent militance.

Particularly because of the violent image of the Black Panthers, many Americans, African American and white, were hostile to the new slogan. For King and his allies, Black Power all too obviously meant repudiation of nonviolent integration. For white leaders like Richard Daley, Black Power meant giving up political authority to African Americans. For Lyndon Johnson, Black Power obviously meant a rejection of his Great Society.

The Youth Rebellion

By the early 1960s many students felt confined and oppressed in overcrowded and impersonal colleges and universities. Moreover, these schools ordered students' lives through rules that governed eating in dining halls, drinking alcohol, keeping cars on campus, and socializing in dorm rooms. Female students were subject to particularly strict rules, including curfews.

Campuses across the country witnessed rebellions against these rules in the 1960s. Demanding greater sexual freedom, students sharply criticized regulations that restricted the mixing of male and female students in dorms. By the end of the decade, students were living together before marriage, to the consternation of college authorities and other adults.

Meanwhile, a much smaller number of students was beginning to see the shortcomings of colleges and universities as symptoms of broader social problems. These youth created the New Left, a radical movement that attempted to confront liberalism and create a more democratic nation. The key organization of the New Left was Students for a Democratic Society (SDS).

During its national convention at Port Huron, Michigan, in 1962, SDS approved an "Agenda for a New Generation" that laid out their developing vision. The Port Huron Statement, as it became known, argued that American society denied people real choice and real power in their lives. The answer, SDS claimed, was "participatory democracy." The members of SDS did not believe that liberalism would promote real democracy in America. Instead, the Port Huron Statement looked to students to lead the way by fighting for control of their schools.

The battle began at the University of California at Berkeley in 1964. That fall, the university's administration banned political speaking and organizing at the one street corner where it had been allowed. When a civil rights activist was arrested for defying the ban in October, hundreds of students sat down around the police cars, trapping the officers for 32 hours. After the stand-off, students created the Free Speech Movement (FSM) to demand greater student involvement in the educational process. When the university refused to accept that demand, students took over the main administration building. The administration eventually succumbed to faculty protests and a student boycott of classes and agreed to new rules on free speech.

Americans had never seen anything quite like the Berkeley protests. Here were privileged students, on their way to comfortable middle-class lives, condemning society, storming a building, and being dragged off by the police. Many people were infuriated; running for governor of California in 1966, the conservative former movie actor Ronald Reagan vowed to "clean up the mess at Berkeley." Many younger Americans were inspired by the FSM; SDS membership rose from 2,500 in December 1964 to 10,000 in October 1965. By then, the New Left had found a perfect issue to dramatize the failings of liberalism—the Vietnam War. Student radicals became the backbone of the antiwar movement.

While the New Left flourished, young people were also creating the rebellious lifestyle that became known as the counterculture. Less politically oriented than the

New Left, the counterculture challenged conventional social values. By the mid-1960s, many younger Americans were condemning conformity, careerism, materialism, and sexual repression as they groped toward an alternative lifestyle.

The counterculture rested on the enjoyment of rock music, drugs, and sexual freedom. Beginning in 1964, the sudden popularity of the Beatles, the Rolling Stones, and other British rock groups brought back a rebellious note to rock and roll. Young Americans loved the Beatles' first movie, *A Hard Day's Night* in 1964, because, a student wrote, "all the dreary old adults are mocked and brushed aside."

Rock also became more socially and politically conscious in the 1960s. Bob Dylan, Simon and Garfunkel, and other musicians rooted in folk music sang about racism, nuclear weapons, and other issues.

Rock music often sang of the virtues of drugs and sex, two more elements of the counterculture. Many young people hoped that the counterculture would weave sex, drugs, and rock into a new lifestyle. Novelist Ken Kesey joined with his followers, the Merry Pranksters, to set up a commune outside San Francisco. The Merry Pranksters used drugs to synchronize with the cosmos and attain a state of ecstasy. By 1965 Kesey had created the "acid test," which fused drugs, rock, and light shows into a multimedia experience. The acid test helped establish the popularity of "acid rock," the "San Francisco sound" of the Jefferson Airplane and the Grateful Dead.

The purest form of the countercultural lifestyle was created by the hippies, who appeared in the mid-1960s. Hippie culture centered in San Francisco. Rejecting materialism and consumerism, hippies celebrated free expression and free love. They wanted to replace competition and aggression with cooperation and community. One group of hippies, the Diggers, tried to transcend the consumer economy by giving away used clothes at their "free store" in Haight-Ashbury, handing out free food, and staging free concerts.

The counterculture had obvious roots in the beat movement and the rebellious style of Elvis Presley and James Dean in the 1950s. The counterculture also had roots in the orthodox culture it attacked. By the close of the 1950s, adults themselves had become ambivalent about consumerism and conventional morality. Sexual freedom for youth was encouraged partly by the greater sexual openness of mainstream culture, the Supreme Court's *Griswold* decision, and the introduction of the oral contraceptive (the "pill") in 1960. Moreover, the countercultural lifestyle itself became a form of consumerism, as young Americans flocked to buy the right clothes and record albums. Nevertheless, the counterculture was a disruptive force in 1960s America. Like the Black Panthers, hippies were a small minority, but they and the counterculture deeply influenced young people and adults. The counterculture encouraged Americans to question conventional values and authority and to seek a freer way of life.

By 1967, the New Left, the counterculture, and the other forms of youth rebellion were upsetting the Great Society. Adults feared that young people were out of control, and a society already divided by race was increasingly divided by generation.

The Rebirth of the Women's Movement

By the 1960s American women were reacting against the difficult social roles enforced on them after World War II. More women than ever went to college, but they were not expected to pursue long-term careers. More women than ever worked outside the home, but they were still expected to devote themselves to home and family. Women also had to put up with the continuing double standard of sexual behavior, which granted men more freedom to seek sexual gratification outside of marriage. As the new decade began, educated middle-class women be-

The counterculture comes together. The three dancers epitomize the joyful quest for freedom at the heart of the youth rebellion of the 1960s; the rest of the crowd is a reminder of how many young people sat and watched.

gan to question their second-class status. In part, they were inspired by the example of the civil rights movement.

Two best-selling books reflected these women's complaints. In *The Feminine Mystique* (1963), journalist Betty Friedan described "the problem that has no name," the growing frustration of educated, middle-class wives and mothers who had subordinated their own aspirations to the needs of men. Meanwhile, journalist Helen Gurley Brown rejected unequal sexual opportunities in her book, *Sex and the Single Girl* (1962). Brown did not challenge male sexual ethics, just as Friedan did not challenge male careerism. Instead, like Friedan, Brown wanted equal opportunity for women, both in and out of marriage. She explained, coyly, that "nice, single girls do."

In 1963 Congress passed the Equal Pay Act, which mandated the same pay for men and women who did the same work, but the measure, full of loopholes, had little impact on women's comparatively low wages and salaries. A year later, Title VII, a provision of the Civil Rights Act of 1964, prohibited employers from discriminating on the basis of sex in hiring and compensating workers. Yet the Equal Employment Opportunity Commission (EEOC) did little to enforce the law.

Male insensitivity and inaction soon pushed women to organize. In 1966 Betty Friedan and a handful of other women, angry at the EEOC, formed the National Organization for Women (NOW). Although frustrated with the Great Society, Friedan and the founders of NOW expressed essentially liberal values. They saw NOW as "a civil rights organization," and wrote a "Bill of Rights" for women that focused on government action to provide rights and opportunities. NOW also demanded access to contraception and abortion.

NOW's platform was too radical for many women and not radical enough for others. Some younger women, particularly activists in the civil rights movement and the New Left, wanted more than liberal solutions to their problems. By the fall of 1967, activists were forming new groups dedicated to "women's liberation." Influenced by the New Left, radical feminists blamed the capitalist system for the oppression of women, but a growing number of radicals saw men as the problem. Like African Americans in the Black Power movement, radical women talked less about rights and more about power and had little interest in collaboration with male liberal politicians.

Few in number, radical feminists nevertheless commanded public attention. In September 1968 New York Radical Women organized a protest against the annual Miss America pageant in Atlantic City, New Jersey. The pageant, they said, was an act of "thought control" intended "to further make women oppressed and men oppressors; to enslave us all the more in high-heeled, low-status roles." The protesters threw bras, girdles, make-up, and other "women-garbage" into a "Freedom Trash Can." Then they crowned a sheep "Miss America."

Not surprisingly, men were generally uncomfortable with radical feminism. Second-wave feminism, like Black Power and the New Left, did not fit comfortably within the political economy of white, male-dominated new liberalism.

1968: A Tumultuous Year

In 1968 the stresses and strains of the Great Society came together to produce the most tumultuous year in the United States since World War II. While Fred Downs lay wounded in an Army hospital, the Viet Cong and North Vietnamese launched bold, sometimes suicidal attacks all over South Vietnam on the first day of Tet, the Vietnamese new year. Although U.S. and South Vietnamese forces inflicted punishing losses on the attackers, the Tet Offensive shocked Americans. If the United States was winning the war, how could the North Vietnamese and the Viet Cong have struck so daringly? Many Americans who had supported the decision to send troops into South Vietnam now began to believe the war was unwinnable.

The Tet Offensive doomed Johnson's increasingly troubled administration. The president needed to send reinforcements to Vietnam, but he knew public opinion would oppose the move. As it was, he could not even pay for more troops. The economy would not support both the war and the Great Society any longer. The political situation was bad, too. On March 12 Senator Eugene McCarthy, an antiwar candidate, nearly beat Johnson in New Hampshire's Democratic primary. Four days later, Senator Robert Kennedy, the younger brother of John Kennedy, announced his own candidacy for the Democratic nomination. Besieged by the war, the economy, and the presidential campaign, Johnson went on television the night of March 31. He announced that he had halted the bombing of much of North Vietnam and indicated his willingness to talk peace with the North Vietnamese. Then Johnson, drained by events, announced that he would not run again for president.

Johnson had painfully accepted new limits on the war, the economy, the Great Society, and his own career. During 1968, Congressional leaders forced him to agree to spending cuts for Great Society programs. Johnson did not have the money or the clout for new welfare programs, new initiatives to improve race relations, or even the space program, that symbol of great liberal dreams. The president continued the Apollo program but abandoned other space projects. The Great Society was coming back down to earth.

Meanwhile, the United States was torn by upheaval and violence. In the first six months of 1968, students carried out demonstrations at 101 colleges and universities. On April 4, Martin Luther King, Jr., was assassinated in Memphis, Tennessee, where he had gone to support striking African-American and white sanitation workers. King's assassination set off riots in more than 100 cities. Forty-one African

Americans and five whites died. African Americans "have had all they can stand," two black psychologists wrote.

The violence soon spread to the presidential campaign. After winning the California Democratic primary on the evening of June 5, Robert Kennedy was shot. Kennedy's death the next morning left Eugene McCarthy to contest the Democratic presidential nomination with Vice President Hubert Humphrey of Minnesota, who still supported the American war effort in Vietnam. Humphrey won the nomination at the Democratic convention in Chicago in August, but the party was deeply divided. Outside the convention hall, Mayor Daley's police battled in the streets with antiwar demonstrators.

The Republican Party nominated Richard Nixon, the man who lost to John Kennedy in 1960. A critic of the Great Society, Nixon promised to end the Vietnam War and unify the country. Nixon tried to exploit the nation's social divisions with promises to speak for "the forgotten Americans, the nonshouters, the nondemonstrators." Running as a third-party candidate, the segregationist former governor of Alabama, George Wallace, reached out even more bluntly to middle- and working-class whites who increasingly resented African Americans and their liberal benefactors.

Like 1960, the 1968 election produced a narrow outcome with large consequences, but this time, Nixon was the winner. Although Humphrey gained in the polls by distancing himself from Johnson's Vietnam policy, the vice president could not overcome the troubles of the Democratic Party and the Great Society. Nixon attracted 43.4 percent of the popular vote to Humphrey's 42.7 percent and Wallace's 13.5 percent. Although the Democrats retained control of the House and Senate, the liberals' eight-year hold on the White House had been broken.

Over the course of 1968, the new liberalism had finally lost its hold on the nation. The Johnson administration could not handle the demands of African Americans, youth, and women, win the war in Vietnam, or stabilize the economy. The violence of 1968 testified to the frustration of many Americans with the Great Society, as did the outcome of the presidential election.

CONCLUSION

In 1960 Nixon's defeat signaled the rise of the new liberalism. In 1968 his victory marked liberalism's fall. The end of liberal dominance marked the end of illusions about limitless American power. John Kennedy's confident America—able to "pay any price, bear any burden, meet any hardship, support any friend, oppose any foe"—had vanished. By 1968 the American economy could no longer "pay any price." The United States could not successfully support its friends in South Vietnam or defeat the North Vietnamese and the Viet Cong. The government could not fulfill the ambitious plans of the New Frontier and the Great Society. Instead, the nation was deeply divided by generation, race, and gender. The assassinations of Robert Kennedy and Martin Luther King, Jr., dramatized the breakdown of the political system. The liberal approach to political economy depended on the state to reform and regulate society, but now the American state no longer seemed to work.

Back in the United States in the spring of 1968, Fred Downs had to deal with his own losses. His left arm, his confidence, and his plans were gone. He had to learn how to use a prosthetic arm and to accept the break-up of his marriage. He had to learn how to deal with a divided, angry America. On the street one day, a man pointed to the hook sticking out of Downs's left sleeve. "Get that in Vietnam?" the man asked. Downs said he had. "Serves you right," the man snapped, and walked away. The United States, like that man, would have a difficult time coming to terms with the events of the 1960s.

CHRONOLOGY

1960	Lunch counter sit-ins at Greensboro, N.C.
	Founding of Student Nonviolent Coordinating Committee (SNCC)
	Formation of Students for a Democratic Society (SDS)
	John Kennedy elected president
1961	Bay of Pigs invasion of Cuba
	First U.S. suborbital space flight, by Alan Shepard
	Freedom Rides
	Beginning of SNCC voter-registration drive in Mississippi
	Beginning of Albany Movement in Albany, Georgia
	Erection of Berlin Wall
	Creation of Peace Corps
1962	Michael Harrington, *The Other America*
	Rachel Carson, *Silent Spring*
	First U.S. orbital space flight, by John Glenn
	Integration of University of Mississippi
	Cuban Missile Crisis
1963	Betty Friedan, *The Feminine Mystique*
	Clean Air Act
	Limited Test Ban Treaty
	Civil rights protests in Birmingham, Alabama
	Civil rights march on Washington, DC
	Assassination of Ngo Dinh Diem
	Assassination of John F. Kennedy in Dallas
	Lyndon B. Johnson succeeds to the presidency
1964	Beatlemania
	Wilderness Act
	Civil Rights Act of 1964

FURTHER READINGS

Terry H. Anderson, *The Movement and the Sixties: Protest in America From Greensboro to Wounded Knee* (1995). A sweeping chronicle of the varieties of protest in the 1960s.

David Farber, *The Age of Great Dreams: America in the 1960s* (1994). Offers a readable account of the decade.

Betty Friedan, *The Feminine Mystique* (1963). Explores the plight of middle-class women that helped produce liberal feminism.

Samuel P. Hays, *Beauty, Health, and Permanence: Environmental Politics in the United States* (1987). A broad study of the emergence of the modern environmental movement.

Announcement of Lyndon Johnson's "War on Poverty"
Economic OpportunityAct
Free Speech Movement
Harlem race riot
Tonkin Gulf incidents
Lyndon Johnson's landslide election as president

1965 Decision to send U.S. troops into battle in South Vietnam
Voting Rights Act of 1965
Creation of Medicare and Medicaid
Elementary and Secondary School Act
Water Quality Act
Watts race riot
Creation of National Endowment for the Arts and National
Endowment for the Humanities
Griswold v. *Connecticut*
Ralph Nader, *Unsafe at Any Speed*

1966 Founding of National Organization for Women (NOW)
Clean Waters Restoration Act
Miranda v. *Arizona*

1967 Air Quality Act
Public Broadcasting Act
Stop the Draft Week

1968 Tet Offensive in Vietnam
Assassination of Martin Luther King, Jr.
Assassination of Robert Kennedy
New York Radical Women's Miss America Protest
Richard Nixon elected president

George C. Herring, *America's Longest War: The United States and Vietnam, 1950–1975* (1996). A balanced overview of the war.

Jim Miller, *"Democracy Is in the Streets": From Port Huron to the Siege of Chicago* (1987). Explores the SDS's efforts to define and promote "participatory democracy."

Howell Raines, *My Soul Is Rested: Movement Days in the Deep South Remembered* (1977). A moving collection of interviews that vividly recreate the struggle against segregation.

 Please refer to the document CD-ROM for primary sources related to this chapter.

CHAPTER

29

Living with Less

1968–1980

"Panic at the Pump," 1973–1974 • A New Crisis: Economic Decline
Confronting Decline: Nixon's Strategy • Refusing to Settle for
Less: Struggles for Rights • Backlash: From Radical Action to
Conservative Reaction • Political Crisis: Three Troubled
Presidencies • Conclusion

"PANIC AT THE PUMP," 1973–1974

Across the country in the fall and winter of 1973–1974, frustrated drivers waited in long lines to buy gasoline. Like most Americans, these men and women took for granted cheap, abundant energy. Suddenly, the price of gas skyrocketed. Many service stations had little or no gas to sell. One news magazine reported about the "Panic at the Pump." Service-station attendants faced curses, threats, guns, and even a hand grenade in one case.

The energy shortage and its effects spread well beyond gas stations. In Pennsylvania, Ohio, and other states, truck drivers blockaded highways to protest the high cost of fuel and low speed limits. Lack of fuel grounded some commercial flights. Heating oil for homes and businesses was also in short supply. Communities opened shelters for people who could not afford to heat their homes.

The crisis dramatized a turning point in American life. Beginning in the early 1960s, the United States had been unable to produce all the oil it needed. By 1974, the nation had to import over a third of its oil, particularly from the Middle East. The energy needs of the United States and other Western countries empowered the Organization of Petroleum Exporting Countries (OPEC), third-world nations that had joined together to get higher prices for their oil. In October 1973 Arab members of OPEC refused to send petroleum to the United States and other nations that supported Israel and raised oil prices nearly 400 percent. The result was the panic at the pump.

Although the Arabs ended the oil embargo in March 1974, the underlying conditions that encouraged it remained. After the soaring liberal hopes of the early 1960s, Americans confronted sobering new realities in the 1970s. The nation did not have enough oil and other natural resources. Its economy, long prosperous, was vulnerable to foreign nations. The federal government was not strong enough to challenge those nations. Americans' consumer lifestyle now seemed as impractical as the big cars built by Detroit. As a magazine concluded, Americans were "Learning to Live With Less."

The 1970s were a difficult period of adjustment for the American political economy. Workers, employers, politicians, and families struggled with the consequences of limited resources and power. This task was made more difficult because of new demands for economic opportunity and political rights from many disadvantaged Americans, who had already lived with less for too long. By the end of the decade, the United States had not solved the problem of equality and the other challenges of living with less.

A New Crisis: Economic Decline

The crises of the 1960s had focused attention on the apparent weaknesses of American politics and government. The Great Society had not established racial harmony and equality; the government had not won the Vietnam War. After the assassinations of John F. Kennedy, Robert F. Kennedy, and Martin Luther King, Jr., Americans even wondered if their society was capable of democratic politics and peaceful change.

The events of the 1970s intensified concerns about the capacity of government to achieve national goals and serve the people. They also focused Americans' attention on a new crisis—the economy. By the end of the 1970s, Americans wondered whether the economy, like the political system, would ever work smoothly again.

The Sources of Economic Decline

There were signs of economic decline almost everywhere. Although the economy continued to grow, the productivity of American workers peaked in 1966 and then began to fall. Corporate profits dropped off after the mid-1960s; the growth rate of the gross national product slowed; poverty remained; unemployment increased; and inflation, which usually dropped when unemployment rose, also increased. The unprecedented combination of high unemployment and high inflation led to the coining of a new word—stagflation.

There were several major reasons for American economic decline. Along with the energy crisis, the United States suffered from increasing competition from Japan, West Germany, and other nations, which, thanks to American aid after World

War II, now had efficient, up-to-date industries. As a result, these nations rivaled the United States not only abroad, but even in the American market.

The rise of Japan was the most dramatic of these developments. By the 1970s, Japan's factories turned out high-quality products. Japanese televisions and other electronic goods filled American homes. Japanese cars—small, well made, and fuel efficient—attracted American buyers worried about the high price of gas.

Because of such competition, the United States fell back in the international economic race. In 1950, the nation had accounted for 40 percent of the value of all the goods and services produced around the globe. By 1970 that figure was down to 23 percent. During these years, the American share of world trade dropped nearly 50 percent. By the end of the 1970s, the United States imported more manufactured goods than it exported.

Long an emblem of security and stability, American corporations suddenly appeared vulnerable. In 1970, the Penn Central Railroad went bankrupt, and only massive aid from the federal government saved the giant Lockheed Aircraft company. Other corporations thrived by becoming multinationals, building factories and other facilities overseas and thus directing jobs and dollars away from the American economy.

The federal government also played a part in the economic predicament. Massive government spending, particularly for defense, had stimulated the economy from the 1940s to the 1960s, but by the 1970s defense spending did not have the same effect. In addition, the government's huge expenditures for the Vietnam War promoted inflation.

In the 1960s, the liberal followers of John Maynard Keynes had been confident that they understood the secret of maintaining prosperity. They believed the federal government could manipulate its budget to stabilize the economy. The economists were unprepared for the novel problem of stagflation. "The rules of economics," admitted the chairman of the Federal Reserve, "are not working quite the way they used to."

The Impact of Decline

Shaped by a broad range of factors, economic decline began to reshape life in the United States. By the 1970s, it seemed as if the industrial revolution was being reversed. As factories closed, Americans witnessed the deindustrialization of their country. Huge steel plants, the symbol of American industrial might, stood empty. Manufacturers switched the production of televisions to Canada, Japan, Taiwan, and Hong Kong. Food-processing companies moved their operations to Mexico. These developments intensified the trend, first evident in the 1950s, toward a service-centered economy. In the 1970s, most new jobs were in the sales and retail sectors.

For American workers, the consequences of deindustrialization were devastating. Heavy industry had been the stronghold of the labor movement. Organized labor lost members, power, and influence. By the late 1970s, less than one in four workers belonged to a union.

The shift away from unionized industrial jobs eroded Americans' incomes. After rising from the 1950s into the 1960s, workers' spendable income began to drop by the mid-1970s. To keep up, more and more women took full-time jobs outside the home, but not all Americans could find work. As the huge baby-boom generation came of age, the economy did not produce enough jobs.

Economic decline accelerated the transformation of America's regions. People and power had been moving from north to south and east to west for a long time.

Population Change

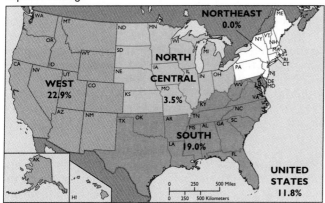

Map 29–1 Movement from Rustbelt to Sunbelt
The percentages track the shift of population (top) and manufacturing jobs (bottom) from the Northeast and the Midwest to the South and West between 1970 and 1980.

Source: D.K. Adams et al., An Atlas of North American Affairs, 2nd ed. (London and New York: Methuen).

Manufacturing Output

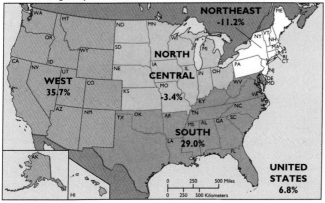

The energy crisis and deindustrialization sped up that movement (see Map 29–1). The Northeast and the Midwest, home to so many aging steel mills and auto plants, suffered especially.

Fleeing deindustrialization, many northerners migrated south to the band of states ranging from Florida to California. As the Sunbelt boomed, farms turned into suburbs and cities such as Orlando, Houston, Dallas, Phoenix, San Diego, and Anaheim exploded in size.

With mild winters, the Sunbelt did not suffer so much from high oil prices. If anything, Texas and the southwestern states, rich in oil and natural gas reserves, profited from the energy crisis. The Sunbelt was also home to new high-technology businesses: aerospace firms, electronics companies, and defense contractors. The Sunbelt was also at the cutting edge of the service economy, with its emphasis on leisure and consumption.

CONFRONTING DECLINE: NIXON'S STRATEGY

Richard Nixon was the first president to confront the decline of America's post-World War II prosperity and power. Nixon and his administration understood that the American political economy would have to live with less. The president also recognized that the failure of the war effort in Vietnam marked the end of America's cold-war pretensions. Nixon would not claim that the nation had unlimited power.

Nixon also recognized that the upheavals of the 1960s had weakened liberalism and its supporters. According to the president, the troubles of Lyndon Johnson's Great Society demonstrated the failings of the activist, liberal approach to the political economy. He believed, too, that the crises of the 1960s created opportunities for new people and new political economic approaches. Abroad and at home, the new president tried to take advantage of those opportunities.

A New Foreign Policy

The president and his national security advisor, Henry Kissinger, still regarded Communism as a menace and saw the cold-war rivalry between the United States and the Soviet Union as the defining reality of the modern world. However, Nixon and Kissinger understood that the relative decline of American power dictated a new approach to the cold war. During Nixon's presidency, the United States pulled back from its promise to intervene around the world to stop the spread of Communism. Nixon moved to ease tensions with the Soviet Union and the People's Republic of China and to end American participation in the Vietnam War. By the end of Nixon's presidency, the role of the United States in the world had changed considerably.

The twin pillars of the new foreign policy were the Nixon Doctrine and détente. In a speech in July 1969, the president announced that the United States "cannot—and will not—conceive all the plans, design all the programs, execute all the decisions and undertake all the defense of the free nations of the world." America would continue to provide a nuclear umbrella, but its allies would have to defend themselves. This Nixon Doctrine amounted to a repudiation of the Truman Doctrine, the 1947 promise "to support free peoples who are resisting attempted subjugation by armed minorities or by outside pressures."

The United States also pursued a new relationship with the Soviet Union and the People's Republic of China. Nixon and Kissinger wanted to lessen the cost of America's rivalry with these two Communist nuclear powers. Separate agreements with the Soviet Union and China would, the American leaders hoped, keep those two nations from combining forces against the United States. Nixon and Kissinger therefore worked to establish détente, the relaxation of tensions.

At the start of Nixon's presidency, the United States had not recognized the legitimacy of the People's Republic of China. Instead, America supported the Communists' bitter foes, the Nationalist Chinese regime on Taiwan. In February 1972, Nixon became the first American president to go to mainland China. He gave the Chinese leaders what they most wanted—a promise that the United States would eventually withdraw its troops from Taiwan. The two sides also made clear that they opposed any Soviet attempt to dominate Asia.

Nixon's trip brought American policy in line with the reality of the 1970s and underscored the gradual ending of anti-Communist hysteria back home in America. As Nixon intended, the trip also left the Soviets with the frightening possibility of a Chinese–American alliance.

Nixon did not want a confrontation with the Soviets. The United States no longer had clear military superiority. Instead, the president sought détente. Above all, he wanted the Soviets to agree to limit their long-range or strategic nuclear arsenals. The Soviets also wished to reduce the expense and danger of the cold war and to counter Nixon's overture to the Chinese. Moreover, they badly needed American grain to help feed their own people.

Under these circumstances, the two sides began talks on the Strategic Arms Limitations Treaty (SALT I) in 1969. In May 1972, three months after his trip to China, Nixon became the first American president to travel to Moscow, where he signed the SALT treaty, limiting for five years the number of each nation's nuclear missiles. An Anti-Ballistic Missile (ABM) treaty sharply limited the number of defensive missiles that the two sides could deploy. Although they did not stop the arms race, the ABM and SALT treaties symbolized the American and Soviet agreement that "there is no alternative to . . . peaceful coexistence."

Ending the Vietnam War

Along with other motivations, the Nixon administration sought better relations with the Soviet Union and the People's Republic of China to help end the Vietnam War. Nixon and Kissinger hoped the Soviets and the Chinese would pressure the North Vietnamese to accept a peace agreement. The president needed such an agreement. Nixon knew the United States could not win the Vietnam War. Meanwhile, the ongoing conflict divided the American people and undermined American prestige and power around the world.

To appease public opinion, Nixon began to bring American soldiers home in 1969. Without those soldiers, he had a hard time persuading North Vietnam to accept the continued existence of South Vietnam. The president attempted to resolve this dilemma with a policy known as "Vietnamization," or encouraging the South Vietnamese to take over their own defense. However, the South Vietnamese military alone could not beat back the Communists.

Accordingly, Nixon turned to U.S. airpower to support South Vietnamese troops. In March 1969, he authorized B-52 raids on North Vietnamese sanctuaries in Cambodia. Because bombing this neutral country might outrage American and world opinion, the president kept the raids secret. However, the Cambodian operation did not force North Vietnam to make peace. Secret negotiations between Henry Kissinger and North Vietnamese diplomats also went nowhere.

Meanwhile, Nixon's actions angered many Americans. News of the secret bombings leaked out. In October, millions of Americans participated in Moratorium Day, a dramatic break from business as usual, to protest the war. In November, more than 250,000 people staged a "March Against Death" in Washington. That month, Americans learned about one of the most troubling episodes of the war. On March 16, 1968, United States soldiers had shot and killed between 200 and 500 unarmed South Vietnamese women, children, and old men in the hamlet of My Lai. This atrocity led to the 1970 court martial and eventual conviction of Lieutenant William Calley, Jr., for mass murder.

Demonstrations and public opinion did not stop the president from using violence to force a peace agreement. When General Lon Nol, the new pro-American leader of Cambodia, appealed for United States aid to stop a Communist insurgency, a joint United States–South Vietnamese force invaded Cambodia in April 1970. The Cambodian invasion produced turmoil in the United States. Students demonstrated on campuses across the country. On May 4, National Guard troops fired at an unarmed crowd of protesters at Kent State University in Ohio. Four students died. Ten days later, state police killed two African-American students at

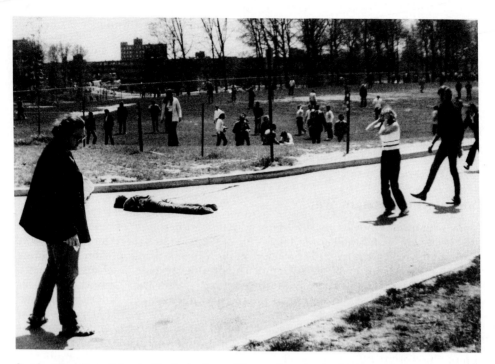

Death at Kent State University: The body of one of four students shot by the Ohio National Guard during protests over the U.S. invasion of Cambodia in 1970.

Jackson State College in Mississippi. These deaths intensified the outrage over the invasion of Cambodia. Students went out on strike at about 450 campuses.

As American troop withdrawals continued, the war and the peace negotiations dragged on. Vietnamization continued to founder. Meanwhile, the *New York Times* began publishing the so-called Pentagon Papers, a secret history of the American involvement in Vietnam. The documents, which made clear that the Johnson administration had misled the American people, further undermined support for the war. The Nixon administration tried unsuccessfully to persuade the Supreme Court to block publication of the papers.

Unable to stop the publication of the Pentagon Papers or secure a peace agreement, Nixon stepped up efforts to pressure North Vietnam into a settlement. When the North Vietnamese Army swept across the border into South Vietnam in March 1972, the president struck back with Operation Linebacker, an aerial attack against North Vietnam. When negotiations stalled again, the president intensified the air raids in December. On January 27, 1973, negotiators signed a peace agreement in Paris. For the United States, at least, the Vietnam War was over.

The United States had gone to war to preserve an anti-Communist South Vietnam, but the peace agreement did not guarantee South Vietnam's survival or require the North Vietnamese to pull their troops out of South Vietnam. The cease-fire came at a heavy cost. Twenty thousand Americans and more than 600,000 North and South Vietnamese soldiers had died since Nixon took office in 1969. The number of civilian casualties will never be known. Nixon had ended U.S. participation in the Vietnam War, but the president's critics asked whether four more years of fighting had really been necessary when the result was such a flawed peace agreement.

Chile and the Middle East

Détente did not end U.S. opposition to Communist initiatives around the world. It also did not restore American power abroad. Nixon, like the presidents before him, refused to accept the establishment of a Communist regime in the Western Hemisphere. In 1970, he ordered the CIA to block the election of Salvador Allende, a Marxist, as president of Chile. Allende was elected anyway. The CIA then destabilized Allende's regime by helping right-wing parties, driving up the price of bread, and encouraging demonstrations. When a military coup murdered Allende and thousands of his followers, the United States denied responsibility and offered financial assistance to the new leader, Augusto Pinochet.

In the Middle East, the Nixon administration also displayed its hostility to Communism and its inability to shape events decisively. During the Six Day War in 1967, Israel defeated Egyptian and Syrian forces and occupied territory belonging to Egypt, Syria, and Jordan. Seeking revenge, Egypt and Syria attacked Israel in October 1973, on Yom Kippur, the holiest day of the Jewish calendar. When the United States sent critical supplies to Israel, Arab countries responded with an oil embargo. Meanwhile, the Soviets supplied the Arabs and pressed for a role in the region. Determined to keep out the Soviet Union, Nixon put American nuclear forces on alert. Kissinger mediated between the combatants, who agreed to pull back their troops in January 1974. Although the embargo ended, American weakness was obvious. Supporting Israel, the United States still needed the Arabs' oil. Nixon and Kissinger held back the Soviet Union, but they could not bring peace to the Middle East.

A Mixed Domestic Record

Nixon had a mixed domestic record. In some areas, his administration shrank the federal government and the Great Society. In others, it accepted new liberal initiatives. Meanwhile, the president had little success in dealing with an ailing economy. The problem of decline, imaginatively addressed in Nixon's foreign policy, proved more difficult to handle at home.

Nixon took office with conventional Republican goals. He wanted the federal government to balance its budget and shed some of its power. In 1969, the president called for a New Federalism, in which Washington would return "a greater share of control to state and local governments and to the people."

During the Nixon years, there were spending cuts for some programs, including defense. The fate of the space program epitomized the new budgetary realities. On July 20, 1969, a lunar landing module touched down on the moon. As astronaut Neil Armstrong set foot on the surface, he proclaimed, "That's one small step for man, one giant leap for mankind." The United States had beaten the Soviets to the moon. This triumph suggested that there was still no limit to what Americans could do. There were, however, firm limits to what the space program could do. The administration slashed NASA's budget.

The New Federalism also put limits on Washington. In 1972 the administration persuaded Congress to pass a revenue-sharing plan that allowed state and local governments to spend funds collected by the federal government. But the president left largely intact the massive New Deal and Great Society programs. By 1971, the unsettled economy and the cost of big government had produced a huge budget deficit.

The president did try to reform the federal welfare system put in place by the New Deal. His administration tried to replace the largest federal welfare program,

Aid to Families with Dependent Children, with a controversial system inspired by presidential aide Daniel Patrick Moynihan, a Harvard sociologist. Moynihan's Family Assistance Plan would have provided poor families with a guaranteed minimum annual income, but it also would have required the heads of poor households to accept any available jobs. Opposed by both liberals and conservatives, the program failed to pass Congress.

Meanwhile, the Nixon administration went along with several liberal initiatives that expanded the government's regulatory powers. By the end of the 1960s, the middle class worried that corporations did not protect workers, consumers, or the environment. A grassroots environmental movement grew rapidly, and in April 1970 tens of millions of Americans celebrated the first Earth Day.

Liberals in Congress responded to popular opinion by establishing three new federal regulatory agencies: the Environmental Protection Agency (EPA), the Occupational Safety and Health Administration (OSHA), and the Consumer Product Safety Commission. These agencies considerably enhanced the government's power over corporations, as did a series of measures to safeguard coastlines and endangered species and to limit the use of pesticides, the strip-mining of coal, and the pollution of air and water.

An Uncertain Economic Policy

Nixon reluctantly accepted liberal policies as he struggled with the economy. The Nixon administration faced inflation, rising unemployment, and falling corporate profits. Beginning in 1970, the president tried unsuccessfully to persuade business to control price increases and organized labor to limit wage demands.

The situation was complicated by the U.S. dollar's role in the international monetary system. Since the Bretton Woods conference during World War II, many other nations had tied the value of their own currencies to the dollar. The value of the dollar, in turn, had been supported by the U.S. commitment to the gold standard. The federal government had promised to give an ounce of gold in return for 35 dollars. By the 1970s, however, strong European economies held too many dollars and the United States held too little gold. If other countries had demanded gold for their dollars, panic could have followed.

In response, Nixon announced his New Economic Policy in August 1971. To prevent a gold crisis, the president took the United States off the gold standard. To strengthen the United States against foreign competition, Nixon lowered the value of the dollar and slapped new tariffs on imports. To slow inflation, he authorized a freeze on wages and prices.

Wage and price controls did not solve the underlying economic problems that caused inflation. The ongoing cost of the Vietnam War, along with the Arab oil embargo, continued to drive up prices. Nixon and his advisers had no domestic counterpart to détente.

REFUSING TO SETTLE FOR LESS: STRUGGLES FOR RIGHTS

In the late 1960s and 1970s, African Americans and women continued their struggles for rights that they had long been denied. Their example and the optimistic promises of liberalism spurred other disadvantaged groups to demand recognition. By the end of the 1970s, American society—however tentatively and reluctantly—was more committed to equality for women and minorities.

African Americans' Struggle for Racial Justice

After the assassination of Martin Luther King, Jr., in 1968, the NAACP, the SCLC, and other civil rights organizations continued to press for integration. By the 1970s, national attention focused on two relatively new and controversial means of promoting racial equality—affirmative action and mandatory school busing.

First ordered by the Johnson administration, affirmative action required businesses, universities, and other institutions receiving federal money to provide opportunities for women and nonwhites. Supporters viewed the policy as a way to make up for past and present discrimination. Opponents argued that affirmative action was itself a form of discrimination that reduced opportunities for whites, particularly white men.

Nixon generally supported the principle of affirmative action. His administration developed the Philadelphia Plan, which encouraged the construction industry to meet targets for hiring minority workers. In 1978, the Supreme Court offered qualified support for affirmative action with its decision in *Regents of the University of California* v. *Allan Bakke.* While the court barred schools from using fixed admissions quotas for different racial groups, it did allow educational institutions to use race as an admissions criteria. By the end of the 1970s, affirmative action had become an important means of increasing diversity in schools and other institutions.

School busing was more controversial than affirmative action. By the late 1960s, the Supreme Court had become impatient with delays in integrating the nation's schools. Even in the North, where there had been no de jure or legal segregation, there was still extensive de facto segregation. In *Swann* v. *Charlotte-Mecklenburg Board of Education,* the court upheld the mandatory busing of thousands of children to desegregate schools. To its advocates, busing seemed to be the best way to ensure equal education for African-American pupils. But many Americans opposed the policy because they did not want integration or because they did not want children taken out of neighborhood schools.

Nixon sided with the opponents of busing. Privately ordering his aides to enforce busing less vigorously, the president publicly called for a "moratorium" on new busing plans. Some communities implemented busing peacefully. Others faced protest and turmoil. In 1974, a federal court ordered busing in Boston. When the white-dominated local school committee refused to comply, a federal judge imposed a busing plan on the community. Working-class and lower middle-class whites protested plans to bus students between the predominantly African-American neighborhood of Roxbury and the largely Irish-American neighborhood of South Boston. In "Southie," whites taunted and injured black students. The violence spread to Roxbury and continued through the fall. With busing and affirmative action, the civil rights movement seemed to have reached its limits.

Women's Liberation

By the 1970s, the movement for women's liberation was flourishing. To commemorate the 50th anniversary of the ratification of the women's suffrage amendment to the Constitution, the Women's Strike for Equality took place on August 26, 1970.

The women's liberation movement, like the struggle for African-American equality, was diverse. Liberal feminist groups, such as the National Organization for Women (NOW), concentrated on equal public opportunities for women. Radical feminists focused on a broader range of private and public issues. Oppression, they insisted, took place in the bedroom and the kitchen as well as the school and the

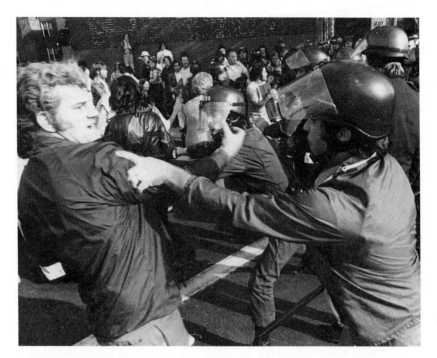

Police break up a crowd of demonstrators opposed to court-ordered busing to integrate public schools in Boston in 1974.

workplace. Some radical feminists blamed women's plight on the inequalities of capitalism; others traced the oppression of women to men. Cultural feminists insisted that women's culture was different from and superior to male culture. They felt that women should create their own separate institutions rather than seek formal equality with men. Some lesbian feminists took this separatist logic one step further to argue that women should avoid heterosexual relationships.

Women's liberation made its mark on the media. In 1972, Gloria Steinem began to publish the feminist magazine *Ms.* On television, popular sitcoms portrayed independent women. Some feminists condemned the availability of pornography, which, they argued, incited violence against women.

In the 1970s, female activists focused on three public issues—access to abortion, equal treatment in schools and workplaces, and passage of the Equal Rights Amendment (ERA) to the Constitution. Abortions were generally illegal and unsafe; in the 1970s, women went to court to challenge the law. In *Roe* v. *Wade* in 1973, the Supreme Court ruled a Texas antiabortion law unconstitutional on the grounds that it violated the "right to privacy" guaranteed by the Ninth and Fourteenth Amendments. With this decision, abortion began to become legal and widely available.

Like the civil rights movement, the women's movement demanded equal treatment in schools and workplaces. Women filed many complaints against discrimination by employers. At first reluctant, the Nixon administration moved to open up government employment to women and to press colleges and businesses to end discriminatory practices. In 1972, Congress approved Title IX of the Higher Education Act, which required schools and universities receiving federal funds to give equal opportunities to women and men in admissions, athletics, and other programs.

The women's movement also continued the long-time struggle to enact the ERA. "Equality of rights under the law," the amendment read, "shall not be denied or abridged by the United States or by any State on account of sex." In 1972 Congress passed the ERA. If 38 states had ratified the amendment within 7 years, it would have become law. Within a year, 28 states had ratified.

Despite this progress, the ERA and women's liberation encountered considerable opposition. To male critics, feminists were a "small band of braless bubbleheads" who suffered from "defeminization." Conservative women activists led a backlash against feminism and equal rights. Phyllis Schlafly organized an effective campaign against the ERA. Although more states ratified the amendment, some rescinded their votes, and the ERA never became law.

The ERA's defeat underscored the challenges that the women's movement faced. Women still did not have full equality in American society. Nevertheless, women had more control over their bodies, more access to education, and more opportunity in the workplace, and women's issues were at the center of American public life.

Mexican Americans and "Brown Power"

In the 1960s and 1970s, Mexican Americans, the second-largest racial minority in the United States, developed a new self-consciousness. Proudly identifying themselves as Chicanos, Mexican Americans organized to protest poverty and discrimination.

Despite the federal efforts to keep out Mexican immigrants, the Mexican-American population grew rapidly. By 1980, at least 7 million Americans claimed Mexican heritage. The great majority lived in Arizona, California, Colorado, New Mexico, and Texas. By the 1970s, most Chicanos lived in urban areas. More than 1 million lived in Los Angeles. Chicanos as a group earned substantially less than did Anglos (white Americans of non-Hispanic descent). One in four Mexican-American families lived in poverty in the mid-1970s.

Chicanos faced racism and discrimination. The media stereotyped them as lazy and shifty. Schools in Chicano neighborhoods were underfunded. In some California schools, Mexican-American children could not eat with Anglo children. California and Texas law prohibited teaching in Spanish.

Although Chicanos were not legally prevented from voting, gerrymandering diluted their political power. Despite its large Mexican-American population, Los Angeles had no Hispanic representative on the city council at the end of the 1960s. The justice system often treated Chicanos unfairly.

The combination of poverty and discrimination marked Chicano life. Many Mexican Americans were crowded into *barrios*, rundown neighborhoods. In the countryside, many lived without hot water or toilets. Infant mortality was high, and life expectancy was low. Nationwide, almost half of the Mexican-American population was functionally illiterate.

Encouraged by the civil rights movement, Mexican Americans protested against poverty and injustice for migrant farm workers. In the fertile San Joaquin Valley of California, the Mexican Americans who labored for powerful fruit growers earned as little as 10 cents an hour and lived in miserable conditions. César Chávez, a former migrant worker influenced by Martin Luther King, Jr.'s nonviolent creed, helped them organize the National Farm Worker Association. In 1965 this union went on strike. The growers, accusing Chávez of Communist ties, called on police, strikebreakers, intimidation, and violence. Chávez's nonviolent tactics, which included a 25-day hunger strike in 1968, gradually appealed to liberals and other

Americans. Chávez also initiated a successful nationwide consumer boycott against grapes. Under this pressure, the grape growers began to settle with the union.

While Chávez turned for inspiration to Martin Luther King, Jr., other Chicanos responded to the nationalism of the Black Power movement. In New Mexico, Reies López "Tiger" Tijerina, a former preacher, favored separatism over integration and nationalism over assimilation. He created the Alianza Federal de Mercedes (Federal Alliance of Land Grants) to take back land that the United States had supposedly stolen from Mexicans. In 1967, Tijerina's raid on a courthouse and other militant acts earned him a jail sentence and a reputation as the Robin Hood of New Mexico.

Chicano activism flourished in the late 1960s. In California in 1969, college students began the Movimiento Estudiantil Chicano de Aztlán (Chicano Student Movement of Aztlán). The organization was known by its initials, MEChA, which spelled the word for "match" in the Spanish dialect of Mexican Americans. MEChA was meant to be the match that would kindle social change for Chicanos. In Crystal City, Texas, a boycott of Anglo businesses led to the formation of La Raza Unida, a political party that won control of the local school board in 1970. Thousands of students marked September 16, 1969, Mexican Independence Day, with the First National Chicano Boycott of high schools.

All these protests and organizations reflected a strong sense of Chicano pride and a desire to preserve Chicano heritage. Protesters wanted bilingual education and Mexican-American studies in the schools and equal opportunity and affirmative action in schools and workplaces. Most fundamentally, Mexican-American activism reflected the desire for empowerment, for what some called "Brown Power."

Asian-American Activism

Asian Americans also pressed for rights and recognition as the 1960s ended. Like Chicanos, Asian Americans confronted a history of discrimination in the United States. They, too, had to contend with denigrating stereotypes and hurtful epithets.

The small size of the Asian-American population limited organization and protest, but the Immigration Act of 1965 had made possible increased Asian migration to the United States. From the 1960s through the 1970s, the war in Southeast Asia, political conditions in the Philippines, and economic opportunity spurred waves of Asian immigration. By 1980 America was home to more than 3 million Asian immigrants, including 812,000 Chinese, 781,000 Filipinos, and 716,000 Japanese. Overall, there were 3.7 million Americans of Asian descent. The majority lived in the Pacific states and in cities.

Asian-American activism followed the pattern of other minority movements. By the late 1960s, Asian Americans were demonstrating a new ethnic self-consciousness and pride. Many Asian Americans saw themselves not only as Chinese or Japanese, inheritors of a particular national and ethnic heritage, but as members of a broader, pan-Asian group.

In 1968, the Asian American Political Alliance (AAPA) emerged on the campus of the University of California at Berkeley to unite Chinese, Japanese, and Filipino students. Asian Americans pushed for Asian studies programs on college campuses. By the end of the 1970s, a number of colleges and universities had responded to Asian-American students' demands for courses and programs.

Asian-American activism spread beyond campuses. In 1974 protests forced the hiring of Chinese-American workers to help build the Confucius Plaza complex in New York City's Chinatown. In San Francisco, activists brought suit against the public school system on behalf of 1,800 Chinese pupils. In *Lau* v. *Nichols* in 1974, the

Supreme Court declared that school systems had to provide bilingual instruction for non-English-speaking students.

Japanese groups demanded compensation for the U.S. government's internment of Japanese Americans during World War II. In 1976 Washington did rescind Executive Order 9066, the 1942 presidential directive that allowed internment to occur. But the federal government did not make a more comprehensive settlement until 1988.

Asian Americans, like Chicanos, made only limited gains by 1980. However, Asian Americans had developed a new consciousness and new organizations; they had also forced real change at the local and national levels.

The Struggle for Native-American Rights

African-American activism also inspired Native Americans. Native Americans' struggle also reflected their distinctive relationship with the federal government.

After many years of decline and stagnation, the Indian population had grown rapidly since World War II (see Map 29–2). By 1970, there were nearly 800,000 Native Americans, half of whom lived on reservations. Native Americans were divided into about 175 tribes and other groups, but, like Mexican Americans and African Americans, they were united by poor living conditions and persistent discrimination. Native Americans had the lowest average family income of any ethnic group. Reservations had especially high unemployment rates. Many Indian children attended substandard schools.

Native-American life was shaped by the Indians' unique relationship with the federal government. Many resented the Bureau of Indian Affairs (BIA), which had long patronized and exploited tribes. Like African-American and Mexican-American separatists, some Native Americans began to see themselves as a nation apart. Calling themselves "prisoners of war," these Native Americans struck an aggressive stance, expressed in such slogans as "Custer Had It Coming" and "Red Power."

Beginning in the 1960s, a Native-American movement emerged to protest federal policy, combat stereotypes, unite tribes, and perpetuate their cultures. Native Americans called for an end to employment discrimination and to the sale of Indian lands and resources to corporations. Native Americans also condemned the use of Indian symbols by schools and sports teams and demanded Indian-centered school curricula.

Some Indians favored more radical action. Copying the Black Panthers, a group of Native Americans in Minneapolis, Minnesota, formed an "Indian Patrol," clad in red berets, to defend against the police. The patrol evolved into the American Indian Movement (AIM), which spread to other cities. In 1969, AIM activists occupied the abandoned federal prison on Alcatraz Island in San Francisco Bay and told the authorities to leave. The occupiers unsuccessfully offered the government "$24 in glass beads and cloth" for the prison, which they planned to convert into a Native-American museum and center. In 1972 and 1973, AIM took over BIA headquarters in Washington and the BIA office in Wounded Knee, South Dakota.

The Native-American rights movement made few gains in a society worried about limited resources and an uncertain future. Through the Indian Self-Determination Act of 1975, the federal government did allow Native Americans more independence on the reservations. Still, Native Americans themselves were divided about their relationship to the government. Many tribal leaders wanted to continue selling off their lands through the BIA, but AIM assailed Native Americans

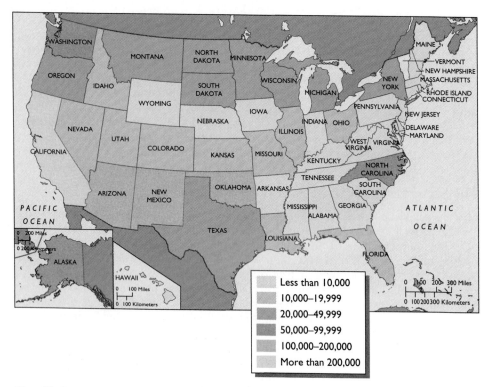

Map 29–2   Native-American Population, 1980
After rapid growth in the years following World War II, the Native-American population remained largest west of the Mississippi River, and above all, across the Southwest. But there were substantial numbers of Native Americans in every region.
Source: Data from Statistical Abstract of the United States, 1973, p. 348; and 1984, pp. 375–376, 463, 760.

who accepted the BIA's authority. Despite such divisions, the movement had forced American society to confront the inequitable treatment of Indians more directly than at any time since the Great Depression.

Homosexuals and Gay Power

Singled out for persecution in the McCarthy era, most homosexual men and women had learned to conceal their sexual identity in public. Mainstream American culture mercilessly ridiculed homosexuals as "faggots," "queers," and "dykes." The medical profession treated homosexuality as an illness. In the late 1960s, that began to change.

A catalyst for change was the struggle of women, racial minorities, and students. Another was a police raid on the Stonewall Inn, a gay bar in New York City's Greenwich Village, in June 1969. Such raids were commonplace, but this time, to the surprise of the police, gay men resisted.

Stonewall became a rallying cry for gay activism. The Gay Liberation Front, the Student Homophile League, and other organizations appeared. Activists picketed companies that discriminated against gays, and homosexuals socialized more openly. On the first anniversary of Stonewall, 10,000 gay men and lesbians paraded down New York's Sixth Avenue. "Two, four, six, eight!" marchers chanted. "Gay is just as good as straight!" Their movement began to have an effect on mainstream culture. In 1974, the American Psychiatric Association decided that homosexuality was not a "mental disorder" and that homosexuals deserved equal rights.

The emerging movements for gay, Native-American, and Chicano rights, along with the ongoing crusades of women and African Americans, made a deep impact on the 1970s. American society could not escape demands for equal rights and opportunities for all people. Women, gays, African Americans, Native Americans, and Chicanos did not win full equality, of course, but these groups made important gains in the 1970s.

BACKLASH: FROM RADICAL ACTION TO CONSERVATIVE REACTION

By the close of the 1960s, American society reverberated with demands to end the war in Vietnam and allow equal rights at home. Surrounded by protests, some hopeful activists believed the United States would be torn apart and remade, but the revolution never came. Radical movements squabbled and fell apart. Many Americans abandoned activism for their own private concerns; others angrily rejected protest movements. Encouraging this backlash, President Nixon won re-election in 1972.

"The Movement" and the "Me-Decade"

Many activists believed that the struggles of women and minorities, along with student protests and the antiwar movement, were creating a single coalition, known simply as "the Movement." At the start of the 1970s, it seemed as if the Movement might take shape, but the different protest groups never merged, and they were often hostile to each other.

In addition, key groups within the Movement fell apart. Plagued by internal divisions, SDS held its last convention in 1969. The violent Weathermen called for "Days of Rage" in the "pig city" of Chicago in October 1969, but only a few hundred protesters showed up. Transient radical groups bombed or burned corporate headquarters and other "establishment" targets but succeeded only in giving the New Left and the Movement a bad name. The FBI secretly penetrated Black Panther chapters and worked to discredit the organization. Panther leaders fled the country, went to jail, or died at the hands of police. Radical feminist groups also declined as women's liberation increasingly focused on liberal demands, such as the ERA.

Some protest movements lost their targets. After the widespread demonstrations of 1970, the antiwar movement declined as the U.S. pulled out of Vietnam. The student movement declined as young people lost some of their grievances. Around the country, colleges and universities eased parietal rules and other regulations. In 1971, the states completed ratification of the Twenty-Sixth Amendment to the Constitution, which lowered the voting age to 18.

The revolution also failed to materialize because many people turned away from activism and political engagement. Some were disillusioned by the failure of the Great Society and the duplicity of the Johnson and Nixon administrations. Others were disappointed by the limited accomplishments of radical movements. Still others found themselves caught up in therapeutic and religious movements, as Americans focused on their inner needs rather than on political change.

The 1970s, announced the writer Tom Wolfe, were the "Me-Decade." Wolfe and other observers believed Americans had become self-absorbed and narcissistic. The cause, explained the historian and social critic Christopher Lasch, was the crisis of capitalism in "an age of diminishing expectations." The fears about the self-absorbed Me-Decade were as exaggerated as the hopes for the revolutionary Movement. People did not stop hoping and working for change, but in a time of economic uncertainty and political disappointment, many Americans felt they could not afford the expansive liberal dreams of the 1960s. They had to look out for themselves.

The Plight of the White Ethnics

The "new American revolution" was a victim of anger as well as apathy. Many lower middle-class and working-class whites rejected the Movement. They felt abandoned by liberal politicians, they believed the Great Society did too little for them and too much for minorities, and they felt threatened by urban renewal projects and court-ordered busing. They resented the students and protesters who had avoided fighting in Vietnam, and many resented the women's movement. Most of all, they feared the consequences of economic decline. In a decade of deindustrialization, they faced the loss of their jobs and their standard of living.

The media painted an unflattering portrait of these Americans. The popular television comedy *All in the Family* derided its main character, the conservative Archie Bunker, who was upset with his feminist daughter, his liberal son-in-law, and all the social change around him. Underneath Archie's outbursts was frustration: "He'll never be more than what he is now," his wife Edith said, "even though he had dreams once."

In reality, the white working and lower-middle classes were not so racist and forlorn. They took renewed pride in the ethnic heritage that set them apart from other Americans. "White ethnics" used their heritage to affirm an alternative set of values—their own counterculture. For them, ethnicity meant a commitment to family, neighborhood, and religion in place of the individualistic American dream and the centralizing federal government. Most important, the white ethnics formed a large potential voting bloc, attractive to politicians.

The Conservative Counterattack

During the 1970s, the white ethnics became an important part of a conservative counterattack against radicalism, liberalism, and the Democratic Party. Assailing the Movement, Richard Nixon and the Republicans put together a coalition of white ethnics in the North and white voters in the Sunbelt. That coalition rewarded Nixon with a landslide re-election in 1972.

The Nixon administration condemned radicalism and demonstrations. "Anarchy," the president fumed, "this is the way civilizations begin to die." The Nixon administration used more than words against protesters. The president ordered IRS investigations to harass liberal and antiwar figures. He used the FBI to infiltrate and disrupt the Black Power movement, the Brown Berets, and the New Left. He made illegal domestic use of the CIA to obstruct the antiwar movement.

To oppose all the forces of disruption, Nixon also called for support from "the great silent majority of my fellow Americans." With his "southern strategy," Nixon reached out to Sunbelt voters by opposing busing, rapid integration, crime, and radicalism. He also tried to create a more conservative, less activist Supreme Court. In 1969, he named the cautious Warren Burger to succeed Earl Warren as chief justice. To fill another vacancy on the court, he nominated first a conservative South Carolina judge, Clement Haynsworth, who had angered civil rights and union leaders, and then Judge G. Harrold Carswell of Florida, a former avowed white supremacist. Both nominations failed, but the president had sent an unmistakable message to the "silent majority" and to white southerners.

The 1972 Election

The conservative counterattack paid off in the 1972 presidential election. The Republican ticket of Nixon and Vice President Spiro Agnew benefited from some unforeseen occurrences in 1972. More than any other politician, George Wallace, the segregationist governor of Alabama, rivaled Nixon's appeal to the "silent majority." But Wallace's campaign for the Democratic nomination came to an end when a would-be assassin's bullet paralyzed him from the waist down. In addition, the Democratic vice presidential nominee, Senator Thomas Eagleton of Missouri, had to withdraw over revelations about his treatment for depression.

Nixon did not really need good luck in 1972. The Democrats chose a strongly liberal senator, George McGovern of South Dakota, as the party nominee for president. McGovern's eventual running mate was another unabashed liberal, Sargent Shriver, a brother-in-law of the Kennedys. The Democratic ticket, which endorsed busing and affirmative action and opposed the Vietnam War, alienated white ethnics, white southerners, and organized labor.

Carrying 49 out of 50 states, Nixon easily won re-election in November 1972. With nearly 61 percent of the popular vote, the president scored almost as big a triumph as Lyndon Johnson in 1964, but Nixon's victory was deceptive. The election had not produced a partisan political realignment. The Democrats still controlled both houses of Congress.

Nevertheless, the 1972 election was a sign that the traditional Democratic coalition was breaking up. More broadly, Nixon's triumph, along with the failure of the Movement, the rise of the white ethnics, and the self-absorption of the Me-Decade, showed that the glory days of liberalism and radicalism were over.

POLITICAL CRISIS: THREE TROUBLED PRESIDENCIES

Nixon's triumph, the 1972 election, soon turned out to be his undoing. The discovery of illegal activities in the president's campaign led to the revelation of other improprieties and, finally, to his resignation. Nixon's successors, Gerald Ford and Jimmy Carter, could not master the problems of a divided nation discovering the limits of its power. The 1970s ended like the 1960s had, with Americans wondering whether their political system still worked.

Watergate: The Fall of Richard Nixon

Nixon's fall began when five men were caught breaking into the offices of the Democratic National Committee in the Watergate complex in Washington, DC, just before 2:00 a.m. on June 17, 1972. The five burglars had ties to Nixon's campaign organization, the Committee to Re-Elect the President (CREEP). They were attempting to repair an electronic eavesdropping device that had been previously planted in the Democrats' headquarters.

At first, Watergate had no impact on the president. He won re-election easily, but gradually, a disturbing story emerged. Two reporters for the *Washington Post*,

Bob Woodward and Carl Bernstein, revealed payments linking the five burglars to CREEP and to Nixon's White House staff. The burglars went on trial with two other former CIA agents, G. Gordon Liddy and E. Howard Hunt, who had directed the break-in for CREEP. Faced with heavy sentences in March 1973, the burglars admitted that "higher-ups" had planned the break-in and orchestrated a cover-up. One of those higher-ups, Nixon's presidential counsel John Dean, revealed his role in the Watergate affair to a grand jury. To emphasize his commitment to justice, Nixon named a special federal prosecutor, Archibald Cox, to investigate Watergate.

A Senate committee, chaired by Sam Ervin of North Carolina, began hearings on Watergate in May 1973. Testifying before the committee, a White House aide revealed that a secret taping system routinely recorded conversations in the president's Oval Office. Claiming "executive privilege," Nixon refused to turn over tapes of his conversations after the break-in. When Archibald Cox continued to press for the tapes, Nixon ordered him fired on Saturday, October 20, 1973. Attorney General Elliott Richardson and a top aide refused to carry out the order and resigned. A third official finally discharged Cox. Nixon's "Saturday Night Massacre" set off a storm of public anger. Nixon had to name a new special prosecutor, Leon Jaworski. The Democratic-controlled House of Representatives began to explore articles of impeachment against the president. "I am not a crook," Nixon insisted.

By 1974, it became clear that the Nixon administration had engaged in a shocking range of improper and illegal behavior. Infuriated by news leaks in 1969, Henry Kissinger had ordered wiretaps on the phones of newspaper reporters and his own staff. Two years later, the White House had created the "Plumbers," a bumbling group of operatives led by Liddy and Hunt, to combat leaks, including the release of the Pentagon Papers. Anxious to win in 1972, Nixon's men had also engaged in dirty tricks to sabotage Democratic presidential aspirants. Nixon's personal lawyer had collected illegal political contributions, "laundered" the money to hide its source, and then transferred it to CREEP.

Nixon himself had ordered the secret and illegal bombing of Cambodia. He had impounded (i.e., refused to spend) money appropriated by Congress for programs he disliked. He had secretly approved the use of federal agencies to hurt "our political enemies."

As a result of the Watergate break-in and other scandals, many of Nixon's associates had to leave office. No fewer than 26, including former Attorney General John Mitchell, went to jail. Vice President Spiro Agnew was found to have accepted bribes as the governor of Maryland in the 1960s. In October 1973 Agnew accepted a plea bargain deal and resigned as vice president. He was replaced by Republican Congressman Gerald R. Ford of Michigan.

Finally, the president himself had to leave office. Under growing pressure to release his tapes, Nixon tried to get away with publishing selected edited transcripts. Revealing a vulgar, rambling, and inarticulate president, the transcripts only fed public disillusionment. In July 1974 the House Judiciary Committee voted to recommend to the full House of Representatives three articles of impeachment—obstruction of justice, abuse of power, and defiance of subpoenas.

Nixon still wanted to fight the charges, but the Supreme Court ruled unanimously that the president had to turn over his tapes to the special prosecutor. The tapes showed that Nixon himself had participated in the cover-up of Watergate as early as June 23, 1972. The president had conspired to obstruct justice and had lied repeatedly to the American people. Almost certain to be impeached, the president agreed to resign rather than face a trial in the Senate. On August 9, 1974, Nixon left office in disgrace. "My fellow Americans, our long national nightmare is over," the new president, Gerald Ford, declared. "Our constitution works."

Gerald Ford and a Skeptical Nation

At first, Gerald Ford was a welcome relief for a nation stunned by the misdeeds of Richard Nixon. Modest and good-humored, the new president seemed unlikely to abuse the authority of the White House. But Ford also seemed stumbling and unimaginative in the face of the nation's declining prosperity and power. Moreover, his administration had no popular mandate. Ford was the first unelected vice president to succeed to the presidency. His vice president, former New York governor Nelson Rockefeller, had not been elected either.

Ford had to govern a nation that had grown skeptical about politicians. Johnson's deceitful conduct of the Vietnam War and Nixon's scandals raised fears that the presidency had grown too powerful. To re-establish its authority, Congress passed the War Powers Act of 1973, which allowed the president to send troops to hostile situations overseas for no more than 60 days without obtaining Congressional consent. In 1975 Congress conducted hearings on the secret operations of the CIA. Amid revelations about the agency's improper roles in domestic spying and the assassination of foreign leaders, the House and Senate created permanent committees to oversee the agency. Ford had to ban the use of assassination in American foreign policy.

Soon after taking office, Ford himself fed public skepticism about the presidency by offering Nixon a full pardon for all crimes committed as president. Ford's popularity dropped immediately and his presidency never fully recovered.

A moderate Republican, Ford did not want the federal government to take an active role in managing the economy. But like Nixon, he could not stop some liberal initiatives. Congress strengthened the regulatory power of the FTC and extended the 1970 Clean Air Act.

Ford had no solutions for deindustrialization and stagflation. Believing inflation was the most serious problem, Ford did little to stop rising unemployment. His anti-inflation program, known as WIN for "Whip Inflation Now," mainly encouraged Americans to control price increases voluntarily. Ford wore a WIN button on his lapel, but inflation continued.

In foreign affairs, the president had to accept limits on American power. Despite the 1973 cease-fire agreement, the fighting continued in Vietnam. Ford promised to protect South Vietnam, but Congress cut the administration's requests for monetary aid to the Saigon government. Sending American armed forces to South Vietnam was out of the question. When North Vietnamese troops invaded early in 1975, panicked civilians fled southward and Congress refused to provide any more aid. As Saigon was overrun, the last Americans evacuated in helicopters. For more than 20 years, the United States had worked to preserve an independent, anti-Communist South Vietnam. Yet, on April 30, 1975, South Vietnam surrendered, and Ford could not prevent the final, ignominious failure of America's Vietnam policy.

The policy of détente with the Soviet Union was supposed to help America cope with its limited power, but détente was clearly in trouble during the Ford administration. The United States and the Soviets failed to agree to a second Strategic Arms Limitation Treaty (SALT II). American critics of détente, including Democratic Senator Henry Jackson of Washington, claimed that the policy sapped

American defenses and overlooked human rights violations by the Soviets. In 1974, Jackson added an amendment to a trade bill linking increased commerce to increased freedom for Soviet Jews to emigrate. The Jackson–Vanik Amendment helped sour the Soviets on détente. In turn, Ford further alienated American conservatives when he traveled to Helsinki, Finland, in 1975 to sign an agreement accepting the post-World War II boundaries of European nations.

Ford's troubles were reflected at the polls. The Democrats made large gains in the Congressional elections in 1974. In 1976, Ford won the Republican nomination for president, replacing Rockefeller with a more conservative vice presidential nominee, Senator Robert Dole of Kansas. The Democrats' presidential choice was former Georgia governor Jimmy Carter, a far cry from the liberal George McGovern. Carter chose a liberal running mate, Senator Walter Mondale of Minnesota, but the Georgian ran as a moderate who could appeal to businessmen and white southerners.

With low turnout at the polls, Carter won 50.1 percent of the vote to Ford's 48 percent. The outcome was less an endorsement of Carter than a rejection of Ford, who became the first sitting president to lose an election since Herbert Hoover.

Jimmy Carter: Why Not the Best?

As he took office in 1977, Jimmy Carter seemed capable and efficient. A graduate of the Naval Academy, he had served as an engineer in the Navy's nuclear submarine program and successfully managed his family's peanut farm before entering politics as a state legislator. Carter's commitment to perfectionism was captured in the title of his autobiography, *Why Not the Best?*

Carter responded more energetically and imaginatively than Ford to the nation's problems, and he had the advantage of working with a Congress controlled by his own party. But Carter came to be seen as a weak, uncertain leader. More important, he faced the same intractable problems that had bedeviled Ford. In the 1970s, it seemed that no president could resolve the nation's economic, political, and diplomatic crises.

Like Ford, Carter had trouble putting to rest the recent past. Carter met angry criticism when he pardoned most American men who had resisted the draft during the Vietnam War, offending many veterans and conservatives.

Carter also had to contend with increasing popular resentment of government. Many Americans believed that government regulation and taxation had gotten out of hand. When the Endangered Species Act of 1973 forced a halt to the construction of a Tennessee dam because it threatened the survival of the snail darter, a small local fish, it seemed as if the federal government worried more about fish than about people's need for electricity and recreation.

The West was the stronghold of antigovernment sentiment in the 1970s. Assailing the bureaucrats in Washington, DC, the Sage Brush Rebellion demanded state control over federal lands in the West. Businessmen in the West also wanted the government to allow more exploitation of oil, forests, and other resources on federal lands. Meanwhile, California became the center of an antitax movement in 1978. Angered by high taxes and government spending, California voters passed Proposition 13, which sharply reduced property taxes.

As always, antigovernment sentiment was inconsistent. Many of the same people who attacked taxes and regulation expected aid and benefits from Washington. When the giant automaker Chrysler faced bankruptcy in 1979, the government had to save the company with a $1.5 billion loan guarantee. When Carter moved to cancel supposedly wasteful federal water projects in the West in 1977, he encountered a storm of protest from the Sage Brush Rebellion.

Carter was most successful when he moved to limit government. By the 1970s, some economists were advocating deregulation of businesses as a way to lower costs, increase competition, and improve services. In 1978, the government removed price controls on the airline industry. In the short run the move lowered fares, but in the long run it drove some airlines out of business.

Deregulation was a sign of a changing balance of political power. Big business, under attack since the 1960s, now lobbied effectively against regulation, organized labor, and taxes. Liberals, meanwhile, had lost influence. As a result, Congress never created the Consumer Protection Agency advocated by consumer activists. Legislation to make labor organization easier also failed. Congress watered down the Humphrey–Hawkins bill, which reasserted the government's responsibility to ensure full employment. When Carter tried to raise taxes on business, Congress instead cut taxes on capital gains and added more loopholes to the tax law.

Carter attempted, with mixed results, to adjust the economy to the realities of living with less. His program of voluntary wage and price controls did not stop soaring inflation. After fuel shortages forced some schools and businesses to close in the harsh winter of 1976–1977, Carter addressed the energy crisis. He proposed the establishment of the Department of Energy, taxes on gas-guzzling automobiles and large consumers of oil, tax incentives to stimulate production of oil and gas, and development of nuclear power. Conservatives thought the program expanded government authority. Liberals and environmentalists objected to its support for nuclear power and oil-company profits. The final plan, passed in 1978, was considerably weakened, but it did encourage conservation.

Nuclear power, a key part of Carter's energy plan, soon lost much of its appeal. In March 1979 a nuclear reactor at Three Mile Island, near Harrisburg, Pennsylvania, nearly suffered a catastrophic meltdown. As 100,000 frightened residents fled their homes, the reactor had to be permanently closed. Around the country, utilities scrapped plans for new nuclear power plants.

Three Mile Island also fed broader anxieties about the environmental damage caused by industrial capitalism. Americans wondered whether their neighborhoods would suffer the fate of Love Canal, located near Niagara Falls, New York. There, hazardous waste buried by a chemical company caused so many health problems that residents had to move away. Despite business concerns about regulation, Washington created a "superfund" of $1.6 billion to clean up hazardous waste sites. The Carter administration also took control of 100 million acres of Alaska to prevent damage from economic development.

At first, Carter had more success with foreign policy than with domestic affairs. Continuing Nixon's de-escalation of the cold war, Carter announced that "we are now free of the inordinate fear of Communism." The president did not abandon Nixon's emphasis on détente with the Soviet Union, but he focused on supporting human rights and building harmony around the world. In 1978, Carter won Senate approval of a treaty yielding ownership of the Panama Canal to Panama at the end of the century. The treaty signaled a new and more respectful approach to Central and Latin America.

In 1978, Carter also mediated the first peace agreement between Israel and an Arab nation. Bringing together Israeli and Egyptian leaders at the Camp David presidential retreat, Carter helped forge a framework for peace that led to Israel's withdrawal from the Sinai Peninsula and the signing of an Israeli–Egyptian treaty. The agreement did not settle the fate of the Israeli-occupied Golan Heights and

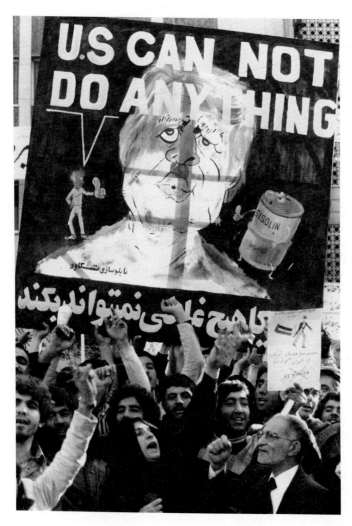

A poster of President Jimmy Carter, carried in a demonstration near the American embassy in Tehran, mocks U.S. weakness during the Iranian hostage crisis in 1979.

Gaza Strip or the future of the Palestinian people, but it did establish a basis for future negotiations in a region torn by conflict for centuries.

Carter's foreign policy suffered from the eventual collapse of détente. The president did reach agreement with the Soviets on the SALT II treaty, but the Senate was reluctant to ratify the agreement. Then, in December 1979, the Soviet Union invaded its southern neighbor, Afghanistan. In response, Carter withdrew the SALT II treaty, stopped grain shipments to the Soviet Union, forbade American athletes to compete in the 1980 Olympics in Moscow, and increased American military spending. These moves had no effect on the Soviet invasion, but détente was obviously over, and the direction of American foreign policy had become unclear.

By 1979, Carter was a deeply unpopular president. He had not stabilized the economy or set out a coherent foreign policy. After pondering the situation at the Camp David retreat for 11 days in July, the president came back to tell a television audience that the nation was suffering a "crisis of spirit." The president offered a number of proposals to deal with the energy crisis, but he spoke most strongly to the state of the nation: "What is lacking is confidence and a sense of community." The speech only seemed to alienate more Americans.

Carter became still more embattled when the Shah of Iran was overthrown by the followers of an Islamic leader, the Ayatollah Ruholla Khomeini, early in 1979. The Shah had long received lavish aid from the United States. Now, the Iranian revolutionaries, eager to restore traditional Islamic values, condemned America for imposing the Shah and modern culture on their nation. In the wake of the revolution, oil prices rose. Once again, Americans had to contend with gas lines and inflation spread through the economy.

The situation worsened when Khomeini condemned the United States for allowing the Shah to receive medical treatment in New York. On November 4, students loyal to Khomeini overran the United States embassy in Tehran, the Iranian capital, and took 60 Americans hostage. Carter froze Iranian assets in the United States, but he could not compel the release of the hostages. As days passed, the United States seemed helpless. In the spring of 1980, the frustrated president ordered a secret military mission to rescue the hostages. On April 24, eight American helicopters headed for a desert rendezvous with six transport planes carrying troops and supplies. However, when two helicopters broke down and another became lost, the mission had to be aborted, and the hostages remained in captivity.

CONCLUSION

The failure of that rescue mission summed up the problems of the United States at the start of the 1980s. The nation was no longer strong enough to protect its own citizens abroad. The presidency seemed weak and ineffectual. The military seemed unable to project its power overseas. The nation had not yet adjusted to the challenges of living with less.

FURTHER READINGS

Stephen E. Ambrose, *Nixon*, 3 vols (1987–1991). A readable narrative of Nixon's many triumphs and ultimate failure.

Terry H. Anderson, *The Movement and the Sixties: Protest in America From Greensboro to Wounded Knee* (1995). A sweeping chronicle of the many protests in both the 1960s and 1970s that created the Movement.

Peter N. Carroll, *It Seemed Like Nothing Happened: The Tragedy and Promise of America in the 1970s* (1983). A fresh, journalistic account that is still the best general social history of the 1970s.

Ronald P. Formisano, *Boston Against Busing: Race, Class, and Ethnicity in the 1960s and 1970s* (1991). Nicely analyzes the white resistance to school desegregation.

Ignacio Garcia, *Chicanismo: The Forging of a Militant Ethos Among Mexican Americans* (2000). Offers a balanced account of the emerging Chicano rights movement.

Seymour Hersh, *The Price of Power: Kissinger in the Nixon White House* (1983). A harsh, fascinating study of the architect of détente.

CHRONOLOGY

1968	My Lai Massacre in South Vietnam Founding of American Indian Movement (AIM)
1969	Secret bombing of Cambodia ordered by President Richard Nixon Stonewall Riot in New York's Greenwich Village *Apollo 11* moon landing Announcement of Nixon Doctrine Founding of Chicano student organization MEChA "Days of Rage" protests by Weathermen in Chicago
1970	First Earth Day Creation of Environmental Protection Agency (EPA) United States–South Vietnam invasion of Cambodia Killing of students at Kent State University and Jackson State College Women's Strike for Equality
1971	Conviction of Lieutenant William Calley, Jr., for role in My Lai Massacre Publication of Pentagon Papers by *New York Times* Nixon takes U.S. off gold standard Ratification of Twenty-Sixth Amendment, lowering voting age to 18 Supreme Court busing decision, *Swann* v. *Charlotte-Mecklenburg Board of Education*
1972	President Nixon's trips to the People's Republic of China and the Soviet Union Strategic Arms Limitation Treaty (SALT I) and Anti-Ballistic Missile (ABM) Treaty signed

Burton I. Kaufman, *The Presidency of James Earl Carter, Jr.* (1993). A fair-minded treatment of a troubled presidency.

Stanley I. Kutler, *The Wars of Watergate: The Last Crisis of Richard Nixon* (1990). A balanced, clear account of the scandal that brought down Richard Nixon.

Eric Marcus, *Making History: The Struggle for Gay and Lesbian Equal Rights, 1945–1980* (1992). Moving, candid oral histories that personalize the gay and lesbian liberation movement.

Winifred D. Wandersee, *On the Move: American Women in the 1970s* (1988). A detailed study of the different social and political phases of women's liberation in the 1970s, including the fight for the Equal Rights Amendment.

Congressional passage of Equal Rights Amendment
Operation Linebacker bombing raids on North Vietnam
Watergate burglary
Re-election of President Nixon

1973   Peace agreement to end Vietnam War signed
Beginning of Arab oil embargo
Supreme Court ruling to legalize abortion, *Roe* v. *Wade*
Resignation of Vice President Spiro Agnew

1974   Beginning of struggle over busing in Boston
Resignation of President Nixon
Succession to presidency by Gerald Ford

1975   Surrender of South Vietnam to North Vietnam
Helsinki Agreement

1976   Announcement of the "Me-Decade" by Tom Wolfe
Jimmy Carter elected president

1977   President Carter proposes energy plan

1978   Camp David peace accords
Supreme Court affirmative action decision, *Regents of the University of California* v. *Allan Bakke*

1979   Accident at Three Mile Island nuclear power plant
Iranian revolution

1980   Failed mission to rescue U.S. hostages in Iran

Please refer to the document CD-ROM for primary sources related to this
chapter.

CHAPTER
30
The Triumph of a New Conservatism
1980–1988

The Trumps' American Dream • **A New Conservative Majority**
The Reagan Revolution at Home • **The Reagan Revolution**
Abroad • **The Battle Over Conservative Social Values**
The Limits of the New Conservatism • **Conclusion**

THE TRUMPS' AMERICAN DREAM

In the 1980s Donald and Ivana Trump were one of the most famous couples in the United States. Rich, glamorous, and powerful, they appeared to prove that the American dream could still come true.

Donald, the son of a prosperous real estate developer, seemed unaffected by recent history. Going into business in New York in the 1970s, Trump refused to be pessimistic about the city's depressed real estate market and uncertain finances. While the nation learned to live with less, Trump aggressively acquired land and buildings at low prices.

Trump's strategy paid off in the 1980s. By 1986, Trump had accumulated one of the largest fortunes in America. He owned apartment houses and hotels. He built the posh Trump Tower on Fifth Avenue, with condominiums priced as high as $10 million. He had a glitzy gambling casino, Trump's Castle, in Atlantic City, New Jersey. He owned an airline, the Trump Shuttle. He owned a football team, the New Jersey Generals. He even had his own bestselling book, naturally titled *Trump*.

Trump's wife, Ivana, lived both an old dream for immigrants and a new dream for women. Born in Austria and raised in Czechoslovakia, she found riches and happiness in the United States. A modestly successful skier and model, Ivana married the man she called "The Donald" in New York in 1977 and became "a stunning prototype of the truly fashionable world-class billionairess."

Ivana's life with "The Donald" seemed to prove that a modern American woman could have it all. After bearing three children she remained, an admiring biographer exclaimed, a "celebration of the body perfect." Ivana gracefully combined family and career, helping to supervise interior decoration for Donald's projects and managing Trump's casino.

To some observers, the Trumps' self-promoting lifestyle was flashy, excessive, and insubstantial. Donald's brash business methods seemed to trample ordinary people. Over the years, tenants accused him of cruel treatment. The U.S. Justice Department charged the Trump Organization with racial discrimination.

Donald and Ivana survived the criticism, but the couple did not avoid personal and financial troubles. Donald removed Ivana as manager of his casino in May 1988 because of lagging profits. Then she discovered his apparent affair with a model. After their much-publicized breakup, she confessed to "a tremendous sense of failure." She wondered, too, about the free-wheeling capitalism that had put the Trumps on top. Meanwhile, that system nearly destroyed Donald's empire. By 1990, he was deep in debt trying to fund his glitziest casino, the Trump Taj Mahal. To stave off bankruptcy, he had to sell the Trump Shuttle and other properties.

The Trumps' story reflected a central theme of the 1980s. Still coming to terms with economic and political decline, the United States turned toward an older, business-centered, conservative vision of the political economy. Rejecting the pessimism of the 1970s, many Americans wanted to believe that success like the Trumps' was still possible. Downplaying the idealism of the 1960s, Americans exalted the material satisfactions of consumerism and favored a more conservative state that promised to restore prosperity and left businesspeople like Donald Trump free to make a fortune.

The trend toward conservatism had wide-ranging consequences. A broad-based coalition elected a conservative Republican, Ronald Reagan, to the presidency. Eager to restore old social, economic, and political values, Reagan set out to recast the American political economy by cutting taxes, reducing government regulation, and diminishing union power to restore economic growth. Abroad, he carried out a foreign policy dedicated to confronting Communism. With Reagan's re-election in 1984, the new conservatism seemed triumphant.

Before the 1980s ended, however, many Americans wondered whether the conservative triumph, like the Trumps' fortune, was real after all. The conservatives' social agenda had met strong opposition. The nation's renewed prosperity seemed fragile and uneven. Like Donald's empire, the wealth of the 1980s depended on borrowed money and shaky deals. And, like Donald's tenants, some Americans found themselves ignored or exploited. By the close of the decade, ordinary people were learning Ivana's lesson: They could not have it all.

A NEW CONSERVATIVE MAJORITY

By 1980, a new conservatism had emerged in the United States. This New Right drew strength from ongoing changes in the economy and Americans' economic values. The rapid growth of a conservative coalition became clear in the 1980 presidential election, when voters sent Ronald Reagan to the White House.

The End of Economic Decline?

The decline of the American economy appeared to halt in the 1980s. The continuing growth of the Sunbelt fueled optimism. Rustbelt industrial cities such as Pittsburgh, Detroit, and Gary, Indiana, lost population, while some counties in Georgia, Florida, and Texas more than doubled in population. The movement of population had political consequences, too. Reapportionment in 1980 gave more Congressional seats and electoral votes to the relatively conservative states of the Sunbelt.

Across the country, technological innovations encouraged hopes for economic revival. Microwave ovens, pocket calculators, compact disc players, cordless telephones, and fax machines were just a few features of a consumer electronics revolution. Videocassette recorders, remote controls, satellites, and cable television transformed Americans' television viewing habits.

The most important new product was the microcomputer. In 1977 a new company, Apple, offered its first microcomputer for sale. Four years later, the computing giant IBM introduced its first personal computer, or PC. By the end of the 1980s, Americans were buying 7 million PCs a year.

These explosive sales produced optimistic visions of the U.S. economy. Computers seemed to promise a way out of national economic decline. Whereas Asian manufacturers built most consumer electronics products, American companies dominated the computer industry. The microcomputer bolstered older companies such as IBM, created new companies such as Apple and Compaq, and fed the growth of the Sunbelt. Compaq's headquarters were in Houston. Apple was one of many computer firms clustered in Silicon Valley just outside San Francisco. The microcomputer also seemed to be reviving parts of the Rustbelt. In Massachusetts, a string of computer companies sprang up around Boston along Route 128 to replace the textile mills and shoe factories that had long since left the state.

The growth of the computer industry rested on the seemingly limitless possibilities of the microcomputer, which inspired utopian dreams of a high-technology society built on the production of knowledge rather than things. Promoting literacy and education, the computer would then lift up the poor and disadvantaged. Unlike the old industrial economy, the computerized economy could cut down on pollution and the consumption of raw materials. By enabling people to work at home, the microcomputer could eliminate commuting and relieve urban congestion.

While the 1980s pointed to a utopian future, the decade also recalled the cutthroat capitalism of the turn of the twentieth century. A wave of corporate takeovers and mergers swept across the economy. Aggressive investment bankers and entrepreneurs such as Michael Milken and Ivan Boesky used a variety of techniques, such as junk bonds, high-risk, high-paying securities, to finance takeovers. Executives agreed to sell their own companies in return for golden parachutes, huge payments these executives received when they lost their jobs. Enormous deals merged some of the largest American corporations. In 1985 General Electric bought RCA for $6 billion. In 1986 alone there were more than 4,000 mergers worth a total of $190 billion. The biggest deal of all came in 1988 when

RJR Nabisco was sold for $25 billion and the company's executives received a $100-million golden parachute.

The takeovers sparked criticism from Americans worried about expensive deals and the concentration of so much economic power. But other observers saw the takeovers as a sign of economic vitality. They argued that the mergers created larger, more efficient companies that could compete more successfully. These observers praised Milken, Boesky, and other wealthy takeover artists as models of entrepreneurial energy and creativity.

The Rehabilitation of Business

The takeover wave, along with the growth of the Sunbelt and the computer industry, encouraged hopes for an economic revival. In turn, those hopes helped rehabilitate business and its values, which had been assailed in the 1960s and 1970s. The media enthusiastically reported the achievements and opinions of Donald Trump, Michael Milken, Ivan Boesky, Bill Gates, and Steve Jobs. Business was more respectable than at any time since the 1950s.

So was materialism. The Trumps and other business figures helped legitimize the pursuit and enjoyment of wealth. There was renewed interest in luxurious living. "Thank goodness it's back," gushed *The New York Times*, "that lovely whipped cream of a word—luxury."

The baby-boom generation reflected the new appeal of business values. Abandoning social action, former 1960s radicals such as the Yippie leader Jerry Rubin took up business careers. By 1983 the media were talking about the emergence of yuppies, young urban professionals. Uninterested in reform, these self-centered baby boomers were supposedly eager to make lots of money and then spend it on BMW cars, Perrier water, and other consumer playthings. The yuppies made up perhaps only five percent of the baby-boom generation. Nevertheless, the yuppie stereotype underscored the resurgence of business values, as many Americans aspired to a more conservative, money-centered way of life.

The Rise of the Religious Right

At the same time American culture celebrated materialism, many Americans still turned to religion to find meaning in their lives. But the ongoing transformation of religious life also reinforced conservative values. Conservative denominations, especially evangelical Christian churches, grew rapidly, and evangelical leaders took conservative stands on social and economic issues. By 1980 they had become a powerful political movement, the religious right.

The rise of the religious right reflected a long-term trend. Such mainline Protestant denominations as the United Methodist Church, the Episcopal Church and the Presbyterian Church, USA, had been dropping sharply in membership since at least 1940. Meanwhile, evangelical churches boomed (see Map 30–1).

The changing balance between mainline and evangelical churches had social and political consequences. The mainline denominations often took moderate or liberal positions on such social issues as civil rights and abortion, but the evangelical churches were much more likely to support conservative positions. Troubled by social change and emboldened by their own growth, evangelicals wanted to spread a conservative message across American culture and politics.

The emergence of so-called "televangelists" was the most obvious result of these efforts. From 1978 to 1989 the number of Christian television ministries grew from

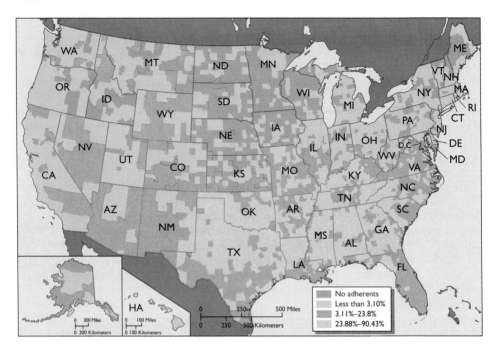

Map 30–1   The Growth of Evangelical Christianity
The Southern Baptist Convention's share of the population, by county, reveals its gradual spread beyond
its traditional base in the South by 1990.

Source: Peter L. Halvorson & William M. Newman, Atlas of Religious Change in America, 1952–1990 (Cincinnati, Ohio; Glenmary
Research Center, 1994), p. 120.

25 to 336. Pat Robertson, a born-again Baptist from Virginia, hosted *The 700 Club* and
ran the Christian Broadcast Network. Jerry Falwell, a fundamentalist who believed in
the literal interpretation of the Bible, hosted *The Old Time Gospel Hour* and founded
Liberty Baptist College in Virginia. He also organized the Moral Majority, a political
pressure group. A televangelist couple, Jim and Tammy Faye Bakker, started Heritage
Park, USA, complete with a hotel and water park, in South Carolina.

Deeply conservative, the televangelists condemned many of the social changes
of the 1960s and 1970s, such as women's liberation, abortion, gay rights, and liberal Great Society programs. They wanted prayer in public schools. Earning millions
of dollars, they praised low taxes, limited government, and financial success. As
materialistic as the Trumps, Jim and Tammy Faye Bakker proudly showed off their
six homes and their air-conditioned doghouse. By 1980, the televangelists were
moving into politics. Through their broadcasts, organizations, and fundraising,
they were creating a conservative political force, a religious right.

The Conservative Counterestablishment

Conservatives and Republicans had long despised the liberal establishment, the
northeastern, Ivy League educated men who supposedly ran Wall Street and Washington. The establishment was never the powerful, tightly knit organization that its
critics imagined, but conservatives endeavored to stop the establishment by creating
their own counterestablishment.

Money helped build the conservative counterestablishment. Wealthy donors, such as brewer Joseph Coors, contributed to conservative organizations and campaigns. Televangelists and such conservative fundraisers as Richard Viguerie collected small contributions from millions of less wealthy Americans.

All this money helped to create and sustain a range of conservative institutions and activities. The John M. Olin Foundation and other philanthropic organizations supported conservative causes and initiatives. The National Conservative Political Action Committee (NCPAC) and other pressure groups lobbied for conservative legislation and supported conservative political candidates. Think tanks such as the Heritage Foundation and the American Enterprise Institute publicized conservative ideas and policies. Conservative publications such as *The Public Interest, Human Events, The National Review*, and *The Wall Street Journal* offered a conservative alternative to establishment news outlets.

Like conservative businessmen and Republicans a century earlier, the New Right praised unrestricted free enterprise and minimal regulation of economic life and blended hostility to activist liberal government with a hatred of Communism. Evangelical Christians wanted to use government power to enforce their views on such social issues as abortion, school prayer, and gay rights, but libertarians believed government should leave people as free as possible. Despite these differences, the conservative counterestablishment offered a powerful cluster of ideas, influenced by economic, social, religious, and political change since the 1960s.

The 1980 Presidential Election

The power of the new conservatism became evident in the presidential election of 1980. The Republican Party nominated a charismatic conservative, Ronald Reagan. Confronting a divided Democratic Party and an unpopular president, Reagan won a stunning victory.

Reagan's life story reflected the rise of the Sunbelt and the new conservatism. Born into a lower middle-class family in Illinois in 1911, Reagan left the Midwest during the Great Depression for California. From the 1930s through the early 1960s, he starred in movies and television shows in Hollywood. A staunch Democrat, he supported Franklin Roosevelt and Harry Truman. Reagan then moved to the right: Angry over high income taxes, he attacked big government while serving as a corporate spokesman for General Electric. In the 1960s, Reagan became a Republican, and his conservative views won him election as governor of California in 1966 and 1970.

The conservative tide carried Reagan along in 1980. Although he chose a moderate running mate, George Bush of Texas, his campaign offered a conservative vision of less government, lower taxes, and renewed military power.

Meanwhile, the Democratic nominee, incumbent President Jimmy Carter, could not overcome the double burdens of a weak economy and the ongoing hostage crisis in Iran. His moderate and sometimes conservative policies alienated liberal Democrats. His poor economic record alienated the party's white ethnics. Moderate Republican Congressman John Anderson of Illinois, who ran as an independent, drew votes away from Carter.

Reagan pulled off the rare feat of defeating an incumbent president (see Map 30–2). The Democrats held on to the House of Representatives, but the Republicans took control of the Senate for the first time since 1952. The nation had turned sharply to the right. Reagan's victory marked the emergence of a conservative majority.

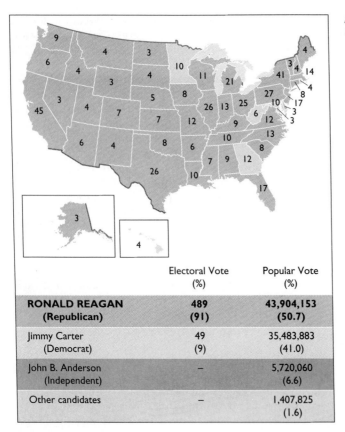

Map 30–2 The
Presidential Election,
1980

	Electoral Vote (%)	Popular Vote (%)
RONALD REAGAN (Republican)	**489** **(91)**	**43,904,153** **(50.7)**
Jimmy Carter (Democrat)	49 (9)	35,483,883 (41.0)
John B. Anderson (Independent)	–	5,720,060 (6.6)
Other candidates	–	1,407,825 (1.6)

THE REAGAN REVOLUTION AT HOME

Ronald Reagan probably shaped American life more decisively than any president since Franklin Roosevelt. Reagan's style—folksy and optimistic—made him popular, but the Reagan years were more than a triumph of style. With some justice, his supporters believed that the president spurred a sweeping conservative transformation of the American political economy.

The Reagan Style

The Reagan Revolution was partly a matter of style. Despite the frustrations of the 1960s and 1970s, Reagan exuded optimism. Rather than teach Americans how to live with less, he embraced luxury. Nevertheless, he retained a common touch. After the troubled presidencies of the 1970s, Reagan made the job seem manageable again.

Reagan's presidency signaled a confident, even opulent, new era. On Inauguration Day, as if to mark the belated end of the frustrating 1970s, the Iranian government finally released its American hostages. In his inaugural address, Reagan firmly rejected pessimism about the nation's future. "We are not," the new president declared, "doomed to an inevitable decline." That night, he and his wife Nancy danced at a series of lavish balls. The Reagan inaugural cost five times more than Jimmy Carter's had four years earlier.

Even while the Reagans continued their lavish lifestyle in the White House, the president remained popular. He knew how to speak simply and effectively to the American people. Although the president did not always master the details of issues, he became known as the "Great Communicator."

Reagan also appeared to enjoy and master his job. Although all his recent predecessors had faded under the pressures of the job, Reagan appeared to delight in the presidency; even though he took office as America's oldest president at the age of 69, he projected an image of vigor and energy.

The president even managed to survive an assassination attempt. On March 30, 1981, John W. Hinckley, a troubled young loner, shot and wounded Reagan, his press secretary, and a policeman. Reagan's chest wound was more serious than his spokesmen admitted, but the president met the situation with good humor. "Honey," he told his wife, "I forgot to duck." The president's popularity soared in opinion polls.

Shrinking Government

Reagan's administration offered a clear conservative alternative to the liberal policies of the New Deal and the Great Society. Above all, Reagan denied that a large, activist federal government could deal with the challenges of American life in the 1980s. Accordingly, he wanted to shrink the government's size and reduce its power.

Reagan's efforts to shrink the federal government met with mixed success. In his 1982 State of the Union address, the president endorsed the New Federalism, a plan to transfer federal programs and tax revenues to the states. Reagan insisted the New Federalism would promote efficiency and economic growth, but governors worried that their states would be saddled with expensive responsibilities. In the end, the federal government passed on only a few programs.

Reagan also created a commission, headed by business executive J. Peter Grace, to explore ways the federal government could save money. The Grace Commission claimed that Washington could save more than $400 billion over three years, partly by making it more difficult for Americans to qualify for welfare, pension, and other benefits. Congress was unwilling to make such reforms. The commission also called for the line-item veto, which would allow a president to reject particular spending programs in Congress's annual budget without having to veto the entire budget bill. Congress was not ready to give Reagan so much new power.

The president had more success when he attacked social welfare programs. Like many other conservatives, Reagan condemned antipoverty programs as a waste of federal resources that sapped the work ethic and the morals of the poor. Reagan and his followers believed that the political economy worked best when workers had to succeed or fail on their own. He wanted reductions in food stamps, school meal programs, and aid to cities. In response, Congress cut appropriations for urban public housing and eliminated job training for the unemployed.

Reagan found it nearly impossible to touch Medicare and Social Security, two expensive and popular programs that benefited most Americans. The Social Security system proved especially difficult to cut. By the 1980s there was growing concern that workers' Social Security payments would eventually not be enough to cover the cost of benefits to retirees. After a long struggle, Congress produced the Social Security Reform Act of 1983, which raised the minimum age for full benefits from 65 to 67 and made retirees pay taxes on some benefits. The measure did little to reduce the total cost of the program, and by 1984 Reagan was promising not to cut Social Security.

Despite his eagerness to reduce the size of government, Reagan did not tear down the federal system of welfare and other benefits. Expenditures for these programs continued to rise, but the Reagan administration managed to slow the growth of welfare. Benefits did not expand dramatically; there were no costly new programs. As expenditures for national defense grew, welfare outlays fell from 28 percent of the federal budget in 1980 to 22 percent by 1987.

Reaganomics

For Reagan and his followers, shrinking the government meant decreasing Washington's role in the economy. They argued that the nation prospered most when government left Americans free to manage their own businesses and keep their own earnings. The Reagan administration worked to lower taxes, deregulate business, and cut federal support for unions. Reaganomics changed the American political economy by reducing the role of the federal government.

Reagan's economic policy drew on a new theory known as supply-side economics. Beginning in the 1970s, economist Arthur Laffer had offered an alternative to the liberal, Keynesian economics that had guided federal policy since the New Deal. While Keynesians believed that increased consumer demand would spur economic growth, Laffer contended that an increased supply of goods and services was the key to growth. He rejected the Keynesian prescription for raising government spending to put more money in the hands of consumers. To promote prosperity, he believed government should cut taxes. By leaving more money in the hands of businesses, government would allow them to invest in more production of goods and services. The increase in supply would stimulate prosperity and increase tax revenues. The tax cut, Laffer concluded, would not even produce a federal budget deficit.

Supply-side economics was controversial. To liberal critics it seemed to be an excuse to let the rich keep more of their money. Even some Republicans doubted that a tax cut would produce more tax revenues. Nevertheless, Reagan asked a joint session of Congress in 1981 to cut taxes dramatically. Impressed by Reagan's popularity and the electorate's increasing conservatism, the Democratic-controlled House joined the Republican-dominated Senate to pass the Economic Recovery Act of 1981 (also known as the Kemp–Roth Bill). This measure cut federal income taxes five percent the first year and then 10 percent in each of the next two years. It especially benefited the wealthy by making the tax structure less progressive and by reducing the tax rate on the highest individual incomes and on large gifts and estates.

Like other conservatives, Reagan believed that federal rules and requirements hamstrung American business and prevented economic growth. Accordingly, his administration stepped up the campaign for deregulation begun by Jimmy Carter. The government cut the budgets of regulatory agencies and made sure that government officials did not strictly enforce regulatory rules and laws. Further, the administration deregulated the telephone industry. In 1982 the government broke up the giant American Telephone and Telegraph Company, allowing new firms such as Sprint and MCI to compete for AT&T's long-distance business.

Reagan moved particularly to lift environmental restrictions on American businesses. His administration made it easier for timber and mining companies to exploit wilderness areas and allowed oil companies to drill off the Pacific coast. The administration also opposed environmentalists' demands for laws to protect against acid rain—air pollution, caused by industrial emissions, that harmed lakes, forests, and crops in the Northeast and Canada.

Reaganomics also meant weakening organized labor. Like most conservatives, Reagan believed that unions obstructed business and limited the freedom of individual workers. Unions were already weakening when Reagan took office. Thanks mainly to deindustrialization, the number of unionized workers dropped from 21 million in 1970 to 17 million in 1986.

Reagan took steps to weaken the labor movement even further. He made probusiness appointments to the National Labor Relations Board. Most important, he took a strong antiunion stance during a strike by the Professional Air Traffic Controllers Organization (PATCO) in 1981. Despite a law forbidding strikes by federal workers, PATCO walked out to protest unsafe conditions in the air traffic control system. Reagan fired the striking controllers, refused to hire them back, and replaced them with nonunion workers.

Reaganomics did not quite have the effect that its supporters anticipated. In the short run, Reagan's measures could not prevent a sharp recession, which began in the fall of 1981. As the Federal Reserve Bank fought inflation by raising interest rates, the economy slowed, and unemployment increased. Reaganomics also increased the federal budget deficit. The supply-side theory that tax cuts would boost tax revenues and balance the budget proved incorrect.

By the spring of 1984, the recession had ended. Thanks largely to the Federal Reserve's monetary policy, the high inflation of the 1970s was over. The economy began a long period of growth and higher employment, and Reagan's supporters gave the president credit. His critics charged that the deficit rather than Reaganomics had produced the boom and that the deficit would ultimately hurt the economy. In the mid-1980s, however, Reaganomics appeared to be a success.

The 1984 Presidential Election

The unclear results of Reaganomics helped to shape national politics. In the depths of the recession, the Republicans lost 26 House seats in the midterm Congressional elections of 1982. With the return of prosperity, and his popularity on the rise, the president was easily renominated in 1984. Reagan ran against a liberal Democratic nominee, former Vice President Walter Mondale of Minnesota. The Democrat, confronting a popular incumbent, made bold moves. Mondale chose the first female vice-presidential nominee of a major party, Representative Geraldine Ferraro of New York. To prove his honesty and openness, Mondale announced that he would raise taxes as president.

Election day revealed both the strength and the weakness of the Reagan Revolution. The contest was a personal triumph for the president. With his conservative message, Reagan polled 58.8 percent of the popular vote and lost only the District of Columbia and Mondale's home state of Minnesota. Reagan's big vote did not translate into a sweeping victory for his party. Holding on to the Senate, the Republicans failed to win a majority in the House of Representatives.

THE REAGAN REVOLUTION ABROAD

Reagan's foreign policy, like his domestic policy, rested on old values. The president rejected the main diplomatic approaches of the 1970s—Richard Nixon's détente with the Soviet Union and Jimmy Carter's support for international human rights. Instead, the Reagan Revolution revived the strident anti-Communism of the 1940s and 1950s. Communism, however, had little to do with such difficult international issues as conflict in the Middle East, terrorism, and economic relations with Japan and developing nations.

Restoring American Power

After losing the Vietnam War, the United States had cut back its armed forces and become reluctant to risk military confrontations abroad. Reagan set out to restore American power in the 1980s.

Like most conservatives, the president did not believe that cutting government spending should include cutting the armed forces. Under Reagan, the nation's defense spending more than doubled, from $134 billion in 1980 to more than $300 billion by 1989. Construction of the B-1 strategic jet bomber, stopped by Jimmy Carter, resumed. Reagan began development of the B-2 Stealth bomber, an innovative plane that could evade detection by enemy radar. He won Congressional approval for the MX Peacekeeper, a nuclear missile with multiple warheads. He also persuaded Congress to authorize work on the neutron bomb, a nuclear weapon that could spread lethal radiation over a half-mile radius.

As he pursued his military buildup, Reagan faced a growing mass movement against nuclear weapons. In both Europe and the United States, millions of people called for a halt to the introduction of new nuclear arms. In June 1982, a crowd of 700,000 gathered in New York to demand a nuclear freeze. The National Conference of Catholic Bishops supported the freeze and declared nuclear war immoral. Reagan rejected the freeze movement as naïve and Communist-infiltrated. The best way to ensure peace, he believed, was to keep developing weapons.

The military buildup was a matter of attitudes as well as weapons and budgets. In the wake of the Vietnam War, many Americans seemed reluctant to endorse U.S. intervention abroad. This Vietnam syndrome threatened the Reagan administration's foreign policy. The president could not afford to let other countries think the United States would not back up its words with action. Accordingly, Reagan used his speeches to stir up patriotic emotion.

By the mid-1980s, Reagan had succeeded in restoring much of America's military power. It remained to be seen, however, whether Americans were willing to use that power abroad.

Confronting the "Evil Empire"

The main purpose of the military buildup was to contain the Soviet Union. Suspicion of the Soviets and their Communist ideology was the heart of Reagan's diplomacy. In the early 1980s, Reagan called the USSR the "evil empire" and insisted that the Soviet Union and its Communist allies were doomed by failing economies and unpopular regimes.

Reagan avoided cooperation with the Soviet Union and held no summit meetings during his first term. The Reagan administration openly supported the *mujahedeen*, the Afghan rebels who were resisting the Soviets.

More important, the president avoided arms-control agreements with the Soviets during his first term. Reagan refused to submit the second Strategic Arms Limitation Treaty, signed by Jimmy Carter, to the Senate for ratification. In response to the United States's deployment of new intermediate-range nuclear missiles in Western Europe, the Soviets walked out of arms-control talks in 1983.

That year, Reagan put even more pressure on the USSR when he announced plans for the Strategic Defense Initiative (SDI), a space-based missile-defense sys-

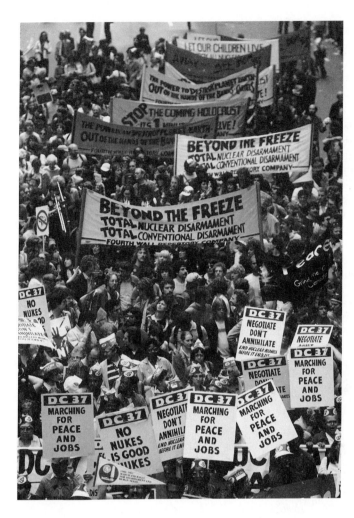

A nuclear freeze rally in New York City in 1982. For a time, the movement to halt the introduction of new nuclear weapons challenged President Reagan's plans for an arms buildup.

tem that would use lasers and other advanced technology to shoot down nuclear missiles launched at the United States. Although funded by Congress, SDI was a long way from reality in 1983. Critics, convinced SDI was science fiction, called the plan Star Wars.

The U.S. initiative pressed the Soviets to expend scarce resources to develop their own SDI. It also seemingly made the USSR more vulnerable to nuclear attack. Since the 1950s, the Americans and the Soviets had relied on the concept of *mutual assured destruction* as a deterrent to nuclear war, but SDI might enable the United States to survive a nuclear attack. The Soviets faced the possibility that the United States, no longer facing assured destruction, might start a nuclear war.

While the United States challenged the Soviets aggressively, the Reagan administration did not confront the other major Communist power, the People's Republic of China. The Chinese, less active in promoting third-world Communism, seemed less of a threat than the Soviets. Instead, Reagan traded visits with China's premier in 1984 and encouraged cultural exchanges, economic cooperation, and a nuclear weapons agreement.

The Reagan Doctrine in the Third World

The Reagan administration also changed American foreign policy toward the third world. Jimmy Carter had wanted the United States to support human rights around the globe, but his successor preferred to support America's national security interests, including anti-Communism.

Reagan, along with other conservatives, had been impatient with the Carter administration's attempts to promote human rights abroad. The United States, conservatives believed, needed to back anti-Communist, pro-American governments, whether or not they respected human rights. Jeane J. Kirkpatrick, who became Reagan's ambassador to the United Nations, called for a distinction between totalitarian regimes hostile to the U.S. and authoritarian governments friendly to American interests. Kirkpatrick's view became known as the Reagan Doctrine.

During the president's first term, his administration applied the Reagan Doctrine aggressively in Central America and the Caribbean (see Map 30–3). Determined to keep Communism out of the Western Hemisphere, the United States opposed the Marxist Sandinista government of Nicaragua and supported the repressive anti-Communist government of neighboring El Salvador.

The Sandinistas had come to power in the late 1970s by overthrowing the dictatorship of Anastasio Somoza with the encouragement of the Carter administration. The Reagan administration believed the Sandinistas were too friendly to the Soviet Union and to leftist rebels in El Salvador. Reagan halted aid to Nicaragua in

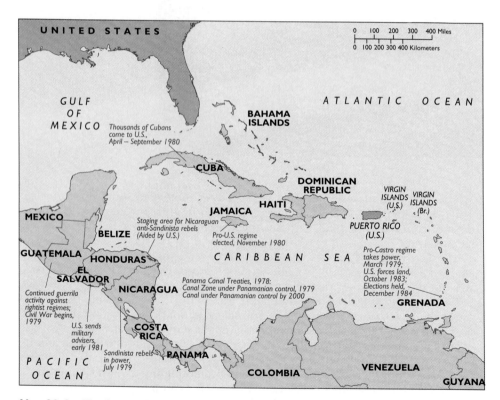

Map 30–3   The Reagan Doctrine in Central America and the Caribbean
Events that shaped Reagan's anti-Communist initiative in the Western Hemisphere.

April 1981 and directed the CIA to train, arm, and supply the Contra rebels who opposed the Sandinistas. Many of the Contras had ties to the oppressive Somoza government, but Reagan praised them as "freedom fighters."

Meanwhile, the president strongly backed the brutal right-wing government of El Salvador. Although the regime engaged in kidnapping and terror, Reagan did not want it to fall to pro-Sandinista and pro-Cuban rebels. El Salvador, the president explained, was "a textbook case of indirect armed aggression by Communist powers."

Despite such anti-Communist rhetoric, the Reagan administration could not persuade Congress to support its Central American policy. Congressional Democrats, like many Americans, did not want to risk another Vietnam War in Central America. They were skeptical about the Communist threat to El Salvador and Nicaragua and troubled by the antidemocratic character of the Salvadoran government and the Contra rebels. In 1983 Congress approved Reagan's Caribbean Basin Initiative, an economic development package, but Reagan did not get the military aid he wanted for the Salvadoran government. Instead, in September 1982 Congress passed the Boland Amendment, which restricted aid to the Contras and banned efforts to topple the Sandinista regime.

The president applied the Reagan Doctrine more successfully in the Caribbean. On October 25, 1983, U.S. troops invaded the small West Indian island of Grenada, supposedly to protect about 1,000 Americans, mostly medical students, from a Marxist regime. The invading force quickly secured the island and replaced the government with a pro-American regime.

The president also implemented the Reagan Doctrine in Africa. The Carter administration had condemned the long-standing policy of *apartheid*—racial separation—pursued by the white government of South Africa. Reagan would not take a similarly strong stance. Rather than impose economic sanctions on the South African regime, the president endorsed a mild policy of diplomatic discussions known as "constructive engagement."

The Middle East and Terrorism

The Reagan Doctrine was not much help in dealing with the Middle East and the growing problem of terrorism. As before, the United States wanted to ensure its supply of oil and to support its longtime ally, Israel. There was no new Arab oil embargo during the Reagan years, but the administration could not bring peace to the Middle East or end the threat of terrorism.

Reagan found it difficult to build on the Camp David Accords between Israel and Egypt, which were supposed to lead to self-government for the Palestinian Arabs who lived in the Israeli-occupied West Bank and Gaza Strip. However, Israel and the Palestine Liberation Organization (PLO) remained at odds. The PLO continued to threaten Israel from bases in neighboring Lebanon. In the spring of 1982, the Israelis invaded Lebanon, which was already convulsed by a civil war between Muslims and Christians.

To end the Israeli invasion and stabilize Lebanon, the United States sent Marines to join an international peacekeeping force. On October 23, 1983, a terrorist killed 241 Americans by driving a truck bomb into Marine headquarters at Beirut. The attack shocked Americans and marked a low point of Reagan's administration. The president pulled out the soldiers in 1984, but there was still no peace in Lebanon and no agreement between the Israelis and the PLO.

The attack on the Marine headquarters illustrated the growing threat of terrorism against the United States and its allies. Reagan vowed to make terrorists "pay for their actions," but terrorism proved hard to stop. Acts of terrorism by Palestinians and Libyans drew quick American reprisals in the 1980s, but the threat of terrorism did not go away.

Reagan also acted to safeguard America's oil supply. During a war between Iran and Iraq, the United States sent Navy ships to protect oil tankers in the Persian Gulf. In May 1987 Iraqi missiles struck the U.S. destroyer *Stark*, killing 37 of its crew. The Reagan administration, unwilling to help Iran, accepted Iraq's apology. In July 1988, the U.S. missile cruiser *Vincennes* accidentally shot down an Iranian airliner, killing 290 passengers. An American apology did little to quell Iranian anger, but the Iran–Iraq war soon ended, and with it the threat to America's oil supply.

The United States and the World Economy

Middle Eastern oil was only one of the economic factors shaping Reagan's foreign policy. The president had to deal with strains on the world economy.

By the end of the 1980s, the developing nations of the third world owed foreign banks more than $1.2 trillion in loan payments. Mexico was more than $100 billion in debt. American banks stood to lose heavily if Mexico and other nations default-ed on loans. American producers stood to lose, too, if these countries could not afford to buy U.S. goods. The Reagan administration nevertheless refused to pro-tect American banks from loan defaults, instead forcing debtor countries to adopt austerity programs in return for new loans.

The Reagan administration had much less power to dictate trade policy with Japan. As Japanese exports flowed into the United States, Americans increasingly resented Japan's domination of the Japanese home market. Congress, believing the Japanese discriminated against American goods, pushed for retaliation. Japan placed voluntary quotas on its export of steel and automobiles to the United States. Although the Reagan administration devalued the dollar to make American goods cheaper, the trade imbalance continued. In 1988 the president signed the Omnibus Trade and Competitiveness Act, which allowed the government to place high tariffs on Japanese goods if Japan continued to discriminate against American goods. However, as long as Americans wanted to buy Japanese products, retaliation was unlikely.

THE BATTLE OVER CONSERVATIVE SOCIAL VALUES

For all of Ronald Reagan's success in the early 1980s, the new conservatism met with considerable opposition. Eager to combat the legacies of the 1960s, many conserva-tives wanted to restore supposedly traditional values and practices. The conservative agenda collided head-on with one of the chief legacies of the 1960s—disadvantaged groups' demands for equal rights and opportunities. Moreover, many Americans were unwilling to abandon the social changes of the last generation. Faced with such opposition, conservatives failed to achieve much of their vision for American society.

Attacking the Legacy of the 1960s

The new conservatism was driven by a desire to undo the liberal and radical legacies of the 1960s. Conservatives blamed federal courts for much of the social change in the United States over the last generation. In the 1960s and 1970s liberal justices with an activist conception of the courts' role had supported defendants' rights, civil rights, affirmative action, busing, and abortion and rejected such conservative causes as school prayer.

Determined to take control of the courts, Reagan appointed many staunch, relatively young conservatives to the federal bench and the Supreme Court. In 1981 Sandra Day O'Connor, a fairly conservative judge from Arizona, became the court's first woman justice. When Chief Justice Warren Burger retired, Reagan replaced him with conservative William Rehnquist. With the appointments of two more conservatives, Antonin Scalia and Anthony Kennedy, the Supreme Court seemed ready to turn away from liberalism.

It did not quite work out that way. In the 1980s the court followed conservative views in limiting the rights of defendants: Ruling in *United States* v. *Leon* and *Nix* v. *Williams* in 1984, the justices made it easier for prosecutors to use evidence improperly obtained by police. However, on a variety of other issues, the court took a moderate stance. In *Wallace* v. *Jaffree* in 1985, the court invalidated an Alabama law that allowed schools to devote a minute each day to voluntary prayer or meditation.

Conservatives believed that the federal government had played too large a role in the schools since the 1960s. Conservative educational reformers wanted to dismantle the federal Department of Education. In addition, they wanted the government to enable parents to choose the best schools—public or private—for their children, by means of a system of federally funded vouchers or tax credits.

Because many Americans were worried about the quality of the schools, conservatives had a golden opportunity. In 1983 a federal study, *A Nation at Risk*, documented American students' shortcomings, especially in math and science. Despite such revelations, Congress refused to adopt the voucher system or to abolish the Department of Education.

In the early 1980s, the sale and use of crack, especially in the cities, led to crime and violence. In 1986 the president and his wife, Nancy, announced a "national crusade" for a "drug-free" America, encouraging young people to "Just Say No" to drugs. Reagan also instituted drug testing for federal employees. The "war on drugs" was controversial. Critics ridiculed the "Just Say No" slogan as naïve and ineffective. Despite the new penalties and expenditures, drug use did not decrease appreciably.

Women's Rights and Abortion

One of the chief legacies of the 1960s was the women's rights movement. Many conservatives, especially evangelical leaders, believed that women were undermining family life by leaving home for jobs and blamed feminists and liberal government for encouraging women to abandon their traditional role. The conservative movement was especially determined to halt federal initiatives, such as affirmative-action programs and the ERA, that used government power to protect women's rights.

The conservative agenda on women's rights met with mixed results. The campaign for the ERA ended unsuccessfully, but affirmative-action programs, designed to promote the hiring of women, continued. So did women's push into the workplace and public life as more and more American families needed two incomes. By 1983 women made up half of the paid work force. As their economic role expanded, American women received more recognition from the political system. Ironically, Reagan himself gave women new public prominence by choosing Jeane J. Kirkpatrick and Sandra Day O'Connor for important offices.

Women still did not enjoy equality in America. They were generally paid less than men doing the same sort of work, and they had less opportunity to break through the glass ceiling and win managerial jobs. Moreover, commentators had begun to note the feminization of poverty. Unmarried or divorced women, many with children, made up an increasing percentage of the poor.

For many conservatives, abortion was the most troubling sign of the changed status of women. A growing Right to Life movement passionately denounced abortion as the murder of the unborn, practiced by selfish women who rejected motherhood and family.

Conservatives failed to narrow abortion rights significantly in the 1980s. Reagan successfully urged Congress to stop the use of federal funds to pay for abortions, but a constitutional amendment outlawing abortion stalled in the Senate. In 1983 and 1986, the Supreme Court made rulings that upheld *Roe* v. *Wade.*

Gays and the AIDS Crisis

The gay rights movement was another legacy of the 1960s that troubled many conservatives. Evangelical leaders such as Jerry Falwell condemned homosexuality on religious grounds. Some people believed that the public acceptance of equal rights for gay men and women would promote immorality and corrupt children.

Despite such opposition, the gay rights movement made progress in the 1980s. By the end of the decade, most states had repealed sodomy laws that criminalized

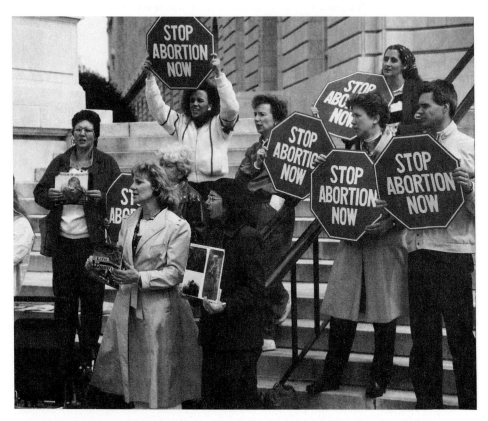

Anti-abortion protestors, part of the Right to Life movement that challenged the legitimacy of the Supreme Court's Roe v. Wade *decision in the 1980s.*

gay sex. In 1982 Wisconsin became the first state to pass a law protecting the rights of gay men and women.

The battle over gay rights took place against a tragic backdrop. In 1981 the Centers for Disease Control began reporting cases of acquired immune deficiency syndrome (AIDS), a disease that destroyed the body's immune system and left it unable to fight off infections and rare cancers. By the mid-1980s, researchers had traced AIDS to different forms of the human immunodeficiency virus (HIV) that were transmitted in semen and blood. By 1990 there were nearly 100,000 recorded deaths from AIDS in the United States.

Because 75 percent of the first victims were gay men, Americans initially considered AIDS a homosexual disease. Some people, including evangelical leaders, believed this "gay cancer" was God's punishment for the alleged sin of homosexuality. As soon became clear, however, AIDS could also be transmitted by heterosexual intercourse, by intravenous drug use that involved sharing needles, and by tainted blood transfusions.

Public understanding of AIDS and HIV gradually increased. Nevertheless, the specter of "gay cancer" promoted homophobia and slowed the public response to the disease. Gay activists pushed for government action. The AIDS Coalition to Unleash Power, known as ACT UP, and other organizations staged demonstrations and acts of civil disobedience to focus attention on the crisis. Nevertheless, the Reagan administration did not fund research on AIDS for several years.

African Americans and Racial Inequality

Conservatives were uneasy with still another legacy of the 1960s, the expansion of African-American civil rights and benefits guaranteed by the federal government. Conservatives believed that the liberal policies of the Great Society hurt, rather than helped, black people. They maintained that individual initiative, and not government action, would promote racial equality. In keeping with these ideas, President Reagan opposed renewal of the Voting Rights Act and condemned busing and affirmative action.

Compared with the 1950s and 1960s, African Americans' crusade for justice and opportunity generally slowed in the 1970s and 1980s. Despite legal equality, African Americans faced persisting racism and discrimination. After years of improvement, African Americans' economic status relative to whites stagnated or declined during the Reagan era. African Americans still made less money than whites did for comparable work and had much less chance to attain managerial positions.

Economic hardship and persistent discrimination did not affect all African Americans equally. Among college-educated Americans, the incomes of black men rose faster than those of whites into the mid-1980s. Meanwhile, working-class African Americans found their wages stagnating or falling compared with those of white workers. In the 1970s and 1980s, poverty rates rose faster among African Americans than among whites. The feminization of poverty hit black families particularly hard. In 1985, 75 percent of poor African-American children lived in families headed by a single female. Observers feared that there was now a permanent African-American underclass living segregated in inner-city neighborhoods with poor schools and widespread crime.

African Americans mobilized to fight for equality and opportunity in the 1980s. Across the country, the number of African-American elected officials increased markedly. The Reverend Jesse Jackson, a protégé of Martin Luther King, Jr., won wide attention. Preaching self-esteem and economic self-help for African Americans, Jackson was the leader of Operation PUSH—People United to Save Humanity. In 1984 Jackson challenged Walter Mondale for the Democratic presidential nomination. His campaign suggested how far American society had come in accepting African-American political participation.

African-American activism made it difficult for Reagan and other conservatives to undo the civil rights revolution, as did the persistence of discrimination and inequality. Most Americans seemed to accept that some federal action was essential to redress the imbalance between races in America. Despite Reagan's opposition, in 1982 Congress voted to extend the Voting Rights Act for 25 years. In 1983 the Supreme Court ruled overwhelmingly against Bob Jones University, an evangelical institution that attempted to retain its tax-exempt status despite discriminatory policies. The court also rejected the Reagan administration's bid to set aside local affirmative-action programs. In other decisions, the justices limited affirmative action somewhat, but this important liberal program survived the Reagan administration.

The battles over the rights of African Americans, gays, and women demonstrated that conservative social values were controversial. Many Americans were not ready to undo the legacy of the 1960s. The result was a stalemate. Disadvantaged groups made relatively little progress in the 1980s, but conservatives also made little progress in their social agenda.

THE LIMITS OF THE NEW CONSERVATISM

The Reagan administration was hurt by policy setbacks, economic woes, and its own scandals. For a time, the conservatives' triumph, like the Trumps' fortune, was seriously in doubt.

Business and Religious Scandals

In the late 1980s the new conservatism suffered from a series of scandals. Even before Donald Trump's fortunes declined in the late 1980s, other famous entrepreneurs were in trouble. In 1986 Ivan Boesky, the swaggering Wall Street dealmaker, was indicted for insider trading, the illegal use of secret financial information. Rather than go to trial, he agreed to give up stock trading, inform on other law breakers, spend two years in jail, and pay a $100-million fine. In 1987 Michael Milken, the junk-bond king, was indicted on fraud and racketeering charges. His eventual plea bargain agreement included a ten-year jail sentence and a stunning $600-million fine.

These scandals provoked second thoughts about the celebration of business and materialism. Critics pointed out that Boesky's and Milken's business methods had hurt the economy by saddling corporations with a great deal of debt and little cash to pay for it. Lavish lifestyles no longer seemed quite so attractive.

Scandal touched religion as well as commerce. Leading televangelists were caught in embarrassing predicaments. In 1987 Americans learned that Jim Bakker had defrauded investors in Heritage Park, USA, and paid hush money to hide an adulterous liaison. The scandal hurt the reputation of Jerry Falwell, who had taken over Bakker's organization. In 1988 Falwell resigned from his own Moral Majority. That same year, televangelist Jimmy Swaggart admitted that he "had sinned" with prostitutes.

Political Scandals

The Reagan administration had its own scandals. Almost from the start, some observers decried its lax ethical standards. Before the end of the president's first term, more than 20 officials of the EPA resigned or were fired over charges of favoritism toward lobbyists and polluters. In 1985 Secretary of Labor Raymond Donovan resigned after becoming the first cabinet officer ever indicted. In 1988 Reagan's friend and attorney general, Edwin Meese III, resigned amid questions about his role in the corrupt awarding of government contracts to a defense firm. To critics of the administration, the president and his followers encouraged fraud and corruption with their contemptuous attitude toward government and their eagerness to please business.

In his second term, Reagan faced much more damaging accusations. In October 1986, Sandinista soldiers in Nicaragua shot down a transport plane attempting to supply the Contra rebels. It soon became clear that the plane had been part of a secret effort by the Reagan administration to violate the Boland Amendment's ban on aid to the Contras. Then, in November, a Lebanese magazine reported that the United States had traded arms to Iran. Despite denials from the president, the government had sold arms to win the release of American hostages held by terrorists in Lebanon. The Reagan administration had broken the president's pledge not to negotiate with terrorists and had violated a ban on arms sales to Iran. Americans soon learned that the arms deal and the Nicaraguan plane crash were connected. Government officials had illegally used proceeds from the arms sale to pay for supplying the Contras.

The scandal that became known as the Iran-Contra affair had the potential to drive Reagan from office. If the president had ordered or known about the arms deal and the supply effort, he might have faced impeachment. The Reagan administration underwent three separate investigations: one by a special commission appointed by the president and headed by former Senator John Tower; one by a special prosecutor appointed by the attorney general; and one by a special Congressional committee. These inquiries made clear that Reagan was probably deeply involved in the Iran-Contra affair, but none turned up enough evidence to impeach him.

Nevertheless, the Iran-Contra affair badly damaged Reagan's reputation. Several of his associates left office and faced jail sentences. Former National Security Adviser Robert "Bud" McFarlane pleaded guilty to withholding information from Congress. His successor, Rear Admiral John Poindexter, was allowed to resign. Poindexter's charismatic aide, Marine Lieutenant Colonel Oliver North, had to be fired. Tried and sentenced for their actions, Poindexter and North had their convictions overturned on technical grounds. Meanwhile, the director of the CIA, William Casey, died in 1987, the day after testimony implicated him in the effort to aid the Contras.

Setbacks for the Conservative Agenda

Against this backdrop of scandal, conservatives faced a series of policy setbacks during Reagan's second term. Even though Democrats controlled the House of Representatives, during his first term Reagan had usually persuaded Congress to back his conservative agenda. The Democrats were less cooperative during his second term. The Democrats became even more combative after winning majorities in both the House and Senate in the Congressional elections of 1986.

Accordingly, Reagan sometimes had to compromise with Congress. In 1985 the president called for a Second American Revolution, a comprehensive overhaul of the income tax system. But the Tax Reform Act that Congress passed in 1986 did not lower and simplify income taxes nearly as much as the president had wanted.

Reagan also met outright defeat in Congress. In 1988, a coalition of Democrats and Republicans passed a bill compelling large companies to give workers 60 days' advance notice of plant closings and layoffs. Reagan opposed this liberal, prolabor measure, but he allowed the bill to become law without his signature.

The president faced repeated defeat on environmental policy. During the 1980s there was growing concern about environmental hazards. In December 1984 the subsidiary of a U.S. corporation accidentally allowed toxic gas to escape from a pesticide plant in Bhopal, India. The emission killed more than 2,500 people and injured 200,000. In April 1986 an explosion and fire allowed radioactive material to escape a nuclear power plant at Chernobyl in the Soviet Union. The accident killed more than 30 people, injured more than 200, exposed countless others to radioactivity, and caused extensive environmental damage.

In this alarming context, Reagan had to accept the extension of the federal Superfund program to clean up hazardous waste in the United States in 1986. The next year, Congress overrode his veto of a bill renewing the Water Quality Control Act. In 1988 the Reagan administration signed an international agreement placing limits on emissions linked to acid rain.

A Vulnerable Economy

Even the economy, the centerpiece of the Reagan Revolution, became a problem during the president's second term. During the 1980s the gap between rich and poor widened sharply. While the average family income, after taxes, of the highest paid tenth of Americans rose 27 percent from 1977 to 1988, the average family income of the poorest tenth fell 11 percent (see Figure 30–1). In the 1980s only the rich earned more and kept more. Other Americans faced economic stagnation or decline.

The falling incomes of the poorest Americans ensured the persistence of poverty. Twenty-nine million Americans lived below the poverty line in 1980. Ten years later, that figure had grown to almost 37 million. Despite Reaganomics, the United States had one of the highest poverty rates among industrialized nations.

One of the most visible consequences of poverty was homelessness. In the 1980s the number of homeless Americans increased markedly. The sight of men and women, their belongings in shopping carts, sleeping on sidewalks, was common during the Reagan years.

Homelessness, poverty, and inequality produced a spirited debate in the 1980s. Democrats and liberals blamed these problems on Reaganomics. The president, they charged, had done nothing to stop the erosion of high-paying factory jobs. His welfare, housing, and job-training cuts hurt the poor, while his tax cuts and deregulation helped the rich.

In response, conservatives and Republicans maintained that activist, liberal government had hurt manufacturing and weakened the economy. Moreover, welfare programs caused poverty by destroying poor people's work ethic and making them dependent on handouts.

Not surprisingly, neither side persuaded the other. In reality, both liberal and conservative policies had produced flawed economic results. Lyndon Johnson's spending for the Great Society, along with the cost of the Vietnam War, had begun

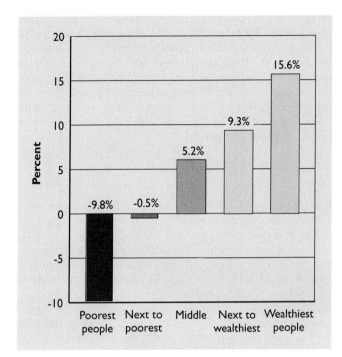

Figure 30–1   Changes in Families' Real Income, 1980–1990

Source: Copyright © 1989 by the New York Times Co. Reprinted by permission.

to undermine the economy in the 1960s. His antipoverty programs had been less effective than liberals wanted to admit, but the Reagan Revolution had offered no solution to poverty, either. Reaganomics did not reinvigorate manufacturing or boost middle-class incomes.

There were other signs of economic vulnerability by the mid-1980s. The federal budget deficit did not disappear. Instead, between 1981 and 1986, as the government cut taxes and increased defense spending, the deficit soared from $79 billion to $221 billion—a staggering new record.

Like poverty and inequality, the deficit was controversial: Some economists believed the deficit was a sign of great economic weakness; others believed it did not matter. Democrats and liberals blamed Reagan for the budgetary red ink. Reagan's supporters blamed Congress for failing to cut the budget.

In fact both the president and Congress were to blame. Neither Republicans nor Democrats wanted to reduce such popular benefits as Medicare and Social Security. Congress enacted the Balanced Budget and Emergency Deficit Control Act of 1985, known as the Gramm–Rudman Act, which promised automatic cuts to balance the budget by 1990. The next year a Supreme Court ruling critically weakened the measure. The deficit remained high during Reagan's last years in office, and the national debt—the total amount owed by the federal government to its creditors—reached $2.6 trillion.

Along with this burgeoning debt, the Reagan years produced a growing international trade deficit. In 1980 the annual value of imports was $25.4 billion greater than the value of the nation's exports. By 1986 that gap had grown to $145.1 billion. Consumers at home and abroad found foreign goods more attractive than ever. Reaganomics had not solved the problem of America's relative decline in the world economy.

Doubts about Reagan's economic policy increased when the stock market plummeted unexpectedly on Monday, October 19, 1987, losing 508 points, or 23 percent of its value. The market drop reflected underlying economic problems including the federal budget deficit, the trade deficit, and deindustrialization, plus lax regulation of Wall Street by the Reagan administration. "What crashed was more than just the market," a journalist concluded. "It was the Reagan Illusion: the idea that there could be a defense buildup and tax cuts without a price, that the country could live beyond its means indefinitely." In the late 1980s, the American economy, like Ivana Trump, apparently could not have it all.

Reagan's Comeback

By 1987 the Reagan presidency, beset by scandals and economic troubles, appeared to be in jeopardy. Reagan's accomplishments, like the Trumps' success, seemed uncertain. Then the president began a comeback.

Reagan benefited from his political skills and his popularity. Continuing economic growth overshadowed the stock market crash and other woes. Most important, perhaps, changes in the Soviet Union led to a dramatic easing of cold-war tensions. By the end of his presidency, Reagan had won back his popularity.

During his second term, Reagan showed a remarkable ability to withstand scandal and defeat. Opponents dubbed him the "Teflon president" because nothing seemed to stick to him. That was a tribute to Reagan's political skills as well as many Americans' real affection for him. After a series of disappointing presidencies, Americans seemed unwilling to let Reagan fail.

The economy also helped the president. Notwithstanding Americans' fears, the stock market crash did not lead to depression or recession. The market soon recovered. The economy continued to grow. The nation was arguably more prosperous than during the 1970s.

Reagan's comeback was probably helped most of all by the transformation of the Soviet Union. By the mid-1980s the USSR suffered from a weakening economy, an unpopular war in Afghanistan, and a costly arms race. At this critical juncture, Mikhail Gorbachev became General Secretary of the Communist Party. The dynamic and charismatic Gorbachev signaled a new era with a series of stunning reforms. At home, he called for restructuring the economy (*perestroika*) and tolerating more open discussion (*glasnost*). Abroad, he sought an easing of tensions with the United States and the West.

Gorbachev's reforms gave the U.S. government a politically popular opportunity to thaw cold-war tensions. Reagan met with the Soviet leader in a series of positive summits beginning in Geneva, Switzerland, in November 1985. Meanwhile, it became apparent that the Soviets were, in fact, changing their foreign policy, as they withdrew their troops from Afghanistan and began to ease control over the Communist regimes of Eastern Europe.

Simultaneously, the United States and the Soviets made striking progress on arms control. In December 1987 Reagan and Gorbachev signed the Intermediate-Range Nuclear Forces Treaty (INF), promising to destroy more than 2,500 intermediate-range nuclear missiles. For the first time, the two powers had agreed to give up a weapon altogether.

The INF treaty signaled a permanent easing of tensions. The cold war, so intense just a few years earlier, suddenly seemed to be ending. Conservatives and Republicans insisted that the president's defense buildup had forced the Soviets to

CHRONOLOGY

1980	Ronald Reagan elected president
1981	Introduction of the IBM personal computer Air traffic controllers' strike Economic Recovery Act passes Appointment of Sandra Day O'Connor to the Supreme Court AIDS cases first publicly reported
1982	Breakup of AT&T Nuclear freeze rally in New York City Passage of the Boland Amendment Extension of the Voting Rights Act
1983	Announcement of Strategic Defense Initiative Congress approves Caribbean Basin Initiative Social Security Reform Act of 1983 U.S. invasion of Grenada Terrorist attack on U.S. Marines in Lebanon Publication of *A Nation at Risk*
1984	Report of the Grace Commission Re-election of Ronald Reagan
1985	General Electric purchases RCA Gramm–Rudman Act
1986	US bombing of Libya Nuclear power plant accident in Chernobyl, USSR Tax Reform Act Indictment of Ivan Boesky Revelation of Iran-Contra affair
1987	Iraqi missile attack on U.S. destroyer *Stark* Indictment of Michael Milken Jim Bakker scandal Stock market crash Intermediate-Range Nuclear Forces Treaty
1988	Omnibus Trade and Competitiveness Act U.S. accidentally shoots down Iranian airliner

capitulate. Democrats and liberals maintained that the buildup and the president's harsh rhetoric had actually slowed the thaw in U.S.–Soviet relations.

As Reagan left office in January 1989, his comeback seemed complete. The economy was growing; the cold war was ending. He had the highest popularity rating of any president since the beginning of modern polling in the 1930s.

CONCLUSION

Reagan's comeback emphasized the triumph of the new conservatism. Americans would debate the nature of that triumph for years to come. Certainly the conservative victory, like the Trumps' success, was never as great as it seemed in the early 1980s. Americans did not embrace much of the conservative social agenda. The Reagan Revolution did not solve such basic economic problems as poverty. It even worsened some problems, such as inequality and the budget deficit.

Nevertheless, the conservative triumph, like the Trumps' fortune, was real. In the 1980s American culture celebrated the wealth and values of Trump and other business figures. A new conservative coalition elected Reagan. Moreover, Reagan combatted the sense of national decline that pervaded America in the 1970s.

The accomplishments of the new conservatism, as Reagan's troubled second term indicated, were fragile. The nation's economic revival was shaky, as was the revival of its spirit. Americans were still worried about the future. "I think," Donald Trump concluded, "the '90s are going to be much trickier than the 1980s."

FURTHER READINGS

Connie Bruck, *The Predators' Ball: The Inside Story of Drexel Burnham and the Rise of the Junk Bond Raiders* (1989). This work vividly describes some of the new, controversial business practices of the 1980s.

Theodore Draper, *A Very Thin Line: The Iran-Contra Affairs* (1991). A careful reconstruction of the major scandal of the Reagan presidency.

Susan Faludi, *Backlash: The Undeclared War Against American Women* (1991). Faludi's book captures the contentiousness surrounding gender issues in the 1980s.

Marshall Frady, *Jesse: The Life and Pilgrimage of Jesse Jackson* (1996). Frady presents a full biography of the most prominent African-American leader of the 1980s.

Paul Freiberger and Michael Swaine, *Fire in the Valley: The Making of the Personal Computer* (1974). An interesting anecdotal account of a critical development in the computer revolution.

Paul Gottfried, *The Conservative Movement* (1993). A balanced analysis, particularly strong on conservative ideas.

Haynes Johnson, *Sleepwalking Through History: America in the Reagan Years* (1991). A journalist's vivid chronicle of major developments in the 1980s.

William E. Pemberton, *Exit With Honor: The Life and Presidency of Ronald Reagan* (1997). One of the first full assessments of Reagan's career by a professional historian.

James M. Scott, *Deciding to Intervene: The Reagan Doctrine and American Foreign Policy* (1996). Scott's book focuses on the anti-Soviet aims of the Reagan administration.

Randy Shilts, *And the Band Played On: Politics, People, and the AIDS Epidemic* (1987). A moving account of the response to AIDS.

 Please refer to the document CD-ROM for primary sources related to this chapter.

CHAPTER

31

A New America?

1989–

Felix Andreev and "The Blessing of America" • **A New Economy**
Political Deadlock • **Struggles Over Diversity and Rights**
From the Cold War to the War on Terrorism • **Conclusion**

FELIX ANDREEV AND "THE BLESSING OF AMERICA"

elix Iosifovich Andreev felt trapped in the Soviet Union. He chafed under the restraints of the Communist political and economic system. A Jew, he resented discrimination against his religion. For years, he had loved American movies, American books, and American jazz. The United States, Andreev believed, was a place of "liberty and generous people." However, for years Soviet immigration law made it impossible for him to leave. Then, in the late 1980s, the Soviet leader Mikhail Gorbachev loosened immigration restrictions, and in 1989, Andreev moved with his family to the Brighton Beach section of Brooklyn in New York City.

From the long perspective of American history, Andreev's story was not unusual. Immigrants, escaping oppression and seeking opportunity, had been migrating to America for centuries. From another perspective, Andreev's arrival in Brooklyn was remarkable. For more than 40 years, the cold war had blocked migration between the Soviet Union and the United States. The emerging crisis of deindustrialization in the 1970s had made the United States a less obvious symbol of economic opportunity. Immigrants had played a lessened role in national life since World War II.

As Felix Andreev's arrival suggested, things were changing. At the end of the 1980s, the cold war was ending. Instead, such forces as immigration were reshaping the nation. Andreev was one of millions of immigrants from Russia, Asia, and Latin America who arrived in the United States in the 1980s and 1990s. These new Americans both changed their adopted country and were changed by it.

Andreev's Brighton Beach showed the process at work. Russian immigrants were transforming this one-and-a-half-mile strip of Brooklyn. Restaurants and stores had signs written in Russia's distinctive Cyrillic alphabet. People spoke Russian in the streets. But the immigrants did not want to re-create the Soviet Union they had left behind. They wanted to share what Andreev called "the blessing of America." But in the early 1990s, the new Russian residents of Brighton Beach struggled to find jobs and make their way. As Andreev's wife admitted, the Russians "do not yet fit into" American society.

Brighton Beach symbolized the promise and the uncertainty of the nation as it ended one century and began another. Despite all the upheavals since the 1960s, the United States still represented freedom and prosperity. The United States, however, was plainly changing. An older nation, defined by the cold war, New Deal liberalism, and heavy industry, was disappearing. A new America had not yet taken its place. Despite the declaration of a new war on terrorism, the nation's role in the world was unclear. As the industrial revolution ran its course, the outlines of a postindustrial economy were still incomplete. In the 2000s, the United States was much like Felix Andreev: The nation had left behind much of its recent past but had not yet defined its future.

A NEW ECONOMY

Felix Andreev and other immigrants were drawn to the United States partly by the promise of its changing economy. As manufacturing played a smaller economic role, the service sector, led by computer companies and other high-technology firms, drove the economy. Like the industrial revolution before it, the computer revolution seemed to have the power to transform American life, but the nature of the new, postindustrial economy remained uncertain at the start of the twenty-first century.

Toward a Postindustrial Economy

Underway since the 1950s, the transition from an industrial to a postindustrial economy picked up momentum in the 1990s. Manufacturing played a smaller role in the economy. American corporations continued to move their manufacturing operations abroad to take advantage of lower wages and production costs. Consequently, workers had less chance to hold relatively high-wage factory jobs.

Those workers were increasingly likely to find employment in the service sector, the fastest growing part of the economy. More and more Americans worked in restaurants, retail stores, and offices instead of factories. By 1994 the service sector accounted for about 70 percent of the nation's economic activity.

Many Americans believed that high technology would dominate the postindustrial economy. In the 1990s the electronics revolution continued to transform communications. More and more Americans carried cellular telephones. High-speed fiber-optic cables and satellite dishes expanded the power and reach of telephone and television systems.

The most powerful symbol of the new economy was still the computer, however. Computers became smaller, faster, more powerful, and more common. By 1999 more than half of the nation's households had at least one computer.

The most dramatic computing development in the 1990s was the explosive growth of the Internet, the communications network linking computer users around the nation and the world. Begun by the Department of Defense in the late 1960s, the Internet had spread through universities and across American society by the end of the century. Originally, people used the Internet to send and receive e-mail, but by the middle of the 1990s millions of Americans began to explore the World Wide Web, the segment of the Internet that blended text, graphics, audio, and video. Americans used the Web to communicate, to do research, to create and exhibit art, to listen to music, and to buy and sell online.

These developments spurred the old utopian dream that the computer would define the postindustrial society. Thanks to the computer and other electronic innovations, the dream held, Americans would process information instead of raw materials. Postindustrial America would be a prosperous information society, sustained by the computerized e-commerce of an "Internet economy."

At the start of the twenty-first century, there were many reasons to believe this utopian dream was coming true. The computer revolution seemed to be repeating the industrial revolution. As in the late 1800s and early 1900s, corporations that best took advantage of new technologies were pushing to the forefront of American capitalism: Microsoft and Oracle, Dell Computer and Intel, Amazon.com and eBay, and America Online. Established companies, meanwhile, rushed to do business online.

Like the industrial revolution, the computer revolution spurred a wave of corporate mergers and acquisitions. The ABC television network, already merged with Capital Cities Communications in the 1980s, was taken over by Walt Disney in 1995. That year, media giant Time-Warner, the product of a merger in 1989, bought out Turner Broadcasting. Then, in a sign of the growing importance of the Internet, America Online arranged to purchase Time-Warner in 2000.

The computer revolution also paralleled the industrial revolution by producing a new, hugely wealthy elite. The most famous of this new corporate elite was Bill Gates, the cofounder of Microsoft, who became the wealthiest American since John D. Rockefeller, the cofounder of Standard Oil, nearly a century before. Like Standard Oil, Microsoft became the target of a federal antitrust suit that ended in a judge's order to break up the company into smaller units.

Like the industrial revolution, the computer revolution also produced uncertainty and fear. At the end of the twentieth century, as at the beginning, many Americans worried about the economic and political power of giant new companies and new fortunes. Microsoft, like Standard Oil, became a symbol of monopoly power, and like Standard Oil, Microsoft became the target of state and federal prosecutors. In 2000, a federal judge ordered that Microsoft, like Standard Oil, be broken up into smaller companies to restore competition. The many parallels between the computer revolution and the industrial revolution seemed to prove that the postindustrial economy had indeed arrived, but in some ways the computerized,

Internet economy remained a dream. Few companies made substantial profits from e-commerce. Many online companies quickly failed. General Motors and Ford— old-fashioned manufacturing companies—remained the largest corporations in America. At the start of the twenty-first century, it was not clear that computers, like machine tools and railroads before them, had boosted the productivity of workers.

Moreover, most new service positions were low paying, involved limited technology, and required little education. As a result, the growth of the service sector inspired fears of a low-tech future as well as dreams of a high-tech utopia.

At the start of the twenty-first century, no one could predict the outcome of America's ongoing economic transformation with much confidence. The postindustrial age had begun, but Americans could not be sure what it would bring.

Toward a Global Economy

There was at least one economic certainty at the start of the new century. The American economy was becoming ever more tightly bound up in a single global economy. Americans owned more stock in foreign companies than ever before, and foreigners had more financial investments in the United States than ever before. U.S. exports and imports both jumped about 50 percent in the five years from 1990 to 1995.

International trade remained intensely competitive in the 1990s. Even though the United States still imported more than it exported, the nation seemed to fare better in its rivalry with other industrial nations. American corporations continued their efforts to become more efficient. By 1993 one study rated the United States, rather than Japan, the most competitive national economy in the world.

International competition involved governments as well as corporations. Since World War II, Western European nations had moved gradually toward economic and political cooperation. That trend culminated with the formation of the European Union in 1993. Through the Union, such nations as France, Germany, and Great Britain planned to coordinate their economic and political policies and create a single vast economic unit. The member countries would then, it was believed, find it easier to trade with one another, and other countries, including the United States, might find it harder to compete in Europe.

The United States responded by creating an economic bloc in North America. In 1992 Canada, Mexico, and the United States announced the North American Free Trade Agreement (NAFTA), which established the world's largest and richest low-tariff trading zone. NAFTA won considerable support from U.S. corporations, but organized labor feared that NAFTA would encourage those corporations to transfer even more jobs from the United States to Mexico. Environmentalists worried that the agreement would weaken the battle against industrial pollution. Despite this opposition, the Senate ratified the agreement in 1993.

Downsizing America

Global competition helped spur a wave of downsizing in the 1990s. Some of America's largest and most advanced corporations announced stunning cutbacks in their operations. For instance, AT&T decided in 1996 to trim 40,000 positions. This and other corporate cutbacks were remarkable for a number of reasons: They came during a period of relative prosperity, they involved some of the largest and seemingly most stable American companies, and they affected many white-collar workers. Large corporations had traditionally been slow to cut loose white-collar workers, but now managers and professionals were vulnerable as well.

Several factors helped produce this situation. Fundamentally, American businesses wanted to cut costs and increase profits. They worried about remaining efficient and competitive in the world economy. Also, the end of the cold war affected American corporations. As the federal government downsized the military, defense contractors had to downsize as well.

Downsizing dramatically affected American workers, particularly members of the middle class, who had to abandon some of their cherished assumptions. In the 1990s the middle class realized what blue-collar workers had known since the 1970s: Even the largest corporations were not as stable and secure as they seemed. Accordingly, middle-class status itself was not as stable and secure as in the past.

An Uneasy Prosperity

In spite of the pangs of downsizing, the productivity of American workers and the vitality of the service sector helped keep the economy expanding throughout most of the 1990s. Inflation was negligible, interest rates were low; unemployment rose during a recession early in the decade, then dropped off to record lows, only to inch up in 2000. Driven by excitement about computer-related companies, the stock market reached one record high after another, until it peaked in early 2000 (see Figure 31–1).

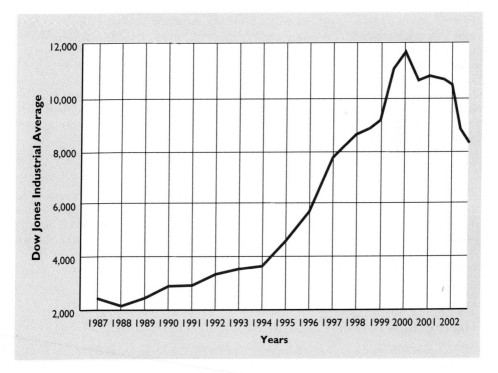

Figure 31–1   The Stock Market, 1987–2002
The Dow Jones Industrial Average had a long, steady rise during the 1990s and a precipitous decline in the early 2000s.

Source: Phyllis S. Pierce, ed., The Dow Jones Averages, 1885–1995 (1996); World Almanac, 1998, p. 510; Standard and Poor's Daily Stock Price Record, NYSE, 1996, vol. 2, and 1997, vol. 2; http://www.forecasts.org/data/data/djiaM.htm.

Despite the good economic news of the 1990s, Americans remained uneasy. Downsizing was one reason; falling wages were another. Allowing for inflation, the average weekly earnings of American workers in 1998 were less than they were in 1970. After 2000, the falling stock market eliminated gains many middle-class people were relying on for retirement.

Americans also worried about whether they could afford the rapidly increasing costs of health care. The United States, almost alone among developed nations, had no national health insurance plan for its citizens. By the 1990s America was spending a greater proportion of its gross domestic product on health care than were the other developed nations. Amid calls for more federal control over health care, many Americans feared the government could not control medical costs without denying people the right to choose their own doctors. As a result, Congress failed to pass a proposal for sweeping health care reform in 1993, and insurance companies were left to attempt to control rising costs. After leveling off in the mid-1990s, by the early 2000s health care costs, including insurance premiums, were again rising rapidly, and the number of uninsured Americans was over 44 million. Congress debated various ways to provide prescription drug coverage to the elderly as part of Medicare, but the larger problem of costs and access was not addressed.

Americans feared, too, that they could not afford retirement. Since the 1980s experts and politicians had debated whether the Social Security system was headed for bankruptcy. With the aging of the baby-boom generation, many people believed there would not be enough money to pay their pensions. Social Security needed reform, but the federal government was reluctant to act. As a result, with a booming stock market, politicians, including George W. Bush, advocated allowing Americans to invest part of their Social Security contributions in stock. A falling stock market silenced that debate, but few other possible reforms were brought forward.

The Social Security and health care issues, along with the corporate downsizing and falling wages, fostered an undertone of anxiety in the midst of prosperity. As the stock market faltered in the early 2000s, Americans were unsure that the future would be prosperous. Leaving the industrial era behind, Americans were not yet sure what the postindustrial era would bring.

POLITICAL DEADLOCK

The economic uncertainty at the start of the twenty-first century was accompanied by a pervasive political deadlock. At the end of the 1980s, conservatives and Republicans believed that Ronald Reagan's presidency had revolutionized the American political economy. The Reagan Revolution had, they expected, realigned politics, government, and the economy for years to come. Despite these hopes, the 1990s brought, instead of a decisive shift to the right, political moderation and uncertainty. No party or philosophy seemed able to mold politics and government—a situation dramatized by a virtual dead heat in the presidential election of 2000.

George Bush and the End of the Reagan Revolution

Conservatives were disappointed even before Reagan left office. The natural choice for his successor, Vice President George Bush of Texas, was a moderate willing to make political compromises. Nevertheless, Bush had loyally served Reagan through two terms, and he had a broad background of government service.

Bush easily won the general election in 1988. Committing himself to Reagan's economic policy, Bush made a popular pledge never to raise taxes. "Read my lips," he vowed. "No new taxes." At the same time, Bush softened the image of the new conservatism by supporting education and the environment. He easily defeated the Democratic nominee, former Governor Michael Dukakis of Massachusetts. Bush polled 53 percent of the popular vote and carried 40 states for a total of 426 electoral votes.

Despite Bush's triumph, the election revealed the weak electoral impact of the Reagan Revolution. Once again, the Republicans had failed to break the Democrats' hold on the House and Senate.

The Republicans' limited victory in 1988 reinforced Bush's instinct for political moderation. Bush disappointed conservatives by signing the Clean Air Act of 1990, which cut emissions from power plants and automobiles, and by signing measures to increase federal funding for education. Above all, he alienated conservatives by agreeing to a tax increase in 1990 to help decrease the federal budget deficit.

Bush's moderation did not ensure his popularity. The abandonment of his no-tax pledge reinforced the sense that he was a weak leader. Then an economic recession in 1991 and 1992 intensified Americans' dissatisfaction with the president.

The Rebellion Against Politics as Usual

Americans' unhappiness with George Bush was part of their broader dissatisfaction with politicians and government. By the 1990s there were signs of a brewing popular rebellion against politics as usual. In 1964, 76 percent of Americans had believed they could trust the government to do what was right always or most of the time. By 1994 only 19 percent of the people felt they could trust government. Americans were troubled by the feeling that politicians were ineffective as well as unethical. During Bush's term, the president and Congress seemed unable to cooperate on critical issues; Bush vetoed legislation more than 40 times. Unable to agree on a budget with Congress, the president shut down "nonessential" government services over Columbus Day weekend in 1990. That episode epitomized many Americans' sense that the government no longer served their needs.

People were still more frustrated because politicians seemed unwilling to reform. By the 1990s there was widespread agreement that money played too large a role in elections. Americans feared that huge donations from special-interest groups and wealthy individuals were corrupting politics. Although Congress and the president talked about the need for campaign finance reform, attempts to reform election spending failed repeatedly.

Americans tried other ways to reform Washington. There was considerable interest in limiting the number of terms that officials could serve in Congress, but Americans settled instead for a more modest reform. For many years the states had not ratified the Twenty-Seventh Amendment to the Constitution, which would keep a Congressional pay increase from taking effect until after the next election. The measure ensured that members of a Congress had to face the voters before getting a raise. Amid the popular anger at Congress, the amendment was finally ratified in 1992.

For a moment that year, it seemed as if popular disaffection was about to revolutionize American politics. Running a tired campaign for re-election in 1992, George Bush faced a sudden challenge from the strongest independent candidate in years, H. Ross Perot of Texas. Perot played to Americans' unhappiness with the political system by promising to end political gridlock, balance the budget, and reform campaign finances.

When voters began to wonder whether the quirky Perot could be an effective president, it was the Democratic nominee, Governor Bill Clinton of Arkansas, who seemed to embody hopes for change. Calling himself a "New Democrat," the charismatic Clinton polled 43 percent of the popular vote to Bush's 37 percent and Perot's surprisingly strong 19 percent. Holding on to African-American support, the Arkansas governor won back many white southerners and workers, the so-called Reagan Democrats. With the Democrats in control of the White House and both houses of Congress, it seemed as if "gridlock" would come to an end.

Bill Clinton and the Disappointment of Reform

In some ways, Clinton's election marked a change in American political life. Clinton was the first of the baby-boom generation to enter the White House. Clinton's rise from modest origins to become a Rhodes Scholar and then the nation's youngest governor reassured an unsettled America that upward mobility was still possible.

Clinton did act like a New Democrat by balancing traditional liberal activism with more conservative efforts to shrink government. Convinced that the federal government could not play an effective social role or maintain prosperity without balancing the budget, the president moved to cut the size of the federal work force. Through budget cuts and tax increases, Clinton and Congress reduced the size of the federal deficit. By 1998 the government posted a budget surplus.

Nevertheless, the promise of the Clinton presidency was limited by the resurgent power of the Republican Party. Clinton's most sweeping liberal proposal, his plan for dramatically increasing the federal role in medical care, went down to defeat. In 1994 voters awarded control of the House of Representatives to Republicans for the first time in 40 years. The new Republican majority chose an outspoken conservative, Newt Gingrich of Georgia, as Speaker of the House. The Republicans vowed to enact a conservative "Contract With America" that featured a balanced budget amendment to the Constitution, term limits, increased defense spending, welfare reform, and tax cuts. The Republicans never won enough popular support to enact key provisions of their "contract." Still, the Republican Party controlled both houses of Congress for the remainder of the decade.

The Republicans' strength forced Clinton to slight key liberal principles and make sometimes controversial compromises with conservatism. Clinton signed a welfare bill in 1996 that significantly reduced federal support for the poor, especially children. Reflecting the conservative vision of political economy, the measure replaced Aid to Families with Dependent Children (AFDC), which had long guaranteed federal payments to the poor, with grants to the states for use as they saw fit. The bill limited welfare recipients to five years of assistance over their lifetime and required heads of households on welfare to find work within two years. To discourage extramarital pregnancies, the bill imposed restrictions on unwed teenage mothers who were receiving benefits and offered bonuses for states with declining rates of illegitimate childbirth. Many Democrats and liberals angrily claimed that the president had betrayed the poor.

Running for re-election in 1996, Clinton benefited from the strength of the economy and the weakness of his opponents. Ross Perot had created a new Reform Party, but his candidacy could not rekindle the enthusiasm of 1992. The Republicans turned to moderate Bob Dole of Kansas, the Senate Majority Leader, who seemed to epitomize the compromising career politician so many Americans distrusted. Clinton won a clear victory with 49 percent of the popular vote. Dole attracted 41 percent of the popular vote and Perot only 8 percent.

Despite his re-election, Clinton no longer seemed like an agent of political change. Damaged by his compromises with conservatism, his reformist image was destroyed by a series of scandals. Soon after taking office, the president, along with the first lady, faced allegations that they had engaged in corrupt deals involving a real estate project, the Whitewater Development Corporation, in Arkansas in the 1970s and 1980s. Meanwhile, there were charges that the Clinton administration had improperly fired White House staff and obtained confidential FBI files on more than 600 people. In 1994, Paula Corbin Jones filed a lawsuit charging Bill Clinton with unwanted sexual advances while he was governor of Arkansas.

Scandal engulfed Clinton's second term. There were charges of illegal fundraising for the president's campaign. Expanding the Whitewater investigation, special prosecutor Kenneth Starr and a grand jury explored whether Clinton had obstructed justice in the Jones lawsuit by covering up an alleged sexual relationship with a young White House page, Monica Lewinsky. After months of denial, Clinton finally admitted to a grand jury in August 1998 that he had had "inappropriate intimate contact" with Lewinsky.

For a time, Clinton's presidency hung in the balance. In November 1998 the president settled Jones's suit by agreeing to pay her $500,000. In December the Republican-dominated House of Representatives voted two articles of impeachment charging Clinton with perjury and obstruction of justice. The following month, he became only the second president to go on trial in the Senate. The Constitution required a two-thirds majority to convict a president, but Republican and Democratic senators alike were well aware that Clinton remained surprisingly popular. In February 1999, the Senate acquitted Clinton on both articles of impeachment.

Like Andrew Johnson in 1868, Clinton held on to the presidency, but he lost the opportunity to make a major impact on public policy in his second term. Clinton's legacy would rest on his shrewd management of the economy and on his attempts to chart a course between liberalism and conservatism. His compromises and personal scandals ensured that his presidency would end with a sense of unfulfilled promise.

Emphasizing the unpopular impeachment issue in the fall elections in 1998, the Republicans barely managed to hold on to their majority in the House of Representatives. In the aftermath of the elections, Speaker of the House Newt Gingrich, plagued by questions about his own ethics, resigned from Congress. His designated successor suddenly admitted extramarital affairs and left as well.

Against this backdrop of frustration, the Republicans nominated George W. Bush, the governor of Texas, for president in 2000. The son of former president George Bush, the candidate benefited from the unity and enthusiasm of Republicans eager to reclaim the White House. He benefited, too, from the decision of the Democratic nominee, Vice President Al Gore of Tennessee, to distance himself from the record of the Clinton administration.

The cautious campaign suddenly became riveting on election night when the contest turned out to be too close to call. As the vote counts stretched into days and then weeks without a clear result, there were fears of a constitutional crisis. The battle turned on the vote in Florida, where Bush held a fluctuating lead of a few hundred votes. Determined to overcome that lead, the Gore campaign called for recounts in key counties, where the votes of his supporters had supposedly been rejected or undercounted. Inevitably, the contest spilled into local courts, the Florida Supreme Court, and the United States Supreme Court. Risking their credibility, the justices of the nation's highest court settled the partisan battle with a close 5-to-4 ruling that effectively halted the recounts. Certified the victor in Florida, George W. Bush became the president-elect.

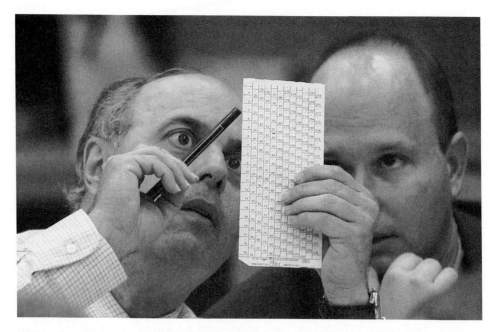

With no clear winner in the presidential election of 2000, attention focused on the closely contested state of Florida. Here, a judge and an observer try to decide how a voter's ballot should be counted in Broward County.

It was nearly the closest presidential election in American history. Gore actually won the popular ballot by 550,000 votes, but Bush won the electoral college, and therefore the election, with 271 votes to Gore's 266. The narrow margin of victory and the narrow differences between the two candidates emphasized the persistence of political deadlock and uncertainty. No party and no philosophy dominated American public life as the new century began.

Struggles Over Diversity and Rights

In the 1990s Americans continued to struggle with the diversity of their society. The wave of immigration made the nation even more heterogeneous than it was during the 1970s and 1980s. Since the 1940s, individuals and groups had been asserting their rights vigorously. In the 1990s the quest for rights took new and sometimes disturbing forms, as some Americans demanded the right to live without government interference.

The Impact of Immigration

Felix Andreev was part of a wave of immigration that took shape in the 1980s and crested in the 1990s. By 1999 the immigrant population had reached 26.3 million, nearly 10 percent of the population, the largest percentage of immigrants since before World War II.

The new immigrants were significant because of their origins as well as their numbers. Only 15 percent were European. In the 1990s more than a quarter of the immigrant population came from Mexico alone. Large numbers also came from the Philippines, China, Cuba, Jamaica, El Salvador, Poland, and the former East Germany.

The shift in immigrant origins should not have been surprising. The people of Eastern Europe and the third world, living with economic and political upheaval, had strong reason to come to the United States. Drawn by a strong job market throughout the United States, the new immigrants settled in all sorts of communities. Mexican immigrants, for instance, settled in small Midwestern towns and cities where semiskilled and unskilled jobs paid 10 and 15 times more than jobs in Mexico.

The majority of immigrants settled in only six states—California, Florida, New York, Texas, Illinois, and New Jersey—and were likely to live in large cities. As a result, the impact of the new immigration was highly concentrated and highly visible.

The effects of large, concentrated, non-western European immigration were especially evident in Miami, Florida. Since the 1960s, migration, particularly from nearby Cuba, had remade this formerly white-majority city. By the 1990s one-third of Miami's 2 million residents had Cuban origins. With substantial numbers of Colombians, Dominicans, Mexicans, Nicaraguans, and Peruvians as well, Miami had become the first major city with a Hispanic majority. The new immigration put considerable strain on Miami. Its schools and hospitals were overcrowded, and many longtime residents resented the new arrivals.

That was what some Americans believed would happen to the United States as a whole. By 2000, non-whites made up one-quarter of the population. Americans of Hispanic origin, both white and non-white, numbered some 35 million—almost 13 percent of the nation's population.

This was a disturbing prospect for some native-born Americans. They worried that immigration would hurt the country. In the short run, the critics of immigration charged, legal and illegal aliens would compete with the native-born population for jobs and drive down wages with their willingness to work cheaply. Native-born Americans complained that they had to pay high taxes to provide health care, education, and welfare for poor immigrants. In the long run, some native-born Americans feared, Spanish would rival English, immigrant cultures would dilute the dominant culture, and whites would lose political power.

Other native-born Americans were not so fearful. Immigration, they believed, had made the United States great in the first place. Instead of undermining the economy, they felt, immigrants would improve it; as in the past, immigrants would invigorate rather than overwhelm the dominant culture. Because of immigrants, the United States would remain a diverse, dynamic nation.

Inevitably, the disagreement over immigration spilled into politics. A new effort to restrict immigration began with the passage of the Immigration Reform and Control Act in 1986, which imposed penalties on Americans who knowingly brought illegal aliens into the country and hired them. The measure also offered amnesty to illegal aliens who had arrived since 1981.

The critics of immigration did not have much success when they tried to go further. In 1990 a revision of the federal immigration law raised the annual quota of immigrants who would be admitted. Illegal aliens were another matter. In 1994 California passed a state referendum denying illegal aliens access to public education and other benefits. In 1996 Congress appropriated more resources to stop the flow of illegal immigrants from Mexico.

Debating Diversity

Disagreements about diversity were at the heart of the immigration controversy. They also drove debates over two other charged issues: the status of the family and American culture. By the 1990s the ongoing transformation of the American family had become unmistakable. Married couples with children, 40 percent of all households as late as 1970, made up only 24 percent by 2000 (see Table 31–1). More Americans were living alone: The percentage of single-person households rose from 17 percent in 1970 to 26 percent in 2000. Families themselves were less likely to fit the traditional model. By 2000, 31 percent of families with children contained one parent rather than two.

A number of factors led to these changes. Americans were marrying later, having fewer children, and having them later in life. The divorce rate doubled from 1960 to 1990. In the 1990s about half of all marriages ended in divorce. As women's wages gradually rose, more women could afford to live alone or to head families by themselves.

Many conservatives and Republicans blamed these developments on the nation's moral decline. Allegedly, the counterculture of the 1960s, liberals, the media, feminists, gays, and others had undermined the nation's "family values." Some defenders of the family suggested that single mothers should receive fewer welfare benefits and that divorce should be made more difficult. Liberals fought back by denying that the family was dying. Instead, they argued, it was simply adapting to change as it always had. The different forms of the family, like diversity in general, were supposedly a good thing.

Liberals and conservatives also fought over the state of culture in America. Since the 1960s, the authority of the Western literary, artistic, and philosophical heritage had been under attack from several directions. Literary critics and other advocates of "deconstruction" had argued that Western culture was revered not because of intrinsic merit but because it reflected the interests of powerful Europeans and Americans. Other people, these critics felt, should be free to place a lesser value on Western culture.

Beginning in the 1960s, several groups did just that. Feminists, African Americans, gays, and other groups maintained that society in general and schools in particular needed to recognize the cultural contributions of the disadvantaged and the oppressed. Instead of worshiping one culture, America needed to practice multiculturalism. That demand horrified conservatives. Western cultural values were, they insisted, vitally important for the well-being of American society. The conservatives charged that the multiculturalists were destroying Western heritage and threatening free speech by making it impossible for anyone to question their positions.

TABLE 31–1

The Changing American Family, 1960–2000*

Year	Households	Families	Married-Couple Families	Single-Parent Families	One-Person Households
1960	52,799	44,905	23,358	3,332	6,917
1970	63,401	51,456	25,541	3,271	10,851
1980	80,776	58,426	24,961	6,061	18,296
1990	93,347	66,090	24,537	7,752	22,999
2000	104,705	72,025	25,248	9,357	26,724

Source: U.S. Census Bureau Web Site:
http://www.census.gov/population/socdemo/hh-fam/tabHH-1.xls and http://www.census.gov/population/socdemo/hh-fam/tabHH-4.xls
*Numbers given in thousands.

The conservatives also attacked the National Endowment for the Humanities (NEH) and the National Endowment for the Arts (NEA) for funding academic and artistic projects that flouted Western values. Liberals, academics, artists, and others defended the NEH, the NEA, and multiculturalism. It was the conservatives, they asserted, who were trying to censor curricula and wipe out diversity.

In the end, the controversies over culture and the family did little to undermine the new diversity of American life. Although Congress cut the budgets of the NEH and the NEA, these agencies survived the conservative attack. States did virtually nothing to make divorce more difficult. The trends toward diverse households and multiculturalism continued, but the controversies revealed just how deeply Americans were divided over diversity.

The Status of African Americans

While Americans debated diversity, individual groups continued to confront their unequal status. From the 1980s into the 1990s, African Americans made economic and political gains. The black middle class continued to grow. African Americans also made progress in electoral politics: In 1992 more than 10,000 African Americans held public office nationwide.

These achievements hardly marked the end to racial injustice and conflict. During the 1990s three episodes, each involving the nation's legal system, dramatized the continuing unequal status of African Americans. In 1991 George Bush nominated an African-American judge, Clarence Thomas, to succeed Thurgood Marshall on the Supreme Court. Thomas's selection proved controversial because of his conservative views, his lack of distinguished credentials, and allegations of sexual harassment made against him by a former subordinate, Anita Hill, an African-American lawyer. Angrily denying her story, Thomas denounced the hearings as "a high-tech lynching for uppity blacks." The Senate confirmed his nomination to the court, but Americans were left to wonder whether Thomas had been singled out for public embarrassment because of his race.

Soon after the Thomas hearings, a second episode exposed the legal system's unequal treatment of African Americans, provoked a race riot, and left lingering questions about the status of African Americans. In Los Angeles in 1991, white police stopped a black motorist, Rodney King, for drunk driving and then savagely beat him. Unknown to the officers, an onlooker had videotaped the beating. Despite the tape, an all-white jury acquitted four of the policemen of all charges on April 29, 1992. The stunning verdict set off rioting in the predominantly African-American community of South Central Los Angeles. Three days of violence left 51 people dead, 1,800 injured, and nearly 3,700 buildings burned.

In the aftermath, Americans debated whether the legal system offered justice to African Americans. They also argued over the cause of poverty and despair in South Central Los Angeles and other black communities. The Bush administration seemed to blame the welfare policy and other liberal programs of the Great Society. Democrats pointed to the welfare cuts and other policies of the Reagan administration. Neither side had concrete solutions for South Central Los Angeles. Subsequent rulings, which convicted two of the police for depriving King of his civil rights and awarded King $3.8 million in damages, failed to wash away the basic messages of the King beating and its violent aftermath. African Americans were less likely than whites to receive fair treatment from the police and the courts. More broadly, society seemed to have no answer for the problems of African-American poverty and inequality.

"We will not rest." In the spring of 1992, rioters in South Central Los Angeles protest the acquittal of white police officers charged with beating an African-American driver, Rodney King.

Less than three months after the damage award to King, another criminal case in Los Angeles raised some of the same questions about race and justice. In June 1994 Los Angeles police charged O.J. Simpson, a charismatic African-American actor, sports announcer, and former football star, with the stabbing murders of his white ex-wife and her male friend. During Simpson's criminal trial for the killings, his lawyers suggested that racist white police had lied and planted evidence. The mostly African-American jury acquitted Simpson in October 1995, but in a civil trial in February 1997, a mostly white jury ordered Simpson to pay millions of dollars in damages to the families of the victims. The Simpson case laid bare deep differences in outlook between whites and African Americans. Most whites believed him guilty; most African Americans believed him innocent.

The Simpson case, the King beating, and the Thomas hearings provoked passionate debate but relatively little action. The federal government did not take sweeping action to deal with African-American inequality. The administrations of both George Bush and Bill Clinton reflected Americans' apparent pessimism about race relations and government activism. Bush disliked affirmative action, but affirmative action programs largely remained in place. The president did sign the Civil Rights Act of 1991, which helped workers sue their employers for discrimination on the basis of race or sex. Although Clinton was supportive of affirmative action and civil rights, his administration did little to deal with the problems dramatized by the Thomas, King, and Simpson episodes.

Contesting Women's Rights

The economic gap between women and men continued to narrow during the decade. The percentage of adult women in the work force rose, as did the percentage of women in high-paying white-collar jobs. Women also played a larger role in government. After the 1992 elections, a record 53 women held seats in Congress.

Clinton selected the first female attorney general, Janet Reno, in 1993; the second female justice of the Supreme Court, Ruth Bader Ginsburg, in 1993; and the first female secretary of state, Madeleine Albright, in 1997.

Nevertheless, women faced continuing discrimination. A woman was likely to make less money than a man. She was also much more likely to live in poverty. Like African Americans, women were still underrepresented in government.

Controversies over sexual harassment also underscored the persistence of gender inequality. Several highly publicized incidents provoked widespread public discussion about the nature of relationships between men and women. The Clarence Thomas confirmation hearings were not only about race; they were also about gender. For many Americans, Thomas's alleged treatment of Anita Hill dramatized the widespread harassment of women in the workplace. President Clinton's affair with Monica Lewinsky further raised the issue of how men exploited their power over women.

As more women entered the military, the armed services also had to deal with the issue of harassment. In 1996 and 1997, the Army was rocked by numerous allegations that drill sergeants had sexually harassed female recruits. Then, in 2000, the Army supported a claim by its highest ranking female general that she had been sexually harassed by a male general.

Despite such revelations, the organized feminist movement did not grow dramatically. Many Americans seemed to accept the expansion of women's rights but to reject feminism. Feminists often found themselves defending earlier accomplishments rather than pushing for new objectives.

Abortion provided a case in point. From the 1980s into the 1990s the conservative Right to Life movement continued its passionate campaign against abortion. Protesters picketed abortion clinics and tried to discourage women from having abortions. Some radicals resorted to violence, including the murder of clinic workers. Meanwhile, George Bush condemned abortion as "murder" and, like Reagan before him, named anti-abortion judges to the federal courts.

In spite of this assault, the right and practice of abortion continued in the 1990s. In *Planned Parenthood* v. *Casey* in 1992, the Supreme Court voted narrowly to uphold much of a Pennsylvania law limiting access to abortions. But the court also declared that a woman's right to choose an abortion was "a component of liberty we cannot renounce." Later that year, Bush's defeat by Clinton, a strongly pro-choice Democrat, made abortion rights seem secure. Nevertheless, the struggle to shut down clinics and overturn *Roe* v. *Wade* continued.

Contesting Gay and Lesbian Rights

In a society struggling over diversity, homosexuality remained perhaps the most controversial difference of all. Like women and African Americans, gay men and lesbian women had made real gains since the 1960s. During the Bush administration, the federal government committed more resources to AIDS research. Meanwhile, gays became more accepted in society. Two openly gay men served in Congress. Many businesses, including Disneyland, welcomed gay customers. Leading corporations, including General Motors and Ford, began providing benefits to the partners of gay employees.

Nevertheless, homosexuals' calls for equal rights met with opposition. Although most Americans believed businesses should not discriminate on the basis of sexual preference, a majority still believed that homosexuality was morally wrong. Every year, there were hundreds of documented instances of violence against gays and lesbians. In 1998, Matthew Shepherd, a gay student at the University of Wyoming in

Laramie, was beaten, robbed, tied to a fence, pistol whipped, and left to die by two homophobic men who were later convicted of murder.

The resistance to gay rights was especially strong in the armed services. Officially barred from serving, homosexuals had long concealed their sexual orientation to remain in the military. By the 1990s, however, many gays called on the armed forces to allow openly homosexual officers and enlisted personnel. Then, in 1992 for the first time, a federal court ordered the Navy to reinstate an openly gay petty officer who had been discharged. Campaigning for president that year, Bill Clinton promised to lift the ban on gays in the armed services. Once in office, he met stiff resistance from military leaders and compromised by instituting a "don't ask, don't tell" policy. The military would no longer ask recruits whether they were gay, and gays and lesbians would continue to conceal their sexual orientation. It was unclear how long this uneasy compromise would survive.

There was no compromise in the struggle over legal protection for gay and lesbian rights in civilian life. In communities and states, homosexuals demanded laws that would prevent businesses from discriminating on the basis of sexual orientation. Conservatives moved to block these measures. In 1992 Colorado voters passed a state referendum forbidding communities to pass laws protecting gay rights, but the state's supreme court declared the referendum unconstitutional. In 1996 Congress passed the Defense of Marriage Act, which denied federal benefits to same-sex couples and allowed states to refuse to recognize same-sex marriages from other states. In 2000, the Supreme Court upheld the right of the Boy Scouts of America to dismiss a homosexual troop leader in New Jersey, despite the existence of a state gay rights law.

New Demands for Rights

While old battles for rights continued, the 1990s also saw new and unsettling demands for rights. A small number of Americans claimed the right for religious or political reasons to live free from governmental authority. That claim inevitably brought them into conflict with the federal government. The result was a series of deadly episodes that raised difficult questions about the way Washington used its power.

In 1992 Randy Weaver, a white separatist, failed to appear for a trial on weapons charges. Federal agents then converged on his remote cabin in Ruby Ridge, Idaho, to arrest him, but Weaver resisted. An 11-day siege, punctuated by two gun battles, ended with the deaths of Weaver's wife, one of his sons, and a federal marshal. For some Americans, Ruby Ridge demonstrated the arrogance and deceitfulness of the federal government. They felt vindicated in 1995 when Weaver was acquitted of assault and the U.S. Justice Department agreed to pay him a $3.1 million settlement. Five federal agents were suspended for misconduct, and one was convicted of obstruction of justice.

In 1993 another tragic siege provoked more charges about the arrogance of federal power. David Koresh, the leader of the tiny Branch Davidian religious sect, had gathered about 100 heavily armed followers in a compound outside Waco, Texas, to wait for the end of the world. When the federal Bureau of Alcohol, Tobacco, and Firearms (ATF) moved to arrest Koresh on weapons charges, a fierce gun battle killed four ATF agents and at least five Branch Davidians. Hundreds of law enforcement officers surrounded the compound. The stand-off continued for 51 days, until April 19, when federal agents pumped tear gas into the compound and it burned down. At least 72 Branch Davidians, including Koresh and 17 children, died—some from bullets fired by members of the sect. Many Americans blamed the horrifying fire on the insanity of Koresh, who considered himself the messiah. Others blamed the federal government, which had refused to delay its assault even though there were children in the compound. For critics of the government, Waco stood as a symbol of Washington's intolerance of personal and religious freedom.

The Waco and Ruby Ridge incidents inspired thousands of people to join right-wing paramilitary groups, known as "Patriots" and "civil militias," which trained with weapons to protect themselves from a supposedly hostile government. Some believed that the federal government, secretly controlled by foreign countries, was planning to take away Americans' guns and freedom. Others denied that local, state, or national government had the right to tax American citizens.

A handful of antigovernment extremists apparently did more than train with guns and denounce Washington. On April 19, 1995—the second anniversary of the Waco tragedy—a car bomb exploded in front of a federal building in Oklahoma City, Oklahoma. The blast killed 169 people, including small children in a day-care center. Americans were stunned over what was then the worst terrorist attack in the

The impact of domestic terrorism: Rescue workers and residents mourn the victims killed in the bombing of the Alfred P. Murrah Federal Building in Oklahoma City in 1995.

nation's history and were shocked when they learned the likely terrorists were not foreigners but Americans. In 1997 Timothy McVeigh, an Army veteran with ties to a right-wing militia group, was convicted of murdering victims of the bombing. A friend of McVeigh's confessed to a role in planning the bombing and another friend was convicted of conspiracy and manslaughter.

The Oklahoma City attack was followed by other incidents that raised fears of domestic terrorism, culminating at the 1996 Olympic games in Atlanta, Georgia, where a bomb went off in a crowded park, killing one person. The leading suspect in the bombing had vague ties to white supremacist, antigovernment groups.

The sudden spread of domestic terrorism emphasized that Americans' sense of rights was unsettling and divisive. The struggles over rights in a diverse society would continue, but Americans would soon be forced to focus on even greater threats from abroad.

From the Cold War to the War on Terrorism

America's role in the world, so plainly fixed for nearly half a century, suddenly became uncertain when the cold war ended with the collapse of Communist regimes in Eastern Europe and the Soviet Union. No longer preoccupied with the Soviet threat, Americans had to reconsider their needs and obligations as the only superpower in a changed world. For a moment in 1991, victory in the Persian Gulf War suggested that the United States might serve as an active international policeman in a "New World Order," but the moment passed. Americans were ambivalent about involvement in crises abroad. Then, in 2001, the worst terrorist attack in the nation's history led to a war on terrorism. As this unprecedented conflict began, it remained to be seen whether a new principle had emerged to guide American foreign policy in the post-cold-war world.

Victory in the Cold War

As President Ronald Reagan left office in 1989, the cold war continued to wind down. Fear and hatred no longer dominated relations between the United States and the Soviet Union. After more than 40 years of cold-war confrontations and crises, most Americans realized that neither the United States nor the Soviet Union was likely to attack the other without provocation. Both sides recognized that the cold war was enormously expensive and potentially tragic.

Reflecting this understanding, George Bush, built cautiously on the initiatives of the second Reagan administration. In 1990 Bush and Soviet leader Mikhail Gorbachev signed an agreement to end production of chemical weapons and reduce existing stockpiles. The next year, Bush and Gorbachev signed the START (Strategic Arms Reduction Talks) Treaty, which called for the United States and the USSR to cut back their arsenals of nuclear weapons by as much as 30 percent. Nuclear war seemed increasingly unlikely.

Gorbachev was willing to cooperate with the United States in part because his regime had grown so weak. In 1989 the Soviet Union could do nothing to stop the collapse of its repressive Communist allies in Eastern Europe. That year, the unpopular Communist regimes in Hungary and Poland had to agree to free elections. Hardline Communist regimes collapsed in Bulgaria, Czechoslovakia, and Romania as well. Most dramatically, a new East German government agreed to allow travel through the Berlin Wall. Intended to keep East Berliners from escaping into non-Communist West Berlin, the wall had long symbolized the cold-war division of Europe. As jubilant Berliners dismantled the wall, it symbolized the collapse of Communism in 1989.

The cold war ends: A man attacks the Berlin Wall, dividing East and West Germany, as onlookers cheer in 1989.

Powerless to stop its allies from abandoning Communism, the Soviet leadership soon found that it could not save itself. Despite Gorbachev's attempts to improve life in the Soviet Union, many people, like Felix Andreev, were still unhappy with the low standard of living, an unpopular war in Afghanistan, and the repressiveness of Communism. In 1990 Russia chose a charismatic president, Boris Yeltsin, who quit the Communist Party, supported independence for the republics, and challenged Gorbachev. The next year, Gorbachev resigned as party leader and president of the Soviet Union. The Soviet parliament suspended the Communist Party. As one republic after another declared its independence, the USSR ceased to exist.

The cold war was over, and the United States and its allies had clearly won. Around the world, capitalism and democracy seemed to be pushing back Communism. The United States now stood as the sole military superpower.

America's Role in a Changed World

With the cold war over, Americans had to reconsider their role in a changed world. Some Republicans called for a new, less internationalist foreign policy, insisting that the United States should no longer provide so much aid and military protection to other countries, especially in Europe.

In contrast, internationalists in both the Democratic and Republican parties believed the United States could protect itself and advance its political and economic interests only by participating actively in world affairs. Even though the cold war was over, America still faced a variety of challenges abroad. The best way to face those challenges was through international cooperation with NATO and the United Nations.

The most powerful internationalist was President Bush, who believed that American commitment to international freedom had won World War II, preserved the peace, and sustained the nation's economy for so many years. With the help of other powerful countries, Bush felt, America should use foreign aid, military strength, NATO, and the United Nations to maintain a stable international system, a New World Order. Like Woodrow Wilson and Harry Truman before him, Bush mixed together idealism and self-interest in his vision of the international political economy: A free world would be good both for other nations and for the United States. However, the president concluded, only American leadership could preserve that world.

The New World Order was a broad, vague concept. Bush and other internationalists had a hard time explaining just what overseas commitments America needed to make. It was also unclear whether the American people would endorse armed intervention abroad. Critics noted a tension between Bush's call for order and his support for democracy. Should the United States protect antidemocratic countries in the name of international stability and national prosperity?

There was also a tension between Bush's commitment to international cooperation and the long-standing tendency for the United States to act alone in its own hemisphere. While the president spoke of the New World Order, he intervened unilaterally in Panama in 1989. Frustrated with General Manuel Noriega, the Panamanian leader who engaged in drug sales to the United States and thwarted democratic elections, Bush dispatched American troops, who captured Noriega and sent him to the United States for prosecution on drug charges. Bush's unilateral action contradicted his rhetoric about international collaboration in the post-cold-war world.

The Persian Gulf War

The test of the New World Order came soon enough. On August 2, 1990, Iraq, led by President Saddam Hussein, overran Kuwait, its oil-rich but defenseless neighbor to the south. Entrenched in Kuwait, Iraq now threatened its much larger western neighbor, oil-producing Saudi Arabia. Hussein's actions clearly jeopardized America's oil supply and its Saudi Arabian ally and challenged George Bush's calls for a stable New World Order of free nations.

The president reacted firmly. Comparing Hussein to Hitler, Bush created an international coalition opposing Iraq. By the end of 1990 more than half a million U.S. troops had joined with forces from more than 30 nations in Operation Desert Shield to protect Saudi Arabia. Meanwhile, the United Nations imposed economic sanctions on Iraq and authorized the use of force if the Iraqis did not withdraw by January 15, 1991. Bush also obtained Congressional approval for the use of force.

When Hussein refused to pull back, Operation Desert Shield became Operation Desert Storm. As television audiences watched around the world on the night of January 17, coalition forces began an intensive air attack against Iraq. Hussein struck back by launching Scud missile attacks against America's ally, Israel, hundreds of miles away. The missiles did little damage and failed to provoke Israeli retaliation that might have split the coalition. Instead, coalition forces, led by U.S. General Norman Schwarzkopf, began a ground attack against the Iraqi army. In just

Saddam Hussein, the Iraqi president, speaks into a bank of microphones at a press conference.

100 hours, Schwarzkopf's solders swept into Kuwait, devastated the Iraqis, and pushed on into Iraq. Bush called a halt before the invasion reached the Iraqi capital of Baghdad and toppled Hussein.

At first, the Persian Gulf War seemed like a great victory. The United States lost only 148 troops while killing thousands of Iraqis. American technology appeared to work perfectly. Bush's popularity soared. The New World Order, at least for a moment, seemed like a practical reality.

Americans' euphoria over the Gulf War did not last, however. Studies showed that U.S. weapons had not worked quite so well, after all. Gulf War veterans began to suffer health problems possibly caused by exposure to Iraqi chemical weapons. Saddam Hussein held on to power and hindered implementation of the agreement ending the war. His aircraft soon encroached on so-called "no-fly" zones over northern and southern Iraq. Hussein also obstructed United Nations inspectors charged with searching for Iraqi chemical and nuclear weapons. In February 2001, the newly inaugurated George W. Bush ordered missile attacks against Iraqi forces in retaliation for violations of the no-fly zones. Despite his father's massive war effort, the goals of the New World Order had not been achieved. Hussein remained a threat to his neighbors and to American interests in the new century. In 2002 George W. Bush again considered the use of American force to topple Saddam Hussein, countered by opposition from within the United States and abroad.

Retreating from the New World Order

After the Persian Gulf War, the United States retreated from George Bush's vision of a New World Order. The American people were reluctant to accept the dangers of involvement abroad. That reluctance was apparent when violence followed the collapse of Communist rule in Yugoslavia in 1990. As this Eastern European country broke apart, three major ethnic groups—Muslim Slavs, Serbs, and Croatians— fought a bitter civil war in the newly independent province of Bosnia-Herzegovina. The remnants of the old Yugoslavia, under the harsh leadership of Slobodan Milosevic, aided the Serbs as they carried out "ethnic cleansing," the forcible expulsion of Muslims and Croats. Faced with the worst mass brutality in Europe since World War II, first George Bush and then Bill Clinton were unwilling to risk military involvement. In 1994 American and NATO planes and missiles attacked Bosnian Serb forces from the air. The following year, the warring parties accepted a peace agreement brokered by the United States. The Clinton administration committed 20,000 troops to join a peacekeeping force.

Yugoslavia posed a challenge again when the Milosevic regime mistreated and attacked ethnic Albanians in the region of Kosovo. The Clinton administration supported a NATO air offensive against the Yugoslavian government in March 1999. The 78-day war killed between 2,000 and 5,000 people, badly damaged Yugoslavia's infrastructure, and forced Milosevic to accept a multinational peacekeeping force. Ultimately, the United States had helped restore some peace to the regions of the former Yugoslavia. Yet, critics charged, millions had suffered and thousands had died before a cautious America had been willing to employ even a minimum of force.

The New World Order depended on maintaining the American power built up during the cold war, but reluctance to spend money and make international commitments diminished that power. As their budget declined, military leaders cut troops, closed bases, and reduced orders for new weapons. In 1993 the government officially abandoned the Strategic Defense Initiative or "Star Wars" project to create a space-based missile defense system. Meanwhile, intelligence operations struggled with tight budgets, low morale, and public criticism. The federal government's foreign aid budget stagnated in the 1990s. Washington also failed to keep up its promised payments to support the work of the United Nations.

The War on Terrorism

As the New World Order faded away, no single overarching principle emerged to direct the nation's diplomacy. After the cold war, anti-Communist passion no longer animated American foreign policy, and economic interests often swayed policy. For years, the United States had withheld diplomatic recognition of the Communist regime in Vietnam, mainly because of the possibility that MIAs—Americans missing in action during the war—might still be held captive. By the 1990s, there was no evidence that MIAs remained alive. Eager for trade with Vietnam, President Clinton announced full diplomatic recognition of this Communist nation in 1995.

Economic interests helped shape policy toward another Asian Communist regime, the People's Republic of China. Although the Chinese leadership clearly violated the human rights of its people, first George Bush and then Bill Clinton proved unwilling to disrupt developing economic ties with the world's most populous country. The Clinton administration pressed Congress to ease trade relations with the Asian nation.

As Clinton's policy toward China suggested, the American commitment to human rights was fairly weak. During Clinton's first term, he offended human rights advocates by sending boatloads of refugees back to Haiti to avoid angering voters who objected to the cost of caring for the new immigrants.

While Americans failed to show much enthusiasm for the New World Order, terrorism gradually forced them to reconsider the nation's foreign policy. In 1993, Middle Eastern terrorism reached into the United States. A car bomb exploded in the underground garage of one of the twin towers of New York City's giant office building complex, the World Trade Center. Six people were killed and more than 1,000 were injured. Investigators traced the attack to followers of a radical Islamic spiritual leader from Egypt, Sheikh Omar Abdel-Rahman. Rahman and more than a dozen associates were convicted for the World Trade Center bombing and other plots. In 1995 and 1996, terrorist bombings killed American soldiers and civilians in Saudi Arabia. In August 1998 bombs killed at least 190 people and wounded 5,000 at U.S. embassies in Kenya and Tanzania. Blaming the embassy attacks on Islamic fundamentalist terrorists funded by Saudi businessman Osama bin Laden, the United States launched missile attacks on targets in Afghanistan and the Sudan linked to bin Laden's organization.

Fire fighters work in the smoking rubble of one of the towers of the World Trade Center in New York City on September 11, 2001.

CHRONOLOGY

1988	George Bush elected president
1989	Collapse of Communist regimes in Eastern Europe Invasion of Panama
1990	Clean Air Act of 1990 signed First assisted suicide involving Jack Kevorkian Partial shutdown of federal government
1991	START (Strategic Arms Reduction Talks) Treaty with Soviet Union Persian Gulf War Civil Rights Act of 1991 Clarence Thomas named to U.S. Supreme Court Collapse of the Soviet Union
1992	Riot in Los Angeles after first Rodney King verdict Ruling in *Planned Parenthood* v. *Casey* Federal confrontation with Randy Weaver in Ruby Ridge, Idaho Bill Clinton elected president Ratification of Twenty-Seventh Amendment
1993	Car bombing of World Trade Center, New York City Burning of Branch Davidian complex at Waco, Texas Family and Medical Leave Act of 1993 signed Cancellation of Strategic Defense Initiative ("Star Wars") Ratification of North American Free Trade Agreement (NAFTA)

Despite these episodes, Americans remained fairly unconcerned about the threat of international terrorism. But on September 11, 2001, small groups of men linked to bin Laden hijacked four U.S. passenger jets soon after takeoff and aimed them at targets in New York City and Washington, DC. As onlookers watched in horror, two of the jets crashed into the upper floors of the World Trade Center's twin towers. Within two hours, both towers collapsed in clouds of smoke and debris, killing and wounding thousands of people. A third jet crashed into the Pentagon, killing and wounding hundreds. The fourth jet, apparently intended for a target in or near Washington, DC, crashed in western Pennsylvania. To stunned Americans, the attacks were a shocking revelation of their nation's vulnerability.

In the aftermath of the attacks, President George W. Bush committed the United States to a war on terrorism around the world. The President sent U.S. military forces to Afghanistan, whose ruling power, the Taliban, had sheltered bin Laden and his organization, Al-Qaeda. With the aid of British forces, the United States quickly drove the Taliban from power and paved the way for a new regime. Using sophisticated weaponry improved by experience in the Gulf War, American forces suffered hardly any casualties. But, as the fighting wound down in 2002, it

1994	Appointment of independent counsel Kenneth Starr in Whitewater affair
	Accusation of sexual harassment against Bill Clinton by Paula Jones
	Murder of Nicole Brown Simpson and Ronald Goldman
	Election of Republican majority to House of Representatives
	Adoption of Proposition 187 in California
1995	Bombing of federal building in Oklahoma City, Oklahoma
	Peace treaty in Bosnia-Herzegovina civil war
	U.S. diplomatic recognition of Socialist Republic of Vietnam
	Repeal of federal 55-mile-an-hour speed limit
	Million Man March
1996	Enactment of welfare reform
	Re-election of Bill Clinton as president
1998	Investigation of Bill Clinton's relationship with White House intern Monica Lewinsky
1999	Acquittal of Bill Clinton in Senate impeachment trial
	NATO air war against Yugoslavia
	Dow Jones Industrial Average over 10,000 for first time
2000	America Online acquisition of Time-Warner
	Breakup of Microsoft ordered by federal court
	Dow Jones Industrial Average begins historic decline
2001	George W. Bush elected president

was unclear whether bin Laden and much of Al-Qaeda had managed to escape to attack the United States again.

The uncertainty about bin Laden's fate was the not the only reason Americans remained fearful about terrorism. The attacks of September 11—known as 9/11—led to changes in American life. Air travelers had to undergo long, careful screening. A new federal agency, charged with protecting homeland security, issued regular alerts about the likelihood of terrorist attacks. Americans discovered, too, that those attacks could take a variety of deadly forms. Not long after 9/11, a series of letters apparently spread anthrax, a deadly bacteria, in postal facilities, federal offices, and newspaper and television news headquarters, killing two people and leaving several others ill.

Although the threat of terrorism changed American life, its impact was not as sweeping or as novel as many people expected. In some ways, the war on terrorism echoed the cold war. Like earlier presidents who confronted communism, George W. Bush did not seek a declaration of war, dramatically alter economic policy, or call on Americans to make major economic sacrifices to fight the new foreign threat. Despite 9/11, the daily routine of most Americans changed very little.

Nevertheless, the war on terrorism was unpredictable. Much as Americans feared terrorist attacks, they also worried about the challenge of combating terrorism. As the campaign in Afghanistan ended, George W. Bush increasingly focused on the threat posed by the regime of Saddam Hussein in Iraq. The president accused Hussein of supporting terrorism and attempting to build weapons of mass destruction. The prospect of war with Iraq underscored how difficult it was to reorient American foreign policy around the confrontation with terrorism. Abroad, American allies warned that an invasion of Iraq would cost the United States political support. At home, even Republican supporters of the Bush administration worried that such an invasion was too costly. It was by no means clear that Americans were ready to accept a war on terrorism as the guiding principle of their nation's foreign policy.

CONCLUSION

At the start of the twenty-first century, Americans lived with uncertainty. An older nation, defined by the cold war, New Deal liberalism, and the industrial economy, was fading away, but the outlines of a new America remained indistinct. For Felix Andreev and other Americans, the United States still meant prosperity and freedom, but how would prosperity and freedom be maintained? There was no sure answer. The postindustrial economy was still evolving, as was the nation's role in the post-cold-war world. American politics, caught between liberalism and conservatism, reflected all these uncertainties. Like so many people before them, Felix Andreev and the rest of the nation would define the meaning of America in a new century.

FURTHER READINGS

Stephanie Coontz, *The Way We Really Are: Coming to Terms With America's Changing Families* (1997). Coontz's book details family life in the 1990s.

Lawrence Freedman and Efraim Karsh, *The Gulf Conflict, 1990–1991: Diplomacy and War in the New World Order* (1993). This work carefully analyzes the international context of the Gulf War.

Raymond L. Garthoff, *The Great Transition: American–Soviet Relations and the End of the Cold War* (1994). A thorough narrative of the end of the US–USSR confrontation.

Jane Mayer and Jill Abramson, *Strange Justice: The Selling of Clarence Thomas* (1994). A journalistic account of the Hill–Thomas confrontation.

New York Times, ed., *The Downsizing of America* (1996). A detailed investigation of the social impact of corporate cutbacks.

Herbert S. Parmet, *George Bush: The Life of a Lone Star Yankee* (1997). The first scholarly biography of George H. Bush by a historian.

Sanford J. Ungar, *Fresh Blood: The New American Immigrants* (1995). A readable account, based on interviews, of the social and political aspects of the new immigration.

 Please refer to the document CD-ROM for primary sources related to this chapter.

APPENDIX

The Declaration of Independence

When in the course of human events it becomes necessary for one people to dissolve the political bands which have connected them with another and to assume, among the powers of the earth, the separate and equal station to which the laws of nature and of nature's God entitle them, a decent respect to the opinions of mankind requires that they should declare the causes which impel them to the separation.

We hold these truths to be self-evident, that all men are created equal; that they are endowed by their Creator with certain unalienable rights; that among these are life, liberty, and the pursuit of happiness. That, to secure these rights, governments are instituted among men, deriving their just powers from the consent of the governed; that, whenever any form of government becomes destructive of these ends, it is the right of the people to alter or to abolish it, and to institute a new government, laying its foundation on such principles, and organizing its powers in such form, as to them shall seem most likely to effect their safety and happiness. Prudence, indeed, will dictate that governments long established should not be changed for light and transient causes; and, accordingly, all experience hath shown that mankind are more disposed to suffer, while evils are sufferable, than to right themselves by abolishing the forms to which they are accustomed. But when a long train of abuses and usurpations, pursuing invariably the same object, evinces a design to reduce them under absolute despotism, it is their right, it is their duty, to throw off such government and to provide new guards for their future security. Such has been the patient sufferance of these colonies, and such is now the necessity which constrains them to alter their former systems of government. The history of the present King of Great Britain is a history of repeated injuries and usurpations, all having, in direct object, the establishment of an absolute tyranny over these States. To prove this, let facts be submitted to a candid world:

He has refused his assent to laws the most wholesome and necessary for the public good.

He has forbidden his governors to pass laws of immediate and pressing importance, unless suspended in their operation till his assent should be obtained; and, when so suspended, he has utterly neglected to attend to them.

He has refused to pass other laws for the accommodation of large districts of people, unless those people would relinquish the right of representation in the legislature, a right inestimable to them and formidable to tyrants only.

He has called together legislative bodies at places unusual, uncomfortable, and distant from the depository of their public records, for the sole purpose of fatiguing them into compliance with his measures.

He has dissolved representative houses, repeatedly for opposing, with manly firmness, his invasions on the rights of the people.

He has refused, for a long time after such dissolutions, to cause others to be elected; whereby the legislative powers, incapable of annihilation, have returned to the people at large for their exercise; the state remaining, in the meantime, exposed to all the danger of invasion from without and convulsions within.

He has endeavored to prevent the population of these States; for that purpose, obstructing the laws for naturalization of foreigners, refusing to pass others to encourage their migration hither, and raising the conditions of new appropriations of lands.

He has obstructed the administration of justice by refusing his assent to laws for establishing judiciary powers.

He has made judges dependent on his will alone for the tenure of their offices and the amount and payment of their salaries.

He has erected a multitude of new offices and sent hither swarms of officers to harass our people and eat out their substance.

He has kept among us, in time of peace, standing armies, without the consent of our legislatures.

He has affected to render the military independent of, and superior to, the civil power.

He has combined with others to subject us to a jurisdiction foreign to our Constitution and unacknowledged by our laws, giving his assent to their acts of pretended legislation—

For quartering large bodies of armed troops among us;

For protecting them, by mock trial, from punishment for any murders which they should commit on the inhabitants of these States;

For cutting off our trade with all parts of the world;

For imposing taxes on us without our consent;

For depriving us, in many cases, of the benefit of trial by jury;

For transporting us beyond seas to be tried for pretended offences;

For abolishing the free system of English laws in a neighboring province, establishing therein an arbitrary government, and enlarging its boundaries, so as to render it at once an example and fit instrument for introducing the same absolute rule into these colonies;

For taking away our charters, abolishing our most valuable laws, and altering, fundamentally, the powers of our governments.

For suspending our own legislatures and declaring themselves invested with power to legislate for us in all cases whatsoever.

He has abdicated government here by declaring us out of his protection and waging war against us.

He has plundered our seas, ravaged our coasts, burnt our towns, and destroyed the lives of our people.

He is, at this time, transporting large armies of foreign mercenaries to complete the works of death, desolation, and tyranny already begun with circumstances of cruelty and perfidy scarcely paralleled in the most barbarous ages, and totally unworthy the head of a civilized nation.

He has constrained our fellow citizens, taken captive on the high seas, to bear arms against their country, to become the executioners of their friends and brethren, or to fall themselves by their hands.

He has excited domestic insurrections amongst us and has endeavored to bring on the inhabitants of our frontiers, the merciless Indian savages, whose known rule of warfare is an undistinguished destruction of all ages, sexes, and conditions.

In every stage of these oppressions, we have petitioned for redress in the most humble terms; our repeated petitions have been answered only by repeated injury. A prince whose character is thus marked by every act which may define a tyrant is unfit to be the ruler of a free people.

Nor have we been wanting in attention to our British brethren. We have warned them, from time to time, of attempts made by their legislature to extend an unwarrantable jurisdiction over us. We have reminded them of the circumstances of our emigration and settlement here. We have appealed to their native justice and magnanimity, and we have conjured them, by the ties of our common kindred, to disavow these usurpations, which would inevitably interrupt our connections and correspondence. They, too, have been deaf to the voice of justice and consanguinity. We must, therefore, acquiesce in the necessity which denounces our separation, and hold them, as we hold the rest of mankind, enemies in war, in peace, friends.

We, therefore, the representatives of the United States of America, in general Congress assembled, appealing to the Supreme Judge of the world for the rectitude of our intentions, do, in the name and by the authority of the good people of these colonies, solemnly publish and declare, that these united colonies are, and of right ought to be, free and independent states: that they are absolved from all allegiance to the British Crown, and that all political connection between them and the state of Great Britain is, and ought to be, totally dissolved; and that, as free and independent states, they have full power to levy war, conclude peace, contract alliances, establish commerce, and to do all other acts and things which independent states may of right do. And, for the support of this declaration, with a firm reliance on the protection of Divine Providence, we mutually pledge to each other our lives, our fortunes, and our sacred honor.

The Constitution of the United States of America

We the people of the United States, in order to form a more perfect union, establish justice, insure domestic tranquillity, provide for the common defense, promote the general welfare, and secure the blessings of liberty to ourselves and our posterity, do ordain and establish this Constitution for the United States of America.

Article I

SECTION 1. All legislative powers herein granted shall be vested in a Congress of the United States, which shall consist of a Senate and House of Representatives.

SECTION 2. 1. The House of Representatives shall be composed of members chosen every second year by the people of the several States, and the electors in each State shall have the qualifications requisite for electors of the most numerous branch of the State legislature.

2. No person shall be a representative who shall not have attained to the age of twenty-five years, and been seven years a citizen of the United States, and who shall not, when elected, be an inhabitant of that State in which he shall be chosen.

3. Representatives and direct taxes[1] shall be apportioned among the several States which may be included within this Union, according to their respective numbers, which shall be determined by adding to the whole number of free persons, including those bound to service for a term of years, and excluding Indians not taxed, three fifths of all other persons.[2] The actual enumeration shall be made within three years after the first meeting of the Congress of the United States, and within every subsequent term of ten years, in such manner as they shall be law direct. The number of representatives shall not exceed one for every thirty thousand, but each State shall have at least one representative; and until such enumeration shall be made, the State of New Hampshire shall be entitled to choose three, Massachusetts eight, Rhode Island and Providence Plantations one, Connecticut five, New York six, New Jersey four, Pennsylvania eight, Delaware one, Maryland six, Virginia ten, North Carolina five, South Carolina five, and Georgia three.

4. When vacancies happen in the representation from any State, the executive authority thereof shall issue writs of election to fill such vacancies.

5. The House of Representatives shall choose their speaker and other officers; and shall have the sole power of impeachment.

SECTION 3. 1. The Senate of the United States shall be composed of two senators from each State, chosen by the legislature thereof,[3] for six years; and each senator shall have one vote.

2. Immediately after they shall be assembled in consequence of the first election, they shall be divided as equally as may be into three classes. The seats of the senators of the first class shall be vacated at the expiration of the second year, of the second class at the expiration of the fourth year, and of the third class at the expiration of the sixth year, so that one third may be chosen every second year; and if vacancies happen by resignation, or otherwise, during the recess of the legislature of any State, the executive thereof may make temporary appointments until the next meeting of the legislature, which shall then fill such vacancies.[4]

3. No person shall be a senator who shall not have attained to the age of thirty years, and been nine years a citizen of the United States, and who shall not, when elected, be an inhabitant of that State for which he shall be chosen.

4. The Vice President of the United States shall be President of the Senate, but shall have no vote, unless they be equally divided.

5. The Senate shall choose their other officers, and also a president pro tempore, in the absence of the Vice President, or when he shall exercise the office of the President of the United States.

6. The Senate shall have the sole power to try all impeachments. When sitting for that purpose, they shall be on oath or affirmation. When the president of the United States is tried, the chief justice shall preside: and no person shall be convicted without the concurrence of two thirds of the members present.

7. Judgment in cases of impeachment shall not extend further than to removal from

[1]See the Sixteenth Amendment.
[2]See the Fourteenth Amendment.

[3]See the Seventeenth Amendment.
[4]See the Seventeenth Amendment.

office, and disqualification to hold and enjoy any office of honor, trust or profit under the United States: but the party convicted shall nevertheless be liable and subject to indictment, trial, judgment and punishment, according to law.

SECTION 4. 1. The times, places, and manner of holding elections for senators and representatives, shall be prescribed in each State by the legislature thereof; but the Congress may at any time by law make or alter such regulations, except as to the places of choosing senators.

2. The Congress shall assemble at least once in every year, and such meeting shall be on the first Monday in December, unless they shall by law appoint a different day.

SECTION 5. 1. Each House shall be the judge of the elections, returns and qualifications of its own members, and a majority of each shall constitute a quorum to do business; but a smaller number may adjourn from day to day, and may be authorized to compel the attendance of absent members, in such manner, and under such penalties as each House may provide.

2. Each House may determine the rules of its proceedings, punish its members for disorderly behavior, and, with the concurrence of two thirds, expel a member.

3. Each House shall keep a journal of its proceedings, and from time to time publish the same, excepting such parts as may in their judgment require secrecy; and the yeas and nays of the members of either house on any question shall, at the desire of one fifth of those present, be entered on the journal.

4. Neither House, during the session of Congress, shall, without the consent of the other, adjourn for more than three days, nor to any other place than that in which the two Houses shall be sitting.

SECTION 6. 1. The senators and representatives shall receive a compensation for their services, to be ascertained by law, and paid out of the Treasury of the United States. They shall in all cases, except treason, felony, and breach of the peace, be privileged from arrest during their attendance at the session of their respective Houses, and in going to and returning from the same; and for any speech or debate in either House, they shall not be questioned in any other place.

2. No senator or representative shall, during the time for which he was elected, be appointed to any civil office under the authority of the United States, which shall have been created, or the emoluments whereof shall have been increased, during such time; and no person holding any office under the United States shall be a member of either House during his continuance in office.

SECTION 7. 1. All bills for raising revenue shall originate in the House of Representatives; but the Senate may purpose or concur with amendments as on other bills.

2. Every bill which shall have passed the House of Representatives and the Senate, shall, before it become a law, be presented to the President of the United States; if he approves he shall sign it, but if not he shall return it, with his objections, to that House in which it shall have originated, who shall enter the objections at large on their journal, and proceed to reconsider it. If after such reconsideration two thirds of that House shall agree to pass the bill, it shall be sent, together with the objections, to the other House, by which it shall likewise be reconsidered, and if approved by two thirds of that House, it shall become a law. But in all such cases the votes of both Houses shall be determined by yeas and nays, and the names of the persons voting for and against the bill shall be entered on the journal of each House respectively. If any bill shall not be returned by the President within ten days (Sundays excepted) after it shall have been presented to him, the same shall be a law, in like manner as if he had signed it, unless the Congress by their adjournment prevent its return, in which case it shall not be a law.

3. Every order, resolution, or vote to which the concurrence of the Senate and the House of Representatives may be necessary (except on a question of adjournment) shall be presented to the President of the United States; and before the same shall take effect, shall be approved by him, or being disapproved by him, shall be repassed by two thirds of the Senate and House of Representatives, according to the rules and limitations prescribed in the case of a bill.

SECTION 8. The Congress shall have the power

1. To lay and collect taxes, duties, imposts, and excises, to pay the debts and provide for the common defense and general welfare of the United States; but all duties, imposts, and excises shall be uniform throughout the United States.

2. To borrow money on the credit of the United States;

3. To regulate commerce with foreign nations, and among the several States, and with the Indian tribes;

4. To establish a uniform rule of naturalization, and uniform laws on the subject of bankruptcies throughout the United States;

5. To coin money, regulate the value thereof, and of foreign coin, and fix the standard of weights and measures;

6. To provide for the punishment of counterfeiting the securities and current coin of the United States;

7. To establish post offices and post roads;

8. To promote the progress of science and useful arts, by securing for limited times to authors and inventors the exclusive right to their respective writings and discoveries;

9. To constitute tribunals inferior to the Supreme Court;

10. To define and punish piracies and felonies committed on the high seas, and offenses against the law of nations;

11. To declare war, grant letters of marque and reprisal, and make rules concerning captures on land and water;

12. To raise and support armies, but no appropriation of money to that use shall be for a longer term than two years;

13. To provide and maintain a navy;

14. To make rules for the government and regulation of the land and naval forces;

15. To provide for calling forth the militia to execute the laws of the Union, suppress insurrections and repel invasions;

16. To provide for organizing, arming, and disciplining the militia, and for governing such part of them as may be employed in the service of the United States, reserving to the States respectively, the appointment of the officers, and the authority of training the militia according to the discipline prescribed by Congress;

17. To exercise exclusive legislation in all cases whatsoever, over such district (not exceeding ten miles square) as may, by cession of particular States, and the acceptance of Congress, become the seat of the government of the United States, and to exercise like authority over all places purchased by the consent of the legislature of the State in which the same shall be, for the erection of forts, magazines, arsenals, dockyards, and other needful buildings; and

18. To make all laws which shall be necessary and proper for carrying into execution the foregoing powers, and all other powers vested by this Constitution in the government of the United States, or any department or officer thereof.

SECTION 9. 1. The migration or importation of such persons as any of the States now existing shall think proper to admit, shall not be prohibited by the Congress prior to the year one thousand eight hundred and eight, but a tax or duty may be imposed on such importation, not exceeding ten dollars for each person.

2. The privilege of the writ of habeas corpus shall not be suspended, unless when in cases of rebellion or invasion the public safety may require it.

3. No bill of attainder or ex post facto law shall be passed.

4. No capitation, or other direct, tax shall be laid, unless in proportion to the census or enumeration herein-before directed to be taken.[5]

5. No tax or duty shall be laid on articles exported from any State.

6. No preference shall be given by any regulation of commerce or revenue to the ports of one State over those of another: nor shall vessels bound to, or from, one State be obliged to enter, clear, or pay duties in another.

7. No money shall be drawn from the treasury, but in consequence of appropriations made by law; and a regular statement and account of the receipts and expenditures of all public money shall be published from time to time.

8. No title of nobility shall be granted by the United States: and no person holding any office of profit or trust under them, shall, without the consent of the Congress, accept of any present, emolument, office, or title, of any kind whatever, from any king, prince, or foreign State.

SECTION 10. 1. No State shall enter into any treaty, alliance, or confederation; grant letters of marque and reprisal; coin money; emit bills of credit; make any thing but gold and silver coin a tender in payment of debts; pass any bill of attainder, ex post facto law, or law impairing the obligation of contracts, or grant, any title of nobility.

2. No State shall, without the consent of the Congress, lay any imposts or duties on imports or exports, except what may be absolutely necessary for executing its inspection laws: and the net produce of all duties and imposts laid by any State on imports or exports,

[5]See the Sixteenth Amendment.

shall be for the use of the treasury of the United States; and all such laws shall be subject to the revision and control of the Congress.

3. No State shall, without the consent of the Congress, lay any duty of tonnage, keep troops, or ships of war in time of peace, enter into any agreement or compact with another State, or with a foreign power, or engage in war, unless actually invaded, or in such imminent danger as will not admit of delay.

Article II

SECTION I. 1. The executive power shall be vested in a President of the United States of America. He shall hold his office during the term of four years, and, together with the Vice President, chosen for the same term, be elected, as follows:

2. Each State shall appoint, in such manner as the legislature thereof may direct, a number of electors, equal to the whole number of senators and representatives to which the State may be entitled in the Congress: but no senator or representative, or person holding any office of trust or profit under the United States, shall be appointed an elector.

The electors shall meet in their respective States, and vote by ballot for two persons, of whom one at least shall not be an inhabitant of the same State with themselves. And they shall make a list of all the persons voted for, and of the number of votes for each; which list they shall sign and certify, and transmit sealed to the seat of the government of the United States, directed to the president of the Senate. The president of the Senate shall, in the presence of the Senate and House of Representatives, open all the certificates, and the votes shall then be counted. The person having the greatest number of votes shall be the President, if such number be a majority of the whole number of electors appointed; and if there be more than one who have such majority, and have an equal number of votes, then the House of Representatives shall immediately choose by ballot one of them for President; and if no person have a majority, then from the five highest on the list the said House shall in like manner choose the President. But in choosing the President, the votes shall be taken by States, the representation from each State having one vote; a quorum for this purpose shall consist of a member or members from two thirds of the States, and a majority of all the States shall be necessary to a choice. In every case after the choice of the President, the person having the greatest number of votes of the electors shall be the Vice President. But if there should remain two or more who have equal votes, the Senate shall choose from them by ballot the Vice President.[6]

3. The Congress may determine the time of choosing the electors, and the day on which they shall give their votes; which day shall be the same throughout the United States.

4. No person except a natural born citizen, or a citizen of the United States, at the time of the adoption of this Constitution, shall be eligible to the office of President; neither shall any person be eligible to the office who shall not have attained to the age of thirty-five years, and been fourteen years a resident within the United States.

5. In case of the removal of the President from office, or of his death, resignation, or inability to discharge the powers and duties of the said office, the same shall devolve on the Vice President, and the Congress may by law provide for the case of removal, death, resignation or inability, both of the President and Vice President, declaring what officer shall then act as President, and such officer shall act accordingly until the disability be removed, or a President shall be elected.

6. The President shall, at stated times, receive for his services a compensation which shall neither be increased nor diminished during the period for which he shall have been elected, and he shall not receive within that period any other emolument from the United States, or any of them.

7. Before he enter on the execution of his office, he shall take the following oath or affirmation:—"I do solemnly swear (or affirm) that I will faithfully execute the office of president of the United States, and will to the best of my ability, preserve, protect and defend the Constitution of the United States."

SECTION 2. 1. The President shall be commander in chief of the army and navy of the United States, and of the militia of the several States, when called into the actual service of the United States; he may require the opinion in writing, of the principal officer in each of the executive departments, upon any subject relating to the duties of their respective offices, and he shall have power to grant reprieves and pardons for

[6]Superseded by the Twelfth Amendment.

offenses against the United States, except in cases of impeachment.

2. He shall have power, by and with the advice and consent of the Senate, to make treaties, provided two thirds of the senators present concur; and he shall nominate, and by and with the advice and consent of the Senate, shall appoint ambassadors, other public ministers and consuls, judges of the Supreme Court, and all other officers of the United States, whose appointments are not herein otherwise provided for, and which shall be established by law; but the Congress may by law vest the appointment of such inferior officers, as they think proper, in the President alone, in the courts of laws, or in the heads of departments.

3. The President shall have power to fill up all vacancies that may happen during the recess of the Senate, by granting commissions which shall expire at the end of their next session.

SECTION 3. He shall from time to time give to the Congress information of the state of the Union, and recommend to their consideration such measures as he shall judge necessary and expedient; he may, on extraordinary occasions, convene both houses, or either of them, and in case of disagreement between them with respect to the time of adjournment, he may adjourn them to such time as he shall think proper; he shall receive ambassadors and other public ministers; he shall take care that the laws be faithfully executed, and shall commission all the officers of the United States.

SECTION 4. The President, Vice President, and all civil officers of the United States, shall be removed from office on impeachment for, and conviction of, treason, bribery, or other high crimes and misdemeanors.

Article III

SECTION 1. The judicial power of the United States shall be vested in one Supreme Court, and in such inferior courts as the Congress may from time to time ordain and establish. The judges, both of the Supreme and inferior courts, shall hold their offices during good behavior, and shall, at stated times, receive for their services, a compensation, which shall not be diminished during their continuance in office.

SECTION 2. 1. The judicial power shall extend to all cases, in law and equity, arising under this Constitution, the laws of the United States, and treaties made, or which shall be made, under their authority;—to all cases of admiralty and maritime jurisdiction;—to controversies to which the United States shall be a party;[7]—to controversies between two or more States;—between a State and citizens of another State;—between citizens of different States;—between citizens of the same State claiming lands under grants of different States, and between a State, or the citizens thereof, and foreign States, citizens or subjects.

2. In all cases affecting ambassadors, other public ministers and consuls, and those in which a State shall be party, the Supreme Court shall have original jurisdiction. In all the other cases before mentioned, the Supreme Court shall have appellate jurisdiction, both as to law and fact, with such exceptions, and under such regulations as the Congress shall make.

3. The trial of all crimes, except in cases of impeachment, shall be by jury; and such trial shall be held in the State where the said crimes shall have been committed; but when not committed within any State, the trial shall be such place or places as the Congress may by law have directed.

SECTION 3. 1. Treason against the United States shall consist only in levying war against them, or in adhering to their enemies, giving them aid and comfort. No person shall be convicted of treason unless on the testimony of two witnesses to the same overt act, or on confession in open court.

2. The Congress shall have power to declare the punishment of treason, but no attainder of treason shall work corruption of blood, or forfeiture except during the life of the person attained.

Article IV

SECTION 1. Full faith and credit shall be given in each State to the public acts, records, and judicial proceedings of every other State. And the Congress may by general laws prescribe the manner in which such acts, records and proceedings shall be proved, and the effect thereof.

SECTION 2. 1. The citizens of each State shall be entitled to all privileges and immunities of citizens in the several States.[8]

2. A person charged in any State with treason, felony, or other crime, who shall flee from justice, and be found in another State, shall on demand of the executive authority of the State from which he fled, be delivered up to

[7]See the Eleventh Amendment.
[8]See the Fourteenth Amendment, Sec. 1.

be removed to the State having jurisdiction of the crime.

3. No person held to service or labor in one State under the laws thereof, escaping into another, shall, in consequence of any law or regulation therein, be discharged from such service or labor, but shall be delivered up on claim of the party to whom such service or labor may be due.[9]

SECTION 3. 1. New States may be admitted by the Congress into this Union; but no new State shall be formed or erected within the jurisdiction of any other State, nor any State be formed by the junction of two or more States, or parts of States, without the consent of the legislatures of the States concerned as well as of the Congress.

2. The Congress shall have power to dispose of and make all needful rules and regulations respecting the territory or other property belonging to the United States; and nothing in this Constitution shall be so construed as to prejudice any claims of the United States, / particular State.

SECTION 4. The United States shall guarantee to every State in this Union a republican form of government, and shall protect each of them against invasion; and on application of the legislature, or of the executive (when the legislature cannot be convened) against domestic violence.

Article V

The Congress, whenever two thirds of both Houses shall deem it necessary, shall propose amendments to this Constitution, or, on the application of the legislatures of two thirds of the several States, shall call a convention for proposing amendments, which in either case shall be valid to all intents and purposes, as part of this Constitution, when ratified by the legislatures of three fourths of the several States, or by conventions in three fourths thereof, as the one or the other mode of ratification may be proposed by the Congress; Provided that no amendment which may be made prior to the year one thousand eight hundred and eight shall in any manner affect the first and fourth clauses in the ninth section of the first article; and that no State, without its consent, shall be deprived of its equal suffrage in the Senate.

Article VI

1. All debts contracted and engagements entered into, before the adoption of this Constitution, shall be as valid against the United States under this Constitution, as under the Confederation.[10]

2. This Constitution, and the laws of the United States which shall be made in pursuance thereof; and all treaties made, or which shall be made, under the authority of the United States, shall be the supreme law of the land; and the judges in every State shall be bound thereby, any thing in the Constitution or laws of any State to the contrary notwithstanding.

3. The senators and representatives before mentioned, and the members of the several State legislatures, and all executive and judicial officers, both of the United States and of the several States, shall be bound by oath or affirmation to support this Constitution; but no religious test shall ever be required as a qualification to any office or public trust under the United States.

Article VII

The ratification of the conventions of nine States shall be sufficient for the establishment of this Constitution between the States so ratifying the same.

Done in Convention by the unanimous consent of the States present the seventeenth day of September in the year of our Lord one thousand seven hundred and eighty-seven, and of the independence of the United States of America the twelfth. In witness whereof we have hereunto subscribed our names.

Articles in addition to, and amendment of, the Constitution of the United States of America, proposed by Congress, and ratified by the legislatures of the several States, pursuant to the fifth article of the original Constitution.

Amendment I

[First ten amendments ratified December 15, 1791]

Congress shall make no law respecting an establishment of religion, or prohibiting the free exercise thereof; or abridging the freedom of speech, or of the press; or the right of the people peaceably to assemble, and to petition the government for a redress of grievances.

Amendment II

A well regulated militia, being necessary to the security of a free State, the right of the people to keep and bear arms, shall not be infringed.

---

[9]See the Thirteenth Amendment.

[10]See the Fourteenth Amendment, Sec. 4.

Amendment III

No soldier shall, in time of peace be quartered in any house, without the consent of the owner, nor in time of war, but in a manner to be prescribed by law.

Amendment IV

The right of the people to be secure in their persons, houses, papers, and effects, against unreasonable searches and seizures, shall not be violated, and no warrants shall issue, but upon probable cause, supported by oath or affirmation, and particularly describing the place to be searched, and the persons or things to be seized.

Amendment V

No person shall be held to answer for a capital or otherwise infamous crime, unless on a presentment or indictment of a grand jury, except in cases arising in the land or naval forces, or in the militia, when in actual service in time of war or public danger; nor shall any person be subject for the same offense to be twice put in jeopardy of life or limb; nor shall be compelled in any criminal case to be a witness against himself, nor be deprived of life, liberty, or property, without due process of law; nor shall private property be taken for public use, without just compensation.

Amendment VI

In all criminal prosecutions, the accused shall enjoy the right to a speedy and public trial, by an impartial jury of the State and district wherein the crime shall have been committed, which district shall have been previously ascertained by law, and to be informed of the nature and cause of the accusation; to be confronted with the witnesses against him; to have compulsory process for obtaining witnesses in his favor, and to have the assistance of counsel for his defense.

Amendment VII

In suits at common law, where the value in controversy shall exceed twenty dollars, the right of trial by jury shall be preserved, and no fact tried by a jury shall be otherwise reexamined in any court of the United States, than according to the rules of the common law.

Amendment VIII

Excessive bail shall not be required, nor excessive fines imposed, nor cruel and unusual punishments inflicted.

Amendment IX

The enumeration in the Constitution of certain rights shall not be construed to deny or disparage others retained by the people.

Amendment X

The powers not delegated to the United States by the Constitution, nor prohibited by it to the States, are reserved to the States respectively, or to the people.

Amendment XI [January 8, 1798]

The judicial power of the United States shall not be construed to extend to any suit in law or equity, commended or prosecuted against one of the United States by citizens of another State, or by citizens or subjects of any foreign State.

Amendment XII [September 25, 1804]

The electors shall meet in their respective States, and vote by ballot for President and Vice President, one of whom, at least, shall not be an inhabitant of the same State with themselves; they shall name in their ballots the person voted for as President, and in distinct ballots, the person voted for as Vice President, and they shall make distinct lists of all persons voted for as President and of all persons voted for as Vice President, and of the number of votes for each, which lists they shall sign and certify, and transmit sealed to the seat of the government of the United States, directed to the President of the Senate;—The President of the Senate shall, in the presence of the Senate and House of Representatives, open all the certificates and the votes shall then be counted;—The person having the greatest number of votes for President, shall be the President, if such number be a majority of the whole number of electors appointed; and if no person have such majority, then from the persons having the highest numbers not exceeding three on the list of those voted for as President, the House of Representatives shall choose immediately, by ballot, the President. But in choosing the President, the votes shall be taken by States, the representation from each State having one vote; a quorum for this purpose shall consist of a member or members from two thirds of the States, and a majority of all the States shall be necessary to a choice. And if the House of Representatives shall not choose a President whenever the right of choice shall devolve upon them, before the fourth day of March next following, then the Vice President shall act as President, as in the case of the death or other constitutional disability of the President. The person having the greatest number of votes as Vice President shall be the Vice President, if such number be a majority of the whole number of electors appointed, and if no person have a majority, then from the two highest numbers on the list, the

Senate shall choose the Vice President; a quorum for the purpose shall consist of two thirds of the whole number of Senators, and a majority of the whole number shall be necessary to a choice. But no person constitutionally ineligible to the office of president shall be eligible to that of Vice President of the United States.

Amendment XIII [December 18, 1865]

SECTION I. Neither slavery nor involuntary servitude, except as punishment for crime whereof the party shall have been duly convicted, shall exist within the United States, or any place subject to their jurisdiction.

SECTION 2. Congress shall have power to enforce this article by appropriate legislation.

Amendment XIV [July 28, 1868]

SECTION I. All persons born or naturalized in the United States, and subject to the jurisdiction thereof, are citizens of the United States and of the State wherein they reside. No State shall make or enforce any law which shall abridge the privileges or immunities of citizens of the United States; nor shall any State deprive any person of life, liberty, or property, without due process of law; nor deny to any person within its jurisdiction the equal protection of the laws.

SECTION 2. Representatives shall be apportioned among the several States according to their respective numbers, counting the whole number of persons in each State, excluding Indians not taxed. But when the right to vote at any election for the choice of electors for President and Vice President of the United States, representatives in Congress, the executive and judicial officers of a State, or the members of the legislature thereof, is denied to any of the male inhabitants of such State, being twenty-one years of age, and citizens of the United States, or in any way abridged, except for participating in rebellion, or other crime, the basis of representation there shall be reduced in the proportion which the number of such male citizens shall bear to the whole number of male citizens twenty-one years of age in such State.

SECTION 3. No person shall be a senator or representative in Congress, or elector of President and Vice President, or hold any office, civil or military, under the United States, or under any State, who having previously taken an oath, as a member of Congress, or as an officer of the United States, or as a member of any State legislature, or

as an executive or judicial officer of any State, to support the Constitution of the United States, shall have engaged in insurrection or rebellion against the same, or given aid or comfort to the enemies thereof. But Congress may by a vote of two thirds of each House, remove such disability.

SECTION 4. The validity of the public debt of the United States, authorized by law, including debts incurred for payment of pensions and bounties for services in suppressing insurrection or rebellion; shall not be questioned. But neither the United States nor any State shall assume or pay any debt or obligation incurred in aid of insurrection or rebellion against the United States, or any claim for the loss or emancipation of any slave; but all such debts, obligations, and claims shall be held illegal and void.

SECTION 5. The Congress shall have the power to enforce, by appropriate legislation, the provisions of this article.

Amendment XV [March 30, 1870]

SECTION I. The right of citizens of the United States to vote shall not be denied or abridged by the United States or by any State on account of race, color, or previous condition of servitude.

SECTION 2. The Congress shall have power to enforce this article by appropriate legislation.

Amendment XVI [February 25, 1913]

The Congress shall have power to lay and collect taxes on incomes, from whatever source derived, without apportionment among the several States, and without regard to any census or enumeration.

Amendment XVII [May 31, 1913]

The Senate of the United States shall be composed of two senators from each State, elected by the people thereof, for six years; and each senator shall have one vote. The electors in each State shall have the qualifications requisite for electors of the most numerous branch of the State legislature.

When vacancies happen in the representation of any State in the Senate, the executive authority of such State shall issue writs of election to fill such vacancies: Provided, That the legislature of any State may empower the executive thereof to make temporary appointments until the people fill the vacancies by election as the legislature may direct.

This amendment shall not be so construed as to affect the election or term of any senator chosen before it becomes valid as part of the Constitution.

Amendment XVIII[11] *[January 29, 1919]*

After one year from the ratification of this article, the manufacture, sale, or transportation of intoxicating liquors within, the importation thereof into, or the exportation thereof from the United States and all territory subject to the jurisdiction thereof for beverage purposes is thereby prohibited.

The Congress and the several States shall have concurrent power to enforce this article by appropriate legislation.

This article shall be inoperative unless it shall have been ratified as an amendment to the Constitution by the legislatures of the several States, as provided in the Constitution, within seven years from the date of the submission hereof to the States by Congress.

Amendment XIX *[August 26, 1920]*

The right of citizens of the United States to vote shall not be denied or abridged by the United States or by any State on account of sex.

Congress shall have the power to enforce this article by appropriate legislation.

Amendment XX *[January 23, 1933]*

SECTION 1. The terms of the President and Vice President shall end at noon on the 20th day of January and the terms of Senators and Representatives at noon on the 3d day of January, of the years in which such terms would have ended if this article had not been ratified; and the terms of their successors shall then begin.

SECTION 2. The Congress shall assemble at least once in every year, and such meeting shall begin at noon on the 3d day of January, unless they shall by law appoint a different day.

SECTION 3. If, at the time fixed for the beginning of the term of president, the President-elect shall have died, the Vice President-elect shall become President. If a President shall not have been chosen before the time fixed for the beginning of his term, or if the President-elect shall have failed to qualify, then the Vice President-elect shall act as president until a President shall have qualified; and the Congress may by law provide for the case wherein neither a President-elect nor a Vice President-elect shall have qualified, declaring who shall then act as President, or the manner in which one who is to act shall be selected, and such person shall act accordingly until a President or Vice President shall have qualified.

SECTION 4. The Congress may by law provide for the case of the death of any of the persons from whom the House of Representatives may choose a President whenever the right of choice shall have devolved upon them, and for the case of the death of any of the persons from whom the Senate may choose a Vice President whenever the right of choice shall have devolved upon them.

SECTION 5. Sections 1 and 2 shall take effect on the 15th day of October following the ratification of this article.

SECTION 6. This article shall be inoperative unless it shall have been ratified as an amendment to the Constitution by the legislatures of three-fourths of the several States within seven years from the date of its submission.

Amendment XXI *[December 5, 1933]*

SECTION 1. The Eighteenth Article of amendment to the Constitution of the United States is hereby repealed.

SECTION 2. The transportation or importation into any State, Territory, or possession of the United States for delivery or use therein of intoxicating liquors in violation of the laws thereof, is hereby prohibited.

SECTION 3. This article shall be inoperative unless it shall have been ratified as an amendment to the Constitution by conventions in the several States, as provided in the Consitution, within seven years from the date of the submission thereof to the States by the Congress.

Amendment XXII *[March 1, 1951]*

No person shall be elected to the office of the President more than twice, and no person who has held the office of President, or acted as President, for more than two years of a term to which some other person was elected President shall be elected to the office of the President more than once.

But this article shall not apply to any person holding the office of President when this article was proposed by the Congress, and shall not prevent any person who may be holding the office of President, or acting as President, during the term within which this article becomes operative from holding the office of President or acting as President during the remainder of such term.

---

[11]Repealed by the Twenty-first Amendment.

This article shall be inoperative unless it shall have been ratified as an amendment to the Constitution by the legislatures of three-fourths of the several States within seven years from the date of its submission to the States by the Congress.

Amendment XXIII [March 29, 1961]

SECTION 1. The District constituting the seat of Government of the United States shall appoint in such manner as the Congress may direct.

A number of electors of President and Vice President equal to the whole number of Senators and Representatives in Congress to which the District would be entitled if it were a State, but in no event more than the least populous State; they shall be in addition to those appointed by the States, but they shall be considered, for the purposes of the election of President and Vice Presient, to be electors appointed by a State; and they shall meet in the District and perform such duties as provided by the twelfth article of amendment.

SECTION 2. The Congress shall have power to enforce this article by appropriate legislation.

Amendment XXIV [January 23, 1964]

SECTION 1. The right of citizens of the United States to vote in any primary or other election for President or Vice President, for electors for President or Vice President, or for Senator or Representative in Congress, shall not be denied or abridged by the United States or any State by reason of failure to pay any poll tax or other tax.

SECTION 2. The Congress shall have power to enforce this article by appropriate legislation.

Amendment XXV [February 10, 1967]

SECTION 1. In case of the removal of the President from office or of his death or resignation, the Vice President shall become President.

SECTION 2. Whenever there is a vacancy in the office of the Vice President, the President shall nominate a Vice President who shall take office upon confirmation by a majority of both Houses of Congress.

SECTION 3. Whenever the President transmits to the President pro tempore of the Senate and the Speaker of the House of Representatives his written declaration that he is unable to discharge the powers and duties of his office, and until he trans-mits to them a written declaration to the contrary, such powers and duties shall be discharged by the Vice President as Acting President.

SECTION 4. Whenever the Vice President and a majority of either the principal officers of the executive departments or of such other body as Congress may by law provide, transmit to the President pro tempore of the Senate and the Speaker of the House of Representatives their written declaration that the President is unable to discharge the powers and duties of his office, the Vice President shall immediately assume the powers and duties of the office as Acting President.

Thereafter, when the President transmits to the President pro tempore of the Senate and the Speaker of the House of Representatives his written declaration that no inability exists, he shall resume the powers and duties of his office unless the Vice President and a majority of either the principal officers of the executive departments or of such other body as Congress may by law provide, transmit within four days to the President pro tempore of the Senate and the Speaker of the House of Representatives their written declaration that the President is unable to discharge the powers and duties of his office. Thereupon Congress shall decide the issue, assembling within forty-eight hours for that purpose if not in session. If the Congress, within twenty-one days after receipt of the latter written declaration, or, if Congress is not in session, within twenty-one days after Congress is required to assemble, determines by two-thirds vote of both houses that the President is unable to discharge the powers and duties of his office, the Vice President shall continue to discharge the same as Acting President; otherwise, the President shall resume the powers and duties of his office.

Amendment XXVI [June 30, 1971]

SECTION 1. The right of citizens of the United States who are eighteen years of age or older to vote shall not be denied or abridged by the United States or by any State on account of age.

SECTION 2. The Congress shall have power to enforce this article by appropriate legislation.

Amendment XXVII [May 8, 1992]

No law, varying the compensation for the services of the Senators and Representatives, shall take effect, until an election of Representatives shall have intervened.

DEMOGRAPHICS OF THE UNITED STATES

Population Growth		
Year	**Population**	**Percent Increase**
1630	4,600	—
1640	26,600	478.3
1650	50,400	90.8
1660	75,100	49.0
1670	111,900	49.0
1680	151,500	35.4
1690	210,400	38.9
1700	250,900	19.2
1710	331,700	32.2
1720	466,200	40.5
1730	629,400	35.0
1740	905,600	43.9
1750	1,170,800	29.3
1760	1,593,600	36.1
1770	2,148,100	34.8
1780	2,780,400	29.4
1790	3,929,214	41.3
1800	5,308,483	35.1
1810	7,239,881	36.4
1820	9,638,453	33.1
1830	12,866,020	33.5
1840	17,069,453	32.7
1850	23,191,876	35.9
1860	31,443,321	35.6
1870	39,818,449	26.6
1880	50,155,783	26.0
1890	62,947,714	25.5
1900	75,994,575	20.7
1910	91,972,266	21.0
1920	105,710,620	14.9
1930	122,775,046	16.1
1940	131,669,275	7.2
1950	150,697,361	14.5
1960	179,323,175	19.0
1970	203,235,298	13.3
1980	226,545,805	11.5
1990	248,709,873	9.8
2000	281,421,906	13.1

Source: Historical Statistics of the United States (1975); Statistical Abstract of the United States (1991 and 2001).
Note: Figures for 1630–1780 include British colonies within limits of present United States only; Native-American population included only in 1930 and thereafter.

Immigration, by origin

(in thousands)

Period	Europe	Americas	Asia
1820–30	106	12	—
1831–40	496	33	—
1841–50	1,597	62	—
1851-60	2,453	75	42
1851-60	2,453	75	42
1861–70	2,065	167	65
1871–80	2,272	404	70
1881–90	4,735	427	70
1891–1900	3,555	39	75
1901–10	8,065	362	324
1911–20	4,322	1,144	247
1921–30	2,463	1,517	112
1931–40	348	160	16
1941–50	621	355	32
1951–60	1,326	997	150
1961–70	1,123	1,716	590
1971–80	800	1,983	1,588
1981–90	706	3,581	2,817
1991–1998	1,086	3,744	2,427

Source: Historical Statistics of the United States (1975); Statistical Abstract of the United States (1991 and 2001)

Racial Composition of the Population

(in thousands)

Year	White	Black	Indian	Hispanic	Asian
1790	3,172	757	(NA)	(NA)	(NA)
1800	4,306	1,002	(NA)	(NA)	(NA)
1820	7,867	1,772	(NA)	(NA)	(NA)
1840	14,196	2,874	(NA)	(NA)	(NA)
1860	26,923	4,442	(NA)	(NA)	(NA)
1880	43,403	6,581	(NA)	(NA)	(NA)
1900	66,809	8,834	(NA)	(NA)	(NA)
1910	81,732	9,828	(NA)	(NA)	(NA)
1920	94,821	10,463	(NA)	(NA)	(NA)
1930	110,287	11,891	(NA)	(NA)	(NA)
1940	118,215	12,866	(NA)	(NA)	(NA)
1950	134,942	15,042	(NA)	(NA)	(NA)
1960	158,832	18,872	(NA)	(NA)	(NA)
1970	178,098	22,581	(NA)	(NA)	(NA)
1980	194,713	26,683	1,420	14,609	3,729
1990	208,741	30,517	2,067	22,479	7,467
2000	226,232	35,307	2,434	32,440	11,159

Source: U.S. Bureau of the Census, U.S. Census of Population: 1940, vol. II, part 1, and vol. IV, part 1; 1950, vol. II, part 1; 1960, vol. I, part 1; 1970, vol. I, part B; and Current Population Reports, P25-1095 and P25-1104; and unpublished data; Statistical Abstract of the United States, 2001.

	Work Force			
Year	Total Number Workers (1000s)	Farmers as % of Total	Women as % of Total	% Workers in Unions
1810	2,330	84	(NA)	(NA)
1840	5,660	75	(NA)	(NA)
1840	5,660	75	(NA)	(NA)
1860	11,110	53	(NA)	(NA)
1870	12,506	53	15	(NA)
1880	17,392	52	15	(NA)
1890	23,318	43	17	(NA)
1900	29,073	40	18	3
1910	38,167	31	21	6
1920	41,614	26	21	12
1930	48,830	22	22	7
1940	53,011	17	24	27
1950	59,643	12	28	25
1960	69,877	8	32	26
1970	82,049	4	37	25
1980	108,544	3	42	23
1990	117,914	3	45	16
2000	140,863	3	47	13.5

Source: Historical Statistics of the United States (1975); Statistical Abstract of the United States (1991, 1996, and 2001).

BIBLIOGRAPHY

This Bibliography contains a selected listing of the extensive body of literature available on American History. It is compiled chapter-by-chapter, enabling the reader to easily find additional references in a given area, and offers an expanded compilation of literature for students who wish to explore topics in fuller detail.

CHAPTER 1

Blackburn, Robin, *The Making of New World Slavery: From the Baroque to the Modern 1492–1800* (1997). Bethell, Leslie, ed., *The Cambridge History of Latin America.* Vol. I (1984). Boucher, Philip P., *Cannibal Encounters: Europeans and Island Caribs, 1492–1763* (1992). Boxer, Charles, *The Portuguese Seaborne Empire: 1415–1825* (1969). Bray, Warwick, ed., *The Meeting of Two Worlds: Europe and the Americas, 1492–1650* (1993). Burkholder, Mark A., and Lyman Johnson, *Colonial Latin America* (2000). Canny, Nicholas, and Anthony Pagden, *Colonial Identity in the Atlantic World, 1500–1800* (1987). Casas, Bartolome de las, *A Short Account of the Destruction of the Indies, with an Introduction by Anthony Pagden* (1992). Chaplin, Joyce E., *Subject Matter: Technology, The Body, and Science on the Anglo-Amercian Frontier, 1500–1676.* (2001). Clayton, Lawrence A., et al., eds., *The De Soto Chronicles: The Expedition of Hernando de Soto to North America in 1539–1543,* 2 vols. (1993). Coe, Michael, Dean Snow, and Elizabeth Benson, *Atlas of Ancient America* (1986). Crosby, Alfred W., Jr., *Ecological Imperialism: The Biological Expansion of Europe, 900–1900* (1986). Denevan, William M., ed., *The Native Population of the Americas in 1492* (1992). Diaz, Bernal, *The Conquest of New Spain* (1963). Dobyns, Henry F., *Their Number Become Thinned: Native American Population Dynamics in Eastern North America* (1983). Dunn, Oliver, and James E. Kelley, Jr., eds., *The Diario of Christopher Columbus's First Voyage to America, 1492–1493* (1989). Elliott, J. H., *Spain and Its World, 1500–1700* (1989). Fagan, Brian M., *Ancient North America: The Archeology of a Continent* (1991). Fage, J. D., *A History of Africa* (1988). Fernandez-Armesto, Felipe, *Columbus* (1991).

Gibson, Charles, *Spain in America* (1966). Gutierrez, Ramon, *When Jesus Came the Corn Mothers Went Away: Marriage, Sexuality, and Power in New Mexico, 1500–1846* (1991). Hanke, Lewis, *The Spanish Struggle for Justice in the Conquest of America* (1965). Hoffman, Paul, *A New Andalucia and a Way to the Orient* (1990). Hulme, Peter, and Neil L. Whitehead, eds., *Wild Majesty* (1992). Jennings, Francis, *The Founders of America* (1993). Kartunnen, Frances, *Between Worlds: Interpreters, Guides, and Survivors* (1994). Klein, Herbert S., *African Slavery in Latin America and the Caribbean* (1986). Kupperman, Karen O., ed., *America in European Consciousness, 1493–1750* (1995). Leon-Portilla, Miguel, ed., *The Broken Spears: The Aztec Account of the Conquest of Mexico* (1990). Liss, Peggy K., *Isabel: The Queen* (1992). Lockhart, James, and Stuart B. Schwartz, *Early Latin America* (1983). Lunenfeld, Marvin, ed., *1492: Discovery, Invasion, Encounter* (1991).

Milanich, Jerald T., and Susan Milanich, eds., *First Encounters: Spanish Explorations in the Caribbean and the United States, 1492–1570* (1989). _____, and Charles Hudson, *Hernando de Soto and the Indians of Florida* (1993). Morison, Samuel Eliot, *The European Discovery of America: The Southern Voyages, 1492–1616* (1974). _____, *Journals and Other Documents on the Life and Voyages of Christopher Columbus* (1963). Nabokov, Peter, ed., *Native American Testimony, 1492–1992* (1999). Oliver, Roland, *The African Experience: Major Themes in African History from Earliest Times to the Present* (1991). Pagden, Anthony, ed., *European Encounters with the New World* (1993). _____, *Lords of All the World: Ideologies of Empire in Spain, Britain and France, c. 1500–1800* (1995). Parry, J. H., *The Age of Reconnaissance: Discovery, Exploration and Settlement 1450–1650* (1963). _____, *The Spanish Seaborne Empire* (1966). Peters, Edward, *Inquisition* (1988). Phillips, J. R. S., *The Medieval Expansion of Europe* (1988). Quinn, David B., *North America from Earliest Discovery to First Settlements* (1975). Rouse, Irving, *The Tainos* (1992). Ruiz, Ramon Eduardo, *Triumphs and Tragedy: A History of the Mexican People* (1992).

Scammell, G. V., *The World Encompassed: The First European Maritime Empires, c. 800–1650* (1981). Solow, Barbara L., *Slavery and the Rise of the Atlantic System* (1991). Trigger, Bruce G., and Wilcomb Washburn, eds., *The Cambridge History of the Native Peoples of the Americas,* Vol. I (1996).

CHAPTER 2

Allen, John Logan, ed., *North American Exploration: A New World* (1997). Anderson, Karen, *Chain Her by One Foot: The Subjugation of Native Women in Seventeenth-Century New France* (1991). Canny, Nicholas P., *The Elizabethan Conquest of Ireland: A Pattern Established, 1565–1576* (1976). Dechêne, Louise, *Habitants and Merchants in Seventeenth-Century Montreal* (1992). Delâge, Denys, *Bitter Feast: Amerindians and Europeans in Northeastern America, 1600–1664* (1993). Dennis, Matthew, *Cultivating a Landscape of Peace: Iroquois-European Encounters in Seventeenth-Century America* (1993). Dickason, Olive Patricia, *Canada's First Nations: A History of Founding Peoples from Earliest Times* (1992). Eccles, W. J., *The Canadian Frontier* (1974). _____, *Essays on New France* (1987).

Gleach, Frederic W., *Powhatan's World and Colonial Virginia: A Conflict of Cultures* (1997). Hoffman, Paul, *A New Andalucia and a Way to the Orient* (1990). Hume, Ivor Noël, *The Virginia Adventure: Roanoke to James Towne: An Archaeological and Historical Odyssey* (1994). Inikori, Joseph, and Stanley L. Engerman, eds., *The Atlantic Slave Trade: Effects on Economies, Societies, and Peoples in Africa, The Americas, and Europe* (1992). Jaenen, Cornelius J., *Friend and Foe: Aspects of French-Amerindian Cultural Contact in the Sixteenth and Seventeenth Centuries* (1976). Jennings, Francis, *The Ambiguous Iroquois Empire: The Covenant Chain Confederation of Indian Tribes with English Colonies* (1984). Klein, Herbert, *African Slavery in Latin America and the Caribbean* (1986). Kupperman, Karen Ordahl, *Settling with the Indians: The Meeting of English and Indian Cultures in America, 1580–1640* (1980).

Merwick, Donna, *Possessing Albany, 1630–1710: The Dutch and English Experience* (1990). Morgan, Edmund S., *American Slavery, American Freedom: The Ordeal of Colonial Virginia* (1975). Morison, Samuel Eliot, *Samuel de Champlain: Father of New France* (1972). Peckham, Howard, and Charles Gibson, eds., *Attitudes of Colonial Powers Toward the American Indian* (1969).

Quinn, David B., ed., *America From Concept to Discovery: Early Explorations of North America* (1979). _____, *North America from Earliest Discovery to First Settlements: The Norse Voyages to 1612* (1977). _____, *Set Fair for Roanoke: Voyages and Colonies, 1584–1606* (1995). Richter, Daniel K., and James H. Merrell, *Beyond the Covenant Chain: The Iroquois and Their Neighbors in Indian North America, 1600–1800* (1987). Rink, Oliver A., *Holland on the Hudson: An Economic and Social History of Dutch New York* (1986). Rountree, Helen C., ed., *Powhatan Foreign Relations* (1993).

Scammell, G. V., *The World Encompassed: The First European Maritime Empires* (1981). Trigger, Bruce, *Natives and Newcomers: Canada's "Heroic Age" Reconsidered* (1985). _____, and Wilcomb E. Washburn, eds., *The Cambridge History of the Native Peoples of the Americas,* Vol. I (1996). Wallace, Anthony F. C., *The Death and Rebirth of the Seneca* (1970). Weber, David, *The Spanish Frontier in North America* (1992). White, Richard, *The Middle Ground: Indians, Empires, and Republics in the Great Lakes Region, 1650–1815* (1991). White, Shane, *Somewhat More Independent: The End of Slavery in New York City, 1770–1810* (1991).

CHAPTER 3

Allen, David Grayson, *In English Ways: The Movement of Societies and the Transferral of English Local Law and Custom to Massachusetts Bay in the Seventeenth Century* (1981). Anderson, Virginia DeJohn, *New England's Generation: The Great Migration and the Formation of Society and Culture in the Seventeenth Century* (1991). Barbour, Philip L., ed., *The Complete Works of John Smith* (1986). _____, *Pocahontas and Her World* (1969). Bernhard, Virginia, "Men, Women and Children at Jamestown: Population and Gender in Early Virginia, 1607–1610," *Journal of Southern History,* LVIII (1992). Blackburn, Robin, *The Making of New World Slavery: From the Baroque to the Modern, 1402–1800* (1997). Bradford, William, *Of Plymouth Plantation, 1620–1647,* ed. Samuel Eliot Morison (1952). Breen, Timothy H., and Stephen Innes, *"Myne Owne Ground": Race and Freedom on Virginia's Eastern Shore, 1640–1676* (1980). Bremer, Francis J., *The Puritan Experiment: New England Society from Bradford to Edwards* (1976). Carr, Lois Green, et al., eds., *Colonial Chesapeake Society* (1988). Delbanco, Andrew, *The Puritan Ordeal* (1989). Demos, John, ed.,

Remarkable Providences: Readings on Early American History (1991). Foster, Stephen, *The Long Argument: English Puritanism and the Shaping of New England Culture, 1570–1700* (1991). _____, *Their Solitary Way: The Puritan Social Ethic in the First Century of Settlement in New England* (1971). Freedman, Estelle B., and John D'Emilio, *Intimate Matters: A History of Sexuality in America* (1988).

Gleach, Frederic W., *Powhatan's World and Colonial Virginia: A Conflict of Cultures* (1997). Greene, Jack P., *Pursuits of Happiness: The Social Development of Early Modern British Colonies and the Formation of American Culture* (1988). Greven, Philip J., *Four Generations: Population, Land, and Family in Colonial Andover, Massachusetts* (1970). _____, *The Protestant Temperament: Patterns of Childrearing, Religious Experience, and the Self in Early America* (1977). Hambrick-Stowe, Charles, *The Practice of Piety: Puritan Devotional Disciplines in Seventeenth-Century New England* (1982). Horn, James, *Adapting to a New World: English Society in the Seventeenth-Century Chesapeake* (1994). Jordan, Winthrop D., *White over Black: American Attitudes Toward the Negro, 1550–1812* (1968). Karlsen, Carol, *The Devil in the Shape of a Woman: Witchcraft in Colonial New England* (1987). Kolchin, Peter, *American Slavery, 1619–1877* (1993). Kupperman, Karen Ordahl, *Providence Island, 1630–1641: The Other Puritan Colony* (1993). _____, *Settling with the Indians: The Meeting of English and Indian Cultures in America, 1580–1640* (1980). Langdon, George D., Jr., *Pilgrim Colony: A History of New Plymouth, 1620–1691* (1966). Lockridge, Kenneth A., *A New England Town, The First Hundred Years: Dedham, Massachusetts 1636–1736* (rev. ed., 1985).

McCusker, John J., and Russell R. Menard, *The Economy of British America, 1607–1789* (1991). McGiffert, Michael, ed., "Constructing Race," *William and Mary Quarterly*, 3d Ser., LIV (1997). Miller, Perry, ed., *The American Puritans: Their Prose and Poetry* (1956). _____, *The New England Mind: The Seventeenth Century* (1939). Morgan, Edmund S., *The Puritan Dilemma: The Story of John Winthrop* (1958). _____, *Visible Saints: The History of a Puritan Idea* (1963). Norton, Mary Beth, *Founding Mothers and Fathers: Gendered Power and the Forming of American Society* (1996). Potter, Stephen R., *Commoners, Tribute, and Chiefs: The Development of Algonquian Culture in the Potomac Valley* (1993). Powell, Sumner Chilton, *Puritan Village: The Formation of a New England Town* (1963). Quinn, David Beers, *North America from Earliest Discovery to First Settlements: The Norse Voyages to 1612* (1977). Rountree, Helen, *Pocahontas's People: The Powhatan Indians of Virginia Through Four Centuries* (1990). _____, ed., *Powhatan Foreign Relations, 1500–1722* (1993). _____, *The Powhatan Indians of Virginia: Their Traditional Culture* (1989). Rutman, Darrett B., *Winthrop's Boston: A Portrait of a Puritan Town* (1965).

Salisbury, Neal, *Manitou and Providence: Indians, Europeans, and the Making of New England, 1500–1643* (1982). _____, "Squanto: Last of the Patuxets," in Gary B. Nash and David W. Sweet, eds., *Struggle and Survival in Colonial America* (1981). Stannard, David E., *The Puritan Way of Death: A Study in Religion, Culture, and Social Change* (1977). Stone, Lawrence, *The Family, Sex, and Marriage in England, 1500–1800* (1977). Stout, Harry S., *The New England Soul: Preaching and Religious Culture in Colonial New England* (1986). Tate, Thad, and David Ammerman, eds., *The Chesapeake in the Seventeenth Century: Essays on Anglo-American Society and Politics* (1979). Thomas, M. Halsey, ed., *The Diary of Samuel Sewall, 1674–1708* (1973.) Ulrich, Laurel Thatcher, *Good Wives: Image and Reality in the Lives of Women in Northern New England, 1650–1750* (1982). Vaughan, Alden T., *New England Frontier: Puritans and Indians, 1620–1675* (1994). _____, ed., *The Puritan Tradition in America, 1620–1730* (1972). Wood, Peter H., Gregory A. Waselkov, and M. Thomas Halsey, eds., *Powhatan's Mantle: Indians in the Colonial Southeast* (1989). Woodward, Grace Steele, *Pocahontas* (1969). Zuckerman, Michael, *Peaceable Kingdoms: New England Towns in the Eighteenth Century* (1970). _____, "Pilgrims in the Wilderness: Community, Modernity, and the Maypole at Merry Mount," *New England Quarterly*, L (1977).

CHAPTER 4

Appleby, Joyce, *Economic Thought and Ideology in Seventeenth-Century England* (1978). _____, *Liberalism and Republicanism in the Historical Imagination* (1992). Bailyn, Bernard, and Philip D. Morgan, eds., *Strangers Within the Realm: Cultural Margins of the First British Empire* (1991). Berlin, Ira D., *Many Thousands Gone: The First Two Centuries of Slavery in North America* (1998). Bonomi, Patricia U., *A Factious People: Politics and Society in Colonial New York* (1971). Boyer, Paul, and Stephen Nissenbaum, *Salem Possessed: The Social Origins of Witchcraft* (1972). _____, ed. *Salem Village Witchcraft: A Documentary Record of Local*

Conflict in Colonial New England (1972). Breen, T. H., *Puritans and Adventurers: Change and Persistence in Early America* (1980). Breslaw, Elaine G., *Tituba, Reluctant Witch of Salem: Devilish Indians and Puritan Fantasies* (1996). Crane, Verner, *The Southern Frontier, 1670–1732*, with a new preface by Peter H. Wood (1981). Craven, Wesley Frank, *White, Red, and Black: The Seventeenth-Century Virginian* (1971). Degler, Carl N., *Out of Our Past: The Forces that Shaped Modern America*, 3rd. ed. (1984). Dunn, Richard S., *Sugar and Slaves: The Rise of the Planter Class in the English West Indies* (1972). Eccles, W. J., *France in America* (1990). Eltis, David, *The Rise of African Slavery in the Americas* (2000). Espinosa, J. Manuel, *The Pueblo Indian Revolt of 1696 and the Franciscan Mission in New Mexico* (1988).

Goodfriend, Joyce, *Before the Melting Pot: Society and Culture in Colonial New York City, 1664–1692* (1992). Greene, Jack P., ed., *Great Britain and the American Colonies, 1606–1763* (1970). Hall, David D., ed., *Witch-Hunting in Seventeenth-Century New England: A Documentary History, 1638–1692* (1991). _____, *Worlds of Wonder, Days of Judgment: Popular Religious Belief in Early New England* (1989). Hall, Gwendolyn Midlo, *Africans in Colonial Louisiana: The Development of Afro-Creole Culture in the Eighteenth Century* (1992). Hammond, George P., and Agapito Reys, eds., *Don Juan de Oñate: Colonizer of New Mexico, 1595–1628* (1953). Hoffer, Peter Charles, *The Devil's Disciples: Makers of the Salem Witchcraft Trials* (1996). Illick, Joseph, *Colonial Pennsylvania: A History* (1976). Jennings, Francis, *The Ambiguous Iroquois Empire: The Covenant Chain Confederation of Indian Tribes with English Colonies* (1984). Johnson, Richard R., *Adjustment to Empire: The New England Colonies, 1665–1715* (1981). Kammen, Michael, *Colonial New York: A History* (1975). Karlsen, Carol, *The Devil in the Shape of a Woman: Witchcraft in Colonial New England* (1987). Klein, Herbert S., *African Slavery in Latin America and the Caribbean* (1986). Kishlansky, Mark, *A Monarchy Transformed: Britain, 1603–1714* (1996). Knaut, Andrew L., *The Pueblo Revolt of 1680: Conquest and Resistance in Seventeenth–Century New Mexico* (1995). Kolchin, Peter, *American Slavery, 1619–1877* (1993). Konig, David Thomas, *Law and Society in Puritan Massachusetts: Essex County, 1629–1692* (1979). Kupperman, Karen Ordahl, ed., *Major Problems in American Colonial History* (2000). Landers, Jane, *Black Society in Spanish Florida* (1999). Leach, Douglas Edward, *Arms for Empire: A Military History of the British Colonies*

of North America, 1607–1763 (1973). Lefler, Hugh T., and William S. Powell, *Colonial North Carolina: A History* (1973). Locke, John, *Two Treatises of Government: A Critical Edition with an Introduction*, ed., Peter Laslett (1960). Lovejoy, David S., *The Glorious Revolution in America* (1972).

Malone, Patrick M., *The Skulking Way of War: Technology and Tactics Among the New England Indians* (1991). Melvoin, Richard I., *The New England Outpost: War and Society in Colonial Deerfield* (1989). Merrell, James H., *The Indians' New World: Catawbas and Their Neighbors from European Contact Through the Era of Removal* (1989). Merwick, Donna, *Possessing Albany, 1630–1710: The Dutch and English Experiences* (1990). Middlekauff, Robert, *The Mathers: Three Generations of Puritan Intellectuals, 1596–1728* (1971). Middleton, Richard, *Colonial America: A History, 1585–1776* (1996). Miller, Perry, *Errand into the Wilderness* (1956). Nash, Gary B., *Quakers and Politics: Pennsylvania, 1681–1726* (1996). _____, *Red, White, and Black: The Peoples of Early America*, 2nd ed. (1982). _____, *Urban Crucible: Social Change, Political Consciousness, and the Origins of the American Revolution* (1979). _____ and Jean Soderlund, *Freedom by Degrees: Emancipation in Pennsylvania and Its Aftermath* (1991). Nobles, Gregory H., *American Frontiers: Cultural Encounters and Continental Conquest* (1997). Nylander, Jane, *Our Own Snug Firesides: Images of the New England Home, 1760–1860* (1993). Oakes, James, *Slavery and Freedom: An Interpretation of the Old South* (1990). Patterson, Orlando, *Slavery and Social Death: A Comparative Study* (1982). Pope, Robert G., *The Half-Way Covenant: Church Membership in Puritan New England* (1986). Quinn, David B., ed., *Early Maryland in a Wider World* (1982). Richter, Daniel K., *The Ordeal of the Longhouse: The Peoples of the Iroquois League in the Era of European Colonization* (1992). Ritchie, Robert C., *The Duke's Province: A Study of New York Politics and Society, 1664–1691* (1977). Robinson, W. Stitt, *The Southern Colonial Frontier, 1607–1763* (1979). Rose, Willie Lee, ed., *A Documentary History of Slavery in North America* (1976). Rosenthal, Bernard, *Salem Story: Reading the Witch Trials of 1692* (1993). Rountree, Helen, *Pocahontas's People: The Powhatan Indians of Virginia Through Four Centuries* (1990).

Simmons, Marc, *The Last Conquistador: Juan de Oñate and the Settling of the Far Southwest* (1991). Sirmans, M. Eugene, *Colonial South Carolina: A Political History, 1663–1763* (1966). Slotkin, Richard, and James K. Folson, eds., *So Dreadfull a*

Judgment: Puritan Responses to King Philip's War, 1676–1677 (1978). Usner, Daniel H., Jr., *Indians, Settlers, and Slaves in a Frontier Exchange Economy: The Lower Mississippi Valley before 1783* (1992). Vaughan, Alden T., ed., *The Puritan Tradition in America, 1620–1730* (1972). Webb, Stephen Saunders, *1676: The End of American Independence* (1984). Weber, David, *The Spanish Frontier in North America* (1992). White, Richard, *The Middle Ground: Indians, Empires, and Republics in the Great Lakes Region, 1650–1815* (1991). Wooten, David, ed., *The Political Writings of John Locke* (1993). Wright, J. Leitch, Jr., *The Only Land They Knew: The Tragic Story of the American Indians in the Old South* (1981).

CHAPTER 5

Ahlstrom, Sydney E., *A Religious History of the American People* (1972). Allison, Robert J., ed., *The Interesting Narrative of the Life of Olaudah Equiano* (1995). Bailyn, Bernard, "The Peopling of British North America: An Introduction," in *Perspectives in American History*. Vol. 2 (1985). _____, *Voyagers to the West: A Passage in the Peopling of America on the Eve of the Revolution* (1986). _____, and Philip D. Morgan, eds., *Strangers within the Realm: Cultural Margins of the First British Empire* (1991). Berlin, Ira, *Many Thousands Gone: The First Two Centuries of Slavery in North America* (1998). _____, and Philip D. Morgan, eds., *Cultivation and Culture: Labor and the Shaping of Slave Life in the Americas* (1993). Bonomi, Patricia, *Under the Cope of Heaven: Religion, Society, and Politics in Colonial America* (1986). Boorstin, Daniel J., *The Lost World of Thomas Jefferson* (1948). Boydston, Jeanne, *Home and Work: Housework, Wages, and the Ideology of Labor in the Early Republic* (1990). Breen, T. H., *Puritans and Adventurers: Change and Persistence in Early America* (1980). Brewer, John, and Roy Porter, eds., *Consumption and the World of Goods* (1993). Bullock, Steven C., *Revolutionary Brotherhood: Freemasonry and the Transformation of the American Social Order, 1730–1840* (1996). Bushman, Richard, *The Refinement of America: Persons, Houses, Cities* (1992). Butler, Jon, *Awash in a Sea of Faith: Christianizing the American People* (1990). _____, *Becoming American: The Revolution before 1776* (2000). Coleman, Kenneth, *Colonial Georgia: A History* (1976). Conroy, David W., *In Public Houses: Drink and the Revolution of Authority in Colonial Massachusetts* (1987). Cott, Nancy F., et al., eds., *Root of Bitterness: Documents of the Social History of American Women* (1996). Davis, Harold E., *The*

Fledgling Province: Social and Cultural Life in Colonial Georgia (1976). Duffy, John, *Epidemics in Colonial America* (1971). Engerman, Stanley L., and Robert E. Gallman, eds., *The Cambridge Economic History of the United States* (1996). Fiering, Norman S., *Jonathan Edwards's Moral Thought and Its British Context* (1981). Franklin, Benjamin, *Writings* (1987).

Gallay, Alan, *The Formation of a Planter Elite: Jonathan Bryan and the Southern Colonial Frontier* (1989). Gilje, Paul A., *The Road to Mobocracy: Popular Disorder in New York City, 1763–1834* (1987). Gordon, Michael, ed., *The American Family in Social-Historical Perspective* (1983). Greene, Jack P., *Pursuits of Happiness: The Social Development of Early Modern British Colonies and the Formation of American Culture* (1988). _____, *The Quest for Power: The Lower Houses of Assembly in the Southern Royal Colonies, 1689–1776* (1976). _____, and J. R. Pole, eds., *Colonial British America: Essays in the New History of the Early Modern Era* (1984). Gross, Robert A., *The Minutemen and Their World* (1976). Hancock, David, *Citizens of the World: London Merchants and the Integration of the British Atlantic Community, 1735–1785* (1995). Heimert, Alan, *Religion and the American Mind, from the Great Awakening to the Revolution* (1968). _____, and Perry Miller, eds., *The Great Awakening: Documents Illustrating the Crisis and Its Consequences* (1967). Henretta, James A., and Gregory H. Nobles, *Evolution and Revolution: American Society, 1600–1820* (1987). Hoffman, Ronald, et al., eds., *Through a Glass Darkly: Reflections on Personal Identity in Early America* (1997). Innes, Stephen A., *Creating the Commonwealth: The Economic Culture of Puritan New England* (1995). _____, ed., *Work and Labor in Early America* (1988). Kammen, Michael, *Colonial New York: A History* (1975). Klein, Herbert, *The Atlantic Slave Trade* (1999). Koch, Adrienne, and William Peden, eds., *The Life and Selected Writings of Thomas Jefferson* (1944). Kulikoff, Allan, *Tobacco and Slaves: The Development of Southern Cultures in the Chesapeake, 1680–1800* (1986). Lambert, Frank, *"Pedlar in Divinity": George Whitefield and the Transatlantic Revivals* (1994). Landers, Jane, "El Gracia de Santa Teresa de Mose: A Free Black Town in Spanish Colonial Florida," *American Historical Review*, 95 (1991). Lewis, Jan, *The Pursuit of Happiness: Family and Values in Jefferson's Virginia* (1983).

Mancall, Peter, *Deadly Medicine: Indians and Alcohol in Early America* (1995). May, Henry F., *The Enlightenment in America* (1976). Matson, Cathy, *Merchants and Empire: Trading in Colonial New*

York (1998). McCusker, John J., and Russell R. Menard, *The Economy of British America, 1607–1789* (1985). Middlekauff, Robert, *The Mathers: Three Generations of Puritan Intellectuals, 1596–1728* (1971). Middleton, Richard, *Colonial America: A History, 1585–1776* (1996). Morgan, Philip D., "Slave Life in Eighteenth-Century Charleston," *Perspectives in American History*, Vol. I (1984). _____, "Work and Culture: The Task System and the World of Lowcountry Blacks, 1700–1800," *William and Mary Quarterly*, 3d Ser., XXXIX (1982). Mullin, Michael, *Africa in America: Slave Acculturation and Resistance in the American South and the British Caribbean, 1736–1831* (1992). Oberg, Barbara B., and Harry S. Stout, eds., *Benjamin Franklin, Jonathan Edwards, and the Representation of American Culture* (1993). Olwell, Robert, *Masters, Slaves, and Subjects: The Culture of Power in the South Carolina Low Country, 1740–1790* (1998). Paine, Thomas, *Collected Writings* (1995). Rawley, James A., *The Transatlantic Slave Trade: A History* (1981). Rediker, Marcus B., *Between the Devil and the Deep Blue Sea: Merchant Seamen, Pirates, and the Anglo-American Maritime World, 1700–1750* (1987).

Sobel, Mechal, *The World They Made Together: Black and White Values in Eighteenth-Century Virginia* (1987). Spalding, Phinizy, *Oglethorpe in America* (1977). Stout, Harry S., *The Divine Dramatist: George Whitefield and the Rise of Modern Evangelicalism* (1991). Thornton, John K., "African Dimensions of the Stono Rebellion," *American Historical Review*, 91 (1994). Ulrich, Laurel Thatcher, *Good Wives; Image and Reality in the Lives of Women in Northern New England, 1650–1750* (1980). Vickers, Daniel, *Farmers and Fishermen: Two Centuries of Work in Essex County, Massachusetts, 1630–1850* (1994). Warner, Michael, *The Letters of the Republic: Publication and the Public Sphere in Eighteenth-Century America* (1990). Whitefield, George, *Sketches of the Life and Labors of the Rev. George Whitefield* (n.d.). Wolf, Stephanie Grauman, *As Various as Their Land: The Everyday Lives of Eighteenth-Century Americans* (1993). Wright, Esmond, *Franklin of Philadelphia* (1986). Zabin, Serena, "Places of Exchange: New York City, 1700–1763," Ph.D. diss., Rutgers University (2000).

CHAPTER 6

Anderson, Fred, *A People's Army: Massachusetts Soldiers and Society in the Seven Years' War* (1984). Bailyn, Bernard, *The Origins of American Politics* (1968). Barrow, Thomas C., *Trade and Empire: The British Customs Service in Colonial America, 1660–1775* (1967). Braund, Kathleen E. Holland, *Deerskins and Duffels: Creek Indian Trade with Anglo-America, 1685–1815* (1993). Breen, T. H., "Narrative of Commercial Life: Consumption, Ideology, and Community on the Eve of the American Revolution," *William and Mary Quarterly*, 3rd Ser., L (1993). Brewer, John, *Party, Ideology, and Popular Politics at the Accession of George II* (1976). Bushman, Richard, *King and People in Provincial Massachusetts* (1985). Dowd, Gregory E., *A Spirited Resistance: The North American Indian Struggle for Unity, 1745–1815* (1992). Draper, Theodore, *A Struggle for Power: The American Revolution* (1996). Eccles, W. J., *France in America* (1990). Ferling, John E., *A Wilderness of Miseries: War and Warriors in Early America* (1980). Flexner, James Thomas, *George Washington: The Forge of Experience, 1732–1775* (1965). _____, *Lord of the Mohawks: A Biography of Sir William Johnson* (1979). Franklin, Benjamin, *Writings* (1987).

Gilje, Paul A., *Rioting in America* (1996). _____, *The Road to Mobocracy: Popular Disorder in New York City, 1763–1834* (1987). Gipson, Lawrence H., *The British Empire before the American Revolution*, 15 vols (1936–1972). Greene, Jack P., *Peripheries and Center: Constitutional Development in the Extended Policies of the British Empire and the United States* (1987). _____, *The Quest for Power: The Lower Houses of Assembly in the Southern Royal Colonies* (1963). Hamilton, Milton W., *Sir William Johnson: Colonial American, 1715–1763* (1976). Hinderacker, Eric, *Elusive Empires: Constructing Colonialism in the Ohio Valley, 1673–1800* (1997). Hoerder, Dirk, *Crowd Action in Revolutionary Massachusetts, 1765–1780* (1977). Holton, Woody, *Forced Founders: Indians, Debtors, Slaves and the Making of the American Revolution in Virginia* (1999). Jefferson, Thomas, *Writings* (1984). Jennings, Francis, *The Ambiguous Iroquois Empire: The Covenant Chain Confederation of Indian Tribes with English Colonies* (1984.) _____, *Empire of Fortune: Crowns, Colonies, and Tribes in the Seven Years' War in America* (1988). Johnson, Susannah Willard, *A Narrative of the Captivity of Mrs. Johnson* (1990). Labaree, Benjamin Woods, *The Boston Tea Party* (1964). Leach, Douglas Edward, *Roots of Conflict: British Armed Forces and Colonial Americans, 1677–1763* (1986).

Maier, Pauline, *From Resistance to Revolution: Colonial Radicals and the Development of American Opposition to Britain, 1765–1776* (1972). McConnell, Michael N., *A Country Between: The Upper Ohio Valley and Its Peoples, 1724–1774*

(1992). Melvoin, Richard I., *New England Outpost: War and Society in Colonial Deerfield* (1989). Middlekauff, Robert, *Benjamin Franklin and His Enemies* (1996). _____, *The Glorious Cause: The American Revolution, 1763–1789* (1982). Morgan, Edmund S. and Helen M., *The Stamp Act Crisis: Prologue to Revolution* (1953). Nash, Gary, *The Urban Crucible: Social Change, Political Consciousness, and the Origins of the American Revolution* (1979). Nobles, Gregory H., *American Frontiers: Cultural Encounters and Continental Conquest* (1997). Peckham, Howard H., *Pontiac and the Indian Uprising* (1947). Pencak, William, *War, Politics, and Revolution in Provincial Massachusetts* (1981). _____, "Warfare and Political Change in Mid-Eighteenth-Century Massachusetts," *The Journal of Imperial and Commonwealth History*, 8 (1980), 51–73. Robinson, W. Stitt, *The Southern Frontier, 1607–1763* (1979).

Sosin, Jack M., *The Revolutionary Frontier, 1763–1783* (1967). Steele, Ian K., *Warpaths: Invasions of North America* (1994). Ulrich, Laurel Thatcher, *Good Wives: Image and Reality in the Lives of Women in Northern New England, 1650–1750* (1982). Vaughan, Alden T., *Roots of American Racism: Essays on the Colonial Experience* (1995). Walton, Gary M., and James F. Shepherd, *The Economic Rise of Early America* (1979). Warden, G. B., *Boston, 1689–1776* (1970). Wood, Gordon S., *The Creation of the American Republic, 1776–1787* (1966). _____, *The Rising Glory of America, 1760–1820* (1990). Wright, Esmond, *Franklin of Philadelphia* (1986). Zobel, Hiller, *The Boston Massacre* (1970).

CHAPTER 7

Alden, John R., *A History of the American Revolution* (1975). Aron, Stephen, *How the West Was Lost: The Transformation of Kentucky from Daniel Boone to Henry Clay* (1996). Bailyn, Bernard, *Faces of Revolution: Personalities and Times in the Struggle for American Independence* (1990). _____, ed., *The Debate on the Constitution*, 2 vols (1993). Beeman, Richard, Stephen Botein, and Edward C. Carter II, *Beyond Confederation: Origins of the Constitution and American National Identity* (1987). Berlin, Ira, and Ronald Hoffman, eds., *Slavery and Freedom in the Age of the American Revolution* (1983). Bernstein, Richard, *Are We to Be a Nation? The Making of the Constitution* (1987). Bloch, Ruth, "The Gendered Meanings of Virtue in Revolutionary America," *Signs*, 13 (1987), 37–58. Bonwick, Colin, *The American Revolution* (1991). Calloway, Colin, *The American Revolution in Indian Country: Crisis and Diversity in Native American Communities* (1995). Carp, E. Wayne, *To Starve the Army at Pleasure: Continental Army Administration and American Political Culture, 1775–1783* (1984). Cooke, Jacob E., ed., *The Federalist* (1961). Countryman, Edward, *The American Revolution* (1985). _____, *A People in Revolution: The American Revolution and Political Society in New York, 1760–1790* (1981). Crow, Jeffrey, and Larry Tise, eds., *The Southern Experience in the American Revolution* (1978). Doerflinger, Thomas M., *A Vigorous Spirit of Enterprise: Merchants and Economic Development in Revolutionary Philadelphia* (1986). Egnal, Marc, *A Mighty Empire: The Origins of the American Revolution* (1988). Engerman, Stanley L., and Robert Gallman, eds., *The Cambridge Economic History of the United States*, Vol. I (1996). Farrand, Max, ed., *The Records of the Federal Convention of 1787*, 4 vols (1966). Fischer, David Hackett, *Paul Revere's Ride* (1994). Flexner, James Thomas, *George Washington and the New Nation (1783–1793)* (1970). _____, *George Washington in the American Revolution (1775–1783)* (1968). Fliegelman, Jay, *Declaring Independence: Jefferson, Natural Language, and the Culture of Performance* (1993). Foner, Eric, *Tom Paine and Revolutionary America* (1976).

Greene, Jack P., *Colonies to Nation, 1763–1789* (1967). _____, and J. R. Pole, eds., *The Blackwell Encyclopedia of the American Revolution* (1991). Gross, Robert A., ed., *In Debt to Shays: The Bicentennial of an Agrarian Rebellion* (1993). _____, *The Minutemen and Their World* (1976). Gruber, Ira D., *The Howe Brothers and the American Revolution* (1972). Hamilton, Alexander, *The Papers of Alexander Hamilton*, ed. Harold C. Syrett et al., 27 vols (1961–87). Higginbotham, Don, *The War of American Independence: Military Attitudes, Policies, and Practice, 1763–1789* (1971). Hoffman, Ronald, and Peter J. Albert, eds., *The Transforming Hand of Revolution: Reconsidering the American Revolution as a Social Movement* (1995). _____, *Women in the Age of the American Revolution* (1989). Hoffman, Ronald, et al., eds., *The Economy of Early America: The Revolutionary Period, 1763–1790* (1988). Jensen, Merrill, *The Articles of Confederation: An Interpretation of the Social-Constitutional History of the American Revolution, 1774–1781* (1970). Jordan, Winthrop D., *White Over Black: American Attitudes Toward the Negro, 1550–1812* (1968). Kaminski, John, and Richard Leffler, eds., *Federalists and Antifederalists: The Debate Over the Ratification of the Constitution* (1989). Ketcham, Ralph, *James Madison: A Biography* (1971). Klein, Rachel N., *Unification of a Slave*

State: Planter Class in the South Carolina Back-country, 1760–1808 (1990). Koistinen, Paul A. C., Beating Plowshares into Swords: The Political Economy of American Warfare, 1606–1865 (1996). Konig, David Thomas, ed., Devising Liberty: Preserving and Creating Freedom in the New American Republic (1995). Kurtz, Stephen G., and James H. Hudson, eds., Essays on the American Revolution (1973). Lee, Jean B., The Price of Nationhood: The American Revolution in Charles County (1994). Lewis, Jan, "The Republican Wife: Virtue and Seduction in the Early Republic," William and Mary Quarterly, 3d Ser., XLIV (1987), 689–721. Lockridge, Kenneth A. "Social Change and the Meaning of the American Revolution," Journal of Social History, 6 (1973), 403–439.

Mackesy, Piers, The War for America, 1775–1783 (1965). Maier, Pauline, American Scripture: Making the Declaration of Independence (1997). _____, The Old Revolutionaries: Political Lives in the Age of Samuel Adams (1980). Main, Jackson Turner, The Sovereign States (1973). Martin, Joseph Plumb, Private Yankee Doodle Dandy (1962). Matson, Cathy D., and Peter S. Onuf, A Union of Interests: Political and Economic Thought in Revolutionary America (1990). Merrell, James H., "Declarations of Independence: Indian-White Relations in the New Nation," in Jack P. Greene, ed., The American Revolution: Its Character and Limits (1987), 197–223. Middlekauff, Robert, The Glorious Cause: The American Revolution, 1763–1789 (1982). Miller, Perry, "From the Covenant to the Revival," in James Ward Smith and A. Leland Jamison, eds., The Shaping of American Religion (1961), 322–368. Morris, Richard B., The Forging of the Union, 1781–1789 (1987). _____, Seven Who Shaped Our Destiny: The Founding Fathers as Revolutionaries (1973). Nash, Gary B., Race and Revolution (1990). _____, The Urban Crucible: Social Change, Political Consciousness, and the Origins of the American Revolution (1979). Norton, Mary Beth, The British-Americans: The Loyalist Exiles in England, 1774–1789 (1972). _____, Liberty's Daughters: The Revolutionary Experience of American Women, 1750–1800 (1980). Onuf, Peter S., "The Origins and Early Development of State Legislatures," in Joel H. Silbey, ed., Encyclopedia of the American Legislative System (1994), 175–194. _____, The Origins of the Federal Republic: Jurisdictional Controversies in the United States, 1775–1787 (1983). _____, Statehood and Union: A History of the Northwest Ordinance (1987). Paine,

Thomas, Collected Writings (1995). Perkins, Bradford, The Cambridge History of American Foreign Relations, Vol I, The Creation of a Republican Empire, 1776–1865 (1993). Rakove, Jack N., The Beginnings of National Politics: An Interpretive History of the Continental Congress (1979).

Smith, Barbara Clark, "Food Rioters and the American Revolution," William and Mary Quarterly, 3d Ser., LI (1994), 3–38. Storing, Herbert J., The Complete Antifederalist, 7 vols (1981). Syrett, Harold C., ed., The Papers of Alexander Hamilton, 27 vols (1961–1987). Szatmary, David P., Shays' Rebellion: The Making of an Agrarian Insurrection (1980). Taylor, Alan, William Cooper's Town: Power and Persuasion on the Frontier of the Early American Republic (1995). Wallace, Anthony F. C., The Death and Rebirth of the Seneca (1969). Washburn, Wilcomb E., ed., History of Indian-White Relations (1988). Weigley, Russell F., Morristown: Official National Park Handbook (1983). _____, The Partisan War: The South Carolina Campaign of 1780–1782 (1970). Wills, Garry, Inventing America: Jefferson's Declaration of Independence (1978). Wood, Gordon S., The Radicalism of the American Revolution (1992). Young, Alfred F., ed., The American Revolution (1976). _____, Beyond the American Revolution: Explorations in the History of American Radicalism (1993).

CHAPTER 8

Appleby, Joyce Oldham, Capitalism and a New Social Order: The Republican Vision of the 1790s (1983). Banning, Lance, The Jeffersonian Persuasion: Evolution of a Party Ideology (1978). _____, The Sacred Fire of Liberty: James Madison and the Founding of the Federal Republic (1995). Beeman, Richard B., The Evolution of the Southern Backcountry: A Case Study of Lunenburg County, Virginia, 1746–1832 (1984). Bemis, Samuel F., Jay's Treaty: A Study in Commerce and Diplomacy (1962). Berkhofer, Robert F., Jr., Salvation and the Savage: An Analysis of Protestant Missions and American Indian Response, 1787–1862 (1965). Berlin, Ira, Many Thousands Gone: The First Two Centuries of Slavery in North America (1998). Buel, Richard, Jr., Securing the Revolution: Ideology in American Politics, 1789–1815 (1972). Calloway, Colin G., Crown and Calumet: British-Indian Relations, 1783–1815 (1987). Cole, Arthur H., ed., Industrial and Commercial Correspondence of Alexander Hamilton (1928). Coxe, Tench, A View of the United States of America Between the Years 1787 and 1794. Cunningham, Noble E., The Jeffersonian Republicans:

The Formation of Party Organization, 1789–1801 (1957). Dillon, Merton L., *Slavery Attacked: Southern Slaves and Their Allies, 1619–1865* (1990). Dorfman, Joseph, *The Economic Mind in American Civilization*, 2 vols (1946). Edmunds, R. David, *Tecumseh: The Quest for Indian Leadership* (1984). Elkins, Stanley, and Eric McKitrick, *The Age of Federalism: The Early American Republic, 1788–1800* (1993).

Hamilton, Alexander, *The Papers of Alexander Hamilton*, ed. Harold C. Syrett et al., 27 vols (1967–87). _____, *The Reports of Alexander Hamilton*, ed. Jacob E. Cooke (1964). Hartz, Louis, *The Liberal Tradition in America: An Interpretation of American Political Thought Since the Revolution* (1955). Henretta, James A., *The Evolution of American Society, 1700–1815: An Interdisciplinary Analysis* (1973). Heyrman, Christine Leigh, *Southern Cross: The Beginnings of the Bible Belt* (1997). Hoffman, Ronald, and Peter J. Albert, eds., *Women in the Age of the American Revolution* (1989). Horsman, Reginald, *Expansionism and American Indian Policy* (1967). Jefferson, Thomas, *Notes on the State of Virginia* (1964). _____, *The Papers of Thomas Jefferson*, ed. Julian P. Boyd, 20 vols (1950). Jordan, Winthrop D., *White Over Black: American Attitudes Toward the Negro, 1550–1812* (1968). Kerber, Linda, *Women of the Republic: Intellect and Ideology in Revolutionary America* (1980). Ketcham, Ralph L., *James Madison: A Biography* (1971). Lee, Jean B., *The Price of Nationhood: The American Revolution in Charles County* (1994).

Malone, Dumas, *Jefferson and His Time* (1948–1981). Marris, Kenneth C., *The Historical Atlas of Political Parties in the United States Congress, 1789–1989* (1989). McCoy, Drew, *The Elusive Republic: Political Economy in Jeffersonian America* (1984). Miller, John C., *The Federalist Era, 1789–1801* (1960). Mittell, Sherman F., ed., *The Federalist: A Commentary on the Constitution of the United States being a Collection of Essays Written in Support of the Constitution agreed upon September 17, 1787, by The Federal Convention* (1937). Nabakov, Peter, ed., *Native American Testimony: I Chronicle of Indian-White Relations from Prophecy to the Present, 1492–1992* (1991). Nelson, John R., Jr., *Liberty and Property: Political Economy and Policy Making, 1789–1812* (1987). Nettels, Curtis P., *The Emergence of a National Economy, 1775–1815* (1962). North, Douglass C., *The Economic Growth of the United States, 1790–1860* (1966). Norton, Mary Beth, *Liberty's Daughters: The Revolutionary Experience of American Women, 1750–1800* (1980). Perdue, Theda, *Slavery and the Evolution of Cherokee Society, 1540–1866* (1979). Peterson, Merrill D., *Thomas Jefferson and the New Nation* (1970). Risjord, Norman K., *Thomas Jefferson* (1994). Rorabaugh, W. J., *The Craft Apprentice, from Franklin to the Machine Age in America* (1986).

Shalhope, Robert E., "Toward a Republican Synthesis: The Emergence of an Understanding of Republicanism in American Historiography," *William and Mary Quarterly*, 3rd Ser. XXXIX (April 1982), 334–356. Sharp, James Roger, *American Politics in the Early Republic: The New Nation in Crisis* (1993). Sheehan, Bernard W., *Seeds of Extinction: Jeffersonian Philanthropy and the American Indian* (1973). Skemp, Sheila L., *Judith Sargent Murray: A Brief Biography with Documents* (1988). Sloan, Herbert, *Principle and Interest: Thomas Jefferson and the Problem of Debt* (1994). Smyth, Albert Henry, ed., *The Writings of Benjamin Franklin* (1907). Sword, Wiley, *President Washington's Indian War* (1985). Taylor, Alan, *Liberty Men and Great Proprietors: The Revolutionary Settlement on the Maine Frontier, 1760–1820* (1990). Ulrich, Laurel Thatcher, *A Midwife's Tale: The Life of Martha Ballard, Based on Her Diary, 1785–1812* (1990). Wallace, Anthony F. C., *The Death and Rebirth of the Seneca* (1970). Watts, Stephen, *The Republic Reborn: War and the Making of Liberal America, 1790–1820* (1987). White, Richard, *The Middle Ground: Indians, Empires, and Republics in the Great Lakes Region, 1650–1815* (1991). Wood, Gordon, *The Creation of the American Republic 1776–1787* (1969). Wright, Donald R., *African Americans in the Early Republic, 1789–1831* (1993). Wright, J. Leitch, Jr., *Creeks and Seminoles: The Destruction and Regeneration of the Muscogulge People* (1986). Yenne, Bill, *The Encyclopedia of North American Indian Tribes: A Comprehensive Study of Tribes from the Abitibi to the Zuni* (1986). Young, Alfred E., *The Democratic Republicans of New York: The Origins, 1763–1797* (1967). Zagarri, Rosemarie, *A Woman's Dilemma: Mercy Otis Warren and the American Revolution* (1995). Zverper, John, *Political Philosophy and Rhetoric: A Study of the Origins of American Party Politics* (1977).

CHAPTER 9

Ambrose, Stephen, *Undaunted Courage: Meriwether Lewis, Thomas Jefferson and the Opening of the American West* (1996). Banning, Lance, *The Jeffersonian Persuasion: Evolution of a Party Ideology* (1978). Beeman, Richard B., *The Evolution of the Southern Backcountry: A Case Study of Lunenburg County, Virginia, 1746–1832* (1984). Bergon, Frank, ed., *The Journals of Lewis and Clark* (1989). Berkhofer, Robert F., Jr., *Salvation and the Savage: An*

Analysis of Protestant Missions and American Indian Response, 1787–1862 (1965). Berlin, Ira, "Time, Space, and the Transformation of Afro-American Society in the United States: 1770–1820" in Elise Marienstras and Barbara Karsky, eds., *Autre Temps, Autre Espace/An Other Time, An Other Place: Études sur l'Amérique pré-Industrielle* (1986). Boles, John B., *Black Southerners, 1619–1869* (1983). _____, *The Great Revival, 1787–1805: The Origins of the Southern Evangelical Mind* (1972). Boyd, Julian P., ed., *The Papers of Thomas Jefferson* (1950). Bruce, Dickson D., Jr., *And They All Sang Hallelujah: Plain-Folk Camp-Meeting Religion, 1800–1845* (1974). Butler, Jon, *Awash in a Sea of Faith: Christianizing the American People* (1972). Cawelti, John G., *Apostles of the Self-Made Man: Changing Concepts of Success in America* (1965). Conklin, Paul K., *Cane Ridge: America's Pentecost* (1990). Curry, Leonard P., *The Free Black in Urban America, 1800–1850: The Shadow of a Dream* (1981). Dillon, Merton L., *Slavery Attacked: Southern Slaves and Their Allies, 1619–1865* (1990). Dowd, Gregory Evans, *A Spirited Resistance: The North American Indian Struggle for Unity, 1745–1815* (1992). Edmunds, R. David, *Tecumseh: The Quest for Indian Leadership* (1984). Egerton, Douglas R., *Gabriel's Rebellion: The Virginia Slave Conspiracies* (1993). Foner, Philip S., *History of Black Americans*. Vol. I, *From Africa to the Emergence of the Cotton Kingdom* (1975).

Henretta, James A., *The Evolution of American Society, 1700–1815: An Interdisciplinary Analysis* (1973). Horsman, Reginald, *Expansionism and American Indian Policy* (1967). Horton, James Oliver, and Lois E., *In Hope of Liberty: Culture, Community, and Protest among Northern Free Blacks, 1700–1860* (1997). Jordan, Winthrop D., *White Over Black: American Attitudes Toward the Negro, 1550–1812* (1968). Litwack, Leon F., *North of Slavery: The Negro in the Free States, 1790–1860* (1961).

Mahon, John K., *The War of 1812* (1972). Malone, Dumas, *Jefferson and His Time* (1948–1981). Marris, Kenneth C., *The Historical Atlas of Political Parties in the United States Congress, 1789–1989* (1989). McCoy, Drew, *The Elusive Republic: Political Economy in Jeffersonian America* (1984). McLoughlin, William G., *Cherokee Renascence in the New Republic* (1986). _____, "Thomas Jefferson and the Beginning of Cherokee Nationalism, 1806–1809," *William and Mary Quarterly*, 3rd Ser., XXXII (1975), 547–580. Melish, Joanne Pope, *Disowning Slavery: Gradual Emancipation and "Race" in New England, 1780–1860* (1998). Nash, Gary B., *Forging Freedom: The Formation of Philadelphia's Black Community, 1720–1840* (1988). Nelson, John R., Jr., *Liberty and Property: Political Economy and Policy Making, 1789–1812* (1987). Nettels, Curtis P., *The Emergence of a National Economy, 1775–1815* (1962). North, Douglass C., *The Economic Growth of the United States, 1790–1860* (1966; first published 1961). Peterson, Merrill D., *Thomas Jefferson and the New Nation* (1970). Risjord, Norman K., *Thomas Jefferson* (1994). Rock, Howard B., *Artisans of the New Republic: The Tradesmen of New York City in the Age of Jefferson* (1984). Rorabaugh, W. J., *The Craft Apprentice, from Franklin to the Machine Age in America* (1986). Ryan, Mary P., *Cradle of the Middle Class: The Family in Oneida County, New York, 1790–1865* (1981).

Scott, Anne Firor, *Natural Allies: Women's Associations in American History* (1992). Shalhope, Robert E., "Toward a Republican Synthesis: The Emergence of an Understanding of Republicanism in American Historiography," *William and Mary Quarterly*, 3rd Ser., XXXIX (1982), 334–356. Sharp, James Roger, *American Politics in the Early Republic: The New Nation in Crisis* (1993). Sheehan, Bernard W., *Seeds of Extinction: Jeffersonian Philanthropy and the American Indian* (1973). Sidbury, James, *Ploughshares into Swords: Race, Rebellion, and Identity in Gabriel's Virginia, 1730–1810* (1997). Sloan, Herbert, *Principle and Interest: Thomas Jefferson and the Problem of Debt* (1994). Smelser, Marshall, *The Democratic Republic, 1801–1815* (1968). Smith, Rogers M., *Civic Ideals: Conflicting Visions of Citizenship in U.S. History* (1997). Stansell, Christine, *City of Women: Sex and Class in New York, 1780–1860* (1986). Stone, Barton W., "A Short History of the Life of Barton W. Stone," in James R. Rogers, *The Cane Ridge Meeting House, to which is Appended the Autobiography of B. W. Stone* (1910). Taylor, Alan, *Liberty Men and Great Proprietors: The Revolutionary Settlement on the Maine Frontier, 1760–1820* (1990). Tucker, Robert W., and David C. Hendrickson, *Empire of Liberty: the Statecraft of Thomas Jefferson* (1990). Ulrich, Laurel Thatcher, *A Midwife's Tale: The Life of Martha Ballard, Based on Her Diary, 1785–1812* (1990). Wallace, Anthony F. C., *Jefferson and the Indians: The Tragic Fate of the First Americans* (1999). Watts, Stephen, *The Republic Reborn: War and the Making of Liberal America, 1790–1820* (1987). White, Shane, *Somewhat More Independent: The End of Slavery in New York City* (1991). Wiebe, Robert H., *The Opening of American Society: From the Adoption of the Constitution to the Eve of Disunion* (1984). Wilentz, Sean, *Chants Democratic: New York City and the*

Rise of the American Working Class, 1788–1850 (1984). Wright, Donald R., *African Americans in the Early Republic, 1789–1831* (1993).

CHAPTER 10

Aaron, Daniel, *Cincinnati, Queen City of the West, 1819–1838* (1992). Ashworth, John, *Slavery, Capitalism, and Politics in the Antebellum Republic.* Vol. I, *Commerce and Compromise, 1820–1850* (1995). Berlin, Ira, *Slaves without Masters: The Free Negro in the Antebellum South* (1974). Blackmar, Elizabeth, *Manhattan for Rent, 1785–1850* (1989). Blassingame, John W., *The Slave Community: Plantation Life in the Antebellum South* (1972). Bleser, Carol, *In Joy and Sorrow: Women, Family, and Marriage in the Victorian South, 1830–1900* (1991). Bolton, Charles C., *Poor Whites of the Antebellum South: Tenants and Laborers in Central North Carolina and Northeastern Mississippi* (1994). Brent, Linda [Harriet Jacobs], *Incidents in the Life of a Slave Girl*, ed. L. Maria Child (1973). Butler, Jon, *Awash in a Sea of Faith: Christianizing the American People* (1990). Carby, Hazel V., *Reconstructing Womanhood: The Emergence of the Afro-American Woman Novelist* (1987). Clark, Christopher, *The Roots of Rural Capitalism: Western Massachusetts, 1780–1860* (1990). Clinton, Catherine, *The Plantation Mistress: Woman's World in the Old South* (1982). Collins, Bruce, *White Society in the Antebellum South* (1985). Conklin, Paul K., *The Uneasy Center: Reformed Christianity in Antebellum America* (1995). Curry, Leonard P., *The Free Black in Urban America, 1800–1850: The Shadow of the Dream* (1981). Dangerfield, George, *The Era of Good Feelings* (1952). Davis, David Brion, *The Problem of Slavery in the Age of Revolution, 1770–1823* (1975). Douglass, Frederick, *Narrative of the Life of Frederick Douglass, an American Slave, Written by Himself*, ed. Benjamin Quarles (1960). Dowd, Gregory, *A Spirited Resistance: The North American Indian Struggle for Unity* (1992). Dublin, Thomas, *Farm to Factory: Women's Letters, 1830–1860*, 2nd ed. (1993). Duncan, John M., *Travels through Part of the United States and Canada in 1818 and 1819*, 2 vols (1823). Escott, Paul D., *Slavery Remembered: A Record of Twentieth-Century Slave Narratives* (1979). Faust, Drew, *James Henry Hammond and the Old South* (1982). Fields, Barbara Jeanne, *Slavery and Freedom on the Middle Ground: Maryland During the Nineteenth Century* (1985). Fox-Genovese, Elizabeth, *Within the Plantation Household: Black and White Women in the Old South* (1988).

Gates, Paul W., *The Farmer's Age: Agriculture, 1815–1860* (1960). Gutman, Herbert G., *The Black Family in Slavery and Freedom, 1750–1925* (1976).

Hahn, Steven, and Jonathan Prude, eds., *The Countryside in the Age of Capitalist Transformation: Essays in the Social History of Rural America* (1985). Harris, J. William, ed., *Society and Culture in the Slave South* (1992). Hudson, Winthrop S., *Religion in America: An Historical Account of the Development of American Religious Life* (1965). Jones, Jacqueline, *Labor of Love, Labor of Sorrow: Black Women, Work, and the Family from Slavery to the Present* (1985). Kolchin, Peter, *American Slavery, 1619–1877* (1993). *Letters of John Pintard to his Daughter Eliza Noel Pontard Davidson, 1816–1833*, 4 vols (1940). Licht, Walter, *Industrializing America: The Nineteenth Century* (1995). Loewenberg, Bert James, and Ruth Bogin, eds., *Black Women in Nineteenth-Century American Life: Their Words, Their Thoughts, Their Feelings* (1976).

McCurry, Stephanie, *Masters of Small Worlds: Yeoman Households, Gender Relations, and the Political Culture of the Antebellum South Carolina Low Country* (1995). Morris, Christopher, *Becoming Southern: The Evolution of a Way of Life, Warren County and Vicksburg, Mississippi, 1770–1860* (1995). Morrison, John H., *History of American Steam Navigation* (1958). Oakes, James, *The Ruling Race: A History of American Slaveholders* (1982). Riley, Glenda, *The Female Frontier: A Comparative View of Women on the Prairie and the Plains* (1988). Rock, Howard B., *Artisans of the New Republic: The Tradesmen of New York in the Age of Jefferson* (1979).

Sellers, Charles, *The Market Revolution: Jacksonian America, 1815–1846* (1991). Shammas, Carole, "Black Women's Work and the Evolution of Plantation Society in Virginia," *Labor History*, 26/1 (Winter 1985), 5–28. Sheriff, Carol, *The Artificial River: The Erie Canal and the Paradox of Progress, 1817–1862* (1996). Stansell, Christine, *City of Women: Sex and Class in New York, 1780–1860* (1986). Tadman, Michael, *Speculators and Slaves: Masters, Traders and Slaves in the Old South* (1989). White, Deborah Gray, *Ar'n't I a Woman? Female Slaves in the Plantation South* (1985). Wilentz, Sean, *Chants Democratic: New York City and the Rise of the American Working Class, 1788–1850* (1984). Wishart, David J., *The Fur Trade of the American West, 1807–1840: A Geographical Synthesis* (1979).

CHAPTER 11

Address of the Republican General Committee of Young Men of the City and County of New York Friendly to the Election of Gen: Andrew Jackson to the Presidency to The Republican Electors of the State of New York (1828). Baxter, Maurice G.,

Henry Clay and the American System (1995). Bellows, Barbara L., *Benevolence Among Slaveholders: Assisting the Poor in Charleston, 1670–1860* (1993). Benson, Lee, *The Concept of Jacksonian Democracy* (1961). Bestor, Arthur, *Backwoods Utopias: The Sectarian Origins and the Owenite Phase of Communitarian Socialism in America, 1663–1829*, 2nd ed. (1970). Butler, Diana Hochstedt, *Standing Against the Whirlwind: Evangelical Episcopalians in Nineteenth-Century America* (1995). Cawelti, John G., *Apostles of the Self-Made Man: Changing Concepts of Success in America* (1965). Clay, Henry, *An Address of Henry Clay, to the Public; Containing Certain Testimony in Refutation of the Charges Against Him, Made by Gen. Andrew Jackson, Touching the Last Presidential Election* (1818). Cole, Donald B., *The Presidency of Andrew Jackson* (1993). Conklin, Paul K., *The Uneasy Center: Reformed Christianity in Antebellum America* (1995). Cott, Nancy F., *The Bonds of Womanhood: "Woman's Sphere" in New England, 1780–1835* (1977). Cross, Whitney, *The Burned-Over District* (1950). Curry, Leonard P., *The Free Black in Urban America, 1800–1850: The Shadow of a Dream* (1981). Feller, Daniel, *The Jacksonian Promise: America, 1815–1840* (1995). _____, *The Public Lands in Jacksonian Politics* (1984). Finney, Charles G[randison], *Autobiography* [Originally Entitled *Memoirs of Charles Grandison Finney*] (1876). Formisano, Ronald P., *The Birth of Mass Political Parties* (1971). Foster, Lawrence, *Women, Family, and Utopia: Communal Experiments of the Shakers, the Oneida Community, and the Mormons* (1991).

Gaustad, Edwin Scott, *A Religious History of America*, Rev. ed. (1966). Ginzberg, Lori D., *Women and the Work of Benevolence: Morality, Politics, and Class in the Nineteenth-Century United States* (1991). Goodrich, Carter, *Government Promotion of American Canals and Railroads, 1800–1890* (1960). Hagan, William T., *The Sac and Fox Indians* (1958). Hall, Thomas Cuming, *The Religious Background of American Culture* (1930). Holt, Michael F., "The Anti-Masonic and Know Nothing Parties," in Arthur M. Schlesinger, Jr., ed., *History of United States Political Parties*, 4 vols (1973). _____, *The Political Crisis of the 1850s* (1978). Horsman, Reginald, *Race and Manifest Destiny: The Origins of American Racial Anglo-Saxonism* (1981). Jackson, Donald, ed., *Black Hawk: An Autobiography* (1955). Johnson, Paul E., *A Shopkeeper's Millennium* (1978). _____, and Sean Wilentz, *The Kingdom of Matthias: The Story of Sex and Salvation in Nineteenth-Century America* (1994). Licht, Walter, *Industrialization in Amer-*

ica: The Nineteenth Century (1995). Litwack, Leon F., *North of Slavery: The Negro in the Free States, 1790–1860* (1961). Loewenberg, Bert James, and Ruth Bogin, eds., *Black Women in Nineteenth-Century American Life: Their Words, Their Thoughts, Their Feelings* (1976).

Matthews, Donald G., "The Second Great Awakening as an Organizing Process, 1780–1830," *American Quarterly*, XXI (1969), 23–43. McCormick, Richard P., *The Second American Party System* (1966). McLoughlin, William G., *Cherokee Renascence in the New Republic* (1986). Mintz, Stephen, *Moralizers and Modernizers: America's Pre-Civil War Reformers* (1995). Nash, Gary B., *Forging Freedom: The Formation of Philadelphia's Black Community, 1720–1840* (1988). Nordhoff, Charles, *The Communistic Societies of the United States: From Personal Observations* (1966). Pollack, Queena, *Peggy Eaton: Democracy's Mistress* (1931). Prucha, Francis P., *The Great Father: The United States Government and the Indians*, 2 vols (1984). _____, *Sword of the Republic: The United States Army on the Frontier, 1783–1846* (1969). Remini, Robert V., *Andrew Jackson and the Course of American Democracy, 1833–1845* (1984). _____, *Andrew Jackson and the Course of American Empire, 1767–1821* (1977). _____, *Andrew Jackson and the Course of American Freedom, 1822–1832* (1981). Roediger, David, *The Wages of Whiteness: Race and the Making of the American Working Class* (1991). Rosenberg, Carroll Smith, *Religion and the Rise of the American City: The New York City Mission Movement, 1812–1870* (1971). Rowe, David, *Thunder and Trumpets: Millerites and Dissenting Religion in Upstate New York, 1800–1850* (1985). Rugoff, Milton, *The Beechers: An American Family of the Nineteenth Century* (1981). Ryan, Mary P., *Cradle of the Middle Class: The Family in Oneida County, New York, 1790–1865* (1981).

Satz, Ronald D., *American Indian Policy in the Jacksonian Era* (1977). Saxton, Alexander, *The Rise and Fall of the White Republic: Class Politics and Mass Culture in Nineteenth-Century America* (1990). Schlesinger, Arthur M., Jr., *The Age of Jackson* (1947). Sellers, Charles, *The Market Revolution: Jacksonian America, 1815–1846* (1991). Smith, Sam B., and Harriet Chappell Owsley, eds., *The Papers of Andrew Jackson*, 6 vols (1980). Spellman, Peter W., and Thomas A. Askew, *The Churches and the American Experience: Ideals and Institutions* (1984). Stansell, Christine, *City of Women: Sex and Class in New York, 1789–1860* (1986). Tanner, Helen Hornbeck, ed., *Atlas of Great Lakes Indian History* (1987). Taylor, George Rogers, ed., *Jackson Versus Biddle: The*

Struggle over the Second Bank of the United States (1949). Van Deusen, Glendon G., *The Jacksonian Era, 1828–1848* (1959). Wallace, Anthony F. C., "Prelude to Disaster: The Course of Indian-White Relations Which Led to the Black Hawk War of 1832," in Ellen M. Whitney, ed., *The Black Hawk War, 1831–1832* (Published as vols 35–38, *Collections of the Illinois State Historical Library* 1970–1978.) I, 1–51. Walter, Ronald G., *American Reformers, 1815–1860* (1978). Ward, John William, *Andrew Jackson—Symbol for an Age* (1953). Watson, Harry L., *Liberty and Power: The Politics of Jacksonian America* (1990). Weddle, David L., *The Law as Gospel: Revival and Reform in the Theology of Charles G. Finney* (1985). Wilburn, Jean Alexander, *Biddle's Bank: The Crucial Years* (1967). Wilentz, Sean, *Chants Democratic: New York City and the Rise of the American Working Class, 1788–1850* (1984).

CHAPTER 12

Billington, Ray Allen, *The Protestant Crusade, 1800–1860: A Study of the Origins of American Nativism* (1938). Blackmar, Elizabeth, *Manhattan for Rent, 1785–1850* (1989). Blumin, Stuart M., *The Emergence of the Middle Class: Social Experience in the American City, 1760–1900* (1989). Boydston, Jeanne, *Home and Work: Housework, Wages, and the Ideology of Labor in the Early Republic* (1990). Carlton, Frank Tracy, *Economic Influences upon Educational Progress in the United States, 1820–1850* (1965). Cawelti, John G., *Apostles of the Self-Made Man: Changing Concepts of Success in America* (1965). Child, Mrs. [Lydia Maria], *The American Frugal Housewife*, 12th ed., (1833). Cole, Donald B., *The Presidency of Andrew Jackson* (1993). Cott, Nancy F., *The Bonds of Womanhood: "Woman's Sphere" in New England, 1780–1835* (1977). Curry, Leonard P., *The Free Black in Urban America, 1800–1850: The Shadow of a Dream* (1981). Davis, David Brion, "The Emergence of Immediatism in British and American Antislavery Thought," *Mississippi Valley Historical Review*, XLIX (September 1962), 209–230. Dew, Thomas R., *Review of the Debate in the Virginia Legislature of 1831 and 1832* (1832). Duberman, Martin, ed., *The Antislavery Vanguard: New Essays on the Abolitionists* (1965). Dudley, William, ed., *Slavery: Opposing Views* (1992). Feller, Daniel, *The Jacksonian Promise: America, 1815–1840* (1995). Foner, Philip S., *From Colonial Times to the Founding of the American Federation of Labor.* Vol. I, *History of the Labor Movement in the United States* (1947). _____, *Women and the American Labor Movement: From the First Trade Unions to the Present* (1979). Freyer, Tony A., *Producers versus Capitalists: Constitutional Conflict in Antebellum America* (1994). Friedman, Lawrence J., *Gregarious Saints: Self and Community in American Abolitionism, 1830–1870* (1982).

Ginzberg, Lori D., "'The Hearts of Your Readers Will Shudder': Fanny Wright, Infidelity, and American Free Thought," *American Quarterly*, Vol. 46, No. 2 (June 1994), 195–226. Griffin, Clifford S., *Their Brothers' Keepers: Moral Stewardship in the United States, 1800–1865* (1960). Jackson, Sidney L., *America's Struggle for Free Schools: Social Tension and Education in New England and New York, 1827–42* (1965). Kaestle, Carl F., *Pillars of the Republic: Common Schools and American Society, 1780–1860* (1983). Katz, Michael B., *The Irony of Early School Reform: Educational Innovation in Mid-Nineteenth-Century Massachusetts* (1968). Lazerow, Jama, *Religion and the Working Class in Antebellum America* (1995).

Mintz, Stephen, *Moralizers and Modernizers: America's Pre-Civil War Reformers* (1995). North, Douglass C., *The Economic Growth of the United States, 1790–1860* (1966; first published 1961). Pease, William H., and Jane H., *The Web of Progress: Private Values and Public Styles in Boston and Charleston, 1828–1843* (1985). Remini, Robert V., *Andrew Jackson and the Course of American Democracy, 1833–1845* (1984). _____, *Andrew Jackson and the Course of American Empire, 1767–1821* (1977). _____, *Andrew Jackson and the Course of American Freedom, 1822–1832* (1981). _____, *The Election of Andrew Jackson* (1963). Roediger, David R., *Towards the Abolition of Whiteness: Essays on Race, Politics, and Working Class History* (1994). _____, *The Wages of Whiteness: Race and the Making of the American Working Class* (1991). Rosenberg, Carroll Smith, *Religion and the Rise of the American City: The New York City Mission Movement, 1812–1870* (1971). Rudolph, Frederick, ed., *Essays on Education in the Early Republic* (1965). Ryan, Mary P., *Cradle of the Middle Class: The Family in Oneida County, New York, 1790–1865* (1981).

Saxton, Alexander, *The Rise and Fall of the White Republic: Class Politics and Mass Culture in Nineteenth-Century America* (1990). Schlesinger, Arthur M., Jr., *The Age of Jackson* (1947). Scott, Anne Firor, *Natural Allies: Women's Associations in American History* (1992). Smith, Sam B., and Harriet Chappell Owsley, eds., *The Papers of Andrew Jackson*, 6 vols (1980). Stansell, Christine, *City* of Women: Sex and Class in New York, 1789–1860 (1986). Vassar, Rena L., ed., Social History of American Education. Vol. I, Colonial Times to 1860 (1965). Walker, David, David Walker's Appeal to the Coloured Citizens of the World (1995). Walters, Ron, American Reformers, 1815–1860 (1978). Welter, Rush, Popular Education and Democratic Thought in America (1962). Wilentz, Sean, Chants Democratic: New York City and the Rise of the American Working Class, 1788–1850 (1984). Yellin, Jean Fagan, and John C. Van Horne, eds., The Abolitionist Sisterhood: Women's Political Culture in Antebellum America (1994).

CHAPTER 13

Ballantine, Betty, and Ian, eds., The Native Americans: An Illustrated History (1993). Bauer, K. Jack, The Mexican War, 1846–1848 (1974). Bergeron, Paul H., The Presidency of James K. Polk (1987). Binkley, William C., The Texas Revolution (1952). Blue, Frederick J., The Free Soilers: Third Party Politics (1973). Brack, Gene M., Mexico Views Manifest Destiny (1976). Butruille, Susan G., Women's Voices from the Oregon Trail (1993). Campbell, Randolph B., An Empire for Slavery: The Peculiar Institution in Texas (1989). Clark, Christopher, The Communitarian Moment: The Radical Challenge of the Northampton Association (1995). Clark, Malcolm, Jr., Eden Seekers: The Settlement of Oregon, 1818–1862 (1981). Clayton, Lawrence R., and Joseph E. Chance, eds., The March to Monterrey: The Diary of Lt. Rankin Dilworth (1966). Dawley, Alan, Class and Community: The Industrial Revolution in Lynn (1976). Dillon, Merton L., Slavery Attacked: Southern Slaves and Their Allies, 1618–1685 (1990). Faragher, John Mack, Women and Men on the Overland Trail (1979). Faust, Drew Gilpin, ed., The Ideology of Slavery: Proslavery Thought in the Antebellum South, 1830–1860 (1981). Foster, Lawrence, Women, Family, and Utopia: Communal Experiments of the Shakers, the Oneida Community, and the Mormons (1991).

Ginzberg, Lori D., Women and the Work of Benevolence: Morality, Politics, and Class in the Nineteenth-Century United States (1990). Graebner, Norman A., Empire on the Pacific: A Study in American Continental Expansion (1955). Holloway, Mark, Heavens on Earth: Utopian Communities in America, 1680–1880, 2nd ed. (1966). Horsman, Reginald, Race and Manifest Destiny: The Origins of American Racial Anglo-Saxonism (1981). Isenberg, Nancy, Sex and Citizenship in Antebellum America

(1998). Jeffrey, Julie Roy, Converting the West: A Biography of Narcissa Whitman (1991). Johannsen, Robert W., To the Halls of Montezumas: The Mexican War in the American Imagination (1985). Johnson, Paul E., and Sean Wilentz, The Kingdom of Matthias: A Story of Sex and Salvation in Nineteenth-Century America (1994). Kohl, Lawrence Frederick, The Politics of Individualism: Parties and the American Character in the Jacksonian Era (1989).

Maffly-Kipp, Laurie F., Religion and Society in Frontier California (1994). Marquis, Thomas B., The Cheyennes of Montana, ed. Thomas D. Weist (1978). Matovina, Timothy M., Tejano Religion and Ethnicity: San Antonio, 1821–1860 (1995). McCaffrey, James M., Army of Manifest Destiny: The American Soldier in the Mexican War, 1846–1848 (1992). Miller, Robert Ryan, ed., The Mexican War Journal and Letters of Ralph W. Kirkham (1991). Mintz, Steven, Moralists and Modernizers: America's Pre-Civil War Reformers (1995). Monaghan, Jay, The Overland Trail (1971). Montejano, David, Anglos and Mexicans in the Making of Texas, 1836–1986 (1987). Morrison, Michael A., Slavery and the American West: The Eclipse of Manifest Destiny and the Coming of the Civil War (1997). Parker, Theodore, The Slave Power (1969). Peterson, Norma Lois, The Presidencies of William Henry Harrison and John Tyler (1989). Prude, Jonathan, The Coming of the Industrial Order: Town and Factory Life in Rural Massachusetts, 1810–1860 (1983). Reidy, Joseph, From Slavery to Agrarian Capitalism in the Cotton Plantation South: Central Georgia, 1800–1880 (1992). Remini, Robert, Martin Van Buren and the Making of the Democratic Party (1959).

Schroeder, John H., Mr. Polk's War: American Opposition and Dissent, 1846–1848 (1973). Seager, Robert, II, And Tyler Too: A Biography of John and Julia Gardiner Tyler (1963). Sellers, Charles, James K. Polk, Continentalist: 1843–1846 (1966). _____, James K. Polk, Jacksonian: 1795–1843 (1957). Sloan, Irving J., ed., Martin van Buren, 1782–1862 (1969). Smith-Rosenberg, Carroll, Disorderly Conduct: Visions of Gender in Victorian America (1985). Stansell, Christine, City of Women: Sex and Class in New York, 1789–1860 (1986). Stephanson, Anders, Manifest Destiny: American Expansion and the Empire of Right (1995). Tijerina, Andrés, Tejanos and Texas under the Mexican Flag, 1821–1836 (1994). Weber, David, The Mexican Frontier, 1821–1846: The American Southwest under Mexico (1982). White, Richard, "It's Your Misfortune and None of My Own"; A History of *the American West* (1991). Wilentz, Sean, *Chants Democratic: New York City and the Rise of the American Working Class, 1788–1850* (1984). Wilson, Major L., *The Presidency of Martin Van Buren* (1984).

CHAPTER 14

Barney, William, *The Road to Secession: A New Perspective on the Old South* (1972). Blumin, Stuart, *The Emergence of the Middle Class: Social Experience in the American City, 1790–1900* (1989). Campbell, Stanley, *The Slave Catchers* (1970). Cooper, William J., Jr., *The South and the Politics of Slavery, 1828–1856* (1978). Craven, Avery, *The Coming of the Civil War*, 2nd ed. (1957). Fehrenbacher, Don E., *Prelude to Greatness: Lincoln in the 1850s* (1952). Fehrenbacher, Don, *The Slaveholding Republic: An Account of the United States Government's Relations to Slavery* (2001). Fishlow, Albert, *American Railroads and the Transformation of the Antebellum Economy* (1965). Fogel, Robert, *Without Consent or Contract: The Rise and Fall of American Slavery* (1989).

Genovese, Eugene D., *The Political Economy of Slavery: Studies in the Economy and Society of the Slave South* (1965). Greenstone, David J., *The Lincoln Persuasion: Remaking American Liberalism* (1993). Hamilton, Holman, *Prologue to Conflict: The Crisis and Compromise of 1850* (1970). Holt, Michael F., *The Rise and Fall of the American Whig Party: Jacksonian Politics and the Onset of the Civil War* (1999). Huston, James, *The Panic of 1857 and the Coming of the Civil War* (1987). Jaffa, Harry V., *Crisis of the House Divided: An Interpretation of the Lincoln-Douglas Debates* (1959). Johannsen, Robert W., *Stephen A. Douglas* (1973). Johnson, Walter, *Soul By Soul: Life Inside the Antebellum Slave Market* (1999).

May, Robert E., *The Southern Dream of a Caribbean Empire, 1854–1861* (1973). McCardell, John, *The Idea of a Southern Nation: Southern Nationalists and Southern Nationalism, 1830–1860* (1979). Morrison, Chaplain W., *Democratic Politics and Sectionalism: The Wilmot Proviso Controversy* (1967). Nevins, Allan, *Ordeal of the Union*, 4 vols (1947–1950). Nichols, Roy F., *The Disruption of American Democracy* (1948). Niven, John, *The Coming of the Civil War, 1837–1861* (1990). Oakes, James, *Slavery and Freedom: An Interpretation of the Old South* (1990). Potter, David M., *The South and the Sectional Conflict* (1969).

Sewell, Richard B., *Ballots for Freedom: Antislavery Politics in the United States, 1837–1860* (1976). Stampp, Kenneth M., *America in 1857: A Nation*

on the Brink (1990). Summers, Mark W., *The Plundering Generation: Corruption and the Crisis of the Union, 1849–1861* (1987). Tadman, Michael, *Speculators and Slaves: Masters, Traders, and Slaves in the Old South* (1996 ed.). Takaki, Ronald, *A Pro-Slavery Crusade: The Agitation to Reopen the African Slave Trade* (1971). Wright, Gavin, *The Political Economy of the Cotton South: Households, Markets and Wealth in the Nineteenth Century* (1978). Zarefsky, David, *Lincoln, Douglas, and Slavery: The Crucible of Public Debate* (1990).

CHAPTER 15

Ball, Douglas B., *Financial Failure and Confederate Defeat* (1990). Barney, William L., *The Secessionist Impulse: Alabama and Mississippi in 1860* (1974). Bernstein, Iver, *The New York City Draft Riots: Their Significance for American Society and Politics in the Age of the Civil War* (1990). Catton, Bruce, *This Hallowed Ground* (1956). _____, *Glory Road* (1952). _____, *Mr. Lincoln's Army* (1951). _____, *A Stillness at Appomattox* (1953). Channing, Steven A., *Crisis of Fear: Secession in South Carolina* (1970). Clinton, Catherine, and Nina Silber, eds., *Divided Houses: Gender and the Civil War* (1992). Connelly, Thomas L., *The Marble Man: Robert E. Lee and His Image in American Society* (1977). Cooper, William J., Jr. *Jefferson Davis: American* (2000). Cornish, Dudley T., *The Sable Arm: Negro Troops in the Union Army* (1977). Current, Richard, *Lincoln and the First Shot* (1963). _____, ed., *Why the North Won the Civil War* (1960). Eaton, Clement, *A History of the Southern Confederacy* (1954). Escott, Paul D., *After Secession: Jefferson Davis and the Failure of Confederate Nationalism* (1978). Faust, Drew Gilpin, *The Creation of Confederate Nationalism* (1988). _____, *Mothers of Invention: Women of the Slaveholding South in the American Civil War* (1996). Fredrickson, George M., *The Inner Civil War: Northern Intellectuals and the Crisis of the Union* (1965).

Glatthaar, Joseph T., *Forged in Battle: The Civil War Alliance of Black Soldiers and White Officers* (1990). Guelzo, Allen C., *Abraham Lincoln: Redeemer President* (1999). Hettle, Wallace, *The Peculiar Democracy: Southern Democrats in Peace and Civil War* (2001). Jaffa, Harry V., *A New Birth of Freedom: Abraham Lincoln and the Coming of the Civil War* (2000). Jones, Howard, *The Union in Peril: The Crisis over British Intervention in the Civil War* (1992). Linderman, Gerald, *Embattled Courage: The Experience of Combat in the American Civil War* (1987).

McPherson, James M., *For Cause and Comrades: Why Men Fought in the Civil War* (1997). _____, *The Negro's Civil War: How American Negroes Felt and Acted During the War for the Union* (1965). _____, *The Struggle for Equality: Abolitionists and the Negro in the Civil War and Reconstruction* (1964). _____, *What They Fought For, 1861–1865* (1994). Mitchell, Reid, *Civil War Soldiers* (1988). _____, *The Vacant Chair: The Northern Soldier Leaves Home* (1993). Neely, Mark E., Jr., *The Fate of Liberty: Abraham Lincoln and Civil Liberties* (1990). Nevins, Allan, *The War for the Union*, 4 vols (1959–1971). Nolan, Alan T., *Lee Considered: General Robert E. Lee and Civil War History* (1991). Oates, Steven B., *A Woman of Valor: Clara Barton and the Civil War* (1994). Paludan, Phillip S., *Victims: A True Story of the Civil War* (1981). Potter, David M., *Lincoln and His Party in the Secession Crisis* (1942). Quarles, Benjamin, *The Negro in the Civil War* (1953). Rable, George C., *Civil Wars: Women and the Crisis of Southern Nationalism* (1989). Roark, James L., *Masters Without Slaves: Southern Planters in the Civil War and Reconstruction* (1977).

Thomas, Emory, *Robert E. Lee: A Biography* (1995). Vinovskis, Maris A., ed., *Toward a Social History of the American Civil War* (1990). Voegli, V. Jacques, *Free But Not Equal: The Midwest and the Negro during the Civil War* (1967). Wiley, Bell Irwin, *The Life of Billy Yank* (1952). _____, *The Life of Johnny Reb* (1943). Wilson, Douglas, *Honor's Voice: The Transformation of Abraham Lincoln* (1998).

CHAPTER 16

Belz, Herman, *Emancipation and Equal Rights: Politics and Constitutionalism in the Civil War Era* (1978). _____, *Reconstructing the Union: Theory and Policy during the Civil War* (1969). Benedict, Michael Les, *A Compromise of Principle: Congressional Republicans and Reconstruction* (1974). Brock, W. R., *An American Crisis: Congress and Reconstruction, 1865–1867* (1963). Cox, LaWanda, *Lincoln and Black Freedom: A Study in Presidential Leadership* (1981). Current, Richard, *Those Terrible Carpetbaggers* (1988). Donald, David, *The Politics of Reconstruction, 1864–1867* (1967). DuBois, Ellen Carol, *Feminism and Suffrage: The Emergence of an Independent Women's Movement in America, 1848–1869* (1978). Edwards, Laura, *Gendered Strife and Confusion: The Political Culture of Reconstruction* (1977). Fields, Barbara Jeanne, *Slavery and Freedom on the Middle Ground: Maryland during the Nineteenth Century* (1985). Foner, Eric, *Freedom's Lawmakers: A Directory of Black Officeholders during Reconstruction* (1993). _____, *Nothing But Freedom: Emancipation and Its Legacy* (1983).

Gillette, William, *Retreat from Reconstruction, 1869–1879* (1979). Hermann, Janet Sharp, *The Pursuit of a Dream* (1981). Holt, Thomas G., *Black over White: Negro Political Leadership in South Carolina during Reconstruction* (1977). Hyman, Harold, *A More Perfect Union: The Impact of the Civil War and Reconstruction on the Constitution* (1973). Jaynes, Gerald David, *Branches without Roots: Genesis of the Black Working Class in the American South, 1862–1882* (1986).

McCrary, Peyton, *Abraham Lincoln and Reconstruction: The Louisiana Experiment* (1978). McFeely, William S., *Grant: A Biography* (1981). _____, *Yankee Stepfather: General O. O. Howard and the Freedmen* (1968). McGerr, Michael, *The Decline of Popular Politics: The American North, 1865–1928* (1986). McKitrick, Eric L., *Andrew Johnson and Reconstruction* (1960). Montgomery, David, *Beyond Equality: Labor and the Radical Republicans, 1861–1872* (1967). Morgan, Lynda J., *Emancipation in Virginia's Tobacco Belt, 1850–1870* (1992). Nieman, Donald L., *To Set the Law in Motion: The Freedmen's Bureau and Legal Rights for Blacks, 1865–1869* (1979). Perman, Michael, *Reunion without Compromise: The South and Reconstruction, 1865–1879* (1973). _____, *The Road to Redemption: Southern Politics, 1868–1879* (1984). Powell, Lawrence N., *New Masters: Northern Planters during the Civil War and Reconstruction* (1980). Rabinowitz, Howard N., *Race Relations in the Urban South, 1865–1890* (1978). Rose, Willie Lee, *Rehearsal for Reconstruction: The Port Royal Experiment* (1964). Royce, Edward, *The Origins of Southern Sharecropping* (1993).

Saville, Julie, *The Work of Reconstruction: From Slave to Wage Laborer in South Carolina, 1860–1870* (1994). Sproat, John G., *"The Best Men": Liberal Reformers in a Gilded Age* (1968). Summers, Mark, *Railroads, Reconstruction and the Gospel of Prosperity: Aid Under the Radical Republicans, 1865–1877* (1984). Trelease, Allen W., *White Terror: The Ku Klux Klan Conspiracy and Southern Reconstruction* (1971). Wayne, Michael, *The Reshaping of Plantation Society: The Natchez District, 1860–1880* (1983). Wiener, Jonathan, *Social Origins of the New South: Alabama, 1860–1885* (1978). Williamson, Joel, *After Slavery: The Negro in South Carolina during Reconstruction, 1861–1877* (1965). Wright, Gavin, *Old South, New South: Revolutions in the Southern Economy Since the Civil War* (1986).

CHAPTER 17

Ayers, Edward L., *The Promise of the New South: Life after Reconstruction* (1992). Bledstein, Burton J., *The Culture of Professionalism: The Middle Class and the Development of Higher Education in America* (1976). Bodnar, John E., *The Transplanted: A History of Immigrants in Urban America* (1985). Brody, David, *Steelworkers in America: The Nonunion Era* (1960). Cochran, Thomas, and William Miller, *The Age of Enterprise: A Social History of Industrial America* (1942). Dubofsky, Melvin, *Industrialism and the American Worker* (1975). Dykstra, Robert R., *The Cattle Towns* (1968). Fite, Gilbert C., *The Farmer's Frontier* (1963).

Goldfield, David, and Blaine Brownell, *Urban America: A History*, 2nd. ed. (1990). Gutman, Herbert G., *Work, Culture and Society in Industrialising America* (1976). Handlin, Oscar, *The Uprooted: The Epic Story of the Great Migrations that Made the American People* (1951, 1973). Hearnden, Patrick H., *Independence and Empire: The New South's Cotton Mill Campaign, 1865–1901* (1982). Jackson, Kenneth T., *Crabgrass Frontier: The Suburbanization of the United States* (1985). Jeffrey, Julie Roy, *Frontier Women* (1979). Johnson, Susan Lee, *Roaring Camp: The Social World of the California Gold Rush* (2000). Josephson, Matthew, *The Robber Barons: The Great American Capitalists, 1861–1901* (1934). Limerick, Patricia Nelson, *Legacy of Conquest: The Unbroken Past of the American West* (1987). Lingenfelter, Richard, *The Hardrock Miners: A History of the Mining Labor Movement in the American West, 1863–1893* (1974).

Montgomery, David, *Workers' Control in America: Studies in the History of Work, Technology, and Labor Struggles* (1979). Rabinowitz, Howard, *Race Relations in the Urban South, 1865–1890* (1978).

Slotkin, Richard, *The Fatal Environment: The Myth of the Frontier in the Age of Industrialization* (1985). Taylor, Philip A. M., *The Distant Magnet: European Emigration to the U.S.A.* (1971). Teaford, Jon C., *City and Suburb: The Political Fragmentation of Metropolitan America, 1850–1970* (1979). Thernstrom, Stephen, *The Other Bostonians: Poverty and Progress in the American Metropolis, 1880–1970* (1973). Utley, Robert M., *The Indian Frontier of the American West, 1846–1890* (1984). Wiebe, Robert, *The Search for Order, 1877–1920* (1967). Wyman, Mark, *Hard Rock Epic: Western Miners and the Industrial Revolution, 1860–1910* (1979).

CHAPTER 18

Addams, Jane, *Twenty Years at Hull House* (1910). Archdeacon, Thomas, *Becoming American: An Ethnic History* (1981). Banner, Lois, *American Beauty* (1981). Barth, Gunther, *City People: The Rise of Modern City Culture in Nineteenth-Century America* (1980). Beisel, Nicola Kay, *Imperiled Innocents: Anthony Comstock and Family Reproduction in Victorian America* (1997). Bodnar, John, *The Transplanted: A History of Immigrants in Urban America* (1985). Boorstin, Daniel J., *The Americans: The Democratic Experience* (1973). Boyer, Paul S., *Purity in Print: The Vice-Society Movement and Book Censorship in America* (1968). Danly, Susan, and Cheryl Leibold, et al., *Eakins and the Photograph* (1994). Fabian, Ann, *Card Sharps and Bucket Shops: Gambling in Nineteenth-Century America* (1999). Fredrickson, George, *The Black Image in the White Mind: The Debate on Afro-American Character and Destiny, 1817–1914* (1971).

Gilfoyle, Timothy, *City of Eros: New York City, Prostitution, and the Commercialization of Sex, 1820–1920* (1992). Gorn, Elliot J., *The Manly Art: Bare-Knuckle Prize Fighting in America* (1986). Graff, Gerald, *Professing Literature: An Institutional History* (1987). Green, Harvey, *Fit for America: Health, Fitness, Sport, and American Society* (1986). Harris, Neil, *Cultural Excursions: Marketing Appetites and Cultural Tastes in Modern America* (1990). Hawkins, Mike, *Social Darwinism in European and American Thought, 1860–1945: Nature as Model and Nature as Threat* (1997). Higham, John, *Send These To Me: Jews and Other Immigrants in Urban America* (1984). Hofstadter, Richard, *Social Darwinism in American Thought* (1992). Lears, T. J. Jackson, *No Place of Grace: Antimodernism and the Transformation of American Culture, 1880–1920* (1981). Lott, Eric, *Love and Theft: Blackface Minstrelsy and the American Working Class* (1993). Lucie-Smith, Edward, *American Realism* (1994).

May, Henry, *Protestant Churches and Industrial America* (1949 and 1963). Mintz, Steven, *A Prison of Expectations: The Family in Victorian Culture* (1983). Nasaw, David, *Going Out: The Rise and Fall of Public Amusements* (1993). Novak, Barbara, *American Painting of the Nineteenth Century: Realism, Idealism, and the American Experience*, 2nd ed. (1979). Rodgers, Daniel, *The Work Ethic in Industrial America, 1850–1920* (1970). Rothman, Sheila M., *Woman's Proper Place: A History of Changing Ideals and Practices, 1870 to the Present* (1978). Rydell, Robert, *All the World's a Fair: Visions of Empire at American International Expositions, 1876–1916* (1984).

Sollors, Werner, *Beyond Ethnicity: Consent and Descent in American Culture* (1986). Toll, Robert, *On with the Show: The First Century of Show Business in America* (1976). Trachtenberg, Alan, *Reading American Photographs: Images as History, Mathew Brady to Walker Evans* (1989).

CHAPTER 19

Baker, Paula C., *The Moral Frameworks of Public Life: Gender, Politics, and the State in Rural New York, 1870–1930* (1991). Beatty, Bess, *A Revolution Gone Backward: The Black Response to National Politics, 1876–1896* (1987). Beisner, Robert L., *From the Old Diplomacy to the New, 1865–1900* (1975). Bordin, Ruth, *Frances Willard: A Biography* (1986). Brock, William R., *Investigation and Responsibility: Public Responsibility in the United States, 1865–1900* (1984). Buhle, Mary Jo, *Women and American Socialism, 1870–1920* (1981). Campbell, Ballard, *Representative Democracy: Public Policy and Midwestern Legislatures in the Late Nineteenth Century* (1980). Campbell, Charles S., *The Transformation of American Foreign Relations, 1865–1900* (1976).

Garraty, John A., *The New Commonwealth, 1877–1890* (1968). Gould, Lewis L., *The Presidency of William McKinley* (1980). Hays, Samuel P., *The Response to Industrialism, 1885–1914*, 2nd ed. (1995). Jensen, Richard J., *The Winning of the Midwest: Social and Political Conflict, 1888–1896* (1971). Keller, Morton, *Affairs of State: Public Life in Late-Nineteenth-Century America* (1977). Kleppner, Paul J., *The Cross of Culture: A Social Analysis of Midwestern Politics, 1850–1900* (1970).

McCormick, Richard L., *The Party Period and Public Policy: American Politics from the Age of Jackson to the Progressive Era* (1986). McMath, Robert C., Jr., *The Populist Vanguard: A History of the Southern Farmers' Alliance* (1975). Mink, Gwendolyn, *Old Labor and New Immigrants in American Political Development: Union, Party, and the State, 1875–1920* (1986). Morgan, H. Wayne, *From Hayes to McKinley: National Politics, 1877–1896* (1969). Nugent, Walter T. K., *Money and American Society, 1865–1880* (1968). Orren, Karen, *Belated Feudalism: Labor, the Law, and Liberal Development in the United States* (1991). Painter, Nell Irvin, *Standing at Armageddon: The United States, 1877–1919* (1987). Peskin, Allan, *Garfield: A Biography* (1978). Reeves, Thomas C., *Gentleman Boss: The Life of Chester Alan Arthur* (1975).

Skowronek, Stephen, *Building A New American State: The Expansion of National Administration Capacities, 1877–1920* (1982). Socolofsky, Homer

Edward, and Allan B. Spetter, *The Presidency of Benjamin Harrison* (1987). Teaford, Jon C., *The Unheralded Triumph: City Government in America, 1870–1900* (1984). Terrill, Tom E., *The Tariff, Politics and American Foreign Policy, 1874–1900* (1973). Tomsich, John, *A Genteel Endeavor: American Culture and Politics in the Gilded Age* (1971). Unger, Irwin, *The Greenback Era: A Social and Political History of American Finance, 1865–1879* (1964).Weinstein, Allen, *Prelude to Populism: Origins of the Silver Issue, 1867–1878* (1970). Welch, Richard E., Jr., *The Presidencies of Grover Cleveland* (1988). Wiebe, Robert H., *The Search for Order, 1877–1920* (1967).

CHAPTER 20

Adams, Henry, *The Education of Henry Adams* (1918). Ayers, Edward L., *The Promise of the New South: Life After Reconstruction* (1992). Bailey, Thomas A., *A Diplomatic History of the American People* (1958). Brands, H. W., *The Reckless Decade: America in the 1890s* (1995). Chernow, Ron, *The House of Morgan: An American Banking Dynasty and the Rise of Modern Finance* (1990). Cochran, Thomas C., and William Miller, *The Age of Enterprise: A Social History of Industrial America* (1961). Dulles, Foster Rhea, *Labor in America: A History* (1960).

Gilbert, James B., *Perfect Cities: Chicago's Utopias of 1893* (1991). Ginger, Ray, *Age of Excess: The United States from 1877 to 1914* (1965). _____, *Altgeld's America: The Lincoln Ideal Versus Changing Realities* (1958). Kanigel, Robert, *The One Best Way: Frederick Winslow Taylor and the Enigma of Efficiency* (1997). Karnow, Stanley, *In Our Image: America's Empire in the Philippines* (1989). Lewis, David L., *W. E. B. Du Bois: Biography of a Race, 1868–1919* (1993).

McCloskey, Robert Green, *American Conservatism in the Age of Enterprise, 1865–1910* (1951). McCormick, Richard L., *The Party Period and Public Policy* (1986). McCormick, Thomas J., *China Market: America's Quest for Informal Empire, 1893–1901* (1967). McDougall, Walter A., *Let the Sea Make a Noise: A History of the North Pacific from Magellan to MacArthur* (1993). McGerr, Michael E., *The Decline of Popular Politics: The American North, 1865–1928* (1986). Montgomery, David, *The Fall of the House of Labor: The Workplace, the State, and American Labor Activism, 1865–1925* (1987). Musicant, Ivan, *Empire by Default: The Spanish American War and the Dawn of the American Century* (1998). Richardson, Dorothy, *The Long Day: The Story of a New York Working Girl*

(1990). Rosenberg, Emily S., *Spreading the American Dream: American Economic and Cultural Expansion, 1890–1945* (1982).

Salvatore, Nick, *Eugene V. Debs: Citizen and Socialist* (1982). Schirmer, Daniel B., *Republic or Empire: American Resistance to the Philippine War* (1972). Slotkin, Richard, *Gunfighter Nation: The Myth of the Frontier in Twentieth-Century America* (1993). Strouse, Jean, *Morgan: American Financier* (1999). Trask, David F., *The War with Spain in 1898* (1981).

CHAPTER 21

Brands, H. W., *T. R.: The Last Romantic* (1997). Bringhurst, Bruce, *Antitrust and the Oil Monopoly: The Standard Oil Cases, 1890–1911* (1979). Clark, Norman H., *Deliver Us from Evil: An Interpretation of American Prohibition* (1976). Cooper, John Milton, Jr., *The Warrior and the Priest: Theodore Roosevelt and Woodrow Wilson in American Politics* (1983). Crichon, Judy, *America 1900: The Turning Point* (1998). Diner, Steven J., *A Very Different Age: Americans in the Progressive Era* (1998). Dulles, Foster Rhea, *Labor in America* (1955). Faulkner, Harold Underwood, *The Quest for Social Justice, 1898–1914* (1931). Filene, Peter G., "Narrating Progressivism: Unitarians v. Pluralists v. Students," *Journal of American History*, 79 (1993) 4, 1546–1561.

Gould, Lewis L., *The Presidency of Theodore Roosevelt* (1991). Harbaugh, William H., *Power and Responsibility: The Life and Times of Theodore Roosevelt* (1961). Kessler-Harris, Alice, *Out to Work: A History of Wage Earning Women* (1982). Lewis, David Levering, *W. E. B. Du Bois: Biography of a Race, 1868–1919* (1993). Lukas, J. Anthony, *Big Trouble: A Murder in a Small Western Town Sets Off a Struggle for the Soul of America* (1997).

McGerr, Michael E., *The Decline of Popular Politics* (1986). McMurry, Linda O., *To Keep the Waters Troubled: The Life of Ida B. Wells* (1998). Ninkovich, Frank, *Modernity and Power: A History of the Domino Theory in the Twentieth Century* (1994). Rodgers, Daniel T., "In Search of Progressivism," *Reviews in American History*, 10 (1982) 4, 113–132. Rosen, Ruth, *The Lost Sisterhood: Prostitution in America, 1900–1918* (1982).

Salvatore, Nick, *Eugene V. Debs: Citizen and Socialist* (1982). Schiesl, Martin J., *The Politics of Efficiency: Municipal Administration and Reform in America, 1800–1920* (1977). Scully, Eileen P., "Taking the Low Road to Sino-American Relations: 'Open Door' Expansionists and the Two China Markets," *Journal of American History*, 82 (1995) 1, 62–83. Shannon, David A., *The Socialist Party of America: A History* (1955). Sklar, Kathryn Kish, *Florence Kelley and the Nation's Work: The Rise of Women's Political Culture, 1830–1900* (1995). Starr, Kevin, *Inventing the Dream: California Through the Progressive Era* (1985). Thelen, David, *Robert M. La Follette and the Insurgent Spirit* (1976). Weibe, Robert H., "The Anthracite Strike of 1902: A Record of Confusion," *Mississippi Valley Historical Review*, 48 (1961) 2, 229–251. _____, *The Search for Order, 1877–1920* (1967).

CHAPTER 22

Bailey, Thomas A., "The Sinking of the Lusitania," *The American Historical Review*, 41 (1935) 1, 54–73. Bird, Kai, *The Chairman: John J. McCloy, The Making of the American Establishment* (1992). Butler, Gregory S., "Visions of a Nation Transformed: Modernity and Ideology in Wilson's Political Thought," *Journal of Church and State*, 39 (Winter 1997) 1, 37–51. Chatfield, Charles, "World War I and the Liberal Pacifist in the United States," *American Historical Review*, 75 (1970) 7, 1920–1937. Clark, Norman H., *Deliver Us from Evil: An Interpretation of American Prohibition* (1976). Clifford, John Garry, *The Citizen Soldiers: The Plattsburg Training Camp Movement, 1919–1920* (1972). Davis, Richard Harding, "The Plattsburg Idea," *Collier's* (October 9, 1915) 7–9. Ferrell, Robert H., *Woodrow Wilson and World War I, 1917–1921* (1985).

Horne, Alistair, *The Price of Glory* (1964). Katz, Freidrich, "Pancho Villa and the Attack on Columbus, New Mexico," *American Historical Review*, 83 (1978) 1, 101–130. _____, *The Secret War in Mexico: Europe, the United States, and the Mexican Revolution* (1981). Levin, N. Gordon, Jr., *Woodrow Wilson and World Politics* (1968).

Miles, Lewis W., "Plattsburgh," *Sewanee Review*, 24 (January 1916) 1, 19–23. Miller, William D., *Pretty Bubbles in the Air: America in 1919* (1991). Page, Ralph W., "What I Learned at Plattsburg," *World's Work* (November 1915), 105–108. Perry, Ralph Barton, "Impressions of a Plattsburg Recruit," *New Republic* (October 2, 1915), 229–231. Rudwick, Elliott M., *Race Riot in East Saint Louis, July 2, 1917* (1964). Russell, Francis, *Tragedy in Dedham: The Story of the Sacco-Vanzetti Case* (1962).

Schaffer, Ronald, *America in the Great War: The Rise of the War Welfare State* (1991). Schoonover, Thomas D., "To End All Social Reform: A Progressive's Search for International Order," *Reviews in American History*, 21 (1993), 647–654. Tuchman, Barbara, *The Guns of August* (1976). Ward, Robert D., "The Origin and Activities of the National Security League, 1914–1919," *Mississippi Valley Historical Review*, 47 (January 1960) 1, 51–65. Wynn, Neil A., *From Progressivism to Prosperity: World War I and American Society* (1986).

CHAPTER 23

Barron, Hal S., *Mixed Harvest: The Second Great Transformation in the Rural North, 1870–1930* (1997). Blee, Kathleen M., *Women of the Klan: Racism and Gender in the 1920s* (1991). Burner, David, *Herbert Hoover: A Public Life* (1979). _____, *The Politics of Provincialism: The Democratic Party in Transition, 1918–1932* (1968). Chandler, Alfred D., Jr., *Strategy and Structure* (1962). Coben, Stanley, *Rebellion Against Victorianism: The Impetus for Change in 1920s America* (1991). Cohen, Warren I., *Empire Without Tears: America's Foreign Relations, 1921–1933* (1987). De Benedetti, Charles, *Origins of the Modern American Peace Movement: 1915–1929* (1978). D'Emilio, John, and Estelle Freedman, *Intimate Matters: A History of Sexuality in America* (1988). Douglas, Ann, *Terrible Honesty: Mongrel Manhattan in the 1920s* (1995). Douglas, Susan J., *Inventing American Broadcasting, 1899–1922* (1987).

Gordon, Linda, *Woman's Body, Woman's Right: A Social History of Birth Control in America* (1977). Griswold, Robert, *Fatherhood in America: A History* (1993). Gutierrez, David, *Walls and Mirrors: Mexican Americans, Mexican Immigrants, and the Politics of Ethnicity* (1995). Hawley, Ellis W., *The Great War and the Search for a Modern Order: A History of the American People and Their Institutions, 1917–1933* (1992). _____, ed., *Herbert Hoover as Secretary of Commerce: Studies in New Era Thought and Practice* (1981). Hogan, Michael J., *Informal Entente: The Private Structure of Cooperation in Anglo-American Economy, 1918–1929* (1977). Hounshell, David A., *From the American System to Mass Production, 1800–1932: The Development of Manufacturing Technology in the United States* (1984). Huggins, Nathan I., *Harlem Renaissance* (1971). Jackson, Kenneth T., *The Ku Klux Klan in the City, 1915–1930* (1967). Kennedy, J. Gerald, *Imagining Paris: Exile, Writing and American Identity* (1993). Kern, Stephen, *The Culture of Time and Space, 1880–1918*

(1983). Koszarski, Richard, *An Evening's Entertainment: The Age of the Silent Feature Picture, 1915–1928* (1990). Ladd-Taylor, Molly, *Mother-Work: Women, Child Welfare, and the State, 1890–1930* (1994). Lears, Jackson, *Fables of Abundance: A Cultural History of Advertising in America* (1994). Leffler, Melvyn P., *The Elusive Quest: America's Pursuit of European Stability and French Security, 1919–1933* (1979). Lemons, J. Stanley, *The Woman Citizen: Social Feminism in the 1920s* (1973). Lichtman, Alan J., *Prejudice and the Old Politics: The Presidential Election of 1928* (1979).

Marsden, George M., *Fundamentalism and American Culture: The Shaping of Twentieth-Century Evangelicalism, 1870–1925* (1980). Meyerowitz, Joanne J., *Women Adrift: Independent Wage Earners in Chicago, 1880–1930* (1988). Montgomery, David, *The Fall of the House of Labor: The Workplace, the State, and American Labor Activism, 1865–1925* (1987). Moore, Leonard J., *Citizen Klansmen: The Ku Klux Klan in Indiana, 1921–1928* (1991). Peretti, Burton W., *The Creation of Jazz: Music, Race, and Culture in Urban America* (1992).

Schlesinger, Arthur M., Jr., *The Crisis of the Old Order: 1919–1933* (1957). Seymour, Harold, *Baseball: The Golden Age* (1971). Singal, Daniel Joseph, *The War Within: From Victorian to Modernist Thought in the South, 1919–1945* (1982). Trani, Eugene P., and David L. Wilson, *The Presidency of Warren G. Harding* (1977). Zunz, Olivier, *Making America Corporate, 1870–1920* (1990).

CHAPTER 24

Badger, Anthony J., *The New Deal: The Depression Years, 1933–1940* (1989). Bernstein, Irving, *The Lean Years* (1960). _____, *The Turbulent Years* (1970). Bernstein, Michael A., *The Great Depression: Delayed Recovery and Economic Change in America, 1929–1939* (1987). Bird, Caroline, *The Invisible Scar* (1966). Brinkley, Alan, *Liberalism and Its Discontents* (1998). _____, *Voices of Protest* (1982). Burns, James MacGregor, *Roosevelt: The Lion and the Fox* (1956). Carnegie, Dale, "Grab Your Bootstraps," *Colliers*, March 5, 1938, 14–15. Carter, Dan T., *Scottsboro: A Tragedy of the American South.* Rev. ed. (1979). Cooke, Blanche Wiesen, *Eleanor Roosevelt*, 2 vols. (1992–1999). Daniels, Roger, *The Bonus March* (1971). Denning, Michael, *The Cultural Front: The Laboring of American Culture in the Twentieth Century* (1997). Edwards, Anne, *Road to Tara* (1983). Eichengreen, Barry, *Golden Fetters: The*

Gold Standard and the Great Depression, 1919–1939 (1995). Ellis, Edward Robb, *A Nation in Torment: The Great American Depression, 1929–1939* (1970). Fraser, Steve, *Labor Will Rule: Sidney Hillman and the Rise of American Labor* (1991). _____, and Gary Gerstle, *The Rise and Fall of the New Deal Order, 1930–1980* (1989).

Galbraith, John Kenneth, *The Great Crash: 1929* (1961). Gourevitch, Peter, *Politics in Hard Times: Comparative Responses to International Economic Crises* (1986). Granberry, Edward, "The Private Life of Margaret Mitchell," *Colliers,* March 13, 1937, 22–24. Greenberg, Cheryl Lynn, *"Or Does it Explode?": Black Harlem in the Great Depression* (1991). Gregory, James, *American Exodus: The Dust Bowl Migration and Okie Culture in California* (1989). Harriman, Margaret Case, "He Sells Hope," *Saturday Evening Post,* August 14, 1937, 12–34. Hofstadter, Richard, *The Age of Reform* (1956). Kelley, Robin D. G., *Hammer and Hoe: Alabama Communists during the Great Depression* (1990). Kennedy, David M., *Freedom from Fear: The American People in Depression and War* (1999). Kindelberger, Charles, *The World in Depression* (1973). Kirby, John B., *Black Americans in the Roosevelt Era* (1980). Klehr, Harvey, *The Heyday of American Communism: The Depression Decade* (1984). Leuchtenberg, William E., *Franklin D. Roosevelt and the New Deal* (1963).

Manchester, William, *The Glory and the Dream* (1973). McElvaine, Robert S., *The Great Depression: America, 1929–1941* (1984). Nelson, Bruce, *Workers on the Waterfront: Seamen, Longshoremen, and Unionism in the 1930s* (1988). Patterson, James, *Congressional Conservatism and the New Deal* (1967). _____, *The New Deal and the States* (1969). Pells, Richard, *Radical Visions and American Dreams: Culture and Social Thought in the Depression Years* (1973). Plotke, David, *Building a Democratic Political Order: Reshaping American Liberalism in the 1930s and 1940s* (1996). Pyron, Darden Asbury, *Southern Daughter* (1991).

Schulman, Bruce J., *From Cotton Belt to Sunbelt: Federal Policy, Economic Development, and the Transformation of the South, 1938–1980* (1991). Sitkoff, Harvard, *A New Deal for Blacks* (1978). Temin, Peter, *Lessons from the Great Depression* (1996). Watkins, T. H., *The Hungry Years* (1999). Williams, T. Harry, *Huey Long: A Biography* (1969). Wilson, Joan Hoff, *Herbert Hoover: Forgotten Progressive* (1975). Worster, Donald, *The Dust Bowl: The Southern Plains in the 1930s* (1979).

CHAPTER 25

Adams, Michael C. C., *The Best War Ever: America and World War II* (1994). Alperovitz, Gar, *The Decision to Use the Atomic Bomb and the Architecture of an American Myth* (1995). Ambrose, Stephen, *American Heritage New History of World War II* (1997). _____, *Citizen Soldiers* (1997). Bendiner, Elmer, *The Fall of Fortresses* (1980). Bergerud, Eric, *Touched with Fire: The Land War in the South Pacific* (1996). Blum, John Morton, *V Was for Victory* (1976). Blumenson, Martin, *Kasserine Pass* (1966). Deighton, Len, *Blood, Tears and Folly: An Objective Look at World War II* (1993). Dower, John W., *War without Mercy* (1986). Feingold, Henry L., *The Politics of Rescue: The Roosevelt Administration and the Holocaust, 1938–1945* (1970). Finkle, Lee, "The Conservative Aims of Militant Rhetoric: Black Protest During World War II," *Journal of American History,* 60 (December 1973) 3, 692–713. Flower, Desmond, and James Reeves, eds., *The War, 1939–1945: A Documentary History* (1997). Fussell, Paul, *Wartime* (1989).

Harris, William H., "A. Philip Randolph as a Charismatic Leader, 1925–1941," *Journal of Negro History,* 64 (Autumn 1979) 4, 301–315. Heinrichs, Waldo, *Threshold of War* (1988). Hobsbawm, Eric, *The Age of Extremes* (1994). Houston, Jeanne Wakatsuki, and James D., *Farewell to Manzanar* (1973). Hynes, Samuel, *Flights of Passage* (1988). Kennedy, Paul, *The Rise and Fall of the Great Powers* (1987). Kimball, Warren F., *The Juggler: Franklin Roosevelt as Wartime Statesman* (1991). Leffler, Melvyn P., *The Specter of Communism* (1994).

Manchester, William, *The Glory and the Dream: A Narrative History of America, 1932–1972* (1973). Milward, Alan S., *War, Economy and Society 1939–1945* (1977). Morison, Samuel Eliot, *Coral Sea, Midway and Submarine Actions* (1949). _____, *The Two-Ocean War* (1963). O'Neill, William L., *A Democracy at War* (1993). Perrett, Geoffrey, *Days of Sadness, Years of Triumph* (1973). Pogue, Forrest C., *George C. Marshall: Ordeal and Hope, 1939–1942* (1965). Prange, Gordon W., *Miracle at Midway* (1982). Rosenberg, Emily S., *Spreading the American Dream: American Economic and Cultural Expansion, 1890–1945* (1982).

Sitkoff, Harvard, "Racial Militancy and Interracial Violence in the Second World War," *Journal of American History,* 58 (December 1971) 3, 661–681. Spickard, Paul R., *Japanese Americans: The Formation and Transformations of an Ethnic*

Group (1996). United States, Federal Bureau of Investigation, "FBI File: A. Philip Randolph" (1990). Weighley, Russell F., *Eisenhower's Lieutenants* (1981). Wright, Gordon, *The Ordeal of Total War, 1939–1945* (1997).

CHAPTER 26

Blackwelder, Julia Kirk, *Now Hiring: The Feminization of Work in the United States, 1900–1995* (1997). Boyer, Paul, *By the Bomb's Early Light: American Thought and Culture at the Dawn of the Atomic Age* (1985). Cumings, Bruce, *The Origins of the Korean War*, 2 vols. (1981–1990). Dalfiume, Richard, *Desegregation of the U.S. Armed Forces: Fighting on Two Fronts, 1939–1953* (1969). Donovan, Robert J., *Conflict and Crisis: The Presidency of Harry S Truman, 1945–1948* (1977). _____, *Tumultuous Years: The Presidency of Harry S Truman, 1948–1953* (1982). Egerton, John, *Speak Now Against the Day: The Generation Before the Civil Rights Movement in the South* (1994). Fried, Richard M., *The Russians Are Coming! the Russians Are Coming!: Pageantry and Patriotism in Cold-War America* (1999).

Gaddis, John Lewis, *The United States and the Origins of the Cold War, 1941–1947* (1972). _____, *We Now Know: Rethinking Cold War History* (1997). Hamby, Alonzo L., *Beyond the New Deal: Harry S. Truman and American Liberalism* (1973). Hartmann, Susan M., *The Home Front and Beyond: American Women in the 1940s* (1982). _____, *Truman and the 80th Congress* (1971). Heller, Francis H., ed., *Economics and the Truman Administration* (1981). Hogan, Michael J., *The Marshall Plan: America, Britain, and the Reconstruction of Western Europe, 1947–1952* (1987). Knox, Donald, *The Korean War: An Oral History*, 2 vols. (1985–1988). Lacey, Michael J., ed., *The Truman Presidency* (1989). LaFeber, Walter, *America, Russia, and the Cold War, 1945–1992* (1993). Lawson, Steven M., *Black Ballots: Voting Rights in the South, 1944–1969* (1976).

May, Lary, ed., *Recasting America: Culture and Politics in the Age of Cold War* (1989). McCoy, Donald, and Richard Ruetten, *Quest and Response: Minority Rights and the Truman Administration* (1973). Meier, August, and Elliott Rudwick, *CORE: A Study in the Civil Rights Movement, 1942–1968* (1973). Merrill, Dennis, ed., *Documentary History of the Truman Presidency*, 20 vols. (1995–1997). Nadel, Alan, *Containment Culture: American Narratives, Postmodernism, and the Atomic Age* (1995). Navasky, Victor S., *Naming Names* (1989). Patterson, James T., *Mr. Republican:*

A Biography of Robert A. Taft (1972). Poen, Monte M., *Harry S. Truman Versus the Medical Lobby: The Genesis of Medicare* (1979). Polan, Dana, *Power and Paranoia: History, Narrative, and the American Cinema, 1940–1950* (1986). Radosh, Ronald, and Joyce Milton, *The Rosenberg File: A Search for the Truth* (1984). Renshaw, Patrick, *American Labor and Consensus Capitalism, 1935–1990* (1991).

Stueck, William, *The Korean War: An International History* (1995). Sugrue, Thomas J., *The Origins of the Urban Crisis: Race and Inequality in Postwar Detroit* (1996). Weiner, Lynn Y., *From Working Girl to Working Mother: The Female Labor Force in the United States, 1820–1980* (1985). Whitfield, Stephen J., *The Culture of the Cold War* (1991).

CHAPTER 27

Baughman, James L., *The Republic of Mass Culture: Journalism, Filmmaking and Broadcasting in America since 1941* (1991). Beschloss, Michael R., *Mayday: Eisenhower, Khrushchev and the U-2 Affair* (1991). Bowie, Robert R., and Richard H. Immerman, *Waging Peace: How Eisenhower Shaped an Enduring Cold War Strategy* (2000). Breines, Wini, *Young, White, and Miserable: Growing Up Female in the Fifties* (1992). Broadwater, Jeff, *Eisenhower and the Anti-Communist Crusade* (1992). Burk, Robert Fredrick, *The Eisenhower Administration and Black Civil Rights, 1953–1961* (1984). Cullather, Nick, *Illusions of Influence: The Political Economy of United States-Philippines Relations, 1942–1960* (1994). Divine, Robert, *The Sputnik Challenge* (1993). Dockrill, Saki, *Eisenhower's New-Look National Security Policy, 1953–1961* (1996). Dudziak, Mary, *Cold War Civil Rights: Race and the Image of American Democracy* (2000). Foreman, Joel, ed., *The Other Fifties: Interrogating Midcentury American Icons* (1997). Fried, Richard M., *Nightmare in Red: The McCarthy Era in Perspective* (1990).

Gardner, Lloyd C., *Approaching Vietnam: From World War II through Dienbienphu* (1988). Gartman, David, *Auto Opium: A Social History of American Automobile Design* (1994). Graebner, William, *Coming of Age in Buffalo: Youth and Authority in the Postwar Era* (1990). Guralnick, Peter, *Last Train to Memphis: The Rise of Elvis Presley* (1994). Gutierrez, David, *Walls and Mirrors: Mexican Americans, Mexican Immigrants, and the Politics of Ethnicity* (1995). Horowitz, Daniel, ed., *American Social Classes in the 1950s: Selections from Vance Packard's The*

Status Seekers (1995). Jackson, Kenneth, *Crabgrass Frontier: The Suburbanization of the United States* (1985). Jones, Gerard, *Honey, I'm Home! Sitcoms: Selling the American Dream* (1992). Karabell, Zachary, *Architects of Intervention: The United States, the Third World, and the Cold War, 1946–1962* (1999). Kluger, Richard, *Simple Justice: The History of* Brown v. *Board of Education and Black America's Struggle for Equality* (1977). Korrol, Virginia Sanchez, *From Colonia to Community: The History of Puerto Ricans in New York City* (1994). Kunz, Diane B., *The Economic Diplomacy of the Suez Crisis* (1991). Lhamon, Ward T., *Deliberate Speed: The Origins of a Cultural Style in the American 1950s* (1990).

May, Elaine Tyler, *Homeward Bound: American Families in the Cold War Era* (1988). Meier, Matt S., and Feliciano Ribera, *Mexican Americans, American Mexicans: from Conquistadors to Chicanos* (1993). O'Neill, William L., *American High: The Years of Confidence, 1945–1960* (1986). Pach, Chester J., and Elmo Richardson, *The Presidency of Dwight D. Eisenhower* (1991). Raines, Howell, *My Soul Is Rested: Movement Days in the Deep South Remembered* (1977). Ramos, Henry A. J., *The American G.I. Forum: In Pursuit of the Dream, 1948–1993* (1998). Rawls, James J., *Chief Red Fox Is Dead: A History of Native Americans Since 1945* (1996). Rupp, Leila J., *Survival in the Doldrums: The American Women's Rights Movement, 1945 to the 1960s* (1987).

Takeyh, Ray, *The Origins of the Eisenhower Doctrine: The U.S., Britain, and Nasser's Egypt, 1953–57* (2000). Watson, Steven, *The Birth of the Beat Generation: Visionaries, Rebels, and Hipsters, 1944–1960* (1995).

CHAPTER 28

Appy, Christian G., *Working-Class War: American Combat Soldiers and Vietnam* (1993). Beschloss, Michael, *The Crisis Years: Kennedy and Khrushchev, 1960–1963* (1991). Blum, John Morton, *Years of Discord: American Politics and Society, 1961–1974* (1991). Brands, H. W., *The Wages of Globalism: Lyndon Johnson and the Limits of American Power* (1995). Brick, Howard, *Age of Contradiction: American Thought and Culture in the 1960s* (2000). Burner, David, *John F. Kennedy and a New Generation* (1988). Carson, Clayborne, *In Struggle: SNCC and the Black Awakening of the 1960s* (1981). Chafe, William H., *Civilities and Civil Rights: Greensboro, North Carolina, and the Black Struggle for Freedom* (1980). Dallek, Robert, *Flawed Giant: Lyndon Johnson and His Times,*

1961–1973 (1991). Davies, Gareth, *From Opportunity to Entitlement: The Transformation and Decline of Great Society Liberalism* (1996). Dickstein, Morris, *Gates of Eden: American Culture in the Sixties* (1977). Dittmer, John, *Local People: The Struggle for Civil Rights in Mississippi* (1994). Douglas, Susan J., *Where the Girls Are: Growing Up Female with the Mass Media* (1994). Downs, Frederick, *The Killing Zone: My Life in the Vietnam War* (1978). Evans, Sara, *Personal Politics: The Roots of Women's Liberation in the Civil Rights Movement and the New Left* (1979). Farber, David, ed., *The Sixties: From Memory to History* (1994).

Garrow, David J., *Bearing the Cross: Martin Luther King, Jr., and the Southern Christian Leadership Conference* (1986). Giglio, James N., *The Presidency of John F. Kennedy* (1991). Halberstam, David, *The Best and the Brightest* (1972). Haley, Alex, *The Autobiography of Malcolm X* (1966). Harrison, Cynthia, *On Account of Sex: The Politics of Women's Issues, 1945–1968* (1988). Harvey, Mark W. T., *A Symbol of Wilderness: Echo Park and the American Conservation Movement* (1994). Hodgson, Godfrey, *America in Our Time: From World War II to Nixon* (1976). Hoffman, Elizabeth Cobbs, *All You Need Is Love: The Peace Corps and the Spirit of the 1960s* (1998). Horne, Gerald, *Fire This Time: The Watts Uprising and the 1960s* (1996). Horowitz, Daniel, *Betty Friedan and the Making of the Feminine Mystique: The American Left, the Cold War, and Modern Feminism* (1998). Jeffreys-Jones, Rhodri, *Peace Now!: American Society and the Ending of the Vietnam War* (1999). Kahin, George McT., *Intervention: How America Became Involved in Vietnam* (1986). Kaiser, David E., *American Tragedy: Kennedy, Johnson, and the Origins of the Vietnam War* (2000). Krepinevich, Andrew F., Jr., *The Army and Vietnam* (1986). Linden-Ward, Blanche, and Carol Hurd Green, *Changing the Future: American Women in the 1960s* (1993).

Macedo, Stephen, ed., *Reassessing the Sixties: Debating the Political and Cultural Legacy* (1997). McAdam, Doug, *Freedom Summer* (1988). McDougall, Walter A., . . . *the Heavens and the Earth: A Political History of the Space Age* (1985). Moïse, Edwin E., *Tonkin Gulf and the Escalation of the Vietnam War* (1996). Paterson, Thomas G., ed., *Kennedy's Quest for Victory: American Foreign Policy, 1961–1963* (1989). Payne, Charles M., *I've Got the Light of Freedom: The Organizing Tradition and the Mississippi Freedom Struggle* (1995). Pearson, Hugh,

The Shadow of the Panther: Huey Newton and the Price of Black Power in America (1994). Ralph, James R., Jr., *Northern Protest: Martin Luther King, Jr., Chicago, and the Civil Rights Movement* (1993). Rorabaugh, W. J., *Berkeley at War: The 1960s* (1989). Rothman, Hal K., *The Greening of a Nation: Environmentalism in the United States since 1945* (1998).

Schlesinger, Arthur M., Jr., *Robert Kennedy and His Times* (1978). Schwartz, Bernard, *Super Chief: Earl Warren and His Supreme Court* (1983). Steigerwald, David, *The Sixties and the End of Modern America* (1995). Summer, Harry G., Jr., *On Strategy: A Critical Analysis of the Vietnam War* (1982). Szatmary, David P., *Rockin' in Time: A Social History of Rock-and-Roll* (1997). Van Deburg, William L., *New Day in Babylon: The Black Power Movement and American Culture, 1965–1975* (1992). Wells, Tom, *The War Within: America's Battle Over Vietnam* (1996).

CHAPTER 29

Adam, Barry D., *The Rise of a Gay and Lesbian Movement*, Rev. ed. (1995). Barnet, Richard J., and Ronald E. Müller, *Global Reach: The Power of the Multinational Corporations* (1974). Bartley, Numan V., *The New South, 1945–1980: The Story of the South's Modernization* (1995). Bernstein, Carl, and Bob Woodward, *All the President's Men* (1974). Bernstein, Michael A., and David E. Adler, eds., *Understanding American Economic Decline* (1994). Bill, James A., *The Eagle and the Lion: The Tragedy of American-Iranian Relations* (1988). Brands, H. W., *Since Vietnam: The United States in World Affairs, 1973–1995* (1996). Campisi, Jack, *The Mashpee Indians: Tribe on Trial* (1991). Carter, Dan T., *The Politics of Rage: George Wallace, the Origins of the New Conservatism, and the Transformation of American Politics* (1995). Chan, Sucheng, *Asian Americans: An Interpretive History* (1990). D'Emilio, John, *Sexual Politics, Sexual Communities: The Making of a Homosexual Minority in the United States, 1940–1970* (1983). Duberman, Martin, *Stonewall* (1993). Engelhardt, Tom, *The End of Victory Culture: Cold War America and the Disillusioning of a Generation* (1995). Espiritu, Yen Le, *Asian American Panethnicity: Bridging Institutions and Identities* (1992). Ford, Daniel F., *Three Mile Island: Thirty Minutes to Meltdown* (1982). Frye, Gaillard, *The Dream Long Deferred* (1988).

Garrow, David J., *Liberty and Sexuality: The Right to Privacy and the Making of* Roe v. Wade (1994). Garthoff, Raymond L., *Détente and Confrontation: American-Soviet Relations from Nixon to Reagan* (1994). Gartman, David, *Auto Opium: A Social History of American Automobile Design* (1994). Greene, John Robert, *The Limits of Power: The Nixon and Ford Administrations* (1992). Isaacs, Arnold R., *Without Honor: Defeat in Vietnam and Cambodia* (1983). Isaacson, Walter, *Kissinger: A Biography* (1992). Jones, Charles O., *The Trusteeship Presidency: Jimmy Carter and the United States Congress* (1988). Kimball, Jeffrey P., *Nixon's Vietnam War* (1998). LaFeber, Walter, *The Panama Canal Crisis in Historical Perspective* (1989). Lasch, Christopher, *The Culture of Narcissism: American Life in an Age of Diminishing Expectations* (1979). Lawson, Steven F., *Running for Freedom: Civil Rights and Black Politics in America since 1941* (1997).

Marin, Marguerite V., *Social Protest in an Urban Barrio: A Study of the Chicano Movement, 1966–1974* (1991). Nagel, Joanne, *American Indian Ethnic Renewal: Red Power and the Resurgence of Identity and Culture* (1996). Rieder, Jonathan, *Canarsie: The Jews and Italians of Brooklyn Against Liberalism* (1985). Rosen, Ellen Israel, *Bitter Choices: Blue-Collar Women In and Out of Work* (1987). Ryan, Paul B., *The Iranian Rescue Mission and Why It Failed* (1986).

Sale, Kirkpatrick, *Power Shift: The Rise of the Southern Rim and Its Challenge to the Eastern Establishment* (1975). Schlesinger, Arthur M., Jr., *The Imperial Presidency* (1973). Schulman, Bruce J., *From Cotton Belt to Sun Belt: Federal Policy, Economic Development, and the Transformation of the South, 1938–1980* (1991). Schur, Edwin, *The Awareness Trap: Self-Absorption Instead of Social Change* (1976). Small, Melvin, *The Presidency of Richard Nixon* (1999). Smith, Gaddis, *Morality, Reason, and Power: American Diplomacy in the Carter Years* (1986). Stern, Kenneth S., *Loud Hawk: The United States versus the American Indian Movement* (1994). Szasz, Andrew, *Eco-Populism: Toxic Waste and the Movement for Environmental Justice* (1994). Takaki, Ronald, *Strangers from a Different Shore: A History of Asian Americans* (1989). Thurow, Lester, *The Zero-Sum Society: Distribution and the Possibilities for Economic Change* (1980). Vigil, Ernesto, *The Crusade for Justice: Chicano Militancy and the Government's War on Dissent* (1999). Wei, William, *The Asian American Movement* (1993). Wicker, Tom, *One of Us: Richard Nixon and the American Dream* (1991). Wilkinson, J. Harvie, III, *From Brown to Bakke: The Supreme Court and School Integration, 1954–1978* (1979). Wolfe, Alan, *America's Impasse: The Rise and Fall of the Politics of Growth* (1981).

CHAPTER 30

Adam, Barry D., *The Rise of a Gay and Lesbian Movement,* Rev. ed. (1995). Anderson, Martin, *Revolution: The Reagan Legacy* (1988). Berman, William C., *America's Right Turn: From Nixon to Bush* (1994). Blumenthal, Sidney, *The Rise of the Counter-Establishment: From Conservative Ideology to Political Power* (1986). Campbell-Kelly, Martin, and William Aspray, *Computer: A History of the Information Machine* (1996). Cannon, Lou, *Ronald Reagan: The Role of a Lifetime* (1991). Davis, Flora, *Moving the Mountain: The Women's Movement in America since 1960* (1991). Ferree, Myra Marx, and Beth B. Hess, *Controversy and Coalition: The New Feminist Movement across Three Decades of Change* (1994). Friedman, Benjamin M., *Day of Reckoning: The Consequences of American Economic Policy under Reagan and After* (1988).

Gallagher, John, *Perfect Enemies: The Religious Right, the Gay Movement, and the Politics of the 1990s* (1996). Garthoff, Raymond L., *Détente and Confrontation: American-Soviet Relations from Nixon to Reagan* (1994). _____, *The Great Transition: American-Soviet Relations and the End of the Cold War* (1994). Gillon, Steven M., *The Democrats' Dilemma: Walter F. Mondale and the Liberal Legacy* (1992). Hill, Dilys M., et al., *The Reagan Presidency: An Incomplete Revolution?* (1990). Hodgson, Godfrey, *The World Turned Right Side Up: A History of the Conservative Ascendancy in America* (1996). Hoeveler, J. David, *Watch on the Right: Conservative Intellectuals in the Reagan Era* (1991). Hurt, Harry, *The Lost Tycoon: The Many Lives of Donald J. Trump* (1993). Jaynes, Gerald David, and Robin M. Williams, Jr., eds., *A Common Destiny: Blacks and American Society* (1989). Fitzgerald, Frances, *Way Out There in the Blue: Reagan and Star Wars and the End of the Cold War* (2000). Jeffords, Susan, *Hard Bodies: Hollywood Masculinity in the Reagan Era* (1994). Jorstad, Erling, *Holding Fast/Pressing On: Religion in America in the 1980s* (1990). Lewis, Michael, *Liar's Poker: Rising Through the Wreckage on Wall Street* (1989). Lofland, John, *Polite Protesters: The American Peace Movement of the 1980s* (1993).

Martin, William C., *With God on Our Side: The Rise of the Religious Right in America* (1996). McGirr, Lisa, *Suburban Warriors: The Origins of the New American Right* (2001). Meyer, Jane, and Doyle McManus, *Landslide: The Unmaking of the President, 1984–1988* (1988). Murray, Charles, *Losing Ground: American Social Policy, 1950–1980* (1984). Noonan, Peggy, *What I Saw at the Revolution: A Political Life in the Reagan Era* (1990). Phillips, Kevin P., *The Politics of Rich and Poor: Wealth and the American Electorate in the Reagan Aftermath* (1990). Rayack, Elton, *Not So Free to Choose: The Political Economy of Milton Friedman and Ronald Reagan* (1987). Reed, Adolph L., *The Jesse Jackson Phenomenon: The Crisis of Purpose in Afro-American Politics* (1986).

Schaller, Michael, *Reckoning with Reagan: America and Its President in the 1980s* (1992). Scheer, Robert, *With Enough Shovels: Reagan, Bush, and Nuclear War* (1982). Taylor, John, *Circus of Ambition: The Culture of Wealth and Power in the Eighties* (1989). Thelen, David P., *Becoming Citizens in the Age of Television: How Americans Challenged the Media and Seized Political Initiative during the Iran-Contra Debate* (1996). Thompson, Mark, ed., *Long Road to Freedom: The Advocate History of the Gay and Lesbian Movement* (1994). Wolters, Raymond, *Right Turn: William Bradford Reynolds, the Reagan Administration, and Black Civil Rights* (1996).

CHAPTER 31

Abramson, Jeffrey, ed., *Postmortem: The O. J. Simpson Case: Justice Confronts Race, Domestic Violence, Lawyers, Money, and the Media* (1996). Beschloss, Michael R., and Strobe Talbott, *At the Highest Levels: The Inside Story of the End of the Cold War* (1993). Bingham, Clara, *Women on the Hill: Challenging the Culture of Congress* (1997). Button, James W., et al., *Private Lives, Public Conflicts: Battles Over Gay Rights in American Communities* (1997). Campbell, Colin, and Bert A. Rockman, eds., *The Clinton Presidency: First Appraisals* (1996). Dertouzos, Michael L., *What Will Be: How the New World of Information Will Change Our Lives* (1998). Drew, Elizabeth, *Showdown: The Struggle Between the Gingrich Congress and the Clinton White House* (1996). Duignan, Peter, and L. H. Gann, eds., *The Debate in the United States Over Immigration* (1998). Dunnigan, James F., and Austin Bay, *From Shield to Storm: High-Tech Weapons, Military Strategy, and Coalition Warfare in the Persian Gulf* (1992).

Gitlin, Todd, *The Twilight of Common Dreams: Why America Is Wracked by Culture Wars* (1995). Gordon, Avery, and Christopher Newfield, eds., *Mapping Multiculturalism* (1996). Green, John C., et al., eds., *Religion and the Culture Wars: Dispatches from the Front* (1996). Greenberg, Stanlwey B., *Middle Class Dreams: The Politics and Power of the New American Majority* (1995). Greene, John Robert, *The Presidency of George Bush* (2000). Haas, Richard N., *The*

Reluctant Sheriff: The United States After the Cold War (1997). Hafner, Katie, and Matthew Lyon, *Where Wizards Stay Up Late: The Origins of the Internet* (1998). Hogan, Michael, ed., *The End of the Cold War: Its Meanings and Implications* (1992). Lind, Michael, *The Next American Nation: The New Nationalism and the Fourth American Revolution* (1995). Lowi, Theodore J., and Benjamin Ginsberg, *Embattled Democracy: Politics and Policy in the Clinton Era* (1995).

Maraniss, David, *First in His Class: A Biography of Bill Clinton* (1995). Matteo, Sherri, ed., *American Women in the Nineties: Today's Critical Issues* (1993). McGuckin, Frank, ed., *Terrorism in the United States* (1997). Morris, Roger, *Partners in Power: The Clintons and Their America* (1996). Newman, Katherine S., *Declining Fortunes: The Withering of the American Dream* (1993). Nolan, James L., Jr., ed., *The American Culture Wars: Current Contests and Future Prospects* (1996). Phillips, Kevin P., *The Politics of Rich and Poor: Wealth and the American Electorate in the Reagan Aftermath* (1990). Posner,

Gerald L., *Citizen Perot: His Life and Times* (1996). Ripley, Randall B., and James M. Lindsay, eds., *U.S. Foreign Policy After the Cold War* (1997). Rivlin, Gary, *The Plot to Get Bill Gates* (1999). Rubin, Lillian B., *Families on the Fault Line: America's Working Class Speaks about the Family, the Economy, Race, and Ethnicity* (1994).

Skocpol, Theda, *Boomerang: Clinton's Health Security Effort and the Turn Against Government in U.S. Politics* (1996). Slessarev, Helene, *The Betrayal of the Urban Poor* (1991). Spain, Daphne, and Suzanne M. Bianchi, *Balancing Act: Motherhood, Marriage, and Employment Among American Women* (1996). Stern, Kenneth S., *A Force Upon the Plain: The American Militia Movement and the Politics of Hate* (1996). Stewart, James B., *Blood Sport: The President and His Adversaries* (1996). Thomas, Evan, et al., *Back from the Dead: How Clinton Survived the Republican Revolution* (1997). Toobin, Jeffrey, *A Vast Conspiracy: The Real Story of the Sex Scandal That Nearly Brought Down a President* (2000). Wray, Matt, and Annalee Newitz, eds., *White Trash: Race and Class in America* (1997).

PHOTO CREDITS

Chapter 1: William R. Iseminger/Cahokia Mounds State Historic Site, 13; Pierpont Morgan Library/Art Resource, N.Y., 18 (left), Pierpont Morgan Library/Art Resource, N.Y., (right); B.N. Manus/O-828 Madrid. Historia de Indias. Herman Cortes y Marina. Diego Duran, 26.

Chapter 2: Bibliotheque Nationale de France, 43; Copyright The British Museum, 55.

Chapter 3: Richard Nowitz Photography, 66 (left), David G. Houser, (right); Ashmolean Museum, Oxford, England, U.K., 67 (left), The New York Public Library Photographic Services, 86.

Chapter 4: Historic St. Mary's City, 100 (left), Historic Mary's City, (right); Beinecke Rare Book and Manuscript Library, Yale University, 110; David Muench Photography, Inc., 117.

Chapter 5: © Collection of The New York Historical Society, 135; The Library Company of Philadelphia, 139.

Chapter 6: J. W. Barber/The Metropolitan Museum of Art, Bequest of Charles Allen Munn, 1924. (24.90.1566a), 175; The Granger Collection, 176.

Chapter 7: The Library Company of Philadelphia, 207.

Chapter 8: © Collection of The New York Historical Society, 224; The William L. Clements Library, 229; The William L. Clements Library, 230; © Collection of The New York Historical Society, 236 (bottom), Library of Congress, 243.

Chapter 9: Collection of The New York Historical Society, 254; The Historical Society of Pennsylvania, Arch Street Ferry, William Birch, Bd 61 B531.1 p1.4, 261; Courtesy of Rhode Island Historical Society, negative number PHix5 22, 263; Smithsonian Institution Photo Services, 269.

Chapter 10: Abby Aldrich Rockefeller Folk Art Museum, Williamsburg, VA, 284; Yeager, Joseph (American), The Procession of the Victuallers, 1821 Philadelphia Museum of Art: Gift of the Estate of Charles M.B. Cadwalader, 299; The Granger Collection, (right bottom).

Chapter 11: Courtesy, American Antiquarian Society, 312; Thomas Gilcrease Institute of American History and Art, 327.

Chapter 12: Courtesy, American Antiquarian Society, 342; Courtesy, American Antiquarian Society, 347; The New York Historical Society, 348; A lecture by James Pollard Espy, Meteorologist, at Clinton Hall. Lithograph. 1841. Museum of the City of New York. 43.368.4 & 6, 355; Courtesy, American Antiquarian Society, 356.

Chapter 13: Courtesy, New York Public Library, 368; CORBIS, 370 (right), Smithsonian American Art Museum, Washington, D.C./Art Resource, N.Y., 378.

Chapter 14: © CORBIS, 399; The New York Public Library Prints Division, 402; John S. Curry/Mrs. John Steuart Curry, 410.

Chapter 15: Culver Pictures, Inc., 433 (top), © CORBIS, 440.

Chapter 16: Moorland Spingham Research Center, 452 (left), Library of Congress, (right); Library of Congress,

455; Courtesy of the Library of Congress, 459; The Museum of the Confederacy, Richmond, Virginia, Photography by Katherine Wetzel, 461; Thomas Nast/Courtesy of the Library of Congress, 469; Napoleon Sarony/Art Resource, N.Y., 471.

Chapter 17: The Denver Public Library, Western History Collection, 491.

Chapter 18: Chicago Historical Society, 520; Black and Tan Dive, Circa 1890, Museum of the City of New York, The Jacob A. Riis Collection, 523; Kaufmann & Fabry/Chicago Historical Society, 1Chi-32364, 530; Thomas Eakins, American, (1844–1916). The Agnew Clinic. University of Pennsylvania Museum, 536 (left), CORBIS, 537.

Chapter 19: The Granger Collection, New York, 545; The Granger Collection, 548; © Bellew/Stock Montage, 552; © B.L. Singley/CORBIS, 556; The Metropolitan Museum of Art, Purchase, Lyman G. Bloomingdale Gift, 1901. (01.7.1), 537.

Chapter 20: Smithsonian Institution/Office of Imaging, Printing, and Photographic Services, 572; Courtesy of the Library of Congress, 580; Courtesy of the Divinity School, Yale University, 585.

Chapter 21: Brown Brothers, 600; Schomburg Center for Research in Black Culture, 610; © Collection of The New York Historical Society, 612; © Lewis W. Hine, CORBIS, 615.

Chapter 22: © Vera Cruz/CORBIS, 630; Erik Overbey Collection/University of South Alabama Archives, 637; The Granger Collection, New York, 640; Library of Congress, 644; Brown Brothers, 649.

Chapter 23: Gaslight Advertising Archives, Inc. N.Y., 663; Collection of Duncan Schiedt, 664; Courtesy of the Library of Congress, 666; © Bettmann/CORBIS, 671; The UT Institute of Texas Cultures, No. 99-573, 672.

Chapter 24: Brown Brothers, 687; Brown Brothers, 688; Hulton Getty/Archive Photos, 690; The Granger Collection, 694; UPI/CORBIS, 697; Brown Brothers, 704.

Chapter 25: The Granger Collection, 718; Culver Pictures, Inc., (top), 722; Hulton/Archive, 739.

Chapter 26: © CORBIS, 747; © Bettmann/CORBIS, 759; Brown Brothers, 762.

Chapter 27: AP/Wide World Photos, 775; Bernard Hoffman/Life Magazine/© 1950 TimePix, 777; Cindy Lewis Photography, 779; AP/Wide World Photos, 792; AP/Wide World Photos, 794.

Chapter 28: The Granger Collection, 807; UPI/CORBIS, 811; Hulton Getty/Archive Photos, 812; Ron Crane/TimePix, 825.

Chapter 29: CORBIS, 843; AP/Wide World Photos, 847; © 1979 Abbas/Magnum Photos, Inc., 861.

Chapter 30: Donald Dietz/Stock Boston, 877; Karen Su/Stock Boston, 883.

Chapter 31: AFP/CORBIS, 909; Alexandra Avakian/TimePix, 910; Carmen Taylor/AP/Wide World Photos, 915; © Kulish L.A. Daily News/CORBIS SYGMA, 919; Kevin Fuji/SIPA Press, 924.

INDEX

SINGLE PC LICENSE AGREEMENT AND LIMITED WARRANTY

READ THIS LICENSE CAREFULLY BEFORE OPENING THIS PACKAGE. BY OPENING THIS PACKAGE, YOU ARE AGREEING TO THE TERMS AND CONDITIONS OF THIS LICENSE. IF YOU DO NOT AGREE, DO NOT OPEN THE PACKAGE. PROMPTLY RETURN THE UNOPENED PACKAGE AND ALL ACCOMPANYING ITEMS TO THE PLACE YOU OBTAINED THEM.

1. GRANT OF LICENSE and OWNERSHIP: The enclosed computer programs ("Software") are licensed, not sold, to you by Prentice-Hall, Inc. ("We" or the "Company") and in consideration of your purchase or adoption of the accompanying Company textbooks and/or other materials, and your agreement to these terms. We reserve any rights not granted to you. You own only the disk(s) but we and/or our licensors own the Software itself. This license allows you to use and display your copy of the Software on a single computer (i.e., with a single CPU) at a single location for academic use only, so long as you comply with the terms of this Agreement. You may make one copy for back up, or transfer your copy to another CPU, provided that the Software is usable on only one computer.

2. RESTRICTIONS: You may not transfer or distribute the Software or documentation to anyone else. Except for backup, you may not copy the documentation or the Software. You may not network the Software or otherwise use it on more than one computer or computer terminal at the same time. You may not reverse engineer, disassemble, decompile, modify, adapt, translate, or create derivative works based on the Software or the Documentation. You may be held legally responsible for any copying or copyright infringement which is caused by your failure to abide by the terms of these restrictions.

3. TERMINATION: This license is effective until terminated. This license will terminate automatically without notice from the Company if you fail to comply with any provisions or limitations of this license. Upon termination, you shall destroy the Documentation and all copies of the Software. All provisions of this Agreement as to limitation and disclaimer of warranties, limitation of liability, remedies or damages, and our ownership rights shall survive termination.

4. LIMITED WARRANTY AND DISCLAIMER OF WARRANTY: Company warrants that for a period of 60 days from the date you purchase this SOFTWARE (or purchase or adopt the accompanying textbook), the Software, when properly installed and used in accordance with the Documentation, will operate in substantial conformity with the description of the Software set forth in the Documentation, and that for a period of 30 days the disk(s) on which the Software is delivered shall be free from defects in materials and workmanship under normal use. The Company does not warrant that the Software will meet your requirements or that the operation of the Software will be uninterrupted or error-free. Your only remedy and the Company's only obligation under these limited warranties is, at the Company's option, return of the disk for a refund of any amounts paid for it by you or replacement of the disk. THIS LIMITED WARRANTY IS THE ONLY WARRANTY PROVIDED BY THE COMPANY AND ITS LICENSORS, AND THE COMPANY AND ITS LICENSORS DISCLAIM ALL OTHER WARRANTIES, EXPRESS OR IMPLIED, INCLUDING WITHOUT LIMITATION, THE IMPLIED WARRANTIES OF MERCHANTABILITY AND FITNESS FOR A PARTICULAR PURPOSE. THE COMPANY DOES NOT WARRANT, GUARANTEE OR MAKE ANY REPRESENTATION REGARDING THE ACCURACY, RELIABILITY, CURRENTNESS, USE, OR RESULTS OF USE, OF THE SOFTWARE.

5. LIMITATION OF REMEDIES AND DAMAGES: IN NO EVENT, SHALL THE COMPANY OR ITS EMPLOYEES, AGENTS, LICENSORS, OR CONTRACTORS BE LIABLE FOR ANY INCIDENTAL, INDIRECT, SPECIAL, OR CONSEQUENTIAL DAMAGES ARISING OUT OF OR IN CONNECTION WITH THIS LICENSE OR THE SOFTWARE, INCLUDING FOR LOSS OF USE, LOSS OF DATA, LOSS OF INCOME OR PROFIT, OR OTHER LOSSES, SUSTAINED AS A RESULT OF INJURY TO ANY PERSON, OR LOSS OF OR DAMAGE TO PROPERTY, OR CLAIMS OF THIRD PARTIES, EVEN IF THE COMPANY OR AN AUTHORIZED REPRESENTATIVE OF THE COMPANY HAS BEEN ADVISED OF THE POSSIBILITY OF SUCH DAMAGES. IN NO EVENT SHALL THE LIABILITY OF THE COMPANY FOR DAMAGES WITH RESPECT TO THE SOFTWARE EXCEED THE AMOUNTS ACTUALLY PAID BY YOU, IF ANY, FOR THE SOFTWARE OR THE ACCOMPANYING TEXTBOOK. BECAUSE SOME JURISDICTIONS DO NOT ALLOW THE LIMITATION OF LIABILITY IN CERTAIN CIRCUMSTANCES, THE ABOVE LIMITATIONS MAY NOT ALWAYS APPLY TO YOU.

6. GENERAL: THIS AGREEMENT SHALL BE CONSTRUED IN ACCORDANCE WITH THE LAWS OF THE UNITED STATES OF AMERICA AND THE STATE OF NEW YORK, APPLICABLE TO CONTRACTS MADE IN NEW YORK, AND SHALL BENEFIT THE COMPANY, ITS AFFILIATES AND ASSIGNEES. HIS AGREEMENT IS THE COMPLETE AND EXCLUSIVE STATEMENT OF THE AGREEMENT BETWEEN YOU AND THE COMPANY AND SUPERSEDES ALL PROPOSALS OR PRIOR AGREEMENTS, ORAL, OR WRITTEN, AND ANY OTHER COMMUNICATIONS BETWEEN YOU AND THE COMPANY OR ANY REPRESENTATIVE OF THE COMPANY RELATING TO THE SUBJECT MATTER OF THIS AGREEMENT. If you are a U.S. Government user, this Software is licensed with "restricted rights" as set forth in subparagraphs (a)-(d) of the Commercial Computer-Restricted Rights clause at FAR 52.227-19 or in subparagraphs (c)(1)(ii) of the Rights in Technical Data and Computer Software clause at DFARS 252.227-7013, and similar clauses, as applicable.

Should you have any questions concerning this agreement please contact in writing: Legal Department, Prentice Hall, One Lake Street, Upper Saddle River, NJ 07458. If you need assistance with technical difficulties, call: 1-800-677-6337. If you wish to contact the Company for any reason, please contact in writing: Humanities Media Editor, Prentice Hall, One Lake Street, Upper Saddle River, NJ 07458.